THE *GEOGRAPHY* OF S.

The *Geography* of Strabo is the only surviving work of its type in Greek literature, and the major source for the history of Greek scholarship on geography and the formative processes of the earth. In addition, this lengthy and complex work contains a vast amount of information on other topics, including the journey of Alexander the Great, cultic history, the history of the eastern Mediterranean in the first century BC, and women's history. Modern knowledge of seminal geographical authors such as Eratosthenes and Hipparchos relies almost totally on Strabo's use of them. This is the first complete English translation in nearly a century, and the first to make use of recent scholarship on the Greek text itself and on the history of geography. The translation is supplemented by a detailed discussion of Strabo's life and his purpose in writing the *Geography*, as well as the sources that he used.

DUANE W. ROLLER is Professor Emeritus of Classics at the Ohio State University. An historian and archaeologist, he is the author of ten books, most recently *Cleopatra: A Biography* (2010) and *Eratosthenes' Geography* (2010), and over a hundred and fifty scholarly articles on topics in archaeology, ancient history, classical studies, and musicology. He has also excavated in Greece, Italy, Turkey, Jordan, and Israel.

THE *GEOGRAPHY* OF STRABO

Translated by

DUANE W. ROLLER

CAMBRIDGE
UNIVERSITY PRESS

CAMBRIDGE
UNIVERSITY PRESS

University Printing House, Cambridge CB2 8BS, United Kingdom

One Liberty Plaza, 20th Floor, New York, NY 10006, USA

477 Williamstown Road, Port Melbourne, VIC 3207, Australia

314-321, 3rd Floor, Plot 3, Splendor Forum, Jasola District Centre, New Delhi - 110025, India

79 Anson Road, #06-04/06, Singapore 079906

Cambridge University Press is part of the University of Cambridge.

It furthers the University's mission by disseminating knowledge in the pursuit of education, learning and research at the highest international levels of excellence.

www.cambridge.org
Information on this title: www.cambridge.org/9781316625675

© Duane W. Roller 2014

First published 2014
Reprinted 2015
First paperback edition 2020

A catalogue record for this publication is available from the British Library

Library of Congress Cataloging in Publication data
Strabo.
[Geographica. English. 2014]
The Geography of Strabo / translated by Duane W. Roller.
pages   cm
Includes bibliographical references and index.
ISBN 978-1-107-03825-7 (hardback)
1. Geography – Early works to 1800.   I. Roller, Duane W., translator.   II. Title.
G87.S9   2014
913–dc23
2014006702

ISBN 978-1-107-03825-7 Hardback
ISBN 978-1-316-62567-5 Paperback

Contents

Preface

The *Geography* of Strabo is known to all, quoted by many, and understood by few. It is a complex, wandering work, the only survivor of its genre in Greek and one of the longest extant works in Greek literature. Generally it is mined for interesting tidbits rather than comprehended as a whole. Previous to this edition it had not been translated into English since the completion of the now-outdated Loeb version in the 1930s (which was thirty years in preparation), and there has been no full English commentary. In the hopes that this fascinating and wide-ranging treatise will become more accessible, this volume is the first of two that together will provide a modern English translation and extensive commentary.

Strabo probably began collecting data for the *Geography* as early as the 20s BC. Yet the work was not completed until sometime in the 20s AD. This half-century that saw the end of the civil war against Antonius and Kleopatra, the entire reign of Augustus, and the first decade of that of Tiberius, was one of immense change in the Mediterranean world. It included a vast expansion of geographical knowledge, especially in western Europe, the Kaspian region, and western North Africa. Strabo built on the existing data from his predecessors (especially the *Geography* of Eratosthenes, the work that created the discipline), as well as the explorations of the late Hellenistic period, such as those which established the sea route to the Indian peninsula. Yet buried within the geographical account is a vast amount of cultural history unavailable from any other extant source. The work is also the beginning of the discipline of topographical research, with Strabo's insightful attempts to locate Nestor's Pylos or the site of Troy.

This project developed out of the translator's previous work in translating and editing geographical texts dependent on Strabo, such as the *Geography* of Eratosthenes and the *Indika* of Megasthenes (*BNJ* #715), as well as Strabo's own *Historical Commentaries* (*BNJ* #91). The study of ancient geography also requires fieldwork, and although visiting every site mentioned by Strabo would probably be impossible, much of the terrain discussed by the geographer has been re-examined.

The sheer length of Strabo's text has meant that it is not feasible to put both a translation and commentary into a single volume, yet this translation is prelude to a complete commentary. Much of this translation was actually created in Santa Fe, in a high desert landscape that Strabo would have found familiar. The translator would like to thank the exceedingly efficient inter-library loan services of the Ohio State University, as well as the Harvard College Library and the libraries of the University of California at Berkeley and the University of New Mexico.

Special thanks also go to the many colleagues whose assistance made this work possible, especially Jeffrey Becker and the staff of the Ancient World Mapping Center, Kai Brodersen, David C. Braund, Stanley Burstein, D. T. Potts, Klaus Geus, David F. Graf, David E. Hahm, Georgia L. Irby, Molly Ayn Jones-Lewis, Susanne Lamm, Henry MacAdam, James D. Muhly, Letitia K. Roller, John Scarborough; Michael Sharp, Samantha Richter, Gill Cloke, Elizabeth Davey, and many others at Cambridge University Press; Richard Stoneman, and Richard Talbert.

Abbreviations

ANRW	*Aufstieg und Niedergang der römischen Welt*
ArchPhilos	*Archives de philosophie*
BNJ	*Brill's New Jacoby.*
BNP	*Brill's New Pauly*
C&M	*Classica et Mediaevalia*
CHL	*Commentationes humanarum litterarum*
CP	*Classical Philology*
CW	*Classical World*
DK	Hermann Diels, *Die Fragmente der Vorsokratiker* (ed. Walther Kranz, sixth edition, Berlin 1951–2)
FGrHist	Felix Jacoby, *Die Fragmente der griechischen Historiker*
FHG	Karl Müller and Theodor Müller, *Fragmenta historicorum graecorum*
G&R	*Greece and Rome*
GB	*Grazer Beiträge*
GGM	Karl Müller, *Geographi graeci minores*
HRF	Hermann Peter, *Historicorum romanorum fragmenta*
IG	*Inscriptiones graecae*
JRS	*Journal of Roman Studies*
LSJ	Liddell, Scott, and Jones, *Greek-English Lexicon*
MediterrAnt	*Mediterraneo Antico*
OGIS	Wilhelm Dittenberger, *Orientis Graeci Inscriptiones Selectae*
OTerr	*Orbis Terrarum*
PIR	*Prosographia imperii romani*
PP	*La parola del passato*
Radt	*Strabons Geographika* (ed. Stefan Radt, Göttingen, 2002–10)
RE	Pauly-Wissowa, *Real-Encyclopädie der classischen Altertumswissenschaft*
RhM	*Rheinisches Museum für Philologie*
ZPE	*Zeitschrift für Papyrologie und Epigraphik*

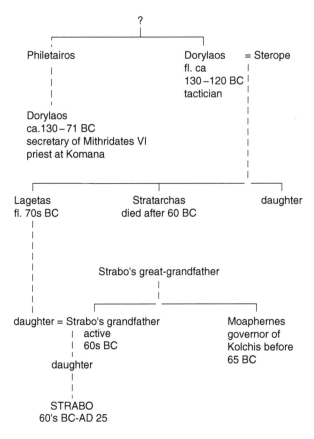

Fig. 1: The stemma of the family of Strabo

Tibios and his son Theophilos cannot be fitted exactly in the stemma. They were both cousins of Strabo's maternal grandfather (and thus cousins of Strabo himself), and were executed in the early 60s BC.

Structural analysis of the Geography

Books 1–2:   Introduction, history of geography, and scientific analysis of the earth

Book 1:   Introduction and predecessors

Part 1. Introduction and purpose of the work
Part 2. Homeric geography
Part 3. Siltation, deposition, and other changes to the earth
Part 4. The surface of the earth

Book 2:   Further Discussion of Predecessors

Part 1. The plan of the inhabited world
Part 2. Poseidonios and the zones
Part 3. Polybios and Poseidonios: The zones and the Ocean
Part 4. Polybios and the Internal Sea
Part 5. The nature of the inhabited world

Books 3–4:   The West

Book 3:   Iberia

Part 1. Introduction and coastal Tourdetania
Part 2. Interior Tourdetania
Part 3. Lusitania
Part 4. Coastal Iberia
Part 5. The islands

Book 4:   Transalpine Keltike

Part 1. Introduction and Narbonitis
Part 2. Aquitania

Books 12–14:   Anatolia

Book 12:   *Central and northern Anatolia*

[an uncertain amount of the start of Book 12 is lost]
Part 1. Introduction to Kappadokia
Part 2. Kappadokia (continued)
Part 3. Paphlagonia and Pontos
Part 4. Bithynia
Part 5. Galatia
Part 6. Lykaonia
Part 7. Pisidia
Part 8. Mysia and Phrygia

Book 13:   *Northwestern and west central Anatolia*

Part 1. The Troad and northern Aiolis
Part 2. Lesbos
Part 3. The remainder of Aiolis
Part 4. Pergamon and Lydia

Book 14:   *Southern Anatolia and Cyprus*

Part 1. Ionia
Part 2. Karia and Rhodes
Part 3. Lykia
Part 4. Pamphylia
Part 5. Kilikia
Part 6. Cyprus

Books 15–17:   The Far East, Egypt, and Libya

Book 15:   *Indike and the Persian plateau*

Part 1. Indike
Part 2. Ariane
Part 3. Persis

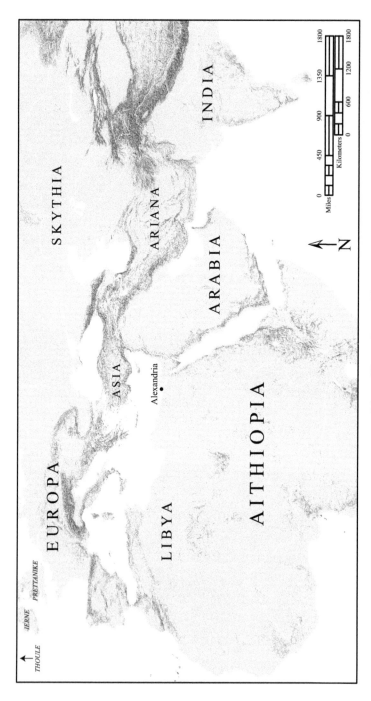

Map 1: The ancient world

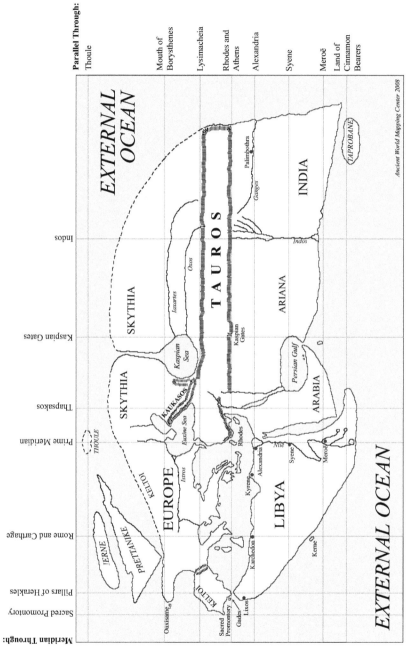

Parallel Through:

Thoule

Mouth of Borysthenes

Lysimacheia

Rhodes and Athens

Alexandria

Syene

Meroë
Land of Cinnamon Bearers

EXTERNAL OCEAN

EXTERNAL OCEAN

TAPROBANE

INDIA

Palimbothra

Ganges

Indos

ARIANA

TAUROS

Oxos

Iaxartes

SKYTHIA

Kaspian Gates

Kaspian Sea

Kaspian Gates

KAUKASOS

SKYTHIA

Euxine Sea

Rhodes

Persian Gulf

ARABIA

Thapsakos

Prime Meridian

THOULE

KELTOI

EUROPE

Istros

Alexandria

Syene

Meroë

Nile

Kyrene

LIBYA

Keme

Rome and Carthage

IERNE

PRETTANIKE

Oxisima

KELTOI

Sacred Promontory

Gades

Likos

Karchedon

Pillars of Herakles

Sacred Promontory

Meridian Through:

Ancient World Mapping Center 2008

Map 2:   The inhabited world in Hellenistic times

Introduction

1. The life of Strabo

All that is known about the life of Strabo is the information that he himself provided in his *Geography*.[1] Not even his full name is preserved, only "Strabo" (actually "Strabon" in the Greek of the sources).[2] Strabon/Strabo could be either a Roman cognomen or a Greek personal name, meaning, in both languages, "Squinter."[3] Yet early citations of the Greek name are rare and dubious, and do not predate the third century BC,[4] when Roman names were already becoming known in the eastern Mediterranean. Although there is the remote possibility that "Strabo" was the geographer's Greek birth name, this seems unlikely. It is more probable that he had a typical Anatolian Greek name, perhaps one of the seven other male names extant from his family (Dorylaos, Philetairos, Lagetas, Stratarchas, Moaphernes, Tibios, and Theophilos).

The geographer's known name was probably from the common Roman cognomen Strabo, first documented with M. Licinius Strabo, military

---

[1] The bibliography on Strabo and his *Geography* is enormous, and only works relevant to the overall composition are cited in this Introduction. The modern editions of the text are discussed below (p. 29). See also Katherine Clarke, *Between Geography and History: Hellenistic Constructions of the Roman World* (Oxford, 1999), esp. 193–336; Johannes Engels, *Augusteische Oikumene Geographie und Universal-Historie im Werk Strabons von Amaseia* (Stuttgart, 1999); Strabo, *Géographie* (ed. Germaine Aujac, François Lasserre, and Raoul Baladié, Paris, 2003), 1: "Introduction générale"; Germaine Aujac, *Strabon et la science de son temps* (Paris, 1966), 221–309; Strabo, *Geographica: Strabon von Amaseia 4* (ed. Wolfgang Aly, Bonn, 1957); E. Honigmann, "Strabon von Amaseia" (#3), *RE* 2. ser. 4 (1931), 76–155; E. H. Bunbury, *A History of Ancient Geography* (London, 1883), esp. pp. 209–337.

[2] *PIR* S673. For convenience, the form "Strabo" is used throughout this edition. References to the *Geography* appear in parentheses in the introduction and in square brackets in the translation.

[3] Pliny, *Natural History* 11.150. But the Greek term seems later than the Latin, and was first documented in medical terminology of the second century AD (Soranos 1.9.52), whereas the Latin was cited as early as the first century BC (Cicero, *Natura deorum* 1.80; Horace, *Satires* 1.3.44). Thus it is probable that the Roman cognomen entered Greek as a descriptive adjective.

[4] The earliest known is from Thasos (*IG* 12.8.294): *A Lexicon of Greek Personal Names* (ed. P. M. Fraser and E. Matthews, Oxford, 1987–), vol. 1, p. 413; vol. 3a, p. 403; vol. 4, p. 317.

tribune of 178 BC.[5] Others with this cognomen included Cn. Pompeius
Strabo (consul 89 BC and the father of Cn. Pompeius Magnus; cf. 5.1.7), and
Julius Caesar Strabo (quaestor in 96 BC and the great-uncle of the Dictator).
It is impossible, however, to determine with certainty where the geographer
might have fit into the inter-related families (which, in the Roman fashion,
were not limited to blood relatives) that used this cognomen. The most
likely branch was that of Seius Strabo, whose members included Aelius
Gallus, prefect of Egypt in the 20s BC, under whom the geographer Strabo
served. Aelius Gallus seems to have adopted Seius Strabo, himself prefect
of Egypt during the reign of Tiberius and father of the notorius Sejanus
(actually L. Aelius Seianus). It is by no means certain, but there is a high
degree of probability that the geographer Strabo was adopted by Aelius
Gallus,[6] yet took part of his name from the family of Seius Strabo, an
example of the common procedure of using names from two closely related
families. Thus, assuming that "Strabo" was the geographer's Roman cognomen, his full name would have been his unknown Greek name coupled with
Aelius Strabo.[7] Yet it is ultimately impossible to tell whether the geographer
had the name Strabo as his birth name or as an adoptive Roman cognomen,[8]
or indeed both, although it would be an odd coincidence if his birth and
adoptive names were the same.[9]

Strabo's birth date falls within a narrow range in the latter 60s BC. He
saw P. Servilius Vatia Isauricus (consul 79 BC), who died at the age of ninety
in 44 BC.[10] Strabo's acquaintance with Isauricus (12.6.2) suggests that he
was an adult – or at least well into adolescence – by that year. Isauricus spent
his last years in Rome, and thus Strabo was probably in the city by the early

---

[5] Livy 41.2.9. For others with the name, see Iiro Kajanto, *The Latin Cognomina* (*CHL* 36.2, 1965), 239.

[6] Interestingly, however, he had little favorable to say about the man who seems to have been his
patron: Aelius Gallus was not only responsible for the disastrous Arabian expedition – something
perfectly obvious in Strabo's account despite attempts to blame it on the Nabataean Syllaios
(16.4.22–4) – but the expedition itself caused a revolt in Aithiopia (due to the lengthy absence
from Egypt of so many Roman soldiers, 17.1.54). Moreover, Gallus had a charlatan, a certain
Chairemon, in his entourage (17.1.29).

[7] On this issue, see G. W. Bowersock, *Augustus and the Greek World* (Oxford, 1965), 128–9. There are
numerous precedents for taking names from two connected families: M. Antonius Lepidus and
C. Julius Lepidus, among others, are documented from the Augustan period.

[8] Sarah Pothecary, "Strabo the Geographer: His Name and Its Meaning," *Mnemosyne* 4th ser. 52 (1999),
691–704.

[9] The name occurs in Greek from the Bosporan city of Gorgippia (Fraser and Matthews, *Lexicon*,
vol. 4, p. 317), one of the most remote Greek settlements, in AD 41, a little more than a decade after the
geographer's death. Gorgippia was well known to him (11.2.10) and was part of the kingdom of
Mithridates VI, whom his family served for many years: it is possible that the existence of this rare
name at this locality reveals a descendant of the geographer.

[10] For details of his career see Karl-Ludwig Elvers, "P. S. Vatia Isauricus," *BNP* 13 (2008), 331.

40s BC. Although his use of "saw" (rather than "knew") to describe the encounter is weak, he probably "saw" many famous people, and it is hard to imagine why he singled out Isauricus unless the contact were of particular importance.[11]

Therefore Strabo was born no later than around 60 BC, perhaps a few years earlier. He frequently used the phrase "our times" to indicate an era after the late 60s BC. These years, which included the eastern campaigns of Pompeius in 65–62 BC and the death of Mithridates VI in 63 BC, with the resultant collapse of the Pontic kingdom, were great turning points in the history of Anatolia and the eastern Mediterranean and seminal events in Strabo's world view: Pompeius is mentioned over fifty times in the *Geography* and Mithridates VI over thirty. "Our times" is not a precise datum for events in the *Geography*,[12] but it is clear that Pompeius' campaigns in the east and the death of Mithridates VI served as a convenient dividing line between the past and the present, the latter being, among other things, Strabo's own era. The best evidence, then, is that he was born between 65 and 60 BC, and thus was close in age both to the emperor Augustus and Kleopatra VII.[13]

There is no doubt as to his place of birth: he told his readers more than once that his hometown was Amaseia (modern Amasya) in Pontos (12.3.15, 12.3.38–9), which had served as a royal residence for the duration of the original Pontic kingdom and had been turned over to Roman control about the time of Strabo's birth, events in which his family was involved. Strabo's description of the city (12.3.39) remains vivid today, and the modern visitor cannot fail to be impressed by its location deep in the dramatic canyon of the Iris River (modern Yeşil Irmak), with the royal tombs rising up the steep slopes opposite the city.

Strabo's background was distinguished.[14] His family had lived in Amaseia for many years, and can be traced back four generations to the brothers Philetairos and Dorylaos (Strabo's great-great-grandfather). Dorylaos was a military tactician and a close associate of Mithridates V Euergetes (ruled 152–120 BC). Relatively late in his reign, the king sent Dorylaos to Thrace, Greece proper, and Crete to enlist mercenaries. While on Crete, Dorylaos

[11] On the problems, see Katherine Clarke, "In Search of the Author of Strabo's *Geography*," *JRS* 87 (1997), 92–110, esp. 101.

[12] Sarah Pothecary, "The Expression 'Our Times' in Strabo's *Geography*," *CP* 92 (1997) 235–46.

[13] Pothecary, "Our Times," 235–46, would argue for a later date, but fails to take into account the matter of Isauricus.

[14] See the stemma on p. x, and Margherita Cassia, "La famiglia di Strabone di Amaseia tra fedeltà mitridatica e tendenze filoromane," *MediterrAnt* 3 (2000) 211–37; G. W. Bowersock, "La patria di Strabone," in *Strabone e l'Asia Minore* (ed. A. M. Biraschi and G. Salmeri, Naples 2000) 15–23.

was chosen to lead Knossian forces in a war against Gortyna, which he prosecuted successfully. Shortly thereafter he learned of the king's death and decided not to return to Pontos. He was greatly honored in Knossos and chose to stay there, marrying a Makedonian woman named Sterope. They had three children: Lagetas (Strabo's great-grandfather), Stratarchas, and a daughter (10.4.10).

Dorylaos' nephew, also named Dorylaos, was a close companion of the new king, Mithridates VI Eupator, who came to the throne in 120 BC. Mithridates was only a boy when he inherited the kingship, and he and Dorylaos were raised together, with the latter becoming an important member of the court: he was both the king's secretary and priest at the famous sanctuary of Pontic Komana (12.3.33).[15] In the First Mithridatic War (89–85 BC), Dorylaos was detailed to take 80,000 men to Greece and to give assistance to the king's commander Archelaos, who was badly pressed by L. Cornelius Sulla.[16] Dorylaos landed at Chalkis and occupied Boiotia, and provoked Sulla into battle, but before long the Romans defeated the Pontic forces at Orchomenos. Dorylaos was also assigned to bring the island of Chios under control, but no details are known and the evidence is contradictory.[17] He continued in the service of the king, but in time allegedly attempted to revolt. The account is confused, and in fact this revolutionary spirit may have been a family myth, because Dorylaos seems still to have been with the king at the battle of Kabeira (near Amaseia) in 71 BC, where he was killed.[18]

His three cousins, the three children of his uncle Dorylaos, had been favored by Mithridates VI after their father's death and had moved from Knossos to Pontos. Little is known about the unnamed daughter or the second son Stratarchas, but the elder son, Lagetas (Strabo's great-grandfather), suggested to the Romans that he would lead a revolt against Mithridates VI if he were made ruler of Pontos (10.4.10), demonstrative of the deteriorating conditions of the last years of Mithridates VI and the abandonment of him by the local aristocracy. Yet this did not happen, and the family survived in reduced circumstances.

Also important at the court of Mithridates VI was Moaphernes, a great-uncle of the geographer, who had been made governor of Kolchis and was involved in mobilizing naval forces during the wars (11.2.18), but after the king's death he was not retained in his governorship. Strabo's grandfather,

---

[15] *OGIS* 372.   [16] Appian, *Mithridatic Wars* 49.
[17] Memnon (*FGrHist* #434), F23; see also Appian, *Mithridatic Wars* 46.   [18] Plutarch, *Lucullus* 17.3.

whom the geographer did not name,[19] also revolted in the last years of the Pontic kingdom, evidently because the king had killed his cousin Tibios and the latter's son Theophilos (12.3.33). Strabo's grandfather caused fifteen fortresses to revolt from the king, but he never received recognition for this from the Romans. The family believed that the matter became tangled in the rivalry between L. Licinius Lucullus, who had been given the command against Mithridates in 74 BC, and Pompeius, who succeeded him in 65 BC. Pompeius, it was felt, would not support anyone who had been associated with Lucullus, and, moreover, convinced the Senate not to ratify Lucullus' acts, which would have included recognition of those who had helped him.

Strabo was born around the time that the Pontic dynasty collapsed with the death of Mithridates VI in 63 BC. As a boy or young man he was able to visit with his great-grandfather's brother Stratarchas, who was very old and was probably the major source for family history (10.4.10). The family seems to have survived the regime change, but did not retain its status under the Romans and left Pontos. Strabo was only an infant at the time of the Roman takeover, and accompanied his family in moving to Nysa in Karia, where they may have had relatives.[20] Nysa was an important cultural and intellectual center, and it was here that Strabo began his education, perhaps in the late 50s BC.

At Nysa Strabo encountered the extremely elderly Aristodemos (14.1.48), from a family of scholars whose patriarch was Menekrates, a student of Aristarchos of Samothrake, the notable philologist who had been librarian at Alexandria in the 150s BC. Aristarchos was one of the first to make critical editions of Greek poetry, especially Homer, a talent that he passed on to his student Menekrates, and the latter to his son Aristodemos, Strabo's teacher. Aristodemos taught Strabo rhetoric and grammar, and, one suspects, Homeric criticism. He may also have given Strabo some connections in Rome, as he had been tutor to the children of Pompeius.

Another teacher was Xenarchos of Kilikian Seleukeia. He left Seleukeia early in his career, and most of his teaching was in Alexandria, Athens, and Rome (14.5.4). At Rome he would become a member of the Augustan

---

[19] Oddly, Strabo named neither his father nor either grandfather, and, in fact, did not mention anyone on his father's side, unless one accepts a variant reading at 12.3.33. All the distinguished ancestors he enumerated were on his mother's side, an unexplained hint at family dynamics.

[20] A certain P. Servilius Strabo, who was a friend of both Cicero and of Ti. Claudius Nero (the father of the emperor Tiberius), was associated with Nysa and was in the city in 51 BC (Cicero, *Letters to Friends* 13.64; see G. C. Richards, "Strabo: the Anatolian Who Failed of Roman Recognition," *G&R* 10 [1941], 79–90, esp. 81–2). If Servilius Strabo were a relative, it raises the interesting possibility that early in life the geographer had a contact with the future imperial family.

intellectual circle. A Peripatetic in outlook, he critiqued the works of
Aristotle and developed his own ideas about motion. There was also
Athenodoros (16.4.21), almost certainly the Stoic scholar from Tarsos who
was the teacher of Octavian,[21] and who would have been a primary source
for the Stoicism that pervades Strabo's writings.[22] Strabo also studied
Aristotelian philosophy and Stoicism with Boethos of Sidon (16.2.24).[23]

Obviously Strabo did not list all his teachers, and the places and dates of
study are uncertain, as are many curriculum details. But as a young man
he had wide-ranging association with the Greek intellectual elite of the era,
many of whom would teach, or had taught, the most prominent people
in Rome. Strabo's studies began at Nysa and then continued in Rome:
his contacts would have eased his ability to move into Greek and Roman
intellectual circles when he came to that city. In Rome he may have come
to know Timagenes of Alexandria, the outstanding Greek historian of the
era (4.1.13, 15.1.57), as well as a younger generation of developing scholars,
such as Nikolaos of Damascus, Dionysios of Halikarnassos, Krinagoras
of Mytilene, and Juba II, the future king of Mauretania, all of whom were
mentioned in the *Geography*.[24] There was also Tyrannion of Amisos (12.3.16),
a grammarian and the cataloger of the library of Aristotle and Theophrastos
(13.1.54). Tyrannion had been established in Rome and well connected to
the Roman elite since before Strabo was born. Of particular interest is that
Tyrannion had some reputation as a geographer, as Cicero had noted as early
as 59 BC,[25] and thus he might have been one of those who pointed Strabo in
that direction. Another academic acquaintance was the poet and historian
Diodoros of Sardeis (13.4.9).

Strabo also took advantage of the cultural opportunities of the city,
including a visit to the temple of Ceres, admiring its painting of Dionysos
by Aristeides of Thebes (8.6.23), one of the works of art that L. Mummius
had brought from Corinth a century previously. The temple of Ceres, on
the lower slopes of the Aventine at the edge of the Circus Maximus, was a

---

[21] Dio 52.36.4.

[22] On Strabo as a Stoic, see Jérôme Laurent, "Strabon et la philosophie stoïcienne," *ArchPhilos* 71
(2008), 111–27; Alexander Jones, "The Stoics and the Astronomical Sciences," in *The Cambridge
Companion to the Stoics* (ed. Brad Inwood, Cambridge, 2003), 328–44, esp. 342–4; Germaine Aujac,
"Strabon et le stoïcisme," *Diotima* 11 (1983), 17–29; W. Aly, "Der Geograph Strabon als Philosoph," in
Miscellanea critica 1 (Leipzig, 1964), 9–19.

[23] Diogenes Laertios 7.54, 143, 148–9.

[24] Dionysios (14.2.16), Krinagoras (13.2.3), and Juba were cited in passing (6.4.2, 17.3.7, 12) and Nikolaos
was actually quoted (15.1.73). See also Bowersock, *Augustus*, 126–7.

[25] Cicero, *Letters to Atticus* #26.

notable depository of art.[26] Strabo's visit was before 31 BC, when both the temple and the painting burned.[27]

Exactly when Strabo moved from Nysa (or elsewhere in Anatolia) to Rome is uncertain. He was probably in the city by 44 BC (the death of Isauricus). He may have seen some of the events surrounding the death of Julius Caesar in March of that year[28] and he obviously was there before 31 BC, as well as when he witnessed the execution of the brigand Selouros (6.2.6), an event of the latter 30s BC.[29] Whether these datum points manifest continuous residence in the city from the mid-40s BC into the late 30s BC cannot be proved. He studied there, became acquainted with the core of Greek scholars and students there, and probably gained some access to the Roman elite. Perhaps at this time he also came into contact with Aelius Gallus and was formally adopted into his family. And during these years he completed the education that he had begun in Anatolia, becoming well grounded in philology (especially Homeric studies), history, geography, and philosophy (oriented toward Stoicism but with extensive Peripatetic training). These were disciplines that would determine his future career. And probably by the 30s BC he had begun to write. He started with a biography of Alexander the Great (2.1.9), parts of which ended up in Books 11, 15, and 16 of the *Geography*.[30] This was a good beginning for a young scholar, and it certainly assisted him in learning geography. He then wrote a history of events "after Polybios," his *Historical Commentaries*. "After Polybios" meant both intellectually and chronologically (after 146 BC). It was forty-three books long. Nineteen fragments survive, the latest describing events in Judaea during 37 BC, and its terminal date may have been 29 BC, the end of the civil war.[31] This work, over twice the length of the *Geography*, serves to remind one that Strabo was in many ways more historian than geographer, something apparent in the historical nature of much of the latter work, especially its valuable material about Anatolia in the first century BC.

---

[26] L. Richardson Jr., *A New Topographical Dictionary of Ancient Rome* (Baltimore, Md., 1992), 80–1.

[27] Dio 50.10.3.   [28] Strabo, *Historical Commentaries*, F19 (= Plutarch, *Caesar* 63).

[29] K. M. Coleman, "Fatal Charades: Roman Executions Staged as Mythological Enactments," *JRS* 80 (1990), 44–73, esp. 53–4.

[30] For example, at 15.2.3 there is an abrupt change from the ethnography of Asia to details of Alexander's expedition, lasting through Section 7. For the *Deeds of Alexander*, see Paul Pédech, "Strabon histoirien d'Alexandre," *GB* 2 (1974), 129–45.

[31] *Historical Commentaries*, T2 (= *Suda*, "Polybios"), F18 (= Josephus, *Jewish Antiquities* 15.8). Josephus identified the author as "Strabo of Kappadokia" (F6, 10, 13, 14, 16, 18), but this is probably not particularly significant, as there was a tendency to use "Kappadokia" to mean much of Anatolia.

Strabo travelled extensively although his scholarly activities may not have been the ultimate reason for his travels. Yet they certainly assisted in his research. He told the readers of the *Geography* about their range:

> Now I will speak of where I have gone by land and sea, and what has been entrusted to the accounts or writings of others. I have gone west from Armenia as far as the regions of Tyrrhenia opposite Sardo, and south from the Euxeinos as far as the boundaries of Aithiopia. You could not find another among the geographers who has travelled over a much farther extent than I have said, for those who have covered more of the western portions have not touched as much of the east, and those in the opposite situation are behind in the west. It is the same in the case of the south and the north [2.5.11].

Although there is a certain polemic tone – one has the feeling that he is commenting on a specific author who is not identified – if the passage is to be taken literally it means that Strabo had visited the entire eastern Mediterranean from Italy east, and far into the interior of western Asia. Travels in Tyrrhenia and the Upper Nile are reflected in the text (5.2.6, 17.1.50). There is no specific reference to having visited the Euxeinos (Black Sea), but such was hardly necessary, as the sea was only a short distance from his hometown of Amaseia and most of its littoral had been part of the Pontic kingdom that his family had served for so long.

Armenia is the most problematic. In Strabo's day, much of the Greco-Roman contact with the territory was military. The region was unstable during most of his lifetime, beginning with the expeditions of Pompeius at the time of his birth, and then Antonius' difficulties in the 30s BC, followed by a lengthy period of rival territories and dynasts. Strabo was fully acquainted with the literature on the region: he made extensive use of Pompeius' chronicler Theophanes (11.2.2, 11.5.1, 11.14.4, 11.14.11, 12.3.28), as well as the notorious Quintus Dellius (11.13.3), who recorded the expeditions of Antonius. Yet it is likely that his personal experience with Armenia was limited to the extreme western regions around the upper Euphrates, the so-called Lesser Armenia, which during his later years was part of the Pontic kingdom of Pythodoris (12.3.28–9).

Some of his travels, such as those in southern Anatolia, occurred early in his life. But most of them were probably after he finished his education. The few that can be dated were in the 20s BC. Yet analysis of them is difficult, because of a lack of diagnostic criteria for determining whether a descriptive passage in the *Geography* is from autopsy or merely from an uncredited source which itself was autoptic, a difficulty in analyzing travel accounts in

Greek literature since that of Herodotos.[32] All topographic authors reflect autopsy without the use of the first person. Strabo's discussion of Egypt is a case in point. First there is a vivid and full description of Alexandria (17.1.6–10), a town that he lived in "for a long time" [2.3.5]. It is hard to imagine that the account is not Strabo's own, but the first person is never used. A voyage up the Nile follows (17.1.14–54), clearly an eyewitness report throughout – although with occasional citation of other sources – but the first person is not introduced until Section 24, in a discussion of lengths of measurement, and then not again until Section 29, when Strabo is at Helioupolis. In fact the first person seems to have been dropped into the narrative irrelevantly and idly, something apparent throughout the *Geography*. Strabo saw the art in the temple of Artemis at Ephesos (14.1.23) but did not record a visit to any other Ionian city, an improbability. His account of Armenia – scattered through Book 11 – has no first person. Thus first person may be valuable in telling where Strabo was but its omission has no meaning at all, and one must assume that the specifics of Strabo's travels were far more extensive than he revealed.

Notices of other journeys are scattered throughout the *Geography*. Strabo was on the obscure Kykladic island of Gyaros when his ship took on a local fisherman whom the villagers had chosen to petition Octavian, who was at Corinth at the time, returning from Egypt to Rome after the deaths of Kleopatra VII and Antonius (10.5.3). This was in the summer of 29 BC.[33] But as is usually the case with Strabo's personal anecdotes, the incident lacks context and the reader never learns why Strabo was crossing the Aigaion that summer. He too may have been on his way to Corinth, a city that he spent time in, climbing Acrocorinth (8.6.19).

Another datable part of his career concerns Egypt. He lived in Alexandria a long time – one would expect this from a scholar – part of which was on the staff of Aelius Gallus, the second prefect of Egypt and probably his Roman patron (2.5.12, 17.1.29–50). C. Cornelius Gallus, the first prefect, had run into difficulty for a variety of reasons and was removed from office, probably in 27 BC.[34] He was then replaced by Aelius Gallus, who made the voyage up the Nile and then a futile Arabian expedition (16.4.22–4) that took over a year: eight months' travel time as well as many additional months sitting at White Village. The Nile voyage would have been a normal

---

[32] For the problems in determining autopsy in an ancient author, see Paul W. Wallace, *Strabo's Description of Boiotia: A Commentary* (Heidelberg, 1979), 168–72.

[33] Dio 51.21.1; Meyer Reinhold, *From Republic to Principate* (Atlanta, Ga., 1988), 155.

[34] Dio 53.23; A. Stein, *Die Präfekten von Ägypten in der Römischen Kaiserzeit* (Bonn, 1950), 14–17.

reconnaissance for a new official, so it was probably in the latter part of 27 BC or early in the following year. Strabo's participation in this expedition, providing so rich an exposure to geographical and cultural lore, may have given him the idea to write about geography. The Arabian expedition was dated to Augustus' tenth consulship (24 BC), but since it took longer than a year, it could have begun as early as the summer of 26 BC.[35] Nothing else is known about Aelius Gallus' career, although his term of office ended soon thereafter because his successor P. Petronius undertook two campaigns in Aithiopia by 21 BC (17.1.54). These were against the Aithiopian queen, Kandake, who sent envoys to Augustus on Samos, where the Princeps spent the winter of 21–20 BC.[36] Strabo stayed in Egypt into Petronius' tenure, perhaps not in any official capacity: the relatively short period that Aelius Gallus was in office (27–24 BC) seems hardly to qualify for the "long time" that he lived in Alexandria.

The only other datable personal vignette was a few years later, when Strabo saw Hermas, a man without arms, who was part of the presentation of Indian ambassadors to Augustus at Daphne in Syria in 20 BC (15.1.73).[37] Yet Strabo did not record where his encounter with Hermas occurred, and there is no indication that he was with Augustus in Daphne.

No other events in Strabo's career can be dated. But the *Geography* repeatedly provides glimpses of the scholar travelling through the eastern Mediterranean and the interior: witnessing the effects of a tidal wave on the eastern Egyptian coast (1.3.17), visiting a glass-blowing establishment in Alexandria (16.2.25), and seeing a very large snake in that city that had come from India (15.1.45). At some time he visited Kyrene, providing a description of his ship approaching the port (17.3.20). There were numerous cities and places in Anatolia familiar to him, as one might expect: Nysa (14.1.48), the sacred city of Komana in Kappadokia (12.2.3), the unusual geological phenomena at Hierapolis in Phrygia (13.4.14), and the striking Pyramos Gorge in Kataonia (12.2.4). He saw Persian rituals somewhere in Kappadokia (15.3.15), left a detailed description of his home town of Amaseia (12.3.15, 12.3.39, 17.1.34), and visited Ephesos (14.1.23).

Strabo also returned to Rome, probably a number of times. His description of the city has an eyewitness flavor (although the first person is absent):

---

[35] Dio 53.29; Shelagh Jameson, "Chronology of the Campaigns of Aelius Gallus and C. Petronius," *JRS* 58 (1968), 71–84; at 77.

[36] Dio 54.7.4; Jameson, "Chronology," 75; Helmut Halfmann, *Itinera principum* (Stuttgart, 1986), 158.

[37] Dio 54.9; Halfmann, *Itinera*, 158.

Most of these [buildings] are in the Campus Martius, which has received, in addition to its natural quality, adornment through foresight. The size of the field is notable, as it provides for simultaneous and indeed unhindered chariot racing and other equestrian activities, as well as for the multitude who exercise with balls, hoops, and wrestling. The constructions located around it, the soil that has grass throughout the year, and the crowns of the hills above the river, coming as far as its stream, show to the eye a stage painting, a view that it is difficult to draw away from [5.3.8].

This account also refers to the Mausoleion of Augustus, so it was written during or after its construction (28–23 BC).[38] In Rome he also saw an exhibition of sacred Egyptian crocodiles (17.1.44), as well as some of the Britons – notable for their unusual physique – who were visible in the city (4.5.2), and it was probably there that he saw a rhinoceros (16.4.15). Over time he expanded his circle of Roman contacts, making the acquaintance of Cn. Calpurnius Piso (consul 7 BC), who provided him with eyewitness information about Africa, where he had served after his consulship (2.5.33). While Strabo was resident in the city he made an excursion to Populonium and the adjacent mining district, and probably the quarries of Luna (5.2.5–6; the description is oriented on Rome), whose fine marble was just becoming popular.[39] But it is not possible to relate these vignettes of Rome and its environs to specific trips, and one suspects that he was in the city repeatedly.

Many other topographical descriptions may also have been eyewitness reports, yet there is nothing that can be dated without question to after 20 BC, although Strabo lived for half a century longer. This raises the issue of what he did during those years. He was constantly working on the *Geography*, but this hardly seems a full-time effort. There is no direct evidence of further service in the Roman government, or any other political position. There is also no record of him teaching students, tutoring the children of the Roman elite, or occupying any scholarly position such as that of a librarian, which were the standard types of employment for a Greek intellectual in the Roman world. Granted evidence of such occupations may not be extant, and in fact Strabo may have had enough inherited wealth not to need a regular income from a patron,[40] yet it seems probable that during most of these years he was busy at something in addition to writing the *Geography*.

---

[38] Richardson, *Topographical Dictionary*, 247–9.   [39] Pliny, *Natural History* 36.14.
[40] David C. Braund, "Polemo, Pythodoris and Strabo," in *Roms auswärtige Freunde in der späten Republik und im frühen Prinzipat* (ed. Altay Coskun, Göttingen, 2005), 253–70; at 254–5.

One professional interest that suggests itself is mining and quarrying, with a corresponding curiosity about geology. Mining, quarrying, and geological phenomena are mentioned remarkably frequently in the *Geography*: over a hundred times and in every book of the treatise. Strabo's descriptions include the famous mines of Iberia (3.2.3, 8–10), the quarries of North Africa (17.3.16), the gold and silver mines of India (15.1.30), and many places in between. Some of these accounts are remarkably detailed (even if derivative), such as that of the wealthy mines in southern Iberia, where there is a description of the entire process, using highly technical vocabulary with words that are rare, unique, or indigenous (3.2.8–10; see also 13.1.56). Strabo was also aware of management issues related to mining, describing the speculation in the price of gold from the eastern Alps and how the problem was only solved by a Roman takeover of the industry (4.6.12). He discussed why certain mines were no longer active (5.1.12); and he knew of developments in technology, pointing out that the original workers at the silver mines in Attika were unable to process all the silver ore because they could not heat their furnaces hot enough, but at a later date, when higher temperatures became possible, the ore in the slag heaps was reheated, producing pure silver (9.1.23). The terrible conditions that miners have always worked under were also noted: in Paphlagonia the air within the mines was so noxious that miners died faster than they could be hired (12.3.40). There is a report on the famous gold-mining ants of India (15.1.44), as well as the asphaltic peculiarities of the Dead Sea (16.2.42), and the matter of living creatures that existed deep in mines (11.14.4). Strabo visited mines that had long been abandoned (5.2.6): one wonders if he had some interest in seeing whether they could be reopened. He was also acquainted with the technical literature on the topic, quoting two mining treatises otherwise unknown: one by a certain Gorgos about India (15.1.30), and the other by Krates of Chalkis about the Lake Kopais region (9.2.18). He even expressed his distaste at writers who failed to pay proper attention to locating silver mines mentioned by Homer (12.3.22).

Related to mining, in a way, was quarrying, and here Strabo also showed an interest beyond ordinary curiosity. There are detailed descriptions of the process, especially at Luna, and how the building programs at Rome and elsewhere affected the industry (5.2.5, 5.3.11). Geology is closely connected to mining and quarrying, and Strabo was extremely interested in the formative processes of the earth. He examined the treatises of Xanthos of Lydia, Straton of Lampsakos, and Eratosthenes of Kyrene – the seminal Greek scholarship on geology – and rarely failed to point out and speculate about places that had undergone geological alteration. His early familiarity with the volcanic regions of southern Anatolia (13.4.11–15) may have been his first contact with these issues, and throughout the *Geography* there are frequent comments on changes in the earth's surface as well as a consideration of their causes: the effects of the tides and differing levels of the ocean (1.3.12), siltation (12.8.17), earthquakes (12.8.18), seashells that are far from the coast (1.3.3–4), and tidal waves as well as places once under the sea but now above it (1.3.17).

Any suggestion as to Strabo's professional interests – beyond scholarship – is highly speculative, yet it seems probable that he did something other than write the *Geography* for fifty years, and that he was in a profession that required an extensive amount of travel. His extraordinary concern for the processes of the earth, mining, and quarrying, and his knowledge of the technical vocabulary and the scholarly literature on those topics, all suggests that Strabo's professional orientation was in this direction, and that he had more than a casual connection with the vast mining and quarrying industry of the early Roman empire.[41]

To be sure, Strabo had other special interests, although these may not have reached the level of professional competence. Both enology and commercial fishing seem to be particular concerns. Fishing is described in detail more than once, especially around the Strait of Messina (1.2.15–16) and in the Black Sea (12.3.11, 19). In addition, Strabo rarely failed to point out the available wines in a given region: in all he cited about forty varieties, from throughout the world, usually providing a qualitative statement.

Although the *Geography* was not designed as an artistic tour of the Greek world (unlike the efforts of Pausanias a century and a half later), Strabo nevertheless had an acute interest in art. He frequently mentioned the sculpture that was visible at the great sanctuaries, such as the Heraion on Samos (14.1.14), and named the most notable sculptors of classical Greece, providing the location of their pieces, including Pheidias (8.3.30, 9.1.16), Myron (14.1.14), Skopas (13.1.48, 14.1.20), Praxiteles (14.1.23), and Lysippos (6.3.1, 10.2.21, 13.1.19). Often he reminded his readers that many of their works had been carried off to Rome.

It is not known when Strabo began to write the *Geography*, but his own statement (1.1.23) that it followed the completion of the *Historical Commentaries* seems to imply soon afterward. Since the history was probably finished by the 20s BC, this suggests that he might have begun the *Geography* by the end of that decade. Yet the issue is complex, and depends

---

[41] On this extensive topic, see Alfred Michael Hirt, *Imperial Mines and Quarries in the Roman World* (Oxford, 2010).

on what one means by "started": collecting data (something that would have occupied much of his life), or beginning to fashion the material into coherent sections. Although it is clear that much work on the *Geography* was done after Tiberius came to power in AD 14, it is probable that Strabo had been working on the project since the latter 20s BC.[42] Thus he continued on the *Geography* for many years, until his death in the 20s AD. Much of his research may have been earlier rather than later in this period, yet he updated the treatise as long as he was able, but not consistently.[43] Thus certain sections seem frozen at a date long before the actual completion of the entire work. This is noticeable in his account of Judaea: he recorded that the ancient city of Samareia had been renamed Sebaste by Herod the Great (16.2.34), an event of 22 BC, but he did not mention the founding of Caesarea at the location of Straton's Tower twelve years later (16.2.27). Since Caesarea was to become the second largest city in the eastern Mediterranean and the main port of entry to the southern Levant, it would be difficult to ignore, and there is much in the *Geography* that is later than 10 BC. This suggests that the Judaean sections – which may in part rely on autopsy, given the full and vivid description of the Dead Sea and its unusual phenomena – were finished before 10 BC and never revised or updated. The description of Rome (5.3.7–8) largely reflects the early years of the Augustan building program but refers to the Theater of Balbus (dedicated 13 BC),[44] the Porticus Liviae (dedicated 7 BC),[45] and the death of Augustus (AD 14). Thus it seems that an original description of the 20s BC was reworked at least twice: in the last decade of the century and after the death of Augustus (the latter perhaps being only a simple insertion). The account of the mountain peoples of interior Iberia (3.3.1–8) relies for the most part on the report of the campaigns of Brutus Callaicus (consul 138 BC) – material probably obtained from Poseidonios[46] – but with an addendum at the end referring to the stationing of three legions there by Tiberius early in his reign. In fact there are several items in the *Geography* that relate to the first decade of Tiberius, such as the German campaigns of that era (7.1.4), or the death of King

---

[42] Sarah Pothecary, "Strabo, the Tiberian Author: Past, Present and Silence in Strabo's *Geography*," *Mnemosyne* 4th ser. 55 (2002), 387–438, would prefer that the *Geography* was not actually started until after AD 17, but this perhaps does not give full credit to the lengthy gestation period of complex writings.

[43] Multiple editions have been suggested (see Richards, "Strabo," 89–90), but this seems unnecessary and unlikely for a work so obscure. Another possibility is some revision after the accession of Tiberius in AD 14 (or even the death of Germanicus five years later), in order to reflect the new reality of the post-Augustan era. See Ronald Syme, *Anatolica: Studies in Strabo* (ed. Anthony Birley, Oxford, 1995), 367; Hugh Lindsay, "Syme's Anatolica and the Date of Strabo's Geography," *Klio* 79 (1997), 484–507.

[44] Dio 54.25.2.   [45] Ovid, *Fasti* 6.637–48; Dio 55.8.2.   [46] Poseidonios, F220, F224.

Archelaos of Kappadokia (12.1.4) around AD 17 or 18.[47] This suggests that much of the final shaping of the *Geography* was done during those years, yet the treatise also reflects an environment when Augustus was still in power, as well as including eyewitness accounts by Strabo (e. g. 12.2.3–4) that were almost certainly gathered during his youthful travels, as early as the 40s BC.

Where Strabo lived during his last years remains unclear. The only place that he specifically mentioned as a residence was Alexandria (2.3.5). He also had a great familiarity with Rome, but there is no evidence that it was his home after the 20s BC. In all probability he retired to Anatolia, perhaps either to his native city of Amaseia or to Sebaste, the royal seat of the Pontic queen Pythodoris (12.3.31), perhaps preferable because Amaseia had become Roman territory (12.3.39).[48] Pythodoris may have been a granddaughter of Antonius, and had inherited the kingdom of Pontos when her first husband Polemon I died about 8 BC. Close to the imperial family, she ruled for many years (probably outliving Strabo) and was treated eulogistically by the geographer ("A wise woman capable of managing the government," 12.3.29–31, 37), who may have seen her as providing intellectual encouragement. Pythodoris' father, Pythodoros, was from Nysa (14.1.42), where Strabo had received much of his education, so he may have known the future queen's family in his youth. Although socially Strabo's superior, the queen shared with the geographer a common interest and involvement in the destiny of Pontos.[49] It is conceivable that Strabo decided to retire and withdraw to his homeland after the disgrace, trial, and suicide of his friend Cn. Calpurnius Piso in AD 20, who was implicated in the peculiar circumstances surrounding the death of Germanicus in the previous year.[50]

Regardless of how much Strabo went back to his manuscript to make adjustments based on the most recent news from throughout the Empire, it all came to an end in the 20s AD. The last certain date in the *Geography* is the death of Juba II of Mauretania, a long-time associate, in AD 23 or 24.[51] The news would have had to come from Mauretania to wherever Strabo

---

[47] Tacitus, *Annals* 2.42; Dio 57.17.

[48] Other suggestions for his final home include elsewhere in Anatolia (J. G. C. Anderson, "Some Questions Bearing on the Date and Place of Composition of Strabo's *Geography*," in *Anatolian Studies Presented to Sir William Mitchell Ramsay* [ed. W. H. Buckler and W. M. Calder, Manchester, 1923], 1–13; at 12–13) or the region of Naples (Syme, *Anatolica*, 293). Neither of these is as probable as in Pontos.

[49] On Pythodoris, see Braund, "Polemo"; Richard D. Sullivan, "Dynasts in Pontus," *ANRW* 2.7 (1980), 913–30; at 920–2.

[50] For Strabo and Calpurnius Piso, see 2.5.33; see also Domitilla Campanile, "Sul ritorno in patria di Strabone," *ZPE* 154 (2005), 267–8.

[51] For the date, see Duane W. Roller, *The World of Juba II and Kleopatra Selene: Royal Scholarship on Rome's African Frontier* (London, 2003), 244–7.

was – a matter of weeks if not months – yet it provides a terminal date for the *Geography* of late AD 23 or during AD 24, perhaps even slightly later if Strabo's statement that Juba's son Ptolemaios was now ruling (17.3.7, 25) reflects the ratification of his accession by the Senate.[52] By any reckoning, Strabo was over eighty years of age – perhaps close to ninety – when he put down the *Geography* for the last time, unpublished (in the ancient sense of the term). The manuscript would disappear for a century, suggesting that Strabo was in a relatively remote place when he died.

2.   The *Geography* of Strabo

The *Geography*[53] of Strabo is a complex and varied work that often can be difficult to understand.[54] Between its beginning outline of the history of geography and its closing summary of the extent of Roman power in the 20s AD, the treatise wanders through a variety of topics, many of which can only marginally be considered geographical. These include Homeric criticism, cultic history, linguistics, biography, autobiography, Jewish religion, and the nature of Roman power. Unique and unusual words are used throughout. The text can be quite repetitive, suggesting a failure to reconcile details of its compositional history. It can also be so digressive and ambiguous that the modern reader can easily lose the thread of the discussion. The gestation period of the *Geography* – during half a century of profound change in the Mediterranean world – means that a consistent tone would have been almost impossible. Its sheer length, one of the longest extant works in Greek literature,[55] also contributes to its difficulty of comprehension. Yet it seems that Strabo was uninterested in a concise summary of world geography. He used the seminal *Geography* of Eratosthenes as his model, yet Eratosthenes' three-book structure was not an influence on Strabo, whose treatise is more than five times as long. The core of Strabo's work remains basic geography – topographic, demographic,

---

[52] Tacitus, *Annals* 4.23–6.

[53] The Greek title is most likely *Geographike*, as cited in various manuscripts, and used by Strabo in the first sentence of the work. The title was also quoted by Athenaios (3.121a), but as *Geographika*. At one point (17.1.1), however, Strabo has *Geographia*, which may be more generic. The English title *Geography*, however, is used in this edition.

[54] Of particular interest on this topic are Johannes Engels, "Die strabonische Kulturgeographie in der Tradition der antiken geographischen Schriften und ihre Bedeutung für die antike Kartographie," *OTerr* 4 (1998), 63–114, and François Lasserre, "Strabon devant l'Empire romain," *ANRW* 30 (1982–3), 867–96.

[55] The only surviving works of comparable length are the histories of Diodoros and Dio, the *Jewish Antiquities* of Josephus, and the *Deipnosophistai* of Athenaios.

and ethnographic data about the inhabited world – yet digressions into other topics are repeated and lengthy, and at times it can be difficult to imagine that the same person wrote the entire treatise.

Although the *Geography* was completed nearly two thousand years ago, much that Strabo mentioned is still accessible to the modern reader. Today one can still enjoy Serrano ham (3.4.11), Hyblaian honey (6.2.2), Falernian wine (5.3.6), retsina (4.6.2), and Jericho dates (16.2.41). The Luna marble quarries (5.2.5) became the Carrara of the Renaissance and remain busy. The present writer can testify to the unusual nature of the cicadas in south Italy (6.1.9). The peculiarities of the Dead Sea (16.2.42) are well known, and the mines in the Rio Tinto district of Spain (3.2.8–10) were active until recently. Water rights are always fought over (4.6.7). Indians still favor bright and unusual colors in their dress (15.1.30), and Druids (4.4.4–5), Corsican bandits (5.2.7), and British fogs (4.5.2) remain elements of popular culture. A surprising amount of the world of today would be familiar to Strabo.

The history of geography and the formative processes of the earth, as well as technical data (from Eratosthenes and Hipparchos) about how to measure the inhabited earth, occupy the first two books, which stand apart from the remaining fifteen. Beginning with Book 3, Strabo progressed through a survey of the inhabited world, starting at the southwest corner of the Iberian peninsula. Yet other topics always intrude. Lurking everywhere is an intense Homeric commentary; although generally geographically oriented, it can overwhelm the flow of the work. Strabo, like Eratosthenes, believed that Homer was the first geographer.[56] Although this provided a rationale for the entire *Geography*, treatment of Homeric topography was theoretically limited to those regions Homer had actually discussed (essentially mainland Greece and Anatolia, with some information on the Levant, North Africa, and southern Italy). Yet Strabo would often stretch his interpretations into regions unlikely to have been mentioned by Homer, such as Iberia (3.2.12). He felt that his topographical research validated Homeric geography, even when data contemporary to Strabo seemed to demonstrate the opposite, such as the location of Pharos in Egypt (1.2.30). Yet Strabo's argumentation is often quite incisive, as in the matter of Odysseus and Skylla (1.2.15–16), or, more importantly, the location of Troy (13.1.5–8, 26–42). His discussions regarding Troy, as well the site of Pylos (8.3.26), are the beginning of

---

[56] See Lawrence Kim, *Homer Between History and Fiction in Imperial Greek Literature* (Cambridge, 2010), 47–84; D. M. Schenkeveld, "Strabo on Homer," *Mnemosyne* 4th ser. 29 (1976) 52–64; Aujac, *Strabon et la science*, 19–36; Francesco Prontera, *Geografia e storia nella Grecia antica* (Florence 2011), 3–14.

topographical scholarship as it is still practiced today. His critical sense was strong, yet his obsession with Homer sometimes drove it in peculiar directions,[57] and what seems an obvious error on the part of Homer would be explained away as faulty transmission of the text (1.1.7, 1.2.16). Nevertheless such an interest in Homeric scholarship and insistence on the poet's importance is to be expected: Strabo had studied at one of the great Homeric schools of his era, that of Aristodemos at Nysa (14.1.48). In fact, it is probable that early in life Strabo wrote his own Homeric commentary, on the model of those by Demetrios of Skepsis and Apollodoros of Athens – both of which were quoted frequently – and inserted portions of it into the *Geography* (e. g. 1.2.4–6). Strabo also had different editions of the Homeric poems at his disposal: the textual variants of the famous Homeric scholars Zenodotos, Zenon, Aristarchos, and Krates were regularly cited.[58]

Other intrusions appear in the treatise. Books 15 and 16, about the easternmost part of the inhabited world, are often based more on the travels of Alexander the Great rather than contemporary geographical data. His route from Baktria to the Indos and back to Babylon is outlined in detail, and later geographical information, such as the reports from the Hellenistic envoys Patrokles and Megasthenes, as well as Eratosthenes' summary, can appear much as an appendage to the description of Alexander's journey. Strabo made extensive use of the writings of those travelling with Alexander, and his account is one of the earliest extant renditions of the king's journey (only that of Diodoros is marginally earlier). In all probability this material is the remnants of Strabo's early treatise *The Deeds of Alexander* (2.1.9), and thus these portions of the *Geography* can have an anachronistic tone, grounded more in the fourth century BC than in Strabo's own era.

The *Geography* also includes components of a personal memoir. This material is scattered throughout the work but is found especially in Books 12–14 (about Anatolia) and 17 (about Egypt), places where Strabo spent a large portion of his life. His desire to recount his family history and education, as well as details about his government service in Egypt, move beyond geography and into the category of autobiography, yet are valuable in outlining the career of an educated and mobile Greek intellectual of the Augustan and early Julio-Claudian periods. Significantly few details are provided about the last half century of Strabo's life, after his Egyptian posting, which ended in the latter 20s BC. If he actually wrote a formal autobiography, it was limited to his ancestry, education, and early professional life,

---

[57] James S. Romm, *The Edges of the Earth in Ancient Thought* (Princeton, N.J., 1992) 190–4.
[58] Zenodotos: 9.2.35, 12.3.8, 25; Zenon: 1.2.34; Aristarchos: 1.2.24, 2.3.8; Krates: 1.2.24, 2.3.8.

much like the one by Augustus, which ended in 25 BC.[59] Strabo's family is of importance historically because of its closeness to the last two Pontic kings, Mithridates V and VI. Thus the *Geography* contains unique information about the final years of that dynasty and the transition to Roman control, as well as the successive era of Caesar, Antonius, and Kleopatra VII. Here the *Geography* is pure history rather than geography, and it is a major source for Anatolia in the immediate pre-Augustan period.

Short digressions on cultic practices appear frequently in the treatise. Yet in two instances Strabo's intent went beyond brief mention of a cult or cultic center. His discussion of the Aitolians breaks off at 10.3.6 for a lengthy examination of the Kouretians. Although there is some evidence that they, or people with a similar name, were an ethnic group in northwest Greece, they are better known as cultic figures who existed mythologically throughout Greece, most notably in the Cretan story of the birth of Zeus. Strabo embarked on a lengthy and intrusive discussion (10.3.7–23) of their cultic history coupled with a general examination of various mystery cults such as the Pythagoreans, Dionysos, Kybele, and others. Then the digression abruptly concludes and the geographical thread picks up at 10.4.1 where it had been interrupted. A similar theological intrusion appears in the description of the southern Levant (16.2.35–9). The topographical account of Judaea is broken off for a history of Jewish religion, concluding with a comparison of Moses and various other religious figures. Then the narrative returns to the topography of Judaea as if the digression had never occurred.

It seems that these two passages are remnants of another part of Strabo's juvenilia: a treatise on cultic practices, with a focus on those that were mystic or inspired in nature. Twice in the digression on the Kouretians (10.3.9, 23) Strabo remarked that the topic was relevant because of its theological importance, a point of view seemingly at odds with geographical theory and which appears nowhere else in the treatise, but which would be relevant in a work on mystery religions. Since one of his ancestors was priest at Pontic Komana (12.3.33), Strabo may have had an early interest in cultic practices.

Yet Strabo always remained a Homeric scholar. His citations of the Homeric poems pervade the *Geography*. They are quoted over seven hundred times, in every book of the treatise, and from every book of the *Iliad* and all but one of the *Odyssey*. In fact, the opening of the *Geography* (1.1.1–11) reads more like the beginning of a Homeric commentary.[60] Although there

---

[59] Suetonius, *Divine Augustus* 85.
[60] Moreover, the following section (1.1.12) reads like the beginning of an actual geographical treatise.

is brief and token recognition of later geographers, Strabo's outline of the inhabited world is, at this point, based totally on Homer, someone so respected that nothing could "be in conflict with him" (8.3.3), an accolade given to no other author. Strabo's intense Homeric exegesis would frequently lead to lengthy grammatical digressions, such as a long discussion of the technique of shortening of a word (apocope), where "opis" and "pedaleia" become "ope" and "peda" (8.5.3), usages that are hardly geographical.[61]

With a work that is so diverse, often frustratingly so, the modern reader can be left wondering what Strabo's purpose was in writing the *Geography*. There is no actual statement to this effect. Strabo outlined why geography was important (1.1.1), but after opening comments he immediately plunged into the history of geography and other issues such as the formation of the earth and how to measure the inhabited world. This was followed by the actual geographical discussion itself. Unlike Eratosthenes (whose treatise began with India and moved west), Strabo moved from west to east, from Iberia to India, and then back west to Egypt, following, more or less, the pattern of *The Circuit of the Earth* of Hekataios of Miletos. This may also have been designed to place Rome at the center of the inhabited world.[62] But instead of continuing west from Egypt across North Africa, the account jumps to the Atlantic coast of Africa and then returns east to finish at Kyrene, perhaps in order to end the geographical description at that great cultural center, the home of Eratosthenes the inventor of the discipline of geography. At the end of the discussion of Kyrene and its territory, there is the definitive statement "this, then, is the situation of the parts of our inhabited world" (17.3.24), immediately followed by a eulogistic summary of the Roman contribution ("since [they] have surpassed all former rulers of whom we have a record"). The final lines of the *Geography* (17.3.25) lay out the division of the world into provinces and allied kingdoms, based on the Augustan settlements of the 20s BC but updated fifty years to the situation after the accession of Ptolemaios of Mauretania in AD 24.

This ending suggests a purpose of the *Geography*: to demonstrate the present state of the inhabited world under Roman control.[63] Yet its long compositional history diffused this motivation somewhat, since things had changed so much over those fifty years, a period spanned even in the last section of the *Geography* with its simultaneous positioning in the early

---

[61] Strabo may have used the *Homeric Problems* of Zenon of Kition (Diogenes Laertios 7.4), a work in five books, as a source.

[62] Clarke, *Between*, 210–28.

[63] For Strabo's position in the Roman world, see Lasserre, *Strabon devant L'Empire romain*, 867–96.

years of Augustus and the middle years of Tiberius. In seeing a world that functioned smoothly under Roman power Strabo was guided to some extent by Polybios – one of his most-cited authors – whose *Histories* sought to recount the rise of Rome in the second century BC.[64] Strabo himself had written his *Historical Commentaries* "after Polybios" (F1 = 11.9.3) and transferred this theme to the *Geography*. Polybios was a significant model for the tone of the *Geography*, and in fact Strabo's concluding statement about the great extent of Roman power (17.3.24) closely echoes Polybios' comments at the beginning of his *Histories*. Yet Strabo was not averse to criticizing Roman policy: in particular, he felt that Pompeius had been unfair to Strabo's family when he failed to honor the commitments of Lucullus regarding its role in the overthrow of Mithridates VI (12.3.33). On a less personal level, he believed that Augustus' refusal to allow his commanders to cross the Albis (Elbe) in retaliation for Germanic incursions only encouraged additional ones (7.1.4), and that the peace that had been established west of the Rhine was largely due to Roman enslavement of the locals (4.4.2). He could also be equally dismissive of Greek culture, noting that their civilization had corrupted the barbarians (7.3.7).

It remains to consider the potential audience of the *Geography*. Strabo wrote that geography was useful for those engaged in political and military activity (1.1.1). His familiarity with the writings of Julius Caesar (4.1.1) and his contact with Roman commanders such as P. Servilius Vatia Isauricus (12.6.2), Cn. Calpurnius Piso (2.5.33), and Aelius Gallus (2.5.12), as well as his family's closeness to the Pontic kings and Lucullus, would make this obvious to him. Strabo had followed this theory in writing his *Historical Commentaries* (F2 = 1.1.23), yet he also suggested that it and the *Geography* would be useful to the general public. Geography was still a relatively new discipline: despite the protestations that Homer had been the first geographer, geographical treatises had only existed for two hundred years when Strabo begin writing. The first work on the topic, by Eratosthenes, had been written in the last half of the third century BC but had not been widely disseminated.[65] Later geographical works were relatively obscure and limited in their scope, such as Hipparchos' highly technical *Against the Geography of Eratosthenes*, from the latter second century BC. As a polemic, it did not have broad appeal. The geographical treatise of Serapion of Antioch, probably slightly later than that of Hipparchos, was so inscrutable

---

[64] Polybios 1.2. He was cited nearly fifty times.
[65] Duane W. Roller, *Eratosthenes' Geography* (Princeton, N.J., 2010), 13–14, 32–3.

that Cicero could hardly understand it.[66] Agatharchides' work on the Erythraian Sea or the Homeric geographical commentaries of Apollodoros of Athens and Demetrios of Skepsis were directed toward limited issues and regions. The geographical section of Polybios' *Histories* and the treatise of Artemidoros of Ephesos, both also from the second century BC, are difficult to assess independently of Strabo, since his *Geography* is the source of many of their fragments. Polybios' geographical digression – Book 34 of his *Histories* – was probably the most accessible in Strabo's day. It was placed at 152 BC in Polybios' chronological scheme[67] and would merely have been a brief summary, far shorter than the work of Eratosthenes and hardly a detailed account of world geography. The *Geography* of Artemidoros of Ephesos, in eleven books, was probably the longest treatment of the subject to date. Written at the very end of the second century BC, it seems to have provided many distances and was perhaps more catalogue than narrative.[68] In the following century Poseidonios of Apameia produced his *On the Ocean*, which was heavily used by Strabo but presumably was limited to the Atlantic coastal regions and perhaps what was beyond.[69]

Thus since Eratosthenes there had been no wide-ranging work on geography that was total in its scope and available to the educated "general public." Strabo insisted that the readers of his own treatise should have passed a basic course in mathematics and be familiar with a globe (1.1.21). The first globe had been created by Krates of Mallos – one of Strabo's sources on the history of the earth – only slightly over a century previously (2.5.10), demonstrating that Strabo believed that his readers should be up-to-date on innovations in the discipline. Yet this "general public" is hard to define. The Roman empire was varied and diverse, and its educated population would itself be diverse. The changes in tone in the *Geography* reflect this. Like his contemporary Dionysios of Halikarnassos, Strabo could create a Greek work of broad appeal to a Roman audience anxious to enjoy the newly elevated status of Greek literature in Rome.[70] For the west (Books 3–4, 7), where Strabo had never travelled but which he had researched intensively (2.5.11), he had to rely on published material, especially Pytheas, Polybios, Poseidonios, Julius Caesar, and the reports of other

---

[66] Cicero, *Letters to Atticus* #24.

[67] F. W. Walbank, "The Geography of Polybius," *C&M* 9 (1947), 155–82; at 168–9.

[68] R. Stiehle, "Der Geograph Artemidoros von Ephesos," *Philologus* 11 (1856), 193–244.

[69] Poseidonios F49 = Strabo 2.2.1. Another work by Poseidonios, *Periploos* or *Periegesis*, is only named with certainty by Pliny (*Natural History* 1.5), and perhaps obliquely mentioned by Strabo [10.3.5], but is otherwise unknown and remains totally obscure. It is unlikely to be the same as *On the Ocean* (*Posidonius 2: The Commentary* [ed. I. G. Kidd, Cambridge, 1985] 275–6).

[70] Jorma Kaimio, *The Romans and the Greek Language* (*CHL* 64 (Helsinki, 1979) 50–2.

Roman field commanders. This part of the *Geography* is a synthesis of previous scholarly reports rather than any new topographical research, yet it brought together all the known evidence for Iberia, the Keltic regions, the Alps, and the north. It reached its final form after Germanicus' victory over the Cherouskians in AD 16 and his triumph the following year (7.1.4), and would have been written for both a Greek and Roman audience that wanted to know the history and current state of the region.

Intruding into the midst of this account of the north and west are two books (5–6) on the Italian peninsula and Sicily. These have quite a different outlook and are designed for an exclusively Greek audience. Romans of the early imperial period hardly needed to be told about the location and function of Ostia (5.2.1) or the early history of Rome (5.3.1–3). But the information might still be novel to a Greek audience, especially one that could not read Latin, and Strabo, like Diodoros of Sicily and Dionysios of Halikarnassos, was willing to illuminate Roman history and culture for Greeks. In fact the different tone of these two books suggests that they may originally have been independent of the *Geography* as a whole: a capsule ethnography and geography of Italy and Sicily for Greeks. The eulogistic summary of Roman power and Augustan peace that ends Book 6 (6.4.1–2) reads like the conclusion of a separate work.

The rest of the *Geography* (Books 8–17) would appeal to an educated general public of either Greeks or Romans. Yet the detailed discussion of Anatolia (Books 12–14) was probably designed more for Romans, providing them with a locally originated report of the changes that had taken place in this part of the world since the later second century BC. Romans would be familiar with their own accounts of these events, but the indigenous view would be different. Strabo rarely missed an opportunity to note the superiority of products from his own homeland (e.g. 3.4.15), and thus he was not a disinterested observer. In fact, he was very much involved, since his family had played a prominent role in the circumstances of the Roman acquisition of the region. He also listed the luminaries from each major city in Anatolia, a subtle reminder to the Romans of the cultural significance of his home region.[71] By contrast, the cultural brilliance of Athens was hardly mentioned (2.3.7), and he was dismissive of Roman intellectual depth (3.4.19). Yet the naming of over two hundred famous Anatolian men and women, many from Strabo's own era, as well as inclusion of his own family history, provides a biographic and hellenocentric element to the *Geography*.

---

[71] Johannes Engels, "Ἄνδρες ἔνδοξοι or 'men of high reputation' in Strabo's *Geography*," in Daniela Dueck *et al.*, *Strabo's Cultural Geography: The Making of a Kolossourgia* (Cambridge, 2006), 129–43.

Thus one of the purposes of the *Geography* was to create a framework for highlighting the cultural predominance of Strabo's own Anatolia of the first century BC. Anatolia, after all, was the site of Troy, the ancestral home of the Romans, and ever since the Trojan War Anatolia had retained a supreme position in history. This continued in Strabo's own era, when the region produced intimates or teachers of Pompeius Magnus, Julius Caesar, Cicero, and the Princeps himself: in other words, of the great Romans of the period. Moreover, Strabo did not allow his audience to forget that Anatolia had also produced Strabo and his own teachers. Anatolia, from the time of the Trojan War to that of Strabo, had made the Roman empire what it was.

3. The sources of the *Geography*

One of the most fascinating elements of the *Geography* is the wide range of sources that Strabo used.[72] Nearly two hundred are mentioned, covering the entire extent of Greek literature from Homer to Strabo's coeval Nikolaos of Damascus. Some Latin literature is also cited. Most major Greek authors familiar today who were contemporary or previous to Strabo were consulted, including epic and lyric poets, tragedians, comic poets, historians, orators, geographers, and natural scientists. Homer alone was quoted over seven hundred times, often in variant readings with a discussion of the scholarship on a particular passage. As expected, geographical authors predominate: after Homer the most commonly cited are Eratosthenes, Poseidonios, Hipparchos, and the geographical portions of the histories of Ephoros and Polybios. In fact, the geographical writings of these five would largely be unknown were it not for Strabo's use of them. He also quoted extensively from *periploi*, the coastal sailing reports that have been a staple of seafaring nations from ancient to modern times. Strabo was able to recover little-known ones, presumably in Alexandria, and frequently fell into their diction (especially at 14.3.1–8 and 16.4.4–14).[73]

More surprising, perhaps, is his familiarity with authors who are not generally considered geographical, but who provided essential nuggets. He used the extensive topographical data in the works of Hesiod, who knew an amazingly wide world from the Istros (Danube) and Phasis (Rioni) to the

---

[72] See the useful list of sources (arranged regionally) in Clarke, *Between*, 374–8, and also Federica Cordano, "Sulle fonti di Strabone per i *Progolomena*," *PP* 61 (2006), 401–16.

[73] Only a few survive from antiquity (the best examples are that of Hanno and the *Periploos of the Erythraian Sea*). See further, Clarke, *Between*, 202.

Nile and the Rhone. There was also material in the plays of Aischylos, Sophokles, and Euripides, whose geographical range – largely quoted from tragedies now lost as well as the *Prometheus Bound* and the *Bacchants* – is astonishing. Other poets are also well represented, among whom are Archilochos, Sappho, Alkaios, and Pindar. There are pre-Sokratic philosophers such as Anaximandros, Parmenides, and Empedokles, as well as the familiar names from classical Athens, not only the tragedians but Herodotos, Thoukydides, Plato, Demosthenes, and Aristotle. Scientific and philosophical authors abound, including, in addition to Anaximandros and Parmenides, Xanthos of Lydia, Demokritos, and Straton of Lampsakos. Technical treatises are also represented, such as that of Gorgos the mining engineer. The comic poet Menandros is cited a number of times. In addition to Sappho, whom Strabo called "an extraordinary person" (13.2.3), he cited another woman author, Hestiaia of Alexandria (13.1.36), who wrote on the *Iliad* and seems to have travelled in the Troad.

In fact, Strabo was quite sensitive to women of accomplishment. In addition to the details about Sappho, Hestiaia, and Pythodoris, there is information about Arete, head of the Kyrenaian school of philosophy in the early fourth century BC (17.3.22), as well as discussions of Queen Amastris of Herakleia, who founded the city of Amastris (12.3.10) and Queen Aba of Olbe in Anatolia, an ally of Kleopatra VII (14.5.10). Moreover there is much unique material about Kleopatra herself (13.1.30, 14.5.3, 17.1.11), including the earliest historical account of her death and the compelling suggestion that she may have died by poison rather than an asp bite (17.1.10). Strabo's interest in women of power and ability may reflect his upbringing: he mentioned his mother and her family (10.4.10, 11.2.18, 12.3.33) but never his father or his family, and thus may have been exposed at an early age to a woman's view of history.

Needless to say Strabo consulted many historians in preparing the *Geography*, in particular obscure ones from the Hellenistic period. The expansive reach of Greek exploration would be virtually unknown were it not for Strabo: he is the primary source for the Arctic voyage of Pytheas of Massalia and the Arabian coastal explorations of Anaxikrates and Androsthenes, and he provided some of the earliest extant and most extensive information on numerous people who explored India with and after Alexander the Great. In fact, the writings of thirteen companions of Alexander are cited,[74] as well as

---

[74] Anaximenes, Androsthenes, Aristoboulos, Gorgos, Kallisthenes, Kleitarchos, Krateros, Kyrsilos, Medios, Nearchos, Onesikritos, Polykleitos, and Ptolemaios (I). For their careers, see the entries in Waldmar Heckel, *Who's Who in the Age of Alexander the Great* (Malden, Mass., 2006).

others in the king's circle who did not join in the expedition.[75] That Strabo was continuing to examine new scholarship as he wrote the *Geography* is shown by his inclusion of the research of his contemporaries such as Timagenes of Alexandria, Nikolaos of Damascus, and Juba II of Mauretania.

Moreover, the richness of the *Geography* is demonstrated by the number of authors Strabo quoted who are unknown elsewhere, such as Gorgos (15.1.30), who seems to have prospected in India for gold and silver, Daes of Kolonai (13.1.62), who wrote on the history of his native city, or Megillos (15.1.18), who described the process of planting rice. The *Geography* is the only source for the writings of King Attalos I of Pergamon (13.1.44), who described the flora of the Troad, and those of King Pausanias of Sparta (8.5.5), who critiqued the laws of Lykourgos. Some of these obscure authors were certainly examined derivatively by Strabo, but nevertheless they are another indication of the depth of his research and his unparalleled use of sources.

Latin literature was also accessible to him. Although his citation of it was limited, this was largely due to a lack of material, rather than a reluctance to do research in Latin. Unlike Plutarch a century later, who was frank about his lack of fluency in the language,[76] and whose professional career, even in Rome, was conducted in Greek, Strabo seems to have had no such issues. In fact, knowledge of Latin may have been a necessity for gathering data on Italy, or on Iberia and the Keltic world, where the field reports of Roman commanders were essential. He regularly explained Latin terms to his Greek audience (e. g. 3.1.4, 9, 5.3.6).

Strabo cited seven Roman authors. Two of them (Q. Fabius Pictor and C. Acilius) are from an earlier era and wrote in Greek. The remaining five (Caesar, Cicero, Asinius Pollio, Q. Dellius, and M. Agrippa) were essentially Strabo's contemporaries – he probably knew some of them – who wrote works that provided insight into current Roman knowledge of geography. A reference to unspecified Roman historians who wrote about northern Iberia (3.4.19), an area of intense Roman activity in his day, indicates his ability at researching the latest Roman views on geography.

Strabo lived in Alexandria a long time, and probably did much of his research there, especially finding the obscure historical and geographical writings that were little known even in his day. The range of his efforts was even deeper than the sources named: in addition to the "Roman historians,"

---

[75] These include Aristotle and Theophrastos, as well as Orthagoras and Anaxikrates, who may or may not have been members of the expedition.

[76] Plutarch, *Demosthenes* 2.2; D. A. Russell, *Plutarch* (New York, N.Y., 1973), 54–5.

there are references to the Atthis historians (5.2.4, 9.1.6), unnamed comic (8.8.1) and iambic (14.2.5) poets, epics about Herakles (15.1.9), and a number of *periploi*. Moreover, he consulted works not specifically mentioned by author or title: knowledge of Euclidian geometry is taken for granted (2.1.10).

And much of the *Geography* relied on material other than literature, including oracles, inscriptions, oral reports from Roman field commanders, and especially Strabo's own conversations with local informants, something particularly apparent in his voyage up the Nile. His contemporary Juba II, whom he probably knew in Rome, seems to have provided unpublished information about Mauretania (17.3.4–7). But it was Strabo's ability to find obscure yet relevant literary material that is remarkable. No previous extant work of ancient literature cites more sources; of those before the era of the Byzantine encyclopedists, only the treatises of Pliny the Elder and Athenaios have more.

4. The later history of the *Geography*

Strabo stopped working on the *Geography* in the 20s AD. The ending of the work (17.3.24–5) indicates that he felt it was complete, yet he had been tinkering with it for many years, and thus one can only assume he was unable to continue working on it, probably due to his own death. Even the latest possible birthdates mean that he would have been over eighty by AD 24. The *Geography* vanished from sight at his death, presumably lying unattended in his study. It was not published (in the ancient sense of creating multiple copies that were placed in private collections or libraries); the failure of the work to be disseminated beyond the author's own manuscript suggests either that he was in a remote place when he died, or that his heirs were indifferent to its significance.[77] The work seems to have been unknown for a century. Pliny the Elder, whose bibliographic research was exhaustive, did not cite it. Plutarch, who might have used it in his biographies of Alexander, Lucullus, Sulla, and Pompeius, was only aware of Strabo's *Historical Commentaries*,[78] which seems to have had a conventional publication in the 20s BC. The geographer Ptolemy, or his source Marinos of Tyre, would have found the work of value but did not quote it.[79] It is

---

[77] Strabo himself cited a tale about indifferent heirs (13.1.54). Neleus of Skepsis, the pupil of Aristotle and Theophrastos, inherited both of their libraries, only to have his own heirs ruin many of the books through improper storage as their only interest was selling them for the maximum price.

[78] Plutarch, *Sulla* 26.3; *Lucullus* 28.7; *Caesar* 63.2.

[79] Aubrey Diller, *The Textual Tradition of Strabo's Geography* (Amsterdam, 1975), 3–24.

only in the second century AD that a copy of the *Geography* emerged from obscurity. In the time of Hadrian, the geographer Dionysios wrote a *Periegesis*, a hexameter description of the known world. Although Strabo was not cited by name, Dionysios' description of Libya[80] closely parallels that of Strabo (2.5.33), which itself was based on oral information from Cn. Calpurnius Piso, the consul of 7 BC who was afterward proconsul of Africa. Piso told Strabo that Libya was like a leopard skin – spotted with oases – a striking image that also appears in Dionysios' *Periegesis*. It is hard to imagine that this anecdotal information which Strabo included in the *Geography* could have been obtained by Dionysios from any other source. Thus Dionysios may somehow have obtained the single copy of Strabo's work and perhaps deposited it in a library, maybe in Byzantion. If, as some believe, he was the son of the imperial librarian Dionysios son of Glaukos, who was active from the time of Nero into that of Trajan,[81] then either the father or the son may have had the obscure bibliographic knowledge that allowed the discovery of Strabo's treatise.

Although copies may still have been limited – perhaps a single one in a library for much of the second century AD – Strabo's *Geography* began to emerge from the shadows. By the end of the century Athenaios, whose bibliographic abilities were unique in their depth, twice quoted the *Geography*.[82] In both cases, as expected, the citations were about food. From this time the *Geography* was used occasionally but regularly, perhaps indicating that copies were still few. It was only in the Byzantine period that references to the work became more frequent. There are over two hundred citations in the *Ethnika* of Stephanos of Byzantion, written in the sixth century. The *Geography* seems finally to have entered the mainstream of scholarship.[83]

Today there are about thirty manuscripts in existence, with a fragmentary palimpsest of the fifth century the earliest (Vaticanus gr. 2306 + 2061 A). Two manuscripts in Paris provide the best extant text: Parisinus gr. 1397 of the tenth century for Books 1–9, and Parisinus gr. 1393 of the thirteenth century for the entire text. The end of Book 7 had been lost sometime in the latter Byzantine period.

---

[80] Dionysios, lines 174–219, especially 181.
[81] Alfred Klotz, "Zu Dionysius Periegetes," *RhM* 64 (1909), 474–5; see also *Suda*, "Dionysios Periegetes."
[82] Athenaios 3.121a, 14.657f.
[83] The limited knowledge of the treatise before late antiquity means that the scholia are few and late (ninth century), and of little interest in illuminating the work or its environment: see Aubrey Diller, "The Scholia on Strabo," *Traditio* 10 (1954) 29–50.

A Latin translation commissioned by Pope Nicolaus V appeared in 1469: this was the edition probably used by Columbus and other early Renaissance explorers.[84] The first printed Greek edition was the Aldine of 1516, and the first text with commentary was produced by Isaac Casaubon in Geneva in 1587. The Teubner edition appeared in 1852–3 under the editorship of August Meineke. There have been only two complete English translations before the present edition (although there are some translations of sections). The earlier is by H. C. Hamilton and W. Falconer (1854–7), in the Bohn's Classical Library series. The other is the Loeb, begun by J. R. Sterrett at the beginning of the twentieth century and completed by H. L. Jones. Publication was between 1917 and 1932. Both of these editions are of minimal value today, since they are based on imperfect texts and a weak understanding of Greek geographical literature. The Loeb is still widely used out of necessity, despite the fact that parts of it are over a century old, yet it has led many people to grief through its unfortunate and misleading interpretations of Strabo's material.

There has been more recent work on the text by French and German scholars. Beginning with the edition of Wolfgang Aly (1957–72), followed by that of Germaine Aujac and others (Budé, Paris 2003) and especially that of Stefan Radt (Göttingen 2002–2011), the Greek text of Strabo has finally been established. But Aly never lived to see the completion of his work, and the Budé seems to have stalled after publishing only the first twelve books, although its commentary, insofar as it is available, is useful. Radt has the best handling of the text, but his commentary, often more philological than geographical, can be astonishingly erratic. And both the Budé and the Radt editions have fallen into the usual trap of making a translation that relies heavily on paraphrase and inadequate handling of toponyms. Often they have substituted a presumed modern equivalent, sometimes accurately, for Strabo's toponyms. The frustrating spelling variants of place names that help in understanding the text and intent of the author are frequently ignored. Translators also have tended to add material in an attempt to make the text less obscure (replacing ambiguity with verbosity); unfortunately this does violence to Strabo's style. One must admit that the obscurities and ambiguities, however frustrating, are part of the treatise. The present translation is based on the recent texts of the *Geography*, especially the editions of Radt, the Budé, and Aly, with the present translator's own emendations.

---

[84] For a list of major editions, see *BNP: Dictionary of Greek and Latin Authors and Texts* (2009) 598–9.

5.   The translation

Translating the *Geography* has always been difficult. The same issues that make understanding of the work problematic also apply to creating a translation. The text is in fairly decent shape, except for the loss of the end of Book 7 and the beginning of Book 12 (the latter either a few words or as much as a paragraph), and an unusually large number of small gaps (often missing toponyms) in Books 8 and 9. Nevertheless there is still the problem of many rare or unique words, extensive paraphrases of earlier authors who are themselves obscure, ambiguities of style, and the sheer length of the work. Moreover, the text can simultaneously be frustratingly elliptical and annoyingly verbose. It is no wonder that it has been translated previously into English only twice and that even the most recent translations of all or part of the work (into German, French, or Italian) can be more paraphrases than accurate renditions.

Toponyms can be a particular problem. The text regularly mixes toponyms and ethnyms, which can be confusing even though this technique was used by Homer.[85] Toponyms can be in varying forms even in close proximity: the Italian town of Pisa appears as both Pisai and Pisa in a single section (5.2.5). The famous city below Mount Vesuvius is both Pompaia and Pompeia (5.4.8, 11). Yet these variants are usually significant and represent both toponymic history and the sources that Strabo was using. The British Isles appear several times as "Prettanike" (2.5.8–16), probably the original Greek spelling used by Pytheas, but elsewhere as "Brettanike," either a later Greek version or a back formation from Latin. Thus it is essential to spell this name as Strabo rendered it in order accurately to understand the text. Such strict fidelity to Greek orthography may seem trivial, but is essential when there are so many slight variants in the text. Yet it is astonishing that even many of the most recent commentators have ignored this crucial subtlety, thereby not only missing the point of the variant but making the translation both inaccurate and even more obscure. In fact, back formations from Latin into Greek occur regularly, some of which may have originated with Poseidonios (e.g. "Tourdoulian," "Mounda," "Lysitania," at 3.3.5–10), but these cannot easily be passed off merely as the hellenizing of a Latin toponym, because the indigenous version (often unknown) may also have figured in creating the Greek one. Strabo could mix forms and would make editorial comments when translating from Latin into Greek. For example, he identified an Iberian plain as

---

[85] For example, *Odyssey* 4.83–5.

both the Spartarian (which is the Latin descriptive name) and the Schoinos (a literal Greek translation), and also included a linguistic explanation (3.4.9). In the Italian sections he often used the Greek form of an indigenous name (bypassing the Latin one that may be more familiar today), such as calling the people generally known today as the Samnites the "Saunitians" (5.2.1 etc.). To render "Saunitians" as "Samnites," as many translators do, is a total misreading and misunderstanding of the text. One cannot deny that handling these toponyms in any language is difficult, as is always the case in moving back and forth between Latin and Greek, or applying names from a third language to either. The present translation attempts to be sensitive to these issues and to avoid "correcting" Strabo's erratic toponyms.

Obviously some conventions apply. A few well-known toponyms have been anglicized (e.g. Athens, Egypt, Rome), and Roman personal names have been rendered in their Latin form. Greek terms for Roman magistracies have tended to be translated into Latin or English. When the meaning is absolutely clear, descriptive toponyms have been translated (e.g. "White Cape" or "Ram's Head"), but those that are ambiguous have been left in the original. In some instances where the ancient and derived modern version of a name refer to different places, Strabo's toponym has been left in the original: the best examples are "Aithiopia" and "Indike," which are not the same as modern Ethiopia and India. "Karchedon" has been retained rather than using the Roman "Carthage." The modern term "Greek" seems inappropriate and misleading, and so Strabo's original "Hellene" has been used, and likewise "Sebastos" instead of "Augustus." Flora, fauna, minerals, and items of material culture can be notoriously difficult to translate, and if uncertain have been left in the original: a glossary of the more obscure terms has been provided (*infra* pp. 778–81). It is hoped that these formulas and conventions have produced the most accurate translation of the *Geography* to date in any language, one that retains, as much as possible, the flavor of Strabo's treatise.

In comprehending the text of the *Geography* the reader should be aware of a few regular idioms. Perhaps the most confusing is "inside" and "outside" to describe locations relative to a fixed point that may be uncertain, a technique originated by Herodotos to describe places inside (west) and outside (east) of the Halys River.[86] Herodotos' use is straightforward, but that of Strabo can be confusing, since the author's topographical perspective is not always clear. Especially obscure to modern readers is "inside" and "outside" of the Tauros Mountains (2.5.31, etc.), where the former is to the north (thereby putting most of Anatolia as well as the remote areas north of the Black Sea "inside"),

---

[86] Herodotos 1.6, 28.

and the latter is to the south (essentially all of the Iranian plateau and Indian
peninsula). This idiomatic formula is based on the false assumption that the
Tauros Mountains run due east and west. "Outside" can also refer to peoples
or places on the coast of the External Sea, or "outside" the Mediterranean-
oriented inhabited world. Another idiom is to describe places "rising opposite" to one another. This was originally nautical terminology (implicit in its
visual context), yet Strabo used it to indicate places on the same latitude or
longitude, even if they were not accessible to one another by any sea voyage
(such as Meroë and southern India). Moreover, "above" can mean "inland,"
which, given the rugged topography of much of the Mediterranean coast,
is sensible. In addition to the four cardinal directions, Strabo often wrote
"toward the sunrise" for east and "toward the sunset" (or "toward the
setting") for west, sometimes modified with "winter" and "summer": thus
"toward the summer sunrise" would mean roughly northeast. Julius Caesar is
regularly "Caesar the God" or "the God Caesar," and Augustus is "Sebastos
Caesar," although in both instances the epithet may be dropped if identi-
fication is clear. In most cases, Homer is merely "the Poet." The Sikelian
Strait (modern Strait of Messina) is often just "the Strait."

Distances and lengths are a problem in any ancient text, and were
ambiguous even in antiquity, as Strabo noted (17.1.24). Generally, the ancient
world had no need for accurate long distances, or an ability to compare a
distance in one part of the world with that in another. In fact, the discipline
of geography, beginning with Eratosthenes, was the first to grapple with
accurate measurements of long distances. Usually it did not matter if the
stadion or *schoinos*, the most common pre-Roman units of distance, varied
from place to place: Strabo commented that at a certain point on the Nile the
schoinos changed from thirty to sixty stadia (17.1.41).

Strabo's primary unit of length was the stadion, about one-eighth of a
Roman mile. But in areas that had been under Persian control, the highly
variable *schoinos* was often preferred, and occasionally the parasang. In
Italy, Sicily, and Iberia, and along Roman roads, he often used Roman
miles. *Schoinoi* or miles were at times given a stadia equivalent by Strabo,
but Strabo was aware of the inconsistencies. Moreover, there are frequent
references to the oldest, yet least precise, of long-distance measurements,
caravan-days and sailing-days.

Although it is difficult to be exact, the following is the best evidence for
modern equivalents of ancient lengths, measures of capacity, and weights,
with the understanding that the data are contradictory:[87]

---

[87] See the useful table in *BNP, Antiquity: Index, Lists and Tables* (2010) 459–66.

stadion: 177.7 to 197.3 m.[88]
schoinos: 30 to 120 stadia, or 5.3 to 23.7 km.
parasang: 30 to 60 stadia, or 5.3 to 10.6 km.
Roman mile: 1480 m.

For shorter lengths Strabo used the following:

daktylos: the width of a finger, perhaps 2 cm.
spithame: 12 *daktyloi*, or about 24 cm.
foot: 16 *daktyloi*, approximately the same as a modern foot or 31 cm.
pechys: 24 *daktyloi*, or about 46 cm.
orgyia: 1.85 m. or 6 feet.
plethron: 31 m. or 100 feet.

In addition, there are four measures of capacity:

kotyle: about 240–75 ml or 8.2–10.7 fluid oz.
choinix (pl. *choinikes*): 4 *kotylai* or about one liter or one quart.
metretes: about 39 liters or 10.3 gallons.
medimnos: about 53 liters or 13.9 gallons.

Weights are as follows:

mina: varying from 480 to 655 gm, or 17–23 oz.
litra: a pound, 327 gm or 11.5 oz.
talent: 28–39 kg. or 62–86 lb.

In the translation, references to Strabo's text have been inserted without attribution (e.g. 1.1.1). References to other ancient texts are identified, although those that are fragmentary have only a fragment or testimonium number (e.g. F1 or T1), insofar as such numbers are available; the sources of the fragments appear on pp. 782–3. Also inserted into the text are the page numbers established by Isaac Casaubon in his 1587 text of the *Geography* (e.g. C564), as these are still cited by some, although they are somewhat anachronistic. Regnal numbers have regularly been added, except for Alexander III the Great, always identified merely as "Alexander." It is intended that this translation stand alone and be accessible without commentary, but a few footnotes have been added where the text is particularly obscure or deficient. Generally, dots in Strabo's actual text indicate that

---

[88] See the discussion of the length of the stadion in Roller, *Eratosthenes*, 271–3.

something is missing in the manuscripts (or too confused to understand); dots within quotations, however, mean that Strabo excerpted them. Square brackets denote explanatory additions to the text, where the Greek cannot be literally translated and retain its meaning or clarity; pointed brackets are additions by editors to the text itself, where it is thought that something is missing.

6.   A note on the maps

An interactive digital map produced by the Ancient World Mapping Center accompanies the translation and is freely accessible (awmc.unc.edu/awmc/applications/Strabo). The map's base outlines the physical landscape of classical antiquity in a seamless arc extending from Ireland to the Indian sub-continent. On this base are marked all the physical features, settlements, and peoples mentioned by Strabo which can be located – over 2,000 of them. Each name on the map is linked to its entry in the Pleiades (Pleiades.stoa.org) and Pelagios (Plagios-project.blogspot.com) databases, where further information is offered; there is also a searchable, sortable gazetteer for the map. In addition, every occurrence of a locatable place in the e-book provides a direct link to it on the map. The map is built upon Open Source software such as Open Layers, and employs a series of custom MapBox tiles created by the Ancient World Mapping Center and hosted by New York University's Institute for the Study of the Ancient World. For users who wish to view the places named by Strabo in relation to today's landscape rather than that of antiquity, there is a link to substitute a modern landscape base as required.

Strabo cited several thousand toponyms and ethnyms used topographically. All that can be located without question appear on the map. Needless to say, many cannot be placed and others are dubious. Moreover, there are instances where Strabo erred in his topography (a notable example is in southern Syria and the Lake Gennesaritis [Sea of Galilee] region [16.2.16]), and on the map the toponyms are placed where they actually are, not where Strabo may have believed they were. Strabo's spellings, however idiosyncratic, have been preserved, although not all variants appear. Features within cities are not shown, and there is no distinction made on the map between a city and its territory.

The translation

BOOK I

Introduction and predecessors

Part 1: Introduction and purpose of the work

(1) What we choose to investigate now, geography, we believe is a discipline [C1]
like others and for the scholar. We believe that this is not inconsequential and
is obvious for many reasons. As Eratosthenes [F1] has said, those who first
dared to begin to consider it were men such as Homer, Anaximandros the
Milesian and his fellow-citizen Hekataios, as well as Demokritos, Eudoxos, [C2]
Dikaiarchos, Ephoros, and a number of others. Moreover, there were those
after them: Eratosthenes, Polybios, and Poseidonios, learned men. Great
learning, which alone makes such a work possible, is attained by no one
other than someone who carefully examines both human and divine matters,
knowledge of which, it is said, is scholarship. Thus the manifest usefulness [of
geography] for political activities and for those of commanders, as well as the
understanding of the heavens and things on the earth and sea (animals, plants,
and fruits, whatever is to be seen in each place), assumes the same type of man
as the one who gives consideration to the art of life and happiness.

(2) We must consider and take up each of these points in greater detail.
First, both I and those before me – among whom is Hipparchos [F1] – assume
correctly that Homer was the originator of the art of geography. He alone
surpassed everyone, both earlier and later, in the excellence of his poetry and –
one might say – his acquaintance with civic life. Thus he was interested not
only in human activities – in order to learn as much about them as possible
and transmit it to those later – but also in each of the places of the entire
inhabited world, both land and sea. Otherwise he would not have gone to its
farthest limits in his writings.

(3) First, he states that it is washed all around by the Ocean, just as it
is. Then he names some of its regions, and alludes to others by certain
hints. He mentions specifically Libya, Aithiopia, the Sidonians, and the
Erembians (by which he probably means the Arabian Trogodytes), but
only hints about those toward the west and east by referring to them as

washed by the Ocean. For he makes the sun rise and set in it, as well as the stars:

> Now Helios was striking the fields from the deep stream of soft-flowing Okeanos [*Iliad* 7.421–2; *Odyssey* 19.433–4]

> ...the bright light of the sun fell into Okeanos, dragging the black night. [*Iliad* 8.485–6]

And he also says that the stars after bathing [rise] from the Ocean [*Iliad* 5.5–6].

(4) Regarding the peoples of the west, he makes clear their prosperity and the good climate of their environment, as he had learned (so it seems) about the Iberian wealth, and how because of it Herakles invaded. Later there were the Phoenicians, who possessed most of it, and after them the [C3] Romans. From there the Zephyrs blow, and there the Poet places the Elysian Plain, where, he says, Menelaos had been sent by the gods:

> but the immortals will send you to the Elysian Plain and the limits of the earth, where fair-haired Rhadamanthys is, where life becomes easiest .... There is no snow, nor any great storms...but Okeanos always sends forth the clear blowing winds of Zephyros. [*Odyssey* 4.563–8, excerpted]

(5) Moreover, the Blessed Islands are to the west of the farthest part of Maurousia, the portion that comes close to the limit of Iberia. From that name it can be seen that they were thought to be prosperous because they lay near such places.

(6) And he makes it clear that the Aithiopians were the farthest on the Ocean, the farthest "Aithiopians, divided in two, the farthest of men" [*Odyssey* 1.23], not saying "divided in two" casually (as will be shown later). They are also on the Ocean: "Zeus went yesterday to Okeanos among the noble Aithiopians for a banquet" [*Iliad* 1.423–4]. He suggests that the farthest land to the north is along the Ocean when he says that the Bear "alone has no part in the waters of Okeanos" [*Iliad* 18.489; *Odyssey* 5.275]. This is because, by the Bear and the Chariot he means the arctic circle. Since so many stars go around in that region which is always visible, he would not have said that it [the Bear] alone has no part in the waters of the Ocean. But it is not good to accuse him of ignorance, that he knew about one Bear rather than two. It is not likely that the other had yet to be classified (as the Phoenicians had designated it and used it for sailing), but that the constellation was still unnoticed by the Hellenes, just as with the Lock of Berenike and Canopus, which were recently named. There are many that are still unnamed, as Aratos [*Phainomena* 145–6, 391] says. Thus Krates is not correct when he says that "it [the arctic circle] alone has no part in the water" [F27], avoiding what need not be avoided.

Herakleitos is better and more Homeric, as he similarly speaks of the Bear in place of the arctic circle: "The Bear is the limit of morning and evening, and opposite the Bear is the boundary of clear Zeus" [F91], since the arctic circle, not the Bear, is the boundary of setting and rising. Thus by the Bear, which he [Homer] also calls the Chariot and which he says [*Iliad* 18.487–8; *Odyssey* 5.273–4] watches Orion, he means the arctic circle, and by Okeanos the horizon into which he makes [the stars] set and from which they rise. Saying that the former rotates without a share in the Ocean, he knows that the arctic circle has as its limit the most northern part of the horizon. Consequently, constructing the poetry in this way, we are obliged (according to our senses) to accept the horizon of the earth as similar to the Ocean, and the arctic circle as touching the earth at the most northern limit of habitation. Thus this part of the earth would also be washed by the Ocean. [C4]

Moreover, he knows about the men who are most toward the north wind, although he does not mention their name (and even still today no common name exists for all of them), but identifies them by their lifestyle, calling them nomads and "noble mare-milkers, milk-drinkers, and the Abians" [*Iliad* 13.5–6].

(7) He shows in other ways that the Ocean lies around the circuit of the earth, as when Hera says this: "I am going to see the limits of the bountiful earth and Okeanos, the progenitor of the gods" [*Iliad* 14.200–1]. He says that the Ocean touches all the limits, and these boundaries lie around the circuit. In the *Making of the Weapons*, he places the Ocean in a circle on the rim of the shield of Achilleus [*Iliad* 18.607–8].

A further indication of his assiduousness is that he was not ignorant of the flood tide and the retreat of the Ocean, speaking of "the Ocean flowing back" [*Iliad* 18.399; *Odyssey* 20.65] and "three times a day it goes up, and three times it is swallowed back" [*Odyssey* 12.105]. Even if it is "three times" and not "twice" – perhaps he has strayed from the record or there is an error in the text – the idea is the same. "Soft-flowing" [*Iliad* 7.422; *Odyssey* 19.434] also has some suggestion of the flood tide, which has a gentle approach without a totally violent flow. Poseidonios [F216] conjectures that when he [Homer] speaks of the covering of the headlands and the laying of them bare, as well as saying that the Ocean is a river, and [speaks of] its flow, he is describing the flood tide. His [Poseidonios'] first suggestion is good but the second is not, for the approach of the flood tide is not like the flow of a river, and the retreat is even less similar. The explanation put forth by Krates [F57] is more plausible: that he [Homer] says the Ocean is deep-flowing and flowing back, and also completely like a river. He further says that a certain part of the Ocean is a river and has the flow of a river – not the whole, but a [C5] part – when he says this: "for when the ship, leaving the stream of the river of Okeanos, and arriving at the swell of the broad sea" [*Odyssey* 12.1–2]. This is not the whole, but the stream of the river that is the Ocean and thus a part of the Ocean, which Krates says is a sort of estuary or gulf that extends toward the south pole from the winter tropic. Moreover, it would be possible to leave this and still be in the Ocean, but to leave the whole and still be in the whole is not possible. Homer thus says "leaving the stream of the river...and arriving at...the sea," which is nothing other than the Ocean. If it is taken otherwise, it becomes "he went out of the Ocean and came into the Ocean." But this is for a longer discussion.

(8) That the inhabited world is an island must be assumed both from the senses as well as experience. Everywhere that it has been possible for men to access the farthest points of the earth, the sea has been found, which we call Okeanos. Wherever it is not possible to make use of the senses, reason shows it. The eastern side (that near the Indians) and the western (that near the Iberians and the Maurousians) can be completely sailed around in the southern or northern portions for a great distance. The remainder that has not been sailed by us up to today, because those who sailed around did not meet each other, is not so great, if one adds together the parallel distances accessible by us. It is not likely that the Atlantic Ocean is divided into two seas, separated by isthmuses so narrow that they prevent sailing around, but rather that it flows together and is continuous. Those who attempted to sail around but turned back say that it was not because they came upon some continent and were prevented from sailing beyond, reversing their direction, but because of the difficulties and the isolation, not that the sea became less open. This agrees better with the properties of the Ocean concerning its ebbing and flooding. Everywhere the same characteristic – or one not greatly varying – is enough for the changes of height and diminution, as if one sea and one cause produced the movements.

(9) Hipparchos [F4] is not credible in refuting this idea on the grounds
that the Ocean is not affected in the same way everywhere, and that even if this were so, it would not follow that the Atlantic Ocean flows around in a complete circle. He uses Seleukos the Babylonian as witness that it is not homogenous. For further discussion about the Ocean and the flood tides we put forth Poseidonios [F214] and Athenodoros [F6a], who have examined the matter sufficiently. In regard to this, I say that at present it is better to assume this homogeneity, and that the heavenly bodies will better be held together by the rising of vapor if the moisture is scattered all around.

(10) Thus the Poet knows and describes clearly the farthest parts of the inhabited world, and what surrounds it, as well as the region of the Internal

Sea. Beginning at the Pillars, it is surrounded by Libya, Egypt, and Phoenicia, and then that around Cyprus, then the Solymians, Lykians, and Karians, and after them the shore between Mykale and the Troad and the islands lying in front (all of which he mentions), as well as those farther, around the Propontis and the Euxeinos as far as Kolchis and the expedition of Jason. Moreover, he knows about the Kimmerian Bosporos, and thus he knows about the Kimmerians, for doubtless if he knew the name "Kimmerians" he thus was not ignorant of them, for in his time or shortly before it they overran everywhere from the Bosporos as far as the land of Ionia. At any rate he suggests that at the latitude of their territory it is gloomy, as he says "they are hidden in mist and cloud, and bright Helios never looks upon them…but deadly night stretches over them" [*Odyssey* 11.15–16, 19, altered]. He knows about the Istros, since he mentions the Mysians (Thracian peoples who live along the Istros). Moreover he knows the coast next to it, which is Thracian as far as the Peneios, for he names the Paionians, Athos, and the Axios, and the islands in front of them. Then there is the coast of Hellas as far as the Thesprotians, all of which he mentions. Moreover, he knows about the promontories of Italia – called Temese and the Sikelian – as well as the promontories of Iberia and its prosperity, as I have just mentioned.

If there appear to be gaps in between these, one might make allowance for them, for the geographer indeed omits many things in the details. One might also make allowance even if he mixes legendary things into his historical and instructive material, and must not censure it. But what Eratosthenes says [cf. F2] is not true, that all poets attempt to amuse rather than to teach. On [C7] the contrary the most learned authorities on poetry clearly state that poetry is a basic kind of philosophy. I will speak about Eratosthenes at greater length later [1.2–3], when I discuss the Poet again.

(11) Let what has now been said be sufficient, that Homer was the beginning of geography. His successors obviously were also notable men and familiar with learning. Eratosthenes [F12] says that the first two after Homer were Anaximandros (a pupil and fellow-citizen of Thales), and Hekataios the Milesian, and that the former was the first to produce a geographical plan, and Hekataios left behind a treatise, believed to be his because of its similarity to his other writings.

(12) Nevertheless, it is necessary to put together a great amount of learning for this, as has been stated. In particular, Hipparchos [F11] demonstrates in his work against Eratosthenes that it is not possible for anyone – whether an amateur or scholar – to undertake geographical research without determination of heavenly phenomena or the eclipses that have been observed. How far Alexandria next to Egypt is north or south of Babylon – or what the distance

is – cannot be determined without an investigation of the latitude. Similarly, the displacement to east or west cannot accurately be learned without comparing the eclipses of the sun and moon. This is what he says about the matter.

(13) Everyone who attempts to talk about the peculiar characteristics of places applies particular attention to heavenly and geometric phenomena, explaining shapes, sizes, intervals, and zones, and also heat and cold, or, simply put, the nature of the atmosphere. A builder constructing a house, or an architect founding a city, would plan for this, and thus no less so would the man who considers the entire inhabited world: these things are more of concern to him. For small regions it is nothing major if their position is moved north or south, but in the entire circuit of the inhabited world, that toward the north is as far as the extreme parts of Skythia or Keltike, and that toward the south is as far as the extreme parts of the Aithiopians. The difference is very large. It is the same for those among the Indians or [C8] Iberians, the former in the extreme east and the latter in the west, and in a certain way the opposites of each other, as we know.

(14) Everything of this type, caused by the movement of the sun and the other stars, and also the tendency toward the center, forces one to look up at the heavens and the phenomena of the heavenly bodies as each appears to us, and one sees in this immense variation in inhabited places. How could someone explain these differences between places, and treat this well and sufficiently, if he did not consider these matters even a little? For if it were impossible for such a treatise to be completely accurate – because it is more political – it would nevertheless be fitting to do so, so that it would be possible for the citizen to follow the discussion.

(15) Thus someone who has once raised his thoughts to the heights would not abstain from the entire earth. It is manifestly ludicrous that someone striving to explain clearly the inhabited world would dare to grasp the heavenly bodies and make use of them for teaching, but would not consider the entire earth (part of which is the inhabited world): neither its size, its characteristics, nor its position in the entire cosmos, or even whether it is inhabited only in the single portion around us or in other places of whatever size, as well as how large the uninhabited portion is and what it is like and why it is so. It seems, then, that in its treatment the nature of geography joins together meteorology and geometry, joining together into one both terrestrial and heavenly matters, as being very near to each other, not separated "as heaven is from the earth" [*Iliad* 8.16].

(16) Now then, let us add to such great learning terrestrial research: that concerning animals, plants, and everything useful or not useful produced on the land and in the sea. I think this will make what I say distinct.

That there is a great advantage to everyone who obtains such information is clear both from ancient memory and reason. At any rate, the poets report that the wisest of the heroes was the one who travelled and wandered in many places, considering it important that "he saw the cities and knew the minds of many men" [*Odyssey* 1.3]. And Nestor exalts because he had an association with the Lapiths, going, when they sent for him, "as they had summoned me from a land so far away" [*Iliad* 1.270], and Menelaos similarly:

> wandering through Cyprus, Phoenicia, and the Egyptians, I came to the Aithiopians, Sidonians, Erembians, and Libya, where the lambs are born with horns. [*Odyssey* 4.83–5]

adding the peculiarity of the region, "for the sheep give birth three times in   [C9]
the course of a year" [*Odyssey* 4.86], "the grain-giving land produces in abundance" [*Odyssey* 4.229], and (about Egyptian Thebes), "it has a hundred gates, and two hundred men go forth from each with horses and chariots" [*Iliad* 9.383–4]. All such things are important preparations for practical understanding, along with learning about the nature of the land and the types of plants and animals. One should also add the sea, for in a certain way we are amphibians and are no more from the land than from the sea. It is probable that Herakles was called "practiced in great deeds" [*Odyssey* 21.26] because of his great experience and knowledge.

Thus what has been said by me from the beginning is witnessed both by ancient memories and reason. Moreover, it seems to me that the other argument can especially be brought forth today, that geography for the most part exists for political needs. The territory of activities on the land and sea where we live is small when it is small and large when it is large, with the largest the entirety that we specifically call the inhabited world, the location of our largest activities. The greatest commanders are those who are able to control both land and sea, and to bring together peoples and cities under a single authority and political administration. Thus it is clear that geography as a whole concerns the activities of the leaders, for it is composed of continents and seas, both those within and outside the entire inhabited world. This situation is in regard to the difference between one thing and another, and what is known or unknown. They can manage things better knowing how large a territory is, where it happens to be situated, and what its peculiarities are in regard to its environment and itself. But they have power in different regions, exercising activities from different locales and starting places and enlarging the extent of their rule. Thus it is equally impossible for them to know everything, and it is the same for geographers, since both see more or less. Indeed, even if the entire inhabited world were all joined together under a single rule and government, it still would not be possible, although the nearer parts would be better known. And it would be proper to discuss these more fully, so that they would be made known, for it would be closer to their needs. Thus it would not be extraordinary if one person were the chorographer for the Indians, another for the Aithiopians, and another for the Hellenes and Romans. How would it be proper for a geographer on the Indians to speak about Boiotia in the way that Homer does ("these lived in Hyrie, rocky Aulis, Schoinos, and Skolos" [*Iliad* 2.496–7])? For me this is proper, but in regard to the Indians it would no longer be so. Necessity, which is the best measure of such a practice, does not invite it.

[C10]

(17) And this is also clear in lesser matters, such as hunting. One will do better in the chase knowing the forest, both its character and extent. Knowing the region, one can best make camp, an ambush, or travel. But it is more conspicuous in greater things, since the prizes from experience and the defeats from ignorance are greater. For example, the expedition of Agamemnon ravaged Mysia instead of the Troad and returned home in disgrace. The Persians and the Libyans, conjecturing that straits were blind narrows, came close to great danger and left behind memorials to their ignorance: the former with the tomb of Salganeus on the Chalkidean Euripos, who was killed because, according to the Persians, he had guided the expedition treacherously from the Malians to the Euripos, and the latter with the memorial of Peloros, whom they executed for the same reason. Hellas is full of shipwrecks resulting from the expedition of Xerxes. Moreover, the settlements sent forth by the Aioleans and Ionians produced many such mistakes. Similarly, there have been successes, and the success was because of acquaintance with the places. For example, it is said that Ephialtes, at the narrows around Thermopylai, showed the Persians the pathway through the mountains and put those with Leonidas in their power, bringing the barbarians inside the Gates. Leaving antiquity, I believe that the contemporary campaign of the Romans against the Parthyaians is sufficient proof, as well as that against the Germans and Kelts, for the barbarians fought using the topography, in marshes and untrodden thickets, and deserted places, making what was near seem farther to the ignorant, as well as concealing the roads and the abundance of provisions and other matters.

(18) Mostly, as has been said, it [geography] relates to the lives and needs of rulers, as ethical philosophy and politics mostly concern the lives of rulers. The proof of this is that we distinguish the differences among states by their governments, calling some forms of rule monarchy (which we also describe as kingship), others aristocracy, and others democracy. And we call govern-

[C11]

ments such names because their structure derives from the following: in some the command of the king is the law, in others that of the best people, and in still others that of the common people. The law is the type and form of government. Because of this, they say that justice is the interest of the more powerful. If, then, political philosophy is largely concerned with the rulers, and geography provides the needs of the rulers, the latter would have an advantage over the former. This advantage, however, is a matter of experience.

(19) Treatment of it also includes no small amount of theory of the arts, mathematics, and natural science, as well as that lying within history and myth, although the latter has nothing to do with practice. If one were to speak about the wanderings of Odysseus, Menelaos, or Jason, it would not seem that he was adding to wisdom (which is what someone of importance seeks) except to mix in useful precedents from what they had been forced to experience. Nevertheless it would provide no poor instruction for someone interested in the places supplied by the makers of myth. Someone of importance seeks this, because it is notable and pleasant, but not very much, for they are eager, rather, for what is useful, as is appropriate. The geographer must take similar care, rather than otherwise. It is the same with history and mathematics, in regard to which the useful and more trustworthy must always be accepted.

(20) Most of all, as has been said, it seems to me that geometry and astronomy must be presumed for this topic, and the need for them is real. Shapes, zones, dimensions, and such other suitable matters cannot be properly determined without this methodology. But just as they show elsewhere that which concerns the measurement of the entire earth, it is necessary here to assume and to believe in what they show. One must assume that the universe is sphere-shaped, and that the surface of the earth is sphere-shaped, and, moreover, what is fundamental to this, that the motion of the [heavenly] bodies is toward the center. It can then be indicated (only in brief summary), whether something is due to sense perception or common knowledge. For example, the suggestion that the earth is sphere-shaped was originally because of the motion toward the center and that each body inclines toward its suspended cord, and more specifically due to the phenomena of the sea and the heavens. Sense perception and common knowledge can be witness to this. [C12] Obviously it is the curvature of the sea that obscures for sailors the perception of distant lights that are raised to an equal level as the eye. But if they are raised higher than the eye they are visible even if they are farther away. Equally, if [the eye] is elevated it can see what was formerly invisible. This is what the Poet revealed, for it is the meaning of "looking ahead exceedingly quickly, lifted on a great wave" [*Odyssey* 5.393]. Moreover, coming into land, the parts always become progressively more visible, and what first appears lower

becomes raised up. The revolution of the heavenly bodies is distinct, especially because of the use of the gnomon, and from it the idea is immediately suggested that such a rotation could not happen if the earth were rooted in the infinite. Regarding the zones, they are discussed along with the inhabited world.

(21) At this time it is necessary to accept some things, especially that which is useful for the political leader and military commander. One must not be so ignorant of matters concerning the heavens and the position of the earth that when someone comes to places where some of the familiar celestial phenomena have changed, he is disturbed and says

> Friends, we do not know where there is darkness or where there is dawn, or where the sun that brings light to mortals goes under the earth or where it rises. [*Odyssey* 10.190–2]

Yet one need not know accurately and absolutely everything about what rises together, what sets together (simultanously passing the meridian), the elevation of the poles, points in the zenith, and everything else one experiences concerning the change of the horizon or the arctic circle, whether visible or physical. One should not consider all these things unless one were to view them as a scholar, but other matters should be believed even if one does not see why, for that is for scholarly investigation alone, something for which there is not sufficient leisure for the political leader, at least not always.

[C13] Someone happening upon this book must not be so simple or idle as not to have seen a globe, or the circles on it, some of which are parallel, others perpendicular to them, and others oblique, or not [to have seen] the position of the tropics, equator, and zodiac, through which the sun is carried, indicating the different zones and winds. For if someone understands the horizons and the arctic circle and other things transmitted in a preliminary course in mathematics, he will be able to follow this treatise. But if he has not learned about a straight line or a curve, the shape of a circle, the difference between a sphere and a plane, or, in regard to the heavens, the seven stars of the Great Bear, or anything else of that kind, he will have no use for this study (at least not now) until he has first come across that without which he cannot be knowledgeable about geography. Thus the ones who have written works on harbors and the so-called *periploi* leave their investigations incomplete if they have not included the learning and celestial matters that are proper to add.

(22) Simply put, this treatise will be equally necessary for the political leader and the general public, as are historical writings. By political leader we do not mean a person who is totally uneducated, but someone who has

taken the customary curriculum for free men or those pursuing knowledge. For one would not be unable to blame or praise it fairly, nor to judge the material that is worthy of recording, unless he has considered virtue and wisdom, and what has been written about them.

(23) Thus, having created my *Historical Commentaries* [F2], which were useful, I suppose, for ethical and political philosophy, I decided also to produce the present work, in the same form and for the same men, especially those of pre-eminence. In the same manner as before, where what happened in the lives of distinguished men was recorded but what is petty and doubtful was omitted, here what is petty and unclear is also rejected, in favor of using what is notable and important, and having within it what is practical, memorable, and pleasant. Just as, in regard to colossal works of art, we do not seek out each detail precisely but rather consider them as a whole, and whether they are pleasing in their entirety, this work must be judged in such a way. It too is a colossal work that only points out great things and the whole, [C14] except for minor things that are able to affect someone who is both fond of learning and practical. Let these things be said, since the present work is serious and worthy of a scholar.

Part 2: Homeric geography

(1) If I were to undertake to speak about something treated by many before me, I could not be blamed unless I were to discuss this in exactly the same way as those writing previously. Yet we assume – although others have accomplished much – that the greater part of the subject still remains. If I am able to add even a small amount to it, this must be considered a sufficient reason for the undertaking.

The contemporary expansion of the dominion of the Romans and Parthyaians has added to such knowledge, just as the expedition of Alexander did previously, as Eratosthenes [cf. F15, 95] has said. For the latter revealed much of Asia to us, as well as all the northern part of Europe as far as the Istros, and the Romans all of western Europe as far as the Albis, the river that divides Germania into two, and beyond the Istros as far as the Tyras River. That beyond, as far as the Maiotis and the coast ending at Kolchis was made known by Mithridates [VI] called Eupator and his generals. The Parthyaians have made that around Hyrkania, Baktriane, and the Skythians beyond them better known to us, areas that were less known to those earlier. Thus something more might be said by me.

This will become most visible in the discussion of my predecessors, not so much the earliest ones, but those after Eratosthenes, and he himself. It is likely that since they were more learned than many, it would be harder for someone later to refute them if they said anything that was wrong. But if we are ever forced to contradict those whom we otherwise follow especially closely, there must be pardon. It is not proposed to contradict everyone, but to omit most of them (those whom it is not worth following) and to pass judgement on those whom we know to have been correct in most things. It is thus unworthy to investigate everyone, but it is good to do so with [C15] Eratosthenes, Poseidonios, Hipparchos, Polybios, and such others.

(2) First, Eratosthenes must be considered, along with the objections of Hipparchos against him. Eratosthenes is not so easily attacked as to say that he never saw Athens, as Polemon [*FHG* vol. 3, p. 130] attempts to show, nor is he as trustworthy as rumored by some. He himself says that he knew notable men. "For," he says,

> it happened at this particular time, as never before within one enclosure or one city, that philosophers flourished, such as those at the time of Ariston and Arkesilas. [*FGrHist* #241, T10]

I do not think that this is sufficient, as there must be a precise judgement as to which of them one should believe. But he places Arkesilas and Ariston at the head of those who flourished in his time. Apelles is also conspicuous to him, as well as Bion, who, he says, was the first to clothe philosophy in flowery dress, but people often said this about him: "Bion [shows] such, from under his rags" [Homer, *Odyssey* 18.74, altered]. In these very statements he demonstrates a significant weakness in his own judgement, for, although he was acquainted in Athens with Zenon of Kition, he does not mention any of his successors, but only speaks of those who differed with him and who could not keep their own school alive and flourishing at the time. His publication titled *On the Good* shows this, as well as his *Exercises* and whatever else he wrote in such a manner: he was thus in the middle between wishing to be a philosopher and lacking the confidence to attempt the undertaking, only advancing far enough to appear to be one, having provided himself an escape from his regular cycle, whether for education or amusement. This is also the fashion in his other writings. But let this pass. Now one must attempt, insofar as possible, to correct his geography, first in the matter that I recently put off.

(3) He [F2] says that all poets attempt to amuse rather than teach. On the contrary, the ancients say that poetry is foremost a pursuit of knowledge, introduced into our life from youth, and which teaches with pleasure about character, emotion, and actions. Moreover, we say that only the poet is wise. For this reason the Hellenic cities educate their youth in poetry first of all,

presumably not for the sake of mere amusement but to learn morality. Even   [C16]
musicians, teaching plucking, lyre playing and flute playing, claim this
virtue, for they say that such an education improves character. One may
hear this said not only by the Pythagoreans, but Aristoxenos [F Ia305]
maintains the same thing. And Homer said that the singers were chastisers,
as in the case of the guardian of Klytaimnestra, "whom Atreides, going
to Troy, strictly commanded to guard his wife" [*Odyssey* 3.267–8]. Aigisthos
was not able to prevail over her before "he took the singer to a deserted
island and left him there...and then willingly led her, willing, to his
home" [*Odyssey* 3.270–2]. Apart from this, Eratosthenes contradicts himself.
Shortly before he said this, at the beginning of his geographical treatise, he
says that from earliest times all of them [the poets] have eagerly placed
themselves in the mainstream of that discipline. For example, whatever
Homer learned about the Aithiopians he recorded in his poem, as well as
about the Egyptians and Libyans. Yet insofar as Hellas and the neighboring
places are concerned, he elaborated excessively, saying that Thisbe is abundant in doves [*Iliad* 2.502], Haliartos is grassy [503], Anthedon is the farthest
[508], and Lilaia is by the Kephissian springs [523], but he also never threw
out a useless qualification. Is someone who does this an entertainer or a
teacher? By Zeus the latter, you say, but that which is beyond perception he
[Homer] and others have filled with legendary marvels. He [Eratosthenes]
should have said that every poet writes for the sake of mere entertainment
and teaching, but he said "merely for entertainment and not for teaching."
He meddles still further when he asks how it contributes to the quality of
the poet to become skilled in places or military command or farming or
rhetoric or whatever else others might wish him to have acquired. The desire
for him to acquire everything would be going beyond the proper limit in
ambition (just as if someone, as Hipparchos [F2] says, were to hang apples
and pears on Attic wreaths, which cannot hold them), burdening him with
all knowledge and every skill. You may be right, Eratosthenes, about that,
but you are not right when you take away from him [Homer] his great
learning, and declare that his creativity is the mythology of an old woman,
who has been allowed to fabricate (as you say) whatever appears for her own   [C17]
amusement.

   Moreover, is nothing contributed to the virtue of those listening to the
poets? I emphasize again that they are experienced in localities, military
command, agriculture, and rhetoric, all of which, as is fitting, the listener
acquires.

   (4) But the Poet has ascribed all this to Odysseus, whom he adorns more
than anyone else with all virtue. Thus he "saw the cities and knew the minds

of many men" [*Odyssey* 1.3], and was "knowledgeable in all kinds of cunning and wise devices" [*Iliad* 3.202]. He is always described as the "sacker of cities" who took Ilion "through his counsel and words and persuasive skill: accompanying me we could both return home from sparkling fire" [*Iliad* 10.246–7, somewhat changed], as Diomedes says. Moreover, he flaunts his skill at farming, in regard to reaping, "in the grass I would have a curved scythe and you one like it" [*Odyssey* 18.368–9], and in regard to plowing, "you should see me, whether I cut an unbroken furrow" [*Odyssey* 18.375].

(5) To be sure, rhetoric is wisdom applied to speaking, which Odysseus shows throughout the work, in the *Trial*, the *Prayers*, and the *Embassy*, where he [Homer] says "when his great voice came from his chest, words like the winter snowflakes, no other mortal could rival Odysseus" [*Iliad* 3.221–3]. Thus not only does Homer understand these things, but everyone enlightened uses the Poet as a witness who speaks correctly, thus demonstrating that such experience particularly leads to wisdom. Who, then, could assume that a poet who is capable of introducing others as public speakers or commanders or other manifestations of virtuous deeds is himself one of the talkers of nonsense or conjurors, only able to bewitch or flatter someone hearing, but not help him? Moreover, we cannot say that the excellence of a poet is superior to his imitation of life through speech. How could one imitate without experience of life and who is a fool? Of course we do not speak of the excellence of a poet as we would of a carpenter or metal worker, for theirs is not due to any beauty or nobility, but that of a poet is coupled with that of a man, and one cannot become a good poet unless previously one was a good man.

(6) Thus to exclude the poet from rhetorical skill is to neglect completely my [position]. What, then, is as rhetorical as the manner of speaking? And

[C18] what is thus poetic? And who is better than Homer in the manner of speaking? By Zeus it is so, but poetic speaking is different in form, just as in poetry the tragic is from the comic, and in prose the historical is from the legal. Moreover, is reasoning not generic, whose forms are either metrical or prosaic? Or is reasoning in such a way, but rhetorical reasoning is not generic, and neither is the style and the quality of reasoning? As it is said, prose reasoning – that which is elaborate – is an imitation of the poetic. Artistic poetry came to be publicly esteemed first of all. Then Kadmos, Pherekydes, and Hekataios [of Miletos] and their followers imitated it, releasing the meter yet otherwise maintaining the poetic style. Then later writers each took away something and brought it down – as if from some height – to its present form. Similarly one could say that comedy takes its structure from tragedy, brought down from the heights to what is called a prosaic form. Moreover, the fact that "sing" was used instead of "declare" in antiquity bears witness to this, proving that poetry was the source and origin of rhetorical expression. For it also required singing in its performance, and this was the ode, or sung speech, from which they began to speak of rhapsody, tragedy, and comedy. Thus, since first of all "declare" described poetic expression, along with the ode, singing was the same as declaring. Having misapplied one of these to poetic discourse, the misuse passed to the other. Moreover, the fact that discourse without meter was said to be "prosaic" shows it had descended from the heights, or from a chariot, to the ground.

(7) But he [Homer] does not speak only of nearby places – as Eratosthenes [F3] says – those within Hellas, but also many far away. Homer tells myths more accurately than later mythological authors, not totally recounting marvels, but for the sake of knowledge, using allegory, revision, and popularity, especially concerning the wanderings of Odysseus, about which he [Eratosthenes] makes many mistakes, maintaining that the commentators and the Poet himself are nonsense. It is worth speaking in detail about these things.

(8) First, the poets were not alone in accepting myths, for much earlier [C19] the cities and lawgivers had considered them useful, seeing the natural condition of the reasoning living being, since man has a love of learning. Thus children listen to tales and take part in them more and more. The reason is that myths are a kind of new language, not describing what is established but something else. What is new is pleasing, as well as something not previously known. This is what makes one eager to learn. When the marvellous and prodigious are added, it increases the pleasure, which is a charm for learning. At first it is necessary to make use of bait, but as [the child] approaches maturity it is led toward the learning of facts, when its intelligence is strengthened and there is no longer a need of flatterers. Every simple and uneducated person is, in a way, a kind of child and thus a lover of myths. The moderately educated person is similar, for he is not strong in reasoning and is attached to childhood habits. Since the prodigious is not only pleasing but also frightening, both types may be used for children and those at maturity. For children, we present the pleasing myths as encouragement and the frightening ones as a dissuasion. Lamia is a myth, and also Gorgo, Ephialtes, and Mormolyke. Most of those living in the cities tend to be encouraged by the pleasing myths, hearing the poets recite mythical deeds of heroism, such as the Labors of Herakles or Theseus, or the honors dispensed to the gods, or, by Zeus, when they see representations, images, or figures that suggest some occurrence in myth. Yet they are dissuaded by

the punishments of the gods, fears, or threats, which are acquired through words or some impression of something seen, or even believing that they have encountered them. For a crowd of women or a common mob cannot be persuaded at all by scholarly reason, or summoned to reverence, piety, or faith, for there is also a need of religious fear, which cannot be without myth-making and marvels. A thunderbolt, aegis, trident, torches, snakes, and thyrsos lances (the weapons of the gods) are myths, as is all ancient theology. But these things were accepted by the founders of states as certain [C20]   hobgoblins against childish minds.

Such is myth-making, directed toward the social and political character of life as well as the history of facts. The ancient ones preserved the educational system of children until maturity, assuming that poetry was sufficient to control every period of life. But much later in time the writing of history and contemporary philosophy have come to the forefront. Yet the latter is for the few, but poetry, especially that of Homer, is more for public use and is able to fill a theater. And the early historians and natural philosophers were also myth writers.

(9) Since the Poet considered myth to be a kind of education, he paid great attention to the truth. But "he placed in it" [*Iliad* 18.541] falsehood for popular favor and to command the masses, although acknowledging it. "Just as when some man pours gold around silver" [*Odyssey* 6.232, 23.159], he placed myth around the perimeter of the truth, sweetening and adorning the style, but seeing the same end as the historian or one narrating facts. Thus he took the Ilian war – which did happen – and adorned it with created myth, as he did with the wanderings of Odysseus, but to fasten an empty story of marvels to something totally untrue is not Homeric. For it happens, as is reasonable, that someone would lie more plausibly if something truthful is mixed in, as Polybios says [34.2.1–3] in his examination of the wanderings of Odysseus, such as in this case: "in speaking he told so many lies that resembled the truth" [*Odyssey* 19.203], not *all*, but *many*, or it would not have "resembled the truth."

The beginnings were taken from history. He says that Aiolos held power over the islands around Lipara, and the inhospitable Kyklopes and Laistrygonians over the region around Aitna and Leontine. Because of this the Strait was unapproachable at that time, and Charybdis and Skyllaion were controlled by brigands. We also observe that others mentioned by Homer were in other places. Knowing that the Kimmerians lived around the Kimmerian Bosporos – a dark region toward the north – he reasonably transferred them to a certain gloomy place down around Hades, as it was useful to his myth-making in the wanderings. That he knew about them is made clear by the chroniclers, who record that the Kimmerian invasion was shortly before him or at about the same time. [C21]

(10) Similarly, because of his knowledge of the Kolchians, of Jason's expedition to Aia, and the myths and accounts concerning Kirke and Medeia (their drugs and their other similarities), he fashioned a kinship between them (although they lived so far apart, one in the recess of the Pontos and the other in Italia), placing both of them out in the Ocean. Perhaps, however, Jason wandered as far as Italia, because certain signs of the wanderings of the Argonauts appear around the Keraunian mountains, the Adria, in the Poseidoniate Gulf, and the islands off Tyrrhenia. In addition there were the Kyaneai, which some call the Symplegades, rocks that made the passage through the Byzantiac mouth rough. It appears believable that Jason sailed through them (comparing Aiaia along with Aia and the Symplegades along with the Planktai, as well as the sail through the rocks near Skyllaion and Charybdis). At that time the Pontic Sea was understood as a kind of second Ocean, and it was believed that those sailing there went beyond the limits of the world, just like those who went far beyond the Pillars. It was considered to be the largest of our [seas], and especially because of this it was named the "Pontos" ["the Sea"], just as Homer was "the Poet." Perhaps because of this he transferred from the Pontos to the Ocean what was acceptable in current opinion. I believe that because the Solymians lived in the highest peaks of the Tauros – those around Lykia as far as Pisidia – and since this appeared to those within the Tauros (particularly those around the Pontos) to be the most conspicuous height to the south, thus because of a certain similarity they were placed out in the Ocean, for he says in regard to [Odysseus] sailing on his raft:

> going from the Aithiopians, the Lord Earth-Shaker saw him from afar, from the mountains of the Solymians. [*Odyssey* 5.282–3]

Perhaps he transferred the one-eyed Kyklopes from the Skythian accounts, for it is said that certain Arimaspians are in such a way, as Aristeas the Prokonnesian [F7] reported in his *Arimaspeia* poem.

(11) Having set forth these preliminaries, it is necessary to ask what is meant by those who say that according to Homer the wanderings of Odysseus were around Sikelia and Italia. This can be understood in two ways, one better and the other worse. The better is to accept that he believed the wanderings of Odysseus were there, and taking this as the truth, elaborated this assumption poetically. One could naturally say this about him, and one can find [C22] vestiges of the wanderings – and those of many others – not only around Italia but in the farthest regions of Iberia. The worse interpretation is to accept the elaboration as historical, because Okeanos, Hades, the cattle of Helios,

hospitality by goddesses, transformations, large Kyklopes and Laistrygonians, the shape of Skylla, the distances sailed, and many other similar things are clearly writings about marvels. But it is not worth refuting someone who is so clearly in error about the Poet, as if one could not say that the return of Odysseus to Ithaka and the Slaughter of the Suitors and the battle in the country between them and the Ithakans happened in that very way. It is also not proper to attack someone who interprets it correctly.

(12) Eratosthenes [F6] has confronted both of these reasons, but not well. In the second case, he believes that he [Homer] attempts to misrepresent something obviously false and unworthy of a lengthy discussion, and in the former, that all poets tell falsehoods and that their experience of places or the arts does not lead to virtue. Myths are related both about uninvented places, such as Ilion, Ida, and Pelion, and also about invented ones, such as where the Gorgons and Geryon are. He [Eratosthenes] says that those mentioned in the wanderings of Odysseus are also a construct, and that those who say they are not invented but substantiated are convicted of falsehood because they do not agree with one another. At any rate, some put the Seirenes on Pelorias, and others on the Seirenoussai, more than two thousand stadia away (allegedly the three-headed promontory that separates the Kymaian and Poseidoniate Gulfs). But this rock is not three-pointed, nor does its summit come at all to a head, but a kind of elbow projects out, long and narrow, from the region of Syrrenton to the strait of Kapria, having the sanctuary of the Seirenes on one side of the mountainous ridge. On the other (toward the Poseidoniate Gulf) lie three deserted and rocky islets that are called the Seirenes. The Athenaion is on the strait itself, from which the elbow is named.

(13) Moreover, even if those who have handed down the account of these places are not in agreement, frankly we should not throw out the entire account, since on the whole it may be more believable. As an example, I would ask whether it is said that the wanderings were around Sikelia or Italia, and that the Seirenes are somewhere around there. The one who [C23] says that they are in Pelorias disagrees with the one putting them on the Seirenoussai, but both of them do not disagree with someone saying that they are around Sikelia and Italia, yet provide him greater credibility, for although they do not point out the same place, nonetheless they do not depart from the region of Italia and Sikelia. If, then, someone were to add that a memorial of Parthenope, one of the Seirenes, is visible in Neapolis, there is even more credibility, although this is mentioning a third place. Moreover, Neapolis lies in this gulf, which Eratosthenes [F6] calls the Kymaian and which is formed by the Seirenoussai, and thus we can believe

even more strongly that the Seirenes were around these places. The Poet did not learn about each accurately, nor do we seek accuracy from him, but nonetheless we do not assume that he learned to sing about the wanderings without [knowing] where or how they happened.

(14) Eratosthenes [F6] infers Hesiod learned that the wanderings of Odysseus were throughout Sikelia and Italia, and believing this, recorded not only those places mentioned by Homer, but also Aitna, Ortygia [Hesiod, F98] (the little island next to Syracuse), and Tyrrhenia [Hesiod, *Theogony* 1016], yet Homer did not know them and did not wish to put the wanderings in known places. Are Aitna and Tyrrhenia well known, but Skyllaion and Charybdis, Kirkaion, and the Seirenoussai not at all? Is it fitting for Hesiod not to talk nonsense and to follow prevailing opinions, yet for Homer "to shout forth everything that comes to his untimely tongue." Apart from what has been said concerning the myth which it was fitting for Homer to relate about a place, most of the prose authors who repeat the same things, as well as the customary local reports about these places, can teach that these are not the fantasies of poets or even prose authors but vestiges of peoples and events.

(15) Yet Polybios [34.2.4–4.8] conjectures correctly about the wanderings. He says that Aiolos – who foretold how to sail through the regions surrounding the Strait, which have places with a constant ebb and flow that are difficult to sail through because of the back flowing – was called the controller of the winds and considered to be their king. Similarly Danaos, who pointed out the reservoirs in Argos, and Atreus [who pointed out] that the path of the sun is opposite to that of the heavens (both of whom were seers and divinators) were appointed kings. Moreover, the priests of the Egyptians, the Chaldaians, and   [C24] the Magoi, being different from the rest in some sort of wisdom, came to be leaders, honored by those before our time. And each one of the gods was honored because he discovered something useful.

With this by way of preface, he [Polybios] does not allow Aiolos to be called a type of myth, nor even the wanderings of Odysseus, but small fictions have been added (as with the Ilian War), and they all have been placed in Sikelia by the Poet and the other writers who speak of the country around Italia and Sikelia. He [Polybios] does not approve of the assertion by Eratosthenes [F5], who says that one will find where Odysseus wandered when you find the cobbler who sewed up the hide of winds. And certainly what happens around the Skyllaion with the hunting of the *galeotes* agrees with what is said about Skylla:

> eagerly searching around the rock, she fishes there for dolphins or dogfish, or whatever larger fish she could take anywhere. [*Odyssey* 12.95–7]

He [Polybios] says that when the schools of tuna are carried along Italia and it happens that they are prevented from reaching Sikelia, they encounter larger animals such as dolphins, dogfish, and other sea creatures. The *galeotes* – called both swordfish and dogfish – are fattened by these animals [the tuna]. This happens here, as with the rising of the Nile and other rivers, and also when there is a fire or conflagration in the woods and the collected animals flee the fire or water and become the prey of those stronger.

(16) Having said these things, he [Polybios] continues about the hunting of the *galeotes* that are associated with the Skyllaion. With a lookout appointed in common, they lie in wait at anchor in many two-oared boats, two men in each little boat, with one directing it and the other standing in the prow holding a spear. When the lookout gives the signal that the *galeotes* have appeared – a third of the animal rises out of the sea – the boat comes nearby and he [the spearman] strikes it at close range, and then draws the spear out of its body, except for the point, for it is barbed and on purpose loosely connected to the spear, having a long small line fastened to it. This is paid out for a while to the wounded [fish] until it becomes tired through its struggles and its attempts to flee. Then it is dragged to the land or taken into the boat, unless its body is altogether too large. If the spear falls into the sea, it is not lost, for it is constructed of both oak and pine, and although the oak sinks because of its weight the remainder rises in the air [C25] and is easily recoverable. It sometimes happens that the rower of the boat is injured because of the size of the sword of the *galeotes*, as the vigor and hunting of the animal is like that of the wild boar.

He [Polybios] says one may conjecture from such things that according to Homer the wanderings occurred around Sikelia, since he ascribed to Skylla the same kind of hunting that is most customary at the Skyllaion. In addition there is what he said about Charybdis, which is similar to what happens at the Strait. But "three times it goes up" [*Odyssey* 12.105], instead of "twice," is either a copyist's error, or one of precision.

(17) Moreover, what is said about Meninx agrees with that about the Lotus Eaters. But if there is no agreement, the reason must be changes, ignorance, or poetic license, which is a combination of information, composition, and myth. The purpose of information is the truth, as is the case in the *Catalogue of Ships*, where the Poet mentions the attributes of each place: that one city is rocky, another is far away, another abounding in doves, and another near the sea. The purpose of composition is stylistic vigor (as when fighting is introduced), and that of myth is pleasure and passion. But to fabricate everything is neither plausible nor Homeric. Everyone believes that his poetry is a scholarly treatise, not like Eratosthenes [F4] says, who

commands us neither to judge the poems in regard to their thought, nor to seek history in them.

It is more plausible that the passage "I was carried along for nine days by destructive winds" [*Odyssey* 9.82] is to be taken as within a small distance (for destructive [winds] do not run in a straight line), than to place it out in the Ocean, as if with continuously blowing fair winds. If one considers the distance from Maleai to the Pillars as 22,500 stadia, and if, as he [Polybios] says, we assume that it was accomplished at an equal speed for the nine days, the sail each day would be 2,500 stadia. But who has ever reported arriving in Alexandria from Lykia or Rhodes on the second day, even though the distance is 4,000 stadia?

Regarding those who further ask how Odysseus could go to Sikelia three times and not sail once through the Strait, he [Polybios] defends this, that it was for the same reason that all later sailors have avoided it.

(18) This is what he [Polybios] has said, and he has generally spoken well. [C26] But when he demolishes placing them out in the Ocean, and reduces the days of sailing to exact measurements and distances, he does not avoid excessive inconsistency. At one point he cites the words of the Poet ("I was carried along for nine days by destructive winds" [*Odyssey* 9.82]), but elsewhere hides things. For the Poet also has this: "when the ship, leaving the stream of the river of Okeanos" [*Odyssey* 12.1–2] and "in the island of Ogygia, where the navel of the sea is" [*Odyssey* 1.50], and that the daughter of Atlas lives there. There is also this about the Phaiakians:

> we live far away on the sea with its many waves, the most distant of peoples, and no other mortals have contact with us. [*Odyssey* 6.204–5]

It is manifestly clear that all these are imagined to be in the Atlantic Ocean. But in hiding these things he [Polybios] does away with what has been said clearly, and that is not right.

Yet he is correct in placing the wanderings around Sikelia and Italia, and this is confirmed by the Poet. When did a poet or prose author persuade the Neapolitans to make a memorial for Parthenope the Seirene, or those in Kyme, Dikaiarcheia, and at Vesuvius[1] for Pyriphlegethon, the Acherousian Marsh, the oracle of the dead at Aornos, or Baios and Misenos, both companions of Odysseus? It is the same with that about the Seirenoussai, the Strait, Skylla and Charybdis, and Aiolos. This must not be scrutinized

---

[1] "Vesuvius" ("Ouesouios") is an emendation; the text has "besbio," which some have emended to "Baiai," given what follows.

carefully or considered without roots or a home, not attached to the truth or any historical benefit.

(19) Eratosthenes [F7] himself suspected this, for he says one might understand that the Poet wished to put the wanderings of Odysseus toward western places, but he set aside the idea because he had not learned about them accurately (or because he chose not to do so), in order to develop each element more cleverly and more marvellously. He [Eratosthenes] understands this correctly, but is wrong in regard to why it was done, since it was not for silliness but for a benefit. Therefore it is proper that he should undergo examination both about this and also why he says that marvellous tales are told about faraway places because it is safe to tell falsehoods about them. For the number of stories of marvels in far distant places is much fewer than those in Hellas or near to Hellas, which include those about the Labors of Herakles and Theseus, the tales set on Crete and Sikelia and the other islands, and those about Kithairon, Helikon, Parnassos, Pelion, and [C27] throughout Attika and the Peloponnesos. No one claims that the myth-makers are ignorant because of their myths. Moreover, they – especially Homer – do not totally create myths, but add a large amount of mythical detail, and someone who seeks what the ancients added in mythical detail does not seek whether the added mythical detail existed or still exists, but rather seeks the truth regarding the places and people of the added mythical detail, such as if the wanderings of Odysseus happened, and where.

(20) By and large, it is not correct to equate the poetry of Homer with that of other poets, and fail to assign him the prerogative, especially in regard to what now lies before us, matters of geography. For if one were to do nothing other than go through the *Triptolemos* of Sophokles or the prologue to the *Bacchants* of Euripides and then compare Homer's care in such matters, one could easily perceive the different approach. Whenever it is necessary to recount places in order, he preserves the order, not only for Hellenic ones but those far away:

> They sought to put Ossa on Olympos, and on Ossa Pelion with quivering foliage. [*Odyssey* 11.315–16]

> Darting Hera left the peak of Olympos and touched on Pieria and lovely Emathia, hurrying over the snowy mountains of the horse-herding Thracians... from Athos to the sea. [*Iliad* 14.225–9]

And in the *Catalogue* he does not mention the cities in order, as it was not necessary, but it was so for the peoples, such as these far away:

> I wandered through Cyprus, Phoenicia, and Egypt, and came to the Aithiopians, Sidonians, Erembians, and Libya. [*Odyssey* 4.83–5]

Hipparchos [F3] also noted this. But both of the others [Sophokles and Euripides] – even where an order is necessary and when the latter is speaking about when Dionysos came to the peoples, and the former about Triptolemos and the sowing of the earth – bring those which are far apart near to each other:

> Having left the fields of the Lydians, rich in gold, the Phrygians, the sun-scorched plains of the Persians, and the walls of Baktria, I have come to the wintry land of the Medes and fortunate Arabia. [Euripides, *Bacchants* 13–16]

Triptolemos does the same.

In regard to the latitudes and winds, Homer further shows his geographical learning, for in his topographical accounts he often speaks of both of them: [C28]

> It [Ithaka] lies near the land, high on the salty sea toward the darkness, but the others are far away toward the dawn and the sun. [*Odyssey* 9.25–6]

> There are two gates, one toward Boreas...and the other toward Notos. [*Odyssey* 13.109–11]

> Whether they go to the right toward the dawn and the sun or to the left toward the misty darkness. [*Iliad* 12.239–40]

In particular, he considers ignorance of these things as confusion about everything:

> Friends, we do not know where there is darkness, where there is dawn, or where the sun... [*Odyssey* 10.190–1]

The Poet spoke accurately: "Boreas and Zephyros, the Thracian winds" [*Iliad* 9.5], but he [Eratosthenes, F11] does not accept this correctly and quibbles about it, as if he [Homer] were speaking generally that the Zephyr blows from Thrace. Yet he is not speaking generally, but about when they come together on the Thracian Sea around the Gulf of Melas, which is a part of the Aigaion itself. For Thrace, where it touches Makedonia, takes a turn to the south, and forms a promontory into the open sea, and it seems to those on Thasos, Lemnos, Imbros, Samothrake, and the surrounding sea that the Zephyrs blow from there, just as for Attika they come from the Skironian rocks, because of which the Zephyrs, and especially the Argestes, are called the Skirones. Eratosthenes did not perceive this, although he suspected it. Nevertheless he told about the turn of the land that I have mentioned. He accepts it [what Homer said] as universal and then accuses the Poet of ignorance, in that the Zephyr blows from the west and Iberia, but Thrace does not extend that far. Is he [Homer] really unaware that the Zephyr blows from the west? But he keeps it in its proper place when he says

"Euros and Notos fell upon each other, and stormy Zephyros and Boreas" [*Odyssey* 5.295–6]. Does he not know that Thrace does not advance beyond the Paionian and Thessalian mountains? But he knows Thrace, and what is next to it, and names both the seacoast and interior, enumerating certain Magnetians, Malians, and the Hellenes beyond them as far as the Thesprotians, as well as those contiguous with the Paionians – the Dolopians, and the Sellians around Dodona as far as the Acheloos – but he does not record any Thracians beyond them. He has a certain fondness for [C29] the sea that is nearest and best known to him, as he says "the assembly stirred like the great waves of the waters of the Ikarian Sea" [*Iliad* 2.144–5].

(21) Some say that there are only two major winds, the Boreas and the Notos, and that the others differ only by a slight displacement: from the summer sunrise there is the Euros, from the winter, the Apeliotes, from the summer sunset the Zephyr, and from the winter, the Argestes. For the fact that there are only two winds [they use] the testimony of Thrasyalkes [F2] and the Poet himself, who assigns the Argestes to the Notos in "of Argestes Notos" [*Iliad* 11.306, 21.334] and the Zephyr to the Boreas in "Boreas and Zephyros, the Thracian winds" [*Iliad* 9.5].

But Poseidonios [F137a] says that none of the authorities (such as Aristotle, Timosthenes [F6], or Bion the astronomer) have reported this about the winds, but the one from the summer sunrise is the Kaikias, and that diametrically opposed is the Lips, from the winter sunset. From the winter sunrise there is the Euros and the opposite is the Argestes. Between these are the Apeliotes and the Zephyr, and when the Poet speaks of "stormy Zephyros" this is what we called the Argestes, and "clear blowing Zephyros" is our Zephyr, and "Argestes Notos" is the Leukonotos, for it makes few clouds, whereas the other Notos does to some extent: "as when Zephyros drives away the clouds of Argestes Notos, striking them with a deep storm" [*Iliad* 11.305–6]. Here he speaks of the stormy Zephyr, which customarily scatters the weak [clouds] gathered by the Leukonotos, for here "Argestes" is used as an epithet of the Notos.

These are the corrections that are to be made at the beginning of the first book of the *Geographika* of Eratosthenes [F11].

(22) Continuing in his assumption about the falsity of Homer, he [Eratosthenes, F10] says that he does not even know that there are several mouths to the Nile, or its name, although Hesiod knows, for he records it [*Theogony* 338]. Concerning the name, it is probable that it was not yet used in his time. In regard to the mouths, if they were unnoticed or only a few knew that there were several rather than one, it might be granted that he did not know this.

But if the river was, and is, the best known and most incredible thing in Egypt, the most worthy of all things to remember and to be recorded, including its rising and its mouths, who would not assume that those who informed him [Homer] about the Aigyptos River, the land, Egyptian Thebes, and Pharos, did not know about them? If they did know about them they did not mention them, since they were in fact well known. But it is still more unbelievable that he mentioned Aithiopia, the Sidonians, Erembians, the External Sea, and that the Aithiopians are divided in two, but not what was near and known. If he did not cite them, this is no proof that he was ignorant of them (he does not cite his own native land or many others), but rather, one would say, he believed that what was especially well known was not worthy of citing to those knowing them. [C30]

(23) How they reproach him [Homer] about this island of Pharos is unreasonable, because he says it is in the open sea, as if he were speaking from ignorance. On the contrary, one might use this as testimony that the Poet was ignorant about nothing that has just been discussed about Egypt. You can understand it this way: everyone who describes his own wanderings is a braggart. Menelaos was one of these, who went up as far as the Aithiopians and learned about the rising of the Nile and the soil that it puts on the land, and the stretch beyond its mouths that has been added to the continent through siltation, so that Herodotos [2.5] was reasonable when he said all Egypt is a gift of the river. Even if this is not the case in its entirety, it is so with that [region] around the Delta called the Lower Territory. He [Homer] learned that Pharos had been in the sea in ancient times, so he falsely added that it was still in the sea, although it was no longer in the sea. It was the Poet who elaborated this, and thus it may be inferred that he knew about the risings and mouths of the Nile.

(24) There is the same mistake about his [Homer's] ignorance of the isthmus between the Egyptian Sea and the Arabian Gulf, in suggesting that he is wrong in speaking of "the Aithiopians, divided in two, the farthest of men" [*Odyssey* 1.23]. It is correct to say this, and later writers do not rebuke him justly. It is hardly true that Homer is ignorant of this isthmus, and thus I say that he not only knows about it but demonstrates this openly, although grammarians beginning with Aristarchos and Krates – the leaders in such knowledge – do not perceive that he speaks about it. The Poet says this: "the Aithiopians, divided in two, the farthest of men" [*Odyssey* 1.23]. Yet there is a dispute concerning the words that follow, as Aristarchos writes "some where Hyperion sets and others where he rises" [*Odyssey* 1.24] but Krates has "living where Hyperion sets and also where he rises," although there is no difference to the story whether the phrase is written one way or the other. [C31]

Following established scientific opinion, the latter says [F37] that the burned zone is occupied by the Ocean and that the temperate one is on either side of it, one part on our side and the other on the other. Just as the Aithiopians are on our side – those who slope toward the south throughout the entire inhabited world – and are said to be the most remote of all, living on the Ocean, he [Krates] believes that there must be certain Aithiopians living across the Ocean, who are the most remote of those in the other temperate zone and live on the shore of this same Ocean, since they are double and divided by the Ocean. He [Homer] adds "living where Hyperion sets and also where he rises" because the zodiac is always in the zenith above the terrestrial zodiac, which, due to its obliqueness, does not extend beyond both Aithopians. It is necessary to believe that the entire solar path is in this expanse and that all its risings and settings occur here, but differently to different people, in one sign or another. This is what he [Krates] says, considering it more astronomically. He could have spoken more simply, yet preserving the matter about the Aithiopians divided in two, as he [Homer] said: that the Aithiopians extend on both sides of the Ocean from the rising to the setting of the sun. What difference is it, in respect to the sense, whether it is read as he [Krates] wrote, or as Aristarchos ("some where Hyperion sets and others where he rises")? This also means that they live toward the setting and the rising, on both sides of the Ocean.

But Aristarchos rejects this hypothesis and believes that those who are said to be divided in two are our Aithiopians, the ones that (to the Hellenes) are farthest to the south. They are not divided in two so as to have two Aithiopias – one to the east and the other to the west – but only one, lying to the south of the Hellenes, located beyond Egypt. The Poet was ignorant of this, just as [he was of] those things that Apollodoros [of Athens, F157e] mentioned in the second book of his *On the Catalogue of Ships*, and he reported false things about those places.

(25) A long discussion would be necessary against Krates, which perhaps would not be of use in the present matter. Yet in this I approve of Aristarchos because he rejects the hypothesis of Krates – about which there are many objections – and conjectures that the text refers to our Aithiopia. Let us consider other things. First, he examines the text minutely in vain. If it is written in either of two ways, it can be adapted to his purposes. What difference is it to say "there are two groups of Aithiopians on our side, one toward the rising and the other toward the setting," or "toward the rising and toward the setting"? Thus he puts forth a false opinion. Suppose that the Poet is ignorant of the isthmus, but mentions Aithopia beyond Egypt when he says "the Aithiopians, divided in two" [*Odyssey* 1.23]. Well! Are they not thus

[C32]

"divided in two" and did the Poet say that in ignorance? Is not Egypt, and are not the Egyptians (beginning with the Delta and as far as Syene) divided in two by the Nile, "some where Hyperion sets and others where he rises" [*Odyssey* 1.24]? What is Egypt other than a riverine island that the water floods? It lies on both sides of the river, toward the rising and the setting. Moreover, Aithiopia is in a straight line with Egypt and resembles it in terms of the Nile and the other characteristics of the place, for it too is narrow, long, and flooded. That which is beyond the flooded region – both what is lying toward the east and toward the west – is desolate and waterless, capable only of scant habitation. Thus is it then not "divided in two"? The Nile appeared worthy of consideration as the boundary separating Asia from Libya, since its length extends to the south more than a myriad of stadia, with such a width that it contains islands with a myriad of people, of which the largest is Meroë, the royal seat and metropolis of the Aithiopians, yet it [the Nile] was not adequate to divide Aithiopia in two! Moreover, the ones who object to those who have the river dividing the continents bring forward as their greatest accusation against them that they tear apart Egypt and Aithiopia, making one part of each Libyan and the other Asiatic, or if they do not wish to do this, they do not divide the continents, at least not with the river.

(26) Apart from this, there may be another way to divide Aithiopia. All those who have sailed along Libya on the Ocean, whether from the Erythra or the Pillars, however far they went, turned back because they were hindered by many strange things, giving to most the impression that what was in between was separated by an isthmus. But the entire Atlantic Sea flows together, especially in the south. All have recorded that the last region to which they sailed was Aithiopia, and have so reported it. How is it thus [C33] unreasonable if Homer, hearing such things, referred to them as divided in two, saying that some were toward the rising and others toward the setting, since it was unknown whether those in between existed or not?

Moreover, Ephoros [F128] mentions another ancient report, and it is not unreasonable that Homer came upon it. He reports the Tartessians say that the Aithiopians overran Libya as far as Dyris, and that some remained there and others occupied much of the coast. He concludes that because of this Homer spoke about "the Aithiopians, divided in two, the farthest of men" [*Odyssey* 1.23].

(27) One might say these things to Aristarchos and his followers, and others more capable, and thus remove the Poet from [a charge of] great ignorance.

I say that according to the opinion of the ancient Hellenes, just as they gave the name Skythians or Nomads (as Homer has) to those who are known to be in the boreal region, and later, when they learned about those toward the

west, they called them Kelts or Iberians, or the compounds Keltiberians or
Keltoskythians – various people assigned a single name through ignorance –
in such a way everywhere to the south near the Ocean was called Aithiopia.
These are the proofs. Aischylos in the *Promethus Unbound* says the following:

> The sacred stream of the Erythran Sea with its red bottom, and the marsh on
> the Ocean, bronze gleaming, all-nurturer of the Aithiopians, where all-seeing
> Helios always refreshed his tired skin and his immortal horses in the hot
> outpourings of soft water. [F192]

Thus the Ocean provides this service and has this relationship to the sun
along the entire southern zone, and he clearly assigns the Aithiopians this
entire position. And Euripides in his *Phaethon* says that Klymene was given

> to Merops, the king of the land that is the first place which Helios, rising in
> his chariot yoked with four horses, strikes with his golden flame. The black
> mortals who live nearby call it the shining stables of Eos and Helios. [F771]

[C34] Here he makes the stables those of both Eos and Helios, but he also says that
they are near to the home of Merops. This is woven into the entire action of
the play, not because it is some peculiarity of Aithiopia near Egypt, but
because of the entire southern zone that extends along the coast.

(28) Ephoros [F30a] also reveals the ancient opinion about Aithiopia, for
in his treatise *On Europe* he says – dividing the regions of the heavens and
earth into four parts – that the Indians will be toward the Apeliotes wind,
the Aithiopians toward the Notos, the Kelts toward the sunset, and the
Skythians toward the boreal wind. He adds that Aithiopia and Skythia are
the larger, for he says it seems that the Aithiopian peoples extend from the
winter sunrise as far as the sunset, and Skythia lies directly opposite them.

It is clear that the Poet agrees with this, for Ithaka lies "toward the
darkness" (which means toward the north), "but the others are far away
toward the dawn and the sun" [*Odyssey* 9.26], meaning the entire southern
side, and also when he says

> whether they go to the right toward the dawn and the sun or to the left
> toward murky darkness [*Iliad* 17.239–40]

and again,

> Friends, we do not know where there is darkness, where there is dawn, or
> where the sun that brings light to mortals goes beneath the earth, or where it
> rises. [*Odyssey* 10.190–2]

This is examined more clearly in the discussion of Ithaka [10.2.11–12].

When he says that "Zeus went yesterday to Okeanos among the noble
Aithiopians" [*Iliad* 1.423–4], it must be [understood] more generally, with

"Okeanos" extending along the entire southern zone, as well as the "Aithiopians," for wherever you turn your attention in this zone, it will be both on the Ocean and in Aithiopia. This is the case when he says "going from the Aithiopians. . .[he] saw him from afar, from the mountains of the Solymians" [*Odyssey* 5.282–3], which is the same as "from the southern places," for he does not mean the Solymians in Pisidia, but, as I have said previously [1.2.10], he creates ones of the same name who lie in an analogous position to the sailor on his raft and those toward his south (who would be Aithiopians), as the Pisidians are in regard to Pontos and the Aithiopians beyond Egypt. His argument about the cranes is also generalized, saying "when they flee the winter and portentous rain, and fly clanging toward   [C35] the streams of Okeanos, bringing slaughter and doom to the Pygmaian men" [*Iliad* 3.4–6]. For the crane is seen moving to the south only in Hellenic places, never in Italia or Iberia, or along the Kaspian or in Baktriane. The extent of the Ocean is along the entire southern coast, to all of which they migrate in winter, and the Pygmaians must mythologically be placed along all of it. And if those later transferred the story about the Pygmaians only to the Aithiopians near Egypt, this would not be something from antiquity. Today we do not say "Achaians" or "Argives" for everyone who made the expedition against Ilion, although Homer thus calls all of them.

What I say about the "Aithiopians divided in two" is nearly the same: that they must be understood as extending along the entire shore of the Ocean from the rising of the sun to the setting of the sun. The Aithiopians who are spoken about in such a way are naturally "divided in two" by the Arabian Gulf (which would be a significant section of a meridian circle) in the manner of a river of about 15,000 stadia in length and a maximum of not much more than 1,000 in width. To this distance must be added that by which the recess of the gulf is separated from the sea at Pelousion – three or four days' journey – which is that occupied by the isthmus. Just as those who are more capable in separating Asia from Libya consider this gulf to be a more natural boundary between the continents than the Nile (for it extends almost entirely from sea to sea, but the Nile is separated from the Ocean by much more, so that it does not separate all Asia from Libya), thus in the same way I assume that the Poet considered the southern portions of the entire inhabited world "divided in two" by this gulf. How, then, can he be ignorant of the isthmus that it makes with the Egyptian Sea?

(29) It is completely unreasonable that if he knew Egyptian Thebes well (which is separated from Our Sea by a little less than 5,000 stadia), he then did not know about the recess of the Arabian Gulf, or the isthmus adjoining

it, whose width is no more than 1,000 stadia. It would seem to be much more unreasonable if he knew that the Nile had the same name as the entire territory but did not know the reasons, for the idea of Herodotos [2.5] would obviously come to mind, that the land was a gift of the river, and for this reason deserved the same name. Moreover, there are the peculiarities of each [region] that are best known and are particularly marvellous and manifest to everyone, such as the rising of the Nile and the silting up of the sea. Just as those going to Egypt learn nothing about this land before the nature of the Nile, because there is nothing the locals can say to foreigners that is more unusual or more famous about their [land] than this (since the entire land, as much as it is, becomes quite clear to someone who has learned about the river), those who hear about it from a distance also learn nothing before this. One can add to this the Poet's fondness of learning and fondness of travel, to which all of those who have written about his life testify, and many examples of which can be obtained from the poems. Thus from many things it is proved that he knows and says specifically what is to be said, but he is silent about what is especially obvious, or uses an epithet.

[C36]

(30) Yet one must be amazed at the Egyptians and Syrians, against whom I am making the present argument, who do not understand him when he is talking about their own territory, but accuse him of ignorance, something that the argument shows they are subject to themselves. In general, not saying something is not a sign of not knowing something. He does not mention the changes of the Euripos, or Thermopylai, or other well-known things among the Hellenes, but he was was not ignorant of them. Yet he speaks of other matters, although to those who affect deafness it does not seem so, and thus the blame must be theirs.

Thus the Poet calls rivers "fallen from Zeus" [*Iliad* 16.174, *Odyssey* 4.477] – not only the winter flow, but all of them in common – because they are all filled by rain water. But the general term becomes specific due to its pre-eminence, for "fallen from Zeus" would be understood in one way in regard to the winter flow and another for the perennial flow, and in this case the pre-eminence is even double. And there are also examples of excess upon excess, such as "lighter than the shadow of a cork," "more cowardly than a Phrygian hare," or "to have farmland smaller than a Lakonian letter," and thus one encounters pre-eminence upon pre-eminence when the Nile is said to be "fallen from Zeus." Although its winter flow exceeds other rivers in terms of having "fallen from Zeus," the Nile when full [exceeds] those winter flows by so much, both in abundance and extent. Thus, since the character of the river was known to the Poet, as we have suggested, and since he had given it this epithet, it must not be in any way other than we have

[C37]

said. Emptying through several mouths is common to several [rivers], and thus he did not consider it worthy of mention to those knowing it, just as Alkaios [F432] did not, although he also says that he visited Egypt.

The siltation can be assumed from the rising as well as from what he [Homer] says about Pharos. For whoever reported to him that Pharos – or rather it was common knowledge – was as far from the mainland as he says (a day's run for a ship) would not have spread abroad such a falsehood. As for the rising and siltation, it is more believable that he had learned this through common knowledge. Thus the Poet concluded from this that the island was somewhat farther from the land when Menelaos was there, and added a distance many times greater for the sake of the fabulous. Myth-making is not done out of ignorance, not even the notices about Proteus or the Pygmaians, or the power of drugs, or anything else that the poets create, for these are told not in ignorance of places but for pleasure and enjoyment. How, then, could he say that it [Pharos] has water when it is without water?

> A harbor is there, with a good anchorage, from which they put the ships into the deep sea, having drawn black water. [*Odyssey* 4.358–9]

It is not impossible that the water source has failed, and, moreover, he does not say that the water source was on the island, only the launching (because of the excellence of the harbor). The water may have been drawn from the mainland opposite, since the Poet to some extent admits to the implication that when he said "the open sea" it was not the truth but for the sake of exaggeration or myth making.

(31) Since what is said about the wanderings of Menelaos seems to imply ignorance of those places, it is perhaps better to set forth the questions in advance, and then separate them and defend the Poet more clearly.

Menelaos, then, says to Telemachos, who has marvelled at the decoration of the palace,

> indeed, after many experiences and many wanderings, I filled my ships and came here in the eighth year. I wandered through Cyprus, Phoenicia, and Egypt, and came to the Aithiopians, Sidonians, Erembians, and Libya. [*Odyssey* 4.81–5]

They ask which Aithiopians, then, did he come to, sailing from Egypt? The [C38] Aithiopians do not live on Our Sea, and ships could not pass the cataracts of the Nile. Who are the Sidonians? They are not those in Phoenicia, for he would not have put the generic before the specific. Who are the Erembians? This is a new name. Aristonikos, a grammarian of our time, in his *On the Wanderings of Menelaos* [F1], has recorded the opinions of many men concerning each of these major points that have been set forth, but for us it will be sufficient to speak briefly. Of those who say that he sailed to Aithiopia, some suggest a circumnavigation past Gadeira as far as Indike, so that the time spent corresponds to the wanderings (as he says, "I came here in the eighth year"), but others [that he went] across the isthmus toward the Arabian Gulf, and others through one of the canals.

A circumnavigation, which Krates proposed [F40], is not necessary – not that it would be impossible (for the wanderings of Odysseus would thus have been impossible) – but because it is of no use either in his mathematical suppositions or in regard to the time spent on the wanderings. For he [Menelaos] was delayed against his will because of the difficulties of sailing – he says that out of sixty ships only five were left to him – and he voluntarily engaged in trade. Nestor says "as he gathered together much sustenance and gold there, wandering with his ships" [*Odyssey* 3.301–2]. Sailing through the isthmus or the canals, if he [Homer] mentioned it, could be considered in the form of a myth, but he did not mention it, and it would be extraordinary and unbelievable for someone to introduce it. I say it would be unlikely, since there was no canal before the Trojan matter, and Sesostris, the one who attempted to make one, is said to have abandoned it because it seemed that the sea appeared to be too high. But the isthmus was also not navigable, and what Eratosthenes [F17] suggests is not correct. He believes that the breakout at the Pillars had not yet happened and that the Internal Sea joined the External Sea, and since it was higher, covered the isthmus, but when the breakout occurred it was lowered and thus uncovered the land around Kasion and Pelousion as far as the Erythra.

[C39] What information, then, do we have concerning the breakthrough, and that it did not yet exist before the Trojan affair? Perhaps the Poet made Odysseus sail through it into the Ocean – as if there already were a breakthrough – at the same time that Menelaos was carried by ship from Egypt into the Erythra, as though [the canal] did not yet exist. Yet he brings Proteus to say to him: "But the immortals will send you to the Elysian Plain and the extremities of the earth" [*Odyssey* 4.563–4]. Where? He says some extreme place in the west, as is shown by citing the Zephyr ("But Okeanos always releases the clear blowing winds of Zephyros" [*Odyssey* 4.567–8]). These things are full of riddles.

(32) If the Poet knew that the isthmus had once been covered, would we not have so much greater belief that the Aithopians were divided in two, as they would be separated by so great a strait? And how could he [Menelaos] have done so much business with the Aithiopians who were outside and along the Ocean? When those with Telemachos marvelled at the adornments of his

palace, they also [marvelled] at their quantity, and that they were "gold, amber, silver, and ivory" [*Odyssey* 4.73]. Except for ivory, there is no abundance of these things among them [the Aithiopians], most of whom are completely without resources and nomadic. But Arabia was near, by Zeus, and the regions as far as Indike. Although the former alone, of all of these, is called "Fortunate," the latter, even though it is not called by that name, is both considered and believed to be most fortunate. Homer did not know about Indike (for if he had known about it he would have recorded it), but [he did know about] Arabia, which today is called Fortunate, yet which was not wealthy in his day, being without resources and mostly having men living in tents. The aromatic-producing region, which obtained this name because such goods are rare and costly among us, is small. Today they are wealthy and rich because their commerce is abundant and plentiful, but it was not likely to have been so at that time. In regard to the aromatics, there might be some amount of wealth from such merchandise for a trader or camel-driver, but it was necessary for Menelaos to receive booty or gifts from kings or dynasts who wished to give him gifts because of his distinction and fame.

The Egyptians, Aithiopians, and Arabians, however, were not totally destitute, nor had they failed to hear about the reputation of the Atreidai, especially because of the successful conclusion of the Ilian War, for there would be the hope of profit from them, just as is said about the breastplate [C40] of Agamemnon: "Kinyras once gave it as a host's gift, having learned in Cyprus about his great reputation" [*Iliad* 11.20–1]. And it must be said that most of his [Menelaos'] wanderings were spent in Phoenicia, Syria, Egypt, Libya, and the region around Cyprus, generally along our coast and the islands. He could acquire gifts from them through hospitality, and also through force and plunder, especially from those who had been allies of the Trojans. But the barbarians outside or far away could offer no such hopes.

Menelaos is said to have come to Aithiopia, as far as the boundary with Egypt. Perhaps at that time the boundary was closer to Thebes, although it is quite near today, beyond Syene and Philai. The former is Egyptian, but Philai is inhabited by both Aithiopians and Egyptians. When he came to Thebes, it is not unreasonable that he also went as far as the boundary of the Aithiopians, or farther, making use of the king's hospitality. Thus Odysseus said that he came to the land of the Kyklopes, going only as far from the sea as the cave, since he says it was located somewhere on the border. And regarding Aiolia, the Laistrygonians, and others (wherever he anchored), he says that he came to them. Thus Menelaos came to Aithiopia, and to Libya, touching certain places, and because of this the harbor at Ardanis above Paraitonion is called Menelaos.

(33) If, in speaking about the Phoenicians, he [Homer] names the Sidonians, their mother city, he is using a familiar figure of speech, such as "he brought the Trojans and Hektor to the ships" [*Iliad* 13.1], and "for the sons of great-hearted Oineus were no more, nor was he, and fair-haired Meleagros was dead" [*Iliad* 2.641–2], and "he came to Ida...to Gagaros" [*Iliad* 8.47–8], and "they held Euboia...Chalkis and Eiretria" [*Iliad* 2.536–7]. Also Sappho [F35]: "either Cyprus or Paphos or Panormos [holds] you."

Moreover, there was another reason that the Poet, although he had already mentioned Phoenicia, repeated it again in a peculiar way: to include Sidon in the catalogue. To recount the peoples in order it was sufficient to say it in this manner: "I wandered through Cyprus, Phoenicia, and Egypt, and came to [C41] Aithiopia" [*Odyssey* 4.83–4]. In order to show that the time spent among the Sidonians was lengthy he thus went back and repeated it, shown by the praise of their prosperity as well as their artistic skill, and also the protection once given by these people to Helen when she was with Alexander. This is why he speaks of many such things stored away at the house of Alexander:

> her richly woven peploi were there, the work of Sidonian women, whom godlike Alexander himself had brought from Sidon...on the journey where he brought back Helen [*Iliad* 6.289–92]

and also in the house of Menelaos, who says to Telemachos:

> I will give you an artistically worked krater; it is completely of silver, with lips finished with gold. It is the work of Hephaistos. The hero Phaidimos, the Sidonian king, gave it to me, when I was sheltered there in his house during my return home. [*Odyssey* 4. 615–19; 15.115–19]

It is necessary to accept the words "the work of Hephaistos" as an exaggeration, just as beautiful things are said to be the work of Athena, the Charites, or the Muses. Those men [the Sidonians] created beautiful works of art, something made clear by the praise of the krater which Euneos gave in exchange for Lykaon, when he [Homer] said:

> in beauty it far surpassed everything else on the earth, for the Sidonians, workers of great skill, had formed it well, and Phoenician men then brought it. [*Iliad* 23.742–4]

(34) Much has been said about the Erembians, and those who believe that he [Homer] said "Arabians" are most persuasive. Our Zenon writes it thus [F275]: "I came to the Aithiopians, Sidonians, and Arabians" [*Odyssey* 4.84, emended]. But it is not necessary to alter the wording, which is old. A better reason is that they changed their name, something that is frequent and manifest among all peoples. It is careless to make changes of certain letters.

What Poseidonios [F280] says seems to be better, with the etymology from the kinship of the peoples and their communality. For the people of Armenia, the Syrians, and the Arabians display a great racial kinship, both in their language and their lives and physical characteristics, particularly where they are adjacent. It is clear that Mesopotamia is where these three peoples come together, and their similarity is particularly manifested. Considering the latitudes, there is a great difference between those toward the north and south and the Syrians in the middle, but common conditions prevail, [C42] and the Assyrians and Arimanians somewhat resemble both each other and the others. He [Poseidonios] infers that the names of these peoples are similar to each other, for those whom we call Syrians are called Aramaians by the Syrians themselves, and there is a resemblance between this [name], and that of the Armenians, Arabians, and Erembians. Perhaps the ancient Hellenes called the latter the Arabians, with the etymology connecting them. Thus most derive it from *eran embainein* ["to go into the earth"], which they later changed to the clearer "Troglodytes." These are the Arabians who are on that side of the Arabian Gulf that inclines toward Egypt and Aithiopia.

Thus it was natural that the Poet was aware of this when he said that Menelaos came to them, in the same manner that he spoke about coming to the Aithiopians, who are also near the Thebais. They were recorded not because of their workmanship nor the business done with them (which would not have been much) but because of the length of his time with them and its distinction, for it was a distinction to have gone so far. Thus "he saw the cities and knew the minds of many men" [*Odyssey* 1.3], and "after many experiences and many wanderings I filled. . ." [*Odyssey* 4.81–2]. Hesiod in the *Catalogue* says: "the daughter of Arabos, whom guileless Hermes bore with Thronia, daughter of lord Belos" [F88]. Stesichoros [F237] says the same. Thus it may be inferred that the land at that time was already called Arabia, although possibly not yet so in heroic times.

(35) Those who suggest that the Erembians are a particular Aithiopian, Kephenian, or, thirdly, Pygmaian people – or a myriad of others – are less believable, since in regard to trustworthiness they manifest a certain confusion between the forms of myth and history. Similar are those who describe Sidonians on the Persian Sea or somewhere else on the Ocean, and place the wanderings of Menelaos out in the Ocean, as well as the Phoenicians.

Not the least reason that they are unbelievable is because their words contradict one another. Some of them say that the Phoenicians and Sidonians near us were settled from those on the Ocean, adding that this is why they are called Phoenicians, because the sea is red. Others have the

[C43]   opposite. Moreover, there are those who transfer Aithiopia to our Phoenicia
        and who say that the matter of Andromeda happened at Iope. Clearly this is
        not said in ignorance of the place but rather in the form of a myth. What
        Apollodoros [of Athens, F157f] alleges from Hesiod and others is the
        same, without realizing how they are being compared to Homer. He
        compares what Homer has about the Pontos and Egypt and accuses him
        of ignorance: that he wished to say what existed but in fact did not speak
        of what existed, and in ignorance had what did not exist instead of what did
        exist. But one would not accuse Hesiod [F101] of ignorance when he speaks
        of the Hemikynians ["Those Who Are Half Dogs"], Makrokephalians
        ["Those With Long Heads"], and Pygmaians. One cannot [say this] when
        Homer discusses them, nor Alkman [F148] when he describes the
        Steganopodians ["Those With Web Feet"], or Aischylos [F431, 441, 434a]
        the Kynokephalians ["Those With Dog Heads"], Sternophthalmians
        ["Those With Their Eyes In Their Chests"], and Monommatians
        ["Those With One Eye"]. Moreover we do not pay attention to those
        who write in prose on many subjects in the form of history, even if they
        do not acknowledge that they are writing myths. It is obviously clear that
        they are intentionally weaving in myths, not through ignorance of what
        existed, but to form the impossible for the sake of the marvellous and
        delightful. Yet they seem to be ignorant, because they tell stories most
        persuasively about the unknown and what is not understood. Theopompos
        [F138] acknowledges this when he says that he will tell myths in his *Histories*,
        and he is better at this than Herodotos, Ktesias, Hellanikos, and those who
        wrote about Indian matters.

        (36) What he [Homer] said about the characteristics of the Ocean is in
        the form of a myth (this is something that a poet must aim at). Charybdis
        was told by him as a myth because of the ebbing and flooding. Even though
        it is not completely Homer's fantasy, he elaborated it from what he had
        been told about the Sikelian Strait. Although it flows back twice each day
        and night, he said three times: "three times a day it goes up and three times
        it is swallowed back" [*Odyssey* 12.105], and he can say it in that way. One
        must not suppose that he is telling the story out of ignorance, but for the
        sake of seriousness and fear, which Kirke attributes through her words
        largely for the sake of turning him [Odysseus] away. Thus falsehood is
        intermingled. At any rate, Kirke said the following in these very words:

> three times a day it goes up and three times it is swallowed back, a fearful
> thing. Do not happen to be there when it sucks down, for no one can protect
> you from this evil, not even the Earth Shaker. [*Odyssey* 12.105–7]

But Odysseus was present when it was swallowed back and he was not destroyed. He himself says [C44]

> the salty sea water was swallowed back, but I grasped an especially tall fig tree high up and clung to it like a bat. [*Odyssey* 12.431–3]

Then waiting for the ship's wreckage and taking hold of it again, he saved himself, and thus Kirke had lied, as she also had in "three times a day it goes up" (instead of twice), although such exaggeration is habitual for everyone, as in saying "thrice-blessed" or "thrice unhappy." And the Poet [says] "thrice-blessed Danaans" [*Odyssey* 5.306], "welcome, thrice prayed-for" [*Iliad* 8.488], and "into three parts, and into four parts" [*Iliad* 3.363, *Odyssey* 9.71]. Perhaps one could suggest that because of the length of time involved he is alluding to the truth in some way, for it is more suitable that the flowing back occurred twice in the double period of a day and a night, rather than three times, since the wreckage of the ship remained underwater for such a time and only came up after a lengthy period, as he was longing for it and kept clinging to the branches:

> I persevered until it disgorged the mast and keel again and they came to my wishes, at the time when a man rises from the agora for the evening meal, the judge of many quarrels, cases pleaded vigorously. At that time the beams came into my view from Charybdis. [*Odyssey* 12.437–41]

All this gives the appearance of a remarkable period of time, especially that it stretched into evening, for he does not say generically that it is when the judge rises up, but when there had been judgements for many quarrels, so that it was somewhat longer. Moreover, he would have been suggesting an implausible escape from the shipwreck if, before he was dragged far away, he was immediately thrown back by the change in the tide.

(37) Apollodoros [of Athens, F157d] agrees with those around Eratosthenes [F9] in censuring Kallimachos [F13], because, although a scholar, he named Gaudos and Korkyra [F413, 470], in opposition to the Homeric assumption that the places where he says the wanderings occurred were located in the External Ocean. If the wanderings never happened anywhere and were completely a fantasy of Homer's, then the criticism is just. Or, if they occurred, but were in other places, it would have been necessary to speak about this straightforwardly and to correct the ignorance. But since, as I have shown, they cannot plausibly be said to be a total fantasy, and no other places are visible that have greater credibility, Kallimachos can be absolved of the accusation. [C45]

(38) Nor is Demetrios the Skepsian [F50] correct, and he is actually the cause of some of the mistakes of Apollodoros [of Athens]. He was especially

eager to refute Neanthes of Kyzikos [F39], who said that the Argonauts, while sailing to Phasis (the journey that Homer and others agree about) dedicated the temple of the Idaian Mother near Kyzikos, for he [Demetrios] says that Homer did not know about the journey of Jason to Phasis. This is at odds not only with the statements of Homer but with his own, for he says that Achilleus ravaged Lesbos and other places, but spared Lemnos and the nearby islands because of his kinship with Jason and his son Euneos who held the island at that time. But how did the Poet know this about Achilleus and Jason (that they were kinsmen, of the same family, neighbors, or related in some way, for no other reason than both happened to be Thessalian, one being Iolkian and the other from Achaian Phthiotis), but did not know how it happened that Jason, being Thessalian and Iolkian, did not leave any successor in his native land, but established his son as master of Lemnos? He knew about Pelias, the daughters of Pelias, and the most beautiful of them, as well as her son

> Eumelos, born to Admetos from Alkestis, noble among women and seen as the most beautiful daughter of Pelias [*Iliad* 2.714–15]

yet concerning what happened to Jason, the Argo, and the Argonauts, he did not hear about what everyone agrees to, and created a voyage from Aietes that was placed in the Ocean yet had no basis in history.

(39) As everyone says, the original voyage to Phasis – that sent forth by Pelias – has a certain plausibility, as well as does the return, the conquering of however many islands on the coastal voyage, and, by Zeus, the farther wanderings (just as in the case of Odysseus and Menelaos). Things are still pointed out today from them, and believed in, and moreover there are the words of Homer. The city of Aia is pointed out near the Phasis, and Aietes – a name that still exists in that region – is believed to have ruled Kolchis. Medeia the sorceress is historical, and the wealth of that land (from gold, silver, and iron), for which Phrixos also went forth on his voyage at an earlier time, suggests a plausible reason for the expeditions. There are also memorials of both expeditions, the Phrixeion on the boundary of Kolchis and Iberia, and the Iasoneia that are pointed out in many places in Armenia, Media, and the [C46] adjacent regions. Moreover, around Sinope and its coast, the Propontis, and the Hellespont as far as Lemnos, there are said to be many signs of the expeditions of Jason and Phrixos. Some of those of Jason and the pursuing Kolchians, as far as Crete, Italia, and the Adria, are noted by Kallimachos in this way: "Aiglete and Anaphe, neighboring Lakonian Thera," saying "I begin with how the heroes sailed from the home of Kytaian Aietes to ancient Haimonia" [F7], and then about those around Kolchis,

they stopped their oars in the Illyrian narrows near the snake stone of fair Harmonia and founded a little town that a certain Graikos would call Phygas ["Flight"], but in their language was Polai. [F11]

Some say that those with Jason sailed up the Istros quite a distance, and others as far as the Adria, the former because of their ignorance of these places, and the latter saying that there is an Istros River that begins at the great Istros and empties into the Adria. What they say otherwise is neither untrustworthy nor unbelievable.

(40) Thus the Poet makes use of such elements as a starting point, agreeing with historical matters, but adds certain myths, keeping to a type of custom that is both common and his own. He agrees with what has been said when he names Aietes, and speaks of Jason and the Argo, and when, in comparison with Aia, he creates Aiaia, and also when he establishes Euneos on Lemnos and makes the island dear to Achilleus, and, moreover, in comparison with Medeia, makes the sorceress Kirke "crafty Aietes' own sister" [*Odyssey* 10.137]. But he adds mythology when he locates the part of the wanderings after the expedition in the Ocean. With this established, it is proper to say "the Argo, famous to all" [*Odyssey* 12.70], since the sea expedition happened in known and populated places. But if it is as Skepsios [F50] says (receiving the report of Mimnermos, who placed the home of Aietes in the Ocean, outside to the east, and says that Jason was sent there by Pelias and carried off the skin), the mission there for the skin would not be believable, a journey to unknown and unseen places through desolate and uninhabited lands remote from us, and neither notable nor famous to all: [C47]

> Jason would never have brought the great fleece back from Aia, completing his painful journey for the sake of arrogant Pelias, completing the difficult task, nor would they have come to the fair stream of Okeanos [Mimnermos F11]

and farther down,

> the city of Aietes, where the rays of swift Helios lie in a golden chamber beside the lips of Okeanos, where divine Jason went. [Mimnermos F11a]

Part 3: Siltation, deposition, and other changes to the earth

(1) Eratosthenes [F13] does not handle the following well: he discusses men not worthy of remembering, sometimes refuting them, and other times believing in them and using them as authorities, such as Damastes and others like him. Even if there is some truth in what they say, we should not use them as authorities or believe them. On the contrary, we should use

only reputable men in this way, those who have generally been correct, and even if they have omitted many things, or not discussed them sufficiently, they have said nothing untrue. But to use Damastes as an authority is no different from invoking as an authority the Bergaian Euhemeros and the others that he [Eratosthenes] quotes in order to discredit their nonsense. He tells one of his pieces of trash, that he [Damastes F8] believes the Arabian Gulf to be a lake, and that Diotimos the son of Strombichos, leading an Athenian embassy, sailed up the Kydnos from Kilikia to the Choaspes River, which flows by Sousa, arriving at Sousa on the fortieth day. He was told this by Diotimos himself. Then he wonders how it was possible for the Kydnos to cut across the Euphrates and Tigris and empty into the Choaspes.

(2) One would not only disapprove of this, but also because he [Eratosthenes] says that the seas were not yet exactly known even in his own time, exhorting us not easily to believe people by chance, and rendering at length the reasons that no one should be believed who tells mythic tales about the Pontos and the Adria. Yet he himself believes people by chance. Although he believed that the Issic Gulf is the most easterly limit of Our Sea, a point at Dioskourias in the extreme recess of the Pontos is farther east by about 3,000 stadia, even from the measurement of stadia that he himself records. In discussing the northern and extreme areas of the Adria, he does not abstain from the fabulous. He also believes many stories about what is beyond the Pillars of Herakles, naming an island called Kerne and [C48] other places that are nowhere visible today, concerning which I will discuss later.

He says that the earliest voyages were for piracy or commerce, and not in the open sea but along the land, like Jason, who abandoned his ships and made an expedition from the Kolchians as far as Armenia and Media. Later he says that in antiquity no one dared to sail on the Euxeinos, or along Libya, Syria, or Kilikia. Now if he means by "in antiquity" those for whom there is no record in our time, I am not about to speak of them and whether they sailed or not. But if he means those who have been recorded, one would not hesitate to say that those in antiquity are shown to have made longer journeys (whether completed by land or sea) than those later, if we pay attention to what has been said. For example, there are Dionysos, Herakles, and Jason himself, and those related by the Poet (Odysseus and Menelaos). It is reasonable that Theseus and Perithoos, having endured long expeditions, left behind the idea that they had gone down to Hades, and that the Dioskouroi were called the guardians of the sea and the saviors of sailors. The thalassocracy of Minos is widely discussed, as well as

Phoenician seamanship, which, shortly after the Trojan matter, went
beyond the Pillars of Herakles and founded cities there and on the central
part of the Libyan coast. Is it not proper to consider Aineias, Antenor, the
Enetians, and, simply, those from the Trojan War who wandered the entire
inhabited world as men of antiquity? Because of the length of the war, it
happened the Hellenes of that time and the barbarians lost what they had
had at home as well as what they had attained while on campaign. Thus,
after the destruction of Ilion, the victors – and even more the defeated who
survived the war – turned because of poverty to piracy. It is thus said that a
large number of cities were founded by them along the entire coast outside
of Hellas, as well as in the interior.

(3) He [Eratosthenes, F15] himself speaks of the great advance made in
the knowledge of the inhabited world by those after Alexander and those in
his own time, and then proceeds to a discussion about the shape, not of the
inhabited world – which would have been more appropriate to his topic –
but of the entire earth. That must also be considered, but not out of its
place. He says, then, that in its entirety it is spherical, not as if turned on a
lathe, but having certain irregularities, and then he lists the numerous   [C49]
changes in its shape that occur because of water, fire, earthquakes, eruptions, and other such phenomena, but here also he does not preserve the
arrangement. The spherical shape of the entire earth results from the state of
the whole, but the changes in form do not alter the earth as a whole (such
small things disappear in great things), although they create in the inhabited
world differences from one time to another, with one and another cause.

(4) He says that this presents a particular issue, for why can one see
mussel, oyster, and scallop shells in many places two or three thousand
stadia from the sea and in the interior, as well as many lagoons, such as, he
says, those around the Temple of Ammon and along the road of 3,000
stadia to it? A large quantity of oyster shells and much salt is still found there
today, and eruptions of salt water spring up to some height. In addition,
pieces of wreckage from sea-going ships are visible, which they say have
been thrown out of a chasm, and there are small columns with dolphins
dedicated on them, having the inscription "Of the Kyrenaian Envoys."

Then he says that he praises the opinion of Straton [F54], the scientist,
and also that of Xanthos the Lydian. Xanthos [F12] says that in the time of
Artaxerxes [I] there was so great a drought that the rivers, lakes, and cisterns
became dry, and he had often seen, far from the sea (among the Armenians,
Matienians, and in Lower Phrygia), stones like mollusk shells, sherds like
combs, the outlines of scallop shells, and a salt lagoon. Because of this he
believed that the plains were once the sea. Straton engages further in the

matter of causes, for he says that he believes the Euxeinos at one time did not have its mouth below Byzantion, but the rivers which empty into it forced it and opened it up, so that the water came out the Propontis and the Hellespont. The same thing occurred in Our Sea, for here the strait beyond the Pillars was broken through when the sea had been filled by the rivers and the former shallows were uncovered by this flooding. He suggests a cause: first, that the External and Internal Seas have a different seabed, and that [C50] even today there is a certain undersea ridge running from Europe to Libya, which shows that formerly the interior and exterior could not have been the same. Around the Pontos it is especially shallow (but the Cretan, Sikelian, and Sardoan Seas are very deep), since the rivers flowing from the north and east are numerous, large, and fill it with sediment, but the others remain deep. This is why the Pontic sea is the sweetest and why it flows out toward the place that its bed slopes. He believes that the entire Pontos will fill up in the future, if such an influx continues. And even now the area on the left side of the Pontos is already covered with shallow water, such as at Salmydessos and the place called by sailors the Breasts (around the Istros), and the Skythian desert. Perhaps the Temple of Ammon was once on the sea but is now in the interior because there has been an outflow of the sea. He suggests that the oracle with good reason became so famous and well known because it was on the sea, but since it is now so far removed from the sea there is no good reason for its fame and reputation. In antiquity Egypt was covered by the sea as far as the marshes around Pelousion, Mount Kasion, and Lake Sirbonis. Even today when the salty lands in Egypt are excavated, the holes are found to contain sand and mussel shells, as though the land had been submerged and all the territory around Kasion and the place called Gerrha had been covered with shallow water, so that it connected to the Erythra Gulf. When the sea gave way they were revealed, although Lake Sirbonis remained, but then it broke through so that there was a marsh. In the same way the shores of what is called Lake Moiris resemble more the shores of the sea than the shores of rivers. One would admit that the greater part of the continents was once flooded at certain times and then uncovered again, and similarly the entire surface of the earth that is now underwater is uneven, just as, by Zeus, that which is above water (on which we live), receives all the changes of which Eratosthenes himself speaks. Thus one cannot accuse Xanthos of saying anything unreasonable.

(5) Against Straton one might say that although there are many actual reasons [for these changes], he ignores them and gives non-existent reasons. He states as the primary cause that the seabed and depth of the Interior and [C51] Exterior Seas are not the same. But this is not the reason for their rising or

falling, and the flooding of certain places and withdrawal from them. It is because the bottom lowers somewhat or rises higher, and at times the seabed rises or at times the sea falls and recedes or abates. When it comes up, it will flood, and when it has risen it runs back to its earlier condition. If it is so, the flooding must occur with a sudden increase of the sea, as when there is a high tide or a rise in the rivers, whether brought in from elsewhere or due to an increase of the water. But the increases are neither simultaneous nor sudden, nor does the high tide remain for any length of time, nor is it irregular, and they do not cause flooding on Our Sea, or anywhere.

It remains, then, that the reason is the seabed, either what lies under the sea or what is flooded, preferably what is underneath. What is watery can more easily be moved and be affected more quickly by changes, for the exhalation, the ultimate cause of such things, is greater there. But, as I have said, the cause of such occurrences is that the seabed rises at times and at times sinks down, and not that some parts are high and others low. He [Straton] takes it this way, believing that what happens with rivers also occurs with the sea, that the flow is away from high places, for he would not have made the seabed the cause of the flow at Byzantion, saying that the [bed] of the Euxeinos is higher than that of the Propontis and the sea that follows. He also added as a reason that its depths are being filled by the mud carried down by the rivers, and thus it is becoming shallow, and that because of this the flow is outward. Through the same argument, the entirety of Our Sea is changing the External, since its seabed is becoming higher than what lies below the Atlantic Ocean, for the former is being filled by many rivers, and is receiving an equivalent accumulation of silt. It is necessary, then, that the inflow at Byzantion be the same as that at the Pillars and Kalpe. But I omit this, because they say that it does happen here but it is diverted by the ebb and flood and is concealed.

(6) I would like to learn what would have prevented it from being filled by rivers, if the bed of the Euxeinos were lower than that of the Propontis and the sea following it (before the opening of the mouth at Byzantion): whether it [C52] was formerly a sea or a lake larger than the Maiotic? If this is conceded, I would further ask this: if its water level and that of the Propontis were such as to be the same, would there be no pressure for an outflow, since the resistance and pressure would be equal, but that when the inner [sea] became higher, would there be pressure that would discharge the excess? Is it not because of this that the outer sea is confluent with the inner, having taken the same level, whether it was formerly a sea or a lake, or later a sea, due to its mixing and prevailing over it? If this is granted, the outflow of today would not be hindered, but it would not be from a higher seabed or a sloping one, as Straton believes.

(7) This, then, is to be transferred to the whole of Our Sea and the External [Sea], attributing the cause of the outflow not to the slope of their beds, but to the rivers. It is not unlikely – according to them – that the whole of Our Sea, even if it were formerly a lake, was flooded by rivers and overflowed, being thrust out through the narrows at the Pillars like a cataract, and that the [external] sea, constantly increased more and more and becoming confluent, would in time come together with it at one level and thus because of its domination it all became sea.

Yet it is completely unnatural to liken the sea to rivers, for the latter are carried down a sloping stream but the former has no slope. But straits have a current for another reason, and not because the silt from the river ends up in the depths. The siltation occurs only at the mouths of rivers, such as at the so-called Breasts of the Istros, the Skythian desert, at Salmydessos (where other torrents contribute to the siltation), around the Phasis and the Kolchian coast (which is sandy, low, and soft), around the Thermodon, the Iris, the whole of Themiskyra (the plain of the Amazons), and most of Sidene. It is the same with others. All of them imitate the Nile, joining the channel that is in front to the mainland, some more and others less: less for those not bringing down much silt and more for those going through territory with soft soil and many torrents, such as the Pyramos, which has [C53] added a great amount to Kilikia, about which this oracle was issued:

> Those in the future will experience the time when silver-eddying Pyramos will pour over its sacred beach and come to Cyprus. [Sibylline Oracle 4.97–8]

It is navigable, and is carried from the middle of the plains of Kataonia, breaking through the narrows of the Tauros into Kilikia, and emptying into the strait between there and Cyprus.

(8) The reason that the dirt brought down by the rivers does not continue to advance into the open sea is that the sea, which is naturally refluent, drives it back. It is like a living being, and just as it breathes in and breathes out continuously, in the same way it has a certain motion from itself and continuously returns back again. This is clear to someone standing on the shore as the waves break, for when the feet are washed they are then bare and then washed again, and this is continuous. In the surf a wave runs in that has more power as it comes in – although it is totally calm – casting all kinds of strange things on the land and "pouring out much seaweed" [*Iliad* 9.7]. This happens more in a wind, but also during a calm and a land breeze, for the wave is nonetheless carried toward the land against the wind, as the sea itself moves with its own motion. Thus "it comes to a swelling head around the promontory, and spits out the salty

foam" [*Iliad* 4.425–6], and "the beach cries out as the salty sea belches forth" [*Iliad* 17.265].

(9) The advance of the wave has a certain force that thrusts away strange things. They say that this is a certain catharsis of the sea, through which dead bodies and shipwrecks are cast up by the waves. But the ebbing does not have such force, and whether it is a corpse, a piece of wood, or the lightest of things, cork, once these have been thrown out of the sea by a wave they fall on the nearby land, wherever they have been taken by the waves. In the same way the silt and the water made dirty by it are thrown out by the waves, and, assisted by their weight, are carried down near the land before going out into the open sea. Indeed, the force of a river ceases shortly beyond its mouth. Thus it is possible that the open sea could be completely silted up, beginning at its shore, if the influx from the rivers were continuous. This would happen even if we were to assume that the Pontos is deeper than the Sardonian Sea, which is said to be the deepest that has been   [C54] measured, about a thousand *orgyiai*, as Poseidonios [F221] says.

(10) One might be less inclined to accept this reasoning, and thus it is necessary to attach the argument to phenomena that are more visible and can be seen every day. Inundations, earthquakes, eruptions, and undersea swelling of the earth raise the sea, and settling lowers it. It is not possible that hot stones and small islands could be lifted up, but that large islands or continents could not. Similarly settlings – both small and large – may happen, if, as they say, chasms and the swallowing of places and villages (such as at Boura, Bizone, and several others) have occurred because of earthquakes. One might suggest that Sikelia, rather than being something broken off from Italia, was thrown up from the depths by the Aitnaian fire and remains there, as is the case with the Liparaians and Pithekoussai.

(11) But he [Eratosthenes, F16] is so ingenuous that even though a mathematician he will not confirm the opinion of Archimedes, who says in his *On Floating Bodies* [Book 1, *Proposition* 2] that all calm and quiet water appears to have a spherical surface, with the sphere having the same center as the earth. Everyone who has ever understood mathematics accepts this point of view. He [Eratosthenes] says that the Internal Sea is a single sea, but he does not believe that it has ever been constituted as a single surface, even in neighboring places. He uses engineers as witnesses for this ignorance, although the mathematicians proclaim that engineering is a part of mathematics. He also says that Demetrios attempted to cut through the Peloponnesian Isthmos to supply a passage for his forces to sail through, but was prevented by the engineers who measured carefully and reported that the sea level of the Corinthian Gulf was higher than at Kenchreai, so that if

he were to cut through the intervening land, the entire strait around Aigina, as well as Aigina itself and the nearby islands, would be submerged and the sailing passage would not be useful. This is why narrow straits have strong currents, especially the narrows of Sikelia which, he says, are similar to the high and low tides of the Ocean, with the flow changing twice each day and

[C55] night, and like the Ocean there are two floodings and two withdrawals. He says that similar to the flood tide is the current that goes down from the Tyrrhenian to the Sikelian Sea, as though from a higher level, which is called "the Descent," and he agrees that it begins and ends at the same time as the high tides. It also begins around the rising and setting of the moon and ceases when it reaches either meridian, that above the earth or below the earth. Like the ebb tide is the opposite current – called "the Ascent" – which begins when the moon is at either meridian, just like the ebb tide, and ceases when it reaches the points of setting and rising.

(12) The flooding and ebbing of the tides has been sufficiently discussed by Poseidonios [F215] and Athenodoros [F6b]. Concerning the rushing back of straits, which is a more scientific discussion than appropriate in this treatise, it is sufficient to say that there is no single explanation for the currents in straits that corresponds to their form, for if so it would not be the case that the Sikelian changes twice a day, as he [Eratosthenes, F16] says, and the Chalkidean seven times, or that the one at Byzantion has no change but continues having only an outflow from the Pontic Sea into the Propontis, as Hipparchos [F6] reports, and at times is stopped. If there were a single explanation, the reason would not be what Eratosthenes says, that each sea has a different surface. This would also not be the case with rivers unless they have cataracts, but even having them, they do not flow back but continuously go lower. Thus it would not flow back, nor would it stand still and remain, even when flowing together, as there is not one level, but one that is higher and the other lower. This also happens because the stream and its surface are inclined. But who would say that the surface of the sea is inclined? This is especially because of the theory that the four bodies – which we would call elements – are made to be spherical. The water is not like the earth, whose state has assumed a solid form, thus having permanent hollows and protuberances, but, through the effect of its weight, is carried upon the earth, having the kind of surface that Archimedes says.

(13) Adding to what he [Eratosthenes, F16] has said about Ammon and Egypt, he believes that Mount Kasion was once washed by the sea and that the entire region (where what is now called Gerrha is), was covered with

[C56] shallow water since it was connected with the Erythra Gulf becoming uncovered when the seas came together. To say that the place was covered with shallows and connected to the Erythra Gulf is ambiguous, since "connected" means "to be near" or "to touch," so that, if it is a body of water, one would flow into the other. I believe that the shallows came near to the Erythra Sea while the narrows at the point of the Pillars were closed, and the withdrawal happened because of the lowering of Our Sea due to the outflow at the Pillars. But Hipparchos [F8] argues that "connected" is the same as Our Sea "flowing into" the Erythra, because of its filling up. Because of the outflow at the Pillars and Our Sea changing its direction, he demands to know why the Erythra, which was flowing into it, remained at the same level and was not lowered. According to Eratosthenes himself the entire External Sea flows together and thus the Western and Erythra Sea are one. Saying this, he insists that the sea outside the Pillars, the Erythra, and even that which flowed together into it, have the same height.

(14) But Eratosthenes [F16] would say he has not reported that the flowing together with the Erythra happened at the time of the filling, but only that they were near to one another. It does not follow that one sea that was kept together would have the same height and same surface, as this is not the case in ours, by Zeus, at Lechaion and around Kenchreai. Hipparchos [F8] indicates this in his treatise against him. Knowing that this is his opinion, let me speak on his own account against him and let him not presume that someone who says that the Exterior Sea is one would agree that its level is also one.

(15) Saying that the inscription of the Kyrenaian envoys on the dolphin is false, he [Hipparchos, F9] provides an implausible reason: that although the founding of Kyrene was in recorded times no one recorded that the oracle was ever on the sea. Even if no one reported this, we can infer from the evidence that the place was once on the coast, since the dolphins were erected and inscribed by the Kyrenaian envoys. He [F10] concedes that with the raising of the bed the sea flooded as far as the location of the oracle, [C57] somewhat more than 3,000 stadia from the sea, but he does not concede that the raised level covered all of Pharos and most of Egypt, as if such a height were not sufficient to cover these also. He also says that if Our Sea were filled to such a level before the outbreak at the Pillars occurred, as Eratosthenes [F16] said, all of Libya and most of Europe and Asia must first have been covered. He then adds that the Pontos would have begun to flow together with the Adria in certain places, since because of the lie of the land the Istros divides in the region of the Pontos and flows into each sea. But the Istros does not have its source in the Pontos region, but on the contrary, in the mountains above the Adria. Moreover, it does not flow into each sea, but only into the Pontos, and it branches only around its mouths. In

common with some of those before him he fails to understand his own ignorance, for they believed that a certain river with the same name as the Istros broke away and emptied into the Adria, from which the people through whom it flows took their name, and by this way Jason made his return voyage from Kolchis.

(16) In order not to marvel at those changes that we have said are the reason for the inundations and happenings which have been mentioned regarding Sikelia, the islands of Aiolos, and Pithekoussai, it is worthwhile to provide things that do occur, or have occurred, in other places. A mass of such examples placed before the eyes will cause a stop to consternation. At present, the unaccustomed troubles the senses and shows ignorance of natural happenings and everything in life, such as if one were to speak about Thera and Therasia – islands situated in the strait between Crete, the Kyrenaia (for Thera is the metropolis of Kyrene), and Egypt – and many such places in Hellas.

Midway between Thera and Therasia, flames arose from the open sea for four days, so that the entire sea boiled and flamed, producing an island that gradually rose as though by a machine, and consisting of a hot mass that was twelve stadia in circumference. After the activity ceased, the first who dared to sail to the place were the Rhodians – during their thalassocracy – who

[C58]   established a sanctuary of Poseidon Asphalios on the island.

Poseidonios [F231] says that in Phoenicia a city above Sidon was swallowed up because of an earthquake, and also that almost two portions of Sidon collapsed, but not all at once, so that not many people were killed. The same activity extended over the whole of Syria, but somewhat moderately. It crossed over to some of the islands, both the Kyklades and Euboia, so that the spring of Arethousa (a fountain in Chalkis) failed, although many days later it gushed out of another mouth. Earthquakes did not cease in parts of the island until a chasm in the earth opened in the Lelanton Plain that vomited a river of fiery mud.

(17) Many have made collections of such incidents, but it is sufficient [to cite] those collected by Demetrios of Skepsis [F48], since they are appropriately set forth. He mentions these verses:

> They came to the fair-flowing fountains, where two springs of whirling Skamandros rise up, one with gentle water. . .the other flows like hail even in summer. [*Iliad* 22.147–51]

He does not allow one to marvel if today the spring of cold water remains but the hot one is not visible. He says that the cause must be the failure of the hot water, and recalls what Demokles [F1] said about this, who recorded

certain great earthquakes, some of which occurred long ago around Lydia
and Ionia as far as the Troad, and which, during the reign of Tantalos,
swallowed up villages and overturned Sipylos.[2] Marshes were created later,
and a wave inundated the Troad.

Pharos in Egypt was once in the sea, but now it has become a sort of
peninsula, and it is the same at Tyre and Klazomenai. When I was living in
Alexandria next to Egypt, the sea around Pelousion and Mount Kasion rose
and inundated the land, making an island of the mountain, so that the road
from Kasion into Phoenicia became navigable. Thus it would be nothing
marvellous if, at some time, the isthmus (the one that divides the Egyptian
Sea from the Erythra Sea) should be separated or undergo subsidence,
revealing a strait and making the outer sea confluent with the inner, just
as happened with the strait at the Pillars of Herakles. This was discussed to
some extent at the beginning of this topic [1.3.4], and it all contributes to a
single thing, to furnish a strong faith in the works of nature and the other
changes that result from them.

(18) They say that the Peiraieus was formerly an island and lay opposite
[*peran*] to the promontory and thus received its name. On the contrary,   [C59]
Leukas became an island when the Corinthians cut a canal through the
isthmus, although formerly it was a promontory. They say that Laertes is
speaking about it: "as it was when I took Neritos, the well-built city, the
promontory of the mainland" [*Odyssey* 24.377–8]. Here a cut has been made
by hand, and elsewhere there are ramps and bridges, just as with the island
next to Syracuse, where today a bridge connects it to the mainland.
Formerly there was a causeway, as Ibykos [F321] said, of chosen stone,
which he calls "selected."

In regard to Boura and Helike, the former disappeared under a chasm,
the latter under waves. At Methone in the Hermionic Gulf a mountain
seven stadia high was thrown up because of a fiery eruption, and it was
inaccesible by day because of the heat and sulphur odor. At night it shone
for a great distance, and the sea boiled five stadia away and was disturbed for
twenty stadia, heaped with broken-off rocks no smaller than towers. Arne
and Mideia were swallowed up by Lake Kopais. They were cited by the Poet
in the *Catalogue*: "some have Arne rich in grapes, and others Mideia" [*Iliad*
2.507]. Around Bistonis and the lake now called Aphnitis there seem to be
certain Thracian cities that were inundated. Some also [add] the Trerians,
believing them to be neighbors of the Thracians. One of the Echinades
Islands, formerly called Artemita, has become part of the mainland, and

---

[2] There may be a gap in the text at this point.

they say that other islets around the Acheloos have experienced the same thing because of the silting of the open sea by the river, and the rest of them are being obliterated, as Herodotos says [2.10]. Certain Aitolian capes were formerly islands, and Asteria has changed, which the Poet calls Asteris:

> There is a rocky island in the middle of the salt sea, Asteris. . .not large, and a harbor on it with a double anchorage. [*Odyssey* 4.844–7]

Today it does not even have a suitable anchorage. In Ithaka there is no cave or Nymphaion such as Homer describes [*Odyssey* 13.103–12]. It is better to make change the reason, rather than ignorance or a false report made about [C60] places in order to be mythic. But there is uncertainty, and I leave it to a general investigation.

(19) Antissa was formerly an island, as Myrsilos [F16] says. Since Lesbos was formerly called Issa, it happened that this island was called Antissa, but now it is a city of Lesbos. Some believe that Lesbos broke away from Ida, just as Prochyte and Pithekoussa did from Misenon, Kapreai from the Athenaion, Sikelia from the region of Rhegion, and Ossa from Olympos. Such changes have occurred in these regions. And the Ladon in Arkadia once ceased its flow. Douris [F54] says that Rhagai in Media was named because the earth around the Kaspian Gates was torn open [*rhageises*] by earthquakes, so that numerous cities and villages were ruined and rivers underwent a variety of changes. Ion in his satyr play *Omphale* says, in regard to Euboia,

> the delicate wave of the Euripos has separated the Euboian land from Boiotia, cutting away a projecting headland by means of a strait. [F18]

(20) Demetrios of Kallatis [F6], describing all the earthquakes ever to occur in Hellas, says that most of the Lichades Islands and Kenaion were submerged, and the hot springs at Aidepsos and Thermopylai, which had stopped for three days, flowed again, and those at Aidepsos burst forth in another spring. At Oreos, the wall next to the sea as well as about 700 houses collapsed, and the greater part of Echinos, Phalara, and Herakleia in Trachis fell in, with the settlement of Phalara overturned from its foundations. Similar things happened to the Lamians and in the Larisaia. Skarpheia was thrown up from its base, and no fewer than 1,700 people were buried, and over half as many Thronians. A wave rose up in three parts, one of which was carried toward Skarphe and Thronion, another toward Thermopylai, and the remainder into the plain as far as Phokic Daphnous. The springs of rivers dried up for several days, the Spercheios changed its course and made the roads navigable, the Boagrios was carried into another ravine, and parts

of Alope, Kynos, and Opous were greatly damaged, with Oion (the fortress lying above the latter) overturned. Part of the walls of Elateia collapsed, and when Alponos was holding the Thesmophoria, twenty-five girls ran up to a tower on the harbor for a view, and the tower fell in, and they fell into the sea. They also say that the central portions of Atalante near Euboia, because [C61] they had been torn apart, received a channel through it, some of the plains were inundated for twenty stadia, and a trireme was lifted out of the shipyards and thrown over the wall.

(21) They also add the changes from migrations (wishing to furnish us with a greater absence of wonder, something celebrated by Demokritos and all the other men of wisdom, who place it alongside of fearlessness, calmness, and intrepidness), such as the movement of the western Iberians to the places beyond the Pontos and Kolchis (not separated from Armenia by the Araxes, as Apollodoros [of Artemita, F2] says, but rather by the Kyros and the Moschikian Mountains), that of the Egyptians to Aithiopia and Kolchis, and that of the Enetians from Paphlagonia to the Adria. This also happened with the Hellenic peoples – the Ionians, Dorians, Achaians, and Aioleans – as well as the Ainianians who now border the Aitolians but lived around Dotion and Ossa among the Perrhaibians. Certain Perrhaibians themselves are immigrants.

The present treatise is replete with such examples. Some of them are readily accessible to most, yet the wanderings of the Karians, Trerians, Teukrians, and Galatians, as well as the distant movements of leaders – such as Madys the Skythian, Tearkos the Aithiopian, Kobos the Trerian, Sesostris and Psammetichos [II?] the Egyptians, and the Persians from Kyros to Xerxes – are not similarly available to all. The Kimmerians whom they call the Trerians – or some of their peoples – often overran the right-hand portions of the Pontos and that adjacent to it, at one time attacking the Paphlagonians and then the Phrygians (when Midas drank bull's blood, they say, and went to his fate). Lygdamis, leading his own men, invaded as far as Lydia and Ionia and took Sardeis, but was killed in Kilikia. Often the Kimmerians and the Trerians made such invasions, but they say that the Trerians and Kobos were finally driven out by Madys, the Skythian king. Let these things be recounted, as they are a suitable discussion of the entire circuit of the earth in general.

(22) I return to what is next, from which I was diverted. In regard to what Herodotos [4.36] said, that there are no Hyperboreans because there are no Hypernotians, Eratosthenes [F20] says that this argument is ludicrous and [C62] would be like the following sophistry: if one were to say that there are none who rejoice at the misfortunes of others because there are none who rejoice

at the good fortune of others. Moreover it so happens that there are Hypernotians, and anyway the Notos does not blow in Aithiopia but farther down. It would be marvellous, since winds blow in every latitude – and the one from the south is called the Notos everywhere – if there were any inhabited place where this does not happen. On the contrary, Aithiopia, as well as every place farther toward the equator, might have the same Notos as we do. Nevertheless, one must accuse Herodotos of interpreting Hyperboreans to mean those where the Boreas does not blow. Even if the poets speak rather mythically, those who interpret them should pay attention to sound opinions, that the Hyperboreans were said to be the farthest north. Their boundary is the north pole, and that of the southern [peoples] is the equator, and the winds have the same boundary.

(23) Next he [Eratosthenes, F19] discusses those who clearly speak of fabricated and impossible things (some of which are in the form of myths and others in the form of history), concerning whom it is not worthy to mention. Yet in this subject matter he should not have considered those who are nonsensical. This, then, is his discussion in the first book of his commentaries.

Part 4:   The surface of the earth

(1) In his second book, he [Eratosthenes, F25] attempts to change the structure of geography and states his own assumptions. If there is any further correction, there must be an attempt to provide it. To introduce mathematics and physics into the topic is well considered, as also is the idea that if the earth is spherical – just as the cosmos – it is inhabited all around, and other such comments. But later writers do not agree as to whether it is as large as he has said, nor do they approve of his measurements. Yet in regard to the signs of the phenomena for each of the inhabited regions, Hipparchos [F35] also makes use of his intervals for the meridian through Meroë, Alexandria, and the Borysthenes, saying that they differ only slightly from the truth. In what follows about its shape, where he proves at length that the nature of the earth (along with its wet portions) is spherical, as are the heavens, he seems to be speaking irrelevantly, for brevity would be sufficient.

(2) In determining the width of the inhabited world, he [Eratosthenes, F35] says that from Meroë it is 10,000 stadia along its meridian to Alexandria, and from there to the Hellespont about 8,100, then 5,000 to the Borysthenes, and then to the parallel that runs through Thoule (which Pytheas [F2] says is six days' sail north of Brettanike and is near the frozen

[C63]

sea) an additional 11,500. Moreover, if we add 3,400 more beyond Meroë, so that we include the Egyptian island, the Cinnamon-Bearer territory, and Taprobane, we have 38,000 stadia.

(3) Let the other distances be granted to him because there is sufficient agreement. Yet would any sensible person grant him the one from the Borysthenes to the circle of Thoule? For the one who records Thoule, Pytheas [F3], has been established as a man of the greatest falsehoods, since those who have seen Brettanike and Ierne have nothing to say about Thoule, although mentioning other islands (the small ones around Brettanike). Brettanike extends alongside Keltike for about an equal distance, no greater than 5,000 stadia, its boundaries marked off by the boundaries that lie opposite. The eastern extremities lie opposite the eastern extremities of the other, and the western [opposite] the western. The eastern are near enough to each other that one may look across from Kantion to the mouth of the Rhenos. Yet he [Pytheas] declares that the extent of the island is more than 20,000 stadia and says that Kantion is several days' sail from Keltike. Concerning the Ostidaians and what is beyond the Rhenos as far as Skythia, anyone who has told such falsehoods about known places would hardly be able to tell the truth about places unknown to everyone.

(4) Hipparchos [F53] and others suggest that the parallel through the Borysthenes is the same as that through Brettanike, because the one through Byzantion is the same as the one through Massalia. Hipparchos says he found at Byzantion the same relationship between the gnomon and its shadow that Pytheas [T2] recorded at the same time at Massalia. Yet from Massalia to the middle of Brettanike is no more than 5,000 stadia. Moreover, if one were to proceed no more than 4,000 from the middle of Brettanike you would find [a region] only somewhat inhabitable (this would be around Ierne), and it would no longer be inhabitable farther on, to where he removes Thoule. By what guesswork he could say that that from [the parallel] through Thoule to that through the Borysthenes is 11,500 [stadia] I cannot see.

[C64]

(5) Since he [Eratosthenes, F37] entirely missed its width, he was also compelled to miss its length. It is agreed by later sources as well as the most talented early ones that its known length is more than twice the known width (I am speaking of that from the extremities of Indike to the extremities of Iberia, and that from the Aithiopians as far as the parallel of Ierne). He has determined the previously mentioned width, that from the farthest Aithiopians to the parallel through Thoule, and has stretched the length more than necessary, so that he can make it more than the previously mentioned width. Moreover, he says that the narrowest part of Indike, up

to the Indos River, is 16,000 stadia – that which extends to the promontories is an additional 3,000 stadia – and to the Kaspian Gates is 14,000, and
then to the Euphrates 10,000, and from the Euphrates to the Nile 5,000,
with an additional 1,300 as far as the Kanobic Mouth, then 13,500 as far as
Karchedon, then as far as the Pillars at least 8,000, a total of 800 beyond
70,000 stadia. Then it is still necessary to add the bulge of Europe outside
the Pillars of Herakles, set against the Iberians and sloping to the west – no
less than 3,000 stadia – as well as all the promontories, especially that of
the Ostidaians (which is called Kabaion), and the surrounding islands,
the farthest of which, Ouxisame, Pytheas [F4] says is three days' sail away.
After mentioning these final places, which in their extent add nothing to its
length, he adds the districts around the promontories, that of the Ostidaians
and Ouxisame and the islands of which he speaks. All these places are
toward the north and are in Keltika, not Iberika, or rather they are fantasies
of Pytheas. He [Eratosthenes] also adds to the previously mentioned length
more stadia, 2,000 to the west and 2,000 to the east, to keep the width from
being more than half the length.

(6) He [Eratosthenes] attempts to reassure us even further when he says
that it is natural to make the interval from east to west greater, and natural
that the inhabited world is longer from east to west, saying that

> we have stated, as do the mathematicians, that it joins together in a circle,
> touching itself with itself, so that, if not prevented by the size of the Atlantic
> Ocean, we could sail from Iberia to Indike along the same parallel (the part
> that remains beyond the previously mentioned interval, which is more than
> one-third of the distance), if the one through Athens, where we have made
> this stated measurement of stadia from Indike to Iberia, is less than 200,000
> stadia. [Eratosthenes, F33]

[C65]

Yet he does not say this well. He might say this about the temperate zone
(ours), according to mathematics, since it is only a portion of the inhabited
earth, yet concerning the inhabited earth – since we call inhabited that
which we inhabit and know – it is possible that in this same temperate zone
there are two inhabited worlds, or more, especially near the circle through
Athens that is drawn through the Atlantic Ocean. Moreover, by persisting
in the proof of the spheroid shape of the earth he receives the same criticism.
Similarly he does not stop disagreeing with Homer about the same things.

(7) Next, saying that there has been much written about the continents,
and that some divide them by rivers, such as the Nile and Tanais (representing them as islands), and others by isthmuses, such as the one between the
Kaspian and Pontic Seas or between the Erythra and the Ekrhegma (saying

that they are peninsulas), he says that he does not see how this examination can result in anything consequential except for those living contentiously in the fashion of Demokritos. If there are no exact boundaries – as with Kolyttos and Melite – such as stelai or enclosures, we can only say that "this is Kolyttos and this is Melite," but do not have the boundaries. It is for this reason that there are often disputes about districts, such as that between the Argives and Lakedaimonians about Thyrea, or between the Athenians and Boiotians about Oropos. The Hellenes named the three continents differently because they did not pay attention to the inhabited world, but only to their own area and what was directly opposite, the Karike, where there are now Ionians and their neighbors. In time, advancing still farther, and learning more about territories, they have focused their division. Were those who first separated the three (so that we begin with his [Eratosthenes'] last point, living contentiously but not in the fashion of Demokritos, but of him) the original men who sought to divide the Karians, lying opposite, from their own territory? Or did they conceive only of Hellas and Karia and the small amount that touched it, but not in the same way about Europe, Asia, or Libya, and were those afterward – travelling through enough to [C66] conceive of the outline of the inhabited world – the ones who divided it into three? How could they not have made the division of the inhabited world? Would someone speaking of three parts and calling each of the parts a continent not think of the whole from which he makes his division? But if he does not conceive of the inhabited world but makes his division of some part of it, what part of the inhabited world would anyone have said that Asia was a part, or Europe, or a continent in general? These things have been said sloppily.

(8) Even more sloppily, he does not see what can be said about the practical result of the investigation of boundaries: to set forth Kolyttos and Melite and then to turn around to the opposite. If the wars about Thyrea and Oropos happened because of ignorance of the boundaries, then the separation of territories results in something practical. Or, in regard to districts, and, by Zeus, the various ethnic groups, is he saying that it is practical to divide them accurately, but for continents this is superfluous? But this is by no means less important, for there might be some great dispute among rulers – one holding Asia and the other Libya – as to which possessed Egypt, specifically that which is called the Lower Territory of Egypt. If anyone were to dismiss this because of its rarity, nevertheless it must be said that the continents are divided according to a major distinction that relates to the entire inhabited world. In regard to this, there must be no concern – if the division is made according to rivers – that certain areas

remain undefined, because the rivers do not extend as far as the Ocean and thus truly do not leave the continents as islands.

(9) Near the end of his treatise he [Eratosthenes, F155] refuses to praise those who separate all the number of humanity into two groups, Hellenes and barbarians, as well as those who advised Alexander to consider the Hellenes as friends but the barbarians as enemies. He says that it is better to make such a distinction between good and bad characteristics, for there are many bad Hellenes or urbane barbarians, such as the Indians or Arians (or, moreover, the Romans and Karchedonians), who administer their governments so marvellously. Because of this, Alexander ignored his advisors, embraced as many distinguished men as possible, and showed them kind- [C67] ness, just as those making this distinction censure some, praise others, and do so because there prevails in some a conformity to lawfulness, education, and speech, but in others the opposite. Thus Alexander did not ignore his advisors but followed their opinion and was guided by them, not the opposite, considering the meaning of their information.

BOOK 2

Further discussion of predecessors

Part 1: The plan of the inhabited world

(1) In the third book of the *Geographika*, establishing the plan of the inhabited world, he [Eratosthenes, F47] divides it into two parts by a certain line from west to east, parallel to the line of the equator. He takes as the extremities of this line the Pillars of Herakles in the west and in the east the farthest summits of the mountains that define the northern edge of Indike. He draws the line from the Pillars through the Sikelian Strait and the southern summits of the Peloponnesos and Attika, as far as the Rhodia and the Issic Gulf. Up to here, he says, the previously mentioned line runs through the sea and the adjacent land (in fact, it lies entirely along the length of Our Sea as far as Kilikia). Then it is thrown out as an approximately straight line along the entire Tauros mountain range as far as Indike, for the   [C68] Tauros runs in a straight line with the sea from the Pillars, dividing Asia lengthwise into two parts, making one the northern part and the other the southern: thus in a similar way it [the Tauros] lies on the parallel through Athens, as does the sea that comes from the Pillars as far as it.

(2) Having said this, he believes it necessary to correct the ancient geographical plan, for according to it the eastern portion of the mountains is greatly twisted toward the north, and Indike is drawn along further to the north than it should be. He offers as his primary proof that many agree the most southerly promontories of Indike rise opposite to the region around Meroë, as demonstrated by the climate and the celestial phenomena. From there to the northern part of Indike, at the Kaukasian Mountains, Patrokles [F2] – who is believed to be most accurate both because of his reputation and because he is not uneducated as a geographer – says is 15,000 stadia, which is about the same as from Meroë to the parallel through Athens. Thus the northern parts of Indike, which touch the Kaukasian Mountains, end at this latitude.

(3) Another proof he offers is that the distance from the Issic Gulf to the Pontic Sea is about 3,000 stadia, going toward the north and the regions

93

around Amisos and Sinope, equal to what is said for the width of the mountains. From Amisos, heading toward the equinoctial sunrise, Kolchis is first, and then the pass to the Hyrkanian Sea, and next the route to Baktra and the Skythians beyond (having the mountains on the right). This line through Amisos, [extended] to the west, is thrown out through the Propontis and the Hellespont. From Meroë to the Hellespont is no more than 18,000 stadia, as much as from the southern side of Indike to the parts around the Baktrians, adding 3,000 to the 15,000, part of which is due to the width of the mountains and part due to that of Indike.

(4) Concerning this assertion, Hipparchos [F12] contradicts it by attacking the proofs: that Patrokles is not trustworthy, since two disprove him, [C69] Deimachos [T3] and Megasthenes [T5], who say that the place is 20,000 stadia distant from the southern sea, or even 30,000. They say this, and the ancient maps agree. Indeed, he thinks it incredible that one must trust Patrokles alone – given those who contradict him – and correct the ancient maps on this matter, rather than to leave them until there is some more accurate information.

(5) I think that the argument can be corrected in many ways. First, although the former [Eratosthenes, F50] used many testimonia, the latter [Hipparchos] says that only one was used, Patrokles. But who said that the southern promontories of Indike rise opposite to the regions of Meroë? Who said that from Meroë as far as the parallel of Athens was such a distance? Again, who said what the width of the mountains was, and that it was the same from Kilikia to Amisos? Who said that from Amisos through Kolchis and Hyrkania as far as Baktria and the regions beyond down to the eastern sea was in a straight line toward equinoctial east, along the mountains that are on the right? Or again that to the west this line was straight toward the Propontis and the Hellespont? Eratosthenes takes all these things as established by those who had been in those places, for he studied many treatises, having them in abundance in a library as large as Hipparchos says that it was.

(6) In addition, the trustworthiness of Patrokles is based on many witnesses: the kings who entrusted him to such a position and those who followed him, whom Hipparchos himself names, for their confidence is proof of what he said. This [statement] of Patrokles [F1] is not untrustworthy, as he says that those on the expedition with Alexander learned about things only cursorily, although Alexander investigated things accurately, since those most experienced in the entire territory recorded it for him, and he [Patrokles] says that this record was later given to him by Xenokles, the treasurer.

(7) Moreover, Hipparchos [F13] records in his second book that Eratosthenes himself [F73] questions the reliability of Patrokles [F3] because of his disagreement with Megasthenes [F6d] about the length of Indike on its northern side, which Megasthenes says is 16,000 stadia, but Patrokles attests is a thousand less. Relying on a certain *Record of Stopping Points*, he [Eratosthenes] distrusts them both because of their disagreement, holding to the *Record*. If Patrokles is untrustworthy because of this disagreement,   [C70] although the difference is merely about 1,000 stadia, how much more must he be mistrusted with a difference of about 8,000 stadia, in contrast to two men who agree with one another and who say that the width of Indike is 20,000 stadia instead of 12,000?

(8) We can say that it was not the bare disagreement that he condemned, but the comparison with the consistency and trustworthiness of the *Record Of Stopping Points*. But it is not surprising if something is more trustworthy than another that is also trustworthy, or if we trust someone in some things more than another, and do not trust him in other things, when something from elsewhere is considered more reliable. It is ludicrous to believe that those who disagree are less trustworthy because of the disagreement. On the contrary, this would rather seem to be the case when the difference is slight. In a treatment that differs only slightly, both among those who are ordinary and those who are somewhat more skilled, the ordinary person would be more likely to be in error and the more scholarly less so, so he is more to be trusted.

(9) All who have written about Indike speak particularly falsely, especially Deimachos [T1]. Second is Megasthenes [T4]. Onesikritos [T11], Nearchos [T14], and such others stammer out some of the truth. This became particularly obvious to me in recording my *Deeds of Alexander* [F3]. Especially worthy of disbelief are Deimachos [F5] and Megasthenes [F27a], for they write about the Enotokoitai ["Those Who Sleep In Their Ears"], the Astomoi ["Those Without Mouths"], and the Arrhinoi ["Those Without Noses"], as well as the Monophthalmoi ["Those With One Eye"], Makroskeles ["Those With Long Legs"], and Opisthodaktyloi ["Those With Fingers Backward"]. They have also revived the Homeric tale about the battle between the cranes and Pygmaians, who, they said, were three *spithamai* tall. There are also the gold-mining ants and Pans with wedged-shaped heads and snakes that swallow both cattle and deer along with their horns. Concerning these things each refutes the other, as Eratosthenes says [F22]. For they were sent to Palimbothra – Megasthenes to Sandrakottos and Deimachos to his son Amitrochades – as ambassadors, and left such writings as reminders of their travels, persuaded to do so for whatever reason.

Patrokles was not such a person at all, and the other witnesses Eratosthenes used are not unreliable.

(10)[1] . . .if the meridian through Rhodes and Byzantion has been taken correctly, then the one through Kilikia and Amisos has also been taken correctly, since from many sources it is shown that lines are parallel if neither of them meets.

[C71]

(11) The voyage from Amisos to Kolchis is thus toward equinoctial east (which is shown by the winds, seasons, crops, and the sunrise itself), as also are the pass to the Kaspia and the route from there to Baktra. Often clarity and total agreement are more trustworthy than an instrument. Hipparchos himself, in regard to the line from the Pillars as far as Kilikia (the fact that it was straight and toward equinoctial east), did not totally make use of instruments and geometry, but he trusted sailors for its entirety from the Pillars to the Straits. Thus he is not accurate in saying

> we cannot say (in regard to either the relation of the longest day to the shortest, or the gnomon to its shadow along the mountainside from Kilikia as far as Indike) whether the slant is a parallel line, but it must not be corrected, preserving the slant that the ancient maps have. [F14]

First, "cannot say" is the same as withholding it, and someone withholding inclines neither way. When he exhorts that it be left alone, just like the ancients, he inclines that way. Rather he would be preserving his consistency if he advised one not to use geography at all, for we "cannot say" what the positions are of the other mountains, such as the Alps, Pyrenaian, Thracian, Illyric, or Germanic. Who would believe that the ancients were more trustworthy than those more recent, since they made all those mistakes in drawing maps that Eratosthenes [F51] has accused them of, none of which Hipparchos objected to.

(12) What follows is full of great difficulties [Hipparchos, F15]. See what paradoxes occur if one did not remove [the assertion that] the Indian capes rise opposite to the region of Meroë, or that the distance from Meroë to the mouth below Byzantion is around 18,000 stadia, yet if one would also make it 30,000 from the southern Indians as far as the mountains. First, if the parallel through Byzantion is the same as that through Massalia – which Hipparchos [F54] said, trusting Pytheas [T4] – and the meridian through Byzantion is the same as that through the Borysthenes, which Hipparchos [F55] sanctions, and if he also sanctions [F59] that the distance from Byzantion to the Borysthenes is 3,700 stadia, this would be the same as

[C72]

[1] There is a gap of uncertain length here.

that from Massalia to the parallel through the Borysthenes, which would be through Keltike along the Ocean, since after approximately this [distance] one comes to the Ocean.

(13) Further, we know that the Cinnamon-Bearer territory is the farthest inhabited place toward the south, and according to Hipparchos [F44] the parallel through there is the beginning of the temperate zone and the inhabited world, about 8,800 stadia from the equator. Since, he says, from the equator to [the parallel] through the Borysthenes is 34,000 stadia, there would remain 25,200 stadia from the boundary of the burned and temperate zones to [the parallel] through the Borysthenes and Keltike along the Ocean. Those today say that the journey from Keltike to the north is the most remote one: the one to Ierne (which lies beyond Brettanike), a miserable place to live because of the cold. Thus what is beyond is considered uninhabitable. They say that Ierne is no farther than 5,000 [stadia] from Keltike, so that the width of the inhabited world would be determined at a total of 30,000 [stadia] or a little more.

(14) Let us, then, go down to that which is opposite the Cinnamon-Bearer territory and lies on the same parallel to the east, that around Taprobane. Taprobane is most strongly believed to be a large island lying in the open sea to the south of Indike. It extends toward Aithiopia for more than 5,000 stadia, as they say, and ivory is taken from there to the Indian markets, as well as tortoise-shell and other goods. If the island is given a width proportionate to its length – and adding the channel between it and Indike – the distance would be no less than 3,000 stadia, which is that from the boundary of the inhabited world to Meroë (if the capes of Indike rise opposite to Meroë) but it is more reasonable to set down more than 3,000. If one were to add this to the 30,000 that Deimachos [F2b] says is as far as the pass over to the Baktrians and Sogdianians, all these peoples would fall outside the inhabited world and the temperate zone.

Who would dare to say this, hearing those both in antiquity and today speak about the temperateness and fruitfulness, especially of the northern Indians, and then that of Hyrkania and Aria, and then Margiane and Baktriane? Although all these are next to the northern side of the Tauros [C73] (and also Baktriane, at least that which is near the pass to the Indians), they are so fortunate that they are very far away from the uninhabitable regions. In Hyrkania they say that the vine produces one *metretes* of wine, the fig sixty *medimnoi*, grain grows forth again from the cut stalks of the crops, bees swarm in the branches, and honey emanates from the leaves. This happens also in Media (part of Matiane) as well as Sakasene (part of Armenia) and Araxene. This is not so remarkable, as they are farther south than Hyrkania and surpass it in temperateness, yet it is more so in regard to the latter. In Margiane they say that it has been discovered that often the base of the vine can only be encircled by the outstretched arms of two men, and a bunch of grapes is two *pecheis* [long]. They say that Aria is similar, but surpassing it in good wine, and that the wine survives there in unpitched vessels to the third generation. Everything except olive oil is produced in Baktriane, which lies alongside of Aria.

(15) But if the portions of these places that are high and mountainous are also cold, this would be not be remarkable. Even in southern latitudes the mountains are cold, and in general so are the highlands, even if plains. At any rate, the parts of Kappadokia next to the Euxeinos are farther north than those next to the Tauros, but Bagadania, an extraordinary plain that falls between the Argaios Mountains and the Tauros, produces fruit trees only scantily – if at all – although it is 3,000 stadia farther south than the Pontic Sea. Yet the suburbs of Sinope, Amisos, and most of Phanaroia are planted with olives. And the Oxos, the boundary between Baktriane and Sogdiane, is so easily navigable, they say, that Indian goods are carried over to it and easily come down to Hyrkania, and then by the rivers to the successive places as far as the Pontos.

(16) What fortune could you find around the Borysthenes and Keltike along the Ocean, where the vine either does not grow or does not bear fruit? In the more southern regions, both on the coast and around the Bosporos, it does bear fruit, although it is small and buried in the winter. The frosts at the mouth of the Maiotic Lake are such that in winter a general of Mithridates [VI] conquered the barbarians in a cavalry battle on ice, [C74] and defeated them on the sea in the summer when the ice had melted. Eratosthenes cites this epigram in the Asklepieion of the Pantikapaians, on a bronze hydria that had been broken by the frost:

> If any man does not believe what can happen here, let him look at this hydria and know, which has been presented by the priest Stratios, not as an honorable dedication to the god but as proof of our great winter. [F61]

Since [the climate] in the region around the Bosporos cannot be compared with that in the places enumerated, not even with Amisos and Sinope (which, we would say, are more temperate), it could hardly lie parallel to the region around the Borysthenes and the farthest Kelts. Moreover, it could scarcely be at the same parallel as the region around Amisos, Sinope, Byzantion, or Massalia, which are agreed to be 3,700 stadia farther south.

(17) If those following Deimachos [F2c] add to the 30,000 [stadia] that to Taprobane and the boundary of the burned zone, which is placed at no less

than 4,000 stadia, they are removing Baktra and Aria to places 34,000 stadia from the burned zone, which Hipparchos says is as much as from the equator to the Borysthenes. Thus they are located 8,800 stadia farther north than the Borysthenes and Keltike, as much as the equator is farther south of the circle that is the boundary between the burned and temperate zones, which we say is drawn approximately through the Cinnamon-Bearer territory.

We were pointing out that the regions beyond Keltike as far as Ierne – no more than 5,000 [stadia] – are scarcely inhabitable. Yet this calculation demonstrates that there is an inhabitable circle 3,800 stadia to the north of Ierne. Baktra will be much farther north than the mouth of the Kaspian – or Hyrkanian – Sea, and about 6,000 stadia from the innermost part of the Kaspian and the Armenian and Median mountains, which seems more to the north than the coast as far as Indike, indicating that a circumnavigation as far as Indike would be possible, as Patrokles [F4a] says, who had a command in these regions. Thus Baktriane stretches 1,000 stadia toward the north. But the Skythian peoples live beyond, in a much larger territory, ending at the northern sea, and although nomadic they nevertheless live there.   [C75]

How, then, can Baktra itself be thrown outside the inhabited world? The distance from the Kaukasos as far as the northern sea [on the line] through Baktra would be slightly more than 4,000 [stadia]. If this is added to the stadia measurement from Ierne to the north, it makes the total distance through the uninhabitable region, on the meridian through Ierne, 7,800 stadia. If one were to leave out the 4,000 stadia, the parts of Baktriane that are next to the Kaukasos would be 3,800 stadia farther north than Ierne and 8,800 stadia [farther north] than Keltike and the Borysthenes.

(18) Hipparchos says [F58, 61], then, that around the Borysthenes and Keltike the light of the sun shines during the entire summer night and circles from the west to the east, and at the winter turning the sun rises at most 9 *pecheis*. This happens more noticeably among those who are 6,300 [stadia] from Massalia (whom he assumes to be Kelts, although I think they are Brettanians, 2,500 stadia farther north of Keltike), and in the winter days the sun rises 6 *pecheis*, but only 4 among those 9,100 stadia from Massalia, and less than 3 among those beyond, who, according to my reasoning would be much farther to the north than Ierne. Yet trusting in Pytheas [T5], he places this inhabited region farther south than Brettanike, and says that the longest day there has 19 equinoctial hours, and 18 where the sun rises only 4 *pecheis*. He says that they are 9,100 stadia from Massalia. Thus the most southerly Brettanians are farther north than them, and they are on the same parallel as the Baktrians near the Kaukasos – or another one near to it – for it

has been said by those following Deimachos that this means the Baktrians near the Kaukasos are 3,800 stadia farther north than Ierne, and if this is added to those from Massalia to Ierne it is 12,500. Who has recorded these places – I mean those around Baktra – and this length of the longest days or meridian height of the sun culminating at the winter turning? All these [C76] things can be seen by an amateur and do not need any mathematical data, so that many could have written them down, both the earliest historians of Persian matters and those later down to our time. How could the fortune of those places correspond to such celestial phenomena? From what I have said it is clear that he [Hipparchos] refutes the proof – although the inquiries are equivalent – taking as proof the inquiry itself.

(19) Moreover, he [Eratosthenes, F67] wishes to demonstrate that Deimachos [F3] is an amateur and inexperienced in such things, for he believes that Indike lies between the autumnal equinox and the winter tropic (contradicting Megasthenes [F7a], who says that in the southern portion of Indike the Bears are hidden and shadows fall in the opposite direction). But he [Deimachos] believes that neither instance occurs anywhere in Indike, and thus in asserting this he speaks with ignorance, for it is ignorant to think that the autumnal differs from the vernal in terms of its distance from the tropic, because the circle and the sunrise are the same at both. Since the distance between the tropic of the earth and the equator – where he had placed Indike – has been shown through careful measurement to be much less than 20,000 stadia, this would turn out to be – even according to him [Deimachos] – exactly what he [Eratosthenes] believes, not what the former believes. If Indike were of that extent – or even 30,000 – it could not fall within that distance, but if it is what he [Eratosthenes] says, it would fall within it. It is the same ignorance to say that nowhere in Indike do the Bears set or the shadows fall in the opposite direction, since it begins to happen as soon as one gets 5,000 [stadia] from Alexandria. But again Hipparchos [F16] is not right in correcting what he [Eratosthenes] says, first taking instead of the winter turning the summer one, and because he believes that one should not use the evidence of a man ignorant of astronomy, just as if Eratosthenes preferred to accept his [Deimachos'] evidence and was not following some general custom against those speaking idly. One way to refute foolish contradictions is to show that their assertions – whatever they are – advance our cause.

(20) Now, with the assumption that the most southern parts of Indike rise opposite to those around Meroë – which many have said and believed – [C77] we have shown the paradoxes that result. But since Hipparchos [F17] at this point does not object to this hypothesis, and later in his second book

does not acquiesce to it, the argument must be considered. He says, then (in regard to places rising opposite to one another which lie on the same parallel), that when the distance between them is great we cannot know the places are on the same parallel without comparing the latitude at the other place. Regarding the latitude of Meroë, Philon [F2], who wrote about his voyage to Aithiopia, records that the sun is at the zenith forty-five days before the summer solstice, and also discusses the relationship of the gnomon to the shadows of both the solstices and equinoxes. Eratosthenes [F40] is closely in agreement with Philon. No one records the latitudes of Indike, not even Eratosthenes. If, as they [Eratosthenes, F68, and Philon] think, both Bears set there, trusting those following Nearchos [F16], then it is impossible that both Meroë and the Indian promontories are on the same parallel. If Eratosthenes agrees with those asserting that both the Bears set, why is it that no one reports on the latitudes in Indike, not even Eratosthenes? For this discussion is about latitude. If he does not agree with them, let him be discharged from the accusation. And he does not agree, for when Deimachos [F3] says that nowhere in Indike are the Bears hidden, nor do the shadows fall in the opposite direction – which Megasthenes [F7a] does in fact assume – he [Eratosthenes] charges him [Deimachos] with ignorance. Thus the entire combination is false, and as granted by Hipparchos himself the falsehood that the shadows do not fall opposite is intertwined with this. Even if the capes of Indike do not rise opposite Meroë, he concedes that they are farther south than Syene.

(21) In what follows, attempting to prove these things, he [Hipparchos, F19] says what has been refuted by me, or uses false assumptions, or imposes erroneous conclusions.

Regarding the fact that from Babylon to Thapsakos is 4,800 stadia, and 2,100 north to the Armenian mountains, one cannot conclude that from Babylon along its meridian to the northern mountains is more than 6,000 [stadia]. Eratosthenes does not say that it is 2,100 stadia from Thapsakos to the mountains, but that there is a remainder that is unmeasured, and thus the following reasoning, from assumptions not proved, cannot be assumed. Eratosthenes nowhere declared that Thapsakos lies more than 4,500 stadia north of Babylon. [C78]

(22) Next, still pleading for the ancient maps, he [Hipparchos, F19] does not bring forth what Eratosthenes said about the third sealstone, but cheerfully creates his own assertion, easily overturned.

Following the thesis about the Tauros and the sea from the Pillars, he [Eratosthenes, F66] divides the inhabited world into two parts by means of this line, calling them the northern part and the southern, and he attempts to divide each again into portions, insofar as possible, calling them "seal-stones." He says that the first sealstone of the southern portion is Indike, and the second Ariane, which are easy to sketch out, as he could render not only the width and length of both, but in a manner to show their shape, as a geometrician would. He says that Indike is rhomboidal because its sides are washed by the sea on the south and east – making shores without major gulfs – and the remainder by the mountains and the river, somewhat preserving there the rectilinear shape. He [Eratosthenes, F79] also sees that Ariane has three sides suitably formed for the creation of a parallelogram, although he cannot mark off the western side by points, because the peoples there alternate with one another, yet he nevertheless indicates it by sort of a line from the Kaspian Gates ending at the promontories of Karmania that touch the Persian Gulf. He calls this side the western and that along the Indos the eastern, but he does not say that these are parallel, nor the others (the ones delineated by the mountain and by the sea), but merely [calls them] the northern and the southern.

(23) Thus he [Eratosthenes, F83] renders the second sealstone by the form of a rough outline, but he renders the third sealstone much more roughly, for several reasons. First, as already mentioned, the side from the Kaspian Gates to Karmania, common to the third and second sealstones, has not been defined distinctly, and then the Persian Gulf breaks into the southern side, as he himself says. Thus he was forced to take the line from Babylon as if it were straight, through Sousa and Persaipolis to the borders of Karmania [C79] and Persis, on which he was able to find a measured route, being in total slightly more than 9,000 stadia. This he calls the southern side but he does not say that it is parallel to the northern. It is clear that the Euphrates, by which he marks off the western side, is nothing like a straight line: after flowing from the mountains to the south it then turns toward the east and then back to the south until it empties into the sea. In showing the shape of Mesopotamia, which is created by the convergence of the Tigris and the Euphrates, and which resembles a rower's cushion (as he says), he makes it clear that the river is not straight. Moreover, he does not have a complete measurement for the western side that is marked off by the Euphrates, and he says that he does not have how much farther the distance is to Armenia and the northern mountains, as it is unmeasured. Because of all this he says that he represents the third portion very roughly. And he says that he collected the distances from many reports of those who had worked out the stopping points, some of which he says were without titles. Thus Hipparchos would seem to be unfair when he refutes this general survey geometrically, although he should have shown gratitude to those who have

reported to us in whatever way the nature of the places. But when he does not even take his geometrical suppositions from what he [Eratosthenes] said, but creates his own, he makes his ambitions more conspicuous.

(24) Thus he [Eratosthenes, F83] says that he has shown the third portion roughly, with a length of 10,000 stadia from the Kaspian Gates to the Euphrates, and in dividing it into portions he set down the measurements as he had found them already recorded, beginning in reverse from the Euphrates and its crossing at Thapsakos. As far as the Tigris, where Alexander crossed it, he writes 2,400 stadia, and then to the successive places through Gaugamela, the Lykos, Arbela, and Ekbatana (by which Dareios [III] fled from Gaugamela to the Kaspian Gates) he fills out with 10,000, having an excess of only 300 stadia. This is how he measures out the northern side, not having placed it parallel with the mountains or with the line through the Pillars, Athens, and Rhodes. For Thapsakos is far away from the mountains, and the mountains and the route from Thapsakos come together at the Kaspian Gates. These are the northern portions of the boundary.   [C80]

(25) Having thus represented the northern side, he says that the southern cannot be taken along the sea because the Persian Gulf breaks into it, but from Babylon through Sousa and Persaipolis to the boundaries of Persis and Karmania it is 9,200 stadia. He calls this the southern side, but he does not say that the southern is parallel to the northern. He says that the difference in length that occurs between the assumed northern and southern sides is because the Euphrates, having up to a point flowed to the south, turns more toward the east.

(26) Of the two flanking sides, he speaks about the western first. What it is like and whether it is one or two [lines] is considered uncertain. He says that from the Thapsakos crossing along the Euphrates to Babylon is 4,800 stadia, and from there to the outlet of the Euphrates and the city of Teredon is 3,000. From Thapsakos to the north it has been measured as far as the Armenian Gates and is about 1,100, but through the Gordyaians and the Armenians it is unknown and thus omitted. The eastern side, that which goes through Persis lengthwise from the Erythra somewhat toward Media and the north, he believes is no less than 8,000, and from certain promontories, over 9,000. The remainder through Paraitakene and Media to the Kaspian Gates is about 3,000. The Tigris River and the Euphrates flow from Armenia to the south, and when they pass the mountains of the Gordyaians they go around a great circle and enclose the large territory of Mesopotamia and then turn toward the winter sunrise and the south, especially in the case of the Euphrates. It constantly becomes closer to the Tigris around the Wall of Semiramis and the village of Opis (from which it is only 200 stadia).

Flowing through Babylon, it empties into the Persian Gulf. Thus it happens, he says, that the shape of Mesopotamia and Babylonia is like a cushion on a rowing bench. This is what Eratosthenes has said concerning the third sealstone.

(27) Certain other errors he makes – which we will point out – are not the ones that Hipparchos [F21] brings up. Let me examine what he says. Wishing to establish what [he said] first, that one must not move Indike farther south, as Eratosthenes believes, he says that it will be particularly [C81] clear from what he himself puts forth. He [Eratosthenes, F84] says that the third portion is bounded on its northern side by a line from the Kaspian Gates to the Euphrates, 10,000 stadia, but later he adds that the southern side, from Babylon to the borders of Karmania, is slightly more than 9,000, and the western side from Thapsakos along the Euphrates to Babylon is 4,800 stadia, and to the outlet 3,000. As for the distance north of Thapsakos, one part has been measured at 1,100, but the remainder is unknown.

Then, he [Hipparchos] says, since the northern side of the third portion is about 10,000 [stadia], and the [line] parallel to it straight from Babylon to the eastern side is calculated at slightly more than 9,000, it is clear that Babylon is not much more than 1,000 stadia farther east than the crossing at Thapsakos.

(28) I would say that this would be so if the Kaspian Gates and the boundary of the Karmanians and the Persians are taken accurately as on the same straight meridian, and at right angles to this previously mentioned straight meridian are [the lines] toward Thapsakos and Babylon. In fact, the line through Babylon, if drawn to meet the straight meridian through Thapsakos, would seem to be equal, or approximately so, to that from the Kaspian Gates to Thapsakos. Thus Babylon would project farther east than Thapsakos, as far as [the line] from the Kaspian Gates to Thapsakos exceeds the one from the Karmanian boundary to Babylon. Yet Eratosthenes [F80] has not said that the line bounding the western side of Ariane lies on a meridian, nor that [the line] from the Kaspian Gates to Thapsakos is at right angles with the meridian through the Kaspian Gates, but rather [mentions the line] marked by the mountain (with which that from Thapsakos makes an angle), since it has been brought down from the same point as that from which the line at the mountain [has been drawn]. Moreover, he has not said that the line to Babylon from Karmania is parallel to the line to Thapsakos. And if it were parallel but not at right angles with the meridian through the Kaspian Gates, there is nothing more to the argument.

(29) Doing this offhand and showing, as he [Hipparchos, F22] thinks, that Babylon, according to Eratosthenes [F63], is farther east than Thapsakos by a little more than 1,000 stadia, he again creates an assumption for his following [C82] argument. And he [Hipparchos] says that if one considers a straight line from Thapsakos to the south, and one perpendicular to it from Babylon, there will be a right-angled triangle consisting of the side from Thapsakos to Babylon, the perpendicular leading from Babylon to the meridian line through Thapsakos, and the meridian itself through Thapsakos. He makes the hypotenuse of this triangle the line from Thapsakos to Babylon, which he says is 4,800 [stadia]. The perpendicular from Babylon to the meridian line through Thapsakos is slightly more than 1,000 stadia, as much as is the excess of [the line] to Thapsakos beyond that up to Babylon. From these he calculates that the remaining [line] of the right angle is much longer than the perpendicular mentioned. He adds to this the one from Thapsakos to the north, running as far as the Armenian mountains (which Eratosthenes says had been measured at 1,100 stadia), but the rest is unmeasured and omitted. He [Hipparchos] assumes at least a thousand, so that both together are 2,100, and adding this to the straight side of the triangle, as far as the perpendicular from Babylon, he calculates a distance of many thousands from the Armenian mountains (or the parallel through Athens), as far as the perpendicular from Babylon, which he places on the parallel through Babylon. He points out that from the parallel through Athens to the one through Babylon it is no more than 2,400 stadia, assuming that the entire meridian is the number of stadia that Eratosthenes says. If so, the mountains of Armenia and those of the Tauros would not be on the parallel through Athens, as Eratosthenes [says], but according to him many thousand stadia toward the north. In addition, making further use of the demolished assumptions about the structure of the right-angled triangle, he [Hipparchos] takes something that is not given: that the hypotenuse in the right angle (the line straight from Thapsakos as far as Babylon) is within 4,800 stadia. But Eratosthenes says that the route is along the Euphrates, and (stating that Mesopotamia along with Babylonia is enclosed by the great circle of the Euphrates and Tigris), he also says that most of the circumference is due to the Euphrates. Therefore the straight line from Thapsakos to Babylon would not be along [C83] the Euphrates or be anywhere near as many stadia. Thus his [Hipparchos'] argument is destroyed. Moreover, it has already been stated that granting two lines drawn from the Kaspian Gates, one to Thapsakos and the other to the part of the Armenian mountains corresponding to Thapsakos (which Hipparchos himself has at least 2,100 stadia from Thapsakos), they could not be parallel to each other or to that through Babylon (which Eratosthenes calls

the southern side). He said that the route along the mountain had not been measured, yet he also said that from Thapsakos to the Kaspian Gates has been, but he added that one is speaking roughly. Moreover, in wishing only to speak about the territory between Ariane and the Euphrates, there is no difference whether one or the other was measured. But when he [Hipparchos] concludes that [the lines] are said to be parallel, he seems completely to charge the man with childish ignorance. Thus he must also be considered childish.

(30) The following are the accusations that one might make against Eratosthenes. Just as the cutting of a limb differs from [the cutting] of a part (because the former removes the parts that are by nature defined by certain joints or a conspicuous shape, about which it has been said "cutting him limb from limb" [*Odyssey* 9.291], but the latter is in no such way), and just as we make use of the proper one, considering the time and necessity, thus in regard to geography it is necessary to cut what is examined into parts, yet imitating the cutting of a limb rather than by chance. Therefore the significant and well-defined is removed, that which is useful for the geographer.

It is well-defined when it is possible [to make use of] rivers, mountains, or seas, people or peoples, or, whenever possible, a particular size or shape. Everywhere, instead of something geometrical, a simple [definition] is totally sufficient. For the size, it is sufficient to state its greatest length and width (as in the case of the inhabited world, a length of about 70,000 [stadia] and a width of less than half its length). For the shape, you can compare it to a certain geometrical figure – such as Sikelia to a triangle – or to other known figures, such as Iberia to a hide or the Peloponnesos to the [C84] leaf of a plane tree. The larger [the region] that is cut up, the rougher the parts will conspicuously be.

(31) He [Eratosthenes, F49, 82] has cheerfully divided the inhabited world into two parts by means of the Tauros and the sea extending to the Pillars. In regard to the southern portion, the borders of Indike have been well delimited in terms of a mountain, river, and sea, and by a single name (that of a single people), so that he correctly calls it four-sided and rhomboidal. Ariane cannot easily be outlined because its western side is confused, but it is bounded by three sides, which are approximately straight, and also by its name, that of one people. But, as it has been determined, the third sealstone is completely undefined, for the common side between it and Ariane is confused, as I have said, and the southern side has been taken most sloppily, for it does not outline the sealstone, since it runs through the middle of it and many portions toward the south are left out. It also does not trace its greatest length, for the northern side is longer. The Euphrates is not the western side, even if it flowed in a straight line, since its extremities do

not lie on the same meridian. How can this be the western rather than the southern? Apart from this, since the remainder to the Kilikian and Syrian Sea is small, it is implausible that the sealstone could not be advanced to there, since Semiramis and Ninos are called Syrians. The former founded Babylon and made it the royal residence, and the latter [founded] Ninos as the metropolis of Syria. Moreover, up to the present the same language exists both outside and within the Euphrates, and to tear in two a most famous people by such a division, joining parts to foreign peoples, would be especially inappropriate.

Nor could he [Eratosthenes] say that he was forced to do this because of the size, for [including the territory] as far as the sea would not make it equal to Indike or Ariane, even adding that as far as the boundary of Fortunate Arabia and Egypt. It would have been much better to extend the third sealstone this far, saying that such [territory] as far as the Syrian Sea has been added to it, so that the southern side is not as he said it was, nor as a straight line, but it extends as one sails straight along the Persian Gulf with the Karmanian coast on the right as far as the mouth of the Euphrates, and touches the boundaries of Mesene and Babylonia, which is the beginning of the isthmus that divides Fortunate Arabia from the rest of the continent, [C85] and then crosses over it and comes as far as the recess of the Arabian Gulf and Pelousion, and even to the Kanobic Mouth of the Nile. This is the southern side; the remaining or western [side] would be from the Kanobic Mouth as far as the Kilikian coast.

(32) The fourth sealstone is composed of Fortunate Arabia, the Arabian Gulf, all Egypt, and Aithiopia [Eratosthenes, F92]. The length of this portion will be that bounded by the two meridians, one of which is drawn through its most western point and the other through the most eastern. The width will be between two parallels, one of which is drawn through the most northern point and the other [through] the most southern, since the size of irregular figures whose sides make it impossible to determine their width and length must be determined in this way.

Generally it must be observed that length and width cannot be described in the same way for a whole as for a part. In regard to a whole the greater distance is called the length and the lesser the width, but with parts the length is that section which is parallel to the length of the whole, and the width is the section that is parallel to the width of the whole, whichever [dimension] is greater, even if the distance taken in the width is greater than the distance taken in the length. Thus, since the inhabited world has a length from east to west, and has a width from north to south – with its length drawn parallel to the equator and the width [parallel to] a meridian – it is necessary in regard to its parts to take as length the sections parallel to the length and as widths those [parallel to] the width. Thus we can better record, first, the size of the entire inhabited world, and then the arrangement and shape of its parts, and through this juxtaposition reveal what is lacking and what is in excess.

(33) Eratosthenes [F56] takes the length of the inhabited world on the line through the Pillars, the Kaspian Gates, and the Kaukasos as if straight, and that of the third section on the one through the Kaspian Gates and Thapsakos, and that of the fourth section on the one through Thapsakos and Heroonpolis as far as the region between the mouths of the Nile, which must come to an end in the region around Kanobos and Alexandria, for the last mouth is there, called the Kanobic or Herakleotic. Whether or not he places these lengths straight with each other or as if making an angle at Thapsakos, it is clear from what he says that neither is parallel to the length [C86] of the inhabited world. He draws the length of the inhabited world straight from the Tauros through the sea as far as the Pillars on a line through the Kaukasos, Rhodes, and Athens, and he says that from Rhodes to Alexandria (along the meridian through them) is not much less than 4,000 stadia: thus the parallels through Rhodes and Alexandria would be this [distance] apart from one another. That at Heroonpolis is about the same [as Alexandria], or somewhat farther south, and thus the line intersecting that parallel and that of Rhodes and the Kaspian Gates, whether straight or deflected, cannot be parallel to either. Thus he has not taken the lengths well, nor has he taken the portions stretching northward well.

(34) Returning first to Hipparchos [F23], let us see what he says next. Again creating his own premises, he geometrically dismantles what he [Eratosthenes] said roughly. He says that he [Eratosthenes, F85] records the distance from Babylon to the Kaspian Gates as 6,700 stadia, and to the borders of Karmania and Persis over 9,000, following a line made straight to equinoctial east. This is perpendicular to the side common with the second and third sealstones, and thus a right-angle triangle is created with the right angle on the boundaries of Karmania and the hypotenuse shorter than one of the sides of the right angle, which necessarily puts Persis into the second sealstone. But I have said [2.1.28] in regard to this that he [Eratosthenes] does not take [the distance] from Babylon to Karmania on a parallel, nor does he say that the straight line that separates the sealstones is a meridian, so he [Hipparchos] cannot speak against him. His [F24] further charge is also not good, since he [Eratosthenes] said that from the Kaspian Gates to Babylon was as already mentioned, and to Sousa 4,900 and from there to Babylon 3,400, but he [Hipparchos] starts from the same hypothesis and

says that an obtuse-angled triangle is established, at the Kaspian Gates, Sousa, and Babylon, with its obtuse angle at Sousa, and the length of its sides as already set forth. Then it follows that according to these assumptions [of Hipparchos] the meridian line through the Kaspian Gates will intersect the parallel through Babylonia and Sousa farther west (by more than 4,400 [stadia]) than the intersection of the same parallel with the straight line running from the Kaspian Gates to the boundaries of Karmania [C87] and Persis, and that this meridian line through the Kaspian Gates would make almost half a right angle with the meridian from the Kaspian Gates to the boundaries of Karmania and Persis, and it will incline midway between the south and equinoctial east. The Indos River will be parallel to this, and thus it does not flow south from the mountains as Eratosthenes [F64] says, but between that direction and equinoctial east, just as it is marked on the old maps.

Who would now agree that the triangle as formed is obtuse-angled, without agreeing that the one surrounding it is right-angled? And who [would agree] that one [of the sides] that forms the obtuse angle – that from Babylon to Sousa – lies on a parallel, without agreeing [it is the same with] the entire [line] as far as Karmania? And that the one from the Kaspian Gates to the boundaries of Karmania is parallel to the Indos? Without this the argument would be empty. And it is without this that he [Eratosthenes] has said that the shape of Indike is rhomboidal, and that just as its eastern side has been pulled far to the east, especially at the farthest promontory (which is thrown to the south compared to the rest of the coast), it is the same with the side along the Indos.

(35) In all these things he [Hipparchos, F18] speaks geometrically, but his test is not believable. He absolves himself from using it by saying that if the test only showed small distances, he could excuse them, but since they clearly are reported to be thousands of stadia, they cannot be excused, as he [Eratosthenes, F54] declares that differences of 400 stadia can be perceived, such as that between the parallels of Athens and Rhodes. Observing this is not something done by a single method, but there is one where the difference is greater and another where it is less. Where it is greater, we can trust our eyes or the crops, or the temperature of the air in judging the latitude, but for the lesser there are instruments such as gnomons or dioptras. Thus when taking the parallels of Athens with a gnomon, and that of Rhodes and Karia, the difference is perceptible, as is expected with so many stadia. But, in a width of 3,000 stadia and a length of 40,000 stadia in the mountains and 30,000 in the sea, when someone makes a line from west to equinoctial east, naming one part the southern and the other the northern, calling them [C88]

"the rectangle" and "the sealstone," we must understand what he means by these terms, as well as "northern sides" or "southern," and, moreover, "western" and "eastern." If he disregards this, he is greatly in error and must be held to account (for it is just), but if it is merely slight, even if he disregards it, he should not be questioned. In this there is no refutation to be made against him [Eratosthenes], since no geometric [proof] would be possible with such a width, and when he [Hipparchos] attempts geometric proofs, he does not use the agreed assumptions, but creates his own.

(36) He [Hipparchos, F26] discusses the fourth portion better, although he imposes his fault-finding and abides by his own assumptions, or similar ones. He rightly objects, because he [Eratosthenes, F62] called the line from Thapsakos to Egypt the length of this portion, as if one were to say that the diagonal of a parallelogram is its length. For Thapsakos and the Egyptian coast do not lie on the same parallel, but on ones far apart from each another, and the line from Thapsakos to Egypt is placed somewhat diagonally and at a slant between them. But when he [Hipparchos] is astonished at how confidently he [Eratosthenes] said that it is 6,000 stadia from Pelousion to Thapsakos (since it is more than 8,000), he is not correct. Taking it as proved that the parallel through Pelousion is more than 2,500 stadia farther south than the one through Babylon – according to Eratosthenes, as he believes – and that the [parallel] through Thapsakos is 4,800 [stadia] farther north than the one through Babylon, he says that this comes to over 8,000 stadia.

How, then, does this establish – according to Eratosthenes – the distance to the parallel through Babylon from that through Thapsakos? He has said that this is [the distance] from Thapsakos to Babylon, but he has not said that this is from the parallel through the former to that [through] the latter, nor that Thapsakos and Babylon are on the same meridian. On the contrary, Hipparchos [F20] himself showed that, according to Eratosthenes, Babylon lies more than 1,000 stadia farther east than Thapsakos. We have also provided the assertion of Eratosthenes that the Tigris and Euphrates encircle Mesopotamia and Babylonia, and that most of this encircling is due to the Euphrates, for, having flowed from the north to the south it turns toward the east and comes out to the south. Its route to the south from the north would be on some meridian, but its turn toward the east and toward Babylon is a deviation from the meridian and is not a straight line because of the previously mentioned encircling. He said that the route to Babylon from Thapsakos is 4,800 stadia and follows the Euphrates, this on purpose so that no one would take it as straight or a measurement of the distance between two parallels. If this is not to be granted, it is futile to point out

[C89]

what seems to follow [Hipparchos, F27], that a right triangle constructed at Pelousion and Thapsakos, and the intersection of the parallel at Pelousion and the meridian of Thapsakos, has one side – that on the meridian – larger than the hypotenuse, that from Thapsakos to Pelousion.

What is connected with this is also futile, because it is constructed from an assumption not conceded. He [Eratosthenes] clearly has not granted that the distance from Babylon to the meridian through the Kaspian Gates is 4,800 [stadia]. It has been proved by me that Hipparchos constructed this from something not conceded by Eratosthenes. In order to weaken what he does concede, he [Hipparchos] assumed that he [Eratosthenes] said it is more than 9,000 [stadia] from Babylon to the line extended from the Kaspian Gates to the boundary of Karmania, and then showed the same thing.

(37) This is not where one must criticize Eratosthenes [F55], but we do say that his loose magnitudes and figures must have some [agreed] measurement, and that in some cases more must be conceded, in others less. Taking the width of the mountains that stretch toward the equinoctial east as 3,000 stadia, and similarly the sea as far as the Pillars, one could agree more easily that the parallels drawn with the same width lie on a single line, rather than those that intersect, and also in regard to the ones that intersect within the same width rather than those that intersect outside. Similarly [considered] are those lines that diverge without extending beyond the width, rather than those extending beyond, and those with greater length rather than those that are shorter. Thus the inequality of the length would be concealed, as well as the dissimilarity of the figures.   [C90]

For example, if the width of the entire Tauros or the sea up to the Pillars is 3,000 stadia, we then perceive a parallelogram that marks the outline of the entire mountain range and the previously mentioned sea. If you were to divide a parallelogram lengthwise into parts, and take the diagonal of the whole and of the portions, then the diagonal of the whole would more easily be considered the same as – parallel and equal to – the length of the side rather than that of one of the parts, and the smaller the parallelogram that is taken as a part, the more this would be the case. The obliquity of the diagonal and the inequality of its length are less visible in large [dimensions], so that you would not be reluctant to say that the diagonal was the length of the figure. But if you make the diagonal more at a slant, so that it falls beyond each side – or one of them – this would no longer be the case. This is what I am saying about having an agreed measurement for a certain width.

But when he takes [the line] from the Kaspian Gates through the mountains themselves and also the one that immediately diverges greatly from the mountains into Thapsakos, as if they led as far as the Pillars on the same parallel, and again throws out [a line] from Thapsakos as far as Egypt, taking in this width, and then measures the length of the figure by this length, he would seem to be measuring the lengths of the rectangle by the diagonal of the rectangle. When it is not a diagonal but a deflected line, he would seem to err much more, for it is a deflected line leading from the Kaspian Gates through Thapsakos to the Nile. This is it against Eratosthenes.

(38) But against Hipparchos [F28] it can be said that, having made accusations against him [Eratosthenes], certain corrections could have been made in regard to his errors, as we are now doing. But he [Hipparchos] – if he gave any thought to this – exhorts us to pay attention to the ancient maps, although they must be corrected much more extensively than is necessary for the map of Eratosthenes.

Moreover, his further attempts have the same difficulty. He takes as assumed what he has fabricated from matters that are not granted (as I have proved [2.1.27]): that Babylon is not much more than 1,000 stadia east of Thapsakos. Even if it is assumed (from what was said by Eratosthenes) that it is more than 2,400 stadia farther east to the crossing of the Tigris (where Alexander crossed) from Thapsakos, that there is a shortcut of [C91] 2,400 stadia, and, moreover, that the Tigris and Euphrates, having circled Mesopotamia, are carried to the east and then turn toward the south and come near to each other and Babylon, then this creates no absurdity in his [Eratosthenes'] argument.

(39) He [Hipparchos, F30] is also mistaken in his next undertaking, in which he wishes to conclude that the route from Thapsakos to the Kaspian Gates (which Eratosthenes [F52] said is 10,000 stadia recorded as a straight line) was not measured in a straight line, with the straight line being much shorter. His attack on him is as follows: he says that according to Eratosthenes himself the meridian through the Kanobic Mouth and through the Kyaneai are the same, and this is 6,300 stadia from the one through Thapsakos, while the Kyaneai are 6,600 from Mount Kaspios, which lies at the pass to the Kaspian Sea from Kolchis. Thus the distance from the meridian through the Kyaneai to Thapsakos is within 300 stadia of being the same as to Kaspios, and therefore, essentially, Thapsakos and Kaspios are on the same meridian. It thus follows that the Kaspian Gates are equidistant from Thapsakos and Kaspios, and Kaspios is much closer to the gates than the 10,000 which Eratosthenes says they are from Thapsakos. Therefore the distance from Thapsakos is much less than the 10,000 of the straight line. Thus the 10,000 that he measures on a straight line from the Kaspian Gates to Thapsakos is circuitous. I say to him [Hipparchos] that

Eratosthenes makes his line loosely, as is proper in geography, and also makes his meridians and lines to the equinoctial east loosely, but he [Hipparchos] critiques them geometrically, as if each had been drawn with instruments. Yet he does not use instruments himself, rather taking [the relationship of the perpendicular and parallel] by guessing. This is one of his mistakes. Another is that he does not put down the measurements that were produced [by Eratosthenes] or put them to the test, but only those created by himself. Thus, although he [Eratosthenes] first said that the distance from the mouth [of the Pontos] to Phasis was 8,000 stadia, added the 600 on to Dioskourias, and then the 5 days' crossing from Dioskourias over to Kaspios (which Hipparchos [F31] represents as 1,000 stadia), so that in all it totals, according to Eratosthenes, 9,600 stadia, he [Hipparchos] makes a short cut and says [C92] that from the Kyaneai to Phasis is 5,600 and from there to Kaspios another 1,000. Thus it is not according to Eratosthenes that Kaspios and Thapsakos are essentially on the same meridian, but according to him [Hipparchos]. But let it be according to Eratosthenes. How, then can it follow that it is an equal [distance] from Kaspios to the Kaspian Gates and from Thapsakos to the same place?

(40) In his second book, he [Hipparchos, F29, 32] takes up again the same inquiry concerning the boundaries along the Tauros, about which I have spoken enough, and then passes to the matter of the northern perimeter of the inhabited world. Then he sets forth what Eratosthenes [F134] has said about the places after the Pontos, that he said there are three promontories coming down from the north: one, on which is the Peloponnesos, the second, the Italian, and the third, the Ligystikian, which cut off the Adriatic and Tyrrhenian Gulfs. Having generally expounded this, he [Hipparchos] attempts to test each statement about them by geometry rather than geography. But the errors made about them by Eratosthenes are so numerous, as well as those by Timosthenes, the writer of *On Harbors*, whom he praises more than the others (although he refutes him, disagreeing on most things), so I do not believe it worthwhile to arbitrate between them, or in regard to Hipparchos, since they are entirely in error. Even he [Hipparchos] passes over their mistakes, not correcting them but only proving that they were false or contradictory. Perhaps one could accuse him [Eratosthenes] of this because he says that there are three promontories of Europe, putting down that which is the Peloponnesos as one, although it is split into many parts. Sounion makes a promontory, just like the Lakonian territory, which is not much less to the south than Maleai and includes a notable gulf. And that from the Thracian Chersonesos up to Sounion cuts off the Melanian Gulf and those as far as the Makedonian. Even if we were to overlook this,

most of the distances are obviously wrong and prove that his ignorance of these places is excessive, without needing any geometrical proofs but only those that are obvious and can be immediately witnessed, such as that the [C93] pass from Epidamnos to the Thermaic Gulf is more than 2,000 stadia. He [Eratosthenes, F65] says it is 900, and that from Alexandria to Karchedon is more than 13,000, although it is no more than 9,000 if Karia and Rhodes are on the same meridian as Alexandria, and the Strait is on the same as Karchedon. All agree that the voyage from Karia to the Strait is no more than 9,000 stadia. In the case of a great interval, the meridian could be taken as the same as the more westerly one, that is, as far west as Karchedon is west of the Strait, but in 4,000 stadia the error is manifest. And he places Rome on the same meridian as Karchedon, although it is more to the west, but he does not admit his excessive ignorance of these regions and of those on toward the west as far as the Pillars.

(41) If Hipparchos were not writing a geographical work, but merely examining what Eratosthenes said in his *Geographia*, it would be fitting to go farther than merely correcting it in detail. For our part, we have thought it necessary in each case to bring forth a proper discussion, not only in regard to where he is right, but especially where he hits a false note, both correcting and absolving him of the charges made against him by Hipparchos, as well as examining Hipparchos himself, whenever he has said something censorious. But in these cases, when I see that he [Eratosthenes] is completely off the mark and that he is accused justly, we assume that it is enough to correct what he said in his *Geographia*. Where the mistakes are continuous and on the surface, it is better not to record them, unless rarely and generally. This is what we will attempt to do in what follows.

But let it now be said that Timosthenes [F18], Eratosthenes [F131], and those even earlier were completely ignorant of the Iberian territory and Keltika, and immensely more so about the German and Brettanikian territory, as well as the territory of the Getians and the Bastarnians. They also happened to be somewhat ignorant of the region of Italia, the Adria, the Pontos, and those portions beyond to the north, although such [statements] are perhaps finding fault. In regard to remote areas, Eratosthenes says that he records the distances that have been handed down, but does not validate them, reporting them as they have been received, although at times adding "by means of a more or less straight line." One cannot put to a strict [C94] test those distances that do not agree with one another. But this is what Hipparchos [F33] attempts to do, both in the examples formerly mentioned, and where he establishes the distances around Hyrkania as far as Baktria and to the peoples living beyond, as well as from Kolchis to the Hyrkanian Sea.

In these matters he should not be scrutinized in the same way as with the continental coast and other places that are well known, and, moreover, as I said, it is not something geometric, but rather geographical.

Making accusations against some of the Aithiopian material, at the end of the second book of his work *Against the Geography of Eratosthenes*, he [Hipparchos, F34] says that in his third book most of the speculation will be mathematical, with a certain amount of geography. Yet it seems clear to me that he does not even have a certain amount of geography, but that it is completely mathematical, although Eratosthenes has given him quite an excuse. Often he [Eratosthenes] slips into something too scholarly for the topic before him, and having slipped into something inaccurate, the conclusions that he makes are roughly done, since in a certain way he is a mathematician among geographers and a geographer among mathematicians, thus giving both an instigation for contradiction. In this section he and Timosthenes provide just occasion [for criticism], so I will abandon any joint examination, as what Hipparchos has said about this is sufficient.

Part 2:   Poseidonios and the zones

(1) Let us see what Poseidonios [F49] says in his *On the Ocean*. In it he seems to concern himself for the most part with geography, as is fitting, but also somewhat mathematically. It is not out of place to treat a few things that he has said, some of it now, and the remainder in the sections, as it occurs, and to have a certain standard. It is proper in geography to assume that the earth as a whole is sphere-shaped – just as the heavens – and to accept what follows from this assumption: that there are five zones.

(2) Poseidonios says that the division into five zones originated with Parmenides [F43], but he represents the extent of the burned zone at almost twice its width, [lying] between the tropics, exceeding both of the tropics, and with its edge in the temperate zones. Aristotle [*Meteorologika* 2.5] defines this zone as that between the tropics, and the temperate zone as that between the tropics and the arctic circles. He [Poseidonios] justly objects to both: the burned is said to be that which is uninhabitable because   [C95] of heat (considering the Aithiopians beyond Egypt), and more than half the width of what is between the tropics is uninhabitable, if that which the equator divides from the other is half the entire width. From Syene, which is on the boundary of the summer tropic, to Meroë is 5,000 [stadia], and from there to the parallel of the Cinnamon-Bearer territory, which is the beginning of the burned zone, is 3,000. All of this distance is measurable, as it is travelled by sea and by land, but the remainder as far as the equator is shown

to be 8,800 stadia, by means of the measurement of the earth made by Eratosthenes [F58]. The relationship of the 16,800 to the 8,800 would be that of the distance between the tropics to the width of the burned zone. If the smallest of the more recent measurements of the earth is introduced – which Poseidonios calculates at around 180,000 [stadia] – this shows that the burned zone is half of what is between the tropics, or slightly more than half, but in no way equal to it. How could someone distinguish the temperate zones, which are unchanging, by means of the arctic circles, which are not visible to all nor the same everywhere? That the arctic circles are not visible to everyone would not be of use in his refutation, because they must be visible to everyone living in the temperate zone, those alone for whom "temperate" is used. It is well taken that it is not the same way everywhere, but changeable.

(3) Dividing the earth into zones, he [Poseidonios] says that five are useful for celestial matters. Two of them (those that are beneath the poles and [extend] as far as the arctic tropics) have shadows all around. The two that are next (as far as those living under the tropics), have shadows in only one direction, and the one between the tropics has shadows both ways. But in regard to human affairs there are two additional narrow ones below the tropics, which have the sun overhead for about half a month and are divided in two by the tropics. These zones have a certain unusual quality, as they are peculiarly without rain, and are sandy and barren except for silphium and certain fiery fruits that are burned up. There are no nearby mountains [C96] that the clouds hit against and make rain, nor do rivers flow through them. Because of this they produce [inhabitants] with curly hair, crumpled horns, prominent lips, and flat noses, for their extremities are twisted. The Fish Eaters also live in these zones. He says that it is clear that these things are peculiar to these zones, since those farther south have a more temperate environment and a more fruitful and better-watered land.

Part 3:   Polybios and Poseidonios: The zones and the Ocean

(1) Polybios [34.1.14] makes six zones, two falling under the arctic circles and two between these and the tropics, and two between them and the equator. Yet it seems to me that the division into five zones is natural and geographical: natural in regard to the heavens and the conditions of the atmosphere, and in regard to the heavens, because of the shadows all around, the shadows in only one direction, and the shadows both ways. This is the best way to distinguish them. One can also determine the appearances of the stars, and thus by a kind of rough division they

undertake their alterations. In regard to the conditions of the atmosphere (because the conditions are judged in regard to the sun), they are affected by three significant differences that influence animals, plants, and everything else beneath the air or in it: too much heat, a lack of it, or a moderate amount. These conditions are properly determined by the division into zones, for the two chilled ones suggest the absence of heat, and indicate a single quality to the atmosphere, the temperate ones are similar in having a single moderate quality, and the remaining single burned one has the remaining [condition].

It is clear that this division is geographical. Geography seeks to determine by boundaries the section of the temperate zone in which we live. On the west and east the limit is the sea, but on the south and north it is the air, for in between it is temperate enough for plants and animals, but beyond it is disagreeable, because of an excess or lack of heat. Because of these three distinctions it is necessary to make the division into five zones. The sphere of the earth is cut in two by the equator, into the northern hemisphere (where we are) and the southern, indicating the three distinctions. At the equator and the burned zone it is uninhabitable because of heat, and at the pole because of cold, but the middle [regions] are temperate and inhabitable. In adding the [zones] beneath the tropic, he does not apply the analogy of the five, or make use of a similar criterion, but seems to have an ethnic   [C97] criterion for the zones, for one is the Aithiopian, another the Skythian and Keltic, and the third the intermediate.

(2) Polybios [34.1.15] is not correct in making the boundary of some of his zones the arctic circles: the two that fall under them and the two between them and the tropics. It has been stated that variable signs cannot define invariables. The tropics must not be used as the boundaries of the burned zone, which also has already been said. Clearly when he divides the burned zone into two parts, he does not appear to have been moved by any careless thought, since because of this we naturally use the equator to divide the entire earth in two: the northern hemisphere, and the southern. It is clear that the burned zone is divided according to this sectioning, conveniently making each of the hemispheres composed of three entire zones, each corresponding to the one in the other hemisphere. Such sectioning makes a division into six zones, but the other not at all. If, at any rate, the earth were cut in two through the poles, each of the hemispheres – the western and eastern – could not easily be cut into six zones, but five would be sufficient, for the similarity of the two sections of the burned zone, which are created by the equator and their contiguousness, makes sectioning of them superfluous and unnecessary. Although the temperate and cold zones

are alike in form, they are not contiguous. Thus, if the entire earth is conceived as such hemispheres, it is sufficient to divide it into the five.

If, as Eratosthenes [F45] says, that which lies under the celestial equator is temperate – and Polybios [34.1.16] agrees with this opinion, although he adds that it is the highest part, and because of this it is rainy, since in the Etesian season the clouds from the north frequently strike against the heights there – it would be much better to consider it a third, narrow, temperate zone, than to introduce two tropical ones. In agreement is what Poseidonios [F49] has recorded in regard to these matters: that the horizontal movement of the sun is quicker, and also that from east to west, for movement at the same speed is quicker where the circle is greater.

[C98]
(3) Poseidonios [F49] resists Polybios [34.1.17] when he says that the inhabited region under the equator is the highest, for no high point appears on a sphere because of its uniformity, and it is not mountainous under the equator, but rather a plain at a level that is about equal with the surface of the sea. The rains that fill the Nile come from the mountains of Aithiopia. Although he said these things, he is in agreement elsewhere, saying that he suspects that there are mountains under the equator and that the clouds from both temperate zones strike against them and make the rains. Yet the inconsistency is obvious. But if one admits that it is mountainous under the equator, something else seems to emerge, for they say that the Ocean flows all around. How, then, can they place mountains at its center, unless they intend to speak of certain islands? However this may be, it falls outside the subject of geography, and perhaps it should be given to someone who proposes a treatise on the Ocean.

(4) Recording those who are said to have circumnavigated Libya, he [Poseidonios] says that Herodotos [4.42] believes that certain men sent by Dareios[2] accomplished the circumnavigation, and that in a dialogue Herakleides of Pontos [F139] also has a Magos who had come to the court of Gelon assert that he had circumnavigated [it].

Saying that these are unattested, he discusses a certain Eudoxos of Kyzikos, an envoy and *spondophoros* for the festival of Kore who is reported to have come to Egypt at the time of the second Euergetes [Ptolemaios VIII]. He became associated with the king and those around him, especially in the matter of the voyages up the Nile, for he was inclined to wonder at unusual places, about which he was not uninformed. It happened that a certain Indian was brought to the king by the guards of the Arabian recess,

---

[2] Although the reading in the text is without question, it was Necho, not Dareios I, who sent forth the expedition, according to Herodotos (4.42).

who said that he had been found half dead, the only survivor of a ship, but who he was and where he came from was unknown, since they did not understand his language. He was given to those who could teach him Hellenic. When he had learned it, he described how, while sailing from Indike, he was shipwrecked due to an error, and although he was saved, he lost his shipmates through starvation. Upon being disbelieved he offered to lead an expedition to the Indians with those selected by the king, among whom was Eudoxos.

He sailed with presents and came back with a return cargo of aromatics and precious stones, some of which the rivers bring down with pebbles and others that are found by digging, solidified from liquid just as our own crystals. But he was deceived in his hopes since Euergetes took the entire   [C99] cargo. After he died, his wife Kleopatra [III] succeeded to the rule, and Eudoxos was sent out again by her with greater preparations. On his return he was driven by winds beyond Aithiopia. Carried to certain places, he won over the people by sharing grain, wine, and preserved fruit – for they had no such things – and in return obtained water and guides. He also recorded some of their words. He found the end of a prow, in wood, from a ship-wreck, which had a horse carved on it, and he found out that this wreckage had come from those sailing from the west, and took it with him when he returned on his journey home. Safely back in Egypt, with Kleopatra [III] no longer reigning, but her son, he again had everything taken away from him, for it was discovered that he had stolen many things. He brought the end of the prow to the market and showed it to the shipowners, who realized that it was Gadeiran, for although their merchants sent out large ships, poor men would have small ones that they called "horses" from the devices on the prows, and would sail in fishing voyages around Maurousia as far as the Lixos River. Some of the shipowners recognized that the end of the prow was from one that had sailed rather far beyond the Lixos River and had not survived.

Putting all this together, Eudoxos realized that a circumnavigation of Libya was possible. He went home, and gathering all his property he set forth. First he went to Dikaiarcheia and then Massalia, and then successive coastal places as far as Gadeira. Everywhere he made a great amount of noise and conducted business. Constructing a large ship along with two rowed barges like those used by pirates, he put on board music girls, physicians, and other artisans, and set sail to Indike, driven on the high seas by the Zephyrs. When his companions tired of the cruise, he unwillingly sailed with a fair wind toward the land, fearing the flood and ebb of the tides. And what he feared actually happened, for the ship ran aground, although gently, so that it was not completely broken apart and they were able to save the cargo and most of the wood on land. From this he was able to construct a third ship, equal in size to a pentakonter, and sailed until he came upon [C100] people who spoke the same language that he had formerly recorded. He also learned that these men were related to the other Aithiopians and that they were neighbors to the kingdom of Bogos [I].

Giving up on the voyage to the Indians, he turned back, and while sailing along the coast he saw an island that was well watered and well wooded but deserted, and made note of it. Safely coming to Maurousia, he disposed of his boats and went on foot to Bogos [I], and advised him to take on the sea expedition, but his friends prevailed upon him to the contrary, suggesting that they feared the land might be exposed to intrigue if the route to it were shown to outsiders who might wish to attack it.

When he [Eudoxos] learned that it was said he was being sent forth on the announced expedition, but in fact was going to be abandoned on some deserted island, he fled to Roman-controlled territory and then crossed over to Iberia. Again he constructed a rounded ship and a long pentakonter, the former to cross the open sea and the latter to explore the coast. He placed on board agricultural instruments, seeds, and builders, and set forth on the same coastal voyage. He planned, if the cruise were delayed, to spend the winter on the island that had been previously observed, and to use the seed and its harvest to complete the cruise that he had planned from the beginning.

(5) "Thus I" – he [Poseidonios, F49] says – "have brought the account of Eudoxos to this point. What happened later, those from Gadeira and Iberia probably know."

Yet he says that from all this it is shown that the inhabited world is encircled by the Ocean flowing around it ("the bonds of a continent do not surround him, but he pours forth boundlessly, and nothing defiles him."). Poseidonios is wonderful in all of this, for he believes the circumnavigation of the Magos, of which Herakleides spoke [F139], to be unsubstantiated, as well as those sent by Dareios[3] whom Herodotos [4.42] records. Nevertheless he puts this Bergaian tale in the category of truth, even though it was either fabricated by him or believed from others who fabricated it.

First, what can be believed about the Indian's reversal of fortune? The Arabian Gulf is narrow like a river, and its length is around 15,000 stadia as far as its mouth, which is completely narrow itself. It is unlikely that the Indians sailing outside of it were pushed aside into the gulf while off course

---

[3] This is the same error as cited in note 2 (2.3.4).

(for the narrowness of the mouth would have shown that they were about to go off course), and if they went purposely into the gulf there would be no excuse about being off course or the uncertain winds. How could they allow [C101] all of them except one to be destroyed by starvation? Having survived, how was he able to guide the ship alone, which was not small, since it was of a size capable of crossing the open sea? How could he learn the language so quickly, well enough to persuade the king that he could lead the expedition? Why did Euergetes have a scarcity of that type of leader, since that sea was already known to many? And why did the *spondophoros* and envoy of the Kyzikenes leave his city and sail to Indike? Why was he entrusted with so important a commission? When he returned, everything was taken from him, contrary to his expectations, and he was in disgrace, so why was he entrusted with a greater shipment of presents? When he returned again and was carried beyond Aithiopia, why did he decide to write down the language, and why did he learn where the piece of prow from the fishing boat had been washed ashore? To learn about this shipwreck sailing from the west would be no accomplishment, since he was about to sail from the west on his return home.

Going, then, to Alexandria, when it was discovered that he had appropriated many things, why was he not punished, but went around questioning shipowners and showing them the part of the prow? And was not the one who recognized it wonderful? And the one who believed him even more wonderful, as he went back home on such a hope, and then made a change of residence to beyond the Pillars? But he could not have set sail from Alexandria without permission, especially if he had appropriated royal property. He also would have been unable to sail out secretly, since the harbor and other exits were barred by a guard, such as we know still remains today (I have lived in Alexandria for a long time), although at present, with the Romans in control, it is loosened, but the royal guard was much stricter.

Then, when he had gone to Gadeira and built a ship in his royal manner and sailed away, and the ship had been wrecked, how could he have built a third boat in a desolate place? And why, when he continued his voyage and found the western Aithiopians who had the same language as the eastern, did he not attempt to complete the remainder of the cruise – being so frivolous in his fondness of travelling abroad and having the expectation that the unknown remaining portion was small – but gave it up and desired that the expedition be at the hands of Bogos [I]? How did he learn about the plot that was secretly contrived against him? And what was the advant- [C102] age to Bogos to destroy the man when he could merely have sent him away? Even if he had anticipated the scheme, how could he have fled to safe places?

Although there is nothing impossible in each case, it is difficult and unlikely even with some good fortune. But he always happened to have good fortune, although he was constantly in danger. Having escaped from Bogos, why was he not afraid to sail again along the coast of Libya when he had preparations capable of settling an island?

This is not so far from the fabrications of Pytheas, Euhemeros, and Antiphanes. They can be pardoned, however, since this is what they practice, like conjurers, but how can he [Poseidonios] who is precise and a scholar, essentially the first contender, be pardoned? He does not do this well.

(6) The rising and settling that the earth undergoes at times, and the changes due to earthquakes and other similar things, which we have enumerated, are correctly laid out by him. It is good that he cites Plato [*Timaios* 24–6] on this, and it is possible that the matter of the island of Atlantis is not fabricated. Concerning this, he reports that Solon – having learned it from the Egyptian priests – said that it once existed but disappeared and was of a size no smaller than a continent. And he [Poseidonios] thinks it is better to say it in that way than how its maker made it disappear, as the Poet [*Iliad* 12.13–33] did with the Achaian Wall.

He also infers that the Kimbrians and their relatives were driven out of their homeland because of an approach of the sea that happened all at once. Also, he suggests that the length of the inhabited world – about 70,000 stadia – is half of the entire circle on which it is taken, so that, he says, someone sailing from the west along its width will come to the Indians in the same number of thousand [stadia].

(7) He attempts to find fault with those who divided the continents in such a way (rather than by using [divisions] parallel to the equator, which would show the variations in animals, plants, and the atmosphere), because some of them approach the cold [zone] and others the burned, and thus the continents are virtually zones. But then he changes again and withdraws his judgement, again approving of the division, thus making it an arbitrary question that serves no purpose.

[C103] Like the differences of nationality or language, such an arrangement is not because of foresight, but due to accident and chance. Arts, qualities, and capabilities, once they have begun, are for the most part strong in any latitude whatsoever, and even in spite of the latitudes. Thus some customs of a people are natural, and others due to training. It is not by nature that the Athenians are fond of learning and the Lakedaimonians are not, or even the nearer Thebans, but rather by training. The Babylonians and Egyptians are scholars not by nature but by practice and habit. The abilities of horses, cows, and other animals are not only because of their location but their training. But he confuses this.

Agreeing on the division of continents as it now is, he uses the example that the Indians differ from the Aithiopians in Libya, for the former are better developed physically and are less burned by the dryness of their atmosphere. This is why Homer, speaking about all of them, divides the Aithiopians into two, "some where Hyperion sets and others where he rises" [*Odyssey* 1.24]. <But Krates [F37] writes "these where Hyperion sets, and those where he rises.">[4] Yet to introduce another inhabited world, which Homer did not know about, is to be a slave to hypothesis, and he [Poseidonios] says that it is necessary to emend it to "both where Hyperion departs," or where he declines from the meridian.

(8) First, the Aithiopians near Egypt are themselves divided in two, for some are in Asia and others in Libya, and not different from one other. Homer divided the Aithiopians in two not because he knew that they were physically similar to the Indians (for Homer probably did not know anything about the Indians, since not even [Ptolemaios VIII] Euergetes, according to the tale of Eudoxos, knew about Indike or the voyage to it), but rather because of the division that we discussed previously [1.2.26]. We have also discussed [1.2.24] the reading suggested by Krates, and there is no difference which way it is read. But he [Poseidonios] says that there is a difference, and it is better to emend it to "both where he departs." How is this different from "where he sets"? The entire section from the meridian to the setting is called "the setting," just like the semi-circle of the horizon. This is what Aratos means in "where the extremities of the settings and the risings mix with one another" [*Phainomena* 61–2]. If the reading of Krates is better, it must be said that the one of Aristarchos is also.

So much for Poseidonios. Many of his points we treat appropriately in   [C104]
what follows, especially geographical matters. What is more about nature must be examined elsewhere, or not considered. There is much inquiry into causes by him, in imitation of Aristotle, that our school avoids because of the concealment of causes.

Part 4:   Polybios and the Internal Sea

(1) Polybios [34.5.1–6] says that in his European chorography he omits those from antiquity in favor of those who refute them, especially scrutinizing

---

[4] Something has fallen out of the text: a citation of Krates' work is assumed from the reference to him in section 8.

Dikaiarchos [F124] and Eratosthenes [F14] (who has produced the ultimate work on geography), and Pytheas [F5], by whom many have been deceived. He asserted that he travelled over the whole of Brettanike that was accessible, reporting that the circumference of the island was more than 40,000 [stadia], and also recorded matters about Thoule and those places where there was no longer any land in existence – and neither sea nor air – but something compounded from these, resembling a sea lung in which, he says, the earth, sea, and everything are suspended, as if it were a bonding for the whole, accessible neither by foot nor ship. He himself saw the lung but tells the rest from hearsay. This is the report of Pytheas, and he adds that when he returned from there he went along the entire ocean coast of Europe from Gadeira to the Tanais.

(2) Now Polybios [34.5.7–6.10] says that this is unbelievable: how could someone who was a private individual and poor have gone such distances by ship and foot? Eratosthenes was at a loss whether to believe these things, but nevertheless believed him about Brettanike and the regions of Gadeira and Iberia. But he [Polybios?] says that it is far better to believe [Euhemeros] the Messenian [T5b] than him, for, he says that he sailed only to one country, Panchaia, but he [Pytheas] closely observed the entire north of Europe as far as the boundary of the world, a report no one would believe even if from Hermes. Eratosthenes called Euhemeros a Bergaian but believes Pytheas, even though Dikaiarchos did not believe him. "Dikaiarchos did not believe him" is an absurd statement, as if it were fitting for him [Eratosthenes] to use as a standard one against whom he has made so many refutations. It has been said [2.1.41] that Eratosthenes was ignorant of the western and northern parts of Europe, but there must be leniency toward him and Dikaiarchos, as they had not seen those places, but who would be lenient toward Polybios or Poseidonios? For it is Polybios who calls what they [Eratosthenes and Dikaiarchos] report about the distances in those regions and other places popular judgements, although he is not free from this when he refutes them. At any rate, Dikaiarchos says that it is 10,000 stadia to the Pillars from the Peloponnesos, and more from there to the recess of the Adria, and allows 3,000 of that to the Pillars from the Strait, so that the remainder is 7,000 from the Strait to the Pillars. Regarding the 3,000, he [Polybios] will take it as either true or false, but not the 7,000, whether measured along the coast or through the middle of the sea, for the coast is much like an obtuse angle, running toward the Strait and the Pillars with its head at Narbon; thus a triangle is created with its base straight through the sea, and the sides made by the previously mentioned angle, of which the one from the Strait as far as Narbon is more than 11,200 [stadia], and the

remaining one a little less than 8,000. It is agreed that the greatest distance from Europe to Libya across the Tyrrhenian Sea is no more than 3,000 stadia, and reduced if taken across the Sardonian [Sea]. But let it be granted, he says, that the latter is also 3,000, and let it be previously assumed that the depth of the gulf at Narbon is 2,000, falling from the head to the base of the obtuse angle. It is thus clear from elementary measurement, he says, that the total coast from the Strait to the Pillars is nearly 500 stadia more than straight through the open sea. Adding the 3,000 from the Peloponnesos to the Strait, the total number of stadia – in a straight line – will be more than twice what Dikaiarchos has said. He [Polybios] also says that it will be necessary to make it more to the Adriatic recess.

(3) But, my dear Polybios [34.6.11–14], one might say, just as the test demonstrates that your words are manifestly false, since you have said that it is 700 [stadia] to Leukas from the Peloponnesos, and the same to Korkyra, and again the same from there to Keraunia, and to Iapydia from the Keraunians, with the Illyrian coast on the right, 6,150 stadia, thus all together it is false, both what Dikaiarchos [F124] said (that it is 7,000 stadia from the Strait to the Pillars), and what you seem to have shown. Most agree in saying that it is 12,000 across the open sea, and this is in harmony with what is asserted about the length of the inhabited world, which most say is 70,000. Its western section, from the Issic Gulf to the capes of Iberia (which are the most western), is a little less than 30,000. This is calculated as follows: from the Issic Gulf to the Rhodia, 5,000; from there to Salmonion, the eastern cape of Crete, 1,000; the length of Crete to the Ram's Forehead, more than 2,000; from there to Pachynon in Sikelia, 4,500; from Pachynon to the Strait over 1,000; then the passage to the Pillars from the Strait, 12,000; and from the Pillars to the extremity of the Sacred Promontory of Iberia, around 3,000. Moreover, he [Polybios] has not taken the perpendicular properly, if Narbon is situated on about the same parallel as that through Massalia (which Hipparchos [F53–5] believes is the same as the one through Byzantion), and [the line] through the sea is the same as that through the Strait and the Rhodia, and from the Rhodia to Byzantion – assuming that both lie on the same meridian – is said to be about 5,000 stadia (for that would be the perpendicular, as has been stated). When they say that the longest passage across this sea from Europe to Libya is 5,000 stadia (from the recess of the Galatic Gulf), this seems to me to be an erroneous statement, or there is a part of Libya that slopes far to the north and touches the parallel through the Pillars. He is again in error in saying that the previously mentioned perpendicular ends near Sardo, for it is not near, but much farther west, leaving most of the Sardoan Sea as well as the

[C106]

Ligystikan in between. And he has also exaggerated the length of the coast, although not by much.

(4) Next, he [Polybios 34.7.1–7] corrects the statements of Eratosthenes [F133], in some cases correctly, but in others what he says is worse. For example, when he [Eratosthenes] says that from Ithaka to Korkyra is 300 [stadia], he [Polybios] says that it is more than 900; [Eratosthenes] set down 900 from Epidamnos to Thessalonikeia, but he [Polybios] says it is more than 2,000. In these he is correct. But when he [Eratosthenes] says that it is 7,000 from Massalia to the Pillars, which are 6,000 from Pyrene, he [Polybios] himself speaks in error in saying that it is more than 9,000 from Massalia and from Pyrene a little less than 8,000, for he [Eratosthenes] is nearer to the truth. Those today agree that if one cuts through the irregu-
[C107] larities of the roads, the length of the whole of Iberia, from Pyrene to its western side, is no more than 6,000 stadia. But he [Polybios] puts the Tagos River at 8,000 in length from its source as far as its mouth, without any of its bends (this is not being geographical), but speaking of a straight line, although the sources of the Tagos are more than 1,000 stadia from Pyrene. On the other hand, he is correct when he proclaims that Eratosthenes is ignorant of Iberika, because he proclaims things that conflict with one another, such as when he says that the exterior as far as Gadeira is inhabited by the Galatians – if they do possess the western part of Europe as far as Gadeira – and then he forgets this and nowhere records the Galatians in his circuit of Iberia.

(5) When he [Polybios, 34.7.8–10] expounds that the length of Europe is less than that of Libya and Asia together, he does not make the comparison correctly. He says that the mouth at the Pillars is at equinoctial west, but the Tanais flows from the summer sunrise, and thus the combined length is less by whatever is between the summer sunrise and the equator, for Asia has precedent to the semicircle from the equinoctial sunrise to the north.

Apart from his stubbornness in regard to matters easy of solution, it is false that the Tanais flows from the summer sunrise, for all those acquainted with these places say that it flows from the north into the Maiotis, and that the mouth of the river and of the Maiotis, as well as the river itself as far as it is known, all lie on the same meridian.

(6) Unworthy of mention are those who have said that its source is in the Istros region, [flowing] from the west, for they have not considered that the Tyras, Borysthenes, and Hypanis – all large rivers – flow between them into the Pontos, one parallel to the Istros and the others to the Tanais. Since the sources of the Tyras have not been observed, nor those of the Borysthenes or Hypanis, places that are farther north would be even less known. Thus the

argument that has the Tanais turn from these regions to the Maiotis (for its mouths are clearly seen at the northern portion of the lake, which is also the most eastern) would be fabricated and an inconclusive statement. Also inconclusive is to say that it flows toward the north through the Kaukasos and then turns toward the Maiotis: this has also been said. No one has said that it flows from the east. If it so flowed, it would not flow opposite to the Nile and in a way diametrically opposed to it, as the more accomplished ones declare, so that both rivers flow on the same meridian or ones lying close to each other.   [C108]

(7) The measurement of the length of the inhabited world is along a parallel to the equator, since its length stretches in the same way. Thus the length of each of the continents must be taken as lying between two meridians. The measurement of these lengths is by stadia, and we seek them out by going through them, or along the roads or water routes that are parallel to them. But he [Polybios] gets rid of this and brings in something new, a section of the northern hemicircle, which is between the summer sunrise and the equator. Yet no one uses rules and measures that are changeable for things that are unchangeable, nor calculations suitable for one thing or another for the same or unchanging things. Length is unchangeable and established, as is the equatorial sunrise and setting, but not that of the summer and winter, which is relative to us. If we move elsewhere, sunset and sunrise (whether equinoctial or tropical) are in a different place, although the length of the continent is the same. It is not out of place to make the Tanais and Nile boundaries, but it is novel [to use] the summer or equinoctial sunrise.

(8) Since Europe extends into a number of promontories, he [Polybios 34.7.11–14] describes it better than Eratosthenes [F135], although not adequately. The latter spoke of only three, the one going down to the Pillars, on which is Iberia, the one to the Strait, on which is Italia, and the third, down to Maleai, on which are all the peoples between the Adria and the Euxeinos and the Tanais. The former sets up two of the promontories in the same way, with a third ending at Maleai and Sounion, on which are all of Hellas and Illyris, and part of Thrace. A fourth consists of the Thracian Chersonesos (where the narrows between Sestos and Abydos are and which is inhabited by Thracians), and a fifth is the Kimmerian Bosporos and the mouth of the Maiotis.

The first two must be granted, as they are surrounded by simple gulfs, one by that between Kalpe and the Sacred Promontory – on which is Gadeira – as well as by the sea between the Pillars and Sikelia, and the other by it and the Adria, although the Iapygian Promontory intervenes, giving Italia two   [C109] peaks and a somewhat different appearance. But the remainder are clearly more complicated with many parts, and require additional division.

Moreover, a division into six has the same objection, since it has been made according to the promontories. In each section we will make the appropriate corrections – both to these and to others – where he is in error about Europe, and in his circuit of Libya.

Now, what has been said about my predecessors is enough, of as many as I would believe are sufficient to be set forth as witnesses that it was proper for me to have undertaken this work, since so many corrections and additions are necessary.

Part 5:   The nature of the inhabited world

(1) Since the undertaking of my project follows what has been said about my predecessors, making another beginning I will say that whoever attempts to produce a chorography must consider as hypotheses much of what is natural and mathematical, and treat what follows through conjecture and faith.

I have said [1.1.13] that no builder or architect would be able to locate a house or city if he did not already know about latitudes, the heavens, figures, dimensions, heat and cold, and other such things. It is no less so for someone [describing] the topography of the entire inhabited world. For to draw on the same single plane Iberika and Indike, and what lies in between, and nonetheless to delineate the setting and rising, or culmination (as though they were in common for everyone), provides a geographical doctrine to someone who had previously considered the arrangement and movement of the heavens, and who understood that the true appearance of the earth is spherical, but in order to see it, it is now devised as a plane. This transmits something geographical to such a person, but to someone else it has no geographical meaning.

It is not like going over the great plains, such as the Babylonian, or over the sea, where everything is placed on a plane before us, behind us, or beside us, providing us with no differing appearance of the heavens or the movement and situation of the sun and the other stars. In regard to geography it must never be in such a way. Someone crossing the sea or travelling through level country is guided by a common imagination that affects both the uneducated and the politically astute, as he is inexperienced in the heavens and ignorant of their difference in appearance. He sees the rising of the sun, its setting, and when it is at the meridian, but he does not consider how this occurs, for it is of no use to what is before him, just as whether or not he stands parallel to someone next to him. Perhaps he does consider it, but has

[C110]

an opinion contrary to mathematical scholarship, just as country people do, for one's situation causes the error.

But the geographer does not create geography for country people, nor for the kind of citizen who has not considered what is peculiarly called mathematical, nor for the harvester or digger, but for someone who can be persuaded that the entire earth is the way the mathematicians say it is, along with everything relating to such a hypothesis. He urges those approaching him to consider such things beforehand, and then to look upon what is next, for he will speak of what follows, and thus if they listen mathematically they will make better and solid use of what has been handed over, but to others he does not speak of geography.

(2) The geographer, in regard to the arrangement of his discipline, must rely on the surveyors who have measured the entire earth, and they on the astronomers, and they on the natural scientists. Natural science is a kind of distinction, and they say that this distinction is absolute, dependent upon itself, and having within itself its own principles and their proofs. What we are shown by the natural scientist is as follows: the cosmos and the heavens are sphere-shaped, and the force of weight is toward the center. The earth, positioned around it, is in the form of a sphere and remains concentric with the heavens, and its axis is also positioned through the center of the heavens. The heavens revolve around it and its axis, from east to west, along with the fixed stars, at the same speed as everything. The fixed stars are carried along parallel circles, and the best known parallels are the equator, the two tropics, and the arctics. The planetary stars, sun, and moon, are on oblique [circles], positioned on the zodiac.

The astronomers believe these things, either completely or in part, and then treat carefully what follows: the movements, revolutions, eclipses, sizes, distances, and a myriad of other things. The geometricians are similar, measuring the entire earth, putting before themselves the opinions of the natural scientists and astronomers, and the geographers are also in such a way regarding the geometricians.   [CIII]

(3) Thus there must be the hypothesis that the heavens are five-zoned, and that the earth is also five-zoned, with these zones having the same names as those above: we have already stated [2.3.1] the reason for this division into zones. The zones are determined by circles drawn parallel to and on both sides of the equator, two that isolate the burned zone, two after these that make the two temperate zones next to the burned zone, and the frigid ones next to the temperate ones. Under each of the celestial circles falls the homonymous terrestrial one, and the zone is the same for each zone. They call temperate those that are suitable for habitation, with the others being

uninhabitable because of the heat or cold. It is in the same way with the tropic and arctic circles (for those who have arctic circles): they are determined by making the terrestrial ones homonymous with those above, as each lies below. Since the equator cuts the entire heavens in two, by necessity the earth is also cut in two by its equator. One of the hemispheres – both the celestial and terrestrial – is called the northern and the other the southern. Since the burned zone is cut in two by the same circle, part will be in the northern and [part] in the southern. It is clear that one of the temperate zones will be the northern and the other the southern, homonymous with the hemisphere it is in. What is called the northern hemisphere contains the temperate zone in which, looking from east to west, the pole is on the right and the equator on the left, or, looking to the south, the west is on the right and the east on the left. For the southern hemisphere it is the opposite. Thus it is clear that we are in one of the two hemispheres (the northern) and it is impossible to be in both, as "in between there are great rivers. . .and first the Ocean" [*Odyssey* 11.157–8], and then the burned zone. But there is no Ocean in the center of our inhabited world, cutting the whole of it, nor does it have a burned place, nor has there been found any portion of it whose latitude is opposite to what has been stated for the northern temperate zone.

(4) Assuming these things, and also using the knowledge from gnomons and other matters shown by the astronomers – through which can be found the parallels to the equator (for each inhabited place), and those cutting at right angles to them, drawn through the poles – the geometrician can measure out the inhabitable places that he visits, and the remainder by calculating the sections. Thus he can find how far it is from the equator to the pole, which is a quarter of the largest circle of the earth, and obtaining this he multiplies it by four, which is the circumference of the earth.

[C112]

Just as someone who measures the earth takes his rules from the astronomer – and the astronomer from the natural scientist – in the same way the geographer must begin with someone who has measured the entire earth, believing in him and in those whom he believed in. He must first explain the inhabited world: its size, shape, and nature, and how it relates to the entire earth. This is the peculiarity of the geographer. Then he must make an appropriate discussion of its parts, both land and sea, and conclude whether it has been discussed insufficiently by those of our predecessors who are most believed to be the best in such matters.

(5) Let us assume that the earth along with the sea is sphere-shaped and that one and the same surface contains the open sea, for the projections on the earth would be concealed because they are small in comparison with its

great size and would escape notice. Thus we call it "sphere-shaped," not as if it were turned on a lathe nor as a surveyor would present it, but in order to perceive it, and this somewhat roughly (Eratosthenes, F30). Let us consider it as five-zoned, with the equator drawn as a circle on it, and another circle parallel to it bordering the cold region in the northern hemisphere, and another at right angles through the poles. Since the northern hemisphere contains two-fourths of the earth, formed by the equator and the [line] passing through the poles, a four-sided area is cut off in each of them. The northern side is half of the parallel next to the pole, the southern side is half of the equator, and the remaining sides are sections of those [lines] passing through the poles, lying opposite to each other and equal in length. In either of these four-sided areas (it would seem to make no difference which one) we say that our inhabited world is placed, washed all around by the sea and like an island. It has been said [1.1.8] that this can be shown through perception and reason. If anyone were not to believe this argument, it would make no difference to geography whether to make it an island or to admit what we understand from experience: that one can sail around both sides, from the east and the west, except for a few areas in the middle. Regarding these, there is no difference whether they are bounded by sea or uninhabitable land, for the geographer attempts to speak about the known parts of the inhabitable world. He omits the unknown parts, as well as that which is outside of it. It will suffice to join with a straight line the farthest   [C113] limits of the coastal voyage on both sides and to fill completely the form of the so-called island.

(6) Let us propose, then, that the island is in the previously mentioned quadrilateral. It is necessary to take as its size what it appears to be, removing our hemisphere from the entire size of the earth, and from this its half, and then from it also the quadrilateral in which we say that the inhabited world lies. It is necessary to understand its shape by analogy and adapt its appearance to the hypotheses. But since the segment of the northern hemisphere that is between the equator and the polar parallel is in the shape of a spindle whorl, and since the polar parallel cuts the hemisphere into two, and also cuts the spindle whorl in two, making the quadrilateral, it will be clear that the quadrilateral in which the Atlantic Ocean lies appears as half the spindle whorl, and that the inhabited world is a chlamys-shaped island in it, less than half the quadrilateral in size. This is clear from geometry, from the size of the sea that spreads around it (which covers the farthest point of the continents at both ends, contracting them to a tapering shape), and, third, from its great length and width. The former is 70,000 stadia, limited for the most part by a sea that still cannot be crossed

because of its size and desolation. The latter is less than 30,000 stadia, bounded by areas that are uninhabitable because of heat or cold. The part of the quadrilateral that is uninhabitable because of heat has a width of 8,800 stadia, and a maximum length of 126,000, which is half the equator. . .and the remainder may be more.[5]

(7) Essentially in agreement with this is what Hipparchos [F36] has said. He says, based on the size of the earth, as Eratosthenes [F34] has stated, that it is necessary to consider the inhabited world separately, for it will not make a great difference in regard to the celestial phenomena for each inhabited region whether his or later measurements are used. Since, according to Eratosthenes [*Measurement of the Earth*, F1–9], the equator is 252,000 stadia, one fourth of it would be 63,000. This is the distance from the equator to the pole, fifteen sixtieths of the sixty [intervals] of the equator.

[C114]   From the equator to the summer tropic is four [sixtieths], and this is the parallel drawn through Syene. Each of these distances is computed from known measurements. The tropic lies at Syene because at the summer solstice there a gnomon has no shadow in the middle of the day. The meridian through Syene is drawn approximately along the course of the Nile from Meroë to Alexandria, which is about 10,000 stadia. It happens that Syene lies in the middle of that distance, so that from there to Meroë is 5,000. Going in a straight line about 3,000 stadia farther south, it is no longer inhabitable because of the heat, so the parallel through these places, the same as the one through the Cinnamon-Bearer territory, must be put as the limit and the beginning of our inhabited world in the south. Since it is 5,000 from Syene to Meroë, adding the other 3,000 the total would be 8,000 to the boundary of the inhabited world. But from Syene to the equator is 16,800 (this is the four sixtieths, with each of them 4,200), so the remainder would be 8,800 from the boundary of the inhabited world to the equator, and 21,800 from Alexandria. Again, everyone agrees that the sea route from Alexandria to Rhodes is in line with the course of the Nile, as well as the sailing route from there along Karia and Ionia to the Troad, Byzantion, and the Borysthenes. Taking, then, the known distances that have been sailed, they consider how far the territories in a straight line beyond the Borysthenes are inhabitable and what the boundary is of the part of the inhabited world toward the north. The Roxolanians, the farthest of the known Skythians, live beyond the Borysthenes, although they are farther south than the remote peoples we know about north of Brettanike. The area lying beyond immediately becomes uninhabitable because of the

---

[5] The thought seems incomplete as preserved.

cold. Farther to the south of them are the Sauromatians beyond the Maiotis and the Skythians as far as the eastern Skythians.

(8) Now Pytheas [F6] the Massaliote says that the region around Thoule, the most northerly of the Prettanidians, is the farthest, and that the circle of the summer tropic is the same as the arctic circle. I have learned nothing about this from anyone else: whether there is a certain island called Thoule, or whether there is habitation up to where the summer tropic becomes the arctic. I believe that the northern boundary of the inhabited world is much farther to the south. Nothing is described beyond Ierne, which lies [C115] to the north of Prettanike and near to it, where men are totally wild and live badly because of the cold, and thus I believe that the boundary is to be placed there.

With the parallel through Byzantion going approximately through Massalia, as Hipparchos [F54] said, believing Pytheas (he says that at Byzantion the relationship of the gnomon to its shadow is the same as what Pytheas reported for Massalia), and with the one running through the Borysthenes about 3,800 from there, considering the distance from Massalia, the circle through the Borysthenes would fall somewhere in Prettanike. But Pytheas, who misleads men everywhere, is totally in error here. That the line from the Pillars to the region of the Strait, and to Athens and Rhodes, lies on the same parallel, is agreed by many. And it is further agreed that the part from the Pillars to the Strait is mostly in the middle of the sea. Sailors [say] that the longest passage from Keltike to Libya – that from the Galatic Gulf – is 5,000 stadia, and this is the greatest width of the sea. Thus from the stated line to the recess of the gulf would be 2,500 stadia, and less to Massalia, for Massalia is farther south than the recess of the gulf. But that from the Rhodia to Byzantion is about 4,900 stadia, and thus [the parallel] through Byzantion would be much farther north than that through Massalia. From there to Prettanike may be in harmony with that from Byzantion to the Borysthenes, but from there to Ierne is no longer known, or whether there are inhabitable regions farther north, nor should this be considered, because of what has been said above [2.5.5].

In regard to knowledge, just as in the southern portion the limit of the inhabitable world was fixed by going 3,000 stadia beyond Meroë (not considered the most accurate limit, but nearly exact), it is sufficient to take nothing farther beyond Prettanike, or a little more, perhaps 4,000. There would be no political advantage to know about such places and their inhabitants, especially if they live in such islands that they are unable to harass or benefit us because of their isolation. The Romans could have held Prettanike but were disdainful, seeing that there was nothing to fear from

[C116] them (for they do not have the strength to cross over to us), and there is no particular benefit to possessing them. It seems that more is derived now from levying them than tribute could provide, removing the military expenses of guarding the island and collecting tribute, which would be even more unprofitable in regard to other places around that island.

(9) If one were to add to the distance from the Rhodia as far as the Borysthenes a distance of 4,000 stadia from the Borysthenes to the northern regions, this is a total of 12,700 stadia, and that from the Rhodia to the southern limit of the inhabited world is 16,600, so the entire width of the inhabited world is less than 30,000 from south to north. The length is said to be about 70,000, that is, from west to east, from the extremities of Iberia to the extremities of Indike, measured in part by land journeys and in part by sea journeys. That this length is within the previously mentioned quadrilateral is clear from the relationship of the parallels to the equator, and thus the length is more than twice the width. It is said to be somewhat chlamys-shaped, for when we travel throughout its regions, a great contracting of width at the extremities is found, especially at the west.

(10) We have now inscribed on a spherical surface the region where we say that the inhabited world is situated. One who also would come closest to imitating the truth by constructed figures must make a sphere of the earth, like that of Krates [F134], and mark off the four-sided figure on it, and put the geographical plan within it. But a large sphere is needed, so that the particular section – which is only a fraction of it – would be sufficient to receive the appropriate portion clearly (the part that belongs to the inhabited world). To supply the proper appearance to those viewing it, it is better to make a construction of as great a size as possible, which would be larger than ten feet in diameter. If one of such size – or not much smaller – is not possible, it should be written on a flat surface of no less than seven feet. It will make only a small difference if we draw the parallels and meridians with straight lines, by which we plainly show the latitudes, winds, and other differences, as well as the positioning of the parts of the earth relative to each other and the heavens, parallel [lines] for the parallels, and ones at right angles for those at [C117] right angles, for the difference can easily be transferred from what is seen by the eye on a flat surface to the form and size carried around the sphere. We can say that the oblique circles and their straight lines are analogous. Although the various meridians drawn through the pole converge on the sphere toward a single point, on the surface of the plan there is no difference if the straight lines converge slightly, but there is often no necessity for this, nor is it obvious when the circumferential and converging lines are transferred to the surface of the plan and drawn as straight lines.

(11) We have set forth the following discussion with the drawing made on a plane surface. Now I will speak of where I have gone by land and sea, and what has been entrusted to the accounts or writings of others. I have gone west from Armenia as far as the regions of Tyrrhenia opposite Sardo, and south from the Euxeinos as far as the boundaries of Aithiopia. You could not find another among the geographers who has travelled over a much farther extent than I have said, for those who have covered more of the western portions have not touched as much of the east, and those in the opposite situation are behind in the west. It is the same in the case of the south and the north.

Yet both I myself and others obtain most of our material by hearsay, and then put together matters of shape, size, and other characteristics, the quality and quantity, just as a thought is put together from mental sensation. The sense of an apple is explained from its shape, color, and size, as well as its odor, feel, and taste, and from this the mind puts together the concept of an apple. It is the same in regard to large figures: sensation perceives only the parts, and the mind creates the whole from what is seen. Men who have a love of learning are in such a way, for they trust as a sense organ what is seen by those who have happened to wander through places, in one or another portion of the earth, putting together in a single geometrical figure the appearance of the entire inhabited world. Thus military commanders, although they do everything themselves, are not everywhere, but accomplish most things successfully through others, trusting the reports of messengers and sending messages in agreement with their commands. Whoever considers useful only what he has seen removes any judgement of what he has heard, although this is much more important than sight for scholarly knowledge.

(12) Certainly those who write today are better informed about the Prettanians and the Germans, those around the Istros – both on this side [C118] and the other – the Getians, Tyregetians, and Bastarnians, as well as those around the Kaukasos, such as the Albanians and Iberians. Information has been reported to us by the writers of Parthian matters, such as those following Apollodoros of Artemita [F3a], who defined these areas better than others, and about Hyrkania and Baktriane. The Romans recently invaded Fortunate Arabia with an army, led by my friend and companion Aelius Gallus, and merchants from Alexandria are sailing on expeditions by means of the Nile and Arabian Gulf as far as Indike, so that these areas are much better known today than to our predecessors. At any rate, when Gallus commanded Egypt, I accompanied him and went up the Nile as far as Syene and the boundary of the Aithiopians, and we recorded that

120 ships sailed from Mussel Anchorage to Indike, but formerly, under the Ptolemaic kings, only a very few dared to sail and to trade merchandise with the Indians.

(13) First and most important, both for scholarly knowledge and governmental needs, is to attempt to state as simply as possible the shape and size that falls on the geographical plan, showing at the same time its nature and what part of the entire earth it is. This is what is proper for the geographer. To describe accurately the entire earth and the whole spindle whorl of the zone of which we are speaking is another discipline (Eratosthenes F51), as is whether the spindle whorl is inhabited in its other fourth portion. If it were, it would not be inhabited by ones like those among us, and it must then be considered another inhabited world, which is believable. But I must speak of what is in our own.

(14) The shape of the inhabited world is somewhat in the form of a chlamys, whose greatest width is marked by the line through the Nile, with its beginning taken at the parallel through the Cinnamon-Bearer territory and the Island of the Fugitive Egyptians as far as the parallel through Ierne (Eratosthenes F53). The length is at right angles, from the west through the Pillars and the Sikelian Strait as far as the Rhodia and the Issic Gulf, going through the Tauros that girdles Asia and ending at the eastern sea between the Indians and the Skythians beyond Baktriane. It is necessary to conceive of a certain parallelogram in which the chlamys-shaped form is engraved so that its greatest length agrees with and is equal to the length [of the parallelogram] and whose width agrees with [and is equal to] its width. This chlamys-shaped form is the inhabited world. Its width, as we have said [2.5.6], is bounded by the farthest sides of the parallelogram, which separate the inhabited and uninhabited parts from one another. These are, on the north, that through Ierne, and in the burned region, that through the Cinnamon-Bearer territory. Extending these to the east and west as far as the portions of the inhabited world that rise opposite to them would make a certain parallelogram, joining up with those at the extremities. It is clear that the inhabited world is within this because neither the greatest width nor length falls outside. The form is chlamys-shaped because the extremities of its length taper on both sides and diminish its width, washed away by the sea. This is clear from those who have sailed around the eastern and western portions on either side. They proclaim that the island of Taprobane is considerably farther south than Indike, but nonetheless inhabited, rising opposite to the Island of the Egyptians and the land of the Cinnamon Bearers, and that the temperature of the air is about the same. The regions around the mouth of the Hyrkanian Sea are farther north than the ultimate

part of Skythia beyond the Indians, and those around Ierne are still farther. Similar things are said about the region beyond the Pillars, that the most western boundary of the inhabited world is the promontory of the Iberians called "Sacred," which lies approximately on the line through the Gadeirans, the Pillars, the Sikelian Strait, and the Rhodia. The *horoskopeia* agree, they say, the winds are favorable in both directions, and the lengths of the longest days and nights [are the same], for the longest days and nights have 14½ equinoctial hours. Occasionally on the coast around Gadeira one can see <Canopus>.[6] Poseidonios [F204] says that from a high house in a city about 400 stadia from these places one can see a star which he considered to be Canopus itself, as those who had gone a short distance south of Iberia agreed that they had seen it, as is also the case from examinations on Knidos, since the observatory of Eudoxos is not much higher than the houses. It is said that he saw the star Canopus from there, and Knidos is on the Rhodian latitude, as are Gadeira and the nearby coastline.

(15) As one sails to the south, there is Libya, whose westernmost portion lies slightly beyond Gadeira. It makes a narrow promontory and then turns back toward the east and south, and becomes slightly broader until it joins the Western Aithiopians. They are the farthest who lie beyond the territory of Karchedon, touching the line through the Cinnamon-Bearer territory. In the opposite direction one sails from the Sacred Promontory as far as those called the Artabrians, and the voyage is toward the north, with Lusitania on the right. The remainder is totally toward to the east, making an obtuse angle as far as the Pyrene Capes that end at the Ocean. The western regions of Prettanike lie opposite to the north, as well as the islands called the Kassiterides, opposite and to the north of the Artabrians, in the open sea lying about the latitude of Prettanike. Thus it is clear how much the extremities of the inhabited world – in regard to its length – have been drawn together and narrowed by the surrounding open sea.

[C120]

(16) Such being the shape of its entirety, it appears useful to take two straight lines, which cut across each other at a right angle, one going throughout the greatest width and the other the length. The first will be one of the parallels and the other one of the meridians. Then one should think of lines parallel to these on either side, which divide the land and the sea that we happen to use. Thus the shape will be somewhat clearer, as we have described, according to the length of the line, with different measurements for both the length and width, and the latitudes will be manifested better, both in the east and west as well in as the south and north. But since these straight lines

---

[6] The text has been emended from the meaningless "*iberas*," based on what follows.

must be taken through known places, as is already the case (I mean the two central ones, for the length and the width, that I previously mentioned), the others will easily be determined by means of these. Using them as a kind of basic element, we can construct the parallel portions as well as the other positions of inhabited places, both on the earth and according to the heavens.

(17) The sea most of all describes the earth and determines its form, by producing gulfs, the open sea, and straits, as well as isthmuses, peninsulas, and capes, with both rivers and mountains providing assistance. The continents, peoples, and the favorable situation of cities are understood through this, as well as the diversity that fills the chorographic plan, including the numerous islands scattered both in the open sea and on the entire coast.

[C121] Various [places] have various virtues and faults, and demonstrate benefits or difficulties, some according to nature but others according to human efforts. Those due to nature must be discussed, for they persist, but what has been imposed undergoes changes. In regard to the latter, it must be pointed out that those which are strong enough to remain for a long time, or which do not [remain] for a long time but nevertheless have a certain distinction or reputation and last into later times, make a certain feature harmonize with the place so that it is no longer considered something created, and must clearly be recorded. One can say about many cities what Demosthenes [*Philippic* 3.26] said about the places around Olynthos that have disappeared: he said that visitors would never know that they had been settled. Nevertheless they find it pleasing to go to such and other places because of a desire to see the traces of memorable deeds, just like the tombs of esteemed men. Thus we have recorded customs and governments that no longer exist (summoned by their usefulness), in the same way as deeds, for the sake of emulation or avoidance.

(18) Taking up the first outline, we say that our inhabited world, surrounded by water, receives into it many gulfs from the External Sea, of which four are the largest. The northern one is called the Kaspian Sea, also called the Hyrkanian. The Persian and Arabian pour from the southern sea, one about opposite the Kaspian and the other [opposite] the Pontic. The fourth, which greatly exceeds the others in size, is formed by what is called the Internal or Our Sea. It takes its beginning from the west at the Herakleian Pillars and is lengthened toward the east but with varying widths, dividing at the end into two gulf-like seas, one on the left that we call the Euxeinos Pontos and the other consisting of the Egyptian Sea, as well as the Pamphylian and Issic. All these gulfs that have been mentioned have narrow entrances from the External Sea, especially the Arabian and that at the Pillars, but the remainder less so.

The land enclosing these is divided into three parts, as I have said. In form, Europe is the most varied of all, but Libya is just the opposite, and Asia has somewhat of a middle situation to both. In all these cases, the reason for this is whether the coastline of the Internal [Sea] is varied or not. Yet that of the External – except for the previously mentioned gulfs – is simple and shaped like a chlamys, as I have said, although other small differences must be omitted, for something small is nothing in relation to large things. Moreover, since research into geography not only inquires into the shapes and sizes of places but their relationship to one another, as I have said, the coastline of the Internal furnishes more variability than that of the External. What is known and temperate, and inhabited by well-governed cities and peoples, is far better here than there. We are anxious to learn about where deeds, governments, the arts, and other matters that produce wisdom have best been handed down, and our needs bring us to where intercourse and associations are available. These are places that are settled, or rather settled well. In all these things, as I have said, Our Sea is greatly advantageous, and thus one must begin the description of the earth there. [C122]

(19) It has been said that the beginning of this gulf is the strait at the Pillars. The narrowest part of it is said to be about 70 stadia, but after one sails through the narrows, which are about 120 stadia, the shores make a sudden divergence, the one on the left more so. Then there appears the impression of a great open sea. It is bounded on the right side by the Libyan coast as far as Karchedon, and on the other by the Iberian territory, Keltike around Narbon and Massalia, and then Ligystike, and finally Italia as far as the Sikelian strait. On the eastern side of the sea are Sikelia and the straits on either side: the one with Italia is 7 stadia, and the one with Karchedon 1,500 stadia.

The line from the Pillars to the 7-stadia [strait] is part of the one to Rhodes and the Tauros, cutting the previously mentioned sea in about the middle. It is said to be 12,000 stadia. This then is the length of the sea, and its greatest width is as much as 5,000 stadia from the Galatic Gulf between Massalia and Narbon, opposite to Libya. The entire portion of this sea along Libya they call the Libyan Sea, and that on the opposite coast the Iberic, Ligystikian, and Sardonian, and finally, as far as Sikelia, the Tyrrhenian.

There are many islands along the coast of the Tyrrhenian Sea as far as Ligystike, with the largest Sardo and Kyrnos, except for Sikelia, which is the largest and best in our region. Left far behind, in the open sea, are Pandataria and Pontia, and near the land are Aithalia, Planasia, Pithekoussa, Prochyte, Kapreai, Leukosia, and such others. On the other side of the Ligystikian [Sea], on the rest of the coast as far as the Pillars, there are not many, but [C123]

among them are the Gymnasiai and Ebysos. Not many are off Libya and
Sikelia, but there are Kossoura, Aigimouros, and the Liparaian Islands, which
some call those of Aiolos.

(20) Beyond Sikelia and the straits on either side another sea adjoins. It
is in front of the Syrtes and the Kyrenaia, and the Syrtes themselves, and
the one formerly called the Ausonian but now the Sikelian, which flow
together. The one in front of the Syrtes and the Kyrenaia is called the
Libyan, and it ends at the Egyptian Sea. The smaller of the Syrtes is about
1,600 stadia in circumference, with the islands of Meninx and Kerkina lying
on either side of its mouth. Eratosthenes [F104] says that the Great Syrtis
has a circuit of 5,000 and is 1,800 deep, from the Hesperides to Automala
and the boundary between the Kyrenaia and the rest of Libya. Others say
that its circumference is 4,000 stadia, with its depth at 1,500, as much as the
width of its mouth. The Sikelian sea is in front of Sikelia and Italia, toward
the eastern regions, and, moreover, in front of the strait between them, from
the Rhegine as far as Lokroi, and from Messenia as far as Syracuse and
Pachynos. It increases toward its eastern portion, as far as the capes of Crete,
and it washes around most of the Peloponnesos and fills what is called the
Corinthian Gulf. On the north [it extends] toward the Iapygian Cape and
the mouth of the Ionian Gulf, and the southern part of Epeiros as far as
the Ambrakian Gulf and the adjoining coast, creating the Corinthian Gulf
and touching the Peloponnesos. The Ionian Gulf is part of what is now
called the Adria. Illyris forms the right side, and Italia the left as far as the
recess toward Aquileia. It is long and narrow, extending to the north and
west, with a length of about 6,000 stadia and a greatest width of 1,200.

[C124]   There are numerous islands off the Illyrian region, including the Apsyrtides,
Kyriktike, and the Libyrnides, as well as Issa, Tragourion, Black Korkyra,
and Pharos. Off Italia are the Diomedeioi. The Sikelian [Sea], to Crete from
Pachynon, is 4,500 stadia, they say, and it is the same to Tainaron in the
Lakonike. From the Iapygian Cape to the recess of the Corinthian Gulf is
less than 3,000, and that from the Iapygian [Cape] to Libya is more than
4,000. The islands here are Korkyra and Sybota off the Epeirotic [coast],
and next, off the Corinthian Gulf, Kephallenia, Ithaka, Zakynthos, and the
Echinades.

(21) Touching the Sikelian Sea are the Cretan, the Saronic, and the
Myrtoan, which is between Crete, the Argeia, and Attika; its greatest width
(from Attika) is 1,200 stadia, and its length is less than double that. In it are
the islands of Kythera, Kalaureia, those around Aigina, Salamis, and some of
the Kyklades. The Aigaion adjoins it, along with the Melanian Gulf and the
Hellespont, as well as the Ikarian and Karpathian [Seas], as far as Rhodes,

Crete, and Cyprus,[7] and the first portions of Asia. The Kyklades Islands are there, the Sporades, and those lying off Karia, Ionia, and Aiolis as far as the Troad: I mean Kos, Samos, Chios, Lesbos, and Tenedos, as well as those lying off Hellas as far as Makedonia and contiguous Thrace, including Euboia, Skyros, Peparethos, Lemnos, Thasos, Imbros, Samothrake, and some others, which I will discuss individually. The length of this sea is about 4,000 [stadia] or a little more, and its width is around 2,000. It is surrounded by the previously mentioned portions of Asia and the coast from Sounion to the Thermaian Gulf as one sails toward the north, and by the Makedonian Gulf as far as the Thracian Chersonesos.

(22) Along it is the 7-stadia [strait] between Sestos and Abydos, through which the Aigaion and Hellespont empty toward the north into another sea which is called the Propontis, and it empties into another known as the Euxeinos Pontos. This is a double type of sea, for about its middle two capes project into it, one from Europe and the northern regions, and the other opposite, from Asia, bringing the strait between them together and creating two large seas. The European promontory is called the Ram's Forehead, and the Asian, Karambis, and they are separated from each other by about 2,500 [C125] stadia. The western sea has a length from Byzantion to the outlet of the Borysthenes of 3,800 stadia and a width of 2,000; the island of Leuke is in it. The eastern is oval-shaped, ending in a narrow recess at Dioskourias, and is 5,000 stadia [long], or a little more, and with a width around 3,000. The circumference of the entire sea is about 25,000 stadia. Some compare the shape of the circumference to a stretched Skythian bow, with the sinew like what is called the right-hand portion of the Pontos. This is the coastal sailing route from the mouth to the recess at Dioskourias, since except for Karambis the entire coast has only small inlets and projections, so it is like a straight line. The rest is the horn of the bow with its double curve, the upper part more rounded and the lower straighter. Thus two gulfs are formed there, with the western one more rounded.

(23) Beyond the eastern gulf to the north lies the Maiotic Lake, whose circumference is 9,000 stadia or a little more. It empties into the Pontos at what is called the Kimmerian Bosporos, and the former into the Propontis at the Thracian, for the Byzantine mouth is called the Thracian Bosporos, which is 4 stadia. The Propontis is said to be 1,500 stadia long from the Troad to Byzantion, and its width is about the same. The Kyzikene island lies in it, and other little islands are around it.

---

[7] "Cyprus" does not fit the geography; "Knidos" or "Karpathos" have been suggested.

(24) This, then, is the character of the extension of the Aigaion Sea toward the north. From the Rhodia the Egyptian Sea is created, as well as the Pamphylian and Issic, stretching toward the east as far as Kilikian Issos, for 5,000 stadia along Lykia, Pamphylia, and the entire coast of Kilikia. Then Syria, Phoenicia, and Egypt encircle the sea on the south and west as far as Alexandria. Cyprus happens to lie in both the Issic Gulf and the Pamphylian, and touches the Egyptian Sea. The passage from Rhodes to Alexandria is about 4,000 stadia with a north wind, but along the coast it is double that. Eratosthenes [F128] says that this is the estimate of sailors regarding the crossing of the sea. Some say this, and others do not shrink from saying [C126] 5,000, but he, using the shadow of a gnomon, found it to be 3,750.

The portion of this sea that is next to Kilikia and Pamphylia, what is called the right-hand side of the Pontic [Sea], and the Propontis and the coast beyond as far as Pamphylia, make a great peninsula and a great isthmus, from the sea at Tarsos to the city of Amisos and to Themiskyra (the Plain of the Amazons). The territory within this line, as far as Karia and Ionia and the peoples living within the Halys, is completely washed by either the Aigaion or the previously mentioned parts of the sea. We distinctly call this Asia, which is the name for the whole.

(25) Saying it briefly, the most southern part of Our Sea is the limit of the recess of the Great Syrtis, and after this Alexandria by Egypt and the mouths of the Nile. The most northerly is the mouth of the Borysthenes, but if the Maiotic Sea is added – and it would be part of it – it is the mouth of the Tanais. The most westerly is the strait at the Pillars, the easternmost the previously mentioned recess at Dioskourias. Eratosthenes [F13] is not correct in saying that it is the Issic Gulf, which lies on the same meridian as Amisos and Themiskyra, or, if one wishes, one can add Sidene as far as Pharnakeia. From these regions, the voyage to the east is more than 3,000 stadia as far as Dioskourias, which will be clearer from the detailed circuit. Such, then, is Our Sea.

(26) One must also sketch out the surrounding lands, making a beginning from the same parts that we described for the sea. As one sails into the strait at the Pillars, Libya is on the right as far as the stream of the Nile, and on the left across the strait is Europe as far as the Tanais. Both end at Asia.

One must begin with Europe, because it is varied in form and the best suited in regard to excellence for men and governments, and because it has given the most of its own good things to others. It is inhabitable in its entirety except for a small portion that is uninhabitable because of the cold. This borders on the Hamaxoikians ["Wagon Dwellers"] around the Tanais, Maiotis, and the Borysthenes. The wintry mountains of the

inhabitable regions naturally cause hardship to the inhabitants, yet the poor
and piratical inhabitants become pacified when given good treatment, just
as with the Hellenes, who occupied mountains and rocks but lived happily
because through forethought they had government, the arts, and wisdom
about life. The Romans acquired many peoples who were savage by nature
because of the harshness of their regions, which were harborless, cold, or for
some other reason were difficult for many to inhabit, and connected them
with others who were isolated, teaching the more savage to live politically.
As much of it [Europe] that is level and temperate has the nature to work
together toward this, for in a happy land everything is peaceful, but in a
wretched place things are warlike and masculine. The peoples from these
receive benefits from each other: those from the latter assist with weapons,
the former with produce, the arts, and character. Yet it is apparent that
they harm each other if they do not assist one another, and the strength of
those carrying arms will give them some advantage unless they are ruled by
the majority. But there is a natural advantage on this continent, for all of it
is scattered with plains and mountains so that everywhere the agricultural,
civilized, and warlike are adjacent. The most numerous of these live in
peace, and thus prevail over all, assisted by those in control, formerly the
Hellenes, then the Makedonians and finally the Romans. Because of this,
it is the most independent in regard to peace and war, for it has a plentiful
warlike population, as well as those who work the land and secure the cities.
It is also different in that it produces the fruits that are the best and a
necessity for life, and many useful metals, and receives fragrances and
expensive stones from abroad, so that life for whom they are scarce is no
worse than those for whom they are abundant. In a general sense, this is the
nature of this continent.

(27) According to its parts, the first of all, from the west, is Iberia, which
resembles an oxhide whose neck portion falls over into adjoining Keltike.
This is what lies toward the east, which is cut off by a chain of mountains
called Pyrene. Otherwise it is surrounded by the sea: ours on the south as far
as the Pillars, and the remainder, as far as the northern capes of Pyrene, by
the Atlantic. The greatest length of this territory is around 6,000 stadia, and
its width 5,000.

(28) After this, Keltike is toward the east, as far as the Rhenos River. On
its northern side it is washed by the entire Brettanike Strait, for that entire
island extends parallel to the whole of it for a length of about 5,000 stadia.
On the east it is limited by the Rhenos River, a stream parallel to Pyrene,
and on the south by the Alps (from the Rhenos) and by Our Sea, the
territory where the so-called Galatic Gulf spreads out and where the most

distinguished cities of Massalia and Narbon are located. Opposite this gulf, and turned in the opposite direction, is another gulf with the same name, also called the Galatic, looking toward the north and Brettanike, where Keltike has its narrowest width, drawn together into an isthmus of less than 3,000 stadia but more than 2,000. Between these is a range of mountains at right angles to Pyrene, called Mount Kemmenon, which ends at the very center of the Keltic Plain. The Alps, which are extremely high and form a curved line, have their convex side turned toward the previously mentioned Keltic Plain and Mount Kemmenon, with the concavity toward Ligystike and Italia. The many peoples in these mountains are Keltic, except for the Ligyans, who are of a different ethnicity but similar in their lifestyle. They live in the part of the Alps that adjoins the Apennine Mountains and also occupy part of the Apennine Mountains. These are a mountain range that extends through the entire length of Italia from the north to the south, ending at the Sikelian Strait.

(29) The first parts of Italia are the plain that falls below the Alps as far as the Adria and the nearby regions, but the remainder is a narrow cape and long peninsula, through which, as I have said, the Apennine Mountains extend for a length of about 7,000 stadia with varying width. What makes Italia a peninsula are the Tyrrhenian Sea (beginning from the Ligystikian), as well as the Ausonian, and the Adria.

(30) After Italia and Keltike is the remainder of Europe toward the east, which is cut in two by the Istros River. It is carried from the west toward the east and the Euxeinos Pontos, leaving the whole of Germania on the left (which begins at the Rhenos), all the Getian region, and the Tyregetians, [C129] Bastarnians, and Sauromatians as far as the Tanais River and the Maiotic Lake, and on the right all of Thrace, Illyris, and, then, finally Hellas.

The islands that I have already mentioned [2.5.15] lie off Europe outside the Pillars (Gadeira, the Kassiterides, and Brettanikai). Inside the Pillars are the Gymnesiai and the other Phoenician islets, and the Massalian and Ligyan, as well as those off Italia, as far as the islands of Aiolos and Sikelia, and all those around Epeirotis and Hellas as far as Makedonia and the Thracian Chersonesos.

(31) After the Tanais and the Maiotis is that lying within the Tauros and then those next, which are outside.[8] It is divided in two by the Tauros Mountains, which stretch from the capes of Pamphylia to the eastern sea at the Indians and the Skythians. The Hellenes call the part of the continent

---

[8] There may be something missing, as the topic has changed from Europe to Asia without any mention of the latter.

that slopes to the north "within the Tauros," and that to the south, "outside."

Adjoining the Maiotis and Tanais are the parts within the Tauros. The first of these parts is between the Kaspian Sea and the Euxeinos Pontos, which on one [side] comes to an end at the Tanais and the Ocean (both the External and that of the Hyrkanian Sea), and on the other at the isthmus where it is narrowest from the recess of the Pontos to the Kaspian. Then there is that within the Tauros beyond Hyrkania as far as the sea at the Indians and the Skythians, and Mount Imaion. The Maiotians are here, as well as those between Hyrkania and the Pontos as far as the Kaukasos: the Iberians, Albanians, Sauromatians, Skythians, Achaians, Zygians, and Henioxians, and, above the Hyrkanian Sea, the Skythians, Hyrkanians, Parthyaians, Baktrians, Sogdianians, and also those lying beyond the Indians to the north. Partly to the south of the Hyrkanian Sea and the entire isthmus between it and the Pontos lie the greater part of Armenia, Kolchis, and all of Kappadokia as far as the Euxeinos Pontos and the Tibaranikian peoples, as well as the territory called that within the Halys, consisting (next to the Pontos and Propontis) of the Paphlagonians, Bithynians, and Mysians (and called Phrygia on the Hellespont, part of which is the Troad). Next to the Aigaion and the sea continuous with it are Aiolis, Ionia, Karia, and Lykia, and then, in the interior, Phrygia (part   [C130] of which includes Galatia called that of the Gallograecians, and "The Acquired"), the Lykaonians, and the Lydians.

(32) Adjoining those within the Tauros are the ones living in the mountains: the Paropamisadians, Parthyaians, Medes, Armenians, the Kilikian peoples, Kataonians, and Pisidians. After those in the mountains are the ones beyond the Tauros. The first of them is Indike, the greatest and most fortunate of all peoples, whose boundaries are at the eastern sea and the southern Atlantic. In this southern sea, lying off Indike, is Taprobane, an island no smaller than Brettanike. If one turns toward the west from Indike and has the mountains on the right, there is an extensive territory whose inhabitants, because of the poverty of the land, are poor and completely barbarian, and are not of the same ethnicity. They are called Arians, extending from the mountains as far as Gedrosia and Karmania. Next, toward the sea, are the Persians, Sousians, and Babylonians, and the small groups living around them who extend down to the Persian Sea. Those next to the mountains or within them are the Parthyaians, Medes, and Armenians, the peoples neighboring them, and Mesopotamia. After Mesopotamia are those within the Euphrates: all of Fortunate Arabia (which is bounded by the entire Arabian Gulf, and the Persian), and all that occupied by the Tent Dwellers

and the phylarchies, down to the Euphrates and Syria. Then there are those beyond the Arabian Gulf as far as the Nile: the Aithiopians and the Arabians, the Egyptians next to them, the Syrians, Kilikians (among whom are the so-called Tracheiotians) and finally the Pamphylians.

(33) After Asia is Libya, which is continuous with Egypt and Aithiopia, and whose shore opposite to us is a straight line almost as far as the Pillars (beginning at Alexandria), except for the Syrtes and perhaps other moderate turns of gulfs and their projecting promontories. Its seacoast from Aithiopia as far as a certain point is parallel to the former, after which it turns toward southern regions in a sharp cape that projects slightly beyond the Pillars, creating approximately the shape of a trapezium. As others have shown, and, moreover, as Gnaeus Piso, who was commander of the territory, related to me, it is like a leopard skin because it is spotted with inhabited places that are surrounded by waterless and desolate land. The Egyptians call such inhabited places "oases." There are certain other differences that [C131] give it a tripartite division. Most of the coastline opposite us is extremely prosperous, especially the Kyrenaia and that around Karchedon as far as Maurousia and the Pillars of Herakles. The coast along the Ocean has only moderate habitation, and the interior, which produces silphium, is poor and for the most part a rough and sandy desolation. It is the same with the straight [coast] extending through Aithiopia, Trogodytike, Arabia, and Gedrosia of the Fish Eaters.

Most of the peoples living in Libya are unknown, for it happens that not much of it is covered by armies, nor men of other tribes, and what they say is neither believable nor extensive. Nevertheless this is what they have said. They assert that the most southern are the Aithiopians, and next to them are the Garamantians, Pharousians, and Nigritians, and next the Gaitoulians. Those who live near the sea, or touching it, next to Egypt, are the Marmaridians, as far as the Kyrenaia. Above it and the Syrtes are the Psyllians, Nasamonians, and certain Gaitoulians, and then the Asbystians and Byzakians as far as Karchedonia. Karchedonia is large. Adjoining it are the nomads, the best known of whom are called the Masylians, and others the Masaisylians. Last are the Maurousians. Everywhere from Karchedon as far as the Pillars is prosperous, although abundant in wild animals, as is the entire interior. It is not unreasonable that some of these were called nomads because in antiquity they were unable to farm because of the many wild animals. But today they excel in the art of hunting – and the Romans join along with them in this, because of their eagerness in fighting wild animals – and are superior both in hunting and farming. This is what we have to say about the continents.

(34) It remains to speak about the latitudes – also only as a general outline – starting with those lines that we have called the elementary ones, I mean those that determine the greatest length and width, especially the width. Astronomers must consider this matter more thoroughly, just as Hipparchos [F39] has, for he recorded, as he himself says, the different aspects of the celestial bodies that exist for each place on earth situated within our quadrant: I mean between the equator and the north pole. Yet nothing that is outside our inhabited world should be considered by geographers, and even in regard to parts of the inhabited world such kinds of differences need not be learned by those politically knowledgeable, for it would be difficult. It is sufficient to set forth the significant and simpler things that he said, with his hypothesis that the size of the earth is 252,000 stadia, as Eratosthenes [*Measurement of the Earth*, F1–9] showed. In regard to the [celestial] phenomena, the difference in the distances between inhabited places will not be large.

[C132]

If the greatest circle of the earth is cut into 360 sections, each of the sections will be 700 stadia, which is what he [Hipparchos] uses for the distances taken on the previously mentioned meridian through Meroë. He begins with those living on the equator, and always using 700 stadia, he goes along the previously mentioned meridian to the inhabited places one after another, attempting to record the [celestial] phenomena for each. For me, one should not begin there. For if they are inhabitable, as some think, it is a peculiar inhabited world, a narrow space stretching through the middle of a region that is uninhabitable because of heat, and not a part of our inhabited world. Yet the geographer examines only this, our inhabited world, whose limits are bounded on the south by the parallel of the Cinnamon-Bearer territory and on the north by that through Ierne. In covering the inhabited world, one should not record every place suggested within this distance, nor position all the [celestial] phenomena, remembering the form of the geographical work. But one must begin, as Hipparchos does, with the southern portions.

(35) He [Hipparchos, F43] says that those who live on the parallel through the Cinnamon-Bearer territory, which lies 3,000 stadia from Meroë toward the south – and the equator is 8,800 from it – live very near to the midpoint between the equator and the summer tropic that passes through Syene, for Syene is 5,000 from Meroë [Eratosthenes, F57]. They are the first for whom the Little Bear is completely within the arctic circle and is always visible, for the bright star at the extremity of the tail, the most southerly, is seated on the arctic circle so that it touches the horizon. The Arabian Gulf lies to the east and approximately parallel to the meridian

[C133]   discussed, and the Cinnamon-Bearer territory is where it empties into the
outer sea, where they hunted the elephant in antiquity. Its parallel is outside
[the inhabited world] and extends on one side somewhat to the south of
Taprobane, or its farthest inhabitants, and on the other through southernmost Libya.

(36) In the region of Meroë and Ptolemais – that among the Trogodytes –
the longest day is 13 equinoctial hours, and this inhabited region is about
midway between the equator and [the parallel] through Alexandria (it is
1,800 more to the equator) [Eratosthenes, F59]. The parallel through Meroë
passes on one side through parts that are unknown and on the other through
the promontories of Indike. At Syene, at Berenike on the Arabian Gulf, and
in Trogodytike the sun is in the zenith at the summer solstice, the longest
day is 13½ equinoctial hours, and almost the entire Great Bear is visible in the
arctic circle, except for the legs, the tip of the tail, and one of the stars in the
square. The parallel through Syene passes, on one side, through the territory
of the Fish Eaters in Gedrosia and through Indike, and on the other side
through territory almost 5,000 stadia farther south than Kyrene.

(37) At every place that lies between the tropic and the equatorial circle
the shadows fall in both directions, toward the north and south, but from
Syene and the summer tropic the shadows fall to the north at noon. Those
of the former [region] are called Amphiskians ["Those With Shadows Both
Ways"], and those of the latter, Heteroskians ["Those With Shadows Either
Way"]. There is another difference about [the regions] under the tropic
that we have mentioned previously in the discussion of the zones [2.2.3]: the
earth is very sandy, silphium-producing, and dry, but the parts farther south
are well-watered and fruitful.

(38) About 400 stadia farther to the south of [the parallel through]
Alexandria and Kyrene, where the longest day is 14 equinoctial hours,
Arcturus is in the zenith, inclined a little toward the south [Eratosthenes,
F60]. At Alexandria the relationship of the gnomon to the equinoctial
shadow is 5 to 3. This is 1,300 stadia farther south than Karchedon, if at
Karchedon the relationship of the gnomon to the equinoctial shadow is
11 to 7. The parallel passes on one side through Kyrene, 900 stadia south
of Karchedon, and as far as the middle of Maurousia, and on the other
[C134]   side through Egypt, Hollow Syria, Upper Syria, Babylon, Sousias, Persis,
Karmania, and Upper Gedrosia, as far as Indike.

(39) In the region of Ptolemais – the one in Phoenicia – and Sidon and
Tyre, the longest day has 14¼ equinoctial hours [Hipparchos, F49]. These
regions are about 1,600 stadia farther north than Alexandria and about
700 from Karchedon. In the Peloponnesos and around the middle of the

Rhodia, around Xanthos in Lykia or a little to the south, and also 400 stadia south of Syracuse, the longest day has 14½ equinoctial hours [Hipparchos, F50]. These places are 3,640 from Alexandria and <2,740 from Karchedon>.⁹ According to Eratosthenes [F60], the parallel runs through Karia, Lykaonia, Kataonia, Media, the Kaspian Gates, and the Indians along the Kaukasos.

(40) In the area around Alexandria Troas, around Amphipolis, Apollonia in Epeiros, and south of Rome but north of Neapolis, the longest day has 15 equinoctial hours [Hipparchos F51]. The parallel is about 7,000 stadia north of the one through Alexandria next to Egypt and more than 28,800 from the equator, 3,400 from the one through Rhodes, and 1,500 south of Byzantion, Nikaia and the region around Massalia. Somewhat to the north is the one through Lysimacheia, which Eratosthenes [F60] says passes through Mysia, Paphlagonia, the region around Sinope, Hyrkania, and Baktra.

(41) In the regions around Byzantion the longest day has 15¼ equinoctial hours and the relationship of the gnomon to its shadow at the summer solstice is 120 to 42 less a fifth [Hipparchos, F52]. These places are 4,900 [stadia] from [the parallel] through the center of the Rhodia and about 30,300 from the equator. For someone sailing into the Pontos and going about 1,400 stadia to the north the longest day is 15½ equinoctial hours [Hipparchos, F56]. These places are equidistant from the pole and the equatorial circle, and the arctic circle is in the zenith, on which the [star] on the neck of Cassiopeia lies, and the one on the right elbow of Perseus is a little farther north.

(42) In the regions 3,800 [stadia] to the north of Byzantion the longest day has 16 equinoctial hours, and thus Cassiopeia appears within the arctic circle [Hipparchos, F57]. These are the places around the Borysthenes and the southern parts of the Maiotis, about 34,100 from the equator. The northern part of the horizon is illuminated almost the entire summer night by the sun after setting, as its light moves back from west to east. The summer tropic is one more than half a twelfth of a zodiacal sign from the horizon, and thus the sun at midnight is the same [distance] below the horizon. Among us, when the sun is that [distance] from the horizon (before daybreak or after sunset), it illuminates the air in the east and west. On winter days there, the sun rises at most to nine *pecheis*. Eratosthenes [F60] says that these regions are a little more than 23,000 [stadia] from Meroë, since it is 18,000 to the Hellespont and then 5,000 to the Borysthenes. About 6,300 stadia from

[C135]

---

⁹ Manuscripts have either "600" or "400" (both impossible) without any toponym.

Byzantion, north of the Maiotis, the sun on winter days rises at most to six *pecheis*, and the longest day has 17 equinoctial hours [Hipparchos, F60].

(43) The regions beyond are already near what is uninhabitable because of the cold, and are of no use to the geographer. Anyone who wishes to learn about them, as well as everything celestial that Hipparchos discusses but which has been omitted by us because it is stated better there than in the present treatise, should consult him [Hipparchos, F62].

Also stated better is what Poseidonios [F208] says about the Periskians ["Those With Shadows All Around"], Amphiskians ["Those With Shadows Both Ways"], and Heteroskians ["Those with Shadows Either Way"]. Nevertheless this must be recounted in order to make the concept understandable, as well as in what way it is useful for the geographer, and in what way it is useless. The issue is about the shadows of the sun, and the sun – as it is perceived – is carried along a parallel, as is the cosmos. Thus when each revolution of the cosmos produces a day and a night (because at one time the sun is carried above the earth and at another under the earth), they are considered Amphiskians or Heteroskians. The Amphiskians are those whose shadows at noon (when the sun is from the south, according to the angle of the gnomon related to the underlying surface) fall at times in one way, and at times in the opposite way when the sun has gone around to the opposite. This occurs only with those who live between the tropics. The Heteroskians are those [whose shadows] always fall toward the north, as with us, or toward the south, as with those living in the other temperate [C136] zone. This is the result for everywhere that the arctic circle is smaller than the tropic. When the former is larger, the Periskians begin, as far as those beneath the pole. There the sun is carried above the earth through the entire revolution of the cosmos, and it is clear that the shadow will be carried in a circle around the gnomon. This is why he called them Periskians, although they do not exist in regard to geography. That region is uninhabitable because of cold, as we have already said in the comments against Pytheas [T10]. Thus one should not consider the size of this uninhabitable region, beyond the fact that those who have the tropic as arctic circle fall below the circle delineated by the pole of the zodiac, according to the revolution of the cosmos, assuming that the distance between the equator and the tropic is four-sixtieths of the greatest circle.

BOOK 3

Iberia

Part 1:   Introduction and coastal Tourdetania

(1) Since I have given a first outline of geography, now it is fitting to have next an examination of each part in order, as I have promised [2.5.4]. It seems that so far the treatise has been divided correctly. But for the same reason it is necessary to begin again with Europe and the parts of it where I was formerly [2.5.27].

(2) The first part of it is the western, or Iberia, as I have said previously [2.5.27]. It is a poor land on which to live, for most of the inhabited region is mountainous, wooded, and has plains with scant earth that are not evenly watered. That toward the north is cold, extremely rugged, and along the Ocean, and moreover is inhospitable and isolated from the others, so that it is an exceedingly disagreeable place to live. This is what that part is like, but the south is almost totally prosperous, especially that which is outside the Pillars. This will be clear in the details, but first we will outline its shape and size.

(3) It resembles an oxhide stretched in length from west to east, having its front parts toward the east, and with its width from north to south. It is a total of 6,000 stadia in length and 5,000 at the greatest width, although in places it is much less than 3,000, especially near Pyrene, which makes the eastern side. The mountains extend unbroken from south to north and form the boundary of Keltike and Iberia. But since the width of Keltike – as well as that of Iberia – is irregular, the narrowest width of both is that between Our Sea and the Ocean closest to Pyrene (the part on either side of it), where gulfs are formed both at the Ocean and Our Sea. The Keltic ones – also called the Galatic – are larger, and the isthmus formed is narrower than the Iberian.

Thus Pyrene forms the eastern side of Iberia. The southern is [formed] by Our Sea from Pyrene to the Pillars, and by the External [Sea] from there as far as the promontory called Sacred. The third side is the western, somewhat parallel to Pyrene, from the Sacred Promontory as far as the Cape of the

[C137]

Artabrians, which is called Nerion. The fourth is from there to the northern capes of Pyrene.

(4) Resuming, let us discuss it in detail, beginning with the Sacred Promontory. This is the most western point, not only of Europe but of the entire inhabited world. The inhabited world is limited in the west by the two continents: the capes of Europe, and the beginnings of Libya (the former held by the Iberians, the latter by the Maurousians). The Iberian territory projects about 1,500 stadia beyond at the previously mentioned promontory. Moreover, the adjacent region is called "Cuneus" in the Latin language, which they take to mean "wedge." The cape itself projects into the sea, and Artemidoros [F13] compares it to a ship (having been at the place, as he says), with three islets assisting in the resemblance, one having the form of a prow and the others (which have reasonable anchorages) like catheads. Concerning Herakles, there is no sanctuary of his to be seen (Ephoros [F130] is wrong about this), nor an altar, or none to any other of the gods. But in many places there are stones in groups of three or four, which, according to a hereditary custom, are rotated by those visiting, and then are moved back after libations are offered. It is not lawful to sacrifice there, or to set foot there at night, for they say that the gods possess it at that time, and those who come to visit spend the night in a nearby village and go there in the daytime, taking water because it is waterless.

[C138]

(5) These things are possible and must be believed, but not so much what he has said that is in agreement with the common masses. Poseidonios [F119] says the masses report that along the Ocean the sun is larger when it sets, with a noise resembling the hissing of the sea, quenching as it falls into the depths, but this is false, as well as that night comes immediately after sunset. For it is not immediate, but a little later, just as on the other large seas. Where it sets into the mountains, the day continues for a long time after sunset because of the indirect light, but there [on the seacoast] it does not follow quickly, although the darkness does not occur immediately, just as it does not in the great plains. Yet it appears to be larger on the seas both at setting and rising, because a great amount of vapor rises from the water. Thus the rays seem broader, as if refracted through a glass, just as when the setting or rising of the sun or the moon is seen through a dry thin cloud, and thus the star appears somewhat red. He says that he proved this false during the thirty days he stayed at Gadeira and carefully observed the sunset. But Artemidoros [F12] says that the setting sun is a hundred times larger, and that night falls immediately. In examining his analysis, however, one must understand that he could not have seen this at the Sacred Promontory, for he says that no one may set foot there at night and thus no one sets foot

there at sunset if night happens immediately. And there is no other place on the coast [for this], since Gadeira is also on the Ocean. Moreover Poseidonios and many others contradict him.

(6) The coast adjacent to the Sacred Promontory is the beginning of the   [C139] western side of Iberia, as far as the outlet of the Tagos River, and of the southern as far as another river, the Anas, and its mouth. Both are carried from eastern regions, but the former runs straight west to its outlet and is much larger than the other, yet the Anas turns to the south and is the boundary of an interfluvial district where mostly Kelts live, as well as some Lusitanians who were removed there from the far side of the Tagos by the Romans. In the upland regions live the Carpetanians, Oretanians, and many Vettonians. This land is moderately prosperous, but that which lies beyond it to the east and south is considered in no way to be behind the entire inhabited earth in terms of the excellence and quality of its land and sea. This is where the Baitis River flows, whose source is in the same districts as the Anas and Tagos, and which is about midway in size between the other two. It resembles the Anas, however, and flows west from its source and then turns to the south, emptying on the same coast, which is called Baitike from the river, and Tourdetania from the inhabitants. The inhabitants are called both Tourdetanians and Tourdoulians, some believing that they are the same, others different. Among the latter is Polybios [34.9.1–2], who says that the Tourdoulians are neighbors to the north of the Tourdetanians, but today there is no distinction to be seen between them. The latter are reputed to be the wisest of the Iberians, and make use of writing, having written works that are 6,000 years [old] (as it is said) that record their antiquity, poetry, and metrical laws. Other Iberians make use of writing, although not of a single type, for there is no single language. The territory extends within the Anas as far east as Oretania and south as far as the coast which is from the mouth of the Anas as far as the Pillars. It is necessary to discuss this and the neighboring regions in greater detail, in order to learn what contributes to the favorability and prosperity of the region.

(7) Between this coast – that on which the Baitis and Anas empty – and the extremities of Maurousia, the Atlantic Ocean breaks in and makes the strait at the Pillars, by which the Internal Sea connects with the External. At that point there is a mountain belonging to those Iberians called the Bastetanians, also called the Bastoulians. It is Kalpe, whose circumference is not large but whose height is so large and steep that from a distance it   [C140] appears to be an island. For someone sailing from Our Sea to the External, it is on the right, and near it, 40 stadia away, is the distinguished ancient city of Kalpe, which was once an Iberian naval station. To some it was a

foundation of Herakles, among whom is Timosthenes [F19], who says that it was called Herakleia in antiquity, and that its large circuit wall and shipsheds are still pointed out.

(8) Then there is Menlaria, with its fish-salting factories, and after that the city and river of Belon. It is from there that most make the crossing to Tingis in Maurousia, and it has trade markets and fish-salting factories. There was also Zelis, a city bordering Tingis, but the Romans resettled it on the opposite coast, and took some from Tingis. They sent some of their own as settlers and named the city Julia Ioza. Then there is Gadeira, an island separated from Tourdetania by a narrow strait, and about 750 stadia from Kalpe, although some say 800. This island is not different from others at all, except for the courage in seamanship of its inhabitants and their friendship with the Romans. They have advanced in all kinds of prosperity so that, although situated at the extremity of the earth, it is the most notable of all. But we will discuss it when we speak about the other islands [3.5.8].

(9) Next is what is called the Harbor of Menestheus, and then the estuary at Asta, and Nabrissa. What are called estuaries are where hollows are filled by the sea at high tides: they are used as rivers to sail into the interior and to the cities on them. Immediately thereafter is the outlet of the Baitis, which is split in two. Surrounded by the mouths is an island that has a coastal boundary of 100 stadia, some say more. Around here is the oracle of Menestheus, and the Tower of Caepio, located on a rock that is washed all around, an impressive construction for the safety of seamen, like the Pharos. The soil discharged by the river creates shallows, and the area in front of it is rocky, so that a conspicuous signal is necessary. The sailing route up the Baitis is from there, as well as the city of Eboura and the shrine of Phosphoros, which is called Loukemdoubia ["Lux Dubia"]. Next are the sailing routes up the other estuaries, and afterward the Anas River, also with two mouths, and the sailing route up from both. Last is the Sacred Promontory, which is less than 2,000 stadia from Gadeira. However some say that from the Sacred Promontory to the mouth of the Anas is 60 miles, and then 100 to the mouth of the Baitis, and 70 from there to Gadeira.

[C141]

Part 2:   Interior Tourdetania

(1) It happens that Tourdetania is situated on the coast within the Anas, and the Baitis River flows through it. Its boundary on the west and north is the Anas River, on the east some of the Carpetanians and Oretanians, and on the south the Bastetanians who live on a narrow part of the coast between Kalpe and Gadeira, and on the neighboring sea[coast] as far as the Anas.

And the Bastetanians, of whom I speak, also belong to Tourdetania, as do those beyond the Anas, and most of their neighbors. The size of this territory – in length and width – is no more than 2,000 stadia, but there is an extremely large number of cities (they say 200). The best known are located on the rivers, estuaries, and the sea, because of their advantages. The ones that have become most important in reputation and power are Corduba – a foundation of Marcellus – and the city of the Gaditanians (because of its seamanship and its conclusion of an alliance with the Romans). The former [is important] because of the excellence and extent of its territory, a great part of which is due to the Baitis River. From its beginning chosen men of the Romans and of the native population have lived there, and moreover this was the first settlement that the Romans sent to those places. After it and that of the Gaditanians, Ispalis is notable, also a Roman settlement – today continuing as a trading center – but Baitis surpasses it in distinction and because the army of Caesar was recently settled there, although it is not notable in terms of population.

(2) After these are Italica and Ilipa, on the Baitis, Astigis (farther away), Carmo, and Obulco. In addition, there are the places where the sons of Pompeius were defeated: Munda, Ategua, Ourson, Tucci, Ulia, and Aegua, all of which are not far from Corduba. In a way, Munda is the metropolis of this region. Munda is 1,400 stadia from Carteia, where Gnaeus fled after he was defeated. He sailed away from there and disembarked in a certain mountainous region overlooking the sea, where he was killed. His brother Sextus escaped from Corduba and waged war among the Iberians for a short time, and then later caused a revolt in Sikelia. Then he departed for Asia and was captured by the commanders of Antonius, and died at Miletos. Konistorgis is the best known [place] among the Kelts, but in the estuaries it is Asta, where the Gaditanians come together, situated not much more than 100 stadia beyond the seaport of the island.

(3) The Baitis has a large number living along it, and can be sailed inland for about 1,200 stadia from the sea as far as Corduba and places a little farther up.   [C142] The region along the river and the islets in the river are extraordinary well cultivated. In addition there is its pleasant appearance, for the landscape is thoroughly worked with groves and gardens. One can sail up as far as Hispalis (not much less than 500 stadia) in especially large merchant ships, in smaller ones to the cities as far as Ilipa, and as far as Corduba in light river boats that at present are well constructed but in antiquity were dugouts. Farther up, toward Castulo, it is not navigable.

There are certain mountain ridges extending parallel to the river, more or less adjoining it on the north, and which are full of mines. Silver is most common in the regions around Ilipa and those around Sisapo (both what is called New and Old). At what is called Cotinae both copper and gold are brought forth. These mountains are on the left as one sails upstream, and on the right is a large plain that is high, fruitful, with large trees, and abundant in pasture.

The Anas can also be sailed up, although not with as large river boats and not as far. Beyond it there are also mountains with mining that reach down to the Tagos. The regions that have mining are by necessity rough and rather poor, particularly those which adjoin Carpetania, and especially those [adjoining] the Keltiberians. Moreover, Baitouria is similar, having dry plains along the Anas.

(4) Tourdetania itself is wonderfully prosperous. It produces everything, and this productivity is doubled by exportation, for the surplus produce is easily sold because of the abundance of ship owners. This is possible due to the rivers, as well as the estuaries, that, as I have said [3.1.9], resemble rivers, and which similarly can be sailed up from the sea to the interior cities not only in small boats but in large ones. Beyond the coast between the Sacred Promontory and the Pillars it is all a large plain. There are many hollows in the interior that the sea reaches, resembling moderate ravines or river channels that extend for many stadia. These are filled by the entry of the sea at the flood tides, so that one can sail inland no less than on rivers – indeed better – for it is like sailing down rivers (as there is no resistance), since one is sent onward by the sea and the flood tide is just like the flow of a river. The rise is greater here than elsewhere because the sea – coming from the great Ocean – is forcibly compressed into the narrows that Maurousia makes with Iberia, and encountering resistance, is carried to those parts of the land that easily give way to it. Certain of these hollows are emptied at the ebb tides – although some are not completely without water – and some of them include islands within them.

[C143]

Such are the estuaries between the Sacred Promontory and the Pillars, having a larger increase than in other places. Such an increase has a certain advantage for the use of seamen, for the estuaries are more numerous and larger, and often can be sailed up for eight stadia[1], so that, in a way, the entire land is navigable and easy for the importation of goods, and their export. But there is also a certain annoyance, since the violence of the flood tides – which press more strongly against the flow of the river – always imposes no small danger to ship captains sailing the river, both in sailing

---

[1] The manuscripts give this number (less than a mile) which seems unlikely and hardly worthy of note. Suggestions include 100, 400, and 800.

downstream as well as upstream. The ebb tides in the estuaries are also dangerous, because they become violent in proportion to the flood tides, and because their swiftness often leaves the ship behind on dry land. Cattle that cross over to the islands in the rivers or estuaries are at times flooded, or at other times cut off. They do not have the strength to make the effort to return and have died. It is said that the cows observe what is happening and wait for the retreat of the sea, and then depart for the mainland.

(5) The people learned the nature of these places and that the estuaries could be of service as rivers, and founded cities and other settlements on them, just as on rivers. Among them are Asta, Nabrissa, Onoba, <Os>sonoba, Maenuba, and a number of others. In places canals have been of assistance, since there are many locations for commercial business, among themselves and externally. Moreover, the flowing together of the high tide over the isthmuses that separate the straits is of great benefit, enabling them to be navigable, so that one can cross from the rivers into the estuaries and back again.

All the commerce is with Italia and Rome, and the sail as far as the Pillars is good except for difficulty around the straits and on the open parts of Our [C144] Sea. The passage is completed through a zone of fair weather (especially on the open sea), which is beneficial to large merchant ships, and the winds on the open sea are regular. Moreover, there is the current peace, and the suppression of piracy, so that there is a complete sense of ease for navigation. Poseidonios [T22] says that he observed a peculiar thing on his return voyage from Iberia, as the Etesian winds which blew as far as the Sardoan Gulf were easterly, and thus it was nearly three months before he docked in Italia, for he was carried both around the Gymnesian Islands and Sardo as well as to the part of Libya that is opposite.

(6) Much grain and wine are exported from Tourdetania, as well as olive oil, not only in quantity but of the best quality. Beeswax, honey, and pitch are also exported, as well as much *kokkos* and red ochre, which is not inferior to the Sinopean earth. Their ship construction is from indigenous wood, and there are salt quarries, and not a few rivers flowing with salt water. Also not unimportant is the industry of fish salting – not only there, but along the entire coast outside the Pillars – which is not inferior to the Pontic [industry]. Previously much clothing came from there, but now it is wool that is mostly raven black. Its beauty is superior: in fact the rams are purchased for breeding at the cost of a talent. Also superior are the delicate woven fabrics that are made by the Saltietians. There is also an abundance of all kinds of cattle and wild game. But there is a scarcity of destructive animals except for burrowing rabbits, which some call *leberides*, and which

cause damage both to plants and seeds by eating the roots. They occur throughout almost the entirety of Iberia, extending as far as Massalia, and are also a problem in the islands. It is said that those living in the Gymnasians once sent an embassy to the Romans to ask for another place because they were being driven away by these animals and were unable to hold out against them because of their numbers. Perhaps such assistance is necessary in so great a war – not always what happens – against a destructive pestilence such as snakes or field mice, but against something moderate many types of hunting have been discovered; in particular, the wild ferrets that are produced in Libya are muzzled and sent into the holes. With their claws, they drag out all [the *leberides*] that they catch, or force them to flee into view, where those stationed hunt them down as they escape.

[C145]

The abundance of exports from Tourdetania is manifested by the size and number of ships, for the large merchantmen sail from there to Dikaiarcheia and Ostia (the port of Rome), and their numbers must be no less than equal to those of the Libyans. . .from multiplication.[2]

(7) The interior of Tourdetania is in such a way, yet one can find that the coast is equal to it, in terms of the quality [of products] from the sea. The many kinds of oysters and mussels are superior in quantity and size along the entire External Sea, but especially so here, because of the increase in the flood and ebb tides, which, due to the activity, are a probable reason for their quantity and size. It is the same concerning all kinds of sea creatures: the snouted, *phalainai*, and the spouters, whose spouting appears – to someone observing from afar – to be a cloud-like pillar. The conger eels are monstrous, much larger in size that those around us, as well as the muraena and many other such [creatures]. In Carteia it is said that there are trumpet and purple shells that hold ten *kotyles*, and in places farther out the conger eels and muraena are larger than eighty *minae*, the polypods a talent, the calamari two *pecheis* long, and so forth.

There are many tuna that are fat and thick which collect here from the external coast. They feed on acorns produced by a certain oak that is completely sunken down in the sea and which bears the fullest fruit. It also grows extensively on the land throughout Iberia, having large roots like a typical oak, and growing less high than a low-lying bush. It produces so much fruit that after its ripening the coast – both within and outside the Pillars – is full of them, as the high tides throw them out. Those inside the Pillars are smaller but are found in greater number. Polybios [34.8.3] says

---

[2] The last part of the sentence makes no sense and most editors have either omitted it or suggested a lost comparison with another geographical region.

that these acorns are thrown ashore as far as Latina, unless, he says, Sardo and neighboring areas produce them. Moreover, the nearer the tuna come to the Pillars, carried from outside, the much leaner they become, since their food fails. Thus they are a type of sea pig, for they enjoy the acorns and become exceedingly fat on them. Where acorns are produced, there is also tuna.

(8) The previously mentioned territory has been abundantly provided with such good things. Not the least – indeed the most – one might admire [C146] and marvel at the richness of its mining operations. All of the Iberian land is full of them, although not all of it is fruitful or prosperous, especially that abundant in mines. It is rare to be fortunate in both, and also rare for the same region to have so much mining in a small territory. Regarding Tourdetania and that which neighbors it, there is no worthy word left for someone who would wish to praise its excellence. Up to this time no gold, silver, copper, or iron of such quality has been discovered anywhere in the world.

Gold is not only mined but drawn out, since rivers and torrents carry down the gold-bearing sand. Moreover, it often exists in waterless places but cannot be seen there, yet in the flooded areas the gold dust gleams. The waterless places are flooded by introducing water and making the dust glitter. They also dig pits and devise other techniques for washing the sand and obtaining the gold, and now there are more places that are called gold washers than gold mines. The Galatians believe that their mines are equal to these, both on Mount Kemmenon as well as those below Pyrene, although those from the former [i.e. Iberia] are more esteemed. They say that in the gold dust nuggets of half a *litra* were once found, which are called *palai* and need only a little purifying. They also say that where the stones are split they find small nuggets that are like nipples. When the gold is refined and purified by means of a type of astringent earth, the residue is called electrum. When this is boiled down – it is a mixture of silver and gold – the silver is burned away and the gold remains. The material is flexible and stone-like. For this reason it is preferable to melt the gold with chaff because the flame, being gentle, is suitable for a substance that is easily dissolved, but charcoal consumes much of it, melting it through its intensity and carrying it away. The earth is carried along in streams and is washed in nearby troughs, or a pit is dug where the accumulation is washed. The silver furnaces are built high, so that the smoke from the ore is removed high into the air, for it is heavy and deadly. Some of the copper mines are called gold mines, from which it is conjectured that gold was formerly dug out of them.

(9) Poseidonios [F239], in his praise of the quantity and quality of the
[C147] mines, does not desist from his customary rhetoric, inspired by the exag-
gerations. He says that he does not disbelieve the story that once when the
thickets had burned up the earth melted – since it contained silver and gold
ore – and boiled over the entire surface, because every mountain and every
wooded hill is money, preserved by a bountiful fortune. He says that in
general anyone who has seen these regions would call them eternal treasuries
of nature, or the infinite storehouse of a government. The land is not only
rich, but rich underneath, he says, and for them it is truly not Hades but
Ploutos who lives in the regions beneath the earth. This is what he says
about these things, in a graceful manner, using much of his language as if
from a mine.

In speaking of the diligence of the miners, he furnishes [Demetrios] the
Phalerian [F35a], who says that in the Attic silver mines the men dig as
intensively as if they expected to bring up Ploutos. Thus he [Poseidonios]
makes it clear that their effort and industriousness are similar, cutting the
passages at an angle and deep, and the rivers that they encounter in them are
often drawn out by the Egyptian screw. Yet the whole situation is never the
same for them as for those in Attika, since he says their mining of the latter is
like the riddle: "what they took up, they did not take, and what they had,
they lost." But for those [in Tourdetania] it is exceedingly profitable, since a
fourth of that brought out of the earth by the copper miners is copper, and
certain private silver miners can take out a Euboian talent in three days.

He says that tin is not found on the surface (despite what the historians
repeat over and over), but by digging. It is produced both among the
barbarians beyond Lusitania and in the Kassiterides Islands, and is carried
to Massalia from the Prettanikians. He says that among the Artabrians, who
are in the farthest northwest of Lusitania, the earth blooms with silver, tin,
and white gold (it is mixed with silver). This earth is carried by the rivers,
and women scrape it away with shovels and wash it in sieves of woven
baskets. This is what he says about mining.

(10) Polybios [34.9.8–11], in discussing the silver mines at New Karchedon,
says that they are exceedingly large and about 20 stadia from the city. They
[C148] encompass a circuit of 400 stadia, and 40,000 workmen remain there
who bring 25,000 drachmas each day to the Roman people. I will omit
everything about the production – for it is lengthy – except that he says the
silver nuggets are washed down, and are crushed and separated in water. The
water is poured off and the sediment is crushed again, strained again,
and crushed. The fifth sediment is smelted, the lead is poured off, and pure
silver is produced. The silver mines are in operation at present, but do not

belong to the state, either here or anywhere else, as they have been privatized. Most of the gold mines are owned by the state. In Castulo and other places there is a particular metal of mined lead that has a small amount of silver mixed in with it which is not profitable to refine.

(11) Not far from Castulo is the mountain from which the Baitis is said to flow, which is called Silver Mountain because of the silver mines on it. Polybios [34.9.12], however, says that both this and the Anas flow from Keltiberia, and are 900 stadia from each other. The Keltiberians, because of their increase in power, made all the neighboring regions have the same name as their own. It seems that the ancients called the Baitis the Tartessos, and Gadeira and its islands Erytheia, and this is supposedly what Stesichoros meant about the cattle of Geryon, who was born

> nearly opposite famous Erytheia, alongside the boundless silver-rooted springs of the Tartessos River, in a hole in the rocks. [F S7]

Since the river has two mouths, they say that a city was established at one time on the land in between, which was called Tartessos, the same name as the river, and the territory Tartessis, where the Tourdoulians now live. Eratosthenes [F153] says that the territory adjoining Kalpe is called Tartessis, and that Erytheia is the Fortunate Island. Artemidoros [F11] contradicts him and says that this is a falsehood by him, just like that the distance from Gadeira to the Sacred Promontory is a five-day sail (although it is no more than 1,700 stadia), that the tides terminate at that point (although they exist around the circuit of the entire inhabited world), that the northerly part of Iberia is an easier means of access to Keltike than sailing by the Ocean, and everything else that he said while relying on Pytheas [T11], because of the latter's false pretensions.   [C149]

(12) The Poet, being someone of many voices and much learning, gives reasons that these places were not unknown to him, if one wished to conclude correctly from both of the statements made about them: a worse one as well as a better and more trustworthy. The worse is that he had heard it was the farthest in the west, where, as he himself says, there falls into the Ocean "the bright light of the sun, dragging the black night over the grain-giving land" [*Iliad* 8.485–6]. It is clear that night is an ill omen and near Hades, and that Hades is associated with Tartessos. One might suggest that because he had heard about Tartessos, he derived Tartaros for the farthest places under the earth, altering the word and preserving the poetic quality. Similarly, as he knew that the Kimmerians lived to the north in gloomy places around the Bosporos, he settled them around Hades, although perhaps it was because of a certain common enmity of the Ionians for this tribe, for it was at the time of

Homer, or a little earlier, that they say the Kimmerian invasion as far as Aiolis and Ionia occurred.

He made the Planktai similar to the Kyaneai, always developing his myths from something factual. He tells the story of certain dangerous rocks, just as the Kyaneai are said to be, and from which they are called the Symplegades ["The Strikers Together"]. For this reason he placed the voyage of Jason near them. But the strait at the Pillars as well as that at Sikelia suggested to him the tale about the Planktai. Thus in regard to the worse [reason], one might have the hint that in the myth-making about Tartaros he had in mind the regions around Tartessos.

(13) The better [reason] is this: the expedition of Herakles (as well as that of the Phoenicians), which came this far, indicated to him [Homer] that they [the Iberians] were rich in some way, and a relaxed people. They became so totally subject to the Phoenicians that most of the cities in Tourdetania as well as nearby places are now inhabited by them. Moreover, the expedition of Odysseus seems to me to have also come this far, providing him [Homer] with an historical pretext. Thus he transferred the *Odyssey* – just as the *Iliad* – from something that had actually happened into a created composition and a mythic invention of a type familiar to poets.

Not only do the places around Italia and Sikelia and certain others indicate such signs, but in Iberia a city of Odysseia is pointed out, as well as a sanctuary of Athena, and a myriad of other traces of his wanderings and those of others that occurred after the Trojan War, which was equally

[C150] disastrous for those who fought as well as those who captured Troy, for the latter happened to obtain a Kadmeian victory. Since the homes had been destroyed, and the spoils that came to each were small, it happened that those who survived departed from the danger and turned to piracy, as the Hellenes did: the former because of the total destruction, and the latter because of the dishonor, since each assumed that "it was dishonorable to remain too long" from one's family "and to go empty-handed" [*Iliad* 2.298] back to them. The wanderings of Aineias are traditional, as well as those of Antenor and the Enetians. Similar are those of Diomedes, Menelaos, Odysseus, and a number of others. Thus the Poet, knowledgeable about so many expeditions to farthest Iberia, and learning about its wealth and other virtues – for the Phoenicians were making this known – imagined that it was the territory of the pious and the Elysian Plain, where Proteus says that Menelaos will settle:

> But the immortals will send you to the Elysian Plain and the extremities of the earth, where fair-haired Rhadamanthys is, and life becomes easiest

for men. There is no snow, nor any great storms, nor rain, but Okeanos always releases the blowing winds of Zephyros to refresh men. [*Odyssey* 4.563–8]

Both the pure air and gentle winds of the Zephyr properly belong to this region, since it is in the west and warm. It is at the extremities of the earth, where Hades is believed to be, as we say. Putting forth Rhadamanthys suggests a place that is near Minos, about whom he says

I saw Minos there, the noble son of Zeus, holding a golden scepter, and giving law to the dead. [*Odyssey* 11.568–9]

Moreover, the poets who came after him repeated similar things over and over: the expedition for the cattle of Geryon, as well as the expedition for the golden apples of the Hesperides, and the naming of certain Blessed Islands, which, as we know, are pointed out not far from the capes of Maurousia that lie opposite Gadeira.

(14) I say that the Phoenicians were his informants, as they possessed the best of Iberia and Libya before the time of Homer, and continued to be masters of those places until the Romans destroyed their power. A [C151] witness to the wealth of Iberia is that the Karchedonians, when they made their expedition along with Barkas, as the historians say, found the Tourdetanians making use of silver mangers and wine jars.

One might assume that it was from their great prosperity that the people there were also named the "Long Lived," especially their leaders, and because of this Anakreon said the following: "I would not wish for the horn of Amaltheia, or to be king of Tartessos for a hundred and fifty years" [F361], and Herodotos [1.163] even recorded the name of the king, calling him Arganthonios. One might take Anakreon literally, or [meaning] an equal time, or more generally as "to be king of Tartessos for a long time." Some consider that Tartessos is modern Carteia.

(15) In addition to the prosperity of the region, a civilized and cultured quality accrues to the Tourdetanians, as well as to the Kelts (because they are neighbors, as Polybios [34.9.3] has said, due to their kinship), but the latter less so because they mostly live in villages. Yet the Tourdetanians, especially those around the Baitis, have completely changed to the Roman manner, and no longer remember their own language. Most of them have become Latins, and have taken Romans as settlers, so they are not far from being completely Roman. The current jointly settled cities include Pax Augusta among the Kelts, Augusta Emerita among the Tourdetanians, Caesaraugusta near Keltiberia, and some other settlements, which manifest the change to the previously mentioned culture. In addition, all the

Iberians in this class are called "*togati*." Among these are the Keltiberians, once considered the most savage of all. This is it about them.

Part 3: Lusitania

(1) Beginning again from the Sacred Promontory, on the other part of the coast toward the Tagos, there is a gulf, and then Barbarion Cape, which is near the mouths of the Tagos, a straight sail of. . .and 10 stadia.[3] There are also estuaries here, one of which is more than 400 stadia from the previously mentioned tower, which is watered[4] . . . . The Tagos has a width of about 20 stadia at its mouth and a great depth, so that 10,000-measure ships can sail up it. When the flood tides occur, two estuaries are formed in the plains lying above it, so that there is a sea for 150 stadia and the plain becomes navigable. In the upper estuary an island of about 30 stadia in width is created, whose width is somewhat less than its length, and which is luxuriant with fine vines. The island lies opposite the city of Moron, which is well situated on a mountain near the river, lying about 500 stadia from the sea. The surrounding country is good and the sail up to it is easy for large boats most of the way and by river boats for the rest. Beyond Moron it is navigable still farther. Brutus called Callaicus used this city as his base of operations when he made war against the Lusitanians and subdued them. At the entrance of the river he fortified Olysipo, so that the voyage inland and the carrying upstream of commodities would be unimpeded. Thus these are the strongest cities around the Tagos. The river has many fish and is full of oysters. It flows from its source in Keltiberia through the Vettonians, Carpetanians, and Lusitanians toward equinoctial west, parallel to the Anas and Baitis up to a certain point, and afterward diverging from them, as they turn off toward the southern coast.

(2) Of those lying beyond the previously mentioned mountains, the Oretanians are the most southern, and they live as far as the coast on the portion within the Pillars. The Carpetanians are after these toward the north, and then the Vettonians and Vaccaeans, through whom the Durius flows, which can be crossed at Akontia, a Vaccaean city. Farthest are the Callaicians, who possess much of the mountainous region. Because they were difficult to fight, they have both provided the surname for the one

[C152]

---

[3] A number is missing: 10 stadia is about a mile, and the distance from the Sacred Promontory to the Tagos is 115 miles.

[4] The manuscripts have meaningless letters here, perhaps a confused rendition of the names of the estuaries.

who subdued the Lusitanians, and it has also resulted that most of the Lusitanians are now called Callaicians. In Oretania the city of Castulo is powerful, as is Oria.

(3) Lusitania, to the north of the Tagos, is the greatest of the Iberian peoples, and those against whom the Romans fought for the longest time. The Tagos surrounds this region on the southern side, the Ocean on the western and northern, and on the eastern are the Carpetanians, Vettonians, Vaccaeans, and Callaicians, well-known peoples. It is not worthwhile to name the others because of their insignificance and obscurity. Contrary to those of today, some also call them the Lusitanians. The Callaicians are bounded on their eastern portion by the Asturian people and the Keltiberians, but the others by only the Keltiberians.   [C153]

Its length is 3,000 stadia and its width much less, created between the eastern side and the coast that lies opposite. The eastern side is high and rugged, but the territory lying below is all plain as far as the sea, except for a few mountains that are not large. Because of this Poseidonios [F220] says that Aristotle [F680] is incorrect in saying that this and the Maurousian coasts are the reason for the flood and ebb tides, and that the flowing back of the sea is because of the height and ruggedness of the capes, which thus receive the waves strongly and give them back with equal force.[5] It is in fact the contrary (for the most part it is sandy and low), as he [Poseidonios] says correctly.

(4) The land of which we speak is prosperous with large and small rivers flowing through it, all of which come from the eastern parts and are parallel to the Tagos. Most of them can be sailed upstream and have large amounts of gold dust. The best known of the rivers beyond the Tagos are the Munda, which can be sailed upstream short distances, and similarly the Vacua. After these is the Durius, which flows from far away and passes Numantia and many other Keltiberian and Vaccaean settlements. It is navigable by large boats for about 800 stadia inland. Then there are other rivers. After them, there is the Lethe, which some call the Limaia and others the Belion. It also flows from the Keltiberians and the Vaccaeans, and after it is the Bainis (some say Minios), the largest by far of those in Lusitania, navigable inland for 800 stadia. Poseidonios [F224] says that it flows from the Cantabrians. An island lies off its mouth, and there are two breakwaters for anchorages.

The nature of these rivers is worthy of praise, because they have high banks that are sufficient to receive the sea within its channel at high tide,

---

[5] The manuscripts actually have "to Iberia" (*teiiberiai*), which may be correct, but a probable emendation is "with equal force" (*teiiseibiai*).

without overflowing or wandering into the plains. This was the limit of Brutus' campaign, although farther on there are many other rivers, parallel to those mentioned.

(5) Lastly, the Artabrians live around the cape called Nerion, which is the end of the western and northern side. The Kelts live around it, related to those on the Anas. It is said that they and the Tourdoulians made an expedition there and quarreled after they crossed the Limaia River. In addition to the quarrel, they lost their leader, and dispersed and remained there, and because of this the river was said to be the Lethe ["Forgetfulness"]. The Artabrians live together in many cities on the gulf which the seamen who know these regions call the Harbor of the Artabrians. Today they call the Artabrians the Arotrebians.

There are about thirty peoples who live in the territory between the Tagos and the Artabrians. The territory is at present prosperous, with produce, cattle, gold, and silver, and much that is similar; nevertheless most of them ceased making their living from the earth but continued with brigandage and waging war against one another and with their neighbors across the Tagos, until the Romans put a stop to it, humbling them and turning most of their cities into villages, although some were improved by being combined. The mountain dwellers began the lawlessness, as is reasonable, for they lived poorly and had few possessions, and desired those of others. The latter defended themselves, but by necessity came to have no power over their own land, so that, instead of farming, they began to wage war, with the result that the land was neglected, becoming barren of good plants and the home of brigands.

(6) They say that the Lusitanians are capable at ambushing, good spies, sharp, nimble, and skillful in maneuvering. They have a small shield two feet in diameter, concave in front, and hung by a strap, for it has neither loops nor handles. They have a knife or a cleaver. Most of them have linen cuirasses, with a few using ones of chain mail and three-crested helmets, but the remainder have sinew helmets. The foot soldiers also have greaves, and each has a number of javelins. Some use spears, with the spear heads made of bronze. They say that some of them who reside near the Durius River live in a Lakonian style, using anointing rooms twice a day, and vapor baths from heated stones, bathing in cold water and eating once a day, in a clean and simple manner.

The Lusitanians make sacrifices, and look closely at the innards. They also look closely at the veins on the side, and perform divination by touching. They also prophesy from the innards of prisoners, whom they cover with coarse cloaks. When they have been struck under the innards by

[C154]

the diviner, the first prophecies are made from their fall. The right hand of those captured is cut off and offered up.

(7) All the mountain people are simple, water drinkers, sleep on the ground, and have their hair streaming down in the fashion of women, although when fighting they use a headband on their forehead. For the most part they eat goat, and they sacrifice a goat to Ares, as well as captives and   [C155] horses, with a hecatomb of each in the Hellenic manner, as Pindar [F170] says, "to sacrifice a hundred of every kind." They hold contests for light-armed troops, hoplites, and cavalry, in boxing, running, skirmishing, and fighting in squadrons. The mountain people use acorns two parts of the year, which are dried and chopped, and then ground and made into bread that can be stored away for a time. They use beer, yet wine is a rarity, and if they have it they consume it quickly, feasting with their kinsmen. Instead of olives they use butter. They eat sitting down, with seats constructed around the walls, and are seated according to age and rank. The meal is carried around. While drinking they dance to the flute and trumpet, in chorus, both leaping up and crouching down. In Bastetania the women mingle with the men and take their hands. All of them dress in black, mostly in coarse cloaks, in which they sleep on beds of leaves. They use wax vessels, just as the Kelts do. The women dress in garments with flowered clothing. Instead of coinage, those[6]. . .far in the interior use barter for goods, or they cut off beaten silver and hand it over.

Those condemned to death are thrown down from rocks, and parricides are stoned beyond the mountains or rivers. They marry just like the Hellenes. They set those who are sick out in the roads – just as the Egyptians did in antiquity – in order to obtain suggestions for those who have experienced the condition. Until the time of Brutus they used boats of prepared hide, because of the flood tides and the shoals, but now even dugouts are rare. Their salt is purple but when beaten it is white.

This is the life of those in the mountains, as I said, I mean those whose boundary is the north side of Iberia, the Callaicians, the Asturians, and the Cantabrians as far as the Vasconians and Pyrene, for the lifestyle of all of them is similar. I shrink from an excess of names, avoiding the unpleasant-ness of writing them, unless it would give someone pleasure to hear Pleutaurians, Bardyetians, Allotrigians, and the others that are worse and more insignificant than these names.

(8) Their restiveness and wild nature does not result solely from warfare, but also because of their remoteness, for whether by sailing or by road it is a

---

[6] There are a number of incomprehensible letters at this point, perhaps a confused toponym or ethnym.

[C156] long way to them, and since they are unsociable they have lost a sense of community and humanity, although this attitude is now diminished because of the peace and the presence of the Romans. But where it occurs less they are more difficult and wilder. As some of them are more disagreeable because of the remoteness of their regions, it is expected that the mountains intensify their uncouthness. But now, as I have said, they have completely ceased warfare, for the Cantabrians, who today still hold the most to brigandage, and their neighbors, have been put down by Sebastos Caesar, and now instead of ravaging the allies of the Romans, they fight for the Romans, both the Koniakians and the[7]. . .who live near the source of the Iber. His successor Tiberius placed three legions in these regions – already assigned by Sebastos Caesar – and thus it has happened that some of them have been made not only peaceful but civilized.

Part 4:   Coastal Iberia

(1) The remainder of Iberia is the coast of Our [Sea] from the Pillars as far as Pyrene, as well as the entire interior lying above it, which is irregular in width, but slightly more than 4,000 stadia in length, although that of the coast is said to be 2,000 stadia more. They say that from Kalpe (the mountain at the Pillars) to New Karchedon is 2,200 stadia, and that this shore is inhabited by the Bastetanians – who are also called the Bastoulians – and in part by the Oretanians. From there to the Iber is about the same distance, and this is held by the Edetanians. Within the Iber as far as Pyrene and the Dedications of Pompeius is 1,600 [stadia]. A few Edetanians live there, and the rest are those known as the Indiketians, divided into four.

(2) In detail, beginning from Kalpe, there is a mountainous ridge of Bastetania and the Oretanians, which has a thick forest full of large trees, and which separates the coast from the interior. In many places here are mines of gold and other metals. The first city on this coast is Malaka, which is the same distance from Kalpe as Gadeira. It is a trading center for the nomads on the opposite coast, and has major fish-salting establishments. Some believe that it is the same as Mainake, which we have heard is the farthest of the Phokaian cities that lie in the west, but this is not so, for it is farther from Kalpe and also has been destroyed, although it preserves the traces of a Hellenic city. Malaka is somewhat nearer and has a Phoenician

---

[7] There are a number of incomprehensible letters at this point, presumably a confusion of the missing ethnym.

appearance. Next is the city of the Exitanians, from which it is said that the salted fish are named.

(3) After this is Abdera, itself a Phoenician foundation. Above these places [C157] in the mountainous country, Odysseia is pointed out, with a sanctuary of Athena in it, as Poseidonios [F247] has said, as well as Artemidoros [F16] and Asklepiades the Myrleian [F7], a man who taught grammar in Tourdetania and published a *Periegesis* about the peoples there. He says that shields and ships' prows have been nailed up in the sanctuary of Athena as a memorial of the wanderings of Odysseus. Some of those who made the expedition with Teukros lived among the Callaicians, and two cities were there, one called Hellenes and the other Amphilochoi, for Amphilochos died there and his companions wandered as far as the interior. He also says that it is recorded some of those with Herakles and from Messene settled Iberia, and part of Cantabria was held by the Lakonians, as he and others say. They say that a city of Okela is there, founded by Okelas, who, along with Antenor and his children crossed over to Italia. And in regard to Libya, some have believed – paying attention to the Gadeiran merchants – as Artemidoros [F77] says, that those living beyond Maurousia next to the Western Aithiopians are called the Lotus Eaters, eating the lotus, a kind of herb and root, and they do not need to drink, or have anything, because of the aridity. They extend as far as the territory of Kyrene. In addition, there are others called the Lotus Eaters who live on Meninx, one of the islands of the Lesser Syrtis.

(4) Thus it is not surprising to anyone that the Poet wrote his stories about the wanderings of Odysseus in such a way that most of what he said about him was placed beyond the Pillars and in the Atlantic Ocean. What he recorded was close [to reality], both in regard to the places and the other things that he created, so that his creations were not unbelievable. Some, believing in these accounts and in the polymathic nature of the Poet, have actually turned to the poetry of Homer as a basis for scholarship, as Krates of Mallos [F75] and certain others have done. Yet others have received such reasoning boorishly and have not only considered the Poet as a ditch digger or harvester, but worthy of expulsion from all such scholarship, assuming that those who undertake such business are mad. But they do not propose defending, correcting, or doing anything else about what the former have said: neither the grammarians nor those clever at scientific matters have any [C158] confidence. But to me it seems possible to defend much of what they said and to correct many other things, especially where Pytheas [T12] has led astray those who believed him, because of their ignorance of places in the west or those toward the north along the Ocean. But let us leave this alone, since the argument is specific and long.

(5) The wandering of the Hellenes to the barbarian peoples may have occurred because the latter were scattered into small groups and dominions that had no interaction with one another – because of their stubbornness – and thus they were weak against those coming from abroad. This stubbornness was particularly intense among the Iberians, since by nature they had fastened onto both wickedness and a lack of openness. Their lifestyle resulted in a readiness to attack and rob, undertaking minor things but never throwing themselves into major ones, because they did not build forces or alliances. If they had been willing to be shield comrades with one another, the Karchedonians would not have been able to subdue them (they attacked most of their territory through their own superiority), or still earlier the Tyrians, then the Kelts who are now called Keltiberians and Beronians, or afterward the brigand Veriathus, or Sertorius, or any others who desired greater power. The Romans made war against the Iberians piecemeal and individually, and continued establishing their power for an extensive period of time, subduing one or the other for so long, until after two hundred years or more they controlled all of them. But I return to my *periegesis*.

(6) After this there is New Karchedon, founded by Hasdrubal who succeeded Barkas the father of Hannibal. It is the most powerful of these cities, for it is adorned with a strong wall that is attractively constructed, harbors, and a lake, and with the silver mines of which I have spoken [3.2.10]. Here and at nearby places there is extensive fish salting. And it is an important emporium for those from the interior, [who obtain] things from the sea, and for everything [going] from there to abroad.

On the coast from there up to the Iber, at a distance of about midway, are the Sucro River, its mouth, and a city with the same name. It flows from the adjoining mountains that connect with the ridge lying above Malaka and the regions around Karchedon. It can be crossed on foot, and is about [C159] parallel to the Iber, slightly less distant from Karchedon than the Iber. Between the Sucro and Karchedon are three small Massaliote cities, of which the best known is Hemeroskopeion, having on its promontory a sanctuary of Ephesian Artemis that is particularly revered, and which was used by Sertorius as a naval base. It is in a strong position and is suitable for pirates, visible for a great [distance] to those sailing against it, and called the Dianium (the same as Artemision). Nearby are good iron mines and the islets of Planesia and Plumbaria, and lying above it is a lagoon whose circuit is 400 stadia. Next is the Island of Herakles, quite near to Karchedon, which is called Skombroaria because of the scomber caught there, from which the best garum is prepared. It is 24 stadia distant from Karchedon.

Again, across the Sucro going toward the mouth of the Iber, is Saguntum, a Zakynthian foundation that Hannibal destroyed in violation of his treaty with the Romans, kindling the second war against the Karchedonians. Nearby are the cities of Chersonesos, Oleastrum, and Cartalia, and at the crossing of the Iber itself is Dertosa. The Iber has its source in Cantabria and flows to the south through a large plain, parallel to the Pyrenaian mountains.

(7) Between the branching of the Iber and the heights of Pyrene (on which the Dedications of Pompeius are set up), the first city is Tarrakon, which has no harbor but is situated on a bay and is sufficiently equipped with everything, today no less populated than Karchedon. It is naturally suited for the residence of the commanders and is the metropolis, so to speak, not only of the territory within the Iber but much of that beyond. The Gymnesian Islands lie nearby, and Ebosos, all notable islands, which suggests that the position of the city is propitious. Eratosthenes [F152] says that it also has a roadstead, but Artemidoros [F26] contradicts him, saying that it is not even fortunate enough to have an anchorage.

(8) The entire distance from the Pillars to this point has a scarcity of harbors, but from here on there are good harbors and the fertile country of the Laietanians and Lartolaietians, and such others, as far as Emporion. This is a Massaliote foundation, which is forty stadia from Pyrene and the boundary between Iberia and Keltike, and it is all fertile with good harbors. [C160] There is also Rhode, a small town of the Emporians, although some say that it was a Rhodian foundation. Both there and in Emporion they honor Ephesian Artemis, and we will discuss the reason in the section on Massalia [4.1.5]. The Emporitians previously lived on a small offshore island, which is now called the Old City, but now they live on the mainland. It is a double city, separated by a wall. Formerly some of the Indiketians were their neighbors, who, although having their own government, wished for the sake of safety to have a common circuit wall with the Hellenes, in two parts, separated by a wall in the middle. In time they came together under the same administration, a mixture of barbarian and Hellenic customs, something that has happened in many other places.

(9) A river flows nearby, whose source is in Pyrene, and whose outlet is the harbor of the Emporitians. The Emporitians are capable linen workers. The inland territory that they hold is fertile in part, but the rest produces a rather useless type of *sparton* and marsh reeds, and is called the Juncarian Plain. Some of them live on the summits of Pyrene as far as the Dedications of Pompeius, by which the route passes from Italia to what is called Farther Iberia, especially Baitike.

This road at times comes near to the sea, and at other times withdraws from it, especially in its western portions. It goes toward Tarrakon from the memorials of Pompeius, through the Juncarian Plain and Betteres, called in the Latin language the Plain of Marathon ["Fennel"], which produces much fennel. From Tarrakon [it goes] toward the crossing of the Iber at the city of Dertosa, and from there, passing through Saguntum and the city of Saitabis, it gradually leaves the sea and joins the Spartarian – called the Schoinous – Plain. It is large and without water, producing the *sparton* for twisting rope, which is exported to everywhere, especially Italia. Previously the road went through the middle of the plain and Egelasta, and was difficult and lengthy, but now it has been constructed more toward the coastal region, only touching the Schoinous gently, yet extending to the same place as before, the area around Castulo and Obulco. The road [goes] through these places to Corduba and Gadeira, the greatest of the trading centers. Obulco is about 300 stadia distant from Corduba. The historians say that Caesar went from Rome to Obulco and the camp there in 27 days, when he was about to

[C161] engage in the battle around Munda.

(10) Such, then, is the entire coast from the Pillars as far as the boundary of the Iberians and the Kelts. The interior that lies beyond – I mean that within the Pyrenaian mountains and the northern side as far as the Asturians – is essentially divided by two mountains. One of these is parallel with Pyrene, beginning from the Cantabrians and ending at Our Sea, and is called Idubeda. The other extends from its middle toward the west, inclining to the south and the coast from the Pillars. At its beginning it is a bare earthy hill, and then it passes through the so-called Spartarian Plain, and joins the forest that lies beyond Karchedon and the regions around Malaka. It is called Orospeda. The Iber River, then, flows between Pyrene and Idubeda, parallel to both mountains and filled by the rivers and the other streams that come down from them. On the Iber there is a city called Caesaraugusta, and also the settlement of Kelsa, where a stone bridge crosses it.

The land is jointly occupied by a number of peoples, of which the best known are those called the Iaccetanians. It begins at the slopes of Pyrene and then broadens into the plain, joining the territories around Ilerda and Osca, those of the Ilergetians, not far away from the Iber. It was in these cities that Sertorius fought for the last time, at Calaguris of the Vasconians, as well as on the coast at Tarrakon and Hermeroskopeion, after he was expelled from Keltiberia. He died at Osca. Later, around Ilerda, Afranius and Petreius, the generals of Pompeius, were defeated by Caesar the God. Ilerda is about 160 stadia from the Iber, for someone going west, about 460 from Tarrakon, to the south, and 540 from Osca, which is to the north. Through these regions is the road from Tarrakon to the farthest Vasconians (on the Ocean), those around Pompaelo, and around the city of Oeaso,[8] which is on the Ocean. It runs 2,400 stadia, as far as the boundaries of Aquitania and Iberia. The [land of the] Iaccetanians is where Sertorius once made war against Pompeius, and later where Sextus the son of Pompeius fought against Caesar. Lying beyond Iaccetania, toward the north, are the Vasconian peoples, among whom there is a city of Pompaelo, that is, Pompeiopolis.

(11) Pyrene itself is well-wooded on the Iberian side with trees of every kind and evergreens, but the Keltic is bare, although the interior contains hollows that provide a good living. These are occupied mostly by the Cerretanians, of the Iberian race, who produce excellent ham, equal to those of the Curicians,[9] and providing them not a small revenue.

[C162]

(12) Crossing the Idubeda, immediately there is Keltiberia, which is large and uneven. Most of it is rough and washed by rivers, for the Anas is carried through it, as well as the Tagos, and a number of rivers one after another that go down to the western sea, and which have their sources in Keltiberia, including the Durius, which goes past Numantia and Serguntia, and the Baitis, whose source is on Orospeda, and which flows through Oretania into Baitike. The Beronians live in the region to the north of the Keltiberians, contiguous with the Cantabrian Coniscians (who also originated in the Keltic region) and whose city is Varia, located at the crossing of the Iber. They are allied with the Bardyetians, who today are called the Bardyllians. On the west are certain Asturians, Callaicians, and Vaccaeans, as well as the Vettonians and Carpetanians. To the south, in addition to the Oretanians, are all those who live on Orespeda, including the Bastetanians and Edetanians. On the east is the Idubeda.

(13) The Keltiberians are divided into four parts. Generally the most powerful are the Arvacians, who are toward the east and south, contiguous with the Carpetanians and the sources of the Tagos. Their most famous city is Numantia. They showed their ability in the Keltiberian War against the Romans, which lasted for 20 years, and in which they destroyed many armies along with their commanders. Finally the Numantians were besieged but endured to the end except for a few who surrendered the walls. The Lusonians live in the east, also contiguous with the sources of the Tagos. The Arvacians have the city of Segeda, and also Pallantia. Numantia is 800 stadia from Caesaraugusta, which, as we said [3.4.10], is situated on the Iber.

---

[8] The text reads "Oidasouna," which does not seem correct.
[9] The manuscripts have the meaningless "kautharikais."

The city of Segobriga is Keltiberian, as well as Bilbilis, around which Metellus and Sertorius made war.

Polybios [34.9.13], in discussing the peoples and places of the Vaccaeans and Keltiberians, includes Segesame and Intercatia with the other cities. Poseidonios [F271] says that Marcus Marcellus exacted a tribute of 600 talents from the Keltiberians, from which one may conjecture that there were many Keltiberians and that they were well-supplied with wealth, although they live in rather poor territory. But when Polybios [25.1.1] says that Tiberius Gracchus destroyed 300 cities, he [Poseidonios] ridicules him, saying that the man did this to gratify Gracchus, calling towers "cities," just as in triumphal processions. Perhaps what he says is not to be disbelieved, for both generals and historians are easily led into such a falsehood, adorning their deeds. Those who assert that there are more than a thousand cities existing in Iberia seem to me to be led into this by calling large villages "cities." The territory is not naturally capable of having many cities because of its poor land, remoteness, and wildness. Also, the life and activities of those [living there] – excluding those living on the coast of Our [Sea] – do not suggest this. They are fierce and live in villages – as do most of the Iberians – and the cities cannot easily tame them, as the majority of them live in the woods to the detriment of their neighbors.

[C163]

(14) After the Keltiberians, on the south are those who live on Mount Orospeda and the territory around the Sucro, who are the Sidetanians (as far as Karchedon), and the Bastetanians and Oretanians (almost as far as Malaka).

(15) The Iberians were once all peltasts, as has been said, having light armor because of their brigandage – as I said [3.3.6] about the Lusitanians – using the javelin, slingshot, and dagger. Mixed among the foot soldiers was a cavalry force, for the horses were taught to climb mountains and to kneel down easily upon order, if necessary.

Iberia has many deer and wild horses. There are marshes in some places, which are teeming with numerous birds, swans, and many bustards. The rivers have beavers, but their castoreum does not have the same strength as that from the Pontos, for the medicinal quality of that from the Pontos is unique, as is the case in many other matters. For example, as Poseidonios [F243] says, Cypriot copper is the only type that produces cadmian stone, chalkanthite, and spodium. Poseidonios says it is unique to Iberia that the crows are black and that the Keltiberian horses, which are somewhat dappled, change their color when transferred to Farther Iberia. They are similar to the Parthian, for they are faster and run better than the others.

(16) They have many roots that are useful for dyeing. Concerning the olive, vine, and fig, and similar plants, the Iberian coast of Our [Sea] thrives with them, and this continues into the interior. But the coast of the Exterior Ocean toward the north is without them because of the cold, as well as most of the remainder because of the negligence of the people and the inadequacy of their lifestyle. They are devoted to their own needs and their animalistic impulses, and are people living in a base way, unless one believes that they have an adequate life bathing in urine that has been aged in cisterns, and washing their teeth in it – themselves and their women – as the Cantabrians and their neighbors are said to do. The Iberians, in common with the Kelts, have both this and their beds on the ground.

[C164]

Some say that the Callaicians are without gods, but the Keltiberians and their northern neighbors <sacrifice>[10] to a certain nameless god on the nights of the full moon in front of their gates, and the entire household dances all night, and that the Vettonians, when they first came to the Roman camp, saw certain of the commanders walking up and down the streets for the sake of exercise, and considering them mad, led them on the path to their tents, as they should remain quietly seated or be fighting.

(17) One would consider the ornaments of some of the women to be barbaric in form, as Artemidoros [F23] reports. He says that they wear iron neckpieces that are curved like a beak over the top of the head, projecting far in front of their foreheads, and, if they wish, they draw their veil down over these beaks so that it spreads into a sunshade for their face, considering this an ornament. They also have a tympanium around them, going around the skull and binding the head as far as the ear lobe, but somewhat thrown back on the top and sides. Others strip away the hair on the front of their head so that it shines more than the forehead, and others place a small rod about a foot high on top and twist their hair around it and then wrap it with a black covering.

In addition to such true matters, many things have been seen and recorded about all the Iberian peoples in general and particularly those in the north, about their courage as well as their crudeness and their animalistic insensibility. For mothers killed their children before being captured during the Cantabrian War, and a small boy, whose parents and brothers had been taken captive, killed them all, having been ordered to do so by his father and obtaining a sword, and a woman did the same to her fellow captives. Someone who was called into the presence of drunken men threw himself onto a pyre. These characteristics are in common with the Keltic

[C165]

---

[10] "Sacrifice" is not in the extant text but seems an obvious emendation.

peoples as well as the Thracian and Skythian. Also common is their courage, both in women and men.

The women are farmers, and upon giving birth they minister to the men, instead of going to bed themselves. On occasion they give birth at their work, turning aside into some stream and bathing and swaddling [the child]. Poseidonios [F269] says that in Ligystike his host, Charmoleon, a Massaliote man, described that he had hired both men and women for digging, and that one of the women, having birthing pains, left her work for a nearby place, and after giving birth returned immediately to her work so that she would not lose her pay. He saw that she was working in pain, but did not know the reason until later. When he did learn it he sent her away, giving her the pay. She carried the infant to a little spring, washed and swaddled it with what she had, and took it safely home.

(18) This is also not unique to the Iberians: they carry two together on horseback, and in battle one of them fights on foot. Also not unique to them are the mice, from whom pestilential diseases often result. This happened to the Romans in Cantabria, so that they barely survived, although mouse-catchers were given a bounty proportionate to what they caught. In addition there was a scarcity of things, especially grain, and they could supply themselves from Aquitania only with difficulty because of the bad roads.

Regarding the insensibility of the Cantabrians, it is said that when some had been crucified, they sang the paean. Such customs would demonstrate a certain savageness, but others that they are not animalistic, although perhaps less than civilized. For example among the Cantabrians the men give dowries to the women, daughters are left inheritances, and brothers are given in marriage by women. It is a sort of rule by women, but not really civilized.

It is also an Iberian custom to have poison available, which is made from an herb that is much like celery, and painless, so as to have it ready for something unexpected. They also devote themselves to whomever they associate with, so that they would even die for them.

(19) Some assert that this territory has been divided into four parts, as we have noted [3.4.13], but others say five. Yet it is not possible to demonstrate [C166] this accurately because of the changes and disrepute of the region. In the well-known and reputable [regions] the population movements and divisions of the territory would be known, as well as the changes in names and other such matters. This is babbled about by many, most of all the Hellenes, who have become the most talkative of all. Those who are barbarian and spread out, and have little land and are scattered, have records that are neither reliable nor numerous, and the ignorance is far greater regarding

those who are far from the Hellenes. The Roman writers imitate the Hellenic, but not to a great extent, for what they say has merely been transferred from the Hellenes, without demonstrating much fondness of learning, so that whenever they [the Hellenes] have left something out, the filling in by the others is not extensive, since most of the distinguished names are Hellenic.

In former times everywhere beyond the Rhodanos and the isthmus bounded by the Galatic Gulfs was called Iberia, but today the boundary is placed at Pyrene, and they speak synonymously of Iberia and Ispania. Earlier, others called only that within the Iber <"Ispania">,[11] and others still earlier that they were Igletians, not occupying much territory, as Asklepiades the Myrleian [F8] says. The Romans called the entire region synonymously Iberia and Ispania, calling one part of it Farther and the other Nearer, dividing it in different ways according to the contemporary political situation.

(20) Today some of the provinces are assigned to the people and Senate and others to the leader of the Romans. Baitike belongs to the people, and a praetor is sent to it, who has a quaestor and a legate. Its boundary on the east has been placed around Castulo. The remainder is Caesar's. He sends to it two legates, one praetorian and one consular; the praetorian one has his own legate and administers justice to the Lusitanians lying alongside Baitike and extending as far as the Durius River and its mouths. At present they call this territory by that name [Lusitania]. The city of Augusta Emerita is also there. The remainder – this is most of Iberia – is under consular rule, having a notable army of about three legions and three legates. One of these, with two legates, guards all the frontier beyond the Durius to the north, which was formerly said to be Lusitanian, but today is called Callaician. Touching this are the northerly mountains, along with the Asturians and Cantabrians.   [C167]

The Melsos River flows through Asturia, and a little farther is the city of Noega, near which is an estuary of the Ocean that separates Asturia from the Cantabrians. Beyond, near the mountains as far as Pyrene, is the second of the legates with the other legion. The third oversees the interior and also protects those already called <*togati*>[12] because of their peaceful nature, having changed to civilized and Italian ways, putting on their *tebennas*. These are both Keltiberians and those who live nearby on both sides of the Iber, as far as

---

[11] "Ispania" has necessarily been added to the text; the profusion of toponyms in this section has meant a certain amount of confusion.

[12] "Togati" is not in the extant text, but is obvious both from what follows and 3.2.15.

the regions next to the sea. The commander himself spends the winters in the region on the sea, primarily in Karchedon and Tarrakon, administering justice, and in summer makes his rounds looking for what requires correction. There are also procurators of Caesar, of equestrian rank, who distribute to the soldiers the materiel for the maintenance of their lives.

Part 5: The islands

(1) Of the islands that lie off Iberia, the two Pityoussai and the two Gymnesiai (also called the Baliarides) lie off the coast that extends between Tarrakon and the Sucro (where Saguntum is situated). They are in the open sea, although the Pityoussai are inclined more to the west than the Gymnesiai. One of the former is called Ebusus, having a city of the same name and a circuit of 400 stadia with a length nearly equal. Ophioussa, lying nearby, is desolate and much smaller. The larger of the Gymnesiai has two cities, Palma and Polentia, one of which, Polentia, is in the east and the other in the west. The length of the island is a little less than 600 stadia and its width 200. Artemidoros [F25] says that the width and length are twice this. The smaller is about 70[13] stadia distant from Polentia. Its size happens to be much less but its fertility is by no means worse, for both are prosperous with good harbors, although rocky at the mouths so that those sailing in must be attentive.

Because of the quality of these regions, the inhabitants, as well as those from Ebusus, are peaceful. Yet because there were a certain few malefactors who joined in common with the pirates on the seas, all of them were slandered, and Metellus called Baliaricus, who founded their cities, went against them. But because of their quality, there are plots against them, although they are peaceful yet nevertheless said to be the best slingshot [C168] users. They have been especially practiced at this, it is said, since the Phoenicians acquired the islands, who are said to have been the first to clothe the people there in a broad-bordered chiton. They used to go out to battle ungirdled, with a goatskin around their arm, or a javelin that had been hardened by fire – occasionally with a small piece of iron on its tip – and three slings around the head, of black reeds (a type of black rope rush from which ropes are woven, as Philetas [F30] has in his *Hermeneia*: "the wretched and filthy chiton, and around the slender waist enclosed by a piece of black rush," as if someone were girdled with rope, hair or sinew):[14]

---

[13] The number is far too small; "370" is the most probable.
[14] The reference to Philetas is generally believed to be an interpolation.

one with long straps for long shots, one with short straps for short shots, and a medium one for the medium shots. They would practice from childhood with the slingshots and children would not be given bread unless they hit it with a slingshot. This is why Metellus, sailing toward the islands, stretched hides over the deck as protection against the slingshots. He brought 3,000 settlers there from the Romans in Iberia.

(2) In addition to the fruitfulness of the earth, no injurious animals are easily found there. They say that even the rabbits are not native, but are descended from a male and female someone brought from the mainland. From the beginning there were so many that they overturned houses and trees by burrowing under them, so that, as I have said [3.2.6], the people were forced to seek refuge with the Romans. Today, however, the hunting of the animal is easy to manage and does not allow it to cause damage, and in fact the owners use the fertility of the earth profitably. These are [the islands] on this side of what are called the Pillars of Herakles.

(3) Near them are two islets, one of which is called Hera's Island, and some call these the Pillars. Outside the Pillars is Gadeira, concerning which I have said [3.1.8] only that it is about 750 stadia distant from Kalpe and is located near the outlet of the Baitis, but there is more to be said about it. Here are the men who equip the most and largest ships, both for Our Sea and the External, although they do not live on a large island, nor do they inhabit much of the mainland or have an abundance of other islands. They live mostly on the sea, with a few living at home or passing time at Rome. In terms of population it does not seem to be less than any city outside of Rome. I have even heard that in one of the censuses from our time five   [C169] hundred men were estimated to be Gadeiran equestrians, an amount nowhere among the Italiotes except at Patavium. Yet they occupy an island not much more than a hundred stadia in length and in places only a stadion in width.

At first the city where they lived was exceedingly small but Balbus Gaditanus, who triumphed, founded another called Nea, and together they are Didyme ["The Twins"], although not more than twenty stadia in circumference and not crowded. Few remain at home because in general they are all at sea. Some live on the mainland, and especially on an islet lying nearby (because of its attractiveness), which they have made a rival city to Didyme, delighting in its location. Yet by comparison only a few live here or in the seaport that Balbus constructed for them on the opposite mainland. The city lies on the western part of the island, and next to it, at the extremity of the islet, is the Kronion. The Herakleion is opposite it, facing the east, where the island happens to touch the mainland most closely, leaving a strait of about a stadion. They say that the sanctuary is twelve miles distant from the city, making the number of miles equal to the Labors, yet it is greater and almost the length of the island. The length of the island is from west to east.

(4) Pherekydes [F18b] seems to say that Erytheia is Gadeira, where the myth-makers have the story of Geryon, but others that it is the island parallel to the city separated by a strait a stadion across, seeing its abundant pasturage, where the milk of the cattle grazing there does not produce whey. In making cheese they mix it with a large amount of water because of its fattiness. The animals choke in thirty days unless a vein is opened for blood. The pasturage on which they graze is dry, but it makes them exceedingly fat, and this is the reason that the myth of the cattle of Geryon was created[15]. . .the entire coast is populated in common.

(5) In telling such stories about the founding of Gadeira, the Gadeirans remember a certain oracle, which, they say, ordered the Tyrians to send a settlement to the Pillars of Herakles. Those who were sent in order to reconnoiter believed that when they came to the strait at Kalpe the capes that formed the strait were the end of the inhabited world and of the expedition of Herakles, and this was what the oracle had called the Pillars. [C170] They took possession of a certain place on this side of the narrows, which is now the city of the Exitanians, and sacrificed there, but the victims were not favorable so they went back. In time, those who were sent later went on about 1,500 stadia outside the strait to an island sacred to Herakles, lying near the Iberian city of Onoba, and believing that the Pillars were here they sacrificed to the god, but again the victims were not favorable and they went back home. On the third expedition those who came founded Gadeira, and they located the temple on the eastern part of the island but the city on the western.

For this reason some believe that the peaks at the strait are the Pillars, others that they are at Gadeira, and others that they lie farther outside of Gadeira. Some assume that the Pillars are Kalpe and Abilyx (the mountain opposite in Libya that Eratosthenes [F106] says is situated among the Metagonians, a nomadic people), and others that they are the islets near each [mountain], one of which is named Hera's Island. Artemidoros [F10] speaks of Hera's Island and her temple, and he mentions another, but neither Mount Abilyx or the Metagonian people. Some transfer the Planktai and Symplegades here, believing these to be the Pillars which Pindar [F256] calls the Gadeiran Gates, saying that they were the farthest

---

[15] There may be something missing here.

point reached by Herakles. And Dikaiarchos [F125], Eratosthenes [F106], Polybios [34.9.4], and most of the Hellenes believe that the Pillars are around the straits. But the Iberians and Libyans say that they are at Gadeira, for the region around the straits does not resemble pillars. Others say that they are believed to be the eight *peches* of bronze in the Herakleion at Gadeira on which the expenses of constructing the sanctuary are inscribed. Those who have ended their voyage and come to sacrifice to Herakles make it loudly known that this is the end of land and sea. Poseidonios [F246] believes this is the most plausible explanation and that the oracle and the many expeditions are a Phoenician falsehood.

Concerning the expeditions, who could assert whether or not they could be proved true, when neither possibility is abnormal? But to deny that the islets or mountains resemble pillars and to search for the properly named pillars, the limits of the inhabited world, and the expedition of Herakles is something reasonable. It was the custom in antiquity to place such boundary pillars: for example the Rhegians set up the column that [C171] is placed at the Strait, a sort of small tower, and lying opposite it is the so-called Tower of Peloros. The altars called those of the Philainians were at about the middle of the Syrtean land. And at the Corinthian Isthmos a column is recorded that was once placed there communally by the Ionians who acquired Attika along with Megaris (having been expelled from the Peloponnesos), and by those who held the Peloponnesos. It has written on the Megarian side "This is not the Peloponnesos but Ionia," and on the other "This is the Peloponnesos, not Ionia." Alexander established altars as the limits of his Indian expedition at the farthest places that he reached among the eastern Indians, imitating Herakles and Dionysos. This was the custom.

(6) It is reasonable that the places would receive the same name, especially when time has destroyed the established landmarks. The Altars of the Philainians no longer remain today, but the place has taken the name instead. They say that in Indike there are no standing pillars to be seen, either of Herakles or Dionysos, but of course certain places were mentioned or shown to the Makedonians who believed them to be pillars, and on which there were certain discovered signs of the record of those with either Dionysos or Herakles. Thus one would not believe that the first [arrivals] did not use handmade landmarks – certain altars, towers, or pillars – in these places, the farthest and most conspicuous places they came to. The most conspicuous are the straits, mountains, and islets situated there, and when these handmade memorials had disappeared their names were transferred to the places, regardless of whether one wishes to say that the islets or capes make the strait.

It is thus difficult to differentiate what the name should be attached to because the term "Pillars" is suitable to both. I say "suitable" because they are both located in places that clearly suggest the extremities, and because of this the strait is called a mouth (it and a number of others). Sailing in, the mouth is the beginning, and sailing out it is the end. Thus the islets in the mouth are remarkably easily defined, and it would not be foolish to compare them to pillars, and the mountains that lie in the strait are in the same way, as they have a certain prominence and visibility like columns [C172] or pillars. Thus Pindar [F256] would be speaking correctly about the Gadeiran Gates, if the Pillars were considered at the mouth, for mouths are like gates.

But Gadeira is not situated at such a place as to manifest an extremity, for it lies at about the middle of a long coast that creates a bay. Yet to consider that they [the Pillars of Herakles] are the pillars in the Herakleion there seems less reasonable. That the origin of the name did not come from merchants but from commanders has the power of persuasive opinion, just as is the case with the Indian pillars. Moreover, the inscription of which they speak does not reveal any establishment of a sanctuary but a total of expenses, and is a witness against the argument, because the Pillars of Herakles should be a memorial of his great achievements, not the expenditures of the Phoenicians.

(7) Polybios [34.9.5–7] says that there is a spring in the Herakleion at Gadeira that has a descent of only a few steps to drinkable water, and that it acts in reverse to the ebb and flow of the sea, ceasing at the time of the flood and filling at the ebb. The reason for this is that the air driven out of the depths of the earth to the surface, if covered by a flood with the approach of the sea, is cut off from its proper outlets and goes back into the interior, blocking up the passages of the spring and creating a lack of water. When it is made bare again, the passages of the spring are set free, so that it gushes forth easily. Artemidoros [F14] speaks against him and gives his own reason, recalling the opinion of Silanos [F9] the historian, but he does not seem to me to have said anything worth recording, since both he and Silanos are laymen in these matters.

Poseidonios [F217] notes that this account is false and says that there are two wells in the Herakleion and a third in the city. When drawing water from the smaller one it immediately fails, but upon leaving it for an interval the water fills up again. Water can be drawn from the larger one for the entire day (although it does diminish, as happens to all wells), yet it fills at night if water is no longer drawn. Since the ebb tide often happens at the time that it is completely full, the locals foolishly believed in the reverse activity. Thus the account that he relates has been believed, and we have accepted it among the paradoxes that are repeated over and over.   [C173]

I have heard that there are other wells, some in the gardens in front of the city and others within it, but because of the bad condition of the water it is common to have water cisterns in the city. Whether any of these wells demonstrates the conjecture of the reversal, I do not know. If it happens in this way, it must be admitted that the causes are a matter of difficulty. It is reasonable that it is as Polybios says, and also reasonable that some of the passages of the spring, moistened from the outside, become relaxed and thus give the water a sideways overflow, rather than forcing it up along the original channel into the spring. If, as Athenodoros [F6c] says, it happens that the flood and ebb tides are similar to inhalation and exhalation, then certain flowing waters that naturally have passages discharging out into the open (which we call the mouths of fountains or springs) and other passages are drawn together into the depths of the sea, and assist in raising it, so that at flood tide when the exhalation occurs, they abandon the proper channel and then withdraw again into their proper channel when it [the sea] makes its withdrawal.

(8) I do not know why Poseidonios – who otherwise represents the Phoenicians as clever – can charge them with foolishness here rather than sharpness. The day and night is measured by the revolution of the sun, at one time below the earth and at another visible above the earth. He says that the movement of the Ocean is controlled by the circuit, like that of the heavenly bodies, since it is daily, monthly, and yearly, in accordance with the moon. When it is above the horizon at the height of a zodiacal sign, the rise of the sea begins to be seen, visibly approaching the land until it [the moon] is in the meridian. But with the declining of the heavenly bodies, the sea withdraws little by little until the moon is at the height of a zodiacal sign above its setting. It then remains at the same place for some time, until the moon touches its point of setting, and even beyond, until it moves beneath the earth as much as a zodiacal sign below the horizon. Then [the sea] rises again until [the moon] is at the meridian below the earth, and then withdraws until the moon goes around to the east and is a zodiacal sign from the horizon. It then remains until [the moon] has risen to a zodiacal sign above the earth, and then [the sea] approaches again. This, he says, is   [C174] the daily circuit.

Regarding the monthly [movement], [he says] that the ebb and flood are largest around the conjunction, and then diminish up to when [the moon] is cut in half, increase again around the full moon, and diminish again until the waning half. From then until the conjunction it increases, and the increase is magnified because of the time and speed.

In the case of the annual [movement], he says that he learned about them from those in Gadeira, who said that at the time of the summer solstice the withdrawal and approach increase the most. He conjectures that they diminish from the solstice to the equinox, and then increase until the winter solstice. Then they diminish up to the spring equinoxes and then increase up to the summer solstice.

These periods occur each day and night, with the sea coming up and retreating twice during both these times together, in an order during both the day and night time. Yet how is it that the filling of the well happens often during the ebb tides but the lack of water is not so often? Or often but not the same number of times? Or the same number of times, for are the Gadeirans not capable of observing closely what happens every day, but observing closely the yearly period from something that happens only once a year? Yet that he [Poseidonios] believes them is clear from his additional conjecture, that the diminutions and the subsequent increases are from one solstice to another solstice, each returning back to the other. And the other matter is not reasonable either, that they closely observed things but did not see what happened, yet believed in what did not happen.

(9) He [Poseidonios, F218] says that Seleukos – the one from the Erythra Sea – speaks of a certain anomaly in this regularity according to the differences of the zodiacal signs. If the moon is in the equinoctial zodiacal sign, the properties are uniform, yet in the solstitial [sign] they are irregular in terms of both quantity and speed, but in each of the others it is in proportion to [the moon's] nearness. He [Poseidonios] says that he spent several days in the Herakleion at Gadeira at the summer solstice around the time of the full moon, yet was unable to see the annual differences. Nevertheless around the conjunction of that month he observed at Ilipa a major difference in the pushing back of the Baitis in relation to what had [C175] happened previously. Formerly it did not wet the banks halfway, yet at this time the water overflowed to the point that the soldiers drew water there (Ilipa is about 700 stadia from the sea). The plains at the sea were deeply covered by the flood tide as far as 30 stadia so that the islands were cut off. The height of the foundation – both of the temple in the Herakleion and of the mole that lies in front of the harbor of Gadeira – was, he says, measured as being covered only by 10 *pecheis* of water. If one were to double this (for the earlier increases), one thus could present the impression produced by the greatness of the flood tide in the plains.

This condition is recorded to be common along the entire circuit of the Ocean, but he says that the Iber is unique and peculiar, for it floods without rain or snow when the north wind is excessive, and the cause of this is the lake through which it flows, since it is driven from the lake by the winds.

(10) He [Poseidonios, F241] mentions a tree in Gadeira that has branches which bend to the ground, and whose leaves are often sword-shaped and eight *pecheis* long but four fingers wide. Around New Karchedon there is a tree whose thorns produce a bark from which most beautiful material is woven. I know of one in Egypt that is similar to that in Gadeira in regard to the bending down of the branches, but different as to the leaves and its lack of fruit, for he says [the one in Gadeira] has [fruit]. Thorn material is also woven in Kappadokia, but it is a low-growing herb that produces the thorn from which the bark occurs, not a tree. In regard to the tree at Gadeira, it is also recorded that milk flows from a branch that is broken, but the cutting of the root produces a red liquid. This is it about Gadeira.

(11) There are ten Kassiterides, lying near to each other in the open sea north of the Artabrian harbor. One of them is deserted, but the others are inhabited by people who wear black cloaks, and chitons that reach to their feet and are girded around their chests. They walk around with wands, like the tragic Avengers. They live off their herds and for the most part are nomadic. They have mines of tin and lead, and in exchange for this and hides they receive ceramics, salt, and bronze objects from traders. Formerly it was only the Phoenicians from Gadeira who engaged in this commerce, keeping the voyage secret from everyone. Once the Romans were closely following a certain ship captain so that they could learn about the trading stations, and the captain maliciously drove his ship willingly into [C176] the shallows and led his followers to the same destruction, and then saved himself on a piece of wreckage and received from the government the value of the cargo that he had lost. The Romans nevertheless often tried to learn all about the voyage. When Publius Crassus crossed over to them and learned that the metals were being mined from only a slight depth and that the men there were peaceful, he immediately made this known to those who wished to trade on this sea, although it is a greater one than that which separates Prettanike. This is it about Iberia and the islands lying off it.

BOOK 4

Transalpine Keltike

Part 1:   Introduction and Narbonitis

(1) Next is Keltike across the Alps. Its shape has already been outlined, as well as its size [2.5.28]. Now it must be discussed in detail.

Some have divided it into three, calling them the Aquitanians, Belgians, and Kelts. The Aquitanians are completely different, not only in language but in their physical characteristics, resembling more the Iberians than the Galatians. The remainder are Galatian in appearance, but not all of them speak the same language, and a few have slight alterations in their language. Moreover, their governments and lifestyle differ slightly. They say that the Aquitanians and Kelts are near Pyrene, but separated by Mount Kemmenon. It has already been said [2.5.28] that this Keltike is bounded on the west by the Pyrenaian Mountains, which touch the sea – both the Inner and Outer – on either side. On the east is the Rhenos, parallel to [C177] Pyrene. As for the parts on the north and south, the former are surrounded by the Ocean, beginning at the northern capes of Pyrene as far as the mouths of the Rhenos, and the opposite side by the sea around Massalia and Narbon, as well as by the Alps beginning at Ligystike as far as the sources of the Rhenos. Mount Kemmenon is drawn at right angles to Pyrene through the middle of the plains, ending at about the center near Lugdunum and extending for about 2,000 stadia.

They say that the Aquitanians are those living in the portions north of Pyrene, from Kemmenon as far as the Ocean, on this side of the Garounna River. The Kelts are in the portions reaching down on the other side to the sea around Massalia and Narbon, and also touching some of the Alpine mountains, and they say that the rest along the coast as far as the mouths of the Rhenos, as well as some of those living along the Rhenos and the Alps, are the Belgians. Thus the God Caesar said in his *Commentaries* [*Gallic War* 1.1].

Sebastos Caesar, however, divided it into four, putting the Kelts into the province of Narbonitis, and the Aquitanians as formerly, although adding to them fourteen peoples residing between the Garounna and the Liger Rivers. The remainder he divided into two, with one within the boundaries of Lugdunum as far as the upper portions of the Rhenos, and the other within the Belgians.

The geographer should speak of all the physical and ethnic divisions, whenever they are worthy of recording, but in regard to the various arrangements made by the commanders because of current political needs it is sufficient to speak of them in summary, conceding precision to others.

(2) The entire territory is watered by rivers, some of which come down from the Alps and others from the Kemmenon and Pyrene, some emptying into the Ocean, and others into Our Sea. The territories through which they pass are mostly plains, and hills with navigable channels. The streams are well placed in regard to each other so that there is transport from one sea to the other, for cargo is carried only a short and easy distance across the plains, but mostly by the rivers, some going upstream and some downstream. The Rhodanos has a certain advantage in this, for it has many tributaries through- out, as has been said, and it connects with Our Sea, which is better than with the Outer [Sea], crossing territory there that is the most favored. The same   [C178] fruits are produced throughout Narbonitis as in Italia. Olive planting and fig planting cease as one proceeds toward the north and Mount Kemmenon, but other things grow. The vine, as one proceeds, comes less easily to maturity. All the rest produces much grain, millet, acorns, and all kinds of livestock. None of it is fallow except where it is hindered by marshes or woods, but even these are heavily settled because of the large population, rather than their diligence. The women are both prolific and good nour- ishers, and the men fight rather than farm, although they are now forced to be farmers since they have laid down their weapons. We are speaking in a general way about all of exterior Keltike, but let me now speak about each of the divisions into fourths, discussing them in summary: first Narbonitis.

(3) Its shape is approximately a parallelogram, marked by Pyrene on the west and Kemmenon on the north. As for the remainder, the sea between Pyrene and Massalia marks the south, and the east partly by the Alps and by the distance taken in a straight line between the Alps and the foothills of Kemmenon that go down to the Rhodanos and make a right angle with the previously mentioned straight line from the Alps. In the southern portion, in addition to the previously mentioned figure, there is the subsequent coast where the Massalians and Sallyans are, as far as the Ligyans to the parts toward Italia and the Varus River. This, as I said previously,[1] is the boundary

---

[1] There is no previous reference to the Varus River in the extant text.

between Narbonitis and Italia. It is small in summer but in winter it widens to as much as seven stadia. From it, the coast stretches as far as the sanctuary of Pyrenaian Aphrodite, and this is the boundary between this province and the Iberian territory, although to some it is the location of the Memorial of Pompeius that marks the boundary between Iberia and Keltike.

From there to Narbon is 63 miles, and from there to Nemausos 88, and from Nemausos through Ugernum and Tarusco to the hot waters called Sextia (which are near Massalia) 53, and then to Antipolis and the Varus River 73, so that all together it is 277 miles. Some have recorded that it is 2,600 stadia from the Aphrodision to the Varus, and others add 200, for there is no agreement regarding the distances.

[C179] The other road – that through the Vocontians and the territory of Cottius – is the same as that from Nemausos as far as Ugernum and Tarusco, but from there to the Vocontian Mountains and the beginning of the climb into the Alps, through Drouentia and Caballio, is 63 miles, and then again to the other boundary of the Vocontians at the territory of Cottius and the village of Ebrodunum, 100 less 1 mile. Then it is the same through the villages of Brigantium and Ecsingomagus to the crossing of the Alps at Ocelum, the end of the land of Cottius. From Ecsingomagus it is said already to be Italia, and from here to Ocelum is 28 miles.

(4) Massalia is a Phokaian foundation, situated on a rocky place. Its harbor is at the foot of a theater-shaped rock that looks to the south. It – as well as the entire city – is well fortified, although it is considerable in size. The Ephesion is located on the headland, as well as the sanctuary of Delphinian Apollo. It is common to all Ionians but the Ephesion is a temple to the Ephesian Artemis.

It is said that when the Phokaians departed from their home, an oracle was delivered to them that they should use on their voyage a guide taken from Ephesian Artemis, and thus some of them went to Ephesos to ask how they could be provided with what the goddess had commanded. In a dream the goddess stood beside Aristarche, one of the most honored of women, and ordered her to go away with the Phokaians, taking a copy of the sacred image of the sanctuary. When this was done and the settlement was finally made, they established the sanctuary, and especially honored Aristarche by appointing her priestess. In their cities settled away from home, this goddess is honored everywhere first of all, and they preserve the representation of the xoanon, and observe all other customs as in the mother city.

(5) The Massaliotes are administered aristocratically, but with the best laws of all, having established a council of 600 men who hold the honor for life and are called Timouchoi. Fifteen are set over the council, to whom is

given the management of matters at hand. Moreover there are three who hold the major power and are placed over the fifteen, with one over them. One cannot be a Timouchos unless he has had children or is descended from three generations of citizens. These are Ionian laws that are made known to the people.

The land is planted with olives and is vine-growing, but is too poor for grain because of its ruggedness, so – trusting the sea rather than the land – they naturally preferred seamanship. Later, however, they prevailed through [C180] their bravery and acquired some of the surrounding plains, with the same strength by which they founded cities and their frontier strongholds in Iberia against the Iberians, where they established the ancestral rites of Ephesian Artemis, so that they would sacrifice in the Hellenic manner, as well as Rho<danousia² and> Agathe (against the barbarians living around the Rhodanos River), and Tauroention, Olbia, Antipolis, and Nikaia, founded against the Sallyan peoples and the Ligyans living in the Alps.

They also have shipsheds and armories. Formerly they had an abundance of ships, weapons, and the instruments useful for seamanship and sieges. Because of these they withstood the barbarians and also acquired the Romans as friends, and were often useful to them, receiving assistance in their own growth. Sextius, then, who put down the Sallyans, founded a city not far from Massalia which he named after himself and the hot waters (some of which, they say, have changed to cold) and settled a Roman garrison there. He also removed the barbarians from the coast that runs to Italia from Massalia, since the Massaliotes had been unable to restrain them completely. But he did not prevail in anything more than having the barbarians withdraw twelve stadia from the sea where there were good harbors, and eight in the rugged areas. What they abandoned he gave over to the Massaliotes.

Much booty has been set up in the city, which they took from defeating in naval battles those who repeatedly and unjustly disputed them at sea. Formerly they were particularly fortunate in all things, especially their friendship with the Romans, in regard to which one may detect many signs. Moreover, the xoanon of Artemis that is on the Aventine was made by the Romans in the same manner as that dedicated by the Massaliotes. When Pompeius made sedition against Caesar, they joined the defeated party and threw away most of their prosperity, although there are traces of

---

² The manuscripts merely have *rhoen*, which many editors delete entirely, although a toponym beginning in such a way would be appropriate for a settlement on the Rhodanos, and "Rhodanousia" is one possibility.

their ancient fervor remaining among the people, especially in the making of instruments and nautical devices. As the barbarians beyond them have been completely tamed, and since instead of war they have turned to government and farming due to the Roman predominance, it may be that [C181] they are no longer as earnest in the matters previously mentioned. This is clear from their present situation: all those of culture have turned to speaking and scholarship, so that the city – which recently was devoted to being a school for barbarians, preparing the Galatians to be so philhellenic that they could write contracts in Hellenic – at present has persuaded the most distinguished Romans who are fond of learning to go abroad there to study instead of Athens. Seeing them and pursuing peace, the Galatians are pleased to arrange their leisure to accommodate such a life, whether as individuals or as a community. At any rate, they welcomed teachers, hired either privately or (for the most part) in common, just as physicians.

This could be considered not the least proof of the simplicity of life and the moderation of the Massaliotes: their maximum dowry is 100 pieces of gold, with five for clothing and five for golden adornment. More is not allowed.

Caesar and the successive commanders acted moderately regarding the wrongs committed in the war and remembered the friendship, preserving the autonomy that the city had had from the beginning, so that it is not subject to the commander sent to the province, neither it nor its subjects. That is it about Massalia.

(6) The mountainous territory of the Sallyans slopes from the west more toward the north, and is removed little by little from the sea. The coast bends toward the west, but a short distance from the city of the Massaliotes – about a hundred stadia – one comes to a good-sized promontory near to some stone quarries, and it begins to curve inland and creates the Galatic Gulf as far as the Aphrodision, the headland of Pyrene. This is also called the Massaliote [Gulf]. It is a double gulf, for two gulfs are outlined within it, bounded by Mount Setion, which juts out, and additionally Blaskon Island, which is situated nearby. The larger of these gulfs, into which the mouth of the Rhodanos discharges, is again properly called the Galatic, and the smaller is from Narbon as far as Pyrene.

Narbon lies above the mouths of the Atax and Lake Narbonitis, and is the largest emporium in the region, although there is a city near the Rhodanos, Arelate, that is an emporium which is not small. These emporia are about the same distance from each other and from the previously mentioned capes, Narbon from the Aphrodision and Arelate from that of Massalia. [C182] Other rivers flow on either side of Narbon, some from the Kemmenon

Mountains, and others from Pyrene, and they have cities to which one sails up – not far – in small boats. From Pyrene come the Ruscino and the Ilibirris, each of which has a homonymous city. The Ruscino has a lake nearby and a small watery district slightly above the sea that is full of salt springs and dug mullets. Digging down two or three feet and putting a trident into the muddy water, one can pierce a fish of notable size that feeds in the mud just like eels. These, then, are the rivers that flow from Pyrene between Narbon and the Aphrodision. On the other side of Narbon are those carried to the sea from Kemmenon (from which the Atax [is carried]), the Orbis and Arauris. On the former is Baiterra, a safe city, near to Narbon, and on the other is Agathe, a Massaliote foundation.

(7) The previously mentioned coast has another marvel in addition to the dug mullets, which is even somewhat greater and will be discussed. Between Massalia and the outlets of the Rhodanos is a plain, a hundred stadia distant from the sea and the same in diameter, and circular in shape. It is called Stony from its characteristics. It is full of stones that can be held in the hand, having *agrostis* growing beneath them, which is exceptional pasturage for livestock. Standing in the middle of it are water, salt springs, and salt. All of the territory that lies beyond is toward the wind that is carried across the plain and rushes down, the Melamboreion, which is violent and shudder-ing. At any rate, they say that the stones are swept and rolled along, and that people are thrown from their vehicles and stripped of weapons and clothing by the force of the wind.

Aristotle [*On the Cosmos* 4 (396a); *Meteorologika* 2.8 (368b)] says that because of the earthquakes called the *brastai* the stones are thrown up into view and fall together in the hollows of the region. But Poseidonios [F229] says that since it was a lake, it solidified during the surging of waves, and because of this it was divided into many stones, just like pebbles in rivers and stones on the shore, and due to this similarity they are smooth and the same size. The causes have been described by both.

Both arguments are plausible. By necessity the stones that have come together have not changed from liquid to solid individually. Nor were they formed from the successive fracturing of great rocks. What was clearly hard to explain, Aischylos, observing carefully or taking it from elsewhere, removed into myth. At any rate, Prometheus, describing to Herakles the roads from the Kaukasos to the Hesperides, says: [C183]

> You will come to the fearless army of the Ligyans and not find fault with battle there, I clearly know, as you are courageous. Yet it is fated that your missiles will fail you, and you will not be able to choose any stone from the

earth, since the entire region is soft. Seeing you at a loss, Zeus will have pity on you and provide a cloud with snowy round stones that will shadow the ground. These you will throw and thus easily break through the Ligyan army. [*Prometheus Unbound*, F199]

Would it not have been better, says Poseidonios, for him [Zeus] to have thrown the stones at the Ligyans himself and to bury them all, rather than to make Herakles need so many stones? Yet he needed so many if the crowd was exceedingly numerous, and thus the writer of myth is more believable than the one who demolishes the myth. Moreover, by saying "it is fated" the poet did not allow conscious fault-finding. For example, in the treatises *On Foresight* and *That Which is Decreed* one could find so many instances in human affairs and natural happenings that one could say this one was much better than that one: for Egypt to be abundant in rain than for Aithiopia to water its land, or for Paris to have a shipwreck while sailing to Sparta rather than later seizing Helen and paying justice to those he had wronged, having caused the destruction of the Hellenes and barbarians, which Euripides attributed to Zeus: "Zeus the father, wishing evil for the Trojans, and misery for the Hellenes, decided on this" [F1082].

(8) Concerning the mouths of the Rhodanos, Polybios [34.10.5] finds fault with Timaios [F70], saying that there are not five mouths but two mouths. Artemidoros [F33] says three. Later Marius, seeing that the mouths had become blind because of siltation and that they were difficult to enter, cut a new channel, admitting most of the river into it, and gave it to the Massaliotes as recognition of their valor in the war against the Ambronians and Toÿgenians. The wealth carried off from this was great, for they exacted a toll both from those sailing up and those sailing down. Nevertheless it remains difficult to sail into because of the current and siltation as well as [C184] the lowness of the land, and thus in bad weather it cannot be seen even when near by. Because of this the Massaliotes erected signal towers, thus appropriating the land in every way. They also established a sanctuary of Ephesian Artemis there, taking a site that the mouths of the river had made into an island.

Lying above the mouths of the Rhodanos is a lagoon called the Mouth Marsh, which has a large quantity of oysters and is also abundant in fish. Some include it among the mouths of the Rhodanos, especially those who say that there are seven mouths, although in neither case are they correct, for there is an intervening mountain that separates the lake from the river. This is the approximate character and extent of the coast from Pyrene to Massalia.

(9) Toward the Varus River and the Ligyans there are the Massaliote cities of Tauroention, Olbia, Antipolis, Nikaia, and the naval station of Caesar Sebastos that is called Forum Julium, which is situated between Olbia and Antipolis, 600 stadia distant from Massalia. The Varus is between Antipolis and Nikaia, about 20 stadia from the latter and 60 from the former, so that according to the presently established boundary Nikaia belongs to Italia, although it is Massaliote, for the Massaliotes founded these places as frontier fortifications against the barbarians who lived beyond, wishing to keep the sea free, since the latter controlled the land. It is mountainous and steep, although there remains next to Massalia some level land of a moderate width, but going toward the east it is completely squeezed out toward the sea, hardly allowing the road to be passable. The Sallyans possess the first [region], and the Ligyans who touch Italia the last, who will be discussed later [4.6.1]. At present this alone must be added, that Antipolis is located in the portion that belongs to Narbonitis, and Nikaia in the Italian, although Nikaia remains under the Massaliotes and is within the province, but Antipolis is enumerated among the Italiotes. There was a judgement against the Massaliotes and thus they have been freed from their orders.

(10) Lying off these narrows, beginning from Massalia, are the Stoichades Islands, three of which are notable and two small. They are farmed by the Massaliotes, who, in antiquity, had a fort there (as they are abundant in harbors), situated to defend against the approach of pirate vessels. After the Stoichades are Planasia and Leron, which are inhabited. On Leron there also [C185] is the heroon of Leron. It lies off Antipolis. In addition there are islets not worth mentioning, some off Massalia itself and others off the previously mentioned shore.

In regard to the harbors, the one at the naval station is notable, as well as that of the Massaliotes, but the others are only moderate, among which is that called Oxybios Harbor, named after the Oxybian Ligyans. This is what we can say about the coast.

(11) The geography of the country lying inland is generally defined by the mountains that lie around it as well as the rivers, especially the Rhodanos, which is the largest and the one having the best upstream sailing, since it is filled by many affluents. But these must be discussed in order.

Beginning from Massalia and going toward the territory between the Alps and the Rhodanos, as far as the Drouentia River, the inhabitants for 500 stadia are the Sallyans. Crossing by ferry to the city of Caballio, the entire country beyond as far as the junction of the Isar with the Rhodanos is that of the Cavarians. This is about where Kemmenon touches the Rhodanos. The length from the Drouentia to here is 700 stadia. The

Sallyans live in their own [territory] in the plains and the mountains lying above, and above the Cavarians are the Vocontians, Tricorians, Iconians, and the Medullians.

Between the Drouentia and the Isar other rivers flow from the Alps into the Rhodanos. Two of these flow around[3]. . .a city of the Cavarians, and in a common stream they join the Rhodanos. A third is the Sulga, which mixes with the Rhodanos near Vindalum, where Gnaeus Domitius Ahenobarbus routed many myriads of Kelts in a great battle. In between are the cities of Avenio, Arausio, and Aeria, which, Artemidoros [F32] says, is actually "aerial" because it is located on a great height. All of it is a plain and good pasturage, except that from Aeria to Avenio, which has narrow and wooded passes. But where the Isar River, the Rhodanos, and Mount Kemmenon come together, Quintus Fabius Maximus Aemilianus, with fewer than 30,000 in all, cut down 200,000 Kelts, and set up a monument there in white stone as well as two temples, one to Ares and the other to Herakles.

From the Isar to Vienna, the metropolis of the Allobrigians, situated on
[C186] the Rhodanos, is 320 stadia. Near to Vienna, and beyond it, is Lugdunum, where the Arar and Rhodanos mingle with one another. It is about 200 stadia by foot through the Allobrigians, but slightly more sailing up the river. Formerly the Allobrigians made frequent war with many myriads, but now they farm the plains and the hollows of the Alps, and they live in villages, except the most notable of them are in Vienna, which was formerly a village – although nevertheless called the metropolis of the people – yet has developed into a city. It is situated on the Rhodanos, which runs from the Alps with great violence, since, although it flows out from Lemenna Lake, its stream is clearly visible for many stadia. Coming down into the plains of the country of the Allobrigians and Segosiavians, it meets the Arar at Lugdunum, the city of the Segosiavians. The Arar also flows from the Alps, dividing the Sequanians from the Aeduans, the Lin<gonians, and the Tri>kasians.[4] Later it takes up the Dubis – which is navigable and comes from the same mountains – and prevails through its name, and consisting of both, it mixes as the Arar with the Rhodanos. Similarly the Rhodanos prevails and runs to Vienna, and makes the rest of its course as far as the sea. At first, then, the three rivers happen to run toward the north, and then toward the west, but as soon as they have come together into one stream it takes another turn and the stream runs to the south as far as its mouths,

[3] The toponym, if Strabo included it, is missing from the text.
[4] The text has "Linkasians," but the emendation is generally accepted.

receiving the other rivers. This is it for what is between the Alps and Rhodanos.

(12) The other side of the river is mostly occupied by the Volcians who are called the Arecomicians. Narbon is said to be their seaport, although it would be more proper to say that it is the one for all of Keltike, for it has greatly excelled in the number who use it as an emporium. The Volcians border on the Rhodanos, and the Sallyans stretch parallel to them on the opposite bank, as well as the Cavarians. The name of the Cavarians prevails and already all the barbarians there are called by that name. Yet they are no longer barbarians, but have mostly been transferred into the form of Romans, in their language and lifestyle, and some in their government. There are other undistinguished and minor peoples alongside the Arecomicians as far as Pyrene.

The metropolis of the Arecomicians is Nemausos, which is much less than Narbon in terms of its foreign crowds and commerce, but surpasses it in its citizenry. It has twenty-four different villages of the same ethnicity subject to it, which are abundant in men and contribute to expenses. It also has what is called the "Latium," so that those who have been considered [C187] worthy to be aedile and quaestor at Nemausos are Roman [citizens]. Because of this, these people are not subject to the order of the commanders sent from Rome.

The city is situated on the road from Iberia to Italia, which is easily travelled in summer, but muddy and flooded in winter and spring. Some of the streams are crossed by ferries and others by bridges, some made of wood and others of stone. But it is the torrents of water that cause difficulty, since after the melting of the snow they come down from the Alps even into summer. This previously mentioned road runs straight into the Alps, as we have said [4.1.3], with a shortcut through the Vocontians. The route through the Massaliote and Ligystikian coast is longer, although the passes into Italia are easier, since the mountains are already lower there. Nemausos is about 100 stadia distant from the Rhodanos (from the little town of Tarusco across the river), and 720 from Narbon.

Adjoining Mount Kemmenon and encompassing its southern side as far as its summits, live those of the Volcians called the Tektosagians, as well as others. We will talk about them and others later.

(13) Those called the Tektosagians come near to Pyrene and touch small areas on the north side of the Kemmenon, and the land that they occupy is rich in gold. It seems that they once were so powerful and abundant in men that when they fell into sedition they drove a large number of their own from home, and some from other peoples made common cause with them.

Among these are those who occupy [the part of] Phrygia that has a common boundary with Kappadokia and Paphlagonia. As proof of this we have those who are still called the Tektosagians. There are three ethnic groups, one of which – around the city of Ankyra – is called the Tektosagians, and the remaining two are the Trokmians and the Tolistobogians. In regard to these – whose emigration from Keltike is indicated by their kinship with the Tektosagians – we cannot determine from what territory they originated, for we have not heard of any Trokmians or Tolistobogians living today either beyond the Alps or on this side of them. But it is likely that nothing is left of them because they departed completely, as has happened with many others. Some say that the other Brennos – the one who attacked Delphi – was Prausian, but we cannot say in what territory the Prausians [C188] formerly lived.

And it is said that the Tektosagians shared in the Delphic expedition, and the treasure that was found in the city of Tolossa by the Roman general Caepio was said to be a part of the goods from there. The people had remitted additional amounts from their personal resources as a dedication and propitiation to the god. Having appropriated them, Caepio ended his life in misfortune, for he was thrown out of his homeland as a temple robber and left behind as his successors only female children, who became prostitutes (as Timagenes [F11] has said), and died in disgrace. But the account of Poseidonios [F273] is more believable, as he says that the amount of goods found in Tolossa was about 15,000 talents – part of it stored in sacred enclosures and part in sacred lakes – and it was unworked, merely gold and silver, but the sanctuary at Delphi at that time was already lacking in such things, as it had been robbed by the Phokians at the time of the Sacred War. But even if something were left, it was distributed among many, and it is not probable that they reached home safely, since after their departure from Delphi they were in a wretched situation and were scattered into groups because of their disagreements. But, as he and many others have said, the country was rich in gold and the people were religious and not extravagant in their lifestyle, so there were treasures in many places. The lakes, especially, provided inviolability, as they put heavy masses of gold and silver down into them. The Romans, then, when they conquered the territory, sold the lakes as state property, and many who purchased them found millstones of hammered silver. The sanctuary in Tolossa was sacred, greatly revered by those living in the area, and because of this its treasures were excessive and dedicated by many, and no one would dare to appropriate them.

(14) Tolossa is located on the narrowest part of the isthmus that separates the Ocean from the sea at Narbon, which Poseidonios [F248] says is less

than 3,000 stadia [across]. But it is worthwhile above everything to indicate – as we have before [4.1.2] – the harmony of this territory in regard both to the rivers and the sea (both the Outer and the Inner). One might find upon some consideration that this is not the least part of the advantages of this region, for I say that the necessities of life are easily interchanged by everyone with everyone, and the benefits that result are common [to all], [C189] especially at this time, when they pursue leisure instead of their weapons, and work the land carefully, building a civilized lifestyle. Thus in such matters one might support that there is confirmation for the working of foresight, since the places are not ordered in a casual way but as if by a certain calculation.

In particular, the Rhodanos can be sailed inland a long distance, and a great part of the territory is accessible to a large amount of goods because of the navigable rivers that receive much of the cargo. It is then received by the Arar and the Dubis (which empties into it), and then it goes by land as far as the Sequana River. From there it goes down to the Ocean and the Lexovians and Caletians, from whom it is less than a day's journey to Prettanike. Since the Rhodanos is swift and difficult to sail up, some of the goods rather go from here by land in covered wagons – what is carried to the Arvernians and the Liger River – although the Rhodanos in places is close to them. The route is level and not long, around 800 stadia, which is an encouragement not to make the sail upstream, since it is easier by land. From there the Liger, which flows from the Kemmenon to the Ocean, naturally receives them. Also, from Narbon one sails inland a short distance on the Atax, and then a longer amount by land to the Garouna River, which is about 800 or 700 stadia. The Garouna also flows to the Ocean.

This, then, is what I have to say about those inhabiting the province of Narbonitis, which was formerly named Keltai. It was from there, I believe, that the Galatians as a whole were called the Kelts by the Hellenes, because of their reputation, but it may also be due to the Massaliotes, because of their proximity.

Part 2: Aquitania

(1) Next there must be a discussion of the Aquitanians and those included within their boundaries, the fourteen Galatic peoples who live between the Garouna and the Liger, some of whom reach the riverine regions of the Rhodanos and the plains of Narbonitis. Speaking simply, the Aquitanians are different from the Galatic race in the physique of their bodies and their language, and are more like the Iberians.

They are bounded by the Garouna River, living beween it and Pyrene. There are more than twenty peoples of the Aquitanians, small and undistinguished, and mostly along the Ocean, with others in the interior and [C190] on the heights of the Kemmenon Mountains, as far as the Tektosagians. Since this was only a small portion, they added to it that between the Garouna and Liger. These rivers are approximately parallel to Pyrene and create with that region two parallelograms, bounded on the other sides by the Ocean and Kemmenon Mountains. The voyage on either of the rivers is about two thousand stadia. The Garouna, increased by three rivers, empties into the region between the Biturigians who are called the Oïskians and the Santonians, both Galatic peoples. The Biturigians are the only peoples situated among the Aquitanians who are of another race and who do not make contributions to them. They have an emporium, Burdigala, on the edge of a certain lagoon that is created by the outlets of the river.

The Liger, however, empties between the Pictonians and Namnetians. Formerly there was an emporium called Korbilon on this river, about which Polybios [34.10.6–7] has said – remembering the mythic stories of Pytheas [T13] – that the Massaliotes who were associated with Scipio, when questioned by Scipio about Prettanike, were unable to say anything worth recording, nor were any of the Narbonians or Korbilonians, although these were the most important cities in that region. Pytheas was bold enough to tell these falsehoods. The city of the Santonians, however, is Mediolanum.

Most of the ocean coast of Aquitania is sandy and poor, growing millet, but it is somewhat unproductive for other crops. The gulf there makes the isthmus that is within the coast of Narbonitis, and is called the Galatic Gulf, homonymous with the other one. The gulf is held by the Tarbellians, among whom the gold mines are the most important of all. In holes excavated to only a slight depth they find flat lumps of gold as large as can be held in the hand and which need only a little refining. The remainder is dust and nuggets that also do not need much working. The interior and mountainous area has better land, next to Pyrene, that of the Convenae – "the assembled" – in which are both the city of Lugdunum and the hot springs of the Onesians, which are most beautiful and have most pleasant water. The territory of the Auscians is also good.

(2) The peoples between the Garouna and the Liger that belong to the Aquitanians are the Elvians, who begin at the Rhodanos, and after them the Vellavians (who were once included within the boundaries of the Arvernians but who are now ranked as autonomous), then the Arvernians, Lemovicians, and Petrocorians. Next to these are the Nitiobrigians, Cadurcians, and the Biturigians called the Cubians. Next to the Ocean are

the Santonians and Pictonians, the former living along the Garouna, as we
have said, and the latter along the Liger. The Rutenians and Gabalians
are near to Narbonitis. Among the Petrocorians are nice iron works (as well
as among the Cubian Biturigians), among the Cadurcians linen works, and
among the Rutenians silver mines. The Gabalians also have silver mines. The
Romans have given the "Latium" to some of the Aquitanians, as with the
Auscians and the Convenae.

(3) The Arvernians are situated on the Liger, and their metropolis is
Nemossos, lying on the river. It flows past Cenabum (which is the emporium of the Carnutians at about the middle of the voyage and is jointly
populated), and then empties into the Ocean. The Arvernians demonstrate
a great proof of their former power in that they often fought against the
Romans, once with 200,000 men and again with double that, as when they
contended under Vercingetorix against Caesar the God, and previously,
with 200,000 against Maximus Aemilianus, and in the same way against
Domitius Ahenobarbus. The fight against Caesar was around Gergovia, a city
of the Arvernians that is located on a high mountain, where Vercingetorix
was from, and also near Alesia, a Mandubian city, who are a people with the
same borders with the Arvernians. This is also situated on a high hill and
is surrounded by mountains and two rivers. Here their commander was
captured and the war came to an end. That against Maximus Aemilianus was
at the junction of the Isar and Rhodanos, where the Kemmenon comes near
to the Rhodanos, and that against Domitius still lower down, at the junction
of the Sulga and the Rhodanos. The Arvernians had extended their power
as far as Narbon and the boundaries of Massaliotis, and ruled peoples as far
as Pyrene and as far as the Ocean and the Rhenos. Luerius, the father of the
Bituitus who made war against Maximus and Domitius, is said to have
been so rich and to have lived in such luxury that at one time – making a
display of abundance to his friends – he rode in a wagon through the
plain, scattering silver and gold coins here and there for those following
him to pick up.

Part 3: Interior Keltike

(1) After the Aquitanian portion and Narbonitis is [the territory] extending
as far as the whole Rhenos, the entirety extending from the Liger River
and the Rhodanos at where the Rhodanos, having come down from its
source, touches Lugdunum. The upper portions of this territory, that next
to the sources of the rivers (the Rhenos and Rhodanos), as far as the middle
of the plains, have been assigned to Lugdunum, and the remaining parts,

including those along the Ocean, are assigned to another portion, granted specifically to the Belgians. We will point out each in a more general way.

[C192]   (2) Lugdunum itself, founded under a hill at the junction of the Arar River and the Rhodanos, is occupied by the Romans. It is the most populous of all except for Narbon, for it is used as an emporium and the Roman governors mint money in gold and silver there. The sanctuary dedicated by all the Galatians in common to Caesar Sebastos is located in front of the city at the junction of the rivers. There is a notable altar in it, on which is written the tribes, sixty in number, and images of each, as well as another large altar.

The city presides over the people of the Segosiavians, who are situated between the Rhodanos and the Dubis. The peoples who stretch toward the Rhenos are bounded by the Dubis and the Arar. These rivers, as I said before [4.1.11], flow down from the Alps and then come together into one stream and flow down into the Rhodanos. There is another that also has its source in the Alps, named the Sequana, flowing to the Ocean, parallel to the Rhenos and through the homonymous peoples who adjoin the Rhenos on their east and the Arar on their opposite side, from where the best salted pork is brought down to Rome. Between the Dubis and the Arar live the Aeduan people, having the city of Kabyllinon on the Arar and the fortress of Bibrax. The Aeduans were named as kindred by the Romans and were the first in that region to apply for friendship and alliance.

Across the Arar live the Sequanians, who for a long time were in disagreement with the Romans and the Aeduans, in the case of the former because they often attached themselves to the Germans when the latter made their attacks on Italy, and showed that their power was not ordinary, as they made them stronger when common with them and weaker when they kept away. They were hostile to the latter for the same reason, intensified by strife around the river that separated them and the Aeduans, as each people considered the Arar their own and that the tolls from those passing through belonged to them. But now everything is under the Romans.

(3) The first of all those living on the Rhenos are the Elvettians, among whom are the sources of the river, on Mount Adoula. It is part of the Alps, and from them, on the opposite side, flows the Adoua, toward Keltike on this side, and it fills Lake Larios on which the city of Comum was founded, and from there it joins the Padus, about which we will speak later [4.6.5].

[C193]   The Rhenos spreads into great marshes and a great lake that is touched by the Rhaitians and Vindolicians, certain Alpine [peoples] who also live beyond the Alps. Asinius [F7] says that the length of the river is six thousand stadia, but it is not, for it would be only a little more than half that in a straight line, and adding a thousand would be sufficient for the bending. It is swift, and thus difficult to bridge, and runs in a level fashion for the rest of the way across the plains after coming down from the mountains. How, then, would it remain swift and violent, if we were to add to its level quality many great bends? He also says that it has two mouths, and complains about those who say that there are more. It and the Sequana circle some territory in their bends, but not that much.

Both flow to the north from the southern portions, and in front of them is Prettanike, which is so near to the Rhenos that Kantion, the eastern cape of the island, is visible, and it is slightly farther from the Sequana. Caesar the God established his shipyard here when he sailed to Prettanike. The voyage on the Sequana by those receiving cargo from the Arar is slightly longer than that on the Liger and Garouna. From Lugdunum to the Sequana is a thousand stadia, and it is less than double this from the entrance to the Rhodanos as far as Lugdunum.

They say that the Elvettians, although rich in gold, nevertheless turned to robbery when they saw the wealth of the Kimbrians, but on campaign two of their tribes – they had three – were eliminated. But there were still many descendants of those remaining, as was made clear in the war against Caesar the God, in which around 400,000 people were killed. The rest were allowed to escape – about 8,000 were let go – so that the territory would not be deserted and given over to the Germans, who bordered on them.

(4) After the Elvettians, the Sequanians and Mediomatrikians live along the Rhenos, among whom are situated the Tribokchians, a German people who crossed over from their home. Among the Sequanians is Mount Iourasios, the boundary between the Elvettians and the Sequanians. Toward the west, beyond the Elvettians and Sequanians, live the Aeduans and Lingonians, and beyond the Mediomatrikians are the Leukians and part of the Lingonians.

Those peoples between the Liger and Sequana Rivers, across the Rhodanos and the Arar, are on the other side (toward the north) of the Allobrigians and those around Lugdunum. The most conspicuous of them are the Arvernians and the Carnutians, through both of whom the Liger is carried as it runs out to the Ocean. The crossing to Prettanike from the rivers of Keltike is 320 stadia: putting to sea at the evening ebb tide, one would land on the island at about the eighth hour of the following day.   [C194]

After the Mediomatrikians and the Tribokchians, the Treverians live along the Rhenos, near whom the bridge was constructed by the Roman commanders who are now making war against the Germans. The Ubians lived on the far side of this region, but they were willingly transferred by

Agrippa to the near side of the Rhenos. The Nervians, also a German peoples, are next to the Treverians. Last are the Menapians, who live on both sides of the river near its mouths, in marshes and forests that are not tall but dense and thorny. The Sougambrians, who are German, are situated opposite them. Lying beyond this entire riverine region are those Germans called the Soebians, surpassing all in power and number, and those driven out have taken refuge on this side of the Rhenos today.[5] Others hold power in different places and succeed to the sparks of war, but the foremost are always put down.

(5) The Senonians and Remians live to the west of the Treverians and Nervians, and farther on are the Atrebatians and Ebouronians. Next to the Menapians, on the sea, are the Morinians, Bellovacians, Ambianians, Souessionians, and Caletians, as far as the outlet of the Sequana River. [The territory of] the Morinians, Atrebatians, and Ebouronians resembles that of the Menapians. Much of it is a forest of trees that are not tall, although not as extensive as writers have said (around four thousand stadia), called the Ardouenna. When they made hostile attacks they would weave together twigs of brush, which were thorny, and thus block any advance. They would also hide behind palisades. They and their households would slink away into the depths, for they had islets in the marshes, a refuge that would be safe during the rains but they would easily be captured in dry periods. Today all those on this side of the Rhenos are at peace and are obedient to the Romans.

The Parisians are around the Sequana River – having an island in the river and a city, Loukotokia – as do the Meldians and the Lexovians, who are by the Ocean. The most notable people in this region are the Remians, and their metropolis is Dourikortora, which is most heavily populated and receives the Roman governors.

Part 4:   The northwestern coast, and ethnography

(1) After these peoples who have been mentioned, the rest of the Belgian people are on the Ocean, among whom are the Venetians who fought the sea battle against Caesar, for they were ready to hinder his voyage to Prettanike, since they were using it as an emporium. He easily beat them [C195] in a sea battle without using ramming (for their timbers were thick), but when they came against him on the wind, the Romans, because of the force of the winds, brought down their sails with halberds, since they were made

---

[5] Many have suggested a lacuna at this point, with "today" belonging to the following sentence.

of leather and were stretched by chains instead of ropes. Because of the ebb tides, they have broad-bottomed boats with high sterns and high prows and made of oak wood, of which they have an abundance. Thus they do not bring the joints of the planks together but leave cracks that they caulk with moss, so that the wood will not lack moisture and dry out when the ship is hauled up on land, as the moss is somewhat moist by nature but the oak is dry and without fat.

I think these are the Venetians who settled on the Adria, for almost all the Kelts who are in Italia migrated from the lands across the Alps, just like the Boians and Senonians, although because of having the same name they are called Paphlagonians. I do not speak with confidence, but likelihood is sufficient in such things.

The Osismians are those whom Pytheas [T14] calls the Ostimnians,[6] living on a promontory that projects very far into the Ocean, although not as far as he and those who have trusted him say. Some of the peoples who are between the Sequana and Liger border on the Sequanians, others on the Arvernians.

(2) The entire race that is now called Gallic or Galatic is intense about war, and high-spirited and quick to fight, but otherwise simple and not malignant. Because of this, when roused to fight they come together in a body for the struggle, openly and without consideration, so that those who wish to defeat them by stratagem can do so easily. If one is willing to provoke them by whatever means on some pretext, they will readily go into danger, having nothing to assist them except strength and courage. But if persuaded, they easily give in to usefulness, so that they engage in education and language. Their strength comes from the size of their bodies and from their numbers. Because of their simplicity and bluntness, they easily come together in a multitude, always having a common anger with their neighbors whom they think have been wronged. At present they are all at peace, since they have been enslaved and live according to the dictates of the Romans who captured them, but we are taking the account from ancient times, as well as the customs that still remain today among the Germans. [C196] They are similar both in nature and government, as well as kindred to one another, and they live in a territory with a common boundary divided by the Rhenos River, and which is similar in most ways. Germania is farther north, but one would compare the southern portions with the southern and the northern with the northern.

---

[6] The manuscripts have only "*timious*"; suggestions include Ostimnians, Ostidaians, and Ostimians.

It is because of this that their migrations occur easily, for they move in a herd with their entire army, or rather remove themselves with their entire household when cast out by those stronger than themselves. The Romans subdued them more easily than they did the Iberians, for the war with the latter began earlier and stopped later, yet meanwhile they defeated all those between the Rhenos and the Pyrenaian Mountains. The former would attack in a body and in large numbers, and thus were defeated in a body, but the latter would store things up and divide the battle, with different people at different times fighting as brigands in different places. They are all fighters by nature and are better as cavalry than infantry: the best Roman cavalry comes from them. Those more toward the north and along the Ocean are always more warlike.

(3) They say that the Belgians are the bravest of these, and they are divided into fifteen peoples living along the Ocean between the Rhenos and the Liger, and thus were the only ones who could hold out against the German invasion by the Kimbrians and Teutonians. They say that the Bellovacians are the bravest of the Belgians, and after them the Souessionians. This is an indicator of their large population: those who have examined this carefully say that formerly there were up to 300,000 Belgians able to bear arms. The number of the Elvettians, Arvernians, and their allies has already been told, from which the size of the population can be shown, and also, as I have said [4.1.2], the excellence of the women in regard to the bearing and nursing of their children.

They wear the *sagos*, let their hair grow, and use tight trousers. Instead of the chiton they wear divided sleeves as far as the genitals and buttocks. Their wool, from which they weave their shaggy *sagoi*, is rough and thick, and called *laenae*. Yet the Romans, even in the most northerly regions, cover their flocks in skins and raise wool that is sufficiently fine. Their weaponry is commensurate with the size of their bodies: a long knife hangs along the right side, and there is a large oblong shield, a number of spears, and the *madaris*, a type of lance. Some of them use bows and slings. There is also a wooden instrument similar to a *grosphos*, thrown by hand rather than by a thong and hitting from farther away than an arrow, used especially for hunting birds.

[C197]

Even now most of them sleep on the ground, and eat seated on beds of straw. They have large amounts of sustenance, including all kinds of meat, but especially pork, both fresh and salted. The boars live out of doors, and are notable in their size, strength, and swiftness. Indeed, it is dangerous for one unaccustomed to them to approach, as with a wolf. The houses are made from timber and wicker, and are large and dome-shaped, with much thatch thrown on them. They have such a large number of sheep and pigsties that they abundantly supply the *sagoi* and salt meat not only for Rome but for most parts of Italia.

Most of their governments were aristocratic, although in antiquity they chose one leader each year, and similarly in war one commander was appointed by the masses. Now they mostly pay attention to the dictates of the Romans. There is a peculiar thing that occurs in their assemblies: if some one raises a noise against the speaker and interrupts him, an official approaches with sword drawn and orders him with a threat to be silent. If he does not stop, it is done a second and third time, and finally as much of his *sagos* is removed as to make the remainder useless. Concerning men and women, they exchange tasks with one another in a manner contrary to us, something that they have in common with other barbarians.

(4) Among all of them there are only three groups who are given particular honors, the Bards, Vates, and Druids. The Bards are singers and poets, the Vates overseers of sacred rites and investigators of nature, and the Druids, in addition to being investigators of nature, practice a love of ethical wisdom. They are considered the most just of people, and because of this they are entrusted with both private and public decisions, so that in former times they would arbitrate matters of war and stop those about to line up for battle, and cases of murder would especially be turned over to them for justice. When these were productive, they believed that the land would also be productive. They and others say that souls and the universe are eternal, although at some time fire and water will prevail.

(5) In addition to their simplicity and high-spirited nature, much foolishness and boastfulness are present, as well as a love of ornamentation. They wear gold-twisted metal around their necks and bracelets around their arms and wrists, and their dignitaries have dyed clothing sprinkled with gold. Because of their lightness of character they are unendurable when victorious but appear panic-stricken when beaten. In addition to their foolishness, there is the barbarity and alienness that is an attribute of most peoples toward the north, so that when going away from a battle they fasten the heads of [C198] their enemies to the necks of their horses and when returning [home] they nail them to their gates. Poseidonios [F274], at any rate, says that he saw this in many places, and at first found it disgusting but later bore it mildly because of its familiarity. Yet the heads of those who were esteemed are embalmed with cedar oil and shown to strangers, and they would not consider returning them even for a ransom of an equal weight of gold. The Romans stopped these things, as well as all the sacrifices and prophecies contrary to our customs. They would strike a man who had been consecrated in the back

with the sword, and prophesy from his convulsions. But they would not sacrifice without the Druids. It is said that there were other forms of human sacrifice: they would shoot some with arrows, or impale them in the sanctuaries, or, having prepared a colossus of straw and wood, would throw cattle, all kinds of wild animals, and people into it as a burnt offering.

(6) He [Poseidonios, F276] says that in the Ocean there is a small island not far out to sea, lying off the mouth of the Liger River. Samnite women live there, who are possessed by Dionysos, and propitiate the god through rites and other festivals. No man sets foot on the island, although the women themselves sail from it, have intercourse with men, and return again. It is their custom once a year to unroof the temple and then roof it again on the same day before sunset, with each bringing a load. If anyone lets her load fall, she is torn apart by the others. They carry the pieces around the temple shouting "euai" and do not stop until their frenzy stops. It always happens that someone is prevailed upon to drop her load.

What Artemidoros [F36] said about ravens is more fabulous. He wrote that there is a certain harbor on the Ocean called "Two Ravens," in which two ravens are seen, whose right wings are somewhat white. Those who have disputes about things come here, put a wooden plank at the place, and then separately throw barley cakes. The birds fly in and eat some and scatter others. The one whose barley cakes are scattered wins. What he says about this is rather fabulous, but that about Demeter and Kore is more believable, for he says that there is an island near Prettanike on which there are religious ceremonies concerning Demeter and Kore similar to those on Samothrake. And it is also believed that in Keltike a tree grows that is like a fig, and the

[C199] fruit it bears is similar to a capital of Corinthian workmanship. An incision will bring forth a deadly juice that is used on arrows. It is also repeated over and over that all the Kelts are contentious, but it is not considered disgraceful to them to be lavish in their youthful vigor.

Ephoros [F131a] says that Keltike is so exceedingly large that he assigns to it most of what we now call Iberia, as far as Gadeira, and he declares that the people are philhellenic, saying many peculiar things about them that are not probable today. It is also peculiar to them that they attempt not to be fat or pot-bellied, and a young man who exceeds a moderate waistline is punished. This is it about Transalpine Keltike.

Part 5: The Keltic islands

(1) Prettanike is in the shape of a triangle, with its longest side parallel to Keltike, not more or less than it in its length, for each is about 4,300 – or

4,400 – stadia. The Keltic [side] is from the outlets of the Rhenos as far as the northern capes of Pyrene near Aquitania, and that from Kantion (which is the easternmost limit of Prettanike, exactly opposite the outlets of the Rhenos) is as far as the western cape of the island, which lies opposite Aquitania and Pyrene. This is the shortest distance from Pyrene to the Rhenos, since it has been said [2.5.28] that the greatest [distance] is 5,000 stadia. But it is probable that there is some convergence from the parallel position of the river and mountains, since both have somewhat of a curve at the extremities near the Ocean.

(2) There are four crossings that are customarily used to go to the island from the continent, which are from the mouths of rivers: the Rhenos, Sequana, Liger, and Garouna. Yet those [living] in places around the Rhenos do not go to sea from its outlets, but from the region of those Morinians who border on the Menapians. Among them is Itium, which Caesar the God used as a naval station when he crossed to the island. He set forth at night and landed on the next day around the fourth hour, having completed 320 stadia in his crossing, and it happened that the grain was in the field.

Most of the island is flat and thickly wooded (although many places have hillocks), and it produces grain, cattle, gold, silver, and iron. These are exported from there, as well as hides, slaves, and dogs suitable for hunting. [C200] The Kelts use both these and native ones in war. The men are taller than the Kelts, less yellow-haired, and looser in their bodies. As an indication of their size, I saw in Rome boys who rose half a foot above the tallest people there, although they were somewhat twisted and not graceful in their structure. Some of their customs are similar to those of the Kelts, but others are simpler and more barbaric, so that some of them who have abundant milk do not make cheese, because of their inexperience, and they have no experience in gardening or other agricultural matters. There are those among them who are politically powerful. For war they mostly use chariots, as do some of the Kelts. The forests are their cities, and they fortify an open circular space with trees that they have felled, and make huts for themselves and for stabling their livestock, but not for a long time. The air is rainy rather than snowy, and when it is clear it is foggy for long periods, so that in an entire day the sun may be seen for only three or four hours around midday. It is the same among the Morinians and Menapians and certain of their neighbors.

(3) Caesar crossed over to the island twice, although he came back quickly without accomplishing anything important or going far into the island, because of quarreling in Keltike – both among the barbarians

and his own soldiers – and the loss of many of his ships at the time of the full moon, with the increase of the ebb and flood tides that occurred. Yet he won two or three victories over the Prettanians, although he carried over only two legions of his army, and he returned with hostages, slaves, and much additional booty. Today, however, some of their leaders have sent ambassadors and favors to Caesar Sebastos, establishing friendship and dedicating offerings on the Capitolium. They have made almost the entire island Roman property. Thus they submit to heavy duties, both on exports from there to Keltike and imports, which include ivory chains, necklaces, *lyngourina*, prepared glass, and other such minor objects, and there is thus no need for a garrison on the island. At the least, one legion and some cavalry would be needed to carry the tribute away from them, and which also would be necessary for the expenses of [C201] situating an army. The duties would have to be decreased if tribute were imposed, and there would be certain dangers everywhere if force were introduced.

(4) In addition to other small islands around Prettanike, there is a large one, Ierne, toward the north but alongside it and rather elongated. I have nothing distinct to say about it, except that those living there are wilder than the Prettanians, and cannibals as well as herb-eaters. When their fathers die they consider it auspicious to eat them, and they have intercourse openly, both with other women and their mothers and sisters. I am saying this even though there are no trustworthy witnesses, although cannibalism is said to exist among the Skythians, and it is said to have been performed by the Kelts, Iberians, and many others, when under the compulsion of sieges.

(5) Concerning Thoule the record is most indistinct because of its remoteness, for it is situated the farthest north of all known [localities]. What Pytheas [T15] has said about it – as well as other places there – has been fabricated, as is clear from regions that are known. Most of them he has reported falsely about, as has been said previously [1.4.3], and thus he is clearly speaking falsely about remote places. Yet it would seem that he [F7] used the facts adequately concerning celestial phenomena and mathematical speculation, but about those living near the frozen zone he said that there is a complete lack or scarcity of domesticated plants and animals, and that they maintain themselves on millet, other legumes, fruit, and roots. Where there is grain and honey they produce a drink from it. Since they have no pure sunshine they beat the grain in large buildings, after gathering in the ears, because threshing floors are useless due to the lack of sun and the rain.

Part 6:   The Alps

(1) After Keltike beyond the Alps and the peoples who occupy that territory, the Alps themselves and those living in them must be discussed, and then Italia in its entirety, preserving in the discussion the same arrangement that is provided by the nature of the territory.

The Alps do not begin at Monoikos Harbor, as some have said, but in the same territory as the Apennine Mountains, around Genua (the emporium of the Ligyans), and what is called Vada ("The Shallows") of Sabata, for the Apennines have their beginning at Genua and the Alps at Sabata. It is   [C202] 260 stadia between Genua and Sabata, and then after 370 is the little town of Albingaunon, whose inhabitants are called Ingaunian Ligyans, and from there it is 480 to Monoikos Harbor. Between them is a good-sized city, Albion Intemelion, where the Intemelians live. Because of these names, proof is clearly established that the beginning of the Alps is at Sabata, for "Alpeia" was formerly called "Albia" or "Alpionia." Even today the high mountain among the Iapodians that almost adjoins Okra and the Alps is called Albion, as the Alps extended as far as there.

(2) The Ligyans were partly Ingaunians and partly Intemelians, and it is reasonable that their settlements on the sea were named Albion (that is, Alpeion) Intemelion, or rather abridged to Albingaunon. Polybios [33.9.8], however, adds the Oxybians and Dekietians to the two previously mentioned tribes of the Ligyans.

Generally this entire coast, to Tyrrhenia from Monoikos Harbor, is windy and inhospitable, except for insignificant roadsteads and anchorages. Lying above it are the extraordinary cliffs of the mountains, which leave only a narrow passage next to the sea. The Ligyans inhabit it, living mostly on livestock, millet, and a drink from barley, with pasturage on the land next to the sea but mostly in the mountains. They have exceedingly large amounts of wood for shipbuilding, trees so large that some of them have a thickness with a diameter of eight feet. Many of them, in their variegation, are no worse than the thyine wood for table making. They are brought down to the emporium of Genua, as well as livestock, hides, and honey, which they exchange in return for olive oil and wine from Italia, for theirs is scant, contains pitch, and is harsh. This is where the so-called *ginnoi* are – horses and mules – but also the Ligystinian chiton and the *sagoi*. There is also an excess of *lyngourion*, which some call electrum. When they make war they are barely capable as cavalry, but good infantry and javelin-throwers, and because they have bronze shields, some consider them to be Hellenes.

(3) Monoikos Harbor, an anchorage neither for large or many ships, has a sanctuary of Herakles called Monoikos. From the name it is reasonable that the coastal voyages of the Massaliotes extended this far. The distance from Antipolis is a little more than two hundred stadia. From there as far as Massalia, or a little farther, live the Sallyan peoples, in the Alps that lie above this coast, mixed up with the Hellenes. The ancient Hellenes called the Sallyans the Ligyans, and the land held by the Massaliotes was Ligystike, but later ones gave them the name Keltoligyans, and assigned to them the level territory as far as Avenio and the Rhodanos, which was divided into ten parts and was from where they would send an army, not only foot soldiers but also cavalry. These were the first of the Kelts across the Alps whom the Romans subdued, making war for a long time against them and the Ligyans, as they had closed the passes to Iberia along the coast. They were raiding by land and sea and were so powerful that passage along the road was hardly possible for a large army. After making war for eighty years, they [the Romans] were barely able to open the road for a width of twelve stadia, for those travelling for the state. After this they defeated all of them and established a government, imposing tribute.

(4) After the Sallyans are the Albieians, Albioikians, and Vocontians, who occupy the northern part of the mountains. The Vocontians stretch alongside as far as the Allobrigians, having notable hollows in the depths of the mountains that are no less than those of the latter. The Allobrigians and Ligyans are assigned to the commanders who come to Narbonitis, but the Vocontians – as we have said [4.1.12] concerning the Volcians around Nemausos – are assigned to themselves. The Ligyans who live on the sea between the Varus and Genua are the same as the Italiotes, but a prefect of equestrian rank is sent to those in the mountains, as is done with others who are completely barbarian.

(5) After the Vocontians are the Iconians and Tricorians, and after them the Medullians, who hold the highest summits. At any rate, they say that the steepest height is an ascent of a hundred stadia, and there is the same descent again to the boundaries of Italia. Up in a certain region that lies in a hollow is a large lake with two springs not far from one another. From one of them comes the torrential Drouentia River, which flows down to the Rhodanos, as well as the Douria, in the opposite direction. It mixes with the Padus, carried down through the Salassians into Keltike on this side of the Alps. From the other, in much lower territory, the Padus itself issues forth, large and swift, although as it proceeds it becomes larger and more gentle. It is increased by many [affluents] and thus has already widened out in the plains, and because of this spreading its flow relaxes and is blunted.

[C203]

[C204]

It empties into the Adriatic Sea, having become the largest of all European rivers except the Istros. The Medullians are situated for the most part above the confluence of the Isar and the Rhodanos.

(6) Toward the other portion – that sloping toward Italia – of the previously mentioned mountains live the Taurinians, a Ligystikian people, and other Ligyans. This is what is called the land of Donnus and Cottius. After these are the Padus and the Salassians, and above them on the summits are the Ceutronians, Catorigians, Varagrians, Nantuatians, Lake Lemenna (through which the Rhodanos flows), and the source of the river. Not far from these are the sources of the Rhenos and Mount Adoula (the mountains from which the Rhenos flows toward the north), and the Adoua, in the opposite direction, which empties into Lake Larios, which is near Comum. Lying beyond Comum, which is situated at the base of the Alps, are, on one side, the Rhaitians and Vennonians, sloped toward the east, and on the other the Lepontians, Tridentinians, Stonians, and a number of other minor peoples, who in former times overran[7] Italia, although brigands and resourceless. Now some of them have been eliminated and others completely pacified, so that the passes through their mountains that were formerly few and hard to cross are now numerous and, through construction, as accessible as possible. In addition to putting down the brigands, Sebastos Caesar constructed the route as much as possible, but he was not able to overpower nature everywhere because of the rocks and the extraordinary cliffs that overhung the route and fell beneath it, so that a small misstep would produce the inevitable danger of falling into a bottomless chasm. The road is so narrow at certain places that dizziness occurs to those travelling by foot, including the beasts of burden unaccustomed to it, although the native ones carry their goods safely. The situation is not curable, as extraordinary slabs of ice slide down that can cut off an entire caravan or throw it all into the chasm below. There are many slabs upon each other, coagulation upon coagulation of icy snow, and those on the surface are always easily released from those within before they are all completely dissolved by the sun.   [C205]

(7) Most of the Salassians are in a deep hollow, with the territory closed in on both sides by mountains, and part of it stretching up to the summits lying above. The road for those from Italia passes over the mountains and through the previously mentioned hollow. Then it forks into two, with one going through what is called Poeninus (which is impassable at the summits

---

[7] The text reads "occupied," but a change of only three letters produces "overran," somewhat more precise, and analogous to the statement in Section 8.

of the Alps by animal teams), and the other more to the west through the Ceutronians. The territory of the Salassians has gold mines, which the Salassians formerly possessed when they were powerful, just as they were masters of the passes. The Douria River was their most important partner in mining – in washing the gold – and because the water was diverted in many places to channels, the normal stream would be emptied. Although this was useful to those hunting for gold, those farming in the plains below were upset as they were deprived of irrigation, because the river used to be able to water the region since its stream was on higher ground. For this reason both peoples were constantly making war against each other. When the Romans gained power, the Salassians were expelled from both the gold mines and the territory, but they still possessed the mountain heights and sold water to the officials who had contracted to work the mines, yet because of the greediness of these officials they were always in disagreement. Thus it resulted that the Romans leading armies who were sent to these places always had pretexts for war against them. Until recent times they were either making a war or ending a war against the Romans, yet they were powerful and were able to cause much damage to those crossing the mountains, because of their habit of brigandage. They exacted a drachma per man from Decimus Brutus when he was fleeing from Mutina. When Messala was spending the winter near them, he paid compensation for wood, both for fuel and for the elm used for javelins and athletic exercises. These men once robbed Caesar of money and threw overhanging rocks down on his camps, with the excuse that they were constructing roads or bridging rivers. Later Sebastos utterly subdued them, and sold all of them as booty, carrying them to Eporedia, a Roman settlement established in the wish that it be a fortress against the Salassians. Those there were able to resist them only slightly until the people were eliminated. The other people numbered 36,000, with 8,000 under arms. Terentius Varro, the commander who subdued them, sold them all under the spear. Caesar sent 3,000 Romans to found the city of Augusta at the place that Varro had made his camp, and now what is within all the neighboring territory as far as the highest summits of the mountains remains peaceful.

[C206]

(8) Next there are those parts of the mountains toward the east, and those that turn toward the south that the Rhaitians and Vindolicians occupy, touching the Elvettians and the Boians, and overlooking their plains. The Rhaitians go down as far as Italia above Verona and Comum. In addition, the Rhaitian wine, which is praised as not inferior to the reputable wines of Italia, is produced in their foothills. They extend as far as the district through which the Rhenos runs. The Lepontians and Camunians are of

this group. Yet the Vindolicians and Noricians occupy much of the territory beyond the mountains, along with the Breunians and the Genaunians, who are Illyrian. All of those would overrun the neighboring territory of Italia, as well as that of the Elvettians, Sequanians, Boians, and the Germans. The most vigorous of the Vindolicians are considered to be the Likattians, Clautenatians, and Vennonians, and, among the Rhaitians, the Rucantians, and Cotuantians. The Estionians are among the Vindolicians, as are the Brigantians and their cities of Brigantium and Cambodunum, as well as Damasia, effectively the akropolis of the Likattians. It is said that these brigands are especially difficult toward the Italiotes since, when they capture a village or a city, they not only slaughter the men from youth upward but go on to the male infants, and do not stop there, but kill all the pregnant women whom their seers say will bear male children.

(9) Immediately after these are those living near the recess of the Adriatic and the regions around Aquileia, who are the Noricians and certain of the Karnians. The Tauriskians are among the Noricians. Tiberius and his brother Drusus stopped them all from their licentious incursions in a single summer, so that for thirty-three years they have been quiet and regularly paying tribute.

Throughout the mountainous Alps there are hilly regions that are capable of good farming, as well as hollows that are well settled, but most of it, especially around the summits – where the brigands gathered – is wretched and unfruitful because of the frosts and the ruggedness of the land. Because of a scarcity of nourishment and other things, they would at times spare those in the plains, so that the latter could supply them, and in return they [C207] would give resin, pitch, pine for torches, wax, cheese, and honey, which they had in abundance.

Above the territory of the Karnians is the Apennine Mountain, which has a lake that flows into the Isara River, which receives another river, the Atagis, and empties into the Adria. From the same lake another river, called the Atesinos, flows into the Istros. And the Istros takes its beginning in these mountains, which have many parts and many summits.

The heights of the Alps extend from Ligystike up to this point and give the appearance of a single mountain. Then they separate and become lower, but rise up again into more parts and more summits. The first is beyond the Rhenos and the lake that slopes toward the east, a moderately high ridge where the sources of the Istros are, near the Soebians and the Herkynian Forest. There are others that turn toward Illyris and the Adria, among which are the Apennine Mountain previously mentioned, and also Tullus and Phligadia, which lie above the Vindolicians, from which come the Douras,

Klanis, and many other torrential rivers flow that join the stream of the Istros.

(10) And the Iapodians – a mixed Illyrian and Keltic peoples – live around these places, and Okra is near to them. The Iapodians were formerly populous and held as their home both sides of the mountain, controlling it through brigandage, but were exhausted through war and completely finished off by Sebastos Caesar. Their cities are Metoulon, Aroupinoi, Monetion, and Vendon.

After them is Segestike, a city in the plain, past which flows the Saos River, which empties into the Istros. This city is naturally situated for war against the Dacians. Okra is the lowest part of the Alps, where it touches the Karnians, through whom goods from Aquileia are carried in covered wagons on a road of not much more than 400 stadia to what is called Pamportos. From there they are carried down the river as far as the Istros and those regions. There is a river that flows by Pamportos, coming from Illyris, which is navigable and empties into the Saos, so that items are easily carried down to Segestike and the Pannonians and Tauriskians. The Kolapis joins the Saos near this city. Both are navigable and flow from the Alps.

The Alps have wild horses and cattle. Polybios [34.10.8–9] says that an [C208] animal of peculiar form is produced there, like a deer in shape except for its neck and growth of hair – in which it resembles a wild boar – and under its chin there is a growth about a *spithame* long with hair at its tip, as thick as the tail of a colt.

(11) Among the passes from Italia to outer and northern Keltike is that leading through the Salassians to Lugdunum. It is double, with one through the Ceutronians, usable by wagons through most of its length, and the other, which is steep and narrow, although shorter, through the Poeninus. Lugdunum is in the center of the territory, as if an akropolis, because the rivers come together there, and it is near all the parts. Because of this Agrippa cut his roads from here, the one through the Kemmenon mountains as far as the Santonians and Aquitania, that to the Rhenos, the third to the Ocean through the Bellovacians and Ambianians, and the fourth to Narbonitis and the Massaliote coast. There is also – on the left leaving Lugdunum and the territory lying above it, in the Poeninus itself – a side road that crosses the Rhodanos or Lake Lemenna and goes into the Elvettian plains, and there is a pass from there to the Sequanians over Mount Iora, and also to the Lingonians. The route through these places divides in two, one toward the Rhenos and the other toward the Ocean.

(12) Polybios [34.10.10–14], moreover, says that in his time there was found right around Aquileia, among the Norician Tauriskians, a particularly

favorable gold mine that would reveal excavated gold if one stripped away the surface of the earth for two feet. The excavations were no more than fifteen feet. Some of the gold would immediately be pure, the size of a bean or lupine, and when only an eighth part was boiled away (although there would need to be more smelting) it was nonetheless greatly profitable. The Italiotes had become fellow workers with the barbarians for two months, when suddenly gold became a third part cheaper in all of Italy. When the Tauriskians learned about this, they threw out their fellow workers and became a monopoly. Yet today all the gold mines are under the Romans. Here, just as in Iberia, in addition to what is dug the rivers carry gold dust, although not much.

The same man [Polybios 34.10.15–21], in telling about the size and height of the Alps, compares them with the largest mountains in Hellas: Taÿgetos, Lykaion, Parnassos, Olympos, Pelion, and Ossa, as well as Haimos, Rhodope, and Dounax in Thrace. He says that each of these mountains can [C209] be climbed in about a day by someone who is active, and similarly an active person can encircle them in a day, but no one could climb any of the Alps in five days. Their length, along their side in the plains, is 2,200 stadia. He names only four passes, that through the Ligyans (nearest to the Tyrrhenian Sea), that through the Taurinians, where Hannibal crossed, that through the Salassians, and the fourth through the Rhaitians, all of which are precipitous. He says that there are a number of lakes in the mountains, three of which are large. Of these, Benakos has a length of 500 stadia and a width of 50, from which the Mincius River flows. Then there is Verbanus, at 400 and narrower in width that the previous one, and which sends forth the Adoua River. Third is Larios, nearly 300 stadia in length and 50 in width, which sends forth the great Ticinus River.[8] All these flow into the Padus. This is what we have to say about the Alpine Mountains.

---

[8] Strabo (or, more probably, Polybios) has interchanged the two lakes. The Verbanus (modern Lago Maggiore) is the source of the Ticinus (Ticino) River; the Larios (modern Lago di Como) is the source of the Adoua (modern Adda).

BOOK 5

Northern and central Italia

Part 1:   Introduction, Padus Valley, and northeastern Italia

(1) After the foothills of the Alps is the beginning of what is now Italia. The ancients called only Oinotria "Italia," which extended from the Sikelian Strait as far as the Tarantine and Poseidoniate Gulfs, but the former name won out and advanced as far as the foothills of the Alps. It took in Ligystike as far as the Varus River and the sea there, from the boundaries of Tyrrhenia, and Istria as far as Pola. One might infer that it was their prosperity that caused those who were first named Italians to transmit it to their neighbors, and then to make further bestowals until the Roman conquest. After a long time, when the Romans had given equal rights to the Italiotes, they decided to assign the same honor to the Alpine Galatians and the Enetians, calling them all Italiotes and Romans, and to send forth many settlements, some earlier and some later, concerning which one cannot easily say that any others were better.

(2) It is not easy to comprehend geometrically (by means of a single figure) what is today the entirety of Italia, yet they say that it is a triangular promontory projecting toward the south and the winter risings, with its head at the Sikelian Strait and its base at the Alps. <The base>[1] must be conceded, as well as one of the sides, that which ends at the Strait and is washed by the Tyrrhenian Sea. A triangle refers peculiarly to a rectilinear figure, yet here the base and the sides are rounded, so that, if I must say "conceded," the base and the side must be put down as a figure with a curved line, and the slant of this side – toward the risings – is also conceded. The rest of what they say is not adequate because they have assumed only a single side from the recess of the Adria to the Strait. We say that a side is a line without an angle, and it is without an angle either when its parts do not converge with one another, or not much. But [the lines] from Ariminum to

[C210]

---

[1] There may be a small lacuna in the text here, but the meaning is clear.

the Iapygian Cape and from the Strait to the same cape converge greatly. I think it is the same with that from the recess of the Adria and that from Iapygia, for they come together around Ariminum and Ravenna and make an angle, or if not an angle, a notable curve. Thus this might be one side – the coastal voyage from the recess to Iapygia – but not straight, and the remainder from there to the Strait would outline another side, and this would also not be straight. Thus one might say that the figure is four-sided rather than three-sided, and in no way a triangle, except in a wrong sense. It is better to agree that figures that are not geographical cannot be rendered by any easy definition.

(3) We can speak by parts as follows. The base of the Alps is curved and like a gulf, with the hollows turned toward Italy. The middle of the gulf is near the Salassians, and the extremities make a turn, one as far as Okra and   [C211] the recess of the Adria, the other as far as Genua on the Ligystikian coast, the emporium of the Ligyans, where the Apennine Mountains join the Alps. But right below them is a notable plain, with its width and length about equal at 2,100 stadia. Its southern side is confined by the coast of the Enetians and the Apennine Mountains that come down to the area of Ariminum and Ankon. These begin in Ligystike and come into Tyrrhenia, leaving only a narrow coast, and then withdraw little by little into the interior. When they are near the Pisatis, they turn toward the east and the Adria until they are near the regions of Ariminum and Ankon, and join the coast of the Enetians in a straight line. Keltike within the Alps is enclosed within these boundaries. The length of the coast. . .of the mountains is 6,300 stadia, and the width is less than 2,000.[2]

The rest of Italy is narrow and oblong, ending in two heads, that at the Sikelian Strait and that at Iapygia, tightened on both sides, on one by the Adria and the other by the Tyrrhenian Sea. The shape of the Adria, and its size, are like that of Italy, marked by the Apennine Mountains and both seas as far as Iapygia and the isthmus between the Tarantine and Poseidoniate Gulfs. The maximum width of both is around 1,300 stadia, and the length not much less than 6,000. The remainder is everything occupied by the Brettians and certain Leukanians. Polybios [34.11.2] says that the coast from Iapygia to the Strait is washed by the Sikelian Sea, and is 3,000 stadia by foot, but by sea it is 500 less. The Apennine Mountains,

---

[2] This sentence is confusing and has been transposed from after "Tyrrhenian Sea" a few lines down. The reference to the mountains seems to have no context and may indicate a lacuna (with possibly an "and" after "coast." The text has also been emended from "1,000" to "2,000" on the basis of the previous "2,100," but the distance depends on where Strabo took his measurement.

after touching the region around Ariminum and Ankon and defining the width of Italia from sea to sea, take another turn and cut the entire territory lengthwise. As far as the Peuketians and Leukanians they do not withdraw from the Adria, but after touching the Leukanians they turn more toward the other sea, and for the remainder pass through the middle of the Leukanians and Brettians, ending at what is called Rhegian Leukopetra.

What is today the entirety of Italia has been described in outline. We will attempt to go back and speak about each portion, first about those at the [C212] base of the Alps.

(4) It is a plain that is very prosperous and diverse in its fruitful hills. The Padus divides it at almost the center, with one side called "that within the Padus" and the other "beyond." That within is everything near the Apennine Mountains and Ligystike, and the rest is beyond. The latter is inhabited by Ligystikian and Keltic peoples, who live both in the mountains and in the plains, and the former by Kelts and Enetians. These Kelts are the same peoples as those beyond the Alps, but there are two accounts about the Enetians. Some say that they are settlers from the homonymous Kelts, who live on the Ocean, and others say that certain Enetians from Paphlagonia were saved with Antenor from the Trojan War. As proof of this they cite their care in the breeding of horses, something that now has been completely abandoned, although formerly it was esteemed by them, and in antiquity they strove to [produce] horses for breeding mules. Homer also alludes to this: "from the Enetians, where the race of wild mules is" [*Iliad* 2.852]. And Dionysios [I], the tyrant of Sikelia, obtained the breeder of his champion horses from there, so that the renown of the Enetian foals was known among the Hellenes and the breed was esteemed for a long time.

(5) All the territory, especially that of the Enetians, is filled with rivers and marshes. These are affected by the actions of the sea, as this is almost the only portion of Our Sea that acts like the Ocean, since both the ebb and flood and tides are similar to it, and because of them most of the plain is a lagoon. It is provided with canals and embankments, like in the territory called Lower Egypt. Some of it has been drained and farmed, and other [portions] can be sailed across. Some of the cities are on islands, and others are partially washed by the sea. The sail up the rivers to those located above the marshes in the interior is marvellous, particularly on the Padus.[3] It is the largest [of these rivers], often filled by rain and snow, although it disperses

---

[3] Some have suspected a lacuna here, as "Padus" is in the nominative but one would expect a prepositional phrase.

into many parts near its outlets, and its mouth is choked with mud and difficult to enter. Yet experience overcomes the greatest difficulties.

(6) In early times, as I was saying, the region around the river was entirely inhabited by Kelts. The most numerous peoples of the Kelts were the Boians, Insoubrians, and the Senonians, who, along with the Gaisatians, once overran the city of the Romans in an onslaught. Later the Romans completely destroyed them, and the Boians were expelled from their [C213] lands. Moving to the lands around the Istros, they lived among the Tauriskians and made war against the Dacians until the entire population was destroyed, leaving their territory, part of Illyris, to their neighbors as a sheep pasture. The Insoubrians, however, still exist today. Their metropolis was Mediolanium, which was a village long ago – as they all lived in villages – but now is a notable city, across the Padus and almost adjoining the Alps. Nearby is Verona, and it also is a large city. Smaller than these are Brixia, Mantua, Regium, and Comum, which was a moderate settlement, but Pompeius Strabo the father of Magnus populated it after bad treatment from the Rhaitians situated above it. Then Gaius Scipio added 3,000, and the God Caesar settled 5,000 more, among whom were 500 of the most distinguished Hellenes, to whom he gave civic rights and enrolled them among the settlers. Yet they did not settle there, although they bequeathed their name on the foundation, for it is said that all were called Neokometai, translated as Novum Comum. Near this place is the lake called Larios, filled by the Adoua River, which then discharges into the Padus. Its source is on Mount Adoula, where [the source of] the Rhenos also is.

(7) These [cities] are situated far above the marshes, and near them is Patavium, the best of all of these. It is said that recently it was enumerated at 500 equestrians, and in antiquity would send forth an army of 120,000. It is apparent from the amount of material sent to the market in Rome – clothing and all kinds of other things – that the city is populated and skilled in the arts. There is a sailing route up from the sea by means of a river running through the marshes, 250 stadia from a large harbor. The harbor is called Medoacus, and the river has the same name.

The largest [city] in the marshes is Ravenna, built entirely of wood and intersected by streams, and provided with bridges and ferries for transportation. At the flood tide it receives not a small portion of the sea, so that all the sewage is washed away by this and the rivers, and therefore the bad air is removed. Thus the place has been shown to be so healthy that the rulers have proclaimed gladiators are to be fed and housed there. It is a marvellous thing about the place that the air in the marshes is harmless, as is also the

[C214] case in Alexandria near Egypt, where in summer the lake loses its bad condition because of the rise of the river and the disappearance of standing water. The behavior of the grapevine is also a marvel worthy of note, for the marshes nourish it and make it produce fruit quickly and abundantly, yet it dies in four or five years.

Altinum is also in a marsh, with a situation similar to that of Ravenna. Between them is Butrium, a town belonging to Ravenna, and Spina, now a small village but long ago a notable Hellenic city. At any rate, a treasury of the Spinitians is visible at Delphi, and it is also recorded that they were masters of the seas. They say that it was once on the sea, although today it is in the interior of the territory about ninety stadia from the sea. It is also said that Ravenna was a Thessalian foundation, but they could not bear the excesses of the Tyrrhenians and willingly received some Ombrians, who hold the city today, but the former returned home. These [cities] are for the most part surrounded by marshes and thus can become flooded.

(8) Opitergium, <Conc>ordia, Atria, and Vicetia, and other such small towns are less troubled by the marshes, and are connected to the sea by small channels. They say that Atria was a notable city, and that the name of the Adria Gulf comes from it, making only a slight change. Aquileia, which is closest to the recess, is a Roman foundation, a fortification against the barbarians situated above it, and one can sail up to it – [a distance of] more than sixty stadia – on the Natiso River in a merchant vessel. It has become an emporium for those Illyrian peoples who live around the Istros, and who carry away in wagons the products of the sea, wine in wooden jars, and olive oil, in return for slaves, cattle, and hides. Aquileia is outside the boundaries of the Enetians. Their boundary is the river flowing from the Alpine Mountains, which one can sail up 1,200 stadia to the city of Noreia, where Gnaeus Carbo engaged the Kimbrians, accomplishing nothing. This place has gold washeries and iron mines.

In the very recess of the Adria is a sanctuary of Diomedes that is worthy of recording, the Timavum. It has a harbor, a remarkable grove, and seven springs of drinkable water that empty immediately into the sea in a wide and deep river. Polybios[4] says that all except one are salt water, and the natives [C215] have named the place the Source and Mother of the Sea. But Poseidonios [F225] says that the Timavus is a river which comes from the mountains and empties into a pit, is carried underground for about 130 stadia, and makes its outlet into the sea.

---

[4] This citation does not appear in either the extant text or published fragments of Polybios' works.

(9) The dominion of Diomedes around this sea is attested by the Diomedeian Islands as well as what is reported about the Daunians and Argos Hippion. I will speak about these insofar as they are historically useful, but it is necessary to let the myths and false reports alone, such as those about Phaethon or the Heliadians who were changed into poplars around the Eridanos (which exists nowhere on earth, although it is said to be near the Padus), the Amber Islands that lie off the Padus, and the guinea fowls on them. None of these things is in those places. It is recorded that certain honors were shown to Diomedes by the Enetians, a white horse is sacrificed to him, and two groves are visible, one to Argive Hera and the other to Aitolian Artemis. But myths have been added, as is reasonable: that in these groves wild animals become tame and deer herd together with wolves who can be approached by people and caressed, and that those chased by dogs are no longer chased when they seek refuge here. It is said that a certain especially well-known person, who would readily give bail and was teased for this, happened upon hunters who had a wolf in their nets. Saying in jest that if he would give bail for the wolf and exclude them from damages, they would set it free and release it from the ropes, he agreed to it. When the wolf was set free, he drove off a sufficient herd of unbranded horses and brought them to the farmstead of the one readily giving bail, who, upon receiving the favor, branded the horses with a wolf and called them the "wolf bearers," notable for their speed rather than beauty. His successors maintained the brand and the name for the breed of horses, but made it customary that the mares would not be exported, so that the legitimate breed would remain solely among them, since that type of horse had become famous. Now, as we have said [5.1.4], the practice has been totally abandoned.

After the Timavum is the coast of the Istrians as far as Pola, which is part of Italia. Between them is the fortress of Tergeste, 180 stadia from Aquileia. Pola is situated in a harbor-like gulf that has small fertile islets with good mooring places. It was founded in antiquity by the Kolchians sent forth after Medeia, but who failed in their attempt and condemned themselves to [C216] exile. "A certain Graikos would call it Phygadon" [Flight], as Kallimachos [F11] said, "but in their language Pola."

The Enetians occupy the lands beyond the Padus, and the <Istrians>[5] as far as Pola. Above the Enetians are the Karnians, Genomanians, Medoakians,

[5] "Istrians" has been added to the text as there is no ethnym preserved after "the".

and Insoubrians. Some of these were hostile toward the Romans, but the Genomanians and Enetians were their allies, both before the campaign of Hannibal – when they made war on the Boians and Insoubrians – and afterward.

(10) Those within the Padus occupy everything that is encircled by the Apennine Mountains toward the Alps as far as Genua and Sabata. Most of it was held by the Boians, Ligyans, Senonians, and Gaisatians. The Boians were driven out, and the Gaisatians and Senonians have disappeared. Only the Ligystikian tribes and Roman settlements are left. The Romans have mixed with the Ombrian tribe, and in some places with the Tyrrhenians. Both these peoples – before the great increase of the Romans – were somewhat contentious with one another for supremacy, and with only the Tiberis River between them they could easily cross to one another. If, it seems, one of them made an expedition against someone else, the other would not fail contentiously to make an excursion to the same place. Thus when the Tyrrhenians prepared an expedition against the barbarians around the Padus and did well, but because of their luxuriousness were quickly cast out again, the other made an expedition against those who had cast them out. Then they disputed the places in succession and made some of the settlements Tyrrhenian and others Ombrian, although more were Ombrian because they were nearer. But the Romans took it upon themselves to send settlers to many places, and preserved the race of the earlier settlers. Yet now they are all Roman, although nevertheless some are said to be Ombrian and others Tyrrhenian, as it is with the Enetians, Ligyans, and Insoubrians.

(11) There are famous cities within the Padus and around the Padus: Placentia and Cremona, which are very near to each other in the center of the territory, and, between these and Ariminum, Parma, Mutina, and Bononia (which is near Ravenna). There are also some small towns in between on the road to Rome: Akara, Regium Lepidum, Makri Campi (where a festival is held every year), Claterna, and Forum Cornelium. Then there are Faventia and Caesena, on the Sapis River and the Rubicon, bordering on Ariminum. Ariminum is an Ombrian settlement, as is Ravenna, although both have received Roman settlers. Ariminum has a harbor and a homonymous river. From Placentia to Ariminum is 1,300 stadia. Beyond Placentia, toward the borders of the land of Cottius, is the city of Ticinum, within 36 miles, and the river of the same name that flows by it and joins the Padus. On a road that branches slightly are Clastidium, Derthon, and Aquae Statiellae. But straight to Ocelum, along the Padus and the Douria Rivers, is mostly precipitous. There are other rivers in

addition – among which is the Drouentia – and it is about <1>60 miles.[6]
Here the Alpine mountains and Keltike begin.

Near the mountains that lie above Luna is the city of Luca. Some of those
living here are in villages. The country is populated and most of the soldiers
are from there, as well of most of the equestrians from whom the Senate is
composed. Derthon is a notable city lying about the midpoint of the road
from Genua to Placentia, 400 stadia distant from each. On this road is also
Aquae Statiellae. That from Placentia to Ariminum has been described.
One can sail down the Padus to Ravenna in two days and nights.

Much of the region within the Padus was occupied by marshes, which
Hannibal went through with difficulty when he was going against
Tyrrhenia. But Scaurus drained the plains by digging navigable channels
from the Padus as far as Parma. Near Placentia the Trebia joins the Padus,
and before that several others, so it is immediately full. This Scaurus is the
one who laid out the Aemilian Road through Pisae and Luna as far as
Sabata, and then through Derthon. There is another Aemilia that succeeds
the Flaminia. Marcus Lepidus and Gaius Flaminius were consular colleagues, and the latter put down the Ligyans and laid out the Flaminia
from Rome through the Tyrrhenians and Ombrike as far as the region
around Ariminum, and the former the continuation as far as Bononia and
from there to Aquileia around the base of the Alps, encircling the marshes.

The boundary of this territory that we call Keltike within [the Alps] and
the remainder of Italia was indicated by the Apennine Mountains that are
beyond Tyrrhenia and the Aisis River, but later by the Rubicon, both of
which empty into the Adria.   [C218]

(12) Proof of the excellence of these places is the population, the size of
the cities, and their wealth, in regard to which the Romans there have
surpassed the rest of Italia in every way. The agricultural land yields much of
all kinds of produce, and the forests have so many acorns that Rome is
largely nourished by the herds of swine from there. The production of millet
is excellent because of the abundant water. It is the greatest remedy for
famine, as it withstands every season of weather and can never fail, even
though there is a scarcity of other grain. There are also outstanding pitch
works. The size of the pithoi is revealing about the wine, for they are
wooden and larger than houses. The abundance of the pitch adds greatly
to the quality of the smearing. The places around Mutina and the Scultanna
River produce soft wool (by far the best of all), and Ligystike and around the
Insoubrians have the rough, from which many Italiote households are

---

[6] The text has "60," far too short.

clothed. The medium, which produces expensive tapestries and *gausapae* and everything of this type that is wool on both or one side, is from Patavium. The mines there are not as energetically worked today because they are not as profitable as those in Keltike across the Alps or Iberia, but formerly they were energetically worked, and there was a gold mine at Vercelli, a village that is near Ictumuli, also a village, both of which are near Placentia. Let this up to here be the description of the first portion of Italia.

Part 2: Northwestern Italia

(1) Let the second be Ligystike that is within the Apennines, situated between the Keltike just spoken about and Tyrrhenia, which has nothing worthy of describing except that they live in villages, tilling and digging rough land, or rather quarrying it, as Poseidonios [F268] says.

The third is that of the Tyrrhenians, contiguous to this, who have the plains as far as the Tiberis River, washed for the most part on the eastern portion as far as its mouth, and on the other side by the Tyrrhenian and Sardoan Seas. The Tiberis flows from the Apennine Mountains and is filled by many rivers, with part of it running through Tyrrhenia itself and separating from it, in order, first Ombrike, then the Sabines, and then the Latins, who are near Rome as far as the coast. These are about parallel to the river and to Tyrrhenia in their width, and to each other in their [C219] length. They go up to the Apennine Mountains that are near to the Adria, with the Ombrians first, afterward the Sabines, and finally the Latins, all beginning at the river. The land of the Latins is between the coast that extends from Ostia as far as the city of Sinoessa and the Sabine territory (Ostia is the seaport of Rome where the Tiberis empties after flowing past it), and it extends lengthwise as far as Campania and the Saunitic Mountains. Sabina extends from the Latins to the Ombrians, and also stretches to the Saunitic Mountains, or rather joins the Apennines that are among the Vestinians, Paelignians, and Marsians. The Ombrians lie between Sabina and Tyrrhenia, and continue as far as Ariminum and Ravenna, across the mountains. The Tyrrhenians cease below the mountains that enclose it from Ligystike to the Adria, having begun at their own sea and the Tiberis. We will go through each, beginning with these.

(2) The Tyrrhenians, then, are called by the Romans Etruscans or Tuscans. Yet the Hellenes, as they say, so named them after Tyrrhenos the son of Atys, who sent settlers there from Lydia. When there was famine and sterility, Atys, who was one of the descendants of Herakles and Omphale and who had two children, by lot kept Lydos but assembled

most of the people and sent them forth with Tyrrhenos. Coming to this land, he called it Tyrrhenia after himself and founded twelve cities, establishing Tarkon as founder – after whom the city of Tarquinia [was named] – who, because of his wisdom is said by the mythographers to have been gray-haired from childhood. When they were subject to a single ruler they were very strong, but in later times this government was dissolved, and yielding to the violence of their neighbors, they were broken up into cities, as seems reasonable, for otherwise they would not have given up a prosperous land and gone to sea as pirates, each turning to different seas. Whenever they were unified it was sufficient for them not only to defend themselves against those who attacked them but to make counter-attacks and long expeditions. After the founding of Rome, Demaratos arrived, bringing people from Corinth, and he was received by the Tarquinians, and through a native woman produced Lucumo. Lucumo was a friend to Ancus Marcius, the king of the Romans, and was made king, changing his name to Lucius Tarquinius Priscus. He also adorned Tyrrhenia, as his father had done   [C220] previously, the latter by an abundance of artisans who had followed him from home and the former through resources from Rome. It is also the case that triumphal and consular ornament, and, simply, that of the rulers, was transferred there from Tarquinia, as well as the fasces, axes, trumpets, sacrificial rites, divination, and whatever music was used in public by the Romans. His son was the second Tarquinius, Superbus, who was the last of the kings and was expelled. Porsinas, the king of the Clusians, a Tyrrhenian city, attempted to restore him by force, but was unable to do so, although any enmity was dissolved and he went away as a friend with honors and great gifts.

(3) This has been about the distinction of Tyrrhenia. There are also the deeds of the Caeretanians. They defeated the Galatians who had taken Rome, attacking them on their return when they were among the Sabines, and taking from them against their will the booty that the Romans had given them. In addition, they saved those who had fled from Rome to them for refuge, as well as the immortal fire and the priestesses of Hestia. The Romans, because of the poor administrators in the city at that time, do not seem to have sufficiently remembered their goodwill, for they gave them civic rights but did not enroll them among the citizens, and others who did not share in political equality were relegated to the Caeretanian Tablets.

Among the Hellenes this city was esteemed because of its bravery and justice, for they abstained from piracy, although they were most capable of it. They established at Pytho a treasury called the Agyllaian. Agylla was the former name of what is now called Caere, which is said to have been founded by Pelasgians who came from Thessaly. When the Tyrrhenians who had changed their name from Lydians made an expedition against the Agyllaians, one of them came to the wall to learn what the name of the city was. One of the Thessalians on the wall, instead of answering, said "chaire" ["greetings"]. The Tyrrhenians accepted the omen, and when the city was captured, changed its name. The city, once so brilliant and distinguished, now preserves only traces, and the nearby hot springs, which are called the Caeretana, have a greater population than it because of those who frequent them for the cure.

(4) Almost everyone agrees that the Pelasgians were an ancient tribe that wandered over all of Hellas, especially among the Aioleans in Thessaly. Ephoros [F113] says he believes that since they were Arkadian in origin they chose a military life and promoted this conduct among many, and thus gave their name to everyone, gaining great distinction among the Hellenes and others, whoever they happened to encounter. And they were the settlers of Crete, as Homer says. At any rate Odysseus says to Penelope:

> One language mixed with others, Achaians are there, great-hearted Eteocretans, Kydonians, the *trichaikes* Dorians, and the divine Pelasgians. [*Odyssey* 19.175–7]

Pelasgian Argos is said to be that between the mouth of the Peneios and Thermopylai as far as the mountainous territory of the Pindos, because the Pelasgians came to rule these places. The Poet calls Zeus of Dodona "Pelasgian": "Zeus, lord, Dodonian, Pelasgian" [*Iliad* 16.233]. Many have said that the Epeirote peoples are Pelasgian, because they came to rule that far. Moreover, many of the heroes were called by the name "Pelasgian," so that later it became the eponym of many peoples. They called Lesbos "Pelasgia," and Homer called the Kilikians in the Troad the "Pelasgians": "Hippothoos leads the tribes of spear-fighting Pelasgians, those who dwell in Larisa, rich in soil" [*Iliad* 2.840–1]. To Ephoros [F113], it was according to Hesiod that the tribe originated in Arkadia, who said that "sons were born to Lykaon, equal to the gods, whom Pelasgos once bore" [F111]. Aischylos [F46] says in his *Suppliants* or *Danaids* that the race was from the Argos that is near Mykenai. And Ephoros says that the Peloponnesos was called Pelasgia, and Euripides in his *Archelaos* says that

> Danaos, the father of fifty daughters. . .came to Argos and lived in the city of Inachos, and he made it the law throughout Hellas that those formerly called Pelasgiotes were to be Danaans. [F228].

Antikleides [F21] says that they were the first to settle around Lemnos and Imbros, and that some of these went with Tyrsenos the son of Atys to Italia.

The Atthis compilers [F1] record that the Pelasgians were also at Athens. Because they were wanderers and inhabited places by chance, like birds, those in Attika called them "Pelargians [storks]."

(5) They say that the greatest length of Tyrrhenia is along the coast from Luna as far as Ostia, about 2,500 stadia, and its width near the mountains is less than half that. To Pisai from Luna is more than 400 stadia, and from the former to Vada Volaterra 280, and again to Poplonion 270, and from Poplonion to Cossa nearly 800, although some say 600 and Polybios [34.11.3] is not correct in saying that the total is 1,430.

Of these, Luna is a city, and there is a harbor that the Hellenes call the Harbor of Selene (as well as the city). The city is not large, but the harbor is very large and attractive, since there are several harbors within it, all of which are deep up to the shore, such as would be fitting for the naval base of a people who had a thalassocracy over so great a sea for so long. The harbor is surrounded by high mountains, from which one can see the open sea, Sardo, and an extensive portion of the coast on either side. Quarries of marble, both white and variegated bluish-gray, are so numerous and of such quality, and produce monolithic slabs and columns, so that most of the remarkable works in Rome and other cities are supplied from there. The stone is easily exported as the quarries lie above and near the sea, and from the sea the loads are received by the Tiberis. Tyrrhenia provides most of the wood supply for the planks in building construction, which are very straight and very long and can be brought right down from the mountains on the river. Between Luna and Pisa is the Makros[7]. . .which many writers consider the boundary between Tyrrhenia and Ligystike.

Pisa was founded by the Pisatai in the Peloponnesos, who made the expedition to Ilion with Nestor and went astray on the sail back, some going to Metapontion and others to the Pisatis, although all were called Pylians. It is situated between two rivers and at their confluence, the Arnus and the Ausar. The former runs from Arretium, and is large and not all together but divided into three, and the latter is from the Apennine Mountains. When they come together into one stream they raise each other so high by such mutual resistance that those standing on the opposite banks cannot see each other. Thus necessarily it is difficult to sail upstream from the sea. The sail upstream is about twenty stadia. The tale is told that when these rivers first began to flow down from the mountains, they were prevented from doing so by the local inhabitants because they might come together and flood the land, and so they agreed not to flood it, and have kept their promise. It

---

[7] After "Makros" the text has "territory," but the Makros is a river, not a region.

seems that the city was once prosperous, and it is not without reputation today because of its fruitfulness, stoneworks, and wood for shipbuilding. They used this in antiquity against the dangers of the sea – for at first they were more warlike than the Tyrrhenians, with the Ligyans urging them on, worthless neighbors alongside them – but most of it today is being consumed by building construction in Rome, as well as for the country homes that are furnished like Persian palaces.

(6) The territory of the Volaterranians is washed by the sea, and their settlement is in a deep ravine. There is a high hill that is steep all around, whose summit is flat and on which the walls of the city are situated. The ascent from the base is fifteen stadia, and it is sharp and difficult all the way. Here some of the Tyrrhenians and those proscribed by Sulla gathered, and when they had filled up four companies they were besieged for two years, and then only gave up the place under a truce.

Poplonion is situated on a high promontory that drops off into the sea and forms a peninsula. It was besieged at about the same time. The town is completely deserted except for the sanctuaries and a few houses, but the port is more inhabited, with a small harbor and two shipsheds at the base of the mountain. It seems to me that this was the only ancient Tyrrhenian city located on the sea itself. The reason for this is the lack of harbors in this territory, which is why the founders totally fled the sea, or projected their defenses toward it, so that they would not be exposed as ready booty to those sailing against them. Beneath the promontory is a lookout for tuna. Looking down from the city, Sardo is barely visible from afar, Kyrnos is nearer – about 60 stadia distant from Sardo – and much more [visible] is Aithalia, which is closer to the mainland, about 300 stadia distant and about the same distance from Kyrnos. This is the best departure point in the district for those three previously mentioned islands. I saw them when I went up to Poplonion, as well as some mines in the district that had failed. I also saw those who work the iron brought from Aithalia, for it cannot be smelted in heating furnaces on the island, and is immediately brought from the mines to the mainland. This island has another curiosity, that the mined excavations have in time filled again, as is said to be the case with the ledges on Rhodes, the marble rock on Paros, and, according to Kleitarchos [F28], the salt among the Indians.

Moreover, Eratosthenes [F151] is not correct when he says that neither Kyrnos nor Sardo can be seen from the mainland, nor is Artemidoros [F48], who says that both are in the open sea within 1,200 stadia, for even if this were the case for some, they could not be seen by me at such [a distance], or were not seen clearly, especially Kyrnos.

[C224]

On Aithalia is Argoos Harbor, from the Argo, as they say. Jason sailed here when he was seeking the home of Kirke, as Medeia wished to see the goddess. At that time the scrapings that the Argonauts made with their strigils congealed, and remain today on the shore as variegated pebbles. Such myth-making is proof of what we have been saying: that Homer did not fabricate everything, but upon hearing such things repeated over and over, situated them at extended and remote distances, just as he cast Odysseus into the Ocean, and similarly Jason, because of certain wanderings by him at that time, as well as by Menelaos. This is it about Aithalia.

(7) Kyrnos is called Corsica by the Romans. It is poorly inhabited, since it is rough and completely impassable in many places, so that those in the mountains who live on brigandage are wilder than animals. At any rate, when the Roman commanders attacked and fell upon their defenses and took a large number of slaves, one could see them at Rome and marvel at the savageness and bestiality manifested among them. Either they cannot endure their lives, or they live in apathy and insensibility, so that they irritate those purchasing them, and whatever was paid for them is regretted. There are nevertheless inhabited portions and some sort of towns, such as Blesinon, Charax, Enikoniai, and Vapanes. The Chorographer [F10–11] says that the length of the island is 160 miles and its width 70. The length of Sardo is 220 and its width 98. Others say that the circumference of Kyrnos is 1,200^8 stadia, and of Sardo, 4,000.

The greater part of it [Sardo] is rough and not peaceful, although there is much land that is prosperous in everything, especially grain. There are a number of cities, notably Caralis and Sulchi. But the virtues of the place are   [C225] set against a certain difficulty, for the island is unhealthy in summer, especially in the fruitful regions. Those regions are continually plundered by the mountaineers called the Diagesbians, formerly named the Iolaans. It is said that Iolaos came here, bringing some of the children of Herakles, and lived with the barbarians who held the island, who were Tyrrhenian. Phoenicians from Karchedon later prevailed over them, and along with them made war against the Romans. When they were defeated everything became subject to the Romans. There are four peoples in the mountains: the Paratians, Sossinatians, Balarians, and Akonitians, who live in caves. If they have some arable land, they do not cultivate it meticulously, but appropriate that which has been worked, not only what is there, but they also sail to those on the mainland, especially the Pisatians. The commanders who are sent to the island at times withstand them, but also at times fail at it,

---

^{8} The text reads "1,200", far too small; "3,200" is the most likely possibility.

since it is not profitable continually to maintain a camp in unhealthy places. What is left to them are certain artful strategems, and as they have observed a certain custom of the barbarians – that they would celebrate for several days after their rampages – they would attack at that time and defeat many of them. There are rams there called *mousmones* that produce goat hair instead of wool, and they [the Sardinians] make their breastplates with their hides. They also use a light shield and a dagger.

(8) The islands can clearly be seen from anywhere between Poplonion and Pisa. The three of them are oblong and approximately parallel, oriented toward the south and Libya. Aithalia falls greatly short of the others in size. The Chorographer [F60] says that from Libya the shortest crossing to Sardo is 300 miles.

After Poplonion is Kossai, a small city above the sea. There is a high *bounos* overlooking the gulf, where the settlement is. Beneath it is the Harbor of Herakles with a lagoon, and on the promontory above the gulf is a tuna viewpoint. The tuna not only follow the acorns but the purple fish, along the land, beginning at the External Sea as far as Sikelia. Along the coastal sail from Kossai to Ostia are the small towns of Gravisci, Pyrgi, Alsium, and Fregena. It is 300 stadia to Gravisci, and a place in between is called Regis Villa. They record that this was once the royal seat of Maleos [C226] the Pelasgian, who, it is said, held power in these places, along with his fellow-settlers the Pelasgians, but then went to Athens. This is the same race as those who possess Agylla. From Gravisci to Pyrgi is a little less than 180 [stadia]. It is the port of the Caeretanians, who are 30 stadia away. It has a sanctuary of Eilethyia – a Pelasgian foundation – which was once rich but was robbed by Dionysios [I] the tyrant of the Sikeliotes when he sailed against Kyrnos. From Pyrgi to Ostia is 260 [stadia], and in between are Alsium and Fregena. This is it about the Tyrrhenian coastline.

(9) In the interior there are cities in addition to those already mentioned: Arretium, Perusia, Volsinii, and Sutrium. In addition there are numerous towns: Blera, Ferentinum, Falerii, Faliscum, Nepita, Statonia, and a number of others. Some of these are organized as they were from the beginning, and others have been settled by the Romans, or have been reduced, as are the case with Veii (which often went to war) and Fidenae. Some say that the Falerians are not Tyrrhenians but Faliscians, a distinct people, and others that the Faliscians have a city with a unique language. They say that Aequum Faliscum is situated on the Flaminian Road between Ocriculi and Rome. The city of Feronia is at the foot of Mount Soraktos, with the same name as a certain indigenous divinity who is particularly honored by the locals, and whose precinct is there and which has a remarkable festival.

Those who are possessed by the divinity walk with bare feet through a great amount of charcoal and ashes without harm, and many people come together at the same time in order to attend the ceremonies (which are held every year), as well as to see what has been described. Farthest in the interior is Arretium, near the mountains. At any rate, it is 1,200 stadia from Rome, although Clusium is 800, and Perusia is near them.

The lakes add to the prosperity of the territory, as they are large and numerous. They are navigable and provide food for many marsh animals and birds. Reeds, papyrus, and flower tufts are sent to Rome by means of the rivers that the lakes send forth as far as the Tiberis. Among these are the Ciminia, the one near Volsinii, the one near Clusium and the one nearest Rome and the sea, the Sabata. Farthest away is the one near Arretium (the Trasumenna), near which are the passes for armies from Keltike into Tyrrhenia that Hannibal used. There are two, this one and the one toward Ariminum through Ombrike. The better one is that toward Ariminum, as the mountains become considerably lower there, but since the passes were carefully guarded, he was forced to choose the more difficult one, and he gained control of it having defeated Flaminius in a great battle. Moreover, there are abundant hot springs in Tyrrhenia, and because they are near to Rome, they are no less popular than those at Baiae, which are the most famous of all. [C227]

(10) Beyond Tyrrhenia to the east is Ombrike, which takes its beginning at the Apennines and extends still farther, to the Adria. Beginning at Ravenna, it occupies what is nearby: successively Sarsina, Ariminum, Sena, and Kamarinon. There are also the Aisis River, Mount Cingulum, Sentinum, the Metauros River, and the sanctuary of Tyche. Around these places is the former boundary between Italia and Keltike (the part near the sea), although this has often been changed by the rulers. Formerly they made the Aisis the boundary, and then the Rubicon River. The Aisis is between Ankon and Sena, and the Rubicon between Ariminum and Ravenna, and both empty into the Adria. Now that everything as far as the Alps is accepted as Italia, it is necessary to disregard these boundaries. Nevertheless everyone agrees that Ombrike itself extends all the way to Ravenna, for they [the Ombrians] live there. From there to Ariminum is about 300 [stadia], they say, and going from Ariminum to Rome on the Flaminian Road through Ombrike the entire route as far as Ocriculi and the Tiberis is 1,350 stadia. This is its length, but the width varies. Cities within the Apennine Mountains and worthy of mention on the Flaminian Road itself are Ocriculi (near the Tiberis), Larolon, and Narnia, through which the Nar River flows, joining the Tiberis a little above Ocriculi and navigable

for small vessels. Then there are Carsuli and Mevania, by which the Teneas flows, which brings [products] from the plain in small vessels down to the Tiberis. There are other settlements that have increased because of the road rather than because of political organization: Forum Flaminium, Nuceria (where wooden implements are made) and Forum Sempronium. On the right of the road, going from Ocriculi to Ariminum are Interamna, Spoletium, Aesium, and Camertes, in those mountains that are the boundary of Picentina. On the other side are Ameria, Tuder (a well-walled city), Hispellum, and Iguvium, which is near the passes over the mountains. The

[C228]   entire territory is prosperous although somewhat mountainous and nourishes its people on zea rather than wheat.

Sabina, which is next, is also mountainous, lying alongside in the same manner as the former does to Tyrrhenia. Much of Latina that is near to this and to the Apennine Mountains is somewhat rough. These two peoples begin at the Tiberis and Tyrrhenia and extend to that part of the Apennine Mountains which lie at a slant toward the Adria, although, as I have said, Ombrike goes beyond them, as far as the sea. This is enough to say about the Ombrians.

Part 3:   Sabina and Latina

(1) The Sabines live in a narrow territory, but its length extends 1,000 stadia from the Tiberis and the town of Nomentum as far as the Vestinians. They have few cities, and those have been reduced because of constant wars: Amiternum and Reate, which is near the village of Interocrea and the cold springs at Cotiliae, which cure diseases by drinking from them and sitting in them. Foruli also belongs to the Sabines, on rocks better suited to revolution than settlement. Kyres is now a village but was a notable city from which the Roman kings Titus Tatius and Numa Pompilius originated. Because of this place public speakers use the name "Kyritians" for the Romans. Treboula, Eretum, and other such settlements should be enumerated as villages rather than cities.

The entire land is especially well planted with olives and vines, and produces many acorns. It is notable for every kind of cattle, and the breed of mules from Reate are remarkably widely known. As they say, Italia is the best rearer of animals and fruits, although different types are pre-eminent in different places.

The Sabines are exceedingly ancient, and are also autochthonic. The Picentinians and Saunitians are settlers from them, the Leukanians from the latter, and the Brettians from them. Their old-fashioned quality could be considered proof of their bravery and other virtues, through which they have survived to the present time. Fabius [F27] the historian says that the Romans understood wealth for the first time when they became established as masters of these people. The Salarian Road has been laid through their region – although it is not long – as well as the Nomentana, which joins with it at Eretum (a Sabine village lying beyond the Tiberis) and which begins at the same gate, the Colline.

(2) Latina is situated next, in which the city of the Romans is, comprising many that were formerly not Latin, including the Aequians, Volscians, Hernicians, the Aborigines who were around Rome itself, the Rutulians who held ancient Ardea, and other groups, larger and smaller, who were [C229] around Rome at the time when the city was first founded. Some of these happened to live autonomously in scattered villages. They say that Aineias, along with his father Anchises and his son Askanios, after landing at Laurentum, which was on the shore near Ostia and the Tiberis, founded a city a little above the sea (within a distance of 24 stadia). They encountered Latinos, the king of the Aborigines, who lived in the place where Rome is now, and who used those with Aineias as allies against the neighboring Rutulians who occupied Ardea (it is 160 stadia from Ardea to Rome). After his victory he founded a city named after his daughter Lavinia. The Rutulians engaged in battle again and Latinos fell, but Aineias was victorious and became king, calling those under him the Latins. After his death, and that of his father, Askanios founded Alba on Mount Albanus, which is the same distance from Rome as Ardea. Here the Romans along with the Latins sacrificed to Zeus – all their collective administration gathered together – and at the time of the sacrifice they established one of their distinguished young men as ruler of the city.

The [stories] about Amollius and his brother Numitor are said to be from 400 years later, and are mythic but closer to the truth. Both succeeded to the rule of Alba from the descendants of Askanios, which extended as far as the Tiberis. Amollius, the younger, elbowed out the elder and ruled. As there were a son and daughter of Numitor, he treacherously killed the former on a hunt. The latter, so that she would remain childless, he made a priestess of Hestia, for the sake of her virginity. She was named Rhea Silva. When it was discovered that she had been seduced (as she bore twin children), instead of killing them he imprisoned her – for the sake of his brother – and exposed them on the Tiberis, by a hereditary custom. According to mythology, however, the children were begotten by Ares, and after they were exposed they were seen to be suckled by a she-wolf. They were taken up and raised by Phaistylos, one of the swineherds of the region (although it is necessary to assume that it was someone important, a subject of Amollius, who took them and raised them), who named one Romulus and the other Remus. When they became adults they attacked Amollius and his children, and upon defeating them and the devolving of the rule upon Numitor, they returned home and founded Rome in a location that was suitable (not by [C230] choice but by necessity). The site was not fortified and it did not have enough suitable land surrounding it that was fitting for a city. People did not live together with them, for they would live by themselves – although almost adjoining the walls of the city being founded – and not even pay attention to the Albans. These were Collatia, Antemnae, Fidenae, Labicum, and other such places that were towns then but are now villages or have been acquired by individuals, all of which are forty stadia or a little more from Rome. At any rate, between the fifth and sixth milestones that mark the distance from Rome is a place called Festi, which is known once to have indicated the boundary of Roman territory. The priests celebrate sacrifices called the Ambarvia there and in many other places considered boundaries, on the same day.

They say that a quarrel arose about the foundation and that Remus was eliminated. After the foundation Romulus collected a promiscuous crowd of men by making a refuge of a precinct between the summit and the Capitolium, and declared as citizens all the neighbors who had fled there. Since no intermarriage occurred, he announced that there would be a horse race sacred to Poseidon, the one that is celebrated today. When a large number had come together, most of whom were Sabines, he told those needing a wife to seize one of the maidens who had come. Titus Tatius, the king of the Kyritians, attempted to avenge the outrage through arms, but agreed with Romulus to have the rule and government in common. After the treacherous death of Tatius at Lavinium, Romulus ruled alone, with the consent of the Kyritians. After him Numa Pompilius, a fellow-citizen of Tatius, succeeded to the rule, receiving it by consent of his subjects. This is the most faithful account of the founding of Rome.

(3) There is another one, older and legendary, in which they say that it was an Arkadian settlement of Euandros. Herakles was entertained as a guest by him when he was driving the cattle of Geryon. Euandros had learned from his mother Nikostrate – who was skilled in prophecies – that Herakles was destined to become a god after completing his labors. He told this to Herakles and dedicated a precinct to him, making sacrifice in the Hellenic manner, something that is still kept today in honor of Herakles. And Acilius [F1], the Roman historian, puts this forth as proof that Rome was a Hellenic foundation and that the hereditary sacrifice to Herakles is in

the Hellenic manner. The Romans also honor the mother of Euandros, considering her as one of the nymphs, although her name was changed to Carmenta.   [C231]

(4) Nevertheless the Latins were few at the beginning, and most of them did not pay attention to the Romans. Later, amazed at the ability of Romulus and the kings after him, they all became subjects. After the putting down of the Aequians, Volscians, and Hernicians, and still earlier, the Rutulians and Aborigines, as well as the Rhaikians, the Argyrouskians, and some Prefernians, their entire territory was called Latina. The Volscians had the Pomentine Plain, on the border of the Latins, and the city of Apiola, which was destroyed by Tarquinius Priscus. The Aequians are the closest neighbors of the Kyritians, and their cities were also sacked by him. His son took Suessa, the metropolis of the Volscians. The Hernicians lived near Lanuvium, Alba, and Rome itself, and Aricia, Tellenae, and Antium were not far away. In the beginning the Albans lived in harmony with the Romans, as they spoke the same language and were Latins, and although they were both ruled by kings they happened to be separate. Yet they intermarried with one another and had sanctuaries – those at Alba – and other political rights in common. Later they went to war and Alba was sacked, except for the sanctuary, and the Albans were judged to be Roman citizens. Regarding the other neighboring cities, some were destroyed and others humbled because of their disobedience, but some were strengthened because of their goodwill. Today the coast to Sinoessa, from Ostia, is called Latina, but formerly it went only as far as the Kirkaion. And formerly it did not possess much of the interior, but later it extended as far as Campania and the Saunitians and Paelignians, and others who live in the Apennines.

(5) All of it is prosperous, producing everything, except for a few districts on the coast that are marshy and unhealthy, such as those of the Ardeatians, those between Antium and Lanuvium as far as Pomentium, and some of the Setine region and that around Tarracina and the Kirkaion or anywhere that is mountainous or rocky. Yet these are not completely unworked or useless but provide abundant pasture or woodland, or certain fruits from what is marshy or rocky. Caecubum, which is marshy, nourishes a tree vine that produces the best wine.

The cities on the sea in Latina include Ostia, a city that is harborless because of siltation from the Tiberis, which is filled by many rivers. The merchant ships anchor in the open sea (which is dangerous because of the swell); nevertheless, conquered by profit and because of the abundance of   [C232] service boats that receive cargo and bring back cargo, they can sail away swiftly before touching the river, or, when they have been lightened somewhat, can sail in and go as far as Rome, 190 stadia. Ostia was founded by Ancus Marcius. Such is this city.

Next is Antium, itself a city without a harbor. It is situated on rocks and is about 260 stadia distant from Ostia. Today it has been given to the rulers for leisure and relief from politics, when they can take the opportunity, and because of this luxurious residences have been established in the city for such visits. Formerly they possessed ships and engaged in piracy along with the Tyrrhenians, although they were already Roman subjects. Because of this Alexander made complaints in earlier times. Later Demetrios, sending the pirates that he had captured back to Rome, said that he was doing these people a favor because of their relationship with the Hellenes, for it was not proper for these men to send out pirates while they were the rulers of Italia and had located in their agora a sanctuary in honor of the Dioskouroi, those whom all name the Saviors, yet at the same time sending plunderers of their native land to Hellas. The Romans stopped such activities.

Midway between these cities is Lavinium, with a sanctuary of Aphrodite common to the Latins, although the Ardeatians, through attendants, take care of it. Then there is Laurentum. Ardea lies beyond them, a foundation of the Rutulians, 70 stadia inland from the sea. There is an Aphrodision nearby where the Latins hold festivals. The Saunitians destroyed these places and only traces of the cities are left, honored both because Aineias visited there and for the sacred rites that they say have been handed down from those times.

(6) After Antium is the Kirkaion, in 290 stadia, a mountain with the form of an island in the sea and marshes. They say that it is abundant in roots, perhaps because of its association with the myth of Kirke. There is a small town, a sanctuary of Kirke, and an altar of Athena, where some bowl is shown that they say belonged to Odysseus. Between these places is the Storas River with an anchorage. Next there is a beach exposed to the Lips wind, where the only harbor is a small one at Kirkaion.

Lying above this in the interior is the Pomentine Plain, and next to it is [C233] where the Ausonians formerly lived, who also held Campania. After these are the Oskans who had a share in Campania, but now everything as far as Sinoessa is held by the Latins, as I said [5.3.4]. There is a certain pecularity with the Oskans and the Ausonian people: although the Oskans have died out, their dialect persists among the Romans, so that at a certain ancestral competition their poems are brought on stage and recited like mimes. The Ausonians never once lived on the Sikelian Sea but the open sea is called "Ausonian."

Next, within a hundred stadia of the Kirkaion, is Tarracina, which was formerly called Trachine because of its character. There is a great marsh in front of it, created by two rivers. The larger one is called the Aufidus. Here the Appian Road first touches the sea, which is the most travelled and was laid from Rome as far as Brentesion. Of the cities on the sea, it touches only Tarracina, those that are next (Formiae, Minturnae, and Sinoessa), and those that are farthest (Taras and Brentesion). Near to Tarracina, as one goes to Rome, a canal runs along the Appian Road, which in many places is filled by water from the marshes and rivers. Most sail on it at night, so they can embark in evening and disembark in the morning, and travel the remainder on the road, but [some] also [travel] by day. They are towed by a mule.

Next is Formiae, a Lakonian foundation, which was formerly called Hormiai because of its good mooring place [*hormos*]. They also named the gulf in between the Kaiatian, for the Lakonians call everything hollow "kaietas." Some say that the eponym of the gulf was the nurse of Aineias. It has a length of 100 stadia, beginning at Tarracina, as far as the homonymous promontory. There are exceedingly large and open caves there that have large luxurious residences in them. From here to Formiae is 40 [stadia]. Midway between it and Sinoessa is Minturnae, about 80 stadia distant from each. The Liris River flows through it, formerly called the Klanis. It runs from the interior, from the Apennine Mountains and the territory of the Vestinians past the town of Fregellae (which was formerly a notable city), and empties into a sacred grove that is greatly honored by those in Minturnae, situated below the city. In the open sea, lying off the caves and visible most of the time, are two islands, Pandataria and Pontia, which are small but well populated, not far distant from one another and 250 [stadia] from the mainland. Caecubum is at the Kaiatian Gulf, and then there is Fundi, a city located on the Appian Road. All these places produce [C234] especially good wines. The Caecubian, Fundanian, and Setinian are distinguished names, as are the Falernian, Alban, and Statanian. Sinoessa is located on the gulf, from which it has its name, as "sinus" means gulf. There are hot baths nearby that are exceedingly useful for certain diseases. These are the cities of the Latins on the sea.

(7) In the interior, the first [city] above Ostia is Rome, the only one situated on the Tiberis, about which it has already been said [5.3.2] that it was founded by necessity rather than choice. It must also be added that those who settled certain additional portions later were unable to master what was better, but were slaves to what was already founded. The first [settlers] walled the Capitolium, Palatium, and Quirinus Hills, which was

so easy for outsiders to ascend that Titus Tatius took it as his approach when he attacked in order to avenge the outrageous seizure of the maidens. Ancus Marcius included Mount Caelium and Mount Aventine, and the plain between them, which were separated from each other and from what was previously walled, acting by necessity, so as not to allow well-fortified hills to be outside the walls for those wishing a good natural fortress. Yet he could not fill out the entire circuit as far as the Quirinus. Servius corrected the omission and filled it up by adding the Esquiline Hill and the Viminalis. These are also easy for outsiders to attack, and thus they excavated a deep ditch and took the earth inside, extending a mound about six stadia along the inner brow of the trench, adding a wall and towers from the Colline Gate to the Esquiline. Below the center of the mound is a third gate homonymous with the Viminalis Hill. Such are the defenses of the city, although other defenses were needed. And it seems to me that the first [settlers] undertook the same consideration both for themselves and those later, so it was appropriate for the Romans that their safety and prosperity were not due to the defenses but their weapons and their own distinction, believing that walls do not protect men but men [protect] the walls. In the beginning the good and extensive land around them belonged to others, the location of the city made it easy to attack, and there was nothing fortunate in the place that could be congratulated. When, through their distinction and hard work, the land became their own, there appeared a [C235] certain concurrence of good things that completely exceeded the natural situation. Because of this, the city, although it has grown so much, endures in its sustenance, as well as wood and stone for house construction, which is incessant because of the collapses, conflagrations, and resales, which themselves are incessant. The resales are voluntary collapses, as they are demolished and rebuilt according to one's wishes, one after another. To implement this, there is a wonderful supply of quarries and woodlands, as well as the rivers that bring [their products] down, first the Anio, flowing from Alba, the Latin city next to the Marsians (through the plain below it, as far as the junction with the Tiberis), then the Nar and Teneas (which run through Ombrike to the same river), the Tiberis, and the Klanis, through Tyrrhenia and the region of Clusium.

Sebastos Caesar paid attention to such deficiencies of the city, organizing a force of freedmen against conflagration, and to assist in the case of collapses, reducing the height of new buildings, and preventing the erection of anything on public roads beyond 70 feet. But these corrections would have been inadequate, except that the quarries, forests, and easy transportation survive.

(8) The nature of the place has supplied these advantages for the city, but the Romans have added others through their foresight. The Hellenes succeeded especially well with their foundations, aiming at beauty, strength, harbors, and fertile land, but the former had particular foresight in what the latter paid no attention to, such as the laying down of roads, the introduction of water, and sewers that are able to wash away the refuse of the city into the Tiberis. They have also laid down roads throughout the country, adding cuts through hills and embankments through valleys, so that covered wagons can ferry freight. The sewers are vaulted with fitted stone, and it is possible for certain fodder wagons to pass through them. Such an amount of water comes in through the aqueducts that rivers flow through the city and sewers, and almost every house has a cistern, pipes, and numerous fountains, something that Marcus Agrippa was most interested in, as well as adorning the city with many other embellishments.

As is said, the ancients took little account of the beauty of Rome,   [C236]
concerned with other greater and more necessary things. Those later – especially today, down to my time – have not fallen behind in this, having filled the city with many beautiful embellishments. Indeed, Pompeius, the God Caesar, and Sebastos, as well as his children, friends, wife, and sister, have surpassed everyone in their eagerness and expense for construction. Most of these are in the Campus Martius, which has received, in addition to its natural quality, adornment through foresight. The size of the field is notable, as it provides for simultaneous and indeed unhindered chariot racing and other equestrian activities, as well as for the multitude who exercise with balls, hoops, and wrestling. The constructions located around it, the soil that has grass throughout the year, and the crowns of the hills above the river, coming as far as its stream, show to the eye a stage painting, a view that it is difficult to draw away from. Because they believed that this was a most sacred place, they constructed here the memorials of their most distinguished men and women. Most remarkable is the so-called Mausoleion, a great mound on a high foundation of white stone, near the river. As far as its summit it is thickly shaded with evergreen trees, and on its top is a bronze image of Sebastos Caesar. Under the mound he, his relatives, and associates are placed, and behind it is a large grove with wonderful promenades. In the center of the field is the precinct of his crematorium, which is of white stone, surrounded by an iron fence and planted inside with black poplars.

Near to this field is another field with a great number of stoas around it, as well as groves, three theaters, an amphitheater, and expensive temples in succession to one another, so it would seem to demonstrate that the rest of the city is incidental. Moreover, if one passes on to the ancient agora, one would see one after another parallel with it, with basilical stoas and temples, and one would also see the Capitolium and the works there, as well as those on the Palatium and in the Promenade of Livia, easily forgetting what was outside. This is Rome.

(9) Regarding the other cities of Latina, some of them are distinguished among themselves, and others would largely be defined by the best-known roads that have been laid through Latina: situated on them, near them, or between them. The best known of these roads are the Appia, Latina, and [C237] Valeria. The former defines the portions of Latina next to the sea, as far as Sinoessa, and the latter the parts of Latina next to Sabina, as far as the Marsians. The Latina is between them, joining the Appia at Casilinum, a city 19 stadia distant from Capua. It begins at the Appia, turning from it to the left near Rome, crossing the Tusculanian Mountains between the city of Tusculum and Mount Albanus, going down to the town of Algidus and the Pictae Inns. There the Labicana joins it, which begins at the Esquiline Gate – as does the Praenestina – and it leaves both it and the Esquiline Plain on the left and continues for more than 120 stadia. Coming near to Labicum, a demolished ancient establishment located on a height, it leaves both it and Tusculum on the right, ending at Pictae and the Latina. This place is 210 stadia distant from Rome. Then, continuing on the Latina itself, there are notable settlements and cities: Ferentinum, Frusino (past which the Cosa River flows), Fabrateria (past which the Trerus flows), Aquinum (which is a large city, past which the Melpis flows, a large river), Interamnium (located at the confluence of two rivers, the Liris and another), and Casinum, which is also a notable city and the last one in Latina. What is called Teanum Sidicinum, located next, shows from its epithet that it belongs to the Sidicinians. They are Oskans, a defunct Campanian people, and thus one could say that this is Campania, although it is the largest city on the Latina. Next is that of the Calenians, itself notable, adjoining Casilinum.

(10) Regarding each side of the Latina, on the right are [the cities] between it and the Appia: Setia and Signia, which produce wine, that of the former one of the most expensive and that of the latter the best astringent for the bowels, called the Signinum. Beyond here are Privernum, Cora, Suessa, Trapontion, Velitrae, and Aletrium. In addition there is Fregellae (past which the Liris flows, which empties at Minturnae), now a village, although it was once notable and possessed many of those just mentioned. Today they come together there to hold a market and certain festivals. After having revolted, it was destroyed by the Romans. Most of these – those on the

Latina and beyond it – are situated among the Hernicians, Aecians and Volscians, and are Roman foundations.

On the left of the Latina are those between it and the Valeria. Gabii, [C238] located on the Praenestine Road, has a stone quarry that is the most useful of all to Rome, equidistant from Rome and Prainestos, about a hundred stadia. Then there is Prainestos, about which we will speak shortly. Then there are those in the mountains above Prainestos: Capitulum – a small city of the Hernicians – Anagnia, a notable city, Cereatae, and Sora, which the Liris passes by, flowing to Fregellae and Minturnae. Then there are certain others, and then Venafrum, where there is the best olive oil. The city is located on a height, and the Volturnus flows past the base of the hill, and going past Casilinum it empties at its homonymous city. Aesernia and Allifae are already Saunitic cities. The former was destroyed in the Marsic War, but the latter continues.

(11) The Valeria begins at Tibur and leads to the Marsians and Corfinium, the metropolis of the Paelignians. On it are the Latin cities of Varia, Carseoli, and Alba, and nearby is the city of Cuculum. Visible to those in Rome are Tibur, Prainestos, and Tusculum. Tibur has a Herakleion and also a waterfall made by the navigable Anio, which falls down from a great height into a deep and wooded ravine near the city itself. From there it passes through an extremely fruitful plain, past quarries of the Tiburtine stone, those in Gabii, and those of what is called the red [stone], so that the removal from the quarries and the transport are especially easy, and thus most of the works in Rome are produced there. Also in this plain flow the so-called Albula waters, which are cold from many springs and healthful for a variety of diseases, both through drinking and bathing. There are also the Labana [waters], not far away on the Nomentana, in the region around Eretum. Prainestos is where the sanctuary of Tyche is, distinguished for its oracle.

Both of these cities happen to be located near the same mountains, about a hundred stadia distant from one another, but from Rome Prainestos is double that and Tibur less. They say that both are Hellenic, and at any rate Prainestos was formerly called Polystephanos. Each is fortified, but Prainestos is more fortified, for it has as a citadel a high mountain above the city which at its rear is disconnected from the continuous mountain range by a neck rising two stadia in a vertical ascent. In addition to this [C239] natural strength, underground passages have been bored through from every side as far as the plains, some for the sake of water and others for secret exits, in one of which Marius was killed while being besieged. In other cities good fortifications are considered a good thing, for the most part, but for the Prainestinians they are a misfortune because of Roman sedition, as those who make revolution flee there for refuge. When it is besieged and forced to surrender, in addition to the suffering in the city, it happens that the region is estranged, and guilt transferred to the guiltless. The Verestis River flows through the region. These above-mentioned cities are to the east of Rome.

(12) Within this mountainous region is another ridge, which leaves a hollow – that around Algidus – that remains high as far as Mount Albanus. Tusculum is situated on it, a city not lacking in constructions. It is adorned with plantings and structures encircling it, especially in its lower parts (those in the portion toward Rome). Here the Tusculanum is a fertile and well-watered hill, which rises in many places to gentle summits that have remarkable constructions in a royal style. Adjoining it are the lower parts of Mount Albanus, with the same quality and constructions. Next are the plains, some touching Rome and its suburbs and others toward the sea. Those toward the sea are less healthy but the others are accommodating and similarly furnished.

After Albanus is Aricia, a city on the Appian Road 160 stadia from Rome. The place is in a hollow, but it has a strong citadel. Above it is Lanuvium, a Roman city, on the right side of the Appian Road, from which the sea and Antium are visible, as well as the Artemision, called Nemos, which is on the left side of the road going up from Aricia[9]. . .and the sanctuary is a copy of Tauropolos, they say, and in fact a certain barbarian and Skythian custom controls the sanctuary. Established as priest is a man who is a runaway slave and has killed with his own hand the former priest. Thus he always has a sword and looks around for the attacks, ready to defend himself. The sanctuary is in a grove, with a lake like a sea lying in front of it. Lying around it in a circle is a mountain brow that is exceedingly high and isolates the sanctuary and the water in a deep and hollow place. One can see the [C240] springs from which the lake is filled – one of them is called Egeria, after a certain eponymous deity – but the outflows are invisible, although they can be seen far outside where they emerge onto the surface.

(13) Near these places there is also Mount Albanus, which rises far above the Artemision and the surrounding brows, although they themselves are high and sufficiently steep. It also has a lake, much larger than that at the Artemision. The previously mentioned cities of Latina are farther away than these. Alba is the farthest in the interior of the cities of Latina, bordering on the Marsians and located on a high crag near Lake Fucinus, which is the size

---

[9] The text is defective at this point.

of an open sea. It is mostly used by the Marsians and all their neighbors. They say that at times it fills almost as far as the mountainous territory and then lowers again, so that marshy areas dry out and can be farmed, due to sporadic and invisible changes to the moisture in the depths, as it flows back again, or the springs fail completely and are compressed back again, just as – it is said – happens with the Amenanos, which flows through Katane and fails for many years but then flows again. It is believed that the springs of the Marcia aqueduct, which provides drinking water for Rome and is the water most favored over others, come from the Fucinus. Because Alba is situated deep in the territory and is well-walled, the Romans have often used it as a prison, there confining those who must be guarded.

Part 4:   The central interior and Campania

(1) Having begun with the peoples next to the Alps, and the Apennine Mountains that are next to them, and then passing over [that region], we have traversed everywhere within that lies between the Tyrrhenian Sea and those Apennine Mountains that incline toward the Adria, as far as the Saunitians and Campanians. We will now go back and disclose those who live in the mountains as well as in the foothills, both outside as far as the Adriatic coast, and within. But it is necessary to begin again at the boundaries of Keltike.

(2) Picentina is after the Ombrian cities that are between Ariminum and Ankon. The Picentinians come from Sabina, with their ancestors led on their way by a woodpecker, from which their name comes, for the bird is named the "picus" and is believed to be sacred to Ares. Where they live begins at the mountains and goes as far as the plains and sea, with the territory increased in length rather than width. It is good for everything, although better for fruit trees than grain. Its breadth – from the mountains [C241] to the sea – is irregular in terms of the intervals, and its length, sailing along the coast from the Aisis River as far as Castrum, is 800 stadia.

The [first of the] cities is Ankon, a Hellenic one, founded by Syracusians fleeing the tyranny of Dionysios [I]. It lies on a promontory, which turns toward the north, enclosing a harbor. It is exceedingly abundant in both wine and wheat. Near it is Auxumum, a city slightly above the sea, and then Septempeda, Pneuentia, Potentia, and Firmum Picenum, whose seaport is Castellum. Next is the sanctuary of Kypra, which was established and founded by the Tyrrhenians, who call Hera "Kypra." Then there is the Truentinus River and its eponymous city, and then Castrum Novum and the Matrinus River, which flows from the city of the Adrianians, and which has on it their eponymous seaport of Adria. It is in the interior, as also is Asculum Picenum, which is a most well-fortified place, and[10]...on which its wall lies, but the surrounding mountains are inaccessible to armies.

Beyond Picentina are the Vestinians, Marsians, Paelignians, Marrucinians, and Frentanians (who are a Saunitic people). They live in the mountainous country, touching the sea only in small areas. These peoples are small in numbers but they are extremely courageous and have often demonstrated this virtue to the Romans: first, when they went to war, second, when they joined them on an expedition, and third, when they needed freedom and civil rights but did not receive them and revolted, thus kindling the so-called Marsic War, proclaiming that Corfinium, the metropolis of the Paelignians, was the common city for all Italiotes (instead of Rome), and the base of operations for the war, changing its name to Italica. There they gathered their followers and appointed consuls and praetors. They held out for two years until they accomplished the partnership for which they had gone to war. It was named the Marsic War because of those who began the revolt, especially Pompaedius.

They live mostly in villages, but they also have cities. Those above the sea are Corfinium, Sulmo, Marruvium, and Teate, the metropolis of the Marrucinians. On the sea itself is Aternum, bordering on Picentina and homonymous with the river that separates Vestina and Marrucina. It flows from Amiternina through the Vestinians, leaving the Marruvinians on the right, who lie above the Paelignians, and it can be crossed on a bridge of [C242] boats. The eponymous town belongs to the Vestinians, and is used as a common seaport by the Paelignians and Marrucinians. The bridge of boats is 24 stadia distant from Corfinium.

After Aternum is Orton, the seaport of the Frentanians, and Buca – which is also Frentanian – bordering on Teanum Apulum. Ortonion is among the Frentanians, on cliffs belonging to pirates, whose homes are put together from the wreckage of ships and who are savage in every way. Between Orton and Aternum is the Sagros River, the boundary between the Frentanians and the Paelignians. The coastal voyage from the Picentinians to those Apulians whom the Hellenes call the Daunians is about 490 stadia.

(3) Next after Latina is Campania, which extends along the sea. Above it in the interior is Saunitis, as far as the Frentanians and Daunians, and then the Daunians themselves and the other peoples as far as the Sikelian Strait.

One must speak first of Campania. There is a good-sized gulf from Sinoessa extending on the coast as far as Misenum, and another gulf,

---

[10] Something is missing here, describing the situation of the wall.

much larger than the former, which they called the Krater, creating a bay from Misenum to the Athenaion, two promontories. Above these coasts lies the whole of Campania, the most fortunate of all plains, as well as the mountains of the Saunitians and the Oskans. Antiochos [F7] says that this territory is where the Opikians live, who are also called the Ausonians. Polybios [34.11.5–7] emphatically believes that they were two peoples, and says that the Opikians and Ausonians live in this territory around the Krater. Others say that the Opikians formerly lived there, as well as the Ausonians. Later the Sidicinians, an Oskan people, possessed it, but they were driven out by the Kymaians and then the Tyrrhenians. Because of its quality the plain became an area of contention, and the latter planted twelve cities there, the chief one of which was named Capua. Due to their luxuriousness they became soft, and just as they had been displaced from the territory around the Padus, they thus conceded this to the Saunitians, who were then driven out by the Romans.

A sign of its fruitfulness is that the best grain is produced here (I am speaking of wheat), from which groats come, much better than any other kind of rice or most grain products. It is reported that annually certain plains are seeded twice yearly with zea, a third time with millet, and a fourth time sown with vegetables. And the Romans obtain the best wine from here, the Falernian, Statanian, and Calenian, yet the Surrentinian is already becoming a match for these, because recent testing shows that it ages well. It is rich in olives everywhere around Venafrum, which is on the border of the plains. [C243]

(4) The cities on the sea after Sinoessa include Liternum, where the memorial of Scipio is, the first one called Africanus. He spent his last days here, giving up politics because of his enmity toward certain people. A homonymous river flows by the city. In the same way the Volturnus is homonymous with the city that lies on it and which is next. It flows through Venafrum and the middle of Campania. Next after these is Kyme, a Chalkidean and Kymaian foundation of greatest antiquity. It is the oldest of all the Sikelian and Italiote [cities]. Those who led the group there, Hippokles of Kyme and Megasthenes of Chalkis, made an agreement with each other that one [place] would be the founder and the other the eponym. Although it is now called Kyme, it is considered to have been founded by Chalkis. Formerly it was prosperous, as is also that which is called the Phlegraian Plain, in which the story of the Gigantes is placed, for no other reason, than it seems that the land would be fought over because of its quality. Later, when the Campanians were established as masters of the city, they committed many outrages against their men, and, moreover, cohabited

with their women. Nevertheless there are many traces of Hellenic attitudes, ceremonies, and customs preserved there. Some say that Kyme is named after the *kymata* ["swells"], because of the surf at the nearby shore. It is the best place for catching large fish.

On this gulf there is a certain forest of shrubs that extends for many stadia across a waterless and sandy area, which is called the Gallinaria Forest. Here the naval commanders of Sextus Pompeius gathered bands of pirates at the time that he caused the revolt in Sikelia.

(5) Near Kyme is the promontory of Misenum, and between them is the Acherousian Lake, a certain effusion of the sea formed by shoal water. After rounding Misenum there is immediately a harbor, at the base of the cape, and after it the shore forms a deep bay, on which are Baiae and the hot [C244] spring waters that are suitable for the luxuriant and also for curing disease. Contiguous to Baiae is the Lokrinos Gulf, and, behind it, Aornos, making a peninsula that cuts off the land as far as Misenum by an oblique line between it and Kyme. There remains an isthmus of only a few stadia through the tunnel to Kyme itself and to the sea next to it.

Those previous to us have recounted that the events of the Homeric *Nekyia* occurred at Aornos, and moreover they related that an oracle of the dead was here and that Odysseus visited it. The Aornos Gulf is deep at the shore and has a good outlet, with the size and nature of a harbor, although it is of no use as a harbor because the Lokrinos Gulf lies in front of it, and is somewhat shallow and large. Aornos is encircled by steep brows that rise up on all sides except where one sails in. Today these have been laboriously cultivated, although formerly they were thickly shaded by a wild and impassable forest of large trees, which, because of superstition, made the gulf shadowy. The locals add the story that birds flying over it fall into the water, killed by the exhalations, as at Ploutonia. It was assumed that this place was a Ploutonion, and only those who sacrificed in advance and propitiated the infernal deities could sail in. The priests holding a contract for the place were there to instruct them. A certain spring of potable water is on the sea there, but everyone kept away from it, believing it to be the water of the Styx, and the oracle is located somewhere around here. Because of this, as well as the nearby hot springs and Acherousia, they recognize it as the Pyriphlegethon. Ephoros [F134a] says that the place was inhabited by the Kimmerians, and that they lived in subterranean houses called *argillai*, coming and going to one another through tunnels, and welcoming strangers to the oracle, which is located far beneath the earth. They subsisted on mining and oracular consultation, and from a stipend provided by their king. Those around the oracle have an ancestral custom never to see the sun and go outside the chasm only at night. Because of this the Poet says the following about them: "bright Helios never looks upon them" [*Odyssey* 11.15–16, altered]. Later the people were destroyed by a certain king because the oracular experience did not turn out well for him. The oracle still survives, although removed to another place. [C245]

Such are the stories told before our time, but now the forest around Aornos has been cut down by Agrippa and the land has been built on, the underground passageway has been cut from Aornos as far as Kyme, and everything has been shown to be a myth, although the Cocceius who made the tunnel there, as well as the one to Neapolis from Dikaiarcheia (near Baiae),[11] rather understood the story just told about the Kimmerians, and perhaps he believed that it was an ancestral custom at this place for roads to be tunnelled.

(6) The Lokrinos Gulf widens as far as Baiae, shut off from the outer sea by a bank eight stadia in length and with the width of a wide wagon road, which, it is said, Herakles built when he was driving the cattle of Geryon. Waves would pass over its surface during storms, and it could not easily be used on foot, and thus Agrippa rebuilt it. One can sail in with light boats, but it is useless as an anchorage, although most excellent for catching oysters. Some say that this is Lake Acherousia, but Artemidoros [F43] that it is Aornos. Baiae is said to be the eponym of Baios, one of the companions of Odysseus, as Misenum[12] .... Next are the promontories around Dikaiarcheia, and the city itself. Formerly it was the Kymaian seaport, situated on a knoll, but at the time of the expedition of Hannibal the Romans made a combined settlement there and changed its name to Puteoli, from the wells [*putei*], although others [say] that it was from the stink [*puteo*] of the water, since the entire region, as far as Baiae and the Kymaia, is full of sulphur, fire, and hot water. Some believe that because of this the Kymaia was called Phlegra, and it is the wounds of the fallen Gigantes – caused by thunderbolts – that put forth the streams of fire and water. The city has become a major emporium, since it has man-made anchorages because of the natural quality of the sand, which is proportionate to the lime and water and creates a strong bonding and coagulation. Therefore by combining the cement with gravel, they can extend moles into the sea and make the open shore into bays, so that the largest merchant

---

[11] The statement about Cocceius' other tunnel is deleted by many editors as a gloss, although its validity seems to be shown by the rest of the sentence.

[12] "As Misenum" is not in all manuscripts; some editors delete it and others add "is from Misenos." If the name should be in the text, the thought as preserved is incomplete.

[C246] vessels can anchor safely. The Agora of Hephaistos lies immediately above the city, a plain enclosed by extremely hot ridges having numerous vents like ovens that are quite foul smelling, and the plain is full of sulphur that has washed down.

(7) After Dikaiarcheia there is Neapolis of the Kymaians. Later it was settled by the Chalkideans, along with some Pithekoussians and Athenians, and because of this it is called Neapolis. A memorial to one of the Seirenes, Parthenope, is visible, and, because of an oracle, a gymnastic contest is celebrated there. Later, certain Campanians were received as settlers, because of dissension, and they were forced to treat their worst enemies as their best friends, since they had become estranged from their friends. This is disclosed by the names of their demarchs, for the first are only Hellenic but later they are Hellenic mixed with Campanian. Numerous traces of Hellenic attitudes are present there, such as *gymnasia, ephebeia, phratriai*, and Hellenic names, although they are now Roman. Today a sacred contest in music and gymnastics is celebrated every fifth year, lasting several days, a match for the most famous ones of Hellas. There is also an underground passageway here, as the mountains between Dikaiarcheia and Neapolis have been excavated as at Kyme, with a road opened for many stadia that is wide enough for opposing teams to pass. Light is visible because frequent windows have been cut into the mountain, down to a great depth. Neapolis has springs of hot water and constructed baths not inferior to those at Baiae, although it is much smaller in population, for a new city has come into existence there, in no way less than Dikaiarcheia, where palaces have been built one after another. Those from Rome who retire there for the sake of leisure are attracted by the Hellenic lifestyle of Neapolis, such as those who have worked in education, or others, who, because of old age or lack of health, long for relaxation. Certain Romans, also, take pleasure in this life, seeing the large numbers of their own men who live that lifestyle, and they gladly become fond of the place and live there.

(8) Next is the fortress of Herakleion, situated on a promontory extend-ing into the sea, marvellously catching the Lips wind, which makes it a
[C247] healthy settlement. The Oskans possessed this place and the next one, Pompaia, which the Sarnus River flows past, and then the Tyrrhenians and Pelasgians and afterward the Saunitians, but they were expelled from those places. Pompaia is the seaport of Nola, Nuceria, and Acherrai (homonymous with a settlement near Cremona), and it is on the Sarnus River, which receives and sends down freight.

Mount Vesuvius lies above these places, which is settled all around with exceedingly attractive fields, except on the summit, whose greater portion is flat but completely unfruitful and ash-like in appearance. It manifests porous hollows in the rock that are sooty in color, as if they had been eaten by fire. Thus one might judge that this region once had been on fire and had craters of fire but was quenched when the fuel failed. Perhaps this is the reason for the surrounding fruitfulness, just as at Katane, it is said, the portion covered with ashes from the dust carried by the Aitnaian fire made the land suitable for the vine. It contains that which enriches both the burned-out soil and produces the fruits, and where there was enough enrichment it suitably burned out, as with all sulphurous matter, and when it had been deprived of moisture and became quenched and burned to ashes, it changed into productiveness.

Next to Pompaia is Syrrenton, of the Campanians, and lying in front of it is the Athenaion, which some call the Seirenoussai Promontory. On the cape is a sanctuary of Athena, built by Odysseus. It is a short sail from here across to the island of Capreae. Going around the cape, one comes to the deserted rocky islets called the Seirenes. On the Syrrenton side one is shown a sort of sanctuary with ancient dedications, as the locals honor the place. The gulf called the Krater comes to an end at this point, bounded by two promontories that look toward the south, Misenum and Athenaion. It is all fully equipped with the cities that I have mentioned, and the dwellings and plantations that are together in succession, thus giving the appearance of a city.

(9) Prochyte island lies off Misenum, broken off from Pithekoussai. Pithekoussai was settled by Eretrians and Chalkideans, who prospered there because of its fruitfulness and gold mines, but left the island because of a disagreement, and were also driven away because of earthquakes and the eruption of fire, the sea, and hot water, for the island has this sort of effluvia.   [C248] Because of this, those sent there by Hieron [I] the Syracusian tyrant also abandoned the island and the fortifications that they had built. The Neapolitans came and took it.

There is also the story in which they say that Typhon lies under the island, and flames and water erupt when he turns over, and at times islets with boiling water. What Pindar [*Pythian* 1.15–28] says is more believable, as he starts with the phenomena, since the entire strait – beginning from the Kymaia and going as far as Sikelia – is inflamed, with certain cavities in the depths that are connected to one another and to the mainland. Aitna also shows such a nature, as everyone records, as well as the Liparaian Islands and the region around Dikaiarcheia, Neapolis, and Baiae, and also Pithekoussai. This is what he had in mind when he said that Typhon lies below the entire place ("Now the sea-fenced heights above Kyme and Sikelia press on his

hairy breast" [*Pythian* 1.17–19]). Timaios [F58] also says that many marvels
are told by the ancients about Pithekoussai, and that shortly before his time
the Epomeus hill, in the middle of the island, was shaken by earthquakes
and threw up fire, thrusting what was between it and the sea into the ocean.
The land that had been burned to ashes was raised to a height and fell down
again onto the island like a whirlwind, and the sea withdrew for three stadia.
After withdrawing, it returned not much later and flowed back, inundating
the island, and thus the fire on it was quenched. Because of the noise, those
on the mainland fled from the coast into Campania. It is believed that the
hot waters there are a cure for stones.

 Capreae had two small towns in antiquity, but only one later. The
Neapolitans also possessed it, but lost Pithekoussai through war and then
regained it, as it was given to them by Sebastos Caesar, although he made
Capreae a private possession and built on it. These are the coastal cities of
Campania and the islands lying off it.

 (10) In the interior, Capua is the metropolis, being the head, as is
indicated by the etymology of its name, for one would consider the other
[C249] towns as small by comparison, except for Teanum Sidicinum, which is
notable. The former lies on the Appian Road, as do the others that lead from
it to Brentesion: Calatia, Caudium, and Beneventum. Casilinum is located
toward Rome on the Volturnus River, where 540 Prainestinian men were
besieged by Hannibal, who was in his prime, and they held out so long that
because of hunger a mouse was sold for two *minai*,[13] and the seller died but
the buyer survived. Seeing them sowing turnips near the wall, Hannibal
wondered – as was reasonable – at their long suffering and whether they
expected to last long enough for the turnips to ripen. Yet they all survived, it
is said, except for a few men who came to an end either through hunger or in
battle.

 (11) In addition to the previously mentioned Campanian cities, there are
Cales and Teanum Sidicinum, separated by the two Tychai situated on
either side of the Latina Road. There are also Suessula, Atella, Nola,
Nuceria, Acherrai, Abella, and other settlements smaller than these, some
of which are said to be Saunitic.

 The Saunitians formerly made expeditions as far as Latina around Ardea,
and afterward, possessing extensive power, ravaged Campania itself. As they
had learned to be ruled by other despots, they quickly submitted to their
commands. Now they [the Saunitai] were completely worn out by others,
last of all by Sulla, the Roman dictator. When he put down the Italiote

---

[13] The text here is uncertain.

revolt through many battles, he saw that they were holding together almost quite alone and were at the borders, so that they could go against Rome, and thus he engaged them in front of the walls. Some of them he cut down in battle – having ordered than none be taken alive – and the others, who had thrown down their weapons (around three or four thousand men, it is said) he brought down to a public encampment in the Campus and imprisoned them. Three days later he sent soldiers against them and cut their throats, and would not stop proscribing them until all the famous Saunitians were destroyed or were thrown out of Italia. To those who accused him of such excessive anger he said that he had learned from experience that not one Roman would survive in peace as long as the Saunitians remained together. Thus their cities have today become villages – and some have been completely abandoned – such as Bovianum, Aesernia, Panna, Telesia (near Venafrum), and such others, none of which is worthy to be considered a city. Yet we will go over them in due measure because of the reputation and power of Italia. Beneventum, however, has survived well, as has Venusia.

[C250]

(12) Regarding the Saunitians, there is a certain story that the Sabines, having been at war with the Ombrians for a long time, vowed – as do certain Hellenes – to consecrate what was produced that year. When they were victorious they sacrificed some of what was produced, and consecrated some. Then a scarcity occurred, and someone said that they should also consecrate their offspring, dedicating the children to Ares. When these became adults, they were sent away to make a settlement, led by a bull. When it lay down to rest among the Opikians (who happened to be living in villages), they were thrown out. The former settled there and slaughtered the bull for Ares (who had given it to them as a guide), according to the pronouncement of their seers. Thus it is reasonable that "Sabellian" is a nickname derived from their parents, but "Samnites," whom the Hellenes call "Saunitians," is for another reason. Some say that Lakonians joined the settlement, and because of this they were philhellenic, with certain of them called Pitanatians. But it seems that the Tarantinians fabricated this to flatter people of great power on their borders and at the same time to conciliate them, since at that time they [the Saunitians] would send forth an army of 80,000 infantry and 8,000 cavalry. They say that there is a law among the Saunitians that is honorable and which stimulates virtue: they are not allowed to give one's daughters to whomever one wishes, but every year ten young women are chosen, as well as ten young men, the best males and the best females, and of these the first girl is given to the first young man, and the second to the second, and so forth. If one receiving this gift of

honor changes and becomes worthless, he is dishonored and what he was given is taken away.

Next are the Hirpinians, who are also Saunitians. Their name is from the wolf that led them to their settlement, for "hirpos" is what the Saunitians call a wolf. They adjoin the Leukanians, who are in the interior. This is it about the Saunitians.

(13) The Campanians, because of the prosperity of the territory, happened to enjoy good and bad things equally. They were over-extravagant and thus would invite gladiators in pairs to dinner, whose number determined the importance of their dinners. When they submitted to Hannibal they received his army into winter quarters. It thus became so soft through pleasures that Hannibal said although he was the victor he was in danger of falling to his enemies because he received back an army of women rather than men. When the Romans conquered them, they were chastened by many wretched things, and later the land was apportioned out. Today, however, they live well, in harmony with the settlers and preserving their ancient reputation, in terms of the size of their city and the quality of their men.

[C251]

After Campania and the Saunitis are, on the Tyrrhenian Sea, the Picentinian people, a small detached portion of the Picentinians on the Adria, who were removed by the Romans to live on the Poseidoniate Gulf, which is today called the Paestanian. The city of Poseidonia, situated on the middle of the gulf, is now Paestus. The Sybarites, to be sure, had established a fortification on the sea, but the settlers removed them farther inland, and later the Leukanians took the city away from them, and then the Romans from the Leukanians. But a river makes the place unhealthy by spreading out into marshes.

Between the Seirenoussai and Poseidonia is Marcina, a Tyrrhenian foundation inhabited by the Saunitians. There is an isthmus of no more than 120 stadia from here to Pompeia via Nuceria. The Picentians extend as far as the Silaris River, which separates this territory from ancient Italia. A peculiarity is reported about it: its water is drinkable but a plant let down into it turns to stone although keeping its color and shape.

The metropolis of the Picentians was originally Picentia, but today they live in villages, having been dispersed by the Romans because of their alliance with Hannibal. Instead of being in the military, at that time they were appointed as couriers and letter carriers for the state, as were also the Leukanians and Brettians, for the same reason. As protection against them the Romans fortified Salernum, which is slightly above the sea. It is 260 stadia from the Seirenoussai to the Silaris.

BOOK 6

Southern Italia and Sikelia

Part 1:   Leukania and Brettia

(1) After the mouth of the Silaris is Leukania and the sanctuary of Argonian [C252]
Hera founded by Jason, and, nearby, within fifty stadia, is Poseidonia. As
one sails on the open sea[1]. . .the island of Leukosia, which is only a short
distance from the mainland. It is named after one of the Seirenes, who was
cast ashore here, according to the myth, after they threw themselves into
the depths. Lying in front of the island is the promontory opposite the
Seirenoussai that makes the Poseidoniate Gulf. As one goes around it, there
is another gulf adjoining, where there is a city that its founders (the
Phokaians) called Hyele, and others Ele from a certain spring, but today
it is Elea. This is where Parmenides and Zenon, the Pythagoreans, came
from. It seems to me that because of them the city was well governed (and
also in earlier times), and thus they held out against the Leukanians and the
Poseidoniates, and returned as masters, although lacking in territory and
number of people. At any rate, they are forced – because their land is most
wretched – to be involved with working on the sea, fish-salting factories,
and other industries. Antiochos [F8] says that after Phokaia had been
captured by Harpagos, the general of Kyros, those who were able to do so
embarked in light boats with their households, under Kreontiades, and
sailed first to Kyrnos and Massalia, but upon being driven away they
founded Elea. Some [say] that the name is from the Elees River. The city
is about 200 stadia distant from Poseidonia.

After this there is the promontory of Palinouros. Off Eleatis are the two
Oinotrides Islands, which have anchorages. After Palinouros is Pyxous, a [C253]
cape, harbor, and river, one name for the three. Mikythos, the ruler of
Messene in Sikelia, settled it, but the settlers, except for a few, went away
again. After Pyxous there is another gulf, river, and city, Laos, the last of

---

[1] The text is confused and something may be missing.

253

those in Leukania, slightly above the sea, a settlement of the Sybarites, 400 stadia from Ele. The entire sail along Leukania is 650 stadia. Nearby is the heroon of Drakon, one of the companions of Odysseus, about whom an oracle was given to the Italiotes: "at some time many people ["laos"] will be destroyed around Drakonian Laos." Those people who campaigned against Laos – the Hellenes of Italia – were defeated by the Leukanians, having been deceived by the oracle.

(2) These are the places on the Tyrrhenian coast that are Leukanian. Formerly they did not reach the other sea, and the Hellenes at the Tarantine Gulf possessed it. Before the Hellenes came, the Leukanians did not yet exist, and the Chonians and Oinotrians occupied these places. After the Saunitians had strengthened greatly and had thrown out the Chonians and Oinotrians, they settled Leukanians in this portion, and at the same time the Hellenes held both coasts as far as the Strait. The Hellenes and barbarians made war against each other for a long time. The tyrants of Sikelia and later the Karchedonians – at one time at war against the Romans for Sikelia and then for Italia itself – treated all of them badly, especially the Hellenes, who later took away much of the interior (something that began at the time of the Trojan matter), and who strengthened to such a point that this [region] and Sikelia were called Greater Hellas. Today all of it – except for Taras, Rhegion, and Neapolis – have become thoroughly barbarized, and are possessed by the Leukanians, Brettians, and the Campanians (in name, but in fact by the Romans, as they have become Roman). Yet he who treats the circuit of the earth must speak about what exists today as well as certain things that have already happened, especially those which are noteworthy.

Those of the Leukanians adjoining the Tyrrhenian Sea have been discussed, as well as those who hold the interior and live above the Tarantine Gulf. But they, the Brettians, and the Saunitians – from whom they originated – are so totally ruined that it is difficult to distinguish their
[C254]   settlements, for the reason that no common organization still remains among any of these peoples. Their characteristics, language, weaponry, dress, and such things, have disappeared, and their settlements – both individually and in detail – are completely obscure.

(3) I will speak generally about what I have heard concerning those living in the interior, without making a distinction between them, as well as the Leukanians and the Saunitians neighboring them. Petelia is considered the metropolis of the Leukanians and has been sufficiently inhabited down to the present. It was founded by Philoktetes, who fled Meliboia because of an uprising. It had such a strong position that the Saunitians once fortified it

against Thourioi. Ancient Krimissa, in the same region, was also [founded] by Philoktetes. Apollodoros [of Athens, F167], in his *On the Ships*, calling to mind Philoktetes, records that some say he came to the Krotoniatis and settled at the promontory of Krimissa and the city of Chone, above it (from which the Chonians were named), and that some of those with him – whom he had sent to the region of Eryx in Sikelia with Aigestes the Trojan – fortified Aigesta. Grumentum and Vertinae are in the interior, as well as Kalasarna and other small settlements, as far as Venusia, a notable city. I think that it and those following after it, going toward Campania, are Saunitic. Beyond Thourioi is located the territory called Tauriana.

The Leukanians are ethnically Saunitic. When they mastered the Posidoniates and their allies, they took over their cities. At other times they were a democracy, but in war they chose a king from those holding magistracies. Now they are Roman.

(4) The Brettians occupy the successive coast as far as the Sikelian Strait, for 1,350 stadia. Antiochos [F3a], in his treatise *On Italia*, says that this was called Italia – and this is what he is writing about – although formerly it was called Oinotria. He proclaims that its boundaries are, on the Tyrrhenian Sea, the same as I have said for Leukania (the Laos River), and on the Sikelian [Sea], Metapontion. The Tarantine, which adjoins Metapontion, he considers outside of Italia, and calls it Iagypia. In still earlier times, he says, those called Oinotrians and Italians were only within the isthmus that slopes toward the Sikelian Strait. The isthmus itself is 160 stadia and [C255] is between two gulfs, the Hipponiate (which Antiochos says is the Napitinos) and the Skylletic. The sail around the territory cut off within the Strait is 2,000 stadia. After this, he says, the name of Italia and Oinotria was extended as far as the Metapontine and the Siritis, as well as to the Chonians, an ordered Oinotrian people, who lived in these places and named the land Chonie. He spoke in a somewhat simple and old-fashioned way, not distinguishing between the Leukanians and the Brettians. Leukania is between the Tyrrhenian and Sikelian coasts, the former from the Silaris as far as the Laos, and the latter from Metapontion to Thourioi, and on the mainland from the Saunitians as far as the isthmus from Thourioi to Kerilloi (near the Laos). The isthmus is 300 stadia. The Brettians are beyond, living on a peninsula, which surrounds another peninsula that contains the isthmus from the Skylletion to the Hipponiate Gulf. The people were named by the Leukanians, for they call rebels "brettioi." They revolted, as it is said, having formerly been shepherds, but later because of a loosening of things they began to act like free men, at the time when Dion made his expedition against Dionysios [II] and

stirred up everyone against everyone. This is what I have to say in its entirety about the Leukanians and Brettians.[2]

(5) The first city after Laos is Brettian Temese. Today it is called Tempsa, an Ausonian foundation that was later settled by the Aitolians under Thoas, but they were thrown out by the Brettians. Afterward Hannibal and then the Romans crushed the Brettians. Near Temese is the heroon – thickly shaded with wild olives – of Polites, a companion of Odysseus, who was treacherously killed by the barbarians. Because of his excessive anger the locals, according to an oracle, collected tribute for him, and thus the proverb[3]. . .are said to have been beset by the hero of Temesa. The story is told that when the Epizephyrian Lokrians took the city, the boxer Euthymos went down against him and defeated him in a fight, forcing the release of the locals from the tribute. It is said that the Poet was calling [C256] this Temese to mind, not Tamassos in Cyprus (it is spelled both ways), with "to Temese for copper" [*Odyssey* 1.184], and copper mines are visible nearby, although they are abandoned today.

Terina is nearby, which Hannibal destroyed, because he was unable to guard it when he had taken refuge in Brettia itself. Then there is Kosentia, the metropolis of the Brettians, and a little above it is Pandosia, a strong fortress, near where Alexander the Molossian was killed. An oracle from Dodona had deceived him, as it told him to be on guard against Acheron and Pandosia, and he was shown [places] with those names in Thesprotia but ended his life here. The fortress has three summits, and the Acheron River flows past it. He was further deceived by another oracle: "three-hilled Pandosia, where you will someday destroy many people," since he clearly believed that the enemy would be killed, not his own people. It is said that Pandosia was once the royal seat of the Oinotrian kings.

After Kosentia is Hipponion, a Lokrian foundation. The Romans took it from the Brettians, who had held it, and changed its name to Vibo Valentia. Because the surrounding country has good meadows, it was believed that Kore had come here from Sikelia to gather flowers, and thus it became the custom among the women to gather flowers and to weave garlands, so that at festivals it is disgraceful to wear purchased garlands. It also has a seaport, which was built by Agathokles the tyrant of the Sikeliotes when he controlled the city.

From there one sails to the Harbor of Herakles, which is where the capes of Italia near the Strait turn toward the west. Medma is on this sailing route,

[2] Some see a lacuna here, or a misplaced sentence, since Section 5 is also about the Brettians.
[3] The text is incomprehensible here.

a city of the Lokrians, with the same name as a large fountain, having a seaport nearby named Emporion. The Metauros River is nearby, and an anchorage with the same name. Lying off this part of the mainland are the Liparaian Islands, 200 stadia distant from the Strait. Some say that they are those of Aiolos, which are mentioned by the Poet in the *Odyssey* [10.1–2]. They are seven in number, and all are in view, visible from both Sikelia and the mainland around Medma. I will speak about them when I talk about Sikelia [6.2.10]. After the Metauros River there is another[4] . . . . Next is the Skyllaion, a high rock that makes a peninsula, with an isthmus that is low and accessible on both sides. Anaxilaos, the tyrant of Rhegion, fortified it against the Tyrrhenians, constructing a naval station, and thus keeping pirates from sailing through the Strait. Kainys is also nearby, 250 stadia distant from Medma, the final cape, which creates the narrows of the Strait, opposite the Sikelian cape of Pelorias. It is one of the three that makes the island triangular, bending toward the summer sunrise, just as Kainys is toward the west, each making a turn away from each other. From Kainys as far as the Poseidonion and the Pillar of the Rheginians is the extent of the narrows of the Strait, about six stadia, with the shortest crossing slightly more. It is a hundred [stadia] from the Pillar to Rhegion, where the Strait widens, proceeding toward the outer sea and the east, the so-called Sikelian Sea.

[C257]

(6) Rhegion is a foundation of the Chalkideans, who, they say, dedicated every tenth man to Apollo because of a shortage of crops, but later emigrated here from Delphi, taking along others from home. Yet Antiochos [F9] says that the Zanklaians sent for the Chalkideans and appointed Antimnestos as their founder. The settlement also included Peloponnesian Messenians fleeing those of the opposing faction, who were unwilling to give justice to the Lakedaimonians because of the assault on the girls that happened at Limnai (they had been sent there for sacred rites), although they had forced themselves on them as well as killing those who came to assist. The refugees withdrew to Makiston and sent to the god, censuring Apollo and Artemis if this were to be their fate in return for honoring them and asking how they might be saved, as they were totally ruined. Apollo ordered them to be sent with the Chalkideans to Rhegion, as well as to be thankful to his sister because they were not ruined but saved, as they would not perish along with their native land (which a little later would be taken by the Spartiates), and they obeyed. Thus the rulers of Rhegion down to Anaxilas were always appointed

---

[4] A phrase has probably dropped out.

from the Messenian race. Antiochos also says that in antiquity all these places were inhabited by the Sikelians and Morgetians, but they crossed to Sikelia later, having been expelled by the Oinotrians. Some say that Morgantion was named from the Morgetians.

[C258]

The city of Rhegion was exceedingly powerful and had many neighboring dependent towns. They were always a stronghold against the island, both in antiquity and in our time, when Sextus Pompeius caused the Sikelians to revolt. It was named Rhegion, as Aischylos says [F402], because of the disaster that this region suffered when Sikelia broke off [*aporrhagenai*] from the mainland due to an earthquake. He and others say that it was called Rhegion because of this. This is demonstrated from what happened around Aitna and in other parts of Sikelia, and on Lipara and the other islands around it, and also on Pithekoussai and the entire neighboring coast, so that it is not unreasonable that this is what occurred. Today the outlets – through which fire is produced and hot masses and water are ejected – are open, but it is said that the earth around the Strait rarely has earthquakes. At that time, however, all the passages to the surface were blocked up, and the fire smouldering beneath the earth, along with the wind, produced violent earthquakes. Thus the localities that were heaved up yielded to the force of the winds and then were broken apart, receiving the sea that was on either side, both here and between the other islands there. In fact Prochyte and Pithekoussai have been torn off from the mainland, as well as Capriae, Leukosia, the Seirenes, and the Oinotrides. There are those that have risen from the open sea, something that occurs today in many places, for it is more believable that they were brought up from the depths, yet it seems reasonable to assume that those lying off promontories or separated only by a strait were broken off.

Nevertheless, it is open to investigation whether it is true that the city received its name in this way or because of the distinction of the city, since the Saunitians might have called it by the Latin word for "royal" ["regium"], because their leaders shared the government with the Romans and generally used the Latin language. Nevertheless it was a city of distinction and founded many cities, producing many men worthy of note, some for their political ability and others for their education. Yet it was destroyed by Dionysios [I], who charged that when he asked for a girl in marriage he was offered the daughter of a public official. His son restored a part of the original foundations and called it Phoibia. At the time of Pyrrhos, the Campanian garrison broke the treaty and massacred most of the inhabitants, and shortly before the Marsic matter earthquakes destroyed much of

[C259]

it. Sebastos Caesar, having thrown Pompeius out of Sikelia and seeing that the city was lacking in population, gave it some from his expedition as settlers, and today it is sufficiently populous.

(7) White Rock Cape, so-called from its color, is a sail of 50 stadia from Rhegion toward the east. It is said to be the end of the Apennine Mountains. Then there is Herakleion, the last promontory, bent toward the south. Going around it one immediately sails with the Lips as far as Cape Iapygia, and then immediately turns away toward the north, and always more and more toward the west, into the Ionian Gulf. After Herakleion there is a cape of the Lokrians called Zephyrion, whose harbor is sheltered from the west winds, from which it is named. Then there is the city of the Epizephyrian Lokrians, settled by the Lokrians who were on the Krisaian Gulf and founded by Euanthes a little later than Kroton and Syracuse. Ephoros [F138a] is not correct when he says that it was founded by the Opountian Lokrians. They lived only three or four years at Zephyrion and then moved the city, with the help of the Syracusians and Tarantinians. A spring is there, Lokria, where the Lokrians made camp. From Rhegion as far as Lokroi is 600 stadia. The city is situated on a brow called Esopis.

(8) They are believed to have been the first to use written laws. After they had had good laws for a long time, Dionysios [II], expelled from Syracuse, treated them the most lawlessly of all. He would seduce women about to be married, entering their bedroom and escorting the bride, or bring together young girls and release doves with cropped wings in a banquet, ordering them to dance around naked, with others having unmatched sandals fastened on – one high and the other low – chasing them all over, for the sake of indecency. He paid the penalty, however, when he went back to Sikelia to take up his rule again, for the Lokrians disbanded his garrison and freed themselves, becoming masters of his wife and children. There were two daughters and his younger son – already an adolescent – since the other, Apollokrates, was on the return campaign with his father. Dionysios [II] – and the Tarantines for him – vigorously pleaded that the people be released in whatever manner they wished, but they would not give them up, [C260] enduring a siege and a sack of their territory. But they poured out most of their anger against the daughters, treating them as prostitutes and then strangling them, burning their bodies, grinding up the bones, and throwing them in the sea.

Ephoros [F139] – discussing the written legislation of the Lokrians, which was drawn up by Zaleukos from Cretan, Lakonian, and Areopagitic models – says that Zaleukos first made this innovation: formerly the penalties for each crime were left to the judges to determine, but he defined them in the laws, believing that among themselves the opinions of the judges would not be the same for the same [crimes], although the <penalties> ought to be. He was also commended for drawing up a simpler contract law. Thourioi, which later wished to become more notable than the Lokrians in precision, became so, yet was inferior, for those who have good laws are not those who guard against all informers in their laws, but those who abide by ones laid down simply. Plato [*Republic* 3.13] has said this: that where there are many laws there are many cases and corrupt livelihoods, just as where there are many physicians there are many diseases.

(9) The Alex River, which is the boundary between the Rhegine and Lokris, passes through a deep ravine, and a peculiar thing happens with the cicadas there: those on the Lokrian side make noise but those on the other are quiet. It is suggested that the cause of the latter is that the land is thickly shaded, and being wet with dew they cannot expand their membranes, whereas those on the sunny side have dry and horn-like membranes and thus can easily send forth noise. In Lokroi a statue of Eunomos the cithara player was visible, with a cicada sitting on the cithara. Timaios [F43b] says that at the Pythian Games he [Eunomos] was once contesting with Ariston of Rhegion and they quarreled about the lots. Ariston asked that the Delphians join in helping him, since his ancestors had been consecrated to the god and the city-foundation had been sent from there. Eunomos said that he had no right even to be in a vocal contest, since in his [territory] the cicadas – the sweetest-voiced of living beings – were mute, but nevertheless Ariston was favored and hoped for the victory. Yet Eunomos won and set up the previously mentioned image in his country, because during the contest one of his strings broke and a cicada landed and supplied the tone.

[C261]

The interior above these cities is held by the Brettians. The city of Mamertion is here, as well as the forests that produce the best pitch (the Brettian) and which are called the Sila. It is both well-wooded and well-watered, and 700 stadia long.

(10) After Lokroi is the Sagra [River],[5] which has a feminine name. On it are altars to the Dioskouroi, near which 10,000 Lokrians, along with the Rheginians, were victorious in a fight with 130,000 Krotoniates, from which arises the proverb said to unbelieving people: "More true than what happened on the Sagra." Some have added the tale that the news was reported at Olympia on the very same day, while the games were happening there, and it was found that the speed of the announcement was true. This misfortune

---

[5] The text reads *sagras* but has been emended to *sagra <potamo>s*.

of the Krotoniates is said to be the reason that the city did not last for much longer a time, as so great a multitude of men fell.

After the Sagra is Kaulonia, an Achaian foundation, formerly called Aulonia because of the hollow [*aulon*] that lies before it. It is deserted, for those possessing it were driven off to Sikelia by the barbarians, and founded Kaulonia there. After it there is Skylletion, a foundation of the Athenians who were with Menestheus, which is now called Skyllakion. Although held by the Krotoniates, Dionysios [I] included it within the boundaries of the Lokrians. The gulf named the Skylletic is named after the city, and creates the previously mentioned [6.1.4] isthmus along with the Hipponiatic Gulf. Dionysios [I] attempted to build a wall across the isthmus when he made war against the Leukanians, on the pretext that it would provide safety for those inside the isthmus against the barbarians outside, but in truth because he wished to dissolve the alliance that the Hellenes had with each other, and thus rule those inside without fear, but those outside came and prevented it.

(11) After Skylletion there is the land of Krotoniatis and the three capes of the Iapygians. After these is the Lakinion, a sanctuary of Hera, which once was rich and full of many offerings. The distances by sea are not recorded clearly, except generally, as Polybios [34.11.9–11] provides 1,300 stadia from the Strait to the Lakinion, and the distance from there to the Iapygian Cape is 700. This is said to be the mouth of the Tarantine Gulf. The sail around the gulf itself is remarkable: 240 miles, as the Chorographer [F43] says, or 380[6]...Artemidoros [F44], and lacking as much in the width [C262] of the gulf. It looks toward the winter sunrise and begins at the Lakinion. Going around it there are immediately the cities of the Achaians, which do not exist today except for that of the Tarantinians. Nevertheless because of the reputation of some of them, they are worthy of extensive mention.

(12) First is Kroton, within 150 stadia from the Lakinion, and then the Aisaros River, a harbor, and another river, the Neaithos, which, they say, was named from what happened there.[7] They say that certain Achaians who had wandered away from the Ilian expedition landed there, and disembarked to examine the territory. When the Trojan women sailing with them learned that the ships were empty of men, they set fire to them, because they were weary of the voyage. Thus the men remained by necessity, although they saw that the land was excellent. Immediately a number of related peoples came and imitated them, and many settlements came into

---

[6] The text is uncertain at this point.
[7] The name Neaithos was believed to mean "to burn the ships" (*neas aethein*).

being, most of which were named for the river. Antiochos [F10] says that when the god told the Achaians to found Kroton, Myskellos went to examine the place, but when he saw that Sybaris had already been founded (having the same name as the nearby river), he judged that it was better and returned and asked the god repeatedly whether he wished him to make his foundation at this place rather than the former, and this was the reply (Myskellos happened to be a hunchback):

> Short-backed Myskellos, in searching outside your place, you are hunting for morsels. It is proper that you approve of what you were given.

He came back and founded Kroton, with Archias, the founder of Syracuse, helping, who happened to be sailing past on his way to found Syracuse.

Formerly the Iapygians lived at Kroton, as Ephoros [F140] says. The city seems to have practiced warfare and athletics. At any rate, in one Olympiad the seven men who were in the lead in the stadium race were all Krotoniates, and thus the saying seems reasonable that the last Krotoniate is the first of all other Hellenes. And they say that there is also a proverb spoken there, that they say "healthier than Kroton," as there is something about the place regarding health and vigor, since it is conducive to so many athletes. They had a large number of Olympian victors, although it was not inhabited for a [C263] long time because of the destruction of so many men who fell at the Sagra. Its reputation was increased by the large number of Pythagoreans as well as Milon, who became the most distinguished of athletes and was a disciple of Pythagoras, who spent a long time in the city. It is said that once, at the common dining room of the philosophers, a column was damaged, and Milon slipped under it and saved them all, and then drew away and [saved] himself. It is probable that because he trusted in this same strength that he brought about the end of his life, as is reported by some. It is said, at any rate, that travelling through a deep forest he went far away from the road, and when he found a large log split by wedges, he put his hands and feet into the separation at the same time, to force it to split completely, but he was only strong enough so that the wedges fell out, and immediately the parts of the log sprang together again, catching him in such a trap that he became food for wild beasts.

(13) Next, within 200 stadia, is Sybaris, an Achaian foundation, between two rivers, the Krathis and the Sybaris. Its founder was[8] . . . . In antiquity the city experienced such prosperity that it ruled 4 neighboring peoples, had

---

[8] The text has *iselikeus*, which seems doubtful.

25 subject cities, and made a campaign with 300,000 men against the Krotoniates. Those living on the Krathis filled a circuit of 50 stadia. Nevertheless, because of their luxuriousness and arrogance, they were deprived of all their good fortune in 70 days by the Krotoniates, for when they took the city they brought on the river and inundated it. Later the few survivors came together and were settling there again, but in time they were destroyed by the Athenians and other Hellenes, who, although they had come there to live with them, despised them and then killed them, removing the city to another place nearby and naming it Thourioi after an eponymous spring. The Sybaris River makes horses that drink from it fearful – thus herds are kept away from it – and the Krathis causes people bathing in it to have yellow hair or white hair, as well as curing many conditions. After the Thourians had prospered for a long time, they were sold into slavery by the Leukanians, and when the Tarantinians took them away from there, they sought refuge among the Romans, who sent settlers to join them (as their number was scant) and changed the name of the city to Copiae.

(14) After Thourioi is the fortress of Lagaria, founded by Epeios and the Phokians, from where the Lagaritanic wine comes, which is sweet and delicate, and greatly esteemed by physicians. The Thourian wine also has [C264] a good reputation. Then there is Herakleia, a city slightly above the sea with two navigable rivers, the Akiris and Siris, on which there was a Trojan city with the same name. In time, when Herakleia was settled from there by the Tarantinians, it became the seaport of the Herakleotes. It is 24 stadia distant from Herakleia and about 330 from Thourioi. The xoanon of Ilian Athena that is set up there is considered as proof of its settlement by the Trojans. The story is told that it closed its eyes when the suppliants were dragged away from the city by the Ionians who captured it. They had come there as settlers fleeing Lydian rule and took the city – which belonged to the Chonians – by force, and called it Polieion. Even today the xoanon is shown closing its eyes. Now it is bold to tell such a story – saying not only that it closed its eyes (just as the one in Ilion turned away when Kasandra was raped), but that it is seen closing its eyes – but it is much bolder to have as many xoana carried away from Ilion as the writers say. At Rome, Lavinium, Luceria, and Siritis, Athena is called "Ilian," as though she had been carried away from there. Moreover, the daring of the Trojan women is known in many places and appears unbelievable although possible.

Some say that Siritis, and Sybaris on the Traeis, were founded by the Rhodians. Antiochos [F11] says that the Tarantinians, at war with the

Thourians and their commander Kleandridas (a fugitive from Lakedaimonia) regarding Siritis, came to an agreement and populated it in common, although it was judged to be a settlement of the Tarantinians. Later it was called Herakleia, changing both its name and its location.

(15) Next is Metapontion, which is 140 stadia from the seaport of Herakleia. It is said to have been a foundation of the Pylians who sailed from Ilion with Nestor. They were so prosperous from farming, they say, that they dedicated a golden harvest at Delphi. They make as a sign of its foundation an offering to the shades of the Neleides. It was obliterated by the Saunitians. Antiochos [F12] says that certain Achaians, sent for by the Achaians in Sybaris, settled the place but were then abandoned. They had been sent for because the Achaians who had been driven from Lakonia had a hatred of the Tarantinians, and so that the adjoining Tarantinians would not rush at the place. There were two cities, with Metapontion the nearer to, and Siritis the farther from, Taras, and the new arrivals were persuaded [C265] by the Sybarites to hold Metapontion, for by holding it they would also have Siritis. But if they turned to Siritis they would add Metapontion to the Tarantinians, as it was alongside it. Later, when they were at war with the Tarantinians and the Oinotrians lying above them, there was a reconciliation regarding the portion of the land that was the boundary between Italia of that time and Iapygia.

The stories of Metapontos, the chained Melanippe and her child Boiotos are located here. Antiochos [F12] believes that the city was formerly called Metabos, with its name slightly changed later, and that Melanippe was not brought to him but to Dios, something proved by the heroon of Metabos, as well as by Asios [F2] the poet, who says Boiotos was the one "whom beautiful Melanippe bore in the megaron of Dios," and thus Melanippe was brought to him, not to Metabos.

The founder of Metapontion was Daulios, the tyrant of Krisa near Delphi, as Ephoros [F141] says. There is another account, that Leukippos was the one sent by the Achaians, and after obtaining the place from the Tarantinians for a day and a night he would not give it up, telling those who asked for it back in the daytime that he had asked for and taken it for the next night, and at night that he had it for the the next day.

Next are Taras and Iapygia, which I will discuss [6.3.1–5], but first I will go through the islands that lie off Italia, according to my original purpose. Since I have always made note of the islands that neighbor various peoples, now, as I have discussed Oinotria in its entirety – which alone those of former times called Italia – it is proper that I preserve the same order in regard to Sikelia and the islands around it.

Part 2:   Sikelia

(1) Sikelia is triangular in shape, and because of this it was formerly
Trinakria, although later this was changed and it was more euphoniously
called Thrinakia. Its shape is determined by three capes, Pelorias, which
along with Kainys and the Pillar of the Rheginians makes the Strait;
Pachynos, which is exposed to the east and is washed by the Sikelian Sea,
looking toward the Peloponnesos and the passage to Crete; and, third,
Lilybaion, that next to Libya, looking both toward it and the winter sunset.
Of the sides, which are marked off by the three capes, two of them are
moderately concave and the third – the one reaching from Lilybaion to   [C266]
Pelorias – is convex and the longest, 1,700 stadia, as Poseidonios [F249]
says, although he adds 20. Of the others, the one from Pachynos to
Lilybaion is longer than the other, and the shortest is that next to the
Strait and Italia (the one from Pelorias to Pachynos), about 1,130 stadia.
Poseidonios reports that the sail around is 4,400 stadia. In the *Chorographia*
[F13] the distances are said to be greater, divided into portions and in miles:
from Pelorias to Mylai, 25, the same from Mylai to Tyndaris, from there to
Agathyrnon 30, the same to Alaisa, and again the same to Kephaloidion
(which are small towns). To the Himeras River (which flows through the
middle of Sikelia) 18, and then to Panormos 35, to the emporium of the
Aigestians 32, and the remainder to Lilybaion 38. Then, going around it to
the adjoining side, it is 75 to the Herakleion, and to the emporium of the
Akragantinians 20, and another 20[9]...to Kamarina, and then to Pachynos
50. Then back along the third side to Syracuse it is 36, to Katane 60, then to
Tauromenion 33, then to Messene 30. On foot it is 168 from Pachynos to
Pelorias, and on the Valerian Road from Messene to Lilybaion is <2>35.[10]
Some are more general, such as Ephoros [F135], saying that the sail around is
5 days and nights.

Poseidonios [F249], marking off the island by latitudes, places Pelorias
toward the north, Lilybaion toward the south, and Pachynos toward the
east. Yet by necessity – since the latitudes are defined by the shape of a
parallelogram – the inscribed triangles (especially those that are unequal and
none of whose sides fits onto [a side] of the parallelogram) would not fit to
the latitudes because of their slant. Regardless, one would say that since
Sikelia lies to the south of Italia, Pelorias is clearly the most northern of the
three corners, and thus we have said what joins it to Pachynos will lie out
toward the east, looking toward the north, making the side along the Strait.

---

[9] At least one toponym and distance have dropped out.   [10] The "35" of the text is far too short.

But it takes a small turn toward the winter sunrise, for the coast bends, going from Katane to Syracuse and Pachynos. The distance from Pachynos [C267] to the mouth of the Alpheios is 4,000 stadia. Artemidoros [F49], however, in saying that it is 4,600 from Pachynos to Tainaron and 1,130 from the Alpheios to Pamisos, seems to me to provide a reason that his statement does not agree with the one who said that it was 4,000 to the Alpheios from Pachynos. That from Pachynos to Lilybaion – which is sufficiently farther west than Pelorias – would slant sufficiently from its southern limit toward the west, and at the same time would look toward the east and toward the south, part being washed by the Sikelian Sea and the other by the Libyan [Sea] that extends to the Syrtes from Karchedon. The shortest crossing from Lilybaion to Libya around Karchedon is 1,500 [stadia]. It is said that someone who was sharp-sighted could from a lookout report the number of boats leaving Karchedon. The side from Lilybaion to Pelorias must slant toward the east and look between west and north, having Italia on the north and the Tyrrhenian Sea and the Aiolean Islands on the west.

(2) The cities along the side that makes the Strait are, first, Messene, and then Tauromenion, Katane, and Syracuse. Those between Katane and Syracuse (Naxos and Megara) are abandoned. There are also the outlets of the Symaithos and Pantakias Rivers, which flow down from Aitna to mouths with good harbors. Here also is the promontory of Xiphonia. Ephoros [F137a] says that these were the first Hellenic cities to be founded in Sikelia, in the tenth generation after the Trojan matter. Before then there was such fear of Tyrrhenian pirates and the savagery of the barbarians in this region, that there was no sailing for commerce. Theokles the Athenian, carried off course to Sikelia by the winds, understood the worthlessness of the people and the quality of the earth, yet upon returning home he could not persuade the Athenians, so he took many Chalkideans from Euboia, some Ionians, and even some Dorians – mostly Megarians – and sailed there. The Chalkideans founded Naxos, and the Dorians Megara, formerly called Hybla. These cities no longer exist but the name of Hybla survives due to the quality of Hyblaian honey.

(3) Among the cities that survive on the previously mentioned side, [C268] Messene lies in a gulf of Pelorias that bends greatly toward the east and makes a sort of an armpit. The distance from Rhegion is 60 stadia, and much less from the Pillar. It was founded by the Messenians of the Peloponnesos, who changed the name, as it was formerly called Zankle because of the crookedness ("crooked" is called "zanklion"), a former foundation of the Naxians near Katane. The Mamertinians, a particular Campanian people, joined the settlement later. The Romans used it as a

base for the Sikelian war against the Karchedonians, and later Sextus Pompeius kept his fleet there in the war against Sebastos Caesar and made his flight from there when he was expelled from the island. Charybdis is visible a short distance in front of the city, in the channel, an extraordinary depth into which the reflux of the Strait cleverly pulls down boats, which are swept away with the twisting around and a great whirling. When swallowed down and broken up, the wreckage is carried along to the Tauromenian shore, which, because of what happens, is called Kopria ["Refuse"]. The Mamertinians prevailed among the Messenians so that the city was theirs, and everyone calls it Mamertinian rather than Messenian. Since the territory has exceedingly good wine, this wine is not called Messenian but Mamertinian, and it is equal to the best in Italia. The city is well populated, although Katane is more so and has also received Romans as inhabitants. Tauromenion is less than either.

Katane was founded by the same Naxians, and Tauromenion by the Zanklaians of Hybla. Katane lost its inhabitants when Hieron [I], the tyrant of the Syracusians, settled others there and called it Aitna instead of Katane. Pindar also records him as its founder when he says "Hold to what I say, he who has the name of the divine sacrifices, father, founder of Aitna" [F105]. After the death of Hieron [I] the Katanians returned, threw out the inhabitants, and razed the tomb of the tyrant. The displaced Aitnaians settled in the hilly region of Aitna called Innesa, and named the territory Aitna – it is 80 stadia from Katane – declaring that Hieron [I] was their founder.

[Mount] Aitna is located right above Katane, which shares most of the effects of the craters, as lava streams are carried down nearly into the [C269] Katanaia. A story is repeated there concerning piety, about Amphinomos and Anapias, who lifted their parents on their shoulders and saved them, carrying them away from disaster. When, according to Poseidonios [F234], the region around the mountain is shaken,[II] the Katanaian territory is deeply covered with ashes. The ashes are an affliction at the moment but are beneficial to the territory at later times, making it productive for the vine and capable of bearing good fruits, as elsewhere it is not good for wine. The roots that have been nourished by the ash-bearing fields make the herds so fat, they say, that they choke, because of which blood is drawn from their ears every four or five days, which, as I have said [3.5.4], also occurs near Erytheia. When the lava changes to a solid, the surface of the earth becomes stone to a sufficent depth, so that quarrying is necessary for those wishing to

[II] This clause is unclear in the text.

uncover the original surface. When the rock in the craters melts and is thrown up, the liquid flows over the summit and black mud flows over the mountain. Upon taking a solid form it becomes millstone, keeping the same color as when it flowed. Ash is created when the stones are burned, as from wood. Just as ash from wood produces rue, thus the ash from Aitna has some advantage suitable for the vine.

(4) Syracuse was founded by Archias, sailing from Corinth about the same time that Naxos and Megara were founded. They say that Archias went to Delphi at the same time as Myskellos, and when they consulted the oracle they were asked by the god whether they chose wealth or good health. Archias chose wealth and Myskellos good health. The former was assigned the foundation of Syracuse and the latter Kroton. Thus it happened that the Krotoniates lived in a city that was healthy, as I have said [6.1.12], and Syracuse fell into such wealth that a proverb was handed down, saying, about the excessively extravagant, that a Syracusian tenth would not be granted.[12] When Archias was sailing to Sikelia he left Chersikrates, of the Herakleidai race, a portion of the command, in order to join in settling what is now called Kerkyra but was formerly Scheria. He

[C270] threw out the Libyrnians, who possessed the island, and Archias occupied Zephyrion. He found some Dorians who had arrived there from Sikelia, coming from the founders of Megara, and included them; in common they founded Syracuse.

The city grew because of the prosperity of the soil and the natural quality of its harbors. The men were capable of command, and thus when the Syracusians were living under the tyrants they dominated the others, and when they were set free they freed those who had been oppressed by the barbarians. Some of the barbarians were indigenous and others had come over from the other side. The Hellenes did not allow them to hold the coast, but were not strong enough to keep them completely away from the interior, and even today Sikelians, Sikanians, Morgetians, and certain others continue to inhabit the island. Among them were Iberians, whom Ephoros [F136] says were recorded as the first barbarian settlers of Sikelia. It is reasonable that Morgantion was settled by the Morgetians; it was a city, but today it does not exist. When the Karchedonians came over, they would not cease treating both them and the Hellenes badly, but nevertheless the Syracusians withstood them. Later the Romans expelled the Karchedonians and took Syracuse by siege. In our time, as Pompeius had treated the other cities badly, and especially Syracuse, Sebastos Caesar sent a settlement and

---

[12] The meaning is obscure and the text may be deficient.

undertook construction in a large portion of the old district. In antiquity it was a pentapolis having a wall of 180 stadia, and although it was not necessary to fill up this entire circuit, he did think it necessary to populate the area near the island of Ortygia, which had a better circumference for a notable city.

Ortygia is connected to the mainland by a bridge[13]. . .and the spring of Arethousa that sends forth a river directly into the sea. The story is told that it is the Alpheios, which begins in the Peloponnesos, flows underground through the open sea as far as Arethousa, and then empties again into the sea. As proof there is the following: a certain phiale thrown into the river at Olympia came up in the spring, which is muddied because of the sacrifice of oxen at Olympia. Pindar follows this when he says "revered resting place of the Alpheios, child of renowed Syracuse, Ortygia" [*Nemean* 1.1–2]. The historian Timaios [F41c] agrees with Pindar. Yet if the Alpheios [C271] fell down into some pit before joining the sea, there would be some plausibility that the stream extends underground as far as Sikelia, preserving potable water unmixed with the sea. But the mouth of the river empties visibly into the sea, and there is no nearby mouth visible within the sea on the crossing that swallows up the stream of the river – and it would not remain sweet (although most of it might if the stream sank down below the earth) – so this is completely impossible. The water of Arethousa testifies against this, since it is potable, and for the stream of the river to remain together through such a crossing without being dispersed into the sea, until it falls into the fabricated stream, is completely mythical. We can hardly believe this about the Rhodanos, whose stream does hold together through a lake, keeping its course visible, but the distance is short there, and the lake does not swell into waves. But in the other case there are extraordinary storms and the surging of waves, and thus the story is in no way suitably believable. Alleging the matter of the phiale only heightens the falsehood, for it would not be obedient to any stream, especially such a one carried through such passages.

There are many rivers throughout the world that flow underground, but not for such a distance. Even if this were possible, that which has been previously mentioned is impossible. The story about the Inachos is similar. "It flows from the heights of Pindos," Sophokles says, "from Lakmos and the Perrhaibians into the Amphilochians and the Arkarnanians, mixing with the waters of Acheloos" [F271], and below, "from there it divides the waves to Argos and comes to the people of Lyrkeion." Such tales of marvels

---

[13] Something is missing here.

are heightened by those who have the Inopos cross from the Nile to Delos.
The rhetorician Zoilos says in his *Eulogy of the Tenedians* [F1] that the
Alpheios flows from Tenedos: he who censures Homer as a writer of myths!
Ibykos [F322] says that the Asopos in Sikyon flows from Phrygia. Hekataios
[of Miletos, F102c] is better, saying that the Inachos among the
Amphilochians, flowing from Lakmos (as the Aias also does), is different
from the one in the Argolid, and it was named by Amphilochos, he who
called the city of Argos Amphilochikos. He also says that it empties into the
Acheloos, but that the Aias flows west into Apollonia.

[C272] On either side of the island [of Ortygia] is a large harbor, of which the
larger is eighty stadia. Caesar rebuilt this city, and also Katane, as well as
Kentoripa, because it contributed so much to the collapse of Pompeius.
Kentoripa lies above Katane, adjacent to the Aitnaian mountains and on the
Symaithos River, which flows into the Katanaia.

(5) Of the remaining sides of Sikelia, the one that extends from Pachynos
to Lilybaion is completely deserted, although it preserves traces of old
settlements, among which was Kamarina, a Syracusian foundation.
Akragas (which is Geloan) and its seaport, as well as Lilybaion, still survive.
This portion was most exposed to Karchedonian attack, and much of it was
destroyed by the long wars that occurred. The last and longest side is also
not populated, but nevertheless sufficiently inhabited. Alaisa, Tyndaris, the
emporium of the Aigestians, and Kephaloidis are small towns, and
Panormos has a Roman settlement. Aigestaia was founded, they say, by
those who crossed over with Philoktetes to the Krotoniatis, as I said in the
Italian section [6.1.3], and who were sent by him to Sikelia with Aigestes the
Trojan.[14] Eryx is also inhabited, a high hill with a sanctuary of Aphrodite
that is especially honored. In antiquity it was full of female temple slaves
who had been dedicated for vows by people from Sikelia and many from
elsewhere. Today, just like the settlement, the sanctuary is lacking in men,
and the multitude of people have abandoned the sanctuary. In Rome an
image of this goddess has been set up before the Colline Gate, in the
sanctuary called Aphrodite Erykina, which has a notable temple and stoa
around it.

(6) In the interior is Enna, where there is a temple of Demeter and only a
few inhabitants, situated on a hill surrounded by broad tablelands that are
arable. It was especially maltreated when the runaway slaves with Eunous
were besieged there, who were barely removed by the Romans. The

---

[14] The remainder of Section 5 has been transposed from Section 6, originally placed after the mention of
the Katanians and Tauromenians.

Katanaians and Tauromenitians, and many others, suffered the same. The rest of the settlements and the interior are held mostly by shepherds. I do not know of any population still in Himera, Gela, Kallipolis, Selinous, Euboia, or a number of other places. Of these, Himera was founded by the Zanklaians of Mylai[15]...Kallipolis by the Naxians, Selinous by the local Megarians, and Euboia by the Leontinians. All of Leontine has been ruined, having belonged to the local Naxians, for they always shared misfortunes with the Syracusians, but it was not always the same with good fortune.[16]
Many of the barbarian [settlements] have also been destroyed, such as   [C273]
Kamikoi, the royal seat of Kokalos, where Minos is said to have been killed by treachery. The Romans, perceiving the desolation, took possession of the mountains and most of the plains, and then gave them over to horse herding, tending cattle, and shepherding. The island was often put into great danger by these shepherds, who at first turned to sporadic brigandage, but later they came together in large numbers and plundered the settlements, such as when those with Eunous took Enna. Recently, in my time, a certain Selouros, called "the son of Aitna" was sent up to Rome because he had led an army and for a long time overran the region around Aitna with repeated plundering. I saw him torn apart by wild animals as part of a gladiatorial contest in the agora. He was placed on a certain high scaffold – as if it were Aitna – that suddenly broke up and collapsed, and he was carried down into an easily opened cage of wild animals that had been prepared under the scaffold.

(7) Why must one speak about the virtues of the territory, since it is talked about by everyone, who declare that it is in no way worse than Italia? In grain, honey, saffron, and certain other things one could even say that it is better. There is also its nearness, as the island is a certain part of Italia, as it were, and supplies Rome easily and without difficulty as though from the Italian fields. It is called the storehouse of Rome, for everything that it produces is brought here – except for a few things that are consumed there – not only fruits, but cattle, hides, wool, and other such things. Poseidonios [F250] says that Syracuse and Eryx are like two akropoleis by the sea, and Enna lies between both of them above the encircling plains.

(8) Near to Kentoripa is the small town of Aitna, mentioned a little previously [6.2.3], whose inhabitants receive and escort those climbing the mountain, for here is the beginning of the mountain ridge. The upper regions are bare and ashy, covered with snow in winter, but the lower are

---

[15] Gela and its founder are missing from the text.
[16] This sentence has been transposed from the end of Section 7.

divided into forests and plantations of every type. The summits of the mountain appear to undergo many changes because of the distribution of the fire, for at one time it is collected into a single crater, and at another it [C274] divides. At one time streams are sent forth, at another flames and fiery smoke, and at still another it blows out masses of rock. The necessary result of these occurrences is that the underground passages change, along with the outlets – sometimes numerous – that appear all around. Some who recently made the ascent told me that they found at the summit a level plain about twenty stadia around, enclosed by an embankment of ash the height of a building wall, so that anyone wishing to go into the plain had to jump down. They saw in the middle of it a mound of ash, like the surface of the plain when looking down onto it. Above the mound was a vertical cloud rising up to a height of two hundred feet, which was motionless – for there was no wind – and resembling smoke. Two of them had the courage to go into the plain, but when the sand they were walking on became hotter and deeper, they turned back, not having been able to perceive anything more extraordinary than what was already visible from a distance. They believed from what they saw that much of what is told is mythical, especially what is said about Empedokles: that he leapt down into the crater and left behind, as a trace of what he experienced, one of the bronze shoes that he wore. It was found a short distance away from the rim of the crater, as though thrown up by the force of the fire. But the place is not to be approached or seen, and it was inferred that nothing could be thrown down into it because of the contrary blasts of wind from the depths, as well as the heat, which, reasonably, is encountered far off before one comes near to the crater. Even if something were thrown down, it would be destroyed before it could be thrown up again[17]...returning in anything like its former form. It is not unreasonable that at some times the winds and fire fail when the fuel fails, but this would not reach such a point that a man could come near to it against such a force. Aitna is situated right above the coast around the Strait and the Katanaia, as well as the region around the Tyrrhenian Sea and the Liparaian Islands. At night there is a bright light from the summit, but in the daytime it is covered with smoke and mist.

(9) The Nebrodes Mountains are over against Aitna, which are lower but surpass it in width. The entire island is hollow underground and full of streams of fire, just as with the Tyrrhenian Sea – as I have said [5.4.9] – as far [C275] as the Kymaia. At any rate, the island has hot water bubbling up in many places, of which that in the Selinountia and around Himera is salty, but that

---

[17] Something seems to be missing here.

in the Aigestaia is potable. Around Akragas there are lakes that taste like the sea but whose nature is different, for those who cannot swim do not sink but float on the surface like wood. The Palikians have craters that throw up water in a tholos-like spray and receive it back in the same recess. A cave around Matauros has a large gallery through which a river flows that is invisible for a great distance, and then it comes up to the surface, as does the Orontes in Syria, which goes down into a chasm between Apameia and Antiocheia called Charybdis, and then rises again in 40 stadia. The Tigris in Mesopotamia and the Nile in Libya are similar to this a short distance from their sources. The water around Stymphalos is carried underground for 200 stadia and then comes out in the Argeia as the Erasinos River. Moreover the [water] near Arkadian Asea is below the surface and then comes out later as both the Eurotas and the Alpheios: there is thus the belief in a certain story that if wreaths are dedicated to each and thrown into the common stream each will reappear in the proper river, according to the dedication. I have already mentioned what is said about the Timavus [5.1.8].

(10) Properties similar both to these and those in Sikelia appear in the Liparaian Islands and on Lipara itself. They are seven in number, with Lipara the largest – a Knidian settlement – which (except for Thermessa) lies closest to Sikelia. It was formerly called Meligounis and commanded a fleet that for a long time opposed the incursions of the Tyrrhenians, holding subject the islands that today are named the Liparaioi, which some call those of Aiolos. It often adorned the sanctuary of Apollo at Delphi with first fruits. It has fertile soil and an alum mine furnishing revenue, as well as hot springs and exhalations of fire.

Approximately between it and Sikelia is what is today called Hiera, entirely rocky, desolate, and fiery. It has three exhalations as if three craters. From the largest the flames carry up masses of rock that have already choked a part of the strait. From observation it is believed that the flames – both here and on Aitna – are provoked by the winds, and when one ceases the other ceases. This is not unreasonable, for the winds are created by the exhalations of the sea, and after they begin they are nourished by them. That the fire is kindled by a related fuel or happening is something that one perceptive about such things should not marvel at. Polybios [34.11.12–20] says that one of the three craters has partially collapsed but the others remain. The largest has a rim five stadia around that reduces to a diameter of fifty feet, whose height above the sea is a stadion, so that it is visible when it is calm, although if one believes this one should also not disbelieve the mythical story about Empedokles. If the south wind is about to blow, he [Polybios] says, a cloudy mist comes down over the circuit of the islet, so

[C276]

that not even Sikelia is visible in the distance. When it is the north wind, pure flames rise high from the previously mentioned crater and a greater roaring is sent forth. The west wind has somewhat of a middle position. The other craters are similar but are lacking in the violence of their eruptions. The difference in the rumbling and the place where the eruption, flames, and smoke begin demonstrate that in three days the wind will blow again. At any rate, those in the Liparai, when sailing was impossible, would predict what the wind would be, he says, and were not mistaken. From this it is clear that what is believed to have been the most mythical of all statements by the Poet was not spoken at random, but he hinted at the truth when he said [*Odyssey* 10.21] that Aiolos was the controller of the winds (which I have previously discussed sufficiently [1.2.9–15]). I will return to what follows from where I digressed.

(11) I have spoken, then, about Lipara and Thermessa. Strongyle ["Round"] is so called because of its shape, and is also inflamed, although its flame is lacking in violence yet extreme in its brilliance. Here, they say, Aiolos lived. The fourth is Didyme ["Twin"], also named after its shape. Of the remainder, Erikoussa and Phoinikoussa are called after plants and are given over to pasture. The seventh is Euonymos ["The Left"], farthest in the open sea and deserted. It is named because for those sailing from Lipara to Sikelia it is the most on the left side.

Often flames have been seen running around the islands on the surface of the open sea, from some passage opened from the cavities in the depths and the forcing out of the fire. Poseidonios [F227] says that in his own memory, about the time of the summer solstice, the sea between Hiera and Euonymos was seen to be raised to an extraordinary height and remained puffed up for some time, continuously and without a pause, and then subsided. Those who dared to sail into it saw dead fish driven by the current, and some of them were stricken because of the heat and odor, and fled. One of the little boats came rather near, and some of those in it were thrown out, and the others barely escaped to Lipara and at times became senseless like epileptics, later regaining their own reason. Many days later mud was seen appearing on the sea, and fire, smoke, and dark flames broke out in many places. Later it solidified and became as hard as millstone. The commander of Sikelia, Titus Flamininus, made this known to the Senate, which sent [a delegation] to make sacrifices to the gods of the underworld and the seas, both on the islet and in the Liparai.

[C277]

The Chorographer [F14] says that from Erikodes to Phoinikodes is 10 miles, and from there to Didyme 30, and from there to the northern part of Lipara 29, and from there to Sikelia 19, but 16 from Strongyle.

Melita – where the little dogs called Melitian come from – lies off
Pachynos, as well as Gaudos, both 88 miles distant from the promontory.
Kossoura is off Lilybaion and off Aspis, a Karchedonian city that is called
Clupea, lying midway between the two and which is the previously men-
tioned distance from both. Aigimouros and other small islets are off Sikelia
and Libya. That is it for the islands.

Part 3: Iapygia and Apulia

(1) As I have gone through ancient Italia as far as Metapontion, the
adjoining areas must be discussed. Iapygia adjoins it. The Hellenes call
it Messapia but to the locals one part is the region of the Salentinians (that
around the Iapygian Cape) and the other that of the Kalabrians. Above
these to the north are the Peuketians and those called in the Hellenic
language the Daunians. The locals call everything after the Kalabrians
Apulia, although some of them are called Poidiklians, especially the
Peuketians. Messapia is a sort of peninsula, enclosed by the isthmus
from Brentesion to Taras, 310 stadia. The sail around the Iapygian Cape
is about 400 stadia.[18]   [C278]

The distance from Metapontion is about 200 stadia,[19] and the voyage is
toward the sunrise. The entire Tarantine Gulf is without harbors, but it
[Taras] has a large and beautiful harbor, enclosed by a large bridge, with a
circumference of 100 stadia. The portion toward the recess makes an
isthmus with the outer sea, and thus the city lies on a peninsula. Ships are
easily hauled overland from either side, as the narrows are low-lying, and the
ground of the city is also low, yet slightly elevated at the akropolis. The old
wall has a large circuit but today most of it around the isthmus is abandoned, yet that around the mouth of the harbor, where the akropolis is,
survives and fills up a city of notable size. It has an exceedingly beautiful
gymnasium and a good-sized agora, in which a bronze colossus of Zeus is
located, the largest except for the Rhodian one. The akropolis is between the
agora and the outlet, but only a few of the dedications that adorned it in
ancient times remain. Most of them were destroyed by the Karchedonians
when they took the city, or carried off as booty when the Romans forcibly
took control, including the colossal bronze Herakles that is on the
Capitolium, a work of Lysippos and dedicated by Fabius Maximus, who
took the city.

[18] This number is far too small, and part of it is probably missing.
[19] After "200" there is an "and" but no other number.

(2) Speaking about its founding, Antiochos [F13] says that when the Messenian War occurred, those Lakedaimonians who did not participate in the expedition were judged to be slaves and were called Helots. All the children born at the time of the expedition were called Parthenians and by judgement were deprived of their civic rights. They did not tolerate this, and since they were numerous they plotted against the citizenry. Learning about this, the latter secretly sent certain ones who, on the pretext of friendship, were to report about what type of plot it was. One of them was Phalanthos,[20] who seemed to be their leader, but was generally not pleased with those joining in the conspiracy. It was agreed that the attack would be made at the Hyakinthioi in Amyklaion, while the games were being celebrated, and when Phalanthos put on his helmet (citizens were recognized by their hair). When those around Phalanthos secretly reported the agreement and the games were underway, the herald came forward and announced that Phalanthos was forbidden to put on a helmet. Perceiving that the conspiracy had been revealed, some ran away and others made supplication. They were told to have courage and were placed under guard, but Phalanthos was sent to the god in regard to emigrating, who said "I give you Satyrion and the rich land of Taras in which to live, to become a calamity for the Iapygians." The Parthenians went there with Phalanthos. They were welcomed both by the barbarians and the Cretans who had previously occupied the place, and who, they say, had sailed with Minos to Sikelia. After his death, which occurred in Kamikoi at the home of Kokalos, they departed from Sikelia, but on the return voyage they were driven off course, although later some went by foot around the Adria as far as Makedonia, and were called Bottiaians. They say that all as far as Daunia are called Iapygians after Iapyx, who was born to Daidalos from a Cretan woman and who was the leader of the Cretans. The city of Taras was named after some hero.

[C279]

(3) Ephoros [F216] says as follows about the founding: the Lakedaimonians were at war with the Messenians, who had killed their king, Teleklos, when he had gone to Messene for a sacrifice. They swore that they would not return home before they destroyed Messene or were all killed. While on the expedition they left behind the youngest and oldest of the citizens to guard the city. Later, in the tenth <year> of the war, the Lakedaimonian women came together and sent certain of themselves to complain to the men that they were not making war against the Messenians on equal terms, for the latter remained at home and were producing

---

[20] Although Strabo's text is ambiguous, it seems that Phalanthos was the disaffected plotter.

children, but the former had abandoned their women to widowhood in making an expedition against the enemy, and there was the danger that the fatherland would lack men. Preserving their oath yet keeping the argument of the women in mind, they sent away from the expedition those who were both the strongest and the youngest, for they understood that these had not participated in the oaths, since they had still been children when they were sent forth with those of age. They were ordered to have intercourse with the women, every man with every woman, thinking that there would be a greater abundance of children. When this happened the children were named the Partheniai. Messene was captured after a nineteen-year war, as Tyrtaios says:

> They fought over it for nineteen years, always unceasingly, having stout-hearted courage, the spearmen who were the fathers of our fathers. In the twentieth, they left their rich lands and fled from the great mountains of Ithome. [F5]

They divided up Messenia, but when they returned home they would not [C280] give the Parthenians civic rights like the others, as they had been born outside of marriage. Allying with the Helots, they formed a conspiracy against the Lakedaimonians and agreed to raise a Lakonian felt cap in the agora as a signal for the attack. Some of the Helots revealed this, yet it was decided that it would be difficult to make a counter-attack – for they were numerous and all were united, believing that they were brothers to one another – and they ordered those about to raise the signal to leave the agora. Learning that they had been betrayed, they held back from action, and were persuaded through their fathers to go and found a settlement. If the place that they took was satisfactory they would remain, but if not, they would return and divide among themselves a fifth part of Messenia. They went forth, encountered the Achaians at war with the barbarians, shared in their dangers, and founded Taras.

(4) At one time the Tarantinians, when they had a democratic government, were exceedingly prosperous. They possessed the largest fleet of all in the region and could send forth 30,000 infantry, 3,000 cavalry, and 1,000 cavalry commanders. They accepted Pythagorean philosophy, especially Archytas, who ruled the city for a long time. Later, because of their prosperity, their luxuriousness became so prevalent that they celebrated more city festivals each year than there were days, and thus their government became worse. Evidence of their poor government is that they made use of foreign commanders, sending Alexander the Molossian against the Messapians and Leukanians, and, earlier, Archidamos [III] the son of Agesilaos [II], and later

Kleonymos, Agathokles, and then Pyrrhos, when they allied with him against the Romans. But they were not well disposed to obey those whom they called in and set them at enmity. At any rate, because of enmity, Alexander attempted to remove to Thourioi the common festival of the Hellenes in that region – which was customarily celebrated at Herakleia in the Tarantine – ordering that a place for the meetings be fortified on the Akalandros River. It was said the misadventure that he later experienced was [C281] because of their ingratitude. About the time of Hannibal they lost their freedom, although later they received a Roman settlement and are living in peace and better than they were earlier. When they made war against the Messapians for possession of Herakleia, they worked with the kings of the Daunians and the Peuketians.

(5) The next part of the Iapygian territory is unexpectedly charming. The surface appears rough but is found to have deep soil when turned over, and although lacking in water it is seen nonetheless to have good pastures and trees. The entire territory was once exceedingly populous and had thirteen cities but now, except for Taras and Brentesion, they are small towns, as they are so worn out.

The Salentinians are said to be Cretan settlers. The sanctuary of Athena, rich at one time, is there, as well as the lookout called Cape Iapygia, extending far out into the open sea toward the winter sunrise, although turning slightly toward the Lakinion, which rises opposite on the west, and with it closing the mouth of the Tarantine Gulf. Along with it the Keraunian Mountains close the mouth of the Ionian Gulf. The crossing from it [Cape Iapygia] is about 700 stadia both to Keraunia and the Lakinion.

The sail from Taras around to Brentesion is 600 stadia as far as the small town of Baris. Today Baris is called Veretum and lies at the extremity of the Salentina. The journey there from Taras is somewhat easier on foot than sailing. From there it is 80 stadia to Leuka, also a small town in which a fountain of foul water is visible. The story is that the Gigantes who survived at the Campanian Phlegra – called the Leuternians – were expelled by Herakles, fled here, and were covered by the earth, with the stream surviving due to their ichor. Because of this, the coast here is called Leuternia. From Leuka to Hydrous, a small town, is 150 [stadia]. From there to Brentesion is 400, and it is the same to the island of Sason, which is located about midway in the crossing from Epeiros to Brentesion. Those who are unable to master the straight voyage put in to the left of Sason at Hydrous, watch for a favorable wind, and continue to the harbor of Brentesion, or they disembark and go on foot by a shorter route via Rhodiai, a Hellenic city [C282] from which the poet Ennius came.

The territory that one sails around from Taras to Brentesion resembles a peninsula. The road from Brentesion to Taras – one day on foot for someone well-girded – makes the isthmus of the previously mentioned peninsula, which most generally call Messapia, Iapygia, Kalabria, or the Salentina, although some divide it up, as I said previously [6.3.1].

(6) This is what can be said about the small towns on the coast. In the interior are Rhodiai, Loupiai, Aletia (slightly above the sea), and on the isthmus, Ouria, where the palace of one of the leaders is still visible. Herodotos [7.170] states that Hyria is in Iapygia, founded by Cretans who wandered from the expedition of Minos to Sikelia, and this must be taken either as here [Ouria] or Veretum.

They say that Brentesion was settled by the Cretans, whether by those who came across with Theseus from Knossos, or those who departed from Sikelia with Iapyx: it is told both ways. They did not remain there, they say, but went to Bottiaia. Later when the city was ruled by kings it lost much of its territory to the Lakedaimonians with Phalanthos. Nevertheless, when he was thrown out of Taras, the Brentesinians accepted him, and when he died they considered him worthy of a magnificent burial. Their territory is better than that of the Tarantinians, for although the soil is thin it bears good fruits, and its honey and wool are particularly praised. Brentesion also has a better harbor, since there are many that are closed by one mouth and sheltered from the waves, for bays are formed inside that resemble in shape the horns of a deer. From this comes the name, for the place, along with the city, greatly resembles the horns of a deer, and in the Messapian language the head of a deer is "brention." The Tarantine one is not completely sheltered from waves, because it lies open and is somewhat shallow within the recess.

(7) The straightest voyage for those crossing from Hellas or Asia is still that to Brentesion, and everyone lands here who takes the road to Rome. There are two: one is the Minucia through the Peuketians (who are called Poidiklians), the Daunians, and the Saunitians, as far as Beneventum. On this road is the city of Egnatia, as well as Caelia, Netium, Canusium, and Herdonia. That via Taras, slightly to the left, which makes a circuit of one more day, is called the Appia and is better as a wagon road. On it are the cities of Ouria and Venusia, the former between Taras and Brentesion and the latter on the boundary of the Saunitians and Leukanians. Both come together near Brentesion and Campania, and then are together as far as Rome. This is called the Appia, through Caudium, Calatia, Capua, and Casilinum as far as Sinoessa (from there has already been described [5.3.5–6]). The total from Rome to Brentesion is 360 miles. There is a third,

[C283]

from Rhegion through the Brettians, Leukanians, and Saunitians to Campania, where it joins the Appia. It is 3 or 4 days longer than from Brentesion, and is through the Apennine Mountains.

(8) The voyage from Brentesion to the opposite side is either to Keraunia and the adjoining coast of Epeiros and Hellas, or to Epidamnos, which is longer than the former (1,000 stadia, while the other is 800) but is used more because the city is well-situated in regard to both the Illyrian peoples and the Makedonians.

As one sails from Brentesion along the Adriatic coast, a voyage with the Notos wind, there is the city of Egnatia, the normal stopping point for those going by sea or foot to Barion. The Peuketians go this far along the sea, and as far as Silvium in the interior. It is all rough and mountainous, since it includes much of the Apennine Mountains, and it seems to have received Arkadian settlers. From Brentesion to Barion is about 700 stadia, and <Egnatia> is about the same distance from both. The Daunians live in the adjoining territory, and then the Apulians as far as the Frentanians. Yet the names "Peuketian" and "Daunian" are not used at all by the locals, except in reference to antiquity, and since the entire territory is now called Apulia, by necessity the boundaries of those peoples cannot be defined exactly. I must not be confidently assertive about them.

(9) From Barion to the Aufidus River, on which is the emporium of the Canusitians, is 400 [stadia], with the sail up to the emporium 90. Also nearby is Salapia, the seaport of the Argyrippenians. Not far above the sea in a fertile plain are situated two cities, which formerly were the largest of the Italiote ones (as is clear from their ancient walls): Canusium and Argyrippa, formerly called Argos Hippion, then Argyrippa, and today Arpi. Both are said to have been founded by Diomedes. In addition to the plain [of [C284] Diomedes], there are many other signs of the power of Diomedes visible in these places, including the old dedications in the sanctuary of Athena at Loucheria, which was an ancient city of the Daunians but is today reduced. In the sea nearby are the two islands called the Diomedeiai, one of which is inhabited and the other one, they say, is deserted. On it, according to certain stories, Diomedes disappeared and his companions were changed into birds, which remain today, tame and living a human type of life, both in their orderly way of living, their fairness toward gentle people and their flight from evil and hateful [people]. What the Enetians have commonly reported about this hero and the honors that were customary for him have already been discussed [5.1.9].

It seems that Sipous was founded by Diomedes, and it is about 140 stadia distant from Salapia. It was named Sepious in Hellenic because of the sepia cast up on the waves. Between Salapia and Sipous is a navigable river and a large lagoon. Produce – especially grain – is brought down from Sipous on both. Visible in Daunia is a hill called Drion, with heroa on it. One, on the height of the summit, is to Kalchas, where those consulting the oracle sacrifice a black ram to the dead and sleep in its hide. The other is to Podaleirios, at the base, and about 100 stadia distant from the sea. A little stream flows from it that is a panacea for diseases of domestic animals. Lying in front of this gulf is a promontory, Garganon, that extends 300 stadia toward the coast into the open sea. When one goes around the cape there is the small town of Ourion and off the cape are the Diomedeian Islands.

The entire country is totally productive and produces much, and is excellent for horses and sheep. The wool is softer than the Tarantine, but less bright. The country is well sheltered because the plains are in hollows. Some say that Diomedes attempted to cut a canal as far as the sea but left this and other activities half finished because he was summoned home, where he ended his life. This is one account of him; a second is that he stayed here until he ended his life, and a third is the mythical version that I mentioned previously which recounts his disappearance on the island. As a fourth one might set down that of the Enetians, for they tell a story that he came to an end among them in some way, which they call his apotheosis.

(10) These distances are laid down as according to Artemidoros [F45].   [C285] The Chorographer [F44] says that from Brentesion as far as Garganon is 165 miles, but Artemidoros gives more. The former says that it is 254 miles from there, but Artemidoros has 1,250 stadia to the Aisis, near Ankon, which is much less. Polybios [34.11.8] says that from Iapygia it has been measured in miles and that it is 562 miles to the city of Sila, and from there to Aquileia 178. They do not agree with the accepted distances along the Illyrian coast from the Keraunian Mountains to the recess of the Adria, since they represent this coastal voyage as over 6,000 [stadia], which makes it even greater, although it is much shorter. But everyone does not agree with everyone else, especially regarding distances, as I have often said. When I am able to make a determination, I will set forth my opinion, but if not, I think I must put down those of others. If I do not have anything from them, then it is not surprising if I omit something, given such a topic, for I would not omit anything important. Small matters are only of slight benefit even when known, and their omission escapes notice and does not weaken the work at all, or not much.

(11) The interval immediately after the Garganon is taken up by a deep gulf. Those who live around it are particularly called Apulians and have the

same language as the Daunians and Peuketians, and today are not in any way different from them, although it is reasonable that they differed in antiquity, from which came the totally variant names that survive. Formerly the whole land was prosperous, but it was laid waste by Hannibal and later wars. Here the matter of Cannae occurred, where the Romans and their allies experienced a great destruction of their people. On the gulf is a lake, and above the lake in the interior is Apulian Teanum, which is homonymous with Sidicinum. It seems that the width of Italia has narrowed considerably, since to the region around Dikaiarcheia there is an isthmus remaining of less than 1,000 stadia from sea to sea. After the lake is the voyage along the coast to the Frentanians and Buca, and it is 200 stadia from the lake to either Buca or the Garganon. I have already discussed what is beyond the region of Buca [5.4.2].

Part 4:　The history of Rome

(1) Italia, then, has such a size and character. Many things have been mentioned, but now I will give the most important indicators concerning [C286] how the Romans rose to such a height. One is that like an island it is safely guarded all around by the open sea except in a few places, which are fortified by mountains and difficult to cross. Second, most of it is harborless and the harbors that do exist are large and marvellous. The former is useful against external attacks and the latter for counter-attacks and of assistance in the abundant commerce. Third, it is affected by many different climates and temperatures, because of which there are the greater variations for living things, plants, and, simply, everything that is useful for life, for better or worse. Its length extends to the south from the north, generally, with Sikelia, itself so extensive, an addition to its length, which is already great. Mild and harsh air temperatures are judged by the cold and heat, and what is in between, and thus necessarily the Italia of today, lying between both extremes and with such a great length, shares in temperateness and many qualities. Moreover, because the Apennine Mountains extend through its entire length, leaving plains and hillocks that are finely fruited on both sides, no part of it fails to enjoy the virtues of both mountains and plains. One can add the size and numbers of its rivers and lakes, and also the eruptions of hot and cold water that have naturally been provided in many places for health, as well as the abundance of all sorts of mines. One cannot adequately speak of the abundant forests and other nourishment provided for men and cattle, and its bearing of good fruits. It is between the largest peoples, Hellas, and the

best parts of Asia,[21] and is superior in virtue and size to those around it, naturally suited to leadership, yet, being near to them, can easily make use of their services.

(2) If it is necessary to add to the discussion of Italia a summary about the Romans who gained possession of it and prepared it as a base of operations for universal leadership, let me add this: after Rome had been founded the Romans wisely continued to be ruled by kings for many generations. But since the last Tarquinius ruled badly he was thrown out, and they constructed a government that was a mixture of monarchy and aristocracy. They treated the Sabines and Latins as partners, but it did   [C287] not always happen that they or other neighbors were conciliatory, and, in a way, they were forced to break them up in order to enlarge their own territory.

Thus as they were slowly advancing, it happened that they suddenly lost the city, contrary to the expectations of everyone, and then contrary to expectation received it back. This happened, as Polybios [1.6.1–3] says, in the nineteenth year after the naval battle at Aigospotamoi, at the time of the Peace of Antalkidas. Having gotten rid of them, the Romans first subjected all the Latins. Then they stopped the Tyrrhenians and Kelts around the Padus from their frequent and unceasing liberties. Then they reduced the Saunitians, and afterward the Tarantinians and Pyrrhos, and then the rest of Italia except that around the Padus. Although this region was still in a state of war, they crossed over to Sikelia and took it away from the Karchedonians, and then went against those around the Padus. While this was still underway Hannibal arrived in Italia: this was the second war that occurred against the Karchedonians. Not much later there was the third, in which Karchedon was destroyed and the Romans gained both Libya and as much of Iberia as they had taken from the Karchedonians.

The Hellenes, Makedonians, and those in Asia within the Halys and the Tauros joined the Karchedonians in revolution, and thus they were persuaded to acquire these regions at the same time, those which belonged to Kings Antiochos [III], Philippos [V], and Perseus. Moreover, the Illyrians and Thracians who were neighbors to the Hellenes and Makedonians began to undertake war against the Romans, and continued to make war until everyone within the Istros and within the Halys had been put down. The

---

[21] Although the manuscripts consistently have "Asia," this seems geographically improbable, and some editors have suggested "Libya."

Iberians, Kelts, and all the rest who are obedient to the Romans experienced the same thing. They did not cease in reducing Iberia by arms until everyone had been overthrown, driving out the Numantinians, and later destroyed Viriathus and Sertorius, and, latest of all, the Cantabrians, whom Sebastos Caesar . . . . In regard to the whole of Keltike (both that within and outside, as well as Ligystike), it originally would come always to their side in parts, but later Caesar the God, and after that Sebastos, won it completely in a general war. Today they are making war against the Germans, starting from these places as the most suitable, and have already [C288] brought several triumphs to the fatherland.

As much of Libya that was not Karchedonian was turned over to subject kings: if they revolted they were deposed. Today Maurousia and many other portions of Libya have devolved upon Juba [II], because of his goodwill and friendship. What happened in Asia was similar. In the beginning it was administered by subject kings, but later when they died (as with the Attalid, Syrian, Paphlagonian, Kappadokian, and Egyptian kings), or when they revolted and were then deposed (as happened with Mithridates [VI] Eupator and the Egyptian Kleopatra [VII]), everywhere within the Phasis and Euphrates, except certain parts of the Arabians, came under Roman power or those subject to them. The Armenians and those lying above Kolchis (the Albanians and Iberians) need only the presence of leaders and act well when ruled, but they revolt when the Romans are otherwise occupied. This is also the case with those beyond the Istros around the Euxeinos, except for those living around the Bosporos and the nomads, for the former are subjects but the latter, because of their great unsociability with everyone, are useless and need only be watched. The remainder are mostly Tent Dwellers and nomads, and are extremely far away. The Parthyaians, although they have a common border with Rome, are very powerful but have also given in to the pre-eminence of the Romans and the leaders of today, so that they not only send the trophies that they had once set up against the Romans to Rome, but Phraates [IV] entrusted his children and his children's children to Sebastos Caesar, thus obsequiously giving hostages in return for friendship. Today they frequently go there [Rome] seeking a king and are about to put their entire power into the hands of the Romans.

Since it has been under the Romans, Italia itself, although often divided by factions, and Rome itself, have been prevented by the quality of their government and rulers from advancing far into error and disorder. But it would be difficult to administer so large a state unless it were turned over to one person, like a father. At any rate, such peace and abundance of good things have never been available to the Romans and their allies as what was provided by Sebastos Caesar, from when he undertook complete authority. It is now provided by his son and successor Tiberius, who has made him the model for his administration and decrees, as are his own children, Germanicus and Drusus, who are assisting their father.

BOOK 7

Northern and eastern Europe

Part 1: Introduction and the territory north of the Rhenos

[C289] (1) Having discussed Iberia, the Keltic and Italian peoples, and the nearby islands, next I will speak about the remaining parts of Europe, dividing it in the approved manner. What remains is, toward the east, that which is across the Rhenos as far as the Tanais and the mouth of the Maiotic Lake, and what is between the Adria and the regions to the left of the Pontic Sea, south as far as Hellas and the Propontis. This is all cut off by the Istros, which divides the previously mentioned territory very nearly into two and is the largest of the rivers of Europe, flowing toward the south at the beginning and then turning straight from the west toward the east and the Pontos. It begins at the western limits of the Germans, near the recess of the Adriatic (about a thousand stadia distant from it) and ends at the Pontos not far away from the outlets of the Tyras and the Borysthenes, bending somewhat toward the north. To the north of the Istros is what is beyond the Rhenos and Keltike: the Galatic and German peoples as far as the Bastarnians, the Tyregetians, and the Borysthenes River, as well as those as far as the Tanais and the mouth of the Maiotis who extend into the interior as far as the Ocean and are also washed by the Pontic Sea. To the south are the Illyrian and Thracian regions, and those of the Kelts and whatever others are mixed in with them, as far as Hellas. I will speak first about those outside the Istros, for they are much simpler than those in the [C290] other portion.

(2) That which is across the Rhenos, immediately after the Kelts, slopes toward the east and is occupied by the Germans, who are slightly different from the Keltic race, as they are much wilder, larger, and have yellower hair, but otherwise are similar. In form, customs, and lifestyle they are as I have described the Kelts [4.4.2–3]. Thus it seems to me that the Romans gave them the name because they wished to consider them genuine Galatians, as "germani" means "genuine" in the Roman language.

(3) The first parts of the territory are those next to the Rhenos, as far as its outlets and beginning at its source. This entire riverine district is about the width of the country on the west. The Romans transferred some of these peoples to Keltike, and others such as the Marsians emigrated deep into the territory. Only a few remain, such as a portion of the Sougambrians.

After those along the river there are other peoples, who are between the Rhenos and the Albis River, which flows toward the Ocean approximately parallel to the others, and crossing no less territory than the former. Between them there are other navigable rivers – including the Amasia, where Drusus won a naval battle over the Broukterians – that also flow from the south toward the north and the Ocean. The country is lifted up toward the south, making a ridge that connects with the Alps and extends toward the east as though it were a part of the Alps. Some declare it to be a part of them because of their previously mentioned position and because they produce the same timber, but this area is not high enough. The Herkynian Forest is also here, and the Soebian peoples, some of whom live in the forest, such as the Quadians. Located among them is Bouiaimon, the royal residence of Marobodos, the place to which he migrated with a number of other peoples, especially his kinsmen the Markommanians. Although previously a private citizen, when he returned from Rome he was placed in a position of control. As a young man he was favored by Sebastos, and when he went back he held power and acquired, in addition to those mentioned, the Lougians – a large ethnic group – and the Zoumians, Goutonians, Mougilonians, and Sibinians, as well as the Semnonians, a large ethnic group of the Soebians. Except for the Soebians, as I have said [4.3.4], these peoples live outside of the forest and have a common boundary with the Getians.

The ethnic group of the Soebians is the largest, extending from the Rhenos as far as the Albis, with a part of them living across the Albis, such as the Hermondorians and the Langobardians. Today every last one of [C291] them has been driven in flight across the river. It is common to all those in this region that they migrate easily because of the simplicity of their life and because they do not farm or store things, yet they are capable of living in small temporary huts, and are nourished for the most part from their domestic animals, like the nomads. In imitation of them they load their possessions onto wagons and with their animals turn to wherever seems best. But the other German peoples are poorer, such as the Cherouskians, Chattians, Gamabrivians, and the Chattouarians, and near the Ocean the Sougambrians, Chaubians, Broukterians, and Kimbrians, as well as the Kaukians, Kaoulkians, Kampsianians, and a number of others.

In the same [direction] as the Amasia flow the Bisourgis and Loupias Rivers, the latter about 600 stadia from the Rhenos and flowing through the lesser Broukterians. There is also the Salas River, and it was between it and the Rhenos that Drusus Germanicus, while successfully waging war, came to an end. He had conquered not only most of the ethnic groups but the islands along the coast, among which is Byrchanis, which he took by siege.

(4) These peoples have become known through their wars with the Romans, in which they would give up and then revolt again, or leave their settlements. They would have become better known if Sebastos had allowed the commanders to cross the Albis and go after those who retreated there. As it is, he assumed that he could more easily wage the war at hand if he could keep those beyond the Albis away, as they were at peace, and not provoke them into making common cause because of their enmity. The Sougambrians, living near the Rhenos, began the war, having Mailon as their leader. From that time different peoples at different times, in succession, would become powerful and would be put down, and then revolt again, abandoning their hostages and their good faith. With them, mistrust has been a benefit, for those who have been trusted have caused the greatest damage, such as the Cherouskians and their subjects, by whom three Roman legions along with their commander, Quintilius Varus, were destroyed by ambush in violation of the treaty. They all paid the penalty and gave the younger Germanicus a most distinguished triumph, the triumph in which there were most notable men and women, including Segimountos, son of Segestes and the leader of the Cherouskians, as well as his sister, the wife of Arminius, who was military commander of the Cherouskians when the [C292] treaty with Quintilius Varus was violated and who is still continuing the war today. Her name was Thusnelda, and there was also her three-year-old son Thoumelikos, as well as Sesithakos the son of Segimeros a leader of the Cherouskians, his wife Rhamis daughter of Veromerus the leader of the Chattians, and Deudorix the son of Baitorix the brother of Mailon, a Sougambrian. Yet Segestes the father-in-law of Arminius, who from the beginning had distanced himself from the latter's plans and took advantage of an opportunity to demonstrate his courage, was present in a position of honor at the triumph over his most loved ones. Libes, a priest of the Chattians, was also in the procession, and other people from the plundered ethnic groups were in the procession: the Kaoulkians, Kampsanians, Broukterians, Usipians, Cherouskians, Chattians, Chattouarians, Landians, and Toubantians. The Rhenos is about 3,000 stadia distant from the Albis, if the roads were straight. Today it is necessary to go circuitously, winding through marshes and forests.

(5) The Herkynian Forest is rather thick and has large trees, enclosing an extensive circuit that is naturally fortified. In the center of it is a territory in which one is able to live, about which I have already spoken [7.1.3]. Near it are the sources of both the Istros and Rhenos, and between them are a lake and the marshes into which the Rhenos disperses. The lake has a perimeter of more than 300 stadia, with the crossing nearly 200.[1] It has an island that Tiberius used as a base of operations in the naval battle against the Vindolicians, and is somewhat south of the sources of the Istros, so that in going from Keltike to the Herkynian Forest one must first cross the lake and then the Istros, and then proceed through more favorable territory to the forest, going across upland plains. Tiberius had gone a day's journey from the lake when he saw the sources of the the the Istros. The Rhaitians adjoin the lake for a short distance, but the Elvettians, Vindolicians, and the desolate region of the Boians are along much of it. All those as far as the Pannonians, especially the Elvettians and Vindolicians, live in upland plains. The Rhaitians and the Noricians rise as far as the Alpine passes and the slopes to Italia, some touching the Insoubrians and others the Karnians and the territory around Aquileia. There is another large forest, Gabreta, on this side of the Soebians – the Herkynian Forest is on the other side – that is held by them.

Part 2:   The Kimbrians and the far north

(1) Concerning the Kimbrians, some things said about them are not correct, and others are most unbelievable. One cannot accept that the reason they became wanderers and brigands is because while living on a peninsula they were driven out of the place by a great flood tide. Today they have the territory that they formerly had, and they sent their most sacred cauldron to Sebastos as a gift, seeking his friendship and an amnesty for their previous offenses, and when they were considered worthy they went away. It is absurd that because of something that is natural and eternal which occurs twice a day they became angry and left the place. It seems a fiction that an excessive flood-tide occurred once, for when the Ocean is affected in this way it is ordered and periodic. Whoever said that the Kimbrians took up arms against the flood tide is also not correct, nor is it that the Kelts, trained to be fearless, submitted to the inundation of their homes and then rebuilt them, or that they suffered greater destruction by water than in war, as Ephoros [F132] says. The regularity of the flood tides and the knowledge

[C293]

---

[1] The numbers are questionable, especially the first, which is far too small.

about the territory that could be inundated would make such absurdities improbable. Since it happens twice each day, how could they not understand and believe at once that the flowing back was natural and harmless, and that it occurred not only among them but everywhere along the Ocean? Kleitarchos [F26] is also in error, for he says that the horsemen, seeing the advance of the sea, rode away and were almost overtaken in flight. We have observed that the onset does not advance with such a speed, but the sea comes imperceptibly, and also what occurs daily and is fresh in the memory of those coming near to it, even before they see it, would not have created such fear as to cause them to flee, as if it had happened unexpectedly.

(2) Poseidonios [F272] is right in finding fault with the historians about these things. He conjectures – not badly – that the Kimbrians, who were brigands and wanderers, made an expedition as far as around the Maiotis, and that the Kimmerian Bosporos was named after them, being the same as Kimbrikos, since the Hellenes named the Kimbrians the Kimmerians. He also says that the Boians formerly lived in the Herkynian Forest, and that the Kimbrians attacked this place but were driven away by the Boians and went down the Istros to the Skordiskian Galatians, then to the Teuristians and Tauriskians (also Galatians), and then to the Elvettians, who were peaceful men rich in gold. When the Elvettians saw that the wealth obtained through brigandage exceeded their own, they – especially the Tigyrenians [C294] and Toÿgenians – became so excited that they rushed forth with them. All of them were put down by the Romans, both the Kimbrians themselves and those who had joined with them, some after they had crossed the Alps into Italia and others while still beyond the Alps.

(3) They describe a certain custom of the Kimbrians, that the women join the expeditions, attended by priestesses who were prophets, grey-haired and dressed in white, with flaxen cloaks buckled on and having bronze girdles and bare feet. With their swords, they would meet captives throughout the camp, and crowning them with wreaths they would lead them to a bronze krater holding about twenty amphoras. They would go up a flight of stairs, each would be lifted over the cauldron, and his throat would be cut after he was raised up. Some would make a certain prophecy from the blood that poured forth into the krater, and others would split them open and examine their entrails, crying out victory for their people. During the battles they would strike the hides that were stretched over the wicker bodies of their wagons, creating an extraordinary noise.

(4) Regarding the Germans, as I have said [7.1.1], those toward the north live along the Ocean, and they are known beginning from the outlets of the Rhenos as far as the Albis. The best known of them are the Sougambrians

and Kimbrians. What is beyond the Albis near the Ocean is totally unknown to us. I know of no one in earlier times who travelled along this coast toward the eastern regions as far as the mouth of the Kaspian Sea. The Romans have not advanced into what is beyond the Albis, and no one has passed through there on foot. Nevertheless the fact that someone going toward the east comes to the regions around the Borysthenes and those to the north of the Pontos is clear from their latitude and the parallel intervals. But what is beyond Germania and that which is next to it – whether one should say the Bastarnians (as most conjecture), or that there are others in between, either the Iazygians, the Roxolanians, or certain other Wagon Dwellers – is not easy to say, nor whether they extend to the Ocean, stretching alongside it for its entire length, whether some of it is uninhabitable because of the cold or another reason, or whether there are other races of people situated successively between the sea and the eastern Germans. This same ignorance exists concerning others successively toward the north, for I do not know about the Bastarnians, Sauromatians, or, simply, those living above the Pontos, and how far they are from the Atlantic Sea, or whether they adjoin it.

Part 3:   Far northeastern Europe

(1) The southern part of Germania beyond the Albis and just touching it is held by the Soebians, and then immediately adjoining is the land of the Getians, which – although narrow at first – extends along the southern [C295] side of the Istros and the opposite, on the mountain slopes of the Herkynian Forest, and possesses a part of the mountains. Then it spreads toward the north as far as the Tyregetians, but I cannot determine the precise boundary. Because of ignorance of these places, consideration is given to those creating stories about the Rhipaia Mountains and the Hyperboreans, and what Pytheas the Massaliote [T16] falsely reported about the territory along the Ocean, using as a screen his knowledge about the heavens and mathematics. Such [people] are to be dismissed. Even if Sophokles, as a tragedian, tells that Oreithyia was snatched up by Boreas and carried

> over the entire Pontos to the farthest part of the earth and the sources of the
> night, the wide expanse of heaven and the ancient garden of Phoibos [F956],

this is not relevant to the present matter and should be dismissed, just as Sokrates did in the *Phaidros* [Plato, *Phaidros* 3]. Let what we say make use of ancient and contemporary research.

(2) The Hellenes assumed that the Getians were Thracian. They lived on either side of the Istros, as did the Mysians (who were also Thracian), those who are today called Moisians. The Mysians who today live between the Lydians, Phrygians, and Trojans originated from them. The Phrygians themselves are Brigians, a Thracian ethnic group, as are also the Mygdonians, Bebrykians, Maidobithynians, Bithynians, Thynians, and, I believe, the Mariandynians. All these have completely abandoned Europe, although the Mysians remain. Poseidonios [F277a] seems to be correct in conjecturing that Homer names the Mysians in Europe when he says

> he turned back his shining eyes and looked far away to the land of the horse-herding Thracians and the hand-to-hand fighting Mysians. [*Iliad* 13.3–5]

If one were to accept this as the Mysians in Asia, the statement would not hang together. When one turns the eyes away from the Trojans toward the Thracian land, to connect it with these Mysians – who are not "far away" but have a common boundary with the Troad and are located behind and on either side of it, separated from Thrace by the "broad Hellespont" [*Iliad* 7.86; *Odyssey* 24.82] – would only be done by someone who confuses the continents and does not understand the wording. "He turned back" generally means to the rear, and he who transfers his view from the Trojans to those who are in their rear or along their side transfers it rather far, but not at [C296] all to [his own] rear. One can produce as witness the fact that he [Homer] connected to them the Mare Milkers, Milk Drinkers, and Abians, who are the wagon-dwelling Skythians and Sarmatians. Today these peoples, as well as the Bastarnians, are mixed together with the Thracians (mostly those outside the Istros but also those within it), as well as those in the Keltike (the Boians, Skordiskians, and Tauriskians). Some call the Skordiskians the Skordistians, and they say that the Tauriskians are Ligyriskians and Tauristians.

(3) Poseidonios says that the Mysians abstain from living things, including their animals, out of piety. They use honey, milk, and cheese, and live peacefully, because of which they are called "god fearing" and *kapnobatai*.[2] Some of the Thracians live apart from women and are called the Founders, and because of their honor are dedicated to the gods and live in freedom from fear. The Poet speaks collectively of all these peoples as "the noble Mare Milkers, Milk Drinkers, and the Abians, the most just of men" [*Iliad* 13.5–6]. He calls them Abians ["Without Lives"] especially because they live apart from women, believing that such a deprived life is only half complete,

---

[2] The meaning of this word, cited only here and in Section 4, is unknown.

just as the house of Protesilaos was half complete because it was deprived [*Iliad* 2.701]. The Mysians are "hand to hand fighters" because they were not subdued, as were all good warriors. It is necessary to write in Book 13 [line 5], "hand-to hand-fighting Moisians," instead of "Mysians".

(4) It is perhaps superfluous to change the wording that has been popular for so many years, for it is more believable that they were called Mysians from the beginning and now. . . . One might accept "Abians" not so much as those who were deprived, but those without hearths who lived in wagons. For the most part injustices are created in regard to contracts and a high esteem for property, so it is reasonable that those who live cheaply on few resources would be called the most just. In fact, the philosophers who place justice nearest to moderation strive most of all for self-sufficiency and frugality, and thus going beyond these limits will push some of them into Cynicism. Regarding the statement that they live deprived of women, he indicates nothing of this sort, particularly with the Thracians and those among them who are Getians. See what Menandros says about them, which one can reasonably assume was not invented, but taken from history: [C297]

> All the Thracians and all of us who are Getians – for I can boast that I am of this race – are not very self- controlled. [F877]

And a little farther down he sets forth an example of their lack of control regarding women:

> We marry not one but ten or eleven women, and some twelve or more. If anyone has only four or five when he dies, he is considered by them to be someone without a nuptial song, unhappy, and without a bride. [Ibid.]

These matters are agreed to by others. Furthermore, it is not reasonable that they consider a life without many women to be unhappy, yet consider it good and just to be completely deprived of women. To consider as god fearing and *kapnobatai* those who are destitute of women is very much opposed to common assumptions. Everyone believes women were the founders of religion and that they call forth the men to greater service to the gods, to festivals, and to lamentations. It would be rare for a man who lives by himself to find these things. See again what the same poet says when he introduces someone annoyed with the expenses made by women in connection with sacrifices, and says:

> The gods afflict us, especially those who are married men, for we must always be celebrating some festival [Menandros F878]

and the Misogynist makes this accusation about these things:

we would sacrifice five times a day, and seven female attendants would beat cymbals around us, while others cried out aloud. [Menandros F237]

Thus to believe that the womanless Getians are particularly reverent is clearly contrary to reason. A feeling for the divine is especially strong among these people – from what Poseidonios [F277a] and other histories generally say – and should not be disbelieved.

(5) It is said that a certain Getian, named Zalmoxis, was a slave of Pythagoras, and had learned from him some things about the heavens, and other matters from the Egyptians, for he had wandered that far. When he returned home the leaders and his people paid close attention to him because he could make predictions from signs. Finally he persuaded the king to take him as a partner in the rule, because he was competent to report about the gods. In the beginning he was established as a priest of the god [C298] most honored among them, and later he was addressed as a god. Having taken possession of a certain inaccessible cave-like place, he spent his life there, rarely meeting anyone from outside except the king and his servants. The king cooperated with him, seeing that the people paid much more attention to him than before, believing that the decrees he put forth were approved by the gods. This custom survived into our time, because some-one could always be found of such character who, although only an advisor to the king, was called a god by the Getians. They took up the idea that the mountain was sacred and call it such, but its name is Kogaionon, homon-ymous with the river flowing by it. When Byrebistas ruled the Getians and Caesar the God was preparing an expedition against him, Dekaineos held the office. The Pythagorean concept of abstaining from living things, handed down by Zalmoxis, still survived.

(6) Such difficulties concerning what is laid down by the Poet about the Mysians and the "noble Mare Milkers" are not a problem. Yet what Apollodoros [of Athens, F157a] says in the preface to the second book of his *On the Ships* is not acceptable. He approves of what Eratosthenes [F8] asserted, that both Homer and other ancient authors knew Hellenic places, but were ignorant of those far away, ignorant of long journeys, and ignorant of sea voyages. In support of this he [Apollodoros of Athens] says that Homer calls Aulis rocky [*Iliad* 2.496], just as it is, Eteonos many-ridged [497], Thisbe abounding in doves [502], and Haliartos grassy [503], but that neither he nor the others knew far-away places. There are about forty rivers that flow into the Pontos, but he does not mention even those that are the best known, such as the Istros, Tanais, Borysthenes, Hypanis, Phasis, Thermodon, or Halys. Moreover, he does not mention the Skythians, but creates certain "noble

Mare Milkers" or the "Milk Drinkers" and the "Abians." Concerning the Paphlagonians of the interior, his report is from those who approached these territories on foot, but he is ignorant of the coast, and naturally so. At that time the sea was not navigable and was called the Axenos ["Inhospitable"] because of its wintriness and the wildness of the peoples living around it, most of all the Skythians, who sacrificed strangers, ate their flesh, and used their skulls as drinking cups. Later, when the Ionians founded cities on its coast, it was called the Euxeinos. Moreover, he is ignorant of matters   [C299] concerning the Egyptians and Libyans, such as the rising of the Nile and the silting up of the sea (which he records nowhere), or the isthmus between the Erythran and Egyptian seas, or Arabia, Aithiopia, and the Ocean, unless one should agree with the scholar Zenon when he wrote [F275] "we came to the Aithiopians and Sidonians and Arabians" [Homer, *Odyssey* 4.84, emended]. But this is not surprising for Homer, for those more recent than him have been ignorant of many things and tell of marvels. Hesiod [F101] speaks of the Half Dogs, Those With Long Heads, and the Pygmaians; Alkman [F148] about Those With Web Feet, and Aischylos [F431, 441, 434a] about the Dog Heads, Those With Eyes in Their Chests, Those With One Eye, and countless others. From these he [Apollodoros of Athens] proceeds against the writers who speak of Mount Rhipaia and Mount Ogyion, and the settlements of the Gorgons and the Hesperides, the Meropian land of Theopompos [F75d], the Kimmerian city of Hekataios [of Abdera, F8], the Panchaian land of Euhemeros [T5c], and Aristotle's river stones formed from sand but melted by rain. In Libya there is the city of Dionysos that no one can find twice. He censures those who say that the wanderings of Odysseus were, according to Homer, around Sikelia, for if so, one must say that although the wanderings were there, they were placed by the Poet in the Ocean for mythological reasons. Although others can be excused, Kallimachos [F13, 470] cannot be at all, in his pretense as a scholar, who says that Gaudos is the Island of Kalypso and Korkyra is Scheria. He [Apollodoros of Athens] accuses others of being mistaken about Gerena, Akakesion, Demos in Ithaka, Pelethronion in Pelion, and Glaukopion in Athens. To this he adds some minor things and then ceases, having transferred most of them from Eratosthenes, and which, as I have said previously [1.2.24], are not correct. In regard to Eratosthenes and him [Apollodoros of Athens], one must grant that the more recent writers are more knowledgeable than the ancient ones, but thus to go beyond moderation, particularly in regard to Homer, seems to me something for which they could justly be rebuked. Indeed one could say the opposite: that when they are ignorant themselves about these things, they reproach the Poet about them. What remains on   [C300] this topic happens to be mentioned at the appropriate places as well as generally.

(7) I was speaking now about the Thracians:

> The hand-to-hand fighting Mysians and the noble Mare Milkers, Milk Drinkers, and the Abians, the most just of men, [Homer, *Iliad* 13.5–6]

wishing to compare what was said by myself and Poseidonios [F277a] with them [Eratosthenes and Apollodoros of Athens]. In the first case, the reasoning that they made is opposite to what they have proposed. They propose to demonstrate that those earlier were more ignorant of places far from Hellas than were those more recent, but they have shown the opposite, not only about far places, but also those within Hellas. But, as I was saying, let us postpone the rest and observe that which is here: they say because of ignorance he [Homer] does not mention the Skythians or their cruelty toward strangers (they sacrifice them and eat their flesh, using their skulls for drinking cups), and because of whom the Pontos was called the Axenos, yet he creates certain "noble Mare Milkers, Milk Drinkers, and the Abians, the most just of men," who are nowhere on earth. How could there be the name "Axenos" if they did not know about their savageness, and that they were the most [savage] of all? These are presumably the Skythians. Were not the Mare Milkers beyond the Mysians, Thracians, and Getians, as well as the Milk Drinkers and the Abians? Even now there are Wagon Dwellers and nomads, as they are called, who live off their animals and milk and cheese, especially that from horses, and do not know about storing things or trading, except goods for goods. How could the poet be ignorant of the Skythians if he spoke of certain Mare Milkers and Milk Drinkers? At that time they were called the Mare Milkers, and Hesiod is a witness to this, in the words that Eratosthenes quotes: "Aithiopians, Ligyans, and also the mare-milking Skythians" [*Catalogue*, F98]. What is there that is marvellous, if – because of the extensive injustices among us concerning contracts – he [Homer] said that those were most just who live the least for contracts and obtaining money, yet possess everything in common except their sword and drinking cup, and most of all have their women and children in common in the Platonic manner? Aischylos is also clearly pleading for the poet when he says [C301] about the Skythians: "the Skythians, with their good laws, eaters of mare's-milk cheese" [F198]. This assumption survives today among the Hellenes, for we believe that the former are the most straightforward and least active in mischief, as well as far more frugal and independent than us. Yet our life has extended a change for the worse to almost everyone, introducing luxury, pleasure, and the base arts that lead to a myriad of excess. Much of such wickedness has fallen onto the barbarians, others as well as the nomads, since having taken up the sea they have become worse – brigands and killers of strangers – and because of their involvement with many peoples they have assumed their extravagance, but they also corrupt and introduce a complexity rather than the ingenuousness that I have just mentioned.

(8) Those previous to us, however, especially those near the time of Homer, were such people as Homer says, and were assumed to be such by the Hellenes. See what Herodotos says [4.127] about the Skythian king against whom Dareios [I] made war, and the messages sent between them. See also what Chrysippos [F692] says about the kings of the Bosporos, those around Leukon. Moreover, the Persian letters, as well as Egyptian, Babylonian, and Indian records, are full of the ingenuousness of which I speak. Because of this, Anacharsis, Abaris, and such others were esteemed by the Hellenes, since they showed national characteristics of contentedness, simplicity, and justice. Yet why should one speak of antiquity? Alexander the son of Philippos [II], on his expedition against the Thracians beyond the Haimos, invaded the Triballians and saw that they reached as far as the Istros and the island of Peuke (which was in it), but the other side was held by the Getians. It is said he went that far but was unable to disembark on the island because of a scarcity of boats (Syrmos the king of the Triballians had taken refuge there and withstood his attempts). He crossed over to the territory of the Getians, took a city of theirs, and returned home swiftly after receiving gifts from the people and Syrmos. Ptolemaios [I] the son of Lagos [F2] says that on this expedition the Kelts around the Adria joined with Alexander for the sake of friendship and hospitality. The king received them in a kindly fashion and asked, while drinking, what they feared the most, thinking that they would say him. They answered that it was no one, except perhaps that the heavens would fall on them, and that they put the friendship of such a man above everything. These are the signs of the ingenuousness of the barbarians: that he [Syrmos] would not acquiesce to the landing on the island yet sent gifts and committed himself to friendship, and that they said they feared no one but placed the friendship of great men above everything. Dromichaites was the king of the Getians at the time of the Successors of Alexander, and when he took Lysimachos alive (who had made an expedition against him), he pointed out the poverty of himself and his people, as well as their independence, and then ordered him not to make war on others, but to consider them friends. Having said this, he received him as a guest and made an agreement of friendship, and then released him.

[C302]

(9) Ephoros [F42], in the fourth book of his history – titled "Europe" (the circuit of Europe as far as the Skythians) – says near the end that the

lifestyles of the Sauromatians and the other Skythians are not alike, for some are cruel enough to be cannibals, yet others abstain from all living things. Others, he says, speak about their fierceness, knowing that the terrible and marvellous are astounding, but one must also speak about the opposite and provide examples. Thus he will discuss those who follow the most just customs, for there are certain Skythian nomads who feed on mare's milk and differ from everyone in their sense of justice, and who are mentioned by the poets. Homer says that Zeus looks down on the land of the "Milk Drinkers and the Abians, the most just of men" [*Iliad* 13.6], and Hesiod in his so-called *Circuit of the Earth* [says] that Phineus was carried by the Harpyioi "to the land of the Milk Drinkers, who live in wagons" [F97]. Then he [Ephoros] accounts for their lifestyle as follows: they are thrifty and not money-getters, law abiding toward each other, and have everything in

[C303]   common (their women, children, and all their kindred), but are unconquerable and incapable of being defeated by outsiders, because they have nothing for which to be enslaved. He cites Choirilos, who said in his *Crossing of the Pontoon Bridge* (the one that Dareios [I] constructed):

> the sheep-herding Sakians, of the Skythian race, who used to live in wheat-bearing Asia and were settlers from the nomads, lawful people. [F5]

When Ephoros calls Anacharsis wise, he says that he is of that race and was considered one of the Seven Wise Men because of his frugality, moderation, and knowledge. He tells of his inventions: the bellows, the double-pointed anchor, and the potter's wheel. I say this knowing well that he does not speak most truthfully about everything, especially about Anacharsis. How could the wheel be his invention if Homer, who was earlier, knew about it ("as when some potter fits the wheel in his hands" [*Iliad* 18.600–1, paraphrased], and so forth)? But in regard to the other matters, I only wish to point out that there was a common report (believed both in antiquity and later) that certain of the nomads – those settled the farthest away from other men – were the Milk Drinkers and the Abians, the most just, and not Homer's fantasy.

(10) Concerning the Mysians, it is proper for Apollodoros [of Athens] to provide a statement regarding what is said in the verses – whether he thinks they are fictitious – when the Poet says "the hand-to-hand fighting Mysians and the noble Mare Milkers" [*Iliad* 13.5], or whether he takes it to refer to those in Asia. If he takes it as those in Asia, he will misinterpret the Poet, as I have said [7.3.2], but if he says that it is a fiction – there were no Mysians in Thrace – he speaks counter to the facts. Nevertheless in our time Aelius Catus transplanted 50,000 persons among the Getians (peoples with

the same language as the Thracians) from the far side of the Istros into Thrace. Today they live there and are called Moisians (whether they were called that in former times) and in Asia the name was changed to Mysians, or (more suitable to what the Poet proclaims) those formerly in Thrace were called Mysians. This is enough on this topic. I return to what is next in my circuit.

(11) Let ancient matters about the Getians be omitted, but this is what there is about our time. Byrebistas, a Getian man, established his dominion over the people and restored them (as the condition of the people had become worse by constant wars), and raised them to such a height by training, sobriety, and obedience to his commands that in a few years he   [C304] had established a great state and subjected to the Getians most of their neighbors. He was regarded with fear even by the Romans because he would confidently cross the Istros and plunder Thrace as far as Makedonia and Illyris, pillaging the Kelts who were mixed with the Thracians and Illyrians, and completely doing away with the Boians under Kritasiros, as well as the Tauriskians. To secure the ready obedience of his people he had as his accomplice Dekaineos, a sorcerer and a man who had wandered throughout Egypt and had completely learned certain prognostics by means of which he would expound divine matters. In a short time he was set up as a god (like I said when discussing Zalmoxis [7.3.5]). As an example of their ready obedience they were persuaded to cut down their vines and live without wine. Yet Byrebistas was deposed by certain men who rose up against him, before the Romans sent an expedition against him, and those who succeeded him divided the state into a number of parts. Today, when Sebastos Caesar sent an expedition against them, there were five parts, although once it happened to have been divided into four.

(12) Such divisions are temporary and variable. But there was another division of the territory that has remained from antiquity. Some are called Dacians and others Getians. The Getians are those who lean toward the Pontos and the east, and the Dacians those in the opposite way, toward Germania and the sources of the Istros. I think that the Dacians were called the Daans in antiquity, from which the household slave names Getas and Daos prevail among those in Attika. This is more believable than that the latter is from the Skythians called the Daans, for they are far away around Hyrkania, and it is not reasonable that slaves were brought to Attika from there. They called their household slaves by the names of the peoples that they came from, such as Lydos or Syros, or addressed them by names prevalent there, such as Manes or Midas for a Phrygian or Tibeios for a Paphlagonian. Although the people were raised up so much by Byrebistas,

they were completely reduced by their own instability and the Romans. Yet today they are capable of sending forth 40,000.

(13) The Marisos River flows through their territory to the Danuvius, on which the Romans would carry the equipment for war. The upper part of the river from near its sources to the cataracts was called the Danuvius, and it goes mostly through the country of the Dacians. The lower portion as far as the Pontos, that past the Getians, they call the Istros. The Dacians have the same language as the Getians. The Getians, however, are better known to the Hellenes because of the continual migrations that they make to either side of the Istros, and because they are mixed with the Thracians and Mysians. The Triballian people, who are also Thracian, have experienced the same thing: movements caused by their neighbors who force the emigration into the territories of those who are weaker. The Skythians, Bastarnians, and Sauromatians on the far side often prevail, so that they cross over and attack those already driven out, with some of them staying there either in the islands or in Thrace. Those in the other portion are generally overpowered by the Illyrians. Nevertheless the Getians and Dacians became exceedingly powerful, so that they could send forth an expedition of 200,000, but today they happen to be reduced to as little as 40,000 and have come near to being obedient to the Romans, although as yet they are not completely under control because of their hopes for the Germans, who are enemies of the Romans.

(14) On that part of the Pontic Sea between the Istros and the Tyras lies the Desert of the Getians, completely flat and without water, in which Dareios [I] the son of Hystaspes was cut off at the time when he crossed the Istros against the Skythians and was in danger of losing his entire army to thirst, but eventually he perceived it and turned back. Later Lysimachos, making an expedition against the Getians and their king, Dromichaites, not only was in danger but was actually taken alive. He came back safely because the barbarian happened to be conciliatory, as I have said formerly [7.3.8].

(15) Near the outlets [of the Istros] is Peuke, a large island. When the Bastarnians took control of it they were called Peukinians. There are other islands that are much smaller, some farther inland and others near the sea, for it has seven mouths. The largest is called the Sacred Mouth, along which one can sail up 120 stadia to Peuke, at whose lower portion Dareios [I] made his pontoon bridge, although it could have been constructed at the upper. This is the first mouth on the left sailing into the Pontos, and the others are in succession on the sail along the coast toward the Tyras. From it to the seventh mouth is about 300 stadia. Islets occur between the mouths. The three mouths that come after the Sacred Mouth are small, but the

[C305]

remainder are much smaller [than the Sacred Mouth] but larger [than the three]. Ephoros [F157] says that the Istros has five mouths. From there to the Tyras, a navigable river, is 900 stadia. In between are two large lakes, one [C306] of which is open to the sea and is usable as a harbor, but the other has no mouth.

(16) At the mouth of the Tyras is what is called the Tower of Neoptolemos and the so-called village of Hermonax. Sailing upstream 140 stadia, there are cities on each side, Nikonia and (on the left) Ophioussa, which those living on the river say is 120 stadia inland. The island of Leuke is a distance of 500 stadia from the mouth and is sacred to Achilleus and is in the open sea.

(17) Then there is the Borysthenes River, which is navigable for 600 stadia. Near it is another river, the Hypanis, and an island off the mouth of the Borysthenes that has a harbor. Sailing up the Borysthenes for 200 stadia, there is a city homonymous with the river (also called Olbia), which is a great emporium and a Milesian foundation. The entire previously mentioned territory lying above – between the Borysthenes and the Istros – is, first, the Desert of the Getians, then that of the Tyregetians, and after it the Iazygian Sarmatians, those called the Basileians, and the Ourgians, who are generally nomads, although a few are engaged in farming (they say that these live along the Istros, often on both sides). In the interior are the Bastarnians who border on the Tyregetians and the Germans, and who are somewhat similar ethnically to the Germans. They are divided into several tribes, some of whom are called Atmonians and Sidonians. Those who possess Peuke – the island in the Istros – are Peukinians. The Roxolanians are the most northern and inhabit the plains between the Tanais and the Borysthenes. The entire territory toward the north from Germania to the Kaspian is a plain, as far as we know. We do not know whether anyone lives beyond the Roxolanians.

The Roxolanians, led by Tasios, made war even against the commanders of Mithridates [VI] Eupator. They came to fight as allies with Palakos the son of Skilouros, and were reputed to be warlike. Yet all the barbarian tribes are weak against an organized and well-armed phalanx. At any rate, they were about 50,000, but were unable to withstand the 6,000 fighting with Diophantes, the commander of Mithridates [VI], and most of them were destroyed. They use helmets and breastplates of untanned oxhide, and carry wicker shields. For defense they have spears, bows, and swords. Most of the others are similar. [C307]

The felt tents of the nomads are fastened to their wagons, in which they pass their lives. Around the tents are the herds that furnish milk, cheese, and meat. They follow their pasturage, continually moving to places that have grass, wintering in the marshes around the Maiotis, but also in the plains in summer.

(18) The entire country has severe winters, as far as the places on the sea that are between the Borysthenes and the mouth of the Maiotis. The most northern places on the sea are at the mouth of the Maiotis, and still farther, that of the Borysthenes and the recess of the Gulf of Tamyrakos, or Karkinitos, which is on the isthmus of the Great Chersonesos. It is obvious that it is cold here, although they live in the plains, for they do not breed asses, an animal that is sensitive to cold. Some of the cattle are born without horns and others have their horns filed off, for this part is sensitive to cold. The horses are small and the sheep are large. Bronze water jars burst and their contents congeal. The vehemence of the frost is most clearly shown by what happens around the mouth of the Maiotis. The passage to Phanagoreia from Pantikapaion is crossed by wagons, so that it is a mud road. Fish that are caught in the ice are dug out with what is called a *gangame*, especially the *antakaioi*, which are about the same size as a dolphin. Neoptolemos, the commander of Mithridates [VI], they say, prevailed in this strait over the barbarians in a sea battle in summer and a cavalry battle in winter. They also say that the vines in the Bosporos are buried during the winter, with much earth heaped over them. It is said, moreover, that the heat becomes excessive, perhaps because their bodies are unaccustomed to it, perhaps because it is never windy on the plains at that time, or perhaps the thick air becomes especially thoroughly heated, like what the parhelia do to the clouds. It seems that Ateas ruled most of the barbarians in this region. He waged war with Philippos [II] the son of Amyntas [III].

(19) After the island off the Borysthenes, next toward the rising sun one sails to the Cape of the Race Course of Achilleus, which is open country but called the Grove and has a sanctuary of Achilleus. Then there is the Race Course of Achilleus, a peninsula projecting into the sea. It is a strip about a thousand stadia long with its length toward the east, and a width of two stadia at the most, and four *plethra* at the least. It is sixty stadia from the mainland on either side of its neck. It is sandy, and water is available by [C308]   digging. The neck is at the center of the isthmus and is about forty stadia. It ends in a cape called Tamyrake, which has an anchorage looking toward the mainland. After this is the Karkinitis Gulf, which is very large, reaching up to the north as much as a thousand stadia. Some say that it is three times as much as the recess ... they are called Taphrians. The gulf is called Tamyrake, homonymous with the cape.

Part 4:   The Tauric Chersonesos

(1) Here is the isthmus that separates the so-called Putrid Lake from the sea. It is 40 stadia [across] and makes the so-called Tauric or Skythian

Chersonesos. Some say that the width of the isthmus is 360 [stadia]. The Putrid Lake is said to be 4,000 stadia, and is the western part of the Maiotis, joined to it by a wide mouth. It is exceedingly marshy and can scarcely be sailed by sewn boats. The winds easily uncover the shallows and then fill them again, so that the marshes are not passable for large boats. The gulf has three islets and some rather shallow places and rocky points along the coast.

(2) Sailing out, on the left is Beautiful Harbor, a small city of the Chersonesites. Next as one sails along the coast is a large cape projecting toward the south, a portion of the entire Chersonesos. Situated on it is a city of the Herakleotes, a settlement of those on the Pontos, which is called Chersonesos. It is 4,400 stadia distant from the Tyras, sailing along the coast. Here is the sanctuary of Parthenos, a certain divinity, and the cape that lies 100 stadia in front of the city is homonymous and is called Parthenion, having a temple of the divinity and a xoanon. Between the city and the cape are three harbors. Then there is Old Chersonesos, which has been razed, and after it a narrow-mouthed harbor where the Taurians, a Skythian people, would generally bring together their pirate bands to attack those who had gone there for refuge. It is called Symbolon Harbor, and with another harbor called Ktenous they make an isthmus of 40 stadia. This is the isthmus that encloses the Little Chersonesos, which, as I have said, is part of the Great Chersonesos, and has the homonymous city of Chersonesos on it.

(3) It was formerly autonomous, but when it was ravaged by the barbarians it was forced to take Mithridates [VI] Eupator as its guardian, who was on an expedition against the barbarians beyond the isthmus, as far as the Borysthenes and the Adria, which was preparation against the Romans. With these hopes, he was glad to send an army to the Chersonesos, and at the same time made war against the Skythians, against both Skilouros and the sons of Skilouros (Palakos and the others, whom Poseidonios [F263] says numbered fifty, but Apollonides [*FHG* vol. 4, p. 310] eighty). At the same time he conquered them by force and established himself as master of the Bosporos, taking it willingly from Pairisades [V], who had held it. From that time until today the city of the Chersonesitians has been subject to the rulers of the Bosporos.

[C309]

Ktenous is equidistant from the city of the Chersonesitians and Symbolon Harbor. After Symbolon Harbor as far as the city of Theodosia there is the Tauric coast, about a thousand stadia in length. It is rough and mountainous, and situated where storms rush down with the north wind. In front of it is a cape projecting far into the open sea – to the south toward Paphlagonia and the city of Amastris – called the Ram's Forehead. Lying opposite it is Karambis, a promontory of Paphlagonia, which divides the Euxine Pontos into two seas by means of the narrowing of the strait on both sides. Karambis is separated from the Chersonesites by 2,500 stadia, but the amount to the Ram's Forehead is much less. At any rate, many who have sailed across the strait say that they can see both capes on either side. In this mountainous region of the Tauros is Mount Trapezous, which is homonymous with the city around Tibarania and Kolchis. Mount Kimmerion is also in the same mountainous region, because the Kimmerians once held power in the Bosporos. The entire strait that extends to the mouth of the Maiotis is called the Kimmerian Bosporos.

(4) The city of Theodosia is located after the previously mentioned mountainous region, in a fertile plain with a harbor suitable for a hundred ships. Formerly this was the border between the Bosporanian and the Taurian territories. Next there is fertile land as far as Pantikapaion, the metropolis of the Bosporanians, situated at the mouth of Lake Maiotis. It is about 530 stadia between Theodosia and Pantikapaion, and the territory produces grain everywhere, with villages and a city called Nymphaion that has a good harbor. Pantikapaion is a hill inhabited on all sides with a circuit of 20 stadia. There is a harbor to the east with a dockyard for about 30 ships, [C310] and also an akropolis. It was a Milesian foundation. For a long time it was a monarchy under the rule of Leukon [I], Satyros [I], and Pairisades [I], including all the neighboring settlements around the mouth of the Maiotis on both sides, until Pairisades [V] handed the rule over to Mithridates [VI]. They were called tyrants but most of them were reasonable, beginning with Pairisades [I] and Leukon [I]. Pairisades [I] was considered a god. The last [ruler] had the same name, but was unable to hold out against the barbarians, who were exacting greater tribute than before, and thus he gave over the rule to Mithridates [VI] Eupator. Since his time the kingdom has been subject to the Romans. The greater part of it is in Europe, although a certain part is in Asia.

(5) The mouth of the Maiotis is called the Kimmerian Bosporos, which is rather wide – about 70 stadia – at its beginning, where one crosses over from the region of Pantikapaion to Phanagoreia, the nearest city in Asia. It ends in a much narrower strait. The narrows separate Asia from Europe, as does the Tanais River, which is directly opposite and flows from the north into the lake and its mouth. There are two outlets into the lake that are about 60 stadia distant from one another. There is also a city homonymous with the river that is the greatest emporium of the barbarians after Pantikapaion.

On the left, sailing into the Kimmerian Bosporos, is the little city of Myrmekion, 20 stadia from Pantikapaion. Twice this distance from Myrmekion is the village of Parthenion, where the entrance is narrowest (about 20 stadia). Lying opposite in Asia is a village called Achilleion. A straight sail from there to the Tanais and the island near its outlets is about 2,200 stadia, and it is slightly more than this amount sailing along Asia. Sailing to the left as far as the Tanais (along the coast where the isthmus is located) is more than three times as much. The sail along this coast – that along Europe – is completely deserted, but it is not deserted on the right. The entire circuit of the lake is reported as 9,000 stadia.

The Great Chersonesos resembles the Peloponnesos in shape and size. It is held by the masters of Bosporos and has been entirely ruined by continual wars. Formerly they held only a small part – that near the mouth of the Maiotis and Pantikapaion as far as Theodosia – and most of it, as far as the [C311] isthmus and the Karkinitic Gulf, was [held by] the Taurians, a Skythian people. This entire territory, as well as nearly almost [all] that outside the isthmus as far as the Borysthenes, was called Little Skythia. Because of the large numbers from there who crossed both the Tyras and the Istros and settled in the land beyond, not a small part of it also came to be called Little Skythia, with the Thracians giving way to them by being forced and also because the land was bad, as most of it was marshy.

(6) The Chersonesos, except for the mountainous region along the sea as far as Theodosia, is a fertile plain everywhere, especially fortunate in its grain. At any rate, it produces thirty-fold if plowed by a digging instrument. They and those in the Asiatic districts around Sindike used to pay a tribute to Mithridates [VI] of 180,000 *medimnoi* and 200 talents of silver. In earlier times the grain supply of the Hellenes was from here, just as their salted fish was from the lake. They say that Leukon [I] sent 2,100,000 *medimnoi* from Theodosia to the Athenians.

These [people] used to be called literally "The Farmers" because those living beyond them were nomads, subsisting generally on meats, and also that from horses, and on mare's cheese, milk, and sour milk, which is outstanding when prepared by them in a specific way. This is why the Poet says that all here are Milk Drinkers. The nomads are warriors rather than brigands, and make war only over tribute. They entrust their land to those wishing to farm it, and are content to receive the tribute that they have assessed for it, which is moderate, not [assessed] for abundance but for the daily necessities of life. If it is not paid they make war on them. Thus the Poet says that these men are just and without resources, for if the tribute were paid regularly they would not go to war. Those who do not pay regularly believe that they are powerful enough easily to ward off attacks or to prevent an attack, just as Hypsikrates [F2] says regarding the time that Asandros walled off the isthmus of the Chersonesos near to the Maiotis for

360 stadia and built ten towers in every stadion. The Farmers here are believed to be more powerful and civilized, but as they are money-getters and connected to the sea they do not desist from piracy or other such injustices and greediness.

(7) In addition to the places in the Chersonesos that have been enumerated, there were also the forts that Skilouros and his sons built, which were used as bases of operations against the commanders of Mithridates [VI]: Palakion, Chabon, and Neapolis. There was also a certain Eupatorion, built by Diophantes the commander of Mithridates [VI]. There is a cape about fifteen stadia distant from the wall of the Chersonesites, which makes an exceedingly large gulf that inclines toward the city. Lying above it is a lagoon with salt works. Ktenous was also here. In order to hold out, the besieged royal officers established a garrison on the previously mentioned cape, fortifying the place, and blocked the mouth of the gulf as far as the city, so that it was easily accessible on foot and in a way became one city instead of two. Thus they could easily drive away the Skythians when they attacked the fortification across the isthmus near Ktenous and filled the ditch with straw. The royal officers at night would set on fire the part that had been bridged by day, and held out until they finally prevailed. Today everything is under the Bosporanian kings whom the Romans appoint.

(8) It is peculiar to the entire Skythian and Sarmatian peoples that they castrate their horses so that they are obedient, for they are small but exceedingly intense and disobedient. The wild animals include deer and wild boars in the marshes, and wild asses and roe in the plains. Another peculiarity is that the eagle does not exist in these places. Among quadrupeds there is the so-called *kolos*, between the deer and the ram in size, white, and quicker in running than they are. It drinks through its nostrils into its head, which is a storehouse for several days so that it lives easily in waterless regions.

This is everything outside the Istros between the Rhenos and the Tanais as far as the Pontic Sea and the Maiotis.

Part 5: Northeastern Europe south of the Istros

(1) The rest of Europe is that within the Istros and the encircling sea, beginning from the recess of the Adriatic and as far as the Sacred Mouth of the Istros. Within it are Hellas and the Makedonian and Epeirote peoples, those above them reaching to the Istros and the seas on either side (the Adriatic and the Pontic). On the Adriatic side are the Illyrians, and on the other (as far as the Propontis and the Hellespont) are the Thracians and whatever Skythians and Kelts are mixed in with them.

The beginning must be made from the Istros, speaking about the places that follow those already encompassed, those adjacent to Italia and the Alps, and the Germans, Dacians, and Getians. This can also be divided into two parts. In a way the Illyrian, Paionian, and Thracian mountains are parallel to the Istros, and almost complete a single line extending from the Adria to the Pontos. To the north of it is the part between the Istros and the mountains, and to the south is Hellas and the adjoining barbarian territory, as far as the mountainous regions. Near the Pontos is Mount Haimos, the largest and highest of those in this region, dividing Thrace almost in the middle. Polybios [24.4] says that both seas can be seen from it, but this is not true, for the distance to the Adria is great and there are many things that are in the way. Almost all of Ardia is near the Adria. Paionia is in the middle and all of it is high. On the side toward Thrace is Rhodope, a mountain whose height is close to that of Haimos, and on the other side toward the north is the Illyrian territory, the country of both the Autariatians and the Dardanike. I will speak first about the Illyrian territory, which joins the Istros and the Alps that lie between Italia and Germania, beginning from the lake around the Vindolicians, Rhaitians, and Toinians.

(2) The Dacians laid waste to a certain part of this territory when they subdued the Boians and Tauriskians, Keltic peoples who were under Ekretosiros, asserting that it was their territory although separated from it by the Marisos River, which flows from the mountains to the Istros near those Skordiskians called the Galatians, who lived mixed with the Illyrian and Thracian peoples. Although the Dacians destroyed the former [Boians and Tauriskians] they often used the latter [Skordiskians] as allies. The remainder is held by the Pannonians as far as Segistike and the Istros, toward the north and east, with portions extending farther in other [directions]. The city of Segistike is Pannonian and at the confluence of several rivers, all of which are navigable, and is a natural base of operations for war against the Dacians. It lies below the Alps that extend as far as the Iapodians, people who are both Keltic and Illyrian. Rivers flow from there that bring [C314] much cargo down to it, both from elsewhere and Italia. Crossing over Okra to Nauportos from Aquileia – the way the wagons come – is 350 stadia, although some say 500. It [Nauportos] is a Tauriskian settlement. Okra is the lowest part of the Alps that extend from the Rhaitians to the Iapodians. From there the mountains rise up again, amidst the Iapodians, and are called the Albia. Similarly there is a pass from Tergeste (a Karnic village) over Okra to what is called the Lougeon Marsh. Near to Nauportos is the Korkoras River, which receives the cargo. It empties into the Sauos, and it into the Drauos, and it into the Noaros around Segistike. Immediately

afterward the Noaros is increased ... also receiving the Kalapis, flowing through the Iapodians from the Albion Mountains, joining the Danuvius near the Skordiskians. The voyage on these rivers is mostly toward the north. The road from Tergeste to the Danuvius is about 1,200 stadia. Near to Segestike are the fortress of Siskia as well as Sirmion, lying on the road to Italia.

(3) The peoples of the Pannonians are the Breukians, Andizetians, Ditionians, Peiroustians, Mazaians, and Daisitiatians (whose leader is Baton), as well as other more obscure and small groups that extend as far as Dalmatia and – going to the south – almost to the Ardiaians. All the mountainous country that extends from the recess of the Adria as far as the Rhizonic Gulf and the land of the Ardiaians falls between the sea and the Pannonian peoples. This is about where one must undertake the beginning of the continuous circuit, with a little of what has been said previously [5.1.1, 5.1.9, 6.3.10]. I said in the circuit of Italia that the Istrians were the first on the Illyrian coast, a continuation of Italia and the Karnians. Because of this the current rulers have advanced the boundary of Italia as far as Pola, an Istrian city. This is about 800 stadia from the recess, and it is the same from the cape in front of Pola to Ankon, keeping the Enetic territory on the right. The entire Istrian coast is 1,300 stadia.

(4) Next is the voyage of 1,000 stadia along the Iapodian coast. The Iapodians are situated on Mount Albion, the last of the Alps, which is exceedingly high, coming down on one side to the Pannonians and the Istros, and on the other to the Adria. They are full of warlike frenzy but have been completely finished off by Sebastos. Their cities are Metoulon, [C315] Aroupinoi, Monetion, and Vendon. The lands are poor, with most people supported by zea and millet. They are armed like the Kelts, and tattooed like the other Illyrians and Thracians. After the Iapodians there is the voyage along the coast of the Libyrnikians, which is 500 stadia longer. On this coastal voyage there is a river that cargo sails up as far as the Dalmatians and the Libyrnian city of Skardon.

(5) There are islands along the entire coast that I have described: the Apsyrtides, around which Medeia is said to have killed her brother Apsyrtos who was pursuing her, Kyriktike, opposite the Iapodes, and then the Libyrnides, about forty in number. Then there are other islands, of which the best known are Issa, Tragourion (founded by the Issians), and Pharos (formerly Paros, founded by the Parians, and where Demetrios the Pharian was from). Then there is the Dalmatian coast and their naval station, Salon. These peoples made war against the Romans for a long time and had up to fifty notable settlements, some of which were cities: Salon, Promon, Ninia,

and Sinotion (both New and Old, which were burned by Sebastos). There is also Andetrion, a fortified place, and Dalmion, a large city, which is the eponym of these people. Nasica made it small and its plain a sheep pasture because of the greed of its people. Peculiar to the Dalmatians is that they make a redistribution of land every eighth year. That they do not use coinage is peculiar compared to others on this coast, but common among other barbarians. Mount Adrion cuts Dalmatike in the middle, with one part toward the sea and one in the other direction.

Then there is the Naron River and those around it: the Daorizians, Ardiaians, and Pleraians, near whom are the island called Black Korkyra and a city founded by the Knidians. Pharos (formerly called Paros, as it was a Parian foundation) is near the Ardiaians.

(6) Later people called the Ardiaians the Vardaeans. The Romans drove them away from the sea into the interior because of their outrages of piracy, and forced them to become farmers. But the country is rough and wretched and not for a farming population, so that these people have been utterly destroyed and have almost ceased to exist. This is what happened to other peoples in this region, since those formerly most powerful were humbled and ceased to exist – the Boians and Skordistians among the Galatians, the Autariatians, Ardiaians, and Dardanians among the Illyrians, and the Triballians among the Thracians – at first warring with one another and later with the Makedonians and Romans. [C316]

(7) Nevertheless, after the coast of the Ardiaians and the Pleraians is the Rhizonic Gulf, the city of Rhizon and other small towns, and the Drilon River, which can be sailed up toward the east as far as Dardanike. It adjoins the Makedonian peoples and Paionians on the south, as do the Autariatians and the Dasaretians, different peoples adjoining each other in different areas[3]. . . . The Galabrians are Dardaniate, and among them is the ancient city of . . . and the Thounatians, who adjoin the Maidians, a Thracian people, on the east. The Dardanians are completely wild – they excavate caves under dung hills and make them their dwellings – but nevertheless they care for music, always using flutes and stringed instruments. But they are in the interior and I will discuss them later.

(8) After the Rhizonic Gulf is the city of Lissos, as well as Akrolissos and Epidamnos, a Kerkyraian foundation that is now called Dyrrhachion, homonymous with the peninsula on which it is located. Then there is the Hapsos River and the Aoos, on which Apollonia is, a most well-governed

---

[3] The text has "autareatais" ("in their self-indulgence"), which does not seem to fit here, and which is probably a confusion of the ethnym "Autariatians," but the passage remains unclear.

city, a Corinthian and Kerkyraian foundation, ten stadia from the river and sixty from the sea. Hekataios [of Miletos, F102b] calls the Aoos the Aias, and he says that from the same place around Lakmon (rather a recess there) the Inachos flows toward the south and Argos, and the Aias toward the west and the Adria. In the territory of the Apolloniates is a certain place called the Nymphaion, a rock that produces fire, and warm bitumenous springs flow beneath, seemingly because the bitumenous lumps are burned. There is a mine of it nearby on a hill, and what is dug out is filled up again in time, for the earth thrown into the excavation is changed into bitumen, as Poseidonios [F235] says. He also speaks of ampelite, the bitumenous earth that is mined at Seleukeia in Pieria as a remedy for infested vines. When rubbed with oil it kills the animals before they can climb the shoots of the roots. This was also discovered on Rhodes when he was serving as *prytanis* [magistrate], but it needed more oil. After Apollonia is Balliake, Orikon and its naval station, Panormos, and the Keraunian Mountains, the beginning of the mouth of the Ionian Gulf and the Adria.

[C317]   (9) The mouth is common to both but the Ionian is different because this is the name of the first part of this sea. The Adria is the inside as far as the recess, yet today it is [the name of] the whole. Theopompos [F129] says that the former name came from a man who ruled the place, a native of Issa, but the eponym of the Adria is a river. It is slightly more than 2,000 stadia from the Libyrnians to Keraunia. Theopompos also says that the whole voyage from the recess is 6 days, and on foot the length of Illyris is 30, although to me this seems too much. He says other unbelievable things: that the seas are connected by a passage since both Chian and Thasian pottery are found in the Naron, that both seas can be seen from a certain mountain, that he puts down the Libyrnian Islands . . . so there is a circuit of 500 stadia, and that one of the mouths of the Istros empties into the Adria. Eratosthenes also has some false stories of this type, popular tales, as Polybios [34.12.1–2] says when discussing him and other writers.

(10) The entire Illyrian coastal voyage has exceedingly good harbors, both on the adjoining shoreline and also on the neighboring islands, although the Italian coast lying opposite is the contrary as it is harborless. They are equally sunny and produce good fruits, and are planted with olives and good vines, except for the rare place where it is totally rough. Although the Illyrian coast is in such a way, formerly it was neglected, perhaps because of ignorance of its virtues, but mostly because of the wildness of the people and their habitual piracy. Everything lying above it is mountainous, cold,

and snowy, especially toward the north, so that the vine is scarce both in the heights and the more level areas. These are the mountain plains that the Pannonians occupy, extending toward the south as far as the Dalmatians and Ardiaians, ending toward the north at the Istros, and on the east adjoining the Skordiskians ... along the mountains of the Makedonians and Thracians.

(11) The Autariatians were the largest and best peoples of the Illyrians. Formerly they were continually at war with the Ardiaians concerning the salt on their borders, which solidified from the water that flowed in a spring at the foot of a certain mountain glen: the salt would solidify if drawn off and stored away for five or six days. They agreed to use the salt works in alternation, but the agreements would be broken and there would be war. At one time the Autariatians had subdued the Triballians –   [C318] who extended from the Agrianians as far as the Istros, a journey of fifteen days – and also ruled the other Thracians and Illyrians. Yet they were destroyed first by the Skordiskians and later by the Romans, who also defeated the Skordiskians themselves, although they had been powerful for a long time.

(12) They lived along the Istros and were divided in two, called the Great and the Little Skordiskians. The former were between two rivers that empty into the Istros: the Noaros (which flows past Segestike) and the Margos (some call it the Bargos). The Little were across it, adjoining the Triballians and Mysians. The Skordiskians also held some of the islands, and increased so much that they advanced as far as the Illyrian, Paionian, and Thracian mountains. They also possessed most of the islands in the Istros and had the cities of Heorta and Kapedounon.

After the country of the Skordiskians, along the Istros is that of the Triballians and Mysians, whom I have discussed previously [7.3.8–13], as well as the marshes of what is called Little Skythia, within the Istros (and I have discussed them [7.4.5]). These, and those called the Krobyzians and Trogodytians live in the region around Kallatis, Tomeus, and Istros. Then there are those around the Haimos and beyond it as far as the Pontos: the Korallians, Bessians, and some Maidians and Dantheletians. All these peoples are brigands, but the Bessians – who live on much of Mount Haimos – are called brigands by the brigands. They live in huts and have a wretched life. They adjoin Rhodope and the Paionians, as well as the Autariatians and Dardanians among the Illyrians. Between them and the Ardiaians are the Dasaretians, the Hybrianians, and other obscure peoples, whom the Skordiskians ravaged until they had depopulated the country and made it full of trackless forests several days across.

Part 6:   The western coast of the Pontos

(1) The remainder between the Istros and the mountains on either side
of Paionia is the Pontic coast from the Sacred Mouth of the Istros as far as
the mountainous country around the Haimos and as far as the mouth at
Byzantion. Just as with going along the Illyrian coast I proceeded as far as
the Keraunian mountains (which fall outside the mountainous country of
Illyria but are a suitable boundary, determining the peoples in the interior
by this, and believing that such limits would be more significant both here
and later), it is the same with the coast, which, although it falls beyond
[C319]   the line of the mountains, will come to an end at an appropriate point (the
mouth of the Pontos) both for the present and what follows.

From the Sacred Mouth of the Istros – keeping the continuous coast on the
right – in 500 stadia there is the small city of Istros, a Milesian foundation.
Then Tomis, another small city, in 250 stadia. Then there is Kallatis in 280, a
Herakleotic settlement, and then Apollonia in 1,300 stadia, a Milesian settlement. Most of this foundation is located on a certain island with a sanctuary of
Apollo, from which Marcus Lucullus took the colossus of Apollo, a work of
Kalamis, and dedicated it on the Capitolium. In the interval between Kallatis
and Apollonia are Bizone – a large part of which was swallowed up by
earthquakes – Krounoi, Odessos (a Milesian settlement), and Naulochos, a
small town of the Mesembrianians. Then there is Mount Haimos, extending
here as far as the sea, and then Mesembria, a Megarian settlement that
was formerly Menebria (that is, "the city of Menas," because its founder was
named Menas, and "bria" means "city" in Thracian, just as the city of Selys
is called Selymbria and Ainos was once named Poltyobria). Then there is
Anchiale, a small town of the Apolloniates, and Apollonia itself. Also on this
coast is Cape Tirizis, a fortified place that Lysimachos once used as a treasury.

Again, from Apollonia to the Kyaneai is about 1,500 stadia. In between
are Thynias, a territory of the Apolloniates, Phinopolis, and Andriake,
which adjoins Salmydessos. This is a desolate and stony beach, harborless
and completely open to the north wind, whose length as far as the Kyaneai
is about 700 stadia. Those who are cast ashore on it are plundered by the
Astians, a Thracian people who are situated above it. The Kyaneai are two
islets near the mouth of the Pontos, one next to Europe, the other to Asia,
separated by a strait of about 20 stadia, and are the same distance from the
sanctuary of the Byzantians and the sanctuary of the Chalkedonians. This
is the narrowest part of the mouth of the Euxeinos, for after proceeding
10 stadia one comes to a cape that makes the strait 5 stadia [in width], and
then it opens more to make the Propontis.

(2) From the cape that makes the Pentastadion to the harbor called Under the Fig Tree is 35 stadia, and it is 5 from there to the Horn of the Byzantians. The Horn is next to the wall of Byzantion and is a gulf that extends toward the west for 60 stadia, resembling the horn of a deer, split into a number of gulfs, as if various branches. The *pelamydes* come down into them and are easily caught because of their quantity and the force of the flow that draws them together. Because of the narrowness of the gulf they are caught by hand. The creature is born in the marshes of the Maiotis, and when it has a little strength it comes down through the mouth in herds and travels along the Asian shore as far as Trapezous and Pharnakeia. Here the first catching of the animal occurs, although it is not large, for it has not yet reached full size. When it comes to Sinope it is mature enough for catching and salting, and when it touches the Kyaneai and passes by them, a certain white rock that projects from the Chalkedonian Cape causes fear in the creature, so that it immediately turns to the opposite side. It is taken by the current there, and since at the same time the nature of the place turns the current of the sea toward Byzantion and the Horn, it is naturally driven there and supplies the Byzantians and the Roman people with a notable income. But the Chalkedonians, situated nearby on the coast, have no share in this abundance since the *pelamydes* do not approach their harbors. Because of this Apollo said the following when the founders of Byzantion consulted the oracle (later than the Megarians founded Chalkedon): they were ordered to make their settlement opposite the blind ones, calling the Chalkedonians blind because they had sailed into these places earlier but had failed to occupy the opposite coast with all its wealth, choosing the poorer side.

[C320]

I have come as far as Byzantion because this famous city very near to the mouth represents a better-known limit to terminate the coastal voyage from the Istros. The Astian peoples lie above Byzantion, among whom is the city of Kalybe, where Philippos [II] the son of Amyntas [III] settled the worst people.

Part 7:   The northern Hellenic peninsula

(1) These are the peoples worth recording of those marked off by the Istros and the Illyrian and Thracian mountains and who possess the entire Adriatic coast beginning at the recess, as well as what is called the Left Side of the Pontos from the Istros River as far as Byzantion. There remains the southern part of the previously mentioned mountainous territory and, next, the lands below it, among which are Hellas and the adjoining barbarians as far as the mountains.

[C321]

Hekataios the Milesian [F119] says that the Peloponnesos was inhabited by barbarians before the Hellenes. But, considering what has been recorded, almost the entirety of Hellas was settled by barbarians in ancient times. Pelops brought people from Phrygia to the Peloponnesos, which was named after him. Danaos was from Egypt, and the Dryopians, Kaukonians, Pelasgians, Lelegians, and such others divided up both what was inside and outside the Isthmos. Attika was held by the Thracians with Eumolpos, Daulis in Phokis by Tereus, the Kadmeia by the Phoenicians with Kadmos, and Boiotia itself by the Aonians, Temmikians and Hyantians. As Pindar [F83] says, "the Boiotian peoples were once called the Swine." Some are shown to be barbarians because of their names: Kekrops, Kodros, Aiklos, Kothos, Drymas, and Krinakos. The Thracians, Illyrians, and Epeirotes are still on the perimeters today – although more so in former times than now – and much of what at present is indisputably Hellas is held by barbarians: Makedonia and certain parts of Thrace are held by the Thessalians, and what is above Akarnania and Aitolia by the Thesprotians, Kassiopaians, Amphilochians, Molossians, and Athamanians, who are Epeirotic peoples.

(2) I have already discussed the Pelasgians [5.2.4]. Some suggest that the Lelegians were the same as the Karians, and others than they were only fellow inhabitants and fellow campaigners with them. This is why certain settlements in Milesian territory are said to be Lelegian, and that in Karia there are tombs of the Lelegians and deserted fortifications said to be Lelegian. All of what is now called Ionia was inhabited by Karians and Lelegians, but the Ionians themselves expelled them and took possession of the territory. Still earlier, those who captured Troy drove the Lelegians from the region around Ida near Pedasos and the Satnioeis River. That they made common cause with the Karians can be considered a sign that they were barbarians. They wandered both with them and apart from them, as is shown by Aristotle in his *Politeiai*. He says in his section on the Akarnanians [F474] that the Kouretians held part of it, with the western portions by the Lelegians and then the Telebians. In his Aitolian section he says [F473] that the Lokrians [C322] of today were called Lelegians and that they possessed Boiotia, and has the same in his section on the Opountians [F560] and Megarians [F550]. In his Leukadian section [F546] he names a certain autochthonous Lelex, as well as Teleboas, his daughter's son, and twenty-two children of Teleboas, some of whom lived in Leukas. One might believe Hesiod when he says about them:

> Indeed Lokros ruled the people of the Lelegians, whom once Zeus the son of Kronos, who knows imperishable skills, gave to Deukalion as pebble-people picked out of the earth, [F251]

for the etymology seems to me to hint that from antiquity they were a mixed collection, and that because of this the race disappeared. One could say the same about the Kaukonians, who today exist nowhere but formerly could be seen in a number of places.

(3) Originally these peoples were small, numerous, and obscure, but because they were populous and ruled by their own kings, it was not at all difficult to comprehend their boundaries. Now much of the country has become deserted, and the settlements, especially the cities, have disappeared, and even if one could determine them accurately, it would be of no use, because of their obscurity and disappearance. This began a long time ago, and because of instability has not completely ceased today in many districts. The Romans camp in their houses, having been placed in power by them. At any rate, Polybios [30.15] says that Paullus, having overthrown the Makedonians and Perseus, destroyed 70 Epeirote cities – most of which were Molossian – and enslaved 150,000 people. Nevertheless, insofar as it is appropriate in my treatise and accessible to me, I will attempt to go across each region, beginning at the coast of the Ionian Gulf. This is where the voyage out of the Adria ends.

(4) The first parts of it are those around Epidamnos and Apollonia. The Egnatia Road goes toward the east from Apollonia to Makedonia. It has been measured out in miles and marked with pillars as far as Kypsela and the Hebros River, which is 535 miles. Calculating, as most do, 8 stadia to the mile, this would be 4,280 stadia, but Polybios [34.12.2a-8] adds 2 plethra (that is a third of a stadion) to the 8 stadia, and thus one must add 178 stadia, the third of the number of miles. Those starting from Apollonia and   [C323] Epidamnos happen to meet at the same distance. The entire road is named the Egnatia, but the first part is called "To Candavia" (an Illyrian mountain), through the city of Lychnidos and Pylon, a place on the road that is the boundary between Illyris and Makedonia. From there it goes through Barnous, Herakleia, the Lynchestians, and the Eordians, into Edessa and Pella, and as far as Thessalonikeia. Polybios says that this length is 267 miles.

Going on this road from the places around Epidamnos and Apollonia, one has on the right the Epeirotic peoples washed by the Sikelian Sea and who are as far as the Ambrakian Gulf, and on the left the mountains of the Illyrians, which I have discussed previously [7.5.1–3], and those peoples living along them as far as Makedonia and the Paionians. Then, from the Ambrakian Gulf – the region that successively inclines toward the east and stretches parallel to the Peloponnesos – is Hellas (which then projects into the Aigaion Sea and leaves the entire Peloponnesos on the right). From the beginning of the Makedonian and Paionian mountains as far as the Strymon River is where the Makedonians live, as well as the Paionians and some of the mountain Thracians. The region beyond the Strymon as far as the mouth of the Pontos and the Haimos is all Thracian except for the coast, which is inhabited by Hellenes, some located on the Propontis, others on the Hellespont and the Melas Gulf, and others on the Aigaion. The Aigaion Sea washes Hellas on two sides: one looking toward the east and stretching from Sounion toward the north as far as the Thermaic Gulf and Thessalonikeia (a Makedonian city that today is the most populous of all), and the other toward the south, the Makedonian, from Thessalonikeia as far as the Strymon. Some assign to Makedonia that from the Strymon as far as the Nestos, since Philippos [II] was especially interested in this territory and appropriated it for himself, creating a large amount of revenue from the mines and other natural resources of the region. From Sounion as far as the Peloponnesos are the Myrtoan, Cretan, and Libyan Seas, and their gulfs, as far as the Sikelian [Sea], which fills out the Ambrakian, Corinthian, and Krisaian Gulfs.

(5) Theopompos [F382] says that there are fourteen peoples of the Epeirotes. Of these, the Chaonians and Molossians are the most notable because at one time they ruled all the Epeirote territory, the Chaonians earlier and the Molossians later, who increased greatly in power because of the family connection of their kings – who were Aiakidai – and because the ancient and famous oracle at Dodona was in their territory.

[C324]

The Chaonians and Thesprotians, and next after them the Kassopaians – who are also Thesprotians – inhabit the coast from the Keraunian Mountains as far as the Ambrakian Gulf, possessing a prosperous territory. The voyage, beginning from the Chaonians and [going] toward the rising sun and toward the Ambrakian and Corinthian Gulfs, having the Ausonian Sea on the right and Epeiros on the left, is 1,300 stadia from the Keraunians to the mouth of the Ambrakian Gulf. In this interval is Panormos, a large harbor in the center of the Keraunian Mountains, and after it another harbor, Onchesmos – the western capes of Korkyra lie opposite it – and still another, Kassiope, from which it is 1,700 stadia to Brentesion. It is the same to Taras from another promontory that is farther south than Kassiope and which is called Phalakron. After Onchesmos are Poseideion, Bouthroton (at the mouth of what is called Muddy Harbor, which is situated at a place that makes a peninsula and has a Roman settlement), and the Sybota. The Sybota are islets a short distance from the mainland, lying off Leukimma, the eastern cape of Korkyra. There are other islets on the coast that are not worthy of recording. Then there is Cape Cheimerion and Sweet Harbor, into which the Acheron River empties, and which flows from the Acherousian Lake and receives several rivers, thus making the gulf sweet. The Thyamis also flows nearby. Kichyros, formerly Ephyra, a Thesprotian city, lies above it, and Phoinike is above the one at Bouthroton. Near to Kichyros is Bouchetion, a small town of the Kassopaians, a short distance above the sea. Elatria, Pandosia, and Batiai are in the interior, although their territory reaches down to the gulf. After Sweet Harbor are two other harbors, with Komaros the nearer and smaller, and which makes an isthmus of 60 stadia with the Ambrakian Gulf and Nikopolis – a foundation of Sebastos Caesar – and the farther, which is larger, and better, near to the mouth of the gulf and about 12 stadia from Nikopolis.

(6) Next is the mouth of the Ambrakian Gulf. The mouth of the gulf is a [C325] little more than 4 stadia and its circumference is 300 stadia, with good harbors everywhere. The Hellenic Akarnanians live on the right as one sails in, and the sanctuary of Aktian Apollo is here, near the mouth. There is a certain hill where the temple is, and a plain below it that has a grove and a dockyard, where Caesar dedicated as first fruits ten ships – from one with a single bank of oars to one with ten banks – but it is said that both the dockyard and the ships have disappeared because of fire. On the left are Nikopolis and the Epeirote Kassopaians, as far as the recess around Ambrakia, which lies a short distance above the recess and was a foundation of Gorgos the son of Kypselos. The Aratthos River flows by it and can be sailed inland from the sea for a few stadia. It begins at Mount Tymphe and the Paroraia. Formerly the city experienced good fortune – at any rate, the gulf has it as an eponym – and Pyrrhos, especially, adorned it and used the place as his royal residence. Later the Makedonians and then the Romans subdued it and others (because of their disobedience) through continual wars, so that finally Sebastos, seeing that the cities had completely failed, settled them into a single one on this gulf that he called Nikopolis, taking the name from the victory in the sea battle in front of the mouth of the gulf over Antonius and Kleopatra [VII] the Egyptian queen, who was also present at the battle. Nikopolis is populous and is increasing each day, having acquired much land and the adornment of the spoils, as well as being provided with a sacred precinct in the suburbs, one part in a grove with a gymnasium and stadium for the quinquennial games, the other lying above the grove on a hill sacred to Apollo. The games have been proclaimed as Olympian and are the Aktia, sacred to Aktian Apollo. The Lakedaimonians are in charge of them. The other settlements are suburbs of Nikopolis. Formerly the Aktia were under the locals (on behalf of the god), a contest with a wreath as the prize, but today Caesar has made them more distinguished.

(7) After Ambrakia is Amphilochic Argos, a foundation of Alkmaion and his children. Ephoros [F123b] says that Alkmaion, after the expedition of the Epigonoi against Thebes, was invited by Diomedes to go with him into Aitolia and to join in acquiring both it and Akarnania. When

[C326] they were summoned by Agamemnon to the Trojan War, Diomedes went but Alkmaion remained in Akarnania and founded Argos, called it Amphilochikon with his brother as eponym, and naming the river that flows through the territory to the gulf the Inachos, after the one in the Argeia. Thoukydides [2.68.3] says that Amphilochos himself, after his return from Troy, was displeased with the situation at Argos and came to Akarnania, and when he inherited his brother's power founded the city named after himself.

(8) The Amphilochians are Epirote, as are those who are situated above them and adjoin the Illyrian mountains, living in rough country: the Molossians, Athamanians, Aithikians, Tymphaians, Orestians, Paroraians, and Atintanians, some of whom are rather near to the Makedonians and others to the Ionian Gulf. It is said that Orestes once possessed Orestias, having fled because of the murder of his mother, and leaving his eponymous territory founded a city that was called Orestian Argos. The Illyrian peoples near the southern portion of the mountainous territory, and those above the Ionian Gulf, are mixed in with them, for the Byllionians, Taulantians, Parthinians, and Brygians live above Epidamnos and Apollonia as far as the Keraunians. Somewhere nearby are the silver mines at Damastion, where the Perisadyans established their power, as well as the Encheleians (called the Sesarethians). Near them are the Lynkestians, Deuriopos, Tripolitanian Pelagonia, the Eordians, Elimeia, and Eratyra. Formerly each of these peoples had power individually, as when the descendants of Kadmos and Harmonia ruled the Encheleians, and stories about them are made known there. These were not ruled by indigenous people, and the Lynkestians became subject to Arrhabaios, who was of the Bakchiad clan (Eurydike the mother of Philippos [II] the son of Amyntas [III] was his granddaughter, a daughter of Sirra). Among the Epeirotes, the Molossians became subject to Pyrrhos the son of Neoptolemos the son of Achilleus and his descendants, who were Thessalian. The remainder were ruled by indigenous people. Because certain of them were always prevailing, everyone became subject to Makedonian rule except a few above the Ionian Gulf. In fact, the region around Lynkos, Pelagonia, Orestias, and Elimeia was called Upper Makedonia, and later Free [Makedonia]. Some call "Makedonia" the entire

[C327] territory as far as Kerkyra, giving as the reason that their usages are similar in regard to their short hair, language, the wearing of the chlamys, and other such things, although some are bilingual. When Makedonian rule came to an end, they fell to the Romans.

The Egnatia Road runs through these peoples, from Epidamnos and Apollonia. Near the road "To Candavia" are the lakes that are around Lychnidos, on which there are independent fish-salting factories. There are also rivers, some of which empty into the Ionian Gulf and others [flow] toward a southerly direction: the Inachos, Aratthos, Acheloos, and Euenos (formerly called the Lykormas). One empties into the Ambrakian Gulf, another into the Acheloos, and the Acheloos itself and the Euenos into the sea, one after crossing Akarnania and the other Aitolia. The Erigon receives many streams from the Illyrian Mountains and the [territories of] the Lynkestians, Brigians, Deuriopians, and Pelagonians, and empties into the Axios.

(9) Formerly there were cities among these peoples: at any rate Pelagonia was once called Tripolitis, one of which was Azoros. All the cities of the Deuriopians on the Erigon were inhabited, including Bryanion, Alkomenai, and Stybara. Kydriai was Brigian, Aiginion (on the borders of Aithikia and Trikke) was Tymphaian. Near to Makedonia and Thessaly, around Mount Poion and the Pindos, are the Aithikians and the sources of the Peneios, disputed between the Tymphaians and the Thessalians who are at the foot of Pindos. There is the city of Oxyneia on the Ion River, 120 stadia distant from Tripolitian Azoros. Nearby are Alkomenai, Aiginion, Europos, and the confluence of the Ion with the Peneios. Although it is full of rough country and mountains (Tomaros, Polyanos, and others), at one time – as I have said [7.7.3] – all Epeiros and Illyris were nonetheless populous. Today most of it is deserted, and what is inhabited survives as villages and ruins. Even the oracle at Dodona, like everything else, is virtually abandoned.

(10) Ephoros [F142] says that it was a Pelasgian foundation. The Pelasgians are said to have been the earliest to hold power in Hellas. The Poet says the following: "Zeus, lord, Dodonian, Pelasgian" [*Iliad* 16.233], and Hesiod: "He came to Dodona and the oak, the seat of the Pelasgians" [F270]. I have spoken [5.2.4] about the Pelasgians in the Tyrrhenian section. Those [C328] living around the sanctuary of Dodona were barbarians, as Homer makes clear from their lifestyle, calling them "those with unwashed feet who sleep on the ground" [*Iliad* 16.235]. Whether they should be called Hellians, as Pindar [F59] does, or Sellians as is conjectured to be the Homeric reading [*Iliad* 16.234], cannot be confirmed as the text is ambiguous. Philochoros [F225] says that the region around Dodona was, like Euboia, called Hellopia, and Hesiod says the following:

There is a certain Hellopia, with many croplands and rich meadows . . . and on its edge a certain city, Dodona, was built. [F181]

Apollodoros [of Athens, F198] says it is believed that it was named because of the marshes [*hele*] around the sanctuary, and he accepts that the Poet clearly did not say Hellians, but Sellians, for those around the sanctuary, since he also called a certain river the Selleeis. He names it when he says, "far away from Ephyra, from the Selleeis River" [*Iliad* 15.531], but[4] . . . this is not Ephyra among the Thesprotians, but the one among the Eleians, for the Selleeis is there, yet there is none among the Thesprotians or the Molossians. The stories about the oak tree and the doves and other such things, like those about Delphi, are from a more poetic environment, yet they are also suitable for contemporary study.

(11) In antiquity Dodona was under the Thesprotians, as was Mount Tomaros, or Tmaros – it is called both – below which the sanctuary lies. Both the tragedians [Aischylos, *Prometheus* 831; Euripides, *Phoenician Women* 982] and Pindar [F60] have called it Thesprotian Dodona. Later it came under the Molossians. It is from Tomaros that those whom the Poet calls the interpreters of Zeus ("those with unwashed feet who sleep on the ground" [*Iliad* 16.235]) are said to be Tomouroi. In the *Odyssey* some write in the following way what Amphinomos says when he advises the suitors not to attack Telemachos before they have asked Zeus:

> if the Tomouroi of great Zeus approve, I myself will kill him and tell all the others to do so, but if the god turns away from it, I tell you to desist. [*Odyssey* 16.403–5]

It is better to write "Tomouroi" than "Themistes," and, at any rate, the oracles are nowhere called "Themistes" by the Poet, but only in decrees, government actions, and ordinances. They are said to be "Tomouroi" as a contraction of "Tomarophylakes." Those more recent say "Tomouroi," but in Homer one should take "Themistes" (and *boulai*) more simply – although misused – as the oracular ordinances and decrees, just like laws. Such is the case with "to listen to the decree [*boule*] of Zeus from the oak with high foliage" [*Odyssey* 14.328].

[C329]

(12) In the beginning the oracular interpreters were men, and perhaps the Poet manifests this, calling them "interpreters" [*hypophetai*], and the prophets [*prophetai*] could be ranked among these. Later, when Dione had been appointed to share the temple with Zeus, three old women were designated. Souidas [F11a], gratifying the Thessalians with mythical stories, says that the

---

4 The source for the following statement is missing.

sanctuary was transferred from Pelasgia around Skotoussa (the Skotoussa of Pelasgian Thessaly), that most of the women, whose descendants are the prophetesses of today, went along, and that because of this Zeus was called Pelasgian. Kineas [F2] is more mythological[5]. . . .

Fragments of the remainder of Book 7

[**Note:** Much of the remainder of Book 7 can be reconstructed from two late collections of excerpts, citations in Eustathios' commentary on the *Odyssey*, and a few comments from other authors. Fragment numbers below are as in Radt's edition. A few that are repetitious or dubious have been omitted, although by necessity what remains is also repetitive, and many of the fragments are merely paraphrases of Strabo's words. What survives is sparse and often lacks much of Strabo's color, especially in terms of mythology and history, yet a substantial part of the gist of the missing portion of Book 7 has been preserved. For a list and concordance of all possible fragments, see the Radt edition, vol. 6, pp. 331–7.]

1a. Formerly the oracular seat was around Skotoussa, a city of Pelasgiotis, but when the tree was set on fire by certain people, it was transferred according to an oracle of Apollo at Dodona. He made his prophecy through certain symbols rather than words, as was the case with the Ammonian one in Libya. Perhaps there was something unusual in the flight of the three doves that the priestesses closely watched and prophesied. It is also said that in the Molossian and Thesprotian language old women are called "peliai" and old men "pelioi," and perhaps the commonly discussed "peleiades" were not birds but the three old women who devoted themselves to the sanctuary.

1b. According to the Geographer a sacred oak is revered at Dodona as the oldest plant created, and the first to nourish man. He also says, in regard to the oracular doves there, as they are called, that the doves are observed for augury, just as some have raven divination. Others say that in antiquity men made the interpretation, but later three old women undertook the divination, and that in the Molossian language they were called "peleiai," as old men were "peleioi."

1c. Among the Thesprotians and Molossians, old women are "peleiai" and old men "peleioi," as it also is among the Makedonians. At any rate, they call those who are honored "peligones" (like the Lakonian and Massaliote

---

[5] All manuscripts break off at or before this point, and do not resume until the beginning of Book 8.

"gerontes"). It is said that this is where the myth about the doves in the Dodonian oak originates.

2. The proverb "the copper cauldron in Dodona" has this origin: there was a copper cauldron in the sanctuary that had a male statue placed above it holding a copper whip, a dedication of the Korkyraians. The whip was threefold and made in chain fashion, having vertebrae hanging from it that would strike the cauldron continuously when swung by the winds. It would produce sounds so long that someone who measured the time from the beginning of the sound to the end would continue to four hundred. From this also comes the proverb "the whip of the Kerkyraians."

3. Paionia is to the east of these people and west of the Thracian Mountains. It lies to the north of the Makedonians where, through the cities of Gortynia and Stoboi, there is a pass to . . . through which the Axios flows, making the passage to Makedonia from Paionia difficult, just as the Peneios runs through Tempe and makes a fortification from Hellas. On the south it borders on the Autariatians, Dardanians, and Ardiaians. Paionia extends as far as the Strymon. The Haliakmon flows into the Thermaian Gulf. Orestis is extensive and has a large mountain that extends as far as Mount Korax in Aitolia and Parnassos. The Orestians themselves live around it, as well as the Tymphaians and those Hellenes outside the Isthmos around Parnassos, Oite, and Pindos. The mountain is generally called by a single name, Boion, but there are many names for its parts. They say that from the highest viewpoints one can see the Aigaion Sea as well as the Ambrakian and Ionian Gulfs, but I think they speak in exaggeration. Pteleon is also rather high, situated around the Ambrakian Gulf, extending on one side as far as the Kerkyraia and on the other to the sea at Leukas.

4a. Korkyra in antiquity was fortunate and had a large naval force, but was destroyed by wars and tyrants. Later it was set free by the Romans, but without any praise, and received as a reproach: "Korkyra is free; relieve yourself where you wish."

5a. The remainder of Europe includes Makedonia, and the adjoining parts of Thrace as far as Byzantion, Hellas, and the nearby islands. Makedonia is [a part] of Hellas. Yet following the places by their nature and shape, I have now considered it apart from the rest of Hellas, joining it with the neighboring parts of Thrace that extend as far as the mouth of the Euxeinos and the Propontis. Then a little farther on there is mention of Kypsela and the Hebros River, delineating a sort of parallelogram that includes all of Makedonia.

5b. Makedonia is bounded on the west by the coast of the Adria, on the east by the parallel meridian line through the mouth of the Hebros River and the city of Kypsela, on the north by the assumed straight line through Mount Bertiskos, and Skardos, Orbelos, Rhodope, and Haimos (for these mountains, beginning at the Adria, extend in a straight line as far as the Euxeinos, making a great peninsula toward the south of Thrace, Makedonia, Epeiros, and Achaia), and on the south by the Egnatia Road running from the city of Dyrrhachion toward the east to Thessalonikeia. Thus the shape of Makedonia is nearly a parallelogram.

6a. What is today called Makedonia was formerly Emathia. It took its name from a certain ancient leader, Makedon. There was also a city of Emathia near the sea.

7a. This land was held by the Epeirotes and Illyrians, but mostly by the Bottiaians and Thracians. The former originated from Crete, it is said, with their leader Botton. Regarding the Thracians, the Pierians inhabited Pieria and the region around Olympos. The Paionians were around the Axios River – because of which it is called the Amphaxitis – and the Edonians and Bisaltians had the remainder as far as the Strymon. Of these the latter are called Bisaltians, but some of the Edonians are Mygdonians, some Edonians, and some Sithonians. Of all of these, those called the Argeadians established themselves as masters, as well as the Chalkideans in Euboia. The Chalkideans in Euboia also came to the territory of the Sithonians and established about thirty cities jointly with them. Later they were thrown out of them and came together into a single city, Olynthos, and they were named the Thracian Chalkideans. The Peneios is the boundary between Lower Makedonia – that on the sea – and Thessaly and Magnesia. The Haliakmon is still [the boundary] of Upper [Makedonia], and along with the Erigon, the Axios, and others is [the boundary] of the Epeirotes and the Paionians. Regarding the coast of Makedonia from the recess of the Thermaic Gulf and Thessalonikeia, one part extends toward the south as far as Sounion and the other to the east as far as the Thracian Chersonesos, making a sort of angle at the recess. As Makedonia reaches both ways, it is necessary to begin with the first [part] mentioned. The first portion, that around Sounion, has Attika lying above it, as well as the Megarike as far as the Krissaian Gulf. After this there is the Boiotian coast facing Euboia, with the rest of Boiotia lying above it toward the west and parallel to Attika. He [Strabo] says that the Egnatia Road from the Ionian Gulf ends at Thessalonikeia. I will mark off the strips of land, he says, beginning with those living on the sea around the Peneios and the Haliakmon.

8a. The Peneios flows from Mount Pindos through the middle of Thessaly toward the east, passes through the cities of the Lapiths and of some of the Perrhaibians, and meets Tempe, receiving a number of rivers, among which is the Europos, which the Poet called the Titaresios [*Iliad* 2.751], since it has its sources in the Titarios Mountains, which are united with Olympos where it begins to determine the boundary between Makedonia and Thessaly. Tempe is a narrow defile between Olympos and Ossa. The Peneios is carried through it for forty stadia having Olympos on the left, the highest mountain in Makedonia . . . near the outlets of the river.

8b. The Peneios River flows through Tempe – having originated in the Pindos Mountains – and through the middle of Thessaly and the Lapiths and Perrhaibians, receiving the Europos River, which Homer calls the Titaresios [*Iliad* 2.751]. It marks the boundary between Makedonia to the north and Thessaly to the south. The sources of the Europos River are in Mount Kitarios which is continuous with Olympos. Olympos is [part] of Makedonia, but Ossa and Pelion are [part] of Thessaly.

8d. The Peneios begins in the Pindos Mountains, according to the Geographer, around where the Perrhaibians are. . . . The following is also said by Strabo about the Peneios: that the Peneios begins in the Pindos and goes past Trikke on the left, is carried around Atrax and Larissa, and receiving the rivers in Thessaly goes through Tempe, that it flows through the middle of Thessaly receiving many rivers, and that the Peneios is carried on, having Olympos on the left and Ossa on the right.

8e. From there the Peneios moves to its outlet in the east, or toward the sunrise.

9a. At the outlets of the Peneios, Gyrton is situated on the right, a Perrhaibian and Magnetian city, where Peirithoos and Ixion ruled. The city of Krannon is 100 stadia distant from Gyrton. They say that when the Poet writes "these two from Thrace" [*Iliad* 13.301–2], he means by the Ephyrians the Krannonians and by the Phlegyans the Gyrtonians. On the other side is Pieria.

10a. The city of Dion is at the base of Olympos. There is a nearby village, Pimpleia. They say that Orpheus the Kikonian spent time here, a sorcerer who at first lived by money from his music, prophecies, and the rites celebrated with initiations. He then believed himself worthy of greater things and acquired a crowd and power. Some received him willingly but others suspected a plot and violence, and rose against him and killed him. Also nearby is Leibethra.

10b. The city of Dion is not on the shore of the Thermaic Gulf but in the foothills of Olympos, as much as 60 stadia away. The city of Dion has a village nearby, Pimpleia, where Orpheus spent time. In antiquity the prophets also practiced music.

11b. After Dion are the outlets of the Haliakmon, then Pydna, Methone, Aloros, the Erigon River, and the Loudias. The former flows from the

Triklarians through the Orestians and the Pellaia, leaving the city on the left and joining with the Axios. The Loudias can be sailed up 108 stadia to Pella. Methone is in the middle, about 40 stadia from Pydna and 70 from Aloros. Aloros is in the innermost recess of the Thermaic Gulf. It is called Thessalonikeia because of its distinction. Aloros is considered Bottaian, and Pydna Pierian. Pella belongs to Lower Makedonia, which the Bottiaians held. In antiquity it was the trading center of the Makedonians. Philippos [II] enlarged it from a small city because he was raised in it. It has a promontory in what is called Lake Loudias (from which the Loudias River comes forth), and it is filled by a certain branch of the Axios. The Axios empties between Chalastra and Therme.

11c. After the city of Dion are the outlets of the Haliakmon River into the Thermaic Gulf. From there, the coast to the north is called Pieria, as far as the Axios River. On it is the city of Pydna, today called Kitron, and then the cities of Methone and Aloros, and the Erigon and Loudias Rivers. From the Loudias up to the city of Pella is a sail of 120 stadia. Methone is 40 stadia from Pydna and 70 stadia from Aloros. Pydna is a Pierian city, and Aloros is Bottaian. In the plain in front of Pydna the Romans made war against Perseus the Makedonian king, and defeated him, and it was in the plains in front of Methone that Philippos [II] the son of Amyntas [III] had his right eye knocked out by a bolt from a catapult during the siege of the city. Pella was formerly small, but Philippos [II] greatly enlarged it because he was raised in it. There is a lake before it, from which the Loudias River flows; the lake is filled by a branch of the Axios. Then there is the Axios, which divides the Bottiaian and Amphaxitian territory. It receives the Erigon River, and discharges between Chalestra and Therme.

12b. On this river there lies a fortified place that is now called Abydon. Homer calls it Amydon, and says that the Paionians went from there to Troy as allies, "from faraway Amydon and the broad-flowing Axios" [*Iliad* 2.849]. It was destroyed by the Argeadians. The Axios is muddy but Homer says that the Axios has the "finest water" [*Iliad* 2.850], perhaps because of the springs called Aia, which discharge the purest water into it, and proving that the current reading of the Poet is wrong.

12c. On the Axios River lies the place that Homer calls Amydon, and he says that the Paionians went to Troy as allies from there, "from faraway Amydon and the broad-flowing Axios" [*Iliad* 2.849]. But since the Axios is muddy, and there is a certain spring that rises in Amydon and mixes the finest water into it, thus the following line, "of the Axios, whose finest water spreads over Aia" [*Iliad* 2.850], is changed to: "of the Axios, over which the finest water of Aia ["the Earth"] is spread," for it is not the water of the Axios that is "finest" and spread over the face of the earth, but that of the earth over the Axios.

12d. In "it is spread over Aia," or "Aian" (it is written in two ways), some believe that Aia is not the earth but a certain spring, as is clear from what the Geographer says, reporting that Amydon in Homer was later called Abydon, but it was destroyed, and there is a spring near Amydon called Aia that empties the purest water into the Axios, which – since it is filled from many rivers – flows full of mud. He says that the current reading ("of the Axios, whose finest water spreads over Aia" [*Iliad* 2.850]) is wrong, because clearly it is not the waters of the Axios that are spread over the spring, but the opposite. Then the Geographer rather irritably censures those who believe that Aia is the earth, and seems disposed to cast such diction completely out of the Homeric poem.

13a. The Echedoros is 20 stadia after the Axios, and then Thessalonikeia, a foundation of Kassandros, is another 40 stadia, as well as the Egnatia Road. He named the city after his wife, Thessalonike, a daughter of Philippos [II] the son of Amyntas [III], after he had destroyed the towns in Krousis and around the Thermaic Gulf (about twenty-six in number), and combined them into one. It is the metropolis of what is now Makedonia. Among those in this combination were Apollonia, Chalastra, Therma, Gareskos, Ainea, and Kissos. Of these one might conjecture that Kissos belonged to the Kissians, of whom the Poet records "Kisses raised him" [*Iliad* 11.223], speaking of Iphidamas.

13b. After the Axios River is the city of Thessalonike, which was formerly called Therme. It is a foundation of Kassandros, who took its name from that of his wife, naming it after the child of Philippos [II] the son of Amyntas [III]. He transferred to it those in the surrounding towns, including Chalastra, Ainea, Kissos, and such others. One might conjecture that it was from this Kissos that Homer's Amphidamas originated, whose grandfather Kisseus raised him "in Thrace," as he says [*Iliad* 11.222], now called Makedonia.

14a. Somewhere around here is Mount Bermion, which was formerly held by the Brigians, a Thracian people, some of whom crossed over into Asia and changed their name to Phrygians. After Thessalonikeia is the rest of the Thermaic Gulf as far as Kanastraion. This is a promontory which is a peninsula rising opposite to the Magnetis. The name of the peninsula is Pallene, and it has a five-stadia isthmus that was cut across. A city lies on it that was formerly Potidaia, a Corinthian foundation, but later was Kassandreia from the same King Kassandros, who restored it after it had been destroyed. The sail around this peninsula is 570 [stadia]. Moreover, they say that formerly the Gigantes were here and this territory was named Phlegra. Some are mythical stories, but others are more believable, telling about a certain barbaric and impious people who occupied the place but were broken up by Herakles when, after capturing Troy, he sailed back home. It is also said that the Trojan women committed an outrage here in burning the ships so that they would not be slaves to the wives of their captors.

14b. The city of Beroia lies in the foothills of Mount Bermion. The peninsula of Pallene, on whose isthmus lies that which was formerly called Potidaia and now is Kassandreia, was called Phlegra still earlier. The mythical Gigantes lived there, an impious and lawless people whom Herakles destroyed. It has four cities: Aphytis, Mende, Skione, and Sane.

15a. Olynthos is 70 stadia distant from Potidaia. After Kassandreia there follows the remainder of the coast of the Toronic Gulf, as far as Derrhis. It is a promontory rising opposite to Kanastraion, making the gulf. Directly opposite Derrhis, toward the east, is the promontory of Athos, and in between is the Singikos Gulf, named after Singis, the completely destroyed ancient city on it. After it is Akanthos, a city lying on the isthmus of Athos, founded by the Andrians. From this many call it the Akanthian Gulf. Athos is high and breast-shaped, so that on its summits the sun has risen and [people] are tired of plowing at the time that the crowing of the cock begins among those living on the coast. On this coast Thamyris the Thracian ruled, who had the same pursuits as Orpheus. Here, in the region around Akanthos, a canal is visible that Xerxes is said to have dug through Athos and which went across from the Strymonic Gulf by bringing the sea into the canal. Demetrios the Skepsian [F46] does not believe that this canal was navigable, for although there is good soil that can be dug as far as 10 stadia, which has been excavated throughout at a width of one *plethron*, yet then there is a high flat rock almost a stadion in length that could not be excavated in its entirety as far as the sea. If it could have been dug that far, it would not have been deep enough to make a navigable passage. This is where Alexarchos the son of Antipatros laid the foundations of the city of Ouranopolis, which had a circuit of 30 stadia. Certain of the Pelasgians from Lemnos settled on this peninsula, and were divided into five towns: Kleonai, Olophyxis, Akrathooi. . . . After Athos is the Strymonic Gulf, as far as the Nestos, the river that is the boundary of Makedonia according to Philippos [II] and Alexander. More accurately, however, there is a certain cape that, along with Athos, makes the gulf, and which has the city of Apollonia on it. First on this gulf after the Akanthian Harbor is Stageira, which is deserted (and which was Chalkidean and the home of Aristotle), and its harbor, Kapros, as well as an islet with the same name. Then there is the Strymon and the sail of 20 stadia up to Amphipolis. It is an Athenian foundation, situated in the place that was called Nine Roads. Then there are Galepsos and Apollonia, which were destroyed by Philippos [II].

15b. The naval station of Olynthos is Mekyperna on the Toronaian Gulf. Near to Olynthos is a hollow place called the Dung-Beetle Killer, from what occurs there, for when the animal called a dung beetle – which is found throughout the territory – touches that place, it dies. Opposite Kanastron, a promontory of Pallene, is Derrhis, a promontory near Kophos Harbor; these mark the boundary of the Toronaian Gulf. Toward the east, again, lies the promontory of Athon, which marks the boundary of the Singitic Gulf. Thus the gulfs of the Aigaion Sea are, in succession extending to the north, the Maliac, Pagasitic, Thermaic, Toronaic, Singitic, and Strymonic. The promontories are: Poseidion (between the Maliac and Pagasitic), and then in succession toward the north, Sepias, then Kanastron (the one on Pallene), then Derrhis, and then Nymphaion (on Athon at the Singitic). Next is Akrathos, the cape that is on the Strymonic. Athon is between these, and Lemnos is to the east. Toward the north Neapolis marks the boundary of the Strymonic. Akanthos, a city on the Singikos Gulf, is on the coast near the canal of Xerxes. Athon has five cities: Dion, Kleonai, Thyssa, Olophyxis, and Akresthooi (which lies near the summit of Athon). Athon is breast-shaped, particularly sharp, and especially high, since those living on the summit see the sunrise three hours before it rises on the coast. The sail around the peninsula from the city of Akanthos as far as Stageiros, the city of Aristotle, is 400 stadia. Here there is a harbor named Kapros and an islet with the same name as the harbor. Then there are the outlets of the Strymon, and then Phagres, Galepsos, and Apollonia, all of which are cities. Then there is the mouth of the Nestos, the boundary between Makedonia and Thrace that Philippos [II] and his son Alexander established in their time.

16a. He [Strabo] says that it is 120 stadia from the Peneios to Pydna. Along the coast of the Strymon are Neapolis, a city of the Datenians, and Daton itself, with its fruitful plains, harbor, rivers, shipyards, and profitable gold mines, from which comes the proverb "Daton of good things," like "a ball of thread of good things." The territory across the Strymon – that which is near the sea and around the territory of Daton – is that of the Odomantians, Edonians, and Bisaltians, both those who are indigenous and those who crossed over from Makedonia, among whom Rhesos ruled. Above Amphipolis are the Bisaltians, as far as the city of Herakleia, which has a fruitful valley that is divided by the Strymon (which originates among the Agrianians around Rhodope). Lying alongside of it is Makedonian Parorbelia, having in the interior (in the valley of Eidomene) the cities of

Kallipolis, Orthopolis, Philippoupolis, and Gareskos. Among the Bisaltians, going up the Strymon River, is situated the village of Berge, about 200 stadia distant from Amphipolis. Going from Herakleia toward the north and the narrows through which the Strymon is carried (having the river on the right), on the left are Paionia and the region around Doberos, Rhodope and Mount Haimos, and on the right is the region around the Haimos. Within the Strymon are Skotoussa, near the river itself, and Arethousa, near Lake Bolbe. Moreover, those around the lake are generally called Mydonians. Not only does the Axios flow from the Paionians, but the Strymon also does, from the Agranians through the Maidians and Sintians, emptying into what is between the Bisaltians and the Odomantians.

16b. There are other cities around the Strymonic Gulf, such as Myrkinos, Argilos, Drabeskos, and Daton, which has a good and fruitful land, shipyards, and gold mines, from which comes the proverb "Daton of good things," like "a ball of thread of good things." There are many gold mines in Krenides, where the city of Philippoi is now situated, near Mount Pangaion. Mount Pangaion itself has gold and silver mines, as does the territory across and within the Strymon River as far as Paionia. They say that those who plow the Paionian land find some bits of gold. The Strymon River begins among the Agrianians around Rhodope.

16c. Thasos, where there were once gold mines, was settled along with Daton, a famous city on the Strymonic coast.

16d. Berge, a Thracian city. Strabo calls it a village, from which the Bergaian Antiphanes came, a *komikos*.

17a. Some say that the Paionians are settlers from Phrygia, and others that they are the original founders. They say that Paionia extended as far as Pelagonia and Pieria, that Pelagonia was formerly called Orgestia, that Asteropaios, one of the commanders who made the expedition from Paionia to Ilion, was not unreasonably called the son of Pelegon, and that the Paionians themselves were called Pelegonians. Since the chanting of the paean [*paianismos*] by the Thracians is called *titanismos* by the Hellenes, in imitation of the sound of the paean, the Titans were called Pelegonians. It appears that in antiquity, as today, the Paionians held much of what is now Makedonia, so that they could lay siege to Perinthos. They also brought under their control all Krestonia and Mygdonis, as well as the territory of the Agrianians as far as Pangaion. Philippoi and the territory around Philippoi lie above that part of the coast of the Strymonic Gulf that is from Galepsos as far as the Nestos. Philippoi was formerly called Krenides and was a small settlement but was enlarged after the defeat of Brutus and Cassius. Two islands lie off this coast, Lemnos and Thasos.

17b. The Asteropaios son of Pelegon who is in Homer [*Iliad* 21.140, etc.] was recorded as being from Paionia in Makedonia. Because of this "son of Pelegon," the Paionians are called Pelegonians. The city that is Philippoi today was called Krenides in antiquity. The Sintians, a Thracian people, inhabit the island of Lemnos. Because of this Homer calls them the Sintians, saying "there the Sintian men . . . me"[6] [*Iliad* 1.594].

18a. After . . . there is Abdera and the mythical tales about Abderos. The Bistonian Thracians lived there, whom Diomedes ruled. The Nestos is not always in the same channel but often floods the territory. Then there is Dikaia, a city situated on a gulf, and a harbor. Lake Bistonis lies above it, which has a circuit of about 200 stadia. They say that this plain was completely a hollow and lower than the sea, and that Herakles – since his horses were inferior when he came for the horses of Diomedes – cut through the shore so that the sea came into the plain, and thus mastered his opponents. The royal residence of Diomedes is visible, which, because of its situation and its strength, is called Strong Village. After the lake – which is in between – are Xantheia, Maroneia, and Ismaros, the Kikonian cities. The last is now called Ismara and is near Maroneia. Nearby is the exit of the Ismaris Lake; the stream is called Odysseion. There is also what are called the Thasian Headlands. The Sapaians are situated above them. Topeira is near the Abderans and Maroneia. Thrace consists of 22 peoples in all, who, although somewhat worked over, are able to send forth 15,000 cavalry and 200,000 infantry.

18b. After the Nestos River, toward the east, is the city of Abdera, whose eponym is Abderos, who was eaten by the horses of Diomedes. Then there is the nearby city of Dikaia, above which lies a great lake, Bistonis, and then the city of Maroneia.

18c. The previously mentioned Ismaros (later Ismara) is, they say, a Kikonian city. It is near Maroneia, where there is a lake whose stream is called Odysseion. A heroon of Maron is there, as the Geographer records.

19. The river in Thrace now called the Rhiginia was called the Erigon.

20a. After Maroneia is the city of Orthagoria and the region around Serrhion, a rough voyage along the coast, and Tempyra (a town of the Samothrakians), and another one, Charakoma. The island of Samothrake lies off it, as well as Imbros, which is not far from it. Thasos is more than twice as far. After Charakoma is Doriskos, where Xerxes enumerated his army. Then there is the Hebros, which can be sailed up 120 stadia to

---

[6] Because of Strabo's excerpting of the quotation, it cannot be rendered grammatically into English.

Kypsela. He [Strabo] says that this was the boundary of Makedonia which the Romans took away from Perseus and later from the false Philippos. Paullus, who captured Perseus, attached the Epeirote peoples to Makedonia and divided the territory into four parts, assigning one to Amphipolis, one to Thessalonikeia, one to Pella, and one to the Pelagonians. The Korpilians live along the Hebros, and, farther up, the Brenians, and farthest, the Bessians (it can be sailed up this far). All these peoples are brigands, especially the Bessians, who, he says, are neighbors of the Odrysians and Sapaians. Bizyes was a royal residence of the Getians. Some define the Odrysians as everyone living along the coast from the Hebros and Kypsela as far as Odessos, over whom Amadokos, Kersobleptes, Berisades, Seuthes, and Kotys ruled. Many say that the gods honored on Samothrake are the same as the Kabeiroi, although they cannot say who the Kabeiroi are, just as with the Kyrbantians, Korybantians, and indeed the Kouretians, and the Idaian Daktyls.

20b. Iasion and Dardanos were brothers who lived on Samothrake. When Iasion was struck by a thunderbolt because of his sin against Demeter, Dardanos, going away from Samothrake, went to live at the foot of Ida, calling his city Dardania, and taught the Trojans the Samothrakian mysteries. Earlier Samothrake was called Samos.

20c. One must understand that this Samos is said to be "Thracian" in order to distinguish it from the other, the Ionian one, as well as the Kephallenian one in the *Odyssey*. The Thracian one is called Samos because of its height, according to the Geographer, for he says that *samoi* means "heights," as is made clear in the . . . of the *Periegetis*.[7] It is also called "Thracian" because it lies opposite to the Thracian mainland and because some Thracians once lived there. The Geographer says that many Samians from Mykale settled on it – for it was deserted because of a lack of crops – and thus it was called Samos. Others also say regarding this settlement that it was a little more than two hundred years after the Trojan matter that Samians from Ionia settled Samothrake, and that these Samians did not call it Samothrake, but rather it was because of the two previous reasons. The Geographer records that formerly Samothrake was called Melite and that it was wealthy. He says that in an attack Kilikian pirates secretly plundered the sanctuary on Samothrake and took away more than a thousand talents.

21a. Near the outlet of the Hebros, which has two mouths, lies the city of Ainos on the Gulf of Melas, a foundation of the Mitylenaians and

---

[7] The antecedent of the prepositional phrase is uncertain; it may refer to excerpts or a commentary on Strabo's work.

Kymaians, and still earlier by the Alopekonnesians. Then there is Cape Sarpedon, and then what is called the Thracian Chersonnesos, which forms the Propontis, Gulf of Melas, and the Hellespont. It is a promontory toward the Euronotos wind, connecting Europe with Asia by the 7-stadia-wide strait between Abydos and Sestos, having the Propontis on the left and the Gulf of Melas on the right, which is so called from the Melas River that empties into it, according to Herodotos [7.58] and Eudoxos [F306]. Herodotos, he says, reports that the stream was insufficient for the army of Xerxes. The previously mentioned promontory is closed by a 40-stadia isthmus. In the middle of the isthmus is situated the city of Lysimacheia, named after the king who founded it. On one side of it lies Kardia, on the Gulf of Melas, the largest of the cities in the Chersonnesos, a Milesian and Klazomenian foundation (later by the Athenians), and on the Propontis is Paktye. After Kardia are Drabos and Limnai, and then Alopekonnesos, at where the Gulf of Melas for the most part ends. Then there is the large Cape Mazousia, and then Elaious, on a gulf, where the Protosilaeion is. Sigeion, the promontory of the Troad, is 40 stadia away. This is approximately the southernmost promontory of the Chersonnesos, slightly more than 400 stadia from Kardia. The remainder, sailing around toward the other part of the isthmus, is a slightly greater distance. On this voyage around, after Elaious, first there is the entrance through the narrows to the Propontis, which is said to be the beginning of the Hellespont. Here is the promontory of the Dog's Grave Monument, although some say it is that of Hekabe, and her tomb is visible after rounding the promontory. Then there are Madytos and the Sestian cape, where Xerxes' pontoon bridge was, and after these, Sestos. From Elaious to the pontoon bridge is 170 [stadia]. After Sestos it is 280 [stadia] to Aigospotamoi, a small town that has been completely destroyed and where, they say, the stone fell at the time of the Persian matter. Then there is Kallipolis, from which the distance to Lampsakos in Asia is 40 [stadia], then Krithote, a small town that has been completely destroyed, then Paktye, then Long Wall, White Cape, the Sacred Mountain, Perinthos (a Samian foundation), and then Selybria. Silta and the Sacred Mountain lie above these places; the latter is honored by the locals and is a sort of akropolis for the territory. It sends forth asphalt into the sea, near the place that Prokonnesos is closest – 120 stadia – to the land. The quarry of white marble is extensive and excellent. After Selybria is the Athyras River and the ... lourias, and then Byzantion and the successive places as far as the Kyanean Rocks.

21b. The Chersonnesos in Thrace makes three seas: the Propontis in the north, the Hellespont in the east, and the Gulf of Melas in the south, where the Melas River empties, having the same name as the gulf. On the isthmus of the Chersonnesos are situated three cities: near the Gulf of Melas is Kardia, near the Propontis is Paktye, and in the interior is Lysimachia. The length of the isthmus is 40 stadia. The city of Eleous is said to be masculine, and perhaps also Trapezous.

22a. From Perinthos to Byzantion is 630 [stadia], and from the Hebros and Kypsela to Byzantion, as far as the Kyaneai, is 3,100, as Artemidoros [F66] says. The entire length from the Ionian Gulf at Apollonia, as far as Byzantion, is 7,320, with Polybios [34.12.9–10] adding 180 more, since he adds a third of a stadion to the 8 stadia to a mile. Demetrios the Skepsian, however, in his *On the Mustering of the Trojan Forces* [F47], says that from Perinthos to Byzantion is 600 stadia, and an equal amount to Parion, with the Propontis represented at 1,400 stadia in length and 500 in width. He says that the Hellespont is 7 stadia at its narrowest and 400 long. There is no agreement among everyone regarding the term "Hellespont," and there are several opinions reported about it. Some call the entire Propontis the Hellespont, and others the portions of the Propontis within Perinthos. Others add to it the open portions of the outer sea that face the Aigaion Sea and the Gulf of Melas. Still others divide it in different ways, some adding that which is from Sigeion to Lampsakos and Kyzikos or Parion or Priapos, and others that from Lesbian Sigrion. Some do not shrink from calling all of the open sea as far as the Myrtoan the Hellespont, as Pindar says in his hymns about those sailing with Herakles from Troy "through the maidenly strait of Hellas" [F33a], who touched the Myrtoan [Sea], and then ran back again to Kos because the Zephyr blew against them. Thus the entire Aigaion Sea as far as the Thermaian Gulf and the sea around Thessaly and Makedonia must deserve to be called the Hellespont, calling upon Homer as witness, who says

> you will see, if you wish and care for it, my ships sailing very early in the morning over the fish-filled Hellespont, [*Iliad* 9.359–61]

but this is refuted by the words "the hero,[8] Imbrasides, who came from Ainos" [*Iliad* 4.520] – the leader of the Thracians – "as many as are shut in by the strong-flowing Hellespont" [*Iliad* 2.845]. Thus he would represent those situated next after these as outside the Hellespont. Ainos lies in what was formerly Apsynthis (now called Korpilike), and the territory of the Kikonians is next toward the west.

---

[8] The text has "the hero" (*heros*), but the generally accepted reading of the *Iliad* is the name Peiros.

24. Amphaxion. Two parts of speech. A city. Those from there are the Amphaxitis. Strabo in the seventh [book].

28. Tetrachoritai: the Bessians. Strabo in the seventh [book].

30. He says in his seventh book of the same treatise that he[9] knew Poseidonios the Stoic philosopher.

---

[9] The antecedent of "he" is uncertain in the text of the source (Athenaios 14.657ef).

BOOK 8

The Peloponnesos

Part 1:   General comments on Hellas

(1) Having gone over the western portions of Europe – those surrounded by   [C332]
the Inner and Outer Sea – I have systematically covered all the barbarian
peoples in it as far as the Tanais, but not much of Hellas. I will now discuss
the rest of the geography of Hellas. Homer was the first to examine it,
followed by a number of others, who have written particularly *On Harbors*,
Periploi, and *The Circuit of the Earth*, or such others, in which Hellas is
included. Still others have published the topography of the continents in
separate portions of their general historical works, as Ephoros and Polybios
did. And even others have added certain material on this topic in a physical
or mathematical work, such as Poseidonios or Hipparchos. It is easy to
decide about these others, but one must consider the statements of Homer
critically, since he is speaking poetically and not about things today, but
about antiquity, which time has largely obscured. Nevertheless this must
be undertaken as far as is possible, beginning from where it was left off. The
treatment ended in the west and north with the Epeirote peoples and the
Illyrians, and in the east with the Makedonians as far as Byzantion.

After the Epeirotes and the Illyrians there are these Hellenes: the
Akarnanians, Aitolians, Ozolian Lokrians, and after them the Phokians
and Boiotians. Across the strait from them is the Peloponnesos, with the
Corinthian Gulf enclosed between them, which creates its shape and is   [C333]
shaped by them. After Makedonia there are the Thessalians as far as the
Malians, and the remainder outside of the Isthmos as well as those inside.

(2) There have been many peoples among them, but the earliest are only
as many as the Hellenic dialects that we have inherited. There are four of
these, and we can say that the "Ias" is the same as the ancient "Atthis," for
the Attic [people] were formerly called Ionians, and from them came the
Ionians who settled Asia and made use of what is now called the Iasic
language. The Doric is the same as the Aiolic. All those outside the Isthmos,

335

except for the Athenians, Megarians, and the Dorians around Parnassos, are today called Aiolians. It is reasonable that the Dorians, being few in number and living in a most rough country unmixed with others, changed their language and their customs so that they are not of the same race (the same race that they were formerly). This also happened to the Athenians, living in a land that was thin-soiled and rough, and remaining unravaged and considered indigenous, as Thoukydides says [1.2.5], always possessing the same territory since no one drove them out of it or even wished to have it. This, it seems, is the reason that they became different in language and customs, although they were few[1] in number. Thus the Aiolic people were predominant in the territory outside the Isthmos, and those inside were formerly Aiolian, but then became mixed, as the Ionians from Attika occupied Aigialos, and the Herakleidai brought the Dorians down, who founded Megara and many of the cities of the Peloponnesos. The Ionians were quickly driven back out by the Achaians, who were Aiolic peoples, so that the only two peoples left in the Peloponnesos were the Aiolians and the Dorians. All those who had less contact with the Dorians, such as the Arkadians and Eleians (as the former were totally mountainous people and were not involved in the allotment, and the latter were considered sacred to Olympian Zeus and had existed for a long time by themselves in peace, and were an Aitolian people and had received the army that had retreated with Oxylos about the time of the return of the Herakleidai) spoke Aiolian, but the rest were a mixture of both, some more Aiolic, some less. I suppose that today the dialects differ somewhat according to each city, although it

[C334] appears that everyone speaks Doric because of its agreed predominance. Such are the peoples of Hellas and their delineation in general, according to their speech. I will speak about them, treating them in the order that is necessary.

(3) Ephoros [F143] says that in its western portions the beginning of Hellas is Akarnania, for it is the first to adjoin the Epeirote peoples. But just as he uses the coast as the limit and makes his beginning there – deciding on the sea as a type of guide to his topography, as otherwise he might have represented the Makedonian and Thessalian land as the beginning of Hellas – thus it is proper for me to follow the nature of the places and to make the sea the advisor. It comes from the Sikelian Sea, on one side pouring to the Corinthian Gulf and on the other producing a large peninsula, the Peloponnesos, closed by a narrow isthmus.

---

[1] Some editors insert a "not" before few.

There are two very large components to Hellas, that inside the Isthmos and that outside, through the Gates as far as the outlet of the Peneios (this is the Thessalian [part]). That within the Isthmos is larger and more distinguished. I suppose that the Peloponnesos is the akropolis of the whole of Hellas, for apart from the magnificence and the power of the peoples who have lived in it, the position of the place itself indicates such authority, through its many and varied capes, gulfs, and – most significantly – the large peninsulas that adorn it, following one after the other in succession. The first is the peninsula of the Peloponnesos, which is closed by an isthmos of 40 stadia. The second includes the former, whose isthmos is from Pagai in the Megaris to Nisaia, the seaport of the Megarians, and which extends 120 stadia across from sea to sea. The third also includes the former, whose isthmos extends from the recess of the Krisaian Gulf as far as Thermopylai, a contrived straight line of about 508[2] stadia, enclosing within it all of <Attika and> Boiotia, and cutting at a slant across Phokis and the Epiknemidians. The fourth is from the Ambrakian Gulf through Oite and Trachinia to the Maliac Gulf and Thermopylai, making an isthmos of about 800 stadia. There is another of more than 1,000 [stadia] extending from the same Ambrakian Gulf through the Thessalians and Makedonians to the recess of the Thermaian [Gulf]. Thus the succession of peninsulas suggests a certain order, and not a bad one. It is necessary to begin with the smallest but most distinguished.

Part 2:   General comments on the Peloponnesos

(1) The Peloponnesos, then, resembles in form the leaf of a plane tree, with its length and width almost equal, at about 1,400 stadia. The former is from the west to the east – that is from Chelonatas through Olympia and the Megalopolitans to the Isthmos – and the latter from the south to the north, from Maleai through Arkadia to Aigion. The perimeter, not following the gulfs, is 4,000 stadia, according to Polybios [34.12.11]. Artemidoros [F59] adds 400. Following the gulfs it is more than 5,600. The Isthmos at the Diolkos (where the crossing is for hauling ships overland from one sea to the other), is 40 stadia, as has already been said.   [C335]

(2) The Eleians and Messenians possess the western part of the peninsula, which is washed by the Sikelian Sea. They also hold the coast in both directions, for Eleia turns toward the north and the beginning of the Corinthian Gulf as far as Cape Araxos. Across the strait from it is Akarnania and the islands

---

[2] The unusually precise number is almost certainly incorrect.

lying in front of it (Zakynthos, Kephallenia, Ithaka, and the Echinades, among which is Doulichion). Most of Messenia opens up to the south and the Libyan Sea as far as the so-called Thyrides near Tainaron. Next after Eleia are the Achaian peoples, facing toward the north and extending along the Corinthian Gulf, ending at the Sikyonia. Next are Sikyon and Corinth, extending as far as the Isthmos. After the Messenian territory are the Lakonike and the Argeia, also as far as the Isthmos. There are gulfs here: the Messenian and Lakonian, and third, the Argolic, fourth the Hermionic and the Saronic, which some call the Salaminiac. Some are filled by the Libyan Sea, others by the Cretan, and others by the Myrtoan. Some call the Saronic a sea. In the middle [of the Peloponnesos] is Arkadia, which adjoins as a neighbor all the other peoples.

(3) The Corinthian Gulf begins at the outlets of the Euenos – although some say that it is those of the Acheloos, the boundary of Akarnania and the Aitolians – and at Araxos. Here the promontories on either side first come remarkably close to one another. As they advance, finally they fall completely together at Rhion and Antirrhion, where they leave a strait of only five stadia. Rhion is Achaian and is a cape projecting into the sea in the shape of a sickle, turning inward, and is also called Drepanon ["Sickle"], lying between Patrai [C336] and Aigion, having a sanctuary of Poseidon. Antirrhion is situated on the boundary of Aitolia and Lokris, and is called Molykrian Rhion. From here both coasts separate somewhat and continue into the Krisaian Gulf. It [the Corinthian Gulf] ends there, closed in by the western ends of Boiotia and the Megaris. The Corinthian Gulf has a perimeter, from the Euenos as far as Araxos, of 2,230 stadia, and from the Acheloos it is about 100 stadia more. From the Acheloos to the Euenos is Akarnanian, and then to Antirrhion it is Aitolian, and the rest as far as the Isthmos belongs to the[3] ... Phokaians, Boiotians, and the Megaris, and is 1,880 stadia. The sea from Antirrhion as far as the Isthmos is called the Alkyonian, being part of the Krisaian Gulf. From the Isthmos to Araxos is 1,030 [stadia]. The position of the Peloponnesos is said to be in such a way in terms of its form, as is also the land lying across the strait as far as the recess. Also in such a way is the gulf that lies in between. I will now discuss each part, making a beginning with Eleia.

Part 3: Eleia

(1) Today all the coast between the Achaians and the Messenians is called Eleia, as well as what is up into the Arkadian interior at Pholoe, the

---

[3] The Lokrians seem to have fallen out of the text.

Azanians, and the Parrhasians. In antiquity it was divided into a number of dominions, and then into two, that of the Epeians and that under Nestor the son of Neleus, just as Homer says when he calls the Epeian territory Elis ("past divine Elis, where the Epeians rule" [*Odyssey* 15.298]). That under Nestor, he says, is Pylos, through which the Alpheios flows ("of the Alpheios, which broadly flows through the land of Pylos" [*Iliad* 5.545]). The Poet also knew Pylos as a city ("they came to Pylos, the well-built city of Neleus" [*Odyssey* 3.4–5]), but the Alpheios neither flows through the city or past it, but another one [flows] past it, which some call the Pamisos and others the Amathos ["Sandy"], from which, it seems, Pylos is called "sandy." The Alpheios flows through the Pylian territory.

(2) The contemporary city of Elis had not yet been founded in Homeric times, and the territory was occupied by villages. It was called Hollow Elis from the situation of the most and the best of it. It was only rather late, after the Persian matter, that the contemporary city of Elis came into existence from many villages. Similarly other places in the Peloponnesos (except a few) that the Poet recorded were named not as cities but as territories, each [C337] composed of several communities which were later joined into the known cities. For example, Mantineia in Arkadia came from the joining together of five Argive communities, Tegea from nine, and from the same [number] Heraia, either by Kleombrotos or Kleonymos. Similarly Aigion became united into one city from seven or eight communities, Patrai from seven, and Dyme from eight. Thus Elis was united into one city from the neighboring towns (one of these[4] ... the Agriadians). The Peneios River flows through the city past its gymnasium, which the Eleians built later, a long time after they obtained the territories that had belonged to Nestor.

(3) These were the Pisatis (of which Olympia is a part), Triphylia, and the Kaukonian territory. The Triphylians were called that because three tribes had come together and joined: the Epeians (there from the beginning), the Minyans (who settled there later), and the Eleians (who dominated last). Some say that it was the Arkadians instead of the Minyans, as the former had often disputed the territory, and thus the same Pylos was called Arkadian or Triphylakian. Homer calls the entire territory as far as Messene "Pylos," the same name as the city. Yet Hollow Elis was distinct from the places subject to Nestor, as is shown by the names of the leaders and their homes in the *Catalogue of Ships*. I say this to bring together both the present and what Homer said. It is necessary to make this comparison because of the reputation of the Poet and our common nurture with him, believing that there is no

---

[4] There is a gap of about five letters.

successful accomplishment of any proposition at present unless nothing is in conflict with him, since there is such belief in his words. It is necessary to speak of what exists, and to apply and to consider the [words] of the Poet, as much as they are relevant.

(4) In Eleia there is a certain cape, Araxos, facing the north, 60 [stadia] from Dyme, an Achaian city. This I put down as the beginning of the Eleian coast. After it, proceeding toward the west, there is the Eleian naval station, Kyllene, where the route inland leads 120 stadia to the present city. Homer records this Kyllene when he says "Otos, the Kyllenian . . . chief of the Epeians" [*Iliad* 15.518–19], for he would not have represented the leader of the Epeians as from the Arkadian mountain. It is a village of moderate size, having the Asklepios of Kolotes, an ivory xoanon that is a marvel to see.

[C338] After Kyllene there is the promontory of Chelonatas, the westernmost point of the Peloponnesos. There is an islet lying off it, and shallows on the border between Hollow Elis and the Pisatians. From here the voyage to Kephallenia is no more than 80 stadia. Somewhere on this previously mentioned border flows the Eleison or Eleisa River.

(5) The Peneios River empties between Chelonatas and Kyllene, as well as the Selleeis (mentioned by the Poet), which flows from Pholoe. On it is the city of Ephyra, which is a fourth one (different from the Thesprotian, Thessalian, and Corinthian ones), lying on the road to Thalasion, and which is either the same as Boinoa (as Oinoe is customarily called), or near to it, at a distance of 120 stadia from the city of the Eleians. From here, it seems, the mother of Tlepolemos the son of Herakles came, as it is said that "he brought her out of Ephyra, from the Selleeis River" [*Iliad* 2.659], for the expeditions of Herakles were there, rather than elsewhere where there is no Selleeis River. Also [it is said], about the corselet of Meges, that "Phyleus once brought this out of Ephyra, from the Selleeis River" [*Iliad* 15.530–1]. The man-killing drugs came from there, for Athena says that Odysseus went to Ephyra "seeking a man-killing drug so that he could coat his arrows" [*Odyssey* 1.261–2] and the suitors [said] about Telemachos:

> or he wishes to go to Ephyra, the rich land, so that he could bring life-destroying drugs from there. [*Odyssey* 2.328–9]

Nestor, in his account of his war against them, introduces the daughter of Augeas the Epeian king as a sorceress when he says

> I was the first to kill a man . . . Moulios the spearbearer, who was a son-in-law of Augeias, having his eldest daughter . . . who had all the drugs nourished by the broad earth [*Iliad* 11.738–41].

There is another Selleeis River around Sikyon, with a village named Ephyra nearby. In Agraia in Aitolia there is a village of Ephyra, whose inhabitants are Ephyrians.

(6) Apollodoros [of Athens, F181], teaching about the manner in which the Poet was accustomed to distinguish the same name, says that he calls Arkadian Orchomenos "rich in herds" [*Iliad* 2.605], the Boiotian one "Minyan" [*Iliad* 2.511; *Odyssey* 11.284], and the Samian as "Thracian" [*Iliad* 13.12–13], connecting it . . . "between Samos and Imbros" [*Iliad* 24.78], so that it is separated from the Ionian. He also says that he [Homer] distinguishes Thesprotian Ephyra by both "far" and "from the Selleeis River" [*Iliad* 2.659]. Yet he [Apollodoros of Athens] does not agree with what Demetrios the Skepsian [F55] says – from whom he has taken most things – who says that there is no Selleeis River among the Thesprotians, but it is in Eleia, going past that Ephyra, as I have said previously. Thus in what he [Apollodoros of Athens] said about Oichalia he lacked perception [*skepsis*], since he says that there is only one, "the city of Oichalian Eurytos." Clearly this is the Thessalian one, about which he [Homer] says "those who held Oichalia, the city of Oichalian Eurytos" [*Iliad* 2.730]. From where, then, did he [Thamyris] set forth when the Muses, near Dorion, "met Thamyris the Thracian and stopped his singing" [*Iliad* 2.595]? He [Homer] then says "he was going from Oichalia, from Oichalian Eurytos" [*Iliad* 2.596]. If it were the Thessalian, the Skepsian is wrong again when he says that it was the Arkadian, now called Andania, but if he is correct, the Arkadian city was also "of Eurytos," and thus there was not only one, but he [Apollodoros of Athens] says that there was only one.

(7) Pylos is situated between the outlets of the Peneios and the Selleeis, near Skollion. This is not the city of Nestor but another one that has nothing in common with the Alpheios or the Pamisos (or the Amathos, if one must call it that). Yet there are some who forcefully seek the reputation and nobility of Nestor. It is recorded that there are three Pyloi in the Peloponnesos, as is said in the proverb, "There is a Pylos in front of Pylos, and even another Pylos": this one, the Lepreatic in Triphylia and the Pisatis, and a third, the Messenian near Koryphasion, each of which attempts to show that it is sandy and to demonstrate that it is the hometown of Nestor. Many of the more recent historians and poets say that Nestor was a Messenian, thus adding support to the one preserved into present times. Those who follow the Homeric wording more closely say that the Pylos of Nestor is the territory that the Alpheios goes through, and it goes through the Pisatis and Triphylia. Yet those from Hollow Elis have supported their own Pylos energetically with tokens of recognition, pointing out places called Geranos, the Geron River,

[C339]

[C340]

and another, the Geranios, believing that the epithet "Gerenian" spoken about Nestor came from there. The Messenians have done the same thing, which appears more believable, for they say that their Gerena is a better known and once-flourishing place. This is the contemporary situation in Hollow Elis.

(8) The Poet divides this territory into four parts with four leaders, yet his words are not spoken clearly:

> They lived both in Bouprasion and divine Elis, as much as is enclosed in Hyrmine and Myrsinos on the borders by the Olenian Rock and Alesion. Of these there were four leaders, with ten quick ships following each man, and many Epeians embarked on them. [*Iliad* 2.615–9]

He calls Epeians both Bouprasians and Eleians, but does not go on to call the Bouprasians the Eleians. It would seem that he is not dividing the Eleians into four parts, but the Epeians, who had previously been divided into two parts. Thus Bouprasion would not be a part of Elis but rather of the Epeians. It is clear that he called the Bouprasians the Epeians, "when the Epeians buried lord Amarynkeus at Bouprasion" [*Iliad* 23.630–1]. Moreover, when he includes them together, saying "Bouprasion and divine Elis" and then divides it into four portions, it seems that he is placing Bouprasion and Elis together. It is likely that there was a notable settlement at Bouprasion in Eleia that is no longer in existence today. Only the territory on the road to Dyme from the present city of Elis is called this. One might suppose that Bouprasion had a certain pre-eminence then, in regard to Elis, just as the Epeians had in regard to them, but that later they were called Eleians instead of Epeians. Although Bouprasion was a part of Elis, they say that Homer, using a sort of poetic figure, includes the part with the whole, as in "throughout Hellas and the middle of Argos" [*Odyssey* 15.80], and "throughout Hellas and Phthia" [*Iliad* 9.395; *Odyssey* 11.496], and "the Kouretians fought, and the Aitolians" [*Iliad* 9.529], and "those from Doulichion and the sacred Echinades" [*Iliad* 2.625] (Doulichion is one of the Echinades). Those who are more recent also make use of this, such as Hipponax, "those who eat the bread of Cyprian and Amathousian wheat" [F125] (the Amathousians [C341] are Cyprians), as well as Alkman ("lovely Cyprus and Paphos surrounded by the sea" [F55]) or Aischylos ("she had Cyprus and Paphos as her allotment" [F402a]). If he [Homer] does not say that the Bouprasians are Eleians, I can say that there are many other things [he does not say], but this is not proof that they were unknown, but only that he did not mention them.

(9) Hekataios the Milesian [F25] says that the Epeians are different from the Eleians, and that, at any rate, the Epeians joined Herakles in his

expedition against Augeas and assisted him in destroying both Augeas and
Elis. He also says [F121] that Dyme is both Epeian and Achaian. Yet the
ancient historians say many things that are not true, because they were
accustomed to falsehoods through their writing of myths, and thus they do
not agree with one another about the same things. But it is not unbelievable –
even if the Epeians were once in disagreement with the Eleians and were of
another ethnic group – that they ruled jointly with them after prevailing
over them, and possessed a common government, prevailing as far as Dyme.
The Poet did not name Dyme, but it is not unreasonable that it was ruled
by the Epeians, and later by the Ionians, or if not them, by the Achaians
who took possession of that territory. Of the four parts, inside of which
Bouprasion is, Hyrmine and Myrsinos are Eleian and the remainder are
already on the boundaries of the Pisatis, as some believe.

(10) Hyrmine was a small town that no longer exists, but near Kyllene
there is a mountain promontory called Hormina or Hyrmina. Myrsinos is
the Myrtountion of today, which reaches to the sea and is situated on the
road from Dyme to Elis, 70 stadia distant from the city of the Eleians. The
Olenian Rock is conjectured to be the Skollis of today, as it is necessary to
infer from probability because both the places and names have changed, and
in many places he [Homer] is not very clear. It is a rocky mountain common
to the Dymaians, Tritaians, and Eleians, bordering another Arkadian mountain, Lampeia, which is 130 stadia distant from Elis, 100 from Tritaia, and the
same from⁵ . . . Arkadian cities. Aleision is the Alasyaion of today, a territory
around Amphidolis where those living in the region come together each
month for a market. It lies on the mountain road from Elis to Olympia and
formerly was a city of the Pisatis, for the boundaries have moved at different
times because of the changes in rulers. The Poet calls Aleision the Hill of
Aleision when he says   [C342]

> until we placed our horses on Bouprasion, rich in wheat, on the Olenian
> Rock of Aleision, where it is called the Hill. [*Iliad* 11.756–8]

It is necessary to take this as a transposition, equal to "and where the Hill of
Aleision is." Some also point out an Aleisios River.

(11) Certain people in Triphylia near Messenia are said to be Kaukonians.
Dyme is said by some to be Kaukonian, and there is a river in the Dymaia
between Dyme and Tritaia that is called the Kaukon. Thus it is questioned
whether two Kaukones are meant, one around Triphylia and the other
around Dyme, Elis, and the Kaukon. It empties into another, called the

---

⁵ There is a gap of about eight letters.

Teutheas, of the masculine gender and having the same name as one of the little towns that were consolidated into Dyme, except that it is called Teuthea, without the sigma, feminine in gender, and with the lengthening of the final syllable. The sanctuary of Nemydian Artemis is there. The Teutheas empties into the Acheloos which flows by Dyme and has the same name as the one in Akarnania. It is also called the Peiros, as Hesiod says: "he lived on the Olenian Rock along the banks of a river, the broad Peiros" [F85]. Some wrongly change it to Poros. They also raise a question about the Kaukonians, because he [Homer] says (in the *Odyssey* when Athena in the form of Mentor, relates the following to Nestor):

> But I will go at dawn to the great-hearted Kaukonians where a debt – neither new or small – is due to me. But you – since he has come to your house – send him forth with a chariot and your son, and give him horses. [*Odyssey* 3.366–9]

He seems to indicate a certain territory among the Epeians that the Kaukonians held, who were different from those in Triphylia and extended as far as the Dymaia. One should not consider it unworthy to ask where "Kaukonian" Dyme originated, and to ask about the Kaukon River, or to question about those Kaukonians to whom Athena says she is going in order to recover her debt. If we take it as speaking about those in Triphylia around Lepreon, I do not know how the account can be believable. Some write as follows: "where a debt – not a small one – is due to me in divine Elis." This will become clearer when I go through the investigation of the following territory, the Pisatis, and Triphylia as far as the Messenian border.

(12) After Chelonatas is the long shore of the Pisatians, and then Cape Phea. There was also a small town "beside the walls of Pheias, around the [C343] streams of Iardanos" [*Iliad* 7.135], for there is a small river nearby. Some say that Phea is the beginning of the Pisatis. An islet and a harbor lie off it, from which the nearest [distance] from the sea to Olympia is 120 stadia. Then there is another cape, projecting a distance straight out to the west, like Chelonatas, from which it is again 120 stadia to Kephallenia.

Then there is the outlet of the Alpheios, which is 280 stadia distant from Chelonatas and 545 from Araxos. It flows from the same region as the Eurotas, a village called Asea in the Megalopolitis, where there are two springs near each other from which the previously mentioned rivers flow. They sink under the earth and rise again after many stadia, and then one of them comes down into the Lakonike and the other into the Pisatis. The stream of the Eurotas rises and shows itself at the beginning of the Bleminatis, and then flows past Sparta itself. It then passes through a certain long hollow, Helos – which is recorded by the Poet [*Iliad* 2.584, 594] – and empties between Gytheion (the Spartan seaport) and Akraiai. The Alpheios, receiving the Ladon, Erymanthos, and others that are more important, is carried through Phrixas, the Pisatis, and Triphylia past Olympia itself and to the Sikelian Sea, emptying into it between Phea and Epitalion. Near its outlet is the grove of Artemis Apheionia or Alpheiousa – it is recorded both ways – about 80 stadia from Olympia. A festival of this goddess is celebrated each year at Olympia, as well as of Elaphia and Daphnia. The entire territory is full of precincts of Artemis, Aphrodite, and the Nymphs . . . of flowers, because they are well watered. There are many Hermeia on the roads, and Poseideia on the capes. In the Alpheionia sanctuary there are paintings by Kleanthes and Aregon, Corinthian men: the *Capture of Troy* and the *Birth of Athena* by the former and the *Artemis Carried Up By a Griffin* by the latter, all exceedingly notable.

(13) Then there is the Triphylian mountain that separates the Makistia from the Pisatis. Then there is another river, the Chalkis, the spring of Krounoi, the settlement of Chalkis, and after these Samikon, where there is the greatly honored sanctuary of Samian Poseidon. There is a grove full of wild olives, which the Makistians manage, who were the ones who proclaimed the so-called Samian armistice. All Triphylians contribute to the sanctuary. In addition, the sanctuary of Athena Skillounta around Skillous is notable, at Phellon near Olympia.[6]

(14) Around these sanctuaries, within thirty stadia or slightly more and lying above the sea, is Triphylian or Lepreatic or Arkadian Pylos, which the Poet calls "sandy" and hands down as the native city of Nestor, as one might judge from his words, whether it is from the river that flows past it toward the north (formerly called the Amathos but now called the Mamaos, so that it [Pylos] was called "sandy" [*emathoeis*]), or because [the river] was called the Pamisos, the same name as two in Messenia. Thus the etymology of the epithet is unclear, for they say it is false that the river or territory was sandy.

[C344]

Near Pylos, to the east, is a mountain named after Minthe, who, according to myth, was the concubine of Hades and was trampled by Kore and changed into garden mint, which some call the sweet variety. Near the mountain is a precinct of Hades that is honored by the Makistians, as well as a grove of Demeter that lies above the Pylian plain. This plain is fertile and adjoins the sea, stretching along the entire distance between Samikon and the Neda River. The shore is sandy and narrow, so that one would not disbelieve that this is why Pylos was named "sandy."

---

[6] This sentence has been transposed from the end of the first paragraph of 8.3.14.

(15) On the northern border of Pylos are two little Triphylian cities, Hypana and Typaneai. The former was combined into Elis, the latter remained. There are two rivers flowing near by, the Dalion and the Acheron, which empty into the Alpheios. The Acheron was named because of its relationship with Hades, for the sanctuaries of Demeter and Kore are greatly honored there, as well as those of Hades, as Demetrios the Skepsian says [F59]. This is perhaps because of the contrast, for although Triphylia is fertile, it also produces rust and rushes, so that instead of a large yield in these places it often happens that there is no yield.

(16) To the south of Pylos is Lepreon. This city was also above the sea, about 40 stadia. Between Lepreon and the Alpheios is the sanctuary of Samian Poseidon, at a distance of 100 stadia from each. This is the sanctuary where the Poet says that Telemachos found the Pylians performing a sacrifice:

> they came to Pylos, the well-built city of Neleus, where on the seashore some were sacrificing to the dark-haired Earthshaker bulls that were completely black. [*Odyssey* 3.4–6][7]

[C345] The Lepreatians had a fertile territory, with the Kyparissians bordering on them. Both these districts were acquired by the Kaukonians, as was Makiston, which some call Platanistous. The name of the town is the same as that of the territory. They say that there is a memorial of Kaukon in Lepreatis, either their founder or someone who for some reason had the same name as the people.

(17) There are a number of accounts about the Kaukonians, for they say that they were an Arkadian people, like the Pelasgians, and like them wanderers. At any rate, the Poet records [*Iliad* 10.429, 20.329] that they came to Troy as allies, but he does not say from where, although it seems to have been from Paphlagonia, for there are certain Kaukonitians there on the borders of the Mariandynians, who are Paphlagonians themselves. I will discuss them more extensively in the material about that place [12.3.5]. At present I must recount additional material about the Kaukonians in Triphylia. Some say that the whole of what is now Eleia, from Messenia as far as Dyme, was called Kaukonia. Antimachos [F27], at any rate, calls everyone both Epeians and Kaukonians, and others [say] that they did occupy the whole, but lived there divided in two, one in Triphylia near Messenia, the other in the Bouprasis and Hollow Elis near Dyme. Aristotle [F493], especially, knew that they were located at the latter. This last assertion agrees better with what Homer says and provides a solution for

---

[7] The manuscripts have at this point the sentence now in 8.3.17 beginning "It is possible for a poet . . ."

the previous question. It is thus established that Nestor lived at Triphylian Pylos, and that what was toward the south and east (that is, what is contiguous to Messenia and the Lakonike), which the Kaukonians held, was subject to him, so that if one travelled from Pylos to Lakedaimon the route necessarily would have been through the Kaukonians. But the sanctuary of Samian Poseidon and the anchorage near it, where Telemachos landed, are toward the north and west. If the Kaukonians only lived here, the account was not preserved by the Poet. It is possible for a poet to fabricate what does not exist, although it is more proper to abstain from it, and when possible he should adjust his words to what exists yet preserve the narrative.[8] The Mentor-Athena, according to Sotades, tells Nestor to send Telemachos to Lakedaimon "with a chariot and your son," toward the parts to the east, but she says that she will travel back to the ship to spend the night, toward the west, and will go "at dawn to the great-hearted Kaukonians" [*Odyssey* 3.365–6], for a debt, going forward again. In what way? It would have been possible for Nestor to say,   [C346]

> the Kaukonians are my subjects and are near the road travelled to Lakedaimon. Why do you not travel with those accompanying Telemachos rather than going back?

At the same time, it would have been proper for someone going to recover a debt that was not small, as she says, from people subject to Nestor, to ask him for some help, in case there were any unfairness – as is customary – regarding the contract. This was not done. Thus if the Kaukonians lived only there, paradoxical things would occur. But if some of them had been dispersed to the regions around Dyme in Eleia, Athena would be talking about her journey there, and there would no longer be anything inconsistent about going down to the ship or separating from her fellow travellers because their roads were opposite to one another. Similarly, the difficulties regarding the matter of Pylos may be appropriately investigated a little later [8.3.26] when the chorography comes to Messenian Pylos.

(18) Part of those in Triphylia were called Paroreatians, occupying mountains around Lepreon and Makiston that come down to the sea near the Samian Posideion.

(19) At their base, on the coast, are two caves, one of the Anigriadian Nymphs, and in the other where the matter about the Atlantides and the birth of Dardanos occurred. Also here are the groves of the Ionaion and the Eurykydaion. Samikon is a fortification, although formerly there was a city

---

[8] This sentence has been transferred from 8.3.16 (see previous note).

called Samos, perhaps because of its height, since high places were called *samoi*. Perhaps it was the akropolis of Arene, which the Poet records in the *Catalogue*: "those who lived in Pylos and lovely Arene" [*Iliad* 2.591]. It is conjectured that Arene is here (although it has not been discovered anywhere with certainty), since the neighboring Anigros River, formerly called the Minyeios, gives no slight indication, as the Poet says "there is a certain Minyeios River that falls into the salty sea near Arene" [*Iliad* 11.722–3]. Near to the cave of the Anigriadian Nymphs is a spring that makes the land lying below it marshy and swampy. The Anigros receives most of the water, and it is deep and flat, creating a lake. The place is muddy and produces a heavy odor for twenty stadia all around, making the fish inedible. Some say that the myths report that certain of the injured Centaurs washed off the poison of the Hydra here, and others that these

[C347] cleansing waters were used by Melampous to purify the Proitides. The baths here cure leprosy, *leuke*, and *leichene*. They also say that the Alpheios was named because it was a cure for leprosy [*alphos*]. Since the flatness of the Anigros and the inflow of the sea produce a persistence rather than a flow in its waters, they say that it was formerly called the Mimneios, although some have changed the name and have made it Minyeios instead. But the etymology has other sources, either from those who went from Minyan Orchomenos with Chloris the mother of Nestor, or from the Minyans, who being descendants of the Argonauts, were driven out of Lemnos into Lakedaimon, and then into Triphylia, and lived around Arene in the territory now called Hypaisia, although it no longer has Minyan settlements. Some of them sailed with Theras the son of Autesion – he was a descendant of Polyneikes – to the island between the Kyrenaia and Crete ("formerly Kalliste but its later name was Thera," as Kallimachos [F716] says), founding Thera, the mother city of Kyrene, and giving the island the same name as the city.

(20) Between the Anigros and the mountain from which it flows the meadow and heroon of Iardanos are visible, as well as the Achaiai, which are cut-off rocks on the same mountain. Above them is Samos, the city that I have already discussed. But Samos is not recorded at all by the writers of the *periploi*, perhaps because it had been torn down in antiquity, and perhaps also because of its location, for the Poseideion is a grove near the sea, as I have said [8.3.13]. A high hill lies above it, in front of the present Samikon, where Samos once was, and thus it could not be seen from the sea. There is also a plain here called the Samikon, because of which there is stronger proof that there once was a city of Samos. The *Rhadine*, which Stesichoros seems to have composed, and which begins

Come, clear Muse, begin the song, the hymn about the beloved children of Samos, voiced with the beloved lyre [F278]

tells about the children of that place. He says that Rhadine, who had been betrothed to the tyrant of Corinth, sailed with the Zephyr from Samos – not presumably, Ionian Samos – and with the same wind her brother went to Delphi as the leader of a sacred embassy. Her cousin, in love with her, went to Corinth in a chariot to see her. The tyrant killed them both and sent their bodies away in a chariot, but repented, called it back, and buried them.   [C348]

(21) From this Pylos and Lepreon it is a distance of about 400 stadia to Messenian Pylos and Koryphasion – which is a fortress situated on the sea – and the adjacent island of Sphagia. From the Alpheios it is 750, and from Chelonatas 1,030. In between are the sanctuary of the Makistian Herakles and the Akidon River. It flows past the tomb of Iardanos and also Chaa, a city that once existed near to Lepreon, where the Aipasian Plain also is. Some say that it was over Chaa that the war of the Arkadians against the Pylians occurred – about which Homer speaks – thinking that one should write

> were that I were in my prime, as when by the swift-flowing Akidon the Pylians and Arkadians gathered together and fought beside the walls of Chaa [*Iliad* 7.133–5, revised]

instead of "Keladon" and "Pheia," for this place is nearer than the other to the tomb of Iardanos and the Arkadian territory.

(22) Kyparissia is on the Triphylian Sea, and so are Pyrgoi, the Akidon River, and the Neda. Today the boundary between Triphylia and Messenia is the Neda, a violent stream that comes down from Lykaion, an Arkadian mountain, and from a spring which, in myth, Rhea caused to break forth so that she could bathe after she had given birth to Zeus. It flows past Phigalia and empties where the Pyrgitians, the last of the Triphylians, are neighbors to the Kyparissians, the first of the Messenians. In antiquity the boundary was different, so that some places across the Neda – the Kyparisseeis and some others on the far side – were subject to Nestor. In such a way the Poet stretches the Pylian Sea as far as the seven cities that Agamemnon provided Achilleus ("all near the sea at the lowest part of sandy Pylos" [*Iliad* 9.153, 295]). This is the same as "near the Pylian Sea."

(23) Next, then, after sailing past the Kyparisseeis toward Messenian Pylos and Koryphasion, is Erana, which some wrongly believe was formerly called Arene (the same name as the Pylian), as well as Cape Platamodes, from which it is 100 stadia to Koryphasion and the place today called Pylos. Here there also is an islet and a small town with the same name, Prote.

Perhaps I would not be examining such ancient things, and it would be sufficient to speak of each as it is now, if there were not certain traditions about them handed down to us from childhood. Since different people say different things, there must be arbitration. The most honored, oldest, and most experienced are the most believed, and it is Homer who has surpassed [C349] everyone in these things. Thus it is necessary both to examine what he has said and to reconcile it with the present situation, as I said recently [8.3.3].

(24) I have examined what Homer has said about Hollow Elis and Bouprasion. Concerning what was subject to Nestor, he says

> those who lived in Pylos and lovely Arene and Thryon, the crossing of the Alpheios, and well-built Aipy, and those living in the Kyparisseeis, and Amphigeneia, Pteleon, Helos, and Dorion, where the Muses met Thamyris the Thracian and stopped his singing while he was going from Oichalia, from Oichalian Eurytos. [*Iliad* 2.591–6]

The investigation is concerned with Pylos, which I will examine shortly. Arene has been discussed [8.3.19]. What he now says is Thryon he called Thryoessa elsewhere: "there is a certain city, Thryoessa, on a steep hill, far away on the Alpheios" [*Iliad* 11.711–12]. He says that it is the ford of the Alpheios because it seems that at this place it could be crossed on foot. Today it is called Epitalion, a place in the Makistia. Regarding "well-built Aipy," some ask which is the epithet and whether the city is the Marganai of today in Amphidolia. The former is not a natural fortress, but another natural [fortress] is visible in the Makistia. Thus someone who suspects that it is the latter believes that he says the name of the city is Aipy ["Sheer"], from what occurs naturally (such as Helos ["Marsh"], Aigialos ["Shore"], and several others), but [someone who suspects] Marganai perhaps does the reverse. Thryon ["Reed"] or Thryoessa, they say, is Epitalion because this entire territory is full of reeds, especially the rivers, particularly visible at the places that the streams are crossed. But they say that perhaps he called the crossing Thryon, and Epitalion "well-built Aipy," for it is naturally fortified. Elsewhere he speaks of a steep hill:

> there is a certain city, Thryoessa, on a steep hill, far away on the Alpheios, the last of sandy Pylos. [*Iliad* 11.711–12]

(25) The Kyparisseeis is around the earlier Makistia, when the Makistia still extended across the Neda, but it is not inhabited, and neither is Makiston. There is another one, Messenian Kyparissia, today called by the same name, Kyparissia, in the singular and feminine. The river is the Kyparisseeis. Amphigeneia is also in the Makistia around the Hypsoeis, where there is a sanctuary of Leto. Pteleon was a foundation from a settlement of [C350] Thessalian Pteleon, as he says about it: "Antron near the sea and grassy

Pteleon" [*Iliad* 2.697]. It is a woody and uninhabited place called Pteleasion. Some say that Helos is a particular place around the Alpheios and others say that it is a city, like the Lakonian one ("Helos, a city on the sea" [*Iliad* 2.584]), but others that it is around the Alorian marsh, where the sanctuary of Eleian Artemis is, managed by the Arkadians, for they had the priesthood. Some say that Dorion is a mountain, others a plain, and still others a little city. Nothing is to be seen today, but some say that the Olouris or Oloura of today, situated in what is called Hollow Messenia, is Dorion. Also somewhere around here is the Oichalia of Eurytos, today Andania, a small Arkadian town with the same name as the Thessalian and Euboian ones. It was from the former that the Poet says Thamyris the Thracian came to Dorion and the Muses deprived him of music [*Iliad* 2.594–5].

(26) From this it is clear that the territory subject to Nestor, all of which he [Homer] calls the Pylian land [*Iliad* 5.545], was on both sides of the Alpheios. Yet the Alpheios nowhere touches either Messenia or Hollow Elis. Thus the fatherland of Nestor is in this territory which we call Triphylian, Arkadian, and Lepreatic Pylos. Other Pyloi are shown to be on the sea, but this one is more than thirty stadia inland, which is clear from the text: a messenger is sent to the ship and the companions of Telemachos, summoning them to hospitality [*Odyssey* 3.423–4]. Telemachos, when he returns from Sparta, does not allow Peisistratos to drive into the city, but to hasten and turn aside to the ship [*Odyssey* 15.195–201], as the road to the city and the anchorage are not the same. Thus the return voyage of Telemachos might properly be described as follows:

> they went past Krounoi and the beautifully flowing Chalkis. The sun set and all the ways became dark, and they came upon the Pheai, exalting in the fair wind of Zeus, and past divine Elis, where the Epeians rule [*Odyssey* 15.295–8].

So far the voyage is toward the north, but then it turns aside in an easterly direction. The ship gives up its original voyage (directly to Ithaka) because the Suitors were positioned for an ambush "in the strait between Ithaka and Samos . . . from there on the contrary he went toward the Thoai islands" [*Odyssey* 15.29, 299]. By the Thoai he means the Oxeiai, which are part of the Echinades, near the beginning of the Corinthian Gulf and the outlet of the Acheloos. Passing beyond Ithaka, having it to the south, he curved back toward the proper course between Akarnania and Ithaka and made his landing on the other side of the island, not in the Kephallenian Strait, which was guarded by the suitors.

[C351]

(27) Thus if one were to suggest that Eleian Pylos is that of Nestor, he [Homer] could not properly say that the ship, after putting to sea from

there, was carried beyond Krounoi and the Chalkis before sunset, and then approached the Pheai at night and sailed past Eleia, for these places are to the south of Eleia: first the Pheai, then the Chalkis, then Krounoi, and then Triphylian Pylos and Samikon. This would be the voyage for someone sailing south from Eleian Pylos. Sailing toward the north, where Ithaka is, all these would be left behind: one must sail past Eleia itself, and before sunset (although he has it after sunset). Moreover, if one were to make another assumption, that Messenian Pylos and Koryphasion are the beginning of the voyage from Nestor's territory, the distance would be more and the time greater. At any rate, it is 400 stadia to Triphylian Pylos and the Samian Posideion, and the first part of the coastal voyage is not past Krounoi and the Chalkis to the Phea (the names of obscure rivers, or rather streams), but past the Neda, then the Akidon, and then the Alpheios, and the places in between. If so, the other places should have been mentioned later, for the voyage was also past them.

(28) In addition, the narrative that Nestor presented to Patroklos about the war that occurred between the Pylians and Eleians [*Iliad* 11.670–761] pleads for what I have been attempting to prove, if one observes the wording. He [Homer] says that since Herakles had ravaged the Pylia and all the youth had been lost, and Nestor, who was exceedingly young, was the only survivor of the twelve sons of Neleus, the Epeians thus despised Neleus because of his age and isolation and they treated the Pylians with contempt and arrogance. In opposition to this Nestor gathered his kinsmen – as many as were possible – and attacked Eleia, as he says, driving away a great deal of plunder ("50 herds of cattle, as many flocks of sheep and as many herds of swine" [*Iliad* 11.678–9], as many herds of goats and "150 bay horses" [*Iliad* 11.680], most of them with foals). He says that "these were driven to Neleian Pylos, to the city at night" [*Iliad* 11.682–3]. Thus it was during the day that the plundering occurred as well as the routing of those coming to assistance (when he says that he killed Itymoneus [*Iliad* 11.672]), and the return occurred at night, and it was during the night when they came to the city. While [the plunder] was being distributed and the sacrifices were taking place, the Epeians, on the third day, gathered together a large number – foot soldiers and cavalry – and went out against Thryon, situated on the Alpheios River. When the Pylians learned about this, they immediately sent out assistance, and spent the night around the Minyeios River near Arene and arrived at the Alpheios "at midday" [*Iliad* 11.726], that is, at noon. They sacrificed to the gods and spent the night at the river, and engaged in battle immediately at dawn. A spectacular rout took place, and they did not stop pursuing and killing them until they set foot on Bouprasion, "on the

[C352]

Olenian Rock of Aleision, where it is called the Hill, where Athena turned
the people back" [*Iliad* 11.757–8], and farther down: "moreover the Achaians
drove the swift horses back from Bouprasion to Pylos" [*Iliad* 11.759–60].

(29) How could one assume from these things whether Eleian or
Messenian Pylos is meant? In regard to the Eleian, if it were being ravaged
by Herakles, the Epeians were [being ravaged] at the same time, who are
in Eleia. How could those ravaged at the same time and who were kindred
acquire such excessive contempt and arrogance toward those who were
mistreated along with them? How could they overrun and plunder their
own homeland? How could Augeas and Neleus both rule the same peoples
simultaneously if they were enemies, if Neleus were

> owed a great debt in divine Elis: four prize-winning horses with their chariots
> had come for the games, and were to run for a tripod, but Augeas, the lord of
> men, withheld them, sending away the driver [*Iliad* 11.698–702]?

If Neleus lived there, Nestor also ruled there. How could it be that among the
Eleians and Bouprasians "there were four leaders, with ten quick ships following each man, and many Epeians embarked on them" [*Iliad* 2.618–19]? The
territory was also divided into four parts, but Nestor ruled none of them, but
over "those who lived in Pylos and lovely Arene" [*Iliad* 2.591], and those after
them as far as Messene. How could the Epeians, marching forth in turn against
the Pylians, set out toward the Alpheios and Thryon? How, after the battle
took place there and they were routed, could they flee toward Bouprasion?

Moreover, if Herakles had ravaged Messenian Pylos, why would those   [C353]
so far away be so arrogant against them, having had many contracts and
defaulting on them by avoiding them, so that war resulted? How could
Nestor, setting forth to plunder them and driving away so much booty –
both pigs and cattle, none of which could travel quickly or far – have
accomplished the more than a thousand stadia to the Pylos at Koryphasion?
Yet "on the third day" [*Iliad* 11.707] they all came to Thryoessa and the
Alpheios River to besiege the fortress. How could these places belong to those
in power in Messenia, when they were held by the Kaukonians, Triphylians,
and Pisatians? And Gerena or Gerenia (it is recorded both ways) was perhaps
named by certain people for a particular purpose, or possibly the place was
named by chance. In general, since it was established that Messenia was
subject to Menelaos, and the Lakonike was also established as subject to
him – as will be clear later [8.4.1] – and since the Pamisos flows through it, as
does the Neda, but the Alpheios nowhere does ("that which flows in a broad
stream through the Pylian land" [*Iliad* 5.545] which Nestor ruled), how could
an account be believable that places him among foreign men and takes away
from him the catalogued cities, making everything subject to someone else?

(30) It remains to speak about Olympia and the transfer of everything to the Eleians. The sanctuary is in the Pisatis less than 300 stadia distant from Elis. A grove of wild olives lies in front of it, in which the stadium is. The Alpheios flows by, which, rising in Arkadia, flows between west and south into the Triphylian Sea. From the beginning it had its fame because of the oracle of Olympian Zeus. After it failed, the reputation of the sanctuary nonetheless continued and it undertook the growth that we know about through its festival and the Olympic Games, in which the prize was a crown and which were sacred, considered the greatest of all. It was adorned by numerous dedications, set up from throughout Hellas, among which was the Zeus of hammered gold, a dedication of Kypselos the tyrant of Corinth. The greatest of these was the image of Zeus made by Pheidias son of Charmides, an Athenian, of ivory and so large that – although the temple was also exceedingly large – the craftsman seems to have missed the proper proportions, making him seated but almost touching the ceiling with his head, thus giving the impression that if he rose up erect, he would unroof [C354] the temple. Certain ones have recorded the measurements of the image, and Kallimachos [F196] told about it in a certain iambic poem. Panainos the painter, a nephew and colleague of Pheidias, helped him greatly in decorating the image with colors, especially the drapery. Many wonderful paintings that are works of his are visible around the sanctuary. It is recorded about Pheidias that when asked by Panainos what model he was going to use for the image of Zeus, he said that he would make his selection from these words of Homer:

> with his dark brows Kronion nodded, the ambrosial mane of the lord rippled from his immortal head, and he caused great Olympos to quiver. [*Iliad* 1.528–30]

This appears to be an especially nice description, because of the brows and other things, since the Poet challenges the imagination to picture a certain great figure and a great power worthy of Zeus, just as with Hera, saying "she shook on the throne and caused high Olympos to quiver" [*Iliad* 8.199], preserving what is suitable for each. Everything that happened when she moved occurred for Zeus merely by moving through nodding his brows, although his hair was also somewhat affected. It is cleverly said that "he alone has seen, or he alone has shown, the image of the gods."

The Eleians are the particular reason for the magnificence and honor given to the Olympian sanctuary. At the time of the Trojan matter (and even before then) they were not prosperous, because they had been reduced by the Pylians, and later by Herakles, when their king Augeas had been overthrown. The evidence is that they sent only forty ships to Troy, but the Pylians and Nestor ninety. Later, after the return of the Herakleidai, it was the opposite. The Aitolians returned with the Herakleidai under Oxylos and, living with the Epeians because of ancient kinship, enlarged Hollow Elis and took much of the Pisatis, so that Olympia was under them. The Olympic Games were their invention and they celebrated the first Olympiad. One must dismiss the ancient tales about the founding of the sanctuary and the establishment of the games: some saying that it was Herakles (one of the [C355] Idaian Daktyls) who founded both, and others that it was the son of Alkmene and Zeus who was the first to compete and win. Such things are described in many ways and can in no way be believed. It is nearer the truth that until the twenty-sixth Olympiad (from the first) – when Koroibos, an Eleian, won in the stadium race – the Eleians managed both the sanctuary and the games. At the time of the Trojan matter there were no games for which the prize was a crown, or they were not notable (neither these or any of the others that are notable today). Homer does not mention them, although he does [mention] certain other funeral games. Yet some believe that he mentions the Olympic Games when he says that Augeas robbed four prize-winning horses that had come for games [*Iliad* 11.698–9]. They say that the Pisatians did not take part in the Trojan War because they were considered to be sacred to Zeus. But the Pisatis – where Olympia is – was not subject to Augeas at that time, but only Eleia was, and the Olympic Games were not celebrated even once in Elis, but always at Olympia. Yet those just mentioned were clearly in Elis, where the debt was owed ("and he was owed a great debt in divine Elis: four prize-winning horses" [*Iliad* 11.698–9]). These were not ones for which the prize was a crown ("they were to run for a tripod" [*Iliad* 11.700–1]), as was the case there. After the twenty-sixth Olympiad the Pisatians, having received back their homeland, celebrated the games, since they saw that they were esteemed. In later times they were transferred back from the Pisatians to the Eleians and thus the management of the games was also transferred back. The Lakedaimonians, after their final defeat of the Messenians, helped them [the Eleians], who had been their allies, but the Arkadians and the descendants of Nestor did the opposite, having joined with the Messenians in the war. They [the Lakedaimonians] helped them so well that the entire territory as far as Messene was called Eleia, which has survived until today, but nothing more than the names of the Pisatians, Triphylians, and Kaukonians has survived. Moreover, those in sandy Pylos were settled in Lepreon, to gratify the Lepreatians, who had been victorious in war, and they destroyed many other settlements, and exacted tribute from those whom they saw as wishing to act independently.

[C356] (31) The Pisatis first became quite widely known because of its rulers, who were most powerful: Oinomaos and his successor Pelops, and his many sons. Salmoneus is also said to have reigned there; at any rate, one of the eight cities into which the Pisatis is divided is called Salmone. Because of this, as well as because of the Olympian sanctuary, the territory has been exceedingly widely reputed. But one should listen to the ancient reports with a particular lack of confidence, because the more recent ones have new opinions about many things, and even say the opposite, such as that Augeas ruled Pisatis, but Oinomaos and Salmoneus were over Eleia, and some combine the peoples into one. One must follow what is agreed to by most. There is no agreement on the etymology of "Pisatis": some have it from the city of Pisa, the homonym of a spring. The spring was called Pisa, like "pistra" ["drinking trough"] or "potistra" ["watering place"], and they show that the city was located on a height between two mountains, Ossa and Olympos, with the same name as those in Thessaly. Some say that there was no city of Pisa (it would have been one of the eight) but only a spring, now called Bisa, near Kikysion, the largest of the eight cities. Stesichoros [F263] calls the territory – named Pisa – a city, just as the Poet [calls] Lesbos the city of Makar [*Iliad* 24.544], and Euripides in his *Ion*, "Euboia, a certain city neighboring Athens" [294], and in his *Rhadamanthys*, "who hold the Euboian land, a neighboring city" [F16], as well as Sophokles in his *Mysians*: "the entirety is called Asia, stranger, but the city of the Mysians is named Mysia" [F411].

(32) Salmone is near a homonymous spring from which the Enipeus flows. It empties into the Alpheios and is today called the Barnichios. They say that Tyro fell in love ("who loved a river, the divine Enipeus" [*Odyssey* 11.238]). Her father Salmoneus ruled there, as Euripides says in his *Aiolos* [F14]. They write the one in Thessaly as Elipeus: it flows from Othrys and receives the Apidanos, which comes down from Pharsalos. Near Salmone is Herakleia, also one of the eight, about forty stadia distant from Olympia and situated on the Kytherios River, where the sanctuary of the Ioniadian Nymphs is, who are believed to cure diseases with the waters.

[C357] Near Olympia is Harpina, also one of the eight, through which the Parthenias River flows, as one goes to Pheraia. Pheraia is in Arkadia, situated above the Dymaia, Bouprasion, and Elis, which means to the north of the Pisatis. There is also Kikysion, of the eight, and also Dyspontion, lying in the plain on the road from Elis to Olympia. It is abandoned, and most of them went to Epidamnos and Apollonia. Pholoe, an Arkadian mountain, lies above and very near to Olympia, so that its foothills are in the Pisatis. All of the Pisatis and most of Triphylia border on Arkadia, and because of this most of the Pylian territory mentioned in the *Catalogue* appears to be Arkadian, although those who are knowledgeable do not say this, for the Arkadian boundary is the Erymanthos, one of the rivers emptying into the Alpheios, and these territories are situated on the outer side of it.

(33) Ephoros [F115] says that Aitolos, after he had been driven out of Eleia into Aitolia by Salmoneus, king of the Pisatians and the Epeians, named the territory after himself and combined the population into one city. His descendant Oxylos, a friend of the Herakleidai around Temenos, led them on the road going down to the Peloponnesos, distributed the territory that was hostile to them, and made proposals about the acquisition of the territory. In return he received the favor of going back to Eleia, his ancestral land. He collected an army and went from Aitolia against the Epeians who held Elis. The Epeians met them with weapons and when the forces were evenly matched Pyraichmes the Aitolian and Degmenos the Epeian came together in single combat, according to the ancient custom of the Hellenes. Degmenos had a bow, without armor, and believed that through his skill in archery he could easily overcome a hoplite, but the other – when he understood the trick – had a slingshot and a pouch of stones, for it happened that the idea of a slingshot had only recently been invented by the Aitolians. The slingshot was able to throw farther, Degmenos fell, and the Aitolians drove out the Epeians and took possession. They also undertook the management of the sanctuary of Olympia, which the Aitolians had held. Because of the friendship of Oxylos with the Herakleidai, it was easily agreed by all under oath that Eleia would be sacred to Zeus, and that [C358] whoever invaded that territory under arms would be under a curse, as well as those who did not come in force to assist. Thus those who later founded the city of the Eleians allowed it to be unwalled, and those going through the territory with an army give over their weapons and receive them back after going beyond its boundaries. Iphitos established the Olympic Games as the Eleians were now sacred. Because of this the people increased in number, for others were always at war with one another, but they alone had complete peace, not only themselves but the foreigners among them. Thus they became the most populous of all. Pheidon the Argive, being tenth from Temenos, surpassed in power everyone of his time, because of which he recovered the entire inheritance of Temenos (which had been broken up into several parts), and also invented the measurements called Pheidonian (weights, and coinage minted from silver and other [metals]). In addition to these things, he attacked the cities that had been taken by Herakles and considered himself worthy of celebrating the games that he had established, including the Olympian. Thus he forcibly invaded and celebrated them

himself, as the Eleians, having no weapons, could not prevent it both because of the peace and because the others were subject to his dominion. The Eleians did not record this occurrence, but because of it they obtained weapons and began to help themselves, with the assistance of the Lakedaimonians, who either envied them because of the prosperity resulting from the peace, or believed that they would have allies in destroying Pheidon, who had deprived them of the hegemony of the Peloponnesos which they had previously possessed. Thus they did help in destroying Pheidon and assisting the Eleians in organizing the Pisatis and Triphylia.

Today the entire voyage along the coast of Eleia, without running into the gulfs, is 1,200 stadia. That is it about Eleia.

Part 4: Messenia

(1) Messenia is contiguous with Eleia, and it mostly inclines toward the south and the Libyan Sea. At the time of the Trojan matter it was classified as subject to Menelaos, being a part of the Lakonike, and was called Messene. The city now named Messene, whose akropolis is Ithome, had [C359] not yet been founded. After the death of Menelaos and when those who had succeeded to the Lakonike had become weakened, the Neleids ruled Messenia. At the time of the return of the Herakleidai and the contemporary division of the territory, Melanthos was king of the Messenians, who were autonomous. Formerly they had been subject to Menelaos, as is indicated by the seven cities on the Messenian Gulf and the adjoining Asinaian [Gulf] – named after Messenian Asine – that Agamemnon offered to give Achilleus:

> Kardamyle, Enope, grassy Hire, divine Pherai, Antheia deep in meadows, beautiful Aipeia, and Pedasos rich in vines. [*Iliad* 9.150–2]

He would not have offered what was subject neither to himself nor his brother. The Poet makes it clear that those from Pherai joined Menelaos in the expedition [*Iliad* 5.541–60], and in the Lakonian Catalogue he includes <Oitylos>,[9] situated on the Messenian Gulf [*Iliad* 2.585]. Messenia is after Triphylia. There is a cape common to both, and after it is Koryphasion. A mountain, Aigaleon, lies seven stadia above it and the sea.

(2) Ancient Messenian Pylos was a city at the foot of Aigaleon, but when it was torn down some of them lived at Koryphasion. The Athenians refounded it as a border fortress against the Lakedaimonians when they sailed the second

---

[9] There is a gap of several letters, but "Oitylos" seems obvious from the citation of Homer.

time to Sikelia under Eurymedon and Sophokles. Messenian Kyparissia is also here, and[10] . . . and the island lying offshore near Pylos called Sphagia (also called Sphakteria), where the Lakedaimonians lost through capture 300 of their men, who were besieged by the Athenians and forced to surrender. Off this coast in the open sea lie two islands of the Kyparissians, called the Strophades, about 400 stadia distant from the mainland in the Libyan and Southern Seas. Thoukydides [4.3] says that this Pylos was the seaport of the Messenians, 400 [stadia] distant from Sparta.

(3) Next is Methone. They say that this is what the Poet calls Pedasos, one of the seven that Agamemnon offered to Achilleus. Here Agrippa, during the Aktian war, after taking the place by sea, put to death Bogos [II], the Maurousian king, who belonged to the faction of Antonius.

(4) Next to Methone is Akritas, the beginning of the Messenian Gulf. It is also called the Asinaian, from Asine, the first town on the gulf, which has [C360] the same name as the Hermionian one. This is the beginning of the gulf at the west, and the east is called Thyrides, which is the border of the Lakonike of today, at Kinaithion and Tainaron. In between, beginning at Thyrides, is Oitylos – called by some Boitylos – then Leuktron, a settlement of the Leuktrians in Boiotia. Then there is Kardamyle, located on a fortified rock, then Pharai, which borders on Thouria and Gerena, the place from which Nestor, they say, was called Gerenian, because he was saved there, as I have previously said [8.3.7]. In the Gerenia a sanctuary of Trikkaian Asklepios is visible, a copy of the one in Thessalian Trikke. It is said that Pelops founded Leuktron, Charadra, and Thalamai (now called Boiotoi) when he gave his sister Niobe to Amphion and brought certain people from Boiotia. Near Pharai is the outlet of the Nedon, which flows through the Lakonike and is different from the Neda. There is a notable sanctuary of Athena Nedousia, and a temple of Athena Nedousia at Poiaessa, named after some place called Nedon, from which they say Teleklos founded Poiaessa, Echeiai, and Tragion.

(5) Of the seven cities that were promised to Achilleus, I have spoken about Kardamyle, Pharai, and Pedasos. Some say that Enope is Pellana, others that it is some place around Kardamyle, and others that it is Gerenia. Hire is visible near the mountain near Arkadian Megalopolis, on the route to Andania, which I said [8.3.6] was called Oichalia by the Poet. Others say that it is what is today called Mesola, which reaches down to the gulf between Taÿgetos and Messenia. Aipeia ["Sheer"] is called Thouria today, which I said borders Pharai. It is situated on a high hill, from which its name

---

[10] There is a gap of about nine letters.

comes. From Thouria is the Thouriates Gulf, on which there was one small city, named Rhion, opposite Tainaron. Some say that Antheia is Thouria, and that Aipeia is Methone, but others that Asine, lying in between, is most properly of the Messenian cities called "deep in meadows" [*Iliad* 9.151]. On its sea is the city of Korone, which some say the Poet called Pedasos. "All [are]

[C361]   near to the sea" [*Iliad* 9.153], with Kardamyle on it, Pharai five stadia away (with a summer anchorage), and the others varying distances from the sea.

(6) The Pamisos River empties near Korone, in about the middle of the gulf. This [city] is on its right, as well as those after it, of which the farthest to the west are Pylos and Kyparissia, with Erana in the middle, which some wrongly believe formerly to have been called Arene. On its left are Thouria and Pharai. It is the largest of the rivers inside the Isthmos, although it [flows] no more than a hundred stadia from its sources, flowing with an abundance of water through the Messenian plain, which is called the Makaria. The river is located fifty stadia from the present city of the Messenians. There is another Pamisos, a small torrent, that flows near Lakonian Leuktron, over which the Messenians sought judgement against the Lakedaimonians at the time of Philippos [II]. I have already spoken about the Pamisos that some call the Amathos [8.3.1].

(7) Ephoros [F116] says that Kresphontes, when he took Messene, divided it into five cities, and since Stenyklaros was in the middle and in the best part of the territory, it was made the royal residence. He sent kings to the others – Pylos, Rhion, Mesola, and Hyameitis – and provided all the Messenians equal rights with the Dorians. This irritated the Dorians, so he changed his mind and acknowledged only Stenyklaros as a city and brought all the Dorians together into it.

(8) The city of the Messenians is similar to Corinth. Above both cities lies a high and sheer mountain enclosed by a common wall, so that it is used as an akropolis. One is called Ithome, the other Acrocorinth. Demetrios the Pharian seems to have spoken suitably to Philippos [V] the son of Demetrios in recommending that he acquire both cities if he desired the Peloponnesos, saying that "if you take both horns you will hold down the cow," with the horns meaning Ithome and Acrocorinth and the cow the Peloponnesos. Thus because of their opportune location these cities have regularly been disputed: Corinth was razed but the Romans rebuilt it again, and Messene was destroyed by the Lakedaimonians but the Thebans – as well as, afterward, Philippos [II] the son of Amyntas [III] – restored it. Both akropoleis remained uninhabited.

[C362]   (9) The sanctuary of Artemis at Limnai, where the Messenians are believed to have committed an outrage against maidens who had come to the sacrifice, lies on the boundary of the Lakonike and Messenia, where both held common festivals and sacrifices. After the outrage and the failure of the Messenians to give justice, they say that the war occurred. The Limnaion in Sparta, a sanctuary of Artemis, was named after this Limnai.

(10) More frequently, they went to war because of the revolts of the Messenians. Tyrtaios [F8] says in his poem that the first acquisition was in the time of his father's fathers, and the second when they chose the Argives, Arkadians, Eleians, and Pisatians as allies and then revolted. The Arkadians provided Aristokrates, king of Orchomenos, as commander, and the Pisatians Pantaleon son of Omphalion. He [Tyrtaios] says that at this time he himself commanded the Lakedaimonians in the war, for he says in his elegy titled *Eunomia* that he came from there:

> Kronion, the spouse of beautifully crowned Hera, Zeus himself, gave this
> city to the Herakleidai, with whom I abandoned windy Erineos and came to
> the broad island of Pelops. [F2]

Either the elegy must be set aside, or Philochoros [F215] cannot be trusted when he says that he [Tyrtaios] was an Athenian from Aphidna, as well as Kallisthenes [F24] and several others, who say that he came from Athens when the Lakedaimonians required him, because an oracle enjoined them to obtain a commander from the Athenians. Thus the second war was in the time of Tyrtaios, but they say that a third and fourth also occurred, in which the Messenians were defeated.

The voyage all around Messenia, going into the gulfs, is about 800 stadia.

(11) But I am going beyond the rule of moderation in pursuing such a number of accounts about a territory that is largely abandoned. The Lakonike is also lacking in men, judging by its ancient population, for other than Sparta there remain only small cities, about thirty in number, yet they say that in antiquity it was called "Hekatompolis" ["Hundred Cities"], and because of this they held an annual Hekatombaia.

Part 5:   Lakonia

(1) Nevertheless, after the Messenian Gulf there is the Lakonikan, between Tainaron and Maleai, which bends slightly from the south toward the east. Thyrides is on the Messenian Gulf 130 stadia from Tainaron, a precipitous cliff that is exposed to the currents. Taÿgetos lies above it, a high and steep   [C363] mountain that is a short distance above the sea, adjoining the Arkadian foothills on its northern portion, in such a way that a hollow is left in between, where Messenia borders on the Lakonike. Sparta lies below Taÿgetos in the

interior, as well as Amyklai – where there is a sanctuary of Apollo – and
Pharis. The site of the city [Sparta] is in a somewhat hollow place, and
although it is surrounded by mountains, no part of it is marshy, yet its
suburb, called Limnai ["Marshes"], was marshy in antiquity. The sanctuary
of Dionysos in Limnai was on damp land, although it is now situated on dry
ground. Cape Tainaron is located in the gulf of the coast, having a sanctuary
of Poseidon situated in a grove. A cave is nearby, through which, according
to the myth, Kerberos was brought up from Hades by Herakles. From here
the sea crossing to the south to Cape Phykous in the Kyrenaika is 3,000
stadia, and to the west to Pachynos, the promontory of Sikelia, is 4,600
(although some say 4,000). East to Maleai is 670, following the gulfs, and to
Onougnathos, a low peninsula somewhat within Maleai, it is 520. Kythera
lies in front of it, 40 stadia away, an island with a good harbor and having a
city of the same name, which Eurykles, the ruler of Lakedaimonia in our
time, acquired as his own property. Lying around it are a number of islets,
some near and others a little farther away. The shortest voyage to Cape
Korykos in Crete is 250 stadia.[II]

(2) After Tainaron, on the voyage to Onougnathos and Maleai, there is
the city of Amathous, and then Asine and Gytheion, the seaport of Sparta,
situated 240 stadia away. The anchorage was dug out, they say. Then there
is the Eurotas, which empties between Gytheion and Akraiai. For a while
there is the voyage along the shore, for 240 stadia, and then a marshy area
lying above the village of Helos, which formerly was a city, as Homer says,
"they held Amyklai and Helos, a city on the sea" [*Iliad* 2.584]. They say that
it is a foundation of Heleios, son of Perseus. There is the plain called Leuke,
and then a city situated on a peninsula, Kyparissia, which has a harbor, then
[C364]   Onougnathos, which has a harbor, then the city of Boia, and then Maleai.
From Onougnathos to here is 150 stadia. There is also a city of Asopos in the
Lakonike.

(3) They say that of the places catalogued by Homer [*Iliad* 2.581–5],
Messe is nowhere to be seen, and that Messoa was not a part of this region
but of Sparta, as were Limnaion and Thornax. Some take it as a cutting
off of Messene, for as I have said [8.3.29], it was a part of the Lakonike.
Examples used by the Poet include *kri, do, maps*, and also "the heroes
Automedon and Alkimos" [*Iliad* 24.474] instead of Alkimedon. Hesiod
[F279] says *bri* for *brithy* and *briaron*, Sophokles [F1086] and Ion [F16] *rha*
for *rhadion*, Epicharmos [F113, 231] *li* for *lian* and "Syrako" for "Syrakousai."
Empedokles has "one vision [*ops*] arises from both" [F152] for *opis*, and

---

[II] The number is far too small; "950" has been suggested.

Antimachos has "the sacred vision [*ops*] of Eleusinian Demeter" [F79] and *alphi* for *alphiton* [F145]. Euphorion [F153] says *hel* for *helos* and Philitas [F18] has "the maidservants brought white wool [*eri*] to put in baskets" for *erion*. Aratos [*Phainomena* 155] says "the rudders [*peda*] toward the wind," for *pedalia*. Simmias [F10] has "Dodo" for "Dodona."

The remainder named by the Poet have either been destroyed, remain only in traces, or have had their names changed, such as Augeiai [*Iliad* 2.583] to Aigaiai (for the one in Lokris no longer survives). Regarding Las, it is reported that the Dioskouroi once took it by siege, from which they were called the Lapersai ["The Las Destroyers"]. Sophokles says somewhere "by the two Lapersai, and third by the Eurotas, by the gods in Argos and around Sparta" [F957].

(4) Ephoros [F117] says that the Herakleidai Eurysthenes and Prokles took possession of the Lakonike, and divided the land into six parts and built cities. One of the portions, Amyklai, was selected to be given to the man who betrayed the Lakonike to them, and who had persuaded the one possessing it to depart under treaty with the Achaians for Ionia. They designated Sparta as a royal residence for themselves and sent kings to the others. These were allowed to accept as fellow settlers any foreigners who so wished, because of the sparsity of population. They used Las as a naval station because of its good harbor, Aigys as a fortress against their enemies, who bordered all around them, and Pharis as a . . . because it was safe against both those inside and outside. All those neighboring were subject to the Spartiates yet had equal privileges, both in the government [C365] and public offices. Agis [I] the son of Eurysthenes took away their equal privileges and ordered them to pay contributions to Sparta. They obeyed, except for the Heleians – those in Helos, called the Helots – who revolted and by force were taken in war and judged to be considered as slaves. Their owners could not set them free or sell them beyond the borders. This was called the War Against the Helots. The later Helot system that persisted until the Roman supremacy was essentially introduced by those around Agis [I], for the Lakedaimonians possessed them in the manner of state slaves, providing them certain places to live and particular public duties.

(5) Concerning the government of the Lakonians and the changes that occurred among them, one might pass over most things because they are known, but there are certain matters worth remembering. They say that the Phthiotian Achaians came down with Pelops into the Peloponnesos and lived in the Lakonike. They excelled so much in virtue that the Peloponnesos – which had been called Argos for a long time – was then called Achaian Argos, a name not only for the Peloponnesos but particularly for the Lakonike

("Where was Menelaos? Was he not in Achaian Argos?" [*Odyssey* 3.249, 251]). This is accepted by some as "was he not in the Lakonike?" At the time of the return of the Herakleidai, when Philonomos gave the territory to the Dorians, they migrated from the Lakonike to Ionia and what is now called Achaia. I will speak of them in my Achaian section [8.7.1]. At first those who possessed the Lakonike were moderate, but when the government was turned over to Lykourgos they so far surpassed the others that they alone of the Hellenes ruled both the land and the sea, and they continued ruling until the Thebans deprived them of the hegemony, and immediately thereafter the Makedonians. They did not yield to them completely, but preserved their autonomy and always continued a struggle for primacy against the other Hellenes and the Makedonian kings. When the latter had been overthrown by the Romans, they committed some slight offense against the commanders sent by the Romans, because at that time they were ruled by tyrants and had a wretched government, but when they recovered they were especially honored

[C366]　and remained free, providing nothing other than friendly public services. But recently Eurykles caused trouble among them, seemingly having abused the friendship of Caesar beyond appropriateness for the sake of his own power. The disturbance quickly ceased, with him retiring to his fate, and his son abandoning all such ambitions. It happened that the Eleutherolakonians ["Free Lakonians"] received a certain type of constitution, since those living in the vicinity, as well as the Helots, were the first to side with the Romans, when the Spartans were ruled by tyrants. Hellanikos [F116] says that Eurysthenes and Prokles drew up the government, but Ephoros [F118] in criticism says that he nowhere mentioned Lykourgos, and that he attributes his deeds to those to whom they do not belong. At any rate, a sanctuary was erected only to Lykourgos and there are sacrifices to him each year. Yet those who were the founders have not been allowed to have their descendants called Eurysthenids and Prokleids, but Agiads after Agis [I] the son of Eurysthenes, and Eurypontids after Eurypon the son of Prokles. They held power justly, but the former accepted foreign people and held power through them. Thus they were not acknowledged as First Leaders, which is given to all founders. Pausanias, a Eurypontid, who was banished by the other house, while in exile put together a treatise on the laws of Lykourgos (who was of the house that banished him), in which he mentions [T3] the oracles that were given to him about most of the panegyrics.

(6) Concerning the nature of the places, both this and the Messenian, one should accept what Euripides [F727e] says about them, for he says that the Lakonike has

> much that is arable, but it is not easy to work, for it is hollow, with mountains encircling it, rough, and difficult for enemies to invade,

but that Messenia is

> rich in fine fruit, watered by a myriad of streams, most abundant in good pasture for cattle and sheep, and neither very wintry in the wintry blasts nor excessively hot due to the four-horse chariots of Helios,

and below, about the lots that the Herakleidai cast for the territory, he says that the first gave "authority over the earth of Lakaine, a poor land," and the second over Messene, "whose excellence is greater than words can say." Tyrtaios [F5] speaks similarly. He [Euripides] also says that the boundary between the Lakonike and Messenia is "the Pamisos, rushing to the sea," but this cannot be granted, for it flows through the middle of Messenia and nowhere touches the Lakonike of today. He is also not correct when he says that Messenia is "far away for sailors," for, like Lakonike, it lies on the sea. Furthermore, he does not have the correct boundary of Elis ("far away, after crossing the river, lies Elis, the neighbor of Zeus"). If he wishes to speak about the current Eleia, which borders on Messenia, the Pamisos does not touch it, just as it does not [touch] Lakonike, for, as I have said, it flows through the middle of Messenia. If he is talking about ancient Hollow [Elis], he departs much farther from the truth, for after crossing the river there is still much of Messenia, and then all of the Kaukonians and Messenians who were called Triphylians. Then there is the Pisatis and Olympia, and then Elis, after 300 stadia. [C367]

(7) Some write "Lakedaimon, the Ketoessan" [*Iliad* 2.581, *Odyssey* 4.1], and others "Kaietaessan." One must ask how to take "Ketoessan" and whether it is from "sea monster" (*ketos*) or merely "large," which seems more believable. Some take *kaietaessan* as "full of mint" (*kalaminthode*), and others say that the fissures from earthquakes are *kaietoi* (the Kaietas is the prison of the Lakedaimonians, as it is a sort of cave). Some prefer to say *kooi* for these cavities, from which comes "mountain-bred [*oreskooisin*] wild beasts" [*Iliad* 1.268]. The Lakonike is subject to earthquakes, and some have recorded that peaks of Taÿgetos have broken away. There are quarries of costly stone – the ancient ones of the Tainarian at Tainaron – and recently some have opened a large mine on Taÿgetos, with the considerable cost supported by the extravagance of the Romans.

(8) The territory and city are called by the same name, Lakedaimon, as Homer makes clear (I say territory, including Messenia). This is clear when he speaks of the bows: "beautiful things that a friend had given him when he was in Lakedaimon, Iphitos Eurytides" [*Odyssey* 21.13–14, variant], and then he adds "both came together in Messene at the home of Ortilochos" [*Odyssey* 21.15–16], meaning the territory of which Messenia was a part. It was of no difference to him whether he said in general "had given him when he was in Lakedaimon" or "both came together in Messene." That Pherai is

the home of Ortilochos is clear from "they came to Pherai, the home of Diokles, son of Ortilochos" [*Odyssey* 3.488–9] – these are Telemachos and Peisistratos – and Pherai is in Messenia. But when, after Telemachos and those with him set forth from Pherai, "they shook the yoke," he says, for "the entire day" [*Odyssey* 3.486], and then says "the sun set . . . and they came to hollow Lakedaimon, the Ketoessan, and then went to the home of [C368] Menelaos" [*Odyssey* 3.497–4.1], the city must be understood, for otherwise it is clear that he is speaking of their arrival at Lakedaimon from Lakedaimon. It is not believable, moreover, that the residence of Menelaos was not in Sparta, for if it were not there, Telemachos would not have said "I am going to Sparta and Pylos" [*Odyssey* 2.214, 359]. But it seems contrary to this that the epithets of the territory[12] . . . unless, by Zeus, one were to concede that it is something poetic[13] . . . and have Messene not as a Lakonian city and not subject to Nestor, not even organized by itself in the *Catalogue* and not sharing in the expedition.

Part 6: The Argolid and Corinthia

(1) After Maleai there is the Argolic Gulf, and then the Hermionic. The former is as far as Skyllaion, sailing facing the east, toward the Kyklades, and the latter is more toward the east, as far as Aigina and the Epidauria. The first part of the Argolid is held by the Lakonians and the remainder by the Argives. Delion is among that [held by] the Lakonians, with a sanctuary to Apollo having the same name as the Boiotian one, and the fortress of Minoa, which has the same name as the one in the Megaris, and Limera Epidauros, as Artemidoros says. Apollodoros [of Athens, F199] records that it is near Kythera, and says that it was shortened and contracted to Limera, the name changed from Limenera (because it has a good harbor). The Lakonian coast, beginning immediately from Maleai, is rough for some distance, but there are anchorages and harbors. The remainder of the coast has good harbors with many islets lying offshore, but not worthy of mentioning.

(2) Prasiai and Temenion are Argive. The latter is where Temenos is buried, and still before it is the territory through which the river called the Lerne flows, with the same name as the marsh in which the myth of the Hydra occurred. Temenion is above the sea, 26 stadia distant from Argos. From Argos to the Heraion it is 40, and from there to Mykenai is 10. After Temenion is Nauplia, the Argive naval station, whose etymology is

---

[12] There is a gap of about nine letters.   [13] There is a gap of about three letters.

because ships can sail to it. Because of this, they say, the matter of Nauplios and his sons has been fabricated by those more recent, for Homer would not have failed to record that Palamedes had shown such wisdom and comprehension and had been unjustly murdered, and that Nauplios had caused the destruction of so many men around Kaphereus. But in addition to its mythical character, the genealogy is in error in terms of its chronology. If one grants that he was the son of Poseidon, how could the son of Amymone still be alive at the time of the Trojan matter? Next after [C369] Nauplia are the caves and labyrinths constructed within them that are called Kyklopean.

(3) Then there are other places, and next the Hermionic Gulf, and since Homer assigns this to the Argeia, not for me[14] . . . portion of the circuit. It begins at the small town of Asine. Then there are Hermione and Troizen, and, as one sails along the coast, the island of Kalauria lying off it, which has a circuit of 30 stadia and is separated from the mainland by a 4-stadia strait.

(4) Then there is the Saronic Gulf. Some call it the open sea, because of which it is also called the Saronic Sea. It is the entire strait from the Hermionic Sea and that around the Isthmos which touches the Myrtoan and Cretan Seas. Epidauros and the island off it, Aigina, belong to the Saronic. Then there is Kenchreai, the naval station of the Corinthians on the east side, and then the harbor of Schoinous, after sailing 45 stadia. From Maleai it is about 1,800 stadia. Near Schoinous is the Diolkos, at the narrowest part of the Isthmos, where the sanctuary of Isthmian Poseidon is. But let us postpone this for now – for it is outside of the Argeia – and take up again the examination of the Argeia.

(5) First, let it be said in how many ways the term "Argos" is used by the Poet, both by itself and with the epithet, calling it Achaian Argos, Iasos, "horsy," Pelasgian, or "horse-pasturing." The city is called Argos ("Argos and Sparta" [*Iliad* 4.52], or "those holding Argos and . . . Tiryns" [*Iliad* 2.559]), as is the Peloponnesos ("in our home in Argos" [*Iliad* 1.30], for the city was not his home). It is also the entirety of Hellas, for he calls all of them Argives, as well as Danaans and Achaians. He defines identical names through epithets, calling Thessaly "Pelasgian Argos" ("now all those living in Pelasgian Argos" [*Iliad* 2.681]), and the Peloponnesos "Achaian" ("if we were to come to Achaian Argos" [*Iliad* 9.141, 283] or "was he not in Achaian Argos?" [*Odyssey* 3.251]). Here he indicates that the Peloponnesians were particularly called Achaians with another meaning. He calls the Peloponnesos "Iasos Argos": "if all the Achaians in Iasos Argos could see"

---

[14] There is a gap of about ten letters.

[C370] [*Odyssey* 18.246] Penelope, she would have had more suitors, for it is not probable that they were from all Hellas but only nearby. But he says "horse pasturing" and "horsy" in a general sense.

(6) There is disagreement about "Hellas," "Hellenes," and "Panhellenes." Thoukydides says (1.3.3) that the Poet nowhere speaks of barbarians "because the Hellenes had not yet been separated off to acquire a single contrasting name." Apollodoros [of Athens, F200] says that only those in Thessaly were called Hellenes ("they were called Myrmidons and Hellenes" [*Iliad* 2.684]), and that, nevertheless, Hesiod [F78] and Archilochos [F102] already knew that they were all called Hellenes and Panhellenes. The former, concerning the Protides, says that the Panhellenes were their suitors, and the latter that "the woes of the Panhellenes came together on Thasos." But others disagree with this, for he [Homer] does speak of barbarians, saying that the Karians are "barbarophonoi" [*Iliad* 2.867], and, about all the Hellenes: "the man whose fame is wide throughout Hellas and the middle of Argos" [*Odyssey* 1.344], and again: "do you not wish to be nourished throughout Hellas and the middle of Argos?" [*Odyssey* 15.80].

(7) The Argive city is situated mostly in flat territory but has a citadel called Larisa, a hill reasonably well fortified with a sanctuary to Zeus. The Inachos flows near the city, a torrential river whose sources are in Lyrkeion, a mountain on the borders of Arkadia. The mythological sources are fabrications of the poets, as has been said [6.2.4]. It is also a fabrication that "Argos was waterless but the Danaans made it well-watered" [Hesiod F76a], as the place is in a hollow, rivers flow through it, and there are marshes, lakes, and many wells that provide abundant water on the surface. Many find fault in this passage: "there is dishonor when I go to Argos, great in thirst" [*polydipsion*] [*Iliad* 4.171]. This is used in place of "much longed-for" [*polypotheton*], or, omitting the delta, "much destroyed" [*polyipsion*], like "the much-destroyed [*polyphthoron*] home of the Pelopidai there" [Sophokles, *Elektra* 10]. *Proïapsai, iapsai,* and *ipsesthai* indicate a type of destruction or damage: "now he is making an attempt, but soon he will oppress [*ipsetai*] the sons of the Achaians" [*Iliad* 2.193], "afflict [*iapsei*] her fair complexion" [*Odyssey* 2.376], "sent away [*proïapsen*] to Hades" [*Iliad* 1.3]. Moreover, he is not speaking of the city of Argos (for he was not about to return there) but the Peloponnesos, which presumably is not thirsty. With the delta, one accepts the transposition and coalescing of syllables with *de*, so that it is "there is dishonor when I go to Argos [*Argosde*], great in thirst" [*polydipsion*]
[C371] for "I go to Argos, great in thirst" [*polyipsion*] instead of "to Argos" [*eis Argos*].

(8) The Inachos is one [river] that flows through the Argeia. There is another river in the Argeia, the Erasinos, which has its beginning at

Stymphalos in Arkadia, in the lake there that is called the Stymphalian, which in mythology is the location of the birds – called the Stymphalides – that were driven out by the arrows and drums of Herakles. They say that the river sinks below the ground and, coming forth in the Argeia, flows into the plain. The Erasinos is also called the Arsinos. There is another of the same name that flows from Arkadia to the seashore around Boura, and there are others in Eretria and in Attika around Brauron. A certain spring, Amymone, is visible around Lerne. Lake Lerne is in the Argeia and the Mykenaia, and is where the story of the Hydra is told. Because of the cleansing that occurred there a certain proverb arose, "Lerne of evils." It is agreed that the territory is well-watered, and although the city is situated in a waterless area, it has an abundance of wells. These are attributed to the Danaids, as they discovered them, from which this phrase comes: "Argos was waterless but the Danaans made Argos well-watered" [Hesiod F76a]. Four of the wells were accepted as sacred and are especially honored . . . introducing a lack of water among abundance.

(9) Danaos is said to have settled the Argive akropolis. He seems to have so surpassed those previously holding power in this region that, according to Euripides "he made it the law throughout Hellas that those formerly called Pelasgiotes were to be Danaans" [F228]. His tomb is in the center of the Argive agora, called Palinthos. I think it was the reputation of this city that prepared the Pelasgiotes and Danaans, as well as the Argives and the rest of the Hellenes, to be called after it. Those more recent say Iasidians, Iasos Argos, Apia, and Apidonians. Homer does not say Apidonians, but has *apia* for those rather far away. [To show] that he says Argos for Peloponnesos one can add the following: "Argive Helen" [*Iliad* 6.323, *Odyssey* 4.296], "Ephyra is a city in the recess of Argos" [*Iliad* 6.152], "the middle of Argos" [*Odyssey* 1.344; 4.726, 816; 15.80], and "he would be lord of many islands and all Argos" [*Iliad* 2.108]. Among those more recent the plain is said [C372] to be Argos, but not once by Homer. But they believe that this is more Makedonian or Thessalian.

(10) After the descendants of Danaos succeeded to power in Argos, and the Amythaonidians, who had come from the Pisatis and Triphylia, had mixed in with them, one should not be astonished if, since they were kinsmen, they first divided the territory into two kingdoms, so that the two cities in which they held power – Argos and Mykenai – were created as metropoleis (although near to each other, situated less than fifty stadia apart) and that the Heraion near Mykenai would be a sanctuary common to both. In it are images by Polykleitos, in technique the most beautiful of all but in cost and size inferior to those of Pheidias. In the beginning Argos

was more powerful, but then Mykenai became greater because of the migration of the Pelopidai there. Everything devolved onto the sons of Atreus, and Agamemnon, the elder, took the office, and through fortune and ability acquired much of the territory – in addition to what he already possessed – adding the Lakonike to the Mykenaia. Menelaos had the Lakonike and Agamemnon took Mykenai and the territory as far as Corinth, Sikyon, and what was then called that of the Ionians and Aigialeans but later of the Achaians. After the Trojan matter, when the rule of Agamemnon had been destroyed, Mykenai decreased, especially after the return of the Herakleidai. When they took possession of the Peloponnesos they expelled its former masters, so that those who held Argos also held Mykenai as a common unit. In later times it was levelled by the Argives, so that today no trace of the Mykenaian city is to be found. Since Mykenai experienced this, one should not wonder if some that were catalogued as subject to Argos have also disappeared by now. The *Catalogue* has the following:

> those holding Argos, and high-walled Tiryns, Hermione and Asine occupying a deep gulf, Troizen, Eïones, and Epidauros rich in vines, and the Achaian youths who hold Aigina and Mases. [*Iliad* 2.559–62]

Of these Argos has been discussed, and one must speak about the others.

[C373] (11) It seems that Proitos used Tiryns as a base of operations, and it was walled by the Kyklopes, who were seven in number and were called "Belly Hands," because they were nourished by their craft. They came by summons from Lykia. Perhaps the caves around Nauplia and their constructions are named after them. The akropolis is Likymna, named after Likymnios. It is about twelve stadia distant from Nauplia, and is deserted, and so is neighboring Midea, different from the Boiotian one, which is Mideia, like Pronoia, and the other Midea, like Tegea. Bordering on it is Prosymna, also deserted, with a sanctuary of Hera. The Argives laid waste to most of these because of their disobedience. The inhabitants of Tiryns went to Epidauros, those from Hermione to Halieis, as it is called, and those from Asine – a village in the Argeia near Nauplia – were resettled in Messenia by the Lakedaimonians, where there is a town with the same name as Argolic Asine. The Lakedaimonians, as Theopompos [F383] says, obtained much that belonged to others and settled on it those who had fled to them and were received[15] . . . from Nauplia withdrew there.

(12) Hermione is not an insignificant city. Its coast is held by the so-called Halieis ["Fishermen"], certain men who are busy with the sea. It is common

---

[15] There is a gap of about six letters.

talk that the descent to Hades among the Hermionians is a short cut, which is why they do not put passage-money with the dead.

(13) They say that <Hermione and> Asine were dwelling places of the Dryopians, whether – since they were from the regions around the Spercheios – they settled here from the Arkadian Dryops, as Aristotle [F482] said, or they were driven out by Herakles from Doris near Parnassos. They say that the Skyllaion at Hermione was named after Skylla the daughter of Nisos, who, out of love for Minos, betrayed Nisaia and, they say, was thrown into the sea by him, and happened to be cast up by the waves here and buried. Eïones was a certain village that the Mykenaians depopulated and made into a naval station[16] . . . is no longer a naval station.

(14) Troizen is sacred to Poseidon, after whom it was once called Poseidonia. It is 15 stadia above the sea and is also not an insignificant city. Lying off its harbor – named Pogon – is Kalauria, an islet with a circumference of about 130 stadia. Here there was an asylum sacred to Poseidon, and they say that this god made an exchange with Leto, giving her Delos in return for Kalauria, and also one with Apollo, giving him Pytho in return for Tainaron. Ephoros also provides the oracle: "for you it is the same to possess either Delos or Kalaureia, most holy Pytho or windy Tainaron" [F150]. There was also a kind of Amphiktyony at this sanctuary for the seven cities that share in the sacrifices. These were Hermion, Epidauros, Aigina, Athens, the Prasians, the Nauplians, and Minyan Orchomenos. The Argives paid for the Nauplians and the Lakedaimonians for the Prasians. The worship of this god was so powerful among the Hellenes that the Makedonians – who already held power this far – in a way guarded its inviolability and were afraid to drag away the suppliants who took refuge on Kalauria. Archias, even with soldiers, did not dare to do violence to Demosthenes, although he had been ordered by Antipatros to bring him in alive, as well as any other orators that he could find who were similarly charged, but could not persuade him, and he [Demosthenes] prevailed by killing himself, taking his life with poison.

[C374]

Troizen and Pittheus, the sons of Pelops, originated in the Pisatis, with the former leaving behind the city named after him, and Pittheus succeeding him and ruling as king. Anthes, who had held it, set sail and founded Halikarnassos. I will speak about this in the Karian and Trojan sections [14.2.16].

(15) Epidauros was called Epitauros, for Aristotle [F491] says that the Karians possessed it, as well as Hermione, but after the return of the

---

[16] There is a gap of about fourteen letters.

Herakleidai the Ionians who had followed them from the Attic tetrapolis to Argos settled there with them. It also is not an insignificant city, especially because of the reputation of Asklepios, who is believed to cure all kind of diseases and whose sanctuary is always full of those who are sick, as well as the dedicated tablets on which the cures are written, just as at Kos and Trikke. The city lies in the recess of the Saronic Gulf, has a coastal circuit of fifteen stadia, and faces the summer sunrise. It is enclosed by high mountains that come down to the sea, so it is naturally furnished all around as a fortress. Between Troizen and Epidauros there is a fortified place called Methana and a peninsula of the same name. In some copies of Thoukydides (4.45.2, 5.18.7) it is "Methone," the same name as in Makedonia, where, in

[C375] the siege there, Philippos [II] had his eye knocked out. Because of this, Demetrios the Skepsian [F67] believes that those are thoroughly deceived who conjecture it was the ones Agamemnon sent here to collect sailors who made a prayer against them that they would never cease building their walls, since they allege that it was not these who refused to submit – in the matter of building walls – but those in Makedonia, as Theopompos [F384] says. It is also unlikely that those so near by would not obey him.

(16) Aigina is a certain place in the Epidauria, and also an island off this part of the mainland, about which the Poet wishes to speak the words just provided [8.6.10]. Because of this, some write "the island [neson] of Aigina," instead of "who held [t'echon] Aigina," distinguishing places with the same name. The island is especially well known: what can one say? Aiakos and his successors were said to be from there. It once ruled the seas and argued with the Athenians about first place in the sea battle around Salamis at the time of the Persian matter. The circumference of the island is said to be 180 stadia. It has a city of the same name facing toward the Lips wind, and is surrounded by Attika, the Megaris, and the Peloponnesos as far as Epidauros, about 100 stadia distant from each. Its eastern and southern portions are washed by the Myrtoan and Cretan seas. There are many islets around it, near the mainland, although Belbina extends to the open sea. The territory has soil at a depth but is rocky on the surface, especially in the plains, and thus is totally bare except for producing enough barley. The Aiginetans were called Myrmidons, not because of the story that when there was a large famine the ants [myrmekes] became human beings due to a prayer by Aiakos, but because, in the manner of ants, they excavated the earth and placed it on the rocks so that it could be cultivated, and also because they lived in dugouts and did not use bricks. In antiquity it was called Oinone, the same name as two Attic demes, one near Eleutherai ("well given to me and my master, you hold Oinone to live in, bordering on

Eleutherai" [Euripides F179]) and the other one of the tetrapolis around Marathon, in regard to which is the proverb "torrential Oinoe." The Argives, Cretans, Epidaurians, and Dorians settled there. Later the Athenians divided the island by lot … settling with the Mendaians at Damastion in Illyris around the silver mines, which I discussed in the Illyrian section [7.7.8]. The Lakedaimonians took it away from the Athenians and gave the island   [C376] back to its ancient settlers. The Aiginetans sent settlers to Kydonia in Crete and to the Ombrians. Ephoros [F176] says that silver was first minted on Aigina, under Pheidon, since it became a great emporium, because the people, due to the wretchedness of the soil, became merchants active on the sea. Because of this minor objects are called "Aiginetan merchandise."

(17) The Poet mentions some places in the order that they are located: "they lived in Hyrie and Aulis" [*Iliad* 2.496], or "those holding Argos … Tiryns, Hermione, Asine … Troizen, and Eïones" [*Iliad* 2.559–61], but at other times not in order: "Schoinos, Skolos … Thespeia, and Graia" [*Iliad* 2.497–8], and mentioning at the same time those on the mainland and the islands: "those who held Ithaka … and lived in Krokyleia" [*Iliad* 2.632–3], for Krokyleia is among the Akarnanians. Here he also connects Mases with Aigina [*Iliad* 2.562], although it is on the mainland in the Argolid.

Homer does not name Thyreai, although others commonly talk about it. Concerning it, a contest occurred between the Argives and Lakedaimonians, three hundred against three hundred. The Lakedaimonians under the command of Othryades won. Thoukydides (4.56.2) says that this place is in Kynouria on the boundary between the Argeia and the Lakonike. There are also Hysiai, a well-known place in the Argolid, and Kenchreai, which lies on the road from Tegea to Argos through Mount Parthenion and Kreopolon. Homer does not know these, nor Lyrkeion or Orneai – villages in Argeia – with the former having the same name as the mountain … and the latter as the Orneai that is located between Corinth and Sikyon.

(18) Of the cities of the Peloponnesos, Argos and Sparta have become the most distinguished, and continue so until today. Since they have been exhaustively discussed, there is no need to speak about them at length, for I would seem to be saying what has already been recounted by everyone. In antiquity Argos was rather more famous, but later, and for all time, the Lakedaimonians surpassed them, and continued preserving their autonomy, unless they happened to stumble slightly at some time. The Argives did not admit Pyrrhos (he fell before the walls when a certain old woman, it seems, threw a tile down on his head) but they became subject to   [C377] other kings. When they joined the Achaian Federation they, along with the

others, came under Roman power, and the city survives today as the second in rank after Sparta.

(19) Let me speak next about the places in the *Catalogue of Ships* that are made subject to Mykenai and Agamemnon. The words are as follows:

> those who held Mykenai, the well-built fortress, and wealthy Corinth and well-built Kleonai, those living in Orneiai and lovely Araithyrea and Sikyon, where Adrastos was originally king, those who held Hyperesia and high Gonoessa and Pellene, and live around Aigion and through all Aigialos and around broad Helike. [*Iliad* 2.569–75]

Mykenai no longer exists. It was founded by Perseus, whom Sthenelos succeeded, and then Eurystheus. The same also ruled Argos. Eurystheus made an expedition to Marathon against the sons of Herakles and Iolaos, with the aid of the Athenians, as it is recounted. He fell in battle, and the rest of his body was buried at Gargettos except for his head, cut off by Iolaos and [buried] at Trikorynthos near the spring of Makaria, below the wagon road. The place is called Eurystheus' Head. Mykenai fell to the Pelopidai who had set forth from the Pisatis, and then to the Herakleidai, who held Argos. After the naval battle at Salamis the Argives, along with the Kleonaians and Tegeatians, utterly destroyed Mykenai and divided up the territory. Because the two cities are quite near to one another, the tragedians mentioned them synonymously, as if one. Even in the same drama Euripides calls the same city at one time Mykenai and at another Argos, as in the *Iphigeneia* and the *Orestes*.

Kleonai is a town lying on the road from Argos to Corinth, on a hill that is completely inhabited all around and is excellently fortified, so that the statement "well-built Kleonai" [*Iliad* 2.570] seems appropriate to me. Nemea is also here, between Kleonai and Phlious, and the grove in which the Argives celebrate the Nemea, as well as the myth of the Nemean lion, and the village of Bembina. Kleonai is 120 stadia distant from Argos and 80 from Corinth. I have observed the settlement from Acrocorinth.

[C378]

(20) Corinth is called "wealthy" because of its commerce. It is located on the Isthmos and is master of two harbors, one to Asia, the other near to Italia, making the interchange of cargo easy between places so far apart. Just as in antiquity the Sikelian Strait was not easy to sail through, so were the open seas, especially beyond Maleai, because of adverse winds. From this comes the proverb "when you round Maleai, forget your home." It was desirable to the merchants both from Italia and Asia to avoid the sail around Maleai, and to land their cargo at Corinth, and to dispose of it. The duties on what was brought out of the Peloponnesos by foot, and what was

imported, fell to those having the keys. This remained completely the case into later times, and more successes accrued to them in later times. The Isthmian Games were celebrated there and brought crowds. The Bakchiads, a rich, numerous, and distinguished family, were tyrants there and held power for nearly two hundred years, increasingly enjoying the fruits of commerce. Kypselos overthrew them and became tyrant himself, and his house lasted for three generations. Evidence of the wealth of the house is the dedication by Kypselos at Olympia, a large statue of hammered gold. Demaratos, one of those who held power in Corinth, fled the uprisings there and carried so much wealth from his home to Tyrrhenia that he became the ruler of the city that received him, and his son became king of the Romans. The sanctuary of Aphrodite was so rich that it possessed more than a thousand temple slaves – hetairas – who had been dedicated to the goddess by both men and women. Because of them the city was crowded and became rich. The shipowners spent freely and easily, and thus a proverb says "the voyage to Corinth is not for all men." The story is told that a certain hetaira said to someone reproaching her dislike of touching wool "in this short a time I have taken down three warps."

(21) The topography of the city, as Hieronymos [F16], Eudoxos [F357],   [C379] and others say, and from what I saw after the recent restoration of the city by the Romans, is as follows. There is a high mountain with a perpendicular height of 3½ stadia and an ascent of 30 that ends in a sharp peak called Acrocorinth. The northern side is the most steep, and the city lies beneath it on a trapezium-shaped level place near the actual base of Acrocorinth. The circuit of the city was 40 stadia, with everything walled that was unprotected by the mountain. The mountain itself, Acrocorinth, was enclosed within the peribolos wherever wall construction was possible. When I went up it, the ruins of the line of the wall were clear. Thus the entire perimeter was about 85 stadia. On the other sides the mountain is less steep but rises considerably and is visible all around. On the summit is a small temple of Aphrodite, and below the summit is the spring of Peirene, which does not overflow but is always full of clear potable water. They say that the spring at the base of the mountain is due to the compressing of certain underground veins, here and elsewhere, and it flows out into the city providing a sufficient water supply. There is also a good supply of wells throughout the city, and also, they say, throughout Acrocorinth, but I did not see the latter. When Euripides says "I have come, abandoning Acrocorinth washed all around, the sacred hill, the city of Aphrodite" [F1084], one should take "washed all around" as in the depths, since there are veins and underground streams extending throughout it, or one should suppose that in antiquity

Peirene came to the surface and flowed down the mountain. Here, they say, Pegasos – the winged horse who sprang up from the neck of Medousa after the cutting off of the Gorgon's head – was caught while drinking by Bellerophon. They say that the same horse caused Hippoukrene ["Horse Spring"] to come up on Helikon, when he struck the rock below it with his hoof. Below Peirene is the Sisypheion, which preserves in white stone no slight remains of a certain sanctuary or royal palace. From the summit Parnassos and Helikon can be seen toward the north, which are high snowclad mountains, and the Krisaian Gulf lying below both, and it is surrounded by Phokis, Boiotia, and the Megaris. Across the strait from Phokis are the Corinthia and Sikyon. To the west is the territory between Corinth and the Asopia, the most attractive within the Isthmos, and to the south is the Teneatis, part of the Corinthian land, as well as Kleonai, one of the Arkadian mountains, and the Phliasia. To the east is the Isthmos and the coasts on both sides of the Isthmos and[17] . . . and the territory as far [C380] as the Megaris, extending from sea to sea. Above all these are the so-called Oneian Mountains, extending as far as Boiotia and Kithairon from the Skironian Rocks and the road along them toward Attika.

(22) The beginning of the coast on each side is at Lechaion and at Kenchreai, a village and harbor about 70 stadia distant from the city. This they use for goods from Asia, and the former from Italia. Lechaion lies below the city and does not have many inhabitants, but long walls have been constructed down to the sea for 12 stadia on both sides of the road to Lechaion. The shore that extends from there to Pagai in the Megaris is washed by the Corinthian Gulf and is concave, and with the other shore makes the Diolkos at Schoinous, near to Kenchreai. In between Lechaion and Pagai there was, in antiquity, the oracle of Hera Akraia, and also Olmiai, the promontory that creates the gulf in which Oinoe and Pagai are, the latter a Megarian fortress and Oinoe a Corinthian one. After Kenchreai there is Schoinous, the narrow part of the Diolkos, and then the Krommyonia. Lying off the shore are the Saronic Gulf and the Eleusinian (which in a certain way are the same), adjoining the Hermionic. On the Isthmos is the sanctuary of Isthmian Poseidon, shaded by a pine grove, where the Corinthians celebrated the Isthmian Games. Krommyon is a village of the Corinthia – formerly in the Megaris – where there is the myth about the Krommyan sow, who they say was the mother of the Kalydonian boar. It has been handed down that the elimination of this sow was one of the labors of Theseus.

---

[17] There is a gap of about ten letters.

Tenea is also a village of the Corinthia, in which there is a sanctuary of Teneatic Apollo. It is said that most of the settlers who set forth with Archias in order to establish Syracuse went from here. Afterward the settlement florished more than the others, and at last it revolted from the Corinthians and formed its own government, went over to the Romans, and survived after the destruction of the city [Corinth]. It is recorded that an oracle was given to a certain person from Asia who asked whether to move his home to Corinth: "blessed is Corinth but I would have the Teneatians." In ignorance some turn it into "I would have the Tegeatians." It is said that Polybos raised Oidipous here. It also seems that there is a certain kinship between them and the Tenedians through Tennes the son of Kyknos, as Aristotle [F594] says, and the similarity among both in the worship of Apollo provides no small indication.

(23) The Corinthians, being under Philippos [V], sided with him and individually were so contemptuous toward the Romans that certain people had the courage to pour filth down on their ambassadors who were going by their house. For this and other offenses they promptly paid the penalty, since a significant army was sent there under Lucius Mummius, and it was utterly destroyed. The other places as far as Makedonia came under the Romans, with different commanders sent to different areas, but most of the Corinthian territory was held by the Sikyonians. Polybios [39.2], who speaks with compassion about the events of the capture, adds that the soldiers had disdain for the works of art and religious dedications. He says that he was present and saw paintings thrown to the ground, and the soldiers playing games on them. Among these he names the figure of Dionysos by Aristeides, about which some record the saying "nothing compares with the *Dionysos*," as well as the *Herakles Afflicted by the Chiton of Deianeira*. This one I have not seen, but I saw the Dionysos set up in the Demetreion at Rome, a most beautiful work, but when the temple recently burned, the painting perished. Essentially, the most and best dedications in Rome came from there [Corinth], with the cities around Rome also having some. Mummius was generous rather than fond of art, they say, and would easily share it with those asking. When Lucullus built the sanctuary of Eutychia and its stoa, Mummius was asked for the use of certain statues to adorn the sanctuary at its dedication, which would be returned. Yet he [Lucullus] did not return them but dedicated them, and then told him [Mummius] to take them away if he wished. But he took it lightly, caring nothing, and thus became more popular than the dedicator.

Corinth remained deserted for a long time, but it was restored again by Caesar the God because of its favorable location. He mostly sent there as

[C381]

settlers those of the freedman class. When they were removing the ruins and also digging up the graves, they found a large amount of ceramic relief work as well as bronzes. Admiring the art, they left no grave unsearched, so that – well supplied with such items and disposing of them expensively – [C382] they filled Rome with "Necrocorinthia," as they called what was taken from the graves, especially the ceramics. In the beginning they were greatly valued, like the bronzes of Corinthian workmanship, but then they ceased to be esteemed, as the supply of ceramics was exhausted and most were not well done.

The city of the Corinthians, then, was always great and wealthy, and abundant in men capable in politics and the techniques of arts and crafts. Both here and in Sikyon painting, sculpting, and other such arts and crafts flourished the most. It had a territory that was not especially fertile, but twisted and rough, because of which everyone has said that Corinth is ridged, as in the proverb "Corinth is ridged and hollowed."

(24) Orneai is named after the river flowing past it. It is now deserted but formerly was well populated, having a sanctuary of Priapos that was honored, because of which Euphronios, the poet of the *Priapeia*, calls the god the Orneatian. It is located above the plain of the Sikyonians, in a territory held by the Argives.

Araithyrea is now called Phiasia, a city with the same name as the territory and near Mount Kelosse. They later moved 30 stadia away from there and founded a city that they called Phlious. A part of Kelosse is Karneates, where the Asopos takes its beginning. It flows past Sikyon and makes the Asopian territory a part of the Sikyonia. There is also an Asopos that flows past Thebes, Plateia, and Tanagra, another in Trachinian Herakleia flowing past a village named Parasopioi, and a fourth on Paros. Phlious lies in the middle of a circle encompassed by the Sikyonia, the Argeia, Kleonai, and Stymphalos. In Phlious and Sikyon the sanctuary of Dia is honored, which is what they call Hebe.

(25) Sikyon was formerly called Mekone, and still earlier Aigialoi. Demetrios removed it about 20 stadia (some say 12) from the sea onto a fortified hill. The old settlement, which has a harbor, is a seaport. The Nemea River is the boundary between the Sikyonia and the Corinthia. Most of the time it was ruled by tyrants, but the tyrants were always reasonable men, with Aratos the most distinguished, who freed the city and ruled the Achaians, as they willingly gave him the authority. He increased the feder- [C383] ation by adding both his native city and other nearby cities. Hyperesia and the cities after it, which the Poet [*Iliad* 2.573] mentions, and Aigialos as far as Dyme and the boundaries of Elis, already belonged to the Achaians.

Part 7:   Achaia

(1) In antiquity the Ionians, who were descended from the Athenians, controlled this territory. It was called Aigialeia in antiquity (and its inhabitants Aigialeans), but later Ionia after the former, just as Attika was after Ion the son of Xouthos. They say that Hellen was the son of Deukalion, and that he was master of those around Phthia, between the Peneios and the Asopos. He gave his rule to the eldest of his sons but sent the others elsewhere to seek their own settlements. One of them, Doros, united the Dorians around Parnassos into one state, named after himself when he died. Xouthos married the daughter of Erechtheus and founded the Attic Tetrapolis (Oinoe, Marathon, Probalinthos, and Trikorynthos). One of the sons, Achaios, involuntarily caused a death and fled to Lakedaimon, resulting in those there being called Achaians. Ion conquered the Thracians under Eumolpos, and thus became so esteemed that the Athenians turned over their government to him. First he divided the population into four tribes, and then into four livelihoods, designated as farmers, craftsmen, religious officials, and the fourth as guards. He made a number of such arrangements and at his death the territory was named after him. The land had become so populous by then that the Athenians sent a settlement of Ionians to the Peloponnesos, and called the land that they possessed after themselves, naming it after the Ionians rather than Aigialos. The men were designated Ionians rather than Aigialeans, and were divided into twelve cities. After the return of the Herakleidai they were driven out by the Achaians and went back again to Athens. From there, they were sent with the Kodridians to the Ionian settlement in Asia, founding twelve cities on the coast of Karia and Lydia and dividing themselves into the same number of parts as they had occupied in the Peloponnesos.

The Achaians were racially Phthiotians, living in Lakedaimon, and when the Herakleidai prevailed, they were taken up by Tisamenos, the son of Orestes, as I have previously said [8.5.5]. They attacked the Ionians and were more powerful, and cast them out and possessed the land themselves, keeping the division of the territory that they had received. They were so [C384] powerful that although the Herakleidai (from whom they had revolted) held the rest of the Peloponnesos, they withstood everyone and named the territory Achaia. From Tisamenos to Ogygos they continued being ruled by kings, as Polybios says [2.41.4–5, 4.1.5]. Then as a democracy they were so esteemed for their government that the Italiotes, after the revolt against the Pythagoreans, took most of their customs for their own usage. After the battle at Leuktra, the Thebans entrusted to them the arbitration of the disputes that the cities had with one another. Later, when their federation was dissolved by the Makedonians, they restored themselves gradually. When Pyrrhos made his expedition to Italia, four cities joined together, including Patrai and Dyme, and then they added some of the twelve, except for Olenos and Helike, as the former did not join and the latter had been destroyed by a wave.

(2) For the sea was lifted up by an earthquake, and it was submerged, as well as the sanctuary of Helikonian Poseidon whom the Ionians still honor today, sacrificing there at the Panionion. Homer, some conjecture, remembers this sacrifice when he says "he breathed out his spirit and bellowed, as when a bull is dragged around the Helikonian lord" [*Iliad* 20.403–4]. They have determined that the Poet was more recent than the Ionian settlements, because he mentions the Panionian sacrifice, in which the Ionians celebrate Helikonian Poseidon in the Prienea, as the Prienians themselves are said to be from Helike, and a young man of the Prienea is appointed as king for this sacrifice, to manage the rites. Moreover, they further determine this by the statement made about the bull, for the Ionians believe that there are good omens from the sacrifice when the bull bellows while being sacrificed. Those who are opposed to transferring these proofs regarding the bull and the sacrifice to Helike assume that they were customary there and the Poet was making a comparison with what was celebrated there.

Helike was submerged two years before Leuktra. Eratosthenes [F139] says that he himself saw the place, and the ferrymen say that a bronze Poseidon stood upright in the strait, with a hippocamp in his hand, a danger to those fishing with nets. Herakleides [F26a] says that the calamity happened in [C385] his time, at night, and although the city was 12 stadia from the sea the entire region and the city were submerged, and 2,000 men sent by the Achaians were unable to recover the bodies. The territory was divided among its neighbors. The catastrophe was because of the anger of Poseidon, since the Ionians who had been driven out of Helike had sent to ask the Helikans especially for the image of Poseidon, or, if that were not possible, for the model of the sanctuary. Neither was given, and they sent to the Achaian council, which voted in favor of them, yet this was not obeyed and the catastrophe occurred the following winter. Later the Achaians did give the model to the Ionians. Hesiod mentions another Helike in Thessaly: "Anthe, the city of the Myrmidons, and famous Iaolkos, Arne, and also Helike" [*Shield of Herakles* 474–5].

(3) For twenty years the Achaians continued to have a common secretary and two commanders each year, and their common council came together at one place (called Hamarion), at which they dealt with common

matters, as the Ionians had formerly. Then they decided to elect only one commander. When Aratos was commander he took Acrocorinth away from Antigonos [II] and added the city to the Achaians, just as he had added his native city. He also took over the Megarians, dissolving the tyrannies in each city and making those who had been freed Achaians. He freed the Peloponnesos from its tyrannies, so that Argos, Hermion, Phlious, and Megalopolis (the largest city in Arkadia) were added to the Achaians. At this time they increased to their greatest power, at the time that the Romans had expelled the Karchedonians from Sikelia and made their expedition against the Galatians around the Padus. The Achaians held together reasonably well until the command of Philopoimen, then it gradually dissolved, as by that time the Romans held all of Hellas and did not make use of it identically throughout, wishing to preserve some and destroy others.

(4) The order of the places in which they settled, dividing it into twelve portions, is this: after Sikyon is Pellene, then Aigeira is second. Third is Aigai, which has a sanctuary of Poseidon, and fourth is Boura. After it there is Helike, where the Ionians fled for refuge after they were defeated in battle by the Achaians, and from where they were finally expelled. After Helike are Aigion, Rhypes, and Patrai and Pharai, then Olenos, past which is the   [C386] Peiros, a large river, and then Dyme and the Tritaians. The Ionians lived in villages but the Achaians founded cities, and later they joined others to certain of these, with some from the other divisions, such as Aigai to Aigeira (the inhabitants were called Aigaians), and Olenos to Dyme. The remains of the old settlement of the Olenians are visible between Patrai and Dyme, as well as the distinguished sanctuary of Asklepios, 40 stadia distant from Dyme and 80 from Patrai.

Having the same name as this Aigai is the one in Euboia, and Olenos [has the same name as] the settlement in Aitolia, which preserves only traces. The Poet does not mention Olenos in Achaia, as is the case with a number of settlements around Aigialos, although he speaks of them generally ("through all Aigialos and around broad Helike" [*Iliad* 2.575]), and he mentions the Aitolian one when he says "they lived in Pleuron and Olenos" [*Iliad* 2.639]. He speaks about both [of the places named] Aigai. There is the one in Achaia ("they brought up gifts for you from both Helike and Aigai" [*Iliad* 8.203]), but when he says "Aigai, where his famous house lies in the depths of the sea ... there Poseidon stopped his horses" [*Iliad* 13.21, 34], it is better to take it as in Euboia, from where the Aigaion Sea was named and the activities of Poseidon during the Trojan War were situated. The Krathis River flows past Achaian Aigai, increased

by two other rivers. It has its name from being mixed [*kirnasthai*], as does
the Krathis in Italia.

(5) Each of the twelve divisions was combined from seven or eight communities, as the territory was so populous. Pellene lies 60 stadia above the sea,
and is a natural fortress. There is also a village of Pellene, where the Pellenian
cloaks come from, which were established as prizes in the games. It lies
between Aigeira and Pellene. Pellana is different, a Lakonian region toward
the Megalopolitis. Aigeira lies on a mound. Boura lies about 40 stadia above
the sea and was swallowed up by an earthquake. They say that it was from the
[C387] spring of Sybaris there that the Italian river was named. Aiga – Aigai is also
called this – is now uninhabited, and the people of Aigion now hold the
territory. Aigion is well populated today. There is the story that Zeus was
nourished there by a goat, just as Aratos says: "the sacred goat, which in the
story held out its breast to Zeus" [*Phainomena* 163]. He also says that "the
interpreters of Zeus call it the Olenian goat" [*Phainomena* 164], making it
clear that the place is near Olenos. Keryneia is also here, situated on a high
rock, the same distance from the sea as Boura. The Aigieans have this place, as
well as Helike and the Hamarion, a grove of Zeus, where the Achaians came
together to deliberate common matters. The Selinous River flows through the
region of Aigion, and has the same name as the one in Ephesos that flows past
the Artemision, as well as the one in the Eleia of today that flows past the land
that Xenophon [*Anabasis* 5.3.7–8] says he purchased for Artemis, according to
an oracle. There is another Selinous that flows past the Hyblaian Megarians,
whom the Karchedonians forced to emigrate.

Of the remaining cities, or divisions of the Achaians, Rhypes is uninhabited, and its territory – called Rhypis – was held by the Aigieans and
Pharians. Aischylos says somewhere "sacred Boura, Keryneia, Rhypes,
Dyme, Helike, Aigion, Aigeira, and high sacred Olenos" [F284]. Myskellos,
the founder of Kroton, was from Rhypes. Leuktron, a deme of Rhypes, is
part of Rhypis. After it there is Patrai, a notable city. Between them are
Rhion, and Antirhion, 40 stadia distant from Patrai. Recently the Romans,
after the Aktian victory, placed an important part of their army there, and
it is especially populated today as a Roman settlement. It has a reasonable
anchorage. Next is Dyme, a city without a harbor, the farthest west, from
which its name comes. Formerly it was called Stratos, and still earlier
Palieia[18]. . . . The Larisos River divides it from Eleia at Bouprasia, and flows
from a mountain. Some locals call it Skollis, but Homer the "Olenian Rock"
[*Iliad* 2.617, 11.757]. Antimachos [F27] says that Dyme is Kaukonian, and

---

[18]   There are twenty-six incomprehensible letters at this point.

some take this to mean an epithet from the Kaukonians, since they extended that far – as I have said above [8.3.11, 17] – but others from the Kaukon River, just as Thebes is Dirkaian and Asopian, Argos is Inacheian, and Troy Simountian. Dyme, shortly before my time, received as inhabitants a mixture of people who survived from the crowd of pirates that Pompeius [C388] had acquired, after he broke up brigandage, settling some at Soloi in Kilikia and others elsewhere, particularly here. Phara borders on the Dymaia, Patrike, and Leontesia (where Antigonos [II] settled the Achaians). Those from Phara are called Pharians, but those from the Messeniake are Pharatians. In the Pharaike there is a spring called Dirke, with the same name as the one in Thebes. Tritaia touches the Pharaike, Leontesia, and Lasionia. In Phokis there is a city with the same name . . . the Kastalia spring . . . Trataia.[19] Olenos is deserted and lies betwen Patrai and Dyme, and the territory is held by the Dymaians. Then there is Araxos, the promontory of Eleia, 1,030 stadia from the Isthmos.

Part 8:   Arkadia, and final comments on the Peloponnesos

(1) Arkadia is in the middle of the Peloponnesos, and most of the territory is defined by mountains. The largest mountain in it is Kyllene. At any rate, some say that its perpendicular height is 20 stadia, although others about 15. It seems that the oldest peoples of the Hellenes are the Arkadians, Azanians, Parrhasians, and such others. But because of complete mistreatment of the territory it would not be proper to write at length about them. Cities that formerly had been notable disappeared due to the continuous wars, and those formerly farming the land have been abandoning it since the time when many came together into what was called Megalopolis, but now even Megalopolis has suffered, as in the comic poet: "Megalopolis has become a great [*megale*] desolation." There is an abundance of pasture for cattle, and especially for horses and the asses used as stallions. The Arkadian breed of horses is the best, like the Argolian and Epidaurian. The deserted parts of Aitolia and Akarnania are suitable for horse racing, no less so than Thessaly.

2) Mantineia was made most famous by Epameinondas, who was victorious over the Lakedaimonians in the second battle, in which he was killed. But it, and Orchomenos, Heraia, Kleitor, Pheneos, Stymphalos, Mainalos, Methydrion, Kaphyeis, and Kynaitha, no longer exist, with hardly any traces of them visible. Tegea still survives moderately, as well as the

---

[19] The manuscripts are exceedingly deficient at this point.

sanctuary of Athena Alea. Slightly honored is the sanctuary of Zeus Lykaios near Mount Lykaion[20]. . . . Of those mentioned by the Poet, "Rhipe, Stratie, and windy Enispe" [*Iliad* 2.606] are difficult to find and when found it is of no advantage because they are deserted.

(3) Notable mountains, in addition to Kyllene, are Pholoe, Lykaion, Mainalos, and the so-called Parthenion, which reaches down from the Tegeatis to the Argeia.

[C389]

(4) I have mentioned the paradoxical situation of the Alpheios and the Eurotas [6.2.9], as well as the Erasinos which today empties from the Stymphalian Lake into the Argeia [8.6.8], but formerly had no outlet, as the sinkholes – which the Arkadians call *zerethra* – were closed and did not admit of an outlet, so that the city of the Stymphalians is now 50 stadia[21] from the lake, although it had been on it. But it was the opposite with the Ladon, since its stream once experienced a blockage because of the stopping of its source. The sinkholes around Pheneos, through which it fell, collapsed because of an earthquake, which stopped the flow as deep as the veins of its source. Thus some say. Eratosthenes [F140] says that around Pheneos the river called the Anias makes a lake in front of the city and flows down into strainers called *zerethra*. When these are stopped up, the water at times overflows into the plains, but when they are opened up again, it comes out of the plains all together and empties into the Ladon and the Alpheus, so that even at Olympia the land around the sanctuary was once flooded and the lake was diminished. The Erasinos, flowing around Stymphalos, goes under the mountain and reappears again in the Argive territory. Because of this Iphikrates, when he was besieging Stymphalos and accomplishing nothing, attempted to block up the sinkhole with many sponges that he provided himself, but ceased because of a sign from Zeus. Around Pheneos is the so-called Water of the Styx, a small stream of deadly water that is believed to be sacred. Let such be said about Arkadia.

(5) Polybios [34.12.12] says that from Maleai north to the Istros is about 10,000 stadia, but Artemidoros [F59a] not unreasonably corrects it, saying that it is a journey[22] of 1,400 [?] to Aigion from Maleai, and from there to Kirrha [?] a voyage of 200, and from there through Herakleia . . . a journey of 500, then to Larisa . . . 340, then through the outlets of the Peneios 240 . . . to Thessalonikeia 660, and then through Eidomene, Stoboi, and the Dardanians 3,000 [?]. . . . Yet according to him [Artemidoros] it is 6,500

---

[20] There is a gap of about nine letters.

[21] The number is far too large: "five" or "four" are the most likely possibilities.

[22] The entire itinerary to the north is full of manuscript gaps and uncertain numbers.

from Thessalonikeia. The reason is that it was not measured by the short route, but one by chance that was taken by a certain commander.

It is not out of place, perhaps, to add the founders of the Peloponnesian settlements after the return of the Herakleidai, as Ephoros [F18b] says: Aletes for Corinth, Phalkes for Sikyon, Tisamenos for Achaia, Oxylos for Elis, Kresphontes for Messene, Eurysthenes and Prokles for Lakedaimon, Temenos and Kissos for Argos, and Agaios and Deiphontes for the region around Akte.

BOOK 9

East Central Hellas

Part 1: Attika

(1) Having gone around the Peloponnesos, which, as I have said [8.1.3], is the first and smallest of the peninsulas of which Hellas consists, the next thing would be to go through what is continuous with it. The second is the one that adds the Megaris to the Peloponnesos. The third includes, in addition to this, Attika, Boiotia, a part of Phokis and of the Epiknemidian Lokrians, so that Krommyon is Megarian and not Corinthian. One must discuss these.

Eudoxos [F350] says that if one considers a straight line extending in an easterly direction from the Keraunian Mountains to Sounion (the promontory of Attika) it would leave the entire Peloponnesos on the right and toward the south, and the continuous coast from the Keraunian Mountains to the Krisaian Gulf and the Megaris, as well as all of Attika, would be on the left and toward the north. He believes that the shore from Sounion to the Isthmos would only be a gulf with a small curve unless one added to this shore of the Peloponnesian territory what is continuous with the Isthmos and makes the Hermionic [Gulf] and Akte. Thus that from the Keraunian Mountains to the Corinthian Gulf would not make such a turn as to be concave in the form of a gulf if Rhion and Antirrhion did not draw together into narrows and create this appearance, as is also the case around the Krisaian recess. It is the same in regard to what surrounds the recess where the Krisaian Sea ceases.

(2) The following is what Eudoxos said, a mathematical person, someone experienced in figures and the zones, and knowledgeable about these places: one must consider this side of Attika along with the Megaris – from Sounion to the Isthmos – as curved, but only slightly. At about the middle of the previously mentioned line is the Peiraieus, the seaport of Athens. It is about 350 stadia distant from Schoinous, at the Isthmos, and 330 from Sounion. The distance to Pagai from the Peiraieus is about as great as that to

Schoinous, although some say that it is about 10 stadia greater. After going around Sounion the voyage is toward the north with an inclination toward the west.

(3) The promontory has seas on both sides and is narrow at first, widening in the interior, although nonetheless it takes a crescent-shaped turn toward Oropos in Boiotia, with its concavity toward the sea. Then there is the second side, the eastern [side] of Attika. The remainder is the northerly side, extending from the Oropia toward the west as far as the Megaris – the mountainous part of Attika – which has many names and separates Boiotia from Attika. Thus, as I have said before [8.1.3], Boiotia, having a sea on both sides, becomes an isthmus of the third previously mentioned peninsula, receiving within it that which is toward the Peloponnesos, the Megaris, and Attika. Because of this, they say, what was called in antiquity the Promontory [*Akte*] or Aktike, is now Attika, with a slight change of name, because the greater part of it lies below the mountains, projects onto the sea, is narrow, and is especially long, thrusting as far as Sounion. I will discuss this in detail, going back to the seacoast where I left off.

(4) After Krommyon, and lying above the promontory, are the Skironides Rocks, which do not allow for a route along the sea. The road to the Megarians and Attika from the Isthmos is above them. But the road is exceedingly near to the rocks, so that it often is on the edge of the precipice because the mountain lying above it is impassable and high. Here the myth is told about Skiron and Pityokamptes, brigands of the previously mentioned mountainous territory, whom Theseus eliminated. The Athenians have given the name Skiron to the Argestes wind, which comes violently down from the heights on the left. After the Skironides Rocks is Cape Minoa, which forms the harbor at Nisaia. Nisaia is the seaport of the Megarians, and is 18 stadia distant from the city, joined to it by long walls [C392] on both sides. It was also called Minoa.

(5) In antiquity, the territory was held by the Ionians, the same who held Attika. Megara had not yet been founded. Thus the Poet does not specifically mention these places, but when he calls all those in Attika "Athenians," he includes them together in the common name, considering them Athenian. When he says in the *Catalogue* "those who held Athens, the well-built city" [*Iliad* 2.546], one must accept this as including the Megarians of today, who also took part in the expedition. This is the proof: in antiquity Attika was called Ionia and Ias, and when the Poet says "there are the Boiotians, and the Iaonians with their long chitons" [*Iliad* 13.685], he speaks of the Athenians, and the Megaris was part of it.

(6) Moreover, the Peloponnesians and Ionians were often disputing about their boundaries, where the Krommyonia – among others – was located, and they came to an agreement and erected a pillar in an agreed-upon place near the Isthmos itself, having inscribed on the side toward the Peloponnesos "This is the Peloponnesos, not Ionia," and toward Megara "This is not the Peloponnesos but Ionia." The *Atthis* writers [F2] disagree about many things, but those who are worth mentioning agree that there were four Pandionides (Aigeus, Lykos, Pallas, and the fourth, Nisos), and that when Attika was divided into four parts, Nisos obtained the Megaris as his portion and founded Nisaia. Philochoros [F107] says that his rule extended from the Isthmos to the Pythion, but Andron [F14] that it was as far as Eleusis and the Thriasian Plain. Different [writers] have divided the four parts in different ways, but it is sufficient to take what Sophokles has recounted: that Aigeus says

> my father determined[1] ... along the coast and dispensing this land to the eldest ... and to Lykos dispensing the garden of Euboia that is parallel, and for Nisos choosing the neighboring land at the shore of Skiron. The land toward the south, the austere one, he who reared giants, Pallas, received. [F24]

That the Megaris was a part of Attika is shown by these proofs.

(7) After the return of the Herakleidai and the division of the territory, it happened that many were driven out of their homes into Attika both by them and the Dorians who were with them, among whom was Melanthos, the king of Messene. He also ruled over the Athenians, with their consent, having been victorious in single combat over Xanthos, the Boiotian king. Attika was now populous because of the exiles, and the Herakleidai were afraid of them. Urged on particularly by those in Corinth and Messene – the former because of their proximity and the latter because Kodros, the son of Melanthos, ruled Attika at that time – they made an expedition against Attika. They were defeated in battle and withdrew from the territory, holding only the Megarike, founding the city of Megara, and making its people Dorian instead of Ionian. They also removed the pillar that marked the boundary between the Ionians and the Peloponnesians.

(8) The city of the Megarians has experienced many changes, but has survived into the present. At one time it was the home of the philosophers called the Megarikoi, the successors of Eukleides, a Sokratic man who was Megarian in origin, just as the Eleatics were the successors of Phaidon the

---

[1] There is a gap of about nine letters, followed in the next line by one of about eight letters.

Eleian, also a Sokratic, among who was Pyrrhon, and the Eretrians were the [successors] of Menedemos the Eretrian. The Megarian territory is rather poor, just like Attika, with the so-called Oneian Mountains stretching over the greater part of it, a kind of ridge that extends from the Skironides Rocks to Boiotia and Kithairon, separating the sea at Nisaia from[2] . . . the so-called Alkyonian.

(9) On the voyage from Nisaia to Attika lie five islets. Then there is Salamis, about 70 stadia in length (some say 80). It has a city with the same name; the deserted ancient one faces toward Aigina and the south, just as Aischylos [F404] said: "Aigina itself lies toward the blasts of the south wind." Today it lies on a gulf, a place like a peninsula that adjoins Attika. In antiquity it was called by different names, such as Skiras and Kychreia after certain heroes. From the former Athena is said to be "Skiras," Skira is a place in Attika, there is a certain festival for Skiros, and there is the month of Skirophorion. From the latter there is the Kychreidian serpent that Hesiod [F143] says was nourished by Kychreus and driven out by Eurylochos because it was causing damage to the island, but was received at Eleusis by Demeter, becoming her attendant. It was also called Pityoussa   [C394] ["Abundant in Pines"] because of the tree. The reputation of the island is because of the Aiakidai, who ruled it (especially Aias the son of Telamon), and because Xerxes was defeated around the island by the Hellenes in a sea battle, and fled home. The Aiginetans shared in this struggle and in driving him away, as they were considered neighbors and provided a notable fleet. On Salamis is a Bokaros River, now called the Bokalia.

(10) Today the Athenians hold it, but in antiquity there was strife between them and the Megarians about it. Some say that it was Peisistratos, and others that it was Solon who interpolated into the *Catalogue of Ships* after the words "Aias brought twelve ships from Salamis" [*Iliad* 2.557] the following: "bringing them, he stationed them next to the position of the Athenian battle line" [*Iliad* 2.558], and then used the Poet as witness that the island had been Athenian from the beginning. But the critics do not accept this because many verses contradict it. Why does Aias appear as the last among the anchored ships, not with the Athenians, but with the Thessalians subject to Protesilaos ("where the ships of Aias and Protesilaos were" [*Iliad* 13.681])? And in the *Visitation*, Agamemnon

> found the son of Peteos, Menestheus the driver of horses, standing with the Athenians, the authors of the battle cry, around him. Moreover, nearby

---

[2] There is a gap of about nine to twelve letters.

stood Odysseus of the many counsels, and around him the lines of the
Kephallenians, [*Iliad* 4.327–30]

and back to Aias and the Salaminians: "he came to the Aiantes" [*Iliad* 4.273],
and, near them, "Idomeneus on the side" [*Iliad* 3.230], not Menestheus. Thus
the Athenians are believed to have alleged such evidence from Homer, and
the Megarians wrote this parody against it: "Aias brought ships from Salamis,
and from Polichne, from Aigeiroussa, Nisaia, and Tripodes," which are
Megarian places. Tripodes is called Tripodiskion, where the Megarian agora
is now located.

[C395]   (11) Because the priestess of Athena Polias will not touch indigenous fresh
cheese – eating only the foreign variety – but will use Salaminian, some say
incorrectly that Salamis is foreign to Attika, for she eats that from other
islands that are agreed to belong to Attika, and those who began this custom
considered foreign everything that was from across the sea. But it seems that
in antiquity what is now Salamis was considered independent, and that
Megara was a part of Attika. The boundaries between the Megarike and
Atthis are placed on the coast opposite Salamis, at the two mountains called
the Horns.

(12) Then there is the city of Eleusis, in which are the sanctuary of
Eleusinian Demeter and the mystic precinct that was constructed by
Iktinos as a theater capable of admitting a crowd. He also built the
Parthenon for Athena on the Akropolis, with Perikles supervising the work.
The city is numbered among the demes.

(13) Then there is the Thriasian Plain, and the shore and deme of the
same name. Then there is Cape Amphiale and the quarry lying above it, and
the passage to Salamis (of about two stadia), across which Xerxes attempted
to construct a mole, but was overtaken by the naval battle and the flight of
the Persians. Here are also the Pharmakoussai, two islets, on the larger of
which the tomb of Kirke is visible.

(14) Above this promontory is a mountain called Korydallos and the
deme of Korydalleis. Then there is the harbor of Phoron and Psyttalia, a
deserted rocky islet, which some have said is the eyesore of the Peiraieus.
Nearby is Atalante – which has the same name as one around Euboia and
one among the Lokrians – and then another islet, similar to Psyttalia, and
this ... then there is the Peiraieus (which is also numbered among the
demes) and Mounychia.

(15) Mounychia is a hill that forms a peninsula, and is hollow and
undermined in many places, in part by nature and in part by purpose, so
that it accepts homes. The entrance is by a small mouth. Three harbors lie

below it. In antiquity Mounychia was walled and inhabited in a similar way to the city of the Rhodians, and included within the peribolos the Peiraieus and the harbors, which were full of shipsheds, as well as the Arsenal, the work of Philon. The naval station was sufficient for 400 ships, which was no fewer than what the Athenians would send forth. To this wall were connected the "legs" that extended down to the sea from the town. These were the long walls, 40 stadia in length, that connected the town with the Peiraieus. The many wars caused the walls and the defenses of Mounychia to become ruined, reducing the Peiraieus to a small settlement around the [C396] harbors and the sanctuary of Zeus Soter. The little stoas of the sanctuary have notable paintings, the works of famous artists, and there are statues in the open courtyard. The long walls have been torn down, originally demolished by the Lakedaimonians and later by the Romans when Sulla took by siege both the Peiraieus and the town.

(16) The town [Athens] is a rock in the plain inhabited all around in a circle. On the rock is the sanctuary of Athena, with the old temple of Polias, where the inextinguishable lamp is, and the Parthenon, which Iktinos constructed, and in which is the ivory Athena, the work of Pheidias.

Yet I hesitate . . . the great number of things that come to mind about this city and that are celebrated and proclaimed, as going too far, for it would happen that the work would digress from its purpose. One might add what Hegesias said:

> I see the Akropolis and the mark of the trident there. I see Eleusis and have become an initiate into the rites. There is the Leokorion, and here is the Theseion. I cannot point them out individually, for Attika belongs to the gods, who took it as a hearth for themselves, and also the ancestral heroes [F24].

Thus he recorded only one landmark on the Akropolis, but Polemon, the guidebook author, wrote four books about the dedications on the Akropolis. The former is correspondingly proportionate in regard to the other parts of the city and territory. He speaks of Eleusis, one of the 170 (or four more, as they say) demes, but names none of the others.

(17) Most of them, if not all, have many stories that are mythical and historical, such as Aphidna, with the seizure of Helen by Theseus, its pillaging by the Dioskouroi, and the recovery of their sister. Marathon has the Persian struggle, Rhamnous the image of Nemesis, which some say is the work of Diodotos and others that of Agorakritos the Parian, and which in its size and beauty was exceedingly successful and a match for the works of Pheidias. Moreover Dekeleia was the base of operations for the Peloponnesians in the

Dekelian War, and Phyle was from where Thrasyboulos brought the citizenry to the Peiraieus and then to the town. In regard to the others there are many historical events, and the Leokorion and the Theseion have . . . as well as the Lykeion and the Olympic stadium, and the Olympion itself, which was left half-finished at the death of the king who dedicated it. Similar are the Akademia, the gardens of the philosophers, the Odeion, the Painted Stoa, and the temples in the city . . . having works of artists.

[C397]

(18) This work would be much longer if one were to review the founders of the settlement, beginning with Kekrops. Moreover everyone does not write the same about them, as is shown from their names. They say that Aktike is from Aktaion, Atthis and Attika from Atthis the daughter of Kranaos (from whom the inhabitants were also Kranaans), Mopsopia from Mopsopos, Ionia from Ion the son of Xouthos, and Poseidonia and Athens from their eponymous gods. I have said [5.2.4] that it is clear the Pelasgian peoples lived here and because of their wandering they were called Pelargians by those in Attika.

(19) The more that there is a fondness of learning about notable things, and the more they are talked about, there will be a greater refutation of them if one has not mastered the historical details. For example, in his *Collection of Rivers*, Kallimachos [F458] says that he would laugh if anyone dared to write that the Athenian virgins "draw the pure bright water of the Eridanos," from which even cattle keep away. Today, as they say, its sources are pure and produce potable water, outside the so-called Diochares Gate, near the Lykeion. In antiquity there was a certain constructed fountain nearby with an abundance of excellent water. If this is not the case today, why should someone wonder if formerly it was abundant and pure and thus also potable, but changed later? Yet it is not possible to delay over such particulars, as they are so numerous, nor to go past them in silence without recording some of them summarily.

(20) It is sufficient to add what Philochoros [F94] says, that when the territory was being ravaged from the sea by the Karians and from the land by the Boiotians (who were called the Aonians), the population was first settled in twelve cities by Kekrops, which were named Kekropia, Tetrapolis, Epakria, Dekeleia, Eleusis, Aphidna (also called Aphidnai, in the plural), Thorikos, Brauron, Kytheros, Sphettos, Kephisia³. . . . Yet later Theseus is said to have brought the twelve together into the single city of today. The Athenians were formerly ruled by kings, and then by a democracy. They were won over by the tyrants – Peisistratos and his sons – but later there was

³ Only eleven cities are listed.

oligarchy, both of the Four Hundred and of the Thirty Tyrants, who were established by the Lakedaimonians. These they easily escaped, and preserved the democracy until the Roman predominance. For even though [C398] they were molested for a short time by the Makedonian kings and were forced to submit to them, they maintained their own general type of government. Some say that they had their best government during the ten years that Kasandros ruled the Makedonians. This man seems to have been more tyrannical toward others, but he was conciliatory toward the Athenians when the city became subject to him. He placed Demetrios of Phaleron over the citizens – a student of the scholar Theophrastos – who did not destroy the democracy but improved it, as is clear from the memoirs that he wrote [F34] about this government. But the envy and hatred was so strong toward the oligarchs that after the death of Kasandros he was forced to flee to Egypt. Those rising in revolt pulled down the more than three hundred statues of him and melted them down (some add that they were made into chamber pots). The Romans, taking over their democracy, preserved their autonomy and freedom. When the Mithridatic War occurred, tyrants were established over them, whomever the king wished. The most powerful of these, Aristion[4] . . . oppressed them and was punished by Sulla, the Roman commander, who took the city by siege. He dispensed a pardon to the city, and to this day it is free and honored by the Romans.

(21) After the Peiraius is the deme of Phalereis, on the coast next to it, and then Halimousioi, Aixoneis, Aixonikian Halaieis, and Anagyrasioi, and then Thoraieis, Lamptreis, Aigilieis, Anaphlystioi, and Ateneis. These are the ones as far as Cape Sounion. Between the previously mentioned demes[5] . . . Zoster, the first after Aixone, and then another after Thorai, Astypalaia. Phabra lies off the former of these and Elaioussa off the latter, and also off Aixone is Hydroussa. Around Anaphlystos are the Paneion and the sanctuary of Aphrodite Kolias, at which place, they say, the waves cast up the last wreckage from the Persian naval battle at Salamis, about which Apollo made the prophecy, "the Koliadian women will cook with oars." The island of Belbina also lies off these places, not far away, and the palisade of Patroklos. Most of these are deserted.

(22) Going around Cape Sounion, there is the notable deme of Sounion, then Thorikos, and then a deme called Potamos, whose people are Potamians. [C399] Then there are Prasiai, Steiria, Brauron (where the sanctuary of Brauronian Artemis is), Araphenidian Halai (where the Tauropolos is), Myrrhinous, Probalinthos, and Marathon, where Miltiades completely destroyed the

---

[4] There is a gap of about seven letters.   [5] There is a gap of about fourteen letters.

power of those who were with Datis the Persian, without waiting for the Lakedaimonians, who were late because of the full moon. Also told here is the myth of the Marathonian bull, which Theseus killed. After Marathon is Trikorynthos, and then Rhamnous, where the sanctuary of Nemesis is. Then there is Psaphis, of the Oropians. Near here is the Amphiareion, an oracle that was once honored, where Amphiaraos in his flight, as Sophokles [F958] says, "was received by a fissure in the Theban dust, with his weapons and four-horsed chariot."

Oropos has often been disputed, for it is situated in the border territory of Attika and Boiotia. Lying off this coast, off Thorikos and Sounion, is the island of Helene, which is rugged and deserted, and oblong with a length of 60 stadia. They say that it was recorded by the Poet in what Alexander says to Helen:

> not even when I first seized you from lovely Lakedaimon and sailed on seafaring ships, and joined with you on the island of Kranae, [*Iliad* 3.443–5]

for he says that Kranae is what is now called Helene because they had intercourse there. After Helene, Euboia lies off the next part of the coast, is similarly narrow and long, and is parallel to the mainland, like Helene. From Sounion to the southern point of Euboia, which is called White Promontory, is a voyage of 300 stadia. Concerning Euboia[6] . . . to speak about the demes in the interior of Attika because of their great number.

(23) The most famous of the mountains are Hymettos, Brilessos, and Lykabettos, and also Parnes and Korydallos. There are excellent marble quarries near the city, the Hymettian and Pentelic. Hymettos also produces the best honey. The silver mines in Attika were originally notable but have now failed. Moreover, the workers, when the mines were going into decline, melted down the ancient tailings and slag and were still able to find pure silver in them, since in ancient times they were ignorant of the heating process. Although Attic honey is the best of all, that around the silver mines is by far the very best, that which is called "unsmoked," from the manner of its preparation.

[C400]

(24) The rivers include the Kephissos, which has its beginning in Trinemeis and flows through the plain (from which comes the bridge and the Gephyrismians), and then through the "legs" that extend from the town to the Peiraieus, emptying into the Phaleric [Gulf]. Mostly it is a torrent, but it lessens completely in summer. The Ilissos is even more so, flowing

---

[6] There is a gap of about fourteen letters.

from the other part of the town to the same coast, from above Agra and the Lykeion, and the fountain celebrated by Plato in the *Phaidros* [4–5]. This is it about Attika.

Part 2:   Boiotia

(1) Next is Boiotia.[7] Concerning what is said about this region and the contiguous peoples, it is necessary to call to mind, for the sake of clarity, what I have said previously [2.5.21, 7.7.4, 9.1.2]. I said that the coast from Sounion as far as Thessalonikeia extends toward the north, inclining slightly toward the west and having the sea on the east. What is above . . . toward the west, as if like a ribbon through the . . . extending parallel to one another. The first is <Attika, along with> Megaris, like a ribbon, with its eastern side the coast from Sounion as far as Oropos and Boiotia. The western is the Isthmos and the Alkyonian Sea, from Pagai as far as . . . around Kreousa. Its remainder is the coast <from Sounion> as far as the Isthmos . . . mountainous, that separates Attika from <Boiotia>. The second is Boiotia . . . extending like a ribbon from east to west, from the Euboian Sea to the sea at the Krisaian Gulf, about equal in length to Attika, or somewhat less. Yet the excellence of the land is greatly superior.

(2) Ephoros [F119] maintains that Boiotia is superior to the territory of neighboring peoples because it alone has three seas and a number of good harbors. In the Krisaian Gulf, and the Corinthian, it receives goods from Italia, Sikelia, and Libya. The coast of the portion toward Euboia branches on either side at the Euripos, one toward Aulis and the Tanagrike, and the other toward Salganeus and Anthedon, with the former sea continuous toward Egypt, Cyprus, and the islands, and the other toward Makedonia, the Propontis, and the Hellespont. He adds that the Euripos has made Euboia somewhat a part of it [Boiotia], since it is narrow and is crossed by a bridge that is two *plethra* long. He praises the territory because of these things, and says that [the Boiotians] are naturally suited for leadership, [C401] but they did not make use of training and education, and thus could not always govern. Whenever they were successful, they remained so for only a short time, as is shown by Epameinondas. After he died the Thebans immediately threw away his hegemony, having had only a taste of it, because they took reason and intercourse with humanity lightly, caring only for military virtues. He [Ephoros] should have added that these things are particularly useful against the Hellenes, although against the

---

[7] There are several gaps and uncertainties in this section, from eight to fourteen letters.

barbarians force is stronger than reason. In antiquity the Romans, warring with the more savage peoples, also did not need any such training, but when they began to have business with more cultured peoples and tribes, they applied themselves to it and thus in this way established themselves as masters of everyone.

(3) Boiotia was formerly inhabited by barbarians, the Aonians and the Temmikians – who wandered from Sounion – and the Lelegians and Hyantians. Then it was held by the Phoenicians with Kadmos, who fortified the Kadmeia and left the rule to his descendants. They founded Thebes, in addition to the Kadmeia, and preserved their rule, leading most of the Boiotians until the expedition of the Epigonoi. At that time they left Thebes for a short while but came back again. Similarly, when they were expelled by the Thracians and Pelasgians, they established their rule in Thessaly, with the Arnaians and for a long time, and thus they were all called Boiotians. Then they returned home, when the Aiolian expedition was in preparation around Boiotian Aulis, the one which the sons of Orestes were sending to Asia. They added the Orchomenia to Boiotia, for it had not been in common with it previously and Homer did not enumerate them with the Boiotians but called them separately the Minyans [*Iliad* 2.511]. Along with them, they drove the Pelasgians to Athens (from whom a portion of the city was called "Pelasgikon," and they lived below Hymettos), and the Thracians to Parnassos. The Hyantians founded the city of Hyampolis in Phokis.

(4) Ephoros [F119] says that the Thracians, having made a treaty with the Boiotians, attacked them at night, as they were encamped rather neglectfully, believing that they were at peace. The latter drove them away, and also charged that they [the Thracians] had broken the treaty. They replied that [C402] they had not broken it because the agreement was for daytime and they had attacked at night. From this is spoken the proverb "a Thracian pretext." The Pelasgians, while the war was continuing, went to consult the oracle at Dodona, as did the Boiotians. What the oracular response given to the Pelasgians was he cannot say, but the prophetess replied to the Boiotians that they would do well by committing sacrilege. The envoys suspected that the prophetess replied in such a way to favor the Pelasgians, because of their kinship, as from the beginning the sanctuary had been Pelasgian. They seized the woman and threw her into a fire, considering that whether or not she had acted wrongly, they were correct in both cases, for if she had given a false oracle she was being punished, but if she had not acted wrongly they were only doing what they had been ordered. Those at the sanctuary did not approve of putting the perpetrators to death unjudged, or to do it in the sanctuary, and thus they were summoned to stand trial before the priestesses

(who were also the prophetesses), those who remained of the original three. They [the Boiotians] said that it was in no way lawful for them to be judged by women, so men equal in number to the women were chosen. The men voted for acquittal but the women for conviction, and since the votes cast were equal they won their release. Because of this, prophecies at Dodona are made to Boiotians only by men, but the prophetesses interpreted the oracle to say that the god had ordered the Boiotians to steal the tripods and each year to send them to Dodona, which they do, always taking down one of the dedicated tripods at night and covering it up with clothing, as if secretly carrying the tripod to Dodona.

(5) Afterward they assisted those with Penthilos in the Aiolian migration, sending most of their people with them, so that it was also called Boiotian. A long time later the Persian War that occurred around Plataiai ruined the territory, but then they recovered to such a point that the Thebans, having defeated the Lakedaimonians in two battles, claimed the rule of the Hellenes. Epameinondas fell in battle and thus they were disappointed in this, but they went to war for the Hellenes against the Phokians, who had pillaged the common sanctuary. After doing poorly in this war, as well as [C403] when the Makedonians attacked the Hellenes, they lost their city through them, which was razed, and then they received it back when it was restored. From then they have always done worse down to our time, not even preserving the impression of a worthwhile village. It is the same with the other cities except for Tanagra and Thespiai, for they, in comparison, have survived adequately.

(6) Next one must begin a circuit of the territory from the coast of Euboia that adjoins Attika, from which I make the change over to the Boiotian section. The beginning is at Oropos and the Sacred Harbor, which is called Delphinion, opposite which is ancient Eretria on Euboia, a crossing of 60 stadia. After Delphinion is Oropos, in 20 stadia, and opposite it is the Eretria of today; the crossing to it is 40 stadia.

(7) Then there is Delion, where the sanctuary of Apollo is, a copy of the one on Delos. It is a small city of the Tanagraians, 30 stadia distant from Aulis. This is where the Athenians, having left the battle, went in headlong flight, and in this flight Sokrates the philosopher, who was fighting on foot since his horse had gotten away, saw Xenophon the son of Gryllos lying on the ground, having fallen from his horse, and he carried him on his shoulders for many stadia, until the flight ceased, thus saving him.

(8) Then there is a large harbor which is called Deep Harbor, and then Aulis, a rocky place of the Tanagraians. It has a harbor suitable for fifty ships, and thus it is reasonable that the naval station of the Hellenes was in

the large harbor. The Chalkidean Euripos is nearby, which is 70 stadia[8] from Sounion. There is a bridge over it two *plethra* long, as I have said [9.2.2], and a tower standing on either side, one on the Chalkidean and the other on the Boiotian, with a passage constructed between them. Concerning the ebb and flow at the Euripos it is sufficient to tell only that they say it changes seven times each day and night. The cause must be investigated elsewhere.

(9) Nearby on a height is situated the place [called] Salganeus, whose eponym, Salganeus, was buried there. He was the Boiotian man who guided the Persians when they sailed into this passage from the Malaic Gulf. They say that he was done away with before they touched the Euripos, by Megabates, the naval commander, who considered him an evildoer because through deceit he had put the expedition into a blind strait of the sea. Yet the barbarian, when he perceived that he had been deceived about this, repented and considered him worthy of burial, as he had been put to death [C404] without cause.

(10) And Graia is a place near Oropos, as well as the sanctuary of Amphiaraos, and the memorial of Narkissos the Eretrian (which is called Sigelos, since those passing by keep silent [*sigosi*]). Some say that it [Graia] is the same as Tanagraia. Aristotle [F613] says the same about Oropos. It lies on the sea and is deserted. Poimandris is the same as the Tanagrike, and the Tanagraians are also called Gephyraians. The Amphiaraion was removed here from Knopia in the Thebais according to an oracle.

(11) And Mykalessos is a village in the Tanagrike. It lies on the road from Thebes to Chalkis, and is called Mykalettos in Boiotian. Harma is also in the Tanagrike, a deserted village near Mykalettos, taking its name from the chariot [*harma*] of Amphiaraos. It is different from the Harma in Attika, which is near Phyle, an Attic deme on the border with Tanagra. Here the proverb originated in which they say "when there is lightning through Harma," since those called the Pythaistai look toward Harma, in accordance with an oracle, for any flash of lightning, and then send the offering to Delphi when they see the lightning. They watch for three months, for three days and nights each month, from the hearth of Zeus Astrapaios, which is within the walls between the Pythion and the Olympion. In regard to Boiotian Harma, some say that Amphiaraos fell in battle from his chariot near the place where the sanctuary is now, and the empty chariot was brought to the place of the same name. Others say that the chariot of Adrastos, when he was fleeing, was shattered there but that he was saved by

---

[8] The number is wrong; it perhaps should be 570 or 670.

Arion. Philochoros [F113] says that he was saved by the villagers, and because of this they received equal rights from the Argives.

(12) To someone going from Thebes to Argos, Tanagra is on the left . . . lies on the right.⁹ Today Hyria is in the Tanagraia – formerly it was in the Thebais – and is where the myth of Hyrieus and the birth of Orion is, of which Pindar speaks in his *Dithyrambs* [F73]. It is located near Aulis. Some say that Hysiai, in the Parasopia below Kithairon and near Erythrai in the interior, is called Hyrie, and that it is a settlement of the Hyrians, a foundation of Nykteus the father of Antiope. There is also a village of Hysiai in the Argeia, and those from there are called Hysiatians. Erythrai in Ionia is a settlement from this Erythrai. Heleon is also a village of the Tanagrike, named for the marshes (*hele*).

(13) After Salganeus is Anthedon, a city having a harbor, the last on the Boiotian coast that is off Euboia, as the Poet says, "farthest Anthedon" [*Iliad* [C405] 2.508]. Still going a little farther, there are two small Boiotian towns: Larymna (near where the Kephissos empties) and, still farther, Halai, with the same name as the Attic demes. Opposite this coast lies, they say, Euboian Aigai, in which there is the sanctuary of Poseidon Aigaios that I mentioned previously [8.7.4]. The distance from Anthedon to Aigai is 120 stadia, but it is much less from the other places. The sanctuary lies on a high mountain, where once there was a city. Orobiai is also near Aigai. In the Anthedonia is Mount Messapion, from Messapos, who, when he came to Iapygia, called the territory Messapia. Here also is told the story of Glaukos the Anthedonian, who, they say, changed into a sea monster.

(14) Near to Anthedon is a sacred Boiotian place that has traces of a city, called Isos, with the first syllable short. Some believe that it should be written "divine Isos and farthest Anthedon" [*Iliad* 2.508], poetically lengthening the first syllable because of the meter, instead of "divine Nisa," for Nisa is seen nowhere in Boiotia, as Apollodoros [of Athens] says in his *On Ships* [F168]¹⁰ . . . if he does not mean Nisa, for there was . . . in the Megarike, settled . . . of Kithairon, but it has been abandoned today. Some write "divine Kreusa," taking it as the Kreousa of today, the seaport of the Thespians on the Krisaian Gulf, but others "divine Pharai," one of the Four Villages around Tanagra (Heleon, Harma, Mykalessos, and Pharai). Others write this: "divine Nysa." Nysa is a village on Helikon. Such, then, is this coast off Euboia.

---

⁹ A gap of thirteen to sixteen letters hides the locality on the right.
¹⁰ There are three gaps in what immediately follows, for a total of about twenty-six letters.

(15) Next are the plains in the interior, which are hollows and surrounded everywhere on their other sides by mountains: those of Attika on the south, and on the north those of the Phokians. On the west Kithairon falls at a slight slant over the Krisaian Sea, having its beginning contiguous with the Megarian and Attic mountains, and then bends into the plain, ending [C406] around the Thebaid.

(16) Some of these plains are marshes, as rivers spread out through them and others fall into them and find an outlet. Some are dried up and are famed in every way because of their fertility. There are underground caves and holes in the depths of the earth, and violent earthquakes often have blocked up some passages and opened up others, some to the surface and others through underground channels. Thus it happens that the waters have some of their streams carried through underground channels and others are on the surface in lakes and rivers. When the passages in the depths are silted up, it happens that the lakes expand as far as the inhabited places, so that they swallow up cities and territories, but when these or others are opened up, they are uncovered. The same places are accessible at some times by boat and at other times by foot, and the same cities at some times are on the lake and at other times are far away.

(17) There are two things that have occurred: either the cities have remained without being moved, when the increase of the waters is less than what would overflow the houses (because of their height), or they have been removed and rebuilt when, because of the dangers due to their proximity, relief is provided from fear by changing to places farther away or on the heights. It follows that those that are rebuilt and keep the same name, although formerly called by names that were locally applicable to the places, [have names that] are no longer applicable. It is probable that Plataiai was so called from the blade [*plate*] of the oars, and that the Plataians made their living from rowing. Now they live far from the lake and the name is no longer applicable. Helos, Heleon, and Heilesion were so called because they were situated near marshes [*hele*], but it is not the same today, as all of them have been rebuilt, or the lake is much smaller because of the later outflow, for this is also possible.

(18) The Kephissos, which fills Lake Kopais, shows this best. When it [Kopais] had filled so much that Kopai (which is named by the Poet [*Iliad* 2.502], and the lake took its name from it) was in danger of being swallowed up, a chasm opened in the lake near Kopai that created a stream under the earth for about thirty stadia which received the river. It then broke onto the surface around Larymna in Lokris (the upper one, for there is another that I have mentioned [9.2.13], the Boiotian one on the sea to which the Romans

attached the upper one). The place is called Anchoe, and there is a lake with [C407]
the same name. From here the Kephissos empties into the sea. At the time
that the flooding ceased there was also a cessation of danger to those living
alongside it, except for the cities that had been swallowed up. The passages
filled up again, and the mining engineer Krates, a Chalkidean man, was
cleaning away the obstacles but ceased because of instability among the
Boiotians, although, as he himself says in his letter to Alexander, many
places had already dried off. Among these, some believe, was the ancient site
of Orchomenos, and according to others Eleusis and Athenai on the Triton
River. It is said that Kekrops[11] . . . when he ruled Boiotia, which at that time
was called Ogygia, but later disappeared because of floods. They say that a
chasm appeared near Orchomenos that admitted the Melas River, which
flowed through the Haliartia, creating the marsh where the reeds for flutes
grow. But it has completely disappeared, either because it is diffused by the
chasm into invisible channels, or it is previously used up by the marshes and
lakes around Haliartos, from which the Poet calls the place "grassy," saying
"grassy Haliartos" [*Iliad* 2.503].

(19) These rivers flow down from the Phokian mountains, and include
the Kephissos, which takes its beginning at Lilaia, a Phokian city, as Homer
says ("those who held Lilaia at the source of the Kephissos" [*Iliad* 2.523]).
Flowing through Elateia, the largest of the cities among the Phokians, and
through Parapotamioi and Phanoteus – also Phokian towns – it continues
to Boiotian Chaironeia, and then through the Orchomenia and the
Koroneiake, emptying into Lake Kopais. There are also the Permessos
and the Olmeios, from Helikon, which join each other and fall into the
same Lake Kopais near Haliartos[12] . . . streams empty into it. It is large,
having a circuit of 380 stadia, but the outlets are nowhere to be seen except
for the chasm that receives the Kephissos and the marshes.

(20) Among the neighboring lakes are Trephia and Kephissis, recorded
by Homer ("he who lived in Hyle, greatly interested in wealth, on the shore
of Lake Kephissis" [*Iliad* 5.708–9]). He does not mean to speak of Lake
Kopais, as some believe, but the one called Hylike (pronounced like *lyrikē*),
from the nearby village that is called Hylai (like *lyrai* and *thyrai*), not Hyde,
as some write ("who lived in Hyde"), which is in Lydia ("below snowy [C408]
Tmolos in the fertile district of Hyde" [*Iliad* 20.385]), but the other is
Boiotian. At any rate, he adds this to "on the shore of Lake Kephissis":
"the other Boiotians lived nearby" [*Iliad* 5.709–10]. It [Kopais] is large and

---

[11] There is a gap of about six letters.   [12] There is a gap of about eight letters.

not in the Thebais, and the other is small, is filled through underground channels, and is situated between Thebes and Anthedon. Homer uses it in the singular, at one point having the first syllable long (as in the *Catalogue*, "Hyle and Peteon" [*Iliad* 2.500]), and elsewhere poetically making it short ("he who lived in Hyle" [*Iliad* 5.708], and Tychios, "the best of leather workers, had his home in Hyle" [*Iliad* 7.221]). Those are not correct who write "Hyde" here, for Aias was not sending for his shield from Lydia.

(21)[13] ... lakes ... the order at the next places ... clearly comprehend in fact because ... in the naming of the places, whether worthy ... it is difficult, with so many that are obscure and in the interior, not to make any error in their order. The coast, however, has a certain advantage in this, for the places are better known and the sea better suggests their order. Thus I will attempt. ... Here I will let this be, and follow the Poet in making the enumeration, adding whatever is useful for us that was omitted by him. He begins with Hyrie and Aulis, of which I have already spoken [9.2.8, 12].

(22) Schoinos is a territory of the Thebaike on the road to Anthedon, about 50 stadia distant from Thebes. The Schoinous River also flows through it.

(23) Skolos is a village in the Parasopia below Kithairon, a rugged place that is difficult to live in, from which there is the proverb "do not go to Skolos or even go there with someone else." They say that this is where Pentheus was brought when he was torn to pieces. Among the cities around Olynthos there is a Skolos with the same name as this one. It has already been said [8.6.24] that there is a certain village called Parasopioi in Trachinian Herakleia, past which an Asopos River flows, and in Sikyon there is another Asopos and a territory of Asopia through which it flows, and there are still other rivers with the same name as this one.

(24) Eteonos changed its name from Skaphlai, and is also in the Parasopia. The Asopos and the Ismenos flow through the plain in front of
[C409]　Thebes. There is also the spring called Dirke, or Potniai, where there is the myth about Glaukos the Potnian, who was torn to pieces below the city by the Potnian mares. Kithairon ends not far from Thebes. The Asopos flows past it, washing its foothills and making a division of the Parasopians into a number of settlements, all of which are subject to Thebes. Others say that Skolos, Eteonos, and Erythrai are in the Plataieia, for it [the Asopos] flows past Plataiai and empties around Tanagra. In the Thebais are also Therapnai

---

[13] The text of section 21 is exceedingly corrupt, with gaps for about seventy letters throughout the passage.

and Teumessos, which Antimachos [F2] has adorned with many words, although he enumerates good attributes that do not exist: "there is a windy little hill" are words that are well known.

(25) He also says Thespeia for the Thespiai of today, for there are many names that are spoken in both the singular and plural – just as in the masculine and feminine – and others in one or the other. It is a city near Helikon, somewhat to the south, with both it and Helikon lying on the Krisaian Gulf. Thespiai has a seaport, Kreousa, which is also called Kreusis.

In the Thespieia, in the part toward Helikon, is Askre, the hometown of Hesiod. It is situated on the right of Helikon, in a high and rugged place, about forty stadia from Thespiai. He satirized it in writing about his father – who earlier had moved here from Aiolian Kyme – saying,

> he settled near Helikon in a wretched village, Askre, bad in winter, difficult in summer, and good at no time. [*Works and Days* 639–40]

In its northern portions Helikon is contiguous to Phokis, and slightly so on the western, around the last harbor of Phokis, which is called Mychos ["Recess"] because of its situation. Lying somewhat above this harbor of the Krisaian Gulf are Helikon and Askre, and also Thespiai and its seaport of Kreousa. This is considered the deepest part of the Krisaian Gulf, and of the Corinthian in general. The coast from the harbor of Mychos to Kreousa is 90 stadia, and from there to the promontory called <Olmiai> is 120. Thus Pegai and Oinoe – about which I have already spoken [8.6.22] – are located in the deepest part of the gulf. Helikon, which is not far distant from Parnassos, is equal to it both in height and circumference. Both mountains [C410] are snow covered and rocky, and they do not circumscribe a large territory. Here are the sanctuary of the Muses and Hippoukrene, and the cave of the Leibethridian Nymphs, which would prove that those who consecrated Helikon to the Muses were certain Thracians, the ones who dedicated Peiris, Leibethron, and Pimpleia to the same goddesses. They were called the Pieres, but they have disappeared and the Makedonians now hold those places. It has been said [9.2.3] that the Thracians were settled in this territory, having used force against the Boiotians, as did the Pelasgians and other barbarians.

Thespiai was formerly well known because of the *Eros* of Praxiteles, which he sculpted and which was dedicated by the hetaira Glykera – who had received it as a gift from the artist – to the Thespians, where she was from. Formerly people would go up to Thespiai – a place not otherwise of note – to see the *Eros*. Today it and Tanagra are the only Boiotian cities still in existence, as the others are ruined and only their names are left.

(26) After Thespiai he [Homer] tells about Graia and Mykalessos, about which I have spoken [9.2.10–11]. He says this about what follows: "those who lived in Harma, Eilesion, and Erythrai, and those who held Eleon, Hyle, and Peteon" [*Iliad* 2.499–500]. Peteon is a village in the Thebais near the road to Anthedon.

Okalee is between Haliartos and Alalkomenion, 30 stadia from each, and a little river of the same name flows past it. Phokian Medeon is on the Krisaian Gulf, 160 stadia distant from Boiotia. The Boiotian ... was named after it, and is near Onchestos at the base of Mount Phoinikion, from which its name has been changed to Phoinikis. It is said to be part of the Thebais – as are Medeon and Okalea – but is seen by some as part of the Haliartia.

(27) He then says "Kopai, Eutresis, and Thisbe abundant in doves" [*Iliad* 2.502]. I have already spoken about Kopai [9.2.18]. It is toward the north, on Lake Kopais, and others are around it. These are Akraiphiai, Phoinikis, Onchestos, Haliartos, Okalea, Alalkomenai, Tilphousion, and Koroneia. In

[C411] antiquity there was no common name for the lake, but it was called by the names of the various settlements on it: Kopais from Kopai, Haliartis from Haliartos, and so forth with the others. Later it was called Kopais in its entirety, through its predominance, for that territory is at its deepest hollow. Pindar [F198b] calls it Kephissis; at any rate, he places it near the spring of Tilphossa, which flows from Mount Tilphossion near Haliartos and Alalkomenai, near which is the memorial of Teiresias and also the sanctuary of Tilphossian Apollo.

(28) Next, after Kopai, the Poet places Eutresis, a small village of the Thespians, where, they say, Zethos and Amphion lived before they ruled Thebes. Thisbe is now called Thisbai. It is a habitation slightly above the sea, bordering the territory of the Thespians and the Koroneiake, lying at the foot of Helikon on its southern portion. It has a seaport at a rocky place full of doves, about which the Poet says "Thisbe abundant in doves" [*Iliad* 2.502]. From here the voyage to Sikyon is 160 stadia.

(29) Next he tells about Koroneia, Haliartos, Plataiai, and Glissas [*Iliad* 2.503–4]. Koroneia was established on a height near Helikon. The Boiotians took it when they returned from Thessalian Arne after the Trojan matter, at which time they also acquired Orchomenos. When they mastered Koroneia, they established the sanctuary of Itonian Athena in the plain before it, named after the one in Thessaly. They called the river flowing past it the Kouarios, having the same name as one there. Alkaios calls it the Koralios, saying "Queen Athena the war-sustaining, who watches over ... of Koroneia in front of the temple ... on the banks of

the Koralios River" [F325].[14] Here the Pamboiotia was also celebrated. Along with Athena, there was a dedication to Hades, for some mystic reason, as they say. Those in Koroneia are called Koronians, but those in Messenia Koronaians.

(30) Haliartos no longer exists today, having been razed during the war with Perseus, and the territory is held by the Athenians, a gift of the Romans. It was situated in a narrow place, between the mountain lying above it and the Kopaic Lake, near the Permessos and Olmeios, and the marsh that produces the reeds for flutes.

(31) Plataiai, which the Poet speaks of in the singular [*Iliad* 2.504], is at the foot of Kithairon, between it and Thebes, along the road to Athens and Megara, and on the borders of Attika and the Megaris. Eleutherai is nearby, which some say is Attic, others Boiotian. It has already been said [9.2.24] that the Asopos flows past Plataiai. Here the forces of the Hellenes completely destroyed Mardonios and his 300,000 Persians. A sanctuary was built to Zeus Eleutherios, and athletic games called the Eleutheria were established, in which the prize was a crown. The state tombs of those who died in the battle are visible. There is also in the Sikyonia a deme of Plataiai, where Mnasalkes the poet was from ("the memorial of Mnasalkes the Plataian" [Theodorides, *Palatine Anthology* 13.21]). He [Homer] then speaks of Glissas, a settlement on Mount Hypaton, which is in the Thebaike near to Teumessos and Kadmeia, and the hillocks called ... that lie below the so-called Aonian Plain, which extend from Mount Hypaton as far as Thebes. [C412]

(32) The following words – "those who held Hypothebes" [*Iliad* 2.505] – some take to mean a little town called Hypothebes, and others Potniai, because Thebes was abandoned due to the expedition of the Epigonoi and did not participate in the Trojan War. Others [say] that they did not participate but were living at that time in the level regions below the Kadmeia after the departure of the Epigonoi, unable to rebuild the Kadmeia. Since the Kadmeia was called Thebes, the Poet said "Hypothebes" for the Thebans of that time, who were living below the Kadmeia.

(33) Onchestos is where the Amphiktyony met, and is in the Haliartia near Lake Kopais and the Teneric Plain. It is situated on a barren height, having a sanctuary of Poseidon that itself is barren. Poets embellish and call all sanctuaries groves even if they are barren, such as what Pindar says about Apollo:

---

[14] Strabo's preserved text has two gaps in the quotation.

he wandered through earth and sea, and on lookouts ... and stood in the mountains, and whirled into recesses, laying the foundations of groves. [F51a]

But Alkaios [F425] is incorrect, for just as he perverted the name of the Kouarios, he falsely reported about Onchestos, placing it near the extremities of Helikon, although it is quite far away from the mountain.

[C413] (34) The Teneric Plain is named after Teneros. The myth is that he was the son of Apollo, from Melia, and was a prophet of the oracle on Mount Ptoion, which the same poet [Pindar] says is three-peaked ("once he took possession of the three-peaked hollows of Ptoion" [F51b]), and he called Teneros "the temple-overseeing prophet, called by the same name as the plains" [F51d]. Ptoion lies above the Teneric Plain and the Kopaic Lake, near Akraiphion. The mountain and the oracle were Theban. Akraiphion itself lies on a height. They say that it is called Arne by the Poet [*Iliad* 2.507], the same name as the Thessalian one.

(35) Some say that Arne was swallowed up by the lake, as Mideia also was. Zenodotos writes "they held Askre rich in grapes" [*Iliad* 2.507, revised], but he does not seem to have come across what Hesiod had said [*Works and Days* 639–40] about his native territory, nor Eudoxos [F353], who says much worse things about Askre. How could anyone believe that such a place was said by the Poet to be "rich in grapes"? This is not correct, and neither are those who write Tarne instead of Arne, for not a single Tarne is pointed out among the Boiotians, although there is one among the Lydians, which Homer records:

> Idomeneus then killed Phaistos, the son of the woodworker Boros, who came from Tarne of the rich soil. [*Iliad* 5.43–4]

The remainder of those worth recording are – lying around the lake – Alalkomenai and Tilphossion, and – among the others – Chaironeia, Lebadeia, and Leuktra.

(36) The Poet mentions Alalkomenai, but not in the *Catalogue* ("Argive Hera and Alalkomenian Athena" [*Iliad* 5.907]). It has an ancient sanctuary of Athena that is greatly honored, and they say that the goddess was born there, just as Hera was in Argos. Because of this the Poet named them both in this way, as these were their native places. It was also because of this, perhaps, that he did not mention the men from there in the *Catalogue*, since they were sacred and released from the expedition. The city always continued unravaged, although neither large or secure in its location, but in a plain. Everyone, because of reverence toward the goddess, avoided any violence, so that the Thebans, at the time of the expedition of the Epigonoi, left their city, it is said, and fled to Mount Tilphossion and the natural

fortification lying above it. At its base is the Tilphossa spring and the monument of Teiresias, who died there during the flight. [C414]

(37) Chaironeia is near Orchomenos. This is where Philippos [II] the son of Amyntas [III] conquered the Athenians, Boiotians, and Corinthians in a great battle and set himself up as master of Hellas. Here the state tombs of those who fell in the battle are visible. In about the same place the Romans prevailed over the many myriads of Mithridates [VI]. Only a few fled to the sea and safety in their ships, and the others either died or were captured.

(38) Lebadeia is where the oracle of Zeus Trophonios is situated. It has a chasm descending under the earth, and the one consulting the oracle descends himself. It is located between Helikon and Chaironeia, near Koroneia.

(39) Leuktra is where Epameinondas defeated the Lakedaimonians in a large battle and began their destruction, since from that time they were no longer able to regain the hegemonic power of the Hellenes which they had formerly held, especially because they did badly in the second engagement around Mantineia. Although they had stumbled in such a way, they remained free of others until the Roman domination, and they have continued in honor among them because of the excellence of their government. The place is to be seen on the road from Plataiai to Thespiai.

(40) Next the Poet records the catalogue of the Orchomenians [*Iliad* 2.511–16], whom he separates from the Boiotian peoples. He calls Orchomenos "Minyeian," from the Minyan peoples. They say that some of the Minyans emigrated from here to Iolkos, because of which the Argonauts were called Minyans. It clearly was a particularly rich and exceedingly powerful city in antiquity. Homer is a witness also to its wealth, for when he enumerates the places that are abundantly rich, he says "not even as much as comes to Orchomenos, nor as much as Egyptian Thebes" [*Iliad* 9.381–2], and its power [is shown] by the [Boiotian] Thebans paying tribute to the Orchomenians and their tyrant, Erginos, who is said to have been put to death by Herakles. Eteokles, one of those who reigned at Orchomenos, established a sanctuary of the Charites and was the first to demonstrate both wealth and power. He honored these goddesses because he was successful in receiving favors [*charites*], or giving them, or both. By necessity, when he had become naturally disposed to [C415] good deeds, he began to honor these goddesses, and thus he already possessed the power, but it was also necessary to have money. One cannot give anything much if one does not have much, and no one could have much if he did not receive much. But if he has both, there is reciprocity, for something that is simultaneously being emptied and filled is always full

for use, yet one who gives and does not receive would not be successful in either. He will cease giving because his treasury fails, and those who give [to him] will cease because he only receives, but grants no favors, and thus he would not be successful in either case. Similar things could be said about power. Apart from the common saying "money is most honored among men, and of everything it has the most power for men" [Euripides, *Phoenician Women* 439–40], it is necessary to consider this by itself. We say that kings have the greatest power [*dynasthai*] – this is why they are called dynasts – and are powerful in leading the masses where they wish, whether through persuasion or force. For the most part they persuade through good deeds, for it is not regal to do so through words, as this is for the orator. We say that regal persuasion is when they produce good deeds and through these obtain what they wish. They are persuasive through good deeds but use force through weapons. Both of these can be bought with money, for the one who has the largest army can support the largest, and the one who acquires the most is able [to produce] the most good deeds.

They say that the place Lake Kopais occupies today was formerly dry and farmed in every way when it was subject to the Orchomenians, who lived near it. This is also considered proof of their wealth.

(41) Some pronounced Aspledon without the first syllable. Then the name both of it and the territory was changed to Eudeielos, perhaps because it offered a peculiar advantage to the homes of those living there, especially regarding the comfort of the winters, as it had an evening (*deilinos*) slope. The extremities of the day are the coldest, and of these the evening is colder than the morning, for as the night draws near it becomes intense, and with its withdrawal it abates. The sun counteracts the cold. Thus the winters are most comfortable where it is warmed most by the sun at the coldest season. It is 20 stadia distant from Orchomenos, with the Melas River in between.

[C416]

(42) Panopeus lies above the Orchomenia, a Phokian city, as well as Hyampolis. Opous borders on these, the metropolis of the Epiknemidian Lokrians. Formerly, they say, Orchomenos was situated on a plain, but when the waters overflowed they migrated up to Mount Akontion, which extends for 60 stadia as far as Parapotamioi in Phokis. They record that the so-called Achaians in Pontos are a settlement of Orchomenians who wandered there with Ialmenos after the sack of Troy. There was also an Orchomenos around Karystos. Those who have written about the ships have made good suggestions for us about such matters, and those are the ones that we follow when they say appropriate things for our treatise.

Part 3: Phokis

(1) Phokis is after Boiotia and Orchomenos, lying parallel to Boiotia on the north, in antiquity almost from sea to sea. At that time Daphnous was part of Phokis, and this split Lokris in two, placed in the middle between the Opountian Gulf and the Epiknemidian coast. The territory is now Lokrian – the town has been razed – so that even here Phokis does not appear to reach the sea around Euboia. It does touch the Krisaian Gulf. Krisa itself is Phokian, situated on the sea, as are Kirrha, Antikyra, and those contiguous places lying above them in the interior near Parnassos – Delphi, Kirphis, and Daulis – as well as Parnassos itself, which is Phokian and forms its boundary on the western side.

In the same way that Phokis is situated alongside Boiotia, Lokris is along Phokis on either side, for it is double, divided in two by Parnassos: the part on the west lying alongside Parnassos and occupying part of it, extending down to the Krisaian Gulf, and that toward the east ending at the sea by Euboia. The Hesperian ["Western"] Lokrians are called Ozolians, and have the Hesperos star engraved on their state seal. The others are somewhat divided into two, the Opountians – from their metropolis – who border on the Phokians and Boiotians, and the Epiknemidians, from Mount Knemis, who are next to the Oitaians and Malians. In the middle of both – the Hesperians and the others – is Parnassos, extending as an oval into the northern portion, from the places around Delphi as far as the junction of [C417] the Oitaian Mountains with the Aitolian, and having the Dorians in between. Again, just as Lokris[15] … is parallel to Phokis, thus <the Oitaians> along with Aitolia and some of the Dorian tetrapolis are in the middle … along with both parts of Lokris, Parnassos, and the Dorians. Immediately above these are <the Thessalians>, the northern Aitolians, the Akarnanians, and some of the Epeirote and Makedonian peoples. … As we said formerly [9.2.1], these previously mentioned territories should be considered as extending parallel to each other from west to east like certain ribbons.

All of Parnassos is considered sacred, since it has caves and other places that are honored and believed to be holy. The best known and most beautiful of these is the Korykion, a cave of the nymphs with the same name as one in Kilikia. In regard to the sides of Parnassos, the Ozolian Lokrians occupy the western, as do some of the Dorians and the Aitolians below the Aitolian mountain called Korax. The other side [is occupied by]

---

[15] There are several gaps for a total of eighteen to twenty-seven letters in the remainder of the paragraph.

the Phokians and most of the Dorians who possess the Tetrapolis, which generally lies around Parnassos, but expands in the areas toward the east.

The long side of the previously mentioned territories and the ribbons of each are all parallel, one being toward the north and the other toward the south.[16] For the remaining ones, the western are not parallel to the eastern, nor is either coast – where these [peoples] come to an end – that of the Krisaian <Gulf> as far as Aktion and toward Euboia as far as <the Makedonian> . . . parallel to each other. One must accept the shape of these regions as if a number of lines . . . the base in a triangle, for those that are cut off . . . parallel to one another . . . sides will be parallel but it is not the case . . . this is a type of rough outline of what remains and which will be gone through next. We will now discuss each successively, beginning from Phokis.

(2) Two cities are the most famous of this region, Delphi and Elateia: Delphi because of the sanctuary of Pythian Apollo and the oracle, which is ancient, since it is said by the Poet that Agamemnon consulted the oracle there, for the citharist is said to have sung

> the quarrel of Odysseus and the son of Peleus, lord, how once they contended . . . Agamemnon, the lord of men, rejoiced in his mind . . . for thus Phoibos Apollo at Pytho had reported that this would be so. [*Odyssey* 8.75–80, excerpted]

[C418]   Delphi is [famous] because of these things, but Elateia because it is the largest of all the cities there, and the best situated, located in a narrows. Whoever has it, holds the passes into Phokis and Boiotia. First there are the Oitaian Mountains, and then those of the Lokrians and Phokians, which are not accessible everywhere to armies making an incursion from Thessaly. There are passes that are narrow and separated that are guarded by the adjacent cities. When they are captured, it happens that the passes are also mastered. Since the distinction of the sanctuary at Delphi has seniority, and the location of its places suggests a natural beginning – these are the westernmost parts of Phokis – one must begin there.

(3) It has already been said that Parnassos is situated on the western boundary of Phokis. The Ozolian Lokrians possess the side toward the west, and Delphi that toward the south, which is a rocky place shaped like a theater, having the oracle and the city on its summit, filling a circuit of 16 stadia. Lykoreia lies above it, the place on which Delphi was formerly situated, above the temple. Now they live near it, around the

---

[16] There are several gaps for a total of thirty-two to forty-four letters in this paragraph.

Kastalian Spring. Kirphis, a precipitous mountain, lies in front of the city beyond its southern side. A ravine remains in between, through which the Pleistos River flows. Kirrha, an ancient city, lies below Kirphis and is situated on the sea, from where the ascent to Delphi is about 80 stadia. It is situated opposite Sikyon. In front of Kirrha is the fertile Krisaian Plain. Next in succession is another city, Krisa, from which is the Krisaian Gulf. Then there is Antikyra, having the same name as that on the Maliac Gulf at Oite which they say produces good hellebore, but at the former it is better prepared, and because of this many travel there in order to be cleansed and cured. In the Phokian [city] a certain sesame-like drug is produced with which the Oitaian hellebore is prepared.

(4) It survives, but Kirrha and Krisa have been destroyed, the latter at a later time by Eurylochos the Thessalian in the Krisaian War. The Krisaians were prosperous because of the duties from Sikelian and Italian products, and harshly assessed those who came to the sanctuary, contrary to the [C419] Amphiktyonic decrees. The same thing happened in regard to the Amphissans – they were Ozolian Lokrians – who came and restored Krisa and returned again to agriculture the plain that had been consecrated by the Amphiktyony. They, however, were worse with foreigners than the Krisaians had formerly been, and thus the Amphiktyony took vengeance on them and gave the territory back to the god.

The sanctuary is exceedingly neglected, although formerly it surpassed . . . The treasuries show this (which were built both by cities and dynasts, and where they deposited valuables that they had dedicated as well as works by the best artisans), as do the Pythian games and the great number of oracles that have been recorded. This is the concept of the founding of cities and the holding of common sanctuaries in high honor: they came together according to cities and peoples, by nature having things in common, and at the same time, because they had a need for each other, meeting at the common sanctuaries for the same reasons, celebrating festivals and holding assemblies. All such things produce friendship, beginning with eating at the same table, drinking together, and being under the same roof. The larger the number coming from more places, so much greater the benefit was believed to be.

(5) They say that the oracle is in a hollow cave that is deep with a rather narrow mouth, and from which a divinely inspired breath rises up. A high tripod is placed over the mouth which the Pythia mounts and, receiving the breath, utters both metrical and unmetrical oracles, with the latter put into meter by certain poets who are in the service of the sanctuary. They say that the first Pythia was Phemonoe, and the prophetess and city were so-called

from "to inquire" (*pythesthai*), although the first syllable was lengthened, as in *athanatos*, *akamatos*, and *diakonos*.

(6) Greater honor resulted for the temple because of the oracle, for it obtained the reputation of being the most truthful of all, and the location of the place also added something. It is almost in the center of the whole of Hellas, both that inside the Isthmos and outside of it. It was also considered [in the center of] the inhabited world, and was called the navel of the earth. A myth was created – which Pindar [F54] tells – that eagles were released by [C420] Zeus and met here, one from the west and the other from the east (some say that they were ravens). A kind of navel is shown in the temple, wearing headbands and having the two images of the myth on it.

(7) With Delphi having such a convenient situation, [people] easily could come together there, especially those who were nearby. In fact, the Amphiktyonic Confederacy was organized from them, to deliberate about common matters and to care for the sanctuary more in common because much money and many dedications were stored there, requiring extensive guarding and religious services. It is not known about antiquity, but Akrisios seems to be the first recorded to administer the offices of the Amphiktyony and to determine the participating cities, giving each a vote in the council – to one individually or together with another or others – and also to make known the Amphiktyonic rights (what the cities had in regard to other cities). Later there were a number of other administrations, until this organization was dissolved, like that of the Achaians. The first cities that came together are said to have been twelve in number, and each sent a Pylagoras. The assembly was twice a year, in spring and late autumn. Later more cities were added. The assembly – both in spring and late autumn – was called the Pylaia, since they came together at Pylai (also called Thermopylai). The Pylagorai sacrificed to Demeter. From the beginning only those nearby took part in this and the oracle, but later those far away came, such as Kroisos, his father Alyattes, and some Italiotes and Sikeliotes, consulting the oracle, sending gifts, and constructing treasuries.

(8) Wealth produces envy, and is difficult to guard even if sacred. Today the sanctuary at Delphi is exceedingly poor in regard to money. Although some of the dedications have been removed, most remain. Formerly the sanctuary was exceedingly wealthy, as Homer said: "nor as much as the stone threshold of the archer Phoibos Apollo shuts up within rocky Pytho" [*Iliad* 9.404–5]. The treasuries show this, as well as the plundering by the Phokians, from which the Phokian, or Sacred, War resulted. This plundering occurred at the time of Philippos [II] the son of Amyntas [III], although an earlier one, in antiquity, is suspected, in which the wealth mentioned by

Homer was carried away. No trace of it was preserved into later times, [C421]
when those with Onomarchos and Phaÿllos plundered the sanctuary. What
was carried away then was the more recent wealth, for what was stored in
the treasuries were dedications of booty that preserved on it the inscriptions
of the dedicators: Gyges, Kroisos, the Sybarites, the Spinetians (those
around the Adria), and such others. It is not[17] ... that the ancient wealth
was mixed in with this, as is clearly indicated by other places pillaged by
these men. Some, however, take "archer" to mean "treasury," and the
"threshold of the archer" as an underground storehouse, saying that the
wealth was buried in the temple and that Onomarchos and those with him
attempted to dig it up at night, but because great earthquakes occurred they
fled outside the temple and stopped their digging, which created a fear in
others of making such an attempt.

(9) Regarding the temples, the "winged" one must be placed among the
myths. The second is said to have been the work of Trophonios and
Agamedes, and the present one was constructed by the Amphiktyonians.
In the precinct the tomb of Neoptolemos is visible, which came into
existence through an oracle, as Machaireus, a man of Delphi, killed him,
because – according to the myth – the former was asking the god for justice
regarding the death of his father, but it was probably because he had
attacked the sanctuary. They said that Branchos, who governed the sanctuary at Didyma, was a descendant of Machaireus.

(10) Regarding the contests at Delphi, in antiquity there was one of
cithara singers, who sang the paean to the god, which the Delphians
established. After the Krisaian War the Amphiktyonians organized, in the
time of Eurylochos, equestrian and gymnastic contests in which the prize
was a crown, and called them the Pythia. In addition to the cithara singers,
there were flute and cithara players who did not sing but played a certain
musical number called the Pythian Melody. It has five parts: the prelude,
trial, encouragement, *iamboi* and dactyls, and the pipes. Timosthenes, the
naval commander of the second Ptolemaios, composed this melody, and he
also wrote *On Harbors* in ten books. He wished in the melody to com-
memorate the contest between Apollo and the serpent, having the prelude
as a preface, the first attack of the contest as the trial, the contest itself as the
encouragement, and the singing of the paean at the victory as the *iambos* and
dactyl, with appropriate rhythms. One was suitable for hymns and the [C422]
other, the *iambos*, for blaming, as in "to lampoon" [*iambizein*]. The pipes

---

[17] There is a gap of nine to twelve letters.

[*syringes*] imitate the death of the serpent, as if ending its life with its final hissing [*syrigmos*].

(11) Ephoros [F31b] (whom we are using the most because he is attentive to these matters, as Polybios [cf. 34.1.3–4] happens to testify), and who is a notable man, seems to me to do the opposite of what he had previously chosen and promised from the beginning. At any rate he censures those who have a fondness for myth in their historical writings. Praising the truth, he puts into his discussion of the oracle an august promise that he believes the truth to be the best in every instance, especially in regard to this subject. He also says that it is paradoxical if we were always to pursue this method in every such thing, yet when speaking of the oracle, which is the most truthful of all, we were to make use of accounts that are unbelievable and false. Having said these things, he immediately adds that it is understood that Apollo, along with Themis, created the oracle because he wished to benefit our race. Then, speaking of its benefits, [he says] that he appealed to gentleness and created temperance by providing oracles to some, enjoining them to do certain things and forbidding them to do other things, yet completely denying admission to others. He says that they believe he [Apollo] controls these things: some say that the god takes bodily form, and others that he transmits to men the intent of his will.

(12) Farther down, discussing who the Delphians were, he says that certain ancient Parnassians, those called the Dytochthonians, lived on Parnassos, and that at this time Apollo, coming into the land, civilized the peoples ... from cultivated fruits and life. Setting forth from Athens to Delphi he went by the same road on which the Athenians today send the Pythais. When he came to the Panopea he destroyed Tityos, a violent and lawless man who possessed the place. The Parnassians joined with him and informed him about another dangerous man named Python, who was also called Drakon, and when he was shot at with arrows they gave encourage-ment with "Hie, paean!" from which comes the singing of the paean that has been handed down as a custom for those about to join the battle line. At that time the tent of Python was burned by the Delphians, just as is still done today, creating a reminder of what happened then. But what would be more mythical than Apollo shooting arrows and punishing Tityoses and Pythons, and travelling from Athens to Delphi and visiting the entire earth? If he [Ephoros] did not take these as myths, how could he say that he was calling the mythological Themis a woman and the mythological Drakon a human being, unless he wished to confuse the types of history and myth? Similar to this is what he says about the Aitolians: saying that they had been unravaged for all time, he then says [F122b] at that one time the Aiolians

[C423]

lived there, having thrown out the barbarians who possessed it, and that at another time Aitolos with the Epeians from Elis[18] . . . from enemies, these subject to Alkmaion and Diomedes. But I return to the Phokians.

(13) Next on the coast after Antikyra is a town called Opisthomarathos, then Cape Pharygion, which has an anchorage, and then the harbor that is called Mychos ["Recess"] from its location, lying below Helikon and Askre. The oracle of Abai is not far from this place, and neither is Ambrysos or Medeon, which has the same name as the Boiotian one. Still farther, in the interior after Delphi and somewhat toward the east, is the town of Daulis, where Tereus the Thracian, they say, held power. The myth about Philomela and Prokne is there, although Thoukydides says that it was at Megara. The place received its name from thickets, for they call thickets "*dauloi*." Now Homer said Daulis [*Iliad* 2.520], but later it was Daulia. And "holding Kyparissos" [*Iliad* 2.519] is taken two ways: some as having the same name as the tree and others, by a slight change, as a village below Lykoreia.

(14) Panopeus, the Phanoteus of today, borders on the regions around Lebadeia, and is the native land of Epeios. The myth about Tityos is located here. Homer says that the Phaiekians "led" Rhadymanthos into Euboia "to see Tityos, the son of Gaia" [*Odyssey* 7.324]. A certain cave, Elarion, named after Elara the mother of Tityos, is visible on the island, as well as a heroon of Tityos, where there are certain honors. Near to Lebadeia is Trachin, a Phokian town with the same name as the Oitaian one, and its inhabitants are called Trachinians.

(15) Anemoreia ["Windy Place"] was named from the condition that it experiences when it [the wind] rushes down from the place called The Lookout, a precipice extending from Parnassos. This place was the boundary between the Delphians and the Phokians when the Lakedaimonians instigated a revolt by the Delphians from the common confederacy of the Phokians and allowed them to have their own government. Some call it [C424] Anemoleia. Then there is Hyampolis, called Hya by some, to which the Hyantians were driven from Boiotia, as we have said [9.2.3]. It is especially far inland, situated near Parapotamioi, and is different from the Hyampeia on Parnassos. There is also Elateia, the largest city of the Phokians, which Homer did not know (as it is more recent than that time). It is well situated up against the passes from Thessaly. Demosthenes [*On the Crown* 169] clearly indicates its natural advantages, speaking of the sudden clamor that

---

[18] There is a gap of about twenty letters.

occurred in Athens when someone reported to the Prytanes that Elateia had been taken.

(16) Parapotamioi is a settlement located on the Kephissos near Phanoteus, Chaironeia, and Elateia. Theopompos [F385] says that this place is about forty stadia distant from Chaironeia, marking the boundary of the Ambrysians, Panopeans, and Daulians. It is situated on a moderately high hill at the pass from Boiotia to Phokis, between the mountains of Parnassos and Hadylion, leaving in the middle an area of about five stadia divided by the Kephissos, providing a narrow passage on either side. It has its beginning at the Phokian city of Lilaia (just as Homer says, "those who held Lilaia at the source of the Kephissos" [*Iliad* 2.523]), and empties into the Kopaic Lake. Hadylion extends over sixty stadia as far as Hyphanteion, where Orchomenos is situated. Hesiod speaks at length about the river and its course, that it flows through all of Phokis in a twisted and serpentine manner: "it winds like a serpent from Panopeus through strong Glechon and through Orchomenos" [F41]. The narrows around Parapotamioi (or Parapotamia, for it is said both ways) were a matter of contention in the Phokian War, since this was the single entrance into Phokis. There is the Kephissos in Phokis, one in Athens and one on Salamis, a fourth and fifth in Sikyon and on Skyros, a sixth in Argos (whose sources are on Lyrkeion), and at Apollonia near Epidamnos there is a spring near the gymnasium that is called Kephissos.

[C425] (17) Daphnous is now razed. It was once a city of Phokis, adjoining the Euboian Sea, and dividing the Epiknemidian Lokrians into a part toward Boiotia and one toward Phokis, which at that time went from sea to sea. A proof of this is the Schedieion there, which, they say, is the tomb of Schedios[19] ... Daphnous once split (*schizein*) Lokris on either side. Later the place was included within the boundaries of the Opountians. This is enough about Phokis.

Part 4: Lokris

(1) Lokris is next, and thus it must be spoken about. It is divided in two, one having the Lokrians toward Euboia, which, as I was saying, was once split on either side of Daphnous. The Opountians were named after their metropolis and the Epiknemidians after a certain mountain, Knemis. The other contains the Hesperian ["Western"] Lokrians who are also called Ozolians. Parnassos (situated between them) and the Dorian Tetrapolis

[19] There is a gap of six to nine letters.

separate them from the Opountians and Epiknemidians. One must begin with the Opountians.

(2) Next after Halai, where the Boiotian coast opposite Euboia terminates, lies the Opountian Gulf. Opous is the metropolis, which is clear from the inscription on the first of the five pillars around Thermopylai, inscribed near the Polyandrion: "Law-abiding Opoeis, the metropolis of the Lokrians, to those who died for Hellas against the Medes." It is about 15 stadia from the sea and 60 from the seaport. Kynos is the seaport, a cape that marks the end of the Opountian Gulf, which is around 40 stadia [in extent]. Between Opous and Kynos is a fertile plain, lying opposite Aidepsos in Euboia, where the hot springs of Herakles are, and separated from it by a strait of 160 stadia. They say that Deukalion lived in Kynos, and the grave memorial of Pyrrha is visible here, although that of Deukalion is at Athens. Kynos is about 50 stadia distant from Knemis. The island of Atalante is also situated opposite Opous, having the same name as the one in front of Attika. It is said that certain people in Eleia are called Opountians, but they are not worthy of recording except that they are renewing the kinship that exists between them and the Opountians. Homer says [*Iliad* 23.83–92] that Patroklos was from Opous, and after an act of involuntary murder he fled to Peleus, but his father Menoitios remained in his native land, for Achilleus said to Menoitios that he would return Patroklos there after coming back from the expedition [*Iliad* 18.324–7]. He was not the king of the Opountians, who was Aias the Lokrian, and whose native land, they say, was Narykon. Aianes was the name of the one killed by Patroklos, and a precinct is visible, the Aianeion, and a certain spring, the Aianis, [named] after him.   [C426]

(3) Next after Kynos are Alope and Daphnous, which, as we have said [9.3.17], has been razed. There is a harbor here, about 90 stadia distant from Kynos, and 120 from Elateia for one going on foot into the interior. Here is the Maliac Gulf, which is continuous with the Opountian.

(4) After Daphnous, in about 20 stadia by sea, is Knemides, a fortified place, which lies opposite Kenaion in Euboia (a cape facing toward the west and the Malian Gulf), and separated from it by a strait of about 20 stadia. These are now the Epiknemidian Lokrians. The three so-called Lichades Islands lie in front, named after Lichas, and there are others along the previously mentioned coast, but we are purposely omitting them. A harbor is 20 stadia after Knemides, above which is Thronion, the same number of stadia in the interior. Then there is the Boagrios River – also called the Manes – which flows past Thronion and empties into the sea. It is winter flowing, so that at times one can cross it on foot without getting

wet, and at others it has a width of two *plethra*. After this, Skarpheia lies 10 stadia above the sea, and 30 stadia from Thronion, and slightly less[20].... Then there are Nikaia and Thermopylai.

(5) Regarding the remaining cities, none of them is worthy of recording except those recorded by Homer [*Iliad* 2.531–3]. Kalliaros ("Beautifully Tilled") is no longer inhabited[21] ... the plain, called from its ease of cultivation. Bessa ["Wooded Glen"], a wooded place, also does not exist, and neither does Augeiai, whose territory is held by the Skarpheians. This Bessa should be written with two sigmas, because it is named from its woodiness, just like Nape ["Woodland Glen"] (in the plain of Methyme), which Hellanikos [F35b] ignorantly calls Lape. But the Attic deme, whose people are called Besaieis, is with one sigma.

(6) Tarphe ["Thicket"] lies on a height, 20 stadia from[22].... The territory is fruitful and well-wooded. It was named from its thickets, but is now called Pharygai, and a sanctuary of Hera Pharygaia is there, from the Pharygai in the Argeia. They say that they are settlers from the Argives.

(7) Homer does not mention the Hesperian ["Western"] Lokrians, or not specifically, but he seems to distinguish them from the others when he says "of the Lokrians who live opposite sacred Euboia" [*Iliad* 2.535], as if there were others, but they have not been chattered about by many. The cities that they held were Amphissa and Naupaktos, of which Naupaktos survives, [C427] near Antirrhion, named from the shipbuilding [*naupegia*] that occurred there, whether the Herakleidai built their equipment there, or, as Ephoros [F121] says, because even earlier the Lokrians had made their preparations there. It is not Aitolian, having been awarded to them by Philippos [II].

(8) Chalkis is there, which the Poet records in the Aitolian *Catalogue* [*Iliad* 2.640], below Kalydon. The hill of Taphiassosis also there, on which the memorial of Nessos and the other Centaurs is. They say that stinking and clotted water flows from under the base of the hill because of their putrefaction, and because of this the people are called Ozolians ["Strong Smelling"]. Molykreia is near Antirrhion and is an Aitolian town. Amphissa is situated at the extremity of the Krisaian plain, and the Amphiktyonians razed it, as we have said [9.3.4][23] ... and Eupalion are Lokrian. The entire voyage along the Lokrian [coast] slightly exceeds 200 stadia.

(9) There is a place named Alope here, among the Epiknemidians, and there is also one in Phthiotis. These are settlers of the Epiknemidians, but the Epizephyrians are [settlers] of them.

---

[20] There is a gap of ten to thirteen letters. [21] There is a gap of fourteen to seventeen letters. [22] There is a gap of about six letters. [23] There is a gap about about twelve letters.

(10) The Aitolians are contiguous with the Hesperian ["Western"] Lokrians, and the Ainianians who possess Oite [border] on the Epiknemidians, with the Dorians in the middle. These are the ones who live in the Tetrapolis, which, they say, is the metropolis of all the Dorians. The cities they possessed were Erineos, Boion, Pindos, and Kytinion. Pindos lies above Erineos, and a river of the same name flows past it and empties into the Kephissos not far away from Lilaia. Some call Pindos Akyphas. Their king, Aigimios, was expelled from his rule but was brought back, as it is recounted, by Herakles, and the former remembered the favor after the latter's death on Oite, for he adopted Hyllos, the eldest of his children, and he and his descendants received the rule. The journey of the Herakleidai down into the Peloponnesos began to set forth from here.

(11) For a while the cities were held in honor, although they were small and had wretched soil, but later they were lightly esteemed. With the Phokian War, and the Makedonian, Aitolian, and Athamanian predominance, it is astonishing that even a trace of them came to the Romans. The Ainianians had the same experience, for they were completely destroyed by the Aitolians and the Athamanians: by the Aitolians when they went to war along with the Akarnanians and were very powerful, and by the Athamanians who were the last of the Epeirotes to have continued with distinction – as the others were already weakened – and who had built up their power through their king Amynandros.

(12) They kept possession of Oite. The mountain extends from Thermopylai in the east as far as the Ambrakian Gulf in the west. In a way, the mountain cuts at a right angle the mountainous territory from Parnassos as far as Pindos and the barbarians situated beyond. Of this, the portion inclining toward Thermopylai is called Oite, 200 stadia long, rugged, and high. It is the highest around Thermopylai, coming to a peak there and ending at the sea in sharp and abrupt cliffs, although it leaves a small passage along the coast for those invading the Lokrian territory from Thessaly. [C428]

(13) The passage is called Pylai ["Gates"], Stena ["Narrows"], and Thermopylai ["Hot Gates"], because there are hot waters nearby that are honored and sacred to Herakles. The mountain lying above it is called Kallidromon, but some call by the name of Kallidromon the remainder that extends through Aitolia and Akarnania as far as the Ambrakian Gulf. Near Thermopylai, inside the narrows, there are forts: Nikaia, toward the Lokrian Sea, and above it Teichious and Herakleia (which was formerly called Trachin), a Lakedaimonian foundation. Herakleia is about six stadia from the old Trachin. Next there is Rhodountia, a natural fortress.

(14) These places are made difficult of access because of the roughness and the numerous streams that create ravines through which they pass. In addition to the Spercheios, which flows past Antikyra, there is the Dyras which, they say, attempted to quench the pyre of Herakles, and another, the Melas, which is 5 stadia from Trachin. Herodotos says [7.199–200] that to the south of Trachin there is a deep gorge through which the Asopos – having the same name as the previously mentioned Asoposes [8.6.24] – empties into the sea outside the Gates after receiving the Phoinix, which joins it from the south and has the same name as the hero, whose tomb is visible nearby. To Thermopylai from the Asopos is 15 stadia.

(15) These places were most highly reputed at the time that they controlled the keys to the Narrows and when there were struggles for primacy among those both outside the Narrows and within it. For example, Philippos [II] used to call Chalkis and Corinth the "shackles of Hellas," viewed from his starting point of Makedonia. Those later called both these and also Demetrias "the bonds," for it controlled the passes around Tempe, [C429] holding both Pelion and Ossa. Later, with everyone having come under a single hegemony, everything is at last open to all.

(16) It was around these Narrows that Leonidas and those with him, as well as a few from neighboring places, held out against such great Persian power, until the barbarians came through paths around the mountains and cut them down. Today their polyandrion and the pillars are there, with the well-known inscription on the Lakedaimonian pillar: "Stranger, announce to the Lakedaimonians that we who have fallen lie here, having obeyed our laws."

(17) There is also a large harbor here and a sanctuary of Demeter, in which the Amphiktyonians performed sacrifices at every Pylaia. From the harbor to Herakleia Trachin is 40 stadia on foot, and the sail to Kenaion is 70. The Spercheios empties immediately outside the Gates. It is 530 stadia from the Euripos to the Gates. Lokris ends there. That which is outside, toward the east and the Maliac Gulf, is Thessalian, and that toward the west is Aitolian and Akarnanian. The Athamanians no longer exist.

(18) The largest and most ancient portion is the Thessalians, some of whom Homer discusses, and others [discuss] most of them. Homer always speaks of the Aitolians by one name, classifying them by cities, not peoples, except for the Kouretians, who in part should be classified as Aitolians. But one must begin with the Thessalians, leaving out what is exceedingly ancient and mythical (and for the most part not agreed upon), as we have done elsewhere, and speaking about what appears appropriate to us.

Part 5: Thessaly

(1) The coast from Thermopylai as far as the outlet of the Peneios and the extremity of Pelion is the part of it [Thessaly] on the sea, facing the east and the northern extremities of Euboia. The Malians and the Achaian Phthiotians possess that which is near Euboia and Thermopylai, and the Magnetians that near Pelion. Let this be called the eastern and coastal side of Thessaly. Regarding the others, one is from Pelion and the Peneios, extending along with Makedonia toward the interior as far as Paionia and the Epeirote peoples, and the other is parallel to the Makedonians, from Thermopylai and the Oitaian and Aitolian mountains, and adjoining the Dorians from Erineos and Parnassos. Let the former – that near the Makedonians – be the northern side and the other the southern. There remains the western, enclosed by the Aitolians, Akarnanians, Amphilochians, and the Athamanian, Ainianian and Molossian Epeirotes, as well as what was [C430] once called the land of the Aithikians and the Tymphaians, or, simply, that around Pindos.

This is the circuit. For the most part Thessaly is flat and bounded on the south, west, and north, except for Pelion and Ossa.[24] These rise up sufficiently but do not enclose much territory and end at the plains.

(2) These [plains] are the middle of Thessaly, a most fortunate territory, except for what is so greatly washed by rivers. The Peneios, which flows through the middle and receives many rivers, often overflows. In antiquity it was totally a lake, as it is reported, since the plain is enclosed by mountains on all sides, and the territory along the coast was higher than the plains. When a fracture occurred because of earthquakes around what is now called Tempe, splitting Ossa from Olympos, the Peneios escaped through it to the sea and dried up this land. There remains Nessonis, a large lake, and Boibeis, which is smaller and closer to the coast.

(3) Being in such a way, it was divided into four parts, which are called Phthiotis, Hestiaiotis, Thessaliotis, and Pelasgiotis. Phthiotis is the southern portion alongside Oite, from the Malaic and Pylaic Gulf extending as far as Dolopia and the Pindos, widening as far as Pharsalos and the Thessalian plains. Hestiaiotis is the western, between Pindos and Upper Makedonia. The remainder are those who live in the plains below Hestiaiotis, who are called Thessaliotes and adjoin Lower Makedonia, as well as those next who fill up the territory as far as the Magnetian coast. Here there will be an enumeration of notable names, especially because of the poetry of Homer.

---

[24] The sentence is unclear and something may be missing.

Only a few of the cities preserve their ancestral reputation, particularly Larisa.

(4) The Poet divides the entirety of what we now call Thessaly into ten parts and dynasties [*Iliad* 2.681–756, 9.484], and he adds certain of the Oitaians and Lokrians, as well as some of what is classified under Makedonia today. He outlines what is common to each territory: that the whole and its parts change according to the power of those who are predominant.

(5) The first whom he catalogues are those subject to Achilleus, who possessed the southern side and were situated alongside Oite and the Epiknemidian Lokrians:

> as many as lived in Pelasgian Argos, who inhabited Alos, Alope, and Trachin, and those who held Phthia and Hellas with beautiful women, those who were called Myrmidons, Hellenes, and Achaians. [*Iliad* 2.681–4]

[C431] With these he couples those subject to Phoinix, and makes the expedition common to both. Nevertheless the Poet does not record a Dolopian army anywhere in the battle around Ilion, nor does he make their leader Phoinix go forth into danger, as is also the case with Nestor. But others speak of him, such as Pindar, who says that Phoinix "led a rash crowd of Dolopians who used the sling and aided the missiles of the horse-taming Danaans" [F183]. This is what one must understand in regard to the Poet, according to the principle of silence, as the grammarians are accustomed to say, for it would be ridiculous if the king took part in the expedition ("I lived in farthest Phthia as lord of the Dolopians" [*Iliad* 9.484]) without his subjects present, for he would not have appeared to have shared in the expedition with Achilleus, accompanying only in the role of a follower or speaker, or perhaps as an advisor. The words are intended to make this clear, as follows: "to be a speaker of words and a doer of deeds" [*Iliad* 9.443]. Thus there are the portions that I mention, one subject to Achilleus and one subject to Phoinix. But those previously mentioned who are subject to Achilleus are disputable: some accept Pelasgian Argos as a Thessalian city once situated around Larisa but now no longer in existence, yet according to others it is not a city but the plain of the Thessalians, called by this name because Abas, who settled there from Argos, gave it the name.

(6) To some, Phthia is the same as Hellas and Achaia, and it is the other (southern) portion of those into which the whole of Thessaly was divided. The Poet seems to make Phthia and Hellas two when he says "those who held Phthia and Hellas" [*Iliad* 2.683] – thus being two – "I fled far away through spacious Hellas and came to Phthia" [*Iliad* 9.478–9] and "there are many Achaian women throughout Hellas and Phthia" [*Iliad* 9.395]. Thus

the Poet makes them two, but it is not clear whether they are cities or territories. Some of those later – speaking of Hellas as a territory – say that it extends to Phthiotic Thebes from Palaipharsalos. In this territory is the Thetideion, near both Pharsaloi (the old and the new). Thus would it not be proof from the Thetideion that this was a part of the territory subject to Achilleus? In regard to others who speak of it as a city, the Pharsalians show a destroyed city 60 stadia from their own city, which they believe to be Hellas, and two nearby springs, Messeis and Hypereia. The Melitaians [say] [C432] that when their own city was named Pyrrha, Hellas was not far from them and situated about 10 stadia across the Enipeus and that it was from Hellas (which is situated in a low region) that the Hellenes migrated to their own city. As a witness to this, there is in their own agora the tomb of Hellen, the son of Deukalion and Pyrrha. It is recorded that Deukalion ruled Phthiotis, and, simply, Thessaly. The Enipeus flows from Othrys past Pharsalos, and empties into the Apidanos, and it into the Peneios. This is it about the Hellenes.

(7) Those subject to Achilleus, and subject to Protesilaos and Philoktetes, were called Phthians. The Poet is a witness to this, for he speaks in the *Catalogue* about those who were subject to Achilleus, including "those who held Phthia" [*Iliad* 2.683]. In the battle at the ships they were made to remain behind in their ships with Achilleus, being at rest, but those subject to Philoktetes were fighting under Medon and those subject to Protesilaos under Podarkes. About these he speaks generally:

> there are the Boiotians, the Iaonians with their long chitons, the Lokrians, the Phthians, and the glorious Epeians [*Iliad* 13.685–6]

and particularly:

> in front of the Phthians was Medon, and also Podarkes, steadfast in war. . . . These were armed, in front of the great-hearted Phthians, and were fighting with the Boiotians, defending the ships. [*Iliad* 13.693, 699–70]

Perhaps those with Eurypylos were also called Phthians, since they were neighbors. Today, however, they believe that the region around Ormenion (which was subject to Eurypylos) belongs to Magnesia, as well as everything that was subject to Philoktetes. But that which was subject to Protesilaos was part of Phthia, from Dolopia and Pindos as far as the Magnesian Sea. That subject to Peleus and Achilleus, beginning at the Trachinian and Oitaian land, is determined as extending as far as the city of Antron, which was subject to Protesilaos and whose name is now written as plural. The Malaic Gulf has about the same length.

(8) Regarding Halos and Alope, there is doubt as to whether he [Homer] does not mean the places that are today placed in the Phthiotian territory, but rather those among the Lokrians, since the dominion of Achilleus went that far, just as it went as far as Trachin and the Oitaia. There are a Halos and Halious on the Lokrian coast, as well as an Alope. Some put Halious in place of Alope and write thus: "those located in Halos, Halious, and Trachin" [*Iliad* 2.682, revised]. Phthiotic Halos is situated below the end of Othrys, a mountain situated to the north of Phthiotis, bordering Typhrestos and the Dolopians, extending along it to near the Maliac Gulf. Halos [masc.] or Halos [fem.] – it is said both ways – is about 60 stadia from Itonos. Athamas founded Halos, but it was obliterated[25] . . . in later times. It lies above the Krokian Plain, and the Amphrysos River flows close to its walls. Below the Krokian is Phthiotic Thebes. Halos is called Phthiotic and Achaian, and adjoins the Malians, just as the spurs of Othrys do, and just as Phylake, which was subject to Protesilaos, is in the part of Phthiotis neighboring the Malians, so is Halos. It is about a hundred stadia distant from Thebes, in between Pharsalos and the Phthiotians. Philippos [II] took it away from the Phthiotians and assigned it to the Pharsalians. It happens that the boundaries and organization of the peoples and places is always changing, as we have said before. Thus Sophokles [F1110] says that Trachin is Phthiotian. Artemidoros [F63] places Halos on the coast, situated outside the Maliac Gulf, but as Phthiotian. He goes from there toward the Peneios, and places Pteleon after Antron, and then Halos, 110 stadia distant from Pteleon. Something has already been said about Trachin [9.4.13–14], and it is named by the Poet [*Iliad* 2.682].

(9) He often mentions the Spercheios as a local river. Its sources are in Typhrestos, a Dryopian mountain formerly called[26] . . . and it empties near Thermopylai (between it and Lamia). Thus it is clear that both what is inside the Gates (as much as belongs to the Maliac Gulf) and what is outside them were subject to him [Achilleus]. The Spercheios is about 30 stadia from Lamia, which lies above a certain plain that extends down to the Maliac Gulf. That the Spercheios is local [is clear] from what he [Achilleus] says about letting his hair grow for it [*Iliad* 23.142–4], and that Menesthios, one of his commanders, was said to be the child of Spercheios and the sister of Achilleus [*Iliad* 16.173–6]. It is reasonable that all those subject to Achilleus and Patroklos – who had accompanied Peleus in his flight from Aigina – were called Myrmidons. The Phthiotians were all called Achaians.

---

[25] There is a gap about about twelve letters.   [26] A name is missing.

[C433]

(10) A number of settlements in the Phthiotic territory that were subject to Achilleus have been enumerated, beginning with the Malians. Among them are Phthiotic Thebes, Echinos, Lamia (around which the Lamian War occurred between the Makedonians under Antipatros and the Athenians, in which Leosthenes the Athenian commander fell, as well as Leonnatos the comrade of King Alexander)[27] . . . Erineos, Koroneia (with the same name as the Boiotian), Meliteia, Thaumakoi, Proerna, Pharsalos, Eretria (with the same name as the Euboian), and Paracheloitai (which also has the same name as the Aitolian). Here also is the Acheloos River, near Lamia, on which the Paracheloitians live. This territory extended toward the north along the most western of the Asklepidians and that of Eurypylos[28] . . . and of Protesilaos, inclining toward the east. In the south is Oitaia (which was divided into fourteen demes), Herakleia, and Dryopis, which was once a tetrapolis (like Doris) and considered the metropolis of the Dryopians in the Peloponnesos. Akyphas, Parasopias, Oineiadai, and Antikyra (with the same name as the one among the Hesperian Lokrians) are also in Oitaia. But I say that this arrangement has not always remained the same, but has undergone various changes. Only the most significant are especially worthy of recording.

(11) The Poet clearly says that the Dolopians were in the farthest part of Phthia, and that both they and the Phthiotians were subject to the same leader, Peleus. He [Homer] says "I [Phoinix] live in farthest Phthia as lord of the Dolopians" [*Iliad* 9.484], a gift of Peleus. They border on Pindos and its surroundings, most of which is Thessalian. Because of the distinction and supremacy of the Thessalians and Makedonians, most of the neighboring Epeirotes – either willingly or unwillingly – were established as part of the Thessalians or Makedonia: the Athamanians, Aithikians, and Talarians were Thessalian, and the Orestians, Pelagonians, and Elimiotians were Makedonian.

(12) Mount Pindos is large and has the Makedonians on the north, the Perrhaibians – a migrant people – on the west, and the Dolopians on the south . . . which is [a part of] Thessaly. The Talarians – a Molossian people and a branch of those around Tomaros – lived on Pindos itself, as did the Aithikians. The Poet says [*Iliad* 2.742–7] that the Centaurs were driven to them by Perithoos, but it is recorded that they are now extinct. "Extinct" can be taken in two ways: either the people have disappeared and the territory is completely desolate, or their ethnic name no longer exists and their government does not survive. When a government totally leaves no

[C434]

[C435]

---

[27] At least one toponym is missing.   [28] There is a gap of about ten letters.

trace today, we do not consider it worthy of recording, either itself or what name it has taken, but when there is a just reason for mentioning it, then it is necessary to speak about the change.

(13) It remains to speak about the order of [places on] the coast subject to Achilleus, beginning at Thermopylai (the Lokrian and[29] ... I have discussed). Thermopylai, then, is separated from Kenaion by a 70-stadia strait, yet sailing along the coast from the Gates it is about 10 stadia from the Spercheios. From there to Phalara is 20, and situated above Phalara, 50 stadia from the sea, is the city of the Lamians. Next, after sailing 100 stadia along the coast, Echinos lies above it. From the next [part of the] coast, in the interior 20 stadia distant from it, is Kremaste Larisa, also called Pelasgia Larisa.

(14) Then there is the islet of Myonnesos, and then Antron, which was subject to Protesilaos. Such, then is the portion subject to Achilleus. Since the Poet has divided Thessaly into many well-known parts – through naming both the leaders and the cities subject to them – and has arranged the entire circuit of it, following him again, as above, we will fill up the remainder of the route around the territory.

He catalogues next after those subject to Achilleus those subject to Protesilaos. These are also the ones who are next after the boundary of the coast subject to Achilleus as far as Antron. Next is that subject to Protesilaos, outside the Maliac Gulf but still inside Phthiotis, yet not[30].... Phylake is near to Phthiotic Thebes, which itself was subject to Protesilaos. Halos, Kremaste Larisa, and Demetrion were subject to him, all being to the east of Othrys. Demetrion, he says [*Iliad* 2.695], has a precinct of Demeter, and he calls it Pyrasos. Pyrasos was a city with a good harbor, and 2 stadia away was the grove of Demeter and the sacred sanctuary, 20 stadia distant from Thebes. Thebes is situated above Pyrasos, and above Thebes is the Krokian Plain (in the interior where Othrys comes to an end). The Amphrysos flows through it. Lying above it is Itonos, where the sanctuary of Itonia is – from which is the one in Boiotia – and the Kouarios River. It was said[31] ... of Arne in the Boiotian section. These are in Thessaliotis, one of the four parts of the whole of Thessaly, in which those places subject to Eurypylos were, as well as Phyllos, the sanctuary of Phyllian Apollo, and Ichnai, where Themis Ichnaia is honored. Kieros was also united with it and[32] ... of Athamania. Below Antron in the Euboian strait there is an undersea reef that is called the Ass of Antron. Then there are

Pteleon and Halos, then the sanctuary of Demeter, and then Pyrasos, which
has been razed. Thebes is above it. Then there is Cape Pyrrha with two islets
nearby, one of which is called Pyrrha and the other Deukalion. Around here
Phthiotis comes to an end.   [C436]

(15) Next he [Homer] catalogues those subject to Eumelos, on the
adjacent coast, which is already Magnesian and Pelasgian land. Pherai is
at the limit of the Pelasgian Plains on the Magnesian side, which extend
as far as Pelion (160 stadia). The seaport of Pherai is Pagasai, 90 stadia
distant from it and 20 from Iolkos. Ancient Iolkos has been razed, but it was
from here that Pelias sent forth Jason and the Argo. It was from the ship
construction [*naupegia*] of the Argo that, according to mythology, the
place was called Pagasai, although it is more plausibly thought that the
name of the place is attributed to the springs [*pegai*], which are numerous
and abundant in flow. Also nearby is Aphetai, as it was the starting point
[*apheterion*] of the Argonauts. Iolkos lies above the sea, 7 stadia from
Demetrias. Demetrias – which Demetrios Poliorketes founded and gave
his own name – is on the sea between Neleia and Pagasai, and was created
by the combining of nearby villages: Neleia, Pagasai, Ormenion, as well as
Rhizous[33] ... Sepias, Olizon, Boibe, and Iolkos, which are now villages
belonging to Demetrias. For a long time this was both a naval station and a
royal residence of the Makedonian kings, and it controlled Tempe and both
the mountains of Pelion and Ossa, as I have already said [9.4.15]. Today it is
reduced but still excels among all the cities of Magnesia. Lake Boibeis is near
to Pherai and adjoins the extremities of Pelion and Magnesia. Boibe is a
place situated on the lake. Just as seditions and tyrannies destroyed Iolkos
after it had greatly increased in power, Pherai was reduced in the same way:
once it had been raised up, and then it was destroyed along with its tyrants.
Near to Demetrias flows the Anauros. The adjoining shore is also called
Iolkos. Here the Pylaia festival was celebrated. Artemidoros [F64] places the
Pagasitic Gulf farther away from Demetrias and among the places subject to
Philoktetes. He says that the island of Kikynethos and a small town with the
same name are in the gulf.

(16) The cities subject to Philoktetes are catalogued next. Methone is
different from the Thracian Methone, which Philippos [II] razed. I have
previously recorded [8.4.3–4, 8.5.3, 8.6.15] the change of name of these
places and those in the Peloponnesos. Others enumerated – Thaumakia,
Olizon, and Meliboia – are on the next part of the coast. There are many
islands lying off the Magnetian shore: the notable ones are Skiathos,

---

[33] A gap of about ten letters indicates that at least one toponym is missing.

Peparethos, Ikos, Halonnesos, and Skyros, which all have homonymous cities. Skyros is the most notable because of Lykomedes' intimacy with Achilleus, and the birth and raising there of Neoptolemos the son of Achilleus. Later, when Philippos [II] had become powerful and saw that the Athenians were dominating the sea and ruling the islands – both these and the others – he made those that were near to him the most notable. Fighting for the hegemony, he always attacked the nearest places first, and just as he made the greater part of Magnetis, Thrace, and the land all around Makedonian, he thus seized the islands around Magnesia, making those that had formerly been known to no one fought over and known. Among these, ancient stories are most associated with Skyros, but there are other matters that make it widely discussed, such as the excellence of the Skyrian goats and the quarries of the variegated Skyrian stone (comparable to the Karystian, Lucullian, and Synnadic). One can see at Rome monolithic columns and great slabs of the variegated stone from which the city is being adorned at public and private expense, which has made the white stone not worth very much.

[C437]

(17) The Poet, having gone this far along the Magnetian coast, returns to Upper Thessaly. Beginning from Dolopia and Pindos, he traverses that which extends along Phthiotis as far as Lower Thessaly, "those who held Trikke and rocky Ithome" [*Iliad* 2.729]. These places are part of Histiaiotis, formerly called Doris, as they say. When the Perrhaibians took possession of it – those who had subdued Histiaiotis in Euboia and forced the people there onto the mainland – because of the large number of Histiaians who had settled in this territory they called it after them. They call it and Dolopia Upper Thessaly, which is in line with Upper Makedonia, just as Lower [Thessaly] is with Lower [Makedonia]. Trikke – where the oldest and most famous sanctuary of Asklepios is – borders on the Dolopians and the places around Pindos. They say that Ithome – which has the same name as the Messenian one – should not be spoken in this way, but without the first syllable, and it was thus called formerly. Now the name has changed to Thamai, a naturally fortified place that is "rocky" [*Iliad* 2.729]. It is situated between four fortresses, as if lying in a square: Trikke, Metropolis, Pelinnaion, and Gomphoi. Ithome is in the territory of the Metropolitans. Formerly Metropolis was a joint settlement of three unimportant towns, but later a number of others were added to it, among which was Ithome.

[C438]

Kallimachos says in his *Iamboi* [F200a] that of the Aphrodites – for there was not merely one of these goddesses – Kastnietis surpasses all in wisdom, for she alone accepts the sacrifice of swine. He was exceedingly learned, if anyone was, through his entire life, as he himself said, "in wishing ears to recount" [F178].[34] Those later have proved that not only this one Aphrodite, but several, accepted this custom, including the one at Metropolis. One of the cities in this settlement transferred it to the Onthyrian custom.

Pharkadon is also in Histiaiotis, and the Peneios and Kouralios flow through its region. Of them, the Kouralios flows past the sanctuary of Itonian Athena and empties into the Peneios. The Peneios itself begins from Pindos, as has already been said [7.F8], and leaving Trikke, Pelinnaion, and Pharkadon on the left it is carried past Atrax and Larisa, and receiving the rivers in Thessaliotis proceeds through Tempe to its outlet.

They record that Oichalia – called "the city of Eurytos" [*Iliad* 2.730] – is in the region, and also on Euboia and in Arkadia (the one in Arkadia has changed its name, as was said in the Peloponnesian section [8.3.6]). They ask about these, especially regarding which one was captured by Herakles, and which one the poet wrote about in *The Capture of Oichalia* [F2]. These places were classified as subject to the Asklepiadai.

(18) Next he speaks of what is subject to Eurypylos:

> those who held Ormenion and the spring of Hypereia, and those who held Asterion and the white peaks of Titanos. [*Iliad* 2.734–5]

Today Ormenion is called Orminion, and it is a village at the foot of Pelion on the Pagasitic Gulf, one of the cities involved in the establishment of Demetrias, as has been said [9.5.15]. Lake Boibeis must also be near by, since Boibe as well as Ormenion were dependencies of Demetrias. Ormenion is 27 stadia by foot from Demetrias, and Iolkos, a place on this road, lies 7 stadia distant from Demetrias and the remaining 20 stadia from Ormenion.

The Skepsian [F68] says that Phoinix was from Ormenion, and that he fled from there and "his father, Ormenian Amyntor" [*Iliad* 9.448] to Phthia and "lord Peleus" [*Iliad* 9.480]. This place was founded by Ormenos the son of Kerphios the son of Aiolos. Amyntor and Euaimos were children of Ormenos, and Phoinix was the son of the former and Eurypylos the son of [C439] the latter. The succession – common to both – was kept for Eurypylos, since Phoinix had gone away from his native land. And he [the Skepsian] also writes "when I first left Ormenion, rich in flocks" [*Iliad* 9.447, revised] instead of "left Hellas of beautiful women." Krates [F10], however, makes Phoinix a Phokian, conjecturing this from the helmet of Meges, which Odysseus used during the *Nightwatch*, about which the Poet says: "Autolykos took it from Amyntor the son of Ormenos, from Eleon, having

[34] There is probably a gap or deficiency in the text, for the quotation is almost incomprehensible.

broken into his solid home" [*Iliad* 10.266–7]. Eleon is a small town on Parnassos, and Amyntor the son of Ormenos is said to have been none other than the father of Phoinix. Autolykos, who lived on Parnassos, broke into the home of a neighbor (not someone far away, as is common with all housebreakers). But the Skepsian says that there is no place called Eleon to be seen on Parnassos, although there is a Neon, which was founded after the Trojan matter, and that housebreaking does not only occur among neighbors. There are other things that one could say but I hesitate to spend more time. Others write "from Heleon," which is in the Tanagrike, which would show the absurdity of saying "I fled far away through Hellas . . . and came to Phthia" [*Iliad* 9.478–9]. The Hypereia fountain is in the middle of the city of the Pheraians. It is absurd. . . . Titanos ["Gypsum"] was named from the situation there, for the territory near Arne and . . . has white earth.[35] Asterion is not far away from these places.

(19) Continuous with this portion are those said to be subject to Polypoites: "those who held Argeisa and lived in Gyrtone, Orthe, Elone, and Oloosson the white city" [*Iliad* 2.738–9]. Formerly the Perrhaibians lived in this territory, inhabiting the portion near the sea and the Peneios, as far as its outlet and the Perrhaibian city of Gyrton. Then they were driven into the riverine interior by the Lapiths (who then possessed the territory) Ixion and his son Peirithoos, who also obtained Pelion and forced out the Centaurs (who held it), a wild tribe, whom "he drove from Pelion to the [C440] Aithikians" [*Iliad* 2.744]. He gave the plain over to the Lapiths, although the Perrhaibians (those near Olympos) retained some of it, and in a few areas lived mixed with the Lapiths.

Argeisa (today Argousa) lies on the Peneios. Atrax lies 40 stadia above it, itself close to the river. The Perrhaibians held the riverine territory between them. Some say that Orthe is the akropolis of the Phalannaians, and Phalanna is a Perrhaibian city on the Peneios near Tempe.

The Perrhaibians, having been oppressed by the Lapiths, mostly went up into the mountainous territory around Pindos and to the Athamanians and Dolopians. Their territory as well as the Perrhaibians who were left behind were acquired by the Larisaians, who lived near the Peneios and were their neighbors, inhabiting the most prosperous part of the plains, only avoiding the exceedingly low-lying area around Lake Nessonis, as the river would overflow into it and carry away some of the arable land of the Larisaians. Later the Larisaians corrected this with embankments. They possessed the Perrhaibia and exacted tribute until Philippos [II] established himself as

---

[35] There are two gaps for a total of about fifteen letters in this sentence.

master of the place. Larisa is also a place on Ossa. There is also Kremaste, which some call Pelasgia. On Crete there is such a city, now joined to Hierapytna, and because of this the plain that is lying below it today is called the Larisian. In the Peloponnesos there is the citadel of the Argives and the Larisos River, which separates Eleia from Dyme. Theopompos [F386] says that there is a city of Larisa lying in their border territory. In Asia there is Phrikonis around Kyme, and one at Hamaxitos in the Troad, Ephesian Larisa, and one in Syria. The Larisaian Rocks are 50 stadia from Mitylene on the road to Methymna. There is a Larisa in Attika, and a village 30 stadia distant from Tralleis, above the city going through the Mesogis toward the Kaystros Plain, and near the sanctuary of the Isodromian Mother. It has a situation and an excellence similar to Kremaste Larisa, for it is well watered and planted with vineyards. Perhaps Larisian Zeus was named after it. Also on the left side of the Pontos is a certain village called Larisa between Naulochos and[36] . . . near the extremity of Haimos.

Oloosson (which is called "white" from the white clay) and Elone are Perrhaibian cities, as well as Gonnos. Elone changed its name to Leimone and is today destroyed. Both are situated below Olympos, not very far from the Europos River, which the Poet calls the Titaresios.

[C441]

(20) The Poet next speaks about it and the Perrhaibians when he says:

> Gouneus led twenty-two ships from Kyphos. The Enienians followed him, and the Perrhaibians steadfast in war, who established their homes around wintry Dodona, and lived on the land around the lovely Titaresios. [*Iliad* 2.748–51]

He says that these places are Perrhaibian, from the portions that they occupied in Hestiaiotis. Those subject to Polypoites were in part Perrhaibian, but he assigned them to the Lapiths because they lived mingled with each other, and – although the Lapiths held the plains and the Perrhaibians who were there were mostly considered subject to them – because the more mountainous territory near Olympos and Tempe was Perrhaibian, such as Kyphos, Dodona, and that around the Titaresios. It flows from Mount Titarios – which connects with Olympos – and into the Perrhaibian territory near Tempe, and has a confluence with the Peneios around there. The water of the Peneios is pure, but that of the Titaresios is oily because of something, and does not mix in, "but runs over it like oil" [*Iliad* 2.754]. Because they lived mingled together, Simonides [F632] calls Perrhaibian and Lapithian all the Pelasgiotes who occupy the eastern

---

[36] There is a gap of about eight letters.

portion, around Gyrton, the outlet of the Peneios, Ossa, Pelion, the region around Demetrias and that in the plain – Larisa, Krannon, Skotoussa, Mopsion, and Atrax – and around Lakes Nessonis and Boibeis. Of these, the Poet records only a few, because they had not yet been settled or were poor settlements because of the occasional inundations. He does not record Lake Nessonis, only Boibeis, because only it survived, although much smaller, but the former seemingly was filled in at irregular times, and at times failed completely. I mentioned Skotoussa in the account of the region of Dodona and the oracle in Thessaly [7.7.12], and that it was originally around these places. Around Skotoussa is a place called Kynoskephalai, where the Romans with the Aitolians and Titus Quinctius defeated Philippos [V] the son of Demetrios, the Makedonian king, in a great battle.

[C442] (21) Magnetis has been treated similarly. Having enumerated many places there, Homer called none of them Magnetian except the following, which are shown dimly and indistinctly: "those living around the Peneios and Pelion with its shaking foliage" [*Iliad* 2.757–8]. But around the Peneios and Pelion lived those holding Gyrton, whom he had already recounted, as well as those [holding] Ormenion and a number of others. There were Magnetians still farther from Pelion, beginning with those subject to Eumelos, according to later people. But they seem – because of continual migrations, changes of government, and mingling – to have confused names and peoples, so that today it presents a difficulty. First, this has happened with Krannon and Gyrton, because formerly the Gyrtonians were called the Phlegyans (from Phlegyas the brother of Ixion), and the Krannonians the Ephyrians, so that it causes difficulty regarding what the Poet wishes to say when he has: "these two from Thrace arm themselves against the Ephyrians or the great-hearted Phlegyians" [*Iliad* 13.301–2].

(22) It is thus the same concerning the Perrhaibians and Ainianians. Homer [*Iliad* 2.749] connected them, as they lived near to one another. Moreover, it is said by those later that the habitation of the Ainianians was in the Dotian Plain for a long time. This is near the just-mentioned Perrhaibia, Ossa, and also Lake Boibeis, and although it is in the middle of Thessaly it is surrounded by its own hills. Hesiod has said this about it:

> Or as the unwedded maiden, who, living in the sacred Didymian hills, in the Dotian Plain in front of Amyros, abundant in grapes, bathed her foot in the Boibiadian Lake. [F164]

Most of the Ainianians were expelled into Oite by the Lapiths and became powerful there, taking away certain portions from the Dorians and the Malians as far as Herakleia and Echinos. Some remained around Kyphos, a

Perrhaibian mountain that had a settlement of the same name. Certain Perrhaibians came together around the western part of Olympos and remained there, becoming neighbors of the Makedonians, but the greater part were driven into the mountains around Athamania and Pindos. Today little or no trace of them is preserved.

The Magnetians mentioned last by the Poet in the Thessalian catalogue should be considered as those within Tempe, from Peneios and Ossa as far [C443] as Pelion, bordering the Makedonian Pieriotians, who held the far side of the Peneios as far as the sea. Homolion or Homole (it is said both ways) should be assigned to them, as it has been said in the Makedonian section that it is near Ossa, where the Peneios begins to go through Tempe. If one were to go along the coast nearest to Homolion, it would be reasonable to assign Rhizous and Erymnai to them, as they lie on the coast that was subject to Philoktetes and to Eumelos. But this must remain uncertain.

The order of the places that are next, as far as Pelion, is not described clearly. Yet these places are undistinguished, and we should not consider the matter important. Nevertheless Cape Sepias was represented in tragedies and later celebrated in hymns because the Persian expedition was destroyed there. It is a rocky cape, and between it and Kasthanaia (a village lying at the foot of Pelion), is the beach where the expedition of Xerxes was lying in wait when a strong east wind drove some of them onto dry land, and others were carried to Ipnoi, a rough place around Pelion, or to Meliboia or Kasthanaia, and were destroyed. The entire sail along the coast of Pelion is rough and about . . . 80 stadia.[37] That along Ossa is similar. Between them there is a gulf of more than 200 stadia, on which is Meliboia. The entire [distance] from Demetrias to the Peneios, following the gulfs, is more than 1,000 [stadia], and 800 more from the Spercheios, and 2,350 from the Euripos. Hieronymos [F17] declares that the circuit of the Thessalian and Magnetian plains is 3,000 stadia, and that it was inhabited by Pelasgians who were driven from there into Italia by the Lapiths. What is today called the Pelasgian Plain includes Larisa, Gyrtone, Pherai, Mopsion, Boibeias, Ossa, Homole, Pelion, and Magnetis. Mopsion is not named after Mopsos the son of Manto the daughter of Teiresias, but from the Lapith who sailed with the Argonauts. But Attic Mopsopia is from another Mopsos.

(23) These are the particulars about Thessaly. In general it was formerly called Pyrrhaia, from Pyrrha the wife of Deukalion, or Haimonia after Haimon, or Thessaly after Thessalos the son of Haimon. Some divide it in two and say that Deukalion obtained the part toward the south and called

---

[37] The extant number is far too small.

[C444] it Pandora after his mother, and the other part was Haimon's and named
Haimonia. The former was changed to Hellas after Hellen the son of
Deukalion, and the latter to Thessaly after the son of Haimon. Some
[say] that the descendants of Antiphos and Pheidippos (the sons of
Thessalos the son of Herakles) came in from Thesprotian Ephyra and
named it after Thessalos, their own ancestor. It has been said that it was
once named Nessonis (like the lake), after Nesson the son of Thessalos.

BOOK 10

West central Hellas and the Hellenic islands

Part 1: Euboia

(1) Since Euboia is parallel to the entire coast from Sounion as far as Thessaly (except for either extremity), it would be suitable to connect the description of the island with what has already been said, and then to pass on to the Aitolian and Akarnanian sections, which are the remaining portions of Europe.

(2) The island is oblong, about 1,200 stadia from Kenaion to Geraistos, and its width is irregular, with a maximum of about 150 stadia. Kenaion is opposite to Thermopylai and slightly to that which is outside Thermopylai, but Geraistos and Petalia are toward Sounion. Thus it is across the strait from Attika, Boiotia, Lokris, and the Malians. Because of its narrowness and previously mentioned length it was named Makris ["Long"] by those in antiquity. It touches the continent at Chalkis, where it projects the most   [C445] in a convexity toward the region of Aulis in Boiotia, creating the Euripos. I have spoken at length concerning it [9.2.2, 8], as well as to some extent about the places opposite to one another across the strait – on the mainland and the island – on either side of the Euripos, both inside and outside. If anything has been left out, we will now explain further. First, that which is between Aulis and the regions of Geraistos is called the Hollows of Euboia, for the coast makes a gulf, but when it comes near to Chalkis it again makes a convexity toward the mainland.

(3) The island was not only called Makris, but also Abantis. At any rate, the Poet mentions Euboia but never calls those who are there Euboians, but always Abantians ("those who held Euboia, the fiercely breathing Abantians" [*Iliad* 2.536]; or "the Abantians followed him" [*Iliad* 2.542]). Aristotle[1] [F601] says that the Thracians, setting forth from Phokaian Aba,

---

[1] It is possible that this citation (as well as the one in 10.1.8) is not from the famous Aristotle, but the little-known Aristotle of Chalkis (*FGrHist* #423).

settled the island and named those holding it the Abantians. Others say that it is from a hero, just as Euboia is from a heroine. Perhaps, just as a certain cave on the coast that is turned toward the Aigaion (where, they say, Io bore Epaphos) is called Boos Aule ["Cow Stall"], the island received its name for the same reason. The island was also called Oche, and the largest mountain there has the same name. It was also named Hellopia after Hellops the son of Ion. They say that he was the brother of Aiklos and Kothos, and is also said to have founded Hellopia, a place in the so-called Oria in Histiaiotis near Mount Telethrion. He also obtained Histiaia, Perias, Kerinthos, Aidepsos, and Orobiai, where there was an oracle that was the most truthful, an oracle of Selinountian Apollo. The Hellopians migrated to Histiaia and enlarged the city, having been forced to do so by the tyrant Philistides after the matter of Leuktra. Demosthenes [*Philippic* 3.33] says that Philistides was also established by Philippos [II] as the tyrant of the Oreitians – for the Histiaians were so named later – and the city was Oreos instead of Histiaia. Some say that Histiaia was settled by Athenians from the deme of Histiaieis, as Eretria was from Eretrieis. Theopompos [F387] says that when Perikles conquered Euboia the Histiaians migrated to Makedonia, according to an agreement, and that 2,000 Athenians, who had formerly been of the deme of Histiaieis, came and lived in Oreos.

(4) It is situated under Mount Telethrion in what is called the Drymos ["Forest"], along the Kallas River on a high rock. Perhaps because the Hellopians – who formerly lived there – were mountaineers [*oreioi*] this name was attached to the city. Some say that Orion was so named because he was raised there, and some say that the Oreitians had their own city, but because the Hellopians made war on them they moved and lived with the Histiaians, and became a single city using both names, just as Lakedaimon and Sparta are identical. As has been said [9.5.17], Histiaiotis in Thessaly was also named after those who had been removed there by the Perrhaibians.

(5) Since Hellopia has led me to begin with Histiaia and Oreos, we will speak about the adjoining places. In this Oreian territory are Kenaion and, near to it, Dion and Athenai Diades, an Athenian foundation lying above the crossing of the strait to Kynos. Aiolian Kanai was settled from Dion. These places are around Histiaia, as well as Kerinthos, a little city on the sea. Near it is the Boudoros River, having the same name as the mountain on Salamis near Attika.

(6) Karystos is at the foot of Mount Oche. Near it are Styra and Marmarion, where the quarry for the Karystian columns is, as well as a sanctuary of Apollo Marmarinos. There is a crossing to Halai Araphenides here. In Karystos there is also a stone that is combed and woven, so that the woven

[C446]

material is made into hand towels which, when they become soiled, are thrown into a fire and cleaned, just like washing away the dirt. They say that these places were settled by those from the Tetrapolis around Marathon and also by the Steirians. Styra was destroyed in the Lamian War by Phaidros, the Athenian commander, but the Eretrians hold the territory. There is another Karystos in the Lakonike, an Aigyan place toward Arkadia, from which the Karystian wine comes that Alkman [F92] mentions.

(7) Geraistos is not mentioned in the *Catalogue of Ships*, but the Poet records it ("at night they landed at Geraistos" [*Odyssey* 3.177–8]). He makes it clear that it is convenient for those crossing from Asia to Attika, as the place lies near Sounion. It has a sanctuary of Poseidon, the most significant in this region, and also a notable settlement.

(8) After Geraistos is Eretria, which, except for Chalkis, is the largest city on Euboia, and then there is Chalkis, which in a certain way is the metropolis of the island, situated on the Euripos itself. Both are said to have been founded by the Athenians before the Trojan matter. After the Trojan [C447] matter, Aiklos and Kothos set forth from Athens, with the former settling Eretria and Kothos Chalkis. There were also some Aiolians from the command of Penthilos who remained on the island, and, in antiquity, Arabians who had crossed over with Kadmos. These cities became exceptionally powerful and sent out notable settlements to Makedonia, for Eretria established the cities around Pallene and Athos, and Chalkis those subject to Olynthos, which were later shamefully maltreated by Philippos [II]. Many places in Italia and Sikelia are also Chalkidean. These settlements were sent out, as Aristotle[2] [F603] says, when the government called the Hippobotai was in power, led by men of wealth who ruled aristocratically. At the time of Alexander's crossing, they enlarged the peribolos of the city, taking within the walls Kanethos and the Euripos, and placing towers, gates, and a wall on the bridge.

(9) The so-called Lelanton Plain lies above the city of the Chalkideans. In it there are outlets of hot water that are suitable for curing disease and which were used by Cornelius Sulla, the Roman commander. There was also a remarkable mine of copper and iron together, which is not recorded as happening elsewhere. Today both have failed. All of Euboia is liable to earthquakes, especially around the strait, which receives blasts through hollow passages, just as in Boiotia and other places, as I previously recorded at great length [9.2.16]. It is said that the city with the same name as the island experienced this and was swallowed up. Aischylos mentions it in

---

[2] *Supra* note 1.

his *Glaukos Pontios*: "Eubois, around the bending promontory of Zeus Kenaios, near the tomb of unhappy Lichas" [F25e]. It is said that in Aitolia there is a like-named Chalkis ("Chalkis on the beach and rocky Kalydon" [*Iliad* 2.640]), and also in what is today Eleia ("they went past Krounoi and the beautifully flowing Chalkis" [*Odyssey* 15.295]: that is, Telemachos and those with him going home from Nestor).

(10) Some say that Euboia was settled from Triphylian Makiston, by Eretrieus, but others from Athenian Eretria, which is now a marketplace. There is also an Eretria around Pharsalos. In the Eretrike there is a city of Tamynai, sacred to Apollo. The sanctuary is said to have been founded by Admetos (they say that the god was his servant), and is near the strait. [C448] Eretria was formerly called Melaneis and also Arotria. The village of Amarynthos is 7 stadia from its walls and belongs to it. The Persians razed the original city, and netted the people, as Herodotos says [6.31], since the barbarians, with their great numbers, were spread around the walls (the foundations are still visible, and it is called Old Eretria). Today it has been refounded. The power that the Eretrians once had is witnessed by the pillar that they erected in the sanctuary of Amarynthian Artemis. Written on it was that they made their procession with 3,000 hoplites, 600 horsemen, and 60 chariots. They ruled over the Andrians, Tenians, Keians, and other islands. They had settlers from Elis, because of whom they frequently used the letter rho – not only at the end of words but in the middle – and thus they have been satirized. There is a villagae of Oichalia in the Eretrike, the remains of a city destroyed by Herakles, having the same name as ones in Trachinia, Trikke, and the Arkadike – which later was called Andania – and in Aitolia around the Eurytanians.

(11) Today it is agreed that Chalkis holds the first place and is said to be the metropolis of the Euboians, with Eretria second. Yet even formerly they were of great distinction, both in war and peace, so that for men of learning they provided a pleasant and undisturbed environment, as witnessed by the Eretrian school of learning of Menedemos and those around him in Eretria, and, still earlier, the time spent by Aristotle in Chalkis, where he ended his life.

(12) These cities were mostly in agreement with one another, and the differences about the Lelanton did not completely hinder ... to carry on war through the stubborness of each, but they came to an agreement among themselves as how to carry on the conflict. The pillar at Amarynthos points out that they were not to use long-distance weapons. In the customs of warfare and the use of weapons there is not – nor has there ever been – any single custom. Some use long-distance weapons, such as archers, slingers,

and javelin throwers, and others fight hand-to-hand, such as those using the sword or the outstretched spear, for the spear is used in two ways, either in the hand or as a missile (just as the pike allows two usages, in close combat and as a thrown missile, like the capabilities of the *sarissa* and javelin).

(13) The Euboians were excellent in standing battle (also called "close combat" or "by hand"), and they used their spears outstretched, as the Poet says: "spearman with outstretched ashen shafts, seeking to break breast-   [C449] plates" [*Iliad* 2.543–4]. It may be that the javelins were different, as perhaps the Pelian ashen spear was, about which the Poet says that "Achilleus alone knew how to brandish" [*Iliad* 16.142, 19.389]. The one [Odysseus] who said "I can throw a spear as far as no one else can an arrow" [*Odyssey* 8.229] meant the hurling spear. Those fighting in single combat are introduced as originally using the hurler, and then continuing with swords. Those fighting hand-to-hand not only use the sword, but also the spear by hand, as he says: "he wounded him with a bronze-tipped shaft and loosened his limbs" [*Iliad* 4.469, 11.260]. He introduces the Euboians as using the same method, but he says the contrary of the Lokrians, that

> they did not care for the work of standing combat ... but with bows and well-twisted sheep's wool, they followed him to Ilion. [*Iliad* 13.713 altered, 716–17]

Also known is an oracle given to the Aigians: "Thessalian horses, Lakedaimonian women, and the men who drink the water of sacred Arethousa," saying that the Chalkideans are the best since Arethousa is there.

(14) Today there are two Euboian rivers, the Kereus and the Neleus, and the animals that drink from the one become white, and from the other, black. The same thing occurs around the Krathis, as has been said [6.1.13].

(15) When the Euboians were returning from Troy, some of them were cast ashore in Illyria, and headed home inland through Makedonia but remained around Edessa, allying in war with those who had received them and founding a city of Euboia. There was also a Euboia in Sikelia, founded by the Chalkideans there, but Gelon drove them out, and it became a Syracusian fortress. On Kerkyra and on Lemnos are places [called] Euboia, and in the Argeia there is a certain hill.

(16) Since to the west of the Thessalians and Oitaians are the Aitolians, Akarnanians, and Athamanians (if these must be called Hellenes), it remains to expound about them, so that we can have the circuit around all of Hellas, and adding the islands that are nearest to Hellas (those that we have not gone through).

Part 2:   Aitolia, Akarnania, and the western islands.

(1) The Aitolians and Akarnanians border each other, having the Acheloos River between them, which flows from the north and the Pindos toward the [C450] south, through the Agraians – an Aitolian people – and the Amphilochians. The Akarnanians hold the western part of the river as far as the Ambrakian Gulf toward the Amphilochians and the sanctuary of Aktian Apollo. The Aitolians have the eastern as far as the Ozolian Lokrians, Parnassos, and the Oitaians. In the interior and northern portions, lying above the Akarnanians, are the Amphilochians, and [above] them the Dolopians and the Pindos. [Above] the Aitolians are the Perrhaibians, Athamanians, and that portion of the Ainianians who hold Oite. The southern side of both Akarnania and Aitolia is washed by the sea that makes the Corinthian Gulf, into which the Acheloos River flows, and which is the boundary between the Aitolian and Akarnanian coast. The Acheloos was formerly called the Thoas. There is another near Dyme that has the same name as this one, as has been stated [8.2.3], and one around Lamia. It has also already been stated that they say the beginning of the Corinthian Gulf is at the mouth of this river.

(2) The cities of the Akarnanians are Anaktorion (situated on a peninsula near Aktion, and today the emporium for Nikopolis, founded in our times), Stratos (a sail up the Acheloos of more than two hundred stadia) and Oineiadai, which is also on the river. The old city, which is uninhabited, is equidistant from the sea and Stratos, and that of today is about seventy stadia distant from the mouth. There are others – Palairos, Alyzia, Leukas, Amphilochian Argos, and Ambrakia – most of which (or rather all) have become dependencies of Nikopolis. Stratos lies midway on the road from Alyzia to Anaktorion.

(3) The Aitolian ones are Kalydon and Pleuron, which are reduced today, although in antiquity these settlements were ornaments of Hellas. Moreover, it happens that Aitolia has been divided in two, one called the Old and the other Epiktetos ["The Acquired"]. The Old was the coast from the Acheloos to Kalydon, reaching greatly into the interior, which is fertile and level. Here are Stratos and Trichonion, which has excellent land. Epiktetos borders the Lokrians toward Naupaktos and Eupalion (it is rather rough and difficult) as far as the Oitaians, the Athamanians, and the mountains and peoples located next toward the north around them.

(4) Aitolia has a very large mountain, Korax, which touches Oite. Of the [C451] others in the middle there is Arakynthos, around the newer Pleuron, the latter founded when the inhabitants left the Old, which was situated near

Kalydon and was fertile and level. This was when Demetrios called Aitolikos ravaged the territory. Above Molykreia are Taphiassos and Chalkis, rather high mountains, on which are the small cities of Makynia and Chalkis (which has the same name as the mountain, and is also called Hypochalkis). Kourion is near Old Pleuron, from which some assume the Pleuronian Kouretians were named.

(5) The Euenos River begins from the Bomieans who are among the Ophians (an Aitolian people, just like the Eurytanians, Agraians, Kouretians, and others). At first it does not flow through the Kouretian territory (which is the same as the Pleuronian), but rather through the more easterly, past Chalkis and Kalydon. It then turns back toward the plains of Old Pleuron, and, changing toward the west, it then turns toward its outlets and the south. It was formerly called the Lykormas. It is said that Nessos, who had been established as ferryman, was killed there by Herakles when he was ferrying Deianeira and attempted to force her.

(6) The Poet names Olenos and Pylene as Aitolian cities [*Iliad* 2.639]. Of those, Olenos – having the same name as the one previously mentioned in Achaia – was razed by the Aiolians. It was near the newer Pleuron, but its territory was disputed by the Akarnanians. Pylene was moved to a higher location and also changed its name, calling itself Proschion. Hellanikos [F118] does not know their history, mentioning them as though the old settlements [still existed], and he catalogues Makynia and Molykreia among the old ones, although they were founded later than the return of the Herakleidai. Almost everywhere in his writings he shows the greatest indifference.

(7) This is the entirety about the territory of the Akarnanians and the Aitolians. Yet the following must be added concerning the coast and the islands lying off it. Beginning from the mouth of the Ambrakian Gulf, the first in the Akarnanian territory is Aktion. It is said that the sanctuary of Aktian Apollo has the same name, as well as the cape that makes the mouth of the gulf and which has a harbor on its outer side. Anaktorion is 40 stadia distant from the sanctuary, situated on the gulf, and Leukas is 240.

(8) In antiquity it was a peninsula of the Akarnanian land. The Poet calls it "a promontory of the mainland" [*Odyssey* 24.378], calling "the mainland" that which is opposite Ithaka and Kephallenia, which is Akarnania. Thus when he says "a promontory of the mainland," it must be taken as a promontory of Akarnania. Nerikos was part of Leukas, which Laertes says that he took: [C452]

> we took Nerikos, the well-built city, the promontory of the mainland, when I was lord of the Kephallenians [*Odyssey* 24.377–8, altered]

as well as those whom he [Homer] mentions in the *Catalogue* ("they lived in Krokyleia and rough Aigilips" [*Iliad* 2.633]).

The Corinthians sent by Kypselos and Gargasousos[3] possessed this promontory and advanced as far as the Ambrakian Gulf, and settled both Ambrakia and Anaktorion. They excavated through the isthmus of the peninsula and made Leukas an island, and transferred Nerikos to the place where the former isthmus is today – a strait crossed by a bridge – and changed its name to Leukas, which, it seems to me, was named after Leukatas. This is a rock, white [*leuke*] in color, that projects from Leukas into the open sea toward Kephallenia, so that it thus took its name.

(9) It has a sanctuary of Apollo Leukatas and The Leap, which is believed to end the longings of love. As Menandros says,

> Sappho is said to have been the first, when through frantic longing she was chasing arrogant Phaon and threw herself from the far-seen rock, through your prayer, master and lord. [*Leukadia*, F1, lines 11–15]

Menandros thus says that Sappho was the first to make the leap, but those more knowledgable in antiquarianism say that it was Kephalos, the son of Deioneus, who was in love with Pterelas. It was the ancestral custom among the Leukadians to throw someone from the overlook every year during the sacrifice to Apollo, in order to turn away evil. Wings and birds would be attached to him, since they would be able to lighten the leap during its flight. Many would be stationed below, all around in small boats, and take him in. When he had been taken up, they would do what they could to have him escape outside their borders.

The author of the *Alkmaionis* [F5] writes that Ikarios, the father of Penelope, had two sons, Alyzeus and Leukadios, and they, along with their father, exercised power over Akarnania. Ephoros [F124] believes that the cities were named after them.

(10) Today only those from the island of Kephallenia are called Kephallenians, but to Homer they were all who were subject to Odysseus, among whom are the Akarnanians. He says, "Moreover, Odysseus led the Kephallenians ... those who held Ithaka and Neriton with quivering foliage" [*Iliad* 2.631–2]. The latter is the conspicuous mountain on it, as in "those from Doulichion and the sacred Echinades" [*Iliad* 2.625] – since Doulichion is part of the Echinades – or "those in Bouprasion and Elis" [*Iliad* 2.615] – as Bouprasion is in Elis – or "those who held Euboia, Chalkis, and Eiretria" [*Iliad* 2.536–7] – for these cities are in Euboia – or "Trojans,

[C453]

---

[3] This does not seem to be a proper name: Gorgos is a possibility.

Lykians, and Dardanians" [*Iliad* 8.173] – as they were Trojans – except after Neriton he says:

> and lived in Krokyleia and rough Aigilips, and those who held Zakynthos and lived around Samos, and those who held the mainland and lived on the other side. [*Iliad* 2.633–5]

By "mainland" he wishes to say those opposite the islands, wishing to include, along with Leukas, the rest of Akarnania, about which he says the following: "twelve herds on the mainland, and as many flocks of sheep" [*Odyssey* 14.100], perhaps because in antiquity Epeirotis extended that far and was commonly called by the name "mainland" [*epeiros*). Samos is the Kephallenia of today, as when he says "in the strait between Ithaka and rugged Samos" [*Odyssey* 4.671, 15.29], for through the epithet he separates those with the same name, and applies the name not only to the city but to the island. The island was a tetrapolis, and one of the four was called either Samos or Same, in either case named with the same name as the island. When he says "all the nobility who prevailed over the islands of Doulichion, Same, and wooded Zakynthos" [*Odyssey* 1.245–6, 16.122–3, 19.130–1], it is clear that he is itemizing the islands and calling Same the island he had formerly called Samos. Apollodoros [of Athens, F201] says that the ambiguity is dispelled through the epithet (that in saying "rugged Samos" the island is meant, and then, again, that one must write "Doulichion and Samos" instead of "Same"), and thus he is clearly putting forth that the city is assumed to have had the name Same or Samos synonymously, but the island was only Samos. But that the city was called Same is clear from the enumeration of the suitors from each city, as he says "from Same there were twenty-four men" [*Odyssey* 16.249], and then from the statement about Ktimene ("they gave her to Same" [*Odyssey* 15.367]). But this is [C454] arguable, for the Poet does not display clarity about either Kephallenia, Ithaka, or other nearby places, and thus the commentators and historians are in disagreement.

(11) For example, when he says about Ithaka: "those who held Ithaka and Neriton with quivering foliage" [*Iliad* 2.631–2], it is clear by the epithet that it is Mount Neriton, and elsewhere it is specifically a mountain: "I live in sunny Ithaka, and in it there is a mountain, Neriton, with quivering foliage and conspicuous" [*Odyssey* 9.21–2]. But whether he means the city or the island of Ithaka is not clear when he says "those who held Ithaka and Neriton," for if one were to accept it precisely one would hear the city, as if one were to say "Athens and Lykabettos" or "Rhodes and Atabyris," or even "Lakedaimon and Taÿgetos," yet if it is poetic, it is the opposite. But in

"I live in sunny Ithaka, and in it there is a mountain, Neriton," it is clear, for the mountain is on the island, not in the city. When, however, he says the following, "we have come from Ithaka, below Neion" [*Odyssey* 3.81], it is unclear whether he is saying that Neion is the same as Neriton, or different, or whether it is a mountain or a district. Someone who writes "Nerikon" instead of "Neriton" (or the opposite) is completely wrong, because the Poet says that the latter has "quivering foliage" [*Iliad* 2.632, *Odyssey* 9.22] but the former is a "well-built city" [*Odyssey* 24.377], and the latter is in Ithaka but the former is a "promontory of the mainland" [*Odyssey* 24.378].

(12) The following seems to reveal a sort of contradiction: "it lies near the land, high above the salty sea" [*Odyssey* 9.25], for "near the land" is low and on the earth, yet "high" is elevated, as he shows in a number of places where he calls it "rugged" [*Odyssey* 1.247, etc.], such as the road from the harbor ("a rough path up through wooded land" [*Odyssey* 14.1–2]), and "none of the islands that lean on the salty sea is sunny or rich in meadows, Ithaka least of all" [*Odyssey* 4.607–8]. The expression has certain incongruities but they are not badly explained away. "Near the land" is not accepted as meaning "low," but "lying nearest to the mainland," as it is exceedingly close. "High" does not mean "lofty," but "high toward the darkness" or extending the farthest of all toward the north, for this is what he wishes to say with [C455] "toward the darkness." The opposite is "toward the south," as in "the other [islands] are away toward the dawn and the sun" [*Odyssey* 9.26], for "away" means "far" and "apart from," as the others incline toward the south and are farther from the mainland, but Ithaka is near and toward the north. He speaks in such a way about the southern portions, as is clear from this:

> whether they go to the right toward the dawn and the sun or to the left toward the misty darkness [*Iliad* 12.239–40]

and more so from this:

> friends, we do not know where there is darkness, or where there is dawn, or where the sun, bringing light to mortals, goes beneath the earth, or where it rises. [*Odyssey* 10.190–2]

One can accept this as the four zones, accepting the dawn as the southern portion – as it has a certain significance – but it is better to believe that what is along the path of the sun is opposite to the northern portion. The statement is intended to show a large change in the celestial phenomena (not merely a concealment of the zones, which must always occur when it is cloudy, whether in the day or night). Celestial phenomena change greatly as we move more toward the south or toward the opposite. This does not create concealment in the west or the east, but in the south or the north, which also happens when it is clear. The pole is at the most northern point but it moves and sometimes is high above us and at other times is below the earth. Thus the arctic [circles] also change, and in such movement at times vanish, so that you cannot know where the northern zone is or where it begins. If this is true, you cannot know the opposite ones either. The circuit of Ithaka is about eighty stadia. This is it about Ithaka.

(13) He [Homer] does not mention Kephallenia – which is a tetrapolis – by its present name, or any of its cities, except for one, either Same or Samos, which no longer exists today, although traces are pointed out in the middle of the crossing to Ithaka. Those from there are called Samaians. The others still exist today, but are small: Paleis, Pronesos, and Kranioi. In our time Gaius Antonius, the uncle of Marcus Antonius, founded another one, when he went into exile after his consulship – which he held with Cicero the orator – and spent time in Kephallenia, subjecting the entire island as though a private possession. But before he completed this settlement he was able to return, and finished his life doing greater things.

(14) Some do not hestitate to say that Kephallenia is Doulichion, and others Taphos – and the Kephallenians are Taphians, or Teleboans – and that Amphitryon made an expedition there with Kephalos the son of Deioneus, an Athenian exile whom he had taken with him. When he [Amphitryon] took possession of the island, he handed it over to Kephalos, and it was named after him, and the cities after his children. But this is not Homeric, for the Kephallenians were subject to Odysseus and Laertes, yet Taphos was subject to Mentes: [C456]

> I profess that I am Mentes the son of Anchialos the skilled, and I am lord over the oar-loving Taphians. [*Odyssey* 1.180–1]

Taphos is now called Taphios. Hellanikos [F144] is not Homeric in saying that Kephallenia is Doulichion, for he [Homer] says [*Iliad* 2.625–30] that it and the rest of the Echinades were subject to Meges. Their inhabitants were Epeians who had come from Elis. Because of this, he calls Otos the Kyllenian "the comrade of Phyleides and ruler of the great-hearted Epeians" [*Iliad* 15.519] but "Odysseus led the great-hearted Kephallenians" [*Iliad* 2.631]. Thus, according to Homer, Kephallenia is not Doulichion, nor is Doulichion a part of Kephallenia (as Andron [F15] says), for the Epeians held it. The Kephallenians held the whole of Kephallenia and were subject to Odysseus, and the others were subject to Meges. Paleis is not called Doulichion by Homer, as Pherekydes [F139] writes. But most opposed to Homer is the one who says that Kephallenia is the same as Doulichion. If, of the suitors, there were "fifty-two from Doulichion" and "twenty-four from Same" [*Odyssey* 16.247, 249], would he not be saying that so many came from the whole but half less two from one of its four [cities]? If one grants this, we would ask what he means by Same when he says "Doulichion, Same, and wooded Zakynthos" [*Odyssey* 1.246]?

(15) Kephallenia lies opposite Akarnania, about 50 stadia – some say 40 – from Leukatas, and about 80 from Chelonatas. Its perimeter is about 300 [stadia]. It is long, reaching toward the Euros wind, and is mountainous. The largest mountain on it is Ainos, on which there is the sanctuary of Zeus Ainesios. Where the island is narrowest it makes a low isthmus that is often washed over from sea to sea. On the gulf near the narrows are Kranioi and Paleis.

(16) The islet of Asteria is between Ithaka and Kephallenia (it is called Asteris by the Poet), which according to the Skepsian [F49] no longer remains in such a way as the Poet says ("there are harbors with a double [C457] anchorage" [*Odyssey* 4.846–7]). Apollodoros [of Athens, F202] says that it remains today, and that there is the small town of Alalkomenai on it, lying on the isthmus itself.

(17) The Poet also calls the Thracian one "Samos," which we today call Samothrake. It is reasonable that he also knows the Ionian one, because he seems to know about the Ionian migration, since he distinguishes those of the same name, specifying Samothrake at one time with the epithet ("high on the uppermost summit of wooded Samos, the Thracian" [*Iliad* 13.12–13]), and at another time by connecting it to the nearby islands ("to Samos, Imbros, and inhospitable Lemnos" [*Iliad* 24.753] and again "between Samos and rugged Imbros" [*Iliad* 24.78]). Thus he knew about it but did not name it, and it was not formerly called by the same name, but was Melamphyllos, then Anthemis, and then Parthenia, from the Parthenios River, whose name was changed to the Imbrasos. At the time of the Trojan matter, then, Kephallenia and Samothrake were called Samos, for Hekabe would not have been introduced as saying that her children, which he [Achilleus] took, would be sold on Samos and Imbros [*Iliad* 24.751–3]. As the Ionian Samos had not yet been settled, clearly it was from one of the earlier ones that had the same name. From this it is also clear that what they write contradicts ancient history when they say that it was after the Ionian migration and the arrival of Tembrion that the settlers came from Samos and named Samothrake "Samos," as this was fabricated by the Samians for the sake of their reputation. Those are more believable who say that the name of the island is found in the fact that high places are called *samoi* ["heights"], since from there "one could plainly see all Ida, and plainly

see the city of Priamos and the ships of the Achaians" [*Iliad* 13.13–14]. Some say that it was called Samos after the Saians, the Thracians who formerly lived there and also held the adjacent mainland, whether they were the same as the Sapaians or the Sintans – the Poet calls them Sintians [*Iliad* 1.594; *Odyssey* 8.294] – or different. Archilochos records them as the Saians: "one of the Saians is adorned with my shield, which I unwillingly left, blameless, beside a bush" [F5].

(18) Zakynthos is the remaining island subject to Odysseus, which inclines more to the west of the Peloponnesos than Kephallenia, and is closer to it.   [C458] The circuit of Zakynthos is 160 stadia, and it is about 60 stadia distant from Kephallenia. It is wooded and fertile, and has a notable city with the same name. It is 3,300 stadia from it to the Libyan Hesperides.

(19) To the east of it and Kephallenia are situated the Echinades Islands. Among them is Doulichion – today called Dolicha – and what are called the Oxeiai, which the Poet says [*Odyssey* 15.299] are the Thoai. Dolicha lies opposite Oiniadai and the outlet of the Acheloos, a hundred [stadia] from Araxos, the promontory of the Eleians. The remainder of the Echinades – there are several of them, all poor and rugged – are off the outlet of the Acheloos, with the farthest 15 stadia away and the nearest 5. Formerly they were in the open sea, but the great amount of silt brought down has joined some of them to the mainland, and will do so to others. This territory was called Paracheloitis ["Along the Acheloos"], since the river overflows it, creating a matter of contention in antiquity, as it confused the boundaries that had long existed between the Akarnanians and the Aitolians. They would decide it by weapons as they did not have arbitrators, and the more powerful would win. This is the reason for the creation of a certain myth that Herakles defeated Acheloos and as the prize of winning the victory married Deianeira the daughter of Oineus, whom Sophokles made to say the following:

> My suitor was the river, I mean Acheloos, who in three shapes would demand me from my father, coming to me in bodily form as a bull, and then as a glittering coiled serpent, and then with the trunk of a man and the face of an ox. [*Trachinian Women* 9–13]

Some add to this, saying that it was the horn of Amaltheia, which Herakles broke off from Acheloos and gave to Oineus as a wedding gift. Others, conjecturing the truth from it, say that the Acheloos, like other rivers, was believed to be like a bull from its sound and the winding of its streams (which were called horns), like a serpent because of its length and twisting, and "with the face of an ox" for the same reason as "bull faced." Herakles, who generally performed good deeds, especially for Oineus (because of the marriage alliance), constrained the problems in the flow of the river by means of embankments and channels, and thus, to the pleasure of Oineus, he gave relief to much of Paracheloitis, and this was the horn of Amaltheia.

[C459]

Regarding the Echinades, or Oxeiai, Homer says that at the time of the Trojan matter they were ruled by Meges,

> whom the horseman Phyleus, a friend to Zeus, produced, he who once moved to Doulichion because of anger toward his father. [*Iliad* 2.628–9]

His father was Augeas, the ruler of the Eleians and the Epeians, and thus the Epeians who went to Doulichion with Phyleus held these islands.

(20) The islands of the Taphians – formerly the Teleboans – among which was Taphos, today called Taphios, were separate from them [the Echinades], not in distance (for they lie nearby), but in that they are marshalled under different commanders, the Taphians and Teleboans. Earlier Amphitryon had made an expedition against them with Kephalos the son of Deioneus, an exile from Athens, and gave the rule over to him. The Poet says that they were marshalled under Mentes [*Odyssey* 1.105, 180–1, 418–19] and calls them brigands [*Odyssey* 15.427, 16.426], as, he says, are all the Teleboans. This is it for the islands off Akarnania.

(21) Between Leukas and the Ambrakian Gulf is a lagoon called Myrtountion. Next after Leukas are Palairos and Alyzia, which are Akarnanian cities, of which Alyzia is 15 stadia distant from the sea, and where there is a harbor sacred to Herakles and a precinct, from where one of the commanders transferred to Rome the *Labors of Herakles*, a work of Lysippos, which was lying out of place because the site was deserted. Next is Cape Krithote, the Echinades, and the city of Astakos, which has the same name as the one around Nikomedeia and the Astakenian Gulf, said in both the singular and plural. Krithote has the same name as a little city in the Thracian Chersonesos. There are good harbors everywhere between these places. Then there are Oiniadai and the Acheloos, and then a lake belonging to Oiniadai called Melite – which is 30 stadia in length and 20 in width – another, Kynia, twice the size of it, both in length and width, and a third, Ouria, which is smaller than them. Kynia empties into the sea but the others lie about half a stadion above it. Then there is the Euenos, which is 670 stadia from Aktion. After the Euenos is Mount Chalkis, which Artemidoros [F57] calls Chalkia, then Pleuron, and then the village of Halikyrna, with Kalydon lying 30 stadia above it in the interior. Around Kalydon is the sanctuary of Apollo Laphrios. Then there is Mount Taphiassos, then the city of Makynia, and then Molykreia, and, nearby, Antirrhion, the boundary between Aitolia

[C460]

and Lokris, which is about 120 stadia from the Euenos. Concerning the mountain – whether it is Chalkis or Chalkia – Artemidoros has it located between the Acheloos and Pleuron, but Apollodoros [of Athens, F203], as I have previously said [10.2.4], has Chalkis and Taphiassos above Molykreia, and he says that Kalydon is located between Pleuron and Chalkis. Perhaps one should assume that there are two, one near Pleuron called Chalkia and the other near Molykreia called Chalkis. There is a certain lake near Kalydon that is large and abundant in fish, which belongs to the Romans in Patrai.

(22) Apollodoros [of Athens, F204] says that in the interior of Akarnania are those called the Erysichaians, whom Alkman [F16] mentions: "neither an Erysichaian ... nor a Kalydonian shepherd, but from the Sardian heights." Olenos, which Homer records [*Iliad* 2.639] in the Aitolian *Catalogue*, was in Aitolia, but only traces of it remain near to Pleuron below Arakynthos. Lysimacheia was near to it – it has also disappeared – situated by the lake today called Lysimacheia, formerly Hydra, between Pleuron and the city of Arsinoë, which was formerly a village called Konopa. It was a foundation by Arsinoë [II], the wife and sister of the second Ptolemaios, well situated at the crossing of the Acheloos. Pylene has experienced something similar to Olenos. When he [Homer] says that Kalydon is "steep" [*Iliad* 13.217, 14.116] and "rocky" [*Iliad* 2.640], one must accept this as the territory, for, as has been said [10.2.3], the territory was divided in two and the mountainous part – Epiktetos – was assigned to Kalydon and the plains to Pleuron.

(23) Today Akarnania and the Aitolians, just as many other peoples, have been worn out and exhausted by continual wars. Yet for an exceedingly long time the Aitolians, along with the Akarnanians, held together against the Makedonians and the other Hellenes, and finally against the Romans, fighting for their autonomy. Since Homer frequently mentions them, as do other poets and writers, at times clearly and understandably, at others less intelligibly – as has been shown in what has already been said about them – one must add some of the older material that has had a basis from the beginning, or is a matter of doubt.   [C461]

(24) Concerning Akarnania, then, Laertes and the Kephallenians acquired it, as we have said [10.2.8], but although many have said who possessed it formerly, they do not agree in what they have said, although well known, and thus it is left for me to make some statement in arbitration about them.

They say that those called the Taphians and Teleboans are said to have lived formerly in Akarnania, and their leader Kephalos, who had been established by Amphitryon as master of the islands around Taphos, became master of these lands. From this they have added the myth that he was considered the first to have made the customary leap from Leukatas, as has been said previously [10.2.9]. Yet the Poet does not say that the Taphians ruled the Akarnanians before the Kephallenians and Laertes arrived, but he says [*Odyssey* 1.417] that they were friends to the Ithakans and thus had not actually ruled over this place and had willingly given it to them, or became fellow inhabitants. It also appears that some from Lakedaimon settled in Akarnania – Ikarios the father of Penelope and those with him – for the Poet handed down in the *Odyssey* that he and her brothers lived there: "they shrink from going to the home of her father Ikarios, for he would have given his daughter in marriage" [*Odyssey* 2.52–3], and, in regard to her brothers, "already her father and brothers urged her to marry Eurymachos" [*Odyssey* 15.16–17]. It is not believable that they were living in Lakedaimon, for Telemachos would not have stayed with Menelaos when he went there, and there is no report of another home. But they say that Tyndareos and his brother Ikarios were driven out of their home by Hippokoon and went to Thestios the ruler of the Pleuronians, and joined with him in acquiring much of the territory beyond the Acheloos, for a share in it. Tyndareos returned home and married Leda the daughter of Thestios, and Ikarios remained, possessing a portion of Akarnania, and, with Polykaste the daughter of Lygaios, had Penelope and her brothers as children.

We have already shown that the Akarnanians were enumerated in the *Catalogue of Ships*, that they took part in the expedition to Ilion, and that among them were those named as "living on the promontory" and those "who held the mainland and lived on the other side" [*Iliad* 2.635]. But the mainland had not yet been named Akarnania, nor the promontory Leukas.

[C462]   (25) Ephoros [F123a] says that they did not join the expedition, for Alkmaion the son of Amphiaraos made an expedition with Diomedes and other Epigonoi, and successfully accomplished the war against the Thebans. Then he joined Diomedes and with him avenged the enemies of Oineus, giving Aitolia to him, and afterward went into Akarnania and subdued it. At the same time Agamemnon attacked the Argives and easily mastered them, since most of them had accompanied Diomedes, but a little later, when the expedition to Ilion came upon him, he was afraid that while he was away on the expedition Diomedes and those with him would come back home – it was heard that a great force had collected around him – and take possession of the sovereignty that most belonged to them, as one was the heir of Adrastos and the other of his father. Thinking this over, he [Agamemnon] intercepted them on their way to Argos and summoned them to join in the war. Diomedes was persuaded to share in the expedition but Alkmaion was displeased and did not consider it. Because of this the Akarnanians alone did not join with the Hellenes in the expedition. Using this story, it seems, the Akarnanians tricked the Romans, as it is said, and managed to retain their autonomy, saying that they alone had not joined in the expedition against their ancestors. They were not mentioned either in the Aitolian *Catalogue* or individually, and their name was not contained in the epics at all.

(26) Ephoros then makes Akarnania subject to Alkmaion before the Trojan matter, proclaiming that Amphilochian Argos was founded by him, and he says that Akarnania was named after his son Akarnan, and the Amphilochians after his brother Amphilochos. Thus what he says is to be cast out as contrary to Homeric history. Thoukydides [2.68.3] and others say that Amphilochos, returning from the Trojan matter, was not satisfied with the situation in Argos, and settled in this territory, some saying that he came to the succession of the political power of his brother, others otherwise.

This is what one can say specifically about the Akarnanians. Now I will speak about them generally, as it is woven in with the Aitolians, discussing next Aitolian matters insofar as we think best in regard to what has already been said.

Part 3: The Kouretians

(1) Some assign the Kouretians to the Akarnanians, others to the Aitolians. Some assert that the race was from Crete and others from Euboia. Since they are recorded by Homer, what he [says] must be investigated first. It is [C463] thought that he says they were Aitolians rather than Akarnanians, if the Porthaonides were "Agrios and then Melas, and the third the horseman Oineus" [*Iliad* 14.117], and "they lived in Pleuron and lofty Kalydon" [*Iliad* 14.116]. These are both Aitolian cities, and are presented in the Aitolian catalogue [*Iliad* 2.639–40]. Thus, since the Kouretians are shown by him to have lived in Pleuron, they would be Aitolian. Those who contradict this are misled by his manner of expression when he says "the Kouretians fought, and the Aitolians steadfast in battle, around the city of Kalydon" [*Iliad* 9.529–30], as it would not be precise to say "the Boiotians and Thebans were fighting each other," or the "Argives and Peloponnesians." But it has been shown previously [8.3.8, 10.2.10] that this mode of expression is Homeric and is in constant use by other poets. Thus this is easy to excuse, but let them explain how the Pleuronians could be catalogued among the Aitolians if they were not Aitolians or of the same peoples.

(2) Ephoros [F122a] says that the Aitolians were people who had never become subject to others, but through all recorded time had remained unravaged because of the roughness of the territory and because of their

training in war. He says that from the beginning the Kouretians possessed the entire territory, yet with the arrival of Aitolos the son of Endymion from Elis, who defeated them in war, the Kouretians withdrew into what is now called Akarnania, but the Aitolians returned with the Epeians and founded the oldest of the cities in Aitolia. In the tenth generation afterward Elis was settled by Oxylos the son of Haimon, who had crossed over from Aitolia. As evidence he puts forth two inscriptions, one from the Thermians in Aitolia – where they have traditionally elected their magistrates – engraved on the base of the image of Aitolos:

> Founder of the territory, once raised beside the eddies of the Alpheios, neighbor of the Olympic stadia, child of Endymion, this Aitolos has been set up by the Aitolians to look upon the memorial of his virtue,

and the other in the agora of the Eleians on the statue of Oxylos:

[C464]

> Aitolos once left the autochthonous people and acquired the land of the Kouretians through his spear and much effort. The tenth generation of this family, Oxylos son of Haimon, founded this ancient city.

(3) Through these inscriptions the kinship of the Eleians and Aitolians with one another is correctly indicated, since they agree, not only in regard to their kinship with each other but that each was the founder of the other. Through this he [Ephoros] convicts well of falsehood those who assert that the Eleians were settled from the Aitolians but the Aitolians were not settled from the Eleians. But he manifests inconsistency in his writing and assertions, as in the matter of the oracle at Delphi that we described [9.3.11]. He says that throughout recorded time all Aitolia was unravaged, and that the Kouretians possessed the territory from the beginning, yet he should have added the following to what he said: the Kouretians continued to possess the Aitolian territory until his time, for only in such a way could he correctly have said that they remained unravaged and that they never became subject to others. He completely forgets his promise and does not add this, but the opposite: when Aitolos arrived from Elis and defeated them in war, the Kouretians withdrew into Akarnania. What is more characteristic of destruction that being defeated in war and withdrawing from the land? The evidence for this is the Eleian inscription, for it says that Aitolos "acquired the land of the Kouretians through his spear and much effort."

(4) Perhaps one could say he meant that Aitolia was unravaged from when it had that name, after the arrival of Aitolos, but the argument supporting this idea was removed when he next said that most of the people who

remained among the Aitolians were these – meaning the Epeians – but that later the Aiolians, who were mixed with the Boiotians, set forth from Thessaly and possessed this territory in common with them. Yet is it believable that without a war they invaded that which belonged to another and divided it up between themselves and those holding it, when the latter had no need of such an association? Or, since this is not believable, that those defeated by weapons ended up as equals? What else is destruction than being defeated by weapons? Moreover, Apollodoros [of Athens, F205] says that it is recorded that the Hyantes went away from Boiotia and settled among the Aitolians. But the former [Ephoros] pronounces – as though successful [in his argument] – that "we are accustomed to examine such things minutely whenever some matter is completely doubtful or falsely conjectured" [F122a].   [C465]

(5) Such is Ephoros, but he is better than many others. Polybios [34.1.3–6] praises him enthusiastically and says that Eudoxos [F328] did well in regard to Hellenic matters, but Ephoros was the best at examining foundations, kinship, migrations, and founders, and he also says that

> we will show things as they now are, concerning both the position of places and the distances between them, for this is most suitable for chorography. [Polybios 34.1.3–6]

But, Polybios, you introduce popular assertions about distances – not only those outside of Hellas but in Hellenic matters – and must submit to examination by Poseidonios, Artemidoros, and a number of others. One also must be lenient toward me and not be scornful – allowing certain mistakes – if much of the history is transferred from such [writers], and be content if most of what I say is better than what others have reported, or if I have added matters that have been overlooked through ignorance.

(6) Concerning the Kouretians, further things are said, some of them closer to the history of the Aitolians and Akarnanians, others farther. Closer are such matters as have been said previously, such as that the Kouretians were living in the territory now called Aitolia, and that the Aitolians with Aitolos drove them into Akarnania. There is also this, that when the Pleuronia was inhabited by the Kouretians and was called the Kouretis, the Aitolians invaded and took it away, driving out those possessing it. Archemachos [F9] the Euboian says that the Kouretians settled at Chalkis and were continually at war over the Lelanton Plain. When the enemy would seize their hair in front and pull them down, they let the hair grow long in back but cut it off in front, and because of the cropping [*koura*] they were called Kouretians. They migrated to Aitolia and possessed the territory around Pleuron, calling those living on the far side of the Acheloos the Akarnanians because they kept their

heads uncut [*akouros*]. Some [say] that each of the tribes was named from a hero, and others that the Kouretians were named from Mount Kourion, which lies above Pleuron, or that they are a certain Aitolian tribe, like the Ophians, Agraians, Eurytanians, or several others. As has been said, when Aitolia was divided in two they say that the region around Kalydon was held by Oineus, and a certain part of Pleuronia was held by the Porthaonides –

[C466]   those with Agrios – ("they lived in Pleuron and lofty Kalydon" [*Iliad* 14.116]), with the mastery over Pleuronia held by Thestios, the father-in-law of Oineus and father of Althaia, and the leader of the Kouretians. When war broke out among the Thestiadai against Oineus and Meleagros, according to the Poet it was "about the head and skin of a pig" [*Iliad* 9.548], following the mythical tale of the boar, but probably it was about a portion of the territory, as it is thus said that "the Kouretians were fighting the Aitolians steadfast in battle" [*Iliad* 9.529]. Such are the closer [accounts].

(7) The proposals that are farther away, but brought into a similarity by the historians, are those based on having the same name, and are called *Kouretika* and *On the Kouretians*, just as if they were matters about those living in Aitolia and Akarnania, but they are different from that and more similar to the accounts about the Satyrs, Silenoi, Bakchoi, and Tityroi. Like these, they say, the Kouretians are called divinities or the attendants of the gods by those handing down Cretan and Phrygian matters, which are interwoven with certain sacred rites – some of which are mystical and some otherwise – about the rearing of the child Zeus on Crete and the celebration of secret rites of the Mother of the Gods in Phrygia and the region of the Trojan Ida. The variation in these accounts is such that some show the Kouretians to be the same as the Korybantes, Kabeiroi, the Idaian Daktyls, and the Telchines, and others that they are related to one another and are defined by small differences from one another. Yet speaking in general, and for the most part, they are all inspired and Bakchic, with martial dances, an uproar, noise, cymbals, drums, and arms, as well as the flute and cries, causing fear through their sacred rites in the manner of religious servants. Thus these rites are considered to have something in common – those among the Samothrakians, on Lemnos, and in a number of other places – because the divine servants are said to be the same. But any such topic of investigation is theological and not alien to the speculations of the philosophers.

(8) Since there is a similarity of name among the Kouretians, the historians have brought unlike things together into a single one. We should not shrink from speaking about them at greater length in a digression, adding an account of their nature as is appropriate for history. Some, however, wish to relate

them to others, and perhaps this happens to be in some way believable. They say that those in Aitolia were named because they wore women's clothing like girls [*korai*], adding that there was a certain rivalry among the Hellenes, [C467] speaking of the "Ioanians with their long chitons" [*Iliad* 13.685; *Hymn to Apollo* 147], and that those with Leonidas were combing their hair when going into battle, so that, they say, they were looked down upon by the Persians, although in the battle they were astonished by them. Simply put, the art of caring for the hair combines its nourishment and cutting [*koura*], suitable for both girls [*korai*] and boys [*koroi*], so that there are various easy ways to obtain the etymology of the Kouretians. It is reasonable that the ritual war dance was first introduced by those adorned in such a way regarding their hair and dress, and called Kouretes. It provided an excuse for those more militaristic than others – who spent their life under arms – and thus they were called by the same name of Kouretes (I mean those in Euboia, Aitolia, and Akarnania). Homer called young soldiers thus:

> choosing the best young men [*kouretes*] of all the Achaians, bring gifts from the quick ships, as many as were promised yesterday to Achilleus, [*Iliad* 19.193–5]

and again, "the Achaian young men [*kouretes*] brought gifts" [*Iliad* 19.248]. This is it for the etymology of the Kouretians. The ritual war dance was militaristic, which is clear by the "pyrrhic" dance and Pyrrhichos himself, who is said to have invented this kind of training in military matters for youths.

(9) Now there must be an examination as to how so many names have been combined into one, and the theology existing in their history. It is common among both the Hellenes and the barbarians to have their sacred rites along with the relaxation of a festival, sometimes with religious frenzy, sometimes without, with or without music, and either mystically or openly. Nature suggests this, for the relaxation draws the mind away from human business and turns it toward the divine, as it should. The religious frenzy seems to provide a kind of divine inspiration similar to that produced by a prophet, and the mystic secrecy of the sacred rites creates reverence for the divine, imitating its nature by avoiding perception by us. Music – with dancing, rhythm, and melody – through its pleasure and technical beauty joins us with the divine for the following reason: it has been well said that people most imitate the divine when they are doing good deeds, although it might be better to say that it is when they are happy, which is rejoicing, taking part in festivals, and engaging in philosophy and music. Otherwise it is abandoned when the hand of the musician turns the art to luxury in symposia, the theatrical, the stage, and such others, yet let us not attack [C468]

the thing itself but examine the nature of education, as it has that as its basis.

(10) Because of this Plato [*Phaidon* 61] – and still earlier, the Pythagoreans – called philosophy music, and they say that the cosmos is constructed according to harmony, assuming that every form of music is the work of the gods. Thus the Muses are goddesses, Apollo is the leader of the Muses, and everything poetic is properly praise. Similarly they attribute to music the building of character, as everything that improves the mind is near to the gods.

Most of the Hellenes attributed to Dionysos, Apollo, Hekate, the Muses, and – by Zeus – to Demeter everything pertaining to secret rites (Bakchic or choral) as well as mystic initiations. They call both Dionysos and the divine leader of the mysteries of Demeter "Iakchos." The carrying of branches, choral dances, and initiations are common with these gods. The Muses are set over the choruses, and Apollo over both these and divination. But all educated people – especially musicians – are servants of the Muses, and these, as well as those connected with divination, belong to Apollo. The initiated, torch-bearers, and hierophants belong to Demeter. The Silenoi, Satyrs, and Bacchants, as well as those called the Lenai, Thyiai, Mimallones, Naiads, and Nymphs belong to Dionysos.

(11) These ceremonies, especially those sacred to Zeus, were performed on Crete, with secret rites and such servants as those who are around Dionysos (the Satyrs). These were called "Kouretes," young men who exhibited martial movements along with dancing, presenting the myth of the origin of Zeus, introducing Kronos as being accustomed to swallow his children immediately after their birth, and Rhea attempting to keep her labor pains secret and, when the baby was born, to get it away and save it through her powers. For this she took the Kouretes as helpers, who, with drums and other such sounds, and the noisy martial dance, protected the goddess and would create panic in Kronos, secretly stealing the child away so that he would be given over to them to be carefully raised. Thus the Kouretes, because they were young men [*koroi*] doing this service, or because they raised the young [*kourotrophein*] Zeus – it is said both ways – were believed worthy of this [C469]   name, as if certain Satyrs of Zeus.

(12) Such are the Hellenes in regard to secret rites. The Berekyntians (a Phrygian tribe), the Phrygians in general, and the Trojans living around Ida honored Rhea and worshiped her in secret rites, calling her the Mother of the Gods, Angdistis, the Phrygian and Great Goddess, as well as (from places) Idaian, Dindymenian, Sipylenian, Pessinountian, and Kybele. The Hellenes call her servants by the same name of Kouretes, but not from the same mythical tale but another, as if they were certain assistants analogous

to the Satyrs. They also call them Korybantes, and through syncope, Kyrbantes.

(13) The poets are evidence for these conjectures. Pindar, in the dithyramb that begins "formerly there walked the song of the dithyramb moving straight ahead" [F70b], records the hymns about Dionysos, both the ancient and later ones, and passing on from these he says:

> for the august and great Mother, the whirling of the cymbals begins among the loud exultation of the rattles, and the torch kindled in the yellow pines. [lines 8–11]

He shows the communality among the Hellenes of the customs around Dionysos, and those of the Mother of the Gods among the Phrygians . . . related to each other. Euripides does the same thing in the *Bacchants*, bringing the Lydian together with the Phrygian, because of their resemblance:

> but those who left Tmolos, the fortress of Lydia, my revelers, women . . . raise up the cymbals native to the Phrygian city, inventions of myself and the Mother of the Gods [lines 55–9, excerpted]

and again:

> O blessed is he who is fortunate and lives a pure life . . . preserving the rites of Great Mother Kybele, and brandishing the thyrsus wreathed with ivy, he who serves Dionysos. Come, Bacchants . . . bring down Bromios, the son of a god, the god Dionysos, from the mountains of Phrygia to the wide streets of Hellas. [lines 72–87, excerpted]

Again, in the following he weaves in Cretan matters:

> O inner room of the Kouretes, sacred interiors of Crete, giving birth to Zeus in the cave where the three-helmeted Korybantes invented for me the drum stretched with hide, and mixed in the intense Bakchic frenzy with   [C470] the sweet-sounding breath of the Phrygian flutes placed in the hands of Mother Rhea, make the noisy Bakchic shout. The maddened Satyrs obtained them from Mother Rhea and added them to the third-year dances that praise Dionysos. [lines 120–34]

In the *Palamedes* [Euripides, F586] the chorus says "of the hair[4] of Dionysos, who rejoices on Ida with his dear mother, with the Iakchic drums."

(14) They bring together into one Silenos, Marsyas, and Olympos as the historical inventors of flutes, again associating Dionysiac and Phrygian

---

[4] The Greek word is uncertain, and given the ambiguities that Strabo has been discussing at great length, it is impossible to determine what Euripides wrote: either "hair" (*koman*), "daughter" (*koran*), or something else.

matters. Often they confuse Ida and Olympos, making them resound as the same mountain. There are four peaks of Ida called Olympos, near Antandria, and there is the Mysian Olympos that borders Ida, but it is not the same. At any rate, Sophokles in the *Polyxena* makes Menelaos eager to sail away from Troy but Agamemnon desirous of remaining behind for a short time in order to propitiate Athena, and introduces Menelaos as saying: "you, remaining here in the Idaian land, collect the flocks of Olympos for sacrifices" [F522].

(15) They invented suitable names for the flute, and for the noise of the rattles, cymbals, and drums, and for the shouting, the Bakchic cries, and foot-stomping, as well as for the servants, choral dancers, and the attendants of the sacred rites – the Kabeiroi, Korybantes, Pans, Satyrs, and Tityroi – calling the god Bakchos, and [calling] Rhea Kybele, Kybebe, and Dindymene, according to the places. Sabazios is also Phrygian and in a way the child of the Mother, as he too transmitted Dionysiac matters.

(16) Similar to these [rituals] are those among the Thracians – the Kotyteian and Bendideian – among whom the Orphic [ritual] began. Those of Kotyto and her instruments are recorded by Aischylos [F57] in his *Edonians*, who speaks of "holding the august rites of Kotyto," immediately adding those around Dionysos:

> one holds in his hand the *bombyx*, the result of great effort with the turning lathe, and it fully fills the fingered melody, the call that brings on the madness. Another makes a loud sound with the bronze-bound *kotylai*, [F57]

[C471] and again:

> the *psalmos* resounds, and fear-inspiring imitators from somewhere invisible bellow in return like bulls, resembling drums, like thunder beneath the earth, terrifyingly carried. [*Ibid.*]

These are like the Phrygian, and it is not unlikely – just as the Phrygians themselves were settlers from Thrace – that their sacred rites were transferred from there. And when they bring Dionysos and the Edonian Lykourgos together, they suggest a similarity of sacred rites.

(17) From the melody, rhythm, and instruments, all Thracian music is considered to be Asiatic. This is clear from the places that the Muses have been honored: Pieria, Olympos, Pimpla, and Leibethron were Thracian places and mountains in antiquity (now they are held by the Makedonians), and Helikon was consecrated to the Muses by the Thracians who settled in Boiotia, those who also consecrated the cave of the Leibethriadian Nymphs. Those who paid attention to ancient music are called Thracians (Orpheus, Mousaios, and Thamyris). Eumolpos ["Sweet-Singer"] was also

named from there. Those who have consecrated to Dionysos the whole of Asia as far as Indike transfer most music from there. Someone says "striking the Asiatic kithara," another calls flutes "Berekyntian" and "Phrygian," and some of the instruments have barbarian names: the *nablas, sambyke, barbitos, magadis*, and a number of others.

(18) The Athenians, just as they continue to be hospitable to other foreign ways, are so in regard to the gods. They admitted so many foreign rituals – especially the Thracian and Phrygian – that they were ridiculed for it. Plato records [*Republic* 1.24] the Bendideian, and Demosthenes [*On the Crown* 259–60] the Phrygian, when he attacks the mother of Aischines and [the man] himself for being with his mother during her initiations, joining her in leading the revels, and often calling out "*euhoi saboi*" and "*hyes Attes hyes*," which belong to the Sabazia and the Mother.

(19) Furthermore, concerning these divinities and their varied names, they were not only called servants of the gods but gods themselves. Hesiod says that five daughters were born to Hekateros and the daughter of Phoroneus:

> from whom sprang the mountain-hunting Nymphs, goddesses, and the race of Satyrs, worthless and unfit for work, and also the Kouretes, sportive gods and dancers. [F11]]

The author of the *Phoronis* [Hellanikos, epic F2a] says that the Kouretes are   [C472]
flute players and Phrygian, and others that they are earth-born with bronze shields. Some [say] that it is not the Kouretes but the Korybantes who are Phrygian, but the former are Cretan, the first on Euboia to put on bronze weapons, because of which they were called Chalkideans ["Brazen"]. Others [say] that the Korybantes, who came from Baktriane (some say from the Kolchians) were given to Rhea by the Titans as armed servants. In the Cretan accounts the Kouretes are called the rearers and guardians of Zeus, having been summoned to Crete from Phrygia by Rhea. Some of the nine Telchines who were on Rhodes accompanying Rhea to Crete and rearing Zeus in his youth were called Kouretes. Kyrbas, one of their companions, was the founder of Hierapytna, and provided an excuse to the Prasians for saying among the Rhodians that the Korybantes were certain divinities, the children of Athena and Helios. Some say, moreover, that the Korybantes were children of Kronos, but others that they were children of Zeus and Kalliope, being the same as the Kabeiroi. They went to Samothrake, formerly called Melite, and performed mystic activities.

(20) The Skepsian [F61] collated the myths, but does not accept the last one, since there is no mystical story about the Kabeiroi told on Samothrake, but nevertheless he provides the opinion of Stesimbrotos the Thasian [F20]

that the sacred rites on Samothrake were performed for the Kabeiroi, and
he says they were so called by them after Mount Kabeiros in Berekyntia.
Some believe that the Kouretes were servants of Hekate and were the same
as the Korybantes.

The Skepsian again says (in contradiction to Euripides [*Bacchants*
120–34]) that on Crete the honoring of Rhea was neither esteemed nor
customary, but only in Phrygia and the Troad, and those who say otherwise
are writing myths rather than history, although perhaps the similarity of
place names contributed to this. Ida is both a Trojan and Cretan mountain,
and Dikte is a place in the Skepsia and a mountain on Crete. Pytna is a
summit of Ida, from which comes the city of Hierapytna. Hippokorona is
Adramyttenian and Hippokoronion is on Crete. Samonion is the eastern
promontory of the island, a plain in the Neandris, and in the Alexandrian
[territory].

(21) Akousilaos the Argive [F20] says that Kamillos is the son of Kabeiro
and Hephaistos, and the three Kabeiroi ... of the Kabeirian Nymphs.
Pherekydes [F48] [says] that there were nine Korybantes – from Apollo
and Rhetia – who lived on Samothrake, that the three Kabeiroi and the
Kabeiridian Nymphs were from Kabeiro the daughter of Proteus and
[C473] Hephaistos, and that sacred rites were instituted for both. It has happened
that the Kabeiroi are most honored on Imbros and Lemnos, but also in
various cities in the region of Troy whose names are secret. Herodotos says
[3.37] that there was a sanctuary of the Kabeiroi in Memphis, as well as one
of Hephaistos, but that they were destroyed by Kambyses. The places where
these deities were honored are uninhabited, both the Korybantion in
Hamaxitia (in what is now the Alexandrian district near Sminthion) and
Korybissa in the Skepsia near the Eureeis River and a village with the same
name, as well as the winter torrent of Aithaloeis. The Skepsian says that it
is plausible that the Kouretes and the Korybantes are the same ... those
who happen to be received as unmarried young men [*koroi*] for the war
dance in the ritual of the Mother of the Gods, and as Korybantes because
they walked butting their heads [*koryptonas bainein*] in the manner of a
dance. The Poet says that they are dancers: "come now, all who are the best
dancers of the Phaiekians" [*Odyssey* 8.250]. Because the Korybantes are
estatic dancers, we say that those who are moved to frenzy are "korybantic."

(22) Some say that the first settlers around the base of Ida were called the
Idaian Daktyls, for the bases of mountains are called feet and the summits
heads, and similar are several extremities around Ida (all sacred to the
Mother of the Gods). Sophokles [F366] believes that the first five were
male, who were the first to discover iron and to work it, as well as many

other things useful for life. There were also five sisters, and they were called Daktyls ["Fingers"] from their number. Others tell the myth in different ways, joining difficulty to difficulty, using differing names and numbers. They name one Kelmis and others Damnameneus, Herakles, and Akmon. To some they are indigenous to Ida, to others they are settlers, but all say that iron was first worked by them on Ida, and all that they were witches and attendants of the Mother of the Gods who lived in Phrygia around Ida (calling the Troad "Phrygia" because the Phrygians, who were neighbors, became its masters after the sack of Troy). They conjecture that both the Kouretes and Korybantes were offspring of the Idaian Daktyls; at any rate the first hundred men born on Crete were called Idaian Daktyls, and they say that their descendants were nine Kouretes, each of whom had ten children called Idaian Daktyls.

[C474]

(23) We have been persuaded to speak about them at length, although not fond of myths in the least, because these facts border on the field of theology. Every account of the gods examines early opinions and myths, since the ancients spoke enigmatically about the physical conceptions regarding the facts, always adding myth to their accounts. It is not easy to solve accurately all the enigmas, but if the greater number of myths is publicly set out – some in agreement and others in contradiction with each other – one might more easily be able to infer the truth from them. They appropriately talk in myths about the wandering in the mountains by those eager for the divine and the gods themselves, and divine inspiration, for the same reason that they believe the gods live in the heavens and show forethought – among other things – for prognostication. Searching for metals and hunting, and seeking what is useful for life, are closely related to wandering in the mountains, but juggling and witchcraft are near to divine inspiration, rituals, and prophecy. In such a way, also, is enthusiasm for the arts, especially the Dionysiac and Orphic rites. But this is enough about this.

Part 4: Crete

(1) Since I have previously gone through the islands of the Peloponnesos, as well as those in the Corinthian Gulf and in front of it, I must speak next about Crete – for it also is part of the Peloponnesos – and whatever is around Crete. Among these are the Kyklades and Sporades, some worthy of recording, others more obscure.

(2) Now we will speak about Crete. Eudoxos [F365] says that it is situated in the Aigaion, but this is not so, for rather it lies between the Kyrenaia and

[the part of] Hellas from Sounion to Lakonike, with its length parallel to those territories from west to east, washed on the north by the Aigaion and Cretan Seas, and on the south by the Libyan, which touches the Egyptian Sea. The western of its extremities is around Phalasarna, and it is 200 stadia wide and divided into two promontories, the southern of which is called the Ram's Forehead and the northern Kimaros. The eastern is Samonion, falling toward the east not much beyond Sounion.

(3) Regarding its size, Sosikrates [F5] – who, Apollodoros [of Athens, F206] says, is accurate about the island – determined its length at more than 2,300 stadia and its width … so that its circuit would be more than 5,000 stadia. Artemidoros [F62] says that it is 4,100 [stadia]. Hieronymos [F18] says that the length is 2,000 stadia, and the width irregular, and thus would say that the circuit is larger than that of Artemidoros. About a third of its length … and then there is an isthmus of about 100 stadia, having a settlement on its northern side, Amphimalla, and, on the southern, Phoinix, which is Lampian. It is widest in the middle. From here it comes together in an isthmus narrower than the former, about 60 stadia, from Minoa of the Lyktians to Hierapytna and the Libyan Sea (the city is situated on a gulf). Then it advances into a deep promontory, Samonion, inclining toward Egypt and the Rhodian islands.

[C475]

(4) The island is mountainous with fertile glens. Regarding the mountains, those toward the west are called Leuka, which are no less than Taÿgetos in height and extend for a length of 300 stadia, making a ridge that ends around the narrows. In the middle, where the island is most spacious, is Mount Ida, the highest one there, circular and 600 stadia in its circuit. There are others about equal to Leuka, some ending toward the south and others toward the north.

(5) The voyage from the Kyrenaia to the Ram's Forehead is 2 days and nights, and from Kimaros it is 700 stadia, with Kythera between them. The voyage from Samonion to Egypt is 4 days and nights – some say 3 – and some state that this is 5,000 stadia, others still less. Eratosthenes [F129] says that from the Kyrenaia to the Ram's Forehead is 2,000 [stadia] and less from there to the Peloponnesos.

(6) "One language mixed with others," as the Poet says, "Achaians are there, great-hearted Eteocretans, Kydonians, the *trichaikes* Dorians, and the divine Pelasgians" [*Odyssey* 19.175–7]. Of these, Staphylos [F12] says that the Dorians possess what is toward the east, the Kydonians the western part, and the Eteocretans the southern. They have the small town of Praisos, where the sanctuary of Diktaian Zeus is. The others, who were stronger, lived in the plains. It is reasonable to assume that the Eteocretans and Kydonians

were autochthonous, and the remainder foreigners, who, Andron [F16a] says, came from Thessaly (that which was formerly called Doris but is now Histiaiotis). The Dorians living around Parnassos set forth from there, as he says, and founded Erineos, Boion, and Kytinion, and because of this the [C476] Poet calls them "threefold [*trichaikes*]" [*Odyssey* 19.177]. But the account of Andron is not accepted at all because he declares that the Dorian tetrapolis is a tripolis, and that the Dorian metropolis is a Thessalian settlement. "Threefold" is taken from the triple crest [*trilophia*] or the crests of the hair [*trichinoi*].

(7) There are several cities on Crete, but three are the largest and most famous: Knossos, Gortyna, and Kydonia. Homer sings of the excellence of Knossos – calling it great and the royal residence of Minos [*Odyssey* 19.178–9] – as do those later. It continued for a long time to carry the first place, and then it was humbled and had many of its rights taken away, and the distinction was removed from it to Gortyna and Lyttos, but later it regained again its old aspect as the metropolis. It is situated in a plain, having an ancient circuit of 30 stadia, between the Lyttia and the Gortynia ... 200 stadia and 120 stadia from Lyttos (to which the Poet gives the name Lyktos [*Iliad* 2.647, 17.611]). Knossos is 25 stadia from the northern sea, Gortyna 90 from the Libyan, and Lyttos itself 80 from the Libyan. Knossos has Herakleion as its seaport.

(8) They say that Minos used Amnisos as his seaport, where there is a sanctuary of Eileithyia. Knossos was formerly named Kairatos, from the river flowing by it. It is recorded that Minos was an excellent lawgiver and was the first to have a thalassocracy. He divided the island into three and founded a city in each part: Knossos in the ... opposite to the Peloponnesos. It also is toward the north. As Ephoros [F147] says, Minos emulated a certain Rhadamanthys, from antiquity, who was a most just man and who had the same name as the former's brother, and who is believed to have been the first to have civilized the island through laws, combining cities, and creating governments, alleging that he had brought from Zeus each of the opinions that he publicly promulgated. In imitation of him, Minos, it seems, would go up to the cave of Zeus every ninth year, spend time there, and return with whatever precepts he had drawn up, which he declared were the edicts of Zeus. For this reason the Poet says the following: "Minos reigned there, who conversed with great Zeus every ninth year" [*Odyssey* 19.178–9]. This is what he says, but the ancients have recorded another story about him – which is contrary to this one – that he was tyrannical, violent, and an exactor of tribute, as represented in tragedy with the Minotaur and the Labyrinth [C477] and what happened to Theseus and Daidalos.

(9) Which of these is more reliable is difficult to say. There is another topic that is not agreed upon, as some say that Minos was a foreigner and others that he was native to the island. The Poet seems to advocate the second view when he says "he first brought forth Minos, the guardian of Crete" [*Iliad* 13.450].

Concerning Crete, it is agreed that from ancient times it had good laws, and made the best of the Hellenes emulate them. First of all it was the Lakedaimonians, as Plato shows in the *Laws*, as well as Ephoros [F33], who recorded their government in his *Europa*. Later it changed greatly for the worse, for they inherited piracy from the Tyrrhenians, who ravaged Our Sea the most. The Kilikians later destroyed this, and it was all put down by the Romans, who made war against Crete as well as the piratical fortresses of the Kilikians. Today Knossos has a Roman settlement.

(10) This is it about Knossos, a city that is not foreign to me, although because of human affairs and the resulting changes and occurrences, the connections that I originally had with the city have ceased. Dorylaos was a tactician and a friend of Mithridates [V] Euergetes. Because of his military experience, he was appointed to recruit mercenaries, mostly in Hellas and Thrace, as well as among the Cretans. This was before the Romans possessed the island and while there was a large number of mercenaries and many soldiers on it, from whom it happened that the pirate bands were mustered. When Dorylaos was living there, war happened to occur between the Knossians and the Gortynians, and he was chosen commander, and successfully accomplished the war, receiving great honor. When, a little later, he learned that Euergetes had been treacherously killed by his friends, through a plot in Sinope, and he heard that his wife and children were his successors, he was in despair about the situation there and remained in Knossos. He had two sons by a Maketian woman named Sterope – Lagetas and Stratarchas (I saw Stratarchas when he was extremely old) – and also one daughter. Euergetes had two sons, one of whom, Mithridates [VI] called Eupator, succeeded to the rule when he was 11 years old. Dorylaos the [C478] son of Philetairos was raised with him, and Philetairos was the brother of the tactician Dorylaos. When the king reached adulthood ... with his companion Dorylaos, that he not only gave him great honors but cared for his kinsmen and sent for those in Knossos. These were those around Lagetas – their father having already died – and as they reached adulthood they left Knossos and went home. A daughter of Lagetas was the mother of my mother. When he prospered, others prospered with him, and when he was destroyed – he was discovered instigating a revolt in the kingdom in favor of the Romans, in which he would be established as its ruler – they

were destroyed with him and humbled. The connections with the Knossians were neglected, as they had undergone a myriad of changes. Such is the account about Knossos.

(11) After it, the city of the Gortynians seems to have been second in power: when the two cooperated they held everyone else subject, and when they were at variance there was sedition throughout the island. Kydonia would be the greatest addition to whichever it attached itself. The city of the Gortynians lies in a plain, and it may have been walled in antiquity – as Homer says "high-walled Gortyna" [*Iliad* 2.646, altered] – but later it lost its walls from the foundations and has remained unwalled for all time. Ptolemaios [IV] Philopator began to build a wall, but it proceeded for only about 8 stadia (it is worth mentioning that the settlement once filled a circuit of 50 stadia). It is 90 stadia distant from the Libyan sea at Leben, which is its emporium, and it has another seaport, Matalon, from which it is a distance of 130 stadia. The Lethaios River flows through the entire territory.

(12) Leukokomas and his lover Euxynthetos were from Leben, whom Theophrastos records in his work *On Love* [F560]. Among the many tasks that Leukokomas assigned to Euxynthetos, one, he says, was to bring back his dog from Praisos. The Prasians border it, about 70 [stadia] from the sea and 180 distant from Gortyn. It has been said [10.4.6] that Praisos belonged to the Eteocretans, and the sanctuary of Diktaian Zeus was there. Dikte is nearby, not, as Aratos has, "close to Mount Ida" [*Phainomena* 33], for Dikte is 1,000 [stadia] from Ida, situated toward the rising sun from it, and 100 from Samonion. Praisos was situated between Samonion and Chersonesos, [C479] 60 stadia above the sea, and the Hierapytnians razed it. Kallimachos is not correct, they say, when he speaks [*Hymn* 3.190–205] about Britomartis, who fled the violence of Minos and leapt from Dikte into fishermen's nets [*diktya*], and that because of this she was called Diktynna by the Kydonians, and the mountain was Dikte. Kydonia is not at all in the neighborhood of these places, but lies near the western end of the island. There is a Mount Tityros in the Kydonia, on which there is a sanctuary, not the Diktaion but the Diktynnaion.

(13) Kydonia is situated on the sea looking toward Lakonike, and is equidistant from Knossos and Gortyn – about 800 stadia – and 80 from Aptera and 40 from the sea in that region. The seaport of Aptera is Kisamos, and the Polyrrhenians border the west of the Kydoniatians, among whom is the sanctuary of Diktynna. They are about 30 stadia distant from the sea and 60 from Phalasarna. They formerly lived in villages, and then the Achaians and Lakonians made a common settlement, building a wall around a natural fortification facing toward the south.

(14) Regarding the three cities united by Minos, the last – this is Phaistos – was razed by the Gortynians. It is 60 [stadia] distant from Gortyn, 20 from the sea, and 40 from its seaport of Matalon. Those who razed it possess the territory. Rhyton, along with Phaistos, belongs to the Gortynians ("Phaistos and Rhyton" [*Iliad* 2.648]). They say that Epimenides, who composed his *Purifications* in poetry, was from Phaistos. Lissen is also Phaistian. The seaport of Lyttos – which we mentioned previously [10.4.7] – is the so-called Chersonesos, where the sanctuary of Britomartis is. The cities catalogued along with it – Miletos and Lykastos – no longer exist, and the Lyttians and Kydonians distributed the territory after they destroyed the city.

(15) Since the Poet says [*Iliad* 2.649] that Crete had a hundred cities at one time, and ninety at another [*Odyssey* 19.174], Ephoros [F146] says that the ten were founded later, after the Trojan matter, by the Dorians who accompanied Althaimenes the Argeian, and that it was Odysseus who said it had ninety cities. This statement is believable, but others say that the ten were razed by the enemies of Idomeneus. Yet the Poet does not say that such existed on Crete at the time of the Trojan matter, but rather in his own time, for he is speaking in his own person, although if the statement were by [C480] someone from an earlier time, such as in the *Odyssey* when he [Odysseus] speaks of the ninety cities, it would be good to accept it. Yet if we concede the former, the latter statement could not be maintained, for it is not likely that these cities were destroyed by the enemies of Idomeneus either at the time of the expedition or the return. When the Poet says

> Idomeneus brought all his companions to Crete, all who escaped from the war, and the open sea robbed him of no one [*Odyssey* 3.191–2]

he would have recorded this incident, although it is clear that Odysseus did not know about the destruction of the cities, since he did not mingle with any Hellenes either during his wanderings or later. The one [Nestor] who accompanied Idomeneus on the expedition and also returned home safe did not know what happened at the latter's home during the expedition, or during the return, for if he [Idomeneus] had been saved with all his companions, he returned in strength, and thus his enemies would not have been strong enough to take ten cities away from him.

(16) This is the circuit of the Cretan territory. Regarding their government, which Ephoros [F149] records, it would be sufficient to go over its most important points. He says that it seems the lawgiver assumed freedom is the greatest thing for cities, for this alone makes goods one's own possessions, but in slavery they belong to the rulers and not to the ruled. Yet those who have it must guard it. Through unanimity all dissension – which produces greed and

luxury – that is encountered is taken away. When everyone lives moderately and simply, one does not encounter envy, arrogance, or hatred toward those who are similar. This is why youths are ordered to frequent the so-called "herds," and those who are grown eat together in common messes, called the Andreia, so that the ones who are poorer are fed at public expense and become equal to the well off. Rather than cowardice, courage rules, and they become familiar from childhood with weapons and hard work, so that they disdain heat, cold, rough and steep roads, and blows in the gymnasium and on the battle line. They practice archery and the war dance, which was first made known by the Kouretes and later Pyrrhichos, who arranged the one that was called after him (the pyrrhic). Thus not even their games failed to provide a share of things useful for war. Moreover, they would use certain Cretan rhythms in their songs, which are exceedingly intense and were invented by Thales, to whom they attribute their paean and other indigenous songs, as well as many of their customs. They also use military dress and shoes, and weapons would be the most honored of gifts for them. [C481]

(17) It is said by some that most Cretan customs are Lakonian, but the truth is that they were invented by the former and perfected by the Spartiates. The Cretans neglected military matters when their cities – especially Knossos – were ruined, but some of their customs were better preserved among the Lyttians, Gortynians, and in certain other small cities. The customs of the Lyttians are presented as evidence for those declaring that the Lakonian ones are older, for as settlers they would preserve the customs of the mother city, especially since it is simplistic to declare that those who are better organized and governed would imitate their inferiors. But this is not said correctly, for one should not conjecture about antiquity from the present arrangement, as both have experienced a reversal. The Cretans were formerly masters of the sea – thus the proverb "a Cretan does not know the sea," for those who pretend not to know what they know – although today they have lost their sea power. Moreover, even though some of the settlements on Crete were Spartiate, they were not forced to retain their customs. At any rate, many settlements do not preserve those of their native land, and many on Crete that are not settlements have the same customs as the settlers.

(18) Lykourgos, the Spartiate lawgiver, was five generations more recent than Althaimenes, who sent the settlement to Crete. It is recorded that he was the son of Kissos, who founded Argos at about the same time as when Prokles united Sparta. It is agreed by all that Lykourgos was the sixth in descent from Prokles. Copies are not earlier than their models, nor are newer things [earlier] than older ones. The dancing that is customary among the Lakedaimonians,

and the rhythms and paeans that are sung according to rules, and many other institutions, are called "Cretan," as if they originated there. Some of the magistracies have the same administration and names, such as the office of the elders and the horsemen, except that the horsemen on Crete happened to possess horses, from which it is presumed that the office of horsemen on Crete is older, as they preserve the true meaning of the word, but the others [Lakedaimonians] do not keep horses. The ephors administer in the same way as the *kosmoi* on Crete, but are named differently. The common messes are still today called the Andreia among the Cretans, but among the Spartiates they do not continue to be called by the same name as formerly. At any rate, this is laid down by Alkman: "in banquets and festivals, among the guests of the Andreia, it is fitting to begin the paean" [F98].

[C482]

(19) It is said by the Cretans that Lykourgos came to them for the following reason. The older brother of Lykourgos was Polydektes. When he died he left his wife pregnant. For a while Lykourgos ruled in place of his brother, and when a child was born he became its guardian, since the rule happened to belong to him. Someone reproached the former [Lykourgos], saying that he clearly knew that he would become king. He understood the implication of such talk: he would be suspected of a plot against the boy. Fearing that if he happened to die he [Lykourgos] would be considered by his enemies to be the cause, he went away to Crete. This is said to be the reason that he went abroad. When he arrived he associated with Thales – a man who was a lyric poet and lawgiver – and was informed by him about the way that in earlier times Rhadamanthys, and later, Minos, put forth laws to men as if from Zeus. He was in Egypt and learned about their customs, and, as some say, meeting with Homer, who was spending time on Chios, he went back home and found when he arrived that the son of his brother, Charilaos the son of Polydektes, was king. Then he set forth to arrange the laws, frequenting the god at Delphi and carrying the decrees away from there, just as Minos and those around him had done from the cave of Zeus, most of them being similar.

(20) He [Ephoros, F149] said that the following are the most important Cretan institutions. All who are selected at the same time from the "herd" of boys are forced to marry at the same time, although they do not immediately take home those whom they have married, but when the girls are sufficiently able to manage household affairs. The dowry – if she has brothers – is half the brother's portion. The children learn writing, the songs that are prescribed, and certain other forms of music. Those who are still younger are taken to the common messes, and they sit together on the ground in cheap and poor clothing – both in winter and summer – serving

[C483]

both themselves and the men. Those from the same mess contend in battle with each other and with those from other messes. A *paidonomos* supervises each Andreion. The older ones are taken to the herds. The most notable and capable of the boys assemble the herds, each collecting as many [boys] as possible. The leader of each herd is usually the father of the assembler, who has the authority to lead them out to hunt and run, and to punish the disobedient. They are fed by the state, and on certain appointed days herd contends with herd, rhythmically battling with flute and lyre, just as is the custom in war, inflicting blows with their hands or by weapons that do not have iron.

(21) There is a peculiar custom regarding love, because it is not by persuasion that they conquer those whom they love, but by abduction. The lover announces to his friends three or more days in advance that he is going to make the abduction, as it is most disgraceful for the boy to be hidden or not allowed to proceed on the appointed road, as if acknowledging that the boy is not worthy of having such a lover. When they come together, if the abductor is equal or superior to the boy in esteem, those pursuing lay hold of him – but moderately – fulfilling the custom. Then they happily give him over to be led away. If the former is not worthy, he is taken away. The pursuit does not terminate until the boy is led to the Andreion of his abductor. They consider worthy of love not someone who is distinctive in beauty, but in manliness and decorum. The lover greets him and gives him presents, and then takes the boy to any place in the territory that he wishes, with those who were present at the abduction pursuing them. After entertaining and hunting with him for two months – he cannot possess the boy for a longer time – they come back down to the city. The boy is sent away after receiving as presents military clothing, an ox, and a drinking cup – these gifts are required by law – and many other extravagant gifts; the friends join in contributing because of the amount of the expense. The ox is sacrificed to Zeus as a banquet for those with him. Then he makes the intercourse with his lover known – whether he was pleased with it or not – as this is permitted by law, so that if there had been any force applied [C484] against him by his lover he could take vengeance through those present and thus be free of him. It is especially disgraceful for those who are attractive in appearance and distinguished in ancestry not to acquire lovers, as this happens due to their character. But the stand-bys (this is what they call those abducted) receive honors, for at the dances and the races they have the most honored places and dress in different clothing from the rest (that was given them by their lovers). Not only then, but when they have grown up, they have distinctive dress, from which it is known that each has become

renowned, for they call the loved one "the renowned" and the lover "the paramour." This is it regarding their customs in love affairs.

(22) They choose ten archons ... concerning the most important issues they make use of counsellors called the Elders.[5] Appointed to this council are those considered worthy of holding the office of *kosmos* and who are otherwise judged acceptable.

I have assumed that the Cretan government is worthy of description because of its peculiar nature and its reputation. Not many of these customs survive, and the administration is through the decrees of the Romans, as happens in other provinces.

Part 5: The smaller islands

(1) The islands around Crete are Thera – the Kyrenaian metropolis and a Lakedaimonian settlement – and, near to it, Anaphe, where the sanctuary of the Aigletian Apollo is. Kallimachos once said the following: "Aiglete and Anaphe, neighbor of Lakonian Thera" [F7], and elsewhere, mentioning Thera, "mother of my homeland, famous for its horses" [F716]. Thera is long, being 200 stadia in circumference, lying opposite Dia, an island near the Knossian Herakleion, but it is 700 stadia distant from Crete. Near to it are Anaphe, Therasia, and the sacred islet that came up during the eruption, as has been said [1.3.16]. One hundred stadia from it is the islet of Ios, on which some say the poet Homer is buried. From Ios toward the west one comes to Sikinos, Lagoussa, and Pholegandros, which Aratos calls [*Katalepton*, F109] "iron worked" because of its roughness. Near to these is Kimolos, from which comes the "Kimolian earth." Siphnos is visible from there, concerning which they say "Siphnian knuckle" because of its cheapness. Still near to Kimolos and Crete is Melos, which is more distinguished than these, 700 stadia distant from the Hermionian Promontory and the Skyllaion, and almost the same from the Diktynnaion. The Athenians once [C485]   sent an expedition there and slaughtered most of them from youth upward.

These are in the Cretan Sea, but in the Aigaion, rather, are Delos, the Kyklades around it, and the Sporades that lie near to them, to which belong the previously mentioned islands around Crete.

(2) Delos has a city situated in the plain, as well as the sanctuary of Apollo and the Letoon. Kynthos, a bare and rugged mountain, lies above the city. The Inopos River flows through the island; it is not large, since the island is

---

[5] This sentence is corrupt with several gaps.

small. From antiquity – beginning in heroic times – it has been honored because of its gods, as the myth is that Leto was relieved there of the birthing pains of Apollo and Artemis. "Formerly it was constantly moving," says Pindar,

> tossed by the waves and all kinds of winds. But when the daughter of Koios, agonizing in the pains of childbirth, set foot on it, then four upright columns with adamant bases sprang up from the foundations of the earth, and held the rock on their capitals. There she gave birth and saw her fortunate offspring. [F33d]

The islands lying around it, called the Kyklades, made it famous, since in its honor they sent at public expense sacred ambassadors, sacrifices, and choruses of maidens, and they would celebrate great festivals there.

(3) Originally they [the Kyklades] were said to have been twelve, but more were added. At any rate, Artemidoros [F60] enumerates them, saying about Helena that it is long, extending from Thorikos to Sounion, about 60 stadia in length. He says that the so-called Kyklades begin from here. He names Keos, which is nearest to Helena, and after it Kythnos, Seriphos, Melos, Siphnos, Kimolos, Prepesinthos, and Oliaros, and in addition Paros, Naxos, Syros, Mykonos, Tenos, Andros, and Gyaros. I consider all these to be among the twelve except for Prepesinthos, Oliaros, and Gyaros. While anchored at Gyaros, I perceived a small village settled by fishermen, and when we departed we took one of the fishermen, who had been chosen as an ambassador to Caesar (Caesar was at Corinth, going to his Aktian triumph). While sailing with us, he said that he had been made ambassador to request a reduction in tribute, for they had been paying 150 drachmas when it was difficult to pay 100. Aratos also makes the poverty clear in his [C486] *Katalepton* [F109]: "Leto, will you soon pass me by, I who am like iron-worked Pholegandros or worthless Gyaros?"

(4) Although Delos had become greatly esteemed, this increased even more when Corinth was razed by the Romans. The merchants moved there, attracted by the immunity of the sanctuary and the convenient situation of the harbor, for it is well situated for those sailing from Italia and Hellas to Asia. Their festival is a sort of commercial occurrence, habituated by the Romans more than anyone else, even when Corinth existed. When the Athenians took the island they cared properly for both the sanctuary and the merchants. But when the commander of Mithridates [VI] and the tyrant who caused the revolt came there, they totally ruined it, and after the king went home the Romans received back a desolate island, and it has remained in an impoverished state up to today. It is possessed by the Athenians.

(5) Rhenaia is a deserted little island within 4 stadia of Delos, where the memorials of the Delians are. It is not allowed to bury or burn a corpse on Delos, and it is not allowed to raise a dog on Delos. Formerly it was named Ortygia.

(6) Keos was originally a tetrapolis, but only two are left, Ioulis and Karthaia, and the remainder were united with them, Poieessa into Karthaia and Koresia into Ioulis. Simonides the lyric poet and his nephew Bakchylides were from there, and after them Erasistratos the physician and Ariston the Peripatetic philosopher and follower of Bion the Borysthenite. It seems that once there was a law established among them, which Menandros records ("the Keian custom is good, Phanias, that one unable to live well should not live badly" [F879]), and which seems to have commanded those over sixty years of age to drink hemlock, so that there would be sufficient nourishment for others. Once, they say, when they were being besieged by the Athenians, they voted that the oldest among them should be put to death, having reached a sufficient limit in years, but the siege came to an end. The city lies on a mountain, about 25 stadia distant from the sea, and its seaport is the place where Koresia was situated, which does not even have [C487] the settlement of a village. Near Koresia (and also near Poieessa) there is a sanctuary of Sminthian Apollo, and between the temple and the ruins of Poieessa is the sanctuary of Nedousian Athena, established by Nestor on his return from Troy. There is an also Elixos River around Koresia.

(7) After it, there are Naxos and Andros – both notable – and Paros. Archilochos the poet was from there. Thasos was founded by the Parians, as well as Parion in the Propontis. On it there is an altar that is said to be worth seeing, a stadion along its sides. Also on Paros is the so-called Parian stone, the best for marble sculpture.

(8) There is Syros – the first syllable is long – where Pherekydes the son of Babys was from (the Athenian is more recent than he). The Poet seems to record this island, calling it Syrie ("there is an island called Syrie above Ortygia" [*Odyssey* 15.403–4]).

(9) There is Mykonos, under which – the myth says – lies the last of the Gigantes destroyed by Herakles. From this comes the proverb "everything under Mykonos," for those who bring under one ascription things that are by nature separated. Moreover, some call bald men Mykonians, as the condition is customary on the island.

(10) There is Seriphos, where the mythical story of Diktys is, who drew up in his nets [*diktyes*] the chest in which Perseus and his mother Danae had been enclosed and thrown into the sea by Akrisios the father of Danae. They say that Perseus was raised there, and brought the head of the Gorgon

there and showed it to the Seriphians, turning them all into stone. He did this to avenge his mother because King Polydektes proclaimed that he would marry her against her will. The island is so rocky that the satirists say this was the action of the Gorgons.

(11) Tenos does not have a large city, but a great sanctuary of Poseidon in a grove outside the city, worth seeing. There are large banqueting halls in it, a sufficient indication of the large number who come together with their neighbors and join them in the sacrifices at the Poseidonia.

(12) Amorgos is one of the Sporades – where Simonides the iambic poet came from – as are Lebinthos and Leros. Phokylides has it thus: "the Lerians are bad, not one but every one except Prokles, and Prokles is a Lerian" [F2]. The people living there were reproached as being malignant. [C488]

(13) Nearby are Patmos and the Korassiai, lying to the west of Ikaria, which is [west] of Samos. Ikaria is deserted but has pastures that are used by the Samians. Although it is in such a way, it is still notable. Lying in front is the Ikarian Sea, named after it, in which it is, as well as Samos and Kos, and those just mentioned (the Korassiai, Patmos, and Leros). Mount Kerketeus, which is on it, is also famous, more than Ampelos, which lies above the Samian city. The Karpathian Sea adjoins the Ikarian on the south, and it [adjoins] the Egyptian, and on the west the Cretan and Libyan.

(14) Also in the Karpathian [Sea] are many of the Sporades, especially between Kos, Rhodes, and Crete. Among these are Astypalaia, Telos, Chalkia, and those that Homer names in the *Catalogue*: "those who held Nisyros, Krapathos, Kasos, and Kos (the city of Eurypylos), and the Kalydnian islands" [*Iliad* 2.676–7]. Except for Kos and Rhodes, which we will speak about later [14.2.5–19], I place them all in the Sporades. I mention them here even though they are near Asia, not Europe, since in some way the narrative has brought about inclusion of the Sporades with Crete and the Kyklades. In the circuit of Asia I will survey and describe the neighboring important islands (Cyprus, Rhodes, and Kos), and those lying next on the coast (Samos, Chios, Lesbos, and Tenedos). Now I will go through the remainder of the Sporades that are worth mentioning.

(15) Astypalaia is exceedingly far out in the open sea, and has a city. Telos extends along the Knidia and is long, high, narrow, and has a perimeter of about 140 stadia and an anchorage. Chalkia is 80 stadia distant from Telos, 400 from Karpathos, and about twice that from Astypalaia. It has a settlement of the same name, a sanctuary of Apollo, and a harbor.

(16) Nisyros is to the north of Telos and about 60 stadia distant from it – also about the same distance from Kos – and is round, high, and rocky with millstones. At any rate, there is an abundance of millstones from there for

the neighbors. It has a city of the same name, a harbor, hot springs, and a sanctuary of Poseidon. Its perimeter is 80 stadia. Near it is the so-called Islet [C489] of the Nisyrians. They say that Nisyros is a piece broken off from Kos, adding the myth that Poseidon, pursuing one of the Gigantes, Polybotes, broke off a lump of Kos with his trident and threw it at him, and the missile became the island of Nisyros, with the Giant lying under it. Some say that he lies under Kos.

(17) Karpathos – the Poet says Krapathos [*Iliad* 2.676] – is high and has a circuit of 200 stadia. It was originally a tetrapolis and its name was notable, from which the sea was named. One of its cities was called Nisyros, the same name as the island of the Nisyrians. It lies opposite the White Cape in Libya, which is about 1,000 stadia distant from Alexandria and 4,000 from Karpathos.

(18) Kasos is 70 stadia from it, and 250 from Samonion, the cape of Crete. It has a circuit of 80 stadia. On it there is a city of the same name, and several islands around it that are called the Kasians.

(19) They say that the Poet calls the Sporades the Kalydnian Islands [*Iliad* 2.677], one of which is Kalymna. But it is reasonable – like those near by and subject to the Nisyrians and Kasians – that those around Kalymna were once called the Kalydnians. Some say that there are only two Kalydnians, Leros and Kalymna, which are mentioned by the Poet. The Skepsian [F17] says that the name was in the plural – Kalymnai – like Athens and Thebes, but the [words of] the Poet must be taken as a transposition, for he does not say "Kalydnian Islands" but "those who held Nisyros, Krapathos, Kasos, and Kos (the city of Eurypylos), and Kalydnai" [*Iliad* 2.676–7, altered]. All the island honey is generally of good quality, a match for that from Attika, but that from these islands is excellent, especially the Kalymnian.

BOOK II

The northeastern part of the inhabited world

Part 1:   Introduction to Asia

(1) Asia adjoins Europe, bordering it along the Tanais River. It is necessary   [C490]
to speak about it next, for clarity dividing it by natural boundaries. We must
do for Asia what Eratosthenes did for the entire inhabited world.

(2) The Tauros passes through the middle of this continent like a girdle,
extending from west to east, leaving part in the north and the other in the
south. The Hellenes call the one "within the Tauros" and the other "outside," as I have already said [2.1.1], but this is for the sake of a reminder.

(3) The mountain generally has a width of 3,000 stadia, and a length as
great as that of Asia, about 45,000 [stadia] from the coast opposite the
Rhodians toward the east to the promontories of Indike and Skythia.

(4) It has been divided into many parts and names, marked off by
boundaries that outline the larger and smaller [areas]. Since certain peoples
are enclosed within the great width of the mountain, some of whom are
without significance and others quite well known (such as Parthyaia, Media,   [C491]
Armenia, and some Kappadokians, Kilikians, and Pisidians), those who are
mostly in the northern portion must be assigned to that part, and in the south
to the southern. Those situated in the middle of the mountains should be
placed in the north because of the similarity of the climate (for it is cold, but
the south is hot). The flow of almost all the rivers there is in opposition – some
to the northern portion and others to the southern (at first, although later
some turn to the east or west) – and thus it is naturally suitable to use the
mountains as boundaries in dividing Asia into two parts, just as the sea within
the Pillars is mostly in a straight line with these mountains and has become
useful in the making of two continents, Europe and Libya, since it is the
important boundary between the two.

(5) Passing from the topic of Europe to that of Asia in geography, the
northern is the first of the two divisions, and thus one must begin with it. Its
first [portion] is around the Tanais, which we have established as the

boundary between Europe and Asia. This, in a way, is a sort of peninsula, surrounded on the west by the Tanais River and the Maiotis as far as the Bosporos and the coast of the Euxeinos that ends at Kolchis, on the north by the Ocean as far as the mouth of the Kaspian Sea, and on the east by the same sea as far as the boundary region of Albania and Armenia where the Kyros and Araxes Rivers empty (the latter flowing through Armenia and the Kyros through Iberia and Albania). On the south it is from the outlet of the Kyros as far as Kolchis, about 3,000 stadia from sea to sea through the Albanians and Iberians, and thus it is said to be an isthmus. Those who have pulled the isthmus together, such as Kleitarchos [F13] – who says that it is flooded from either sea – are not worthy of mention. Poseidonios [F206] says that the isthmus is 1,500 [stadia], as much as from Pelousion to the Erythra. "I believe," he says, "that from the Maiotis to the Ocean it is not much different."

(6) Yet I do not know how he can be trusted about uncertain things when he speaks so unreasonably about what is visible, even though he was a [C492] friend of Pompeius, who made an expedition against the Iberians and the Albanians as far as both seas, the Kaspian and the Kolchian. At any rate, they say that when Pompeius came to Rhodes, about to go to war against the pirates (immediately afterward he was to set forth against Mithridates [VI] and the peoples as far as the Kaspian), he happened to be present at a lecture by Poseidonios, and when leaving asked if he had any suggestions. He replied "always be the best and pre-eminent above all" [*Iliad* 6.208, 11.784]. In addition to this he wrote a history of him, and because of this he should have been more considerate of the truth.

(7) The second portion is that beyond the Hyrkanian Sea – which we call the Kaspian – as far as the Skythians near the Indians. The third portion adjoins the previously mentioned isthmus and is in sequence after it to the Kaspian Gates, within the Tauros and nearest to Europe (Media, Armenia, Kappadokia, and what is in between). The fourth is the land inside the Halys, and that within the Tauros and outside it, which falls within the peninsula that is formed by the isthmus separating the Pontic and Kilikian Seas. In the other areas outside the Tauros we place Indike, Ariane as far as the peoples reaching down to the Persian Sea, the Arabian Gulf, the Nile, and the Egyptian and Issic Seas.

Part 2:   The Territory north and east of the Euxeinos

(1) Having established this, the first portion is inhabited in the portions toward the north and the Ocean by certain Skythian nomads and the

Wagon Dwellers. More within than these are the Sarmatians – they are Skythians – and the Aorsians and Sirakians, who extend toward the south as far as the Kaukasos Mountains. Some of them are nomads, and others live in tents and are farmers. The Maiotians are around the lake. Sindike is on the sea, on the Asian side of the Bosporos, after which are the Achaians, Zygians, Heniochians, Kerketians, and Makropogonians. Lying above them are the narrows of the Phtheirophagians. Kolchis is beyond the Heniochians, lying at the foot of the Kaukasian (or Moschikian) Mountains. Since the Tanais River is established as the boundary of Europe and Asia, we will begin our detailed description there.

(2) It is carried from northern parts, not flowing diametrically opposite to the Nile, as most think, but more from the east, and, similarly, its sources   [C493] are not known. Much of the latter is known, as it goes through territory that is completely accessible and can be sailed inland a long distance. But although we know the outlets of the Tanais – there are two, in the north-ernmost portion of the Maiotis, 60 stadia distant from each other – beyond the outlets little is known because of the cold and the poverty of the territory. The indigenous people can bear this, who, in nomadic fashion, are nourished on flesh and milk, but other peoples cannot endure it. Moreover, the nomads, disinclined to mingle with others, and excelling in numbers and power, have shut off the passable parts of the territory and whatever rivers can be sailed up. For this reason some have assumed that its sources are in the Kaukasian Mountains, and that it is carried greatly to the north and then turns back, emptying into the Maiotis (Theophanes of Mitylene [F3] agrees with them), and others that it is carried from the upper portion of the Istros, although there is no evidence that it flows that far or from another latitude, as if it were impossible to come both from nearby and the north.

(3) On the river and the lake is situated a city with the same name, Tanais, a foundation of the Hellenes who held the Bosporos. Recently King Polemon [I] pillaged it for disobedience. It was an emporium common to both the Asiatic and European nomads and those sailing on the lake from the Bosporos, the former bringing slaves, hides, and other such nomadic things, in return for clothing, wine, and other such products of a civilized life. Lying 100 stadia off the emporium is the island of Alopekia, a settle-ment with mixed population. There are also other islets nearby on the lake. The Tanais is 2,200 stadia distant from the mouth of the Maiotis, by a sail straight to the north. It is not much more going along the coast.

(4) Sailing along the coast, one comes first (800 stadia from Tanais) to the so-called Great Rhombites, in which there are the largest number of fish

suitable for salting. Then, 800 more, is the Lesser Rhombites, a cape, and fisheries. Those who were previously around the former had small islands as their bases, but those who work the small Rhombites are the Maiotians themselves, for the Maiotians live along the entire coast and are farmers, although no less warlike than the nomads. They are divided into a number of peoples, with those near the Tanais somewhat wild, but those adjoining the Bosporos rather subdued. From the Small Rhombites it is 600 stadia to Tyrambe and the Antikeites River, and then 120 to the village of the Kimmerians, which is a starting point for sailing on the lake. On this coast there are certain lookouts that are said to be Klazomenian.

(5) Kimmerikon was a city that was formerly situated on a peninsula, closing the isthmus with a ditch and an embankment. The Kimmerians once possessed great power in the Bosporos, which is why it was named the Kimmerian Bosporos. These are the ones who overran the interior along the right portion of the Pontos as far as Ionia. They were driven out of the region by the Skythians, and then the Skythians by the Hellenes who founded Pantikapaion and other cities in the Bosporos.

(6) Then it is 20 [stadia] to the village of Achilleion, where the sanctuary of Achilleus is. Here is the narrowest crossing across the mouth of the Maiotis – about 20 stadia or a little more – and on the opposite shore is the village of Myrmekion. Nearby are Herakleion and Parthenion.

(7) Then it is 90 stadia to the memorial of Satyros. This is an earthen mound on a cape, for a man who was one of the most prominent of those holding power in the Bosporos.

(8) There is a nearby village, Patrasys, from which it is 130 [stadia] to the village of Korokondame. This is the limit of what is called the Kimmerian Bosporos. The narrows at the mouth of the Maiotis are called that because of the narrows at Achilleion and Myrmekion, extending as far as Korokondame and a small village named Akra that lies opposite it in the land of the Pantikapaians, separated from it by a strait of 70 stadia. Crystallizing also extends this far, for the Maiotis is frozen at the time of the frosts and can be crossed on foot. These narrows have good harbors everywhere.

(9) Lying above Korokondame is a good-sized lake, which is called Korokondamitis from it. It empties in the sea 10 stadia from the village. A branch of the Antikeites River empties into the lake and makes a kind of island that is washed all around by this lake, the Maiotis, and the river. Some call this river the Hypanis, just like the one near Borysthenes.

(10) As one sails into the Korokondamitis, there is Phanagoreia, a notable city, and Kepoi, Hermonassa, and Apatouron (a sanctuary of Aphrodite). Of these, Phanagoreia and Kepoi are situated on the previously mentioned

[C494]

[C495]

island, on the left as one sails in, and the remainder are on the right, across the Hypanis in the Sindike. Gorgippia is also in the Sindike, the royal residence of the Sindians, near the sea, and also Aborake. All those who are subject to Bosporian power are called Bosporanians, and Pantikapaion is the metropolis of the European Bosporanians, and that of the Asians is Phanagoras (the city is also called in that way). Phanagoreia seems to be the emporium for what comes down from the Maiotis and the barbarian territory lying above it, and Pantikapaion for what is carried up from the sea. In Phanagoreia there is also a distinguished sanctuary of Aphrodite Apatouros. The etymology of the epithet of the goddess is suggested by a certain myth in which the Gigantes attacked the goddess there. She called upon Herakles and hid him in a certain hole, and then she admitted the Gigantes one by one and gave them over to Herakles to be treacherously killed by deceit [*apate*].

(11) The Sindians themselves are among the Maiotians, as well as the Dandarians, Toretians, Agrianians, and Arrhechians, and also the Tarpetians, Obidiakenians, Sittakenians, Doskians, and a number of others. There are also the Aspourgianians, who live between Phanagoreia and Gorgippia (within 500 stadia[1]). King Polemon [I] attacked them, pretending friendship, but this did not escape notice and they made war against him, and taking him alive, killed him. The Asian Maiotians in general were subjects of those who possessed the emporium on the Tanais, or of the Bosporanians. In that period different peoples revolted at different times. Often the Bosporanian rulers held possession as far as the Tanais, especially the latest ones, Pharnakes [II], Asandros, and Polemon [I]. Pharnakes is said to have once brought the Hypanis through the Dandarian territory in an old canal that he cleaned out, inundating the territory.

(12) After the Sindike and Gorgippia there is, on the sea, the coast of the Achaians, Zygians, and Heniochians, which is mostly without harbors and mountainous, being a part of the Kaukasos. They live by robbery at sea, and have boats that are light, narrow, and quick, holding about twenty-five people, although occasionally they can hold thirty in all. The Hellenes call them *kamarai* ["vaults"]. They say that the Phthiotian Achaians on Jason's expedition settled in this Achaia, and the Lakonians in Heniochia, whose leaders were Rhekas and Amphistratos, the charioteers [*heniochoi*] of the Dioskouroi, and thus the Heniochians were probably named after them. They would equip fleets of *kamarai* and at times sail against merchant vessels, and at times against certain territories or cities, and thus they would

[C496]

---

[1] The number is probably wrong as the two cities are much closer together than 500 stadia.

be masters of the sea. At times those holding the Bosporos gave assistance, supplying anchorages, agoras, and disposing of their booty. When they returned to their own territory, as they had no place to anchor, they would put the *kamarai* on their shoulders and carry them into the forests where they live and work on poor land. They carry them down again when it is time to sail. They do the same elsewhere, for they know wooded places in which they can hide the *kamarai*, and then they wander night and day on foot for the sake of kidnapping. Those whom they have taken they easily set free for ransom, informing those left behind when they have sailed away. In the places under local domination there will be assistance by the rulers against those who have been wronged, as they often make a counter-attack and sink the *kamarai* and their men. But that which is under the Romans offers less of a remedy because of the negligence of those sent there.

(13) Such is their life. They are ruled by leaders called "staff bearers," who are subject to tyrants or kings. At any rate, the Heniochians had four kings when Mithridates [VI] Eupator, fleeing from his ancestral territory to the Bosporos, went through this country. He found it passable – as he had despaired of going through that of the Zygians because of the rough ground and their savageness – but it was difficult along the coast. Yet going mostly along the sea, he came to the Achaians. Received by them, he completed his journey from Phasis, which was not much less that 4,000 stadia.

(14) The voyage from Korokondame is straight toward the east, and the Sindian harbor and city is in 180 stadia. Then, in 400 [stadia] is what is called Bata, a village and harbor. It is believed that Sinope lies almost opposite the coast toward the south, just as Karambis is said [to be opposite] the Ram's Forehead. After Bata, Artemidoros [F138] speaks about the coast of the Kerketians, which has anchorages and villages for about 850 stadia. Then there is that of the Achaians, for 500 stadia, then that of the Heniochians, for 1,000 stadia, and the Great Pityous ... 360 [stadia] as

[C497] far as Dioskourias. The historians of Mithridatic affairs – those with whom one must agree the most – first mention the Achaians, then the Zygians, then the Heniochians, then the Kerketians, Moschians, Kolchians, the Phtheirophagians who are above them, the Soanians, and other lesser peoples around the Kaukasos. At first the coast, as I have said, extends toward the east and faces the south, but from Bata it gradually takes a turn so that it faces the west and ends at Pityous and Dioskourias, for these places adjoin the previously mentioned coast of Kolchis. After Dioskourias there is the remainder of the Kolchian coast and the contiguous Trapezian, which makes a notable bend, and then, extending in an approximately straight line, creates the right side of the Pontos, which faces north. The entire coast of the Achaians and the others, as far as Dioskourias, and the places straight toward the south in the interior, fall at the foot of the Kaukasos.

(15) This mountain lies above both seas – the Pontic and the Kaspian – and makes a wall that extends across the isthmus that separates them. Toward the south it marks the boundary between Albania and Iberia, and toward the north, of the plains of the Sarmatians. It is well wooded with all kinds of timber, especially that used for shipbuilding. Eratosthenes [F113] says that the Kaukasos is called the Kaspios by those living there, perhaps derived from the Kaspians. There are certain arms projecting toward the south, which include the middle of Iberia and join the Armenian mountains with those called the Moschikian, and also the Skydisian and Paryadrian. These are all parts of the Tauros, which makes the southern side of Armenia, broken off in some way from it on the north and projecting as far as the Kaukasos and the coast of the Euxeinos that extends to Themiskyra from Kolchis.

(16) As Dioskourias lies in such a gulf at the easternmost point of the entire sea, it is is called the recess of the Euxeinos and is the farthest voyage. The author of the proverbial statement "to Phasis, which is the farthest journey for ships" cannot be accepted as meaning the river in his iambic verse, or even the city of the same name as the river, but the [whole of] Kolchis (from the part), since there remains from the river and city a straight sail into the recess of no less than 600 stadia. This same Dioskourias is the [C498] beginning of the isthmus between the Kaspian and the Pontos, as well as the common emporium for the peoples situated above and near it. At any rate seventy peoples come together there – some say three hundred, but they have no care for the facts – all of whom have different languages because they are scattered and live without mingling due to their stubbornness and fierceness. Most of them are Sarmatians, but they are all Kaukasians. This is it about the region of Dioskourias.

(17) Most of the rest of Kolchis is on the sea. The Phasis flows through it, a large river that originates in Armenia, receiving the Glaukos and the Hippos, which come down from the neighboring mountains. One can sail up it as far as Sarapana, a fortress that is capable of admitting the inhabitants of a city, and from where one can go to the Kyros in four days by wagon. On the Phasis is situated the city of the same name, an emporium of the Kolchians, defended by the river, a lake, and the sea. From there it is a sail of three or two days to Amisos and Sinope . . . because the coasts are soft and the outlets of the rivers. The country is excellent in terms of its produce – except for its honey, which is generally bitter – and in terms of everything regarding shipbuilding, for it yields a large amount of wood

that is brought down on the rivers. It produces much linen, hemp, wax, and pitch. The linen industry is often talked about, for it was exported to foreign places, and some rely on this who wish to show a kinship between the Kolchians and Egyptians. Above the previously mentioned rivers in the Moschic territory is the sanctuary of Leukothea, a foundation of Phrixos, and his oracle, where no ram is sacrificed. It was originally wealthy, but was stripped in our time by Pharnakes [II], and a little later by Mithridates of Pergamon. When a country has been badly affected, "divine matters are diseased and should not be honored," as Euripides says [*Trojan Women* 27].

(18) This territory had such distinction in antiquity, as the myths reveal obscurely that the expedition of Jason proceeded as far as Media, and, even previously, there was that of Phrixos. After this, kings succeeded to power, since the territory was divided into staff-bearing commands, which did moderately well. When Mithridates [VI] Eupator became more powerful, [C499] the territory devolved upon him, and he would always send one of his friends as subcommander or administrator of the territory. One of these was Moaphernes, the uncle of my mother on her father's side. It was here that most of the services for naval power were provided to the king. When Mithridates [VI] came to an end, everything subject to him was also broken up and distributed to many people. Finally Polemon [I] possessed Kolchis, and since his death his wife Pythodoris has ruled, queen of the Kolchians, Trapezous, and Pharnakeia, and the barbarians living above them, about whom I will speak later [12.3.38–9].

The Moschike, where the sanctuary is, is divided into three parts: one is held by the Kolchians, one by the Iberians, and one by the Armenians. There is also a small city in Iberia, the city of Phrixos, now Ideessa, a well-fortified territory on the boundary of Kolchis. The Chares River is around Dioskourias.

(19) Among the peoples who come together at Dioskourias are the Phtheirophagians ["Lice Eaters"], who have taken their name because of their squalor and filth. Near to them are the Soanians, who are no better in terms of filth, although better in power, in fact nearly the strongest in strength and power. At any rate, they are the masters of most around them and possess the heights of the Kaukasos above Dioskourias. They have a king and a council of 300 men, and they bring together, as they say, an army of 200,000, for all the people are warlike, although not organized. It is said that in their region gold is carried down by the torrents, which the barbarians obtain by using perforated troughs and skins lined with wool, from which comes the myth of the skin lined with gold . . . unless they are called Iberians, the same name as those in the west, because both have gold

mines. The Soanians use remarkable poisons for their arrow points, and those not injured by the poisoned missiles suffer pain from the odor.

The peoples in the vicinity of the Kaukasos have poor and scanty land, but the Albanian and Iberian peoples, who fill much of the previously mentioned isthmus, could also be said to be Kaukasian, and they have prosperous land and are able to live exceedingly well.

Part 3:   Kaukasian Iberia

(1) Moreover, most of Iberia is so well settled in regard to cities and farmsteads that their roofs are tiled, and their homes, agoras, and other public buildings are constructed with architectural skill.

(2) Parts of the country are surrounded by the circuit of the Kaukasian Mountains, for, as I have said, arms project to the south. They are fruitful, [C500] encompass the entirety of Iberia, and border on Armenia and Kolchis. In the middle there is a plain intersected by rivers, the largest of which is the Kyros. Beginning from Armenia, it flows immediately into the previously mentioned plain, receiving the Aragos – which flows from the Kaukasos – and other streams, and empties through a riverine narrows into Albania. Between here and Armenia it is carried intensively through plains that are exceedingly abundant in pastures, and receives more rivers, including the Alazonios, Sandobanes, Rhoitakes, and Chanes, all of which are navigable. It empties into the Kaspian Sea and was formerly called the Koros.

(3) The plain of the Iberians is inhabited by ones somewhat inclined to farming and to peace, who equip themselves both in the Armenian and Median styles. Most – those who are warlike – occupy the mountainous region, living in the manner of Skythians and Sarmatians, of whom they are neighbors and kinsmen, but they also engage in farming. They bring together many myriads, from both their own and others, when anything alarming occurs.

(4) There are four entrances into the territory. One is through Sarapana, a Kolchian fortress, and then through the narrows there, through which the Phasis flows, roughly and violently, down to Kolchis. The route has been made passable by 120 bridges (because of the windings), as the place is full of many ravines due to the abundance of rain. It originates in the mountains lying above it, and is filled by springs. In the plains it also receives other rivers, among which are the Glaukos and the Hippos. Filled, and having become navigable, it goes out into the Pontos and has on it a city of the same name with a lake near it. Such, then, is the route from Kolchis into Iberia, closed in by rocks, natural defenses, and rivers running through ravines.

(5) From the nomads on the north it is a difficult ascent of three days, after which there is a riverine narrows on the Aragos River with a single-file road for four days. The end of the road is guarded by a fortification that is difficult to capture. The route of access from Albania is first hewn out of rock, and then is through a marsh made by a river coming down from the Kaukasos. From Armenia, there are the narrows on the Kyros and those on the Aragos. Before they meet each other, fortified cities on the rocks are situated along them, about 16 stadia distant from each other. On the Kyros there is Harmozike and on the other Seusamora. These routes of access were first used by Pompeius when he set forth from the Armenians, and afterward by Canidius.

[C501]

(6) There are four classes of people living in the territory. One, and the first, is that from which they appoint their kings (one who is nearest in kinship and the oldest, and a second who administers justice and leads the army). The second [class] is the priests, who tend to matters of justice with the neighbors. The third is the soldiers and farmers, and the fourth the people, who are royal slaves and perform all the services regarding life. Their possessions are held in common according to kinship. The oldest rules and manages them. Such are the Iberians and their territory.

Part 4: Albania

(1) The Albanians are more shepherd-like and closer to nomadic people, except that they are not savage, and because of this they are only moderately warlike. They live between the Iberians and the Kaspian Sea, touching the sea on the east and bordering the Iberians on the west. Of their remaining sides, the north is protected by the Kaukasian mountains, which lie above the plains, with those next to the sea called the Keraunia. The southern is formed by Armenia, which lies alongside it, much of which is plains and much of it mountains, like the Kambisene, where the Armenians adjoin the Iberians and the Albanians.

(2) The Kyros, which flows through Albania, and the other rivers that fill it, add to the excellence of the land, and deprive the sea. The silt falls down and fills the channel, so that the offshore islets are joined to the mainland and create shallows that are irregular and difficult to avoid. This irregularity is augmented by the recoil of the flood tides. Moreover, they say that the outlet is divided into twelve mouths, some of which are blind and others completely flat, not even leaving an anchorage. At any rate, although the coast is washed on all sides for more than 60 stadia by the sea and the rivers, every part of it is unapproachable, and the silt stretches as much as

500 stadia, making the coast sandy. The Araxes empties nearby, which is rough and comes out of Armenia. Its silt is pushed forward, making the stream navigable, but this is made up by the Kyros.

(3) Perhaps such a type of people do not need the sea. They do not use their land according to its value, which bears all fruit – even the most   [C502] cultivated – and every plant, even producing evergreens. Not even slight attention happens to be paid to it, "but everything is produced without tilling and plowing" [*Odyssey* 9.109], and those who have made expeditions there say that they possess a sort of Kyklopeian life. At any rate, the land, when sown only once, produces two or three crops, the first with a yield of fifty-fold, unplowed and never cut with iron but with a wooden plow. The entire plain is better irrigated with its rivers and other water than the Babylonian or Egyptian ones, and thus always retains a grassy appearance, because of which it is good pasture. In addition, the air is fresher there. The vines are not dug around but remain complete, yet are cut in the fifth year, and the new ones produce fruit in the second year, and when grown they yield so much that a large part is left on the branches. Their cattle flourish, both domesticated and wild.

(4) The people are especially attractive and large. They are straight-forward and not mercenary, for in general they do not use coinage and do not know any number larger than a hundred, but they make exchanges of goods. In everything they have a carefree life. They are unacquainted with accurate measures and weights, and have no advance consideration for war, government, or farming. Yet they fight on foot and horseback, both in light armor and in full armor, just like the Armenians, and they send forth a larger army than the Iberians.

(5) They have 60,000 infantry and 22,000 cavalry, as much as when they risked everything against Pompeius. The nomads join with them in war against outsiders, just as they do with the Iberians, for the same reasons. They also often attack the people, so that the latter are prevented from farming. They have javelin-throwers and archers, and breastplates and oblong shields, with caps of wild beasts, similar to those of the Iberians.

Kaspiane is [part] of the Albanian territory, named after the Kaspian peoples, as was the sea, but they have disappeared today. The access from Iberia into Albania is through Kambisene, which is waterless and rough, to the Alazonios River. They and their dogs are hunters to excess, not so much because of their skill but their eagerness for it.   [C503]

(6) The kings are . . . today one rules everything, but formerly . . . each was ruled separately, according to their language. They have twenty-six languages, because of which they are not accessible to one another.

The land produces certain deadly reptiles, scorpions, and *phalangia*. Some of the *phalangia* cause death while [the victims] are laughing, or wailing while yearning for their family.

(7) They honor the gods Helios, Zeus, and Selene, especially Selene. Her sanctuary is near Iberia. The man who is most honored after the king is the priest, who is in charge of the sacred land – which is extensive and well populated – and of the temple slaves, many of whom are divinely inspired and give prophecies. Anyone who is possessed in such a way for a long time and wanders alone in the forest is seized by the priest, who binds him with sacred chains and maintains him luxuriously for a year. Then he is led to the sacrifice for the goddess, anointed, and sacrificed with the other victims. The manner of the sacrifice is this: someone who is not inexperienced in this and is holding a sacred spear – with which it is the custom to make the human sacrifice – comes forward from the crowd and strikes him through the side into the heart. When he falls, they observe certain prophetic signs from the fall and make them known to the people. When the body is carried away to a certain place they all walk on it, using it as a purification.

(8) The Albanians honor old age exceedingly greatly, including others as well as their parents. It is not religiously proper to think about or to remember those who have died. In fact, they bury their possessions with them, and because of this live in poverty, having no inheritances. This is it about the Albanians.

It is said that Jason, along with Armenos of Thessaly, on his voyage to the Kolchians, pushed on as far as the Kaspian Sea, coming to Iberia and Albania, and much of Armenia and Media, as witnessed by the Iasoneia and many other memorials. Armenos was from Armenion, one of the cities around Lake Boibeis between Pherai and Larisa, and he and those with him lived in Akilisene and Syspiritis, as far as Kalachane and Adiabene, leaving behind the name of Armenia after himself.

Part 5:   The Amazons and the Kaukasos

(1) In the mountains above Albania the Amazons are said to live. Theophanes [F4], who made the expedition with Pompeius and was among the Albanians, says that between the Amazons and the Albanians live the Gelians and Legians, who are Skythian, and that the Mermadalis River flows between them and the Amazons. Others, among whom are Metrodoros the Skepsian [F7] and Hypsikrates [F3], who were also not unacquainted with the place, say that they [the Amazons] live on the boundary of the Gargarians, the northern foothills of the Kaukasian mountains, which are called Keraunia.

[C504]

They spend much of the time by themselves, working at their own tasks: plowing, planting, and pasturing, especially tending to horses. The bravest are involved mostly in hunting and practicing warlike matters. The right breasts of all are burned off in infancy, so that they can easily use the arm for every purpose, especially throwing the javelin. They use the bow, *sagaris*, and light shield, and make caps, clothing, and girdles from the hides of wild animals. Two months are chosen in the spring when they go up into the neighboring mountain that separates them from the Gargarians. The latter also go up there, according to an ancient custom, to sacrifice and to come together with the women in order to produce children, unseen and in darkness, anyone with anyone, and after they make them pregnant they are sent away. They [the Amazons] keep the females who are born, but the males are brought to them [the Gargarians] to be raised. Each who is brought one considers him to be his own son, because of not knowing.

(2) The Mermadalis rushes down from the mountains through the territory of the Amazons and Sirakene and the deserted country in between, emptying into the Maiotis. They say that the Gargarians went up into this region from Themiskyra with the Amazons, and then revolted, and along with some Thracians and Euboians who had wandered this far, made war against them. Later they broke off the war and made the agreement as mentioned, that they would join together only for offspring, but live separately from each other.

(3) Something unusual has happened to the account of the Amazons. In regard to others, a distinction is drawn between the mythic and historical, for what is ancient, false, and marvellous is called myth, yet history wishes for the truth – whether ancient or recent – and has nothing marvellous, or only rarely. But concerning the Amazons, the same things are said today and in antiquity, although marvellous beyond belief. Who could believe that an army of women, or a city, or a people, could ever be organized without men, and not only be organized, but make attacks upon others, and not only conquer those near them (so that they would go as far as what is now Ionia) [C505] but even send an expedition across the sea as far as Attika? This is like saying that the men were women then, and the women were men. But even today these things are said about them. This intensifies the peculiarity and the belief in antiquity rather than in today.

(4) At any rate, they are said to have founded cities and named them – Ephesos, Smyrna, Kyme, and Myrina – and there are also tombs and memorials. Everyone calls Themiskyra, the plains around Thermodon, and the mountains above them "Amazonian," but they say that they were driven out of there. As to where they are now, only a few declare it – without

proof and unbelievably – such as in the matter of Thalestria, who was the leader of the Amazons and with whom, they say, Alexander associated in Hyrkania, and had intercourse with her for the sake of offspring, but this is not agreed to. The historical writers who are most careful about the truth do not say this, those who are most trustworthy do not record it, and those who do speak about it do not say the same thing. Kleitarchos [F16] says that Thalestria set forth from the Kaspian Gates and Thermodon, and came to Alexander, but from the Kaspian to Thermodon is more than 6,000 stadia.

(5) All the talk about his reputation that is accepted by everyone was fabricated by those who considered flattery rather than the truth. They transferred the Kaukasos from the mountains that lie above Kolchis and the Euxeinos to the Indian mountains and the eastern sea that is near them. These are the mountains that the Hellenes named the Kaukasos, more than 30,000 stadia distant from Indike. Here they told the story about Prometheus and the binding of him, for these were the farthest toward the east that they knew about at that time. The expeditions of Dionysos and Herakles to the Indians appear to be a myth created at a later date, because Herakles is said to have released Prometheus a thousand years later. It gave greater esteem to Alexander to have subdued Asia as far as the Indian mountains rather than only as far as the recess of the Euxeinos and the Kaukasos, but the reputation of the mountain and its name, the belief that Jason and those with him had accomplished the longest of expeditions – as far as the vicinity of the Kaukasos – and the tradition that Prometheus [C506] was bound at the farthest point of the earth in the Kaukasos, led to the assumption that it would be a favor to the king to transfer the name of the mountains to Indike.

(6) The highest parts of the Kaukasos are the most southern, those next to Albania, Iberia, the Kolchians, and the Heniochians. Those living there, as I have said [11.2.16], assemble at Dioskourias, assembling there mostly for the sake of salt. Some of these occupy the mountain ridges, and others live in the ravines and subsist mostly on the flesh of wild animals, wild fruits, and milk. The summits are impassable in winter, but in summer they ascend them by wearing broad pieces of oxhide, like drums, with spikes for the snow and ice. They, with their goods, come down seated on skins and slide down, as happens in Atropatian Media and on Mount Masion in Armenia, where they place small wooden discs with spikes under the soles of their shoes. These, then, are the heights of the Kaukasos.

(7) As one comes down to the foothills, it slopes more toward the north, but it becomes milder and adjoins the plains of the Sirakians. There are some Troglodytes ["Cave Dwellers"] here, who live in holes because of the

cold, and among them there is a lack of barley. After the Troglodytes there are the Chamaikoitians ["Those Who Sleep on the Ground"] and Polyphagians ["Those Who Eat Much"], as they are called, and the villages of the Eisadikians, who are able to farm because they are not completely exposed to the north.

(8) Those next between the Maiotis and the Kaspian are nomadic: the Nabianians, Panzanians, and then the Sirakian and Aorsian peoples. The Aorsians and Sirakians are believed to be fugitives from those farther up, and the Aorsians are farther north. Abeakos, king of the Sirakians at the time that Pharnakes [II] held the Bosporos, sent 20,000 horsemen, and Spadines of the Aorsians 20[0,000], but the Upper Aorsians sent more, for they were masters of more land and essentially ruled most of the Kaspian coast, and thus they imported by camel Indian and Babylonian goods, receiving them from the Armenians and Medes. Because of their prosperity they wore gold ornaments. The Aorsians live along the Tanais, and the Sirakians along the Achardaios, which flows from the Kaukasos and empties into the Maiotis.

Part 6:   The Kaspian Sea

(1) The second portion begins from the Kaspian Sea, where the first comes to an end. The same sea is also called the Hyrkanian. It is necessary to speak first about the sea and the people living around it. It is the gulf that extends from the Ocean to the south, somewhat narrow at its entrance but becoming wider as it goes inland, especially around its recess, where it is about 5,000 stadia. Sailing from the entrance to the recess would be slightly more, since it nearly touches the uninhabited region. Eratosthenes [F110] says that the circuit of this sea was well known to the Hellenes, that the portion along the Albanians and Kadousians is 5,400 stadia, the portion along the Anariakians, Mardians, and Hyrkanians to the mouth of the Oxos River is 4,800, and from there to the Iaxartes, 2,400. It is necessary to pay attention more generally to matters about this portion and the remote regions, especially concerning distances.

[C507]

(2) Sailing in, on the right are the Skythians and Samartians who live adjoining Europe between the Tanais and the sea, mostly nomads, about whom I have spoken [11.2.1]. On the left are the Skythians toward the east, also nomads, who extend as far as the eastern sea and Indike.

The ancient historians of the Hellenes called all those toward the north generally Skythians or Keltoskythians. Those still earlier distinguished between those living above the Euxeinos, the Istros, and the Adria – whom they called Hyperboreans, Sauromatians, and Arimaspasians – and those across the Kaspian Sea, some of whom were called Sakians and others Massagetians. They could not speak accurately about them, although they recorded a war by Kyros against the Massagetians. But they have not been accurate or truthful about them, nor have they been believable about the antiquity of the Persians, Medes, or Syrians because of the simpleness and fondness for myths of the historians.

(3) Seeing that those who were clearly writers of myths were esteemed, they thought that they could produce writings which were pleasing if they were to speak in the fashion of history about what they had never seen or heard – or not from anyone knowledgeable – and only to examine what those listening would find pleasurable and marvellous. It would be easier to [C508] believe Hesiod or Homer in their accounts of the heroes, or the tragic poets, than Ktesias, Herodotos, Hellanikos, and such others.

(4) It is also not easy to believe most of those who have written the history of Alexander, for they are reckless because of the reputation of Alexander and because his expedition reached the extremity of Asia, far from us. Material about things far away is difficult to refute. The domination of the Romans and that of the Parthyaians has disclosed more than previously had been handed down. Those writing the history of lands and peoples where things have happened are more trustworthy than those formerly, for they have looked into them more.

Part 7:   Hyrkania

(1) The nomads living on the left as one sails into the Kaspian Sea are today called the Daans, who are also named the Parnians. Then, deserted territory lies in front and between them and Hyrkania (which is next), from where it forms an open sea as far as where it touches the Median and the Armenian mountains. Their shape is crescent-like along their foot-hills, which end at the sea and make the recess of the gulf. Living on this side of them, beginning at the sea and as far as their heights for a short distance, are part of the Albanians and Armenians, but mostly the Gelians, Kadousians, Amardians, Ouitians, and Anariakians. They say that some of the Parrhasians lived with the Anariakians, who today are called Parsians, and that the Ainianians had a walled city among the Ouitians, which is today called Ainiana. Hellenic implements, bronze vessels, and graves are visible there. They say that there is a city of Anariake there, in which a sleeping-oracle is visible, and some other ... people more inclined to brigandage and warfare than farming. The ruggedness of the place causes this. Most of the coast around the mountains, however, is occupied by the

Kadousians, for almost 5,000 stadia, as Patrokles [F7] says, who believes this sea to be equal to the Pontos.

(2) These regions are poor. But Hyrkania is exceedingly prosperous and extensive, mostly a plain, and includes distinguished cities, among which are Talabroke, Samariane, Karta, and the royal residence of Tape, which they say is situated slightly above the sea and 1,400 stadia distant from the Kaspian Gates. Because of the nature of its prosperity its signs ... the vine produces a *metretes* of wine, the fig 60 *medimnoi*, grain is produced from the seeds that have fallen from the stalks, bees swarm in the trees, and honey [C509] flows from the leaves. This also occurs in Matiane in Media, and in Sakasene and Araxene in Armenia. Yet neither it [Hyrkania] nor the sea named after it have been given proper attention, as the latter is without ships and idle. There are islands that could be settled and which – some say – have gold ore. The reason is that the first governors of the Hyrkanians, who were Medes and Persians, as well as the last, who were Parthyaians and inferior, were barbarians, and also all of the neighboring territory was full of brigands and nomads, and was desolate. The Makedonians ruled it for a short period, but they were involved in wars and were unable to pay more attention to it. Aristoboulos [F19] says that Hyrkania is wooded and has the oak, but does not produce the *peuke*, fir, or *pitys*, although Indike has many of them. Nesaia is in Hyrkania, although some put Nesaia down as by itself.

(3) The rivers flowing through Hyrkania are the Oxos and Ochos, which empty into the sea. Of these, the Ochos also flows through Nesaia, but some say that the Ochos empties into the Oxos. Aristoboulos [F20] says that the Oxos is the largest that he had seen in Asia, except those among the Indians. He also says that it is navigable (he and Eratosthenes [F109] took this from Patrokles [F5]), and that many Indian goods come down it to the Hyrkanian Sea, and from there are carried over to Albania by means of the Kyros River, brought down through the successive places to the Euxeinos. The Ochos is not named at all by the ancients. Apollodoros [of Artemita, F4], however, who wrote the *Parthika*, names it continually, and that it flows very close to the Parthyaians.

(4) Many false things were further imagined about this sea because of the ambition of Alexander. Since it was agreed by all that the Tanais River separated Asia from Europe, and that which was between the sea and the Tanais (a greater part of Asia), had not fallen to the Makedonians, it was reported in such a way as to show that Alexander had conquered that region. They combined the Maiotic Lake (which receives the Tanais) and the Kaspian Sea, calling it a lake, and insisting that there was a passage from one to the other so that each was a part of the other. Polykleitos [F7] offers

[C510] proofs that the sea is a lake (it produces serpents and the water is sweetish) and he judges that it is nothing other than the Maiotis because the Tanais empties into it. The Ochos and Oxos and many others come from the same Indian mountains that the Iaxartes flows, which is the most northerly of all and like the rest empties into the Kaspian Sea. This they named the Tanais, and as an additional proof that it was the Tanais of which Polykleitos spoke, they note that across the river the fir tree exists and that the Skythians there use fir arrows. This is their proof that the territory across the river is part of Europe and not Asia, for upper and eastern Asia do not produce the fir tree. But Eratosthenes [F24] says that the fir tree also grows in Indike and that Alexander built his ships there out of fir. Eratosthenes attempts to reconcile many other such issues, but let what I have said about them be enough.

(5) Among the marvels of Hyrkania, recorded by Eudoxos [F344a] and others, is that there are some promontories projecting into the sea that have caves beneath them, and between them and the sea lies a low beach. Rivers flowing from the cliffs above are carried forward with such force that when they reach the promontories they hurl the water forth into the sea, keeping the beach unsprinkled so that armies can pass by sheltered from the stream. The locals often come down to the place for feasting and sacrifice. Sometimes they recline below in the caves, and sometimes they bask in the sun under the stream itself, different people enjoying themselves in different ways, with the sea and the shore visible on either side. The latter is grassy and flowery because of its moisture.

Part 8:   East of the Hyrkanian Sea

(1) Proceeding east from the Hyrkanian Sea, on the right are the mountains that the Hellenes call the Tauros, stretching as far as the Indian Sea. Beginning from Pamphylia and Kilikia they proceed this far continuously from the west, and have one name or another. Near the northern portion first live the Gelians, Kadousians, and Amardians, as has been said [11.7.1], and some of the Hyrkanians, and then the Parthyaian peoples, the Margianians, and the Arians. Then there is deserted territory that is separated by the Sarnios

[C511] River from Hyrkania, as one goes east and toward the Ochos. What extends from Armenia to here, or a little less, is called Parachoathras. It is about 6,000 stadia from the Hyrkanian Sea to the Arians. Then there are Baktriane and Sogdiane, and finally Skythian nomads. The Makedonians called "the Kaukasos" all the mountain that followed after the Arians, but according to the barbarians, the promontories on the north of the Paropamisos were Emoda and Imaon, with such other names applied to the separate parts.

(2) On the left and lying opposite to these are the Skythian and nomadic peoples, who fill up the northern side. Most of the Skythians, beginning at the Kaspian Sea, are called the Daans, but those more to the east are the Massagetians and the Sakians. The others are called by the general name of Skythians, although each has its own. For the most part they are all nomads. The best known of the nomads are those who took Baktriane away from the Hellenes – the Asians, Pasianians, Tocharians, and Sakaraukians – who came from the opposite side of the Iaxartes, which was opposite the Sakians and Sogdianians and was possessed by the Sakians. Regarding the Daans, some are called Parnians, other Exarthrians, and others Pissourians. The Parnians are situated the closest to Hyrkania and the sea along it, but the rest extend as far as the territory stretching parallel to Aria.

(3) Between them, Hyrkania, and Parthyaia, as far as the Arians, lies a great waterless desert, which they crossed by long journeys and then overran Hyrkania, Nesaia, and the Parthyaian plains. They collected tribute, and the tribute allowed them to overrun the territory at certain appointed times and to carry off booty. But when they exceeded the agreement there was war, and it came to an end and then war began again. Such is the life of the other nomads, who are always attacking those nearby and then reconciling again.

(4) The Sakians, however, made attacks similar to those of the Kimmerians and Trersians, some farther away and others nearer. They possessed Baktriane, and acquired the best land in Armenia, and left it named after themselves, Sakasene. They advanced as far as the Kappadokians, especially those near the Euxeinos, who are now called the Pontikians.   [C512] When they were having a festival because of their booty, they were obliterated at night by Persian commanders, who were there at that time and piled up earth over a certain rock in the plain, completing it in the form of a hill and placing a wall on it. They established a sanctuary of Anaitis and the gods sharing her altar, Omanos and Anadates, Persian divinities, instituting an annual sacred festival, the Sakaia, which is still celebrated today by those in Zela (this is what the place is called). It is a small city mostly of temple slaves. Pompeius added a notable amount of territory to it and settled its inhabitants within the walls, since it was one of the cities that he organized after he put down Mithridates [VI].

(5) This is what some say about the Sakians. Others [say] that Kyros made an expedition against the Sakians but was defeated in a battle and fled. He encamped at the place where he had left his supplies – a great abundance of everything, especially wine – rested his army for a short time, and went away in the evening as though in flight, leaving the tents full and going as far as

seemed expedient. They [the Sakians] came and found the camp deserted of men but full of enjoyable things, and they filled themselves with abandon. He [Kyros] turned back and found them drunk and in a stupor, and some were cut down while in a heavy sleep and others fell to the weapons of the enemy while dancing and reveling naked. All except a few died. He considered this good fortune as something divine, and consecrated the day to his ancestral goddess and called it the Sakaia. Wherever there is a sanctuary of this goddess, the feast of the Sakaia is the custom, a kind of Bakcheia, where they dress in the Skythian style and drink and cavort day and night with each other and with the women who are drinking with them.

(6) The Massagetians revealed their excellence in the war against Kyros. Many talk about it repeatedly, from whom it is necessary to learn about it. The following is said about the Massagetians: that some of them live in the mountains, others in the plains, others in the marshes formed by the rivers, and others on islands in the marshes. They say that the territory is inundated the most by the Araxes River, which has numerous branches and [C513] empties by other mouths into the other sea on the north, although by one into the Hyrkanian Gulf. They consider Helios their only god and sacrifice horses to him. Each marries one woman, but they use those of each other, not secretly, for the man having intercourse with another's woman hangs his quiver on the wagon and has intercourse openly. Among them it is considered the best death to be cut up with the meat of sheep and eaten mixed up with it, when they are old. Those who die through disease are thrown out as profane and worthy of being eaten only by wild animals. They are good horsemen and foot soldiers, and use bows, daggers, breastplates, and bronze *sagareis*. In battle they use belts and diadems of gold, and their horses have bridles studded with gold and golden girths. Silver is not found among them, but there is a little iron and plentiful copper and gold.

(7) Those in the islands have nothing to sow and use roots and wild fruit. They clothe themselves with the bark of trees (for they have no cattle) and drink what they squeeze from the fruit of trees. Those in the marshes are fish eaters and clothe themselves in the skins of the seals that run up from the sea. Those in the mountains also live on wild fruits, but they also have a few sheep, and thus do not butcher them but spare them for their wool and milk. They variegate their clothing by painting it with colors whose richness does not easily fade. Those in the plains, although they have land, do not farm it, but live on sheep and fish, in the manner of Skythian nomads. There is a certain method of life common to all such people, about which I often speak, and their burials, customs, and entire lives are similar. They

are mischievous, wild, and warlike, but in business they are straightforward and without deceit.

(8) Among the Massegetian and Sakian peoples are the Attasians and Chorasmians, to whom Spitamenes fled from the Baktrianians and Sogdianians. He was one of the Persians who ran from Alexander, as did Bessos. Later Arsakes [I], when he fled from Seleukos [II] Kallinikos, went on to the Apassiakians.

Eratosthenes [F108] says that the Arachotians and Massagetians are alongside the Baktrians to the west along the Oxos, and that the Sakians and Sogdianians and all their lands lie opposite to Indike, although the Baktrians only for a small distance, as they are mostly along the Paropamisos. The Sakians and Sogdianians are separated by the Iaxartes, and the Sogdianians and Baktrianians by the Oxos, and the Tapyrians live between the Hyrkanians and the Arians. In a circuit around the sea, after the Hyrkanians are the Amardians, Anariakians, Kadousians, Albanians, Kaspians, and Ouitians, and perhaps others, until the Skythians are reached. On the other side of the Hyrkanians are the Derbikians, and the Kadousians touch the Medes and the Matianians below Parachoathras.

[C514]

(9) He says that these are the distances: from Kaspios to the Kyros is about 1,800 stadia, and then to the Kaspian Gates 5,600, to Alexandria among the Arians, 6,400, then to the city of Baktra, also called Zariaspa, 3,870, then to the Iaxartes River, to which Alexander came, about 5,000, a total of 22,670. He also says that the distances from the Kaspian Gates to the Indians are as follows: they say it is 1,960 to Hekatompylos, to Alexandria among the Arians 4,530, then to Prophthasia in Drange 1,600 (others say 1,500), then to the city of the Arachotians 4,120, then to Ortospana and the meeting of three roads from Baktra, 2,000, and then to the borders of Indike 1,000, a total of 15,300.[2] It must be believed that the length of Indike is a distance in a straight line, that from the Indos as far as the eastern sea. This is it about the Sakians.

Part 9: Parthyaia

(1) Parthyaia is not large. At any rate, in Persian times it paid tribute along with the Hyrkanians, and for a long time afterward when the Makedonians were in power. In addition to its smallness it is wooded, mountainous, and

---

[2] As is often the case in ancient texts, both the sums in this section do not equal the totals of the individual distances.

poor, and because of this the kings send their multitudes through it quickly, since the land is unable to support them even for a short time. Today it has become stronger. Parts of Parthyaia include Komisene and Chorene, and essentially that as far as the Kaspian Gates, Rhagai, and the Tapyrians, which was formerly Median. Around Rhagai are the cities of Apameia and Herakleia. From the Kaspian Gates to Rhagai is 500 stadia, as Apollodoros [of Artemita, F5a] says, and to Hekatompylos, the Parthyaian royal seat, is 1,260. They say that Rhagai ["Fissures"] was named from the earthquakes that occur there, because of which numerous cities and 2,000 villages were ruined, as Poseidonios [F233] says. They say that the Tapyrians live between the Derbikians and Hyrkanians. It is recorded about the Tapyrians that it

[C515]   was their custom to give their wives in marriage to other men, when they had had two or three children, just as in our time Cato gave Marcia to Hortensius at his request, according to an ancient Roman custom.

(2) When there were uprisings in the territories outside the Tauros (because the kings of Syria and Media – who possessed them – were involved with others), those entrusted with them (those around Euthydemos [I]) first caused a revolt in Baktriane and everywhere near it. Then Arsakes [I], a Skythian man, and some of the Daans (those called the Parnians, nomads living along the Ochos) invaded Parthyaia and conquered it. In the beginning he was weak, as he was continually at war with those he had deprived of territory, both he himself and his successors. Later they became stronger and were always taking away the territory of their neighbors – through their success in war – so that finally they were established as masters of everything within the Euphrates. They also took a portion of Baktriane, having forced it from the Skythians, and still earlier from Eukratides [I] and those around him. Today they rule so much land and so many peoples that, in a way, they have become rivals of the Romans in the size of their empire. The reason for this is their lifestyle and their customs, which have much that is barbarian and Skythian, and more that is useful for political supremacy and success in war.

(3) They say that the Parnian Daans migrated from the Daans around the Maiotis, who are called Xandians or Parians. But there is not complete agreement that certain Daans were among the Skythians above the Maiotis. Some say that Arsakes [I] derived his origin from them, but others say that he was Baktrianian, and that when he fled from the increase in power of Diodotos [I] he caused the Parthyaians to revolt. But I have said much about Parthian customs in the sixth book of my *Historical Commentaries* [F1], in the second book of events after Polybios, and thus we will pass over it here so that we would not seem to repeat what already has been said,

although I will only say that the Parthyaian council, as Poseidonios [F282] says, is double, one consisting of the kinsmen and the other of the wise men and Magoi, and the kings are appointed from both.

Part 10:   Aria and Margiane

(1) Aria and Margiane are the most powerful territories in this region, as they are enclosed by mountains and have their habitations in the plains. The mountains are occupied by certain tent-dwellers, and the plains are irrigated by rivers flowing through them, partly by the Arios and partly by the Margos.   [C516]

Aria borders on Baktriane and was under Stasanor, who held Baktriane. It is about 6,000 stadia distant from Hyrkania. Drangiane as far as Karmania was joined with it, which mostly lies below the southern part of the mountains, although some parts come near to the northern regions opposite Aria. Arachosia is not far away, also lying below the southern parts of the mountains and stretching as far as the Indos River, being a part of Ariane. The length of Aria is about 2,000 stadia and the width of the plain 300. The cities are Artakaena, Alexandria, and Achaia, named after their founders. The land is exceedingly good in wine, which lasts for three generations in unpitched vessels.

(2) Margiane is similar, although the plain is surrounded by deserts. Marvelling at its fertility, Antiochos [I] Soter enclosed a circuit of 1,500 stadia with a wall and founded the city of Antiocheia. The land is good for the vine; at any rate they say that a trunk is often found that it would take two men to embrace, and the bunches are two *pecheis*.

Part 11:   Baktria and Sogdiane

(1) A certain part of Baktria lies alongside Aria to the north, although most of it lies above it to the east. Most of it has everything except oil. The Hellenes who revolted became so powerful because of the quality of the territory that they became the masters of both Ariane and the Indians (as Apollodoros of Artemita [F7a] says), subduing more peoples than Alexander, especially under Menandros [I], if he did cross the Hypanis toward the east and went as far as the Isamos. Some he [subdued] himself and others [had been subdued] by Demetrios [I] the son of Euthydemos [I], the king of the Baktrians. They possessed not only Patalene but the rest of the coast, what are called the kingdoms of Saraostos and Sigerdis. On the whole, he says that Baktriane is the ornament of Ariane. They extended their empire as far as the Serians and the Phaunians.

(2) Their cities were Baktra, which is called Zariaspa (through which flows a river of the same name that empties into the Oxos), Darapsa, and a number of others. Among them was Eukratideia, named after the ruler.

[C517]   The Hellenes took possession of it and divided it into satrapies, of which the Parthyaians took Aspiones and Tourioua away from Eukratides [I]. They also held Sogdiane, lying above Baktriane toward the east between the Oxos River – which is the boundary between the Baktrians and the Sogdians – and the Iaxartes, which itself is the boundary between the Sogdians and the nomads.

(3) In antiquity the Sogdianians and Baktrianians were not much different in lifestyle and customs from the nomads, although the Baktrianians were a little more civilized. Those following Onesikritos [F5] do not say the best things about them and the other [peoples], for he says that those who are old or sick are thrown out to be eaten by dogs kept for that purpose, which are called "undertakers" in their native language, and although what is outside the walls of the metropolis of the Baktrians appears clean, most of that inside is filled with human bones, but Alexander brought an end to the custom. What he [Onesikritos] records about the Kaspians is somewhat similar, that when parents have gone past seventy years they are shut in and starved. This is more tolerable and is similar to a custom of the Keians, although it is Skythian. That of the Baktrianians is much more like the Skythians. If it is reasonable to be in doubt about what Alexander was finding in his own time, what can one presume in regard to the customs that were appropriate to the first Persians and the still earlier rulers?

(4) They say that Alexander founded eight cities in Baktriane and Sogdiane, and that he razed some, including Kariatai in Baktriane (where Kallisthenes was seized and placed under guard), Marakanda in Sogdiane, and Kyra, the farthest foundation of Kyros, situated on the Iaxartes River, which was the boundary of the Persian empire. He razed the settlement because, although it was fond of Kyros, it was continuously in revolt. He took the strongly fortified rocks of Sisimithres in Baktriane – where Oxyartes kept his daughter Rhoxane – and Oxos (others say Ariamazes) in Sogdiane. They record that Sisimithres is 15 stadia high and 80 in circuit, and it is level and fertile on top, and can support as many as 500 men. Here Alexander received extravagant hospitality and married Rhoxane the daughter of Oxyartes. They say that the one in Sogdiane is

[C518] twice as high. In this region he destroyed the city of the Branchidians, whom Xerxes had settled there and who had voluntarily come together from their native land because they had handed over the possessions and treasuries of the god at Didyma. He [Alexander] destroyed it because he loathed the sacrilege and the betrayal.

(5) Aristoboulos [F28a] calls the river flowing through Sogdiane the Polytimetos, a name established by the Makedonians, just as they instituted many others, some new and others slightly changed. It waters the territory and empties into a deserted and sandy land, absorbed by the sand, flowing, like the Arios, through the Arian territory. They say that those digging near the Oxos River found a spring of oil. It is reasonable – just as some natron and astringent, bituminous, and sulphurous liquids flow through the earth – that oily ones are also found, but their rarity is astonishing. Some say that the Ochos flows through Baktriane, and others that it is alongside it. Some [say] that it is different from the Oxos as far as its mouths, and farther to the south – although they both have their outflow into the sea in Hyrkania – and others that it is different from its source but that they (the stream of the Ochos and the Oxos) join into one which is often at a width of 6 or 7 stadia. The Iaxartes, however, is different from the Oxos from its beginning to its end. Although it ends in the same sea the mouths are different, separated by about 80 parasangs from each other, as Patrokles [F6] says. Some say that the Persian parasang is 60 stadia, others 30 or 40. When we were sailing up the Nile, they used different measurements at different places, so that when they spoke of the *schoinoi* from city to city, the same number of *schoinoi* would mean a longer voyage in one place, a shorter in another. Thus what was handed down from the beginning has been preserved until today.

(6) The peoples extending from Hyrkania toward the rising sun as far as Sogdiane – those outside the Tauros – became known first to the Persians, then the Makedonians, and afterward the Parthyaians. Those beyond in a straight line are compared to the Skythians, because of their similar nature, although there have been no expeditions against them known to us, just as is the case with the most northern nomads. Alexander attempted to lead an expedition against them when he went after Bessos and Spitamenes, but when Bessos was brought back alive and Spitamenes was killed by the barbarians he ceased the attempt. It is not agreed that peoples have sailed from Indike to Hyrkania, but Patrokles [F4b] says that it is possible.   [C519]

(7) It is said that the farthest part of the Tauros, which is called Imaion and adjoins the Indian Sea, does not go farther east than Indike, nor into it. As one goes to the northern side [of Indike] the sea continually reduces its length and width, so that a tapering appears toward the east in the portion of Asia now being outlined, which the Tauros cuts off from the Ocean that fills the Kaspian Sea. The maximum length of this portion from the Hyrkanian

Sea to the Ocean opposite Imaion is about 30,000 stadia, the route being along the mountainous portion of the Tauros, and the width less than 10,000. It has been said [2.1.4] that it is around 40,000 stadia from the Issic Gulf as far as the eastern sea among the Indians, and to Issos from the western cape at the Pillars another 30,000. The recess of the Issic Gulf is only slightly farther east than Amisos, if at all, and from Amisos to the Hyrkanian land is around 10,000 stadia, parallel to what was previously mentioned from Issos to the Indians. There remains 30,000 stadia as the previously mentioned length toward the east of the portion already described. Again, the greatest width of the inhabited world (which is chlamys-shaped) is around 30,000 stadia – the distance near the meridian drawn through the Hyrkanian and Persian Seas – if the length of the inhabited world is 70,000 stadia. If it is 8,000 stadia from Hyrkania to Artemita in Babylonia, as Apollodoros of Artemita [F6] says, and from there to the mouth of the Persian Sea is the same, and again if it is the same or a little less to the same parallel as the promontories of Aithiopia, there would remain of the previously mentioned width of the inhabited world that from the recess of the Hyrkanian Sea to its mouth, as I have already said [2.1.17]. This segment of the earth tapers toward the eastern parts, and its shape would be similar to a kitchen cleaver, with the mountain in a straight line and considered as the edge of the knife, and the coast from the Hyrkanian mouth to Tamaron as the other side, ending in a tapering line that is carried around to a point.

(8) One must mention some incredible things that are chattered about those who are completely barbarian, such as those around the Kaukasos and the other mountainous regions. One of their customs is mentioned by Euripides:

[C520]

> To lament those born for so many evils that they will encounter, but those who are dead and who have ceased from their suffering are carried from their homes with pleasure and triumph. [F449]

Others do not kill their greatest wrongdoers but only banish them and their children, which is the opposite of the Derbikians, who slaughter them even for slight offenses. The Derbikians worship the earth and do not sacrifice or eat anything female. Men who become over seventy years of age are slaughtered and their flesh is consumed by their nearest relatives. The old women are strangled and then buried. Those who die under seventy are not eaten, merely buried. The Siginnians imitate the Persians in everything, except that they use small shaggy horses that are unable to carry a rider but are yoked into a four-horse team driven by women so trained from childhood. The best driver lives with whomever she wishes. They say that some practice making their heads appear as long as possible and making their foreheads project, so that they are beyond their chins. Among the Tapyrians the men dress in black and wear their hair long, and the women dress in white and wear their hair short. They live between the Derbikians and the Hyrkanians. The Kaspians starve those over seventy years of age and place them in the desert and watch from a distance. If they see them dragged from their biers by birds, they are considered fortunate, less so if by wild animals or dogs, and if by nothing, they are possessed by an evil divinity.

Part 12:   The Tauros

(1) Since the northern portion of Asia is created by the Tauros – that which is called "within the Tauros" – we have chosen to speak about it first, including all or most of the regions in the mountains themselves. That which is more to the east of the Kaspian Gates can be outlined more simply because of the wildness of its inhabitants, and it would not make much difference whether they were catalogued in this or that latitude. Yet all those to the west provide abundant material to describe them. Thus one must proceed with that lying along the Kaspian Gates. Media lies alongside to the west, a territory at one time both extensive and powerful, situated in the middle of the Tauros, split into many parts, including large valleys as also occur in Armenia.

(2) This mountain begins in Karia and Lykia, and does not show any notable width or height there. It first becomes quite high opposite the Chelidoniai, which are islands at the beginning of the Pamphylian coast. It [C521] stretches toward the east, receiving the large valleys of Kilikia. Then the Amanos splits off from it on one side, and on the other the Antitauros (in which Komana is situated, in so-called Upper Kappadokia). The latter ends in Kataonia, but Mount Amanos projects as far as the Euphrates and Melitene, where Kommagene lies beside Kappadokia. It is succeeded on the far side of the Euphrates by mountains that are continuous with those previously mentioned, except that they are cut by the river flowing through their middle. It greatly increases in height and width, and divides into many branches. Nevertheless the more southerly one is the Tauros, which divides Armenia from Mesopotamia.

(3) Both of the rivers flow from there (the Euphrates and the Tigris, which nearly touch each other in Babylonia and empty into the Persian Sea). The Euphrates is the larger and, with its winding stream, passes through more territory. Its sources are in the northerly portion of the

Tauros, and it flows toward the west through Greater Armenia, as it is called, to Lesser [Armenia], having it on its right, and on its left Akilisene. Then it turns toward the south, and at the turn touches the boundaries of Kappadokia. It leaves both these and the region of Kommagene on the right, and Akisilene and Sophene (a part of Greater Armenia) on the left. Advancing into Syria, it makes another bend into Babylonia and the Persian Gulf. The Tigris is carried from the southern portion of the same mountain to Seleukeia, nearly touching the Euphrates and creating with it Mesopotamia, and then it goes into the same gulf as the other. The sources of the Euphrates and Tigris are about 2,500 stadia distant from each other.

(4) There are many branches of the Tauros toward the north, one of which is called the Antitauros (that so named surrounds Sophene, which is in a valley lying between it and the Tauros). On the other side of the Euphrates near Lesser Armenia and next to the Antitauros (toward the north) extends a large mountain with many branches, one of which is called Paryadres, another the Moschian Mountain, and another with various names, and these surround all of Armenia as far as Iberia and Albania. Then others rise toward the east, those lying above the Kaspian Sea as far as [C522] Atropatian and Greater Media. All the parts of these mountains are called Parachoathras, as well as those as far as the Kaspian Gates and extending still farther toward the east and touching Aria. This is what the mountains toward the north are called. Those on the south, on the other side of the Euphrates, stretching toward the east from Kappadokia and Kommagene, are at the beginning of the Tauros itself, which separates Sophene and the rest of Armenia from Mesopotamia. Some call these the Gordyaia Mountains. Among them is Masion, the mountain that lies above Nisibis and Tigranokerta. Then it [the Tauros] rises higher and is called Niphates. Somewhere around here are the sources of the Tigris, on the southern side of the mountainous territory. Then from Niphates the ridge extends still farther and farther and forms Mount Zagrion, which separates Media and Babylonia. Next after Zagrion is – above Babylonia – the mountainous territory of the Elymaians and the Paraitakenians, and, above Media, that of the Kossaians. In the middle are Media and Armenia, which encompass many mountains, many tablelands, and similarly plains and large valleys with numerous peoples living around about, who are small in number and mountaineers and mostly brigands. Thus we place Media, in which the Kaspian Gates are, within the Tauros, as well as Armenia.

(5) According to me, then, these peoples would be toward the north, but Eratosthenes [F48], who made the division into a southern part and a northern, calling some of his previously mentioned "sealstones" northern

and others southern, declares that the Kaspian Gates are the boundary between the two latitudinal regions. Reasonably, he would declare the southern part that which is more southerly than the Kaspian Gates, stretching toward the east, among which are Media and Armenia, and the northern part the more northerly, since this happens regardless of the distribution of sections. But perhaps it did not occur to him that no part of either Armenia or Media is south or outside of the Tauros.

Part 13:　Media

(1) Media is divided in two, one of which is called the Greater, whose metropolis is Ekbatana, a large city that was the royal residence of the Median state. The Parthyaians continue to use it today as a royal residence, and their kings spend the summer there, for Media is cold. Their winter quarters are at Seleukeia on the Tigris near Babylon. The other part is Atropatian Media, which was named after the commander Atropates, who　　[C523] prevented it from becoming subject to the Makedonians, since it was a part of Greater Media. After he was proclaimed king, he organized this territory separately, and his successors have preserved it until today, the later ones having contracted marriages with the kings of Armenia, Syria, and afterward the Parthyaians.

(2) The territory lies to the east of Armenia and Matiane, to the west of Greater Media, and to the north of both. It lies alongside the region around the recess of the Hyrkanian Sea with Matiane on the south. It is not small, considering its power, as Apollonides [*FHG* vol. 4, pp. 309–10] says, for it can supply 10,000 horsemen and 40,000 foot soldiers. It has a lake, Spauta, in which salt appears on the surface and solidifies. It causes itching and is painful, but the condition is cured by olive oil, and by sweet water for brittle clothing, if through ignorance one should dip them in for washing. They have powerful neighbors, the Armenians and the Parthyaians, by whom they are often plundered, but they hold out against them and receive back what has been taken, just as they received back Symbake when the Armenians became subject to the Romans. They have the friendship of Caesar, but at the same time are courting the Parthyaians.

(3) The summer royal residence is situated in the plain at Gazaka . . . in a strong fortification called Ouera, which was besieged by Antonius on his expedition against the Parthyaians. It is a distance of 2,400 stadia from the Araxes River, which is the boundary between Armenia and Atropatene, as Dellius [F1], the friend of Antonius, says, who wrote the history of his Parthyaian expedition, on which he was present and was a commander.

All the regions of this territory are prosperous, although the part toward the north is mountainous, rough, and cold. This is where the Kadousian mountaineers live, as well as the Amardians, Tapyrians, Kyrtians, and such others, who are migrants and brigands, for the Zagros and Niphates scatter these peoples. In Persis the Kyrtians and Mardians (as the Amardians are called), and those in Armenia who are still called today by the same name, are of the same type.

(4) The Kadousians are only slightly less than the Arianians in the number of their foot soldiers. Their javelin men are excellent, and in rough areas the foot soldiers fight, instead of the horsemen. But it was not the nature of the territory that made the expedition difficult for Antonius, but his guide for the route, the Armenian king Artavasdes [II], who was plotting against him yet was made his advisor and the master of judgements about the war. He was punished, but too late, after he was responsible for many offenses against the Romans (not only he himself, but the other one, who had made the route from Zeugma on the Euphrates as far as the border of Atropatene 8,000 stadia – more than twice the direct route – through mountains, places with no roads, and circuituous ways).

(5) In antiquity Greater Media ruled all of Asia, after it destroyed the Syrian empire, but later, in the time of Astyages, it was deprived of that authority by Kyros and the Persians, although retaining much of its ancestral status. Ekbatana was a winter residence[3] for the Persians, and similarly for the Makedonians who brought them to an end and possessed Syria. Today it still provides the same advantages and security for the Parthyaian kings.

(6) It is bounded on the east by Parthyaia and the mountains of the Kossaians, who are a brigand peoples. They once provided the Elymaians – with whom they were allied against the Sousians and Babylonians – 13,000 bowmen. Nearchos [F1g] says that there were four brigand peoples, and that the Mardians were next to the Persians, the Ouxians and Elymaians next to the former and the Sousians, and the Kossaians [next to] the Medians. All exacted tribute from the kings, and the Kossaians also received gifts when the king, having spent the summer in Ekbatana, went down to Babylonia. Alexander brought their excessive boldness to an end when he attacked them in winter. Thus it is bounded on the east by these and also by the Paraitakenians (who adjoin the Persians and also are mountaineers and brigands), on the north by the Kadousians (who live above the Hyrkanian

[C524]

---

[3] It is unlikely that cold snowy Ekbatana was a winter residence; "winter" is probably an error for "summer" (see sections 1 and 6) or "royal."

Sea) and the others that we have just described, toward the south wind by Apolloniatis (which the ancients called Sitakene) and the Zagros, where Massabatike is situated (which is Median, although some say Elymaian), and toward the west by the Atropatians and some Armenians.

There are also Hellenic cities in Media, founded by the Makedonians, including Laodikeia, Apameia (the one near Rhagai), and Rhagai itself, which was founded by [Seleukos I] Nikator, who named it Europos (but the Parthians Arsakia), being about 500 stadia to the south of the Kaspian Gates, as Apollodoros of Artemita [F5b] says.

(7) Much of it is high and cold, as are the mountains lying above Ekbatana and around Rhagai and the Kaspian Gates, and the northern portion in general from these to Matiane and Armenia. What is below the Kaspian Gates – low ground and hollows – is exceedingly prosperous and produces everything except the olive, which, if grown anywhere, is poor and dry. This, as well as Armenia, is important for "horse-pasturing" [*hippobotos, Iliad* 2.287 etc.], and there is a certain meadow there called Hippobotos, passed through by those travelling from Persis and Babylon to the Kaspian Gates. They say that in the time of the Persians 50,000 mares were pastured there, and these were the royal herds. Some say that the breed of Nesaian horses, which the kings used because they were the best and the largest, were from here, and others that they were from Armenia. They are peculiar in form – as are the ones today called Parthian – in comparison to the Helladic and the others among us. Moreover, we call the pasturage that is the best nourishment for horses "Medic" because it is common there. The territory also produces silphium – from which comes what is called Median juice – which is not greatly inferior to the Kyrenaian, and sometimes superior, because of differences as to place, a change in the form of the plant, or due to those who extract and prepare the juice so that it is preserved for storage and use.

(8) Such is the land. Regarding its size, the width and length are about equal. The greatest width of Media seems to be 4,100 stadia, from the crossing over the Zagros – called the Median Gate – to the Kaspian Gates, through Sigriane. Reports about the tribute agree with the size and power of the country, for Kappadokia paid each year to the Persians, in addition to a tax on silver, 1,500 horses, 2,000 mules, and 50,000 sheep, yet the Medes paid almost twice as much.

(9) Most of their customs and those of the Armenians are the same, because of the similarity of the territories. Yet they say that the Medes originated them, and, still earlier, for the Persians, who took them over and succeeded to power in Asia. What is today called the Persian robe, their

[C525]

eagerness for archery and horsemanship, the attention paid to their kings, their ornaments, and their divine reverence toward their rulers came to the Persians from the Medes. That this is true can best be seen from their dress, for the type of tiara, headdress, felt cap, the sleeved chiton, and the trousers are suitable to be worn in cold and northerly places (where the Medes are), but not at all in southern ones. Yet most of the Persian settlements were situated on the Erythran Sea, farther south than the Babylonians and the Sousians. After bringing the Medes to an end they acquired certain regions that were attached to Media. But the customs of the conquered appeared so stately and suitable for royal dignity that instead of going naked or lightly dressed they submitted to wearing women's clothes and entirely covered themselves.

(10) Some say that Medeia introduced this type of dress when she held power in these places along with Jason, hiding her face when she went forth in place of the king, that the Jasonian heroa greatly honored by the barbarians are memorials of Jason (there is a large mountain above the Kaspian Gates, on the left, called Iasonion), and that the dress and the name of the territory are from Medeia. It is said that her son Medos succeeded to the rule and left his name on the territory. In agreement with this are the Iasoneia in Armenia and the name of that territory, and a number of other matters which we will discuss.

(11) This is also Median: to choose the bravest man as king, but not from everyone, only the mountaineers. More common is that the kings have many wives; this is the custom of the mountaineers and of all the Medes, for it is not permitted to have fewer than five. Moreover, they say that the women consider it honorable that their men be allotted as many as possible, considering fewer than five a misfortune.

The rest of Media is prosperous, but the northern mountainous part is poor. At any rate, they are fed from the fruit of trees, making cakes from dried and cut apples, and bread from roasted almonds. They squeeze wine from roots and use the meat of wild animals, but do not raise domesticated animals.

This is what we say about the Medes. We will speak about the customs that are common to all of Media – since they are the same as the Persian ones because of the Persian conquest – in the appropriate section [15.3.13].

Part 14: Armenia

(1) The southern parts of Armenia are protected by the Tauros, which separates it from the entire territory between the Euphrates and the Tigris

(called Mesopotamia). The eastern parts adjoin Greater Media and [C527] Atropatene, and on the north are the mountains of Parachoathras that lie above the Kaspian Sea, the Albanians, Iberians, and the Kaukasos (which encircles these peoples and adjoins the Armenians, and also adjoins the Moschian and Kolchian mountains as far as the so-called Tibaranians). On the west are these peoples and Paryadres and Skydises, as far as Lesser Armenia and the riverine area of the Euphrates, which separates Armenia from Kappadokia and Kommagene.

(2) The Euphrates has its beginning on the north side of the Tauros, and flows first toward the west through Armenia, and then turns toward the south and cuts through the Tauros between the Armenians, Kappadokians, and Kommagenians. Then it comes out into Syria and turns toward the winter sunrise as far as Babylon, and along with the Tigris forms Mesopotamia. Both end in the Persian Gulf.

This is the circuit, and almost all of it is mountainous and rough, except the small amount that inclines toward Media. The previously mentioned Tauros makes a new beginning on the far side of the Kommagenians and Melitenians, [territory] that the Euphrates creates. Mount Masion lies above the Mygdonians in Mesopotamia, on the south, in which Nisibis is. Sophene lies in the northern portion, between Masion and the Antitauros, which makes its beginning from the Euphrates and the Tauros, and ends toward the eastern part of Armenia, enclosing the middle of Sophene, and having on the other portion Akilisene, situated between the Tauros and the riverine area of the Euphrates, before it turns toward the south. The royal city of Sophene is Karkathiokerta. Lying above Masion, far toward the east opposite Gordyene, is Niphates, and then Abos, from which the Euphrates and the Araxes flow, the former toward the west and the latter toward the east. Then there is Nibaros, which extends as far as Media.

(3) The manner in which the Euphrates flows has been described. The Araxes is carried toward the east as far as Atropatene and then bends toward the west and toward the north, and flows first past Azara, then Artaxata (Armenian cities), and then through the Araxene Plain, emptying into the Kaspian Sea.

(4) In Armenia itself there are many mountains, and many mountain [C528] plains in which the vine will not easily grow. There are many valleys, some moderately and others exceedingly prosperous, such as the Araxene Plain, through which the Araxes River flows to the extremities of Albania and then empties into the Kaspian Sea. After it there is Sakasene – which also lies near Albania and the Kyros River – and then Gogarene. All of this territory is full of fruits, cultivated trees, and evergreens, and produces the olive. There are

also Phauene (a province of Armenia), Komisene, and Orchistene (which provides the most cavalry). Chorzene and Kambisene are the most northern and the most covered with snow, adjoining the Kaukasian mountains, Iberia, and Kolchis. They say that there are places in the mountain passes where entire caravans are swallowed up by the snow when major snow-storms occur. They carry staffs against such danger, which they thrust up to the surface in order to breathe clearly and to point themselves out to those approaching, so that they can be helped. They say that hollow lumps of ice form that have good water, which can be drunk by splitting open their covering. Animals breed in them, which Apollonides [*FHG* vol. 4, pp. 309–10] calls earthworms and Theophanes [F5] woodworms, and the origin of these animals is similar to the gnats that come from the flames and sparks in mines.

(5) It is recorded that Armenia, although formerly small, was enlarged by Artaxias [I] and Zariadris, former commanders of Antiochos [III] the Great. Later, after he weakened, they became kings, the former of Sophene, Amphissene, Odomantis, and other places, and the latter of the territory around Artaxata. Together they enlarged [their kingdoms] by cutting off portions of surrounding peoples: Kaspiane, Phaunitis, and Basoropaida from the Medes; from the Iberians, that on the mountainside of Paryadres, Chorzene, and Gogarene, which is across the Kyros; from the Chalybians and Mosynoikians, Karenitis and Xerxene, which are on the borders of Lesser Armenia or are parts of it; Akilisene and that around the Antitauros from the Kataonians; and Tamoritis from the Syrians. Because of this they all speak the same language.

(6) The cities of Armenia are Artaxata (which is also called Artaxiasata, [C529] founded by Hannibal for King Artaxias [I]) and Arxata, both on the Araxes. Arxata is near to the borders of Atropatene, and Artaxata is near the Araxene Plain, a beautiful settlement and the royal residence of the territory. It is situated on a peninsula-like elbow, and its walls have the river as protection all around except at the isthmus. The isthmus is enclosed by a ditch and a palisade. Not far away from the city are the treasuries of Tigranes [II] and Artavasdes [II?] and the strong fortresses of Babyrsa and Olane. There were others on the Euphrates. Ador, its commandant, caused Artagerai to revolt, but the commanders of Caesar took it after besieging it for a long time and removed its walls.

(7) There are a number of rivers in the territory, the best known of which are the Phasis and the Lykos, which empty into the Pontic Sea (Eratosthenes [F119] has wrongly put down the Thermodon instead of the Lykos), the Kyros and Araxes into the Kaspian, and the Euphrates and Tigris into the Erythran.

(8) There are large lakes in Armenia, one of which is Mantiane, which is translated as Kyane ["Dark Blue"]. They say that it is the largest body of salt water after the Maiotis. It extends as far as the Atropatia and has salt works. There is also Arsene, which is called Thonitis. It contains natron and tears up and shreds clothes, because of which the water is undrinkable. The Tigris rushes from this mountainous territory near the Niphates, and the flow remains unmixed [with Lake Thonitis] because of its quickness, from which comes its name, since the Medes call an arrow "tigris." And while it has many types of fish, there is only one type in the lake. Around the innermost recess of the lake the river falls into a pit and flows underground for some distance, coming up around Chalonitis. From there it goes down toward Opis and the so-called Wall of Semiramis, leaving the Gordyaians and all Mesopotamia on the right, but the Euphrates, on the contrary, has the same territory on the left. Coming near to one another and producing Mesopotamia, the former runs through Seleukeia to the Persian Gulf and the latter through Babylon, which I said [2.1.26] somewhere in my discussion against Eratosthenes [F89] and Hipparchos.

(9) There are gold mines in Hyspiratis near Kaballa, to which Alexander sent Menon with soldiers, who was led up to them by the locals. There are other mines, especially of what is called *sandyx* (also called "Armenian color," like purple). The territory is especially good for "horse pasturing" [*Iliad* 2.287 etc.], no less so than Media, so that the Nesaian horses [C530] are produced there, which were used by the Persian kings. The satrap of Armenia sent 20,000 foals every year to the Persian [king], at the time of the Mithrakana. Artavasdes [II], when he invaded Media with Antonius, showed him – apart from the rest of the cavalry – 6,000 armored horses in battle array. Not only do the Medes and the Armenians esteem this type of cavalry, but also the Albanians, who likewise use them in full armor.

(10) Regarding the wealth and power of the territory, it is no small sign of it that when Pompeius assessed Tigranes [II], the father of Artavasdes [II], six thousand talents of silver, he immediately distributed the following to the Roman forces: to the soldiers fifty drachmas per man, to each centurion a thousand, and to each hipparch and chiliarch a talent.

(11) Theophanes [F6] gives the size of the territory as a width of a hundred *schoinoi* and the length twice that, putting the *schoinos* at 40 stadia, but what he says is too much. It is nearer the truth to put down the length as the stated width and the width as half or a little more. Such is the nature and power of Armenia.

(12) There is an ancient story about these people, as follows: Armenos from Armenion – a Thessalian city that, as I have said [11.4.8], lies between Pharai and Larisa on Boibe – made the expedition with Jason into Armenia. Those following Kyrsilos the Pharsalian [F1] and Medios the Larisian [F1] – men who made the expedition with Alexander – say that Armenia was named after him, and that some of those with Armenos settled in Akilisene (which formerly was subject to the Sophenians), and others in Syspiritis, as far as Kalachene and Adiabene, outside the Armenian mountains. They also say that Armenian clothing is Thessalian, such as the long chitons, which are called "Thessalian" in the tragedies and are girded around the breast, as well as the cloaks with which the tragedians also imitate the Thessalians. It was necessary to apply some such adornment, and the Thessalians especially used full robes, probably because they lived the farthest north of all the Hellenes and in the coldest places, and thus it was most suitable for the actors to imitate them in their preparation for their representations. They also say that the eagerness for horsemanship is Thessalian, both theirs and equally that of the Medes. Witness to this are the expedition of Jason, and the Iasoneia, some of which those in power also razed to the ground, as Parmenion did with the temple of Jason at Abdera.

[C531]

(13) It is believed that the Araxes was ambiguously named by those with Armenos, because of its similarity to the Peneios, which was also called the Araxes, for it cut off [aparaxai] Ossa from Olympos, breaking through Tempe. They say that in antiquity the one in Armenia came down from the mountains and spread out, making a sea in the plains lying below, but there was no outlet. Jason, in order to make it like Tempe, created the fissure through which the water today rushes down to the Kaspian Sea. Because of this, the Araxene Plain, through which the river flows to its sharp descent, was exposed. This account of the Araxes River can be said to have some plausibility, but the Herodotean one [1.202.3] none at all, for he says that after flowing from the Matienians it splits into forty rivers, dividing the Skythians from the Baktrians. Kallisthenes [F38] follows him.

(14) It is said that certain of the Ainianians settled in Ouitia, and others above the Armenians, above Abos and Nibaros (these are parts of the Tauros). Of these, Abos is near the road coming into Ekbatana past the temple of Baris. They say that certain Thracians – those called the Saraparians – settled above Armenia near to the Gouranians and Medes, and were wild and disobedient people, mountaineers, scalpers, and beheaders (this is what "Saraparians" means). Matters about Media have been discussed in the Median section [11.13.1–11]. Thus all this suggests that

the Medes and the Armenians are related in some way to the Thessalians and descended from Jason and Medeia.

(15) This is the account from antiquity. The more recent one, that from Persian times continuously to our own, can be said appropriately and summarized as follows. The Persians and the Makedonians held Armenia, and afterward those who held Syria and Media. The last was Orontes, the descendant of Hydarnes, one of the seven Persians. Then it was divided in two by Artaxias [I] and Zariadris, the commanders of Antiochos [III] the Great, who was making war against the Romans. They ruled, since it was turned over to them by the king, but when he was defeated they joined the Romans and were considered autonomous and called kings. Tigranes [II]   [C532] was a descendant of Artaxias and held what is specifically called Armenia, which adjoined Media, the Albanians, and Iberia, as far as Kolchis and Kappadokia on the Euxeinos. But the Sophenian, Artanes, was a descendant of Zariadris and held the southern portions and those rather to the west. He was put down by Tigranes [II], who established himself as master of all, and who experienced varied fortunes. First he was a hostage among the Parthians, and then through them he gained his return, with them taking the lease of seventy valleys in Armenia. When he had increased in power he took back this territory and ravaged theirs around both Ninos and Arbela. He made subject the Atropatenian and Gordyaian [rulers], and with them and the rest of Mesopotamia he crossed the Euphrates and vigorously took both Syria itself and Phoenicia. Exalted in such a way, he founded a city near Iberia,[4] between it and Zeugma on the Euphrates, which he called Tigranokerta, bringing together people from twelve Hellenic cities that he evacuated. But Lucullus – who had been waging war against Mithridates [VI] – arrived before he finished it and discharged the inhabitants to their various homes. The foundation was still only half-finished, but he attacked it and pulled it down, leaving it a small village, and drove him [Tigranes II] out of Syria and Phoenicia. His successor Artavasdes [II] prospered for a while as a friend of the Romans, but when he betrayed Antonius to the Parthyaians in his war against them, he paid the penalty, for he was taken by him to Alexandria and paraded thoroughout the city in chains. For a time he was kept under guard but was killed when the Aktian war occurred. After him several kings ruled under Caesar and the Romans, and today it is still held together in the same way.

(16) All the sacred rites of the Persians are honored by the Medes and Armenians, but those of Anaitis particularly by the Armenians, who have

---

[4] "Iberia" seems unlikely to be correct.

established her in various places, especially in Akilisene. Here they dedicate male and female slaves, which is not remarkable, but the most distinguished men among the people dedicate their daughters while still virgins. It is customary for them to be prostituted at the sanctuary of the goddess for a long time, and after this to be given in marriage. No one considers it unworthy to live with such a woman (Herodotos says [1.93.4] something like this about Lydian women, all of whom prostitute themselves). They treat their lovers so kindly that they demonstrate hospitality and exchange gifts, often more than they receive, as those from wealthy homes are well supplied. They do not accept any stranger, but preferably those of equal status.

[C533]

Central and northern Anatolia

Part 1:   Introduction to Kappadokia

(1) . . . and Kappadokia has many parts and has experienced many changes.[1] Those who speak the same language are mostly those bounded on the south by the so-called Kilikian Tauros, on the east by Armenia, Kolchis, and those peoples in between who speak other languages, on the north by the Euxeinos as far as the outlets of the Halys, and on the west by the Paphlagonian peoples and the Galatians who settled in Phrygia, as far as the Lykaonians and the Kilikians who possess Rough Kilikia.

(2) Regarding those speaking the same language, the ancients place the Kataonians by themselves, distinguished from the Kappadokians as different peoples. In the enumeration of the peoples they place Kataonia after Kappadokia, and then the Euphrates and the peoples across it, so that Melitene is placed under Kataonia, which lies between it and the Euphrates, adjoining Kommagene. According to the division of Kappadokia into ten districts, this is a tenth part of the territory. In this way the kings in our time (before Archelaos) were appointed to the rule of [C534] Kappadokia. Kataonia is also a tenth part of it. In our time each had its own commander, but there is no visible difference in language among the Kappadokians, or in any of their customs, and it is remarkable that the signs of differing ethnicity have completely disappeared. They were once separate but were added by Ariarathes [III], the first to be called king of Kappadokia.

(3) It is as if the isthmus of a large peninsula bounded by two seas, that of the Issic Gulf as far as Rough Kilikia, and the Euxeinos as far as Sinope and the Tibarenian coast. I consider the peninsula everything that is within the isthmus and west of Kappadokia, which Herodotos calls (1.6, 1.28, 5.102) "within the Halys." This in its entirety was ruled by Kroisos, whom he

---

[1] The beginning of the sentence seems to be missing.

describes as "tyrant of the peoples within the Halys River" [1.6]. Those of today say that which is within the Tauros is Asia, calling it by the same name as the entire continent. It consists of the first peoples toward the east, the Paphlagonians, Phrygians, and Lykaonians, and then the Bithynians, Mysians, and Epiktetos, as well as the Troad and the Hellespont, and, after these, on the sea, the Aiolians and Ionians – who are Hellenes – and, among the others, the Karians, Lykians, and the Lydians in the interior.

(4) We will speak about the others later. Kappadokia had been divided into two satrapies by the Persians when the Makedonians obtained it. They allowed one part willingly and the other part unwillingly to change to kingdoms instead of satrapies. One they named Kappadokia itself, or "Near the Tauros," or, by Zeus, Greater Kappadokia, and the other Pontos (to some it was Kappadokia Near the Pontos). We do not yet know the current organization of Greater Kappadokia, for after it was known that King Archelaos had come to the end of his life, Caesar and the Senate made it a Roman province. Under the king and his predecessors the territory had been divided into ten districts. There were five considered near the Tauros – Melitene, Kataonia, Kilikia, Tyanitis, and Garsauritis – and the remaining five were Laouiansene, Sargarausene, Saraouene, Chamanene, and Morimene. Later the Romans gave an eleventh district from Kilikia to [C535] the predecessors of Archelaos: the territory around Kastabala and Kybistra as far as Derbe (that of Antipatros the brigand), and to Archelaos himself, Rough Kilikia around Elaioussa and everywhere that had been involved in piracy.

Part 2:   Kappadokia (continued)

(1) Melitene is similar to Kommagene, for it is the only part of Kappadokia that is entirely planted with cultivated trees, so that it produces the olive and the Monarite wine, which is a match for the Hellenic. It is situated opposite Sophene, with the Euphrates River between it and Kommagene, which borders it. On the far side there is a noteworthy fortress of the Kappadokians, Tomisa. It was sold to the ruler of Sophene for a hundred talents, and later Lucullus presented it as a gift to the ruler of Kappadokia for his valor when he joined in the war against Mithridates [VI].

(2) Kataonia is a wide and hollow plain that produces everything except evergreens. It is surrounded by the mountains, with the Amanos on the southern side (which are severed from the Kilikian Tauros), and with the Antitauros breaking off in the opposite direction. The Amanos extends from Kataonia toward the west and south to Kilikia and the Syrian Sea, and

separates the confines of the entire Issic Gulf and the Kilikian plains that are between it and the Tauros. The Antitauros inclines toward the north and goes slightly toward the east, and then comes to an end in the interior.

(3) In this Antitauros there are deep and narrow valleys, in one of which is situated Komana, the sanctuary of Enyo (who they named Ma). It is a notable city, but most of those in it are the divinely inspired people and the temple slaves. The inhabitants are Kataonians, who are generally classified as subject to the king, but for the most part answer to the priest. He is the master of the sanctuary and the temple slaves, of whom there were more than six thousand, men and women, when I stayed there. Much territory is attached to the sanctuary, and the priest enjoys the revenue. He is second in honor in Kappadokia after the king, and for the most part the priests are from the same family as the kings. Orestes – along with his sister Iphigeneia – is believed to have brought these rites (those of Artemis Tauropolos) here from Tauric Skythia, and deposited here the hair [*kome*] of mourning, from which the name of the city came. The Saros River flows through the city and through the narrow glens of the Tauros, passing into [C536] the Kilikian Plain and to the sea lying below.

(4) The Pyramos is navigable and [flows] through Kataonia, with its sources in the middle of the plain. There is a notable pit into which one can look down and see the water passing underground, hidden for a long interval and then rising to the surface. The force of the water resists a javelin put down into the pit, so that it can hardly be immersed. Because of its immense depth and width it is carried along, and with strength, but when it reaches the Tauros, it undergoes a remarkable contraction. Remarkable also is the cleft in the mountains through which the stream is carried, for just as with rocks that have been broken and split in two, the projections on either side agree with the recesses on each side, so that they could be fitted together. It was thus with the rocks that I saw lying above the river on either side, extending almost to the ridge of the mountain at a distance of two or three *plethra* from each other, and with the cavities corresponding to the projections. The foundation in between is completely rocky, with a deep and extremely narrow cleft through the middle, so that a dog or a hare could jump across. This is the stream of the river, completely full to the edge. In width it resembles a channel, but because of its crookedness and such a contraction, and the depth of the chasm, a thunderous noise is heard from far away by those approaching. In passing down through the mountains it carries much silt down to the sea, some from Kataonia and some from the Kilikian plains, so that an oracle is said to have been issued as follows:

Those in the future will experience the time when silver-eddying Pyramos
will pour over its sacred beach and come to Cyprus. [Sibylline Oracle 4.97–8]

Something similar occurs in Egypt, as the Nile is always turning the sea into
dry land through siltation. Thus Herodotos says that Egypt is "the gift of the
river" [2.5], and the Poet that Pharos was formerly in the open sea [*Odyssey*
4.356–7], but today it is near the shore of Egypt.[2]

[C537]   (6) Neither the plain of the Kataonians nor Melitene has a city, but there
are fortified citadels in the mountains, Azamora and Dastarkon, around
which the Karmalas River flows. It has a sanctuary of Kataonian Apollo,
which is honored throughout the whole of Kappadokia, where they have
made copies of it. None of the other districts – except two – have cities. Of
the remaining districts, Sargarausene has a small town, Herpa, and the
Karmalas River, which itself empties into the Kilikian [Sea]. In the others
are Argos, a high fortress near the Tauros, and Nora, today called Neroassos,
in which Eumenes resisted a siege for a long time. In our time it was near the
treasury of Sisenes, who attacked the Kappadokian empire. He also had
Kadena, a royal residence fitted out like a city. On the borders of Lykaonia is
the town of Garsaueira, which is also said once to have been the metropolis
of the territory. In Morimene there is the sanctuary of Ouenasian Zeus,
which has a settlement of almost three thousand temple slaves and a fruitful
sacred territory, giving the priest a yearly revenue of fifteen talents. He holds
[the office] for life, just like the one among the Komanans, and is considered
to be the second in honor.

(5) The third is the priesthood of Zeus Dakeios [?], which is inferior to
the previous but is nonetheless notable. There is a cistern of salt water there
that has a circumference of a notable lake, enclosed by embankments so
high and steep that they go down in ladders. They say that the water neither
increases nor visibly sinks down.

(7) Only two districts have cities. Tyanitis has Tyana, which lies at the
foot of the Tauros at the Kilikian Gates, the easiest and most commonly
used pass for everyone into Kilikia and Syria. It is called Eusebeia near the
Tauros, and is mostly good and level. Tyana is situated on a mound of
Semiramis and is beautifully fortified. Not far from it are Kastabala and
Kybistra, towns that are still nearer to the mountain. In Kastabala there is
the sanctuary of the Perasian Artemis, where, they say, the priestesses walk
with naked feet over burning coals without suffering. Some talk here about

---

[2] Section 5 has been moved to after section 6, preserving Strabo's sequence of the three priesthoods.

the account of Orestes and Tauropolos, and say that she was called Perasian because she was brought from the other side [*perathen*].

Tyana is in the district of Tyanitis (one of the ten previously mentioned). We are not enumerating those acquired in addition: Kastabala, Kybistra, and the places in Rough Kilikia, where Elaioussa, a fertile islet, was notably founded by Archelaos, who spent most of his time there. Mazaka, the metropolis of the people, is in what is called Kilikia. It is also called [C538] Eusebeia, with the surname "near Argaios," as it is situated at the foot of Argaios, the highest mountain of all, whose summit is never free of snow. Those who climb it – and these are few – say that in clear weather both seas are visible (the Pontos and the Issic). It [Mazaka] is an unsuitable place to found a city, because it is without water and in open territory. Due to the neglect of its leaders, it is without walls. Perhaps this was intentional, so that those living in the plain (with hills above them that were not within range of missiles) would not trust too much in fortifications and engage in brigandage. The territory all around is completely barren and uncultivated, although level, and sandy and rocky underneath. Proceeding a little farther, there are plains over many stadia that are volcanic and full of pits of fire; thus the necessary supplies come from far away. What seems advantageous is dangerous, for although almost all of Kappadokia is without timber, Argaios has forests all around it, and thus there is lumbering nearby, but the places lying below the forests often have fire and cold water under the surface, which is mostly grassy. In some places the ground is marshy and flames are found on it at night. Those who are familiar with it are able to do the lumbering, but guardedly, as it is dangerous for many, especially for flocks and herds, which fall into the unseen fire pits.

(8) There is a river in the plain in front of the city, called the Melas – about 40 stadia distant from the city – whose source is in a region somewhat lower than the city. Because of this it is useless to them, as the stream does not lie above and disperses into marshes and lakes, making the air around the city bad in summer, and the quarries difficult to work although they are otherwise useful. There are ledges from which the Mazakenians acquire a plentiful amount of fine stone for their buildings, but when the slabs are hidden by water it is the opposite. These marshes are volcanic everywhere. Since the Melas had an outlet through a narrows into the Euphrates,[3] King Ariarathes [V?] blocked it and made the neighboring plain into a lake that was like a sea. He isolated certain islets as if creating the Kyklades and created youthful amusements for himself. But the barrier [C539]

---

[3] Here and below the text has "Euphrates," but almost certainly "Halys" is meant.

broke all at once, the water washed away again, and the Euphrates was filled with much of Kappadokia, carrying away settlements and obliterating numerous fields, ruining no small part of the territory of the Galatians in Phrygia. In return for the damage, a penalty was exacted of 300 talents, with the judgement entrusted to the Romans. The same thing happened in regard to Herpa, for there he blocked the stream of the Karmalas, then the mouth broke and the waters destroyed certain regions of Kilikia around Mallos, and he paid damages to those who had been wronged.

(9) Since the territory of the Mazakenians is in many ways naturally unsuitable for habitation, the kings seem to have chosen it especially because it was the nearest of all places to the middle of the region that had timber and stone for buildings, as well as pasturage – of which they needed a large amount, as they kept cattle – for the city was, in a way, an encampment. Their safety – both for their bodies and their possessions – was due to their fortresses, of which there were many, some royal and others belonging to their friends. Mazaka is about 800 stadia from the Pontos, toward the south, slightly less than twice that from the Euphrates, and a route of 6 days via Tyana from the Kilikian Gates and the camp of Kyros. Tyana is situated at the middle of the route, 300 stadia distant from the Kybistrians. The Mazakenians use the laws of Charondas and choose a law-singer, who expounds the laws, like the legal advisors among the Romans. Tigranes [II] the Armenian treated them badly when he overran Kappadokia. He made everyone depart for Mesopotamia, settling Tigranokerta mostly from there. Later, after the capture of Tigranokerta, those who could went back again.

(10) The size of the territory, in width, from the Pontos to the Tauros, is about 1,800 stadia, and in length, from Lykaonia and Phrygia as far as the Euphrates (toward the east) and Armenia, is about 3,000. It is good in terms of fruits, but especially in grain and all kinds of cattle. It is farther south than Pontos but colder. Bagadania, although a plain and the farthest south of all – it is at the foot of the Tauros – produces hardly any fruit trees, but is grazed by wild asses, both it and most of the rest, especially that around [C540] Garsaueira, Lykaonia, and Morimene. The so-called Sinopean red ochre, the best of all (although the Iberian is a match for it) occurs in Kappadokia. It was named Sinopean because merchants were accustomed to bring it down to Sinope before the emporium of the Ephesians penetrated as far as those people. It is said that slabs of crystal and onyx stone were found by the miners of Archelaos near the Galatians. There was also a certain place with white stone, resembling ivory in color and producing something like a not very large whetstone, from which they made the handles of daggers.

Another place yielded lumps of transparent [stone] so large that they were sent abroad. The boundary of Pontos and Kappadokia is a mountainous region parallel to the Tauros, which has its beginnings at the western extremities of Chamanene – where the precipitous fortress of Dasmenda is located – as far east as Laouiansene.

(11) When the Romans, after conquering Antiochos [VIII], first administered Asia and were making friendships and alliances with the peoples and the kings, in other cases they gave this honor to the king alone, but in Kappadokia to him and to the people in common. When the royal family came to an end, the Romans gave them autonomy, according to the agreement of friendship and alliance with the people. Yet those sent on the embassy rejected the freedom – they said that they would not be able to bear it – for they were worthy of being assigned a king. They [the Romans] were astonished that they would renounce freedom, and allowed them to choose by a show of hands whomever they wished from their own. They chose Ariobarzanes [I], but during the third generation his family died out, and Archelaos, although unrelated, was appointed by Antonius.

This is it about Greater Kappadokia. Concerning Rough Kilikia, which was added to it, it is better to discuss it in the section on the whole of Kilikia [14.5.1].

Part 3:   Paphlagonia and Pontos

(1) Mithridates [VI] Eupator was established as king of Pontos, and he held what was bounded by the Halys as far as the Tibaranians and Armenians, as well as that within the Halys as far as Amastris and certain parts of Paphlagonia. He also acquired the coast: its western portion as far as Herakleia (the home of Herakleides the Platonist), and in the opposite direction as far as Kolchis and Lesser Armenia, which he added to Pontos. Pompeius, after putting him down, received this territory within these boundaries. Those parts toward Armenia and around Kolchis he distributed to the dynasts who had fought on his side, and the remainder he divided into eleven political entities and added them to Bithynia, creating a single province from both. He gave the kingship over certain Paphlagonians in the interior to the descendants of Pylaimenes, just as that over the Galatians was to tetrarchs from that family. Later the Roman commanders made different divisions at different times, establishing kings and dynasts, liberating some cities and placing others in the hands of dynasts, and leaving others subject to the Roman people. In what follows let us speak in detail of how it is today, and touch slightly on former times

[C541]

where this is useful. We will begin from Herakleia, the most western place in this region.

(2) Sailing into the Euxine Sea from the Propontis, on the left lies what adjoins Byzantion, which is Thracian and is called "The Left Side of the Pontos." On the right is what adjoins Chalkedon. The first of these is Bithynian, and then it is Mariandynian (some say Kaukonian). Then it is Paphlagonian as far as the Halys, and then Kappadokian (those near the Pontos), and those next as far as Kolchis. All of these are called "The Right Side of the Pontos." [Mithridates VI] Eupator ruled over all this coast, beginning from Kolchis as far as Herakleia, but what was farther, as far as the mouth and Chalkedon, remained with the king of Bithynia. When the kings had been put down, the Romans preserved the same boundaries, so that Herakleia belonged to Pontos, and that which was farther was joined to Bithynia.

(3) That the Bithynians were formerly Mysians, but had their name changed by the Thracians, who were immigrants – the Bithynians and Thynians – is agreed by most, and they put forth as evidence of the Bithynian people that to this day certain people in Thrace are called Maidobithynians, and (about the Thynians) that there is the promontory of Thynias near Apollonia and Salmydessos. The Bebrykians, who settled [C542] here before the Mysians, were also Thracian, as I conjecture. It is said that the Mysians themselves are settlers from those who are today called the Moisians.

(4) Such is what is said. But not everyone agrees about the Mariandynians and Kaukonians. They say that Herakleia is situated among the Mariandynians and is a Milesian foundation, but nothing is said about who they are or where they came from. They do not appear different from these people in dialect or ethnicity, although they are similar to the Bithynians. It seems, then, that this tribe was originally Thracian. Theopompos [F388] says that Mariandynos ruled part of Paphlagonia – which was ruled by many dynasts – and invaded and took possession of the territory of the Bebrykians, but what he had abandoned remained named after himself. It is also said that the Milesians who first founded Herakleia forced the Mariandynians – who had previously held the place – to be Helots, so that they sold them, but not across their boundaries (there was an agreement between them), just as the so-called *mnoia* class served the Cretans and the *penestai* the Thessalians.

(5) It is reported that the Kaukonians settled on the coast next to the Mariandynians, as far as the Parthenios River, having the city of Tieion. Some say that they were Skythians, others certain Makedonians, and others

from the Pelasgians. Something has already been said about this previously [8.3.17]. Kallisthenes [F53] wrote these words in his *Battle Order*, after "Kromna, Aigialos, and the high Erythinoi" [*Iliad* 2.855], putting "the Kaukonians were led by the noble son of Polykles, who lived on their famous lands around the Parthenios River," for they extended from Herakleia and the Mariandynians to the White Syrians (whom we called Kappadokians), and the Kaukonian race around Tieion was as far as the Parthenios, with the Enetians (who held Kytoron), next to them beyond the Parthenios. Even today there are certain Kaukonitians around the Parthenios.

(6) Herakleia is a city with a good harbor, and it is otherwise notable. It has sent forth settlements, for Chersonesos and Kallatis are its settlements. It was autonomous, and then ruled for a while by tyrants, and then gained back its freedom. Later it was ruled by kings. It became subject to the Romans and received a Roman settlement in a portion of the city and territory. Adiatorix, son of Domnekleios, the tetrarch of the Galatians, received from Antonius a portion of the city that the Herakleiotes possessed.   [C543] Slightly before the Aktian matter he attacked the Romans at night and cut their throats, with, as he said, the permission of Antonius. After the victory at Aktion he was led in the triumph and sacrificed along with his son. The city is part of the province of Pontos, which was united with Bithynia.

(7) Several rivers flow between Chalkedon and Herakleia, among which are the Psillis, Kalpas, and Sangarios, which is recorded by the Poet [*Iliad* 3.187, 16.719]. It has its sources near the village of Sangia, about 150 stadia from Pessinous (passing through most of Phrygia Epiktetos and a certain part of Bithynia, so that it is a little more than 300 stadia from Nikomedeia), where the Gallos River joins it, which begins at Modra in Phrygia on the Hellespont. This is the same as Epiktetos, which the Bithynians formerly held. It has increased and has become navigable – although in antiquity it was not navigable – and at its outlets it is the boundary of Bithynia. The island of Thynias also lies off this coast. Aconite is produced in the Herakleiotis. The city is about 1,500 stadia from the Chalkedonian sanctuary and 500 from the Sangarios.

(8) Tieion is a small town that has nothing worth recording except that Philetairos, the founder of the dynasty of Attalid kings, was from there. Then there is the Parthenios River, which is carried through flowery territory and thus received its name. Its sources are in Paphlagonia proper. Then there are Paphlagonia and the Enetians.

Some ask what the Poet means when he says: "The shaggy heart of Pylaimenes led the Paphlagonians from the Enetians, where the race of wild mules is" [*Iliad* 2.851–2], for they say that today no Enetians are visible among the Paphlagonians, although they also say that there is such a village on the Aigialos ten *schoinoi* distant from Amisos. Yet Zenodotos writes "from Enete" and says that it is clearly the Amisos of today, and others that a certain tribe on the border of the Kappadokians made an expedition with the Kimmerians and then were driven out to the Adria. It is generally agreed that the Enetians were the most notable tribe of the Paphlagonians, from which Pylaimenes was, and also that they made the expedition with him in a large group. Having lost their leader, they crossed over to Thrace after the capture of Troy and wandered, coming to what is today Enetike. Some say [C544] that Antenor and his children shared in this expedition and settled at the recess of the Adria, as we have recorded in the Italian section [5.1.4]. It is reasonable that because of this the Enetians disappeared and are not visible in Paphlagonia.

(9) The Halys River is the Paphlagonian boundary to the east, which "flows from the south between the Syrians and Paphlagonians and empties . . . into the sea called the Euxeinos," according to Herodotos [1.6]. By Syrians he means Kappadokians, who are still today called White Syrians, while those outside the Tauros are said to be Syrians. In comparison with those within the Tauros they have a burned appearance, but the former do not, and thus received the extra name. Pindar says that the Amazons "engaged the far-reaching Syrian army" [F173], and thus it is clear that they lived in Themiskyra. Themiskyra is among the Amisenians, which is White Syrian, and after the Halys. On the east, then, the Halys is the boundary of the Paphlagonians. On the south the Phrygians and the Galatians settled among them, on the west the Bithynians and Mariandynians (for the Kaukonian race has been completely destroyed everywhere), and on the north is the Euxeinos. This territory was divided into the part in the interior and that on the sea, each extending from the Halys to Bithynia. [Mithridates VI] Eupator held the coast as far as Herakleia, and also held the nearest part of the interior, parts of which extended across the Halys. The boundary of the province of Pontos has been defined by the Romans as going this far. The remainder was subject to chieftains, even after the end of Mithridates [VI]. We will speak later [12.3.41–2] about the Paphlagonians in the interior, who were not subject to Mithridates [VI]. Now it is proposed to go through the territory subject to him called Pontos.

(10) After the Parthenios River, there is Amastris, named after the woman who founded it. It is situated on a peninsula and has harbors on each side of the isthmus. Amastris was the wife of Dionysios, the tyrant of Herakleia,

and the daughter of Oxyathres, the brother of the Dareios [III] at the time of Alexander. She established the city from four settlements, Sesamos, Kytoron, and Kromna (which Homer records in the Paphlagonian marshalling [*Iliad* 2.853–5]). The fourth is Tios. It promptly revolted from the communality, but the others remain together. Sesamos is called the Akropolis of Amastris. Kytoron was once the emporium of the Sinopeans, named after Kytoros the child of Phrixos, as Ephoros [F185] says. The most [C545] and best boxwood grows in the Amastriane, especially around Kytoron. The Aigialos is a long coast of more than a hundred stadia, and it has a village of the same name. The Poet records it when he says "Kromna, Aigialos, and the high Erythinoi" [*Iliad* 2.855], although some write "Kromna and also Kobialos." They say that the Erythinoi are called the Erythrinoi today from their appearance. They are two rocks. After the Aigialos is Karambis, a large promontory stretching toward the north and the Skythian Chersonesos. We have mentioned it frequently, as well as the Ram's Forehead, which lies opposite it [2.5.22, 7.4.3, 11.2.14]. These make the Euxeinos Sea a double sea. After Karambis are Kinolis, Antikinolis, Abonouteichos (a small city), and Armene, about which there is the proverb "whoever had no work walled Armene." It is a village of the Sinopeans and has a harbor.

(11) Then there is Sinope itself, which is 50 stadia distant from Armene. It is the most notable city in that region. It was founded by the Milesians, who built a fleet there, and it ruled over the sea within the Kyaneai, and shared with the Hellenes in many struggles outside them. It was autonomous for a long time but finally could not preserve its freedom and was taken by siege and enslaved, first by Pharnakes [I], and then by his successors down to [Mithridates VI] Eupator and the Romans who put him down. Eupator was born and raised there, and he gave it special honor and considered it the metropolis of his kingdom. It is well furnished both by nature and foresight, situated on the neck of a certain peninsula with (on either side of the isthmus) harbors, naval stations, and the marvellous *pelamydes* fisheries. We have spoken about them [7.6.2], how the Sinopeans have the second catch and the Byzantines the third. The peninsula is protected all around by promontories with breakers that have hollows in them – as if rocky holes – that are called *choinikides*. They are filled when the sea rises and thus the region is not easy of access (also because the entire surface of the rocks is prickly and not easy for bare feet). Higher up, however, above the city, the ground is fertile and adorned with a variety of field gardens, especially in the suburbs. The city itself is beauti- [C546] fully walled and magnificently adorned with a gymnasium, agora, and stoas. Even so it was taken twice, first by Pharnakes [I], who attacked it suddenly

and unexpectedly, and later by Lucullus and the tyrant who was within it, thus besieged both from inside and outside. Bakchides, who had been established by the king as garrison commander, always suspected some treason from those inside, and was committing many outrages and murders. Thus he made the people weary of either being unable to defend themselves nobly or to agree to an arrangement, and it was taken. Lucullus preserved the other adornments of the city, but took the sphere of Billaros and the *Autolykos* (a work of Sthenis), whom they considered their founder and honored as a god. There was also an oracle of him. It seems that he sailed with Jason and took possession of this place, but later the Milesians, seeing its suitability and the weakness of the inhabitants, appropriated it to themselves and sent settlers. Today it has also received a Roman settlement and a part of the city and the territory are theirs. It is 3,500 stadia from the Hieron, 2,000 from Herakleia, and 700 from Karambis. It has produced excellent men: the philosophers Diogenes the Cynic and Timotheos Paparion, the comic poet Diphilos, and the historian Baton, who wrote the *Persika*.

(12) The outlet of the Halys River is next. It was named from the saltworks [*halai*] that it flows past. Its sources are in Pontic Greater Kappadokia near Kamisene. It is carried with great force toward the west, and then turns toward the north through the Galatians and Paphlagonians, and forms the boundary between them and the White Syrians. The Sinopitis and all the mountainous territory as far as Bithynia, lying above the previously mentioned coast, have wood for ship building that is good and easily transported. The Sinopitis also produces maple and the mountain nut, from which they cut tables. All the farmland above the sea is planted with olives.

(13) After the outlet of the Halys is the Gadilonitis, as far as Saramene, a fertile territory that is level everywhere and has everything. They have sheep that wear skins and produce soft wool, of which there is an exceedingly great scarcity in the whole of Kappadokia and Pontos. It also produces gazelles, which are rare elsewhere. The Amisenians have [part] of this country, but the rest Pompeius gave to Deiotaros [I], as well as that around Pharnakeia and Trapezousia as far as Kolchis and Lesser Armenia. He was made king of these regions, already possessing his ancestral Galatian tetrarchy, that of the Tolistobogians. After his death there have been many successors to him.

[C547]

(14) After Gadilon are Saramene and Amisos, a notable city about 900 stadia distant from Sinope. Theopompos [F389] says that it was first founded by the Milesians ... the ruler of the Kappadokians, enlarged it.

Third, it was settled by Athenokles and the Athenians and had its name changed to Peiraieus. The kings took possession of it, and [Mithridates VI] Eupator adorned it with sanctuaries and built an additional portion. Lucullus besieged it and forced it to surrender, as Pharnakes [II] did later, when he crossed over from Bosporos. It was given its freedom by Caesar the God, and given to the kings by Antonius. Then the tyrant Straton managed it badly. After the Aktian matter it was freed again by Caesar Sebastos, and today it is well composed. In addition to the rest of its beautiful territory, it has Themiskyra – the home of the Amazons – and Sidene.

(15) Themiskyra is a plain, washed on one side by the sea (which is about 60 stadia distant from the city). On the other side it is at the foot of the mountainous territory, which is well wooded and has rivers flowing through it whose sources are in it. A single river, called the Thermodon, is filled by all these and goes through the plain. Another one, almost equal, flows from so-called Phanaroia and goes through the same plain, and is called the Iris. Its sources are in Pontos itself, and it flows through the middle of the city of Pontic Komana and through the Dazimonitis, a prosperous plain, toward the west, and then turns back toward the north past Gazioura itself, an old royal residence, now deserted. It then turns back again toward the east and receives the Skylax and other rivers, and is carried past the wall itself of Amaseia – my home town and a most strongly fortified city – and goes on into Phanaroia. There the Lykos joins it, which has its beginnings in Armenia, and it becomes the Iris itself. Then Themiskyra receives the stream, and the Pontic Sea. Because of this, the plain is always moist and grassy, and can support herds of both cattle and horses. It allows the sowing of a great amount of millet and grains, even unlimited in quantity. The abundance of water greatly surpasses any drought, so that [C548] there is never any famine touching these people, not even once. The territory on the side of the mountain produces such fruit – natural and wild – including grapes, pear, apples, and nuts, that at any time of the year those who go into the woods can easily obtain enough, for at one time the fruit still hangs from the trees and at another lies on the fallen leaves or beneath them, which are deep and have dropped in profusion. Also numerous are the catches of all kinds of wild animals, because of the abundance of nourishment.

(16) After Themiskyra is the Sidene, a prosperous plain, although not as well watered. It has fortified territory on the coast, including Side (from which the Sidene was named), Chabaka, and Phabda. The Amisene extends this far. It has produced men worthy of recording because of their education: the mathematicians Demetrios son of Rhathenos and Dionysodoros

(who had the same name as the ... geometrician[4]), and the grammarian Tyrannion, whom I heard lecture.

(17) After the Sidene is Pharnakeia, a fortified town, and after it Trapezous, a Hellenic city, to which the voyage from Amisos is about 2,200 stadia. From there to Phasis it is about 1,400, so that all together from the Hieron to Phasis it is about 8,000 stadia, slightly more or less. As one sails on this coast from Amisos, the Herakleian Cape is first, then another cape, Iasonion, and Genetes, then the town of Kotyoros, from which Pharnakeia was settled, then Ischopolis, which is in ruins, then a gulf, on which are the moderate settlements of Kerasous and Hermonassa, then (near Hermonassa) Trapezous, and then Kolchis. Somewhere around here is the settlement called Zygopolis. Kolchis and the coast lying above it have already been described [11.2.14–15].

(18) Lying above Trapezous and Pharnakeia are the Tibaranians, Chaldaians, Sannians (formerly called the Makronians), and Lesser Armenia. The Appaitians, who were formerly the Kerkitians, are in the general vicinity of these regions. Extending through them is Skydises, an exceedingly rugged mountain that adjoins the Moschian Mountains above Kolchis (whose heights are occupied by the Heptakometians), and also Paryadres, which extends as far as Lesser Armenia from the places [C549] around Sidene and Themiskyra, making the eastern side of the Pontos. All the mountaineers are completely wild, but the Heptakometians exceed the others. Some of them live in trees or towers, because of which the ancients called them the Mosynoikians, as they called towers *mosynoi*. They live on the flesh of wild animals and tree fruit, and they attack travellers, leaping down on them from their scaffolds. The Heptakometians cut down three of Pompeius' maniples when they were passing through the mountainous territory, for they mixed bowls of malignant honey that is produced by the branches of trees, and set it out. When the men drank it they were driven mad, and were attacked and easily killed. Some of these barbarians were called Byzerians.

(19) The Chaldaians of today were named the Chalybians in antiquity. Pharnakeia is situated exactly opposite them, and since it is on the sea it is well situated for *pelamydes* fishing, for it is here that they are first caught. There are mines on this land, today iron but earlier silver. The seacoast in this area is on the whole extremely narrow, for the mountains – full of mines and forest – lie immediately above. Not much of it is farmed. The livelihood

---

[4] The manuscripts have "*hikeni*," which is not a known toponym.

from the mines remains for the miners, and the fishing for those working on the sea, especially *pelamydes* and dolphins, for the latter follow the groups of fish – *kordyle*, tuna, and the *pelamydes* themselves – and become fat and easy to catch because they rather rashly come near to the land and are enticed by bait. These are the only ones who cut up dolphins and use their great amount of fat for everything.

(20) I believe these are the ones whom the Poet calls Halizonians ("Those Living on the Sea"), in the *Catalogue of the Paphlagonians*: "Odios and Epistrophos led the Halizonians, from far-away Alybe, where the birthplace of silver is" [*Iliad* 2.856–7], with the wording changed from "far-away Chalybe," for formerly the people could have been Alybians, instead of Chalybians, but it is not possible today that they were called Chaldaians (from Chalybians), if formerly they were not Chalybians instead of Albyians, even accepting that there are many changes of name, especially among barbarians. Some of the Thracians were called Sintians, then Sintans, and then Saians, among whom Archilochos says that he threw away his shield: "one of the Saians is adorned with my shield, which I unwillingly left, blameless, beside a bush" [F5]. The same are now named [C550] Sapaians, and all of them have their home around Abdera and the island of Lemnos. Similarly the Brygians, Brigians, and Phrygians are the same, and the Mysians, Moisians, Maionians, and Meionians, but it is not necessary to go further. The Skepsian [F45] is suspicious of the change from Alybians to Chalybians, for he does not consider what follows and what is in harmony with it (especially why he [Homer] calls the Chalybians Halizonians), and rejects the opinion. Let us contrast and compare our [opinion] with his, and consider the assumptions of others.

(21) Some change the text to Alazonians, and others make it Amazons. For "from Alybe" they have "from Alope" or "from Alobe," assuming that the Skythians beyond the Borysthenes are Alazonians, Kallipidians, and other names that Hellanikos [F186], Herodotos [4.17] and Eudoxos [F345] keep on chattering to us about. Ephoros [F114a] – whose home was near Kyme – considers that the Amazons are between Mysia, Karia, and Lydia. This is perhaps a reasonable opinion, for he may be talking about what was later settled by the Aiolians and Ionians, and previously the Amazons. They say that there are certain cities named for them: Ephesos, Smyrna, Kyme, and Myrina. But how could Albye – or, as with some, Alope or Alobe – be considered among these places? How about "far away"? How about "the birthplace of silver"?

(22) This he [Ephoros] solves by changing the words, writing as follows: "Odios and Epistrophos led the Amazons and came from Alope, where the

Amazons were born" [*Iliad* 2.856–7, rewritten]. But in solving this he has fallen into another fiction, because Alope is found nowhere nearby, and his change of the text and writing contrary to the old tradition seems to be such capriciousness. The Skepsian does not accept this opinion, nor that of those who assume it to be the Halizonians around Pallene, whom we recorded in the Makedonian section. He is also in doubt as to how anyone could come from the nomads around the Borysthenes to be allies of the Trojans, and he approves especially of the opinions of Hekataios the Milesian, Menekrates the Elaian (a man who is identified with Xenokrates) and Palaiphatos. The first of these says in his *Circuit of the Earth*: "Then the city of Alazia. The Odrysses River flows from the west, out of Lake Daskylitis through the plain of Mygdonia, and empties into the Rhyndakos" [F217]. He

[C551] also says that Alazia is deserted today, but that many villages of the Alazonians are inhabited, through which the Odrysses flows, and in these Apollo is particularly honored, especially on the border of the Kyzikenians. Menekrates [F3] in his *Circuit of the Hellespontic Regions* says that lying above the territory of Myrleia there is an adjoining mountainous district where the Halizonian people live. It is necessary, he says, to write it with two lambdas, but because of the meter the Poet writes it with one. Palaiphatos [F4] says that it was from the Alazonians who lived in Alope (but now in Zeleia) that Odios and Epistrophos made their expedition. How can one give approval to their opinions? Apart from the fact that they move away from the old wording, they do not point out the silver mines (which are in the Myrleatis), or how those who went from there to Ilion were from "far away," even if one were to grant that there actually was an Alope or Alazia, which are much nearer to the Troad than the places around Ephesos. Demetrios [the Skepsian, F45] says that those who say the Amazons are around Pygela – between Ephesos, Magnesia, and Priene – talk nonsense, for "far away" does not suit that region. How much more unsuited it is to the region of Mysia and Teuthrania.

(23) By Zeus, he says that certain things must be accepted as having been inserted improperly, such as "from far Askania" [*Iliad* 2.863], and "Arnaios was his name, which his august mother gave him" [*Odyssey* 18.5], and Penelope "took the curved key in her thick hand" [*Odyssey* 21.6]. Let this be granted. But one cannot grant what Demetrios suggests in making a believable reply to those who must say "from far-away Chalybe," for if he agrees that even if the silver mines are not among the Chalybians of today, it is possible that they once did exist. Yet he does not agree that they were famous and notable, like the iron mines. One might ask what would prevent them from being famous like the iron mines? Can an abundance

of iron make a place capable of being distinctive, but not silver? If the silver mines had become famous, not in the time of the heroes but of Homer, how could anyone censure the decision of the Poet? How could their reputation have come to the Poet? How about the copper mines at Temese in Italiotis [*Odyssey* 1.184], or the wealth of Thebes in Egypt [*Iliad* 9.381–2; *Odyssey* 4.126–7], although he was about twice the distance from Thebes in Egypt than from the Chaldaians? But he [Demetrios the Skepsian] does not even agree with those whom he advocates. In fixing the topography around   [C552] Skepsis, his home town, he says that the village of Ainea, as well as Argyria and Alazonion, are near Skepsis and the Aisepos. These places, if they exist, would be near the sources of the Aisepos, but Hekataios says that they are beyond its outlets. Palaiphatos, who says that they formerly lived in Alope, but now in Zeleia, does not say the same as the others. If Menekrates does, he does not point out what Alope or Alobe – or however they wish to write it – are, and neither does Demetrios himself.

(24) Apollodoros [of Athens] discusses the same topic in his *Trojan Marshalling* [F171] and much has been said previously on this [7.3.6], but it is necessary to speak about it now. He does not think one must accept that the Halizonians are outside the Halys, for no allies came to the Trojans from the far side of the Halys. First, we must inquire of him who are the Halizonians within the Halys, "from far-away Alybe, where the birthplace of silver is" [*Iliad* 2.857]? He will be unable to say. Then what is the reason he does not concede that some allies came from the far side? If all the others happened to be within the river, except for the Thracians, nothing would prevent these alone coming from the far side, from beyond the White Syrians. Or was it possible for those fighting against them to cross over from both these places and from ones still beyond – as they say that the Amazons, Trerians, and Kimmerians did – yet those who were their allies could not? The Amazons were not allies, because Priamos, as an ally of the Phrygians, had fought against them:

> then they were camped on the banks of the Sangarios ... on the day when the Amazons came, a match for men. [*Iliad* 3.187, 189]

Priamos says "as I was their ally, I was numbered among them" [*Iliad* 3.188]. Those bordering them were not far enough away to make a difficulty when they [the Trojans] sent for help, and thus, as I believe, there was no underlying enmity to prevent an alliance.

(25) He [Apollodoros of Athens] should not have had such an opinion about the ancient sources, saying that all of them together agreed that no one from the far side of the Halys joined in the Trojan War. One could find

evidence to the contrary. At any rate, Maiandrios [F4] says that the Enetians set out from the White Syrians and became allies of the Trojans, and that they went away with the Thracians and settled around the recess of the Adria, but the Enetians who did not share in the expedition became Kappadokians. It might seem to be in agreement with this account [C553] that all of Kappadokia near the Halys extending along Paphlagonia uses two languages that are abundant in Paphlagonian names: Bagas, Biasas, Ainiates, Atotes, Zardokes, Tiberos, Gassys, Olgassys, and Maes. These names are common in Babamonitis, Pimolisitis, Gazalouitis, Gazakene, and most of the other regions. Apollodoros [of Athens] himself reproduces what Zenodotos wrote: "from Enete, where the race of wild mules is" [*Iliad* 2.852, revised], and he says that Hekataios the Milesian [F199] takes it as Amisos. But it has been stated [12.3.9] that Amisos is White Syrian and outside the Halys.

(26) It is also stated by him [Apollodoros of Athens, F157b] somewhere that the Poet had heard about the Paphlagonians in the interior from some who had passed through the country on foot, but he was ignorant of the coast (as well as the rest of the Pontic [coast]) for he would have named it. On the contrary, one can come back and say, from the circuit that has now been laid out and explained, that he went over the entire coast, leaving out nothing that was worth recording at that time. If he does not speak of Herakleia, Amastris, and Sinope, which had not yet been founded, it is not remarkable, and it is not extraordinary if he does not speak of the interior. Moreover, his failure to name many of the known places is not a sign of ignorance, as we have previously indicated [1.2.14, 19; 7.3.6–7; 8.3.8]. He [Apollodoros of Athens] says that he was ignorant of many things around the Pontos – such as rivers and peoples – for he would have named them. One might grant this in regard to certain very remarkable things such as the Skythians, the Maiotis, and the Istros. He would not have spoken about the nomads through their characteristics – such as "Milk Drinkers and the Abians, the most just of men" [*Iliad* 13.6], and the "noble Mare Milkers" [*Iliad* 13.5] – yet fail to say that they were Skythians, Sauromatians or Sarmatians (if they were so named by the Hellenes) nor (when he mentions the Thracians and the Mysians near the Istros [*Iliad* 13.4–5]) pass by the greatest of rivers in silence, especially when he is inclined to mark the boundaries of places by rivers, nor, in speaking about the Kimmerians [*Odyssey* 11.14] pass by the Bosporos and the Maiotis.

(27) But regarding those that are not so remarkable – neither at that time nor in regard to his material – how could one find fault? For example, there is the Tanais, which is known for no other reason than it is the boundary

between Asia and Europe. But at that time neither Europe or Asia had been   [C554]
named, nor had the inhabited world been divided into three continents, for
he would have named them somewhere, because they were exceedingly
remarkable, as is Libya and the Lips, the wind that blows from the west of
Libya. But the continents had not yet been determined and thus it was not
necessary to record the Tanais. Many things were worthy of recording, but
he did not make use of them, for there is a great nature of casual occurrence
in words and deeds.

From all this it is clear that everyone who makes a judgement from the
failure of the Poet to mention what he is ignorant about is using fallacies as
evidence. It is necessary to refute this fallaciousness through a number of
examples, for many make great use of them. They must be stopped when
they bring such things forward, even if we repeat what has been said. In
regard to rivers, if anyone were to say that he was ignorant of one because he
does not name it, we will say that his argument is simplistic. He does not
name the Meles River, which flows past Smyrna, said by most to be his
home town, although he names the Hermos and Hyllos [*Iliad* 20.392].
There is no Paktolos, which empties into the same stream as these two and
begins from Tmolos, which he does record [*Iliad* 2.866, 20.385]. He does
not speak of Smyrna itself, nor the other Ionian cities, nor most of the
Aiolian ones, but speaks of Miletos, Samos, Lesbos, and Tenedos, but
not the Lethaios, which flows past Magnesia, nor the Marsyas, both of
which empty into the Maiandros (which he names [*Iliad* 2.869]), as well as
[naming] "the Rhesos, Heptaporos, Karesos, Rhodios" [*Iliad* 12.20],
and others, most of which are no more than streams. He names many
territories and cities, some mentioned along with rivers and mountains,
and others without [them]. At any rate he does not mention those in Aitolia
or Attika, or a number of other places. If he mentioned those that were
far away and did not record those quite near, surely he was not ignorant
of them, as they were known to others. It is the same with the nearer
[peoples], some of which he names and others he does not, such as the
Lykians and Solymians but not the Milyans, Pamphylians, or Pisidians; the
Paphlagonians, Phrygians, and Mysians but not the Mariandynians, nor
Thynians, Bithynians, or Bebrykians. He mentions the Amazons but not
the White Syrians, Syrians, Kappadokians, or Lykaonians; yet he repeatedly
mentions the Phoenicians, Egyptians, and Aithiopians. He speaks about the   [C555]
Aleian Plain and the Arimoi but is silent about their peoples. Such a test,
then, is false, but it is true only when it shows that he has said something
false. He [Apollodoros of Athens] has not been shown to be correct in
having the confidence to say that the noble Mare Milkers and Milk

Drinkers were fantasies. So much for Apollodoros. I return to the next part of the circuit.

(28) Above the places around Pharnakeia and Trapezous are the Tibarenians and the Chaldaians, who extend to Lesser Armenia. This territory, like Sophene, is sufficiently prosperous and was always held by the dynasts, who at times were friendly to the other Armenians and at times acted independently. They had as subjects the Chaldaians and Tibarenians, and thus their sovereignty extended to Trapezous and Pharnakeia. When Mithridates [VI] Eupator increased in power, he established himself as the master both of Kolchis and all these places, which were yielded to him by Antipatros son of Sisis. He cared so much for these places that he constructed seventy-five fortresses in them, where he entrusted most of his treasure. The most notable of these were Hydara, Basgoidariza, and Sinoria (close to the borders of the territory of Greater Armenia, which is why Theophanes [F7] changed the name to Synoria ["Border Land"]). The entire mountainous territory of the Paryadres has many suitable places, as it is well watered and wooded, broken up in many places by sheer ravines and cliffs. It was here that most of the fortified treasuries were built. Finally, with the invasion of Pompeius, Mithridates [VI] fled into these farthest parts of the Pontic kingdom. He seized a well-watered mountain near Dasteira in Akisilene. The Euphrates was nearby, which separates Akisilene from Lesser Armenia. He lived there until he was besieged and forced to flee through the mountains to Kolchis, and from there to the Bosporos. Pompeius founded the city of Nikopolis near this place, in Lesser Armenia, and it survives today and is well populated.

(29) Lesser Armenia was held by different peoples at different times – whomever the Romans wished – and finally by Archelaos. The Tibarenians and the Chaldaians as far as Kolchis, and Pharnakeia and Trapezous, are held by Pythodoris, a wise woman capable of managing the government. [C556] She is the daughter of Pythodoros of Tralleis, and became the wife of Polemon [I], reigning with him for a time. When he died, she succeeded to the rule among the so-called Aspourgianians, the barbarians around Sindike. She had two sons with Polemon, and a daughter, who was given to Kotys [VIII] the Sapaian, but he was treacherously killed. She remained a widow, since she had had children with him. The oldest is now in power. One of the sons of Pythodoris is now, as a private individual, administering the state with his mother, and the other has recently been established as king of Greater Armenia. She married Archelaos and remained with him until the end, but is now a widow, possessing the territories already mentioned and others more elegant, which we will discuss next.

(30) Sidene and Themiskyra adjoin Pharnakeia. Above them lies Phanaroia, which is the strongest part of Pontos, planted in olives and abundant in wine and every other virtue. On its eastern portion it is protected by Paryadres, with its length parallel to it, and on the west by the Lithros and Ophlimos. It is a valley notable in its length and width. The Lykos flows through it from Armenia, and the Iris from the narrows around Amaseia. They both come together around the middle of the valley, and at the junction a city, Eupatoria, is located, named after the one who first subjugated it. Pompeius found it half finished and added territory and settlers to it, calling it Magnopolis. It lies in the middle of the plain, and Kabeira is situated on the actual side of the Paryadres about 150 stadia farther south than Magnopolis, the same that Amaseia is farther west. At Kabeira the palace of Mithridates [VI] was constructed, as well as the water mill and menagerie, and nearby were the hunting grounds and mines.

(31) Also here is what is called the New Place, a rock that is naturally fortified and sheer, less than 200 stadia distant from Kabeira. On its summit is a spring that sends up much water, and a river and a deep ravine at its base. The height of the rock is immense ... of the neck, so that it cannot be besieged. It has been remarkably walled, except for what the Romans pulled down. Everywhere all around is thickly forested, mountainous, and waterless, so that it is impossible to make an encampment within 120 stadia. The most valuable treasures of Mithridates [VI] were here, which are now located on the Capitolium, a dedication of Pompeius. [C557]

Pythodoris has this entire territory, which is adjacent to the barbarian [territory] that is held by her. Pompeius had made Kabeira into a city called Diospolis, and she built further in it, and changed its name to Sebaste, using the city as a royal residence. It also has the sanctuary of Men of Pharnakes [I], as it is called, the village city of Ameria, which has many temple slaves and a sacred territory, whose crops are always consecrated. The kings honored this sanctuary so greatly that they declared what was called their royal oath as "By the fortune of the king and the Men of Pharnakes." There is also a sanctuary of Selene, similar to the ones among the Albanians and in Phrygia, that of Men in the place of the same name, of Askaios near Antiocheia (near Pisidia), and that in the land of the Antiocheians.

(32) Above Pharnaroia is Komana in Pontos, having the same name as the one in greater Kappadokia, consecrated to the same goddess and copied after it. The method that they have used in their sacred rites, divine inspiration, and the honor shown to their priests, is almost the same, especially in the time of the earlier kings, when twice a year during the so-called Procession

of the Goddess the priest would wear a diadem and be second in honor after the king.

(33) Previously I mentioned [10.4.10] Dorylaos the military tactician, who was the great-grandfather of my mother, and another Dorylaos – his nephew and the son of Philetairos – who received all the greatest honors from [Mithridates VI] Eupator, especially the priesthood at Komana. He was discovered instigating a revolt in the kingdom in favor of the Romans, and was overthrown and his family was accused with him. After a long time Moaphernes, my mother's uncle, became distinguished (just before the kingdom was dissolved), but again he – and his friends – were unfortunate along with the king, except for some who had previously revolted, such as my grandfather. He saw that things were going badly for the king in the war against Lucullus, but at the same time because of anger he was alienated from the former, who had recently put to death his cousin Tibeios and his son Theophilos. Thus he set out to avenge both them and himself. Taking [C558] assurances from Lucullus, he handed over fifteen fortresses. Great promises were made in return for this, but when Pompeius, his successor in the war, went there, he considered all who had favored the former as his enemies, because of the hatred that had developed between them. He finished the war and returned home with such a victory that the honors Lucullus had promised to certain Pontians were not approved by the Senate. It was considered unjust that when the war had been successfully completed by one person, the prizes and the distribution of awards should be handled by another.

(34) Komana was administered in the way described at the time of the kings. When Pompeius received the authority, he appointed Archelaos priest and included with the sanctuary a circuit of two *schoinoi* and ordered those living there to obey his rule. He was their commander, and master of the temple slaves who lived in the city, except that he could not sell them (they were no less than 6,000 here). He was the son of the Archelaos who had been honored by Sulla and the Senate, and was also a friend of Gabinius, a certain consular. When the latter was sent to Syria, he [Archelaos] also went there in the hope of sharing in his preparations for a Parthian war, but the Senate would not allow this. He set aside this hope and found a greater one. It happened that Ptolemaios [XII], the father of Kleopatra [VII], had been banished by the Egyptians, and his daughter, the older sister of Kleopatra, held the kingdom. A man from a royal family was being sought for her, and he offered himself to her agents, pretending to be a son of Mithridates [VI] Eupator. He was accepted but ruled only six months. Gabinius killed him in battle during the restoration of Ptolemaios [XII].

(35) His son succeeded to the priesthood, and then later Lykomedes, who was assigned an additional 400 *schoinoi*. Now he has been deposed and it is held by Dyteutos the son of Adiatorix, who seems to have received the honor from Caesar Sebastos because of his distinction. Caesar led Adiatorix in triumph, along with his wife and children, and resolved to do away with him and the oldest of his children. He [Dyteutos] was the oldest. The second oldest of the brothers said to the soldiers leading them away that he was the oldest. There was a quarrel between the two of them for a long time, until the parents persuaded Dyteutos to yield victory to the younger, for given the age of the former, he would be a more suitable guardian for his mother and the remaining brother. Thus [the younger] was put to death with his father and [the elder] was saved and given the honor. When Caesar learned about this – after the men had already been done away with – he was upset and considered the survivors worthy of kindness and attention, and gave them this honor. [C559]

(36) Komana is populous and a notable emporium for those from Armenia. At the time of the Procession of the Goddess people come together from everywhere for the festival, from the cities and the territory, men and women. Others, because of a certain vow, always live there, performing sacrifices for the goddess. The inhabitants live luxuriously, with all their property planted with vines. There is a large number of women who work with their bodies, most of whom are consecrated. In a certain way the city is a lesser Corinth, for there also, because of the large number of hetairas, who were consecrated to Aphrodite, many visitors would come for a holiday at the place. The merchants and soldiers would exhaust their funds completely, so that this proverb arose: "the voyage to Corinth is not for all men." This is it about Komana.

(37) Pythodoris holds all of the surrounding area, including Phanaroia, Zelitis, and Megalopolitis. Phanaroia has been discussed [12.3.30–1]. The Zelitis has the city of Zela, which is fortified on a mound of Semiramis and has the sanctuary of Anaitis, whom the Armenians also revere. The sacred rites here are performed with a greater ritual, and here all the Pontians make their oaths concerning the greatest things. The large number of temple slaves and the honors of the priests were, in the time of the kings, of the same type as we have previously stated, but today everything is dependent on Pythodoris. Many had mistreated and reduced the amount of both the temple slaves and other resources. The surrounding territory was also reduced, having been divided into a number of dominions (the so-called Zelitis), for in antiquity the kings administered Zela not as a city but as a sanctuary of the Persian gods, with the priest as master of everything. It was

inhabited by the large number of temple slaves and the priest, who had a great abundance. The sacred territory of the priest and the many around

him were subject to him. Pompeius included many provinces within the boundaries of the place and named it and Megalopolis cities, bringing together into one the latter, Kouloupene and Kamisene (which border on Lesser Armenia), and Laouiansene. It has both excavated salt and the ancient fortress of Kamisa, which is destroyed today. Later the Roman commanders assigned part of these two states to the priest of Komana, part to the priest of Zela, and part to Ateporix, a certain dynast who was a man of the family of the tetrarchs of Galatia, but since he has died, his portion – which was not large – is subject to the Romans and is called a province. This little town is a government in itself, having Karana joined with it, from which the territory is called Karanitis. The remainder is held by Pythodoris and Dyteutos.

(38) What remains is the part of Pontos between this territory and that of the Amisenians and Sinopians, which extends toward Kappadokia, the Galatians, and the Paphlagonians. After the Amisenians is Phazemonitis (as far as the Halys), which Pompeius named Neapolitis, proclaiming the settlement at the village of Phazemon a city and naming it Neapolis. Gadilotos and the land of the Amisenians enclose it on the northern side of this territory, the Halys on the western side, Phanaroia on the eastern side, and on the remainder my land of the Amasians, which is the largest and the best. The portion of Phazemonitis toward Phanaroia contains a lake that is the size of a sea, called Stiphane, abundant in fish and having plentiful pasturage of every kind all around. A strong fortress is situated on it, Ikizari, today deserted, and nearby is a destroyed royal residence. The remaining territory is pasture land and is greatly productive of grain. Lying above the territory of the Amasians are the hot springs of the Phazemonitians, which are exceedingly healthful, and Sagylion, which has a fortress located on a steep and high mountain that extends up to a sharp peak. It has an abundant reservoir, which is now neglected, although it was useful to the kings for many reasons. Here Arsakes, one of the sons of King Pharnakes [II] was captured and put to death. He was acting as a dynast and attempting revolution without the permission of the commanders. He was not captured by force (although the fortress was taken by Polemon [I] and Lykomedes, both kings), but by hunger, for he fled up the mountain without preparations and was shut out of the plains. He found the reservoirs closed up with great rocks, something Pompeius

had undertaken, who had ordered that the fortresses be destroyed and not left useful for those wishing to flee up into them for brigandage. He arranged the Phazemonitis in this way, but later it was distributed among the kings.

(39) My city lies in a large and deep valley, through which the Iris is carried. By foresight and nature it is marvellously furnished, as it can be useful simultaneously as a city and a fortress. It is on a high rock that is steep all around and which falls down to the river, having the wall on the edge of the river where the city is located, and then it runs up either side to the peaks, which are two, naturally joined to one another and beautifully furnished with towers. Within this peribolos are the royal palace and the memorials of the kings. The peaks have a neck that is exceedingly narrow, and five or six stadia in height on either side, as one goes up from the river bank to the suburbs. From the neck to the peaks there remains a further approach of a stadion, which is sharp and superior to all kinds of force. There are reservoirs within it, whose [supply] cannot be taken away since two pipes have been cut, one toward the river and the other toward the neck. There are bridges across the river, one from the city to the suburbs and the other from the suburbs to the territory outside, for the mountain lying above the rock leaves off at this bridge. There is a valley extending from the river, not very wide at first, but later it widens out and creates the so-called Plain Of a Thousand Villages. Then there are Diakopene and Pimolisene, all fertile territory, as far as the Halys. This is the northern part of the Amasian territory, a length of about five hundred stadia. Next is the remainder, much longer than this, as far as Babamonon and the Ximene, the latter extending as far as the Halys. This is the length of it, and the width from north to south is to Zelitis and Greater Kappadokia, as far as the Trokmians. In the Ximene there are salt works [*halai*] where salt is excavated, from which it is inferred that the Halys River was named. There are a number of demolished fortresses in our territory, and much deserted land, because of the Mithridatic War. Nevertheless it is all well forested, with horse pasturing, and also suitable for other domesticated animals, and all beautifully inhabitable. Amaseia was given to the kings but today it is a province.

(40) There remains the territory of the Pontic province within the Halys that is around Olgassys, which adjoins the Sinopis. Mount Olgassys is [C562] extremely high and impassable. The Paphlagonians hold the sanctuaries that have been established everywhere on the mountain. There is fairly good territory around it, Blaene and Domanitis, through which the Amnias River flows. Here Mithridates [VI] Eupator completely destroyed the power of Nikomedes [IV] of Bithynia, although he was not present, but through his commanders. Although he [Nikomedes] safely fled with a few to his

homeland and then sailed to Italia, he was followed and Bithynia was taken in an attack, as well as Asia as far as Karia and Lykia. A city was created here, Pompeioupolis. There are realgar works in it, not far away from Pimolisa, a royal fortress that has been razed, from which the territory on the other side of the river is called the Pimolisene. The realgar works are a hollow mountain, because of the mining, and the works have excavated great passages under it. The works were publicly owned, and slaves sold in the agora because of their crimes were used as miners. In addition to the painfulness of the work, they say that the air in the mines is deadly and hard to bear because of the heavy odor of the lumps, so that the workers have a quick death. Moreover, the mine is often abandoned because of its unprofitability, as the more than two hundred workmen are continually used up by disease and death. This is what can be said about Pontos.

(41) After Pompeioupolis is the remainder of the interior of Paphlagonia, extending toward the west as far as Bithynia. It is small, and had a number of rulers shortly before our time. Now the Romans possess it, as the family of kings has died out. That which borders Bithynia is named Timonitis, the territory of Gezatorix, and Marmolitis, as well as Sanisene and Potamia. There was also a certain Kimiatene, in which Kimiata was, a strong fortress lying below the mountainous region of Olgassys, which was used by Mithridates [I] called Ktistes as his base when he established himself as master of Pontos, and his succession was preserved as far as [Mithridates VI] Eupator. The last ruler of Paphlagonia was Deiotaros [IV] the son of Kastor [II], surnamed Philadelphos, who held Gangra, the royal residence of Morzeos, both a small town and a fortress.

(42) Eudoxos [F329] says that fish are excavated in dry places in Paphlagonia, but he does not distinguish the place, and he says [F335] that they come from moist places around the Askanian Lake, below Kios, but he does not say anything clear.

Since I am expounding on the part of Paphlagonia that borders on Pontos, and the Bithynians border the Paphlagonians toward the west, I will attempt to go over them. Then, taking another beginning from there and the Paphlagonians, I will weave together those that are next toward the south as far as the Tauros, parallel to Pontos and Kappadokia, for such an order and division is indicated by their nature.

Part 4: Bithynia

(1) The Paphlagonians, Mariandynians, and some of the Epiktetians are the boundary of Bithynia on the east, the Pontic Sea on the north (from the

outlets of the Sangarios as far as the mouth at Byzantion and Chalkedon), on the west the Propontis, and toward the south Mysia and Phrygia called Epiktetos (the same is called Hellespontine Phrygia).

(2) Chalkedon, a Megarian foundation, is situated at the mouth of the Pontos, as well as the village of Chrysopolis and the Chalkedonian sanctuary. The territory has a spring, Azaritia, slightly above the sea, where small crocodiles are reared. Then the so-called Astakenian Gulf follows the Chalkedonian shore (a part of the Propontis), on which Nikomedeia was founded, named after one of the Bithynian kings who founded it. Many were given the same name, just as with the Ptolemies, because of the reputation of the first. On the gulf itself is the city of Astakos, a foundation of the Megarians and Athenians, and later of Doidalses, and after which the gulf was named. It was razed by Lysimachos and the inhabitants transferred to Nikomedeia by its founder.

(3) Continuous with the Astakenian is another gulf that stretches more toward the rising sun, on which Prousias is, formerly called Kios. Philippos [V], the son of Demetrios and the father of Perseus, razed Kios, and gave it to Prousias [I] the son of Zelas, who had assisted in razing both it and Myrleia, a neighboring city that is also near Prousa. He restored it from the ruins and named it Kios Prousias after himself, and [named] Myrleia after his wife Apameia. This is the Prousias who received Hannibal, who withdrew there after the defeat of Antiochos [III], having removed himself from Hellespontine Phrygia through an agreement with the Attalids. It was formerly called Lesser Phrygia, but they called it Epiktetos ["Acquired"]. A mountain lies above Prousias, called Arganthonion. Here there is the myth of Hylas, one of the companions of Herakles, who sailed with him on the Argo and who, when going out for water, was seized by nymphs. Kios – also a companion of Herakles and on the voyage with him – returned from Kolchis and remained here, establishing the city named after him. A kind of festival is still celebrated today among the Prousians, in which they wander through the mountains celebrating Bakchic rites and calling upon Hylas, as though making an expedition into the woods seeking him. The Prousians were well-disposed toward the Roman government and received their freedom, and the Apameians accepted a Roman settlement. Prousa is situated on Mysian Olympos and is a well-ordered city, on the boundary of Phrygia and Mysia, and was founded by the Prousias who made war against Kroisos. [C564]

(4) It is difficult to determine the boundaries between the Bithynians, Phrygians, and Mysians, and even the Dolionians around Kyzikos, and the Mygdonians and Trojans. Thus it must be agreed that each tribe is apart from the others. In regard to the Phrygians and Mysians there is the proverb

"the boundaries of the Mysians and Phrygians are apart," and it is difficult to determine them. The reason is that the foreigners there – barbarians and soldiers – did not hold what they conquered firmly, but were mostly wanderers, driving others out and being driven out. One might conjecture that all these peoples were Thracian, because they inhabited the opposite side and because those on either side are not much different.

(5) Nevertheless, as much as can be conjectured, one might put Mysia in between Bithynia and the outlet of the Aisepos, touching the sea and extending as far as almost all of Olympos, with Epiktetos lying around it in the interior but nowhere touching the sea and stretching as far as the eastern part of the Askanian Lake and territory (the lake and territory are called by the same name). Part of this was Phrygian and part Mysian, but the Phrygian was farther from Troy. One must understand the Poet, when he says, "Phorkys and godlike Askanios led the Phrygians from far Askania" [*Iliad* 2.862–3], as [referring to] the Phrygian one, near present Nikaia, since there is another Askania, the Mysian one, which he records when he says

> Palmys, Askanios, and Morys the son of Hippotion, leader of the Mysians, the hand-to-hand fighters, who came as relief from Askania with its large clods. [*Iliad* 13.792–4]

It is not remarkable that he speaks of a certain Askanios as leader of the Phrygians from Askania, and then mentions another Askanios as leader of the Mysians from Askania, for having the same name is frequent with him, as well as surnames from rivers, lakes, and places.

(6) The Poet himself gives the Aisepos as the boundary of the Mysians, for after cataloguing the region on the Trojan mountainside above Ilion that was subject to Aineias, which he calls Dardania, he puts Lykia next to the north, which was subject to Pandaros, and in which Zeleia is. And he says

> those who inhabited Zeleia, under the lowest foot of Ida, wealthy Trojans, who drink the black water of the Aisepos. [*Iliad* 2.824–6]

Lying below Zeleia and near the sea, on this side of the Aisepos, are the Adrasteian Plain, Tereia, and Pitya (generally the Kyzikene of today near Priapos), which he catalogues next. Then he returns back to the parts toward the west and on the opposite side, indicating that he believes what is as far as the Aisepos is the northern and eastern limit of the Troad. Mysia and Olympos are after the Troad.

Ancient memory suggests this is the position of the peoples. But today many changes have resulted because there have been different masters at different times, some bringing some together and others separating others. The Phrygians and the Mysians were the masters after the sack of Troy, and later the Lydians, along with the Aiolians and Ionians, and then the Persians and Makedonians, and finally the Romans, under whom most have lost their dialects and their names, since the territory has been divided differently. But one must rather consider these matters when speaking of how things are now, and also to pay proper attention to ancient history.

(7) In the interior of Bithynia are Bithynion, which lies above Tieion and possesses the territory around Salon (where the best pasturage for cattle is and the Salonitic cheese is from) and Nikaia, the metropolis of Bithynia, on Lake Askania, surrounded by a large and especially fertile plain that is not at all healthy in summer. It was a foundation of Antigonos [I] the son of Philippos, who called it Antigoneia, and then of Lysimachos, who changed the name to that of his wife, Nikaia, the daughter of Antipatros. The circuit of the city is 16 stadia, in the shape of a tetragon. It has four towers and is situated in a plain, divided by streets at right angles so that from a single [C566] stone situated in the middle of the gymnasium one can see the four gates. The small town of Otroia is slightly above Lake Askania, toward the east on the borders of Bithynia. It is conjectured that Otroiai was named in early times after Otreus.

(8) That Bithynia was a Mysian settlement is first testified by Skylax the Karyandian [F11], who says that Phrygians and Mysians lived around Lake Askania, and then by the Dionysios who wrote the *Foundations* [F7], who says that the narrows at Chalkedon and Byzantion, today called the Thracian Bosporos, was formerly the Mysian Bosporos. This might be put down as evidence that the Mysians were Thracians. When Euphorion says "beside the waters of Mysian Askanios" [F73], and the Aitolian Alexander: "those who have their homes on the Askanian streams, on the lip of the Askanian Lake, where Dolion, the son of Silenos and Melias, lived" [F9], they are evidence for the same thing, since Lake Askania is to be found nowhere except here.

(9) Bithynia has produced men notable in culture: the philosopher Xenokrates, the dialectician Dionysios, Hipparchos, Theodosios and his sons (the mathematicians), Kleophanes the Myrlean rhetorician, and Asklepiades the Prousian physician.

(10) To the south of the Bithynians are the Mysians around Olympos (whom some call Olympenians and others Hellespontians), and Hellespontian Phrygia. [To the south] of the Paphlagonians are the Galatians, and still farther south of these is Greater Phrygia and Lykaonia,

as far as the Kilikian and Pisidian Tauros. Since what is continuous with
Paphlagonia lies next to Pontos and Kappadokia and the peoples already
gone through, it would be appropriate first to finish off the neighboring
portions and then to point out the places that are next.

Part 5:   Galatia

(1) The Galatians are to the south of the Paphlagonians. There are three
ethnic groups, two of which are named after their leaders (the Trokmians
and Tolistobogians), and the third, the Tektosagians, from the Keltic
peoples. The Galatians possessed this territory after wandering for a long
time, and they were overrunning the territory of the Attalid and Bithynian
kings until they willingly took what is now Galatia, also called Gallograecia.
It seems that their chief leader during the crossing over to Asia was
[C567]   Leonnorios. The three ethnic groups spoke the same language and differed
from each other in no way. Each was divided into four portions called
tetrarchies, each of which had its own tetrarch, one judge, and one commanding officer – both considered subject to the tetrarch – and two
subcommanders. The council of the twelve tetrarchs had three hundred
men, who assembled at the place called Drynemeton. The council adjudi-
cated homicides, but the tetrarchs and judges the other [crimes]. This was
the organization in antiquity, but in our time the power was with three
rulers, then two, and then one, Deiotaros [I], and then his successor
Amyntas. Today the Romans have both this and the entirety that was
subject to Amyntas, brought together into one province.

(2) The Trokmians possess what is near Pontos and Kappadokia, the
strongest of that which the Galatians live in. They have three walled
fortresses: Taouion (the emporium of that region, where there is a colossal
bronze of Zeus and his inviolable precinct), and Mithridation, which
Pompeius gave to Brogitaros, having separated it from the kingdom of
Pontos. The third is Posala[5] where Pompeius and Lucullus had their meeting, the former succeeding the latter in the war, who gave over his authority
and departed to celebrate his triumph. The Trokmians possess these portions, and the Tektosages that [portion] near Greater Phrygia around
Pessinous and Orkaorkoi. They had the fortress of Ankyra, which has the
same name as the little Phrygian town toward Lydia around Blaudos. The
Tolistobogians border the Bithynians and Phrygia called Epiktetos. Their

---

[5] The name is not consistent in the manuscripts. Other variants are Posdala and Danala.

fortresses are Bloukion and Peion: the former was the royal residence of Deiotaros [I] and the latter his treasury.

(3) Pessinous is the greatest emporium in that region, having a sanctuary of the Mother of the Gods, which is greatly revered. They call her Angdistis. In antiquity the priests were essentially the masters and benefited from a great priesthood, yet today these honors have been greatly reduced, although the emporium remains. The precinct was developed by the Attalid kings in a manner befitting a sacred place, with a temple and stoas of white stone. The Romans made the sanctuary famous when they sent for the image of the goddess, according to an oracle of the Sibyl, just as they had with the Asklepios at Epidauros. There is a mountain lying above the city, Dindymon, from which comes Didymene, just as Kybele was from Kybela. The Sangarios River has its stream nearby, on which are the ancient dwell-   [C568] ings of the Phrygians, of Midas and Gordios (who was still earlier) and certain others. There are no traces of cities but only villages slightly less small than the others, such as Gordion and Gorbeus, the royal residence of Kastor [I] the son of Saokondarios. This was where his father-in-law Deiotaros [I] killed him and his own daughter. He razed the fortress and ruined most of the settlement.

(4) After Galatia, toward the south, are Lake Tatta (which lies alongside Greater Kappadokia near the Morimenians, a part of Greater Phrygia), and that which is contiguous as far as the Tauros, most of which was held by Amyntas. Tatta is a natural salt pit, and the water easily congeals around everything dipped into it, so that wreaths of salt are drawn up when rings of rope are put down into it, and birds that touch the water with their wings are caught, falling on the spot because of the congealing of the salt.

Part 6: Lykaonia

(1) Tatta and the region around Orkaorkoi and Pitnissos, as well as the Lykaonian mountain plains, are cold, bare, and grazed by asses. Water is exceedingly scarce, and where it can be found the wells are the deepest that exist, just as in Soatroi (a village city near to Garsaoura), where water is sold. Although the territory is without water, it is remarkably productive of sheep. Although their wool is rough, some have acquired great wealth from them. Amyntas had over 300 flocks in this region. There are two lakes, the larger being Koralis and the smaller Trogitis. Ikonion is also somewhere around here, which has been united into a small town and is a territory more prosperous than the previously mentioned region grazed by asses. It was held by Polemon [I]. The Tauros is near to these regions, which

separates Kappadokia and Lykaonia from Rough Kilikia, lying above them. The boundary between the Lykaonians and Kappadokians is between Koropassos, a Lykaonian village, and Garsaoura, a Kappadokian town. The distance beween these fortresses is about 120 stadia.

(2) The Isaurike is also in Lykaonia, near the Tauros itself, which has Isaura, two villages with the same name, one called the Old ... well-fortified. Many other villages were subject to them, and they were all settlements of brigands. They caused much concern for the Romans, especially to Publius Servilius, called Isauricus, whom I saw. He subjected [C569] them to the Romans and eliminated most of the pirate strongholds on the sea.

(3) Derbe is on the side of Isaurike, which is closest to Kappadokia ... and was the home of the tyrant Antipatros Derbetes, who also held Laranda. In our time Amyntas held both Isauras and Derbe. He attacked and removed Derbetes and received the Isauras from the Romans. He destroyed old Isaura and built a royal palace there. He was constructing a new wall in the same place, but did not survive to complete it, as the Kilikians killed him when he invaded the Homonadians, for he was taken by ambush.

(4) He possessed Antiocheia near Pisidia as far as the Apollonias near Apameia in Kibotos, part of the Paroreios and Lykaonia, and was attempting to overrun the Kilikians and Pisidians from the Tauros who were destroying this territory, which was Phrygian and Lykaonian. He took many places that formerly had been unravaged, including Kremna. But he did not attempt to take Sandalion, which lies between Kremna and Sagalassos.

(5) Roman settlers possess Kremna, and Sagalassos is under the same Roman commander as is all the kingdom of Amyntas. It is a day's journey distant from Apameia, a descent of about 30 stadia from the fortress. It is also called Selgessos. This city was taken by Alexander. Amyntas took Kremna and passed on into the Homonadians, who were considered the most difficult to capture. He established himself as master of most of the places and removed their tyrant, but was taken through the treachery of the tyrant's wife. They put him to death, but Quirinius laid waste to them through starvation, capturing 4,000 men alive and settling them in the nearby cities, leaving the territory deserted of those in their prime.

In the middle of the high portions of the Tauros, which are very steep and precipitous, there is a hollow and fertile plain that is divided into several valleys. It is farmed, but the inhabitants live on the overhanging brows and in caves. They were mostly armed and would overrun others, with the mountains as walls for their territory.

Part 7: Pisidia

(1) Continuous to these are the Pisidians and Selgians, the most notable of the Pisidians. The greater part of them possess the ridges of the Tauros, but some, who are above Side and Aspendos (Pamphylian cities) possess hilly [C570] places that are planted everywhere with olives. The Kotennians are in the mountainous region above this, and they border on the Selgians and Homonadians, and the Sagalassians that are inside [the Tauros] toward Milyas.

(2) Artemidoros [F119] says that the Pisidian cities are Selge, Sagalassos, Petnelissos, Adada, Timbriada, Kremna, Tityassos, Amblada, Anaboura, Sinda, Aarassos, Tarbassos, and Termessos. Some of these are completely in the mountains and others reach as far as the foothills on either side, to Pamphylia and Milyas, bordering on the Phrygians, Lydians, and Karians, all peaceful people although toward the north. The Pamphylians, who share much with the Kilikian tribe, do not completely avoid the business of brigandage and do not allow those on their borders to live in peace, although they occupy the southern portions of the foothills of the Tauros. On the borders of the Phrygians and Karia are Tabai, Sinda, and Amblada, from which the Ambladian wine is exported, which is suitable for a medicinal diet.

(3) The other mountain Pisidians, whom I have mentioned, are divided according to tyrannies, like the Kilikians, and practice brigandage. They say that in antiquity the Lelegians, a wandering people, mingled with them and remained there because of similar characteristics. Selge was a city originally founded by the Lakedaimonians, and still earlier by Kalchas, but later it remained independent, having strengthened because of its lawful government, so that at one time it had 20,000 men. The nature of the region is remarkable, for among the summits of the Tauros there is a territory that can support myriads and which is exceedingly fertile, so that it is planted with olives in many places and has fine vineyards and unenvied pasturage for all kinds of cattle. Lying above this, all around, are varied forests of timber. They produce the styrax the most, a tree that is not large but tall, from which styracine javelins are made, similar to those of *kraneia*. A type of wood-eating worm is produced in the trunk that eats through the wood as far as the surface and first pours forth shavings that are like bran or sawdust, which create a pile at the roots. After this, a certain liquid drips out that easily solidifies into a gum-like substance. Part of it goes down to the shavings at the roots and mixes with them and earth, except some of it solidifies on the surface and remains pure, and some is fixed on the trunk [C571]

that it flows down and is also pure. They make a mixture from it that is not pure, mixing it with the wood and earth. It is more fragrant than what is pure but otherwise has an inferior strength (unnoticed by most), but is used in quantity as incense by those who are religious.

The Selgic iris is also praised, and its ointment. There are only a few approaches to the city and territory of the Selgians, as it is mountainous and full of cliffs and ravines that are formed by various rivers – including the Eurymedon and the Kestros – which flow from the Selgic mountains and empty into the Pamphylian Sea. There are bridges situated on their roads. Because of their natural strength, the Selgians have never once come under others, either earlier or later. Without fear they have enjoyed the benefits of the entire territory, although they would always war with the kings over what was below them in Pamphylia and inside the Tauros. They sent an embassy to Alexander, saying that they would accept his commands as friends. In regard to the Romans, they possess the territory under certain rules. They are wholly subject to them today, and are included in what was formerly subject to Amyntas.

Part 8:   Mysia and Phrygia

(1) Bordering on the Bithynians, toward the south, as I have said [12.4.4–5], are the Mysians and the Phrygians, who live around what is called Mysian Olympos. Each of these peoples is divided into two parts. There is the Phrygia called Greater, over which Midas reigned, part of which was possessed by the Galatians, and there is Lesser, which is on the Hellespont and around Olympos, called Epiktetos. Mysia is in a similar situation, with the Olympene (continuous with Bithynia and Epiktetos and which Artemidoros [F131] says was settled by Mysians from across the Istros) as well as that around the Kaikos and Pergamene as far as Teuthrania and the outlets of the river.

(2) These have undergone changes with one another – as we have often said [12.4.4] – so that it is not clear whether that around Sipylos, which was called Phrygia in antiquity (that of Phrygian Tantalos, Pelops, and Niobe) was a part of Greater or Lesser. Whichever it was, the changes are clear, for the Pergamene and Elaitis (where the Kaikos empties), and Teuthrania (which is between them, where Teuthras was and Telephos was raised), are between the Hellespont and the territory around Sipylos, and Magnesia is at its foot. Thus, as I have said, it is an effort to [C572]   determine the boundaries ("the boundaries of the Mysians and Phrygians are apart").

(3) The Lydians and the Maionians – whom Homer calls the Meionians – are in some way confused both with these and each other, because some say that they are the same and others that they are different. Some say that the Mysians were Thracians but others that they were Lydians. According to what the ancient historians Xanthos the Lydian [F15] and Menekrates the Elaian [F2] wrote, the name of the Mysians has its etymology from what the Lydians named the beech tree. The beech tree is common around Olympos, where they say those decimated were put out, and their descendants were the later Mysians, named from the beech tree. Their dialect is evidence for this, for it is mixed Lydian and Phrygian, since they lived around Olympos for a long time. When the Phrygians crossed over from Thrace and killed the ruler of Troy and of the nearby territory, they came to live there, with the Mysians above the sources of the Kaikos near Lydia.

(4) Contributing to such myth making is the confusion of peoples there and the prosperity of the territory within the Halys, particularly on the coast, because of which attacks were made against it from all sides, and continually from the mainland, or those nearby would go against each other. The invasions and migrations occurred especially at the time of the Trojan matter and afterward, since both the barbarians and Hellenes were impelled in some way to acquire the possessions of others. It was the same before the Trojan matter. The Pelasgian tribe existed then, as well as the Kaukonians and the Lelegians. It has been said [5.2.4, 8.3.17] that they happened to wander frequently over much of Europe. The Poet makes them Trojan allies, but not from the mainland. What is said about the Phrygians and Mysians is older than the Trojan matter. The doubling of the Lykians suggests that they were of the same race, whether it was the Trojans or those near Karia who settled the territory of the other. Perhaps it was the same in regard to the Kilikians (they too were doubled), but we do not have the same evidence that the Kilikians of today existed before the Trojan matter. Telephos might be considered to have come from Arkadia with his mother, and with her marriage he was accepted and welcomed by Teuthras, and, acknowledged by him, succeeded to the rule of the Mysians.

(5) The Karians were formerly islanders, and the Lelegians, as they say, became mainlanders with the help of the Cretans, who founded Miletos, taking Sarpedon from the Cretan Miletos as their founder. They settled the Termilians in what is now Lykia, with Sarpedon having brought the settlers from Crete. He was the brother of Minos and Rhadamanthys, and named those formerly called the Milyans the Termilians, as Herodotos says [1.173]. Still earlier they were the Solymians, but when Lykos the son of Pandion

[C573]

went there he named them Lykians after himself. This account shows that the Solymians and Lykians were the same, but the Poet distinguishes them. At any rate, Bellerophontes set forth from from Lykia, and "fought with the glorious Solymians" [*Iliad* 6.184], and in the same way, Ares (as he says) "while doing battle with the Solymians killed" [*Iliad* 6.204] his son Peisandros. He also says [*Iliad* 6.196–9] that Sarpedon was a native of Lykia.

(6) That the fertility of the country of which I am speaking was set before the powerful as a prize stands on many things . . . after the Trojan matter. The Amazons had such confidence, against whom Priamos and also Bellerophontes are said to have made an expedition. This is confirmed by the ancient cities named after them. In the Ilian plain there is a hill "which men address as Batieia, but the immortals the tomb of much-leaping Myrina" [*Iliad* 2.813–14], whom they record as one of the Amazons, judging from the epithet (for they say that horses are "well-leaping" because of their speed, and she was "much-leaping" because of the speed that she drove her chariot). Myrina, then, is said to have its name from her. The neighboring islands experienced the same thing because of their quality: among them, Rhodes and Kos were already inhabited by the Hellenes before the Trojan matter, as Homer clearly testifies [*Iliad* 2.653–4, 677].

(7) After the Trojan matter, everything was confused and disturbed by the migrations of the Hellenes and Trerians, the attacks of the Kimmerians and the Lydians, then those of the Persians and Makedonians, and finally those of the Galatians. Uncertainty has arisen not only because of these changes but because of the disagreements of the historians, who do not say the same things about these matters, and call the Trojans Phrygians (just as the tragedians do), and the Lykians Karians, and so forth. The Trojans, who [C574] became strong from having been small, so that they became kings of kings, provided a reason for the Poet to consider what must be called Troy. He generally calls "Trojans" all those who fought together, just as their opponents were Danaans and Achaians, but clearly we would not speak, by Zeus, of Paphlagonia, Karia, or neighboring Lykia, as Troy. I mean when he says as follows: "the Trojans came, shouting shrilly" [*Iliad* 3.2], or, of their opponents, "the Achaians came in silence, breathing with fierceness" [*Iliad* 3.8]. In many other places he speaks in different ways. Although such is the case, one must attempt to arbitrate each as capably as possible. If anything in ancient history escapes notice, it must be let alone, for this is not the task of the geographer, and one must speak of things as they are today.

(8) There are two mountains lying above the Propontis, Mysian Olympos and Ida. The Bithynian region is at the foot of Olympos, and Troy lies between Ida and the sea, adjoining the mountain. We will discuss

it and the area around it later, as well as what is contiguous toward the south [13.1.34–5]. Now we will discuss that around the Olympene and what is next as far as the Tauros, parallel to what has been traversed before.

Olympos, then, is well settled all around, and has extraordinary forests on its heights, and well-fortified places that can support groups of brigands. Among them there arise tyrants who can often remain in power for a long time, such as Kleon, who in our time was the leader of the groups of brigands.

(9) He came from the village of Gordion, which he later enlarged, making it a city and calling it Ioulioupolis, but from the beginning he used the strongest place, named Kallydion, as a base for brigandage and his operations. He became useful to Antonius, since he attacked those levying money from Labienus when the latter held Asia, and hindered his preparations. In the Aktian matter – having revolted from Antonius – he joined the commanders of Caesar and was honored more than he deserved, receiving in addition to what Antonius had given him, what Caesar [gave him]. Thus, instead of being a brigand, he was invested with the appearance of a dynast. He became the priest of Abrettenian Zeus (a Mysian god) and held subject a part of the Morene (which is also Mysian, like the Abrettene), and, finally, received the priesthood of Komana in Pontos, although within the time of a month from when he went down there his life came to an end. He was carried off by an acute disease, which afflicted him due to unceasing over- [C575] eating, or, as those around the sanctuary said, because of the wrath of the goddess, for the dwelling of both the priest and priestess is within the peribolos of the precinct, and the precinct, apart from its sanctity in other matters, is most conspicuously free from eating the meat of swine (as is the entire city, for swine cannot be brought into it). But at first he showed the character of a brigand, as soon as he first arrived, by violating this custom, as if he had not come as a priest but to corrupt the sanctity.

(10) Such is Olympos. Toward the north it is inhabited all around by the Bithynians, Mygdonians, and Dolionians, and the remainder by the Mysians and Epiktetians. Those around Kyzikos, from the Aisepos as far as the Rhyndakos and the Daskylitis Lake, are mostly called Dolionians. Those who are next after these as far as the Myrleanian territory are Mygdonians. Above Daskylitis are two other large lakes, Apolloniatis and Miletopolitis. Near Daskylitis is the city of Daskylion, near Miletopolitis is the city of Miletoupolis, and near the third is what is called Apollonia on the Rhyndakos. Today most of these are Kyzikian.

(11) Kyzikos is an island on the Propontis, connected with the mainland by two bridges. It is excellent in its quality, and in size has a perimeter of

about five hundred stadia. There is a city of the same name near the bridges, two harbors that can be closed, and more than two hundred shipsheds. Part of the city is on level ground and part is near a mountain called Bear Mountain. Another, Dindymon, lies above it, with a single summit, and having a sanctuary of Dindymene, the Mother of the Gods, established by the Argonauts. The city is a match for the first in Asia in its size, beauty, and good order, both in peace and war. Its adornment seems to be similar to that of the Rhodians and Massaliotes, or the ancient Karchedonians. Passing over most things, there are three directors of building projects who care for public buildings and equipment, and three who are in charge of the treasuries (one of whom has weapons, one equipment, and one grain). Chalkidean earth is mixed with the grain to keep it fresh. The benefit of this preparation was demonstrated in the Mithridatic War. The king came against them unexpectedly with 150,000 and much cavalry, and took possession of the mountain lying opposite them called Adrasteia, as well as the suburb. When he moved to the neck above the city and was fighting

[C576] both on foot and by sea with 400 ships, the Kyzikenians held out against everything, and almost took the king alive in a ditch (as in return they had dug one against him), but he moved to save himself by withdrawing outside of his own ditch. The Roman commander Lucullus eventually sent a certain force by night to assist. A famine that afflicted this great army was also of assistance, something the king did not foresee, and thus he lost many before he left. The Romans honored the city, and it is free to this day and holds a large territory, not only what it had from antiquity, but also what was given to it by the Romans. It has the part of the Troad around Zeleia across the Aisepos and the Adrasteian Plain, and they also have part of Lake Daskylitis (the Byzantians have the rest). In addition to the Dolionis and the Mygdonis, it occupies much of what is as far as Lake Miletopolitis, and Apolloniatis itself. The Rhyndakos River flows through this territory, having its beginning in the Azanitis. It receives others from Abrettenian Mysia – including the Mekestos, which [flows] from Ankyra in Abaeitis – and it empties into the Propontis at the island of Besbikos. On the Kyzikenian island there is a well-wooded mountain called Artake, with an islet in front of it that has the same name. Nearby is a promontory called Melanos, which is passed on the coastal voyage to Priapos from Kyzikos.

(12) The cities of Azanoi, Nakoleia, Kotiaeion, Midaion, Dorylaion, and Kadoi are in Phrygia Epiktetos. Some say that Kadoi is in Mysia. In the interior Mysia reaches from the Olympene to the Pergamene, and to the so-called Plain of the Kaikos. Thus it lies between Ida and the Katakekaumene, which to some is Mysian and to others Maionian.

(13) Greater Phrygia is above Epiktetos, toward the south, which leaves on the left Pessinous, that around Orkaorkoi, and Lykaonia, and on the right the Maionians, Lydians, and Karians. Within it are Phrygia called Paroreios, that toward Pisidia, and that around Amorion, Eumeneia, and Synnada. Then there are Apameia called Kibotos and Laodikeia, which are the largest Phrygian cities. Around these are towns and ... Aphrodisias, Kolossai, Themisonion, Sanaos, Metropolis, and Apollonias. Still farther away than these are Peltai, Tabai, Eukarpia, and Lysias.   [C577]

(14) Paroreia has a kind of mountain ridge extending from the east to the west. A certain large plain lies below it on either side, and there are nearby cities. Toward the north is Philomelion, and on the other side Antiocheia called "near Pisidia." The former lies completely in a plain and the latter is on a hill and has a Roman settlement. The Magnesians near the Maiandros founded it, and the Romans freed them from the kings when they gave over to Eumenes [II] all of Asia within the Tauros. There was also a priesthood of Men Askaios here, which had a number of temple slaves and sacred places, but it was dissolved after the death of Amyntas by those sent to succeed to his inheritance.

Synnada is not a large city. There is a plain of about 60 stadia in front of it, planted with olives. Beyond it is the village of Dokimeia and the quarry of the Synnadic stone (as the Romans call it, but to the locals it is Dokimitic or Dokimaian). In the beginning the quarry produced small blocks, but because of the present extravagance of the Romans great monolithic columns are now taken from it, which are variegated and similar to the alabastrite stone. Although movement of such loads to the sea ... both columns and slabs, remarkable for their size and beauty, are carried away to Rome.

(15) Apameia is a great emporium of Asia (in the specific sense), second after Ephesos, for it is a common storehouse for things from both Italia and Hellas. Apameia is situated at the outlets of the Marsyas River; the river flows through the middle of the city and has its sources ... of the city, carried down to the suburb, and then with an exceedingly steep downward flow joins the Maiandros, which receives another river, the Orgas, and is carried gently and softly across level territory. When it has become navigable, the Maiandros is carried for a while through Phrygia and then forms the boundary between Karia and Lydia at what is called the Maiandros Plain, where it is excessively crooked (from which everything crooked is called "meandering"). Finally it flows through Karia itself, which is now occupied by the Ionians, and then makes its outlet between Miletos and Priene. It begins on a certain hill in Kelainai, on which there is a city with

[C578]   the same name as the hill. It was from there that Antiochos [I] Soter
removed people to the present Apameia, the city to which he gave the
name of his mother Apama, the daughter of Artabazos and who was given in
marriage to Seleukos [I] Nikator. Here is told the myth of Olympos and
Marsyas, and the quarrel that arose between Marsyas and Apollo. A lake
lies above it that produces the reed suitable for the mouthpieces of flutes.
They say that two springs pour forth from it, that of the Marsyas and the
Maiandros.

(16) Laodikeia was formerly small but became powerful in our time and
in that of our fathers, even though it had been maltreated under Mithridates
[VI] Eupator. But the quality of its territory and the prosperity of its citizens
made it great. First there was Hieron, who left the people an inheritance of
more than 2,000 talents and adorned the city with many dedications. Later
there was Zenon the rhetorician and his son Polemon [I], who was considered worthy of a kingdom because of his character, first by Antonius and
later by Caesar Sebastos. The places around Laodikeia produce excellent
sheep whose wool is not only soft but different from the Milesian, and
which has the appearance of a crow, so that they receive outstanding
revenue from them (as do the Kolossenians, who live nearby, from the
color named after them). Here the Maiandros is joined by the Kapros and
the Lykos, which is a good-sized river, from which [the city] is called
Laodikeia on the Lykos. Mount Kadmos lies above the city, from which
the Lykos flows (and another with the same name as the mountain). It
mostly flows underground and then comes up and falls together with other
rivers, showing that the territory is porous and liable to earthquakes. If
anywhere is liable to earthquakes, it is Laodikeia, as well as neighboring
Karoura.

(17) Karoura is the boundary between Phrygia and Karia. It is a village
with inns and fountains of hot water, some of which are in the Maiandros
River and others above its banks. They say that once a brothel keeper was
staying in the inns with a large number of women, and an earthquake
occurred at night and they all disappeared together.

Almost all the territory around the Maiandros is liable to earthquakes and
[C579]   is undermined by fire and water, into the interior. Beginning at the plains
these conditions extend throughout the territory, as far as the Charonia (the
ones at Hierapolis, at Acharaka in the Nysais and near Magnesia and
Myous). The earth is easily broken and crumbling but is salty and easily
burned. Perhaps this is why the Maiandros is winding, because it frequently
changes its stream and carries much silt down, adding it at different times to
different parts of the shore, although some of it is forced out into the sea. In

fact, the alluvial deposits extend 40 stadia and have made Priene inland, although it was formerly on the sea.

(18) The Katakekaumene ["Burned Up"], which is held by Lydians and Mysians, happened to be named for some such reason. In Philadelphia, the city near it, the walls are not safe but are shaken and separated every day. The locals are always attentive to the condition of the earth and make their constructions accordingly. Among other cities, Apameia often had earthquakes before the expedition of Mithridates [VI]. The king, when he went there and saw that it was in ruins, gave a hundred talents for reconstruction. It is said that the same thing had happened at the time of Alexander. This is probably why Poseidon is honored among them although they are in the interior, and why it was called after Kelainos ["Black"], the son of Poseidon from Kelaino one of the Danaids ... the city was named, or because of the black stone due to the conflagrations. The matter of Sipylos and its destruction is not to be put down as a myth, for recently Magnesia, at its foot, was thrown down by an earthquake, at the time that Sardeis and other most distinguished places were ruined in many locations. The Princeps sent money, just as his father had, when the Trallianians experienced misfortune, as the gymnasium and other areas had collapsed. This was also the case with Laodikeia.

(19) One can also hear the ancient historians, such as Xanthos [F13] who wrote the *Lydian Matters* and describes the changes that were frequent in this territory, which we have recorded previously somewhere [1.3.4]. They tell the myth here of the suffering of Typhon and the Arimians, and say that this is the Katakekaumene. They do not hesitate to suspect that everything between the Maiandros and the Lydians is in such a way because of the number of lakes and rivers and the frequent holes in the earth. The lake [C580] between Laodikeia and Apameia, although like a sea, has effluvia that is muddy and is from underground. They say that proceedings are brought against the Maiandros for changing its territory when the headlands are broken away, and the penalties are ordered to be taken from the tolls of the ferries.

(20) Between Laodikeia and Karoura is a sanctuary of Men Karos, as it is called, which is notably honored. In our times a school of Herophilian physicians was established by Zeuxis, and afterward by Alexander Philalethes, just as in the time of our fathers there was the Erasistratian in Smyrna, under Hikesios. Today it does not survive in the same manner.

(21) It is said that certain Phrygian tribes are no longer to be seen, such as the Berekyntians. Alkman says that "he played the flute and the Kerbesian melody, the Phrygian" [F126]. A certain pit that has deadly effluvia is said to

be Kerbesian, and it can be seen, but the people are no longer called that. Aischylos in his *Niobe* is confused: she [Niobe] says that she will remember the family of Tantalos, "for whom there is an altar of paternal Zeus on the Idaian hill" [F162], and again "Sipylos in the Idaian land" [F163], and Tantalos says,

> I sow the land for a journey of ten days, that of the Berekyntians, where the site of Adrasteia is, and where Ida resounds with the bellowing and bleating of herds, all the Erechtheian plain. [F158]

BOOK 13

Northwestern and west central Anatolia

Part 1:   The Troad and northern Aiolis

(1) Let this far mark the boundary of Phrygia. Going back to the Propontis   [C581]
and the coast that is next after the Aisepos, we will return to the same
arrangement of the circuit. The Troad is first on the coast, whose notoriety –
although left in ruins and deserted – produces an extraordinary loquacity in
writings. In regard to this one must request pardon so that those coming
across it would not attach the cause for its length to me, but rather on those
eagerly yearning after knowledge of notable and ancient things. Additionally
this length is due to the large number of those settling in the land, both
Hellenes and barbarians, as well as the historians who do not write the same
about the same things, nor always clearly. Among the first of these is Homer,
who makes inferences about most things. It is necessary to arbitrate between
him and others, after first outlining summarily the nature of the places.

(2) The coast of the Propontis is from the Kyzikene and the places around
the Aisepos and the Granikos as far as Abydos and Sestos. That around
Ilion, Tenedos, and Alexandria Troas is from Abydos as far as Lekton.
Mount Ida lies above all this, and extends down to Lekton. From Lekton as
far as the Kaikos River and the so-called Kanai are the places around Assos,
Adramyttion, Atarneus, Pitane, and the Elaitic Gulf (with the island of the
Lesbians stretching parallel to all of them). Next, then, are those around   [C582]
Kyme as far as the Hermos and Phokaia, which is the beginning of Ionia and
the boundary of Aiolis.

Such are these places. The Poet suggests [*Iliad* 2.816–39] that the Trojans
ruled the territory from the places around the Aisepos and the present
Kyzikene as far as the Kaikos River, divided by dominions into eight or
nine parts, with most of their troops numbered among the allies.

(3) Those later do not speak of the same boundaries and use different
names, providing a number of choices. The settlements of the Hellenes,
especially of the Aiolians, furnish the primary reason (less so those of the

Ionians, for they were separated greatly from the Troad). They were scattered through its entirety, from the Kyzikene as far as the Kaikos, and they occupied that beyond, between the Kaikos and the Hermos. They say that the Aiolian settlements were four generations earlier than the Ionian, but they had delays and took a longer time. Orestes began the expedition, but his life came to an end in Arkadia. His son Penthilos succeeded him and advanced as far as Thrace, sixty years after the Trojan matter, at the time of the return of the Herakleidai to the Peloponnesos. Then Archelaos – his son – took the Aiolian expedition across into the present Kyzikene around Daskylion. Gras, his youngest son, advanced to the Granikos River, and, because he was better prepared, crossed over to Lesbos with most of his army and occupied it. Kleues the son of Doros, and Malaos – both descendants of Agamemnon – collected an army at about the same time as Penthilos (the expedition of Penthilos had previously crossed over from Thrace to Asia), and delayed a long time around Lokris and Mount Phrikion, crossing later and founding Phrikonian Kyme, named after the Lokrian mountains.

(4) Thus the Aiolians were scattered through the entire territory, which, as we have said, was called "Trojan" by the Poet. Some of those later called all Aiolis by this name, others only a portion, others the whole of Troy, and still others a portion of it, not completely agreeing with each other. Thus, in regard to the places on the Propontis, Homer [*Iliad* 2.825] makes the Troad begin at the Aisepos, but Eudoxos [F336] at Priapos and Artake (the place on the Kyzikene island that lies opposite Priapos), thus reducing its boundaries. Damastes [F9] reduces it still more (from Parion), and he extends it as far as Lekton. Others are different. Charon of Lampsakos [F13] begins at Praktios and diminishes it by another 300 stadia (this is the amount from Parion to Praktios), yet he extends it to Adramyttion. Skylax of Karyanda [F12] has it begin at Abydos, and similarly Ephoros [F163a] says that Aiolis is from Abydos as far as Kyme. Others are different.

[C583]

(5) The topography of Troy, in the best sense, is marked by the position of Ida, a high mountain that looks toward the west and that sea, but which turns slightly toward the north and that coast, that of the Propontis, from the narrows around Abydos to the Aisepos and the Kyzikene. The western sea is that of the outer Hellespont and the Aigaion Sea. Ida has many spurs, shaped like a scolopendra, and is defined by the extremities of the promontory around Zeleia and the one called Lekton, the former ending in the interior slightly above the Kyzikene (Zeleia today is part of the Kyzikene): "those who live in Zeleia under the lowest foot of Ida" [*Iliad* 2.824]. Lekton comes down to the Aigaion Sea, lying on the coastal voyage sailing from Tenedos to Lesbos. In:

they came to Ida with its many springs, the mother of wild animals, Lekton,
where they first left the sea [*Iliad* 14.283–4]

this is Hypnos and Hera. The situation of Lekton is described properly
by the Poet (that Lekton is a part of Ida) since it is the first disembarkation
point for those going up from the sea to Ida, and that it has "many springs,"
for the mountain is especially well-watered there, as is shown by the large
number of rivers "all that flow forth from the Idaian mountain to the sea,
the Rhesos and the Heptaporos" [*Iliad* 12.19–20], as well as the following
ones about which he speaks and which can be seen by us today. He says,
then, that Lekton and Zeleia are the most extreme spurs in either direction,
yet he properly distinguishes from them the ridge that he calls the summit
of Gargaron. Today Gargaron is a place visible on the upper portions of
Ida, from which comes the present Gargara, an Aiolian city. Between Zeleia
and Lekton, beginning from the Propontis, is [the territory] as far as the
narrows at Abydos, and then, outside the Propontis, that as far as Lekton.

(6) As one curves around Lekton, a large gulf spreads out that is created   [C584]
by Ida in its withdrawal from Lekton to the mainland, as well as by Kanai,
which is the promontory lying opposite Lekton on the other side. Some
call this the Idaian Gulf, others the Adramyttenian. On it are the Aiolian
cities, as far as the outlets of the Hermos, which we have mentioned [13.1.2].

Previously it was said [2.5.7] that the voyage sailing from Byzantion
toward the south is a straight line, first to Sestos and Abydos through the
middle of the Propontis, and then along the coast of Asia as far as Karia. It
is necessary to keep this supposition in mind in listening to the following,
and when we speak of certain gulfs on the coast one must consider that the
capes which form them lie on the same line, as if a meridian.

(7) Those who have considered more carefully what the Poet has said
about these things conjecture from it that this entire coast became subject
to the Trojans, divided into nine dominions under Priamos at the time of
the Ilian War, and which was called Troy. This is clear from his specific
points. For example, Achilleus and those with him saw at the beginning that
the Ilians were enclosed by walls and attempted to make war outside, going
around in order to take away the surrounding territory:

> twelve cities of men I have destroyed with my ships, and I say eleven by foot
> throughout Troy with its rich soil. [*Iliad* 9.328–9]

He says "Troy" for the mainland that he ravaged. Along with other places, he
ravaged that lying opposite Lesbos around Thebe, Lyrnessos, and Pedasos
(of the Lelegians), and also that of Eurypylos son of Telephos ("but such
was Telephides, whom he [Neoptolemos] killed with bronze, the hero

Eurypylos" [*Odyssey* 11.519–20]), and "he sacked Lyrnessos and Pedasos" [*Iliad* 20.92], and "he utterly destroyed Lyrnessos and the walls of Thebe" [*Iliad* 2.691]. He [Homer] says that these were destroyed, as well as Lesbos ("he took well-built Lesbos" [*Iliad* 9.271]). Briseis was taken from Lyrnessos ("taken away from Lyrnessos" [*Iliad* 2.690]), and at her capture – he says [*Iliad* 2.692] – Mynes and Epistrophos fell, as is shown when Briseis lamented over Patroklos:

> you would not allow me to weep, not even, when swift Achilleus killed my man and sacked the city of divine Mynes. [*Iliad* 19.295–7]

[C585] In saying that Lyrnessos was "the city of divine Mynes," he indicates that he was dynast over it and fell in battle there.

Chryseis was taken from Thebe ("we went to Thebe, the sacred city of Eetion" [*Iliad* 1.366]), and he says that Chryseis was part of what was taken from there. . . .

> Andromache, the daughter of great-hearted Eetion, Eetion who lived under wooden Plakos in Thebe Hypoplakia, master of the Kilikian men. [*Iliad* 6. 395–7]

This is the second Trojan dominion after that of Mynes. Fitting with this is the following said by Andromache:

> Hektor, I am wretched. We were both born to one fate, you at Troy in the house of Priamos, but I at Thebe [*Iliad* 22.477–9]

which is not meant to be heard literally ("you at Troy in the house of Priamos, but I at Thebe"), but as a transposition ("both at Troy, you in the house of Priamos but I at Thebe").

The third was the Lelegians, also Trojan ("Altes lord of the Lelegians, lovers of war" [*Iliad* 21.86]), whose daughter Priamos joined with, producing Lykaon and Polydoros. Moreover, those assigned to Hektor in the *Catalogue* are called Trojans: "the Trojans were led by great Hektor with the flashing helmet" [*Iliad* 2.816]. Then there are those under Aineias ("the Dardanians were led by the noble son of Anchises" [*Iliad* 2.819]), who were also Trojans; at any rate he [Homer] says "Aineias, advisor to the Trojans" [*Iliad* 5.180, etc.]. Then there are the Lykians under Pandaros, whom he also called Trojans:

> those who live in Zeleia, under the lowest foot of Ida, the Aphneians, who drink the dark water of the Aisepos, the Trojans, whom Pandaros led, the famous son of Lykaon. [*Iliad* 2.824–7]

This is the sixth dominion.

Thus those between the Aisepos and Abydos were Trojans, for that around Abydos was subject to Asios:

> those who live around Perkote and Praktios, and held Sestos, Abydos, and divine Arisbe, who then were led by Asios Hyrtakides. [*Iliad* 2.835–7]

But a son of Priamos spent time at Abydos pasturing horses, clearly those of his father:

> he hit Demokoon, the bastard son of Priamos, who had come from Abydos, from his swift horses. [*Iliad* 4.499–500]

In Perkote a son of Hiketaon was pasturing cattle, and these cattle belonged [C586] to no one else [than Priamos]:

> first he rebuked strong Melanippos Hiketaonides, who had once fed the cattle with rolling gait in Perkote. [*Iliad* 15.546–8]

Thus this would be the Troad, as well as what is next, as far as Adrasteia, whose leaders were "the two sons of Merops of Perkote" [*Iliad* 2.831]. Everyone, then, from Abydos as far as Adrasteia, was Trojan, although divided in two, one part under Asios and the other under the Meropidai, just as Kilikia was divided into the Thebaike and the Lyrnessis.

As the ninth [dominion] one could consider that under Eurypylos, next to Lyrnessis. But that Priamos ruled all these is clearly demonstrated by Achilleus' words to Priamos:

> You, old man, were formerly blessed, we hear, with as much as is enclosed above Lesbos (the city of Makar), by Phrygia in the upland, and the unbounded Hellespont. [*Iliad* 24.543–5]

(8) It was in such a way at that time, but later all kinds of changes followed. The Phrygians settled in the regions around Kyzikos, as far as Praktios, and the Thracians around Abydos. Still earlier than these two were the Bebrykians and Dryopians. The Trerians – who were also Thracians – possessed that which is next, and in the Plain of Thebe were the Lydians (at that time called Meionians) and the survivors of the Mysians who were formerly subject to Telephos and Teuthras.

Thus when the Poet puts Aiolis and Troy together into one, and since the Aiolians held everything from the Hermos as far as the coast at Kyzikos and also founded cities, we would not be going through it unnaturally by putting together Aiolis – now so-called properly, and extending from the Hermos as far as Lekton – with that next as far as the Aisepos. In the specifics we will separate them again and set forth both as they are today and as they were described by the Poet and others.

(9) The beginning of the Troad is after the city of the Kyzikenes and the Aisepos, according to Homer. He says this about it:

> those who live in Zeleia, under the lowest foot of Ida, the Aphneians, who drink the dark water of the Aisepos, the Trojans, whom Pandaros led, the famous son of Lykaon. [*Iliad* 2.824–7]

[C587] He also calls them Lykians. They are considered to be Aphneians (from Lake Aphnitis, as Daskylitis is called by that name).

(10) Zeleia is on the farthest slopes of Ida, 190 stadia distant from Kyzikos, and about 80 from the nearest sea, where the Aisepos empties. He enumerates in order the places along the coast after the Aisepos:

> those who held Adrasteia and the district of Apaisos, and held Pitya and the steep mountain of Tereia, were led by Adrestos and Amphios of the linen breastplate, the two sons of Merops of Perkote. [*Iliad* 2.828–31]

These territories lie below Zeleia and are held by the Kyzikenians and Priapenians as far as the coast. The Tarsios River is around Zeleia, and is crossed twenty times by the same road, like the Heptaporos, which the Poet mentions [*Iliad* 12.20].

(11) About ... stadia above the outlet of the Aisepos there is a hill on which the tomb of Memnon the son of Tithonos is shown. Nearby is the village of Memnon. The Granikos flows between the Aisepos and the Priapos, mostly through the Adrasteian Plain, on which Alexander defeated the satraps of Dareios [III], who had come together in force, and thus he took everything within the Tauros and the Euphrates. On the Granikos is the city of Sidene, which has a large territory with the same name, but today it is destroyed. On the boundary between the Kyzikene and the Priapene is a place, Harpagia ["Seizure"], from which, according to the myth, Ganymedes was seized. According to others it was around the Dardanian Cape, near Dardanos.

(12) Priapos is a city on the sea and a harbor. Some say that it was a Milesian foundation, settled at the same time as Abydos and Prokonnesos; others that it was Kyzikene. It was named after Priapos, who was honored by them. Either his sanctuary was transferred from Orneai near Corinth, or the people there were inspired to honor the god because it was said that he was the son of Dionysos and a nymph (since there is a significant abundance of vines both in their territory and those neighboring it, that of the Parianians and the Lampsakenians). At any rate, Xerxes gave Lampsakos

to Themistokles for wine. But he [Priapos] was proclaimed a god by those more recent, as Hesiod does not know about Priapos, and he is similar to the Attic [divinities] Orthannes, Konisalos, Tychon, and such ones. [C588]

(13) This territory was called the Adrasteia and the Plain of Adrasteia according to a custom of naming the same place twice, such as Thebe and the Plain of Thebe, or Mygdonia and the Plain of Mygdonia. Kallisthenes [F28] says that it is from King Adrastos, who was the first to establish a sanctuary of Nemesis, called the Adrasteia. The city is between Priapos and Parion, and has a plain of the same name lying below it, in which there was an oracle of Aktaian Apollo and Artemis toward[1]. . . . The furnishings and stone of the sanctuary were demolished and removed to Parion, and an altar was constructed, the work of Hermokreon and greatly worthy of memory because of its size and beauty. The oracle was abandoned, just like the one at Zeleia. Here there is no sanctuary of Adrasteia visible, nor any of Nemesis, although there is a sanctuary of Adrasteia near Kyzikos. Antimachos says the following:

> There is a great goddess, Nemesis, who obtained all these things from the Blessed Ones. Adrestos was the first to place an altar to her on the stream of the Aisepos River, where she is honored and called Adresteia. [F131]

(14) Parion is also a city on the sea, having a larger harbor than Priapos and augmented from it. The Parians served the Attalids, to whom the Priapene was assigned, and with their permission cut off a large portion. Here there is the myth that the Ophiogenians ["Serpent Born"] have some relationship to serpents. They say that the males cure those who are bitten by snakes through continuous touching, like enchanters, first transferring the lividity to themselves and then stopping both the inflammation and the pain. According to the myth, the founder of the race was a certain hero who had changed from a serpent. Perhaps he was one of the Libyan Psyllians, whose power survived in his race until that time. Parion was a foundation of the Milesians, Erythraians, and Parians.

(15) Pitya ["Pines"] is in Parian Pityous, below a mountain that is abundant in pines. It lies between Parion and Priapos, near Linos, a locality on the sea, where the Linousian snails – the best of all – are caught.

(16) On the coastal voyage from Parion to Priapos are Old Prokonnesos and the Prokonnesos of today, which has a city and the quarries of the white stone that is greatly esteemed. At any rate, the most beautiful works [C589]

---

[1] The manuscripts have the meaningless "*tykaten.*"

in those cities, especially in Kyzikos, are from this stone. Aristeas was from here, the poet of the so-called Arimaspeian epic, a charlatan if anyone was.

(17) Some say that Mount Tereia is the mountain in Peirossos that the Kyzikenians hold, adjoining Zeleia. A royal hunting preserve was established on it by the Lydians, and later by the Persians. Others show a hill 40 stadia from Lampsakos, on which there is a sanctuary sacred to the Mother of the Gods, called the Tereia.

(18) Lampsakos is also a city on the sea, with a good harbor and which is notable and continues to be attractive, like Abydos. It is about 170 stadia distant from it and was formerly called Pityoussa, just like Chios, they say. On the opposite shore of the Chersonesos is the small town of Kallipolis. It lies on the cape that projects far toward Asia, toward the city of Lampsakos, so that the crossing of the channel is no more than 40 stadia.

(19) Between Lampsakos and Parion was Paisos, a city and a river, but the city is destroyed. The Paisenians changed their home to Lampsakos, as they were also Milesian settlers, just like the Lampsakenians. The Poet speaks of it in two ways: adding the syllable "a" ("the district of Apaisos" [*Iliad* 2.828]) and omitting it ("he lived in Paisos, and was exceedingly rich" [*Iliad* 5.612–13]); the river is called this today.

Kolonai is also Milesian, and is above Lampsakos in the interior of the Lampsakene. There is another one on the outer Hellespontine Sea, 140 stadia distant from Ilion, where, they say, Kyknos was from. Anaximenes [of Lampsakos, F25] says that there are places named Kolonai in Erythraia, Phokis, and Thessaly.

In the Pariane is Iliokolone, and in the Lampsakene a place abundant in vines, Gergithion. There was also a city of Gergitha, from Kymaian Gergithes, as there was a city there called Gergithes – in the feminine plural – where the Gergithian Kephalon was from. Today there is still a place, Gergithion, in the Kymaia near Larisa.

The glossographer Neoptolemos, worthy of remembering, was from Parion. From Lampsakos were Charon the historian, Adeimantos, Anaximenes the rhetorician, and Metrodoros the companion of Epikouros. Epikouros himself was, in a certain way, a Lampsakenian, as he spent time in Lampsakos and had as friends the best men in that city (Idomeneus, Leonteus, and those around them). Agrippa took *The Fallen Lion*, a work of Lysippos, from here and dedicated it in the grove between the lake and the Euripos.

[C590]

(20) After Lampsakos are Abydos and the localities in between. The Poet puts them together with the Lampsakene and part of the Pariane (for their

cities were not yet in existence at the time of the Trojan matter) and says about them:

> those who live around Perkote and Praktios, and held Sestos, Abydos, and divine Arisbe, who then were led by Asios Hyrtakides, whose large fierce horses brought him from Arisbe, from the Selleeis River. [*Iliad* 2.835–9]

In speaking in such a way, he seems to represent Arisbe – from where he says Asios came – as his royal residence. But these localities are so obscure that researchers do not agree about them, except that they are around Abydos, Lampsakos, and Parion, and that Old Perkote ... the place changed its name.

(21) In regard to the rivers, the Poet says that the Selleeis flows by Arisbe, if Asios came "from Arisbe" and "from the Selleeis River." The Praktios is a river. Some believe that there is also a city, but none is to be found. It also flows between Abydos and Lampsakos. Thus "live around ... Praktios" must apply to the river, as well as the following: "those who live around the divine Kephisos" [*Iliad* 2.522] and "those who lived on their renowned lands around the Parthenios River" [*Iliad* 2.854]. There was also a city of Arisba on Lesbos, whose territory was held by the Methymnaians, and there is an Arisbos River in Thrace, as has been previously said,[2] near which the Thracian Kebrenians are. There are many identical names among the Thracians and Trojans, such as the Thracians who are called the Skaians, the Skaios River, Skaian Wall, and the Skaian Gates at Troy. There are Thracian Xanthians and the Xanthos River at Troy. There is an Arisbos that empties into the Hebros, and an Arisbe at Troy. There is a Rhesos River at Troy and a Rhesos who was king of the Thracians. There is also another Asios, with the same name, according to the Poet:

> Asios, who was the maternal uncle of Hektor the tamer of horses and Hekabe's own brother, the son of Dymas who lived in Phrygia on the stream of the Sangarios. [*Iliad* 16.717–19]

(22) Abydos was a Milesian foundation, with the permission of Gyges the Lydian king, for this district and all the Troad were under him. There is a certain promontory named Gygas near Dardanos. It lies at the mouth of the Propontis and the Hellespont, equidistant (about 170 stadia) from Lampsakos and Ilion. Here is the Heptastadion, which Xerxes bridged, separating Europe and Asia. The European promontory that makes the narrows at the bridge is called the Chersonesos ["Peninsula"} because of its   [C591]

---

[2] The reference was presumably in the lost part of Book 7.

shape. Sestos lies opposite Abydos, the best of the cities in the Chersonesos. Because of its proximity it was assigned the same commander, when commands had not been separated by continents. Abydos and Sestos are separated from each other by about 30 stadia – from harbor to harbor – but the bridge was shorter, at an angle between the cities, toward the Propontis from Abydos and in the opposite direction from Sestos. There is a place named Apobathra ["Gangway"] near Sestos where the pontoon bridge was attached. Sestos is farther into the Propontis, lying above the stream that flows out of it. Thus it is easier to cross from Sestos, sailing a short distance to the Tower of Hero, and then sending the ships across to the other side assisted by the current. Those who cross from Abydos must sail in the opposite direction for about 8 stadia, to a tower directly opposite Sestos, and then cross at an angle, so as not to be completely opposed to the current.

After the Trojan matter Thracians lived at Abydos, and then Milesians. When the cities (those in the Propontis) were burned by Dareios [I] – the father of Xerxes – Abydos had the same misfortune. He burned them because he learned after his return from the Skythians that the nomads were preparing to cross, in order to avenge what they had suffered, and he was afraid that the cities would supply ferries for their army. This, the other changes, and the passage of time are the reasons for the confusion regarding the places. We have previously discussed Sestos and the entire Chersonesos in the Thracian section [7.F21]. Theopompos [F390] says that Sestos is small but well fortified, connected to its harbor by a long wall of two *plethra*, and because of this – as well as the current – it is mistress of the passage.

(23) Lying above the Abydenian territory in the Troad is Astyra, which today is Abydenian, and is a city that is completely destroyed. Formerly it was independent and had gold mines, which are now scant, having been exhausted like those on Tmolos around the Paktolos. They say that from [C592] Abydos to the Aisepos is about 700 stadia, but less by a straight sail.

(24) Outside is the territory around Ilion: that on the coast as far as Lekton and the Trojan Plain, and that on the slopes of Ida which was subject to Aineias. The Poet names these in two ways, at one time saying "the Dardanians were led by the noble son of Anchises" [*Iliad* 2.819], calling them Dardanians, and another time Dardanans ("Trojans, Lykians, and Dardanans fought hand-to-hand" [*Iliad* 8.173 etc.]). It is reasonable that in antiquity this was the site of the Dardania mentioned by the Poet: "first Dardanos, begotten by Zeus the cloud-gatherer, founded Dardania" [*Iliad* 20.215–16]. Today there is no trace of a city preserved there.

(25) Plato [*Laws* 3.677–8] infers that after the floods three stages of culture came to be formed: the first on the mountain summits (which was

simple and wild, in fear of the waters whose height covered the plains), the second in the foothills (where gradually there was courage, because the plains were beginning to become dry), and the third in the plains. One might also speak of a fourth, fifth, or more, with the last on the coast and in the islands, when they were released from all such fear. The greater or lesser courage in coming near to the sea would indicate a number of cultural stages and customs, just as the wild customs were the foundation for the simplicity that still remained in some way during the second stage. But there is also a certain difference – that between the rustic and semi-rustic cultural stages – from which the gradual . . . ended in urbanity and the best customs, with the change in customs for the better as well as the changes in places and lifestyle.

These differences, Plato says [*Laws* 3.680], are suggested by the Poet, who puts forth as an example of the first stage of culture the life of the Kyklopes, who passed their lives on natural fruits, occupying the summits in caves. "But everything is produced without tilling and plowing" [*Odyssey* 9.109], he says, for they have

> no counselling assemblies, nor laws, but they live on the peaks of high mountains in hollow caves, and each is lawgiver to his children and partners. [*Odyssey* 9.112–15]

The second is in the time of Dardanos, who

> founded Dardania, since sacred Ilion had not yet been built in the plain as a   [C593]
> city for articulate men, for they were still living on the foothills of Ida with its
> many springs. [*Iliad* 20.216–18]

The third is that in the plains at the time of Ilos, who was the traditional founder of Ilion, and from whom the city took its name. It is reasonable that because of this he was buried in the middle of the plain, as he was the first who dared to put his settlement in the plains: "they drove past the tomb of ancient Ilos, son of Dardanos, through the middle of the plain past the wild fig tree" [*Iliad* 11.166–7]. But he was not totally courageous, for he did not establish the city where it is now, but about 30 stadia higher toward the east, toward Ida and Dardania, at what is now called the Village of the Ilians. But the Ilians of today, seeking honor and wishing that theirs was the ancient one – for it does not seem to be the one mentioned by Homer – have provided an argument for those seeking proof from the poetry of Homer. Others have determined that the site of the city has changed several times, but finally remained in this place from about the time of Kroisos. I assume that such changes to the lower portions occurring then demonstrate differences in lifestyle and cultural stage, but this must be investigated at another time.

(26) They say that the present city of Ilion was a village for a time, having a sanctuary of Athena that was small and cheap, but when Alexander went up there after his victory at the Granikos he adorned the sanctuary with dedications and called it a city, ordering its managers to erect buildings and judging it to be free and exempt from tribute. Later, after the Persians were overthrown, he sent them a friendly letter, undertaking to make it a great city with a most distinguished sanctuary, and proclaiming sacred games. After his death, Lysimachos gave particular care to the city, building a temple and a circuit wall of about 40 stadia, joining the surrounding cities to it, which were old and in a poor situation. He also gave care to Alexandria, which had already been joined into one city under Antigonos [I] and called Antigoneia, but had changed its name. It seemed pious for the successors of Alexander to found cities named after him before themselves.

[C594]   The city survived and became large, and today has a Roman settlement and is one of the most reputed of cities.

(27) Present-day Ilion was a type of village-city when the Romans first landed in Asia and expelled Antiochos [III] the Great from within the Tauros. At any rate, Demetrios the Skepsian [F21] says that when he lived in the city as a youth, about the same time, he saw that the settlement was so neglected that there were no tile roofs, and Hegesianax [F3] [says] that when the Galatians crossed over from Europe they went up into the city because they needed a fortified place, but immediately left because it was unwalled. Later it was greatly restored, but then it was ruined again by the Romans under Fimbria, who took it by siege during the Mithridatic War. Fimbria had been sent there as quaestor along with the consul Valerius Flaccus, when the latter was assigned against Mithridates [VI], but he rose in revolt and killed the consul in Bithynia, setting himself up as master of the army. When he came to Ilion, the Ilians would not receive him (as he was considered a brigand), but he applied . . . and took it on the eleventh day. He boasted that he had subdued on the eleventh day the city that Agamemnon had barely taken in the tenth year, although having a fleet of a thousand ships and the whole of Hellas on his expedition. One of the Ilians then said "There was no Hektor." Sulla came across and removed Fimbria, sent Mithridates [VI] home by agreement, and encouraged the Ilians through much restoration. In our time Caesar the God was much more considerate, and also emulated Alexander. The latter had set out to provide for them through a renewal of kinship and his fondness of Homer. At any rate, it happens that there was a certain edition of the poetry of

Homer called "that of the casket," which Alexander, along with Kallisthenes and Anaxarchos, went through and annotated somewhat. Then he placed it in a richly wrought casket that he had found among the Persian treasure. It was because of his zeal for the Poet and his kinship with the Aiakidai – those who ruled the Molossians, among whom, it is recounted, Andromache the wife of Hektor ruled as queen – that Alexander was kindly disposed toward the Ilians. Caesar was also fond of Alexander but had a better-known proof of kinship with the Ilians, and thus was encouraged toward kindnesses in a youthful manner. It became better known because he was Roman, and   [C595] the Romans believe that Aineias was their founder, and also because Julius was from an ancestor, a certain Iulus, who had this surname from Ilos one of the descendants of Aineias. He [Caesar] allotted them territory and preserved their freedom and exemption from taxation, and until today they continue to preserve them.

That this is not the site of ancient Ilion (if one considers it according to Homer) is shown by the following. But before that one must describe the places, beginning from on the coast where we previously left off.

(28) After Abydos there is the Dardanian Cape that I mentioned previously [13.1.11], and the city of Dardanos, which is 70 stadia distant from Abydos. The Rhodios River empties between them, and opposite it in the Chersonesos is the Kynossema ["Dog Grave"], which is said to be the tomb of Hekabe. Some say that the Rhodios empties into the Aisepos. It is one of the rivers mentioned by the Poet, as follows: "the Rhesos, Heptaporos, Karesos, and Rhodios" [*Iliad* 12.20]. Dardanos was an ancient settlement, but it was so despised that often the kings removed the settlers to Abydos and then resettled others again on the ancient foundation. Here Cornelius Sulla the Roman commander and Mithridates [VI] called Eupator met and agreed with one another on the ending of the war.

(29) Nearby is Ophrynion, above which is the grove of Hektor, in a conspicuous place, and next is Lake Pteleos.

(30) Then there is Rhoiteion, a city situated on a hill, and adjoining Rhoiteion is the seashore on which the memorial and sanctuary of Aias are, and a statue of him, which Antonius took and carried away to Egypt. Sebastos Caesar gave it back to the Rhoiteians, as he did with others. The former took the most beautiful dedications from the most distinguished sanctuaries to gratify the Egyptian woman, but the latter gave them back to the gods.

(31) After Rhoiteion are Sigeion – a destroyed city – and the naval station and harbor of the Achaians, the Achaian camp, the so-called Stomalimne ["Mouth of the Lake"], and the mouths of the Skamandros. After the

Simoeis and Skamandros come together in the plain, they carry down much sediment and silt up the coast, creating a blind mouth, lagoons, and marshes. Opposite the Sigeian Cape on the Chersonesos are the Protesilaeion and Elaioussa, which we discussed in the Thracian section.

(32) The length of this coast – in a straight voyage from Rhoteion as far as Sigeion and the memorial of Achilleus – is 60 stadia. All of it lies below Ilion, both the present one (which is about 12 stadia distant from the harbor of the Achaians) and the earlier one, about 30 stadia farther inland in the direction of Ida. Near Sigeion are a sanctuary and memorial of Achilleus, as well as memorials of Patroklos and Antilochos, and the Ilians offer sacrifice to all of them as well as to Aias. They do not honor Herakles for the reason that they were ravaged by him. But one can say that although he did ravage them, he left it a city for those who completely ravaged it later. Thus the Poet says "he emptied the city of Ilion and widowed its streets" [*Iliad* 5.642], and widowing is a loss of the men, not a complete extermination. But the others completely destroyed it, those whom they consider worthy of offering sacrifice to and honoring as gods. Perhaps the reason for this is that they waged a just war, but he [Herakles] was unjust "because of the horses of Laomedon" [*Iliad* 5.640]. But set against this is the story that it was not because of the horses but because of the reward for Hesione and the sea monster. Yet let us ignore this, as they degenerate into arguments about myths, and perhaps we do not notice some more believable reasons as to why the Ilians came to honor some and not others. It seems that the Poet, in what he says about Herakles, has the city appear small, since "with six ships and fewer men he ravaged the city of Ilion" [*Iliad* 5.641–2]. This is clear when he says that Priamos, once small, became a great king of kings, as we have said [12.8.7, 13.1.7]. Continuing a little farther along this coast there is the Achaiion, opposite the Tenedian shore.

(33) These are the places on the sea, above which lies the Trojan Plain, which reaches inland in the eastern direction for many stadia as far as Ida. The district alongside the mountains is narrow, stretching toward the south as far as the locality of Skepsis, and toward the north as far as the Lykians around Zeleia. The Poet [*Iliad* 2.819–23] makes this subject to Aineias and the Antenoridai, and calls it the Dardania. Below it is the Kebrenia, which is mostly level territory, approximately parallel to the Dardania. There was once a city called Kebrene. Demetrios [of Skepsis, F22] suspects that the region of Ilion subject to Hektor extended this far, reaching from the naval station as far as the Kebrenia. He says that the tomb of Alexander is pointed out there, as well as that of Oinone, who is recorded as the wife of Alexander before Helen was seized. The Poet also says "Kebriones, the bastard son of

[C596]

glorious Priamos" [*Iliad* 16.738], after whom it is reasonable that the region   [C597]
was named, or, more believably, the city. The Kebrenia extends as far as the
Skepsia, with the boundary at the Skamandros, which flows in between.
The Kebrenians and Skepsians were hostile and at war until Antigonos [I]
settled both in what was then Antigoneia, now Alexandria. The Kebrenians
remained with the others in Alexandria, but the Skepsians returned home
with the permission of Lysimachos.

(34) In this region, he [Demetrios] says, two spurs extend from the Idaian
mountain to the sea, one straight to Rhoiteion and the other to Sigeion,
together making a semicircular line. They end on the plain at the same
distance from the sea as the present Ilion, which is thus between the ends of
the spurs that have been mentioned. The old settlement is between their
beginnings. They include within them the Simoeisian Plain, through
which the Simoeis is carred, and the Skamandrian, through which the
Skamandros flows. This is specifically called the Trojan Plain, and here
the Poet represents that most of the fighting occurred, for it is wide. Here we
see pointed out the places that he named: the wild fig tree [*Iliad* 6.433 etc.],
the tomb of Aisyetes [*Iliad* 2.793], Batieia [*Iliad* 2.811–14], and the grave of
Ilos [*Iliad* 10.415 etc.]. The Skamandros and Simoeis Rivers, after flowing
near to Sigeion and Rhoiteion respectively, come together a little in front
of the present Ilion, and then empty near Sigeion and create what is called
the Stomalimne ["Mouth of the Lake"]. The previously mentioned plains
are separated from one another by a great neck of the mentioned spurs . . . in
a straight line (starting from the present Ilion), which is connected to them,
and stretches as far as the Kebrenia, along with both spurs, forming the
letter epsilon.

(35) A little above this is the Village of the Ilians, where it is thought that
ancient Ilion was formerly situated, at a distance of 30 stadia from the
present city. Kallikolone – 10 stadia above the Village of the Ilians – is a
particular hill 5 stadia from which the Simoeis flows. Thus, first, the
reference to Ares becomes reasonable:

> Ares called forth from the other side, like a dark storm, sharply urging on the
> Trojans from the highest part of the city, and again speeding along the
> Simoeis above Kallikolone. [*Iliad* 20.51–3]

If the battle took place on the Skamandrian Plain it would be plausible that   [C598]
at one time Ares would make his encouragement from the akropolis and
at another from the nearby localities of the Simoeis and Kallikolone, for it is
reasonable that the battle extended to them. But since Kallikolone is 40
stadia distant from the present Ilion, how could it have been useful to bring

in places so far away that the battle arrangement would not have extended to them? Thus "the Lykians were allotted that toward Thymbra" [*Iliad* 10.430] is more suitable to the ancient settlement, for the plain of Thymbra is nearby, and the Thymbrios River flows through it and empties into the Skamandros at the sanctuary of Thymbraian Apollo, but it is as much as 50 stadia distant from the present Ilion. Erineus ["wild fig tree"] is a rough locality with wild fig trees that lies below the ancient foundation, so that Andromache can appropriately say: "station the men by the wild fig tree, where the city can best be climbed and the wall is easily accessible" [*Iliad* 6.433–4], but it is situated a distance from present Ilion. Phegos ["oak tree"] is a little below Erineus, about which Achilleus says:

> as long as I was making war along with the Achaians, Hektor did not wish to make battle away from the wall, but would only come to the Skaian Gate and the oak tree. [*Iliad* 9.352–4]

(36) The naval station – as it is still called today – is so near to the present city that one could suitably wonder at the senselessness of one side and the faintheartedness of the other. Senselessness, if it was unwalled for such a time, being near to the city and to so many people (both there and among the allies), for he says [*Iliad* 7.436–7] that the wall had been constructed recently (or not at all but fabricated and then made invisible by the Poet, as Aristotle [F162] says). Faintheartedness, if, when the wall was built, they could rush into the naval station and attack the ships, but did not have the courage to go besiege it while it was unwalled, when it was only a slight distance away, for the naval station is near Sigeion and the Skamandros empties near it, and it is a distance of 20 stadia from Ilion. If one says that what is now called the Harbor of the Achaians is the naval station, this would be speaking of a closer place, about 12 stadia distant from the city, even adding the plain that lies before the city on the sea, because in its entirety it is an alluvial deposit of the rivers. Thus if it is now 12 stadia between them, at that time it would have been less than half. The fabricated story told to Eumaios by Odysseus indicates that the distance between the city and naval station is great, for "we led our ambush beneath Troy" [*Odyssey* 14.469], and (he says lower down) "we went exceedingly far from the ships" [*Odyssey* 14.496]. Spies are sent to learn whether they will remain "far away from the ships," – far separated from their own walls – "or withdraw back to the city" [*Iliad* 10.209–10]. Poulydamas says "on both sides, friends, consider it, for I urge you to go now to the city . . . as we are far from its walls" [*Iliad* 18.254–6]. Demetrios [of Skepsis, F26] provides the Alexandrian Hestiaia as witness, who wrote about Homer's *Iliad* and asked

[C599]

whether the war took place around the present city and the Trojan plain, which the Poet asserts is between the city and the sea, since the one seen before the present city is due to the later siltation of the river.

(37) Polites, "who was a lookout for the Trojans, trusting in his swift feet, on the highest point of the mound of old Aisyetes" [*Iliad* 2.792–3], was foolish, for even though he was on the highest point, he might have had as a lookout the higher summit of the akropolis, from about the same distance, with no need of his swift feet for safety, for the mound of Aisyetes that is visible today is 5 stadia away on the road to Alexandria. The running circuit of Hektor around the city is also not possible, as there is no running circuit today because of the ridge that adjoins it, but the ancient site has a running circuit.

(38) No trace of the ancient city survives, as is natural, for although the surrounding cities were pillaged, they were not completely destroyed, yet it was demolished from its foundations and all the stones were taken up and transferred to the others. At any rate, they say that Archeanax the Mitylenaian built a wall at Sigeion with its stones. The Athenians sent Phrynon the Olympian victor to take possession of it, although the Lesbians had a legal claim to almost the entire Troad. Most of the settlements there were founded by them, some surviving today and others having disappeared. Pittakos of Mitylene, one of the so-called Seven Wise Men, sailed [C600] against Phrynon the commander and carried on the war for a while, but managed it poorly. The poet Alkaios says that he threw away his weapons and fled at this time, as he was doing poorly in a battle. He says to a certain herald, whom he had ordered to say to those at home: "Alkaios is safe . . . the Attikans hung in the Glaukopian sanctuary" [F428].[3] Later, challenged to single combat by Phrynon, he took up his fishing equipment and ran to him, throwing his net around him, and attacked and killed him with his trident and dagger. But the war continued and Periandros was chosen by both sides as arbiter and ended the war.

(39) Demetrios [of Skepsis, F27] says that Timaios [F129] is mistaken in recording that Periandros fortified Achilleion against the Athenians with stones from Ilion in order to assist those with Pittakos, for this place was fortified by the Mitylenaians against Sigeion, yet not with these stones and not by Periandros. How could someone carrying on a war against them be chosen as arbiter? Achilleion is the place where the memorial of Achilleus is, a small settlement. But Sigeion was razed by the Ilians because of disobedience, for the latter held the entire coast as far as Dardanos, but today it is

---

[3] The text of the quotation is so uncertain that it is not fully comprehensible.

subject to the former. In antiquity it was mostly subject to the Aiolians, so that Ephoros [F163b] does not hesitate to call everything from Abydos as far as Kyme "Aiolis." Thoukydides [3.50.3] says that Troy was taken from the Mitylenaians by the Athenians during the Peloponnesian War at the time of Paches.

(40) The Ilians of today say that the city was not completely destroyed when the Achaians captured it, and that it was never abandoned. At any rate, beginning a little later, the Lokrian maidens were sent there every year. But this is not Homeric, for Homer does not know about the rape of Kasandra, only that she was a maiden at about that time:

> he struck down Othryoneus, who had arrived from Kabesos, coming because of the report of war, seeking the most beautiful of the daughters of Priamos, Kassandra, without a dowry, [*Iliad* 13.363–6]

[C601] but he does not record any force against her or that the destruction of Aias in the shipwreck was because of the wrath of Athena or for any such reason, saying [*Iliad* 4.502–11] that although he was hated by Athena in general – since all of them committed sacrilege against her sanctuary she hated them all – he was destroyed by Poseidon because of his boastfulness. It happens that the Lokrian maidens were sent when the Persians were in power.

(41) This is what the Ilians say, but Homer specifically says that the city was destroyed: "there will be a day when sacred Ilios will be destroyed" [*Iliad* 4.164, 6.448], and "we completely destroyed the lofty city of Priamos" [*Odyssey* 3.130, etc.], and "through counsel and words, in the tenth year the city of Priamos was destroyed" [*Iliad* 12.15, altered]. Other proofs of this are set forth, such as the present xoanon of Athena is now seen to be standing, but Homer shows it as sitting, for it is ordered that the peplos "be put on Athena's knees" [*Iliad* 6.92] (such as "a dear child would never sit on his knees" [*Iliad* 9.455]). It is better to accept it thus, as some do, rather than putting it beside her knees, as in "she sits on the hearth in the light of the fire" [*Odyssey* 6.305] instead of "beside the hearth." How could one consider dedicating a peplos beside the knees? Others change the pronunciation – *goundsin*, like *thyidsin* (whichever way it is accepted) – endlessly talking. . . . Many of the ancient xoana of Athena are seen to be sitting, such as those at Phokaia, Massalia, Rome, Chios, and a number of other places. Those more recent argue that the city was destroyed, including the orator Lykourgos, who says about the city "who has not heard . . . that after it was razed by the Hellenes . . . it was uninhabited" [*Against Leokrates* 62].

(42) It is inferred that those who later considered rebuilding it thought that the place was ill-omened, either because of its misfortune or because,

according to an ancient custom, Agamemnon had cursed it, just as Kroisos (after he took Sidene, where the tyrant Glaukias had fled for refuge) put a curse on anyone who should fortify the site again. Thus they recoiled from the site and fortified another. The Astypalaians who held Rhoiteion were the first to settle Polion – today called Polisma – on the Simoeis, but not at a secure site, and it was quickly razed. It was under the Lydians that the present settlement was founded, as well as the sanctuary. It was not a city, but a long time later it gradually grew, as I have said [13.1.26]. Hellanikos [F25b], to please the Ilians – "such is the temperament of that man" [*Iliad* 15.94] – agrees with them that the present city is the same as the former one. When the city was destroyed, its territory was divided up between those possessing Sigeion, Rhoiteion, and other places in the neighborhood, but it was given back when it was refounded.

[C602]

(43) "With many springs" [*Iliad* 8.47 etc.] is believed particularly to mean Ida because of the large number of rivers that flow from it, especially in the Dardanike that lies below it as far as Skepsis and the region of Ilion. Demetrios [of Skepsis, F29] was acquainted with the region, as he was a native, and he says the following: there is a hill of Ida, Kotylos, that lies about 120 stadia above Skepsis, from which the Skamandros flows, as well as the Granikos and Aisepos, the latter two toward the north and the Propontis – with streams collected from a number of sources – but the Skamandros toward the west from a single source. All of them are close to one another, encompassing a distance of 20 stadia, but the end of the Aisepos stands the farthest away from its beginning, approximately 500 stadia. What the Poet says creates a problem:

> they come to the two fair-flowing fountains, where the two sources of whirling Skamandros rise up, for one flows with gentle water

– that is "hot" – and he adds

> around it smoke is produced from it, as though a fire. The other flows cold even in summer, like hail or snow. [*Iliad* 22.147–52]

But today there is no hot spring to be found at the site, nor is the source of the Skamandros there, but in the mountain, and there is only one, not two. It is reasonable, then, that the hot spring has failed, and the cold one has flowed out from underneath the Skamandros through a passage and comes up to the surface here, or that because of its proximity to the Skamandros the water is said to be the source of the Skamandros, since several sources are said to belong to the same river.

(44) The Andeiros joins it from Karesene, a mountainous district settled with many villages and beautifully cultivated. It extends alongside the Dardanike, as far as the localities of Zeleia and Pityeia. They say that the territory was named after the Karesos River, which the Poet names ("the Rhesos, Heptaporos, Karesos, and Rhodios" [*Iliad* 12.20]), and that the city with the same name as the river was razed.

Again, he [Demetrios of Skepsis, F31] says the following: the Rhesos River is today called the Rhoeites (unless the river that empties into the Granikos is the Rhesos). The Heptaporos ["Seven-Crossing"], also called [C603] the Polyporos ["Many-Crossing"], is crossed seven times by someone going from the district of the Beautiful Pine to the village of Melainai and the Asklepieion that was founded by Lysimachos. Concerning the Beautiful Pine, King Attalos the First writes as follows: he says that its circumference is 24 feet and its trunk is a height of 67 feet and splits into 3, equidistant from one another, and then comes together again into a single crown, completing a total height of 2 *plethra* and 15 *pecheis*. It is 180 stadia distant from Adramyttion, to the north. The Karesos flows from Malous, a place lying between Old Skepsis and the Achaiion (on the Tenedian coast), and it empties into the Aisepos. The Rhodios comes from Kleandria and Gordos, which are 60 stadia distant from the Beautiful Pine, and it empties into the Ainios.

(45) In the hollow of the Aisepos, on the left of the stream, first there is Polichna, a place enclosed by walls, then Old Skepsis, and then Alazonion (which was fabricated for the hypothesis of the Halizonians, which we have discussed [12.3.20–7]). Then there is Karesos, which is deserted, and the Karasene and the river of the same name, which makes a notable hollow, although smaller than that of the Aisepos. Then there are the plains and mountain plains of Zeleia, which are beautifully cultivated. On the right of the Aisepos, between Polichna and Old Skepsis, are the villages of Ainea and Argyria, which again is a fabrication for the same hypothesis, to preserve "the birthplace of silver" [*Iliad* 2.857]. Where is Alybe, or Alope, or whatever they wish to call it? They should also have fabricated it – having rubbed their faces – and not allowed it to be lame and easy to disprove, having already made a bold venture. These things have their objections, but we can accept the others – or most of them – and we must pay heed to this man [Demetrios of Skepsis] as a native and from this place, who took enough care to write thirty books of commentary on slightly more than sixty lines, the *Catalogue of the Trojans*. He says that Old Skepsis is a distance of 50 stadia from Ainea and 30 from the Aisepos River, and that from Old Skepsis the same name was extended to a number of other places. But we return to the coast where we left off.

(46) After the Sigeian Promontory and the Achilleion there is the Tenedian
coast, the Achaiion, and Tenedos itself, which is no more than 40 stadia
distant from the mainland. It has a circumference of about 80 stadia,
and has an Aiolian city, two harbors, and a sanctuary of Apollo Smintheus,
just as the Poet testifies ("you, Smintheus, rule over mighty Tenedos"
[*Iliad* 1.38–9]). Several islets lie around it, two of which are called the
Kalydnai, situated on the voyage to Lekton. Some say that Kalydna is
Tenedos itself, others that it is Leukophrys. The story about Tennes is
there (from whom the island was named), and also that about Kyknos, a
Thracian by birth who some have as the father of Tennes and the king of
Kolonai.

(47) Larisa and Kolonai were adjacent to the Achaiion (what was formerly
the Lesbian coast). Then there is the present Chrysa, which is on a rocky
height, and then Hamaxitos, which is situated below and adjacent to Lekton.
Today Alexandria is adjacent to the Achaiion, and those towns, as well as
some of the other fortresses, have been incorporated into Alexandria –
including Kebrene and Neandria – and it possesses their territory. The
place where Alexandria now lies was called Sigia.

(48) In this Chrysa is the sanctuary of Apollo Smintheus ["Mouse-
Killer"], and the symbol that preserves the etymology of the name, the
mouse, lying at the foot of the xoanon. These are the works of Skopas of
Paros. The history – or myth – about the mice is associated with this place.
When the Teukrians came from Crete (Kallinos [T4] the elegiac poet was
the first to hand this down, and many have followed him), there was an
oracle that they should make their settlement where "the earthborn" would
attack them. He says that this happened around Hamaxitos, for at night a
large number of field mice burst forth and ate up all the leather in their
weapons and equipment. They remained there, and were the ones who
named Ida, after the one on Crete. Herakleides Pontikos [F142a] says that
the mice who spread throughout the sanctuary were considered sacred,
and thus the xoanon was made stepping on the mouse. Others say that a
certain Teukros came from the deme of Troes – today called Xypetaiones –
in Attika, but that no Teukrians came from Crete. Another sign of the
intermixture of those from Attika with the Trojans is that Erichthonios
was a founder of both. This is what those more recent say, but more in
agreement with the works of Homer are the traces pointed out in the
Theban Plain and at the Chrysa that once was founded there, which we
are about to discuss [13.1.63]. Today they call the sanctuary Sminthion. The
name Smintheus exists in many places, for around Hamaxitos – in addition
to the sanctuary of Sminthion – there are two places called Sminthia, and

there are others in the nearby Larisaia. In the Pariane there is a locality called Sminthia, as well as on Rhodes and Lindos and in many other places.

... and the Halesian Plain, which is not large and is inland from Lekton and the Tragasaian salt works near Hamaxitos, where it naturally congeals due to the Etesian winds. At Lekton an altar of the Twelve Gods is visible, said to have been founded by Agamemnon. These places are in sight of Ilion, within 200 stadia or a little more, and it is the same with those around Abydos on the other side, although Abydos is a little nearer.

(49) Going around Lekton, next there are the most reputed cities of the Aiolians, and the Gulf of Adramyttene, on which the Poet places most of the Lelegian settlements and the double Kilikians. The Mitylenaian shore is also here, with certain villages held by the Mitylenaians who are on the mainland. This same gulf is called the Idaian, since the ridge that extends from Lekton to Ida lies above the first part of the gulf. The Poet has the Lelegians first settling here [*Iliad* 10.429].

(50) They have been discussed previously [7.7.2, 12.8.4, 13.1.17]. One must add that he speaks about Pedasos, one of their cities, as assigned to Altes: "Altes lord of the Lelegians, lovers of war, holding rugged Pedasos on the Satnioeis" [*Iliad* 21.86–7]. The site of the city is visible today and is deserted. Some write incorrectly "at the foot of the Satnioeis," as though the city lay at the foot of a Mount Satnioeis, but there is no mountain called Satnioeis there, only a river, on which the city is situated. The Poet names the river:

> he wounded Satnios with his spear ... the son of Oinops, whom a noble nymph, a Naiad, bore to Oinops who was tending his cattle on the bank of the Satnioeis [*Iliad* 14.443–5]

[C606] and again, "he lived by the banks of the fair-flowing Satnioeis in steep Pedasos" [*Iliad* 6.34–5]. The Satnioeis was later called the Saphnioeis. It is a large winter torrent but it has been made worthy of mention because the Poet named it. These places are continuous with the Dardania and the Skepsia, as if another Dardania, but lower.

(51) The Assians and Gargarians now possess that which is as far as the sea toward Lesbos, surrounded by the Antandria, and the Kebrenians, Neandrians, and Hamaxitians. The Neandrians lie above Hamaxitos and also within Lekton, although farther inland and nearer to Ilion (they are 130 stadia distant). Above them are the Kebrenians, and [higher] than them are the Dardanians – as far as Old Skepsis – and Skepsis itself. Alkaios called Antandros the city of the Lelegians ("Antandros, first city of the Lelegians" [F337]). The Skepsian [F33] places it among the adjacent

ones, so that it would fall among the Kilikians, who are continuous with the Lelegians and mark off the southern side of Ida somewhat more. They are low and adjoin the coast, rather near Adramyttion. After Lekton there is a place called Polymedion, in 40 stadia, and then in 80 is Assos, a little above the sea, and then in 140 is Gargara. Gargara lies on a promontory that forms what is actually called the Adramyttenian Gulf. It is said that the entire coast from Lekton as far as Kanai has this particular name, which also includes the Elaitic [Gulf]. In particular, however, they say "Adramyttenian" only for what is enclosed by the cape on which Gargara is, which is called Cape Pyrrha, on which an Aphrodision is situated. The width of the mouth from cape to cape is a distance of 120 stadia. Antandros is within it, above which lies a mountain that is called Alexandria, where they say that the goddesses were judged by Paris. There is also Aspaneus, the timber market for Idaian wood, for it is brought down to here and distributed to those needing it. Then there is Astyra, a village and a grove sacred to Artemis Astyrene. Especially near by is Adramyttion, a city settled by the Athenians that has a harbor and a naval station. Outside the gulf and Cape Pyrrha is Kisthene, a deserted city that has a harbor. Above it in the interior is [C607] a copper mine, and Perperena, Trarion, and other such settlements. On the next part of the coast are the Mitylenaian villages – Koryphantis and Herakleia – and after them Attea, then Atarneus, Pitane, and the outlets of the Kaikos. This is already on the Elaitic Gulf. On the far side are Elaia and the rest of the gulf as far as Kanai. But we will go back and discuss each, if anything worthy of recording has been passed over, and first that around Skepsis.

(52) Old Skepsis is above Kebren on the highest part of Ida near Polichna. It was called Skepsis ["Viewing"] then, whether for another reason or because the place can be seen all around, if one must derive Hellenic words from names used at that time by the barbarians. Later they were resettled 60 stadia farther down at the present Skepsis, by Skamandrios the son of Hektor and Askanios the son of Aineias. The descendants of these two are said to have ruled Skepsis for a long time. Afterward they changed to an oligarchy. Then Milesians settled with them as fellow citizens and it became a democracy. But the descendants nonetheless were called kings and had certain honors. Then Antigonos [I] incorporated the Skepsians into Alexandria, and then Lysimachos released them and they returned home.

(53) The Skepsian [F35] believes that Skepsis was the royal residence of Aineias, since it is midway between what was subject to Aineias and Lyrnessos, where he fled, it is said, when he was being pursued by Achilleus. At any rate Achilleus says:

Do you not remember when you were alone and I chased you from the cattle, with swift feet down the Idaian mountains? . . . you fled from there to Lyrnessos but I pursued you and sacked it. [*Iliad* 20.188–92]

But the chattering about Aineias today does not agree with the reports mentioned about the founding of Skepsis. They say that he survived the war because of his enmity toward Priamos: "he always had resentment against divine Priamos, because although he was brave among men, he would not honor him" [*Iliad* 13.460–1]. His fellow rulers, the Antenoridai and Antenor himself, [survived] because of the hospitality that they showed [C608] Menelaos. At any rate, Sophokles says that when Troy was sacked a leopard skin was placed before Antenor's doors as a sign that his house was to be left unpillaged. Antenor and his children crossed over to Thrace with the surviving Enetians, and from there slipped away to the so-called Enetike on the Adria. Aineias, along with his father Anchises and his son Askanios, collected a large number of people and set sail. Some say that he settled around Makedonian Olympos, and others that he founded Kapyai near Mantineia in Arkadia (taking the name of the town from Kapys), and still others that he landed at Aigesta in Sikelia with Elymos the Trojan and took possession of Eryx and Lilybaion, naming the rivers around Aigesta the Skamandros and the Simoeis, and then he went into Latina and remained there according to an oracle that he should stay where he ate his table. This happened in Latina around Lavinium where a large piece of bread was put down instead of a table – because one was lacking – and it was consumed along with the meat. Homer, however, does not seem to agree with any of this, or what was previously mentioned about the founding of Skepsis. He indicates that Aineias remained in Troy and succeeded to the rule, handing the succession over to the sons of his sons, as the family of Priamos had been obliterated:

already the race of Priamos was hated by Kronion, and now mighty Aineias will rule the Trojans, and the sons of his sons, those who will come afterward. [*Iliad* 20.306–8]

Thus the succession of Skamandrios cannot be saved. He [Homer] disagrees far more with the others who say that he wandered as far as Italia and who would have him end his life there. Some write "the family of Aineias will rule everyone, and his son's sons," as the Romans say.

(54) From Skepsis came the Sokratics Erastos, Koriskos, and Koriskos' son Neleus, a man who heard both Aristotle and Theophrastos, and also received the library of Theophrastos, which included that of Aristotle. At any rate, Aristotle gave his to Theophrastos (and also left him his school),

who was the first, as far as we know, to collect books and to teach the kings of Egypt how to arrange a library. Theophrastos gave it to Neleus, who took [C609] it to Skepsis and gave it to his heirs, who were ordinary people who locked up the books and did not store them carefully. When they learned that the Attalid kings – to whom the city was subject – were seeking books to furnish the library at Pergamon, they hid them underground in a kind of trench. They were damaged by moisture and moths, and after a long time the books of Aristotle and Theophrastos were sold to Apellikon of Teos for a large amount of money. Apellikon was a bibliophile rather than a scholar, and seeking to restore what had been eaten through, he made new copies of the writings, filling things in wrongly, and letting the books out full of errors. Thus the older Peripatetics – those immediately after Theophrastos – did not have any books except for a few, mostly esoteric, and therefore could not philosophize about anything practical, but only declaim in a hollow manner about propositions. Those later, after these books came forth, could better philosophize and Aristotelianize, but were forced mostly to infer from probabilities because of the large number of errors. Rome also contributed much to this. Immediately after the death of Apellikon, Sulla, who had captured Athens, took the library of Apellikon home with him. Tyrannion the grammarian, an admirer of Aristotle, acquired it by paying attention to the caretaker of the library, as also did certain booksellers who used bad copyists and would not collate them, something that happens with books that are copied to be sold, both there and in Alexandria. Enough about this.

(55) Demetrios was also from Skepsis, whom I often mention, the grammarian who produced *The Battle Order of the Trojans*, and who was born at about the same time as Krates and Aristarchos. Later there was Metrodoros, a man who changed his life from philosophy to politics, and practiced rhetoric, for the most part, in his writings. He made use of a new style of speaking that was astonishing to many. Because of his reputation, he married with distinction in Chalkedon, although poor, and he came to act like a Chalkedonian. He paid attention to Mithridates [VI] Eupator, and went away, along with his wife, to Pontos. He was honored greatly [C610] and appointed to a judgeship, one from which there was no appeal of the judgement to the king. He did not continue in his prosperity, however, because he incurred the enmity of people who were less just than himself. He revolted from the king during an embassy to Tigranes [II] the Armenian, who sent him back against his will to Eupator, already in flight from his ancestral lands. But his life came to an end on the road, either by order of the king or due to disease (it is reported both ways). This is it about the Skepsians.

(56) After Skepsis are Andeira, Pioniai, and Gargaris. There is a stone around Andeira that when burned becomes iron, and then when heated in a furnace with a type of earth distills false silver, and with the addition of copper produces what is called the "mixture," which some call mountain copper. False silver is also found around Tmolos. These are places held by the Lelegians, as well as those around Assos.

(57) Assos is strong and well-watered, and the ascent to it from the sea and the harbor is steep and long, so that it seems what Stratonikos the citharist said is appropriate: "go to Assos, so that you may quickly come to destruction." The harbor is created from a large mole. Kleanthes the Stoic was from here, who succeeded to the school of Zenon of Kition, and left it to Chrysippos of Soloi. Aristotle also spent time here because of his marriage connection with the tyrant Hermias. Hermias was a eunuch, the slave of a certain banker, and when he came to Athens he heard both Plato and Aristotle. When he returned he shared the tyranny with his master – who had previously taken both Atarneus and Assos – and then succeeded him and sent for both Aristotle and Xenokrates and cared for them, marrying his brother's daughter to Aristotle. Memnon the Rhodian, who was a commander for the Persians at that time, pretended friendship and summoned him [Hermias] on the pretence of both hospitality and business, but seized him and sent him up to the king, who put him to death by hanging. The philosophers safely fled the territory, which the Persians took.

(58) Myrsilos [F17] says that Assos was founded by the Methymnaians, and Hellanikos [F16o] says that it was Aiolian, just as Gargara and Lamponia were also Aiolian. Gargara was an Assian foundation, but it was not well [C611] populated, for the kings brought in settlers from Miletoupolis when it was destroyed, so that – Demetrios the Skepsian [F36] says – it was semi-barbarian instead of Aiolian. According to Homer, however, all these are Lelegian, whom some represent to be Karian. Homer separates them: "toward the sea are the Karians and the Paionians with crooked bow, and the Lelegians and Kaukonians" [*Iliad* 10.428–9]. Thus they were different from the Karians, living between those subject to Aineias and those whom the Poet calls Kilikians. When they were pillaged by Achilleus they emigrated to Karia and took possession of the territory around present Halikarnassos.

(59) The city of Pedasos, today abandoned by them, is no longer in existence, but inland of Halikarnassos there was a city of Pedasa, named by them, and the territory is today called Pedasis. They say that eight cities were settled in this territory by the Lelegians, who formerly were so numerous that they took possesion of Karia as far as Myndos and Bargylia, but also cut off a large part of Pisidia. Later they made expeditions with the Karians

and became distributed throughout the whole of Hellas, and the ethnic group disappeared. Regarding the eight cities, Mausolos united six into one, Halikarnassos, as Kallisthenes [F25] records, but preserved Syangela and Myndos. These are the Pedasians of whom Herodotos says [1.175] that when anything disagreeble was about to happen to them and their neighbors, the priestess of Athena would grow a beard, and this happened three times. There is also a town named Pedason in the present region of Stratonikeia. Tombs and fortifications are visible throughout Karia and in Miletos, as well as traces of Lelegian settlements.

(60) After the Lelegians, the Kilikians lived on the next part of the coast, according to Homer. Today the Adramyttenians, Atarnians, and Pitanaians possess it, as far as the outlet of the Kaikos. The Kilikians were divided into two dominions, as we have said [13.1.7, 49], one under Eetion and one under Mynes.

(61) He [Homer] says that Thebe is the city of Eetion ("we went to Thebe, the sacred city of Eetion" [*Iliad* 1.366]) and he clearly indicates that Chrysa . . . which had the sanctuary of Apollo Smintheus, if Chryseis was taken at Thebe, for he says:

> we went to Thebe . . . and completely destroyed it and brought everything here. They divided it well among themselves, but they chose Chryseis for Atreides. [*Iliad* 1.366–9] [C612]

Mynes held Lyrnessos, since Achilleus "utterly destroyed Lyrnessos and the walls of Thebe" [*Iliad* 2.691], killing both Mynes and Epistrophos, so that when Briseis says

> you would not allow me to weep, not even, when swift Achilleus killed my man and sacked the city of divine Mynes [*Iliad* 19.295–7]

he [Homer] cannot be speaking of Thebe (for it belonged to Eetion), but Lyrnessos. Both were in what was later called the Plain of Thebe, which, because of its quality, was formerly fought over, they say, between the Mysians and Lydians, and later between the Hellenes who settled there from Aiolis and Lesbos. Most of it is now held by the Adramyttenians, for both Thebe and Lyrnessos (a fortified place) are here, although both are deserted. The former is 60 stadia distant from Adramyttion and the latter 88, in the opposite direction.

(62) Chrysa and Killa are also in the Adramyttene. At any rate, still today there is said to be a certain place near Thebe called Killa, where there is a sanctuary of Apollo Killaios. The Killaios River flows past it, coming from Ida. These are near the Antandria. Killaion in Lesbos is named after this

Killa, and there is a Mount Killaion between Gargara and Antandros. Daes of Kolonai [*FHG* vol. 4, p. 376] says that the sanctuary of Apollo Killaios was first founded in Kolonai by Aiolians sailing from Hellas. They also say that Apollo Killaios was established at Chrysa, but it is not clear whether this is the same as Smintheus or different.

(63) Chrysa was a town on the sea, having a harbor. Thebe is near by and above it. Here was also the sanctuary of Apollo Smintheus, and Chryseis. Today the place is completely deserted and the sanctuary was transferred to the present Chrysa, near Hamaxitos, at the time that the Kilikians were expelled, some to Pamphylia and others to Hamaxitos. Those less experienced in ancient history say that Chryses and Chryseis were there and that Homer records this place. But there is no harbor there, and he says "they arrived within the exceedingly deep harbor" [*Iliad* 1.432], and the sanctuary is not on the sea, although he locates the sanctuary on the sea:

[C613]   Chryseis stepped out of the seafaring ship, and Odysseus of many counsels
                  led her to the altar and placed her in the arms of her dear father. [*Iliad*
                  1.439–41]

It is not near Thebe (although he has it near by), yet he says at any rate [*Iliad* 1.366–9] that Chryseis was captured there. Also, there is no place of Killa pointed out in the Alexandrian territory, nor any sanctuary of Apollo Killaios, but the Poet joins the two together ("you who protect Chrysa and sacred Killa" [*Iliad* 1.37–8]). Yet the Plain of Thebe is visible near by. The voyage from Kilikian Chrysa to the naval station is around 700 stadia, about a day's journey, the amount that it appears Odysseus sailed, for immediately upon disembarking he rendered the sacrifice to the god, and since he was overtaken by evening he remained there and sailed away in the morning. But from Hamaxitos the distance is scarcely a third of what is mentioned, so that Odysseus upon arrival could have completed the sacrifice and sailed back to the naval station on the same day.

The memorial of Killos is near the sanctuary of Apollo Killaios and is a large mound. They say that he was the charioteer of Pelops and ruled over these places, from whom, perhaps, comes Kilikia, or the reverse.

(64) The matter of the Teukrians and the mice – from which Smintheus comes, since *sminthoi* means mice – must be transferred here. They justify a surname from something small by the following: it is said to be from locusts – which the Oitaians call *kornopes* – that Herakles Kornopion is honored among them, because he drove the locusts away. Among the Erythraians who live in Mimas he is Ipoktonos ["Worm Killer"] because he destroyed the vine-eating worm, and these are the only Erythraians

among whom the creature is not found. The Rhodians have a sanctuary of Apollo Erythibios ["Rust"] – "erysibe" they call "erythibe" – and the Asian Aiolians call a certain month Pornopion – which is what the Boiotians call locusts – and make sacrifice to Apollo Pornopion.

(65) The territory around Adramyttion is Mysian, although it was once subject to the Lydians. Today a gate at Adramyttion is called the Lydian, because, as they say, the Lydians founded the city. They say that the neighboring village of Astyra is Mysian. It was once a small town, which had a grove with the sanctuary of Artemis Astyrene, managed – along with its rituals – by the Antandrians, who were near neighbors. It is 20 stadia distant from ancient Chrysa, which also had a sanctuary and a grove. The Palisade of Achilleus was also here. Thebe, now deserted, is in the interior fifty stadia away. The Poet says that it is "under wooded Plakos" [*Iliad* 6.396   [C614] etc.] but no Plakos or Plax is recorded there and no woods lie above it, although it is near Ida. Thebe is as much as 70 stadia distant from Astyra and sixty from Andeira, but all these are names of deserted or lightly populated places, or winter rivers, talked about only because of their ancient history.

(66) Assos and Adramyttion are both notable cities. Adramyttion suffered in the Mithridatic War, because the commander Diodoros cut the throats of the citizen council in order to please the king. He pretended to be a philosopher of the Academy, a dispenser of justice, and a teacher of rhetoric. He went with the king to Pontos, but when the king was overthrown he paid the penalty for his injustice, since at the same time many charges were brought against him. He was unable to bear the shame and disgracefully starved himself to death in my own city. Another famous Adramyttenian man was the rhetorician Xenokles. He was of the Asiatic type, a debater like none other, who spoke before the Senate on the matter of Asia at the time when it was charged with Mithradatizing.

(67) Near Astyra is a precipitously deep lake called Sapra, which breaks out onto a surf-filled sea beach. Below the Andeirans is a sanctuary of the Andeirene Mother of the Gods, and a cave that is underground as far as Palaia. Palaia is a settlement so-named at a distance of 130 stadia from the Andeirans. The underground passage became known because a goat fell into its mouth and was found the next day near Andeira by a shepherd who happened to come to make sacrifice.

Atarneus is the seat of the tyrant Hermias. Then there is Pitane, an Aiolian city with two harbors, and the Euenos River, which flows past it, from which an aqueduct has been constructed by the Adramyttenians. Arkisilaos is from Pitane, who along with Zenon of Kition was a fellow student of Polemon.

In Pitane there is also a place on the sea called Atarneus Under Pitane, opposite the island called Elaioussa. They say that in Pitane bricks float on water, as also occurs on an islet in Tyrrhenia, for the earth is lighter than an equal bulk of water, so it floats. Poseidonios [F237] says that in Iberia he [C615] saw bricks molded from a clayey earth, by which silver plate is cleaned, and they floated. After Pitane there is the Kaikos River, which empties in 30 stadia into the so-called Elaitic Gulf. On the far side of the Kaikos – 12 stadia distant from the river – is the Aiolian city of Elaia, which is also a Pergamene seaport, and 120 stadia distant from Pergamon.

(68) Then there is Kane, in 100 stadia, a promontory rising opposite Lekton that forms the Adramyttenian Gulf, of which the Elaitic is a part. Kanai is a small town of Lokrians from Kynos, lying in the Kanaia opposite the southermost capes of Lesbos. This extends as far as the Arginousai and the cape lying above them, which some name Aiga ["Goat"], the same name as the animal. But the second syllable is to be considered long (Aigan, like "aktan" and "archan"), for it was the name of the entire mountain that is now called Kane or Kanai. The sea surrounds the mountain on the south and west, and the Kaikos Plain lies below it on the east, and the Elaitis on the north. It is sufficiently contracted, although it slopes toward the Aigaion Sea, from which it was named. Later the promontory was called Aiga, such as by Sappho [F170], but the rest was Kane or Kanai.

(69) Teuthrania lies between Elaia, Pitane, Artaneus, and Pergamon. It is no more than 70 stadia distant from any of them and is within the Kaikos. It is related that Teuthras was the king of the Kilikians and Mysians. Euripides [F696] says that Auge, with her child Telephos, was put into a chest by Aleos, the father of Auge, and was submerged into the sea – because he detected that she had been seduced by Herakles – yet due to the providence of Athena the chest was carried across and cast up at the mouth of the Kaikos. Teuthras took the people up and considered her as his wife and the child as his own. This is the myth, but something else must have happened for the daughter of an Arkadian to have come together with the Mysian king, and for the son to have received the kingdom. It is believed that both Teuthras and Telephos ruled the territory around Teuthrania and the Kaikos. The Poet only records the story as follows:

> such was Telephides, whom he killed with bronze, the hero Eurypylos, and many comrades were slain around him, Keteians, because of the gifts of a woman. [*Odyssey* 11.519–21]

[C616] Thus an enigma is set before us instead of a clear statement, for we do not know how we must understand either the "Keteians" or "the gifts of a woman," but the grammarians have thrown in mythic traditions more for their ingenuity in argumentation rather than to solve questions.

(70) Let us leave this, and say – taking that which is more obvious – that according to Homer, Eurypylos clearly reigned in the places around the Kaikos. Thus a part of the Kilikians was subject to him, and there were not only two dominions among them, but three. This is supported by the fact that in the Elaitis a torrential stream is visible, the Keteios, which empties into another like it, and then another, and they end in the Kaikos.

But the Kaikos does not flow from Ida (as Bakchylides [F49] says). Euripides says incorrectly that Marsyas "lives in widely known Kelainai, in the farthermost places of Ida" [F1085], for Kelainai is very far from Ida, and the sources of the Kaikos are also far. They are visible in the plain. Temnon is a mountain that makes the boundary between it and what is called the Plain of Apia, which lies in the interior above the Plain of Thebe. The Mysios River flows from Temnon and empties into the Kaikos below its springs. Some accept that because of this Aischylos said at the beginning of the prologue of his *Myrmidons* "O Kaikos and the Mysian influxes" [F143]. Near the springs is the village of Gergitha, to which Attalos [I] transferred those in the Troad, when he destroyed their territory.

Part 2: Lesbos

(1) Since the island of Lesbos, which is worthy of major discussion, stretches alongside the coast from Lekton as far as Kanai, and has some islets lying around it – some outside it and others between it and the mainland – it is now the proper time to speak about them, for they are Aiolian, and Lesbos is essentially the metropolis of the Aiolian cities. It is nessary to begin from the point opposite to where we were on the coast.

(2) As one sails from Lekton to Assos, the Lesbia begins at Sigrion, its northern cape. Around here is Methymna, a Lesbian city that is 60 stadia from the coast extending from Polymedion to Assos. The entire island fills a perimeter of 1,100 stadia. The various [distances] are as follows: from Methymna to Malia, the southernmost cape if one has the island on the right (where Kanai lies most directly opposite the island and comes to an [C617] end with it) is 340 stadia. Then to Sigrion, which is the length of the island, is 560, and then 210 to Methymna.

Mitylene lies between Methymna and Malia, and is the largest city. It is 70 stadia distant from Malia, 120 from Kanai, and the same from the Arginousai, which are three islands that are not large and are near to the mainland, lying alongside Kanai. Between Mitylene and Methymna, near the village called Aigeiros in the Methymnaia, the island is the narrowest, with a passage of 20 stadia over to the Pyrrhaian Euripos. Pyrrha is situated on the western side of Lesbos, 100 [stadia] distant from Malia. Mitylene has two harbors, the southern of which can be closed . . . fifty triremes, and the northern is large and deep, protected by a mole. An islet lies off both, which has on it the part of the city that is settled there. It is well furnished with everything.

(3) It has had distinguished men. In antiquity there were Pittakos, one of the Seven Wise Men, and the poet Alkaios, and his brother Antimenidas, who, Alkaios says, won a great struggle when fighting along with the Babylonians, rescuing them from their difficulties by killing, as he says, "a fighting man who was one palm less than five royal *pecheis*." (F350). Sappho also flourished at the same time, an extraordinary person. We do not know in all the time that has been recorded any woman who could rival her even slightly in poetry. At that time the city was ruled by a number of tyrants because of dissension, about which there are the so-called "Stastiotic [Factional]" poems of Alkaios. Pittakos was also one of the tyrants. Alkaios would reproach both him and the others – Myrsilos, Melanchros, the Kleanaktidai, and certain others – but he was not free himself from attempts at revolution. Pittakos himself used the monarchy to overthrow those in power, and then, when it had been overthrown, returned independence to the city. Diophanes the rhetorician was born at a much later time, and in our time there were Potamon, Lesbokles, Krinagoras, and the historian Theophanes, who was also a politician and became a friend of Pompeius Magnus, mostly through his ability, and helped him in the proper execution of all his deeds. Because of this he adorned his native land – both through him [Pompeius] and himself – and was shown to be the most distinguished of all the Hellenes. He left a son, Marcus Pompeius, whom Caesar Sebastos once established as administrator of Asia, and who now is considered one of the primary friends of Tiberius. The Athenians were in danger of falling into an incurable disgrace when they voted that the Mitylenaians from youth upward should have their throats cut, but they changed their minds, and their vote reached the commanders only one day before the order for execution was to be carried out.

[C618]

(4) Pyrrha is destroyed, but its suburb is inhabited and it has a harbor. There is a passage of 40 stadia from it to Mitylene. Then after Pyrrha is Eressos, situated on a hill and extending down to the sea. Then, in 28 stadia, is Sigrion. Both Theophrastos and Phanias, the Peripatic philosophers who were acquaintances of Aristotle, were from Eressos. Theophrastos was originally called Tyrtamos, but Aristotle changed his name to Theophrastos

["Divine Speaker"], both avoiding the cacophony of his former name and recognizing the eagerness of his speech. Aristotle made all his pupils eloquent, but Theophrastos was the most eloquent. Antissa, a city having a harbor, is next after Sigrion. Then there is Methymna, from which Arion came, who, according to the story told by those following Herodotos [1.23–4], safely went to Tainaron on a dolphin, after being thrown into the sea by brigands. He was a citharodist. Terpandros is also said to have been skilled in the same type of music and to have been born on the same island. He was the first to use a seven-stringed lyre, instead of the four-stringed, as is said in the words attributed to him: "having set aside the four-toned song, we will sound for you new hymns with a seven-toned instrument" [F5]. Hellanikos the historian was a Lesbian, as well as Kallias, the interpreter of Sappho and Alkaios.

(5) In the strait between Asia and Lesbos there are about twenty islets, but Timosthenes [F35] says forty. They are called the Hekatonnesoi, a compound like "Peloponnesos," with the customary repetition of the letter nu in such forms, as is said in Myonnesos, Prokonnesos, and Halonnesos. Thus these are the Hekatonnesoi – that is, the Apollononnesoi, as Hekatos is Apollo. Along this entire coast Apollo is greatly honored, as far as Tenedos, and is called Smintheus, Killaios, Gryneus, or other titles. Pordoselene is near them, which has a city of the same name on it, and in front of the city is [C619] another island, larger and with the same name,[4] which is deserted and has a sanctuary of Apollo.

(6) Some, to avoid the bad form of the names, say that one should read "Poroselene" here, Aspordenon – the mountain around Pergamon that is rough and wretched – as "Asporenon [Barren]," and the sanctuary of the Mother of the Gods as "Asporene." What do we say, then, about *pordalis*, *saperdes*, Perdikkas, and Simonides' "he was banished with damp [*pordakoisin*] clothing"[5] – instead of "moist" – and, in the old comedy, "the damp [*pordakon*] place" [Aristophanes, *Peace* 1148] instead of "marshy"? Lesbos is equidistant from Tenedos, Lemnos, and Chios, somewhat less than 500 stadia.

Part 3: The remainder of Aiolis

(1) Since the Lelegians and Kilikians were related to the Trojans, it is questioned why they are not catalogued along with them in the *Catalogue*.

---

[4] The passage as it appears in the manuscripts seems confused, and there may be a lacuna or some repetition.
[5] This citation is generally attributed to Semonides of Amorgas (F21) rather than Simonides of Keos.

It is reasonable that because of the death of their leaders and the destruction of their cities the few remaining Kilikians were made subject to Hektor. Both Eetion and his sons are said to have been killed before [the time of] the *Catalogue*:

> indeed my father was killed by divine Achilleus, who sacked the city of the Kilikians . . . Thebe of the high gates . . . my seven brothers who were in our megara all went on the same day, went to the house of Hades, all killed by swift-footed Achilleus. [*Iliad* 6.414–23, excerpted]

In the same way those subject to Mynes lost both their leader and their city: "he cast down Mynes and Epistrophos" [*Iliad* 2.692] and "sacked the city of divine Mynes" [*Iliad* 19.296]. But he makes the Lelegians present at the fights when he says this: "toward the sea are the Karians and the Paionians with crooked bow, and the Lelegians and Kaukonians" [*Iliad* 10.428–9], and again:

> he wounded Satnios with his sharp spear, the son of Oinops, whom a noble nymph, a Naiad, bore to Oinops who was tending his cattle on the bank of the Satnioeis. [*Iliad* 14.443–5]

They had not so totally disappeared that they did not have some structure of their own, as their king still survived ("Altes lord of the Lelegians, lovers of war" [*Iliad* 21.86]), and their city had not been completely destroyed, for he adds "who holds rugged Pedasos on the Satnioeis" [*Iliad* 21.87]. Yet they [C620] have been omitted from the *Catalogue*, for their structure was not considered sufficient to be organized in the *Catalogue*, and they are catalogued under Hektor as is appropriate. Lykaion, a brother of Hektor, says:

> my mother Laothoe bore me for a short life, she who was the daughter of old Altes, Altes lord of the Lelegians, lovers of war. [*Iliad* 21.84–6]

Such are the inferences from probabilities in these things.

(2) It is also inferring from probabilities if one were to ask what the exact boundaries were to which the Kilikians extended, according to the Poet, as well as the Pelasgians and even the so-called Keteians who were under Eurypylos and who were between them. Concerning the Kilikians and those under Eurypylos, what is possible has already been said, that they are in general bounded by the the region of the Kaikos. Regarding the Pelasgians, it is reasonable to place them next, both from what Homer says and other accounts. He says as follows:

> Hippothoos led the tribes of Pelasgians who fight with the spear, those who lived in Larisa with its large clods. Hippothoos and Pylaios the offspring of

Ares, the two sons of Pelasgian Lethos the son of Teutamos, ruled them. [*Iliad* 2.840–3]

From this he clearly shows that the number of Pelasgians was notable, for he says "tribes" not "tribe" and declares that their home was in Larisa.

There are many Larisas, but it is necessary to understand that it was one which was near, and it is perhaps best to assume correctly it was the one near Kyme. Of the three that existed, the one near Hamaxitos was in actual sight of Ilion and very near it (about 200 stadia away). Thus one could not plausibly say that Hippothoos fell in the fight against Patroklos "far from [this] Larisa" [*Iliad* 17.301], but rather from the one near Kyme, as there is about 1,000 stadia between them. The third Larisa is an Ephesian village in the Kaystros Plain, which is said to have been formerly a city with a sanctuary of Larisenian Apollo, and closer to Tmolos than Ephesos. It is 180 stadia distant and thus might be considered subject to the Meionans. But the Ephesians, having grown in power, later cut off much of the Meionians, whom we now call Lydians. Thus this would not be Pelasgian Larisa either, but rather another one. And we have no strong proof that this Larisa in the Kaystriane existed at that time (nor for Ephesos). But all Aiolian history, coming into existence shortly after the Trojan matter, is a witness to [C621] the one near Kyme.

(3) They say that those who set forth from Phrikion, the Lokrian mountains above Thermopylai, landed at the place where Kyme now is, and they found the Pelasgians doing badly because of the Trojan War, although still possessing Larisa, which was about 70 stadia distant from Kyme. On their frontier they built a fortification that is still called today the New Wall, thirty stadia from Larisa, and when they captured it they founded Kyme and settled there those people who survived. It is called Kyme Phrikonis after the Lokrian mountains, as is Larisa, but the latter is now deserted.

They say that history in general bears witness to the fact that the Pelasgians were a great people. At any rate, Menekrates of Elaia, in his *On Foundings*, says [F1] that the entirety of what is now the Ionian coast beginning at Mykale, as well as the neighboring islands, was formerly inhabited by Pelasgians. The Lesbians say that they were placed under the command of Pylaios, whom the Poet calls the ruler of the Pelasgians [*Iliad* 2.842], and from whom their mountain is still called Pylaion. The Chians, also, say that the Pelasgians from Thessaly were their founders. But the people frequently were wandering and departing, and they greatly increased and then disappeared as a group, especially when the Aiolians and Ionians crossed over to Asia.

(4) A peculiarity with the Larisaians (the Kaystrenian and Phrikonian ones, and third, those in Thessaly) is that they all held land that was deposited by rivers, by the Kaystros, Hermos, and Peneios. It is at Phrikonian Larisa that Piasos is said to have been honored, who, they say, was ruler of the Pelasgians and fell in love with his daughter Larisa, using force against her and paying the penalty for his outrage. She observed him looking into a pithos of wine and took him by the legs, raised him up, and dumped him into the pithos.

(5) Such are the ancient accounts. To the present Aiolian cities must also be added Aigai as well as Temnos, where Hermagoras, the author of the rhetorical handbook, was from. These cities are situated in the mountainous territory that lies above the Kymaian, Phokaian, and Smyrnaian territory, along which the Hermos flows. Magnesia is not far from these cities, at the foot of Sipylos, and which the Romans have judged to be a free city. It has been damaged by [C622] recent earthquakes. In the opposite direction, sloping toward the Kaikos, it is 70 stadia from Larisa across the Hermos to Kyme. Then it is 40 to Myrina, and the same from there to Grynion, and from there to Elaia. According to Artemidoros [F129], one goes from Kyme to Adai, and then, after forty stadia there is the cape called Hydra, which, along with the opposite cape, Harmatous, forms the Elaitic Gulf. The width of its mouth is about 80 stadia, but, including the bays, it is 60 stadia to Myrina, an Aiolian city with a harbor. Then there is the Harbor of the Achaians, where there are altars of the Twelve Gods, and then the Myrinaian town of Grynion, and a sanctuary of Apollo (an ancient oracle and an expensive temple of white stone) at a distance of 40 stadia. Then it is 70 to Elaia, which has a harbor and a naval station of the Attalid kings, founded by Menestheus and those Athenians who joined him in the expedition to Ilion. What comes next has already been discussed, that around Pitane, Atarneus, and other places [13.1.66].

(6) Kyme is the largest and best of the Aiolian [cities], and along with Lesbos is more or less the metropolis of the other cities, about thirty in number, of which not a few have disappeared. Kyme is ridiculed for its lack of astuteness, because, as some say, they were reputed not to have had tolls for their harbor until 300 years after their foundation, and thus the people previous to that time did not enjoy the use of this revenue. They obtained the reputation of learning late that they were living in a city on the sea. There is also another story, that they borrowed money for the state, using their stoas as security. When they did not pay on the appointed day, they were kept from walking in them. When it rained, the creditors – through a sort of shame – told them through a herald to go under the stoas. Thus the herald announced "Go under the stoas," but the story spread that

the Kymaians did not understand that they could go under the stoas when it rained without being given a sign by the herald. Ephoros, a man indisputably worthy of remembering, was from this city. He was acquainted with Isokrates the rhetorician and wrote a *History* and *On Discoveries*. Still earlier there was Hesiod the poet, who said that his father Dios left Aiolian Kyme and emigrated to Boiotia:

> he lived near Helikon in a wretched village, Askre, bad in winter, difficult in summer, and good at no time. [*Works and Days* 639–40]

There is no agreement regarding Homer, for many lay claim to him. But the name of the city was established from an Amazon, just as Myrina was (from the one who lies in the Trojan plain below Batieia: "which indeed men call Batieia but the immortals the mound of much-bounding Myrina" [*Iliad* 2.813–14]). Ephoros, also, is ridiculed because he does not speak of the deeds of his native land while enumerating the deeds of others, but he is unwilling that it should fail to be remembered, and thus proclaims "at the same time the Kymaians enjoyed peace" [F236].   [C623]

Since we have gone through both the Trojan and Aiolian coasts, next one should go over the interior as far as the Tauros, keeping to the same order of approach.

Part 4:   Pergamon and Lydia

(1) Pergamon holds a type of hegemony over these plains. It is a distinguished city and prospered under the Attalid kings, and it is necessary to begin the next circuit here. First, it must briefly be shown how those kings started and how they came to an end.

Pergamon was a treasury of Lysimachos the son of Agathokles, who was one of the successors of Alexander. The settlement is on the very summit of a mountain (the mountain is conical and ends in a sharp top). The custody of this fortress and its money (which was nine 9,000 talents) was entrusted to Philetairos, a man from Tios, who was a eunuch from childhood, for it happened that at a certain burial where there was a spectacle – at which many were present – the attendant who was rearing Philetairos (who was still a youth) was cut off by the crowd so that the child was mutilated and became a eunuch. Although he was a eunuch he appeared to be well trained and worthy of trust. For a time he continued to be well disposed toward Lysimachos, but had differences with his wife Arsinoë [II], who slandered him. Thus he caused the territory to revolt and administered it for a time, seeing that it was suitable for political change. Lysimachos was inflicted with domestic difficulties and was forced to kill his son Agathokles. Seleukos [I] Nikator invaded and overthrew him, and then was overthrown himself and treacherously killed by Ptolemaios Keraunos. During these troubles the eunuch continued at the fortress and always administered it through promises and other services to anyone strong who was nearby. At any rate, he continued master of the fortress and the money for twenty years.

[C624] (2) He had two brothers. The older was Eumenes and the younger Attalos. Eumenes had a son of the same name as his father, Eumenes [I], who succeeeded to Pergamon, and was already master of the surrounding territory, so that near Sardeis he fought Antiochos [I] son of Seleukos [I] in a battle and was victorious. His life ended after a reign of twenty-two years, and Attalos [I], the son of Attalos and Antiochis the daughter of Achaios, succeeded to the rule and was the first to be proclaimed king, having conquered the Galatians in a great battle. He became a friend of the Romans and fought along with them and with the Rhodian fleet, joining in the war against Philippos [V]. He died in old age, having ruled as king for forty-three years, and left four sons by Apollonis (a Kyzikene woman): Eumenes [II], Attalos [II], Philetairos, and Athenaios. The younger ones remained private citizens, but Eumenes [II], the elder of the other two, ruled. He fought along with the Romans against Antiochos [III] the Great and against Perseus, and he received from the Romans everything within the Tauros that had been subject to Antiochos [III]. Previously the territory of Pergamon had not included many places even extending as far as the sea around the Elaitic and Adramyttenian Gulfs. He built up the city, planting Nikephorion with a grove, and made dedications and libraries, and through a love of splendor established Pergamon as it now is. After a reign of forty-nine years, he left it to his son Attalos [III] (from Stratonike, the daughter of Ariarathes [IV] the king of Kappadokia). He established his brother Attalos [II] as guardian of his son – who was extremely young – and of the rule, who, after ruling twenty-one years, died as an old man, having been successful in many things. Along with Alexander [Balas] – the son of Antiochos [IV] – he helped make war against Demetrios [I] the son of Seleukos [IV], and fought with the Romans against the false Philippos. He overthrew Diegylis king of the Kainians, having made an expedition into Thrace, and killed Prousias [II], after raising up his son Nikomedes [II] against him. He left the rule under a guardian to Attalos [III], who ruled for five years and was called Philometer, ending his life through disease, having left it to the Romans as his heirs. They proclaimed it a province, calling it Asia, the same as the continent.

The Kaikos flows by Pergamon, through the so-called Kaikos Plain,
[C625] going through exceedingly prosperous land, about the best in Mysia.

(3) Pergamene men have become notable in my time: Mithridates the son of Menodotos and Adobogiona, who was from the family of the tetrarchs of Galatia and was said to have been a concubine of King Mithridates [VI]. Because of this her friends gave the child the name of Mithridates, pretending that he had been produced by the king. He became a friend of Caesar the God and received such honor from him that he was appointed tetrarch from his mother's family and king of the Bosporos and elsewhere. He was overthrown by Asandros, who killed King Pharnakes [II] and took possession of the Bosporos. He [Mithridates] was thus considered worthy of a great name, as was Apollodoros the rhetorician who wrote about that art and led the Apollodorian school (whatever that is, for there were many prevailing, such as the Apollodorian and Theodorian schools, and to make a judgement is more than is possible for us). But the friendship of Caesar Sebastos has especially raised up Apollodoros, as he was his teacher in speaking. He had a notable student in Dionysios, surnamed Attikos, his fellow citizen, who was a capable sophist, historian, and prose writer.

(4) Proceeding from the plain and the city toward the east, there is a city, Apollonia, that is situated on an elevated site. Toward the south there is a mountainous ridge, and crossing it, as one proceeds to Sardeis, on the left there is the city of Thyateira, a Makedonian settlement, which some say is the farthest Mysian one. On the right is Apollonis, which is 300 stadia distant from Pergamon and the same from Sardeis. It is named after the Kyzikene Apollonis. Next are the Hermos Plain and Sardeis. The territory to the north of Pergamon is mostly held by the Mysians – that on the right of the so-called Abaeitians – and Epiktetos adjoins them as far as Bithynia.

(5) Sardeis is a great city, and although it is more recent than the Trojan matter, it is still old and has a secure citadel. It was the royal city of the Lydians, whom the Poet calls the Meionians (those later the Maionians). Some represent that they are the same as the Lydians, and others that they are different, but it is better to say that they are the same. Tmolos lies above Sardeis, a fortunate mountain with a lookout on its peak, which is an exedra of white stone, the work of the Persians. From it one can look all around to the plains below, especially the Kaystrianian. Lydians, Mysians, and Makedonians live around it. The Paktolos flows from Tmolos, and they say that in antiquity a large amount of gold dust was carried down, from [C626] which, they say, the well-known wealth of Kroisos and his ancestors became famous. Today the dust has ceased. The Paktolos is carried down to the Hermos, into which the Hyllos – today called the Phrygios – also empties. These three – and others less notable – come together and empty into the sea around Phokaia, as Herodotos says [1.80.1]. The Hermos begins in

Mysia on the sacred mountain of Didymene, and is carried through the Katakekaumene into the Sardiane and adjoining plains (as has been said), as far as the sea. Below the city lies the Sardianon Plain and that of the Kyros, the Hermos, and the Kaystrianian, which are contiguous and the best of all plains. Forty stadia from the city is Gygaia, mentioned by the Poet [*Iliad* 2.865, 20.390–1], a lake whose name was later changed to Koloe, where there is a sanctuary of Koloenian Artemis, which has a great sanctity. They say that at the festivals the baskets dance, but I do not know why they tell incredible things instead of the truth.

(6) These are about how the verses of Homer stand:

> The Meionians were led by Mesthles and Antiphon, the two sons of Palaimenes born from Lake Gygaia, and they led the Meionians, born at the foot of Tmolos. [*Iliad* 2.864–6]

Some also write this as a fourth verse: "under snowy Tmolos in the rich land of Hyde." There is no Hyde to be found among the Lydians. Some also place Tychios there, of whom the Poet says "the best of leather workers, who was in Hyde" [*Iliad* 7.221]. They add that the place is woody and subject to lightning, and the Arimians are there. After "among the Arimians, where they say the bed of Typhon is" [*Iliad* 2.783] they put "in a woodland place, in the rich land of Hyde." Others locate the myth in Kilikia, and some in Syria, and others in the Pithekoussai (those who say that among the Tyrrhenians apes [*pithekoi*] are called *arimoi*). Some call Sardeis Hyde, and others its akropolis. Skepsios [F39] considers the most believable those who place the Arimians in the Katakekaumenian territory of Mysia. Pindar associates the Pithekoussai (those off the Kymaia as well as those in Sikelia) with those in Kilikia, for he says that Typhon lies below Aitna:

[C627]
> Once he was nourished in a famous Kilikian cave, but now his woolly breast is pressed by the sea- surrounded bank above Kyme and Sikelia, [*Pythian* 1.16- 19]

and again "Aitna with its arrogant bonds lies around him" [F92], and again "once among the Arimians father Zeus alone of the gods by necessity ravaged terrible Typhon of the fifty heads" [F93]. Some accept the Syrians as the Arimians, now called the Aramaians, and that the Kilikians in Troy migrated and settled again in Syria, cutting off from the Syrians what is today called Kilikia. According to Kallisthenes [F33] the Arimians, after whom the nearby mountains are called the Arima, are near Kalykadnos and the Sarpedonian Cape near the Korykian Cave.

(7) Lying around Lake Koloe are the memorials of the kings. Near Sardeis is the great mound of Alyattes on a high base, built, as Herodotos

says [1.93], by the people of the city, with most of the work accomplished by the prostitutes. He says that all the women prostituted themselves, and some say that the tomb is a monument to prostitution. Some report that Koloe is an artificial lake, to contain the flooding that occurs when the rivers are full. Hypaipa is a city that one comes to, [going] from Tmolos to the Kaystrian Plain.

(8) Kallisthenes [F29] says that Sardeis was first taken by the Kimmerians and then by the Trerians and Lykians – as is shown by Kallinos [T5] the elegiac poet – and taken last in the time of Kyros and Kroisos. When Kallinos says that the attack of the Kimmerians occurred against the Esionians, at which time Sardeis was taken, the Skepsian [F41] and his followers conjecture that he called the Asionians the Esionians (in Ionic), for perhaps, he says, Meionia was called Asia, as Homer says ("on the Asian meadow around the streams of the Kaystrios" [*Iliad* 2.461]).

The city was later restored in a notable manner because of the quality of its territory and was in no way less than any of the neighboring cities, although recently it has lost many of its buildings because of earthquakes. Through the forethought of Tiberius – our ruler at this time – and his good deeds, it has been restored, this one and many others, all those that shared the same misfortune at the same time.

(9) Notable men of the same family were born at Sardeis, including the two Diodoroi, rhetoricians, of whom the elder was called Zonas, a man [C628] who frequently argued the cause of Asia. At the time of the attack of King Mithridates [VI] he was accused of attempting to make the cities revolt from him, but acquitted himself of the charge. The younger was a friend of mine and wrote historical works, as well as melic and other poems that adequately show the old style of writing. Xanthos, the ancient historian, is called a Lydian, but we do not know whether he was from Sardeis.

(10) After the Lydians are the Mysians and the city of Philadelphia, full of earthquakes. The walls of the houses are broken and separated, as different parts of the city suffered at different times. Because of this few live in the city and many spend their lives as farmers in the country, having prosperous soil. One may be astonished at the few who are so fond of the place but whose homes are so precarious, and one might marvel still more at its founders.

(11) After this is the so-called Katakekaumene ["Burned"] territory, which has a length of 500 stadia and a width of 400, whether it should be called Mysia or Meionia (both are said). It is entirely without trees except for the vine that produces the Katakekaumenitic wine, which is no less in quality than the most reputable ones. The surface of the plains is ashy and the mountainous and rocky portions are black, as if burned. Some

conjecture that this occurred from thunderbolts and whirlwinds, and do not hesitate to locate the mythical story about Typhon here. Xanthos [F13] says that a certain Arimous was king of this place, but it is not reasonable that this territory experienced a conflagration all at once because of such things, but rather that it was by an earth-born fire, whose sources are exhausted today. Three pits are visible there, which are called "the bellows" and are about 40 stadia distant from each other. Rough hills lie above them, which are reasonably suggested to be heaps of stones that have been blown out. One might understand that such soil is good for the vine from the situation in the Katanaia, where ashes are heaped up and produce an abundance of excellent wine. Some wittily say – using such places as proof – that it is suitable to speak of Dionysos as "fire-born."

(12) The next portions, toward the south as far as the Tauros, are so interwoven with each other that the Phrygian, Karian, Lydian, and even the [C629] Mysian portions fall into one another and are difficult to distinguish. This confusion has been increased in no small way because the Romans did not divide them by tribes, but arranged their administration in another way, in which they have their assemblies and jurisdiction. Tmolos comes together somewhat and has only a moderate circumference, with its portions bounded by the Lydians. The Mesogis extends in the opposite direction as far as Mykale, beginning at Kelainai, as Theopompos [F391] says, so that some of it is occupied by the Phrygians (that around Kelainai and Apameia), some by Mysians and Lydians, and some by Karians and Ionians. The rivers also – especially the Maiandros – mark the boundaries between peoples, but where they flow through the middle it makes an exact distinction difficult to comprehend. The same is said of the plains that are on either side of the mountainous or riverine territory. We should not consider such things as a surveyor, but must record only as much as has been handed down by our predecessors.

(13) Adjoining the Kaystrianian Plain on the east, which lies between the Mesogis and Tmolos, is the Kilbianian Plain. It is large and well-settled, and is an excellent territory. Then there is the Hyrkanian Plain, which the Persians named, bringing settlers from there (similarly the Persians named the Plain of Kyros). Then there is the Peltenian Plain – already in Phrygia – and the Killanian and Tabenian, whose towns have both a mixed Phrygian population and some Pisidians, after whom the plains were named.

(14) After crossing the Mesogis, between the Karians and the Nysaia (which is a territory across the Maiandros as far as the Kibyratis and the Kabalis), there are cities near the Mesogis and directly opposite Laodikeia. There is Hierapolis, where there are hot springs and the Ploutonion, both of

which are something marvellous. The water easily solidifies and turns into stone, so that streams are carried along that make fences of a single stone. The Ploutonion is below a small brow of the mountainous territory above it and is a moderately sized opening, large enough to be capable of admitting a man, but which is very deep. A quadrilaterial railing is in front of it, about half a *plethron* in circumference, and it is full of a thick mist-like cloud, so that one can scarcely see the surface. For those who come near to the railing, the air around it is harmless, since it is free from the cloud when it is calm, remaining within the enclosure, but all animals that pass within die imme-   [C630] diately. At any rate, bulls that are led to it fall in and are dragged out dead, and I threw in sparrows and they immediately breathed their last and died. But the Galloi, who are castrated, go into it without suffering, so that they come near to the opening and bend over it, going down to a certain depth, although holding their breath as much as they can (I could see by their appearance that they were experiencing a kind of choking): whether this is the case with all who are mutilated in this way or only those around the sanctuary, whether it is divine providence (as would be suitable with religious ecstasy), or whether certain powers are antidotes. The petrification, they say, occurs with waters around Laodikeia, although there it is potable. The water at Hierapolis is remarkably useful for the dyeing of wool, and thus what is dyed with roots is equal to that with the coccus or marine purple. The supply of water is so abundant that the city is full of natural baths.

(15) After Hierapolis are the places across the Maiandros. Those around Laodikeia, Aphrodisias, and as far as Karoura, have already been discussed (12.8.13–17). Next are the portions toward the west, the city of Antiocheia on the Maiandros (already in Karia), and that toward the south, Greater Kibyra, Sinda, and Kabalis, as far as the Tauros and Lykia. Antiocheia is a city of moderate size situated on the portion of the Maiandros near Phrygia, where there is a bridge over the river. It has a large territory on both sides of the river and is prosperous everywhere. It produces in large amounts the so-called Antiocheian dried fig, also named the "three-leafed." This place is also full of earthquakes. A distinguished sophist was produced among them, Diotrephes, whom Hybreas, the greatest rhetorician of my time, heard.

(16) They say that the Kabalians are the Solymians. At any rate, the hill that lies above the citadel of the Termessians is called Solymos, and the Termessians themselves are called the Solymians. Nearby is the Palisade of Bellerophon, and the tomb of his son Peisandros, who fell in a battle against the Solymians. This agrees with the words of the Poet, who said the following about Bellerophon: "second, he fought with the glorious Solymians" [*Iliad* 6.184], and, about his son: "Ares, insatiable for war, killed   [C631]

his son Peisandros, fighting with the Solymians" [*Iliad* 6.203–4]. Termessos is a Pisidian city lying directly above and near to Kibyra.

(17) It is said that the Kibyratians are descendants of the Lydians who possessed Kabalis. Later the neighboring Pisidians settled there and transferred it to another site that was well fortified and about 100 stadia in circuit. It became strong because of its good order, and its villages extended alongside from Pisidia and neighboring Milyas as far as Lykia and the Rhodian coast. Three bordering cities were added to it: Boubon, Balboura, and Oinoanda, and collectively they were called a tetrapolis. Each had one vote but Kibyra two, for they could send forth 30,000 foot soldiers and 2,000 horsemen. It was always ruled by tyrants, but with moderation. The tyranny came to an end in the time of Moagetes, when Murena overthrew it and included Balboura and Boubon within the boundaries of Lykia. Nevertheless the Kibyratic territory is considered the largest administration in Asia. The Kibyratians used four languages: Pisidian, Solymian, Hellenic, and Lydian, but there is no trace of Lydian in Lydia. The easy embossing of iron is peculiar to Kibyra.

Milya extends from the narrows at Termessos and from the pass through them to within the Tauros toward Isinda, as far as Sagalassos and the territory of the Apameians.

BOOK 14

Southern Anatolia and Cyprus

Part 1: Ionia

(1) It remains to speak about the Ionians and Karians, and the coast outside [C632] the Tauros that the Lykians, Pamphylians, and Kilikians possess. Thus the entire circuit of the peninsula can be completed, which, as we have said [12.1.3], is an isthmus crossing from the Pontic Sea to the Issic.

(2) The coastal voyage along the land of Ionia is about 3,430 stadia, because of the gulfs and peninsulas throughout the territory, but the straight length is not great. At any rate, from Ephesos to Smyrna in a straight line is a route of 320 stadia (120 stadia to Metropolis and the remainder to Smyrna), but the coastal voyage is a little less than 2,200. The limits of the Ionian coast are from the Poseideion of the Milesians and the Karian boundary as far as Phokaia and the Hermos.

(3) Concerning it, Pherekydes [F155] says that Miletos, Myous, and that around Mykale and Ephesos were formerly Karian, and the adjoining coast, as far as Phokaia, Chios, and Samos (which Ankaios ruled) was Lelegian. Both were driven out by the Ionians into the remaining portion of Karia. He says that Androkles, the legitimate son of Kodros the Athenian king, led the Ionian settlement, which was later than the Aiolian, and he became the founder of Ephesos. Because of this, they say that the royal seat of the Ionians was [C633] established there. Even today his descendants are called kings and have certain honors, such as the front seats at the games, purple as a sign of royal descent, a staff instead of a scepter, and the rites of the Eleusinian Demeter. Neleus, who came from Pylos, founded Miletos. The Messenians and the Pylians pretend a kind of kinship – because of which the more recent poets say that Nestor was Messenian – and they say that many Pylians came along with Melanthos the father of Kodros and those with him to Athens, and all these people, in common with the Ionians, sent forth the migration. An altar, a foundation of Neleus, is visible at the Posideion. Kydrelos, the bastard son of Kodros, founded Myous; Lebedos was by Andropompos, who took over a place called

Artis; Kolophon was by the Pylian Andraimon (as Mimnermos says in his *Nanno* [F10]); Priene was by Aipytos the son of Neleus, and then later by Philotas, who brought people from Thebes; Teos was originally by Athamas (because Anakreon [F463] calls it Athamantis), and then at the time of the Ionian settlement by Nauklos, the bastard son of Kodros, and after him by Poikes and Damathos, who were Athenians, and Geren from Boiotia; Erythrai was by Knopos, also a bastard son of Kodros; Phokaia was by the Athenians under Philogenes; Klazomenai was by Paralos; Chios was by Egertios, who brought a mixed crowd with him; and Samos was by Tembrion and later by Prokles.

(4) These are the twelve Ionian cities, but Smyrna was added at a later time, urged by the Ephesians to join the Ionikon, for in antiquity they were fellow inhabitants, when Ephesos was called Smyrna. Somewhere Kallinos uses that name, and he calls the Ephesians Smyrnaians in his work on Zeus ("have pity on the Smyrnaians" [F2]), and again "remember if the Smyrnaians ever burned beautiful thighs of oxen for you" [F2a]. Smyrna was an Amazon who took possession of Ephesos, from whom came the name of both the people and the city, just as certain Ephesians were said to be Sisyrbitians from Sisyrba. A certain Ephesian place was called Smyrna, as Hipponax makes clear: "he lived behind the city, in Smyrna, between Trechea and the Lepre Promontory" [F50], since Preon – which lies above the present city and has part of its wall on it – was called the Lepre Promontory. At any rate, the property behind Preon is [C634] called today, In the Opistholepria ["Territory Behind Lepra"], and that alongside and above Koressos was called Tracheia ["Rough"]. In antiquity the city was around the Athenaion, which today is outside the city, around the so-called Hypelaios. Thus Smyrna was near the present gymnasium, behind the former city, "between Trechea and the Lepre Promontory." When they left the Ephesians, the Smyrnaians advanced to the place where Smyrna is today, which was held by the Lelegians. Driving them out, they founded ancient Smyrna, about 20 stadia distant from the present one. Later they were driven out by the Aiolians and fled for refuge to Kolophon, and returned with them to their own [territory] and took it back, just as Mimnermos points out in his *Nanno*, recording that Smyrna was always fought over:

> Then leaving Pylos, the Nelean city, we came by ship to lovely Asia, and with overwhelming force took beloved Kolophon and settled there, led by painful insolence. We started from the...River[1] and through the will of the gods took Aiolian Smyrna. [F9]

---

[1] The manuscripts have "diasteentos," which does not seem to preserve the name of the river.

This is it about this. But we must go back over each of the parts, beginning with the more important places, where the first foundations were: I am saying those around Miletos and Ephesos, for they are the best and most notable cities.

(5) Next after the Posideion of the Milesians is the oracle of Apollo Didymeus among the Branchidai, 18 stadia inland. It was burned by Xerxes, as were the other sanctuaries, except that at Ephesos. The Branchidai handed over the treasury of the god to the Persian, and departed with him in flight so that they would not receive justice for the sacrilege and betrayal. Later the Milesians constructed the largest temple of all, although because of its size it remained without a roof. At any rate, the peribolos of the sacred enclosure has a village settlement, and there is an extravagant grove both inside and outside. There are other sacred enclosures for the oracle and the sacred objects. Here there is the myth about Branchos and the love of Apollo. It is adorned with the most expensive dedications of ancient art. From there to the city is not far, whether by road or sea.

(6) Ephoros [F127] says that the foundation [of Miletos] was originally Cretan and that it was fortified above the sea, where Old Miletos is now. The inhabitants were brought from Cretan Miletos by Sarpedon, who named [C635] the city after the name of the city there. The place was formerly held by the Lelegians. Later Neleus and those with him fortified the present city. Today it has four harbors, only one of which is sufficient for a fleet. There are many deeds associated with this city, with the most important the number of its settlements. Everywhere in the Euxeinos Pontos has been settled by them, as well as the Propontis and a number of other places. At any rate, Anaximenes of Lampsakos [F26] says that the Milesians settled the islands of Ikaros and Leros, and – around the Hellespont – Limnai in the Chersonesos, Abydos, Arisba, and Paisos in Asia, Artake and Kyzikos in the Kyzikene, and Skepsis in the interior Troad. We have spoken in the detailed section about others that he omitted.

Milesians and Delians call upon Apollo Oulios, as *oulein* means "to be healthy," from which are *oule* and "health and great rejoicing" [*Odyssey* 24.402], for Apollo is the healer. Artemis is from "artemeas" ["safe and sound"]. The sun and the moon are associated with them, since they are the reason for the mildness of the air. Both pestilential diseases and unexplained death are attributed to these gods.

(7) Notable men who are remembered from Miletos include Thales, one of the Seven Wise Men, and the first among the Hellenes to begin the scholarly study of nature and mathematics, and his student Anaximandros, and that of the latter, Anaximenes. There was also Hekataios, who put

together a history, and in my time Aischines the rhetorician, who remained in exile until the end because he spoke frankly and immoderately before Pompeius Magnus.

The city was unfortunate because it shut out Alexander and was taken by force – as was Halikarnassos – and earlier by the Persians. Kallisthenes [F30] says that Phrynichos the tragedian was fined 1,000 drachmas because he produced a play called the *Sack of Miletos by Dareios*. The island of Lade lies in front of it, near to the Tragaian islets, where there is an anchorage for pirates.

(8) The Latmian Gulf is next, on which Herakleia called Below Latmos is, a small town with an anchorage. It was first called Latmos, the same name as the mountain lying above it, which Hekataios [of Miletos, F239] asserts to be the same name as that which the Poet calls the mountain of the Phtheirians [*Iliad* 2.868], for he says that Mount Phtheiron lies above [C636] Latmos. Some say that it is Grion, which lies about parallel to Latmos, extending from the Milesia toward the east through Karia to Euromos and Chalketores. It lies above it and is high. At a slight distance away, after having crossed the little river that is near Latmos, the tomb of Endymion is visible in a cave. Then it is a voyage of about 100 stadia from Herakleia to the small town of Pyrrha.

(9) The voyage from Miletos to Herakleia, going through the gulfs, is a little more than 100 stadia, but the straight voyage to Pyrrha from Miletos is only 30 [stadia] (the voyage is much longer along the land). But in regard to notable places one must endure such irritating items of geography.

(10) From Pyrrha to the outlet of the Maiandros is 50 [stadia], a place with shoal waters and marshes. Sailing inland 30 stadia in rowboats there is the city of Myous, one of the Ionian twelve, which today is slight in population and has been incorporated into Miletos. It is said that Xerxes gave it to Themistokles for food, Magnesia for bread, and Lampsakos for wine.

(11) Within 4 stadia is the Karian village of Thymbria, which is near a sacred cave that is without birds and called the Charonion, as it has deadly exhalations. Magnesia on the Maiandros lies above it, a settlement of the Magnesians of Thessaly and Crete, about which we will speak shortly [14.1.39–40].

(12) After the outlets of the Maiandros is the Prienian coast, and Priene is above it, as well as Mount Mykale, which is rich in wild animals and trees. It lies above the Samia and makes a 7-stadia strait along with it, beyond the so-called Promontory of Trogilion. It is said by some that Priene is

Kadme, since Philotas, its founder, was Boiotian. Bias, one of the Seven Wise Men, was from Priene, about whom Hipponax [F123] says "stronger in making judgement than Bias of Priene."

(13) An islet of the same name lies off Trogilion. From there the shortest crossing to Sounion is 1,600 stadia. At first, on the right, are Samos, Ikaria, and Korsiai, and the Melantian Rocks on the left, and the rest is through the middle of the Kykladic islands. The Trogilion Promontory is a kind of spur of Mykale. Mount Paktyes lies in front of Mykale in the Ephesia. The Mesogis comes to an end there.

(14) From Trogilion to Samos is 40 stadia. It and its harbor face the south, and it has a naval station. Most of it is a plain, having been washed [C637] by the sea, but a portion goes up onto the mountain lying above. On the right as one sails to the city is the Posideion, a promontory that along with Mykale creates the 7-stadia strait. It has a temple of Poseidon, with a little islet, Narthekis, lying in front of it. On the left is a suburb that is near the Heraion, and the Imbrasos River. The Heraion is an ancient sanctuary with a large temple and is now a picture gallery. Apart from the number of paintings placed there, there are other picture galleries and some shrines full of ancient art. It is open to the air and full of the best statues, of which there were three colossal works of Myron situated on a single base. Antonius took them away, but Sebastos Caesar put two back on the same base – the Athena and the Herakles – yet transferred the Zeus to the Capitolium, having erected a small shrine for it.

(15) The voyage around the island of the Samians is 600 stadia. Formerly it was called Parthenia, when inhabited by the Karians, then Anthemous, then Metamphyllos, and then Samos, whether from some local hero or someone who settled there from Ithaka or Kephallenia. There is a promontory called Ampelos that approximately faces Drepanon in Ikaria, but the entire mountain that makes the whole island mountainous is called by the same name. It does not have good wine, although good wine is produced in the surrounding islands (such as Chios, Lesbos, and Kos), and almost all of the adjacent mainland produces the best wine. The Ephesian and Metropolitan are good, and the Mesogis, Tmolos, Katakekaumene, Knidos, Smyrna, and other less distinguished places produce various good wines, whether for enjoyment or medicinal reasons. Samos is not completely fortunate in regard to wine, but in other things it is fortunate, as is clear because it was fought over. Those who praise it do not hesitate to apply to it the proverbial saying "it even produces birds' milk," as Menandros [F880] says somewhere. This was the reason that tyrannies were established there, and why they were hostile to the Athenians.

(16) The tyrannies reached their greatest peak at the time of Polykrates and his brother Syloson. The former was so illustrious both in his fortune and power that he held control over the sea. It is set down as a sign of his good fortune that he expressly threw into the sea his ring – which had an expensive stone and engraving – and that a little later one of his fishermen brought him the very fish that had swallowed it, and when it was cut open the ring was found. The Egyptian king, upon learning about this, frankly said in a sort of prophecy that anyone who had been raised so high in good fortune would shortly be overturned and end his life without good fortune. And this is what happened, for he was taken in treachery by the Persian satrap and hanged. Anakreon the melic poet lived with him and all his poetry is full of mention of him. It is recorded that Pythagoras, seeing that the tyranny was flourishing, left the city then and went away to Egypt and Babylon because of his fondness for learning. When he came back he saw that the tyranny still survived, so he sailed to Italia and spent the rest of his life there. This is it about Polykrates.

[C638]

(17) Syloson was left a private citizen by his brother. In order to gratify Dareios [I] the son of Hystaspes, he gave him an article of clothing that he was wearing which the latter saw and desired. He was not yet king, but when he became king he gave the former the tyranny in return. But he ruled so harshly that the city became depopulated, from which the proverb arose "on account of Syloson there is open space."

(18) The Athenians originally sent Perikles as commander, and with him Sophokles the poet, who through a siege put the disobedient Samians into a difficult situation. Later they sent 2,000 cleruchs from themselves, among whom was Neokles the father of Epikouros, whom they say was a schoolmaster. They say that the latter grew up here, as well as on Teos, and became an ephebe at Athens. Menandros the comic poet became an ephebe at the same time. Kreophylos was also a Samian, who, they say, once hosted Homer and received from him as a gift the dedication of his poem called *The Capture of Oichalia*. Kallimachos indicates the opposite in one of his epigrams, that it was written by the former but dedicated to Homer because of the hospitality mentioned:

> I am the hard work of the Samian, who once received in his home divine Homer. I celebrate Eurytos, as much as he suffered, and fair Ioleia. I am called the writing of Homer. For Kreophylos, dear Zeus, this is something great. [*Epigram* 6]

Some say that he was the teacher of Homer, but others that it was not he but Aristeas of Prokonnesos.

[C639]

(19) The island of Ikaria extends alongside Samos, from which is the Ikarian Sea. It is named after Ikaros the son of Daidalos, who, they say, having joined with his father in flying (both having been furnished with wings), fled from Crete and fell here, having lost control of the course, for he rose too close to the sun and his wings fell off due to the melting of the wax. The entire island is only 300 stadia in perimeter and has no harbors, only anchorages, of which the best is called Histoi. It has a promontory that extends toward the west. There is a sanctuary of Artemis, called Tauropolion, on the island, and a small town called Oinoe and another named Drakanon, with the same name as the promontory on which it is situated, and which has an anchorage. The promontory is 80 stadia distant from the Samian promontory called Kantharion, and this is the shortest distance between them. Today, however, there are only a few inhabitants and the Samians mostly pasture cattle there.

(20) After the Samian strait, near Mykale, as one sails toward Ephesos, the Ephesian coast is on the right, part of which the Samians held. The Panionion is first on this coast, lying 3 stadia above the sea, where the Panionia – a festival common to the Ionians – takes place, as well as sacrifices to Helikonian Poseidon. The Prienians serve as the priests, but this has been discussed in the section on the Peloponnesos [8.7.2]. Then there is the city of Anaia, which was formerly Ephesian but is now Samian, exchanged for Marathesion, the nearer for the farther. Then there is the small town of Pygela, which has a sanctuary of Artemis Mounychia, a foundation of Agamemnon that was inhabited by a portion of his people. Some of them had the condition of buttock pain [*pygalgea*], and were so-called. Because they were sick with this disease they remained there, and thus the place was appropriately named. Then there is the harbor called Panormos with a sanctuary of Ephesian Artemis, and then the city.

Ortygia is on the same coast, slightly above the sea, a magnificent grove of an abundance of trees, especially the cypress. The Kenchrios River flows through it, where, they say, Leto bathed herself after her birthing pains. Here is the myth of the birth, and of Ortygia her nurse, the shrine in which the birth was, and the nearby olive tree where, they say, the goddess rested after being relieved from the birthing pains. Mount Solmissos lies above the grove, where, they say, the Kouretes were stationed, who, through the noise of their weapons, frightened Hera (who was jealously watching) and thereby assisted Leto in hiding the birth. There are several temples in the place, some ancient and others later. In the ancient ones are ancient xoana and in the more recent ones the works of Skopas. There is Leto holding a scepter, with Ortygia standing beside her holding a child on each arm. A festival is

[C640]

held there every year, and through a certain custom the young men show their enthusiasm, especially in the splendid feasting. At that time a group of the Kouretes gathers for symposia and performs certain mystic sacrifices.

(21) Both Karians and Lelegians inhabited the city [Ephesos], but Androklos drove them out and settled most of those who had come with him around the Athenaion and the Hypelaios, also including that around the slopes of Koressos. It was inhabited in such a way until the time of Kroisos, but later they came down from the mountain slopes and lived around the present sanctuary until Alexander. Lysimachos built a wall around the present city but the people were not agreeable to the change. He watched for a downpour of rain and made use of it, blocking up the sewers so that the city was flooded, and then they were pleased to make the change. He called it Arsinoë after his wife [Arsinoë II] but nevertheless the old name prevailed. It had a gerousia that was registered, and associated with it were those called the Epikletoi ["Those Summoned"] who administered everything.

(22) Chersiphron was the first architect of the temple of Artemis, and then someone else enlarged it. When a certain Herostratos set it on fire, they built another and better one, having collected the ornaments of women and their own property, and disposing of the earlier columns. The proof of what happened is in the decrees from that time. Artemidoros [F126] says that because Timaios of Tauromenion [F150b] was ignorant of them – and was envious and argumentive (because of which he was called Epitimaios ["Fault Finder"]) – he says that they provided for the restoration of the sanctuary from Persian funds deposited there. But there was nothing deposited at that time, and even if there had been, they would have been burned along with the temple. After the fire, who would have wished to have things deposited there, when the roof had been destroyed and the sacred precinct was open to the air? Alexander suggested that he would [C641] pay the Ephesians for both past and future expenses, if he were credited on the inscription, but they were unwilling, and they would have been far more unwilling to acquire a reputation for sacrilege and robbery. He [Artemidoros] praises the Ephesian who said to the king that it was not proper for a god to construct a dedication to gods.

(23) After the completion of the temple, which he says was the work of Cheirokrates, the same man who built Alexandria and who suggested to Alexander that he put his likeness on Athos (pouring an offering from a vessel into a bowl), and to make two cities, one on the right of the mountain and the other on the left, with a river flowing from one to the other: after the temple [was completed] the large number of dedications were obtained by

the honor given the artists, but almost the entire altar was filled with the works of Praxiteles. They showed me some by Thrason, such as the *Hekatesion*, the *Spring² of Penelope*, and the old woman, *Eurykleia*. The priests were eunuchs who were called the Megabyxoi – they were always seeking those from other places worthy of this – and they held them in great honor. It was required that maidens join in the rites. Today some of the customs are preserved but others are not, yet the sanctuary remains an asylum, as previously. The boundaries of the asylum have often been changed: Alexander extended them for a stadion, Mithridates [VI] shot an arrow from a corner of the foundation that seemed to go slightly more than a stadion, and Antonius doubled this and included within the asylum part of the city. But this appeared to be harmful and put the city in the power of criminals, so Sebastos Caesar invalidated it.

(24) The city has both a dockyard and a harbor, which was made narrower by the architects, but they were deceived, along with the king who ordered it. This was Attalos [II] Philadelphos, who thought that the entrance, as well as the harbor, would be deep enough for large merchantmen – previously there were shallows because of siltation from the Kaystros – if a mole were placed alongside the mouth, which was extremely wide. Thus he ordered the mole to be constructed. But the opposite happened, because the silt was held in and the entire harbor became shallower as far as the mouth. Previously the ebb and flow of the sea was sufficient to remove the silt and draw it outside. Such is the harbor. The city, because of the prosperity of its location, increases each day and is the largest emporium in Asia within the Tauros.   [C642]

(25) Notable men from here include, in antiquity, Herakleitos called The Obscure, and Hermodoros, about whom the former says:

> Let the Ephesians strangle their notable youths, they who banished their useful man, Hermodoros, saying "Let no one of us be useful. If not, let him be elsewhere and with others." [F2, 143]

The man is believed to have written certain laws for the Romans. Hipponax the poet was from Ephesos, as well as Parrhasios the painter, and Apelles, and more recently Alexander the rhetorician, called Lynchos, who was a politician and wrote history and left poems on the arrangement of the heavenly bodies and the geography of the continents, each in its own poem.

(26) After the outlet of the Kaystros is a lake that overflows from the sea – called Selinousia – and next there is another that flows together with it, both providing a large income. Although these were sacred, the kings took them

---

² This seems unlikely to be correct.

away from the goddess, but the Romans gave them back. Again the tax collectors forcibly appropriated the duties for themselves, and Artemidoros [F127] was sent on an embassy, as he himself says, and received the lakes back for the goddess and also won at Rome a judgement against the Herakleotis, which was in revolt. In return the city erected a golden image of him in the sanctuary. In the deepest recess of the lake is the sanctuary of the King, which they say was established by Agamemnon.

(27) Then there are Mount Gallesion and Kolophon, an Ionian city, and before it the grove of Apollo Klarios, in which there was once an ancient oracle. It is said that the prophet Kalchas, along with Amphilochos the son of Amphiaraos, went there on foot after his return from Troy. Near Klaros he happened to meet someone who was better than he was, Mopsos the son of Manto the daughter of Teiresias, and died of grief. Hesiod somewhat revises the myth, having Kalchas ask Mospos this question:

> I am amazed in my heart at how many fruits there are on this fig tree, even though it is small. Can you say the number? [F214]

and the latter replied:

> They are a myriad in number, and they measure a *medimnos*, but there is one beyond the number that you cannot put in. Thus he spoke, and the number was seen to be the truth. And then the sleep of death covered Kalchas. [Ibid.]

[C643] Pherekydes [F142] says that Kalchas asked about a pregnant sow and how many piglets she had, and he [Mopsos] replied that it was ten, one of which was female, and when it was the truth, the former died of grief. Some say that Kalchas asked the question about the sow, and the other about the figs, and the latter spoke the truth but the former did not and died of grief according to a certain oracle. Sophokles [F180] tells it in his *The Demanding Back of Helen* – that he was destined to die when he happened to meet a prophet better than himself – but he transfers the rivalry and the death of Kalchas to Kilikia. Such are the ancient matters.

(28) The Kolophonians once possessed notable naval and cavalry forces, in which they surpassed others so much that whenever there were wars that were difficult to bring to an end, the Kolophonian cavalry would serve as allies and the war would come to an end. From this the proverb arose "he put Kolophon to it," said whenever a certain end is put to a matter.

Kolophonian men who have been remembered include Mimnermos, who was both a flute player and elegiac poet, and Xenophanes the natural philosopher, who composed in poetry the *Silloi*. Pindar speaks of a certain Polymnastos who was one of the highly reputed musicians ("you know the voice, common to all, of Polymnastos, a Kolophonian man" [F188]). Some say that Homer was from there. On a straight voyage it is 70 stadia from Ephesos, but going into the gulfs it is 120.

(29) After Kolophon there is Mount Korakion and an islet sacred to Artemis, to which, it has been believed, deer swim across to give birth. Then there is Lebedos, 120 stadia distant from Kolophon. This is the assembly and settlement of the Dionysiac artists both in Ionia and as far as the Hellespont, and where a festival and games are given for Dionysos every year. They formerly lived in Teos, the next Ionian city, but when sedition broke out they fled for refuge to Ephesos. Attalos [III?] settled them in Myonnesos – between Teos and Lebedos – but the Teians sent an embassy asking the Romans not to wait until Myonnesos was fortified against them. They then migrated to Lebedos, and the Lebedians gladly received them because they themselves were low in population. Teos is also 120 stadia distant from Lebedos, and in between is the island of Aspis (some call it Arkonnesos). Myonnesos is settled on a height that forms a peninsula. [C644]

(30) Teos is also situated on a peninsula, and it has a harbor. Anakreon the melic poet was from here, in whose time the Teians abandoned their city (as they were unable to bear Persian insolence) and emigrated to Abdera, a Thracian city, about which he said "Abdera, beautiful settlement of the Teians" [F505a]. Some of them went back at a later time. It has been said [13.1.54] that Apellikon was himself a Teian, and the historian Hekataios was from the same city. There is another harbor toward the north, 30 stadia from the city, and called Gerrhaiidai.

(31) Then there is the Chalkideis and the isthmus of the peninsula of the Teians and Erythraians. The latter live within the isthmus, but the Teians and Klazomenians are on the isthmus itself. The southern side of the isthmus – the Chalkideis – is next to the Teians, and the northern next to the Klazomenians, where they adjoin the Erythraians. Hypokremnos is a place lying at the beginning of the isthmus, divided by the Erythraia within it and the Klazomenians outside. Above the Chalkideis is a grove that Alexander the son of Philippos [II] consecrated, and games – the Alexandria – are proclaimed by the Ionian Federation and are celebrated there. The crossing over of the isthmus from the Alexandreion and the Chalkideis as far as Hypokremnos is 50 stadia, but the sail around is more than 1,000. Erythrai is somewhere about the middle of the sail around, an Ionian city having four islets lying off it called the Hippoi.

(32) Before coming to Erythrai, first there is the small town of Airai, which is Teian, and then Korykos, a high mountain, and a harbor at its foot, Kasystes, another harbor called Erythras, and a number of others afterward.

They say that the voyage along the coast of Korykos had pirates everywhere, called the Korykaians, who had found a new way of attacking those sailing on the sea. They would scatter themselves among the harbors and arrive before the merchants had anchored. They would overhear what they carried and to where they were sailing, and then come together and set upon the men, attacking them and seizing them. Because of this we call a Korykaian anyone who is a meddler and who attempts to overhear discussions that are secret and private, and we say in a proverb "then a Korykaian heard this," when one believes that he was doing or saying something in secret, but failed because of those who spy on him and inquire curiously about what does not concern them.

[C645] (33) After Korykos is the islet of Halonnesos. Then there is Argennon, an Erythraian promontory that is exceedingly close to the Posideion of the Chians, and forms a strait of about 60 stadia. Mimas is between Erythrai and Hypokremnos, a high mountain that is abundant in game and well forested. Then there is the village of Kybeleia and a promontory called Melaina, which has a millstone quarry.

(34) The Sibyl was from Erythrai, a woman of antiquity who was inspired and a prophetess. In the time of Alexander there was another woman from the same city who was a prophetess in the same way, called Athenais. In my time there was Herakleides, the Herophileian physician, a fellow pupil of Apollonios Mys.

(35) The voyage around Chios is 900 stadia, going along the land. It has a city with a good harbor and a naval station for 80 ships. On the sail around it from the city, having the island on the right, there is the Posideion, then Phanai, a deep harbor, and a temple of Apollo and a grove of palm trees, then Notion, with a beach for an anchorage, then Laious, also with a beach for an anchorage, from which there is an isthmus of 60 stadia to the city, but the sail around, which I have gone through, is 360. Then there is the Melaina Promontory, opposite which is Psyra, an island 50 stadia from the promontory that is high and has a city of the same name. The circuit of the island is 40 stadia. Then there is Ariousia, a rugged and harborless territory of about 30 stadia which produces the best of the Hellenic wines. Then there is Pelinaios, the highest mountain on the island. The island has a quarry of marble stone.

Men in high repute from Chios include Ion the tragedian, Theopompos the historian, and Theokritos the sophist. The latter two were political opponents of each other. The Chians are in dispute about Homer, producing strong evidence that those called the Homeridai are his descendants, those whom Pindar records: "just as the Homeridai, the singers of words sewn together, mostly" [*Nemean* 2.1 – 2]. At one time the Chians possessed a fleet, and flourished through their rule of the sea and their freedom. From Chios it is about 400 stadia with the Notos wind to Lesbos.

(36) Chyton is a place after Hypokremnos, where Klazomenai was later settled. Then there is the present city, which has eight cultivated islets lying off it. A distinguished man from Klazomenai was the natural philosopher Anaxagoras, a disciple of Anaximenes of Miletos. The natural philosopher Archelaos and the poet Euripides heard him. Then there is a sanctuary of Apollo and hot springs, and the gulf and the city of the Smyrnaians.   [C646]

(37) Next there is another gulf, on which Old Smyrna is, 20 stadia distant from the one of today. After the Lydians had razed Smyrna, the inhabitants continued in villages for about 400 years. Then Antigonos [I] and later Lysimachos reconstructed it, and today it is the most beautiful of all. Part of it is on a mountain and is walled, but most of it is on the plain near the harbor, near the Metroon, and near the gymnasium. The division into streets is excellent, with straight alignments as far as possible, and the streets are paved with stone. There are large quadrilateral stoas with both lower and upper stories. There is also a library and the Homereion, a quadrilateral stoa with a temple and xoanon of Homer, for they lay special claim to the Poet, and a copper coin of theirs is said to be a "homerion." The Meles River flows near to its walls. In addition to the other fixtures of the city, it has a closed harbor. There is one defect – not a small one – attributed to the architects, for when they paved the streets they did not give them underground drainage, and thus sewage is on the surface, especially during rain, when the sewage is let loose. Here Dolabella captured by siege and killed Trebonius, one of those who treacherously murdered Caesar the God, and he destroyed many parts of the city.

(38) Leukai is a small town after Smyrna. After the death of Attalos [III] Philometor, Aristonikos incited it to revolt. He was believed to be related to the royal family and intended to obtain the kingdom. He was thrown out after being defeated by the Ephesians in a naval battle near the Kymaia, but he went up into the interior and quickly assembled a large number of resourceless people and slaves, whom he appealed to through freedom, and whom he called the Heliopolitai. First he unexpectedly moved into Thyateira, then took Apollonis, and then went against other fortresses. But he did not survive long, as the cities immediately sent a large number against him, assisted by Nikomedes [II] the Bithynian and the Kappadokian kings. Then five Roman ambassadors came, afterward an army under the consul Publius Crassus, and after that Marcus Perperna, who brought the war to an end, taking Aristonikos alive and sending him to Rome. He ended his life in

a prison, Perperna died of disease, and Crassus – attacked by certain people around Leukai – fell in battle. Manius Aquillius came as consul with ten legates and organized the province into the form of government that still survives today.

[C647]

After Leukai there is Phokaia, in a gulf, concerning which we have spoken in the section about Massalia [4.1.4]. Then there is the boundary of the Ionians and the Aiolians, which also has been discussed [13.1.2].

In the interior of the Ionian coast there remains the territory around the road from Ephesos as far as Antiocheia and the Maiandros. These places are Lydian and Karian mixed with Hellenes.

(39) Magnesia is the first after Ephesos, an Aiolian city, called "On the Maiandros," for it is situated near it. It is much nearer to the Lethaios, which empties into the Maiandros and has its beginning on Paktyes, the mountain of the Ephesians (there is another Lethaios in Gortyna and one around Trikke – where Asklepios is said to have been born – and still another among the Western Libyans). It lies in a plain near the mountain called Thorax on which Daphitas the grammarian is said to have been crucified because he abused the kings in a distich: "Purple stripes, scraps of the treasure of Lysimachos, you rule the Lydians and Phrygians." It is said that an oracle was put forth that he should be on guard against Thorax.

(40) The Magnetians are believed to be the descendants of Delphians who settled in the Didyma mountains of Thessaly, concerning which Hesiod says:

> or as the unwedded maiden who, living in the sacred Didymian hills in the Dotian Plain in front of Amyros, abundant in grapes, bathed her foot in the Boibiadian Lake. [F164]

The sanctuary of Dindymene, the Mother of the Gods, was also here. It is handed down that the wife of Themistokles – some have his daughter – was priestess here. Today the sanctuary is no longer in existence because the city has been transferred to another site. In the present city there is the sanctuary of Leukophryene Artemis, which, in the size of its temple and the quantity of its dedications, is inferior to that at Ephesos, but the harmony and skill of the construction of the shrine are far superior. In size it surpasses all in Asia except two, that at Ephesos and that at Didyma. In antiquity it happened that the Magnetians were utterly destroyed by the Trerians (a Kimmerian people), although they had been prosperous for a long time, and in the following year the Milesians occupied the place. Kallinos [T1] records that the Magnetians were still prosperous and successful in their war against the Ephesians, but clearly Archilochos already knows about the misfortune they experienced ("lamenting the misfortunes of the Thasians, not the Magnetians" [F20]), from which he can be proved to have been more recent [C648] than Kallinos. Kallinos records an earlier Kimmerian invasion when he says "now the Kimmerian army comes, violent in its deeds" [F5], in which he clearly refers to the capture of Sardeis.

(41) Well-known Magnetians are Hegesias the rhetorician, who more than anyone began the so-called Asiatic fervor and thus corrupted the established Attic custom; Simos the melic poet, who established the Simoidia and also corrupted the method of the earlier melic poets, [corrupted] even more so by the Lysioidoi, Magoidoi, and Kleomachos the boxer, who fell in love with a certain *kinaidos* and a young female slave who was kept by the *kinaidos*. (Sotades was the first to talk in the manner of the *kinaidoi*, and then Alexander the Aiolian, those only in bare speech but Lysis with music and still later Simos.) Anaxenor the citharodist was exalted in the theater, but especially by Antonius, who appointed him tax collector in four cities and provided him soldiers. Moreover his native land honored him notably, dressing him in purple as sacred to Zeus Sosipolis, as is clearly shown by his painted image in the agora. There is also a bronze image of him in the theater with the inscription: "surely this is beautiful, to listen to a singer such as this one, resembling the gods in voice" [*Odyssey* 9.3–4]. But the inscriber did not calculate correctly and left out the last letter of the second verse – the base not being sufficiently wide – so that the city was charged with ignorance because of the ambiguity of the writing as to whether the last word should be taken as nominative or dative, for many write the dative without the iota, rejecting the usage as having no natural reason.

(42) After Magnesia there is the road to Tralleis, with Mesogis on the left, and on the road itself and on the right is the Maiandros Plain, in which Lydians and Karians live, as well as Ionians (Milesians and Myesians) and also the Aiolians of Magnesia. The same kind of topography exists as far as Nysa and Antiocheia.

The city of the Trallianians is situated on a certain tableland with a fortified height, and the places around it are especially secure. It is as well populated as [C649] anywhere else in Asia, and the people are resourceful. Some of them always hold the first places in the province and are called Asiarchs. One of these was Pythodoros, originally a Nysaian man, who moved there [Tralleis] because of its distinction, and with a few others became prominent as a friend of Pompeius. He acquired the wealth of royalty – more than 2,000 talents – which Caesar the God sold but he redeemed because of his friendship toward Pompeius, and left it undiminished to his children. His daughter was Pythodoris, who is now queen of Pontos, about whom I have spoken

[12.3.29–37]. Thus he flourished in our time, as did Menodoros, an educated man who was serious and dignified, and who held the priesthood of Zeus Larisios. He was overthrown by the friends of Domitius Ahenobarbus, who killed him, for he believed through informants that he had caused the fleet to revolt. There were also distinguished rhetoricians from here: Dionysokles, and after him Damas Skombros. Tralleis is said to have been an Argive foundation, along with some Thracian Trallians (from whence the name). For a short time a tyranny was established in the city under the sons of Kratippos, at the time of the Mithridatic matter.

(43) Nysa is situated near to Mesogis and is mostly located on the slopes of the mountain. It is a double city, for a certain cataract that makes a gorge flows through it, which has a bridge over it joining the two cities. It is also adorned by an amphitheater with a hidden underground passage for the torrential waters. There are two peaks near the theater, and the gymnasium of the youths lies at the foot of one, and at the foot of the other is the agora and the senate. The plain lies to the south of the city, just as with Tralleis.

(44) On the road between Tralleis and Nysa is the Nysaian village of Acharaka, not far from the city, where there is a Ploutonion with an expensive grove and temples of Plouton and Kore, and the Charonion, a cave lying above the grove, marvellous by nature. They say that those who are sick and pay attention to the cures of the gods frequent it, and live in a village near the cave among experienced priests, who sleep in it for them and prescribe cures through their dreams. They also call on the healing power of the gods, often bringing [the sick] into the cave and placing them there to remain quietly, as if hibernating, and without food, for many days. The sick may pay attention to what they see in their own sleep, but they also use others as priests to initiate them into the mysteries and to advise them. The place is not to be entered by others and is deadly. A festival is celebrated every year by the Acharakians, and then those attending the festival can especially see and hear about these things. At that time, about noon, the young men and ephebes of the gymnasium, nude and anointed with oil, take up a bull and quickly carry him into the cave. He goes a short distance ahead, falls, and breathes his last.

[C650]

(45) Thirty stadia from Nysa, crossing over Mount Tmolos and Mesogis in the portion toward the south is the place called Leimon ["Meadow"], where the Nysaians and those around them go out to celebrate their festivals. Not far away is an outlet sacred to the same gods, which is said to extend down as far as Acharaka. They say that this meadow is named by the Poet when he says "on the Asian meadow" [*Iliad* 2.461], and a heroon of a certain Kaystrios and Asios is pointed out, and the Kaystros flows nearby.

(46) It is recorded that three brothers, Athymbros, Athymbrados, and Hydrelos, came from Lakedaimon and founded the cities named after them, which later became lacking in population, and today the Nysaians consider Athymbros to be their founder.

(47) These are the notable settlements situated in the vicinity: across the Maiandros are Koskinia and Orthosia, within it are Brioula, Mastaura, and Acharaka, and above the city in the mountains is Aroma, where the best wine of the Mesogitis comes from, the Aromeus.

(48) Notable Nysaian men include Apollonios the Stoic philosopher who was the best pupil of Panaitios, Menekrates the student of Aristarchos, his son Aristodemos (whom I heard extensively at Nysa when he was extremely old and I was young), Sostratos the brother of Aristodemos, and another Aristodemos who was his cousin and who taught Pompeius Magnus. They were distinguished philologists. Mine had two schools, one on Rhodes and the other in his homeland, and taught rhetoric in the morning and philology in the afternoon, but at Rome as the tutor of the children of Magnus it was enough to teach philology.

Part 2: Karia and Rhodes

(1) On the far side of the Maiandros – what remains in the circuit – it is entirely Karian, as the Lydians are no longer mixed in with the Karians, who [C651] possess it by themselves, except that some of the coast is Milesian and Myousian. The beginning of Karia is the Rhodian Shore on the sea, and the end is the Posideion of the Milesians. In the interior are the extremities of the Tauros as far as the Maiandros. It is said that the beginning of the Tauros lies above the so-called Chelidonian islands, which lie off the border territory of Pamphylia and Lykia, for there the Tauros rises up to a height. But the truth is that all of Lykia, toward what is outside and in the southern portion, is separated from the Kibyratian territory as far as the Rhodian Shore by a mountainous ridge of the Tauros. The mountainous part adjacent to here is much lower and is no longer considered the Tauros – nor are those outside and inside – because the prominences and hollows are scattered equally throughout the width and length of the entire territory and are in no way a dividing wall. The entire voyage around, going into the gulfs, is 4,900 stadia, and that of the Rhodian Shore is nearly 1,500.

(2) Daidala – a Rhodian locality – is the beginning of it, and the so-called Mount Phoinix the end, which is also in the Rhodia. The island of Elaioussa lies off it, 120 stadia distant from Rhodes. Between them – sailing toward the west from Daidala, in a straight line with the coast of Kilikia, Pamphylia,

and Lykia – there is first the gulf called Glaukos, with a good harbor, then the Artemision, a promontory and sanctuary, and then the grove of Leto, above which, and above the sea, is the city of Kalynda, in 60 stadia. Then there is Kaunos and the nearby and deep Kalbis River, which one can go up, with Pisilis between them.

(3) The city [Kaunos] has dockyards and an enclosed harbor. Imbros lies above the city on a fortified height. The territory is prosperous, but it is agreed by all that the city has bad air in summer and autumn because of the burning heat and the abundance of produce. And in fact various little stories are chattered about, such as the one about Stratonikos the citharist, who saw that the Kaunians were quite pale, and said it was like the phrase of the Poet, "just as the race of leaves is that of man" [*Iliad* 6.146]. When he was blamed for mocking the city as if diseased, he said "would I dare say that they are [C652] sick, where even the corpses walk around?" The Kaunians once revolted from the Rhodians, but by a judgement of the Romans they were restored back to them, and there is a work by Molon, *Against the Kaunians*. They say that they speak the same language as the Karians and came from Crete but make use of their own customs.

(4) Next is Physkos, a small town with a harbor and a grove of Leto. Then there is Loryma, a rough coast, and Phoinix, the highest mountain in the region. On its summit is a fortress with the same name as the mountain. Elaioussa lies in front of the mountain, an island 4 stadia away that is about 8 stadia in circumference.

(5) The city of the Rhodians lies on the eastern promontory. In harbors, roads, walls, and other constructions it is so much better than other places that I cannot speak of any other that is equal or even superior to this city. It is marvellous because of its good order and its attention to political and, especially, naval matters, because of which it was master of the sea for a long time, overthrowing piracy and becoming a friend of the Romans and the kings who were friendly to the Romans and the Hellenes. Thus it has remained autonomous but has been adorned with many dedications, which are mostly located in the Dionysion and the gymnasium, as well as in other places. The best of these includes the Colossus of Helios, about which the iambic poet says "seven times ten *pecheis*, which Charos of Lindos made." Today it lies fallen due to an earthquake, broken at the knees. It was not re-erected, because of a certain oracle. This is the most excellent of the dedications: at any rate, it is agreed to be one of the Seven Wonders. There are also the paintings of Protogenes: his *Ialysos* and his *Satyr Standing by a Pillar*. A partridge stood on the pillar, which (when the painting had recently been put up) the people – as is fitting – gaped at in wonder, ignoring the Satyr,

although it was quite successful. Partridge breeders were still more amazed and would bring domesticated ones and place them right next to it, since the partridges would call to the painting and attract a crowd. Protogenes, seeing that the main work had become subordinate, begged those in charge of the precinct to allow him to go in and obliterate the bird, and he did so.

The Rhodians have concern for their people although they are not a democracy, but they wish to care for the large number of poor people. The people are supplied with provisions and the wealthy support those in need, [C653] according to an ancestral custom. There are certain public offices that furnish provisions so that a poor person receives support and the city does not become lacking in its needs, especially for its naval expeditions. Some of the naval stations were kept hidden and inaccessible to the people, and the penalty was death for anyone spying on them or going within their boundaries. Here, just as at Massalia and Kyzikos, matters concerning the construction, making of materials, storage of weapons, and everything else are exceptionally maintained, much more so than elsewhere.

(6) They are Dorians, like the Halikarnassians, Knidians, and Koans. The Dorians founded Megara after the death of Kodros, and some remained there, others joined Althaimenes the Argive in settling Crete, and others went to Rhodes and the cities just mentioned. This is more recent than the statement Homer made. Knidos and Halikarnassos were not yet in existence, although Rhodes and Kos were, but inhabited by Herakleidai. When Tlepolemos had grown to manhood

> he immediately killed his own father's dear uncle, Likymnios, who was growing old...and quickly built ships, and when he had gathered many people he went in flight. [*Iliad* 2.662–5]

He then says: "wandering, he came to Rhodes where they settled in three divisions by tribes" [*Iliad* 2.667–8], and he names the cities of that time: "Lindos, Ielysos, and bright-shining Kamiros" [*Iliad* 2.656], the city of the Rhodians not yet having been incorporated. Nowhere here does he name the Dorians, but perhaps he indicates the Aiolians and the Boiotians, if Herakles and Likymnios settled there. Yet if Tlepolemos departed from Argos and Tiryns, as others say, the emigration there could not have been Dorian, because it occurred before the return of the Herakleidai. About the Koans, "Pheidippos and Antiphos led them, the two sons of lord Thessalos son of Herakles" [*Iliad* 2.678–9], which indicates Aiolian peoples rather than Dorian.

(7) Formerly Rhodes was called Ophioussa and Stadia, and then Telchinis after the Telchinians, who settled on the island. They say that

[C654] they are sorcerers [*baskanoi*] and wizards who pour the water of the Styx mixed with sulphur onto animals and plants in order to destroy them. Others say that they excelled in craftsmanship and were maligned [*baskanthenai*] by rival craftsmen and this resulted in their bad reputation, and that they first came from Crete to Cyprus and then to Rhodes. They were the first to work iron and bronze, and in fact crafted the sickle for Kronos. They have been discussed previously [10.3.7, 19], but the numerous myths about them make it necessary to go back to them and fill things up, if I have omitted anything.

(8) The Heliadians, according to the myth, took possession of the island after the Telchinians. To one of them, Kerkaphos, and [to] Kydippe, were born children who founded the cities named after them ("Lindos, Ielysos, and bright-shining Kamiros" [*Iliad* 2.656]). Some say that Tlepolemos founded them and gave them the same names as certain daughters of Danaos.

(9) The present city was founded at the time of the Peloponnesian matter by the same architect – they say – who [founded] the Peiraieus. But the Peiraieus no longer survives, having been badly maltreated first by the Lakedaimonians, who tore down the long walls, and then by Sulla, the Roman commander.

(10) It is recorded by the Rhodians that they were prosperous due to the sea, not only in the time since they founded the present city, but many years before the establishment of the Olympics, as they would sail far from their home for the security of their people. Since then they have sailed as far as Iberia, founding Rhode there – which the Massaliotes later possessed – Parthenope among the Opikians, and, along with the Koans, Elpiai among the Daunians. Some say that the Gymnesian Islands were founded by them after their departure from Troy. Timaios [F65] says that the larger of these is the largest after the Seven (Sardo, Sikelia, Cyprus, Crete, Euboia, Kyrnos, and Lesbos), but he does not speak the truth, as there are others much larger. They say that the light-armed soldiers [*gymnetes*] were called *balearides* by the Phoenicians, from which the Gymnesiai were called the Balearides. Some of the Rhodians settled around Sybaris in Chonia. The Poet seems to testify to the prosperity that the Rhodians experienced from antiquity immediately after the first founding of the three cities:

> When they settled in three divisions by tribes and were loved by Zeus, lord over gods and men, Kronion poured over them marvellous wealth. [*Iliad* 2.668–70]

[C655] Others reduce these words to a myth and say that gold rained on the island when Athena was born from the head of Zeus, as Pindar says [*Olympian* 7.34–7]. The island has a circuit of 920 stadia.

(11) Lindos is first as one sails from the city, with the island on the right. It is a city located on a mountain that extends far toward the south, approximately toward Alexandria. There is a famous sanctuary of Athena Lindia, established by the Danaids. Formerly the Lindians had their own government, as did the Kamirians and Ialysians, but afterward they all came together into Rhodes. Kleoboulos, one of the Seven Wise Men, was from here.

(12) After Lindos is the district of Ixia, and Mnasyrion, then Atabyris, the highest of the mountains there, with a sanctuary of Zeus Atabyrios, then Kamiros, then Ialysos (a village), above which is an akropolis called Ochyroma, and then the city of the Rhodians in about 80 stadia. Between them is Thoanteion, a promontory, and the Sporades and the Chalkia lying around them are generally in front of it, as we have previously recorded (10.5.14).

(13) There are many men notable of recording, both commanders and athletes, among whom were the ancestors of Panaitios the philosopher. Among politicians, and those in speaking and philosophy, there are Panaitios himself, Stratokles, Andronikos (one of the Peripatetics), Leonides the Stoic, and, still earlier, Praxiphanes, Hieronymos, and Eudemos. Poseidonios was a political leader on Rhodes and taught there (although he was from Apameia in Syria), as also did Apollonios Malakos and Molon, who were Alabandians, pupils of the rhetorician Menekles. Apollonios moved there earlier, and when Molon came later, the former said to him "coming late [*molon*]." Peisandros, the poet who wrote the *Herakleia*, was a Rhodian, as were, in my time, Simmias the philologist and Aristokles. Dionysios the Thracian and Apollonios who wrote the *Argonautika*, although Alexandrians, were called Rhodians.

(14) This is enough to say about Rhodes. The Karian coast after Rhodes, from Elaioussa and Loryma, bends back toward the north, and the voyage afterward is in a straight line as far as the Propontis, making a meridian line of about 5,000 stadia or slightly less. The remainder of Karia is on it, as well as the Ionians, Aiolians, Troy, and that around Kyzikos and Byzantion.

(15) After Loryma is Kynossema and the island of Syme, and then Knidos, which has two harbors – one of which can be closed and is for triremes – and is a naval station for twenty ships. An island of about 7 stadia in circumference lies off it that is high and theater-shaped, connected by moles to the mainland, making Knidos, in a way, a kind of double city. A large portion live on the island, which shelters both harbors. Nisyros is opposite it in the sea. Notable Knidian men are, first, Eudoxos the mathematician (one of the companions of Plato), then Agatharchides, one of the Peripatics and an historian, and in our time Theopompos, a friend of Caesar the God, who

was of great influence, and his son Artemidoros. Ktesias the physician of Artaxerxes [II], who wrote an *Assyrika* and *Persika*, was also from there.

(16) Then after Knidos are Keramos and Bargasa, small towns above the sea. Then there is Halikarnassos, the royal residence of the dynasts of Karia, which was formerly called Zephyria. Here is the tomb of Mausolos, one of the Seven Wonders, a work that Artemisia erected for her husband, and the spring of Salmakis, which has been slandered – I do not know why – as making those who drink from it effeminate. It seems that the reason for softness in men is believed to be the air or water, but that is not the reason for softness, for it is due to wealth and intemperate lifestyle. Halikarnassos has an akropolis, and Arkonnesos lies in front of it. Its settlers were, among others, Anthes, along with Troizenians. Men coming from there are Herodotos the historian, who was later called Thourian because he joined in the settlement of Thourioi, Herakleitos the poet (the companion of Kallimachos), and, in my time, Dionysios the historian.

(17) This city also blundered when Alexander seized it by force. Hekatomnos, the king of Karia, had three sons, Mausolos, Idrieus, and Pixodaros, and two daughters. Mausolos, who was the eldest brother, married the elder daughter Artemisia, and Idrieus, the second son, [married] the other sister, Ada. Mausolos became king and when he died childless he left the rule to his wife, who built the previously mentioned tomb. She wasted away and died through grief for her husband, and Idrieus became ruler. His wife Ada succeeded him after he died of disease. Pixodaros – the [C657] last son of Hekatomnos – threw her out. Taking the side of the Persians, he sent for a satrap to rule in common with him, and when he departed from life the satrap took over Halikarnassos. His wife was Ada, the daughter of Pixodaros by Aphneis, a Kappadokian woman. When Alexander came he withstood a siege. But Ada the daughter of Hekatomnos, whom Pixodaros had thrown out, beseeched Alexander and persuaded him to restore her to the kingdom that had been taken away from her, promising to join in helping him against the areas in revolt, for those holding them were her relatives. She also gave him Alinda, where she was living. He agreed and proclaimed her queen. When the city, except for the heights (it was double), had been taken, he gave her the siege of it. The heights were taken a little later, the siege having become a matter of anger and hatred.

(18) Next there is the promontory of Termerion, which is Myndian. Skandaria, a promontory of Kos, lies opposite, 40 stadia distant from the mainland. There is a place, Termeron, above the promontory.

(19) The city of the Koans was called Astypalaia in antiquity and was settled on another site that was also on the sea. Because of internal strife they

moved to the present city, around Skandarion, and changed the name to Kos, the same as the island. The city is not large but is the most beautiful settlement of all, and has a pleasant situation as one sails into it. The size of the island is about 550 stadia. It is fertile everywhere, and best in terms of its wine, like Chios and Lesbos. There is a promontory toward the south, Laketer, from which it is 60 [stadia] to Nisyros. Near Laketer is the district of Halisarna. On the west are Drekanon and a village called Stomalimne. The former is about 200 stadia distant from the city, but Laketer adds 35 to the length of the voyage. In the suburb is the Asklepieion, an exceedingly notable sanctuary with many dedications, including the *Antigonos* of Apelles. The *Aphrodite Anadyomene* was also there but it is now dedicated to the God Caesar at Rome, as Sebastos dedicated to his father the female founder of his family. They say that the Koans had a hundred talents of their assigned tribute remitted for the painting. They also say that the regimens practiced by Hippokrates came mostly from the cures set up there. He, then is one of the notable Koan men, as well as Simos the physician, Philitas – both poet and critic – and, in my time, Nikias who was tyrant over the [C658] Koans and heard Ariston the Peripatic and was his heir. There was also Theomnestos, a renowned harpist and a political opponent of Nikias.

(20) On the coast of the mainland near the Myndian territory are the promontory of Astypalaia and Zephyrion. Then, immediately, is Myndos, which has a harbor, and after it is Bargylia, also a city. Between them is Karyanda, a harbor and city having the same name, where the Karyandians lived. Skylax, the ancient historian, was from here. Near Bargylia is the sanctuary of Artemis Kindyas, where it is believed that the rain only falls around it. There was once a territory of Kindye. A highly regarded man was from Bargylia, the Epicurean Protarchos, who was the teacher of Demetrios called Lakon.

(21) Then Iasos lies on an island lying before the mainland. It has a harbor, and most of their livelihood comes from the sea, which is abundant in fish, but the land is rather poor. In fact, various tales are fabricated about it. When a citharodist was giving a performance, everyone listened to him for a while, but when the bell for the sale of fish was heard, they left and went away to the food, except for someone who was hard of hearing. The citharodist went up to him and said: "Sir, I am very thankful to you for your honor toward me and your love of music, for the others went away as soon as they heard the bell." And the man said, "What are you saying? Has the bell already rung?" And when the former said that it had, the latter said "Good wishes to you," and got up and went away. The dialectician Diodoros was from here. He was called Kronos, originally by error, for it

was Apollonios his overseer who was called Kronos, but it was transferred to him because of the ignorance of the true Kronos.

(22) After Iasos is the Posideion of the Milesians. In the interior are three notable cities: Mylasa, Stratonikeia, and Alabanda. There are others around these or on the coast, including Amyzon, Herakleia, Euromos, and Chalketor. There is less to be said about them.

(23) Mylasa is situated in an exceedingly fertile plain, with a mountain forming a peak above it that has an excellent quarry of white stone. This is of no small benefit, since there is plentiful building stone nearby for construction, especially for the preparation of sanctuaries and other public

[C659] works. Thus it is beautifully adorned – as much as anywhere – with stoas and temples. One marvels at the irrational people who founded it under a vertical and overhanging cliff. One of the commanders, amazed at the situation, is reported to have said, "if the founder of this city was not afraid, was he not even ashamed?" The Mylasians have two sanctuaries of Zeus, one called Osogos and the other the Labrayndenian. The former is in the city. Labraynda is a village on the mountain near the pass from Alabanda to Mylasa, far from the city. An ancient temple and a xoanon of Zeus Stratios is there, honored by those all around and by the Mylasians. There is a paved road of almost 60 stadia from the city, called "Sacred," on which the sacred processions are conducted. The priesthoods are always held by the most distinguished citizens, and for life. These are distinctive to the city, but there is a third sanctuary of Karian Zeus that is common to all Karians and which is shared by the Lydians and Mysians, as they are brothers. It is recorded that it was a village in antiquity, but was the native land and royal residence of the Karians of [the family of] Hekatomnos. The city is nearest to the sea at Physkos, which is its seaport.

(24) Mylasa had notable men in my time, including the rhetoricians and civic leaders Euthydemos and Hybreas. Euthydemos inherited great wealth and reputation from his ancestors, and added his own cleverness to these. He was not only great in his native land but was considered worthy of the foremost honor in Asia. Hybreas would recount in school – and the citizens agreed – that his father left to him only a wood-bearing mule and a muledriver. Managing with these, he heard Diotrephes of Antiocheia for a short time, and then returned and gave himself over to being clerk of the agora. When he had rolled around with this and had made a little money, he entered politics and paid attention to the activities in the agora. He quickly became powerful and was already considered amazing while Euthydemos still lived, but especially after his death, becoming master of the city. Yet while the latter [Euthydemos] lived, he prevailed, being both powerful and

useful to the city, and even if he were something of a tyrant, it was relieved by being attended with what was useful. As any rate, what Hybreas said near the end of a public speech is praised: "Euthydemos, you are a necessary evil for the city, for we cannot live with you or without you." He [Hybreas] became very strong and was esteemed as a good citizen and rhetorician, yet he stumbled in his political opposition to Labienus. Others – when Labienus was coming against them with arms and a Parthian alliance (for at that time the Parthians possessed Asia) – yielded to him, as they were without weapons and peaceful, but Zenon of Laodikeia and Hybreas, both rhetoricians, would not yield. Hybreas also provoked him [Labienus] with a certain statement, for the latter was a boy who was irritable and full of folly, and when he announced that he was emperor of the Parthians, the former said "Then I call myself the Karian emperor." He advanced toward the city with a body of Roman soldiers that had already been organized in Asia. He did not seize the former [Hybreas], however, since he had withdrawn to Rhodes, but he shamefully maltreated his home with its expensive furnishings, and plundered it. He also treated the entire city badly. Although the former had abandoned Asia, he came back and restored both himself and the city. That is it about Mylasa. [C660]

(25) Stratonikeia is a Makedonian settlement. It too was adorned with expensive furnishings by the kings. There are two sanctuaries in the territory of the Stratonikeians, of which the most famous is that of Hekate at Lagina, which has a great festive gathering each year. Near to the city is that of Zeus Chrysaoreus, common to all Karians, where they come together to make sacrifice and to deliberate on common matters. Their federation is called the Chrysaorian, and it consists of villages. Those who supply the most villages are preferred in the vote, such as the Keramietians. The Stratonikeians share in the federation although they are not of Karian stock, because they have villages of the Chrysaorian Federation. Here a notable man, the rhetorician Menippos, was born in the time of our fathers. He was called Kotokas, and especially praised the Asian rhetoricians that he had heard, as Cicero says in one of his writings [*Brutus* 315], comparing him with Xenokles and the others who flourished at that time. There is another Stratonikeia, called "Near the Tauros," a small town situated on the mountain.

(26) Alabanda is also situated at the foot of hills, two that are joined together in such a way that they give the appearance of a loaded pack ass. Apollonios Malakos ridiculed the city both in regard to this and the large number of scorpions there, saying that it was a pack ass loaded with scorpions. This city and the Mylasian one are full of these creatures, as well as the entire mountainous country between them. It is a place of people who are luxurious [C661]

and debauchers, and of many female harpists. Alabandian men worthy of note are the two rhetoricians, the brothers Menekles (whom we mentioned a little above [14.2.13]) and Hierokles, and also Apollonios and Molon who moved to Rhodes.

(27) Of the many accounts that have been reported about the Karians, the one most agreed on is that the Karians were structured under Minos and were once called Lelegians and lived in the islands. Then they became mainlanders and gained possession of much of the coast and the interior, taking it away from those who had possessed it (who were mostly Lelegians and Pelasgians), and in turn the Hellenes – the Ionians and Dorians – took part of the territory away from them. Evidence for their military fervor is demonstrated through the shield holders, shield devices, and crests that everyone calls Karian. Anakreon, in fact, says "come, put your arm through the shield holder, work of the Karians" [F401], and Alkaios has "shaking the Karian crest" [F388].

(28) When the Poet says the following: "Masthles led the Karians, of barbarian speech" [*Iliad* 2.867], although he knew of barbarian peoples there is no reason why the Karians alone are of barbarian speech, but not barbarians. Thus Thoukydides [1.3.3] is incorrect, for he says that he [Homer] failed to say barbarian "because the Hellenes had not yet ... been distinguished by a single name as opposed to them," for the Poet refutes "the Hellenes had not yet" as a falsehood by saying "the man whose fame is spread throughout Hellas and the middle of Argos" [*Odyssey* 1.344], and "if you wish to be nourished throughout Hellas and the middle of Argos" [*Odyssey* 15.80]. If they were not called barbarians, how could they correctly be called "of barbarian speech"? Thus he [Thoukydides] is not correct, nor is the philologist Apollodoros [of Athens, F207], that the Hellenes used it abusively as a specific name against the Karians, especially the Ionians, who hated them because of their enmity and continuous military expeditions. Thus they would be named barbarians. But I ask why he calls them "of barbarian speech," but not even once barbarians? Because, he [Apollodoros of Athens] says, the plural does not fall in the meter, and because of this he does not call them barbarians. This form does not fall in it, but the nomi-

[C662]   native [*barbaroi*] is no different from "Dardanoi" ("Trojans, Lykians, and Dardanans" [*Dardanoi: Iliad* 8.173, etc.]), and also in "what kind of Trojan [*Troioi*] horses" [*Iliad* 5.222, 8.106]. It is not that the language of the Karians is exceedingly harsh, for it is not, and it has many Hellenic words mixed into it, as Philippos – who wrote the *Karika* – says [F1]. I think that in the beginning "barbarian" was pronounced onomatopoetically to mean those who spoke with difficulty, harshly, or roughly, like *battarizein* ["to stutter"], *traulizein* ["to lisp"], and *psellizein* ["to speak inarticulately"]. By nature we name sounds by similar sounds because of the homogeneity. Onomatopoeia is thus common, such as *kelaryzei* ["gurgle"], *klange* ["clang"], *psophos* ["noise"], *boe* ["cry out"], and *krotos* ["rattle"], most of which are now used properly. As all who spoke thickly were called barbarians, it appeared that the speech of other peoples was the same way (I am speaking of those who were not Hellenes). Those whom they peculiarly called barbarians, at first in ridicule, were those who spoke thickly and harshly. Then we misused it as a general ethnic name, thus logically distinguishing the Hellenes. But because of much intercourse and entanglement with the barbarians, this appeared not to occur due to a thickness of speech or something unnatural in their vocal organs, but because of the peculiarity of their languages. Moreover, there were those who appeared to speak our language with bad pronunciation, thus speaking like a barbarian, speaking Hellenic and not doing it correctly, yet saying words in the way barbarians beginning to learn Hellenic would, but not be able to do it properly, as when we speak other languages. This particularly happened with the Karians, although others were not mingling much with the Hellenes or attempting to live in the Hellenic manner or learn our language, except for the rare ones who by chance and individually were with a few Hellenes, such as those who wandered throughout Hellas serving in the military for pay. Thus barbarian speech was strong because of their expeditions in Hellas, and it prevailed afterward when they lived in the islands with Hellenes. When they were pushed from there into Asia they were still unable to live separately from the Hellenes (when the Ionians and Dorians crossed over). For the same reason there is the term "barbarize," which we are   [C663] accustomed to say about those who speak Hellenic badly, not those who talk in Karian. Thus "to speak barbarian" and "barbarian speakers" must be those who speak Hellenic badly. It was from "karianize" that "barbarize" was used differently in the treatises on the art of speaking Hellenic, as was "solecize," whether the word is from Soloi or created in another way.

(29) Artemidoros [F125] says that going from Physkos on the Rhodian Shore to Ephesos it is 850 stadia as far as Lagina and then another 250 to Alabanda, and 160 to Tralleis. But the road to Tralleis is at the crossing of the Maiandros, about the middle of the route, at the boundaries of Karia. In its entirety, from Physkos to the Maiandros along the Ephesos road, it is 1,180. Again, from the Maiandros next going the length of Ionia on the same road, it is 80 from the river to Tralleis, and then 140 to Magnesia, 120 to Ephesos, 320 to Smyrna, and less than 200 to Phokaia and the boundaries of Ionia. Thus the straight length of Ionia would be – according to him – slightly more than 800. There is a sort of common road used by everyone

travelling from Ephesos toward the east, and he goes along it. To Karoura, the Karian boundary toward Phrygia, through Magnesia, Tralleis, Nysa, and Antiocheia, is a route of 740 stadia. The Phrygian part is through Laodikeia, Apameia, Metropolis, and Chelidonia. At the beginning of the Paroreios is Holmoi, about 920 stadia from Karoura, and at the end of the Paroreios near Lykaonia, through Philomelion, is Tyriaion, which is slightly more than 500. Then there is Lykaonia, as far as Koropassos, through Laodikeia Katakekaumene, in 840. From Koropassos in Lykaonia to Garsaoura, a small town in Kappadokia situated on its border, is 120. Then to Mazaka, the metropolis of the Kappadokians, through Soandos and Sadakora, is 680, and from there to the Euphrates as far as Tomisa (a place in Sophene) through Erpha, a small town, is 1,440. The places lying in a straight line as far as Indike are the same in Artemidoros as Eratosthenes [F88]. Polybios [34.13] says that in regard to this the latter must be trusted, who begins from Samosata in Kommagene, which lies at the crossing and at Zeugma, saying that it is 450 stadia to Samosata from the boundaries of Kappadokia around Tomisa across the Tauros.

[C664]

Part 3: Lykia

(1) After the Rhodian Shore, whose boundary is Daidala, Lykia is next, on the sail toward the rising sun. It lies as far as Pamphylia, and then there is Pamphylia itself, as far as the Rough Kilikians, and those places [extend] as far as the other Kilikians around the Issic Gulf. These are parts of the peninsula, whose isthmus – as we have said [12.1.3] – is the route from Issos to Amisos (or Sinope, according to some), outside the Tauros on the narrow coast from Lykia as far as the region around Soloi, today Pompeioupolis. Then immediately there is the coast on the Issic Gulf that spreads into the plains, beginning at Soloi and Tarsos. After having gone through this, the account of the entire peninsula will have been systematically completed. Then we will pass on to the other portions of Asia outside the Tauros, and finally we will expound about Libya.

(2) After Rhodian Daidala there is a Lykian mountain that has the same name, Daidala, from where the entire sail along the Lykiakos has its beginning. It is 1,720 stadia and rough and difficult, but exceedingly well supplied with harbors and occupied by reasonable people. The nature of the territory is similar to that of the Pamphylians and the Rough Kilikians, but they used their localities as bases for brigandage, whether they were pirates themselves or supplied the pirates with places either for the selling of booty or for naval stations. In Side, at any rate, a Pamphylian city, the shipyards

were available to the Kilikians, who would sell their captives there by auction, yet agreeing that they were free people. The Lykians continued living in a civilized and moderate way – although through their good fortune they mastered the sea as far as Italia – and thus they were not moved to disgraceful profit, but remained in the ancestral district of the Lykian Federation.

(3) There are twenty-three cities that share in the vote. They come together from each city – those cities that were declared eligible – to a common council. The largest cities control three votes each, the middle-sized two, and the others one. In the same manner they make their [C665] contributions and other services. Artemidoros [F122] says that the six largest were Xanthos, Patara, Pinara, Olympos, Myra, and Tlos (located near the pass to Kibyra). At the council they first choose a Lykiarch and then other officers of the federation, and the common courts of justice are proclaimed. Formerly they deliberated about war, peace, and alliances, but today this is not reasonable since by necessity such matters are handled by the Romans, except when they are given permission or it is useful for them. Similarly the judges and magistrates are proportionately chosen by vote from each city. Since they were under such a good government they remained free under the Romans, retaining their ancestral customs, and experiencing the complete elimination of piracy (originally by Servilius Isauricus at the time that he destroyed Isaura, and later by Pompeius Magnus when he set fire to more than 1,300 boats and eradicated their settlements). He brought some of the men who survived the battles down to Soloi, which he named Pompeioupolis, and others to Dyme, which was lacking in population. Today it is occupied by a Roman settlement. The poets – especially the tragedians – are confused about the peoples, such as the Trojans, Mysians, and Lydians, whom they call Phrygians, and they also have the Lykians as Karians.

(4) After Daidala (the Lykian mountain), Telmessos is nearby, a Lykian town, and Telmessis, a promontory with a harbor. Eumenes [II] took the place from the Romans in the war against Antiochos [III], but when his kingdom was dissolved the Lykians received it back.

(5) Next is Antikragos, a steep mountain, where Karmylessos is, an inhabited place in a ravine, and after this is Kragos, which has eight promontories and a city of the same name. Around these mountains is the myth of the Chimaira, and not far away is the chasm of Chimaira, which extends up from the shrine. Pinara, which is one of the largest cities in Lykia, lies in the interior at the foot of Kragos. Pandaros is honored here, perhaps from the same family as the Trojan hero, who is said to have been from Lykia.

(6) Then there is the Xanthos River, formerly called the Sirbis. After
[C666] sailing up in a small boat for ten stadia there is the Letoon. Going 60 [stadia]
beyond the sanctuary is the city of the Xanthians, the largest in Lykia. After
Xanthos is Patara, also a large city, having a harbor and a sanctuary of
Apollo, a foundation of Pataros. Ptolemaios [II] Philadelphos restored it and
called it Arsinoë In Lykia but the original name prevailed.

(7) Then there is Myra, in 20 stadia, above the sea on a high hill. Then
there is the outlet of the Limyros River and, going 20 stadia inland on
foot, the small town of Limyra. In between, on the coastal voyage previously
mentioned there are small islets and harbors, including the island of Megiste
and a city of the same name, and Kisthene. In the interior are the places of
Phellos, Antiphellos, and Chimaira, which I mentioned above.

(8) Then there is the Sacred Promontory and the Chelidoniai, which are
three rough islands about equal in size and about 5 stadia distant from
each other. They lie about 6 stadia from the land. One of them has an
anchorage. Here, most believe, the Tauros takes its beginning because of the
high promontory that goes down from the Pisidian mountains that lie above
Pamphylia, and because of the islands that lie off it which make a rather
conspicuous sign in the sea in the manner of an edge. Yet in truth the
mountainous territory is continuous from the Rhodian Shore to the portions near Pisidia, and this is also called the Tauros. The Chelidoniai are
believed to lie approximately opposite to Kanobos, and it is said that the sea
passage is 4,000 stadia. From the Sacred Promontory to Olbia there remains
367 stadia, and on this portion are Krambousa, the large city of Olympos,
and the mountain of the same name, which is also called Phoinikous. Then
there is the shore of Korykos.

(9) Then there is Phaselis, which has three harbors, a notable city, and a
lake. Solyma lies above it, a mountain, and Termessos, a Pisidian city that lies
at the narrows, through which there is a pass to Milyas. Alexander destroyed it
because he wished to open the narrows. Around Phaselis there are narrows
running down to the sea, through which Alexander led his army. There is a
mountain here called Klimax, which lies near the Pamphylian Sea and leaves a
narrow passage on the shore. When it is calm it is bare, so that it is passable for
travellers, but at the flood tide of the sea it is largely hidden by the waves. The
pass through the mountain is circuitous and steep, and the beach is used in
fair weather. Alexander fell into the stormy season, and as one who greatly
[C667] trusted in fortune, he set forth before the waves receded. During the entire
day the journey was in water up to their navels. This city is also Lykian,
situated on the border toward Pamphylia, but it does not partake in common
Lykian matters and is associated only with itself.

(10) The Poet mentions the Solymians as different from the Lykians, for when Bellerophontes was sent by the Lykian king to the second fight "he fought with the glorious Solymians" [*Iliad* 6.184]. Others assert that the Lykians were formerly called the Solymians, but later Termilians, who came from Crete along with Sarpedon and who were afterward Lykians from Lykos the son of Pandion. After being expelled from his home, he was received by Sarpedon into a portion of his rule. They do not agree with Homer. Those are better who assert that the Solymians mentioned by the Poet are the ones now called the Milyans, about whom I have spoken [12.8.5].

Part 4: Pamphylia

(1) After Phaselis there is Olbia, the beginning of Pamphylia and a large fortress, and after this there is the so-called Kataraktes, a river that rushes down [*kataratton*] from a high rock so greatly and torrentially that the noise can be heard far away. Then there is the city of Attaleia, named after its founder [Attalos II] Philadelphos, who also settled Korykos, a small neighboring town, surrounding the settlement with a larger circuit wall. They say that Thebe and Lyrnessos are pointed out between Phaselis and Attaleia, part of the Trojan Kilikians having been driven from the Plain of Thebe into Pamphylia, as Kallisthenes [F32] says.

(2) Then there is the Kestros River, which one can sail up 60 stadia to the city of Perge. Nearby on a high location is the sanctuary of Artemis Pergaia where a festival is celebrated every year. Then, about 40 stadia above the sea, is Syllion, a high city that is visible from Perge. Then there is an exceedingly large lake, Kapria, and after it the Eurymedon River, which one can sail up for 60 stadia to Aspendos, a sufficiently well-populated city and an Argive foundation. Petnelissos lies above it. Then there is another river with numerous islets off it, and then Side, a Kymaian settlement, which has a most notable sanctuary of Athena. The coast of the Lesser Kibyratians is near to it. Then there is the Melas River and an anchorage, and then the city of Ptolemais. After it are the boundaries of Pamphylia and also Korakesion, the beginning of Rough Kilikia. The entire voyage along Pamphylia is 640 stadia.

(3) Herodotos [7.91] says that the Pamphylians belong to the mixed crowd of people from Troy who followed along with Amphilochos and Kalchas, most of whom remained here but some of whom were scattered everywhere on earth. Kallisthenes says that Kalchas died in Klaros, but the crowd of people with Mopsos went over the Tauros. Some remained in

[C668]

Pamphylia, and others were distributed throughout Kilikia and Syria as far as Phoenicia.

Part 5:   Kilikia

(1) The part of Kilikia outside the Tauros is called Rough [Tracheia] and the other is Level [Pedias]. The coast of Rough is narrow and has hardly any level ground. Moreover it lies beneath the Tauros, which is poorly inhabited as far as its northern side around Isaura and the Homonadeis as far as Pisidia. It is also called Tracheiotis and its inhabitants Tracheiotes. Level is from Soloi and Tarsos as far as Issos, beyond which on the north side of the Tauros are the Kappadokians. This territory is mostly a plain supplied with good land. As some of it is within the Tauros and other parts outside, and those inside have been discussed, I will speak about those outside, beginning with the Tracheiotes.

(2) In Kilikia there is first a fortress, Korakesion, situated on an abrupt rock that was used by Diodotos called Tryphon as a base when he caused Syria to revolt from the kings and was fighting it out with them, sometimes successfully and sometimes stumbling. Antiochos [VII] son of Demetrios [I] shut him in at a certain place and forced him to kill himself. Tryphon was the reason – as well as the worthlessness of the kings at that time who had successively been set over Syria as well as Kilikia – that the Kilikians began to organize their piratical groups. Because of his attempts at revolution, others also attempted revolution along with him, dividing brothers against each other and making the territory come under the control of those attacking it. The exportation of slaves encouraged this evil business most of all since it was especially profitable, as they were easily captured and the emporium was not very far away and was large and exceedingly wealthy. This was Delos, which could receive and send away a myriad of slaves on the same day, from which comes the proverb "Merchant, sail in and unload, everything has been sold." The reason for this was that the Romans, having become wealthy after the destruction of Karchedon and Corinth, made use of many slaves, and the pirates saw how easy it was and thus flourished in large numbers, both plundering and dealing in slaves. The kings of Cyprus and Egypt cooperated in this as they were enemies of the Syrians, and Rhodians were also unfriendly toward them and thus would not help them. At the same time the pirates, pretending to be slave dealers, were unrestrained in their evil business. The Romans were not yet considering matters outside the Tauros, but they sent Scipio Aemilianus to inspect the people and cities, and later there were others. They decided that it was due to the

[C669]

bad quality of the rulers, but, since they had ratified the hereditary succession from Seleukos [I] Nikator, they were ashamed to remove it. This is what made the Parthyaians masters of the territory, who possessed that beyond the Euphrates, and eventually the Armenians, who had also taken that outside the Tauros as far as Phoenicia, and overthrew the kings and the entire royal family as much as possible, but they gave the sea over to the Kilikians. Then the Romans, when they had increased in power, were forced to destroy them by war and with an army, although they had not hindered their increase in power. It is difficult to condemn them of negligence, since because of matters that were nearer and more at hand they were unable to observe what was farther away. I have decided to say this as a brief digression.

(3) After Korakesion there is the city of Arsinoë, and then Hamaxia, a settlement on a mound with an anchorage, where ship material is brought down. This is mostly cedar, and it seems that this region is more abundant in the cutting of wood. Because of this Antonius assigned the territory to Kleopatra [VII], since it was useful for the building of her fleets. Then there is Laertes, a fortress on a breast-shaped hill, with an anchorage. Then there is the Selinous River, then Kragos, a rock that is steep all around near the sea. Then there is Charadrous, a fortification, also with an anchorage (Mount Andriklos lies above it). The coast alongside it, called Platanistos, is rugged. Then Cape Anemourion, where the mainland is closest to Cyprus, toward Cape Krommyon in a crossing of 350 stadia. The Kilikian coastal voyage to Anemourion from the borders of Pamphylia is 820 stadia, and the rest as far as Soloi is a voyage along the coast of about 500 stadia. [C670]

Nagidos is the first city after Anemourion. Then there is Arsinoë, which has an anchorage, and then a place, Melania, and Kelenderis, a city having a harbor. Some put this, not Korakesion, as the beginning of Kilikia, among whom is Artemidoros [F116]. He says that from the Pelousiac mouth it is 3,650 stadia to Orthosia, 1,130 to the Orontes River, to the Gates that follow 520, and to the Kilikian borders 1,900.

(4) Then there is Holmoi where the Seleukeians of today formerly lived, but when Kalykadnos Seleukeia was founded they migrated there. Immediately there is the mouth of the Kalykadnos, where the shore curves around making a cape called Sarpedon. Near the Kalykadnos is Zephyrion, also a cape. The river can be sailed inland to Seleukeia, a well-populated city far removed from the Kilikian and Pamphylian styles. Notable men were born here in my time: the Peripatetic philosophers Athenaios and Xenarchos. Of these, Athenaios was politically active and was for a time the leader of the people in his native land. Then, after he fell into friendship with Murena he was captured along with him while in flight when the plot

contrived against Sebastos Caesar was discovered, but he was clearly guiltless and was released by Caesar. When he returned from Rome, he said the following (from Euripides) to the first who happened to greet and question him: "I have come, having left the hiding place of the dead and the gates of darkness" [*Hekouba* 1–2]. He survived only a short time, as he was killed when the house he was living in collapsed at night. Xenarchos, however, whom I heard, did not stay long at home, but chose the life of a teacher in Alexandria, Athens, and Rome. He enjoyed the friendship of Areios, and afterward Caesar Sebastos, and continued to be held in honor into old age. Shortly before the end he lost his sight, and then his life ended through disease.

(5) After the Kalykadnos is the rock called Painted, which has a rock-cut stairway leading to Seleukeia. Then there is Cape Anemourion, having the same name as the previous one, the island of Krambousa, and Cape Korykos, 20 stadia above which is the Korykian Cave, in which the best [C671] saffron grows. It is a large circular hollow, having a rocky brow lying around it that is quite high everywhere. Going down into it, there is a small surface that is irregular and quite rocky but full of shrub-like brush that includes both evergreen and domesticated types. Scattered around are the surfaces on which the saffron is produced. There is also a cave with a large spring which sends forth a river of pure and transparent water that immediately falls under the earth and then is carried invisibly and empties into the sea. It is called Bitter Water.

(6) Then after Korykos there is the island of Elaioussa, lying close to the mainland, which Archelaos settled and prepared as a royal residence, after he had received all of Rough Kilikia except Seleukeia, in the same way that Amyntas formerly had it, and still earlier Kleopatra [VII]. The place was naturally useful for piracy, both by land and sea: by land because of the height of the mountains and the peoples living beyond them who have large plains and farmlands that can easily be overrun, and by sea because of the abundance of shipbuilding timber, harbors, fortresses, and coves. Because of this it was thought better in every way that the place be ruled by kings rather than Roman commanders sent to administer justice, who would not always be present or under arms. Thus Archelaos received – in addition to Kappadokia – Rough Kilikia, whose boundary is the Lamos River and the village of the same name between Soloi and Elaioussa.

(7) Near the ridges of the Tauros is the pirate stronghold of Zeniketes, Olympos, a mountain and fortress of the same name from which one can look over all Lykia, Pamphylia, Pisidia, and Milyas. When the mountain was taken by Isauricus, he burned himself up with his entire household. He

also held Korykos, Phaselis, and many places in Pamphylia, all of which were taken by Isauricus.

(8) After the Lamos there is Soloi, a notable city, and the beginning of the other Kilikia, that around Issos. It was a foundation of Achaians and Rhodians from Lindos. Because it was lightly populated, Pompeius Magnus settled the surviving pirates in it whom he believed worthy of being saved and nurtured, and changed its name to Pompeioupolis. Men of note from there are Chrysippos the Stoic philosopher, whose father had moved there from Tarsos, Philemon the comic poet, and Aratos who wrote the *Phainomena* in verse.

(9) Then there is Zephyrion, which has the same name as the one near the Kalykadnos. Then, a little above the sea, is Anchiale, which, Aristoboulos [C672] [F9b] says, was a foundation of Sardanapallos. The memorial of Sardanapallos is there, a stone relief with the fingers of the right hand coming together as if snapping, and the following inscription in Assyrian letters:

> Sardanapallos the son of Anakyndaraxes built Anchiale and Tarsos in one day. Eat, drink, and play, for everything else is not worth this,

meaning the snapping. Choirilos also records it, and these words are generally known:

> I love most what I have eaten, what I have indulged, and the delights of love that I have experienced. I have left behind all the blessings.

(10) Kyinda lies above Anchiale, a fortress that once was a Makedonian treasury. The funds were taken by Eumenes when he revolted from Antigonos [I]. Above here and Soloi it is mountainous, where there is the city of Olbe and a sanctuary of Zeus, a foundation of Aias the son of Teukros. Its priest became dynast of Tracheiotis, and then there were many tyrants in the territory, and the pirate bands were formed. After these were overthrown in my time they called it the dominion or priesthood of Teukros, and most of the priests were named Teukros or Aias. Aba, the daughter of Zenophanes (one of the tyrants), came into this family through marriage and took possession of the rule, her father having previously received it in the manner of a guardian. Later both Antonius and Kleopatra [VII] showed favor to her, because of her services and earnest pleas. When she was overthrown the rule remained with her descendants.

After Anchiale there are the outlets of the Kydnos near the so-called Rhegma. It is a place that forms a lake and has ancient dockyards. The Kydnos flows through the middle of Tarsos, and its sources are in the city of Tauros that lies above it. The lake is also the seaport of Tarsos. [C673]

(11) The entire coast this far, beginning at the Rhodian Shore, extends toward equinoctal sunrise from the sunset of the same name. Then it bends toward the winter sunrise as far as Issos and immediately makes a turn toward the south as far as Phoenicia. The rest is toward the sunset as far as the Pillars, where it ends. The truth is that the isthmus of the peninsula that has been gone around is from Tarsos and the mouth of the Kydnos as far as Amisos, for this is the shortest distance from Amisos to the boundaries of Kilikia. From there to Tarsos is 120 stadia, and no more to the outlet of the Kydnos. And in fact there is no other road to Issos and its sea from Amisos that is any shorter than the one through Tarsos, and Tarsos is no nearer Issos than the Kydnos is. Thus it is clear that in truth this would be the isthmus, but it is said that it is actually as far as the Issic Gulf, a deception because of its significance. Due to this very matter we have brought the line from the Rhodia down as far as the Kydnos and have represented it as the same as the one as far as Issos, not making a distinction. We also assert that the Tauros extends in a straight line as far as Indike.

(12) Tarsos lies in a plain, a foundation of the Argives who wandered with Triptolemos seeking Io. The Kydnos flows through its middle and right past the gymnasium of the youths. Its springs are not far away, and the stream goes through a deep chasm and then immediately comes out into the city, with a flow that is both cold and fast. Because of this it is beneficial both to animals and people for swollen sinews, if they make use of its rushing.

(13) The people there are so eager about philosophy and everything else in terms of general education that they have surpassed Athens and Alexandria or any other place that can be named where there have been schools or discourses of philosophers. But it is different, for those who study there are all natives, as foreigners do not readily stay. Moreover, the former do not remain there, but finish abroad, and having finished they are pleased to live abroad, although a few return. With the other cities that I have just mentioned – except Alexandria – it is the opposite, for many frequent them [C674] and are pleased to pass time there, but you would not see many natives frequenting foreign places or eager about learning at home. With the Alexandrians both occurs: they accept many foreigners from everywhere and send away not a few of their own. There are all kinds of schools in the art of speaking there [Tarsos], and it is well populated and most powerful, having the reputation of a metropolis.

(14) Those born there include the Stoics Antipatros, Archedemos, and Nestor, and also the two Athenodoroi, one of whom, called Kordylion, lived with Marcus Cato and died in his home. The other was the son of Sandon,

whom they called Kananites after some village. He was the teacher of Caesar and was greatly honored by him. When he returned to his homeland as an old man, he dissolved the established government, which was being badly handled by Boethos (and others), a bad poet and a bad citizen who had become strong mostly due to bribery. Antonius had raised him up, in the beginning having favorably received the poem that he had written on the victory at Philippoi, and moreover the ease by which he could improvise unceasingly on the spot about any topic that he was given, something prevalent among the Tarsians. Moreover, the Tarsians were promised a gymnasiarch, but he was appointed instead of a gymnasiarch and entrusted with the expenses. But he was caught appropriating olive oil and other things, and when he was being questioned by his accusers in front of Antonius he deprecated the latter's anger, saying, among other things,

> Just as Homer celebrated Achilleus, Agamemnon, and Odysseus, I have done the same for you. Therefore it is unjust that I should be brought before you on such charges.

When his accuser heard the statement, he said "Homer did not steal Agamemnon's olive oil, nor that of Achilleus, but you did and should be punished." Nevertheless he evaded his [Antonius'] anger through his services and continued in power, plundering the city until the overthrow of Antonius. Finding the city in such a situation, Athenodoros attempted for a while to have him [Boethos] and his followers change their course, but they would not abstain from any kind of arrogance, and thus he used the authority given to him by Caesar and expelled and exiled them. At first they wrote on a wall "work for youth, counsels for middle age, and flatulence for the old." He [Athenodoros] took it as a kind of joke and ordered that "the thunder of old men" be inscribed beside it. But someone who was disdainful and had loose bowels splattered extensively on the door and wall of his house while passing by at night, and he, making accusations against the faction in the assembly, said "One can see the sickness and disaffection of the city in many places, but especially from its excrement." [C675]

These then were Stoics, but the Nestor of my time was an Academic. He was the teacher of Marcellus the son of Octavia the sister of Caesar, and he was also a leader in the government, the successor of Athenodoros, and continued to be honored by the authorities and those in the city.

(15) Other philosophers from here "whom I could well recognize and note their names" [*Iliad* 3.235] are Ploutiades and Diogenes, who wandered around and managed schools ably. Diogenes also wrote poems, mostly tragic ones, through inspiration when provided with a subject. Philologists whose writings

are extant include Artemidoros and Diodoros. The best tragic poet – who is numbered in the Pleiades – was Dionysiades. The great number of scholars from here is best demonstrated in Rome, for it is full of Tarsians and Alexandrians. This is Tarsos.

(16) After the Kydnos is the Pyramos, which flows from Kataonia and which I have mentioned previously [12.2.4]. Artemidoros [F115] says that from there to Soloi is a straight voyage of 500 stadia. Mallos is nearby, situated on a height, a foundation of Amphilochos and Mopsos the son of Apollo and Manto, about whom many myths are told. I have discussed them in the account of Kalchas and the quarrel that occurred between Kalchas and Mopsos over their prophetic powers [14.1.27]. Some – especially Sophokles [F180] – transfer this quarrel to Kilikia (which he, in the fashion of tragedians, calls Pamphylia, just as Lykia is Karia and Troy and Lydia are Phrygia). Sophokles and others hand down that Kalchas died there. But, according to the myth, the quarrel was not only about prophetic powers but also the rule. They say that Mopsos and Amphilochos came [C676] from Troy and founded Mallos, and then Amphilochos went away to Argos, but he was displeased with the situation there and returned. Yet then he was excluded from joining into a partnership and so fought Mopsos in single combat. Both fell and were buried out of sight of one another. Today their tombs are visible around Magarsa near the Pyramos. Krates the philologist was from here, of whom Panaitios is said to have been a pupil.

(17) The Aleian Plain is above this coast, through which Philotas took the cavalry of Alexander when the latter led the phalanx along the coast from Soloi, going from the Mallotis against Issos and the forces of Dareios [III]. They say that Alexander offered sacrifices to Amphilochos because of his kinship with the Argives. Hesiod [F215] says that Amphilochos was done away with at Soloi by Apollo, but others that it happened around the Aleian Plain, and others in Syria after he left the Aleian due to the quarrel.

(18) After Mallos is Aigaiai, a small town with an anchorage, and then the Amanian Gates, with an anchorage, where Mount Amanos ends. It comes down from the Tauros and lies above Kilikia toward the eastern portion. The region was always ruled by powerful tyrants, and in our time a notable man became master of it all and was named king by the Romans because of his virtue and character. This was Tarkondimotos [I], who passed the succession to those after him.

(19) After Aigaiai is Issos, a small town with an anchorage, and the Pinaros River. Here the struggle between Alexander and Dareios [III] occurred. The gulf is called the Issic. On it are the cities of Rhosos, Myriandros, Alexandria, Nikopolis, Mopsou Hestia, and what are called the Gates, the boundary

between Kilikia and Syria. In Kilikia there is also the sanctuary and oracle of Sarpedonian Artemis, and the responses are told by those who are divinely inspired.

(20) After Kilikia the first Syrian city is Seleukeia in Pieria, near which the Orontes River empties. From Seleukeia to Soloi in a straight voyage is a little less than a thousand stadia.

(21) The Kilikians at Troy, whom Homer records, are far away from the Kilikians outside the Tauros. Some proclaim that those at Troy were the founders of the others and point out certain places in Pamphylia, such as Thebe and Lyrnessos. Those who have a contrary opinion point out an Aleian Plain there. Although the parts of the previously mentioned peninsula outside the Tauros have been gone through, the following must be added.   [C677]

(22) Apollodoros [of Athens], in his *On the Ships* [F170], says the following: all the allies of the Trojans from Asia were enumerated by the Poet and said to be inhabitants of the peninsula, whose narrowest isthmus is between the recess at Sinope and Issos. He says that the exterior sides make a triangular shape but are unequal, one extending from Kilikia to the Chelidoniai, one from there to the mouth of the Euxine, and one from there back to Sinope. That they lived only in the peninsula can be proved false by what I said previously (12.3.24), that they did not live only within the Halys. The places around Pharnakeia where the Halizonians were are outside the Halys, as I said, and are also outside the isthmus if they are outside the narrows between Sinope and Issos (not only these, but the true narrows between Amisos and Tarsos). He incorrectly determines the isthmus and its narrows since he places the former for the latter, and he is most simplistic when he says that the peninsula is triangular in shape, representing the exterior sides as three in number, but in speaking of the exterior sides he is content to exclude what is along the narrows as if a side, yet one that is neither exterior or on the sea. If these narrows were shortened, so that the sides ending at Issos and that at Sinope lacked a small amount of touching each other, one might say that the peninsula comes together into a triangular shape. But now there are 3,000 stadia left on the narrows mentioned by him, and it is ignorant to say that such a four-sided figure is in the shape of a triangle. This is not suitable for chorography. Yet he produced in comic meter a chorography titled *Circuit of the Earth*. The same ignorance remains even if one were to reduce the distance of the isthmus to the least possible, one half of the total, or 1,500 stadia – as those who are the most deceived say, as well as Artemidoros [F114] – but this does not bring it together enough to create a triangular form. The exterior sides are not correctly separated when

he speaks of that from the Issos to the Chelidoniai, because the entirety of the Lykian coast remains in straight alignment with it, as well as the Rhodian Shore as far as Physkos. There the mainland takes a bend and begins to make the second or western side, as far as the Propontis and Byzantion.

[C678]   (23) Ephoros [F162] says that the peninsula was inhabited by sixteen peoples, three of which were Hellenic and the rest barbarian, except for those who were mixed. On the sea were the Kilikians, Pamphylians, Lykians, Bithynians, Paphlagonians, Mariandynians, Trojans, and Karians. The Pisidians, Mysians, Chalybians, Phrygians, and Milyans were in the interior. Apollodoros [of Athens, F170] investigates this and says that the Galatians – who are more recent than Ephoros – are a seventeenth. Of those previously mentioned, the Hellenes were not yet settled there at the time of the Trojan matter, and the barbarians are greatly confused because of the length of time. The Poet catalogues the Trojans and those now named the Paphlagonians, and the Mysians, Phrygians, Karians and Lykians, the Meionians instead of the Lydians, and others who are unknown such as the Halizonians and Kaukonians. Outside the *Catalogue* there are the Keteians, Solymians, Kilikians from the Plain of Thebe, and the Lelegians, but he does not name the Pamphylians, Bithynians, Mariandynians, Pisidians, Chalybians, Milyans, or Kappadokians. Some had not yet settled in these places and others were included among other peoples, such as the Idrieians and Termilians among the Karians, and the Dolionians and Bebrykians among the Phrygians.

(24) It is sufficient that he [Apollodoros of Athens] does not consider the assertion of Ephoros, and thus confuses and falsifies what the Poet says. He should first have asked Ephoros why he placed the Chalybians within the peninsula, when they were located far away, east of Sinope and Amisos. Those who say that the isthmus of the peninsula is the line from the Issos to the Euxeinos establish it as a sort of meridian, which some believe should be [the line] to Sinope and others the one to Amisos, but no one that to the Chalybians, which would be completely at a slant. The meridian through the Chalybians would be drawn through Lesser Armenia and the Euphrates, cutting off within it all of Kappadokia, Kommagene, Amanos, and the Issic Gulf. If we concede that the slanting line marks the boundary of the isthmus, most of these places – especially Kappadokia – would be cut off within it, including what is now distinctly called Pontos, a part of Kappadokia toward the Euxeinos. Thus if the Chalybians must be set down as part of the peninsula, more so should Kataonia, both Kappadokias, and Lykaonia, which he disregards.

And why did he place the Chalybians in the interior, whom the Poet
[C679]   called the Halizonians, as we have already shown [12.3.20]? It would have

been better to divide them and have one part appear on the sea and the other in the interior. This also should be done with Kappadokia and Kilikia, but he does not name the former and speaks only of the Kilikians on the sea. Concerning those subject to Antipatros of Derbe, the Homonadians, and a number of others adjoining the Pisidians – "men who do not know the seas and do not eat food mixed with salt" [*Odyssey* 11.122–3] – how should they be positioned? Nor does he say whether the Lydians or Meionians are two or are the same, or whether they are separate by themselves or encompassed by another people. It would be impossible for such a significant people to be hidden, and if he [Ephoros] does not speak about them, would it not seem that he has omitted something most important?

(25) Who are the mixed peoples? In regard to the previously mentioned places, we cannot say whether those considered to be mixed were named or omitted by him, or whether any of those whom he has mentioned or omitted were [mixed]. If they had been combined, either the Hellenic or barbarian would become dominant, and we do not know any third peoples who could be mixed in.

(26) How can there be three Hellenic peoples living in the peninsula? If it is because the Ionians and Athenians were the same in antiquity, let the Dorians and Aiolians also be the same, and thus there would be only two peoples. If one were to divide them according to later customs, such as by dialects, then there would be four peoples, like the dialects. But inhabiting this peninsula – especially according to the determinations of Ephoros – there are not only Ionians, but also Athenians, as has been shown in each instance [14.1.3].

It is worthwhile then, in regard to Ephoros, that this be a matter of discussion. Yet Apollodoros [of Athens] gave it no consideration and added to the sixteen peoples a seventeenth, the Galatians, something useful to say but unnecessary in regard to consideration of what Ephoros omitted saying. The former gives the reason himself: that all this is at a time later than him.

(27) Passing on to the Poet, he [Apollodoros of Athens] correctly says that because of many changes there is much confusion regarding the barbarian peoples from the time of the Trojan matter to today. Some of them have been added to, others have gone out of existence, others have dispersed, and still others have been combined into one. But he incorrectly proclaims two reasons why the Poet does not record some of them: either [a region] was [C680] not yet inhabited by a particular tribe, or it was included within another. Yet he [Homer} fails to mention Kappadokia, Kataonia, and also Lykaonia for neither of these [reasons], for we have no such history for any of them. It is ridiculous that he [Apollodoros of Athens] should consider why he omitted

the Kappadokians and Lykaonians and defend him, yet pass over why
Ephoros passed over them – and this when he had put forward the statement of the man in order to examine it and judge it – as well as to teach why
Homer said Meionians instead of Lydians but not to say that Ephoros
indicates neither the Lydians or the Meionians.

(28) Saying that the Poet records certain peoples, he [Apollodoros] then
correctly names the Kaukonians, Solymians, Keteians, Lelegians, and the
Kilikians of the Plain of Thebe. Yet the Halizonians are his fabrication, or
rather of the first ones who did not know who the Halizonians were and
transcribed the name in various ways, fabricating the birthplace of silver
and many other mines, all of which have failed. To further their ambitions,
they collected the stories put together by the Skepsian [F44], taken from
Kallisthenes [F54] and certain others who were not free of the false ideas
about the Halizonians. Similarly the wealth of Tantalos and the Pelopidai
came from the mines around Phrygia and Sipylos, that of Kadmos from
those around Thrace and Mount Pangaion, that of Priamos from the gold
mines at Astyra near Abydos (small remains of which survive today, for much
was thrown out, and the excavations are evidence for ancient mining), that of
Midas from around Mount Bermion, and that of Gyges, Alyattes, and Kroisos
from Lydia and between Atarneus and Pergamon, where there is a deserted
small town and whose lands have been emptied of ore.

(29) One might censure Apollodoros [of Athens] still more, because when
those more recent made many changes that are contrary to the statements of
Homer, he is accustomed to test them frequently. Yet in this matter he has
not only made light of them but has put together opposing things that were
not meant to be the same. Xanthos the Lydian [F14] says that it was after the
Trojan matter that the Phrygians came from Europe and the left side of the
Pontos, led by Skamandrios from the Berekyntians and Askania. Apollodoros
[of Athens, F170] adds that Homer records this Askania of Xanthos
("Phorkyas and godlike Askanios led the Phrygians from far away, from
[C681]   Askania" [Iliad 2.862–3]). If this is so, the migration happened later than the
Trojan matter, but the assistance to the Trojans mentioned by the Poet
was from the far side, from the Berekyntians and Askania. Who were the
Phrygians, "camped on the banks of the Sangarios" [Iliad 3.187], when
Priamos says "I was an ally, numbered among them" [Iliad 3.188]? How
could Priamos have sent for the Phrygians from the Berekyntians – with
whom he had no agreement – and yet neglect those on his borders with whom
he previously had had an alliance? After speaking this way about the Phrygians,
he [Apollodoros of Athens] adds something about the Mysians that is not in
agreement with it: he says that there is a village in Mysia called Askania, near a

lake of the same name, from which the Askanios River flows, and which is mentioned by Euphorion ("by the waters of Mysian Askanios" [F73]) as well as Alexander the Aitolian:

> who have their homes by the Askanian stream, on the lips of the Askanian Lake, where Dolion lived, the son of Silenos and Melia. [F9]

He also says that the territory around Kyzikos – going up to Miletoupolis – is called Dolionis and Mysia. If this is so – and there is the evidence of the places now pointed out, and of the poets – what prevented Homer from recording this Askania and not the one mentioned by Xanthos? This has been stated previously in the Mysian and Phrygian section [7.3.2–3, 12.4.4–8], so let this be the end.

Part 6: Cyprus

(1) It remains to go around the island of Cyprus, which lies alongside the peninsula on the south. It has been said [2.5.18] that the sea surrounded by Egypt, Phoenicia, Syria, and the rest of the coast as far as the Rhodia, consists approximately of the Egyptian and Pamphylian Seas, and the Issic Gulf, which Cyprus is in, with its northern parts adjoining Rough Kilikia – where it is closest to the mainland – its eastern on the Issic Gulf, its western washed by the Pamphylian Sea, and its southern by the Egyptian. This flows together on the west with the Libyan and Karpathian Seas, but on its southern and eastern portions there is Egypt and the adjoining coast as far as Seleukeia and Issos, and on its north Cyprus and the Pamphylian Sea. This is surrounded on the north by the extremities of Rough Kilikia, Pamphylia, and Lykia, as far as the Rhodia, on the west by the Rhodian island, on the east by Cyprus near Paphos and Akamas, and on the south it flows together with the Egyptian Sea. [C682]

(2) The circuit of Cyprus is 3,420 stadia, going through the gulfs. The length by foot from the Kleides to Akamas, travelling from east to west, is 1,400 stadia. The Kleides are two islets lying off Cyprus, off the eastern part of the island, 700 stadia distant from Pyramos. Akamas is a promontory with two breasts and much timber, lying in the western part of the island, extending toward the north and nearest to Selinous in Rough Kilikia, a passage of 1,000 stadia. To Side in Pamphylia is 1,600 and to the Chelidoniai 1,900. The shape of the island as a whole is an oblong, with some isthmuses on the sides that delimit its width. There are several portions, which will be described briefly, beginning with what is the closest point to the mainland.

(3) I have said somewhere [14.5.3] that the promontory of the Cyprians, Cape Krommyon, lies 350 stadia opposite Anemourion, the cape of Rough Kilikia. The sea voyage from there to the Kleides, having the island on the right and the mainland on the left, is a straight sail to the northeast of 700 stadia. In between is Lapathos, a city with an anchorage and dockyards, a foundation of the Lakonians and Praxandros. Opposite it is Nagidos. Then there is the Aphrodision, where the island is narrow, for the crossing to Salamis is 70 stadia. Then there is the Achaian Cape, where Teukros first anchored, the founder of Salamis in Cyprus. They say that he was banished by his father Telamon. Then there is the city of Karpasia, which has a harbor, lying opposite the Sarpedon Promontory. The passage from Karpasia across the isthmus to the Karpasian Islands and the southern sea is 30 stadia. Then there are a cape and a mountain. The promontory is called Olympos and has a temple of Aphrodite Akraia that cannot be entered or seen by women. The Kleides lie off it, nearby, and several others. Then there are the Karpasian Islands and after them Salamis, from which Aristos the historian came. Then there is Arsinoë, a city and a harbor. Then there is another harbor, Leukolla, and then Cape Pedalion, above which lies a hill that is rough and high, shaped like a table and with a sanctuary of Aphrodite, and which is 680 stadia from the Kleides. Then there is the largely winding and rough coastal voyage to Kition. It has a harbor that can be closed. Zenon, the founder of the Stoic system, and the physician Apollonios were from here. From here to Berytos it is 1,500 stadia. Then there is the city of Amathous, and in between is a small town called Palaia and the breast-shaped mountain of Olympos. Then there is Cape Kourias, in the shape of a peninsula, which is 700 stadia from Thronoi. Then there is the city of Kourion, which has a roadstead and was an Argive foundation.

[C683]

Thus one can see the indifference of the poet who wrote the elegy that begins "Sacred to Phoibos, we deer came swiftly here, escaping the arrows rushing across many waves," whether it was Hedylos or someone else. He says that the deer set forth from the Korykian ridges and from "the Kilissan beach," and swam across to the Kouriadian shore. He further writes: "it is a myriad of wonders for men to perceive how we ran over the impassable stream because of the soft Zephyr." Although there is a voyage around from Korykos to the Kouriadian shore, without the Zephyr or having the island either on the right or the left, there is no sea passage.

At any rate, Kourion is the beginning of the westerly voyage looking toward Rhodes. Immediately there is a promontory, from which those who touch the altar of Apollo are thrown. Then there are Treta, Boosoura, and Old Paphos, which is situated about 10 stadia above the sea, having an anchorage and the ancient sanctuary of Paphian Aphrodite. Then there is the Zephyria Promontory, which has an anchorage, and then another Arsinoë, which also has an anchorage, a sanctuary, and a grove. Hierokepia is a short distance from the sea. Then there is Paphos, a foundation of Agapenor, which has a harbor and well-constructed sanctuaries. It is 60 stadia distant from Old Paphos by foot, and every year men and women come together on this road from other cities to celebrate the festival at Old Paphos. Some say that it is 3,600 stadia to Alexandria from Paphos. Then Akamas is after Paphos, and then after Akamas, voyaging toward the east, is the city of Arsinoë and a grove of Zeus. Then there is Soloi, a city having a harbor, river, and a sanctuary of Aphrodite and Isis. It was a foundation of the Athenians Phaleros and Akamas, and the inhabitants are called Solians. Stasanor was from here, one of the companions of Alexander, a man believed worthy of a command. The city of Limenia lies above it in the interior. Then there is Cape Krommyon.

(4) Why should one wonder at the poets, especially those who were totally eager about their manner of expression, when one compares what Damastes [F10] says, who gives the length of the island as running from north to south, from Hierokepia, as he says, to Kleides? Nor is Eratosthenes [F130] correct, although complaining about him, when he says that Hierokepia is not in the north, but the south. It is not in the south, but the west, as it lies on the western side, where Paphos and Akamas are. Such is the location of the position of Cyprus. [C684]

(5) It is not inferior to any other island in excellence, for it is good in wine and good in olives, and sufficient in grain for its use. There are abundant copper mines at Tamassos, in which chalkanthite is produced, and also verdigris of copper, useful for its medicinal purposes. Eratosthenes [F130] says that formerly the plains were overrun with woods, and thus there were thickets spread over them that were uncultivated. Mining helped this a little, since the trees would be cut down to burn the copper and silver, and in addition there was shipbuilding, for sailing on the sea was safe through sea power. Yet because it was not possible to prevail, those wishing or able were allowed to cut them down and to possess the cleared land as private property, tax free.

(6) Formerly the Cyprian cities were ruled by tyrants, but when the Ptolemaic kings were established as the masters of Egypt, Cyprus came to them, with the Romans often assisting. When the last Ptolemaios ruled – the brother of the father of Kleopatra [VII], who was queen in my time – he was considered to be outrageous and ungracious toward his benefactors and was deposed, and the Romans took possession of the island, and it became a praetorian province in itself. The major reason for the ruin of the king was

Publius Claudius Pulcher. He had fallen into the hands of the Kilikian pirates – who were in their prime at that time – and when he was asked for a ransom he wrote to the king, requesting that he send it and rescue him. He did send it, but it was so small that the pirates were ashamed to take it and sent it back, releasing him without the ransom. He was saved and remembered the favor of both. When he became plebeian tribune he was so powerful that he sent Marcus Cato to take Cyprus from its possessor, [C685] who killed himself by his own hand. Cato went and took Cyprus, disposing of the royal property and carrying the money away to the public treasury of the Romans. From then the island was a praetorian province, just as it is now, although for a short time in between Antonius gave it to Kleopatra [VII] and her sister Arsinoë [IV], but when he was overthrown all his arrangements were overthrown with him.

BOOK 15

Indike and the Persian plateau

Part 1:   Indike

(1) The remainder of Asia outside the Tauros – except Kilikia, Pamphylia, and Lykia – is that from Indike as far as the Nile, lying between the Tauros and the External Sea on the south. After Asia there is Libya, which I will speak about later [17.3.1–23]. One must now begin with Indike, which is the first and largest territory lying out toward the east.

(2) It is necessary to hear about it sensibly, for it is the farthest away and not many of our people have observed it. Those who have seen it have only seen certain parts, most of what they report is from hearsay, and what they did see they learned from a hurried military passage. Thus the same account has not been produced about the same things, although written down as if most carefully investigated. Some were on the same expeditions with each other, and travelled together – such as those who assisted Alexander in the subjugation of Asia – but often each speaks in contradiction to one another. If they are so different about what they actually saw, what must one think about material from hearsay?

(3) Moreover, most of those who wrote about it did so a long time later, and those who voyage there today do not produce anything accurate. At any rate, Apollodoros [of Artemita, F7b], who wrote the *Parthika*, when he mentions the Hellenes who made Baktriane revolt from the Syrian kings – those after Seleukos [I] Nikator – says that when they became powerful they also attacked Indike, yet he discloses nothing beyond what was formerly known and even contradicts it, saying that they subjugated more of Indike than the Makedonians, and that Eukratides [I], at any rate, had a thousand cities under him. Others, however, [say] that the peoples between the Hydaspes and Hypanis were nine in number and had five thousand cities, none of which was smaller than Meropian Kos, and that Alexander subjugated the entire territory and handed it over to Poros.

(4) It is rare for the merchants who today sail from Egypt by means of the Nile and the Arabian Gulf as far as Indike to sail around as far as the Ganges,

[C686]

and they are laymen and are of no use for the history of the places. But there
was a single king from a single place – Pandion or another Poros – who came
with gifts and an embassy to Caesar Sebastos. There was also the Indian
sophist who burned himself up at Athens, just like Kalanos, who had made a
display of himself with the same performance before Alexander.

(5) If one were to set this aside and look at the records before the expedition
of Alexander, one would find the material even more obscure. It is reasonable
that Alexander believed them because he was blinded by such good fortune.
At any rate, Nearchos [F3b] says that due to his fondness for victory he led his
expedition through Gedrosia because he had learned that both Semiramis and
Kyros had made an expedition against the Indians, yet the former had turned
back in flight with only twenty people and the latter with seven. He believed
that it would be glorious, after their reverses, to bring an army safely and
victoriously through the same peoples and places.

(6) Yet how can we truly believe things about Indike from the expeditions
of Kyros or Semiramis? Megasthenes [F11a], moreover, agrees with this point
of view when he urges disbelief in the ancient accounts of the Indians, for no
army was ever sent outside by the Indians, nor did any from outside invade
and conquer them, except the ones with Herakles and Dionysos and now with
the Makedonians. But Sesostris the Egyptian and Tearkon the Aithiopian
[C687]   advanced as far as Europe, and Nabokodrosoros, esteemed more among the
Chaldaians than Herakles, went as far as the Pillars, and Tearkon also went
that far and led an army from Iberia into Thrace and to Pontos. Idanthyrsos
the Skythian overran Asia as far as Egypt, but none of these touched Indike,
and Semiramis died before the attempt. The Persians sent for the Hydrakians
from Indike as mercenaries, but did not make an expedition there, only
coming near to it when Kyros attacked the Massagetians.

(7) Regarding the tales about Herakles and Dionysos, Megasthenes and a
few others consider them trustworthy, but most, including Eratosthenes
[F21], find them not to be trusted, but legendary, like the tales among the
Hellenes. In the *Bacchants* of Euripides, Dionysos youthfully states:

> Leaving the gold-rich fields of the Lydians and the Phrygians, I have come to
> the sun-scorched plains of the Persians, the walls of Baktria, the wintry land
> of the Medes, Fortunate Arabia, and all of Asia. [13–17]

There is also someone in Sophokles who sings about Nysa as the mountain
sacred to Dionysos:

> Where I looked down on renowned Nysa, where mortals are in Bakchic
> frenzy, where ox-horned Iakchos dwells, his sweetest midwife: what bird
> does not cry out there? [F959]

And so forth. He is also called Thigh-Bred. The Poet says the following about Lykourgos the Edonian: "he who once chased the nurses of raging Dionysos down most holy Nyseion" [*Iliad* 6.132–3]. Such is it concerning Dionysos. Concerning Herakles, some record that he went only in the opposite direction, to the western limits, and others to both.

(8) From these things some have named a Nysaian people, a city of Nysa among them – a foundation of Dionysos – and a mountain above the city, Meros ["Thigh"]. They give as the reason the ivy there and the vines that do not grow to maturity, since due to the unceasing rain the bunches of grapes fall off before turning dark. The Sydrakians are [said to be] the descendants of Dionysos because of the vines among them and their expensive processions, as their kings make foreign expeditions in a Bakchic manner, and all their other [C688] processions have the beating of drums and flowered clothing, something that is prevalent among the other Indians. When Aornos – a certain rock at whose base the Indos flows, near its sources – was taken by Alexander in a single attack, those exalting him said that Herakles had attacked this rock three times and was driven away three times. The Sibians were the descendants of those sharing in this expedition, who retained tokens of their descent, for they wore skins just like Herakles, and carried clubs and branded their cattle and mules with a club. They also establish this myth from the matter of the Kaukasos and Prometheus, for they transferred it from the Pontos on a slight pretext: having seen a sacred cave among the Paropamisadians, they point it out as the prison of Prometheus where Herakles came to free Prometheus, and that this was the Kaukasos, which the Hellenes asserted was the prison of Prometheus.

(9) That these are fabrications of the flatterers of Alexander is clear, especially because the historians do not agree with one another, with some speaking about them but others simply not recording them. It is unreasonable that matters so notable and full of delusions were unknown, or if known were not considered worthy of recording even by the most trustworthy. Moreover those situated in between – through whom it would have been necessary for Dionysos, Herakles, and those with them to reach the Indians – show no evidence that a journey was made through their land. In addition, such equipment of Herakles is much more recent that the record of the Trojan matter, a fabrication of those creating the *Herakleia*, either Peisandros or someone else. The ancient xoana are not so equipped.

(10) In such matters one must accept everything that is nearest to believability. We made an investigation in our first discussions about geography [2.1.1], as much as possible. Now we shall use them as in hand, and add other things that seem necessary for clarity. From my former discussion, that

which was expounded by Eratosthenes [F69] in the summary of the third book of his *Geographika*, concerning what was believed to be Indike when Alexander invaded, particularly seems most trustworthy. The Indos was the boundary between it and Ariane, which is to the west and was then a Persian possession. Later the Indians held much of Ariane, having taken it from the Makedonians.

[C689]

(11) This is what Eratosthenes says about it: Indike is bounded on the north, from Ariane to the eastern sea, by the extremities of the Tauros, whose various parts the inhabitants call the Paropamisos, Emodon, Imaon, and other names, but the Makedonians call it the Kaukasos. On the west is the Indos River, and the southern and eastern sides, much larger than the others, are thrust into the Atlantic Ocean. Thus the shape of the territory becomes rhomboidal, with each of the larger sides having the advantage over the opposite sides by 3,000 stadia, which is as much as the promontory common to the eastern and southern coast thrusts out equally on either side beyond the remaining shore. The western side from the Kaukasian Mountains to the southern sea is said to be about 13,000 stadia, along the Indos River to its outlets. Thus the opposite – eastern – side, adding the 3,000 to the promontory, will be 16,000 stadia. These are the least and greatest widths of the territory. The length is from west to east, and one may speak with certainty about it as far as Palibothra, for it has been measured with lines, and there is a royal road of 10,000 stadia. Beyond, it is known only by guess, by means of the voyage from the sea on the Ganges River as far as Palibothra, which would be about 6,000 stadia. The entire extent, at least, is 16,000 stadia, which Eratosthenes says that he took from the most trusted record of stopping points. <Megasthenes [F6c]> agrees, although Patrokles [F3b] says 1,000 less. The fact that the promontory thrusts out farther west into the sea adds to this distance, and these 3,000 stadia make the greatest length. This is how it is from the outlets of the Indos River along the successive shore to the previously mentioned promontory and the eastern boundary. Those living there are called the Koniakians.

(12) From this it can be seen how much the various opinions differ. Ktesias [F49b] says that Indike is no smaller than the rest of Asia, Onesikritos [F6] that it is one-third of the inhabited world, and Nearchos [F5] that it is a four-month journey simply through the plain. But Megasthenes [F6c] and Deimachos [F2a] are somewhat more moderate, for they make it over 20,000 stadia from the southern Ocean to the Kaukasos, although according to Deimachos it is over 30,000 at some places, but I have refuted them previously [2.1.4]. Now it is sufficient to say that this agrees with those asking for pardon if whatever they say about Indike is not done with confidence.

[C690]

(13) All of Indike is watered by rivers, some of which flow into the two largest, the Indos and the Ganges, and others empty into the sea through their own mouths. All begin in the Kaukasos and first run toward the south, and although some continue in the same direction, especially those that join the Indos, others turn toward the east, such as the Ganges. It flows down from the mountains and when it reaches the plain it turns toward the east and flows past Palibothra, a very large city, and then continues toward the sea and a single outlet. It is the largest of the Indian rivers. The Indos empties by two mouths into the southern sea, encompassing the land called Patalene, similar to the Egyptian Delta. It is because of the rising of vapors from these rivers and the Etesian winds, as Eratosthenes says [F74], that Indike is inundated by summer rains and the plains become lakes. At the time of the rains, flax and millet are sown, and in addition sesame, rice, and *bosmoron*. In the winter season there are wheat, barley, pulse, and other edible crops unknown to us. Almost the same animals that are in Indike appear in Aithiopia and throughout Egypt, and there are the same ones in the Indian rivers except the hippopotamus, although Onesikritos [F7] says that this horse is also there. The people in the south are the same as the Aithiopians in color, but in regard to eyes and hair they are like the others (because of the moisture in the air their hair is not curly). Those in the north are like the Egyptians.

(14) They say that Taprobane is an island in the Ocean, seven days' sail to the south from the southernmost part of Indike (the territory of the Koniakians). Its length is 8,000 stadia, toward Aithiopia, and it has elephants. This is what Eratosthenes [F74] reports. But this work will be made more pleasant by adding material from others, whenever they have something accurate.

[C691]

(15) Concerning Taprobane, Onesikritos [F12] says that its size is 5,000 stadia (but he does not distinguish length or width), that it is twenty days' voyage distant from the mainland (a difficult sail for ships that are poorly rigged and constructed without bilge spanning pieces on both sides), and that there are other islands between it and Indike, although it is the farthest south. Amphibious sea creatures are found around it, which are like cattle, horses, or other land animals.

(16) Nearchos [F17], in regard to the alluvial soil from the rivers, gives these examples: the plains of the Hermos and Kaystros, as well as the Maiandros and Kaikos, are so named because the piling on of soil increases the plains, or rather they are created by what is carried down from the mountains, as it is fertile and soft. It is carried down by the rivers so that the plains are their offspring, and it is well said that the plains are theirs. This is

the same as what Herodotos said [2.5.1] about the Nile and the land along it, that it is its gift. Because of this Nearchos correctly says that the Nile had the same name as Egypt.

(17) Aristoboulos [F35] says that it rains and snows only in the mountains and the foothills, but that the plains are free of both rain and snow, and are flooded only with the rising of the rivers. The mountains have snow in the winter, and at the beginning of spring the rains start and always increase still more. During the Etesians they pour forth incessantly and violently night and day, until the rising of Arcturus. The rivers are filled from the snow and the rain, and they water the plains. He says that both he and others experienced this when they set forth for Indike from the Paropamisadai after the setting of the Pleiades. They spent the winter near the mountainous territory in the Hypasian land and that of Assakanos, and at the beginning of spring went down into the plains to the large city of Taxila, and then to the Hydaspes and the land of Poros. In winter there was no water to be seen, but only snow, and the first rain was among the Taxilians. When they had gone down to the Hydaspes and defeated Poros, their route was toward the east to the Hypanis and then back to the Hydaspes, and it rained continually, especially during the Etesians, but it stopped when Arcturus rose. They spent time on the Hydaspes during the construction of their ships and began their voyage not many days before the setting of
[C692] the Pleiades. They passed all autumn, winter, and the coming spring and summer sailing down and came to Patalene around the rising of the Dog. Thus the voyage down took ten months, and they experienced rain nowhere, not even at the height of the Etesians. The plains were flooded when the rivers were filled, the sea was not navigable when the winds were blowing against them, and there was no wind from the land following it.

(18) Nearchos [F18] also says this, but he does not agree about the summer. He says that the plains have rain in the summer but are without rain in the winter. Both speak about the rising of the rivers. Nearchos says that when they were encamped near the Akesines they were forced to move to a higher place because of the rising, which happened at the time of the summer turning. Aristoboulos provides the height of the rising – forty *pecheis* – of which twenty was the filling of the stream above its previous depth to the edge and the other twenty the outflow into the plains. They agree that cities situated on top of mounds become islands, just as in Egypt and Aithiopia. After the rising of Arcturus the flooding ceases, when the waters recede. The land is sown when half-dry, after being cut into furrows by a digging implement, and the fruit comes to maturity and is excellent. Aristoboulos says that the rice stands in watery enclosures in beds, with the

plant at a height of four *pecheis*, having many ears and much fruit. The harvest is around the setting of the Pleiades, and it is winnowed like zea. It also grows in Baktriane, Babylonia, and Sousis, as well as growing in Lower Syria. Megillos says that the rice is sown before the rains, but must be irrigated and transplanted, and watered in enclosures. Onesikritos [F15] says that *bosmoron* is a smaller grain than wheat, growing between rivers. It is roasted when threshed, since it is sworn beforehand that it will not be carried away from the threshing floor unroasted, in order that the seed is not removed.

(19) Aristoboulos sets forth the similarities of the region with both Egypt and Aithiopia, as well as the differences – such as that the flooding of the Nile is from southern rains but the Indian rivers are from the northern – and [C693] asks why the places in between have no rain, not in the Thebais as far as Syene and near Meroë, nor in Indike from Patalene as far as the Hydaspes. But the portions of the territory above there, in which there are both rain and snow, are farmed in a way similar to the land outside Indike, watered from rain and snow.

It is reasonable to assume from what he says that the land is liable to earthquakes, since it is weakened by the great amount of moisture and subject to breaking up, so that the beds of rivers are changed. At any rate, he says that when he was sent on a certain mission he saw a territory of more than a thousand cities, along with villages, that had been abandoned because the Indos had left its proper bed, turning aside into another on the left that was much deeper, and therefore it was like a cataract. Thus, through its overflowing, it no longer watered the abandoned territory on the right, since this was higher than not only the new stream but its overflows.

(20) The flooding of the rivers and the absence of winds blowing on the land agrees with what Onesikritos [F8] has recorded, for he says that the coast is covered with shoal water, especially at the mouths of rivers, because of the silt, the flood tides, and the strength of the sea winds.

Megasthenes [F8] demonstrates the prosperity of Indike through its two yearly harvests and crops, as Eratosthenes [F75] also says, who mentions the winter sowing and that of the summer, as well as the rain. He says that no year is found to be without rain in both seasons, resulting in prosperity with the earth never barren. There are many fruit trees and plant roots, especially the large reeds that are sweet both by nature and when boiled, since the water is warmed by the sun, both that falling on account of Zeus and in the rivers. In a way, then, he wishes to say that what is called by others ripening – whether of fruits or juices – they call heating, and this is as effective as using fire to produce a good taste. In addition, he says that the branches of trees used in wheels are flexible, and for the same reason wool blooms on some. Nearchos [F19] says that finely woven garments are produced from it, which the Makedonians use in place of stuffing and for saddle blankets. The [C694] material of the Serika is the same, with *byssos* carded from a type of bark. Concerning the reeds, he says that honey is made from them although there are no bees, and that there are fruit-bearing trees from whose fruit honey is created, but those who eat the fruit raw become intoxicated.

(21) Indike also produces many incredible trees, including the one whose branches bend down and whose leaves are no smaller than a shield. Onesikritos [F22] rather elaborately discusses the territory of Mousikanos, which, he says, is the most southern part of Indike. He describes large trees whose branches have grown to twelve *pecheis* and then, having grown, go downward as though bent down until they touch the earth. Then, having spread these around, they take root underground beneath the earth from which they put forth trunks, which bend down again as they grow and make more roots, and again, and thus successively, so that from a single tree a large sunshade is created, like a tent with many pillars. He says that the tree is of such a size that five men would have difficulty embracing the trunk. In [discussing] the Akesines and its confluence with the Hyarotis, Aristoboulos [F36] speaks of those whose branches are bent downward and are of such a size that 50 horsemen (the former [Onesikritos] has 400) can spend the middle of the day in the shade of a single tree. Aristoboulos [F37] also says that there is another tree that is not large and has pods like a bean, 10 *daktyloi* in length, that are full of honey. Those who eat it are not easily saved. In regard to the size of trees, everything is surpassed by those who say that men have seen on the far side of the Hyarotis a tree which makes a shadow of 5 stadia at noon. Regarding the wool-bearing trees, he says that the flower has a kernel that is removed, with the remainder carded like wool.

(22) He speaks of a wild grain similar to wheat, in the territory of Mousikanos, and a vine that produces wine, although others say that Indike has no wine. Thus, according to Anacharsis [F A23B], there are no flutes or any other musical instruments except cymbals, drums, and rattles, which are possessed by conjurers. He [Aristoboulos] and others speak of the abundance of drugs and roots that are both curative and the opposite, as well as the richness of colors. He also adds there is a law that anyone who discovers something deadly is put to death unless he also discovers its cure. [C695] If he discovers it, he is honored by the kings. There are cinnamon, nard, and other aromatics in the southern lands of Indike, as in Arabia and Aithiopia, as it is similar to them in terms of the sun, although surpassing them in regard to its abundance of water, so that the air is both humid and more

nourishing, and both the land and water are more productive. Because of this, land and water animals are found to be larger among the Indians than elsewhere. But the Nile is more productive than others of large creatures, especially amphibians. Egyptian women can bear quadruplets. Aristotle [F284] records that someone bore septuplets, and he also calls the Nile prolific and nourishing because of the moderating heat of the sun that preserves the nurturing while vaporizing what is superfluous.

(23) He also says that it is probably for the same reason that the water of the Nile boils at half the fire of other rivers. He further says that its waters go straight through an extensive and narrow territory, passing through many latitudes and many climates, but the Indian streams spread into plains that are large and broad, remaining for a long time in the same latitudes, and thus they are in such a way more nourishing. Because of this, the river creatures are larger and more numerous, and moreover the water is already boiling when it pours from the clouds.

(24) Those following Aristoboulos do not agree to this, as they say that there is no rain in the plains. Onesikritos [F22] believes that the water is the reason for the peculiarities of the animals. He uses as evidence that the color of foreign cattle who drink it changes to that of the native ones. He is correct about this, but not when he gives the reason for the black color and curly hair of the Aithiopians as merely due to the water, censuring Theodektes, who refers to the sun as the reason, since he says:

> Helios, near to their borders, driving his chariot, colored the bodies of men with a dark bloom of flame and twisted their hair, fusing it with unincreasable forms of fire. [F17]

But he [Onesikritos] might have an argument, for he says that the sun is no nearer to the Aithiopians than to others, but it is more perpendicular, and burns more because of this. Thus it is incorrect to say that the sun is near to their borders, since it is equidistant from everyone. Moreover, the heat is [C696] not the reason for the condition, since this is not the case for those in the womb who are not touched by the sun. Those are better who give as the reason a great deficiency of moisture in the skin because of the sun and its burning. I have said [15.1.13] that because of this the Indians do not have curly hair and their skin is not abundantly burned, since they have in common a humid atmosphere. In the womb, because of the seminal distribution, they already have become like their parents, for congenital conditions and other similaries are explained in the same way. Moreover, it is said through perception, not reason, that the sun is equidistant from everyone, and through perceptions that are not by chance, but, as we say, in regard to the observation that the earth is merely a point in comparison to the sphere of the sun, since the perception through which we comprehend heat – more when it is near and less when far away – is not equal, and thus the sun is said to be near to the borders of Aithiopia, but not in the way that Onesikritos believes.

(25) Those who maintain its similarity to Egypt and Aithiopia agree that the plains which are not inundated are unfruitful because of a lack of water. Nearchos [F20] says that the question formerly asked about the Nile – where its flooding is from – is explained by the Indian rivers: a result of the summer rains. When Alexander saw crocodiles in the Hydaspes and Egyptian beans in the Akesines, he believed that he had found the sources of the Nile, and made preparations for an expedition to Egypt and to sail on this river as far as there, but learned a little later that he could not do what he hoped, since "in between there are great rivers and terrible streams, and first the Ocean" [*Odyssey* 11.157–8], into which all the Indian rivers empty. Then there are Ariane, the Persian and Arabian Gulfs, Arabia, and Trogodytike. This is what is said about the winds and the rains, the flooding of the rivers, and the inundation of the plains.

(26) It is necessary to speak in detail about the rivers, insofar as it is useful for geography and as much as we have received regarding their history. The rivers, especially, being natural boundaries for the size and shape of the territories, are extremely suitable for the entirety of the present topic. Yet the Nile and the Indian ones have a certain advantage over others because the land is uninhabitable without them, as they are both navigable and useful for farming. Otherwise it cannot be travelled or inhabited at all.

[C697]

Let us record the rivers that flow down into the Indos which are worthy of mention, and the regions through which they flow, but for the rest there is more ignorance than knowledge. At the beginning, when those who had deceitfully killed Dareios [III] set out to cause Baktriane to revolt, Alexander – who uncovered these areas the most – decided that it would be most desirable to pursue and overthrow them. Thus he came near to Indike through Ariane, but leaving it on his right crossed over the Paropamisos to the northern portions and Baktriane, subduing everything there that was subject to the Persians, and even more. He immediately reached out to Indike, for many had mentioned it to him, although not with clarity. He turned back, crossing the same mountains, but by other and shorter routes. Keeping Indike on his left, he then immediately turned toward it, its western boundaries, and the Kophes River, as well as the Choaspes, which empties into the Kophes near the city of Plemyrion, having flowed past Gorys (another city), and going through Bandobene and Gandaritis. He learned that the most habitable and fertile region was the mountainous territory toward the north, but that the south was partly without water and partly washed by rivers, yet exceedingly hot and more suitable for wild beasts than people. He set forth to gain possession of what was first commended to him, at the same time considering that the rivers that needed to be crossed would be easier near their sources, since they flow crosswise and cut across the land that he was going through. At the same time he heard that several flowed together into one, and this was always more so as they advanced forward, so that they became more difficult to cross, especially with a lack of boats. Fearing this, he crossed the Kophes and subdued the mountainous territory stretching toward the east.

(27) The Indos was after the Kophes, then the Hydaspes, then the Akesines and the Hyarotis, and finally the Hypanis. He was prevented from going farther partly because of certain oracles, and because his army prohibited it, forced by their suffering, especially in regard to the water, as they were continually distressed by the rain. Thus the eastern portions of Indike within the Hypanis are known to us and whatever is on the farther [C698] side of the Hypanis has been added to the record by those after him, who went as far as the Ganges and Palibothra.

The Indos flows after the Kophes. Between these two rivers are the Astakenians, Masianians, Nysaians, and Hypasians. Then there is the territory of Assakanos, where the city of Masoga is, the royal seat of the region. Near the Indos again is another city, Peukolaitis, near which the army crossed by an existing bridge.

(28) Between the Indos and the Hydaspes is Taxila, a large and most well-ordered city. The country lying around it is extensive and exceedingly fertile, immediately adjoining the plains. The people and their king, Taxiles, received Alexander in a friendly manner and obtained from him more than they provided, so that the Makedonians were begrudging and said that it seemed Alexander did not have anyone to show kindness to before he crossed the Indos. Some say that this territory is larger than Egypt. Above it in the mountains is the land of Abisares, who raised two serpents – according to the ambassadors who came from him – one of which was 80 *pecheis* and the other 140, as Onesikritos [F16a] says, who would not so much be called the chief pilot of Alexander as of incredible things. All those around Alexander preferred to accept the marvellous instead of what was true, but he seems to surpass them in his telling of marvels. Yet he says some things that are believable and worthy of recording, and thus they are not to be passed over even if unbelievable. Others speak of the two serpents, and that they are hunted in the Emodon Mountains and raised in caves.

(29) Between the Hydaspes and the Akesines is the territory of Poros, which is extensive and good, and has about 300 cities and a forest near the Emodon Mountains from which Alexander cut and brought down to the Hydaspes a large amount of fir, pine, cedar, and all kinds of other logs for shipbuilding. From this he built a fleet on the Hydaspes near the cities that he had founded on either side of the river, where he had crossed and defeated Poros. One of these he named Boukephalia after his horse, who had fallen during the battle with Poros. He was called Boukephalas ["Ox-Head"] because of the width of his forehead, and was a good fighter [C699] and was always used by him in battle. The other he called Nikaia after his victory.

In the previously mentioned forest, the number and size of long-tailed monkeys are described in an extraordinary manner. The Makedonians, once seeing many of them standing on some bare ridges, formed before them as if in a battle line (for the animal is most human in its intelligence, like elephants), imagined that they were an army, and set forth against them as if an enemy, but learned the truth from Taxiles (who was then with the king) and desisted. The animal is hunted in two ways. It is imitative, and flees up into the trees. The hunters, when they see one situated in a tree, place a bowl of water in sight and anoint their own eyes with it. Then they put down a bowl of birdlime instead of water, leave, and lie in wait some distance away. The animal leaps down and anoints itself with the birdlime. When he falls asleep his eyes become sealed, and they approach and take him alive. This is one way but there is another. They put on loose clothing like trousers and then go away, leaving behind others that are shaggy and smeared inside with birdlime, and when these are put on, they are easily taken.

(30) Some put Kathaia and the territory of Sopeithes (one of the regional chieftains) between these rivers, but others on the far side of the Akesines and the Hyarotis, bordering on the territory of the other Poros who was a cousin of the one taken by Alexander. The land subject to him is called Gandaris. In Kathaia a most unusual regard for beauty is recorded, as it is exceptionally honored in horses and dogs. Onesikritos [F21] says that they choose the most beautiful person as their king and that a child is judged in public when it is two months old as to whether it has the lawful form and is worthy to live or not, judged by the appointed magistrate as to whether it will live or die. They dye their beards with many flowery colors in order to beautify themselves (this is assiduously practiced by many other Indians because the region produces marvellous colors), as well as their hair and clothing, for the people are shabby in other ways but are fond of ornament.

Recorded as peculiar to the Kathaians is that the groom and bride choose each other themselves. Wives are burned up with their dead husbands for this reason: if they were to fall in love with young men they would do away with their husbands or poison them. Thus this was established as a law in [C700] order to stop the poisoning, but the law is not stated well, nor is the reason given. They say that in the land of Sopeithes there is a mountain of excavated salt that could be sufficient for the whole of Indike. Gold and silver mines are reported not to be far away in other mountains, and also to be excellent, as Gorgos the mining engineer has shown. But the Indians are inexperienced in mining and smelting and do not know what resources they have, and handle the matter rather simply.

(31) In the land of Sopeithes the quality of the dogs is said to be remarkable. Alexander received a hundred and fifty dogs from Sopeithes, and in order to test them two were let loose against a lion, and when they were being overpowered two others were let loose. Then, since it had become equally matched, Sopeithes ordered that one of the dogs be taken by the leg and dragged away, and if he did not obey to cut it off. At first Alexander would not agree to cutting it off, sparing the dog, but when the former said "I will give you four in place of it," he did agree, and the dog saw the slow cutting off of his leg before he gave up biting.

(32) The route as far as the Hydaspes was mostly toward the south, but from there as far as the Hypanis it was more toward the east, and as a whole more in the foothills than the plains. Alexander, when he returned from the Hypanis to the Hydaspes and the naval station, equipped the fleet and then sailed on the Hydaspes. All these previously mentioned rivers – the last of which is the Hypanis – come together into one, the Indos. They say that fifteen notable ones all flow together into it, and after having been filled by all of them it is widened in some places to as much as a hundred stadia, according to what those who are immoderate say. Those who are more moderate have fifty at the most and seven at the least. There are many peoples and cities all around. It empties into the Southern Sea through two mouths and forms the island called Patalene. Alexander had this idea after giving up the eastern portions, first because he had been prevented from crossing the Hypanis, and also because he had learned through experience that the report with which he had previously been preoccupied (that the regions and the plains were burning hot and better for the habitation of animals than humans) was false. Thus he set forth, giving up the others, and this became better known than the other regions.

(33) There are said to be nine peoples between the Hypanis and the Hydaspes, and five thousand cities, no smaller than Meropian Kos, although [C701]

the amount stated seems to be excessive. Those living between the Indos and the Hydaspes who are worthy of recording have already been approximately stated [15.1.28]. Next below are the so-called Sibians, whom we have previously recorded [15.1.8], and the Mallians and Sydrakians, who are extensive peoples. It was among the Mallians that Alexander was in danger of death, having been wounded in the capture of some small town. We have already mentioned the Sydrakians as mythologically related to Dionysos. They say that near to Patalene in the territory of Mousikanos and that of Sabos . . . Sindomana and also that of Portikanos and others. All of these were conquered by Alexander – those living along the Indos river valley – and last there is Patalene, where the Indos divides into two mouths. Aristoboulos [F48] says that they are 1,000 stadia distant from each other, but Nearchos [F21] adds 800. Onesikritos [F26] has each side of the detached island, which is triangular in shape, at 2,000, and the width of the river where it branches into mouths at about 200. He calls the island Delta and says that it is equal to the Egyptian Delta, a statement that is not true. The Egyptian Delta is said to have a base of 1,300 stadia, with each side shorter than the base. In Patalene there is a notable city, Patala, from which the island is named.

(34) Onesikritos says that most of this coast is abundant in shoals, especially at the mouths of rivers, because of the silt, the flood tides, and the lack of land winds, as these places mostly have winds from the open sea. He also speaks [F24] about the land of Mousikanos, praising it at length. Some things recorded about it are common to other Indians, such as their longevity – which is thirty years beyond a hundred (and some say that the Serians live still longer) – and their simple life and healthiness, even though their country is abundant in everything. Peculiar to them is common dining in the Lakonian style (in which they eat in public with food from what they have hunted), that they do not use gold or silver although having mines, and that they use young men in the prime of life instead of slaves, as the Cretans use the Aphamiotians and the Lakonians the Helots. They do not investigate knowledge accurately (except for medicine), since too much practice of it is considered by them to be malignant, especially military and similar [C702] matters. They have no legal proceedings except for murder and violence. One cannot avoid experiencing these, whereas contracts are in one's own hands, for one must bear it if anyone were to overstep faith, as well as pay attention to who must be trusted and not fill the city with legal proceedings.

(35) This is what those say who made the expedition with Alexander. A letter from Krateros [F2] to his mother Aristopatra has also been published that tells many other incredible things and agrees with no one else, especially that Alexander went as far as the Ganges. He says that he himself saw

the river and the creatures in it. . .and a size, width, and depth that is far from, rather than near, believability. It is the largest known on the three continents, and after it is the Indos, and the third and fourth the Istros and the Nile: this is sufficiently agreed. But details are stated differently: some that its least width is 30 stadia and others three, and Megasthenes [F9b] that on average it widens to 100 with its minimum depth at 20 *orgyiai*.

(36) Palibothra was established at the junction of it and another river. It is 80 stadia in length and 15 across, shaped like a parallelogram, surrounded by a perforated wooden construction, so that one can shoot arrows through the holes. In front is a ditch for defense used as a reservoir for what flows out of the city. The ethnic group that lives in this city is called the Prasians, the most distinguished of all. The ruling king must be named after the city, called Palibothros in addition to his personal family name, such as Sandrokottos, to whom Megasthenes [F18b] was sent. It is the same among the Parthyaians, as all are called Arsakes, but personally Orodes, Phraates, or something else.

(37) It is agreed that everything beyond the Hypanis is the best, but there is no accuracy, since because of ignorance and distance everything is said to be greater or more marvellous, such as the gold-mining ants and other animals and humans of peculiar form that have altered properties, or such as the Serians, who are said to be long-lived, surviving over 200 years. There is said to be a type of aristocratic arrangement of the government, composed of 5,000 councillors, each of whom provides the state with an elephant. [C703] Megasthenes says [F21a] that the largest tigers are among the Prasians, nearly twice the size of lions, and so powerful that a tame one led by four men seized a mule by the hind leg and dragged it to itself by force; and that the long-tailed monkeys are larger than the largest dogs and are white except for their faces, which are black – it is the reverse elsewhere – and have tails longer than two *pecheis*, and are exceedingly tame and not malicious regarding attacks and thefts. Stones are dug up that are the color of frankincense and sweeter than figs or honey. Elsewhere there are snakes two *pecheis* long with membranous wings like bats, who fly at night, discharging drops of urine or perspiration that putrifies the skin of someone not on guard. There are winged scorpions that are excessively large, ebony also grows, and there are brave dogs who do not let go of what they have bitten until water is poured down their nostrils. Some bite with such eagerness that their eyes become twisted and in some cases fall out. A lion was overcome by a dog, and even a bull, and the bull, held by the nose, was killed before he could be released.

(38) There is a Silas river in the mountains, in which nothing floats. Demokritos [F12] did not believe this, although he had wandered through

much of Asia. Aristotle also did not believe it, although the air can be so thin
that no winged creature can be carried on it. Moreover, there are certain
vapors that are drawn in to themselves and absorb that which flies over
them, such as amber with chaff and the lodestone with iron, and perhaps
there is such a power in water. But these things are a matter of natural causes
and the study of floating bodies, and thus must be examined there. Here
the following must now be added, as well as whatever is close to the matter
of geography.

(39) He [Megasthenes, F19b, 20b, 23b] says, then, that the people of
Indike are divided into seven classes, and the first is the philosophers, largest
in honor but least in number. They are used by private individuals in
making sacrifices or offerings to the dead, and in public by the kings at
what is called the great assembly, where, at the new year, all the philosophers
come together at the doors of the king. What each has written or observed as
useful regarding the prosperity of either crops or living things, and concerning the state, he brings forward in their midst. Anyone who is found to
be false three times is expected to remain silent for the rest of his life, but the
one who is correct is judged exempt from taxes.

[C704]

(40) The second class is that of the farmers, which is the most numerous
and most capable, exempted from military service and secure in their work.
They do not come to the city either because of public disturbance or any
other business. Nevertheless it often happens that when some are drawn up
in battle and under risk from the enemy, they are plowing or digging
without danger, with the others fighting in front of them. All the land is a
royal possession, and it is worked for rent, a fourth of the produce.

(41) The third is the shepherds and hunters, who are the only ones
allowed to hunt, keep cattle, and purchase and rent teams of oxen. In return
for freeing the land from wild beasts and birds that pick up seeds, they are
allotted grain from the king, and undergo a wandering tent-living existence.
Horses and elephants cannot be kept by private persons, as possession of
either is a royal privilege, and there are those who tend them.

(42) Hunting of the animals [elephants] is as follows. They dig a deep
ditch for four or five stadia around a bare space and bridge the entrance with
an exceedingly narrow bridge. Then they admit three or four of the tamest
females, and lie in ambush in hidden huts. The wild animals do not come in
the daytime but make their entrance at night one by one, and when they
have gone in, the entrance is secretly closed. The most aggressive of the
tamed combatants are led in to fight with them, and simultaneously they are
also subdued through hunger. When they are exhausted, the most courageous of the drivers dismount secretly and slip under the belly of their own

riding animals and then dart under the wild animal and tie its feet together. When this is done the domesticated ones are ordered to beat those whose feet have been bound until they fall to the ground. When they have fallen, their necks are fastened with straps of raw oxhide to those of the domesticated ones. So that they cannot shake those attempting to mount them and shake them off, cuts are made in a circle around their throats, and straps are attached in the actual incisions so that they yield to their bonds because of the pain and are quiet. They reject from the captured ones those too old or young to be useful, and take away the rest to stables and tie their feet to one another and their necks to a well-grounded pillar, taming them through hunger, and reviving them with green reeds and grass. After this they are [C705] taught to obey commands, some through words and others charmed by certain songs and the beating of drums. It is rare that they are hard to tame, for by nature their disposition is mild and gentle, so that they are nearly rational animals. Some have lifted up their riders who have fallen in battle through loss of blood and saved them from the fighting, and others have fought for and saved those who have crept under their forefeet. If one kills his food-bearer or teacher through anger, he longs for him so much that through grief he keeps away from food and even starves to death.

(43) They have intercourse and give birth like horses, mostly in the spring. It is the season for the males when they are possessed by madness and anger; at that time a kind of fat comes out of the breathing holes that are on the side of their forehead. It is when this same passage happens to be open in the females. They are pregnant for eighteen months at most, sixteen at least, and the mothers nurse for six years. Most live as long as the longest-lived humans, and some even survive for 200 years. They have many diseases that are difficult to heal. A remedy for eye conditions is to wash them with cow's milk, but for most diseases they drink dark wine. For injuries there is liquid butter – which draws out the iron – and swine's flesh is burned for wounds. Onesikritos [F14] says that they live as long as 300 years, and in rare cases as long as 500. They are most powerful around the age of 200, and are pregnant for ten years. He and others say that they are larger and more powerful than the Libyan ones. At any rate, by means of their trunk they tear down battlements and pull up trees by the roots, while standing on their hind feet. Nearchos [F22] says that in hunting for them, foot traps are placed where their routes come together, and the wild ones are driven into them by the tame ones, who are stronger and are ridden. They are so easy to tame that they have learned to throw stones at any object and to use weapons. They are excellent swimmers. An elephant chariot is considered a great possession, and they are

driven under a yoke … camels. A woman is highly esteemed if she receives the gift of an elephant from a lover, but this statement does not agree with the one that said [15.1.41] that horses and elephants were possessed only by the kings.

(44) He [Nearchos, F8b] also says that he saw the skins of the gold-mining ants which are like those of leopards. Megasthenes [F23b] says the [C706] following about the ants: that among the Derdians, a large group of Indians who live toward the east in the mountains, there is a table-land about 3,000 stadia around. Lying below it are gold mines where the miners are ants, animals no smaller than foxes that are exceedingly fast and live on their prey. They dig in the ground in winter and pile it up at the mouths, like moles. The gold dust requires only a small amount of refining. Those living nearby go after it secretly with beasts of burden, for if they go openly, they [the ants] fight with them and pursue them when they flee, and if they catch them they do away with them and their beasts of burden. To escape notice they set out pieces of animal meat and when they [the ants] are lured away, they then take the dust and distribute it unrefined to traders as they can, since they do not know how to smelt it.

(45) Since we have recorded in this account of hunters and wild animals what Megasthenes and others have said, it is necessary to continue with this. Nearchos [F10b] marvels at the number of reptiles and their perniciousness, who flee up from the plains into the settlements that escape the inunda-tions, and fill the houses. Because of this beds are made high up, and they even move out of their homes if there is an abundance of them. If the greater number of them were not destroyed by the waters the country would be abandoned. The small size of some is a difficulty, as well as the excessive size of others: the former because it is difficult to guard against them and the latter because of their strength. Vipers of sixteen *pecheis* are to be seen, and there are singers who wander around and are believed to heal, and who are almost the only hope of medicine. They do not have many diseases because of the simplicity of their lifestyle and their absention from wine. If it happens, they are cured by the wise men. Yet Aristoboulos [F38] says that he did not see any of the large ones that are talked about everywhere, except a viper of nine *pecheis* and a *spithame*. I saw one in Egypt of the same size that had been brought from there. He says that there are many which are much smaller, as well as asps and large scorpions, but none of these is as troublesome as the little snakes no larger than a *spithame* long that are found hidden in tents, equipment, and thickets. Those who are bitten bleed in anguish from every opening and die unless they are helped immediately, but [C707] this help is easy because of the quality of Indian roots and drugs. He also

says that crocodiles – which are neither numerous nor harmful to people – are found in the Indos. Most other animals that occur in the Nile exist there, except for the hippopotamos, but Onesikritos [F7] says that it also occurs. Aristoboulos says that because of the crocodiles nothing comes into the Nile except the *thrissa*, *kestreus*, and dolphins, but a large number are found in the Indos. The small *karides* come up as far as the mountains but the large ones as far as the confluence of the Indos and the Akesines. This is what is said about wild animals. Returning to Megasthenes [F19], let us continue the discussion from where I left off.

(46) After the hunters and shepherds there is the fourth class, the workmen, craftsmen, tradesmen, and those who work with their bodies. Some of these pay taxes and provide prescribed public services, but those who make weapons and build ships are given pay and sustenance by the king, and work for him alone. The commanding officer provides weapons for the soldiers, and the naval commander rents the ships to sailors and merchants.

(47) The fifth is the warriors, who otherwise pass their lives at leisure and drinking, supported by the royal treasury, so that their expeditions – when necessary – are made quickly, since they provide nothing of their own other than their bodies.

(48) The sixth is the overseers, who are assigned to inspect what happens and report in secret to the king, making colleagues of the hetairas, those in the city using the ones in the city and those in the military camps using those there. The best and most trustworthy people are appointed.

(49) The seventh is the advisors and councillors to the king, from whom come the magistrates, judges, and administrators of everything. It is not possible to marry someone from another class or to change one's business or work from one to another, or to practice several, except for the philosophers, who are allowed to do so because of their virtue.

(50) Some of the magistrates are *agoranomoi*, others city commissioners and others are in charge of the military. The former work on the rivers and carefully measure the land, as in Egypt, and inspect the enclosed canals from which water is distributed into the irrigation ditches, so that all may have equal use of the water. They are also in charge of the hunters and have the [C708] power to reward or chastise them appropriately. They levy taxes and watch the crafts throughout the land: the wood cutters, carpenters, bronze workers, and miners. They build the roads and place pillars every ten stadia showing the turnoffs and distances.

(51) The city commissioners are divided into six groups of five each. One of these inspects the craftsmen, and another entertains strangers, assigning them lodging and following closely their activities, giving them attendants,

and either sending them or the possessions of those who die on their way, as well as caring for them when they are sick and burying them when they die. The third group examines births and deaths – when and how – both because of taxes and so that the births and deaths are known, for better or worse. The fourth group concerns itself with retail trade and barter, caring for measures and seasonable produce, so that it can be sold with the stamps. It is not possible for the same man to barter more than one thing without paying double taxes. The fifth group is in charge of the products of artisans and sells them by stamps, the new separately from the old, and anyone mixing them is penalized. The sixth and last collect a tenth part of what is sold, with death the penalty for the thief. Each group has these distinctions, but in common they care for private and public affairs as well as repairing public works, honors,[1] markets, harbors, and temples.

(52) In addition to the city commissioners there is a third joint administration, concerning military affairs, which is also divided into six groups of five. One of these is stationed with the naval commander, and another with the ox teams, which carry implements and food for them and their animals, and the other necessities for the army. They also provide for the servants, drum beaters, and bell carriers, as well as the grooms, engineers, and their subordinates. They send out foragers to the sound of bells, and through reward and punishment establish speed and safety. The third cares for the infantry, the fourth for the horses, the fifth for the chariots, and the sixth for the elephants. There are royal stables for both the horses and the animals, [C709] and the armory is also royal. The soldier hands over his equipment to the armory, that of his horse to the horse stables, and the animal likewise. They are without bridles. The chariots are drawn by oxen on the road, but the horses are led by halter so that their legs are not chafed by rubbing and their eagerness with the chariots is not dulled. There are two men in the chariot in addition to the driver, but the driver is the fourth on the elephant, as there are also three archers.

(53) All Indians live thriftily, especially on military expeditions. They do not take pleasure in an extravagant crowd, but behave in an orderly fashion. Their greatest self-restraint is in regard to theft. Megasthenes says [F32] that when he was in the camp of Sandrakottos, he did not see on any day reports of thefts worth more than 200 drachmas – and this among those with only unwritten laws – although the number [of people] settled there was 400,000. They have no knowledge of written characters but manage everything from memory, yet they flourish because of their simplicity and thriftiness.

---

[1] This word (Greek *timon*) seems oddly out of context and may be an error.

They do not drink wine, except at sacrifices, but concoct a drink made from rice rather than barley, and most of their food is a rice gruel. In their laws and contracts their simplicity is demonstrated, since they are not litigious, for there are no lawsuits regarding mortgages or deposits, and they do not need witnesses or seals, but trust those to whom they commit their interests. Also, they generally leave their houses unguarded.

These things are a matter of temperance, but no one else would accept always passing one's life alone without a common time for dinner and breakfast rather than what pleases each: the other way is better for a social and political life.

(54) They approve most of rubbing for exercising, and among other ways they smooth their bodies with small sticks of smooth ebony. Their funerals are simple and their burials mounds small. But a contrast to their simplicity is how they adorn themselves. They use clothing with gold ornamentation, set with precious stones, wearing flowery linen and accompanied by sun shades. They honor beauty and thus practice whatever embellishes their appearance. They approve equally of truth and virtue, and thus do not give any privileges to men in their old age, unless they have an advantage in wisdom. They marry many wives, purchasing them from their parents (receiving them in exchange for a yoke of oxen), some for the sake of ready obedience, others for pleasure and many children. The women may prostitute themselves if they are not forced to be temperate. No one wears a [C710] wreath while sacrificing or uses incense or makes libations, or cuts the throat of the victim, but they strangle it so that it is not mutilated but given to the god in perfect condition. Anyone convicted of perjury has his hands and feet cut off, and whoever maims someone not only suffers the same thing in return but also has his hands cut off, and if he deprives a craftsman of his hand or eye, he is put to death. He [Megasthenes] also says that no Indian makes use of slaves, but Onesikritos [F25] declares that this is peculiar to those in the territory of Mousikanos, and quite successful, just as he tells of many other successes in that region, which is especially well governed.

(55) The care of the body of the king is done by women who are purchased from their fathers. The bodyguards and the rest of the soldiers are outside the doors. A woman who kills the king when he is drunk has the privilege of consorting with his successor, and their children succeed. The king does not sleep in the daytime, and at night is forced to change his bed at times because of plots. When he departs – other than for war – it is to the courts, where he spends the entire day hearing cases, no less so even if the time comes to care for his body. This is done by rubbing him with small sticks (while he is hearing cases he is rubbed by four men who stand around

and rub him). A second departure is for the sacrifices. A third is to a sort of
Bakchic hunt where women crowd around him in a circle, with the spear
bearers outside. The roadway is fenced off, and it is death for anyone to
come inside to the women. They are preceded by drum beaters and bell
carriers. He hunts from the enclosures, shooting with a bow from a platform
(with two or three armed women standing beside him), and also from an
elephant in unfenced hunting preserves. Some of the women ride in
chariots, some on horses, and some on elephants, and, as is also the case
when they join in military expeditions, they are supplied with all kinds of
weapons.

(56) Compared to our attitudes, these things are exceedingly strange, but
what follows is even more so. He [Megasthenes, F27b] says that those living
in the Kaukasos have intercourse with women in public and that they eat
the bodies of their relatives; that long-tailed monkeys roll rocks, and lurking
on precipices roll them down on their pursuers; and that most of the
animals that are tame to us are wild to them. He says that there are one-
horned horses with the head of a deer, and also reeds, some of which are
[C711] thirty *orgyiai* straight up and others that lie on the ground for fifty, so that
they are three *pecheis* in diameter, or twice that.

(57) Going beyond into the mythic, he says that there are men five
spithamai tall and others who are three *spithamai*, some without nostrils,
but with only two breathing holes above their mouths. Those three *spithamai* tall make war against cranes (which Homer recounts [*Iliad* 3.3–6]) and
partridges, which are as large as geese. They pick out the eggs from where
the cranes lay their eggs and destroy them. Because of this one does not find
cranes' eggs anywhere, or their nestlings. Often a crane is driven away from
fighting with a bronze arrow in it. Similar are the tales of the Enotokoitai
["People Who Sleep in Their Ears"] and wild men and other marvels. The
wild men could not be brought to Sandrakottos for they would starve
themselves to death, and they have their heels in front and the flat of their
feet and toes behind. Some mouthless ones were brought, tame people, who
live around the source of the Ganges and who nourish themselves with the
odors of roasting meat and the scents of fruits and flowers, since instead of
mouths they have only breathing holes. They are upset by bad odors, and
because of this can hardly survive, especially in a military camp. Others were
described by the philosophers, who reported on the Okypodes ["Those
With Swift Feet"], who are faster than horses; the Enotokoitai, whose ears
reach to their feet so that they can sleep in them, and who are strong enough
to tear up trees and to break bowstrings. Others are the Monommatoi
["Those With One Eye"], who have dog's ears and their eye in the middle of

the forehead, hair standing on end, and shaggy breasts, and the Amykteres ["Those Without Nostrils"] who eat everything including raw meat and live only a short time, dying before old age, and whose upper lips are much more prominent. In regard to the Hyperboreans who live a thousand years, he says the same as Simonides [F570] and Pindar [*Pythian* 10.41–2] and the other tellers of tales. There is also a tale that Timagenes [F12] reports, that bronze rained in bronze drops and was swept away. But Megasthenes comes closer to believability in saying that the rivers carry down gold scrapings and from it a tax is paid to the king; the same happens in Iberia.

(58) In regard to the philosophers, he [Megasthenes, F33] says that those living in the mountains sing praises of Dionysos, showing the wild grapevine, which only grows there, and the ivy, laurel, myrtle, boxwood, and other evergreens, none of which is found elsewhere beyond the Euphrates except occasionally in *paradeisoi* and which survive only with great care. [C712] Also Dionysiac is the wearing of linen, headbands, ointments, and flowery clothing, and for the king to have bell carriers and drummers on his sorties. Yet those in the plains honor Herakles. These things are considered mythical and refuted by many, especially about the grapevine and the wine, for the far side of the Euphrates includes much of Armenia, all of Mesopotamia, Media as far as Persis and Karmania, and a large part of the territory of each of these peoples is said to be rich in grapevines and good wine.

(59) He makes another division in regard to the philosophers, saying that there are two types, one called the Brachmanes, the other the Sarmanes. The Brachmanes are somewhat more distinguished, for they are more in agreement as to their beliefs. While still in the womb one is under the care of learned men who are allegedly thought to go and charm the mother and the unborn child for a happy birth, but in truth give temperate advice and counsel. The women who hear these things with the greatest pleasure are believed to be most fortunate in their births. After birth, one after another succeeds to their care, and they always obtain more capable teachers as their age becomes greater. The philosophers spend time in a grove outside the city, in a suitable enclosure, living simply on beds of straw and skins, keeping away from animate things or sexual matters, listening to serious words, and communicating with whomever wishes. Those hearing are not allowed to chatter, clear their throats, or even spit, or they will be expelled from the company for that day as being undisciplined. After they live this way for thirty-seven years, each retires to his own property, where they live freely and somewhat less restrained, wearing linen clothing and having modest golden ornaments in their ears and on their hands, and consuming the flesh of living beings that are not of use in work, but keeping away from

pungent and seasoned foods. They marry many wives in order to have many children, for many would produce a larger number of excellent children. Since they are without slaves they must draw more from their children, as they are the nearest. The Brachmanes do not share their wisdom with their wedded wives, because if they were unenlightened they might say something improper to the profane, and if they were enlightened, they might leave their husbands, because no one who has contempt for pleasure and labor, and also for life and death, wishes to be subject to another. Such are [C713] the enlightened man and the enlightened woman. They talk mostly about death, believing that the life here is the culmination of gestation, and that death for the philosophers is birth into the true and happy life. Thus they mostly train to be ready for death. Nothing that happens to men is either good or bad, since otherwise some would not be upset and others would be pleased at the same things, having dream-like assumptions, as the same people cannot be at one time grieved and then change and be pleased by the same things. Concerning the natural world, he says that they exhibit simplicity because they are better in deeds than words, believing most things through myths. They are of the same opinion as the Hellenes about many things, such as that the cosmos was born and is perishable, as they also say, and that it is spherical in shape, and that the god who controls it and made it permeates it. The first principles of all things are diverse, but water is the maker of the cosmos. In addition to the four elements there is a fifth natural one from which the heavens and stars come. The earth is placed in the middle of everything. Similar things are said concerning the seed and the soul as well as other matters. They also weave in myths, like Plato [*Phaidon* 57; *Gorgias* 523a1], about the immortality of the soul and the judgements in Hades and other things. This is what he says about the Brachmanes.

(60) Regarding the Sarmanes, he says that the most honored of them are the Hylobians ["Those Living in the Woods"], who live in the forests on leaves and wild fruits, clothed with the bark of trees, without sexual pleasure and wine. They associate with the kings, who ask through messengers about causes and through them serve and pray to the divinity. Second in honor to the Hylobians are the physicians, who are, so to speak, philosophers concerning humans, frugal (but who do not live in the open), and who feed on rice and barley, which are furnished to them by everyone whom they ask or who offers them hospitality. They have the power to produce many offspring, either male or female children, by means of drugs. Their treatment for the most part is accomplished through grains rather than drugs. The most esteemed of their drugs are their ointments and plasters, but the rest involve a good deal that is injurious. This and the other [classes] practice

patience, in work and in inactivity, so that they can spend the entire day immovable in a single position. There are also prophets and enchanters who are skilled in the rites and customs of the dead, and go begging throughout the villages and cities, and there are others more capable and charming, but they do not desist from the chatter about Hades, insofar as it is believed to be reverent and sacred. Some women study philosophy and also abstain from sexual pleasure.   [C714]

(61) Aristoboulos [F41] says that he saw two of the wise men in Taxila, both Brachmanes, and the elder was shaved but the younger had long hair. Both were followed by students. They spent their free time in the agora and were honored as advisors and had the authority to take as a gift whatever merchandise they wished. Whomever they came upon would pour sesame oil on them, so that it flowed down into their eyes. There was much honey and sesame set out, and they made cakes and were nourished by this gift. They came up to the table of Alexander and dined while standing. They practiced endurance by going to a nearby place where the elder fell onto his back and bore the sun and the rains – for it was already raining, as spring had begun – and the other stood on one leg holding up a piece of wood of about three *pecheis* in both hands, and when the leg tired he changed to standing on the other, continuing this the entire day. The younger showed greater mastery, for he followed the king for a short distance and then quickly turned back toward home, and when he was followed, he ordered him [the king] to come if he happened to want anything. But the other went and was with him to the end, changing his method of dress and lifestyle in order to be with the king. When he was censured by some he said that he had completed the forty years of training that he had undergone, and that Alexander had given his children a gift.

(62) He [Aristoboulos, F42] also tells about novel and unusual customs at Taxila. Those who, because of poverty, are unable to marry off their daughters lead them in the prime of their age to the agora with mussel trumpets and drums – those that signal a battle – and thus summon a crowd. To anyone coming forward they first expose her back side up to the shoulders and then her front, and if she is pleasing and he is persuaded, they live together as agreed. The dead are thrown out to the vultures, and to have several wives is common, as it also is among others. He says that he heard that wives were pleased to be burned along with their husbands, and not to accept this would be contemptible. This is also mentioned by others.

(63) Onesikritos [F17a] says that he was sent to converse with these wise men. Alexander had heard that these people were always naked and devoted themselves to endurance, and were held in great honor. They would not   [C715]

come to others when summoned, but summoned the others to visit them who wished to take part in what they did or said. Since it did not seem fitting to him [Alexander] to visit them or to force them to do anything contrary to their ancestral traditions, he [Onesikritos] said that he was sent. He found fifteen men 20 stadia from the city, each in a different posture (standing, sitting, or lying down), naked and motionless until evening, when they went back to the city. It was exceedingly difficult to endure the sun, which was so hot that at noon no one could easily endure walking on the ground with bare feet.

(64) He conversed with one of them, Kalanos, who accompanied the king as far as Persis and died there, and who, according to his ancestral custom, was placed on a pyre. He happened to be lying on stones. He says that he came and greeted him, saying that he had been sent by the king to hear their wisdom and report to him about it to him. If there were no envy, he was ready to listen. When he [Kalanos] saw the chlamys, *kausia*, and boots that he wore he laughed at him and said:

> In antiquity everything was full of barley meal and wheat meal, but now it is as if dust. Springs flowed with water, others with milk, honey, or wine, and some with oil, but because of abundance and luxury people fell into arrogance. Zeus hated this condition and destroyed everything, establishing a life of hard work. When moderation and other types of prosperity returned to them again, there was an abundance of good things. But now matters are already near satiety and arrogance, and there is the danger of the destruction of existence.

He [Onesikritos] says that he was exorted – if he wished to listen to him – to remove his clothing and to lie down naked on the same stones, in order to partake in the discourse. While he remained in uncertainty, Mandanis, who was the oldest and wisest of them, chastised him [Kalanos] as arrogant – and also that he was doing this while denouncing arrogance – and summoned him [Onesikritos], saying that he applauded the king because he was administering so great a state yet was desirious of wisdom, and was the only philosopher under arms that he had ever seen. It was the most beneficial of all if those who were wise had the power to persuade those wishing to act in moderation, as well as forcing those who were unwilling. He also sought pardon for speaking through three interpreters who – except for language – were acquainted with nothing more than any of the masses, and thus he was unable to make anything known that would be useful, as if water could flow cleanly through mud.

[C716]

(65) At any rate, what he said was directed toward this statement: the best teaching is that which removes pleasure and pain from the soul, and that

pain and hard work are different, for the former is hostile and the latter friendly, since bodies are trained for hard work in order to strengthen judgement, through which dissension ceases and advice about good things is available to all, both in public and private. He had now advised Taxiles to receive Alexander, for if he received someone better than himself he would be well persuaded, but if inferior he would handle him well. Having said this, he asked whether such ideas were taught among the Hellenes. When he [Onesikritos] replied that Pythagoras [F9] taught such things (and also urged abstention from living beings), as well as Sokrates and Diogenes (whom he himself had heard) the other replied that he thought this seemed to be sensible but was wrong in one respect: placing custom before nature, for they would not be ashamed to be naked, as he was, and spend their life frugally, for the best house is the one that requires the least repair.

He [Onesikritos] also said that they examine many things about nature, such as foretelling the future, rain, drought, and diseases. When they go into the city they scatter to the agoras, and whenever they happen upon someone carrying figs or a bunch of grapes, they take some as a willing gift, but if it is oil it is poured over them and they are anointed with it. The entirety of a wealthy home is open to them, as far as the women's apartments, and they go in and take part in the meals and discussion. They consider bodily disease to be most disgraceful, and anyone who suspects that he has it releases himself by heaping up a funeral pyre, and, anointing himself, he sits on the pyre and orders that it be lit underneath, and burns without moving.

(66) Nearchos [F23] says the following about the wise men: the Brachmanes are active in politics and attend the king as advisors, but the others investigate matters of nature (Kalanos was one of these). Their wives join with them in the study of philosophy. The lifestyle of all of them is harsh.

Concerning the customs of the others, he makes the following known: their laws are unwritten, and some are public and others private. They have customs that are strange when compared to those of others. Virgins are set forth as a prize for the victor in boxing, so that they marry without a dowry.   [C717] In addition, others work crops in common according to kinship, and when they gather them in, they each take a load as sustenance for a year, burning the rest in order later to have work and not idleness. They are armed with bows and arrows (which are three *pecheis* long), javelins, shields, and a sword three *pecheis* long. Instead of bridles they use nosebands that are slightly different from muzzles, with studs driven through the lips.

(67) In regard to the obvious craftsmanship of the Indians, he says that when they saw sponges among the Makedonians they imitated them by sewing hairs, light cords, and threads through wool and compressing it and

removing them, and then dyeing it with colors. Numerous makers of strigils and lekythoi also quickly appeared. They write letters on linen that is exceedingly well beaten (others say that they do not use writing). They use cast bronze that is not forged, but he does not state the reason, although he mentions the extraordinary thing that happens when it falls to the ground, as it shatters like pottery.

Concerning what is said about Indike there is also this: instead of prostrating themselves it is the custom to offer prayers to the kings and to all in authority and who are superior. The territory produces precious stones, crystals, and all kinds of *anthrakes*, as well as pearls.

(68) Regarding inconsistency among the writers, let us consider the example of the story of Kalanos. They all agree that he was with Alexander and that he died willingly in his presence by means of fire, but they do not give the same account of the mode of death or the cause for it. Some say as follows: he went along as a eulogizer of the king, going outside the boundaries of Indike, contrary to the common custom of their philosophers, who only attend their kings there, guiding them in matters about the gods, as the Magoi did for the Persians. At Pasargadai he became sick – the first illness that he had ever had – and released himself from his struggle in his seventy-third year, not paying attention to the entreaties of the king. A pyre was made and a golden couch was placed on it, and he lay on it and covered himself and was burned up. Others have that a wooden house was constructed, filled with leaves, and a pyre was constructed on its roof. He was shut in it, as he had ordered – after a procession in which he had participated – and threw himself on it.[2] He was [C718] burned up with the house like a roofbeam. But Megasthenes [F34a] says that doing away with oneself is not a belief of the philosophers, and that those who do so are judged to be impetuous. Some who are strong by nature throw themselves at a weapon or over a cliff. Others who do not tolerate pain plunge into the depths, those who are greatly suffering hang themselves, and some who are fiery throw themselves into fire. Such was Kalanos, a man who was undisciplined and enslaved by the table of Alexander. Thus he was censured, but Mandanis was commended, for when the messengers of Alexander summoned him to the son of Zeus and promised him gifts if he complied – and that he would be punished if he disobeyed – he said that he [Alexander] was not the son of Zeus, since he did not even rule over the smallest part of the earth. Nor did he need any gifts, as there were not enough for anyone,[3] and he did not fear threats, since Indike would give him sufficient nourishment while he was alive, and when he died he would be released from flesh wasted by old

---

[2] Something is confused in the text here.   [3] This phrase is not clear.

age and transferred to a better and purer life. And so Alexander commended him and acquiesced.

(69) The historians also say that the Indians worship Zeus the Bringer of Rain, the Ganges River, and local divinities. When the king washes his hair, they have a great festival and send great gifts, each striving in rivalry with his wealth. They say that some of the gold-mining ants have wings. The gold scrapings are brought down by the rivers, as with the Iberian ones. Many elephants take part in the festival processions, adorned with gold and silver, as well as many four-horse chariots and ox teams, and then the equipped army, and golden vessels (large cauldrons and bowls an *orgyia* in size). Of Indian bronze . . . and tables, thrones, drinking cups, and washtubs, most of which are set with precious stones (emeralds, beryls, and Indian *anthrakes*). There is clothing embroidered with gold . . . leopards, tamed lions, and a number of colored and sweet-voiced birds. Kleitarchos [F20] says that there are four-wheeled chariots carrying large-leafed trees on which tame birds hang, and he says that the *orion* has the sweetest voice of these, but the so-called *katreus* has the most splendid appearance and is the most colored, most similar to the peacock. One must obtain the remainder of the description from him.

(70) Among the philosophers, the Pramnai are in opposition to the Brachmanes. They are contentious and disputatious. The Brachmanes study natural phenomena and astronomy but are ridiculed by the former as boastful and foolish, of whom some are called Mountainous, the others Naked, City, or Neighboring. The Mountainous wear deerskins and have pouches full of roots and drugs, pretending to cure by means of witchcraft, enchantment, and charms. The Naked pass their life naked, as their name shows, mostly in the open air, and practice endurance – as we have said previously – for thirty-seven years. There are women associated with them, but they do not have intercourse. These are marvelled at exceptionally. [C719]

(71) The City wear linen clothing and live in the city or in the fields, and put on fawn or gazelle skins, but it is generally said that the Indians wear white clothing – white linen or cotton – contrary to those who say that they wear brightly colored garments. They all have long hair and let the beard grow, and they braid their hair and surround it with a band.

(72) Artemidoros [F109] says that the Ganges River flows down from the Emodon Mountains toward the south, and when it comes to the city of Gange it turns toward the east as far as Palibothra and the outlet to the sea. He calls one of its tributaries the Oidanes. It produces crocodiles and dolphins. He says certain other things but they are confused and unpolished and should not be considered.

(73) One might add Nikolaos of Damascus [F100] to this. He says that at Antiocheia near Daphne he happened to meet the Indian ambassadors who came to Caesar Sebastos. It was clear from their letter that there had been more, but only three survived, whom he says that he saw. The others had died largely because of the length of the journey. The letter was in Hellenic and written on leather, and it showed that it had been written by Poros, who was the ruler of six hundred kings but especially wanted to be a friend of Caesar's and was ready to allow him passage whenever he wished and also to cooperate in whatever was proper (he says that this is what the letter said). The gifts that had been brought were presented by eight naked servants in loincloths sprinkled with aromatics. The gifts were Hermas, whose arms had been removed at the shoulders in youth – whom I saw – and large vipers, a snake ten *pecheis* in length, a river tortoise of three *pecheis*, and a partridge larger than a vulture. Also with them, he says, was the one who [C720] burned himself up at Athens. Some of them do this when they are in poor condition, seeking release from their present situation, but others when they are flourishing, as was the case with him. Although he had done well in everything according to his opinion, up to the present, it was necessary to leave, as something not according to his wishes might occur if he lingered. Thus he laughed, having anointed his body with oil – he was naked except for a loincloth – and leapt onto the pyre. This was inscribed on his tomb: "Zarmanochegas lies here, an Indian from Bargosa, who made himself immortal according to the ancestral customs of the Indians."

Part 2: Ariane

(1) Ariane is after Indike, the first portion subject to the Persians after the Indos River and the upper satrapies outside the Tauros, bounded on the south and north by the same sea and the same mountains as Indike, and the same river, the Indos, from which it stretches toward the west as far as the line drawn from the Kaspian Gates to Karmania, so that its shape is a quadrilateral. The southern side begins at the outlets of the Indos and at Patalene and ends at Karmania and the mouth of the Persian Gulf, having a promontory stretching considerably to the south, and then making a turn into the gulf toward Persis. First there are the Arbians (named like the Arbis River, which is the boundary between them and the next people, the Oreitians), who have a seacoast of 1,000 stadia, as Nearchos [F24] says. This is a part of the Indians. Then there are the Oreitians, an autonomous people. The sail along the seacoast is 1,800 stadia, along the next peoples, the Fish Eaters, 7,400, and along the Karmanian territory as far as Persis, 3,700, so that the total is 12,900.

(2) The territory of the Fish Eaters is on the shore and is mostly without trees, except for palms, a kind of thorn, and tamarisk. There is a scarcity both of water and cultivated nourishment. They and their animals use fish and rain and well water. The meat of their animals smells like fish. They mostly make their homes using the bones of sea creatures and oyster shells, with the ribs as beams and supports, and the jawbones as doorposts. They use the vertebrae as mortars, in which they pound the fish after roasting it in the sun. Then they make bread from this with a small amount of grain mixed in, for they have mills but no iron. This is not astonishing, for   [C721] although they could import them from elsewhere, how could they recut them when worn away? They say that it is by means of the stones through which they sharpen arrows and javelins that have been heated by fire. They bake some of their fish in covered earthen vessels but mostly eat it raw, and catch them in nets of palm bark.

(3) Gedrosia lies above them, which is less torrid than Indike, but more so than the rest of Asia, and lacking in fruits and water, so it is not much better than the territory of the Fish Eaters. It produces aromatics, especially nard and myrrh, so that the army of Alexander used them for roofing and covering while en route, and thus at the same time they had fragrances and healthier air because of them. Therefore they decided to return from Indike in the summer, when there are rains in Gedrosia and the rivers and waterholes are full, as they fail in winter. The rains fall in the upper portions toward the north and near the mountains, and when the rivers are full the plains near the sea are watered and the waterholes abundant. The king sent before himself into the desert those who excavated waterholes and prepared anchorages for himself and his fleet.

(4) He divided his forces into three. He himself set forth through Gedrosia, keeping at most 500 stadia from the sea, so that he could prepare the coast for use by the fleet, and he often came near to the sea although there were impassable and rough promontories. He sent those under Krateros through the interior, who was both to subdue Ariane and advance to the localities toward which Alexander was marching. He gave the fleet to Nearchos and Onesikritos – the latter was his chief pilot – ordering them to take a proper position and to follow and to sail along with the expedition.

(5) In addition, Nearchos [F1a] says that while the king was completing his journey, he himself began his own voyage, in autumn at the evening rising of the Pleiades, although the winds were not yet suitable. The barbarians had attacked them and driven them out, for they took courage with the departure of the king and acted like free people. Krateros started from the Hydaspes and went through the Arachotians and Drangians into

[C722] Karmania. Alexander was in great distress for the entire journey, as he was going through wretched territory. He was supplied only at a distance, in small quantities, and rarely, so that the army was hungry, the beasts of burden failed, and equipment was left behind on the roads and in the camps. Their salvation was the palms, both the fruit and the hearts. He [Nearchos, F3b] says that since it was generally believed that Semiramis had escaped in flight from the Indians with only twenty men and Kyros with only seven, Alexander, due to his fondness of victory, wanted to be able to save such an army in such territory and be victorious, although he knew about the shortages.

(6) In addition to these problems, the burning heat was harsh, as well as the depth and heat of the sand. There were dunes so high that in addition to the difficulty of lifting one's limbs as if from the depths, there were ascents and descents. It was necessary, because of the waterholes, to make long stages – two or three hundred stadia, or even six hundred– and mostly at night. They would camp far from the water holes (often thirty stadia) so that they would not fill themselves up due to their thirst. Many would fall in with their weapons and drink. . .as those below the surface would come up filled and having expired, and would corrupt the shallow waterholes. Others, exhausted by thirst, would lie down in the sun and in the middle of the road, and then, trembling and with a throbbing of their hands and legs, would die like those with chills and shivering. Some would turn aside from the road and fall asleep, overpowered by sleep and exhaustion. Others would lag behind and die either by wandering from the routes or due to a lack of everything as well as the heat, yet still others survived after many hardships. Many people and much equipment were overwhelmed by a torrent that fell upon them at night, and much of the royal furnishings were destroyed. When the guides, through ignorance, turned away far into the interior, so that the sea could no longer be seen, the king immediately realized this and set out to look for the coast. When he found both it and potable water (through digging), he sent for the army. He remained near to the coast for seven days, well provided with water, and then went again into the interior.

(7) There was a type of plant similar to a laurel that would cause a beast of burden which tasted it to die through a seizure and foaming. There was also [C723] an acanthus whose fruit was on the ground like gourds and which was full of juice. Drops of it striking the eye would blind any animal. Unripe dates choked many. There was also a danger from snakes, for herbs grew on the dunes under which they slipped unnoticed and killed those whom they struck. It was said that the arrows of the Oreitians were rubbed with a

deadly poison – they were wooden and hardened in the fire – and that Ptolemaios [I] was wounded and in danger. Someone standing beside Alexander in his sleep showed him a root together with a branch, and ordered him to crush it and apply it to the wound. When he awoke from sleep he remembered the vision and looked for and found the root, which grew extensively. He made use of it – both himself and the others – and when the barbarians saw that the remedy had been discovered they became subject to the king. It is reasonable to assume that someone who knew about it had revealed it, and the mythical part was added for the sake of flattery. He came to the royal seat of the Gedrosians on the sixtieth day from the Orians, and with a brief rest the multitude set off for Karmania.

(8) The southern side of Ariane is the location of the coast and the lands that lie above it and nearby, those of the Gedrosians and Oreitians. It is large, and Gedrosia extends into the interior until it touches the Drangians, Arachotians, and Paropamisadians, concerning which Eratosthenes [F78] has spoken as follows (for I cannot say it any better): he says that Ariane is bordered on the east by the Indos, on the south by the Great Ocean, on the north by the Paropamisos and the mountains continuing up to the Kaspian Gates, and on the west by the same boundaries that separate Parthyene from Media and Karmania from Paraitakene and Persis. The width of the territory is the length of the Indos from the Paropamisos to its outlets, 12,000 stadia (although some say 13,000), and the length from the Kaspian Gates is recorded in the treatise *Asiatic Stopping Points* in two ways. As far as Alexandria of the Arians, from the Kaspian Gates through the Parthyaians there is one route, and then there is a straight route through Baktriane and over the mountain pass into Ortospana to the meeting of three roads from the Baktrians, which is among the Paropamisadians. The other route turns slightly from Aria toward the south to Prophthasia in Drangiane, and the rest of it then goes back to the Indian boundaries and the Indos. This route through the territory of the Drangians and Arachosians is longer, 15,300 stadia in its entirety. If one were to remove 1,300, the remainder would be a [C724] straight line and the length of the territory would be 14,000. The seacoast is not much less, although some increase it and in addition to the 10,000 add Karmania with 6,000, including the gulfs or the seacoast of Karmania within the Persian Gulf. The name Ariane is extended to a certain part of Persis and Media as well as to the Baktrians and Sogdianians toward the north, who speak roughly the same language, only slightly different.

(9) The arrangement of the peoples is as follows: along the Indos are the Paropamisadians, above whom is the Paropamisos. Then, toward the south, are the Arachotians, and next toward the south the Gedrosenians along with

the others on the seacoast, and with the Indos lying alongside all of these. Part of these places along the Indos are possessed by certain Indians, but formerly were Persian. Alexander took them away from the Arians and established his own foundations, and Seleukos [I] Nikator gave them to Sandrakottos, concluding an intermarriage and receiving 500 elephants in return. Lying to the west of the Paropamisadians are the Arians, and the Drangians [are west] of the Arachotians and Gedrosians, but the Arians also lie to the north of the Drangians, as well as to the west, almost encircling a small part of them. Baktriane lies to the north of Aria and then there are the Paropamisadians, through whom Alexander passed over the Kaukasos pushing toward Baktra. To the west, next to the Arians, are the Parthyaians and the territory around the Kaspian Gates, and to the south is the Karmanian desert, and then the rest of Karmania and Gedrosia.

(10) One would understand still better the accounts of the previously mentioned mountainous region by means of the route Alexander used in pursuing Bessos into Baktra from Parthyene. He came into Aria, and then to the Drangians, where he put Philotas the son of Parmenion to death, whom he had discovered involved in a plot. He also sent people to Ekbatana to put the father to death, as he shared in the plot. They say that they accomplished in eleven days a route of thirty or forty days, using dromedary camels, and completed their deed. The Drangians, who in other ways imitate the Persians in their lifestyle, have a scarcity of wine, but there is tin among them. Then, from the Drangians, he went to the Benefactors – so named by Kyros and the Arachotians – and then through the Paropamisadian territory when the

Pleiades were setting. It is mountainous and was covered with snow at that time, so that they travelled with difficulty. Yet frequent villages, well supplied with everything except oil, received them and relieved their problems. They had the mountainous ridges on their left. Indika and Ariana have the southern portion of the Paropamisos Mountains, but on the north, those on the western are Baktrian ... to the barbarians among the Baktrians. He spent the winter here, having Indike above him and on the right, and founded a city. Then he climbed over into Baktriane, along routes that were barren except for a few shrubby terebinths, which were so lacking in nourishment that it was necessary to make use of the flesh of the animals, which was raw because of no wood. The silphium that grew there was used for digesting the raw food. On the fifteenth day after founding the city and leaving the winter quarters, he came to Adrapsa, a city in Baktriane.

(11) Somewhere around these parts is what borders on Indike and Choarene. This is the closest that the Parthyaian subjects are to Indike, separated by 19,000 stadia from Ariane through the Arachotians and the

previously mentioned mountainous territory. Krateros went through this region, simultaneously subduing those who were disobedient and going as quickly as possible as he was eager to join the king. In fact, both infantry forces gathered together in Karmania at about the same time. A little later those with Nearchos sailed into the Persian Gulf, having had much hardship because of the hardships and the large sea creatures.

(12) It is reasonable that those who went by sea would frequently chatter in exaggeration, yet at the same time what they have said suggests the suffering that they endured, and that through their inexperience there existed apprehension rather than danger. What was most troubling was the spouting that produced great streams and a large body of mist from the eruptions, so that they could not see the area in front of them. The leaders of the voyage made known to the frightened men the reason that they could not see: it was due to creatures, which would quickly go away upon hearing trumpets and noises. Thus Nearchos led his ships toward the roaring and was blocked, but at the same time frightened them with trumpets. The creatures plunged down and then came up at the sterns, so that they presented the struggle of a sea battle, but immediately departed.

(13) Those who now sail to the Indians speak of the size of the creatures and their appearance, but also that they are not in crowds and do not attack frequently, and are scared away by shouts and trumpets and depart. They [C726] say that they do not come close to the land, but when the bones of those that have died are stripped bare they are easily cast up by the waves and furnish the Fish Eaters with the previously mentioned [15.2.2] material for making their huts. Nearchos [F1b] says that the size of the beasts is twenty-three *orgyiai*.

Nearchos [F1c] also says he determined that something totally believed by those in the fleet was false: that there was an island in the passage where those anchored near it disappeared. A certain light boat that came to the island was no longer seen, and those sent to seek it did not have the courage to land on the island, but called loudly to the people, yet no one answered, and they returned. Although everyone gave the island as the reason, he said that he sailed to it and anchored, disembarking with a portion of those who had sailed with him, and went around the island. He did not find any trace of those he was seeking and gave up and returned. He informed his people that the island had been falsely accused – for he and those with him would have experienced the same destruction – and that the disappearance of the boat occurred in another way, as there was a myriad of possibilities.

(14) Karmania is the last place on the seacoast from the Indos, although much farther north than the outlet of the Indos. Its first promontory,

however, stretches to the south, toward the Great Ocean, making the mouth of the Persian Gulf, along with the promontory extending from Fortunate Arabia (which is in view), and it bends toward the Persian Gulf until it touches Persis. It is large and extends in the interior between Gedrosia and Persis, although it deviates more to the north than Gedrosia. This is clear from its fruitfulness, for it produces everything, has large trees (except the olive), and is well watered with rivers. Gedrosia is only slightly different from the territory of the Fish Eaters and thus is often barren, because of which they preserve the annual crop and dispense it over several years. Onesikritos [F32] says that there is a river in Karmania that carries down gold scrapings, as well as mines that excavate silver, copper, and red ochre, and two mountains, one of *arsenikon* and the other of salt. It also has a desert that immediately adjoins Parthyaia and Paraitakene. It has farming similar to the Persians, especially the vine, as the "Karmania" (as it is called by us) comes from here, which has clusters of two *pecheis* that are thick with

[C727]   large grapes; it is reasonable that it flourishes more there. Most of them use asses for war because horses are scarce. They sacrifice an ass to Ares, who is the only god that they worship, and they are warlike. No one marries before he has cut off the head of an enemy and brought it to the king, who sets up the skull in the palace, minces the tongue, and mixes it with meal. After tasting it he gives it to the one who brought it and his family to be eaten up. The one to whom the most heads have been brought is the most honored. Nearchos [F1f] says that most of the customs and the language of the Karmanians are Persian and Median. The crossing of the mouth of the Persian Gulf is no more than a single day.

Part 3:   Persis

(1) Persis is after Karmania. Much of it is on the coast of the gulf that is named after it, but much more is in the interior, especially its length, from the south and Karmania toward the north and the Median people. There are three parts, due both to its nature and the temperature of its air. The coast is exceedingly hot, sandy, and sparse in fruits except for dates. It is estimated at 4,400 or 4,300 stadia, ending at the largest river in the region, called the Oroatis. Next, that above it is all-productive, level, good for the rearing of animals, and abundant in rivers and lakes. The third portion is toward the north and is wintry and mountainous. The camel herders are in its farthest portions. According to Eratosthenes [F86], the length of the territory toward the north and the Kaspian Gates is about 8,000 stadia, or 9,000 advancing by certain promontories, and the remainder to the Kaspian Gates

is no more than 2,000. The width, in the interior, from Sousa to Persaipolis, is 4,200 stadia, and from there to the border of Karmania an additional 1,600. The tribes living in the country are the so-called Pateischorians, the Achaimenidians, and the Magoi (who have chosen a certain holy life), but the Kyrtians and Mardians are piratical, and the others are farmers.

(2) Sousis is almost a part of Persis, lying between it and Babylonia, and having a most notable city, Sousa. The Persians and Kyros, having mastered the Medes, saw that their own land was situated rather at the extremities, and that Sousis was farther in and nearer to Babylonia and the other peoples. Thus they established the royal seat of their empire there, at the same time approving both of the fact that it bordered their territory, and the reputation of the city. Third, Sousis never had anything in itself but shared [C728] in a larger situation, always subject to others but having been organized as part of a larger political unit, except perhaps in antiquity in the time of the heroes. It is said to have been a foundation of Tithonos the father of Memnon, and had a circuit of 120 stadia, oval in shape. The akropolis was called the Memnonion. The Sousians are also called Kissians, and Aischylos [F405] has Kissia as the mother of Memnon. Memnon is said to have been buried around Paltos in Syria, on the Badas River, as Simonides [F539] says in his dithyramb *Memnon*, one of his Delians. The wall, sanctuaries, and palace of the city were constructed similar to the Babylonian manner, of baked brick and asphalt, as some say. Polykleitos [F2] says that the circuit is 200 and it is unwalled.

(3) They adorned the palace at Sousa more than any of the others, yet they honored those at Persaipolis and Pasargadai no less highly, since the treasure, wealth, and memorials of the Persians were there, in ancestral places that were better fortified. There were other palaces: those at Gabai somewhere in the upper portions of Persis, and those on the coast around what is called Taoke. These were the ones at the time of the Persian empire, but those later used others that were cheaper, as was appropriate, since Persis had become weaker due to the Makedonians, and still more due the Parthyaians. The Persians are still ruled by kings and have their own king, but their power is greatly weakened and they are subject to the Parthyaian king.

(4) Sousa lies in the interior on the Choaspes River beyond the bridge, but its territory extends as far as the sea. Its coast extends as far as the outlets of the Tigris from the boundaries of the Persian coast, about 3,000 stadia. The Choaspes flows through the territory, and ends at the same coast, having its beginning among the Ouxians. There is a rough and precipitous mountainous territory that falls between the Sousians and Persis, which has narrows that are difficult to enter, and containing men who are brigands and

who would exact payments even from the kings when they passed from Sousis into Persis. Polykleitos [F6] says that the Choaspes, Eulaios, and also the Tigris come together in a kind of lake and then empty into the sea, and

there is an emporium near the lake, since the rivers cannot receive anything from the sea nor bring anything down because of constructed cataracts. Thus mercantile traffic is by foot, as it is 800 stadia to Sousis. Others say that the rivers through Sousa become one stream (that of the Tigris) between the canals of the Euphrates, and because of this the outlets are called the Pasitigris ["Universal Tigris"].

(5) Nearchos [F25] says that there are shoals as one sails along the coast of Sousis, which has its end at the Euphrates River. At the mouth there is an inhabited village that receives goods from Arabia, for the Arabian coast adjoins the mouths of the Euphrates and the Pasitigris, with everything in between occupied by a lake that receives the Tigris. As one sails up the Pasitigris, in 150 stadia there is the pontoon bridge that leads from Persis to Sousa, 60 stadia distant from Sousa. The Pasitigris is about 2,000 stadia distant from the Oroatis. The sail through the lake to the mouth of the Tigris is 600 stadia, and near the mouth there is an inhabited Sousian village, 500 stadia from Sousa. The sail up from the mouth of the Euphrates as far as Babylon – through a well-settled land – is more than 3,000 stadia. Onesikritos [F33] says that everything empties into the lake – the Euphrates and the Tigris – but the Euphrates comes out of the lake again and joins the sea through its own mouth.

(6) There are a number of other narrows that pass through the territory of the Ouxians around Persis itself, through which Alexander went by force (both at the Persian Gates and other places) when he was going through the territory and was eager to reconnoiter the most powerful portions and the treasuries, which had become filled during all the time that the Persians collected tribute from Asia. He crossed a number of rivers that flowed through the territory and were carried down into the Persian Gulf. After the Choaspes there is the Kopratas and the Pasitigris, which also flows from Ouxia. There is also a Kyros River, flowing through so-called Hollow Persis around Pasargadai, and the king took its name, calling himself Kyros rather than Agradates. He [Alexander] crossed the Araxes near Persaipolis itself. Persaipolis was the most beautifully constructed city (after Sousa) and the largest, having a splendid palace, especially in regard to its expensive furnishing. The Araxes flows from the Paraitakians, and the Medos – rushing from Media – joins it. They are carried through a thoroughly productive valley that adjoins Karmania and the eastern por-

tions of the territory, as Persaipolis itself does. Alexander burned the palace at Persaipolis to avenge the Hellenes, because the Persians had destroyed their sanctuaries and cities by fire and sword.

(7) Then he went to Pasargadai, which was also an ancient royal residence. He also saw the tomb of Kyros there, in a *paradeisos*. It was a tower that was not large and concealed in a thicket of trees, solid below but with a chamber and the sepulcher above, and having an extremely narrow entrance. Aristoboulos [F51b] says that he entered it, ordered by the king to adorn the grave, and that he saw a golden couch, a table with drinking cups, a golden sarcophagus, and much clothing and adornment set with precious stones. He saw these things on his first visit, but later it was plundered and everything had been carried away except the couch – which had only been broken – and the sarcophagus. The corpse had been removed elsewhere, and from this it was clear that it was the work of plunderers – not the satrap – since they left behind what was impossible to carry away easily. This happened even though a guard of the Magoi was situated around it, who took as their maintenance a sheep every day and a horse each month. The remoteness of Alexander's expedition – into Baktra and the Indians – brought about many acts of revolution, and this was one of those acts of revolution. This is what Aristoboulos says, and he also recorded this inscription: "Sir, I am Kyros, who acquired the empire for the Persians and was king of Asia. Do not begrudge me my memorial." Onesikritos [F34], however, says that the tower had ten stories and that Kyros lay in the uppermost story, and there was an inscription in Hellenic, carved in Persian letters ("I lie here, Kyros, king of kings") and another in Persian with the same meaning.

(8) Onesikritos [F35] also records this inscription in the tomb of Dareios [I]: "I was a friend to my friends, the best horseman and archer. I prevailed as a hunter, and I was pleased to do everything." Aristos of Salamis [F1] is a much more recent writer than these, but he says that the tower has two stories and is large, constructed when the Persians obtained the succession, and that the tomb was guarded and had the quoted inscription in Hellenic and another in Persian with the same meaning. Kyros honored Pasargadai because he conquered Astyages the Mede there in the final battle and transferred the rule of Asia to himself. He founded the city, and constructed a palace as a memorial of the victory.

(9) He [Alexander] transferred all the wealth in Persis to Sousa – which   [C731] was also full of treasuries and equipment – yet he did not consider it his royal residence, but Babylon, which he intended to furnish still further. There were treasuries there as well. They say that apart from those in Babylon and those obtained in the camp around Gaugamela, what was in

Sousa and Persis was calculated at 40,000 talents – although some say 50,000 – and others that everything from everywhere was brought together at Ekbatana and totalled 180,000 talents. That which was carried away by Dareios [III] in his flight from Media – 8,000 talents – was taken by those who killed him.

(10) Nevertheless Alexander preferred Babylon, seeing that it surpassed the others in size and everything else.

Sousis is prosperous, but it has a fiery and burning atmosphere, especially around the city, as he[4] says. At any rate, when the sun is in its prime of heat, at noon, lizards and snakes cannot cross the streets in the city without being burned to death in the middle. This occurs nowhere in Persis, although it is more to the south. Cold bath water is placed outside and is immediately heated, and barley spread out in the sun leaps up like when it is parched in ovens. Because of this, earth is placed on roofs, up to two *pecheis*, and due to the weight they are forced to make their houses narrow and long: although lacking long beams they need large houses because of the stifling heat. There is a certain peculiarity that the palm beam has, for although it is solid, when it ages it does not give way but swells in an upward direction because of its weight, and thus holds up the roof better. It is said that the reason for the burning heat is the high mountains that lie above to the north and which intercept all the north winds. They blow from the summits and fly high over the plains, not touching them, although they rush toward the more southern parts of Sousis. But it is calm there, especially when the Etesians cool the rest of the land that is burned by the heat.

(11) There is a great abundance of grain, and barley and wheat regularly produce a hundredfold and even two hundredfold, because of which the furrows are not cut close together, since the closeness of the roots hinders growth. The vine did not grow there before the Makedonians introduced it, both there and at Babylon, but they did not make ditches but inserted stakes [C732] whose points were plated with iron and then removed them, immediately putting in the twigs. Such is the interior, but the coast is shallow and without harbors. On this matter, at any rate, Nearchos [F26] says that he did not come across any local guides when he was sailing along the coast with his fleet to Babylonia from Indike, so that there were no anchorages and he was unable to find experienced people to guide him.

(12) Neighboring Sousis is the part of Babylonia that was formerly Sitakene but is now called Apolloniatis. Lying above both, on the north and toward the east, are the Elymaians and the Paraitakenians, who are a

---

[4] The antecedent of "he" (Strabo's source) is not clear.

brigand people and trust in the rugged mountainous territory. The Paraitakenians lie rather near to the Apolloniatians and thus treat them worse. The Elymaians make war against both them and the Sousians, and the Ouxians against them, but less so today, seemingly because of the strength of the Parthyaians, to whom everyone there is subject. When they do well, all the subjects do well, but when there is insurrection – as happens frequently even in our times – the result is different at different times and not the same for all. The disorder is beneficial to some, but others find it contrary to their expectations.

(13) Such is the teritory of Persis and the Sousiane. Persian customs are the same as theirs [the Sousians], those of Medes, and several others. Several have spoken about them, but it is necessary for me to comment on what is appropriate. The Persians do not set up dedications or altars, but sacrifice on a high place and consider the heavens as Zeus. They honor Helios (whom they call Mithra), Selene, Aphrodite, fire, earth, the winds, and water. They sacrifice with earnest prayers in a pure place, presenting the victim crowned. When the Magos who has led the ceremony has divided the meat, they go away with what they have received, not distributing any portion for the gods, for they say that the god only accepts the soul of the victim and nothing else. Some say that they place a small part of the omentum on the fire.

(14) They sacrifice especially to fire and water. To fire they add dry wood without the bark and place fat on top on it, pouring oil and lighting it from below, not blowing on it but fanning it. Those who blow on it or place anything dead or any dung on the fire are put to death. Regarding water, they go to a lake, river, or spring, and excavate a trench to it, killing a victim and guarding that none of the nearby water should become bloody, as this would be pollution. Then they place the meat on myrtle or laurel, and the Magoi touch it with small wands and make incantations, pouring out oil mixed with milk and honey, not into fire or water but onto the ground. They make the incantations for a long time, holding a bundle of small tamarisk wands. [C733]

(15) In Kappadokia – where the clan of the Magoi (who are also called the Pyraithians) is numerous and there are many sanctuaries to the Persian gods – they do not sacrifice using a dagger but a kind of tree trunk, beating as with a club. There are also the Pyraitheia, certain notable enclosures, with an altar in the middle of them, in which there are many ashes and an inextinguishable fire that the Magoi guard. They go in each day and make incantations for about an hour, holding the bundle of wands before the fire, having felt tiaras wrapped around them that come down their cheeks on either side far enough to cover their lips. These are celebrated in the sanctuaries of Anaitis and Omanos, which also have enclosures, and the

xoanon of Omanos is carried in procession. I have seen this myself, but other matters and what follows are recorded in the histories.

(16) The Persians neither urinate, wash, or bathe in a river, or throw into one anything dead or anything else that is considered polluted. They first pray with fire to whatever god they make sacrifice.

(17) They are ruled by hereditary kings. Anyone who is disobedient has his head and arms cut off and is cast out. They marry many women and at the same time have a number of concubines for the sake of raising many children. Each year the kings establish prizes for many children, but the offspring are not brought into the sight of their own parents until the age of four. Marriages are accomplished at the beginning of the vernal equinox, and they go to the bridal chamber having eaten an apple or camel marrow but nothing else on that day.

(18) From five years of age until twenty-four they are taught to use the bow, to throw the javelin, to ride horseback, and to speak the truth. They use their wisest people as teachers of knowledge, who weave in the mythical and produce something useful. Both with and without song and through odes they present the deeds of gods and the best men. They bring them together in one place, having raised them before dawn with the noise of a bronze implement, as if they were preparing for a hunt. They are arranged [C734] into groups of fifty with one of the sons of the king or of a satrap as leader, and they are ordered to follow him in a race, having marked off a distance of thirty or forty stadia. They are required to make a statement about each thing that they have learned, and at the same time are trained in loud speaking, breathing, and use of their lungs, as well as heat, cold, rain, and the crossing of torrents so that their weapons and clothing are kept dry, and to tend flocks and to live in the open and make use of wild fruits such as terebinth, acorns, and wild pears. They are called Kardakians, as they are nourished by theft, and "karda" means "manly" and "warlike." Their daily regimen after the gymnastic training is bread, barley cake, cardamom, lumps of salt, and meat roasted or boiled in water, and their drink is water. They hunt by throwing javelins from horses and with bows and slings. In the afternoon they are trained in gardening, gathering roots, making weapons, and the art of fishing and hunting nets. The boys do not touch what they have hunted but it is customary to bring it home. The king establishes prizes for running and the pentathlon. The boys are adorned in gold, since they hold its fiery appearance in honor, and because of this they do not apply it to a corpse, as is also the case with fire.

(19) They serve in the army and hold commands for twenty to fifty years, both as foot soldiers and cavalry. They do not make use of an agora, for they

neither sell nor buy things. They are armed with a rhomboidal wicker shield, and in addition to quivers they have *sagareis* and *kopides*, and on their heads a felt hat like a tower. Their breastplate is made of scales. The clothing of the commanders is triple trousers and a double sleeved chiton as far as the knees, with the undergarment white and the upper brightly colored. In summer they wear a purple or violet-colored himation and in winter a brightly colored one. Their tiaras are similar to those of the Magoi, and they wear a deep double shoe. Most of the men have a double chiton reaching as far as the middle of the leg, and a strip around the head, and each has a bow and sling.

The Persians dine extravagantly, putting out a large variety of complete animals, and their couches are brilliantly adorned, as well as their drinking cups and everything else, shining with gold and silver.

(20) They deliberate the best with wine, assuming that matters are more certain than when sober. When they meet on the streets, they approach and kiss acquaintances who are equals, and to those lower they present the cheek and accept a kiss, but those who are still lower only make obeisance. They bury the bodies of the dead plastered with wax, yet do not bury the Magoi – who by ancestral custom have intercourse with their mothers – but leave them to be eaten by birds. Such are their customs.   [C735]

(21) Perhaps what Polykleitos [F3a] says is also a matter of custom. In Sousa each of the kings prepared for himself on the akropolis a dwelling, treasuries, and storage places for the tribute that was exacted, as memorials of his government. They exacted silver from those on the coast, and from those in the interior that which each territory produced, such as dyes, drugs, hair, wool, or other things, as well as animals. The tribute was arranged by Dareios [I?] the Long Armed, who was the most attractive of men except for the length of his upper and forearms, for they touched his knees. Most of the gold and silver is in equipment, but not much of it is coinage, as they consider the former more agreeable for gifts and depositing in treasuries. Yet they have what coinage is sufficient enough for their needs, and they strike only what is commensurate with their expenditures.

(22) Their customs are generally temperate by nature, but because of their wealth the kings degenerated into luxury, so that they sought wheat from Aiolian Assos, Chalybonian wine from Syria, and water from the Eulaios, which is the lightest of all, so that an Attic *kotyle* weighs a drachma less.

(23) The Persians became, to the Hellenes, the most notable of the barbarians, because none of the others ruling in Asia ruled Hellenes, nor were they known to them, or the Hellenes to the barbarians, except only briefly by distant hearsay. At any rate, Homer did not know about the

Syrian or Median empires. Since he mentions Egyptian Thebes and the wealth there and in Phoenicia [*Iliad* 9.380–1, 23.740–7; *Odyssey* 4.126–7, 615–19], he would not have passed over Babylon, Ninos, and Ekbatana in silence. The Persians were the first to rule over Hellenes. The Lydians had ruled over them, but did not rule the whole of Asia, only a certain small part within the Halys, and this for a short time under Kroisos and Alyattes. They were mastered by the Persians and whatever reputation they had was eliminated by them. The Persians, from the time when they put down the Medes, immediately mastered the Lydians and obtained the Hellenes in Asia as subjects, and later even crossed over into Hellas. Although they were [C736] defeated frequently in many battles, they persevered in Asia, holding places as far as those on the sea, until put down by the Makedonians.

(24) Kyros was the one who established their hegemony. He was succeeded by his son Kambyses, who was put down by the Magoi. The Seven Persians eliminated them, and gave the empire over to Dareios [I] the son of Hystaspes. His successors ended with Arses, who was killed by Bagoos the eunuch, and who established Dareios [III], not related to the royal family. Alexander deposed him and ruled for ten or eleven years. Then the hegemony of Asia was divided among his various successors and their descendants, and then they came to an end, having lasted about two hundred and fifty years. Today the Persians are organized on their own, but their kings are subject to other kings, formerly the Makedonians and now the Parthyaians.

BOOK 16

Assyria, Phoenicia, and Arabia

Part 1: Assyria

(1) The Assyrians adjoin Persis and Sousiane. This is what Babylonia and much of the surrounding land is called, which in part is also Atouria. Here are Ninos, Apolloniatis, the Elymaians, Paraitakians, Chalonitis around Mount Zagros, the plains around Ninos, Dolomene, Kalachene, Chazene, and Adiabene as well as the Mesopotamian peoples around the Gordyaians, the Mygdonians around Nisibis as far as the bridge across the Euphrates, and also much of that across the Euphrates which is occupied by the Arabians and those today particularly called the Syrians, as far as the Kilikians, Phoenicians, [C737] Libyans, and the sea opposite the Egyptian Sea and the Issic Gulf.

(2) It seems that in antiquity the name "Syrian" extended from Babylonia as far as the Issic Gulf, and from it as far as the Euxeinos. At any rate, both groups of Kappadokians – those near the Tauros and those near the Pontos – have been called the White Syrians down to the present, as though some Syrians were black (those who are outside the Tauros). I say that the name "Tauros" should be extended as far as the Amanos. Those who have written histories of the Syrian empire say that when the Medes were overthrown by the Persians, and the Syrians by the Medes, they spoke of the Syrians only as those who built the palaces at Babylon and Ninos. Of these, Ninos founded Ninos in Atouria, and his wife Semiramis succeeded her husband and founded Babylon. They mastered Asia, and many works of Semiramis – in addition to those at Babylon – are visible throughout almost the entirety of this continent. There are the mounds (called those of Semiramis), walls, the constructed fortifications with passages, reservoirs, and ladders in them, channels in rivers and lakes, roads, and bridges. They left the empire to those afterward until the time of Sardanapallos and Arbakes, and later it went over to the Medes.

(3) The city of Ninos was destroyed immediately after the overthrow of the Syrians. It was much greater than Babylon and was situated in the plain

of Atouria. Atouria borders the locality of Arbela, with the Lykos River between them. Arbela is an independent province of Babylonia, and the territory across the Lykos is the plains of Atouria, which lie around Ninos. The village of Gaugamela is in Atouria, where Dareios [III] was conquered and lost his empire. This is a notable place, as is its name, which is translated as "House of the Camel." Dareios [I] the son of Hystaspes so named it, creating it as a location for the sustenance of the camels that were of great assistance on the journey through the Skythian desert with the loads for the sustenance of the king. Yet the Makedonians, seeing that it was a shabby village but that Arbela was a notable settlement (founded, as they say, by Arbelos the son of Athmoneus) put forth that the battle and victory were near Arbela and thus transmitted this to the historians.

(4) After Arbela and Victory Mountain – a name applied by Alexander after his victory in the battle around Arbela – there is the Kapros River, which is the same distance away as is the Lykos. The territory is called [C738] Artakene. Near Arbela is the city of Demetrias, and then there are a spring of naphtha, fires, the sanctuary of Anaia, Sadrakai (the royal seat of Dareios [I] the son of Hystaspes), the cypresses, and the crossing of the Kapros, which borders on Seleukeia and Babylon.

(5) Babylon is also in a plain, and the circuit of its wall is 385 stadia. The thickness of the wall is 32 feet, the height between the towers 50 *pecheis*, and the towers 60. The passage on the wall is such that four-horse chariots can easily pass one another. Because of this it is called one of the Seven Wonders, as the Hanging Garden also is, which is quadrilateral in shape with each side four *plethra*. It consists of arched vaults on terraced foundations one after another in the shape of cubes. The terraces are hollowed out and are full of earth, so that they accept the planting of the largest trees. They are constructed of baked brick and asphalt, both the terraces themselves and the foundations. There are stairways for access to the uppermost roof, and alongside them are screws through which the water is continually sent up from the Euphrates to the garden by those posted there. The river flows through the middle of the city and is a stadion in width, and the garden is on the river.

The tomb of Belos is also here, today razed to the ground (they say that Xerxes demolished it). It was a quadrilateral pyramid of baked brick, a stadion in height and with each side a stadion. Alexander planned to repair it, a large project that would have taken a long time (for the clearing of the mound was the work of a myriad of men for two months), and he could not complete what he had attempted, for immediately disease and death fell upon the king. No one later considered it. The remains were neglected and the city fell into ruins, in part due to the Persians and in part due to time and the neglect of the Makedonians regarding such things, especially when Seleukos [I] Nikator fortified Seleukeia on the Tigris, about 300 stadia from Babylon. He and all those after him were attentive to this city and transferred the royal seat to it. Moreover, today it has become larger than Babylon, but most of the latter is deserted, so that one would not hesitate to say what the comic poet said about Megalopolis ["Great City"] in Arkadia: "The Great City is a great desert."

[C739]

Because of the scarcity of wood, their buildings are completed with beams and columns of palm wood. They put reed ropes around the columns, and then smeared painted colors over them, with asphalt on the doors. They are high, as are the houses, and all are vaulted because of the lack of wood. Most of the territory is bare and has only brush, except for the palm tree, which is most common in Babylonia, but there are also many in Sousa, on the coast of Persis, and in Karmania. They do not use tiles, for there is no rain, and it is similar in Sousa and Sitakene.

(6) There is a settlement in Babylon marked off for the local philosophers, who are called the Chaldaians. Mostly they study astronomy, but some of them pretend to be astrologers. The others do not accept them. There is also a certain Chaldaian tribe and a territory inhabited by them in Babylonia, near the Arabians and the sea called the Persian. There are also a number of groups of Chaldaian astronomers, some of whom are called Orchenians, Borsippenians, and a number of others, as if considered different sects, each with their own dogma about the same things. The mathematicians record some of these men, such as Kidenas, Nabourianos, and Soudines. Seleukos of Seleukeia was a Chaldaian, as were a number of other notable men.

(7) Borsippa is a city sacred to Artemis and Apollo, and it has large linen factories. It is abundant in bats, which are much larger than in other places and are caught and salted for eating.

(8) The land of the Babylonians is surrounded on the east by the Sousians, Elymaians, and Paraitakenians, on the south by the Persian Gulf and the Chaldaians as far as the Alesenian Arabians, on the west by the Tent-Dwelling Arabians as far as Adiabene and Gordyaia, and on the north by the Armenians and Medes as far as the Zagros and the peoples around it.

(9) The land has a number of rivers flowing through it, with the largest the Euphrates and the Tigris. After the Indian ones, these rivers are said to have second place in the southern portion of Asia. One can sail up the latter to Opis and the present Seleukeia (the village of Opis is the emporium of the surrounding plains), and up the former to Babylon, more than 3,000

[C740] stadia. The Persians wished to prevent any capability of sailing up them – in fear of foreign invasion – and constructed artificial cataracts, but Alexander, when he went against them, dismantled as many as possible, especially those at Opis. He also paid attention to the canals. The Euphrates floods at the beginning of summer, starting in the spring when the snow in Armenia melts, so that by necessity it creates lakes and inundates the fields, unless the excess flow and surface water is distributed through channels and ditches, as with the Nile in Egypt. This is the origin of the canals, but they require a great amount of work, since the earth is deep, soft, and yielding, so that it is easily swept away by the streams. Thus the plains become bare, with the canals filled and silt easily blocking their mouths. This again produces an overflow of the waters that empty into the plains near the sea, creating lakes, marshes and beds of reed, from which come the reeds that produce all kinds of woven materials, some of which – when smeared with asphalt – hold moisture. Others are used in a bare state. They also make reed sails, similar to reed mats or wicker work.

(10) It is not possible, perhaps, to prevent such flooding completely, but good leaders provide whatever assistance can be produced. The assistance is this: to prevent much of the overflowing by barriers, and [to prevent] the silt from filling up, as well as to keep the canals cleared and their mouths open. The clearing is easy but the barriers require many hands, for the earth yields easily and is soft, not supporting the silt that is put onto it, but it gives way and is drawn along, making the mouth hard to dam up. It is necessary to be quick and close the canals quickly, so that all the water does not drain out of them. When they dry up in summer, they also dry up the river, and when it is lowered it cannot supply the sluices at the proper time, since it is most needed in summer when the land is fiery hot and burning. There is no difference whether the crops are inundated by an abundance of water or are destroyed by thirst and want of water. Moreover, the voyages upstream, with their many advantages, were always being ruined by both of the previously mentioned reasons. It would not be possible to correct this unless the mouths of the canals were quickly opened and quickly closed, with the canals always regulated so that the water in them was neither excessive nor lacking.

[C741] (11) Aristoboulos [F56] says that Alexander himself, when he was sailing up and piloting the boat, inspected the canals and with his multitude of followers cleared them out, blocking up some of the mouths and opening others. When he observed that the one which extended most directly toward the marshes and lakes in front of Arabia had a mouth that was difficult to manage and could not easily be blocked because of the yielding and soft soil, he opened up a new one 30 stadia away, having chosen a rocky place, and diverted the stream there. Moreover, in doing this he foresaw that it would not be difficult to accomplish an entrance to Arabia by the lakes or even the marshes, since it was already becoming an island because of the abundance of water. He intended to gain possession of that territory and had already prepared fleets and bases, having constructed ships in Phoenicia and Cyprus. They were fastened with bolts and could be broken apart, and were carried for seven days to Thapsakos and then brought down the river as far as Babylon. Others were constructed in Babylonia, from the cypresses in the groves and *paradeisoi*, for there is a scarcity of wood there, although there is a moderate abundance among the Kossaians and certain others. He [Aristoboulos] says that he [Alexander] alleged that the cause of the war was that the Arabians were the only ones of all who did not send ambassadors to him, but the truth was that he was grasping at being the master of everyone. When he learned that they honored only two gods – Zeus and Dionysos, those who provide what is most important for life – he assumed that he would be honored as the third if he mastered them and also allowed them to retain the ancestral independence that they previously had. Thus Alexander busied himself with the canals and examined the tombs of the kings and rulers, most of which are around the lakes.

(12) Eratosthenes [F96], mentioning the lakes near Arabia, says that when the water is unable to exit, it opens underground passages and flows underground as far as Hollow Syria, pressing into the region of Rhinokoroura and Mount Kasion, creating lakes and pits there. I do not know whether what he says is believable. The overflow of the Euphrates that creates the lakes around Arabia and the marshes is near the Persian Sea, but the isthmus that separates them is neither extensive or rocky. Thus it is more probable that the water would force its way into the sea – either underground or on the surface – than that it would complete more than 6,000 stadia through such a waterless and dry region with mountains – such as the Libanos, the Antilibanos, and Kasion – situated in the midst of it. [C742]

(13) This is what they say. Polykleitos [F5] says that the Euphrates does not flood, for it is carried through large plains, and the mountains are 2,000 stadia away from it (although the Kossaians are scarcely a thousand), but they are neither very high or intensively snowy and do not produce sudden melting of the snow, since the heights of the mountains are in the portions above Ekbatana, toward the north, but toward the south they split, broaden, and become much lower, and at the same time much of their water is received by the Tigris. This last statement is manifestly absurd, for it comes down into the same plains, and the previously mentioned

heights of the mountains are different. Those toward the north are more elevated and those toward the south broadened out, and moreover the snow is not only due to the height but the latitude. The same mountain will have more snow in its northern portion than its southern, and the snow remains longer in the former than in the latter. The Tigris receives the water from the snow in the southernmost part of Armenia, which is near Babylon. But this is not much, as it is from the southern side, and thus it would be flooded less. Yet the Euphrates receives it from both portions, and not from one mountain but many, as we made clear in the description of Armenia [11.12.2–3, 11.14.2]. The length of the river is defined as that going through Greater and Lesser Armenia: that from Lesser Armenia and Kappadokia passing through the Tauros as far as Thapsakos (where it forms the boundary between Lower Syria and Mesopotamia), and that of the remainder as far as Babylon and the outlet, as much as 36,000 stadia. Such is it about the canals.

(14) The territory produces more barley than anywhere else (they say 300-fold), and the palm provides the rest, including bread, wine, vinegar, honey, and meal. All kinds of woven material come from it. The metalworkers use its stones instead of charcoal, and when soaked these are food for cattle and sheep. They say that there is a Persian song that enumerates 360 benefits from it. They mostly use sesame oil. In Artemita there blooms . . . called . . . but this plant is rare in all other places.

[C743]

(15) A large amount of asphalt is produced in Babylonia, about which Eratosthenes [F90] says that the liquid kind, which is called naphtha, is found in Sousis, but the dry kind, which can be solidified, is in Babylonia. There is a fountain of the latter near the Euphrates, and at the time of flooding by snow-melt it fills and overflows into the river. Large lumps are formed that are suitable for structures of baked brick. Others say that the liquid kind also occurs in Babylonia. They say that the dry kind is particularly useful in building construction, and they say that boats are woven, but when smeared with asphalt they become solid. The liquid kind, which is called naphtha, has a nature contrary to expectation, because if naphtha is brought near to fire it takes away the fire, and if a body is smeared with it and brought toward it, it burns and it is impossible to quench it with water (it burns even more) unless there is a large amount, although it can be extinguished and quenched with mud, vinegar, alum, or birdlime. They say that Alexander, making an experiment, poured naphtha on a boy in a bath and brought a lamp to him, and then the boy was on fire and came near to death, except that those standing around poured an exceedingly great amount of water over him which prevailed and saved the boy. Poseidonios

[F236] says that some of the naphtha springs in Babylonia are white while others are black, and that some of those (I mean those that are white) have liquid sulphur – these attract the flames – and the black have liquid asphalt, which is burned in lamps instead of oil.

(16) In antiquity Babylon was the metropolis of Assyria, but today it is Seleukeia, the one called "On the Tigris." Nearby is a large village called Ktesiphon, which the Parthyaian kings have made their winter residence, sparing the Seleukeians, so that they would not be oppressed by having Skythian tribes or soldiers quartered among them. Due to the Parthian power it is a city instead of a village, and it is of a size to accept large numbers and has been furnished by them with constructions, as well as provided with goods for sale and suitable crafts. The kings are accustomed to spend the winter there because of the freshness of the air, but their summer is at Ekbatana and in Hyrkania because of the strength of their ancient reputation. Just as we call the territory Babylonia, the men from there are Babylonians, taken not from the city but from the territory. Yet this is not the case with someone   [C744] from Seleukeia, such as Diogenes the Stoic philosopher.

(17) There is also the notable city of Artemita, 500 stadia distant from Seleukeia generally toward the east, as Sitakene also is. It is large and fertile, situated between Babylon and Sousis, so that the entire journey going from Babylon to Sousa is through Sitakene and toward the east. From Sousa to the interior of Persis through Ouxia is also toward the east, as it is from Persis to the middle of Karmania. Persis – which is large – encircles Karmania on the north, and adjoining it on the north are Paraitakene and Kossaia, as far as the Kaspian Gates, with mountainous and brigand peoples. Elymais also [borders] Sousis, most of which is rugged and has brigands, and [bordering] Elymais are both the region around Zagros and Media.

(18) The Kossaians are mostly archers – like the neighboring mountaineers – and are always foraging, for they have a territory that is small and poor, so by necessity they live on others and by necessity are strong and all warriors. At any rate, 13,000 joined the Elymaians in battle when they were making war against the Babylonians and Sousians. But the Paraitakenians care for the land more than the Kossaians, yet even so they do not avoid brigandage. The Elymaians have a larger and more varied history, and as much of it as is fertile is inhabited by farmers. The mountainous region nourishes soldiers, mostly archers. It is extensive and provides so large an army that its king, who possesses a great amount of power, does not consent to be subject to the Parthyaian king like the others, and was formerly disposed toward the Makedonians when they ruled Syria. When Antiochos [III] the Great attempted to plunder the sanctuary of Belos, he was attacked and killed by

the neighboring barbarians all by themselves. In later times the Parthyaian [king], although chastened by what had happened, heard that the sanctuaries there were wealthy. Seeing that the inhabitants were disobedient, he invaded with a large force and took both the sanctuary of Athena and that of Artemis (Azara), taking a treasure of a myriad of talents. Seleukeia on the Hedyphon River, a large city, was also taken; formerly it was called Soloke. There are three natural entrances into the territory: from Media and the places around the Zagros through Massabatike, from Sousis [C745] through Gabiane (Gabiane and Massabatike are provinces of Elymaia), and the third from Persis. Korbiane is also a province of Elymais. The Sagapenians and Silakenians, small states, border on these.

Such are the numbers and the nature of the peoples situated above the Babylonians toward the east. As we have said, Media and Armenia are on the north, and Mesopotamia on the west.

(19) Most of Adiabene is plains, and it also is a part of Babylonia, but has its own ruler and adjoins Armenia in some places. The Medes and the Armenians and, third, the Babylonians – the greatest peoples there – were situated in such a way from the beginning and continue to be so, and thus they would attack each other when it was opportune and suitable, and then put an end to it, which continued until the domination of the Parthyaians. The Parthyaians rule over the Medes and Babylonians, but have never [ruled] over the Armenians, who were often attacked but could not be taken by strength. Tigranes [II] forcefully opposed such strength, as was said in the Armenian section [11.14.15]. Such is Adiabene, and the Adiabenians are also called Sakkopodians.

Next we will speak about Mesopotamia and the peoples toward the south, after going briefly over what has been previously said about the customs of the Assyrians.

(20) Generally they are similar to those of the Persians, but peculiar to them is the establishment of three wise men as rulers of each tribe, who present the marriageable girls to the people and sell them by auction to the bridegrooms, with the most honored always the first. Thus unions are accomplished. Whenever they have intercourse with one another, they get up and offer incense apart from each other. In the morning they bathe before they touch any vessel, for just as a bath is the custom after approaching a corpse, it is the same after intercourse. It is the custom, according to a certain oracle, for all Babylonian women to have intercourse with a foreigner, going to the Aphrodision with many attendants and a crowd. Each woman is crowned with a string. The man who approaches her places a good amount of money on her knees and then, going far away from the precinct, has intercourse. The

money is considered sacred to Aphrodite. There are three magisterial boards (in addition to those appointed by the king): those who have already been discharged from the army, those who are the most distinguished, and those who are old men. The last gives maidens in marriage and determines judge- [C746] ments in matters of adultery, another in regard to theft, and the third in regard to use of force. They place the sick at the meeting of three roads and question those passing by, if by chance someone can tell the cure for their condition. No one passing by is so indifferent as to fail to suggest something when he meets them, if he has any remedy in mind. Their clothing is a linen chiton reaching to the feet, a wool outer garment, and a white himation. Their hair is long and their shoes are like slippers. They also carry a seal and a scepter that is not plain but which has a device on it: an apple, rose, lily, or some such on top. They anoint themselves with sesame. They lament the dead, like the Egyptians and many others, and bury them in honey, smearing them with wax. Three of their clans lack grain and are in the marshes and eat fish, living similar to those in Gedrosia.

(21) Mesopotamia is named from what it is. As I have said [11.14.2], it lies between the Euphrates and Tigris, and thus the Tigris washes only its eastern side, and the Euphrates its western and southern. To the north is the Tauros, which separates Armenia from Mesopotamia. The greatest distance that they are apart from one another is toward the mountains, and this would be the same as Eratosthenes [F87] has said, 2,400, from Thapsakos – where the ancient bridge over the Euphrates was – to the crossing of the Tigris where Alexander himself crossed. The least is slightly more than 200 somewhere around Seleukeia and Babylon. The Tigris flows through the lake called Thopitis, through the middle of its width, and going to the opposite edge sinks under the earth with a great noise and upward blasts. It is invisible for a distance, and then appears again not far from Gordyaia. It thus runs through it so vehemently, as Eratosthenes says, that although it is generally salty and without fish, this part is sweet, with a strong current, and full of fish.

(22) The contracting of Mesopotamia goes on for a great length, some-what like a boat, with the Euphrates making most of the circumference, and it is 4,800 stadia from Thapsakos as far as Babylon, as Eratosthenes says. From Zeugma in Kommagene, where Mesopotamia begins, to Thapsakos is [C747] no less than 2,000 stadia.

(23) The territory along the mountains is sufficiently prosperous. That near the Euphrates and the bridge – both the present one in Kommagene and the old one near Thapsakos – is held by the Mygdonians, who were named by the Makedonians. Nisibis is among them, which is also called Antiocheia in Mygdonia. It lies at the foot of Mount Masion, as do

Tigranokerta and the region around Karrhai, Nikephorion, Chordiraza, and Sinnaka, where Crassus was killed, treacherouly captured by Sourenas the Parthyaian commander.

(24) Near the Tigris are the localities of the Gordyaians, whom the ancients called Kardouchians. Their cities are Sareisa and Satalka, as well as Pinaka (a most powerful fortress with three citadels, each fortified with its own wall, so that it is like a triple city). The Armenian [king] held it in subjugation and the Romans took it by force, although the Gordyaians were exceptional builders and skilled in the construction of siege machines. Because of this Tigranes [II] used them for such things. The rest of the riverine territory became subject to the Romans, and Pompeius assigned to Tigranes [II] everywhere that was notable. The territory is abundant in pasturage and flourishing, so that it produces evergreens and an aromatic called amomum. It nourishes lions and produces naphtha and the *gangitis* stone, which reptiles avoid.

(25) It is said that Gordys the son of Triptolemos lived in Gordyene, and later the Eretrians who were carried away by the Persians. We will soon make it clear about Triptolemos, in the Syrian section [16.2.5].

(26) The portions of Mesopotamia that incline toward the south and are farther from the mountains are waterless and poor, and are held by the Tent-Dwelling Arabians, who are brigands and shepherds, and easily move to another place when pasturage and plunder fail. Therefore those living along the mountains are treated badly by them, as well as by the Armenians, who are situated above them and through their strength oppress them. Thus they are most subject to them or the Parthyaians, who are also on the sides and hold both Media and Babylonia.

(27) Another river flows between the Euphrates and the Tigris, the Basileios, and yet another, the Aborras, is around Anthemousia. The road for those travelling from Syria to Seleukeia and Babylon is through the territory of the Tent Dwellers – today called Malians by some – and through their desert. The crossing of the Euphrates is near Anthemousia, a place in Mesopotamia. Lying four *schoinoi* above the river is Bambyke, called Edessa or the Sacred City, where the Syrian goddess Atargatis is honored. After the crossing, the road is through the desert to Skenai ["Tents"], a notable city on the borders of Babylonia, situated on a canal. The journey from the crossing to Skenai is twenty-five days. There are camel drivers who have stopping places, some of which are well provided with waterholes (for the most part cisterns), or sometimes they use water from elsewhere. The Tent Dwellers are peaceful and moderate in the exacting of tribute, and because of this going along the river is avoided. Thus [travellers] expose themselves

[C748]

to the desert, leaving the river on their right for a journey of about three days. The chieftains living on both sides of the river live in territory that is not abundant – yet less lacking in abundance [than elsewhere] – and each is surrounded by his own dominion and has his own tolls, which are not moderate. It is difficult with so many – and so many who are stubborn – for a common standard to be established that is advantageous to the merchant. Skenai is eighteen *schoinoi* distant from Seleukia.

(28) The Euphrates and that beyond it are the boundary of the Parthyaians. That within it as far as Babylonia is held by the Romans or the Arabian chieftains. Some of them are connected to the former and others to the Romans, whom they are adjacent to. The Tent Dwellers near the river are less connected to them, but more so are those who are farther away and near Fortunate Arabia. The Parthyaians once considered friendship with the Romans, but they defended themselves against Crassus, who began a war against them, and then in turn they began a battle when they sent Pakoros into Asia, but met with equal misfortune. Antonius used the Armenian [king] as an advisor, but was betrayed and did badly in the war. His successor Phraates [IV] was so eager for friendship with Caesar Sebastos that he sent him the trophies which the Parthyaians had set up against the Romans. He called Titius (who was then in charge of Syria) to a conference and put into his hands as hostages four of his legitimate sons – Seraspadanes, Rhodaspes, Phraates [V], and Vonones, and two of their wives and four of their sons, fearing sedition and attempts against himself. He knew that no one could [C749] prevail against him without supporting someone of the family of Arsakes [I] because the Parthyaians were extremely devoted to the Arsakids. Thus he sent his children away, seeking to deprive evildoers of that hope. The children who survived were royally cared for in Rome at public expense, and the successive kings have continued to send ambassadors and come to conferences.

Part 2:   Syria

(1) Syria is bounded on the north by Kilikia and the Amanos. From the sea to the bridge of the Euphrates (which is the boundary on the side mentioned) is not less than 1,400 stadia. On the east it is the Euphrates and the Tent-Dwelling Arabians (those within the Euphrates), on the south Fortunate Arabia and Egypt, and on the west the Egyptian and Syrian Seas as far as Issos.

(2) We set down as parts of it – beginning at Kilikia and the Amanos – Kommagene and the so-called Syrian Seleukis, and then Hollow Syria, and finally Phoenicia on the coast and Judaea in the interior. Some divide the whole of Syria into the Hollow Syrians, Syrians, and Phoenicians, and they

say that four other peoples are mixed up with them: the Judaeans, Idumaeans, Gazaians, and Azotians, some of whom (such as the Syrians and the Hollow Syrians) are farmers, and others (such as the Phoenicians) are merchants.

(3) Thus it is in general. In detail, Kommagene is somewhat small and has a fortified city, Samosata, where the royal seat was. Today it has become a province, and the surrounding territory is exceedingly fertile but small. The Euphrates bridge is here now, and Seleukeia is situated nearby, a Mesopotamian fortress that Pompeius included within the boundaries of Kommagene and where Tigranes [II] killed Kleopatra [V] called Selene after imprisoning her for a time, when she had been expelled from Syria.

(4) Seleukis is the best of the previously mentioned portions, and is called a tetrapolis, and is one because of the prominent cities in it. There are several, with four as the largest: Antiocheia near Daphne, Seleukeia in Pieria, Apameia, and Laodikeia. They were called sisters of each other because of their unanimity, and they were foundations of Seleukos [I] Nikator. The largest was named after his father, the best fortified after himself, and the others were Apameia [C750] after his wife Apama, and Laodikeia after his mother. The Seleukis, with the tetrapolis, was divided into four satrapies, as Poseidonios [F251] says, the same as Hollow Syria, although Mespotamia was only one.

Antiocheia is also a tetrapolis, since it was put together from four parts. Each settlement is fortified by the common wall and its own. Nikator founded the first of them, transferring the settlers from Antigoneia, which had been fortified nearby by Antigonos [I] the son of Philippos a short time previously. The second was a foundation of a large number of settlers, the third by Seleukos [II] Kallinikos, and the fourth by Antiochos [IV] Epiphanes.

(5) It is also the metropolis of Syria, and the royal seat of the rulers of the territory was located here. In power and size it is not much inferior to Seleukeia on the Tigris or Alexandria near Egypt. Nikator settled the descendants of Triptolemos here, whom we mentioned a little previously [16.1.25]. Because of this the Antiocheians honor him as a hero and celebrate a festival on Mount Kasion near Seleukeia. They say that he was sent by the Argives seeking Io – who first disappeared in Tyre – and he wandered through Kilikia. Some of the Argives with him separated from him there and founded Tarsos, but others accompanied him on the successive coast and gave up the search in despair, remaining with him in the riverine territory of the Orontes. Gordys the son of Triptolemos and some of the people with his father emigrated to Gordyaia, and the descendants of the rest became fellow inhabitants with the Antiocheians.

(6) Daphne lies 40 stadia above it, a moderate settlement having a large thickly shaded grove with the waters from springs running through it. In the

middle of it is an asylum precinct and a temple of Apollo and Artemis. It is the custom here for the Antiocheians and their neighbors to have a festival. The circuit of the grove is 80 stadia.

(7) The Orontes River flows near the city. Its sources are in Hollow Syria, and then after being carried underground and coming up again the stream proceeds through the region of Apameia to Antiocheia. Coming near to the city it is carried down to the sea around Seleukeia. It was formerly called the Typhon, but the name was changed because Orontes built a bridge across it. Somewhere around here was the myth of Typhon being struck with a thunderbolt and the Arimians, about which we have spoken pre- [C751] viously [12.8.19, 13.4.6]. They say that he (who was a serpent), when struck by the thunderbolt, fled and sought a descent underground, and cut furrows into the earth, creating the bed of the stream, as well as descending under- ground, which caused the spring to break out. The river received its name from this.

On the west, the sea lies below Antiocheia and Seleukeia (near which the Orontes makes its outlets), which is 40 stadia distant from the outlets, and 120 from Antiocheia. One sails up from the sea to Antiocheia on the same day.

To the east of Antiocheia are the Euphrates, and Bambyke, Beroia, and Herakleia, small towns once ruled by the tyrant Dionysios son of Herakleon. Herakleia is 20 stadia distant from the sanctuary of Athena Kyrrhestis.

(8) Then there is the Kyrrhestike, as far as the Antiochis. Near to it on the north are the Amanos and Kommagene. The Kyrrhestike adjoins them and extends that far. The city of Gindaros is here, which is the akropolis of Kyrrhestike and naturally suited for brigands, Nearby is the so-called Herakleion. It was around these places that Pakoros, the oldest son of the Parthyaian [king], was killed by Ventidius, when the former made an expedition against Syria. Adjoining Gindaros in the Antiochis is Pagrai, a fortified locality situated near the pass over the Amanos that goes from the Amanian Gates to Syria. The Antiocheian Plain lies below Pagrai, through which the Arkeuthos River flows, as well as the Orontes and Labotas. In this plain is the Palisade of Meleagros and the Oinoparas River, on which Ptolemaios [VI] Philometer conquered Alexander Balas in a battle but died from a wound. A hill lies above here called Trapezon ["Table"] because of its similarity, on which Ventidius had the battle with Phranikates the Parthyaian commander. Seleukeia is seaward of these places, as well as Pieria – a mountain continuous with the Amanos – and Rhosos, which is situated between Issos and Seleukeia. Formerly Seleukeia was called Rivers

of Water. The city is a notable fortress, too strong to be forced, and because of this Pompeius, after excluding Tigranes [II] from it, judged it to be free.

To the south of the Antiocheians is Apameia, situated in the interior, and [to the south] of the Seleukeians are the outlets of the Orontes, then Mount Kasion and Antikasion, and still farther after Seleukeia is the Nymphaion – a kind of sacred cave – and then Kasion. Next is the small town of Poseideion and then Herakleia.

(9) Then there is Laodikeia on the sea, a city that is most beautifully constructed with a good harbor, having a territory abundant in wine and [C752] other good crops. It provides most of the wine for the Alexandrians, since the entirety of the mountain lying above the city, almost as far as the summits, is covered in vines. The summits are very far from Laodikeia, and they slope up gently and gradually. They are high above Apameia and extend to a perpendicular height. It [Laodikeia] was immoderately afflicted by Dolabella, who fled to it for refuge and was besieged there by Cassius until he died, having destroyed both himself and many parts of the city.

(10) Apameia has an <akropolis> that is extremely well-fortified, a beautifully walled hill in a hollow plain that the Orontes makes into a peninsula, with a large lake situated nearby and broad marshes spreading into large meadows for cattle and horse pasturing. Thus the city is securely located and was called Chersonesos ["Peninsula"] because of its position, supplied with a fertile and fortunate territory in every way, through which the Orontes flows and in which there are many suburbs. Seleukos [I] Nikator maintained 500 elephants and most of his army here, as did the later kings. It was originally called Pella by the first Makedonians because most of the Makedonians on the expedition lived there, and because Pella, the home city of Philippos [II] and Alexander, had become the metropolis of the Makedonians. The military offices and horse breeders were also there. There were more than 30,000 royal mares and 300 stallions, as well as the horse breakers and the weapon instructors, and also all those hired to teach about warfare.

Its power is clearly shown by the rise of Tryphon surnamed Diodotos, who attacked the Syrian kingdom and made it [Apameia] his base of operations. He was born at Kasiana, a fortress in the Apameian land, and was raised at Apameia, connected to the king and those around him. When he began his revolution, he started from that city and those around it – Larisa, Kasiana, Megara, Apollonia, and other similar ones – which were all tributary to Apameia. He was proclaimed king and held out for a long time. Caecilius Bassus with two legions caused Apameia to revolt and endured a siege by two large Roman armies for so long a time that he did not come out

until he voluntarily entrusted himself to them in a way that he wished. The   [C753]
land supported his army and he had an abundance of allies, including the
neighboring chieftains who had fortresses, among which was Lysias, situated
above the lake near Apameia, and Arethousa, belonging to Sampsikeramos
and his son Iamblichos, chieftains of the Emisenian peoples. Not far away
were Helioupolis and Chalkis, which was subject to Ptolemaios the son of
Mennaios, who held Massyas and the mountainous territory of Itouraia.
Among the allies of Bassus were Alchaidamnos the king of the Rhambaians,
who were nomads inside of the Euphrates. He was a friend of the Romans,
but he believed that he was being treated unjustly by their commanders, so
he departed for Mesopotamia and was then hired by Bassus. Poseidonios the
Stoic, the man who was the most learned scholar of my time, was from there.

(11) Bordering on the Apameian territory, on the east, is the territory of
the Arabian chieftains called the Parapotamia, as well as the Chalkidike,
which reaches down from Massyas and all. . . . The territory south of the
Apameians has mostly tent-dwelling men, who are similar to the nomads in
Mesopotamia. Those nearer to the Syrians are always more civilized, and the
Arabians and Tent Dwellers less so, for the former have better-ordered
governments, such as those of Sampsikeramos, Gambaros, Themellas, and
such others.

(12) Such is the interior of the Seleukis. The remainder along the coast
from Laodikeia is as follows: near to Laodikeia are three towns, Posideion,
Herakleion, and Gabala, and then immediately there is the coast opposite
the Aradians, with Paltos, Balanaia, and Karanos (which is the seaport of
Arados and has a small harbor), and then Enydra and Marathos, an ancient
destroyed Phoenician city. The Aradians divided this territory among
themselves, as well as Ximyra, the next locality. Orthosia is contiguous
with it, and also the Eleutheros (the nearby river), which some make the
boundary between the Seleukis toward Phoenicia and Hollow Syria.

(13) Arados lies off a coast that is full of surf and without harbors,
approximately between its naval station and Marathos, 20 stadia distant
from the land. It is a rock washed all around by the sea, about 7 stadia in
circuit and full of dwellings. It has had such a large population, even until
today, that they live in houses with many stories. It was founded, as they
say, by exiles from Sidon. They obtain their water supply from the rains and
water cisterns, as well as from the mainland. During wars their water supply   [C754]
comes from the strait a small distance in front of the city, which has a
plentiful spring of water, and into which an inverted wide-mouthed funnel
made of lead is let down from a water boat. It contracts into a narrow base
with a moderately sized opening. A leather pipe – unless one should call it a

bellows – is bound tightly all around the base, and it receives the water that is forced from the spring into the funnel. The first that is forced up is from the sea, but they wait for the flow of pure potable water and take as much as necessary in prepared receptables and ferry it to the city.

(14) In antiquity the Aradians were independently ruled by kings, as was each of the other Phoenician cities. Then the Persians, Makedonians, and today the Romans changed them to their present arrangement. The Aradians, along with the other Phoenicians, became subject to the Syrian kings as friends. Then, when there was a disagreement between two brothers, Kallinikos Seleukos [II] and Antiochos Hierax, they sided with Kallinikos and made an agreement so that they could receive exiles from the kingdom and not give them up unwillingly, although these were not allowed to sail away without the king permitting it. Great advantages resulted for them from this, for those seeking refuge with them were not ordinary but the ones who had been trusted the most and were in the greatest fear. They were entertained by them as guests and considered those who received them as their benefactors and saviors, and remembered the favor, especially when they returned home. Because of this they [the Aradians] gained possession of a large part of the mainland, most of which they hold today, and they have otherwise prospered. To this good fortune they added forethought and industriousness in regard to their seafaring. Seeing that the neighboring Kilikians were organizing piracy, they would not join even once with them in such an enterprise.

(15) After Orthosia and the Eleutheros is Tripolis, which has taken its name from the fact that it is a foundation from three cities, Tyre, Sidon, and Arados. Contiguous with Tripolis is Theouprosopon, which is the end of Mount Libanos, and between them is the locality of Trieres.

(16) There are two mountains, Libanos and Antilibanos, which are about parallel and create the so-called Hollow Syria. They both begin slightly above the sea, with Libanos around Tripolis and nearest to Theouprosopon, and Antilibanos around Sidon. They come to an end in other mountains that are hilly and fruitful, near the Arabian mountains above the Damaskene and the so-called Trachones there. They leave a hollow plain between them whose width (near the sea) is 200 stadia, and whose length (from the sea to the interior) is about twice that. Rivers flow through it, watering a prosperous and totally productive territory. The largest is the Jordan. There is also a lake that produces aromatic rushes and reeds as well as marshes. It is called Lake Gennesaritis, and balsam is produced there. Among the rivers is the Chrysorrhoas, which begins at the city and territory of the Damaskenians and is almost entirely consumed by irrigation, watering a large region that is

[C755]

exceedingly deep. The Aradians sail up the Lykos and the Jordan, mostly with freight.

(17) The first of the plains from the sea is called the Makras, or the Makra, Plain. Poseidonios [F244] records that a dead serpent was seen here, whose length was about a *plethron*, and so thick that horsemen positioned on either side could not see one another. Its gaping mouth admitted someone on horseback and each of its horny scales was larger than an oblong shield.

(18) After the Makras is the Massyas, which has some mountainous portions, including Chalkis, essentially the akropolis of the Massyans. Its beginning is at Laodikeia near Libanos. All the mountainous portions are held by Itouraians and Arabians, all evildoers, but those in the plains are farmers, and when they are maltreated by the former, they require different kinds of help at different times. They use strong positions as bases of operations, such as those holding the Libanos have. Above, on the mountain, are Sinna, Borrama, and other similar ones, and below, Botrys, Gigartos, the caves on the sea, and the fortress constructed on Theouprosopon, which Pompeius destroyed. From these places they overran Byblos and, next to it, Berytos, which are situated between Sidon and Theouprosopon. Byblos, the royal seat of Kinyras, is sacred to Adonis. Pompeius freed it from the tyrant by killing him with an ax. It is situated on a height a slight distance from the sea.

(19) Next are the Adonis River, Mount Klimax, and Old Byblos, and then the Lykos River and Berytos. It was destroyed by Tryphon, and now it [C756] has been restored by the Romans, receiving two legions that were settled there by Agrippa, who added much of the territory of Massyas to it, as far as the springs of the Orontes (which are near to the Libanos), Paradeisos, and the Egyptian Wall in the Apameian land.

(20) These are the places on the sea. Above Massyas is the so-called Royal Valley and the Damascene territory, which is exceptionally praised. Damascus is a notable city, perhaps even the most famous in the region at the time of the Persians. The two hills called the Trachones lie above it. Then, toward the Arabian portions – with the Itouraians mixed in – are mountains that are difficult to cross, where there are caves with deep mouths, one of which can accept 4,000 people in case of raids, which are made against the Damaskenians from many places. For the most part, however, the barbarians have been robbing the merchants from Fortunate Arabia, but this has become less today since the brigands around Zenodoros have been broken up because of the good government of the Romans and the security nourished by the soldiers in Syria.

(21) Everything above the Seleukis, toward Egypt and Arabia, is called Hollow Syria, but especially that bounded by the Libanos and the

Antilibanos. The remainder of the coast, from Orthosia to Pelousion, is called Phoenicia – which is narrow and coastal – and the interior above it, as far as the Arabians, between Gaza and the Antilibanos, is called Judaea.

(22) Since we have gone through what is especially called Hollow Syria, we will go on to Phoenicia. That from Orthosia to Berytos has already been discussed. After Berytos there is Sidon in about 400 stadia, and between them are the Tamyras River, a grove of Asklepios, and Leontonpolis. After Sidon is Tyre, the largest and oldest in Phoenicia, which is equal to the former in its size, reputation, and antiquity, as is handed down in many myths. The poets chatter more about Sidon (Homer does not mention Tyre), but the settlements of the latter in Libya and Iberia, as far as outside the Pillars, sing rather about Tyre. Yet both have been esteemed and illustrious, in antiquity as well as today. It is disputed by both which one should be called the metropolis of the Phoenicians. Sidon is situated on the mainland at a good natural harbor.

[C757]   (23) Tyre is completely an island – populated in a similar way to Arados – and is joined to the mainland by an embankment, which Alexander constructed during his siege. It has two harbors, one that can be closed and the other, called the Egyptian, is open. They say that the houses have many stories, more than in Rome. Because of this, when an earthquake occurred it was only slightly lacking in destroying the city. It was also unfortunate when it was taken in a siege by Alexander. Yet it became stronger through its misfortunes and restored itself through its seamanship – in which the Phoenicians have generally always been superior to everyone – and its purple dye works, for Tyrian purple is considered the most beautiful of all. The creatures are caught nearby, and everything suitable for dyeing is easily obtained. The large number of dye works makes the city unpleasant to live in, but it is rich because of such hardiness. They are judged to be autonomous, not only by the kings but by the Romans (at small expense), when they confirmed their decrees. Herakles is greatly honored by them. The number and size of the foreign settlements of the city is proof of its maritime power.

(24) They are in such a way. It has been handed down that the Sidonians are skilled in making many beautiful works of art, as the Poet makes clear [*Iliad* 6.289–92, 23.743], and moreover that they are scholars in astronomy and arithmetic, which originated both from their calculations and their night sailing, for both of these are of concern to merchants and shipowners, just as, they say, geometry was invented by the Egyptians for the measurement of land, brought about because the Nile, when it rises, obliterates the boundaries. It is thus believed to have come from the Egyptians to the

Hellenes, and astronomy and arithmetic from the Phoenicians. Today the greatest amount of every kind of scholarship is, by far, taken from these cities. If one is to believe Poseidonios [F285], the ancient dogma about atoms came from a man of Sidon, Mochos [F6], before the time of the Trojan matter. But let us be done with ancient things. In our time there have been many notable philosophers from Sidon, including Boethos (with whom I studied Aristotelian matters) and his brother Diodotos, and, from Tyre, Antipatros and (a little before our time) Apollonios, who published a catalogue of the Zenonian philosophers and their books.

Tyre is no more than 200 stadia from Sidon, and between them is a [C758] town called the City of Birds, and then there is another river that empties near Tyre. After Tyre is Old Tyre, in 30 stadia.

(25) Then there is Ptolemais, a large city, which was formerly named Ake. The Persians used it as a base against Egypt. Between Ake and Tyre there is a sandy beach that produces vitreous sand. They say that it is not melted there but is taken to Sidon and processed. Some say that the Sidonians have the vitreous sand that is suitable for fusing, and others that any from anywhere can be poured. I heard from the glass workers in Alexandria that there was a vitreous earth in Egypt without which many-colored and expensive designs could not be completed, just as other places need different compounds. At Rome they say that many discoveries have been made both for the colors and also for ease in production, as in the case of transparent crystal. There one can purchase a bowl or small drinking cup for a bronze piece.

(26) Something incredible that is exceedingly rare is recorded on this shore between Tyre and Ptolemais, at the time when the Ptolemies, joining battle with the commander Sarpedon, were left there after a brilliant rout had occurred. A wave from the sea, like a flood tide, inundated the fugitives, some of whom were snatched away by the sea and destroyed, and others remained dead in hollow places. Then the ebb tide uncovered them again, revealing the bodies lying mixed in with dead fish. This is similar to what happens around Kasion near Egypt, where the land, through a single sharp convulsion, changes suddenly and falls on both sides, so that the elevated portion brings on the sea and the collapsed receives it, and then it changes back to its old position and returns to its location. At times there is a complete interchange and at times not. Perhaps such occurrences are connected to some cycle unknown to us, as it is said that it is the same with the rising of the Nile, which is variable but due to some unknown regularity.

(27) After Ake is the Tower of Straton, which has an anchorage. Between them is Mount Karmelos and towns for which there is nothing more than

the names: Sykaminonpolis, Boukolon, and Krokodeilonpolis, and others
[C759]   that are similar, and then a large forest.

(28) Then there is Iope, where the coast from Egypt makes a remarkable
turn toward the north, having formerly extended toward the east. Here,
according to certain myths, Andromeda was set out for the sea creature, for
the place is so high that, they say, one can see Hierosolyma, the Judaean
metropolis, from it, and the Judaeans have used it as a seaport when they go
as far as the sea (but the seaports of brigands are clearly brigand retreats).
Karmelos as well as the forest were possessed by them, and the place
was so well populated that 40,000 could be put under arms from the
neighboring village of Iamneia and the settlements around it. From there
to Kasion near Pelousion it is a little more than 1,000 stadia, and Pelousion
itself is 300 farther.

(29) In between is the Gadaris, which the Judaeans appropriated to
themselves, and then Azotos and Askalon. From Iamneia to Azotos and
Askalon is about 200 stadia. The land of the Askalonites is good for onions,
although it is a small town. The philosopher Antiochos was from there, who
lived a little before our time. From Gadara were Philodemos the Epicurean,
Meleagros, Menippos the satirist, and Theodoros, a rhetorician of our time.

(30) Next is the harbor of the Gazaians. The city is above it, 7 stadia
inland. It was once notable but was destroyed by Alexander, and remains
deserted. It is said that there is a route of 1,260 stadia from there to Ailana,
a city located in the recess of the Arabian Gulf, which is double:
one stretching toward the region of Arabia and Gaza – which is called the
Ailanitic from the city on it – and the other toward the region of Egypt and
Heroonpolis, to which the route from Pelousion is shorter. The journeys are
on camels through deserted and sandy places, and there are many reptiles
in them.

(31) After Gaza is Rhaphia, where a battle occurred between the fourth
Ptolemaios and Antiochos [III] the Great. Then there is Rhinokoloura
["Clipped Nose"], so called from the people with mutilated noses who
were established there in antiquity. A certain Aithiopian invaded Egypt,
and instead of doing away with the wrongdoers he cut off their noses and
settled them there, so that they would no longer dare to do anything wrong
because of the disgrace to their faces.

(32) Everything beyond Gaza is poor and sandy, but even more is
[C760]   that lying next above it, which has Lake Sirbonis lying about parallel to
the sea (with a short passage in between as far as the Outlet, as it is called),
about 200 stadia in length, with its greatest width at 50. The Outlet

has been filled with earth. Then there is another area of this type that is contiguous, to Kasion and Pelousion.

(33) Kasion is a sandy hill without water that creates a promontory. The body of Pompeius Magnus lies there, and there is also a sanctuary of Zeus Kasios. Magnus was slaughtered there, treacherously murdered by the Egyptians. Then there is the road to Pelousion, on which are Gerrha, the so-called Palisade of Chabrias, and the pits near Pelousion that are formed when the Nile pours in, as the places are naturally hollow and marshy.

Such is Phoenicia. Artemidoros [F116] says that it is 3,650 stadia to Pelousion from Orthosia, going through the gulfs, and from Melainai or Melaniai in Kilikia, near Kelenderis, to the common boundary of Kilikia and Syria, it is 1,900. From there to the Orontes is 520, and then it is 1,130 to Orthosia.

(34) The western extremities of Judaea toward Kasion are occupied by the Idumaeans and the lake. The Idumaeans are Nabataeans but because of sedition they were expelled and joined with the Judaeans, adopting their customs. Sirbonis occupies most of the region near the sea, along with what is contiguous as far as Ierosolymna, which is also near the sea and is visible from the seaport of Iope, as has been stated. This is toward the north, and generally and in particular it is inhabited by mixed tribes of Egyptian, Arabian, and Phoenician peoples, as are those who hold Galilaia, Hierikous, Philadelphia, and Samareia, which Herod named Sebaste. Although they are mixed in such a way, the most prevalent report of those regarding the sanctuary of Hierosolyma demonstrates that the ancestors of the so-called Judaeans of today were Egyptian.

(35) Moses was one of the Egyptian priests and held a part of the so-called territory of . . . but he went away from there, as he was disgusted with the situation, and many went with him who honored the Divinity. He said and taught that the Egyptians were not correct in presuming that the Divinity was in the form of animals and cattle, nor were the Libyans, and that Hellenes were also wrong with their anthropomorphizing. God [C761] is the only one who surrounds us all, as well as the earth and sea, what we call the heavens, cosmos, or the nature of existence. Who then would dare to consider fashioning an image similar to anything among us? One should be finished with all forms of images, and set apart a precinct and a notable enclosure, and give honor and worship without a statue. Those who had good dreams should sleep in it, both for themselves and also for everyone else, and those who live moderately and with justice should always expect a gift or sign from the god, but others should not expect anything.

(36) He said such things, and persuaded not a few reasonable men, and then went away to the place where the settlement of Hierosolyma is now. He took possession easily, since it was not a place that was envied or over which anyone would fight. It is rocky, and although well supplied with water, the territory around it is poor and waterless, and it is rocky underneath within 60 stadia. Instead of using weapons, he put forward his sacrifices and the Divinity, seeking a worthy location for him and promising to deliver a ritual and ceremonies that would not trouble those with him with expenses, ecstasy, or other unnatural business. He was highly esteemed by them, and organized a government that was unusual, and everyone all around easily joined with him because of his association with them and what he offered.

(37) For some time his followers continued in the same way, acting justly and religiously. Yet later, superstitious men were first appointed to the priesthood, and then tyrannical people, and from superstition came the abstention from meat (and today it is common to abstain from it), circumcision, excision, and other such practices. The brigands came from the tyrannies, for some revolted and maltreated the territory and that of their neighbors, and others – cooperating with the rulers – seized the property of others and subjected much of Syria and Phoenicia. But nevertheless there was a certain dignity to their akropolis, and it was not loathed as a place of tyranny but revered and honored as sacred.

(38) For this then is natural, and common to the Hellenes and barbarians. They exist in a political community and live under common decrees, for otherwise it would not be possible for the masses to do any single thing joined together with each other – which is what it is to be a citizen – or to live [C762] a common life in any other way. The decrees are double: from gods and from mankind. Those in antiquity worshipped and exalted the gods more, and because of this, those who consulted the oracles at that time were numerous: those who ran to Dodona "to hear the decree of Zeus from the oak with high foliage" [*Odyssey* 14.328], using Zeus as their advisor, and also to Delphi "to learn by inquiry whether the child that had been exposed was no longer alive" [Euripides, *Phoenician Women* 36–7], but the child itself "was going to the home of Phoibos to learn about its parents" [Euripides, *Phoenician Women* 34–5], and Minos among the Cretans, who "reigned there, and who conversed with great Zeus every nine years" [*Odyssey* 19.179]. Every nine years, as Plato says [*Minos* 319e, *Laws* 1.624b], he would go up to the cave of Zeus and receive decrees from him and carry them to the people. Lykourgos, his emulator, did the same, for repeatedly, as it seems, he would go abroad to ask the Pythia what was proper to announce to the Lakedaimonians.

(39) These matters – whatever truth there was in them – were believed and sanctioned by the people, and because of this the prophets were honored, so much so that they were considered worthy of being kings, as they transmitted to us the precepts and corrections from the gods, both when alive and also when dead, such as Teiresias: "to whom even in death Persephoneia gave his senses, so that he alone had understanding, yet the others darted as shadows" [*Odyssey* 10.494–5]. Also in such a way were Amphiaraos, Trophonios, Orpheus, Mousaios, the god among the Getai (who in antiquity was Zalmoxis, a Pythagorean, and in our time there was Dekaineos, the prophet of Byrebistas), Achaikaros among the Bosporenians, the Gymnosophists among the Indians, the Magoi among the Persians (as well as the necromancers, and also those called the dish-diviners and water-diviners), the Chaldaians among the Assyrians, and the Tyrrhenian astrologers among the Romans. Moses was such a person, as well as his successors, who did not have a bad beginning but turned out for the worse.

(40) When Judaea was manifestly under the rule of tyrants, Alexander was the first to declare himself king instead of priest, and his sons were Hyrkanos [II] and Aristoboulos [II]. When they differed about the rule, Pompeius went there and overthrew them, and tore down their fortifications, and in particular took Hierosolyma by force. It was a rocky and well-built fortress, and well supplied with water inside it, but outside it was completely dry. There was a rock-cut trench, 60 feet in depth and 250 in [C763] width (the wall of the sanctuary was fitted with towers made from the stone that had been hewn out). He took the city, as they say, after watching for the day of fasting when the Judaeans abstained from all work, and filled up the trench and threw ladders across it. He ordered that all the walls be torn down, and destroyed as much as possible the brigand retreats and the treasuries of the tyrants. There were two of these in the passes above Hierikous – Threx and Tauros – and also Alexandreion, Hyrkaneion, Machairous, Lysias, and those around Philadelphia as well as Skythopolis in Galilaia.

(41) Hierikous is in a plain surrounded by a sort of mountainous territory that slopes toward it, somewhat in the form of a theater. The Phoinikon is here, which is mixed with other cultivated and fruitful trees, although mostly palms. It is 100 stadia in length with streams flowing through it everywhere and is also full of dwellings. There is also a palace here, as well as a balsam *paradeisos*. It is of the shrubby type, similar to *kytisos* and terebinth, and is aromatic. They cut into the bark and catch the juice in vessels, which is similar to a sticky milk. When a mussel-shell full is taken up, it becomes solid. It is marvellous for its cure of headaches, the early stage

of cataracts, and dimness of sight. Thus it is expensive, and also because it is produced only here. It is also the same way with the Phoinikon, which is the only place with the date palm, except for the Babylonian and those east of there. Thus the income from it is great, and they use balsam wood as an aromatic.

(42) Lake Sirbonis[1] is large – some say that it is 1,000 stadia in circuit – and extends along the coast for a length reaching slightly more than 200 stadia. It is deep at the shore and has water that is so exceedingly heavy there is no need for divers, for someone going into it proceeds as far as his navel and is immediately raised up. It is full of asphalt, which is produced at irregular intervals from the midst of the depths, along with bubbles – as if the water were boiling – and its surface is convex and gives the appearance of a hill. A great amount of soot is also raised up, which is smoky but cannot be seen by the eye. It tarnishes copper, silver, and everything that glistens, even gold. Those living around it knew that when their materials were becoming tarnished the asphalt was beginning to rise, and they prepared to

[C764]   mine it with rafts made of reeds. The asphalt is a lump of earth that is moistened by heat which comes up and is dispersed, and then changes again into a hard solid substance because of the cold, which is the kind of water that the lake has. Then it must be cut and chopped, and it floats on the surface because of the nature of the water, due to which, as we said, there is no need for divers, and no one going into it can be immersed but is raised up. They sail to the asphalt on rafts, and cut it up and carry away as much as they can.

(43) Such is the way that it happens. Poseidonios [F279] says that the people are sorcerers and pretend to be enchanters, using urine and other foul liquids, which they pour over the asphalt and then squeeze. It then solidifies and is cut. But it is possible that there is something useful in urine, such as *chrysokolla*, which is produced in the bladder when there are stones and in the urine of children. It is reasonable that such a situation would occur in the middle of the lake, because the source of the fire and most of the asphalt is in the middle. But the upward blowing is irregular, because, like many other blasts, the movement of the fire has no order that is revealed to us. It is also in such a way at Apollonia in Epeiros.

(44) There are many other proofs that demonstrate the region was exposed to fire. Around Moasada rough rocks that have been scorched are visible, as well as porous rock, ashy soil, drops of pitch dripping from smooth cliffs,

---

[1] Although the text has "Lake Sirbonis," the description is garbled, and it is clear (after the first sentence at least) that Lake Asphaltitis (the Dead Sea) is meant.

boiling rivers that are foul smelling far away, and scattered settlements that have been destroyed. Thus what the local people chatter about is believed: that there were once thirteen inhabited cities there, whose metropolis was Sodom, but a circuit of about 60 stadia was saved. Because of earthquakes and eruptions of fire, and hot waters with asphalt and sulphur, the lake rushed forward and rocks were seized by fire. Some of the cities were swallowed up and others abandoned by those who could flee. Eratosthenes [F18] says the contrary, that the territory formed a lake, most of which was uncovered by an outbreak, as in Thessaly.

(45) In the Gadaris, also, there is disagreeable marsh water, and when animals taste it they lose their hair, hooves, and horns. At what is called Taricheai ["Salting Factory"] the lake produces nice fish for salting, and the land produces fruit-bearing trees similar to apples. The Egyptians use asphalt for preserving the dead.

(46) Pompeius cut off some [of the territory] that had been forcibly appropriated by the Judaeans for themselves, and appointed Hyrkanos [II] [C765] to the priesthood. Later his descendant, a certain Herod, a local man, crept into the priesthood, but was so different from his predecessors, especially in his intercourse with the Romans and his government, that he was given the title of king, first through the authority of Antonius and then later by Caesar Sebastos. He killed some of his sons on the grounds that they were plotting against him, and at his own death left others as his successors, having given portions over to them. Caesar also honored the sons of Herod, his sister Salome, and her daughter Berenike. But the sons were not fortunate and there were charges made against them. One remained thereafter in exile, taking up residence among the Allobrigian Galatians, but the others, through their great services, found (with difficulty) that they could return, and each was appointed to a tetrarchy.

Part 3: The Persian Gulf

(1) The entirety of Arabia lies above Judaea and Hollow Syria, as far as Babylonia and the riverine valley of the Euphrates, and toward the south except for the Tent Dwellers in Mesopotamia. Mesopotamia and the people living there have already been discussed [16.1.26–8], and in regard to the portions on the far side of the Euphrates, the Babylonians and the Chaldaian peoples (who also have been discussed [16.1.6]) live near its outlets. What is next to Mesopotamia as far as Hollow Syria (that near the river), as well as Mesopotamia itself, is held by the Arabians called the Tent Dwellers, divided into small dominions that are poor territories lacking in water. They farm

little, or not at all, but they have herds of all kinds of animals, especially camels. There is a large desert above them, but that which is still farther south is held by those inhabiting what is called Fortunate Arabia. Its northern side is the previously mentioned desert, the eastern is the Persian Gulf, the western the Arabian, and the southern the great sea that is outside both gulfs, which is collectively called the Erythra.

(2) The Persian Gulf is also called the Persian Sea. Eratosthenes [F94] says the following about it: he says that its mouth is so narrow that from Harmozai, the promontory of Karmania, one can look across to that of Makai in Arabia. From its mouth the right-hand coast, being curved, is at first turned slightly to the east from Karmania, and then bends toward the north, and afterward toward the west as far as Teredon and the mouth of the Euphrates. It consists of the Karmanian coast, and part of the Persian, [C766] Sousian, and Babylonian, about 10,000 stadia, concerning which I have already spoken [15.2.14]. From there to its mouth is the same distance. This, he says, is according to Androsthenes the Thasian [F2], who sailed with Nearchos and also by himself. Thus it is clear that this sea is only slightly smaller than the Euxeinos Sea. He [Eratosthenes] says that he [Androsthenes], who sailed around the gulf with an expedition, said that beyond Teredon – having the continent on his right and sailing along the coast – is the island of Ikaros, with a temple on it sacred to Apollo and an oracle of Tauropolos.

(3) After sailing along Arabia for 2,400 stadia there is the city of Gerrha, lying on a deep gulf, where Chaldaians exiled from Babylon live. The land is salty and they have houses of salt, and since flakes of salt come away because of the heat of the sun and fall off, they sprinkle the walls with water and keep them solid. The city is 200 stadia from the sea. The Gerrhaians trade mostly by land for Arabian goods and aromatics. In contrast Aristoboulos [F57] says that the Gerrhaians generally travel on rafts to Babylonia for trade, sailing up the Euphrates to Thapsakos with their goods, and distributing them to everywhere by land from there.

(4) Sailing farther, there are other islands, Tyros and Arados, that have temples like those of the Phoenicians. Those living there say that the islands and cities with the same names are Phoenician settlements. These islands are ten days' sail from Teredon and one day from the mouth at the promontory of Makai.

(5) Both Nearchos [F27] and Orthagoras [F5] say that the island of Tyrine[2] lies toward the south on the Ocean at a distance of 2,000 stadia, and

---

[2] The text has "Tyrine" but this is almost certainly an error for "Ogyros" (see section 7).

the grave of Erythras is visible on it, a large mound planted with wild palms. He was king of that region and left the sea named after himself. They say that this was pointed out to them by Mithropastes son of Arsites the satrap of Phrygia, who had been exiled by Dareios [III] and passed his time on the island, joining them when they landed in the Persian Gulf and through them attempting to return home.

(6) Along the entire coast of the Erythran Sea are trees in the depths that are like laurel and olive, completely visible at low tide but completely covered at high tide, although the land lying above is without trees, thus intensifying the peculiarity. Concerning the region of the Persian Sea, [C767] which, as I have said, forms the eastern side of Fortunate Arabia, this is what Eratosthenes has said.

(7) Nearchos [F28] says that they happened upon Mithropastes along with Mazenes, and that Mazenes ruled an island in the Persian Gulf, and the island was called Dorakta. Mithropastes took refuge and obtained hospitality here after he departed Ogyros, and he met with Mazenes in regard to suggesting him to the Makedonian fleet, and Mazenes became the guide for the voyage. He [Nearchos] also says that there is an island at the beginning of the Persian Gulf on which there are many valuable pearls, and that on others there are pebbles that are transparent and bright. In the islands off the Euphrates trees grow that smell like frankincense, and juice flows from the roots when they are broken. There are large crabs and sea urchins, which are common in the entire External Sea. Some of them are larger than a *kausia*, and others have a measure of two *kotylai*. He also saw a sea creature on the shore that was 50 *pecheis*.

Part 4: Arabia

(1) Mesene is the beginning of Arabia, going from Babylonia. The desert of the Arabians lies in front of it on one side, on another are the marshes near the Chaldaians – which are created by the overflow from the Euphrates – and on the other is the Persian Sea. It has bad air and is misty, rainy, and exceedingly hot, but nevertheless produces fine fruit. The vine grows in the marshes, with as much earth thrown on reeds as the plant needs, so that it often wanders away and then is pushed back with poles to its proper place.

(2) But I return to Eratosthenes [F95], who sets forth what he knows about Arabia. He says, concerning its northerly or desert part – which is between Fortunate Arabia, Hollow Syria, and Judaea as far as the recesses of the Arabian Gulf (from Heroonpolis, which is at the recess of the Arabian Gulf near the Nile) – that it is 5,600 stadia from Nabataean Petra to

Babylon, entirely toward the summer sunrise, through the adjacent Arabian tribes, the Nabataeans, Chaulotaians, and Agraians. Beyond these is Fortunate [Arabia], which extends for 12,000 stadia toward the south as far as the Atlantic Ocean. The first people there, beyond the Syrians and Judaeans, are farmers. Beyond these the land is very sandy and wretched, with a few palm trees, a thorny plant, and the tamarisk, with water from digging, just [C768] as in Gedrosia. The tent-dwelling Arabians and camel herders are there. The extremities, toward the south, rising opposite to Aithiopia, are watered by summer rains and have two sowings, like Indike, and the rivers are consumed by plains and lakes. It is fertile and abundant in honey production. It has plenty of fatted animals (except for horses, mules, and pigs), and all kinds of birds except geese and chickens. The four most numerous peoples living in the extremity of the previously mentioned territory are the Minaians, in the district toward the Erythran Sea, whose largest city is Karna or Karnana; next to these are the Sabaians, whose metropolis is Mariaba; third are the Kattabanians, extending to the narrows and the crossing of the Arabian Gulf, and whose royal seat is called Tamna; and, farthest toward the east are the Chatramotitians, whose city is Sabata.

(3) All are monarchies and prosperous, beautifully furnished with temples and palaces. Their houses are like those of the Egyptians regarding the joining of the beams. The four districts have more territory than the Egyptian Delta. No child succeeds to the kingship of his father: rather it is the child of a distinguished person who was the first born after the accession of the king. At the same time that someone accedes to the throne, the pregnant wives of distinguished men are recorded and guards are placed. The son who is born first to one of them is by law adopted and raised in a royal fashion to be the successor.

(4) Kattabania produces frankincense, and Chatramotitis myrrh, and these and other aromatics are traded with merchants. They come there from the Ailanians, arriving in Minaia in seventy days. Ailana is a city on the other recess of the Arabian gulf, the one opposite Gaza called the Ailanitic, as I have already said [16.2.30]. The Gerrhaians, however, arrive at Chatramotitis in forty days. The part of the Arabian Gulf along the side of Arabia, beginning at the Ailanitic recess, was recorded by those around Alexander, especially Anaxikrates, as 14,000 stadia, although this is said to be too much. The part opposite the Trogodytic territory, which is on the right when sailing from Heroonpolis, as far as Ptolemais and the elephant-hunting territory, is 9,000 stadia to the south and slightly toward the [C769] east, and then, as far as the narrows, 4,500 somewhat more to the east. The narrows toward Arabia are created by a promontory called Deire, and a

small town with the same name, in which the Fish Eaters live. Here, it is said, there is a pillar of Sesostris the Egyptian that records his crossing in hieroglyphics. It appears that he was the first to subdue the Aithiopian and Trogodytic territory, and then he crossed into Arabia and proceeded against all Asia. Because of this, what are called the fortifications of Sesostris are identified everywhere, as well as reproductions of temples to the Egyptian gods. The narrows at Deire contract to 60 stadia, yet these are not called the narrows now. As one sails farther along, where the passage between the continents is about 200 stadia, there are six islands that come in succession and fill up the crossing, leaving extremely narrow passages through which boats carry goods across, and these are called the narrows. After the islands, the next sailing, following the bays along the myrrh-bearing territory toward the south, and east as far as the Cinnamon-Bearer territory, is about 5,000 stadia. It is said that until now no one has gone beyond this region. There are not many cities on the coast, but many beautiful settlements in the interior. This, then, is the account of Eratosthenes about Arabia.

(5) Artemidoros [F96] says that the promontory on the Arabian side lying opposite Deire is called Akila, and that those living there have their penis mutilated. Sailing from Heroonpolis there is, in Trogodytike, a city of Philotera, named after the sister of the second Ptolemaios. It was a foundation of Satyros, who had been sent to investigate the elephant hunts and Trogodytike. Then there is another city, Arsinoë, and then an outlet of hot water that is bitter and salty and empties from a high rock into the sea. Nearby there is a mountain in a plain that is as red as ochre. Then there is Mussel Anchorage – also called the Anchorage of Aphrodite – a large harbor that has a winding entrance. There are three islands off it, two of which are shaded with olive trees and the other less so and full of guinea fowls. Then the Unclean Gulf is next, which, like Mussel Anchorage, also lies on the same latitude as Thebes, and it is indeed unclean, for it is made rough by undersea reefs and rocks, and at most times by winds that rush down in a storm. Here, in the depth of the gulf, is situated the city of Berenike.   [C770]

(6) After the gulf is an island called Ophiodes ["Snaky"], from its situation, but the king freed it from the reptiles, both because the animals killed the people who landed there and because of the *topazos*. It is a transparent stone that shines with a golden luster, but one cannot easily see it in the daytime because it is eclipsed by the superior light. Those who collect it see it at night, putting a vessel over it as a sign so that it can be dug up in the daytime. There was a group of people appointed to guard both the stone and its collection, paid by the kings of Egypt.

(7) After this island there are many clans of Fish Eaters and nomads. Then there is Savior Harbor, so called by some commanders who happened to have been saved from great dangers. After this there are many changes in the coast and the gulf, for the sail along the coast is no longer rough and in a way touches Arabia. The sea is shallow (about two *orgyiai*) and it appears grassy with seaweed and other weeds showing through. This is more common at the strait, where trees grow among them below the water. The strait also has a large number of sea dogs. Then there are the Bulls, two mountains that from far away give the impression of being similar to the animals. Then there is another mountain that has a sanctuary of Isis, a copy of one by Sesostris. Then there is an island that floods and is planted with olives. After this is Ptolemais, near the hunting area for elephants, a foundation of Eumedes, who had been sent to the hunting grounds by [Ptolemaios II] Philadelphos, and who secretly enclosed a kind of peninsula with a ditch and peribolos, and then won over as friends rather than enemies those hindering the construction.

(8) In between, a branch of the river called the Astaboras empties, whose source is in a lake and empties part of its waters, but mostly joins the Nile. Then there are the six islands called the Quarries, and then the so-called Sabaitic Mouth, and in the interior there is a fortress, a foundation of Tosouchos. Then there is the so-called Olive Harbor and the island of Straton, and then Saba Harbor and an elephant-hunting area of the same name. The land deep in the interior is called Tenessis, and it is held by the Egyptians who were exiled by Psammetichos [II]. They are called [C771] Sembritians – as they were foreigners – and are ruled by a woman, to whom Meroë, an island in the Nile in that region, is also subject. Above this island, not far away, is another in the river, a settlement of the same exiles. From Meroë to this sea is a journey of fifteen days for someone who is well-girded. Around Meroë is the confluence of the Astaboras and the Astapous, as well as that of the Astasobas with the Nile.

(9) The Root Eaters and Marsh Dwellers live alongside them, so-called because they cut roots from the bordering marshes and crush them with stones, forming them into cakes and baking them in the sun and eating them. The region is a territory for lions, and on the days of the rising of the Dog the animals are driven out of the place by large gnats. The Seed Eaters are nearby, who are nourished on acorns when the seeds fall, preparing them in a similar way as the Root Eaters do roots.

After Olive [Harbor] there are the Lookouts of Demetrios and the Altars of Konon, and in the interior many Indian reeds grow. The territory is called that of Korakios. Deep in the interior is a certain Endera, a settlement of naked people who use bows made of reeds and arrows hardened by fire. Generally they shoot wild animals from trees, but sometimes from the ground. There are a large number of wild cattle among them, whose meat they live on, as well as that of other wild animals. When they take nothing from hunting they bake dry skins over charcoal and are satisfied with such nourishment. It is their custom also to have archery contests for young men who are not yet adults.

After the Altars of Konon is Apple Harbor, above which lie the fortress called Koraos, the hunting area of Koraos, another fortress, and a number of hunting areas. Then there is Antiphilos Harbor, and above it, the Meat Eaters, whose males have their penises mutilated and the women are excised in the Judaean manner.

(10) Farther above them and toward the south are the Dog Milkers, who are called Agrians by the locals, and who have hair that falls down, long beards, and raise quite large dogs, with which they hunt the Indian cattle that come in from the neighboring region, either driven there by wild animals or because of a scarcity of pasturage. Their onslaught is from the summer turning until the middle of winter.

Next after Antiphilos Harbor is the so-called Grove of the Mutilated, the city of Berenike near Sabai, and Sabai, an exceedingly large city. Then there is the Grove of Eumenes. Lying above it are the city of Darada and the elephant hunting ground called "The One Near the Cistern." These are inhabited by the Elephant Eaters, who obtain the animals in the following way: when they see from the trees a herd moving through the forest, they do [C772] not attack them, but follow them secretly and hamstring those who have wandered away from the rear. Some kill them with arrows dipped in the bile of snakes. The archery is performed by three men: two of them come forward and hold the bow with their feet, and the other draws the string. Others make note of the trees beside which they are accustomed to rest and approach them from the other side, cutting into the trunks. When the animal approaches and leans against it, the tree falls, and it does too, and it is unable to get up because its legs have a continuous and rigid bone. They leap down from the tree and cut it up. The nomads call these hunters the Unclean.

(11) The Strouthophagians, a group of people that is not very large, lie above them. Among them there are birds the size of deer, who are unable to fly but run swiftly like ostriches. Some hunt them with bows, and others cover themselves with the skins of *strouthoi*, hiding the right hand in part of the neck and moving it in the same way that the animal moves its neck. With the left they pour forth seeds from a pouch hanging alongside, and

with them they entice the animals and force them together into ravines, where men with sticks stand over them and cut them down. Their skins are used for coverlets and spreads. The Aithiopians called the Flat-Nosed make war against them, using the horns of gazelles as weapons.

(12) The Locust Eaters are neighbors to them, who are blacker than others, shorter, and the shortest-lived. They rarely survive more than forty years, since their flesh has become full of wild creatures. They live on locusts, which in spring are driven into these places by the strong Lips and Zephyr winds. They throw smoky wood into gullies, light it slightly from underneath, and when they [the locusts] fly above the smoke they are blinded and fall. They are pounded with salt and made into cakes and used. Above them lies a large uninhabited region with abundant pastures. It was abandoned because of many scorpions and spiders – the so-called "four-jawed" – that once prevailed and caused a complete flight of the people.

[C773] (13) After the Harbor of Eumenes, as far as Deire and the narrows opposite the six islands, live the Fish Eaters, the Meat Eaters, and the Mutilated People, as far as the interior. There are several hunting areas for elephants here, insignificant cities, and islands off the coast. Most are nomads and few are farmers. Not a small amount of styrax grows in some places. The Fish Eaters collect the fish at low tide, throw them on the rocks, and bake them in the sun. They remove the bones and spine and pile them up, and then walk on the flesh and make it into cakes, and bake them again in the sun and eat them. During winter, when they are unable to collect the fish, they pound the bones that they have piled up and mold them into cakes and use them, and drain them when fresh. Some who have shellfish fatten their flesh by throwing them into pits and pools of the sea. Then they throw little fishes as nourishment for them, and use them when there is a scarcity of fish. They have all kinds of places for the raising of fish, which they dispense. Some of those who live on the waterless coast go inland every five days to waterholes, with their households singing the paean, and throw themselves face downwards and drink like cattle until their stomachs have swollen like a drum, and then go back to the sea. They live in caves or in pens covered with beams and rafters of the bones of sea creatures, fish spines, and olive branches.

(14) The Tortoise Eaters are sheltered by shells so large that they can sail in them. Since seaweed is thrown out in large amounts and makes high hill-like heaps, some dig beneath them and live under them. They throw out their dead as nourishment for the fish, taken up by the flood tides.

There are three islands that are situated in succession, called that of the Tortoises, of the Seals, and of the Hawks. The entire coast – not only that within the narrows, but most of that outside – has palm trees and olive and laurel groves. There is also Philippos Island, opposite and above of which is the elephant-hunting area called that of Pythangelos. Then there is Arsinoë, a city and a harbor, and after these, Deire, above which lies a hunting area for elephants. Next after Deire is the aromatic-producing region, the first that produces myrrh (which belongs to both the Fish Eaters and the Meat Eaters), and it also produces the *persea* and the Egyptian mulberry. The hunting area for elephants called Lichas lies above it. There are often pools of rain water, and when these dry up the elephants dig wells with their trunks and tusks and discover water. On this coast, as far as Pytholaos [C774] Promontory, are two good-sized lakes, one of which has salt water and is called a sea. The other is sweet and supports both hippopotami and crocodiles, and has papyrus around its edges. The ibis is also seen around this place. Those near to Cape Pytholaos have their bodies complete.

Next there is the frankincense-bearing territory, and here there is a promontory and a sanctuary with poplars. In the interior is what is called the riverine territory of Isis, and another which is that of the Nile, both of which produce myrrh and frankincense along them. There is also a cistern filled with water from the mountains, and afterward the Lookout of Leon and Pythangelos Harbor. The following region also has false cassia. There are a number of riverine districts in succession that have frankincense along the rivers, as far as the Cinnamon-Bearer territory. The river that borders them produces a very great number of flowering plants. Then there is another river, Daphnous Harbor, and the so-called riverine district of Apollo, which produces myrrh and cinnamon (more common in places deep in the interior), in addition to frankincense. Then there is Mount Elephas, which projects into the sea, a trench, and next the large Drying Harbor, the so-called Watering Place of the Dog-Headed People, and then the last promontory on this coast, the Horn of the South. After rounding it toward the south, he[3] says that there is no longer any record of harbors or places, because no more is known about the successive coast.

(15) There are also the pillars and altars of Pytholaos, Lichas, Pythangelos, Leon, and Charimortos on the known coast from Deire to the Horn of the South, but the distance is unknown. The territory is abundant in elephants and the lions called ants, which have their genitals backward and are golden in color, but are less hairy than the Arabian ones. It also produces fierce leopards and the rhinoceros. The rhinoceros is only slightly smaller than the elephant in size, not in its length to its tail, as Artemidoros [F97] says (although he says that he saw it in Alexandria), but somewhat less in its

---

[3] Probably Artemidoros is meant, but this is by no means certain.

height (according to the one that I saw). Its color does not resemble box-wood, but rather that of the elephant. It is the size of a bull, but its shape is nearest to the wild boar, especially in its front parts, except for its nose, which has a snub horn larger than any bone. This is used as a weapon, just as the wild boar uses its tusks. It also has two calluses that coil around like [C775] serpents located from its lower back to its belly, one on the back of its neck and the other on its loins. I am saying this from the one that I saw, but he explains further that the animal fights especially with the elephant for pasture, putting its front parts underneath and tearing up the belly, unless it is anticipated by the trunk and tusks.

(16) The camelopard occurs in this region, which is not like a leopard. Its variegated color seems more like a fawn, marked with dappled spots, and its hind parts are much lower than its foreparts, so that it seems to be seated on its tail portion, which has the height of an ox. Its forelegs are no shorter than those of camels, and its neck rises high and straight, with its head flying much higher than those of a camel. Because of this lack of symmetry I do not think that the speed of the animal can be as much as Artemidoros [F98] has stated, who says that it cannot be surpassed. It is not a wild animal, but rather domesticated, for it shows no aggressiveness. He says that there are also the sphinx, the dog-head, and the *kebos*, which has the face of a lion but its remaining body is like a panther, and it is the size of a gazelle. There are wild carnivorous bulls, greatly surpassing those among us in size and speed, and reddish in color. The *krokottas* is a mixture of wolf and dog, as he says. But what Metrodoros the Skepsian says in his book *On Customs* [F5] seems to be mythical and is not to be considered. Artemidoros also speaks of serpents thirty *pecheis* in length that overpower elephants and bulls, and this measurement is moderate, for the Indian ones are rather fabulous, as well as those in Libya that are said to have grass growing on them.

(17) The life of the Trogodytes is nomadic, and collectively they are ruled by tyrants. Their women and children are held in common except for those of the tyrants. The penalty for anyone who seduces the wife of a tyrant is a sheep. The women paint their eyes carefully with kohl, and they wear little mussel shells as amulets around their necks. They will make war over pasturage, at first pushing through with their hands and then with stones, and, when a wound is inflicted, with arrows and daggers. The women put an end to this by going into the middle and making entreaties. Their nourish-ment is flesh and bones that are cut up together and wrapped in skins and then baked, or often prepared in many other ways by the cooks (who are [C776] called unclean). Thus they not only eat the flesh, but eat the bones and the skin. They also use the blood mixed with milk. Most of them have as a drink

an infusion of paliurus, but the tyrants have a honey mixture, with the honey pressed out of some flower. It is winter when the Etesians blow, and then the rains fall, but the remaining time is summer. They are continually naked, wear skins, and carry clubs. They are not only mutilated but some are also circumcised, just like the Egyptians. The Megabarian Aithiopians have iron knobs on their clubs, and use javelins and shields of rawhide, but the other Aithiopians have bows and arrows. In regard to burial, some of the Trogodytes bind up the necks of the corpses to the legs with shoots of paliurus, and then immediately with cheerful laughter throw stones until the body is hidden from sight. Then they place a ram's horn on it and go away. They make journeys by night, fastening bells to the male animals, in order to drive away the wild animals with the noise. They also use lights and bows against the wild animals, and for the sake of the herds they lie awake, singing a song near the fire.

(18) After saying these things about the Trogodytes and the neighboring Aithiopians, he [Artemidoros, F99–100] returns to the Arabians, first those who border the Arabian Gulf and are situated opposite the Trogodytes, beginning from Posideion. He says that it lies farther in than the Ailanitic recess, and that contiguous to Posideion there is a well-watered palm grove that is highly honored because everything around it is exceedingly hot, waterless, and without shade. Here the fruitfulness of the palms is wonderful. A man and a woman manage the grove, having been appointed through their ancestry. They wear skins and are nourished from the palms, but they sleep in a hut in the trees because of the number of wild animals.

Next, then, is Seal Island, named for the quantity of the animal that is there. Nearby is a promontory that extends to Petra of the Nabataean Arabians, as they are called, and then to the Palestinian territory, to which the Minaians, Gerrhaians, and all the neighboring peoples carry their loads of aromatics. Then there is another coast, formerly called that of the Maranitians (some of whom were farmers and others Tent Dwellers), but now that of the Garindaians, who destroyed them by treachery. They attacked while the former were celebrating some fifth-year festival and destroyed them, as well as attacking and completely doing away with the rest of them. [C777]

Then there is the Ailanitic Gulf and Nabataea, a populated territory abundant in pasturage. They also live on nearby islands lying offshore. Formerly they were peaceful, but later, using rafts, they would plunder those sailing from Egypt. They paid the penalty for this when a fleet went and sacked them. Next there is a plain abundant in trees and water, full of all kinds of domestic animals including mules and others. There are also many wild camels, deer, and gazelles, as well as numerous lions, leopards, and wolves. There is an island called Dia lying offshore. Then there is a gulf of about 500 stadia, enclosed all around by mountains and with a mouth that is difficult to enter. Living around it are men who hunt the animals that are on the land. Then there are three deserted islands that are full of olive trees, not like ours, but indigenous, called the Aithiopic, whose sap has medicinal powers.

Next there is a stony beach and after that a rough coast that is difficult to sail along, of about 1,000 stadia, lacking in harbors and anchorages. A rough and high mountain extends along it. Then there are foothills that are rocky as far as the sea, especially at the time of the Etesians and the heavy rains, which present a danger beyond help. Next there is a gulf with scattered islands, and continuous with it are three exceedingly high piles of black sand, and afterward Charmothas Harbor, about 100 stadia in circuit, whose entrance is narrow and dangerous to all boats. A river flows into it, and in the middle there is an island that is abundant in trees and is arable. Then there is a rugged coast, and afterward certain gulfs and a region of nomads whose livelihood is from camels. They make war from them, travel on them, and use their milk and flesh for nourishment. A river flowing through the territory brings down gold dust, but they do not know how to work it. They are called the Debans; some are nomads and some are farmers. I am not saying the names of most of the other peoples because they are obscure and because of the absurdity of their pronunciation.

Next there are men who are more civilized, and who live in a temperate land. It is well-watered and abundant in rain. They find gold through [C778] digging, not dust but nuggets of gold that do not require much cleaning. The smallest are the size of a fruit pit, the medium that of a medlar, and the largest that of a nut. They make necklaces from them, perforating them and stringing them on thread, alternating with transparent stones and placing them around their necks and wrists. They sell the gold cheaply to their neighbors, giving it in return for three times the amount of bronze, twice the amount of <iron, and ten times the amount> of silver, because of their inexperience in working it and the scarcity of what they receive back, which is more necessary for the needs of life.

(19) Adjoining them is the exceedingly fertile territory of the Sabaians, a large ethnic group, among whom there are myrrh, frankincense, and cinnamon. There is balsam on the coast, and another kind of exceedingly fragrant herb that swiftly loses its odor. There are also fragrant palms, reeds, and snakes a *spithame* long and red in color that can jump as far as a hare and make an incurable bite. Because of the abundance of fruits, the people are lazy and idle in their lifestyle. Most of the people sleep on the roots of trees that they

have cut out. When they are stupefied by the sweet odors they relieve the torpor through asphalt incense and goats' beard.

The city of the Sabaians, Mariaba, lies on a well-wooded mountain, and it has a king who has the power over judgements and other matters. It is not lawful for him to go out of the palace, otherwise the masses stone him on the spot, according to some oracle. He and those around him live in effeminate luxury. Most of the people are farmers, but some are aromatic merchants, dealing in both the local variety and those from Aithiopia (they sail across the narrows in hide boats). Those near to one another continually receive the goods and deliver them to those after them, as far as Syria and Mesopotamia. They have them in such abundance that they use cinnamon, cassia, and the others instead of sticks and combustible wood. Among the Sabaians there is also *larimnon*, a most fragrant incense. From their trade, they and the Gerrhaians have become the richest of all, and they have a multitude of golden and silver possessions, such as couches, tripods, and bowls, along with drinking cups and expensive houses, whose doors, walls, and roofs are variegated with ivory, gold, and silver and with precious stones set in. This is what he [Artemidoros] says. The rest is in part similar to what Eratosthenes says, and in part set forth by other historians. [C779]

(20) Some say [Artemidoros, F102][4] that the sea is called Erythra ["Red"] from the color that it displays through reflection, whether from the sun when it is at its peak, or from the mountains that have become red from the scorching heat. It is conjectured both ways. Ktesias the Knidian [F66] records a spring that empties into the sea with reddish and ochre water. Agatharchides [F5b], a fellow citizen of his, records from a certain Boxos, of Persian nationality, that a Persian, Erythras, built a raft and was the first to cross over to a certain island, at the time that a herd of horses, pressed as far as the sea by a frenzied lioness, was driven to this island. Seeing that it was beautiful for habitation, he drove the herd back to Persis and sent forth settlers to it and the other islands off the coast, causing the sea to be named after him. Some proclaim that Erythras was the son of Perseus and ruled these places. It is said by some that from the narrows of the Arabian Gulf to the extremity of the Cinnamon-Bearer territory is five thousand stadia, but without being clear whether this is toward the south or west. It is also said that emeralds and beryl are found in the gold mines. There are also fragrant salts in Arapsis, as Poseidonios says. [F238]

---

[4] Although the following has been identified as a fragment of Artemidoros' text, the attribution is not certain.

(21) The first who live in Fortunate Arabia above the Syrians are the Nabataeans and the Sabaians, who often overran them before the Romans appeared, but today they and the Syrians are subject to the Romans. The metropolis of the Nabataeans is called Petra. It is situated in a place that is otherwise flat and level, but is fortified all around by rocks, with the outside being precipitous and sheer, and the inside having abundant springs, both for water usage and gardens. Outside the circuit, most of the territory is deserted, especially toward Judaea. Here also there is the shortest route – three or four days – to Hierikous (five to the Phoinikon). It is always ruled by a king from the royal family, and the king has as administrator one of his companions, someone called the "Brother." It is exceedingly well governed. At any rate, Athenodoros [F5], a scholarly man and companion of mine, who had been among the Petraians, described them with admiration. He said that he found many Romans and many other foreigners spending time there, and he saw that the foreigners often had legal disputes with each other and with the locals, but the locals did not make accusations against each other, and in every way they kept peace with one another.

[C780]

(22) The expedition of the Romans against the Arabians, recently and in our time, of which Aelius Gallus was commander, learned many things about the peculiarities of the territory. Sebastos Caesar sent him to reconnoiter these peoples and places, as well as the Aithiopians, seeing that Trogodytike, which is contiguous with Egypt, is neighboring to them, and the Arabian Gulf that separates them from the Trogodytes is exceedingly narrow. Thus he had in mind developing a relationship with them, or subjecting them. Moreover, it had been heard for all time that they were exceedingly wealthy, disposing of aromatics and the most expensive stones for gold and silver, and they never spent on outsiders what they received. He hoped to have dealings with wealthy friends or subdue wealthy enemies. The hope of assistance from the Nabataeans encouraged him, as they were friends and promised to cooperate in every way.

(23) With these considerations, Gallus set forth on the expedition, but the Nabataean administrator, Syllaios, who was to provide guidance on the route, supplies, and cooperation, deceived him and acted treacherously in every way. He did not indicate either a safe coastal or land route, but inflicted on him circuitous routes without roads and through places lacking in everything, with rocky shores, or full of undersea rocks and covered with shoals. In such places the flood tides, as well as the ebb tides, particularly caused distress.

The first error was to build large ships, since there was no naval war, for the Arabians are not very good warriors even on land – much less on the sea – as they are rather hucksters and merchants. But he built no fewer than 80 two-banked galleys, triremes, and *phaseloi* at Kleopatris, which is near the old canal from the Nile. When he realized that he had been completely deceived, he built 130 transport vessels, on which he sailed with about a myriad of infantry, Romans in Egypt as well as allies, including 500 Judaeans and 1,000 Nabataeans under Syllaios.

After many difficulties and much suffering, in fifteen days he came to White Village in the Nabataean land, a large emporium. He had lost many ships (some with their men), not due to an enemy but because of difficult sailing. This was caused by the malevolence of Syllaios, who said that it was impossible for an expedition to go to White Village by foot, and yet [C781] the camel expeditions travel safely and easily to there from Petra, and from Petra to there, with so many men and camels that it is no different from an army.

(24) This occurred because their king, Obodas [II or III] did not pay attention to public affairs, especially those concerning the military (this is common to all the Arabian kings) and put everything under the administration of Syllaios, who acted treacherously in every way as a commander. He was seeking, as I think, to reconnoiter the territory himself and to eliminate some of its cities and peoples – with Roman help – and then to establish himself as master of everything, as they would disappear through hunger, exertion, disease, and whatever other suffering he contrived.

He [Gallus] landed at White Village, with his army sorely tried and with gum disease and lameness, which are native ailments, a kind of paralysis, the former of the mouth and the latter around the legs, both resulting from the water and the plants. He was forced to spend the summer and winter there for them to recover their strength. Goods used to be carried from White Village to Petra, then to Rhinokoloura (which is in Phoenicia near Egypt), and then to elsewhere. Today, for the most part, they go by the Nile to Alexandria, landing from Arabia and Indike at Mussel Anchorage, and then are carried by camels over to Koptos in the Thebaid, located on a canal of the Nile, and then to Alexandria.

Gallus, then, moved his headquarters and army from White Village and proceeded through regions of such a kind that water had to be carried by camels, because of the incapacity of those guiding him on the route. Thus it took many days to come to the land of Aretas, a kinsman of Obodas [II or III]. Aretas received him in a friendly manner and offered him gifts, but the treachery of Syllaios made it difficult to travel through the territory. At any rate it took thirty days to go through it, because it was without roads, and had only zea, a few palm trees, and butter instead of oil.

Next he went through a region of nomads, most truly a desert, called Ararene. Its king was Sabos. He spent fifty days passing through it, as it was without roads, going as far as the city of the Agranians and a territory that was peaceful and prosperous. Their king had fled and the city was taken on the first attack. Six days from there, he came to a river where the barbarians joined in battle with the Romans and about ten thousand of them fell [C782] but only two Romans. They used their weapons in an inexperienced way and were completely unwarlike, using bows, javelins, swords, and slings, although most of them used a double ax. Immediately he took their city, called Aska, which had been abandoned by its king.

From there he came to the city of Athroula and mastered it without a struggle. He placed a garrison in it and made preparations . . . of grain and dates, advancing to the city of Marsiaba, among the Rhammanitian peoples, who were subject to Ilasaros. He attacked and besieged it for six days, but desisted through lack of water. He was only two days' journey away from the aromatic producers – as he heard from his captives – but he had wasted six months on his journey because of bad leadership. He realized this when he turned back, and thus learned of the treachery, as he returned on other routes. On the ninth day he came to Anagrana, where the battle had occurred, and on the eleventh to the Seven Cisterns, so called from its situation. Then he went through peaceful territory and arrived at the village of Chaalla and again another, Malotha, which is situated near a river. Then the route was through deserted territory that has few waterholes, as far as the village of Egra, which belonged to Obodas [II or III] and lies on the sea. He accomplished the return journey in sixty days, but he had consumed six months on the beginning of the journey.

Then he crossed the army over to Mussel Anchorage, within eleven days, and then went over to Koptos with those who were able to do so, and came down to Alexandria. He had lost the rest not to enemies, but through disease, exertion, hunger, and the difficulty of the routes, for it happened that only seven were killed in war. For these reasons, the expedition did not gain a great amount of knowledge about these places, yet it made a small contribution. But Syllaios, who was the reason for this, paid with justice at Rome, as he had pretended friendship yet was convicted of this and other crimes and beheaded.

(25) They divide the aromatic-producing region into four parts, as we have said [16.4.2], and in regard to the aromatics, they say that frankincense and myrrh are produced from trees, and cassia from the marshes. According to some, most of the latter is from the Indians, and the best frankincense is from Persis. According to another division, all of Fortunate [Arabia] is split

into five kingdoms, one of which is the warriors, who fight for everyone, then the farmers, who provide food to the others, then the technical artisans, then the myrrh-producing territory and the frankincense-producing territory, [C783] although some regions produce cassia, cinnamon, and nard. The occupations are not changed from one to another, but each remains within that of their fathers.

Most of their wine is from the palm. Brothers are honored more than children. The descendants [of the royal family] not only rule as kings according to seniority but also hold other offices. Property is held in common by all kinsmen, but the oldest is master. There is one woman for all, and the one who goes in first has intercourse, placing his staff before the door (for by custom each man must carry a staff), but she spends the night with the eldest. Thus all are brothers of all. They also have intercourse with their mothers, and the penalty for an adulterer is death. An adulterer is merely someone from another family. A daughter of one of the kings was admired for her beauty, and had fifteen brothers, who were all in love with her, and thus went to her unceasingly, one after the other, so that she became distressed and made use of the following plan: she made staffs like theirs, and whenever one left her, she would always put one like his outside the door, and a little later another, and then another, assuming that whoever came next would not have a similar one. Once when all of them were in the agora, one went to her door, and seeing the staff, presumed that someone was there. Because he had left all his brothers in the agora, he suspected that it was an adulterer. He ran to their father and brought him there, but was proved to have accused his sister falsely.

(26) The Nabataeans are prudent and acquisitive, so much so that they penalize anyone who has diminished his possessions and honor someone who has increased them. They have few slaves, and are served mostly by their own kind, by each other, or serve themselves. This custom even extends to the kings. They make common meals for thirteen people, with two singers for each banquet. The king holds many symposia in a great fashion, but no one drinks more than eleven cups, each time drinking from a different golden one. The king is so egalitarian that, in addition to serving himself, he serves others. He often gives a public account of himself to the people, and may be examined about his lifestyle. Their homes are expensive, because of the use of stone, yet the cities are not walled because of peace. Most of it is fertile, except for the olive, as they use sesame oil. The sheep [C784] have white fleeces and the oxen are large. The territory produces no horses, as camels provide services instead. They go out without chitons, but with girdles around them and slippers, even the kings, who are clad in purple. Some things are totally imported, but others not in entirety, especially what

is indigenous, such as gold, silver, and many aromatics, but copper, iron, purple clothing, styrax, saffron, *kostaria*, embossed work, and molded work are not native. They regard dung equally with dead bodies – as Herakleitos [F116] says, "the dead are more to be cast out than dung," – and thus they bury even their kings in dung heaps. They worship the sun, and construct an altar in their houses, pouring libations to it each day and burning frankincense.

(27) When the Poet says "I came to the Aithiopians, Sidonians, and Erembians" [*Odyssey* 4.84], they are at a loss whether one should speak of the Sidonians as certain inhabitants on the Persian Gulf (from whom the Sidonians near us were settlers), just as they record certain island-dwelling Tyrians there, and Aradians (saying that those among us were settlers), or whether they are the Sidonians themselves. The inquiry about the Erembians is more serious, for one must suspect either that the Troglodytes are meant, as do those who force the etymology from *eram embainei* – that is, "to go into the earth" – or that they are the Arabians. Our Zenon [F275] changed it to: "and to the Sidonians and Arabians." Poseidonios [F281a], more plausibly, writes – with only a small change – "to the Sidonians and Arambians," as though the Poet called the present Arabians thus, the same as they were named by others in his time. He [Poseidonios] also says that there were three tribes situated adjacent to each another that show a homogeneity with each another because they are called by similar names: the Armenians, Aramaians, and Arambians. Just as one can accept that they were divided into three tribes, according to the differences in latitude, which always vary, thus they used a number of names instead of one. Those who write "Eremnians" are not believable, for that is more peculiarily Aithiopian. The Poet also speaks of the Arimians [*Iliad* 2.783], which, as Poseidonios says, must be accepted not as in some place in Syria or Kilikia or elsewhere, but Syria itself, for those there are Aramaians, although perhaps the Hellenes called them Arimaians or Arimians. The changes in names, especially among the barbarians, are many, just as Dariekes is called Dareios, Pharziris Parysatis, and Athara Atargatis, yet Ktesias [F1d] calls her Derketo.

One might even make Alexander a witness to the fortunateness of Arabia, since he intended, as they say, to make it his royal seat after his return from the Indians. All his plans were dissolved after the sudden end of his life, but this was one of his plans. Either they would accept him willingly, or if not, he would go to war. When he saw – either earlier or later – that they had not sent ambassadors to him, he prepared for war, as we have said previously [16.1.11].

[C785]

BOOK 17

Egypt, Libya, and conclusion

Part 1: Egypt and the Upper Nile

(1) In making the rounds of Arabia, I have included the gulfs that tighten it up and make it a peninsula – the Persian and Arabian – and at the same time I have gone around parts of Egypt and Aithiopia, that of the Trogodytes and those beyond them as far as the Cinnamon-Bearer territory. The remainder that touches these peoples must be set forth, the regions around the Nile. Afterward I will go across Libya, which is the last topic of the entire *Geographia*. The assertions of Eratosthenes [F98] must also be expounded.

(2) He says that the Nile is 900 or 1,000 stadia west of the Arabian Gulf, and is similar to the shape of a backward letter nu, for, he says, after flowing from Meroë toward the north for about 2,700 stadia, it turns back toward the south and the winter sunset for about 3,700 stadia, and after coming almost opposite the location of Meroë and projecting far into Libya, it makes the second turn and is carried 5,300 stadia north to the great cataract, turning aside slightly toward the east, then 1,200 to the smaller one at Syene, and then 5,300 more to the sea. There are two rivers that empty into it, which come from certain lakes to the east and encircle Meroë, a good-sized island. One of these is called the Astaboras, flowing on the eastern side, and the other the Astapous (although some call it the Astasobas, saying that another is the Astapous), flowing from certain lakes to the south, and this one makes almost the entire straight body of the Nile, created by being filled with summer rains. Seven hundred stadia above the confluence of the Astaboras and the Nile is Meroë, a city with the same name as the island. There is another island above Meroë which is held by the Egyptian fugitives who revolted at the time of Psammetichos [II], called the Sembritians, which means "foreigners." They are ruled by a woman but are subject to those in Meroë. In the lower districts on either side of Meroë, along the Nile toward the Erythra, live the Megabarians and Blemmyans, subject to the Aithiopians and bordering the Egyptians. Along the sea are the Trogodytes.

[C786]

The Trogodytes opposite Meroë lie ten or twelve days' journey from the Nile. On the left side of the course of the Nile in Libya live the Nubians, a large group of people who begin at Meroë and extend as far as the bends, not subject to the Aithiopians but divided into a number of separate kingdoms. The extent of Egypt along the sea from the Pelousiac to the Kanobic mouth is 1,300 stadia. Eratosthenes has these things.

(3) It is necessary to speak at greater length, first about what is around Egypt, so that we proceed from that which is better known to those next. The Nile provides certain common things for this territory – both what is continuous with it and what is above it (most of the Aithiopians) – for it waters them at the time of the rising, and only leaves the parts that have been covered in the flooding habitable. It merely passes through all the higher parts that lie above its flow, which are uninhabitable and desert on [C787] both sides because of the lack of water. But the Nile does not pass through all of Aithiopia, neither alone, in a straight line, or through that which is well inhabited, but it alone [passes through] Egypt, through all of it and in a straight line, beginning from the little cataract above Syene and Elephantine – which is the boundary of Egypt and Aithiopia – to its outlets at the sea. In fact, the Aithiopians generally live a nomadic and difficult life because of the poverty of the land and the unharmonious climate, and their remoteness from us. In regard to the Egyptians, everything is the opposite, for from the beginning they have lived a civilized and cultivated life, and have been settled in known places, so that their organization is remembered. They are believed to have used the prosperity of their territory commendably and worthily, having divided it well and paid care to it.

When they had appointed a king, the people were divided into three groups, calling one the soldiers, another the farmers, and another the priests. The last cared for sacred matters and the others for human ones, some in matters of war and others in peace, both working the earth and having trades, from which income was collected for the king. The priests practiced philosophy and astronomy, and were associates of the king. The territory was divided first into nomes, with ten in the Thebais, ten in the Delta, and sixteen in between (some have the total of nomes the same as the halls in the Labyrinth, but these are fewer than thirty). The nomes were cut up again, most of them divided into toparchies, and these cut up into others, with the smallest portion the *arourai*. This accurate and refined division was necessary because of the continual confusion of the boundaries caused by the Nile at the time of the increases, since it takes away and adds, and changes the forms, hiding the signs that distinguish one's own from that of another. Thus it is necessary to remeasure again and again. Here, they say, geometry was devised, just as accounting and arithmetic was by the Phoenicians because of their trade. Like the entirety of the population, each nome was divided into three, as the territory itself was in three parts.

The preoccupation with the river is carried so far as to conquer nature through careful attention. By nature it produces more fruits, even more when watered, and naturally more land is watered by a greater rise of the [C788] river. Attention has often made it possible (when nature has failed at the time of the smaller rises) to water as much land as at the time of the greater ones by means of canals and embankments. At any rate, during the time before Petronius, the crop and the rise were the largest when the Nile rose fourteen *pecheis*. When it was only eight, there would be hunger, but during his rule over the country, when the Nilometer was only filled to twelve *pecheis* the crop was the largest, and once when it was only filled to eight, no one experienced hunger.

(4) Such is its organization. We will now speak of what is next. The Nile flows from the Aithiopian boundary straight toward the north as far as the region called the Delta, and then it is split at the head, as Plato says [*Timaios* 21e], creating there the head of a triangle with the sides of the triangle being the streams that split in either direction and go down as far as the sea, the one on the right to Pelousion and that on the left to Kanobos and the neighboring Herakleion, as it is called, with its base the coast between Pelousion and the Herakleion. An island has been formed by the sea and both streams of the river, called the Delta because of the similarity of its shape. The territory at the head has been called by the same name because it is the beginning of the previously mentioned figure. The village there is also called Delta.

These are two of the mouths of the Nile – one of which is called the Pelousiac and the other the Kanobic or Herakleotic – but in between there are five other outlets (those that are notable), and several smaller ones. From the first portion there are many parts that break off through the entire island, making many streams and islands, so that it is navigable in its entirety, with canals cut into canals, which are sailed so easily that some use ferries made of ceramics. The entire island has a perimeter of about 3,000 stadia, and they call it, along with the opposite riverine territory of the Delta, the Lower Territory. At the rising of the Nile it is all covered and becomes a lake, except for the inhabited portions, which are situated on natural hills or mounds, containing notable cities and villages, and when seen from a distance are like islands. The water remains for over [C789] forty days in summer and then goes down gradually, just as it rose. In sixty days the plain is completely dry, and the sooner the drying the sooner the ploughing and sowing: it is sooner where the heat is greater.

Those above the Delta are watered in the same manner, except that the river flows straight for 4,000 stadia in a single stream, unless some island intervenes – of which the most notable is that which comprises the Herakleotes Nome – or where there is some turning aside by a canal into a large lake or a region that it can water, as with the watering of the Arsinoites Nome and Lake Moeris, as well as that pouring over the Mareotis. In summation, Egypt is said to be limited to the riverine territory on both sides of the Nile, and is scarcely anywhere a continuous inhabitable region as wide as about 300 stadia, beginning at the boundaries of Aithiopia and extending as far as the head of the Delta. In its length and with its many turns it resembles an unwound bandage. The shape of the riverine area, about which I am speaking, is that of the territory, and is created by the mountains on either side (going down from the places around Syene as far as the Egyptian Sea), for as they extend alongside or are separated from one another, the river is contracted or dispersed, shaping the uninhabitable territory differently. That beyond the mountains is uninhabited for a long distance.

(5) The ancients conjectured, for the most part, but those later perceived through autopsy that the Nile was filled by summer rains, when upper Aithiopia was inundated, especially in its farthest mountains, and when the rains ceased the flooding gradually did also. This was especially clear to those sailing the Arabian Gulf as far as the Cinnamon-Bearer territory, and to those sent out to hunt elephants or on any other business that had provoked the Ptolemaic kings of Egypt to assign men there. They considered such matters, especially the one called [Ptolemaios II] Philadelphos, who was curious, and because of the sickness of his body was always looking for new amusements and pleasures. The ancient kings did not concern themselves at all with such things, although they were sympathetic to learning (both they and the priests, with whom they spent much of their lives). Thus this is worthy of astonishment, as well as that Sesostris went through the entirety of Aithiopia as far as the Cinnamon-Bearer territory, and that memorials of his expedition – pillars and inscriptions – are still visible today. When Kambyses took possession of Egypt he advanced with the Egyptians as far as Meroë, and in fact they say that he gave the name to the island and the city because his sister Meroë died there (some say that it was his wife). It was given the name in honor of the woman.

[C790]

Starting from such things, it is astonishing that they did not have clear information then about the rains, since the priests rather officiously report in the sacred books whatever reveals any extraordinary information and then store it away. They should have investigated – if they did anything at all – what is investigated still today: why the rains fall in summer and not in winter, and why in the southernmost portions but not in the Thebais and the region around Syene. That the rising is from the rains need not have been investigated, nor did this need such witnesses as Poseidonios [F222] mentions. He says Kallisthenes [F12b] states that the reason is the summer rains, something taken from Aristotle [F246], and he from Thrasyalkes the Thasian (one of the ancient natural philosophers), and he from someone else, and he from Homer, who calls the Nile "fallen from Zeus" ("back to the river of Egypt, fallen from Zeus" [*Odyssey* 4.581]).

But I let this go, as it has been discussed by many, of whom it is sufficient to reveal two who produced books about the Nile in our own time, Eudoros [F1] and Ariston the Peripatetic [F1]. Except for the arrangement, everything laid out by either is the same in terms of the mode of expression and technique, but at any rate I was lacking copies with which to compare each copy with the other. Who appropriated from the other could only be discovered by Ammon. Eudoros accused Ariston, but the style is more like that of Ariston.

Those in antiquity called "Egypt" only that which was inhabited and watered by the Nile, beginning from around Syene, and extending as far as the sea. Those later – down to the present – have added onto the eastern portion approximately everything between the Arabian Gulf and the Nile (the Aithiopians do not make use of the Erythran Sea at all), onto the western that as far as the oases, and onto the coast that from the Kanobic [C791] Mouth as far as the Descent and the dominion of the Kyrenaians. The kings after Ptolemaios [I] became so powerful that they gained possession of the Kyrenaia and assigned Cyprus to Egypt. The Romans, their successors, separated these into provinces and restored Egypt to its own boundaries. The Egyptians call "oases" the inhabited regions surrounded by large deserts, like islands in the open sea. There are many of them in Libya, three of which are near Egypt and are classified with it. This, then, is what we have to say in general, and primarily, about Egypt, and now we will go through each part and its virtues.

(6) Since Alexandria and what is around it are the largest and most important part of this topic, one must begin there. The coast from Pelousion, as one sails toward the west as far as the Kanobic Mouth, is about 1,300 stadia (which is the base of the Delta, as we have said [17.1.4]). From there to the island of Pharos is another 150 stadia. Pharos is an oblong islet, against the mainland, making a harbor with two mouths. The shore is in the form of a bay, putting forward two promontories into the open sea, and the island is situated between them and closes the bay, for its length is parallel to it. The

eastern promontory of Pharos is more toward the mainland and its promontory (called Lochias Promontory), and thus makes a small mouth. In addition to the narrowness of the passage in between, there are also rocks, some under water and others projecting from it, which at all hours make the waves that strike them from the open sea rough. The extremity of the islet is also rock, washed all around, and there is a tower on it marvellously constructed of white stone, with many stories and named after the island. Sostratos the Knidian, a friend of the kings, dedicated it for the safety of sailors, as the inscription says. The coast was without a harbor and was low on either side, having hogbacks and shallows, so those sailing in from the open sea needed a high and clear sign

that they were on course for the entrance of the harbor. The western mouth is not easy to enter, but it does not need as much forethought. It forms a second harbor, called Eunostos, which lies in front of the man-made enclosed harbor. The one that is entered from the previously mentioned Pharos tower is the Great Harbor, and the others are beside it, continuous in their depth and separated from it by the mole called the Heptastadion. The mole is a bridge extending from the mainland to the western part of the island, leaving only two passages open to the Eunostos Harbor, which are bridged. It was not only a bridge to the island when it was inhabited, but also an aqueduct. Now the God Caesar laid it waste in his war with the Alexandrians, since they were drawn up with the kings. A few seamen, however, live near the tower. The Great Harbor is beautifully enclosed by the mole and by nature. It is deep near the shore – so that the largest ship can anchor at the steps – and is cut up into a number of harbors.

The earlier Egyptian kings were content with what they had and did not need imports at all, and were suspicious of all those who sailed, especially the Hellenes (since due to a scarcity of land they destroyed and desired that belonging to others). They put a guard over this place which was ordered to drive away those entering. They were given as a residence what was called Rhakotis, which today is the portion of the city of the Alexandrians that lies above the shipsheds, but was a village then. They gave what was around the village to herdsmen, who were also able to prevent the approach of outsiders. Alexander came there and saw its appropriateness, and decided to fortify the city on the harbor. They record as a sign of the good fortune that later attended the city what occurred at the time of the outlining of the foundations: when the architects were marking out the lines of the enclosure with white earth, the earth ran short. When the king arrived, the administrators provided a portion of the barley that had been prepared for the workmen, by means of which the streets were laid out, even more in number. They said that this occurrence was a good omen.

(7) The advantages of its situation are various. The region is washed by seas on both sides: on the north by the so-called Egyptian, and on the south by Lake Mareia, also called the Mareotis. The Nile fills it through many canals, from above and on the sides, and through them much more is imported than from the sea, so that the lake harbor was richer than the one on the sea. What is exported from Alexandria here is greater than what is imported. One can perceive (either at Alexandria or Dikaiarcheia), when seeing the merchant vessels at their arrival or departure, how much heavier or lighter they are as they sail to or from here. In addition to the wealth of what is brought down from both – into the sea harbor and the lake one – the freshness of the air is worthy of note. This happens because it is washed on both sides, as well as the advantages of the rising of the Nile. In other cities situated on lakes, the air is heavy and stifling in the heat of the summer because the lakes become marshy on their edges due to the rising vapors caused by the sun. Thus when so much filthy moisture rises up, the air that one inhales is unhealthy and causes pestilential diseases. But at Alexandria, in the beginning of summer, the Nile is full and fills the lake, leaving nothing marshy to corrupt what rises up. Also, at that time the Etesian winds blow from the north and from an extensive sea, so that the Alexandrians pass the summer most pleasantly.

[C793]

(8) The shape of the plan of the city is like a chlamys. The long sides are those washed by the water – having a diameter of about 30 stadia – and the short ones are the isthmuses, each of 7 or 8 stadia, that are pressed together by the sea on one [side] and the lake on the other. As a whole, it is cut up by streets that are suitable for riding horses and driving chariots. Two of them are exceedingly wide – spread out more than a *plethron* – which cut each other into two at right angles. The city has the most beautiful precincts and royal palaces, which are a fourth or third part of the entire circuit. Each of the kings, from a love of splendor, made some adornment to the public monuments, and would also expand his own residence in addition to what already existed, so that today (with the Poet), "there is another on another" [*Odyssey* 17.266]. Everything is connected with one another, the harbor, or what is outside it. The Mouseion is part of the palaces, with a walkway, an exedra, and a large structure in which there is the common mess of the scholarly men who share the Mouseion. This assembly has both common property and a priest for the Mouseion, once appointed by the kings but now by Caesar.

[C794]

The so-called Sema is a part of the palaces, which is the enclosure where the tombs of the kings are, as well as that of Alexander. Ptolemaios [I], the son of Lagos, forestalled Perdikkas in taking the body when it was being brought down from Babylon, and turned it away through his presumptiousness and appropriation of Egypt to himself. The latter was destroyed, killed by his soldiers when Ptolemaios [I] attacked him and blockaded him on a deserted island. He died, having been impaled by *sarissas* when the soldiers attacked him. Those with him . . .and the kings, as well as Aridaios, the children of Alexander, and his wife Rhoxane, went away to Makedonia. Ptolemaios [I] took the body of Alexander and buried it in Alexandria, where it still lies today, although not in the same sarcophagus but one of glass (the former was of gold). The Ptolemaios [XII] called Kokkes and Pareisaktos stripped it. He had come over from Syria but was immediately expelled so that the plunder was unprofitable for him.

(9) In the Great Harbor, at its entrance and on the right, are the island and tower of Pharos, and on the other hand the hogbacks and the Lochias Promontory, with a palace on it. As one sails in, on the left are the inner palaces, continuous with those on Lochias, having numerous many-colored buildings as well as groves. Lying below them is an excavated harbor that is enclosed – a private one for the kings – and also Antirrhodos, an islet lying off the excavated harbor that has a palace and a small harbor. It was called this as if a rival to Rhodes. The theater lies above it, and then the Posideion, which is a sort of elbow projecting from the so-called Emporion and which has a sanctuary of Poseidon. Antonius added a mole to it that projected still farther into the middle of the harbor, and constructed a royal dwelling on it called the Timoneion. This was the last thing that he did, when, abandoned by his friends, he came to Alexandria after the failure at Aktion, deciding to live his remaining life at the Timoneion, planning to spend it without his friends. Then there is the Kaisareion, the Emporion, and the warehouses, and afterward the shipsheds, as far as the Heptastadion. This is it for that around the Great Harbor.

[C795]

(10) The Harbor of Eunostos is after the Heptastadion, and the excavated one is above it, which is called Kibotos and also has shipsheds. Farther in there is a navigable canal, extending as far as Lake Mareotis. Outside the canal only a small part of the city is left, and then there is the suburb of Nekropolis, where there are many gardens, graves, and structures suitable for the embalming of the dead. Inside the canal are the Sarapeion and other ancient precincts, now abandoned because of the new constructions at Nikopolis – such as an amphitheater and a stadium where quinquennial games are celebrated – but its ancient ones are neglected.

In short, the city is full of dedications and sanctuaries, but the most beautiful is the Gymnasium, whose stoas are longer than a stadion. In the middle are the lawcourts and groves. There is also the Paneion, a man-made height in the shape of a pine cone, similar to a rocky hill, ascended by a spiral. From its summit one can look over the entire city, which lies below on all sides.

From Nekropolis the length of the broad street extends past the Gymnasium as far as the Kanobic Gate, and then there is the so-called Hippodrome, and those [streets] that lie parallel as far as the Kanobic Canal. After the Hippodrome one comes to Nikopolis, a settlement on the sea, no smaller than a city. It is 30 stadia from Alexandria. Sebastos Caesar honored this place because here he conquered in battle those who had come out with Antonius against him. When he had taken the city in his attack, he forced Antonius to kill himself and Kleopatra [VII] to come into his power alive. A little later she killed herself secretly while imprisoned, through the bite of an asp or a poisonous ointment – it is said both ways – and the rule of the Lagids, which had survived for many years, was dissolved.

(11) For Ptolemaios [I] the son of Lagos had succeeded Alexander, and then there was [Ptolemaios II] Philadelphos and [Ptolemaios III] Euergetes, then [Ptolemaios IV] Philopator the son of Agathokleia, and then [Ptolemaios V] Epiphanes, and then [Ptolemaios VI] Philometor, a son always succeeding a father. But he was succeeded by a brother, the second Euergetes [Ptolemaios VIII] – who was also called Physkon – and he by [Ptolemaios IX] Lathouros, and he in our time by [Ptolemaios XII] Auletes, who was the father of Kleopatra [VII]. All those after the third Ptolemaios were corrupted by luxury [C796] and governed badly, but the worst were the fourth, seventh, and the last, Auletes ["Flute Player"], who, apart from his general licentiousness, practiced accompanying choruses on the flute, and because of this exalted himself so much that he did not hesitate to celebrate contests in the palaces, at which he would come forward himself to contend with the participants. He was expelled by the Alexandrians, and since he had three daughters, of which only one, the eldest, was legitimate, she was proclaimed queen. His two sons were infants and at that time were completely excluded from providing any services. When she had been established, they sent a salted-fish dealer from Syria for her, who pretended that he was from the family of the Syrian kings. The queen had him strangled in a few days, unable to bear his vulgarity and rudeness. In place of him there came someone who had pretended to be the son of Mithridates [VI] Eupator, a certain Archelaos, who was in fact the son of the Archelaos who had carried on a war against Sulla and was afterward honored by Pompeius and was the grandfather of the one who later, in our time, ruled Kappadokia and was the priest of Komana in Pontos. At that time he [the son] had been spending time with Gabinius, hoping to join his expedition against the Parthyaians, but unknown to him was brought by certain people to the queen and proclaimed king.

At this time Pompeius Magnus had received [Ptolemaios XII] Auletes, who had arrived in Rome, introduced him to the Senate, and effected his restoration and also the destruction of most of the ambassadors – a hundred in number – who had made an embassy against him, including Dion the Academic, who had been chief ambassador. Ptolemaios [XII], restored by Gabinius, killed both Archelaos and his own daughter. But before he had added much time to his reign, he died of disease, leaving two sons and two daughters, of which the eldest was Kleopatra [VII]. The Alexandrians proclaimed the elder of the boys and Kleopatra as monarchs, but the associates of the boy revolted and banished Kleopatra, and she went with her sister to Syria. At this time Pompeius Magnus came to Pelousion and Mount Kasion, in flight from Old Pharsalos. He was treacherously killed by those around the king. When Caesar came he killed the boy, and summoned Kleopatra from exile and made her queen of Egypt, and proclaimed her

[C797] remaining brother ruler with her, although he was exceedingly young. After the death of Caesar and the matter of Philippoi, Antonius crossed to Asia and honored Kleopatra so greatly that he chose her for his wife and had children by her. He took part in the Aktaian battle with her and fled with her, and afterward Sebastos Caesar followed them and destroyed both of them, bringing the drunken violence of Egypt to an end.

(12) Today it is a province, paying a notable tribute and being administered by prudent men, the prefects who are always sent there. The one who is sent has the rank of the king, and under him is a judicial legate, who is the master over most of the lawsuits. Another is the one called the controller, who examines that which is without an owner and is due to fall to Caesar. Freedmen and household managers of Caesar attend them, and they are entrusted with greater or lesser matters. There are also three legions of soldiers, one stationed in the city and the others in the country. Apart from this there are nine Roman cohorts: three in the city, three on the borders of Aithiopia at Syene – as a guard for the region – and three elsewhere in the territory. There are also three cavalry squadrons, which are stationed at various critical places. Of the indigenous officials in the city, there is the interpreter (who is dressed in purple and has hereditary honors and cares for the needs of the city), the recorder, and the chief judge. The fourth is the night commander.

These officials existed in the time of the kings, but the kings were running the government badly and the prosperity of the city was vanishing through lawlessness. At any rate Polybios, who was in the city, loathed the conditions at that time and said [34.14] that three groups lived in the city: the Egyptian or indigenous tribe – who were sharp and litigious – and the mercenaries (because by an ancient custom they maintained foreign men at arms, taught by the worthlessness of the kings to rule rather than be ruled), who were violent, numerous, and dissolute. Third was the race of the Alexandrians who were not favorable toward politics, for the same reasons, although they were better. Even though they were mixed, they were Hellenes by origin and remembered the common Hellenic customs. But after this mass had been removed, largely by [Ptolemaios VIII] Euergetes Physkon (in whose time Polybios went to Alexandria) – for Physkon a number of times ran down   [C798] the masses with soldiers sent against them and destroyed them – he says the city was in such a state that there only remained what the Poet has, "to go to Egypt, a long and painful journey" [*Odyssey* 4.483].

(13) It was in such a way, if not worse, under the later kings. But the Romans have corrected most things to the best of their ability and organized the city, as I have said, having appointed those called *epistrategoi*, nomarchs, and ethnarchs throughout the region, who were considered worthy of administering matters that were not of major importance.

The greatest advantage of the city is that it is the only place in all of Egypt naturally good in both ways: that from the sea (through the good harbor) and that from the country, because the river easily carries everything that comes together into this region, the greatest emporium in the inhabited world.

One might say that these are the virtues of the city. Cicero points out the revenues of Egypt, saying in some speech [*De rege Alexandrino*, T3] that a tribute of 12,500 talents was paid annually to [Ptolemaios XII] Auletes the father of Kleopatra [VII]. If someone who administered the kingdom so badly and carelessly had such an income, what must one think that it would be today, when it is managed so carefully and when trade with the Indians and Trogodytes has increased so much? Formerly no more than twenty ships dared to pass through the Arabian Gulf in order to have a view outside the narrows, but today large fleets are sent as far as Indike and the Aithiopian extremities. From these places the most valuable cargo is brought to Egypt and then sent out again to other places, so that double duties are collected, on both imports and exports, and things that are expensive have a heavy duty. There are also monopolies, for Alexandria is not only the receptacle for such things, for the most part, but also the supplier for those outside it

Moreover, one can better observe these natural qualities through travelling around the region, beginning first with the coast from the Descent (for it is Egypt this far). Next are the Kyrenaia and the neighboring barbarians, the Marmaridians.

(14) From the Descent to Paraitonion, sailing straight, is a run of 900 stadia.
[C799] It is a city and a large harbor (of about 40 stadia). Some call it Paraitonion,
others Ammonia. In between is the Egyptian Village, the Ainesisphyra
Promontory, and the Tyndareian Rocks, which are four islets with a harbor.
Next are the Drepanon Promontory and Ainesippeia, an island with a harbor,
and the village of Apis, from which it is 100 stadia to Paraitonion and a
journey of five days to Ammon.

From Paraitonion to Alexandria is about 1,300 stadia. In between there
is first a promontory of white earth called White Cape, and then there is
Phoinikous Harbor and the village of Pnigeus. Then there is Sidonia, an
island that has a harbor, and then Antiphrai, a little above the sea. The entire
region is without good wine, since the vessels receive more sea than wine,
which they call "Libyan," and which, along with beer, is what the entire
tribe of Alexandrians uses. Antiphrai is ridiculed the most. Then there is
Derrhis Harbor, called because of the black rock nearby that resembles a
curtain [derrhis]. The neighboring place is also called Zephyrion. Then
there is another harbor, White Shield, and then the Dog Monument. Then
there is Taposeiris, which is not on the sea and which holds a large festival
(there is another Taposeiris far on the other side of the city), and nearby there
is a rocky place on the sea where many celebrate a banquet on the shore at all
seasons of the year. Then there are Plinthine, the village of Nikias, and the
fortress of Chersonesos, which is already near to Alexandria and Nekropolis
(70 stadia). Lake Mareia extends this far and has a width of over 150 stadia
and a length of less than 300. It has eight islands and is well inhabited all
around. The wine from these places is so good that the Mareotic wine is
poured off in order to age it.

(15) Papyrus grows in the Alexandrian marshes and lakes, as well as the
Egyptian bean, from which the *kiborion* comes. Their stalks are almost
equal in height (about ten feet). The papyrus is a bare stalk having foliage on
top, but the bean produces leaves and flowers in many parts and a fruit like
our bean, different only in size and taste. The bean fields present a pleasing
sight and provide pleasure to those wishing to feast lavishly in them. They
[C800] have lavish feasts in *thalamegos* boats, on which they enter the thick bean
fields and take shade under the leaves, which are so extremely large that they
are used both for drinking cups and bowls, as they have a concavity suitable
for this. The workshops of Alexandria are full of them – where they are used
as vessels – and the country people have this (that from the leaves) as one
source of income. Such is the bean. The papyrus does not grow as extensively here – for it is not cultivated – but it is extensive in the lower parts of
the Delta, with one type inferior and the other (the hieratic) better. Here

those who wished to enhance their income used the skill that the Judaeans had devised in regard to the palm (particularly the date and balsam), for they did not allow it to grow in many places, and because of its scarcity they set a price that would increase the income, although this corrupts its common use.

(16) On the right of the Kanobic Gate (as one goes out) is the canal to Kanobos that is connected to the lake. One sails on it to Schedia and to the great river, as well as to Kanobos, although Eleusis is first. It is a settlement near Alexandria and Nikopolis, situated on the Kanobic Canal itself, having lodging and views for those wishing to engage in revelry – both men and women – a beginning of the "Kanobic life" and the wantonness there. At a slight distance away from Eleusis, on the right, is the canal that leads up to Schedia. Schedia is four *schoinoi* distant from Alexandria and is a settlement of the city with the naval station for the *thalamegos* boats that the commanders use to sail up to the Upper Territory. The customs station for things brought down from above and also brought up is there, for which pontoons (*schedia*) bridge the river, and from which the place has its name. After the canal that leads to Schedia, the next voyage is to Kanobos, parallel to the coast from Pharos to the Kanobic Mouth. There is a narrow ribbon that extends between the sea and the canal on which, after Nikopolis, is Little Taposeiris and Zephyrion, a promontory having the shrine of Aphrodite Arsinoë. In antiquity, they say, there was a city of Thonis here, named after the king who received Menelaos and Helen with hospitality. At any rate, the Poet speaks of Helen's drugs as follows: "good ones, which Polydamna, the bedfellow of Thon, gave her" [*Odyssey* 4.228]).   [C801]

(17) Kanobos is a city 120 stadia from Alexandria going by foot, named after Kanobos the pilot of Menelaos, who died there. It has a sanctuary of Sarapis, honored with a great ceremony, which produces such cures that the most distinguished men believe in it and sleep there (themselves and for others). Some record the cures, and others the virtues of the oracles there. In contrast, there is the crowd that goes down from Alexandria to the festivals on the canal, for every day and every night it is full of people on the boats playing the flute and dancing without restraint and with extreme licentiousness – both men and women – often including those in Kanobos itself, who have lodgings situated on the canal suitable for such relaxation and feasting.

(18) After Kanobos is the Herakleion, which has a sanctuary of Herakles. Then there is the Kanobic Mouth and the beginning of the Delta. That on the right of the Kanobic Canal is the Menelaites Nome, from the brother of the first Ptolemaios and not – by Zeus – from the hero, as some, including

Artemidoros [F87], say. After the Kanobic Mouth is the Bolbitine, and then the Sebennytic and the Phatnitic, which is the third in size after the first two that are the boundaries of the Delta. Not far from the head it has a split that goes into the Delta. The Mendesian adjoins the Phatnitic, and then there is the Tanitic and finally the Pelousiac. There are also others in between these, as if insignificant pseudo-mouths. The mouths have entrances, yet are not suitable for large boats but only for service boats, because they are shallow and marshy. It was the Kanobic Mouth that was mostly used for the emporium, since the harbors at Alexandria were closed, as we have previously said [17.1.6].

After the Bolbitine Mouth there is a low and sandy promontory that projects rather far, called Agnoukeras. Then there is the lookout of Perseus and the Milesian Wall. In the time of Psammetichos [I] – this was in the time of Kyaxares the Mede – the Milesians, with thirty ships, put into the Bolbitine Mouth, and then disembarked and fortified the previously mentioned settlement. In time they sailed up to the Saites Nome and defeated the city of Inaros in a naval battle and founded Naukratis, not far above [C802] Schedia. After the Milesian Wall (as one proceeds toward the Sebennytic Mouth) there are two lakes – one of which, the Boutic, is named for the city of Boutos – then the Sebennytic city, and Saïs, the metropolis of the Lower Territory, in which Athena is worshipped. In her sanctuary lies the tomb of Psammetichos [I]. Around Boutos is Hermoupolis, situated on an island, and in Boutos there is an oracle of Leto.

(19) In the interior above the Sebennytic and Phatnitic mouths is Xoïs, both an island and a city in the Sebennytes Nome. Here also are Hermoupolis, Lykonpolis, and Mendes, where they worship Pan, and among animals a goat. As Pindar says, the goats have intercourse with women there:

> Mendes, along the crags of the sea, the farthest horn of the Nile, where the goat-mounting goats have intercourse with women. [F201]

Near Mendes is Diospolis. There are lakes around it, and Leontonpolis, and then, farther up, the city of Bousiris and the Bousirites Nome and Kynonpolis. Eratosthenes [F154] says that banishment of foreigners is common among all barbarians, but the Egyptians are censured for this because of the tales concerning Bousiris. Those later wish to accuse this place of inhospitality, but, by Zeus, there was no king or tyrant named Bousiris. Moreover, this is quoted as a reproach: "To go to Egypt, a long and painful journey" [Odyssey 4.483]. The lack of harbors adds greatly to the problem, and also that one could not enter the single existing harbor, the one at Pharos, because it was guarded by shepherds who were pirates, and who would attack those coming to anchor. The Karchedonians would drown any foreigner who sailed past them to Sardo or the Pillars. Because of this most things about the west are not believed. Moreover, the Persians would deceitfully guide ambassadors over circuitous roads and through difficult places.

(20) Adjoining it are the Athribites Nome, the city of Athribis, and also the Prosopites Nome, in which the city of Aphrodite is. Above the Mendesian Mouth, and the Tanitic, are a large lake and the Mendesios Nome and the Leontopolites, the city of Aphrodite, and the Pharbetites Nome. Then there is the Tanitic Mouth – which some call the Saitic – and the Tanites Nome. In it is Tanis, a large city.

(21) There are lakes between the Tanitic and Pelousiac [Mouths], and large continuous marshes that have many villages. Pelousion also has marshes lying around it – some of which are called "The Pits" – as well as ponds. It is [C803] situated more than 20 stadia from the sea and has a wall of 20 stadia around it. Its name is from the mud [*pelos*] of the ponds. Egypt is also difficult to enter here: from the eastern regions toward Phoenicia and Judaea, and from the Arabia of the Nabataeans which borders it. The road to Egypt is through these places. Arabia is between the Nile and the Arabian Gulf, and Pelousion is situated at its extremity, but it is all desert and impassable for an army. The isthmus between Pelousion and the recess at Hieroonpolis is 1,000 stadia, but Poseidonios [F207] says that it is less than 1,500. In addition to being waterless and sandy it has many sand-burrowing reptiles.

(22) From Schedia as one sails up to Memphis, there are a large number of villages on the right as far as Lake Mareia, among which is the so-called village of Chabrias. On the river is Hermoupolis, then the City of Women, the Gynaikopolites Nome, and next Momemphis and the Momemphites Nome. In between there are a number of canals into the Mareotis. The Momemphitians worship Aphrodite and a sacred cow is tended there, like Apis in Memphis and Mneuis in Helioupolis. They are considered gods but those elsewhere – for there are many both in the Delta and outside of it, where the male or female animal is tended – are not considered gods, merely sacred.

(23) Above Momemphis there are two nitre pits that have a very large amount of nitre, and the Nitriotes Nome. Sarapis is honored here, and they are the only ones in Egypt who sacrifice sheep. Near by is the city of Menelaos and, on the left, in the Delta and on the river, is Naukratis. Saïs is about two *schoinoi* distant from the river, and a little above it is the Asylum of Osiris, in which they say Osiris lies, although many dispute this, particularly the inhabitants of Philai above Syene and Elephantine. There is the mythical tale that Isis placed coffins of Osiris under the earth in

many places, but only one of them held Osiris, unknown to all. She did this because she wished to hide it from Typhon, fearing that he might come upon it and cast the body out of its tomb.

(24) This is the description from Alexandria to the head of the Delta. [C804] Artemidoros [F88] says that the sail up is 28 *schoinoi*, which is 840 stadia, calculating the *schoinos* at 30 stadia. When I made the voyage different measurements were used by different people, in giving the distance in *schoinoi*, so that 40 stadia or even more was agreed upon, according to the places. That the measure of the *schoinos* among the Egyptians is uncertain was made clear by Artemidoros himself in the following: he says that from Memphis to the Thebais each *schoinos* is 120 stadia, and from the Thebais to Syene 60. He also says that sailing up from Pelousion to the head [of the Delta] is 25 *schoinoi*, or 750 stadia using the same measurement.

The first canal (going from Pelousion) is the one that fills the lakes called At the Marshes, which are two and lie on the left of the great river above Pelousion, in Arabia. He also speaks of other lakes and canals in the same portions outside the Delta. There is also the Sethroites Nome by the second lake, which he numbers as one of the ten in the Delta. Two other canals come together in the same lake.

(25) There is another that empties into the Erythra and the Arabian Gulf near the city of Arsinoë, which some call Kleopatris. It flows through the so-called Bitter Lakes, which were formerly bitter, but when the previously mentioned canal was cut they changed because they became mixed with the river, and now they are abundant with fish and also full of lake birds. The canal was first cut by Sesostris before the Trojan matter – although according to some it was the son of Psammetichos – who only began the work and then ceased his life, and later by the first Dareios, who succeeded to the following work. He had been persuaded by a false idea and gave the work up, although it was already near completion. He was persuaded that the Erythran Sea was higher than the Egyptian, and if the isthmus in between were cut through, Egypt would be inundated by the sea. The Ptolemaic kings, however, did cut through it and enclosed the strait, so that when they wished they could sail out unhindered into the sea and back in again. The matter of the level of the waters has already been mentioned in my first treatises [1.3.8–10].

(26) Near Arsinoë are Heroonpolis (in the recess of the Arabian Gulf [C805] toward Egypt) and harbors and settlements, with a number of canals and lakes nearby. Here also is the Phagroriopolites Nome and the city of Phagrorionpolis. The beginning of the canal that empties into the Erythra starts at the village of Phakoussa, which is contiguous to the village of

Philon. The canal is a hundred *pecheis* wide and of a depth sufficient for ships with a capacity of ten thousand.

(27) These places are near to the head of the Delta. There is the city of Boubastos and the Boubastites Nome, and above it is the Heliopolites Nome. Helioupolis is in it, situated on a notable mound and having the sanctuary of Helios and the ox Mneuis, who is tended in a kind of precinct and who is considered by them to be a god, like Apis in Memphis. There are lakes in front of the mound that have the overflow from the neighboring canal. Today the city is completely deserted, but it has the ancient sanctuary constructed in the Egyptian style and which shows the madness and sacrilege of Kambyses, who by fire and sword thoroughly outraged the sanctuary, mutilating and burning it all around, just as [he did] with the obelisks. Two of them were brought to Rome, as they were not completely ruined, but others are still there and in Thebes, today Diospolis. Some are still standing, others have been totally devoured by fire, and still others are lying down.

(28) The arrangement of the construction of the sanctuaries is as follows. At the entrance to the precinct there is a floor paved with stone that is about a *plethron* wide, or less, and with a length three or four times as large, or sometimes more, that is called the dromos, as Kallimachos says ("This is the sacred dromos of Anubis" [F715].). Throughout its entire length there are stone sphinxes situated on either side, in succession, twenty *pecheis* or a little more distant from each other, so that one row of sphinxes is on the right and the other on the left. After the sphinxes there is a large propylon, and then, as one proceeds, another, and then another, but there is no deter- mined number of either propyla or sphinxes, and it is different in different sanctuaries, as are the widths and lengths of the dromoi. After the propylaia there is the temple – which has a large and notable pronaos – and a cella of commensurate size, in which there is no xoanon (or rather none that is anthropomorphic, but only one of some unreasoning animal). What are called wings project on either side of the pronaos, with two walls equal in height to the temple. At first their distance from one another is a little more [C806] than the width of the foundation of the temple, but as one proceeds forward their lines converge for fifty or sixty *pecheis*. These walls have large images in low relief, like the Tyrrhenian ones and the very ancient Hellenic works of art. There is also a structure with many columns – as at Memphis – having a barbarian construction. Except for the fact that the columns are large and numerous, and in many rows, it has nothing pleasing or picturesque, but rather shows labor in vain.

(29) In Helioupolis I saw the large houses in which the priests lived. They say that in antiquity this settlement was especially one of priests who were

men of philosophy and astronomy, but today both this organization and its practices have disappeared. No one was shown to me as an authority on such practices, but only those who performed the sacrifices and explained the sacred matters to strangers. When Aelius Gallus the commander sailed up into Egypt he was accompanied by someone from Alexandria named Chairemon, who pretended to have some such knowledge, but was generally ridiculed as a charlatan and layman. The houses of the priests were pointed out there, as well as the haunts of Plato and Eudoxos. Eudoxos went up there with Plato, and they spent thirteen years with the priests – as is said by some – who were extraordinarily knowledgeable about the heavens, although secretive and reluctant to show it. In time, after being earnestly cultivated, they recounted some of their speculations, but the barbarians kept most things hidden, although going over the portions of the day and the night that exceed the 365 days which fill the time period of the year. The period of a year was unknown then to the Hellenes – as were many other things – until later astronomers obtained it from those who had translated into Hellenic the treatises of the priests. Today they still obtain things from them as well as from the Chaldaians.

(30) Here the Nile is above the Delta. What is on the right, as one sails up, is called Libya – as is that around Alexandria and the Mareotis – and what is on the left, Arabia. Helioupolis is in Arabia, but the city of [C807] Kerkesoura is in Libya, lying near the observatories of Eudoxos. A certain observatory is visible in front of Helioupolis, just like the one in front of Knidos, where he would examine certain movements of the heavens. The Letopolites Nome is here. As one sails up, there is the fortress of Babylon, to which some Babylonians withdrew and then obtained a settlement here from the kings. Today it is the camp of one of the three legions that guard Egypt. There is a ridge reaching from the camp to the Nile, on which water comes up from the river by means of wheels and screws, and a hundred and fifty captive men work it. The pyramids are conspicuously seen from Memphis on the far side, and are nearby.

(31) Memphis itself – the royal residence of the Egyptians – is also nearby, for it is only three *schoinoi* from the Delta. It has sanctuaries, including that of Apis (who is the same as Osiris), where the Apis bull is tended in a kind of precinct, and who is considered a god, as I have said [17.1.22]. His forehead and other small parts of his body are quite white but the rest is black, and from these markings they always choose the one suitable for the succession when the one holding the honor has died. There is a courtyard in front of the precinct, in which there is another precinct for the mother of the bull. They release Apis into the courtyard at a certain hour, especially

so that he can be shown to foreigners, although he can be seen through a window in the precinct. But they also wish him to be seen outside. After he has capered there for a short time he is taken back to his own stall.

Thus the sanctuary of Apis is there – which lies near the Hephaisteion – as is the Hephaisteion itself, an expensive structure in terms of the size of its temple and other things. There is a monolithic colossus lying in front of the dromos, and it is the custom to have bulls fight with one another in this dromos, and certain ones raise them for this purpose, like those who raise horses. They are released and join in battle, and the one considered stronger obtains a prize. There is also a sanctuary of Aphrodite in Memphis, who is considered to be a Hellenic goddess, although some say that it is a sanctuary of Selene.

(32) There is also a Sarapeion, in an exceedingly sandy place where the wind piles up heaps of sand, so that the sphinxes we saw were buried as far as the head, and others were only half visible. From this, one could suppose the danger that would exist if someone walking toward the temple encountered a bad storm. The city is large and populous, second after Alexandria, and with a mixed population, like those who have settled at the latter. There are lakes in front of the city and the palaces, which are destroyed and deserted today. They are situated on a height and extend down to the level of the city below. Adjoining them are a grove and a lake.   [C808]

(33) When one proceeds 40 stadia from the city there is a kind of mountainous brow, and on it are many pyramids – the graves of the kings – three of which are notable. Two of them are numbered among the Seven Wonders. They are a stadion in height, quadrilateral in shape, with their height a little greater than the length of a side. One of them is a little larger than the other. High up, approximately in the middle between the sides, is a removable stone. When it is raised up, there is a twisted passage to the tomb. They are near to one another and on the same level. Farther away, on a greater height of the mountainous ridge, is a third that is smaller than the two, although constructed at much greater expense. From the foundations – almost as far as the middle – it is of black stone (that from which mortars are constructed) which was brought from far away (from the mountains of Aithiopia). Because it is hard and difficult to work, it made the matter exceedingly expensive. It is called the Tomb of the Hetaira, built by her lovers. She was the one whom Sappho [F202] the melic poetess calls Doricha, the beloved of her brother Charaxos, who brought Lesbian wine to Naukratis as merchandise. Others call her Rhodopis. They tell the tale that while she was bathing, an eagle snatched one of her sandals from her maid and carried it to Memphis where the king was administering justice (in the open air),

and when it was over his head it threw the sandal into his lap. He, due to the shapeliness of the sandal and the incredible occurrence, was moved to send throughout the territory seeking the woman who wore it, who was found in the city of Naukratis. She was brought and became the wife of the king, and when she died she received the previously mentioned tomb.

(34) One of the incredible things that I saw at the pyramid cannot be omitted. There are heaps of stone chips lying in front of the pyramids, among which are found shavings that are like lentils in shape and size, and under them are some that are like half-peeled winnowed grain. They say that these are the petrified remains of the food of the workmen, and this is not impossible. At my home there is an oblong hill that is full of lentil-shaped pebbles of *poria* stone. The pebbles from the seas and the rivers present the same difficulty: these can ingeniously be explained by the movement due to the current, but the speculation with the former is more difficult.

[C809]

It has been stated elsewhere that around the quarry which produced the stones for the pyramids (it is in sight of the pyramids, across in Arabia) there is a very rocky mountain called "Trojan." There are caves at its foot, a village near them, and a river called the Troia, an ancient settlement of the Trojan captives who came here with Menelaos and remained.

(35) After Memphis there is the city of Akanthos (also in Libya), the sanctuary of Osiris, and a grove of Theban acanthus, from which gum comes. Then there is the Aphroditopolites Nome, and the homonymous city in Arabia, where a sacred cow was tended. Then there is the Herakleotes Nome, on a large island where (on the right) is the canal into Libya and the Arsinoïtes Nome. Thus the canal has two mouths, with a part of the island intervening. This nome is the most notable of all in regard to its appearance, quality, and condition. It also is planted with olives that are large, with full trees and fine fruit, and if harvested well there is good oil. But they are neglectful of this, and although they make a large quantity of oil, it has a wretched odor. The rest of Egypt is without olives except for the gardens at Alexandria, which are sufficient to furnish olives but do not provide oil.

It produces not a small amount of wine, grain, pulse, and numerous other seeds. It also has the wonderful lake called Moiris, which is the size of an open sea and like a sea in color. Its shores are also seen to resemble those of a sea. One could conjecture the same about this as about the places around Ammon – and they are not exceedingly far from one another, or from Paraitonion – so that, just as one could suppose from much evidence that that sanctuary was formerly situated on the sea, similarly these regions were also formerly on the sea. Lower Egypt and that as far as Lake Sirbonis were once a sea, which happened perhaps to be confluent with the Erythra at Heroonpolis and the Ailanitic Recess.

(36) This has been discussed at great length in the first treatise of the *Geography* (1.3.4, 13). Now it is necessary to make mention of the work of nature and at the same time that of forethought, as they come together into one. That of nature is this: everything converges into the middle of the whole, and creates a sphere around this. The densest and most central is the earth, and what is less so and is next is water. Each is a sphere, the former   [C810] solid and the latter hollow (as the earth is within it). That of forethought – as it is an embroiderer and artisan of a myriad of works – is that it has willed among its first things to create life, as superior to everything else, and among them the strongest (gods and people), because of whom everything else has been contrived. The heavens were assigned to the gods and the earth to people. These are the extremities of the parts of the cosmos, and the extremities of the sphere are the middle and outermost. But since water surrounds the earth and man is not an aquatic animal, but a land one who partakes of air and much light, numerous elevations and hollows have been made on the earth so that all or most of the water is received and hides the earth beneath it, with the earth projecting and hiding the water beneath itself (except for as much as is used by the human race, as well as by the living creatures and the plants around it). Since everything is continually in motion and there are great changes – for it is not otherwise possible for such things of such quantity and size in the universe to be controlled – it must be understood that the earth is not always in such a state that it is always of such a size, adding nothing to itself, or taking anything away, and neither is the water. Neither one remains in the same place because the change of one into the other is most natural and most at hand. Much of the earth changes into water and much of the latter becomes dry land in the same way as the earth, where there are such variations. Some is easily broken, or solid, or rocky, or contains iron, and so forth with the rest. It is the same with liquid substances: one is salty, another sweet and potable, another contains drugs that are either curative or deadly, and another is cold or hot. Why is it astonishing if some parts that are inhabited today were formerly in the sea, and what are now the seas were formerly inhabited, just as springs of former times have given out, and others have come up, and rivers and lakes as well as mountains and plains have changed into each other? But I have previously spoken about this extensively (1.3.4, 12–15), so let what has been said now be sufficient.

(37) Lake Moiris, because of its size and depth, is sufficient to bear the floods of the rising, and not to overflow into the inhabited and planted

regions, and then, with the withdrawal, to return the excess by the same
canal – at each of the mouths – and to retain (both in itself and the canal)
what is useful for irrigation. This is what is natural, yet locks have been
placed at the mouths of both canals by which the superintendents control
the inflow and outflow of the water.

In addition, there is the Labyrinth, a work equal to the pyramids. Lying
nearby is the tomb of the king who built the Labyrinth. Near the first
entrance to the canal, proceeding about 30 or 40 stadia, there is a flat, table-
like place which has a village and a large palatial complex of as many palaces
as there were formerly nomes. There are this many courtyards surrounded
by colonnades that are continuous with one another in a single row and all
along one wall, so that it is a long wall with the courtyards lying in front of it.
The roads to them are exactly opposite to the wall. In front of the entrances
are large and numerous crypts that have winding passages connected with
one another, so that no stranger can go into or out of any courtyard without
a guide. It is astonishing that the roofs of each structure are monolithic, and
the width of the crypts also have monolithic roofs that are flat and excel in
their size. No wood or any other timber is mixed in anywhere. Going up to
the roof – it is no greater than one story in height – one sees a stone plain, of
stones of such a size, and then going back into the courtyard one sees that
they lie one after another, supported by twenty-seven monolithic columns.
The walls are also composed of stones no smaller in size. At the end of this
structure – which comprises more than a stadion – is the tomb, a quadrilateral pyramid whose sides are each about four *plethra* and equal in height.
The name of the one buried there is Imandes. It is said that so many
courtyards were constructed because it was the custom that all the nomes
would assemble there, according to rank, with their own priests and priestesses, in order to sacrifice, to give gifts to the gods, and to administer justice
on the greatest matters. Each of the nomes was brought down to its
appointed court.

(38) After sailing along for a hundred stadia there is the city of Arsinoë,
which was formerly called Crocodile City. In this nome they worship the
crocodile greatly, and there is a sacred one there that is tended by itself in
a lake, and is tame to the priests. It is called Souchos, and is fed on grain,
meat, and wine, which are always being fed to it by the foreigners who go
there to see it. At any rate, our host – one of those honored there – was
guiding us and went with us to the lake carrying from our meal a small cake,
some roasted meat, and a vessel with a honey mixture. We found the animal
lying on the banks, and when the priests went to it, some of them opened its
mouth, and another put in the cake, then the meat, and then poured down

the honey mixture. It leapt down into the lake and went across to the far side. When another foreigner arrived, also with first fruits, they went around at a run, took hold of it, and offered what they carried in the same way.

(39) After the Arsinoites and Herakleotes Nomes is the City of Herakles, where they honor the ichneumon. This is the opposite of the Arsinoitians, who worship the crocodile – because of which both their canal and Lake Moiris are full of them, for they are revered and keep away from them – but the former [honor] the ichneumon, which is most destructive toward the crocodile. They are the same toward the asp, whose eggs they destroy, as well as the animal itself. They cover themselves with an armor of earth, rolling in it and letting it dry in the sun, and then they seize the asps either by the head or tail and take them down to the river and kill them. They also lie in wait for the crocodiles, and when they are sunning themselves with their mouths open, they throw themselves into the gaping mouth and eat through their innards and stomachs and emerge from their dead bodies.

(40) Next is the Kynopolites Nome and the City of Dogs, in which Anubis is honored, and where feeding and a type of ritual has been organized for dogs. On the far side is the city of Oxyrhynchos and the homonymous nome. They worship the oxyrhynchus, and there is a sanctuary of the oxyrhynchus, although other Egyptians in common worship the oxyrhynchus. Certain animals are worshipped by all Egyptians in common, such as three land animals (the bull, dog, and cat), two birds (the hawk and ibis), and two aquatic ones (the scaly fish and the oxyrhynchus). There are others that are worshipped separately by others, such as the sheep by the Saitians and Thebaians, the *latos* (a Nile fish) by the Latopolitans, the wolf by the Lykopolitans, the *kynokephalos* by the Hermopolitans, the *kebos* by the Babylonians around Memphis (the *kebos* has a face like a satyr, but otherwise is between a dog and a bear, and comes from Aithiopia), the eagle by the Thebaians, the lion by the Lentopolitans, the female and male goat by the Mendesians, the field mouse by the Athribitians, and others by others, [C813] but they do not speak in agreement about the reasons.

(41) Next there is the Hermopolitic guard station, a kind of customs house for things brought down from the Thebais. Here is the beginning of the 60-stadia *schoinos*, as far as Syene and Elephantine. Then there are the Thebais guard station and the canal that leads to Tanis, and then Lykonpolis, Aphrodites, and the City of Pan, an old settlement of linen and stone workers.

(42) Then there is the city of Ptolemais, the largest in the Thebais, no smaller than Memphis, and which has a political system in the Hellenic manner. Above it is Abydos, where the Memnoneion is, a marvellous royal

structure constructed completely of stone and with the same building technique that I mentioned about the Labyrinth, although not as complex. There is also a well that lies at a great depth, so that one goes down to it through monolithic curved vaults of outstanding size and workmanship. There is a canal that leads to the place from the great river, and around the canal is a grove of Egyptian acanthus, sacred to Apollo. Abydos seems to have been a great city at one time, second only to Thebes. Today it is a small settlement. If, as they say, Memnon is called Ismandes by the Egyptians, the Labyrinth would also be a Memnoneion and a work of the same person as those in Abydos and the Thebais, for it is said that there are certain Memnoneia there. Beyond Abydos is the first of the three previously mentioned [17.1.5] oases in Libya, which is seven days' distance through the desert. It is a settlement abundant in water and abundant in wine, and sufficient in other things. The second is around Lake Moiris and the third is around the oracle at Ammon. These are notable settlements.

(43) Much has been said about Ammon, but I wish to add that prophecy in general as well as oracles were more greatly honored among those in antiquity, but now there is much neglect of them, since the Romans are content with the oracles of the Sibyl and the Tyrrhenian prophecies from innards, the flight of birds, and signs from Zeus. Because of this the oracle at Ammon has almost been abandoned, yet formerly it was held in honor, something most clearly shown by those recording the deeds of Alexander. Although they add many forms of flattery, they do manifest some things worthy of belief. Kallisthenes [F14a] says that Alexander, with his love of glory, especially wanted to go up to the oracle, since he had heard that Perseus and Herakles had formerly done so. He started from Paraitonion, and although the south winds fell upon them, he forced his way. When he lost the route because of the clouds of dust, he was saved by rainfall and through being guided by two ravens. This assertion, however, is flattery, as is what follows: that the priest allowed only the king to go into the temple in his habitual dress, but the others put on other clothes, that everyone except Alexander heard the oracles from outside but he was inside, that the oracular responses were not as at Delphi and Branchidai (through words), but by nods and tokens, as according to Homer ("with his dark brows Kronion nodded" [*Iliad* 1.528]) – the prophet playing the role of Zeus – and that the man specifically said to the king that he was the son of Zeus. Kallisthenes also adds in tragic style that the oracle of Apollo at Branchidai had ceased to sound when the sanctuary had been plundered by the Branchidians (who had sided with the Persians at the time of Xerxes), and the spring had also ceased, but then the spring emerged and many oracles were carried by

[C814]

Milesian ambassadors to Memphis concerning Alexander's descent from Zeus, his future victory around Arbela, the death of Dareios [III], and the revolutions in Lakedaimon. He also says that the Erythraian Artemis proclaimed words about his high descent, for she was like the ancient Sibyl of Erythraia. Such it is from the historians.

(44) At Abydos they honor Osiris, and in the sanctuary of Osiris neither a singer, flute player, or harp player may begin the sacrifice to the god, unlike the custom with other gods. After Abydos there is the city of Little Diospolis and then the city of Tentyra. There, differing from other Egyptians, the crocodile is dishonored and considered the most hateful of all animals. Others know about the bad qualities of the creature and how destructive it is to the human race, yet they revere it and keep away from it, but these track them down and destroy them in every way. Some say that just as there is a certain natural antipathy of the Psyllians in the Kyrenaia against reptiles, it is the same between the Tentyritians and the crocodile, who suffer nothing from them, even swimming without fear and crossing over [the river], although no one else dares it. When crocodiles were brought to Rome for   [C815] exhibition, Tentyritians accompanied them. They made a reservoir and a kind of stage above one of the sides, so that the animals could go out of the water and have a sunning place. Going together into the water, they would then drag them together into a net to the sunning place, so that they could be seen by the spectators, and then pull them back to the reservoir. They worship Aphrodite, and behind the temple of Aphrodite is a sanctuary of Isis. Then there is what is called Typhonia (and the canal to Koptos), a city common to the Egyptians and the Arabians.

(45) Then there is an isthmus, to the Erythra and the city of Berenike, which has no harbor, but because of the convenient situation of the isthmus it has suitable landing places. It is said that [Ptolemaios II] Philadelphos was the first, by means of an army, to cut this road (which is without water) and to construct stations – for mercantile travel on camels – doing this because the Erythra was difficult to sail on, especially for those setting sail from its recess. The usefulness of it was shown through experience to be large, and now all Indian goods, as well as Arabian and Aithiopian ones, are carried down through the Arabian Gulf and brought to Koptos, where the emporium is for such goods. Mussel Anchorage is not far from Berenike, a city that has the naval station for sailors. Not far away from Koptos is what is called the City of Apollo, so that the boundaries of the isthmus are the two cities on either side. Today Koptos and Mussel Anchorage are highly esteemed, and the places are in use. Formerly the camel merchants travelled by night, looking at the stars, and like sailors carried water as they travelled.

Today water holes have been constructed, excavated to a great depth, and although rainwater is scarce, they have made cisterns. The journey is six or seven days. On the isthmus there are also *smaragdos* mines – the Arabians excavate passages that are deep underground – and those of other precious stones.

(46) After the City of Apollo is Thebes (today called Diospolis): "it has a hundred gates, and two hundred men go forth from each with horses and chariots" [*Iliad* 9.383–4]. Thus Homer, and he also speaks of its wealth: "nor as much as Egyptian Thebes, where the greatest possessions lie in houses"

[C816] [*Iliad* 9.381–2]. Others say such things, making this the metropolis of Egypt. Today only traces of its greatness are visible. Its length is 80 stadia, and there are a number of sanctuaries, most of which Kambyses mutilated. Today it is a collection of habitations in villages, part of which is in Arabia, where the city was, and part on the far side, where the Memnoneion is. There are two monolithic colossi there, near to each other. One is preserved but the upper portions of the other, from the seat, fell due to an earthquake, as they say. It is believed that once each day a noise, as if from a slight blow, is produced from the part that remains on the throne or its base. I was present at the place with Aelius Gallus and the multitude of those with him, both friends and soldiers, and heard the noise at about the first hour, but whether it was from the base, or the colossus, or whether the noise was made on purpose by someone standing around the base, I cannot assert with confidence. Because of the complete uncertainty of the reason one comes to believe anything other than that the sound came from stones arranged in such a way. Above the Memnoneion are the tombs of the kings, in rock-cut caves, about forty in number. They are marvellously constructed and are worth seeing. In the Thebais are inscriptions on some obelisks that show the wealth of the kings at that time, as well as their dominion (extending as far as the Skythians, Baktrians, Indians, and what is today Ionia), the tribute, and the size of their army (about a hundred myriads).

The priests there are said to have been mostly astronomers and philosophers, and it is because of them that the days are calculated not by the moon but by the sun, adding five days each year to the twelve months of thirty days. To fill out the whole – since a portion of a day runs beyond the length of the year – they put together a period from whole days and whole years, so that the portion running over makes an entire day. They attribute all such wisdom to Hermes. To Zeus, whom they honor the most, a maiden of the greatest beauty and most illustrious ancestry (they are called *pallades* by the Hellenes) is dedicated and becomes a ritual concubine with whomever she wishes, until the natural cleansing of her body occurs. After the cleansing she is given to a man, but before she is given, after the time of her concubinage, a period of mourning occurs.

(47) After Thebes there is the city of Hermonthis, where both Apollo and [C817] Zeus are honored. Then there is the City of Crocodiles, where the animal is worshipped, and then the City of Aphrodite, and afterward Latonpolis, which honors Athena and the *latos*. Then the City of Eileithyia and a sanctuary, and on the far side is the City of Hawks, where the hawk is worshipped, and then the City of Apollo, which also makes war against the crocodile.

(48) Regarding Syene and Elephantine, the former is a city on the borders of Aithiopia and Egypt, and the latter an island in the Nile, half a stadion in front of Syene, as well as a city on it that has a sanctuary of Knouphis and a Nilometer, like at Memphis. The Nilometer is a well constructed of fitted stones on the bank of the Nile. There are marks on it showing the highest, lowest, and mean rises of the Nile, for the water in the well rises and lowers with the river. Notations on the wall of the well are measures of the completed rises, and the others. Those who observe these indicate them to others so that they may know. Long in advance they know from such signs and the dates what the future rising will be, and they tell it beforehand. This is useful to the farmers – in regard to the management of the water, embankments, canals, and other such things – and also to the commanders in regard to the revenue, for a greater rising indicates greater revenue. At Syene there is also the well that marks the summer tropic, because these regions lie under the tropic circle. From our regions – I mean the Hellenic – proceeding toward the south, this is where the sun is first over our heads, causing the gnomons to have no shadow at noon. By necessity, when it is over our heads, its rays are thrown down in the wells as far as the water, even if they are exceedingly deep. We stand perpendicular, as is the excavation of wells. Here three Roman cohorts are stationed as a guard.

(49) A little above Elephantine is a little cataract on which the boatmen put on a performance for the commanders. The cataract is in the middle of the river and is a brow of rock that is flat on top, so that it receives the river, but it ends in a dropoff, over which the water flows down. On either side toward the land there is a stream, which generally can be navigated up. They [C818] sail up here and then drift down to the cataract, and are thrust with the boat over the dropoff but are saved without harm. A little above the cataract is Philai, a common settlement of Aithiopians and Egyptians, constructed like Elephantine and equal in size, having Egyptian sanctuaries. Here a bird is honored that is called a hawk but it does not appear similar to the hawks among us and in Egypt, as it is far larger and greatly different in its coloration. They say that it is Aithiopian, and one would be brought from

there whenever the former one died. The one shown to us was nearly dead of disease.

(50) We went to Philai from Syene by wagon, about a hundred stadia through an exceedingly level plain. Along the entire road one could frequently see rocks like Hermaia on both sides that were large, round, quite smooth, and nearly sphere-shaped, of the black and hard stone that produces mortars: one stone lying on a larger one and on it another one. Some of the rocks were by themselves. The largest had a diameter of not less than twelve feet, although all were greater than half this. We crossed to the island by a *pakton*. The *pakton* is a small boat fabricated of willow branches, so that it resembles something woven. Although standing in water or seated on planks, we crossed easily, yet unreasonably fearful, since there is no danger if the ferry has not become overloaded.

(51) In the entirety of Egypt the palm is not of high quality, and in the places around the Delta and Alexandria it produces fruit that is not good to eat, but the palm in the Thebais grows better than the others. It is worthy of astonishment how a territory of the same latitude as Judaea and bordering it – that around the Delta and Alexandria – differs so much, since the former produces the caryotic palm (in addition to this one), which is much better than the one in Babylonia. There are two kinds in the Thebais as well as in Judaea, the other and the caryotic. The Thebaian is harder but more agreeable to the taste. There is also an island that especially produces the best ones, providing a particularly large revenue for the commanders. It used to be royal – shared by no private person – and now belongs to the commanders.

(52) Herodotos [2.28] and others talk nonsense, adding marvels to their accounts, as if a kind of melody or rhythm or sweetener. They say that the sources of the Nile are around islands near Syene and Elephantine (there are several) and the channel at this place is bottomless in depth. The Nile has very many islands scattered along it, some of which are completely covered at the rising and others partially, of which the portions rising out of the waters are irrigated by screws.

[C819]

(53) From the beginning Egypt was generally peaceful, because of the self-sufficiency of the territory and the difficulty of invasion by those outside. It was protected on the north by a harborless coast and the Egyptian Sea, and on the east and west by the deserted Libyan and Arabian mountains, as we have said [17.1.4]. The remainder, toward the south, have the Trogodytians, Blemmyans, Nubians, and Megabarians (the Aithiopians above Syene). These are nomads and are not numerous or warlike. In antiquity they were thought to be so, because, like brigands, they would often attack those who were defenseless. Those Aithiopians who reach toward the south and to

Meroë are themselves not numerous nor collected together, for they live in a long, narrow, and winding riverine territory, as we have previously said [17.1.3 – 4]. They are not well prepared for war, or any other kind of life.

Today all the land is similarly disposed. An indication of this is that this region is sufficiently guarded by the Romans with only three cohorts, which are not complete. When the Aithiopians dared to attack them, they put their own land in danger. The remaining forces in Egypt are not as large as these, and the Romans have not used them collectively all at once, for the Egyptians themselves are not warriors (although they are very numerous), nor are the surrounding peoples. Cornelius Gallus, the first whom Caesar appointed to be prefect of the territory, went against Heroonpolis, which had revolted, and took it with only a few, and in only a short time broke up a revolt over tribute that had occurred in the Thebais. Later Petronius, when so many myriads of Alexandrians rushed against him and were throwing stones, went against them with only his own soldiers, and after killing one of them caused the rest to stop. Aelius Gallus, when he invaded Arabia with a part of the guard from Egypt – as has been stated [16.4.23–4] – demon-strated in this way that the people were unwarlike. If he had not been betrayed by Syllaios he would have subdued all of Fortunate [Arabia].

(54) Since the Aithiopians were encouraged when a portion of the forces in Egypt were away with Aelius Gallus making war against the Arabians, they attacked the Thebais and the garrison of three cohorts at Syene, and were able to take Syene, Elephantine, and Philai through this sudden attack, enslaving the inhabitants and pulling down the statues of Caesar. Petronius went out against 30,000 men with fewer than a myriad of foot soldiers and 800 cavalry. He first forced them to flee up to Pselchis, an Aithiopian city, and sent ambassadors to demand back what they had taken and the reasons for beginning the war. They said that they had been treated unjustly by the nomarchs, yet he said that they were not the rulers of the territory, but it was Caesar. When they requested three days for deliberations but did not do what was necessary, he attacked them and forced them into battle. He quickly turned them, as they were badly organized and armed. They had large oblong shields – these were of raw oxhide – and for defense some had axes, others pikes, and others swords. Some were driven together into the city and others fled into the desert, and still others went onto neighboring islands, crossing the channel, for there were not many crocodiles there because of the current. Among them were the commanders of Queen Kandake who was ruler of the Aithiopians in our time, a masculine sort of woman who was mutilated in one eye. He captured all of them alive, sailing after them in rafts and ships, and

[C820]

immediately sent them down to Alexandria. He also went against Pselchis and took it. If one added to those taken the multitude that fell in battle, those who were saved would be quite few in number. From Pselchis he went to Premnis, a fortified city, passing through the dunes that had poured down on the army of Kambyses when the wind fell on them. He attacked and took the fortress in the onslaught and afterward set forth for Napata. This was the royal residence of Kandake, and her son was there. She was located at a nearby place, and she sent ambassadors for friendship and to give back the captives and statues from Syene, but he attacked and took Napata, from which her son had fled, and razed it to the ground. He enslaved its inhabitants and turned back again with the booty, having decided that to go farther would be a difficult journey. He fortified Premnis better and threw in a garrison of four hundred men, with supplies for two years, and then set [C821] out for Alexandria. The captives were sold as booty, and a thousand were sent to Caesar, who had recently returned from the Cantabrians. Diseases destroyed the rest.

Meanwhile Kandake went against the garrison with many myriads. Petronius set out to give aid and arrived at the garrison first. When he had made the place secure through various preparations, ambassadors came. He ordered them to make their embassy to Caesar. They said that they did not know who Caesar was, or where they must go. He gave them escorts and they went to Samos, as Caesar was there, about to go to Syria, after sending Tiberius to Armenia. They obtained everything that they needed, and he remitted the tribute that had been imposed.

Part 2: Aithiopian and Egyptian Customs

(1) In the previous portion many things were said about the Aithiopians, so that it could be described at the same time as Egypt. One can say that the extremities of the inhabited world, which lie alongside what is not temperate and is uninhabitable because of the heat or cold, must be deficient and inferior to that which is temperate, which is clear from the lifestyle and the lack of necessities of the inhabitants. They live a hard life, are naked, and are mostly nomads. Their domestic animals – sheep, goats, and cattle – are small, and their dogs are small although fast and belligerent. Perhaps because they are naturally small, Pygmaians have been conceived of and fabricated, since no man worthy of belief has recorded seeing them.

(2) They [the Aithiopians] live on millet and barley, from which they make a drink. For oil they use butter and fat. They do not have fruit trees except for a few palms in the royal gardens. Some of them have grass as food,

as well as soft twigs, lotus, and the roots of reeds. They also use meat, blood, milk, and cheese.

They revere their kings as gods, who are generally shut up in their homes. Meroë is their greatest royal residence, a city having the same name as the island, which they say is like an oblong shield in shape. It is said that its size – perhaps exaggerated – has a length of about 3,000 stadia, and its width is about 1,000. It[1] has many mountains and large thickets, and is inhabited by nomads, hunters, and farmers. There are copper mines, iron mines, and gold, and varieties of precious stones. It is surrounded on the Libyan side by large dunes, on the Arabian by continuous cliffs, and up in the south by the confluence of rivers (the Astaboras, Astapous, and Astasobas). Toward the north is the onward stream of the Nile, as far as   [C822] Egypt, along the previously mentioned windings of the river [17.1.2]. The houses in the cities have walls of split palm woven together, or of brick. They excavate salt, as do the Arabians. The palm, *persea*, ebony, and carob are the abundant plants. They hunt elephants, lions, and leopards. There are also the elephant-fighting serpents and many other wild animals, who flee for refuge from the more burning and arid regions to those that are moist and marshy.

(3) Psebo lies above Meroë, a large lake having a rather well-settled island. Since the Libyans have what is on the western riverbank of the Nile, and the Aithiopians on the opposite side, they dominate in turns the islands and the riverine territory, each being driven out by the other and giving way to whomever is stronger.

The Aithiopians use bows of four *pecheis* that are wooden and hardened in the fire. The women are armed, and most of them have a copper ring through the lip of their mouth. They wear sheepskin – as they do not have wool – and their sheep are hairy like goats. They are naked, or are girdled with sheepskins of well-woven hair. They believe in an immortal god – the cause of everything – and also a mortal one, who is unnamed and not manifest. For the most part they consider their benefactors and kings to be gods, and of these the kings are the common saviors and guardians of all, and as private individuals are the same, in a special sense, to those who have experienced good things from them. Some of those in the burned regions are considered without gods. They say that they hate the sun and speak badly of it when they look at its rising, since it burns them and makes war on them, and they flee for refuge into the marshes. Those in Meroë revere Herakles, Pan, Isis, and some other barbarian god. Some throw the dead

---

[1] The antecedent may be lost.

into the river, others pour glass around them and keep them, and some bury them around the sanctuaries in clay coffins. They call upon them in oaths, and consider them the most sacred of all.

They appoint as kings those who are unusual in their beauty, their keeping of cattle, courage, or wealth. The priest had the highest rank at Meroë in antiquity, and would command the king, sometimes sending a messenger [C823] [to tell him] to kill himself, and appointing another in place of him. Later one of the kings brought this custom to an end by going with armed men to the sanctuary – where the golden temple is – and cutting the throats of all the priests. It is also an Aithiopian custom that if one of the kings is mutilated in any part of his body, those closest around him undergo the same thing, and they die with him. Because of this the king is guarded especially well by them. This is sufficient about the Aithiopians.

(4) There must be added to the Egyptian account what is peculiar to it. There is the so-called Egyptian bean, from which the *kibarion* comes, and papyrus, which is only here and among the Indians. The *persea* is only here and among the Aithiopians, a large tree with fruit that is sweet and also large. There is also the mulberry that produces the fruit called a *sykomoros*, which resembles a fig, although it is not valued for its taste. There is also the *korsion*, a sweet fruit like a pepper but a little larger. There are many fish in the Nile, of different types, that are special and indigenous. The best known are the oxyrhynchus, *lepidotos, latos, alabes, korakinos, choiros,* and *phagrorios* (also called the *phagros*), and also the silurus, *kitharos, thrissa, kestreus, lychnos, physa,* and *bous*. The shellfish include a large snail that makes a sound like a frog croaking. Egyptian indigenous animals include the ichneumon and the asp, which is peculiar in regard to others. There are two kinds, one of which is a *spithame* in length and causes death quickly, and the other is nearly an *orgyia*, as Nikandros, who wrote the *Theriaka* stated [168–9]. Among the birds are the ibis and the Egyptian hawk, which is tame like the cat, when compared to those elsewhere. The night raven here is also distinctive, for among us it is the size of an eagle and makes a deep sound, but in Egypt it is the size of a jackdaw and makes a different sound. The ibis is the tamest, and is like a stork in shape and size. There are two colors, one of which is like the stork and the other completely black. Every road intersection in Alexandria is full of them, and they are useful in a way, but in another way they are not useful. They are useful because they pick out every animal[2] as well as the by-products from the meat and

---

[2] "Harmful" or a similar word may have fallen out of the text.

food shops, but they are inconvenient because they eat everything and are unclean, and only with difficulty can they be kept away from clean things and anything that is not polluted.

(5) The statement of Herodotos [2.36] is also true, that it is an Egyptian custom to knead mud with the hands, but the dough for breadmaking with the feet. *Kakeis* is a special kind of bread that stops the bowels, and the   [C824] *kiki* is a fruit that is sown in the fields, from which oil is pressed for lamps, and which is used by almost everyone in the region, and also as an unguent for those who are poorer and more hard-working, both men and women. *Koukina* is Egyptian wicker-work from some plant similar to rushes or palms. They prepare beer in a peculiar way: it is common to many, but the preparation varies among each. Most zealously they raise all children who are born and circumcise the males and cut the females, as is the custom among the Judaeans, who were originally Egyptians, as we said in that section [16.2.34].

Aristoboulos [F39] says that because of the crocodiles no fish comes up from the sea into the Nile except the *kestreus*, *thrissa*, and dolphin: the dolphin because it is stronger, and the *kestreus* because it is escorted by *choiroi* along the banks through a natural affinity. The crocodiles keep away from the *choiroi*, since they are round and have spines on their heads that are dangerous to the animals. The *kestreus* runs up in the spring, carrying its offspring, but comes down in groups to give birth a little before the setting of the Pleiades. This is when they are captured, since their groups are surrounded by nets. Such a reason can also be conjectured in the case of the *thrissa*. This is it for Egypt.

Part 3:   Libya, and conclusion

(1) Next I will speak about Libya, which is the remaining part of the entire *Geography*. I have previously said much about it [2.3.4, 2.4.3], but now additional appropriate matters must also be mentioned, adding what has not previously been said. Those who have divided the inhabited world into continents have divided it unequally, for the division into three parts suggests three equal ones, but Libya is so much lacking in being a third part of the inhabited world that even if it were combined with Europe it would not seem to be equal to Asia. Perhaps it is smaller than Europe, and greatly so in regard to its importance, for much of the interior and of the coast along the Ocean is desert, dotted with small settlements that are for the most part scattered and nomadic. In addition to the desert, it abounds in wild beasts that drive [the inhabitants] away even from areas capable of habitation, and it occupies much of the burned zone. However, all of the   [C825]

coast opposite us – that between the Nile and the Pillars – is prosperously settled, especially what was subject to the Karchedonians, although even here portions are found without water, such as those around the Syrtes, Marmaridai, and the Descent.

It is in the shape of a right-angled triangle as conceived on a level surface, having as its base the seacoast opposite us from Egypt and the Nile as far as Maurousia and the Pillars. The side perpendicular to this is that which is formed by the Nile as far as Aithiopia and extended by us to the Ocean, and the hypotenuse to the right angle is the entire coast of the Ocean between the Aithiopians and the Maurousians. What is at the extremity of the previously mentioned triangle, lying somewhat within the burned zone, we can only speak about from conjecture because it is inaccessible, so we cannot speak of the greatest width of the land, although we have said in a previous section [1.4.2] this much: going south from Alexandria to Meroë, the royal capital of the Aithiopians, is about 10,000 stadia, and from there in a straight line to the boundaries between the burned and inhabited regions is another 3,000. At any rate, this should be put down as the greatest width of Libya – 13 or 14,000 stadia – with its length slightly less than double that. This then is the totality of Libya, but I must speak about each [region], beginning from the western parts, the most famous.

(2) Here live those whom the Hellenes call the Maurousians, and the Romans and locals the Maurians, a numerous and prosperous Libyan peoples on the strait opposite Iberia. Here also is the strait called the Pillars of Herakles, of which I have often spoken. Going outside the strait at the Pillars, having Libya on the left, there is the mountain that the Hellenes call Atlas and the barbarians Dyris. Something projects from it farthest toward the west of Maurousia, called the Koteis. Nearby is a small town above the sea that the barbarians call Trinx, but Artemidoros [F76] calls it Lynx and Eratosthenes [F100] Lixos. It lies across the strait from the Gadeirans, 800 stadia across the sea, which is about as far as each lies from the strait at the Pillars. To the south of Lixos and the Koteis lies the

[C826] gulf called Emporikos, which has settlements of Phoenician merchants. The entire seacoast encompassed by this gulf is indented, according to the triangle shape that I have outlined, but the gulfs and projections should be removed. One must conceive that the continent becomes larger to the south and east. The mountain that extends through Maurousia from the Koteis as far as the Syrtes is inhabited, both it and the others that are parallel, first by Maurousians but deep within the territory by the most numerous of the Libyan peoples, who are called the Gaitoulians.

(3) The historians, beginning with the *Periploos* of Ophelas [T1], have added many fabrications about the exterior coast of Libya. We have mentioned these somewhere previously [1.1.5, 3.2.13], and now let me speak about them, seeking leniency for the telling of marvels, if we are forced to degenerate into such things, thus avoiding rejecting them completely in silence and in a way mutilating the research. They say that the Emporikos Gulf has a cave that allows the sea to come into it at flood tide as far as 7 stadia, and that lying in front of it is a low and level place with an altar of Herakles which, they say, is not inundated by the flood tide. I consider this to be one of the fabrications. Similar to this is the statement that the successive gulfs had ancient settlements of Tyrians that are deserted today, no less than 300 cities, which the Pharousians and Nigritians pillaged. They say that these are thirty days' journey from Lynx.

(4) Everyone agrees that Maurousia is a fertile territory, except for a small amount of desert, and provided with rivers and lakes. The size and numbers of its trees are surpassing, and it produces everything. At any rate, it supplies the Romans with the very large variegated tables made of a single piece of wood. They say that the rivers have crocodiles and other types of animals resembling those in the Nile. Some think that the sources of the Nile are near the extremities of Maurousia. In a certain river lampreys are found, seven *pecheis* long, having gills that are perforated so that they can breathe. They also say that this region produces a vine so thick that it can hardly be encircled by two men, and it yields bunches of about one *pecheis*, and that the herbs (vegetables, arum, *drakontion*, the stalks of *staphylinoi*, horse fennel, and *skolymos*) are 12 *pecheis* high and four palms thick. There are also   [C827] serpents, elephants, gazelles, antelopes, and similar animals, and the country nourishes lions and leopards in every way. It produces weasels that are the same size as cats and similar to them (except that their noses project farther), and many very large apes, about which Poseidonios [F245] says that when he was sailing from Gadeira to Italia he was carried close to the Libyan coast and saw a forest projecting into the sea full of these animals, some in the trees and others on the ground. Some had their young and were giving them their breast, but he laughed when he saw some with heavy breasts, some with bald heads, and others ruptured or showing other such injuries.

(5) Above it, on the External Sea, is the land of the so-called Western Aithiopians, which is mostly poorly settled. Iphikrates says that camelopards and elephants are found here, as well as the so-called *rhizeis*, which have the form of a bull but in their life style, size, and strength in battle are like elephants. He speaks of serpents so large that grass grows on them. Lions attack the offspring of elephants, but after they have drawn blood,

they flee when the mothers approach, who, when they see them bloodied, kill them, and the lions come back to the corpses and eat them. Bogos [II], the king of the Maurousians, went up against the Western Aithiopians, and sent down to his wife reeds as a gift, similar to Indian ones, of which each joint contained eight *choinikes*, and there was also asparagus similar in size.

(6) As one sails into the Inner Sea from Lynx, there is the city of Zelis, then Tinga, then the Memorial of the Seven Brothers, and the mountain lying above named Abile, which is abundant in animals and large trees. The length of the strait at the Pillars is said to be 120 stadia, and the minimum width, at Elephas, is 60. On sailing in, next there are a number of cities and rivers as far as the Molochath River, which forms the boundary between the Maurousian and Masaisylian lands. A large promontory lies near the river, as well as Metagonion, a place that is waterless and wretched, and one might say that the mountain from the Koteis extends as far as here. The length from the Koteis to the boundaries of the Masaisylians is 5,000 stadia. Metagonion is across from New Karchedon on the far side, but [C828] Timosthenes [F11] incorrectly says that it is across from Massalia. The crossing from New Karchedon to Metagonion is 3,000 stadia, and the voyage along the coast to Massalia is more than 6,000.

(7) The Maurousians inhabit, for the most part, territory that is exceedingly prosperous, but even to this time most live a nomadic life. They beautify themselves by braiding their hair, having beards, wearing gold, cleaning their teeth, and paring their nails. Rarely do you see them touch each other while walking, in order that the adornment of their hair may remain intact. Their horsemen fight mostly with a javelin, and use reins of twisted rushes for the horses, which are bare. They also have daggers. The foot soldiers have elephant skins in front of them as shields, and clothe themselves and sleep in those of lions, leopards, and bears. One might say that they, the Masaisylians (who are next), and the Libyans in general, mostly dress alike, and are similar in other matters, using small horses that are sharp and obedient, so much so that they are guided by a small rod. They have collars of wood or hair, from which the reins hang, although some follow without being led, like dogs. They have small shields of leather, small broad and pointed [spears], ungirdled chitons with broad borders, and – as I have said – skins as cloaks and shields. The Pharousians and the Nigretians, who live above them toward the Western Aithiopians, also use bows, and, like the Aithiopians, scythe-bearing chariots. The Pharousians rarely mingle with the Maurousians when going through the desert, and have skins of water bound under the bellies of their horses. At times they come to Kirta, through certain places with marshes and lakes. They say that

some of them live like Troglodytes, excavating in the earth. It is said that the summer rains are prevalent here, but the winter is without water. Some of the barbarians here use snake and fish skins as clothing and bed coverings. Some say that the Maurousians are the Indians who came here with Herakles. A little before our time the families of Bogos and Bokchos held the land, who were friends of the Romans. When they came to an end, Juba [II] succeeded to the rule, having been given it by Sebastos Caesar, as well as his ancestral rule. He was the son of the Juba [I] who, along with Scipio, made war against Caesar the God. Juba [II] came to the end of his life recently, and his son Ptolemaios succeeded to the rule, born from the daughter of Antonius and Kleopatra [VII].   [C829]

(8) Artemidoros [F77] disagrees with Eratosthenes [F107] because the latter says that a certain city near the western extremities of Maurousia is Lixos rather than Lynx, that there are a large number of Phoenician cities that have been destroyed and of which there are no traces to be seen, that he says the air among the western Aithiopians is brackish, and that the air at the hours of daybreak and the afternoon is thick and misty. How can this be in places that are dry and very hot? But he [Artemidoros] speaks much worse about these places. He recounts that certain wanderers, the Lotus Eaters, would inhabit the waterless [regions] and eat the lotus, a kind of herb and root, and because of it they do not need to drink. They extend as far as the places above Kyrene. Those who are there also drink milk and eat meat, although they are at the same latitude. Gabinius [F1], the Roman historian, does not avoid telling marvels about Maurousia. He records the memorial of Antaios near Lynx, and a skeleton extending sixty *pecheis*, which Sertorius exposed and then covered again with earth. He also tells mythic tales about elephants, saying that other animals flee from fire but elephants make war against it and defend themselves because it destroys the forest, that they fight with humans and send out scouts, and when they see them fleeing they also flee. When they are wounded, as suppliants they hold out branches, webs, or dust.

(9) After the land of the Maurousians, there is that of the Masaisylians, which takes its beginning at the Molochath River and ends at the promontory called Treton, the boundary between the Masaisylians and the Masylian land. It is 6,000 stadia (some say less) from Metagonion to Treton. The coast has a number of rivers and cities, and naturally good land, but it is sufficient to record only that which is notable. The city of Siga is 1,000 stadia from the previously mentioned boundaries. It was the royal residence of Sophax, although today destroyed. After Sophax, Masanasses possessed the land, then Mikipsas, and then his successors, and in our time Juba [I]

the father of the Juba [II] who recently died. Zama, his royal residence, was destroyed by the Romans. After Siga is the Harbor of the Gods, in 600 stadia, and then other insignificant places. Those places deep in the territory are mountainous and deserted ... at times scattered, which the Gaitoulians hold, as far as the Syrtes. Those near the sea are fertile plains with many cities, [C830]   rivers, and lakes.

(10) I do not know whether Poseidonios [F223] tells the truth when he says that only a few small rivers flow through Libya, for those mentioned by Artemidoros [F79] – between Lynx and Karchedon – he says are numerous and large. The statement is more truthful in regard to the interior, and the former says the reason for this is that no rain falls in the northern portions, just as they say about Aithiopia. Because of this, pestilence often occurs due to the droughts, as the lakes are filled with mud and locusts are common. He further says that the eastern regions are moist, for the sun passes quickly when rising but the western ones are dry because it turns back there. Moisture and dryness are a matter of abundance or scarcity of water, as well as the effect of the sun. He wishes to speak about the effect of the sun, which everyone defines by the northern or southern latitude. Moreover, the eastern and western regions – speaking in regard to the inhabitable areas – differ according to each habitation and the change in horizons, so that it is not possible to speak generally in regard to an incomprehensible number [of places] as to whether the western are moist and the eastern dry. Yet if he were to make such statements about the entire inhabited world and such extremities as Indike and Iberia, perhaps he could make such a decision. But what plausibility is there is giving such a cause? In the revolution of the sun, which is continual and incessant, what would be the turning back? The speed of its movement is everywhere equal. Moreover, it is contrary to perception to say that the extremities of Iberia or Maurousia – those in the west – are the dryest places of all, for they have a temperate atmosphere and are greatly abundant in water. And if the turning back is taken to mean that it is the last above the inhabited world there, how does this relate to the aridity? For there, and in the other parts of the inhabited world in the same latitude, it departs for an equal time of night and then returns again and warms the earth.

(11) Somewhere there is a spring of asphalt as well as copper mines. A large number of scorpions – winged and wingless – are also mentioned, in size having seven vertebrae. Similarly there are spiders that are exceptional in size and number, and lizards that they say are two *pecheis*. On the side of the mountain are found, they say, the so-called *lychnites* and Karchedonian stones, and in the plains there are many oyster and scallop shells, similar to

what we mentioned in the section about Ammon [1.3.4]. There is a tree   [C831]
called the honey lotus, from which wine is prepared. Some have land that
produces two crops and yields two harvests, one in summer and the other
in spring. The stalk is five *pecheis* in height and the thickness that of the little
finger, producing a yield of 240 times. In the spring they do not sow, but
harrow the ground lightly with bundles of paliurus, and are satisfied with
what falls out of the earth at harvest, for a summer crop comes to maturity.
Because of the number of animals, they work wearing leggings and with
leather on their other portions. When they lie asleep they smear the foot of
the beds with garlic and tie paliurus around them, because of the scorpions.

(12) On this coast there is a city named Iol, which Juba [II] the father of
Ptolemaios refounded and changed its name to Kaisareia. It has a harbor,
with a small harbor in front of the harbor. Between Kaisareia and Treton is a
large harbor called Salda, which is the boundary between what is subject to
Juba [II] and what is subject to the Romans.

The divisions of the territory have been made in various ways, since there
have been a number of different inhabitants whom the Romans treated in
a different manner, some as friends and some as enemies, so that parts have
been taken away and given to others, but not in the same manner. That
toward Maurousia was more productive and more powerful, and that toward
Karchedonia and the Masylians more flourishing and better equipped,
although it had been in a bad situation, first because of the Karchedonian
matter and then because of the war against Jugurtha. He took Adarbal by
siege (who was a friend of the Romans) at Ityke and killed him, thus filling
the territory with war. Then other wars upon others occurred, ending with
what happened between Scipio and Caesar the God, in which Juba [I] was
killed, and the cities disappeared along with their leaders, such as Tisiaous,
Vaga, Thala, and also Kapsa (the treasury of Jugurtha), Zama, Zincha, and
those near where Caesar made war against Scipio. He was first victorious
at Rhouspinon, then near Ouzita, and then near Thapsos and the nearby lake
and marshes. Also nearby are the free cities of Zella and Acholla. Caesar
captured in his onslaught the island of Kerkinna as well as Thena, a town
on the coast. Of all these, some were completely destroyed and others left
half torn down. Phara was burned by the cavalry of Scipio.   [C832]

(13) After Treton there is the territory of the Masylians, and then that of
the Karchedonians, which is similar. Kirta, the royal residence of Masanasses
and his successors, is in the interior, and is a city that was excellently fortified,
especially by Mikipsas, who settled Hellenes there and made it so that he
could send forth a myriad of cavalry and twice as many infantry. Kirta, then,
is here, and the two Hippos, one near Ityke and the other farther away, rather

toward Treton. Both are royal residences. Ityke was second after Karchedon in size and reputation, and when Karchedon was destroyed it was the metropolis of the Romans and their base of operations for activities in Libya. It is situated in the same gulf as Karchedon, near one of the promontories that makes the gulf, of which the one near Ityke is called Apollonion and the other Hermaia. The cities are in sight of one another. The Bagradas River flows through Ityke. From Treton as far as Karchedon is 2,500 stadia, but neither this distance nor that as far as the Syrtes is agreed upon.

(14) Karchedon is on a peninsula, comprising a circuit of 360 stadia, and having a wall. The neck occupies 60 stadia of its length, extending from sea to sea, and this, an open place, is where the Karchedonians had their elephant stalls. The akropolis, which they called Byrsa, was in the middle of the city, a fairly steep ridge inhabited all around and having an Asklepeion at its summit. When the city was captured, it was burned by the wife of Hasdrubal along with herself. The harbors lie below the akropolis, as well as Kothon, a circular islet that is surrounded by a strait with boathouses around it on both sides.

(15) It was founded by Dido, who brought people from Tyre. External settlements were so successful for the Phoenicians – this one and the others as far as Iberia (both the rest and those inside the Pillars) – that still today the best part of the continent of Europe and the adjacent islands are inhabited by Phoenicians, as well as all the entire part of Libya where one can live without being nomadic. From this dominion they built a city to be a rival of Rome and fought three great wars against it.

Their power would be quite clear from the last war, in which they were brought to an end by Scipio Aemilianus and the city was completely wiped [C833] out. When they began to fight this war they had 300 cities in Libya and 700,000 people in the city. When they were besieged and forced to surrender, they gave up as reparations 200,000 suits of armor and 3,000 catapult machines so that they could not make war. When they decided to initiate the war again, they instantaneously established the making of arms, and each day produced 140 finished oblong shields, 300 daggers, 500 spears, and 1,000 catapult missiles, with the women servants providing hair for the catapults. Moreover, although 50 years previously they had only 12 ships, according to the agreement at the time of the second war (and although at that time they had fled for refuge into the Byrsa), in two months they constructed 120 cataphract ships. Since the mouth of the Kothon was guarded, they excavated another mouth and the fleet sailed out suddenly. Old timber had been stored away and a large number of craftsmen, maintained at public expense, were in waiting.

Although Karchedon was in such a way, it was nevertheless captured and razed. The Romans proclaimed the territory (that which had been subject to the Karchedonians) a province, and appointed Masanasses and his descendants (those around Mikipsas) as dynasts for the rest. Masanasses was especially respected by the Romans because of his virtue and friendship. It was he who turned the nomads into citizens and farmers, and taught them to be soldiers instead of brigands. A peculiar thing had happened with these people: they lived in a territory that was prosperous except for its abundance of animals. Yet they would not allow their destruction – in order to work the land without anxiety – and they would turn against each other and abandon the land to the animals. Because of this they experienced a wandering and migratory life, no less than those in a difficult or poor location or climate are surrounded by such a life. Thus the Masaisylians are called Nomadians, having obtained this as their special name. By necessity, such people have a poor life, and are more root eaters than meat eaters, nourished by milk and cheese. For a long time Karchedon was desolate – for about the same period of time as Corinth – but it was restored at about the same time by Caesar the God, who sent there the Roman settlers who chose to go, as well as some soldiers. Today it is as attractive a settlement as any city in Libya. [C834]

(16) In the middle of the mouth of the Karchedonian Gulf is the island of Kossoura. Sikelia is on the opposite side of the strait from these places, around Lilybaion, at a distance of about 1,500 stadia (this is what it is said to be from Lilybaion to Karchedon). Not far distant from either Kossoura or Sikelia are various islands, including Aigimouros.

Sailing across from Karchedon to the adjoining coast is 60 stadia, from which the journey inland to Nepheris is about 120 stadia. It is a fortified city established on a rock. On the same gulf as Karchedon is the city of Tynis, as well as hot springs and quarries. Then there is the rough promontory of Hermaia and a city on it with the same name. Then there is Neapolis, and then the Taphitis Promontory and a hill on it called Aspis ["Shield"] from the resemblance, which the tyrant of Sikelia, Agathokles, settled at the time that he sailed against the Karchedonians. These cities were demolished by the Romans together with Karchedon. There is an island of Kossouros 400 stadia from Taphitis, off the Selinous River of Sikelia, with a homonymous city. It is 150 stadia in circuit and about 600 stadia distant from Sikelia. There is also the island of Melite 500 stadia from Kossouros. Then there is the city of Adrymes, where there were shipyards, and then the so-called Taricheiai, several islets close to one another. Then there is the city of Thapsos, and after it Lopadoussa, an island in the open sea. Then there is the promontory of Ammon Balithon, near which there is a tuna lookout.

Then there is the city of Thena, lying near the beginning of the Little Syrtis. In between are many other small towns not worth mentioning. Lying near the beginning of the Syrtis is the oblong island of Kerkinna, which is rather large and has a city of the same name. There is also a smaller one, Kerkinnitis.

(17) Adjoining these is the Little Syrtis, which is called the Syrtis of the Lotus Eaters. The circuit of the gulf is 1,600 stadia, and the width of the mouth is 600. At each of the promontories that make the mouth are islands close to the mainland: the previously mentioned Kerkinna and Meninx, which are about equal in size. Meninx is considered to be the land of the Lotus Eaters mentioned by Homer [*Odyssey* 9.82–104], and certain tokens of this are visible, both the altar of Odysseus and the fruit itself, because the tree called the lotus is common there, and has the sweetest fruit. There are a number of towns there, one of which has the same name as the island. [C835] There are also some small towns on the Syrtis itself, and in its recess is an exceedingly large emporium with a river that empties into the gulf. The effect of the ebb and flood tides extends this far, and at the proper times the inhabitants eagerly go out to catch the fish.

(18) After the Syrtis there is Zouchis, a lake of 400 stadia. It has a narrow entrance and is near a city of the same name that has purple dye factories and all kinds of pickling factories. Then there is another lake that is much smaller, and after this the city of Abrotonon and some others. Adjoining these is Neapolis, which is also called Leptis. From here the crossing to the Epizephyrian Lokrians is 3,600 stadia. Next there is a river, and after it a kind of dividing wall that the Karchedonians constructed to bridge some clefts that go up into the interior. There are some harborless places here, although the rest of the coast has harbors. Then there is a high wooded promontory that is the beginning of the Great Syrtis, called the Heads. To this promontory from Karchedon is a little more than 5,000 stadia.

(19) Lying above the coast from Karchedon as far as the Heads and the Masaisylians is the Libyphoenician land, which extends to the mountainous country of the Gaitoulians, and which is already Libya. The land above the Gaitoulians is that of the Garamantians, lying parallel to it, from where the Karchedonian stones are brought. They say that the Garamantians are nine or ten days' journey from the Aithiopians who live on the Ocean, and fifteen from Ammon. Between the Gaitoulians and our coast there are many plains, many mountains, large lakes, and rivers, some of which sink below the earth and become invisible. They are exceedingly simple in their lifestyle and adornment, with many women and children, and are otherwise similar to the nomadic Arabians. Their horses and cattle have longer necks than

others. Horse keeping is such an exceptional interest of their kings that the number of foals is estimated at a hundred thousand each year. Their sheep are raised on milk and meat, especially near Aithiopia. This is it about the interior.

(20) The Great Syrtis has a circuit of about 930³ stadia, and a diameter, in the innermost recess, of 1,500, which is the same as the width at the mouth. The difficulty with both this Syrtis and the Little [Syrtis] is that often the depths have shallows, so that with the ebb and flood of the tides one may fall [C836] into the shallows and go aground, and it is rare that a boat is saved. Because of this, one sails far from the coast, taking care not to be caught off guard and driven by the winds into the gulfs. Nevertheless people take risks and will attempt to do anything, especially in regard to sailing along the coast of the land.

As one sails into the Great Syrtis, on the right after the Heads is a lake about 300 stadia in length and 70 in width that empties into the gulf and contains islets and an anchorage in front of its mouth. After the lake there is the place [called] Aspis and the best harbor in the Syrtis. Adjoining this is the Euphrantas Tower, the former boundary between the Karchedonian territory and the Kyrenaia as it was under Ptolemaios [II?]. Then there is another place called Charax, which the Karchedonians used as an emporium, taking wine there and receiving as return cargo silphium juice that had been brought secretly from Kyrene. Then there are the Altars of Philainos and after them Automala, a fortress that has a garrison, situated at the innermost recess of the entire gulf. The parallel of this recess is slightly to the south (about a thousand stadia) of the one through Alexandria, and less than two thousand from the one through Karchedon, but it would fall on the one through Heroonpolis on the recess of the Arabian Gulf and the one through the interior of the Masaisylians and Maurousians.

The remainder of the coast, to the city of Berenike, is 1,500 stadia. Lying inland along its length, extending as far as the Altars of Philainos, are the so-called Nasamonians, a Libyan peoples. In the distance between them there are not many harbors and a scarcity of waterholes. There is a promontory called Pseudopenias, on which Berenike is placed, near a certain lake, Tritonis, which particularly has an islet with a sanctuary of Aphrodite on it. There is also the Lake of the Hesperides and the Lathon River that empties into it. Farther inside than Berenike is a small promonotory called Boreion, which, along with the Heads, makes the mouth of the Syrtis. Berenike lies directly down from the promontories of the Peloponnesos, directly down

---

³ The number is far too small: 3,930 or 4,930 have been suggested.

from what is called the Fish, and the Chelonatas, and directly down from Zakynthos at a distance of 3,600 stadia. From this city Marcus Cato went around the Syrtis on foot in 30 days, leading an army of more than a myriad of men, dividing them into portions because of the scarcity of water holes. He travelled on foot in deep sand and burning heat.

[C837]   After Berenike there is the city of Taucheira, which is also called Arsinoë, and then the former Barke, now Ptolemais. Then there is Phykous Promontory, which is low and projects the most toward the north of anywhere on the Libyan coast. It lies directly down from Tainaron in Lakonia at a distance of 2,800 stadia. There is also a small town with the same name as the promontory. Not far away from Phykous (about 170 stadia) is the seaport of the Kyrenaians, Apollonia. It is 1,000 from Berenike and 80 from Kyrene, a large city lying on a table-shaped plain, as I saw it from the sea.

(21) It is a foundation of the Theraians, a Lakonian island that was called Kalliste in antiquity, as Kallimachos says:

> Formerly it was Kalliste, but its later name was Thera, the mother of our fatherland, famed for its horses. [F716]

The seaport of the Kyrenaians lies down from the Ram's Forehead, the western promontory of Crete, at a distance of 2,000 stadia. The voyage is made with the Leukonotos wind. Kyrene is said to have been a foundation of Battos, and Kallimachos asserts that he was his ancestor. It increased in power because of the quality of its territory, for it is excellent in the breeding of horses and the beauty of its fruit. It had many notable men whose power was capable of notably defending its freedom and strongly resisting the barbarians living above them. In antiquity the city was independent, and then the Makedonians, who had taken possession of Egypt, increased in power and attacked them, led by those with Thibron, who had killed Harpalos. It was ruled by the kings for some time and then came under Roman power, today joined with Crete in a single province. Apollonia, Barke, Taucheira, Berenike, and other nearby towns are suburbs of Kyrene.

(22) Bordering the Kyrenaia is the territory producing silphium and the Kyrenaian juice, which is produced from silphium. It came near to giving out when the barbarians (who are nomads) invaded because of some enmity and destroyed the roots of the plant.

Kyrenaians who became notable include Aristippos the Sokratic, who laid the foundations of the Kyrenaian philosophy, his daughter, named Arete and who was his successor in the school, and again her successor and son Aristippos, called Metrodidaktos ["Mother Taught"], and Annikeris [C838]   who revised the Kyrenaian school and introduced the Annikereian.

Kallimachos and Eratosthenes were Kyrenaians, both honored by the Egyptian kings, the former a poet and an enthusiastic scholar, the latter superior in these things as well as philosophy and mathematics, if anyone was. There was also Karneades – agreed to be the best of the Academic philosophers – as well as Apollonios Kronos, who was the teacher of Diodoros the dialectician, also called Kronos, as some transferred the epithet from the teacher to the pupil.

After Apollonia there is the remainder of the Kyrenaian coast as far as the Descent, 2,200 stadia, not at all an easy coastal voyage. There are few harbors, anchorages, settlements, or watering places. The best-known places along the coast are the Roadstead, Zephyrion (which has an anchorage), another Zephyrion, and the Chersonesos Promontory, which has a harbor. This lies directly down from Kaudos in Crete, and the crossing is 1,500 stadia with the Notos wind. Then there is sort of a sanctuary of Herakles, and above it the village of Paliouros. Then there is the harbor of Menelaos, and Ardanixis, a low promontory having an anchorage. Then there is the Great Harbor, which is situated directly down from the Chersonesos on Crete, the passage between them being a distance of about 2,000 stadia. One could almost say that Crete, being narrow and long, as a whole lies opposite and parallel to this coast. After the Great Harbor there is another harbor, Plynos, and above it the Four Towers. The place is called the Descent, and the Kyrenaia goes this far. The remainder, as far as Paratonion and then to Alexandria, we have already mentioned in the Egyptian section [17.1.14].

(23) The Libyans occupy the territory deep in the interior above the Syrtis and the Kyrenaia, which is rather poor and dry. First there are the Nasamonians, then the Psyllians, certain Gaitoulians, and the Garamantians. Still more toward the coast are the Marmaridians, who for the most part border the Kyrenaia and extend as far as Ammon. They say that those travelling from the recess of the Great Syrtis, from around Automala, approximately toward the winter sunrise, come to Augila on the fourth day. This place resembles Ammon, producing palms and being well watered. It lies above the Kyrenaia toward the south. For as far as a hundred stadia the land produces trees, and for another hundred it is only sown, although because of its dryness the land does not produce roots. Above this is the silphium-producing territory, and then the uninhabited territory of the Garamantians. [C839] The silphium-producing territory is narrow, oblong, and somewhat arid, and with a length – as one goes approximately toward the east – of about 1,900 stadia, and 300 or a little more in width, as far as is known. It is possible to conjecture that everywhere lying in continuous succession on the same parallel is similar in regard to climate and the production of plants. Since a

number of deserts intrude, we do not know all these places. Similarly the regions above Ammon and the oases as far as Aithiopia are unknown. We cannot speak about the boundaries of Aithiopia and Libya: not even clearly about what is near Egypt, and much less about that which is near the Ocean.

(24) This, then, is the situation of the parts of our inhabited world. Since the Romans occupy the best and the most known, and have surpassed all former rulers of whom we have a record, it is worthwhile to speak briefly about them. It has been stated [6.4.2] that setting forth from the single city of Rome, they came to possess all Italia through war and statesmanlike rule, and that, after Italia, they also gained that which was around it, making use of the same qualities. Of the three continents, they have almost all of Europe except that outside the Istros and that along the Ocean betwen the Rhenos and Tanais. The entire coast of Libya that is toward us is subject to them, and the rest of it is uninhabited, or inhabited wretchedly or nomadically. Similarly the entire coast of Asia that is toward us is under their control, unless one considers the Achaians, Zygians, and Heniochians, who live piratically and nomadically in narrow and wretched places. Regarding the interior, and that deep within, they have a part, and the Parthyaians and those barbarians beyond them another. On the east and north are Indians, Baktrians, and Skythians, and then Arabians and Aithiopians, but something is always being handed over from them. Some of this entire territory subject to the Romans is ruled by kings, but they [the Romans] have what are called provinces and send commanders and tax collectors to them. There are also some free cities, some of which came originally as friends, and others which were set free as an honor. There are also dynasts, chieftains, and priests subject to them, but who live according to certain ancestral laws.

[C840]

(25) The provinces have been divided in different ways at different times, although at present they are as Sebastos Caesar arranged them. When his native land had been turned over to him with authority as its leader, and he was established as master in war and peace for life, he divided the entire territory into two parts, assigning one to himself and the other to the people. He had for himself that which needed a military guard, that which was barbarian, and that adjacent to those peoples who were not yet subdued, or which was poor and difficult to farm and – being lacking in everything yet well provided with defenses – would throw off the reins and rebel. The rest – that which was peaceful and easy to rule without weapons – was for the people. He divided the two portions into a number of provinces, some of which are "of Caesar" and the others "of the people." Caesar sends to those "of Caesar" commanders and procurators, dividing the territory in different ways at different times, and administering them according to the

occasion. The people [send] to those "of the people" praetors or consuls, and these are divided differently when circumstances require it. At the beginning he arranged them by creating two that were consular: Libya (insofar as it was subject to the Romans, except for that formerly subject to Juba [II] and now his son Ptolemaios), and Asia within the Halys and the Tauros, except for the Galatians and those people who had been subject to Amyntas, as well as Bithynia and the Propontis. There were ten that were praetorian. In Europe and the islands near it there were the so-called Outer Iberia (what is around the Baitis River and the Anas) and Narbonitis in Keltike. Third was Sardo along with Kyrnos, fourth Sikelia, fifth and sixth Illyris next to Epeiros and Makedonia, seventh Achaia along with Thessaly, the Aitolians, the Akarnanians, and certain Epeirotic peoples who border Makedonia, eighth Crete along with the Kyrenaia, ninth Cyprus, and tenth Bithynia along with the Propontis and certain parts of the Pontos. Caesar holds the rest of the provinces, and to some he sends consular men as inspectors, to others praetorians, and to others equestrians. The kings, dynasts, and decarchies are, and always have been, in his portion.

Glossary of untranslated words

This glossary includes words that are of uncertain meaning (often flora and fauna), foreign words (including Latin words not translated by Strabo), and other terms that cannot easily be translated without explanation. It does not include words translated by Strabo or proper names. For weights and measures see pp. 32–3.

agoranomos: the clerk of the agora, but used by Strabo for a more general Indian magistracy.

agrostis: a wild grass, perhaps Cynodon daktylon.

alabes: a Nile fish.

antakaios: a type of sturgeon.

anthrax (pl. *anthrakes*): a category of dark red precious stones.

argillai: the underground homes in the vicinity of the Bay of Naples. Seemingly from argillos, a type of clay.

aroura: arable land, but also a land measure in Egypt of 100 Egyptian pecheis square (Herodotos 2.168).

arsenikon: a yellow mineral, probably arsenic trisulphide.

barbitos: a many-stringed instrument.

bombyx: a deep flute.

bosmoron: an Indian grain.

bounos: a hill, used by Herodotos (4.199) as a Kyrenaian localism but by Strabo to describe a feature on the coast north of Rome.

bous: "cow," a Nile fish.

brastes: an earthquake that raises the earth up vertically.

byssos: Normally flax, but Strabo implied silk.

choinikides: literally a cavity, used by Strabo for tidal rock cavities in the vicinity of Sinope.

choiros: a young pig, but also either a variety of Nile fish or perhaps a river hog.

chrysokolla: "gold solder," defined as a liquid flowing along veins of gold (Pliny, Natural History 33.86), but to Strabo something found in urine.

drakontion: perhaps edder wort.

epistrategos: a senior Ptolemaic and Roman provincial official in Egypt.

gangame: a fisherman's implement. Seemingly a net, although this is hard to explain in the context.

gangitis: perhaps lignite or jet.

gausapa: a Latin word meaning a cloth of woollen frieze.

ginnos: properly the offspring of a mare and a mule, but seemingly used by Strabo to mean a small equine.

grosphos: a Keltic word for a type of javelin.

horoskopeion: an instrument for telling time, whether a sundial or water clock.

iambos: a type of meter, and also a type of poem using that meter.

kakeis: a type of Egyptian bread.

karis (pl. karides): a general term for small crustaceans.

katreus: an Indian bird, perhaps a pheasant.

kausia: a Makedonian felt hat, part of the regalia of royalty.

kebos: a long-tailed monkey.

kestreus: a type of fish, probably a mullet.

kiborion: the seed vessel of the Egyptian bean, used as a drinking cup.

kiki: probably the bean of the castor plant.

kinaidos: a male prostitute.

kitharos: an Egyptian fish with a body striped like the strings of a lyre.

kokkos: a red dye obtained from the kermes oak (Quercus coccifera).

kolos: "stump-horned," a hornless goat native to the northern parts of the inhabited world.

komikos: a comedian, used both for a writer and performer.

kopis (pl. kopides): a broad curved knife.

korakinos: a black Nile fish.

kordyle: a type of fish, perhaps a young tuna.

korsion: a tuber, perhaps from the water lily.

kosmos: a Cretan magistrate (in the plural, a body of such magistrates).

kostarion: an aromatic plant, probably the same as Latin costus, perhaps derived from Sanskrit kushtha, Saussurea lappa from Kashmir.

kotyle: a small vessel; also a measure of capacity (see p. 33).

koukina: a type of palm fiber (the exact form of the word is uncertain).

kraneia: a tree, perhaps the cornelian cherry (Cornus mas).

krokottas: perhaps a hyena.

kynokephalos: "doghead," proably the dog-faced baboon (Simia hamadryas).

kytisos: a shrub, perhaps Medicago arborea.

laena: the Latin world for a cloak (used to translate the Keltic sagos).

larimnon: the Sabaian word for frankincense.

latos: an Egyptian fish, perhaps the perch.

leberis *(pl. leberides)*: a Massalian word for a type of rabbit.

leichene: a lichen-like skin disease.

lepidotos: a scaly Nile fish.

leuke: "whiteness," a disease like leprosy.

lychnites: "luminous," an African stone.

lychnos: "light," a Nile fish.

lyngourina: a Prettanikian variant of lyngourion.

lyngourion: red amber from Ligystike.

madaris: a Keltic word for a type of javelin.

magadis: a Lydian twenty-stringed instrument.

mnoia: a vassal class on Crete.

mousmon: a Sardinian ovine, probably ovis musimon.

nablas: a stringed instrument (probably a Phoenician word).

Nekyia: "The Summoning of the Spirits," the ancient term for Book 11 of the Odyssey.

orion: an Indian bird.

paidonomos: a magistracy on Crete and elsewhere supervising education.

pakton: a Nile boat made of wicker.

pala: an Iberian word for a nugget (used by Strabo for a nugget of gold).

pallas (pl. *pallades)*: a virgin priestess.

paradeisos: a formal garden in the Persian style.

pelamydes: a young tuna fish.

penestai: a vassal class on Crete.

periegesis: a geographical description, also the title of some geographical treatises.

periploos: originally a circumnavigation (Herodotos 6.95); later a literary genre that describes a coastal voyage.

persea: a fruit tree from the coast of the Red Sea and Aithiopia.

peuke: a generic word used for different types of pine trees.

phagrorios (or *phagros)*: a Nile fish.

phalaina: a type of whale.

phalangion: a type of venomous spider.

phaselos: a Latin term for a light boat, so named for its resemblance to a bean pod.

physa: "bellows," a Nile fish.

pitys: a generic word used for different types of pine trees.

pordalis: probably a variant of pardalis, the leopard.

poria (poreia?): a stone native to Pontos, perhaps a porous limestone or tufa.

prytanis a presiding magistrate

psalmos: a stringed instrument as well as the sound made by it.

rhizis (pl. rhizeis): "root-like," an northwest African animal of uncertain type, similar to a rhinoceros or elephant.

sagaris: a weapon used by Skythians and others.

sagos: a coarse cloak, perhaps a Keltic word.

sambyke: a triangular stringed instrument (a Semitic word).

sandyx: an arsenical (?) ore that produces a red color.

sarissa: a Makedonian long pike.

skolymos: a type of thistle.

smaragdos: an emerald

sparton: literally a cord or rope, but used by Strabo for a type of esparto grass.

spondophoros: the officer in charge of announcing festivals or games, in particular Eudoxos of Kyzikos.

staphylinos: carrots or parsnips.

strouthos: normally an ostrich, but Strabo seems to apply the term to a different but similar bird.

sykomoros: the sycamore fig.

tebenna (pl. tebennas): a standard Greek term for the Roman toga; of uncertain origin (perhaps Etruscan).

thalamegos: a lavish Egyptian houseboat, most familiar as the state boat of the Ptolemies (the "Cleopatra's barge" of Shakespeare).

thrissa: a type of fish.

togati: "Wearers of the toga" (Latin), used to describe locals in the Keltic territory who have become totally romanized both culturally and legally.

topazos: a Trogodyte word for a green gemstone, probably chrysolite or peridot.

trichaikes: a Homeric word (Iliad 19.177) of uncertain meaning, either "threefold" or "shaking crests" (or something similar: see LSJ).

The sources of the fragments

The following is a list of the fragment collections used in the translation. Fragments are cited by F and a number, or occasionally a T and a number (for testimonia). In the case of authors preserved both in actual texts and fragments, the following list only includes the sources for the fragments. Dates of the more obscure figures may be uncertain. Many of the fragment collections in *FGrHist* are now available in the ongoing *BNJ*.

Acilius, C. (second century BC): *FGrHist* #813.

Agatharchides of Knidos (second century BC): Agatharchides of Cnidus, *On the Erythraean Sea* (trans. and ed. Stanley M. Burstein, London, 1989).

Agrippa, M. Vipsanius (first century BC): see "The Chorographer."

Aischylos (fifth century BC): *Tragicorum graecorum fragmenta* 3: *Aeschylus* (ed. Stefan Radt, Göttingen, 1985).

Akousilaos (sixth century BC): *FGrHist* #2.

Alexander of Aitolia (third century BC): *Hellenistic Collection* (ed. and trans. J. L. Lightfoot, Cambridge, Mass., 2009).

Alkaios (seventh century BC): *Greek Lyric* 1: *Sappho and Alcaeus* (ed. and trans. David A. Campbell, Cambridge, Mass., 1982).

Alkmaionis (fifth century BC?): *Greek Epic Fragments* (ed. and trans. Martin L. West, Cambridge, Mass., 2003).

Alkman (seventh century BC): *Greek Lyric* 2 (trans. David A. Campbell, Cambridge, Mass., 1988).

Anacharsis (sixth century BC): Jan Fredrick Kindstrand, *Anacharsis: the Legend and the Apophthegmata* (Uppsala, 1981).

Anakreon (sixth century BC): *Greek Lyric* 2 (trans. David A. Campbell, Cambridge, Mass., 1988).

Anaximenes of Lampsakos (fourth century BC): *FGrHist* #72.

Andron (fourth century BC): *FGrHist* #10.

Androsthenes (fourth century BC): *FGrHist* #711.

Antikleides (*c.* 300 BC): *FGrHist* #140.

Antimachos (*c.* 400 BC): Victor J. Matthews, *Antimachus of Colophon: Text and Commentary* (Leiden, 1996).

Antiochos of Syracuse (fifth century BC): *FGrHist* #555.

Apollodoros of Artemita (first century BC): *FGrHist* #779.

Apollodoros of Athens (second century BC): *FGrHist* #244.

Apollonides (first century BC): *FHG* vol. 4, pp. 309–10.

Apollonios Molon (first century BC): *FGrHist* #728.

Aratos of Soloi (second century BC): *Supplementum hellenisticum* (ed. Hugh Lloyd Jones and Peter Parsons, Berlin, 1983).

Archemachos (third century BC?): *FGrHist* #424.

Archilochos (seventh century BC): *Greek Iambic Poetry* (ed. and trans. Douglas E. Gerber, Cambridge, Mass., 1999).

Aristeas (seventh century BC?): J. D. P. Bolton, *Aristeas of Proconnesus* (Oxford, 1962).

Aristoboulos of Kassandreia (fourth century BC): *FGrHist* #139.

Ariston (writer on the Nile, first century BC?): *FGrHist* #649.

Aristonikos (first century BC?): *FGrHist* #53.

Aristos of Salamis (third century BC?): *FGrHist* #143.

Aristotle of Chalkis (fourth century BC?): *FGrHist* #423.

Aristotle of Stageira (fourth century BC): *Qui ferebantur librorum fragmenta* (ed. V. Rose, Stuttgart, 1967).

Aristoxenos (fourth century BC): Stefan Ikarus Kaiser, *Die Fragmente des Aristoxenos aus Tarent* (Zürich, 2010).

Artemidoros of Ephesos (*c.* 100 BC): R. Stiehle, "Der Geograph Artemidoros von Ephesos," *Philologus* 11 (1856), 193–244.

Asinius Pollio, C. (first century BC): *HRF*, pp. 262–5.

Asios (sixth century BC?): *Greek Epic Fragments* (ed. and trans. Martin L. West, Cambridge, Mass., 2003).

Asklepiades of Myrleia (first century BC): *FGrHist* #697.

Athenodoros of Tarsos (first century BC): *FGrHist* #746.

Atthis historians (fifth–fourth centuries BC): *FGrHist* #329.

Bakchylides (fifth century BC): *Greek Lyric* 4 (ed. and trans. David A. Campbell, Cambridge, Mass., 1992).

Capture of Oichalia (sixth century BC?): *Greek Epic Fragments* (ed. and trans. Martin L. West, Cambridge, Mass., 2003).

Charon of Lampsakos (fifth century BC): *FGrHist* #262.

Choirilos of Samos (fifth century BC): *Poetae Epici Graeci* (ed. A. Bernabé, Leipzig-Berlin-Munich, 1987–2007).

"The Chorographer" (first century BC): Alfred Klotz, "Die Geographischen Commentarii des Agrippa und Ihre Überreste," *Klio* 24 (1931) 38–58, 386–466.

Chrysippos of Soloi (third century BC): *Stoicorum veterum fragmenta* (ed. J. van Arnem, Leipzig, 1903–5).

Cicero, M. Tullius (first century BC): Jane W. Crawford, *M. Tullius Cicero: The Fragmentary Speeches* (Atlanta, Ga., 1994).

Daes of Kolonai (fourth century BC): *FHG* vol. 4, p. 376.

Damastes (fifth century BC): *FGrHist* #5.

Deimachos (third century BC): *FGrHist* #716.

Dellius, Q. (first century BC): *FGrHist* #197.

Demetrios of Kallatis (third century BC): *FGrHist* #85.

Demetrios of Phaleron (fourth–third centuries BC): *FGrHist* #228.

Demetrios of Skepsis ("The Skepsian," second century BC): *BNJ* #2013.

Demokles (fifth or fourth century BC?): Robert L. Fowler, *Early Greek Mythography* 1 (Oxford, 2000).

Demokritos (fifth century BC): *DK* 68.

Dikaiarchos (fourth century BC): *Dicaearchus of Messana: Text, Translation, and Discussion* (ed. William W. Fortenbaugh and Eckart Schütrumpf, New Brunswick, N.J., 2001).

Dionysios, author of *On Foundations* (fourth century BC?): *FHG* vol. 4, pp. 393–6.

Douris (fourth–third centuries BC): *FGrHist* #76.

Empedokles (fifth century BC): Daniel W. Graham, *The Texts of Early Greek Philosophy* (Cambridge, 2010).

Ephoros (fourth century BC): *FGrHist* #70.

Epicharmos (fifth century BC): *Poetae Comici Graeci* (ed. R. Kassel and C. Austin, Berlin, 1983–2001).

Eratosthenes (third century BC). *Geographika, Measurement of the Earth*: Duane W. Roller, *Eratosthenes' Geography* (Princeton, N.J., 2010). Other works: *FGrHist* #241.

Eudoros (first century BC?): *FGrHist* #650.

Eudoxos of Knidos (fourth century BC): *Die Fragmente des Eudoxos von Knidos* (ed. François Lasserre, Berlin, 1966).

Euhemeros (fourth–third centuries BC): *FGrHist* #63.

Euphorion (third century BC): *Hellenistic Collection* (ed. and trans. J. L. Lightfoot, Cambridge, Mass., 2009).

Euripides (fifth century BC): *Fragments* (ed. and trans. Christopher Collard and Martin Cropp, Cambridge, Mass., 2008).

Fabius Pictor, Q. (third century BC): *FGrHist* #809.

Gabinius (first century BC?): *HRF* pp. 372–3.

Hegesianax (third–second century BC): *FGrHist* #45.

Hegesias (fourth–third centuries BC): *FGrHist* #142.

Hekataios of Abdera (fourth century BC): *FGrHist* #264.

Hekataios of Miletos (*c.* 500 BC): *FGrHist* #1.

Hellanikos (fifth century BC). Historical writings: *FGrHist* #4. *Phoronis: Greek Epic Fragments* (ed. and trans. Martin L. West, Cambridge, Mass., 2003).

Herakleides of Pontos (fourth century BC): *Heraclides of Pontos, Texts and Translations* (ed. Eckhart Schütrumpf, New Brunswick, N.J., 2008).

Herakleitos of Ephesos (*c.* 500 BC): Daniel W. Graham, *The Texts of Early Greek Philosophy* I (Cambridge, 2010).

Hesiod (*c.* 700 BC): *The Shield, Catalogue of Women, and Other Fragments* (ed. and trans. Glenn W. Most, Cambridge, Mass., 2007).

Hieronymos of Kardia (fourth–third centuries BC): *FGrHist* #154.

Hipparchos (second century BC): D. R. Dicks, *The Geographical Fragments of Hipparchus* (London, 1960).

Hipponax (sixth century BC): *Greek Iambic Poetry* (ed. and trans. Douglas A. Gerber, Cambridge, Mass., 1999).

Hypsikrates (first century BC?): *FGrHist* #190.

Ibykos (sixth century BC): *Greek Lyric* 3: *Stesichorus, Ibycus, Simonides, and Others* (ed. and trans. David A. Campbell, Cambridge, Mass., 1991).

Ion of Chios (fifth century BC): *Tragicorum graecorum fragmenta* I (ed. Bruno Snell, Göttingen 1986).

Kallimachos (third century BC): *Callimachus* (ed. R. Pfeiffer, Oxford 1949).

Kallinos (seventh century BC): *Greek Elegiac Poetry* (ed. and trans. Douglas E. Gerber, Cambridge, Mass., 1999).

Kallisthenes (fourth century BC): *FGrHist* #124.

Kineas (fourth–third century BC): *FGrHist* #603.

Kleitarchos (fourth century BC): *FGrHist* #137.

Krateros (fourth century BC): *FGrHist* #153.

Krates of Mallos (second century BC): *I frammenti* (ed. Maria Broggiato, La Spezia, 2001).

Kreophylos (eighth–seventh century BC?): *Greek Epic Fragments* (ed. and trans. Martin L. West, Cambridge, Mass., 2003).

Ktesias (late fifth century BC): *FGrHist* #688.

Kyrsilos (fourth century BC): *FGrHist* #130.

Maiandrios (fourth century BC?): *FGrHist* #491.

Medios (fourth century BC): *FGrHist* #129.

Megasthenes (fourth–third centuries BC): *FGrHist* #715.

Menandros (fourth century BC): *Poetae Comici Graeci* (ed. R. Kassel and C. Austin, Berlin, 1983–2001).

Menekrates the Elaian (fourth century BC): *FHG* vol. 2, p. 342.

Metrodoros of Skepsis (first century BC): *FGrHist* #184.

Mimnermos (seventh century BC): Archibald Allen, *The Fragments of Mimnermus* (Stuttgart, 1993).

Mochos of Sidon (pre-Greek?): *FGrHist* #784.

Myrsilos (third century BC): *FGrHist* #477.

Neanthes (third century BC): *FGrHist* #84.

Nearchos (fourth century BC): *FGrHist* #133.

Nikolaos of Damascus (first century BC): *FGrHist* #90.

Onesikritos (fourth century BC): *FGrHist* #134.

Ophelas (third–second centuries BC?): *BNJ* #2033.

Orthagoras (fourth century BC?): *FGrHist* #713.

Palaiphatos (fourth century BC): *FGrHist* #44.

Parmenides (fifth century BC): Daniel W. Graham, *The Texts of Early Greek Philosophy* (Cambridge, 2010).

Patrokles (fourth–third century BC): *FGrHist* #712.

Pausanias of Sparta (fifth century BC): *FGrHist* #582.

Pherekydes of Athens (fifth century BC): *FGrHist* #3.

Philetas (Philitas) of Kos (fourth–third century BC): *Hellenistic Collection* (ed. and trans. J. L. Lightfoot, Cambridge, Mass., 2009).

Philippos, author of *Karika* (third century BC): *FGrHist* #741.

Philochoros (fourth–third century BC): *FGrHist* #328.

Philon, Ptolemaic envoy (third century BC): *FGrHist* #670.

Phokylides (sixth century BC): *Greek Elegiac Poetry* (ed. and trans. Douglas E. Gerber, Cambridge, Mass., 1999).

Pindar (fifth century BC): *Pindari Carmina* 2 (ed. H. Maehler, Leipzig, 1989).

Polemon of Ilion (second century BC): *FHG* vol. 3, pp. 108–48.

Polykleitos of Larissa (fourth century BC): *FGrHist* #128.

Poseidonios (second–first century BC): *Posidonius* 1: *The Fragments* (ed. L. Edelstein and I. G. Kidd, second edition, Cambridge, 1989).

Ptolemaios I (fourth–third centuries BC): *FGrHist* #138.

Pythagoras: Hermann Diels, *Die Fragmente der Vorsokratiker* (ed. Walther Kranz, sixth edition, Berlin 1951–2).

Pytheas of Massalia (fourth century BC): *On the Ocean* (ed. Christina Horst Roseman, Chicago, Il., 1994).

Sappho: (seventh century BC): *Greek Lyric* 1: *Sappho and Alcaeus* (ed. David A. Campbell, Cambridge, Mass., 1982).

Semonides of Amorgas (seventh century BC): M. L. West, *Iambi et Elegi Graeci* (Oxford, 1987–92).

Sibylline Oracles (second–first centuries BC): *Old Testament Pseudepigraphia* (ed. James H. Charlesworth, New York, N.Y., 1983).

Silanos (third–second centuries BC): *FGrHist* #175.

Simmias (third century BC): *Collectanea Alexandrina* (ed. J. E. Powell, Oxford, 1925).

Simonides (sixth–fifth centuries BC): *Poetae melici graeci* (ed. D. L. Page, Oxford, 1962).

The Skepsian, or Skepsios: see Demetrios of Skepsis.

Skylax of Karyanda (sixth century BC): *FGrHist* #709.

Sophokles (fifth century BC): *Tragicorum graecorum fragmenta* 4: *Sophocles* (ed. Stefan Radt, Göttingen, 1999).

Sosikrates (second century BC): *FGrHist* #461.

Souidas (fourth century BC?): *FGrHist* #602.

Staphylos (second century BC?): *FGrHist* #269.

Stesichoros (sixth century BC): *Greek Lyric* 3: *Stesichorus, Ibycus, Simonides, and Others* (ed. and trans. David A. Campbell, Cambridge, Mass., 1991).

Stesimbrotos (fifth century BC): *FGrHist* #107.

Strabo (first century BC–early first century AD): *Deeds of Alexander, Historical Commentaries*: *FGrHist* #91.

Straton of Lampsakos (fourth–third centuries BC): *Strato of Lampsacus, Text, Translation, and Discussion* (ed. Marie-Laurence Desclos and William W. Fortenbaugh, New Brunswick, N.J., 2011).

Terpandros (seventh century BC): *Greek Lyric* 2 (trans. David A. Campbell, Cambridge, Mass., 1988).

Theodektes (fourth century BC): *Tragicorum graecorum fragmenta* 1 (ed. Bruno Snell, Göttingen, 1986).

Theophanes (first century BC): *FGrHist* #188.

Theophrastos (fourth–third centuries BC): *Theophrastus of Eresus: Sources for His Life, Writings, Thought and Influence* 2 (ed. William W. Fortenbaugh *et al.*, Leiden, 1992).

Theopompos (fourth century BC): *FGrHist* #115.

Timagenes (first century BC) *FGrHist* #88.

Timaios of Tauromenion (fourth–third centuries BC): *FGrHist* #566.

Timosthenes (third century BC): Emil August Wagner, *Die Erdbeschreibung des Timosthenes von Rhodus* (Leipzig, 1888).

Tyrtaios (seventh century BC): *Iambi et Elegi Graeci* 2 (ed. M. L. West, Oxford, 1987–92).

Xanthos of Lydia (fifth century BC): *FGrHist* #765.

Zenon of Kition (fourth–third centuries BC): *Stoicorum veterum fragmenta* (ed. J. van Arnem, Leipzig, 1903–5).

Zoilos (fourth century BC): *FGrHist* #71.

Bibliography

Agatharchides of Knidos, *On the Erythraean Sea* (trans. and ed. Stanley M. Burstein, London, 1989).

Allen, Archibald, *The Fragments of Mimnermus* (Stuttgart, 1993).

Aly, Wolfgang, "Der Geograph Strabon als Philosoph," *Miscellanea critica* 1 (Leipzig, 1964), 9–19.

Anderson, J. G. C., "Some Questions Bearing on the Date and Place of Composition of Strabo's *Geography*," in *Anatolian Studies Presented to Sir William Mitchell Ramsay* (ed. W. H. Buckler and W. M. Calder, Manchester, 1923), 1–13.

Aristotle, *Qui ferebantur librorum fragmenta* (ed. V. Rose, Stuttgart, 1967).

Aujac, Germaine, *Strabon et la science de son temps* (Paris, 1966).

"Strabon et le stoïcisme," *Diotima* 11 (1983), 17–29.

Balsdon, J. P. V. D., *Romans and Aliens* (Chapel Hill, N.C., 1979).

Bolton, J. D. P., *Aristeas of Proconnesus* (Oxford, 1962).

Bowersock, G. W., *Augustus and the Greek World* (Oxford, 1965).

"La *patria* di Strabone," in *Strabone e l'Asia Minore* (ed. A. M. Biraschi and G. Salmeri, Naples, 2000), 15–23.

Braund, David C., "Polemo, Pythodoris and Strabo," in *Roms auswärtige Freunde in der späten Republik und im frühen Prinzipat* (ed. Altay Coskun, Göttingen, 2005), 253–70.

Bunbury, E. H., *A History of Ancient Geography* (London, 1883).

Campanile, Domitilla, "Sul ritorno in patria di Strabone," *ZPE* 154 (2005), 267–8.

Cassia, Margherita, "La famiglia di Strabone di Amaseia tra fedeltà mitridatica e tendenze filoromane," *MediterrAnt* 3 (2000), 211–37.

Clarke, Katherine, *Between Geography and History: Hellenistic Constructions of the Roman World* (Oxford, 1999).

"In Search of the Author of Strabo's *Geography*," *JRS* 87 (1997), 92–110.

Coleman, K. M., "Fatal Charades: Roman Executions Staged as Mythological Enactments," *JRS* 80 (1990), 44–73.

Collectanea Alexandrina (ed. J. E. Powell, Oxford, 1925).

Cordano, Federica, "Sulle fonti di Strabone per i *Prolegomena*," *PP* 61 (2006), 401–16.

Crawford, Jane W., *M. Tullius Cicero: The Fragmentary Speeches* (Atlanta, Ga., 1994).

Dicks, D. R., *The Geographical Fragments of Hipparchus* (London, 1960).

Dikaiarchos, *Dicaearchus of Messana: Text, Translation, and Discussion* (ed. William W. Fortenbaugh and Eckhart Schütrumpf, New Brunswick, N.J., 2001).

Diller, Aubrey, "The Scholia on Strabo," *Traditio* 10 (1954), 29–50.

The Textual Tradition of Strabo's Geography (Amsterdam, 1975).

Dueck, Daniela, *Strabo of Amaseia: A Greek Man of Letters in Augustan Rome* (London, 2000).

Elvers, Karl-Ludwig, "P. S. Vatia Isauricus," *BNP* 13 (2008), 331.

Engels, Johannes, "Ἄνδρες ἔνδοξοι or 'Men of High Reputation' in Strabo's *Geography*," in Daniela Dueck *et al.*, *Strabo's Cultural Geography: The Making of a Kolossourgia* (Cambridge, 2006), 129–43.

Augusteische Oikumene Geographie und Universal-Historie im Werk Strabons von Amaseia (Stuttgart, 1999).

"Die strabonische Kulturgeographie in der Tradition der antiken geographischen Schriften und ihre Bedeutung für die antike Kartographie," *OTerr* 4 (1998), 63–114.

Eudoxos, *Die Fragmente des Eudoxos von Knidos* (ed. François Lasserre, Berlin, 1966).

Euripides, *Fragments* (ed. Christopher Collard and Martin Cropp, Cambridge, Mass., 2008).

Fowler, Robert L., *Early Greek Mythography* (Oxford, 2000).

Fraser, P. M. and E. Matthews (eds.), *A Lexicon of Greek Personal Names* (Oxford, 1987–).

Graham, Daniel W., *The Texts of Early Greek Philosophy* (Cambridge, 2010).

Greek Elegiac Poetry (ed. Douglas E. Gerber, Cambridge, Mass., 1999).

Greek Epic Fragments (ed. and trans. Martin L. West, Cambridge, Mass., 2003).

Greek Iambic Poetry (ed. and trans. Douglas E. Gerber, Cambridge, Mass., 1999).

Greek Lyric (ed. and trans. David A. Campbell, Cambridge, Mass., 1982–93).

Halfmann, Helmut, *Itinera principum* (Stuttgart, 1986).

Heckel, Waldmar, *Who's Who in the Age of Alexander the Great* (Malden, Mass., 2006).

Hellenistic Collection (ed. and trans. J. L. Lightfoot, Cambridge, Mass., 2009).

Herakleides of Pontos, *Heraclides of Pontus: Texts and Translations* (ed. Eckhart Schütrumpf, New Brunswick, N.J., 2008).

Hesiod, *The Shield, Catalogue of Women, and Other Fragments* (ed. and trans. Glenn W. Most, Cambridge, Mass., 2007).

Hirt, Alfred Michael, *Imperial Mines and Quarries in the Roman World* (Oxford, 2010).

Honigmann, E., "Strabon von Amaseia" (#3), *RE* 2. ser. 4 (1931), 76–155.

Iambi et Elegi Graeci 2 (ed. M. L. West, Oxford, 1972).

Jameson, Shelagh, "Chronology of the Campaigns of Aelius Gallus and C. Petronius," *JRS* 58 (1968), 71–84.

Jones, Alexander, "The Stoics and the Astronomical Sciences," in *The Cambridge Companion to the Stoics* (ed. Brad Inwood, Cambridge, 2003), 328–44.

Kaimio, Jorma, *The Romans and the Greek Language* (CHL 64, 1979).

Kaiser, Stefan Ikarus, *Die Fragmente des Aristoxenos aus Tarent* (Zürich, 2010).

Kajanto, Iiro, *The Latin Cognomina* (*CHL* 36.2, 1965).

Kallimachos, *Callimachus* (ed. R. Pfeiffer, Oxford, 1949).

Keyser, Paul T., "The Geographical Work of Dikaiarchos," in *Dicaearchus of Messana: Text, Translation, and Discussion* (ed. William W. Fortenbaugh and Eckhart Schütrumpf, New Brunswick, N.J., 2001) 353–72.

Kim, Lawrence, *Homer Between History and Fiction in Imperial Greek Literature* (Cambridge, 2010).

"The Portrait of Homer in Strabo's *Geography*," *CP* 102 (2007), 363–88.

Kindstrand, Jan Fredrick, *Anacharsis: The Legend and the Apophthegmata* (Uppsala, 1981).

Klotz, Alfred, "Zu Dionysius Periegetes," *RhM* 64 (1909), 474–5.

"Die geographischen commentarii des Agrippa und ihre Überreste," *Klio* 24 (1931), 38–58, 386–466.

Krates of Mallos, *I frammenti* (ed. Maria Broggiato, La Spezia, 2001).

Lasserre, François, "Strabon devant l'Empire romain," *ANRW* 30 (1982–3), 867–96.

Laurent, Jérôme, "Strabon et la philosophie stoïcienne," *ArchPhilos* 71 (2008), 111–27.

Lindsay, Hugh, "Syme's Anatolica and the Date of Strabo's Geography," *Klio* 79 (1997), 484–507.

Matthews, Victor J., *Antimachus of Colophon: Text and Commentary* (Leiden, 1996).

Old Testament Pseudepigraphia (ed. James H. Charlesworth, New York, N.Y., 1983).

Pédech, Paul, "Strabon historien d'Alexandre," *GB* 2 (1974), 129–45.

Pindar, *Pindari Carmina* (ed. H. Maehler, Leipzig, 1989).

Poetae Comici Graeci (ed. R. Kassel and C. Austin, Berlin, 1983–2001).

Poetae Epici Graeci (ed. A. Bernabé, Leipzig-Berlin-Munich, 1987–2007).

Poetae Melici Graeci (ed. D. L. Page, Oxford, 1962).

Poseidonios, *Posidonius* 1: *The Fragments* (ed. L. Edelstein and I. G. Kidd, second edition, Cambridge, 1989).

Posidonius 2: *The Commentary* (ed. I. G. Kidd, Cambridge, 1989).

Pothecary, Sarah, "The Expression 'Our Times' in Strabo's *Geography*," *CP* 92 (1997), 235–46.

"Strabo the Geographer: His Name and its Meaning," *Mnemosyne* 4th ser. 52 (1999), 691–704.

"Strabo, the Tiberian Author: Past, Present and Silence in Strabo's *Geography*," *Mnemosyne* 4th ser. 55 (2002), 387–438.

Prontera, Francesco, *Geografia e storia nella Grecia antica* (Florence, 2011).

Pytheas of Massalia, *On the Ocean* (ed. Christina Horst Roseman, Chicago, Il., 1994).

Reinhold, Meyer, *From Republic to Principate* (Atlanta, Ga., 1988).

Richards, G. C., "Strabo: The Anatolian Who Failed of Roman Recognition," *G&R* 10 (1941), 79–90.

Richardson Jr., L. *A New Topographical Dictionary of Ancient Rome* (Baltimore, Md., 1992).

Roller, Duane W., *Eratosthenes' Geography* (Princeton, N.J., 2010).

    The World of Juba II and Kleopatra Selene: Royal Scholarship on Rome's African Frontier (London, 2003).

Romm, James, *The Edges of the Earth in Ancient Thought* (Princeton 1992).

    Review of Dueck *et al.* (eds.), *Strabo's Cultural Geography, CW* 101 (2007), 107–8.

Russell, D. A., *Plutarch* (New York, N.Y., 1973).

Schenkeveld, D. M., "Strabo on Homer," *Mnemosyne* 4th ser. 29 (1976), 52–64.

Stein, A., *Die Präfekten von Ägypten in der Römischen Kaiserzeit* (Bonn, 1950).

Stiehle, R., "Der Geograph Artemidoros von Ephesos," *Philologus* 11 (1856), 193–244.

Stoicorum veterum fragmenta (ed. J. van Arnem, Leipzig, 1903–5).

Strabo, *Geographica* (ed. Wolfgang Aly, Bonn, 1957–72).

    Géographie (ed. Germaine Aujac, François Lasserre, and Raoul Baladié, Paris, 2003).

    Geography (trans. Horace Leonard Jones, Cambridge, Mass., 1917–32).

    Strabons Geographika (ed. Stefan Radt, Göttingen, 2002–11).

Straton of Lampsakos, *Strato of Lampsacus: Text, Translation, and Discussion* (ed. Marie-Laurence Desclos and William W. Fortenbaugh, New Brunswick, N.J., 2011).

Sullivan, Richard D., "Dynasts in Pontus," *ANRW* 2.7 (1980), 913–30.

Supplementum hellenisticum (ed. Hugh Lloyd Jones and Peter Parsons, Berlin, 1983).

Syme, Ronald, *Anatolica: Studies in Strabo* (ed. Anthony Birley, Oxford, 1995).

Theophrastos, *Theophrastus of Eresus: Sources for His Life, Writings, Thought and Influence* 2 (ed. William W. Fortenbaugh et al.) Leiden, 1992.

Thomson, J. Oliver, *History of Ancient Geography* (reprint, New York, N.Y., 1965).

Tragicorum graecorum fragmenta (ed. Bruno Snell and Stefan Radt, Göttingen, 1985–99).

Van der Vliet, Edward Ch. L., Review of Dueck *et al.* (eds.), *Strabo's Cultural Geography* (Cambridge, 2006), *Mnemosyne* 4th ser. 61 (2008), 690–3.

Wagner, Emil August, *Die Erdbeschreibung des Timosthenes von Rhodus* (Leipzig, 1888).

Walbank, F. W., "The Geography of Polybius," *C&M* 9 (1947), 155–82.

Wallace, Paul W., *Strabo's Description of Boiotia: A Commentary* (Heidelberg, 1979).

West, M. L., *Iambi et Elegi Graeci* (Oxford,1987–92).

List of passages cited

Greek and Latin Authors

Acilius, C.
  F1 234
Agatharchides
  F5b 725
Agrippa, M.: see The Chorographer
Aischylos
  Prometheus
    831 320
  F25e 438
  F46 226
  F57 458
  F143 585
  F158 554
  F162 554
  F163 554
  F192 64
  F198 296
  F199 192
  F284 382
  F402 258
  F402a 342
  F404 389
  F405 681
  F431 72, 295
  F434a 72, 295
  F441 72, 295
Akousilaos
  F20 460
Alexander of Aitolia
  F9 541, 641
Alkaios
  F325 405
  F337 576
  F350 586
  F388 624

  F425 406
  F428 571
  F432 67
Alkmaionis
  F5 442
Alkman
  F16 449
  F55 342
  F92 437
  F98 468
  F126 553
  F148 72, 295
Anacharsis
  F A23B 652
Anakreon
  F361 163
  F401 624
  F463 600
  F505a 609
Anaximenes of Lampsakos
  F25 562
  F26 601
Andron
  F14 388
  F15 445
  F16a 463
Androsthenes
  F2 714
Antikleides
  F21 226
Antimachos
  F2 403
  F27 346, 382
  F79 363
  F131 561
  F145 363

Index

Ethnyms may be indexed with their toponyms. Romans are generally listed under their *nomen*, except for a few (e.g. Cicero, the emperor Tiberius) much better known by another name.

Many toponyms in the *Geography* appear in a number of variants. Often these are significant and represent the history of the name or its form in different languages, but in other cases they may simply indicate differences between Strabo's sources or even errors. Nevertheless, in the interest of thoroughness and clarity, many variants appear in this index. Moreover, it is not always possible to determine whether repeated mentions of the same toponym in the same region are identical or different places.

Lightning Source UK Ltd.
Milton Keynes UK
UKHW021542210921
390601UK00019B/489